November 2–4, 2011
Berlin, Germany

Association for
Computing Machinery

Advancing Computing as a Science & Profession

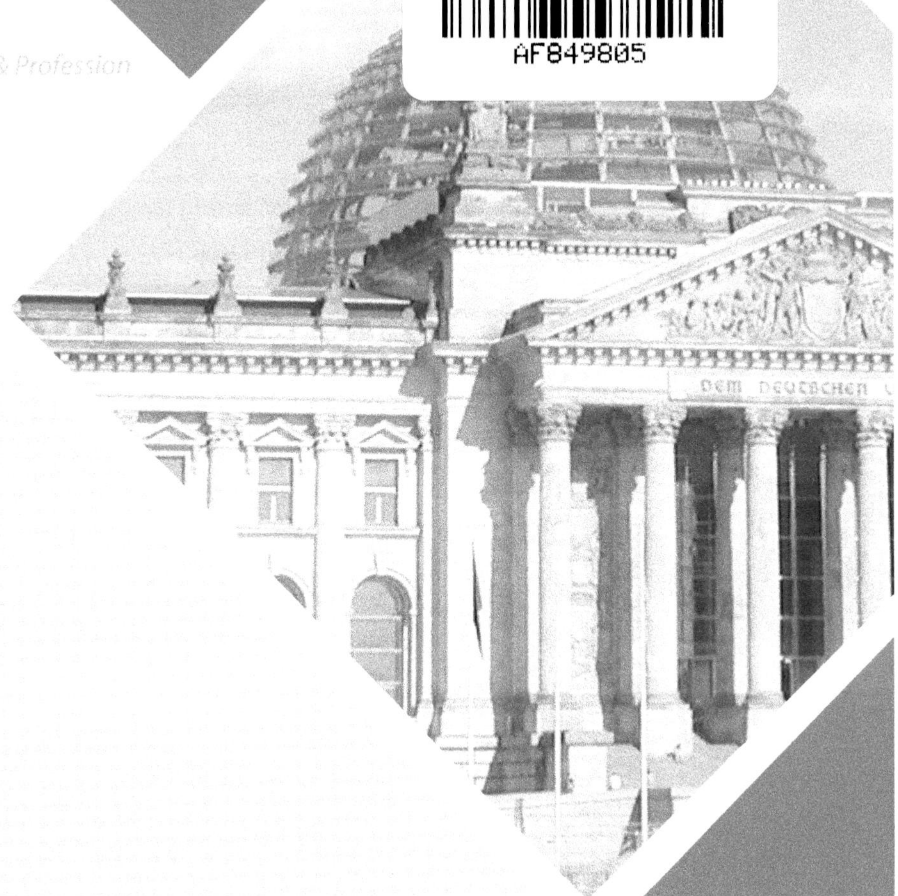

IMC 2011

Proceedings of the 2011 ACM SIGCOMM on
Internet Measurement Conference

Sponsored by:

ACM SIGCOMM & ACM SIGMETRICS

In cooperation with:

USENIX

Supported by:

Endace, NSF, Akamai, AT&T, Technicolor, Hewlett-Packard, Telefonica, Narus, Sprint, & IBM Research

Association for
Computing Machinery

Advancing Computing as a Science & Profession

The Association for Computing Machinery
2 Penn Plaza, Suite 701
New York, New York 10121-0701

Notice to Past Authors of ACM-Published Articles

ACM intends to create a complete electronic archive of all articles and/or other material previously published by ACM. If you have written a work that has been previously published by ACM in any journal or conference proceedings prior to 1978, or any SIG Newsletter at any time, and you do NOT want this work to appear in the ACM Digital Library, please inform permissions@acm.org, stating the title of the work, the author(s), and where and when published.

ISBN: 978-1-4503-1013-0 (Digital)

ISBN: 978-1-4503-1398-8 (Print)

Additional copies may be ordered prepaid from:

ACM Order Department
PO Box 30777
New York, NY 10087-0777, USA

Phone: 1-800-342-6626 (USA and Canada)
+1-212-626-0500 (Global)
Fax: +1-212-944-1318
E-mail: acmhelp@acm.org
Hours of Operation: 8:30 am – 4:30 pm ET

Printed in the USA

Foreword

It is our great pleasure to welcome you to the *2011 Internet Measurement Conference - IMC'11*. What started in 2001 as a small workshop, organized by a handful of dedicated individuals and sponsored by ACM SIGCOMM, has quickly grown into the premier venue for the dissemination of measurement-driven networking research. In putting together this year's program, we explicitly tried (with varying degrees of success) to uphold IMC's best traditions – encouraging reappraisal of previous results, fostering papers that assess emerging uses (or mis-uses) of the Internet, and promoting the development of innovative new methodologies for increasing our understanding of the Internet and related networked communication systems. As in the recent past, the program consists of a mix of short and long papers to encourage both early exposure to new ideas and deep treatment of topics.

The following IMC "facts and firsts" are all signs of a vibrant and thriving community. This year we received a record submission of 221 papers (111 long and 110 short papers). This represents an increase of 5% over 2010 and is comparable to the total number of submissions received by the annual ACM SIGCOMM Conference. The technical program was chosen by a highly skilled and dedicated program committee (PC) of 34 researchers from academia and industry and is the outcome of a thorough reviewing process. During the first round of this process, each paper received three reviews. The resulting 100 or so most competitive submissions received two additional reviews during a second round, after which some 64 papers were chosen to be discussed for inclusion in the final program at the PC meeting, held at the Shannon Laboratory at AT&T Labs-Research in Florham Park, NJ, on July 22, 2011. This meeting was attended by all but five PC members and resulted in 42 accepted papers (28 long and 14 short papers) that will be presented as part of this year's three-day conference in Berlin. Paper notifications were emailed within hours of the end of the PC meeting.

To increase the transparency and accountability of the IMC reviewing process, IMC'11 performed a first-of-its-kind reviewing experiment whereby authors of accepted papers were given a choice to have the significant (verbatim) portions of the reviews that their papers received during the reviewing process (together with a short response from the authors) published alongside the final version of their papers. With the full backing of the IMC's steering committee and the enthusiastic support of the entire PC for this experiment, we are happy to inform you that all but one set of authors opted for participating in this experiment. As a result, readers of this year's IMC Proceedings have a unique opportunity to see the IMC reviewing process "in action" and we hope that this level of transparency provides some useful insight into how IMC reviewers assess the relevance or importance of work in this area while remaining anonymous. IMC is considering adopting this experimental reviewing process as a new standard, so we would greatly appreciate any feedback in any form from readers, authors, or PC members about their views or experience with this approach to improving transparency and accountability.

Separate from the technical program, IMC'11 will also experiment with a new one-hour "News and Community Feedback Session". The session will consist of short presentations or announcements on topics that are relevant to the IMC audience and is intended to "take the pulse" of the community in terms of efforts, activities and topics that should be encouraged to maintain a vibrant community engaged in relevant and cutting-edge measurement-driven networking research.

Last but not least, we wish to thank the many people who have contributed their time, energy, and ideas to support this year's IMC program. For one, our thanks go to the hundreds of authors who chose to submit their latest research to IMC'11 and, in doing so, ensure the vitality and continued growth of this community. We also thank the IMC steering committee members for their trust and support throughout this year's process. A special "thank you" goes to the PC members who all devoted much of their time to review submissions, write thoughtful and constructive reviews, engage in fruitful discussions, and travel to the PC meeting just in time to experience the few 100+ degree days which New Jersey faced this summer. We also like to thank Eddie Kohler, the author of the reviewing software HotCRP that greatly simplified our tasks as PC chairs, Bernhard Ager and Steve Uhlig who installed and maintained the software on one of their TU Berlin servers, and Oliver Hohlfeld who served as scribe during the PC meeting.

We hope that you will find this year's program exciting and thought-provoking and that the conference provides you with a rewarding forum for fruitful discussions with colleagues from around the world. Enjoy the program and the conference!

Patrick Thiran
IMC'11 PC Chair
EPFL, Switzerland

Walter Willinger
IMC'11 PC Chair
AT&T Labs-Research, USA

Table of Contents

Session 5: Analyzing IPTV Systems and Their Usage

Session 6: Users Behaving Badly

Session 7: Web Traffic Revisited

Session 8: Social Media (YouTube) and the Web

IMC 2011 Conference Organization

Program Chairs: Patrick Thiran *(EPFL, Switzerland)*
Walter Willinger *(AT&T Labs-Research, USA)*

Local Arrangements Chairs: Anja Feldmann *(TU Berlin/Deutsche Telekom Laboratories)*
Georgios Smaragdakis *(TU Berlin/Deutsche Telekom Laboratories)*
Steve Uhlig *(TU Berlin/Deutsche Telekom Laboratories)*

Steering Committee: Mark Allman *(International Computer Science Institute, USA)*
Paul Barford *(University of Wisconsin at Madison, USA)*
Chen-Nee Chuah *(University of California at Davis, USA)*
Renata Teixeira *(CNRS and UPMC Sorbonne, France)*

Program Committee: Katerina Argyraki *(EPFL, Switzerland)*
Martin Arlitt *(HP Labs and University of Calgary, Canada)*
Suman Banerjee *(University of Wisconsin, USA)*
Bobby Bhattacharjee *(University of Maryland, USA)*
Fabian Bustamante *(Northwestern University, USA)*
Augustin Chaintreau *(Columbia University, USA)*
Xenofontas Dimitropoulos *(ETH Zurich, Switzerland)*
Lixin Gao *(University of Massachusetts, USA)*
Alexandre Gerber *(AT&T Labs-Research, USA)*
Srikanth Kandula *(Microsoft Research, USA)*
Thomas Karagiannis *(Microsoft Research, UK)*
Sachin Katti *(Stanford University, USA)*
Ramana Kompella *(Purdue University, USA)*
Christian Kreibich *(ICSI, USA)*
Nikolaos Laoutaris *(Telefonica Research, Spain)*
Olaf Maennel *(Loughborough University, UK)*
Ratul Mahajan *(Microsoft Research, USA)*
Z. Morley Mao *(University of Michigan, USA)*
Hung X. Nguyen *(University of Adelaide, Australia)*
Antonio Nucci *(Narus, USA)*
Konstantina (Dina) Papagiannaki *(Telefonica Research, Spain)*
Lili Qiu *(University of Texas, USA)*
Reza Rejaie *(University of Oregon, USA)*
Pablo Rodriguez *(Telefonica Research, Spain)*
Matthew Roughan *(University of Adelaide, Australia)*
Vyas Sekar *(Intel Labs, USA)*
Rob Sherwood *(Deutsche Telekom Labs, USA)*
Georgios Smaragdakis *(TU Berlin and Deutsche Telekom Labs, Germany)*
Joel Sommers *(Colgate University, USA)*
Neil Spring *(University of Maryland, USA)*
Renata Teixeira *(CNRS and UPMC Sorbonne Universités, France)*
Steve Uhlig *(TU Berlin and Deutsche Telekom Labs, Germany)*
David Wetherall *(University of Washington, USA)*
Lixia Zhang *(UCLA, USA)*

IMC 2011 Sponsors & Supporters

Sponsors: acm sigcomm — ACM SIGMETRICS

In Cooperation with: USENIX

Platinum Supporters: endace — NSF

Gold Supporters: Akamai — at&t

Silver Supporters: technicolor — hp

Telefonica — NARUS®

Sprint

Other Supporter: IBM Research

Analysis of Country-wide Internet Outages Caused by Censorship

Alberto Dainotti
University of Napoli Federico II
alberto@unina.it

Claudio Squarcella
Roma Tre University
squarcel@dia.uniroma3.it

Emile Aben
RIPE NCC
emile.aben@ripe.net

Kimberly C. Claffy
CAIDA/UCSD
kc@caida.org

Marco Chiesa
Roma Tre University
chiesa@dia.uniroma3.it

Michele Russo
University of Napoli Federico II
mic.russo83@gmail.com

Antonio Pescapé
University of Napoli Federico II
pescape@unina.it

ABSTRACT

In the first months of 2011, Internet communications were disrupted in several North African countries in response to civilian protests and threats of civil war. In this paper we analyze episodes of these disruptions in two countries: Egypt and Libya. Our analysis relies on multiple sources of large-scale data already available to academic researchers: BGP interdomain routing *control plane* data; unsolicited *data plane* traffic to unassigned address space; active macroscopic traceroute measurements; RIR delegation files; and MaxMind's geolocation database. We used the latter two data sets to determine which IP address ranges were allocated to entities within each country, and then mapped these IP addresses of interest to BGP-announced address ranges (prefixes) and origin ASes using publicly available BGP data repositories in the U.S. and Europe. We then analyzed observable activity related to these sets of prefixes and ASes throughout the censorship episodes. Using both *control plane* and *data plane* data sets in combination allowed us to narrow down which forms of Internet access disruption were implemented in a given region over time. Among other insights, we detected what we believe were Libya's attempts to test firewall-based blocking before they executed more aggressive BGP-based disconnection. Our methodology could be used, and automated, to detect outages or similar macroscopically disruptive events in other geographic or topological regions.

Categories and Subject Descriptors

C.2.3 [**Network Operations**]: Network Monitoring;
C.2.5 [**Local and Wide-Area Networks**]: Internet

General Terms

Measurement, Security

Keywords

Outages, Connectivity Disruption, Censorship, Darknet, Network Telescope, Internet Background Radiation

1. INTRODUCTION

On the evening of January 27, 2011 Egypt—a population of 80 million, including 23 million Internet users [41]—vanished from the Internet. The Egyptian government ordered a complete Internet shutdown amidst popular anti-government protests calling for the resignation of Egyptian President Hosni Mubarak. The order followed reports on the previous day (25 January) of blocked access to Twitter [24], although an Egyptian government official denied blocking any social media web sites [48]. In addition to mainstream media reporting of traffic disruption [49], several commercial Internet measurement companies posted technical data analyses on their blogs [16, 32, 50]. The heavy-handed attempt to block communications in the country did not quell the protests, and may have even increased the number of people in the streets; protests intensified and continued even after Internet connectivity was restored five days later. Under political pressure from inside and outside Egypt, President Hosni Mubarak resigned, turning command over to the military on February 11.

Four days later, similar protests erupted in Libya, calling for an end to the Gaddafi regime. On February 17 major protests took place across the country [44], and that evening YouTube became inaccessible from Libya [25]. On the night of February 18 (Friday) the government imposed an "Internet curfew", blocking all Internet access until morning (08:01 local time), and repeating it the next day (Saturday) [16, 32, 63]. In the following days, Libyan traffic to popular sites like Google increased steadily [26] until Internet access was disabled again, this time for nearly four days. Figure 1 presents a brief chronology of the events.

Wide-scale Internet service disruptions are nothing new [12, 15, 57, 66–69], even politically-motivated interference with Internet access in order to hinder anti-government organization [3, 8]. But the scale, duration, coverage, and violent context of Egypt's and Libya's disruptions has brought the Internet "kill switch" issue into new critical light.

In this paper we analyze the Internet disruptions that took place in Egypt and Libya in early 2011. These two events are of historical as well as scientific interest. Access to publicly available Internet measurement data that cover the outage intervals allows empirical

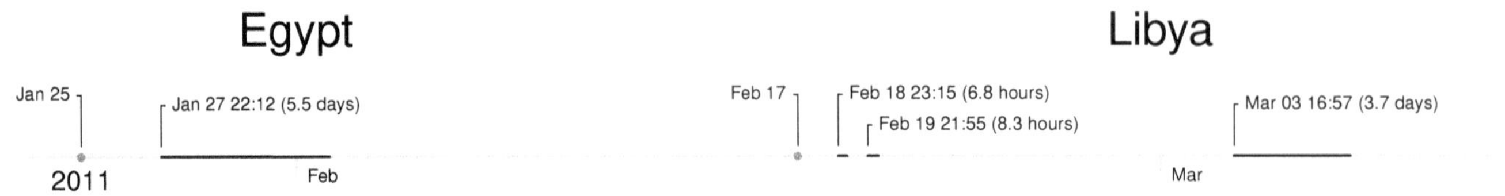

Figure 1: Timeline of Internet disruptions described in the paper. Times in figure are UTC (Egypt and Libya are UTC+2). The pair of red dots indicate the start of major political protests in the respective countries.

study of what it takes to bring down an entire country's communications infrastructure, which has security relevance for every nation in the world. We were also able to observe surprisingly noticeable effects of such large scale censorship on ongoing global measurement activities, suggesting how similar events could be detected and/or documented in the future. Our analysis relies on multiple measurements and vantage points:

- **Traffic to unassigned address space**, specifically data collected from the UCSD network telescope [7], reveal changes in background Internet traffic from the affected regions.
- **BGP data** from RouteViews [59] and RIPE NCC's Routing Information Service (RIS) [6] provide a view of BGP activity during the events.
- **Active traceroute probing** from Ark [2] reveals forward path information and can reveal additional types of filtering, e.g. firewalling, not observable via BGP, as well as help calibrate BGP observations.

We focus on two episodes of Internet disruption, although the same global data sources and our proposed methodology could illuminate the study of similar events in other countries. The main contributions of this paper are:

- We document a rich view of the disruptions using three types of measurement data sources.
- We demonstrate how to use unsolicited background traffic to identify country-level blocking events.
- We report previously unknown details of each event, including the use of packet filtering as well as BGP route withdrawals to effect the disruption.
- We sketch a general methodology for the analysis of some types of of disruptions that combines multiple measurement data sources available to researchers.
- Our methodology and findings can form the basis for automated early-warning detection systems for Internet service suppression events.

The rest of this paper is organized as follows. Section 2 gives technical background on network disruption, limiting its focus to the paper's scope. Section 3 summarizes related work. Section 4 describes our measurement and analysis methodology. Section 5 presents the results of our analysis. Section 6 discusses our findings and concludes the paper.

2. BACKGROUND

Disabling Internet access is an extreme form of Internet censorship in which a population's Internet access is blocked completely, a coarse but technically more straightforward approach than the selective blocking used in most Internet censorship regimes. It can be implemented by simply powering down or physically disconnecting critical equipment, although this approach typically requires physical co-location with the communications equipment, which may be spread over a wide area. A more flexible approach is to use *software* to disrupt either the *routing* or *packet forwarding* mechanisms.

Routing disruption. While *forwarding* is the mechanism that advances packets from source to destination, the *routing* mechanism determines which parts of the network are reachable and how. On the Internet, global routing is coordinated at the level of Autonomous Systems (ASes) – administratively distinct parts of the network – using BGP as the interdomain routing protocol. Routers exchange BGP information (*BGP updates*) regarding which destination addresses they can reach, and continually update their forwarding tables to use the best available path to each contiguous block of destination addresses.[1] Disabling the routing process on critical routers or suppressing BGP information transmission can effectively render large parts of a network unreachable.

Packet filtering. Packet filtering intervenes in the normal packet forwarding mechanism to block (i.e., not forward) packets matching given criteria. Today packet filtering of varying complexity is a standard security feature of network equipment from switches to dedicated firewalls.[2]

Disabling a network's connectivity to the Internet through BGP routing disruption is easily detectable, since it entails changes in the *global* routing state of the network, i.e., in the *control plane*. Previously advertised prefixes must be withdrawn or re-advertised with different properties in order to change global routing behavior. Detecting packet filtering is harder; it requires either active probing of the forward path, or monitoring traffic (the *data plane*) from the affected parts of the network for changes.

We also note that BGP-based traffic control and packet-filtering are only two of many layers where censorship of connectivity and content may occur. A taxonomy of blocking technologies would include a range of approaches, including physical layer disconnection, content blocking based on deep packet inspection by an ISP, DNS-based blocking or manipulation at multiple granularities, and end-client software blocking in an enterprise or household.

3. RELATED WORK

An Internet blackout is put into effect by a government when more selective forms of censorship are either impractical or ineffective. Governments use selective censorship to restrict Internet traffic for political, religious, and cultural reasons. Recent studies have found that Internet censorship is widespread and on the rise [3, 8]. Unsurprisingly, there is also growing interest in analyzing the technical aspects of censorship, and methods to circumvent them.

[1] Destination addresses are advertised as *prefixes*, ranges of addresses represented as a set of fixed high-order bits and varying low-order bits. A prefixes is written as an IP address in dotted quad notation followed by a "/" and the prefix length. For example, the prefix 132.239.0.0/17 represents IP addresses 132.239.0.0 to 132.239.127.255.

[2] Because of their versatile packet filtering capabilities, firewalls can flexibly implement many types of selective censorship: address filtering, protocol filtering, and simple content filtering.

In [14] Clayton et al. analyzed the keyword filtering mechanism of the "Great Firewall of China" (GFC) and found that it was possible to circumvent it by simply ignoring the forged TCP packets with the reset flag set sent by the firewall. In [21], Crandall et al. disproved the notion that the GFC is a firewall strictly operating at the border of China's Internet. They showed that filtering can occur at different hops past the Chinese border (cases of up to 13 IP address hops were observed), suggesting that filtering happens at the AS level. They also proposed *ConceptDoppler*, a system for monitoring which keywords are filtered over time. In more recent work on censorship in China [64], Xueyang Xu et al. explored the AS-level topology of China's network and probed the firewall to find the locations of filtering devices. They found that two major ISPs in China had different approaches to the placement of filtering devices, either decentralized or in the backbone. Results also showed that most of the filtering happened in "border ASes", that is, ASes that peer with foreign networks. In [53] Skoric et al. provided a detailed analysis of how social media platforms (e.g., Facebook), as well as traditional media were used to organize a student protest against censorship in Singapore. They found that activists used social media to engage rather than circumvent traditional media stakeholders, in order to amplify their impact. Trying to prevent such amplification was a likely motivation for the Internet blackouts we analyzed in this study.

The scientific study of Internet interdomain routing has a longer and richer history (thus far) than the study of Internet censorship. Academic researchers have used BGP data to support scientific study of Internet dynamics for over a decade, including Labovitz et al.'s studies in the late 1990's of several root causes of high levels Internet routing instability [35, 36]. They traced a large fraction of unnecessary ("pathological") BGP update volume to router vendor software implementation decisions, and their research convinced router vendors to modify BGP parameters, decreasing the volume of Internet routing updates they observed a year later by an order of magnitude. More recently researchers have explored the use of spatial and temporal correlations among the behaviors of BGP prefixes to detect and hopefully predict instabilities [23, 30].

In [51] Sahoo et al. used simulations to estimate BGP recovery time for networks with a range of topological characteristics undergoing large-scale failure scenarios, such as those caused by disastrous natural or man-made events. They showed that topological properties, especially the node degree distribution, can significantly affect recovery time. In [38] Li and Brooks proposed an *Internet seismograph* to consistently measure the impact of disruptive events such as large-scale power outages, undersea cable cuts and worms, to enable quantitative comparison of the impact of different events. Other researchers have also used BGP monitoring infrastructure to analyze the impact of these types of disruptive events on the routing system [19, 20, 37]. In [61] Tao Wan and Van Oorschot used data from the RouteViews project [59] during Google's outage in 2005, showing what was probably a malicious BGP advertisement of a Google network prefix by another AS.

Several analysis and real-time BGP monitoring tools have also been developed. In [56] Teoh et al. presented BGP Eye, a tool for root-cause analysis and visualization of BGP anomalies based on clustering of BGP updates into events that are compared across different border routers. The visualization helps to show events that may affect prefix reachability and hijacking. In [29] Katz-Bassett et al. introduced Hubble, a prototype system that operated continuously for a couple of years to find Internet reachability problems in real-time, specifically for situations where routes exist to a destination but packets are unable to reach the destination. While the Hubble system detected unreachability of prefixes, it did not aggregate results beyond a single AS. Dan Massey's group at Colorado State is maintaining BGPMon, a real-time BGP routing instrumentation system [65] designed to scalably monitor BGP updates and routing tables from many BGP routers simultaneously, while also allowing user-defined real-time "notification" feeds of specific subsets of the data.

Regarding the specific blackouts we describe in this paper, several commercial Internet measurement companies posted technical data analyses on their blogs during and following the outages [11,16–18,31–34,60]. Most of them analyzed flow-level traffic data or BGP updates seen by their routers, providing timely news and technical insights, although omitting specifics about the proprietary data and analysis methodologies used.

Our work combines multiple different data sources available to academic researchers to analyze in detail the characteristics of two large-scale censorship episodes that occurred early this year. None of the data analysis studies described above were designed to detect phenomena at a country granularity, nor to integrate traffic, topology, and routing data, although their techniques could complement the ones we present in this paper to improve detection of country-wide network disruptions. Moreover, while BGP data has often been used to monitor network infrastructure dynamics during outages, we are not aware of any previous work using unsolicited (sometimes called darknet or telescope) traffic to monitor such outages, although we proposed it in March 2011 [10]. Our approach facilitated the discovery of important technical aspects of the outages not previously reported: the combination of packet filtering techniques with BGP disruption, and disruption of satellite Internet connectivity.

4. DATA SOURCES AND METHODOLOGY

4.1 Internet Geography

To properly observe the effects of a blackout in a given country, we first need to identify which Internet numbering resources are under the control of, or related to, those countries. In this section we explain how we used geolocation data to select the relevant set of IP addresses, BGP prefixes, and AS numbers to monitor for visibility into Egypt and Libya during the blackout intervals.

4.1.1 IP Addresses

Five Regional Internet Registries (RIRs) manage the allocation and registration of Internet resources (IP prefixes and autonomous system numbers) to entities within five distinct regions of the world, and publish lists of the Internet resources they delegate, which include the country hosting the headquarters of the receiving entity. Egypt and Libya are in the AfriNIC (Africa's) region [1]. The first row of Table 1 lists the number of IPv4 addresses delegated to Egypt and Libya by AfriNIC. Additionally, IP addresses nominally allocated to a different country may be used within Egypt and Libya if a foreign ISP provides Internet access in those countries. The second row of Table 1 lists the IP addresses geolocated in Egypt and Libya according to the MaxMind GeoLite Country database [40]. We used these two sources of data to construct the list of IP address ranges (prefixes) that geolocated to Egypt and Libya.

Although there are accuracy issues in all geolocation databases [27, 46, 52], at a country granularity these databases almost always agree with (sometimes because they are based on) the RIR-delegation file information. Countries with either low Internet penetration or a small population (Libya has both) may only have few IPs officially RIR-delegated to them, in which case IP geolocation database information can provide useful additional information. Satellite con-

	Egypt	Libya
AfriNIC delegated IPs	5,762,816	299,008
MaxMind GeoLite IPs	5,710,240	307,225

Table 1: IPv4 address space delegated to Egypt (as of January 24, 2011) and Libya (as of February 15, 2011) by AfriNIC (top half) as well as additional IPv4 address ranges associated with the two countries based on MaxMind GeoLite database (as of January 2011).

nectivity, which at least one ISP uses to serve Libya, is another source of IP geolocation discrepancy.

4.1.2 AS Numbers and BGP-announced prefixes

Once we had derived a set of IP address ranges to monitor, we mapped these to BGP-announced prefixes and ASes announcing those prefixes, using a database constructed from publicly available BGP data from RouteViews and RIPE NCC RIS [6,59] for the week preceding the outages, up to and including the first day of the outage. The allocated address ranges might not map precisely to a BGP prefix boundary, since ASes may implement complex routing policies to accomplish traffic engineering and other business objectives, which may involve splitting BGP prefixes into smaller chunks, or aggregating prefixes into larger chunks to reduce routing table sizes. Thus, different views of the routing system (BGP monitors) may have different BGP prefixes covering a given set of IP addresses. Once we gather BGP events within the time window we want to observe, we compute the set of *covering* prefixes P for address space S as follows:

- We look up the address space in the BGP database described above, to find an exactly matching BGP prefix;
- We find all the more specific (strict subset, longer) prefixes of this prefix;
- if the two previous steps yielded no prefix, we retrieve the longest BGP prefix entirely containing the address space S.

For each AS we show results only for the IP ranges or BGP prefixes that are solely related to the country under analysis, e.g., traffic whose source addresses are included in prefixes announced by that AS *and* are geolocated or delegated to the country under analysis.

4.2 BGP Data

BGP routing changes can rapidly induce global effects, including coarse-grained filtering that may be indistinguishable from complete physical disconnection of infrastructure. Using BGP data in conjunction with data-plane measurements such as traceroute or traffic flows can yield a rich understanding of the type of censorship strategy being used.

The two main sources of BGP updates used throughout our analysis are the already mentioned Route Views Project [59] and RIPE NCC's Routing Information Service (RIS) [6], respectively maintained by University of Oregon and RIPE NCC. Both services rely on routers that establish BGP peering sessions with many ISPs around the world. The available data reveal a broad and global though necessarily incomplete view of BGP connectivity over time, at a announced-prefix granularity. We analyzed this data at the finest possible time granularity – BGP updates – to detect and isolate events observed during the outages. However, BGP updates only provide information about *changes* in routing state. Each route collector also periodically dumps a snapshot of its entire control plane table, called a *RIB*, containing all known routing information related to prefixes that are reachable at that point in time. We used these periodic dumps in conjunction with the fine-grained updates to track a precise view of prefix reachability over the duration of the outage intervals.

Each source of data also has a graphical tool to query for specific prefixes, BGPlay [58] for Route Views and BGPviz [4] for RIS. An online service called REX [5] allows coarse-grained analysis of historical BGP events in RIS data, based on snapshots taken every 8 hours of the RIB table dumps. (Routeviews RIBs are dumped every two hours.)

To perform chronological analysis of the outages, we first identified the time window during which disconnection activity was observed, using previous reports [16, 17], BGPlay and BGPviz. We extended this window to one hour before and one hour after the main events we observed to detect possible early symptoms of the outage and late reconnection patterns. We used the last RIB table dumps from both RouteViews and RIS just before this interval as the starting point, and used BGP updates and subsequent BGP table dumps to reconstruct the routing history during the time window under examination.

For each prefix we processed the downloaded data to build a set of routing histories, one for each route collector peer (that is, an AS feeding its BGP updates to a route collector). We marked a prefix as *disappeared* if it was withdrawn during the blackout interval for each of the above routing histories, i.e., no longer observable from any route collector peer, and remained so for the duration of the interval. We chose the earliest of those withdrawals as the event representing the initial disconnection of the prefix. This approach provides an overview of the prefixes going down over time, as well as the first signs of disconnection for each withdrawn prefix.

We used a similar approach to study the end of the outage, focusing instead on when BGP prefixes become reachable again via announcements seen in BGP updates. BGPlay and BGPviz were also useful to visualize the transition periods, to see which prefixes were still visible as the outage information propagated and to see peers reconverge to secondary backup paths. We visualized the reconnection as well, with peers reverting to primary paths as prefixes were re-announced.

Note that the collected data is subject to uncertainty, especially regarding timing of events, so we cannot obtain a perfect understanding of BGP dynamics. BGP messages are sometimes delayed (aggregated) by routers in order to minimize control traffic. Furthermore, router clocks are not necessarily synchronized, so one cannot be sure of the exact interleaving sequence of events occurring at different routers. However, empirical analysis of data coming from different collectors generally shows good correlation in terms of time values. While imperfect, our methodology provides a consistent way to approximate the timing of BGP withdrawals during an outage.

4.3 Darknet Traffic

Unsolicited one-way Internet traffic, also called *Internet background radiation (IBR)* [45], has been used for years to study malicious activity on the Internet including worms, DoS attacks, and scanning address space looking for vulnerabilities to exploit. Such a vast number of computers generate such background radiation, mostly unbeknownst to their legitimate users, that the resulting traffic aggregate has proven a useful source of data for observing characteristics of the malware itself [22, 42, 43] not revealed by other types of data.

Researchers observe IBR traffic using *network telescopes*, often called *darknets* if the IP addresses are not being used by devices. We collected and analyzed traffic arriving at the UCSD network telescope [7], which observes a mostly unassigned /8, that is,

1/256th of the entire IPv4 address space. We used the same IP-AS databases described in Section 4.1 to determine the levels of unsolicited traffic throughout the outages in Egypt and Libya. Although the unsolicited traffic from these countries exhibited a typical diurnal pattern, sudden changes in the packet rate suggest start and end times of several of the outages (see Figure 2).

There are three primary causes of IBR traffic: (i) *backscatter* from spoofed denial-of-service (DoS) attacks, (ii) scans, or (iii) bugs and misconfiguration [45]. Different types of IBR traffic induce separate sources of packet rate dynamics, which can heavily affect the amount of traffic observed from a specific country to the network telescope. Our methodology identifies and separates these sources of IBR-induced dynamics to avoid misinterpreting them.

Packets associated with denial-of-service attacks represent a special category, because they cause substantial packet rate variation, especially for countries with few IP addresses such as Egypt and Libya. A DoS attack attempts to overwhelm a victim with traffic or transaction requests in order to reduce or prevent his ability to serve legitimate requests. When the source IP addresses in attacking packets are randomly spoofed, the response packets (e.g. *SYN-ACK* TCP packets in reply to *SYNs* from the attacker) are sent back to the spoofed addresses, producing *backscatter*, which will be captured by telescopes [43] that happen to contain (and thus observe traffic to) those spoofed addresses. To identify and characterize these attacks we used the methodology in [43], separating potential backscatter packet flows (i.e. TCP packets with SYN-ACK or RST flags on, ICMP echo replies) by sender (potential victims of the attack), then classifying any such flows above predefined volume or duration thresholds as backscatter reflecting a denial-of-service attack. Of course, DoS attacks to a country in civil unrest may themselves be of interest; we did notice attacks on some government web sites approximately when the protests began and a short time before the outage (see Sections 5.1.3 and 5.2.3.)

Automated (e.g. from worms) or manually initiated random scanning of address space in search of victims is another component of IBR [22,42]. On 21 November 2008, the amount of unsolicited traffic grew dramatically with the advent of the Conficker worm [9], which widely infected Windows hosts and actively scanned for hosts to infect on TCP port 445. Sufficiently pervasive network scanning such as done by Conficker reveals surprisingly detailed insights into global Internet behavior. In particular, geolocation of all IP source addresses of such scanning packets makes it easy to detect country-wide outages [10], since an entire country disappears from this category of traffic. We identified Conficker scanning traffic by selecting TCP SYN packets with destination port 445 and packet size 48 bytes.

Misconfiguration of systems can also induce IBR traffic, for example by setting the wrong IP address on a DNS or proxy server. Bugs in network applications and router firmware and software e.g., getting byte ordering wrong, can assign incorrect network addresses to a device, triggering unsolicited traffic in response.

We further analyzed the unsolicited traffic by Autonomous System (AS) coming from within each of the two countries, revealing AS-specific behavior. IP address space that has been withdrawn from the global BGP routing table will not be able to receive traffic from the Internet default-free zone anymore, but may be able to successfully send outbound traffic in the absence of packet filtering. Analysis of background radiation, especially Conficker-like scanning, reveals some of this leaked traffic.

4.4 Active forward path probing

We made limited use of active measurements taken during the outages in Egypt and Libya, toward address space in these countries. The measurements consisted both of ad-hoc measurements using standard ping and traceroute, and of structured global IPv4 address probing from CAIDA's IPv4 Routed /24 Topology Dataset [28] collected on CAIDA's Ark infrastructure [2]. We used the IPv4 topology data set to observe surprising 2-way connectivity surviving the outage intervals that span more then a day. This data does not provide sufficient granularity to analyze the shorter outages due to Ark's low probing rate (one cycle of /24 IPv4 prefixes in about 3 days) and the relatively few IP prefixes in each country.

5. ANALYSIS

In this section we present our analysis of the Internet blackouts from the perspectives of the control plane (BGP data) and the data plane (traffic and traceroute data). Section 5.1 discusses the outage in Egypt; Section 5.2 discusses the several disconnections in Libya. To prevent unintentional harm to those involved in these episodes of censorship or their circumvention, we have anonymized most AS numbers in this paper as described in Appendix A.

5.1 Egypt

5.1.1 Overview

According to Greg Mahlknecht's cable map web site [39], which might have dated information, Egypt's Internet infrastructure is dominated by state ownership, consisting primarily of a few large players with international connectivity through the major submarine cable systems that run through the Suez canal. Most, if not all, submarine fiber-optic circuits are backhauled to the Ramses Exchange [62], which is not only the main connection facility for the Egyptian-government-controlled telecommunications provider, but also the location of the largest Internet exchange point in North Africa or the Middle East. Both the small number of parties involved in international connectivity, and the physical connectivity under control of the state telecommunications provider, facilitate manipulation of the system by a state actor, as shown by the events described below.

Renesys reported that on January 27, around 22:34:00 GMT, they observed the *"virtually simultaneous withdrawal of all routes to Egyptian networks in the Internet's global routing table"* [16]. The packet rate of unsolicited traffic from Egypt seen by the UCSD telescope (Figure 2) suddenly decreased at almost the same time, on January 27 around 22:32:00 GMT. In terms of BGP, the methodology explained in Section 4 identifies the outage as a sequence of routing events between approximately 22:12:00 GMT and 22:34:00 GMT. The outage lasted for more than five days, during which more active BGP IPv4 prefixes in Egypt were withdrawn. In Figure 3 each step represents a set of IPv4 prefixes at the point in time when they first disappeared from the network.

The UCSD darknet traffic returned to packet rates comparable to those preceding the outage at 10:00:00 GMT on February 2. The unsolicited traffic level from Egypt to the telescope was roughly consistent with our BGP analysis, which found that the first set of re-announcements of Egyptian connectivity after the crisis occurred around 09:29:31 GMT. Figure 4 shows the BGP connectivity reappearing.

5.1.2 Outages in detail

BGP data reveals a dramatic drop in reachability for many Egyptian IPv4 prefixes during the outage. It is not obvious which event should be considered the first sign of the outage. The leftmost end of the graph in Figure 3 shows 2928 IPv4 prefixes visible via BGP at 20:00:00 GMT. A noticeable loss of connectivity is first seen by RouteViews and RIS route collectors on January 27 at 20:24:11

GMT, related to 15 IPv4 prefixes routed by EgAS2.[3]. Further losses of BGP connectivity are visible in the next two hours, summing up to 236 withdrawn IPv4 prefixes. The biggest disruption then appears as an almost vertical drop in Figure 3, with the initial step at 22:12:26 GMT, after which roughly 2500 prefixes disappear within a 20 minute interval. At 23:30:00 GMT only 176 prefixes remain visible.

Figure 5 shows the same sequence of events separated by the six main Egyptian ASes. Although the image seems to suggest a time sequence for the interleaving BGP withdrawals, we can make no safe assumption on the chronology of underlying decisions.

Contrary to IPv4 prefixes, there was no major change in visibility for IPv6 prefixes. Of the six IPv6 prefixes in AfriNIC's delegated file, only one is seen in RIS and this prefix of length /32 is announced by IntAS1, a major international carrier. This prefix stayed visible during the outage, as did all its more specific prefixes seen in RIS (20 /48s announced by EgAS4 and 1 /48 by EgAS6).

Figure 6 shows a breakdown of the traffic observed by the UCSD network telescope in three categories: *conficker*, *backscatter*, and *other*. Conficker refers to TCP SYN packets with destination port 445 and packet size 48 bytes. While we assume that these packets are generated by systems infected by the Conficker worm scanning for new victims, we cannot be absolutely certain, although our inferences are valid if the majority of packets satisfy this assumption. The most important implication of the assumption is that the source IP addresses are not spoofed; if they were, the geolocation mapping would be meaningless.

The backscatter category of traffic requires careful treatment. When an attacker uses fake source IP addresses in a denial-of-service attack targeting a victim in the address space we are trying to observe, backscatter traffic from the victim IP addresses can increase suddenly and dramatically, jeopardizing our inferences about background traffic levels coming from this address space. So our methodology must identify and filter out this backscatter traffic.

The *other* category represents all other packets composing the background radiation [45] captured by the network telescope: worms, generic scanning and probing activity, misconfigurations, etc.

Figure 6 reveals the diurnal patterns of activity in Conficker traffic, which are typical of (infected) PCs that are not kept on 24 hours per day. Conficker traffic is the dominant component, and stays partially alive even during the outage, for two reasons: (i) some prefixes are still visible via BGP and (ii) outbound connectivity still works for some networks. For a given network, BGP withdrawals are a consequence of either propagation of a withdrawal from elsewhere in the network, or a data-plane failure immediately adjacent to the router. In the former case the network is unreachable from the outside world, but may still be able to send packets in the outbound direction. In the same figure, the *backscatter* traffic has some spikes related to a couple of denial-of-service attacks which we discuss in Section 5.1.3.

The *other* category of traffic in Figure 6 is most interesting: soon after the Egyptian networks are again BGP-reachable, the packet rate of this traffic grows much higher than before the outage. By analyzing traffic from the entire Internet reaching the UCSD darknet, we found that a large UDP/TCP scan targeted toward a specific service was conducted from thousands of hosts all around the world.[4] The diurnal pattern suggests this traffic was a coordinated scan operated by a botnet, which started on January 31st (based on global traffic to the telescope) and lasted several days. It looks like the Egyptian hosts infected by the botnet lost communication with the botnet control channel during the outage, but after BGP connectivity returned, they started to participate in the coordinated scan. The interesting insight is that scanning activities under botnet control cannot operate in the absence of bidirectional connectivity (since the bots cannot communicate with their controller) but random scans from worm-infected hosts still do, and are still visible by the telescope when the senders are not BGP-reachable but still connected to the network. Such gaps between what the telescope can see globally versus from a specific country can help define criteria for the automated detection and classification of such events.

More than 3165 IPv4 prefixes are delegated to Egypt and managed by 51 ASes. In order to sketch per-AS observations by the network telescope, we classify the traffic observed from Egyptian IP addresses by the AS responsible for ("originating") the IP addresses. Figure 7 shows the packet rate of traffic observed by the telescope from two major ASes in Egypt: EgStateAS, and EgAS4. EgStateAS is the largest Egyptian Internet service provider.

Figure 5 shows that many of the prefixes announced by EgStateAS via BGP were withdrawn on or shortly after January 27. A small set

[3]AS numbers anonymized, see Appendix A

[4]The UDP packets sent during this scan have specific properties that allow us to recognize them, but details are beyond the scope of the paper

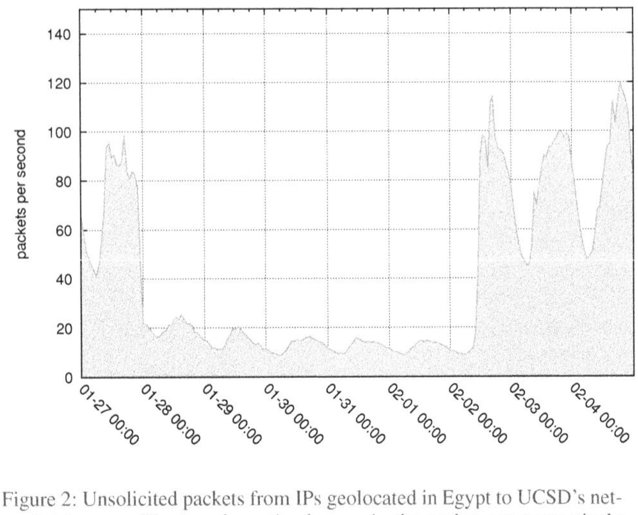

Figure 2: Unsolicited packets from IPs geolocated in Egypt to UCSD's network telescope. The two dramatic changes in the packet rate respectively match the withdrawals and reannoucements of BGP routes to Egyptian networks.

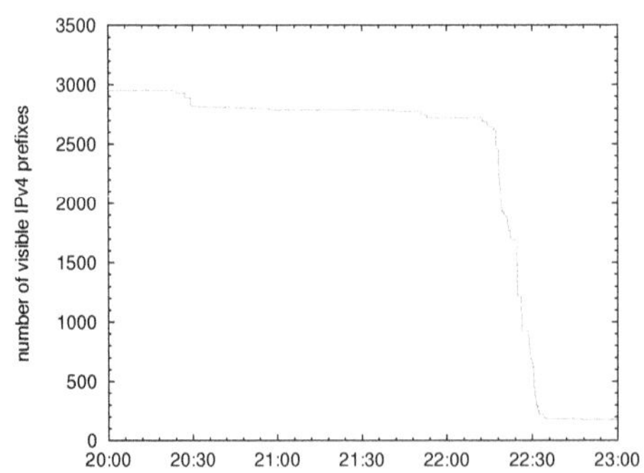

Figure 3: Disconnection of Egyptian IPv4 prefixes via BGP during the outage on January 27, based on data from RouteViews and RIPE NCC's RIS. For each disconnected prefix, the red line drops down at the instant in which a lasting (i.e., not temporarily fluctuating) BGP withdrawal is first observed.

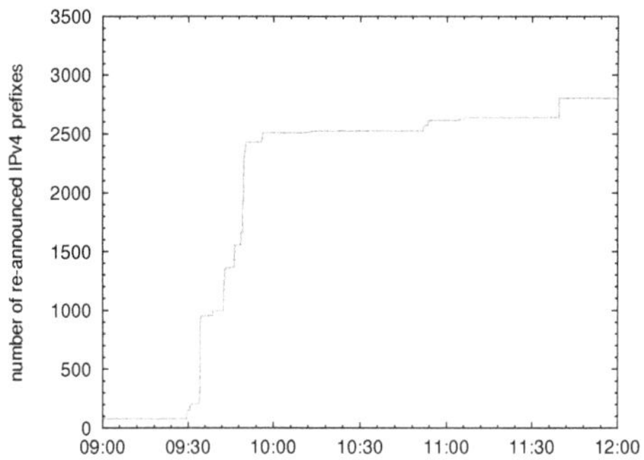

Figure 4: Re-announcement of Egyptian IPv4 prefixes via BGP at the end of the outage on February 2, based on data from RouteViews and RIPE NCC's RIS. For each re-announced prefix, the red line goes up at the instant in which a stable BGP announcement is first detected.

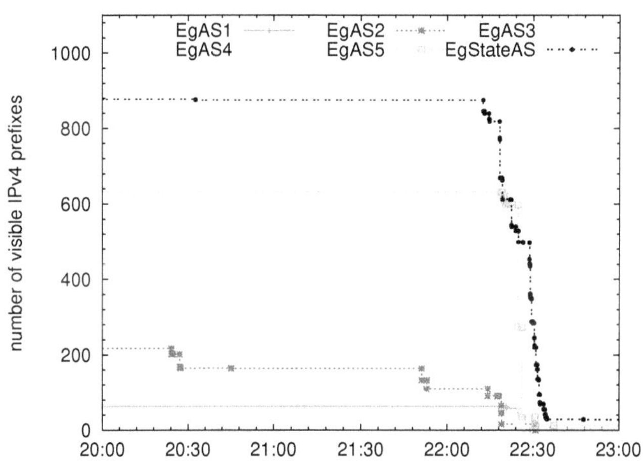

Figure 5: Visibility of main Egyptian Autonomous Systems via BGP during the outage on January 27 (based on data from RouteViews and RIPE NCC's RIS). Each AS is plotted independently; as in Figure 3, each line drops down at the instant in which a lasting (i.e., not temporarily fluctuating) BGP withdrawal is first observed.

of IPv4 prefixes remained visible during the outage, including some not announced in the previous months. For this reason we still observe darknet traffic coming from this AS, whereas the prefixes of EgAS4 were all withdrawn. A closer look at EgStateAS reveals that several of the visible IPv4 prefixes were reachable through IntAS2 or IntAS3, either because they were already served by those two Autonomous Systems or they rerouted to paths using those ASes after the massive disconnection. Figures 8(a) and 8(b) illustrate this behavior, where a prefix previously using IntAS4 as its only externally visible upstream switches to IntAS2 once the outage begins.

Finally, we ran ad-hoc active measurements during the outage to some related prefixes. In particular, we sent ICMP echo requests on 1 February at 09:00:00 GMT from GARR (the Italian Research and Academic Network), the replies to which revealed that at least three IPv4 prefixes, among those announced by EgStateAS and not withdrawn during the outage, were actually reachable. Traceroute probes simultaneously issued toward the same destinations went through IntAS2.

Another interesting case is that of EgAS7. As also reported by Renesys [16], the 83 prefixes managed by this AS remained untouched for several days during the Egyptian Internet outage. There was speculation that this AS retained Internet connectivity due to its high-profile, economically-relevant customers, including the Egyptian stock exchange, the National Bank of Egypt, and the Commercial International Bank of Egypt. However, at a certain point the censorship was tightened in Egypt: we observed the withdrawals of all 83 prefixes, almost simultaneously, on Monday, January 31, 20:46:48 GMT until the end of the outage, when all the Egyptian routes were restored. Figure 9 shows a perfect match between our telescope observation of Egyptian traffic from EgAS7 and the BGP reachability of its prefixes.

Figure 10 plots reachability statistics of active measurements from CAIDA's Ark infrastructure, revealing that during the outage, 1% of measurements to IPv4 prefixes geolocated in Egypt reached a responding destination, whereas on normal days it is closer to 16-17%. Examination of the specific IP addresses that retained bi-directional connectivity throughout the outage confirms that they all match BGP prefixes that were not withdrawn.

At the end of the outage, a steady reconnection is observed via

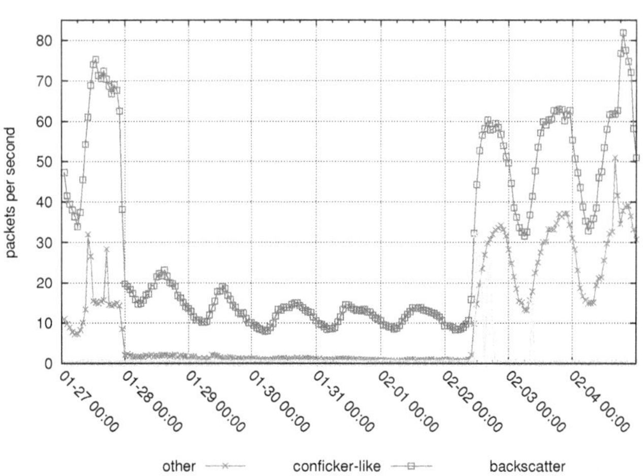

Figure 6: Categories of unsolicited packets from IPs geolocated in Egypt to UCSD's network telescope: other, conficker-like, backscatter. Spikes in backscatter traffic reflect large denial-of-service attacks against hosts in Egypt.

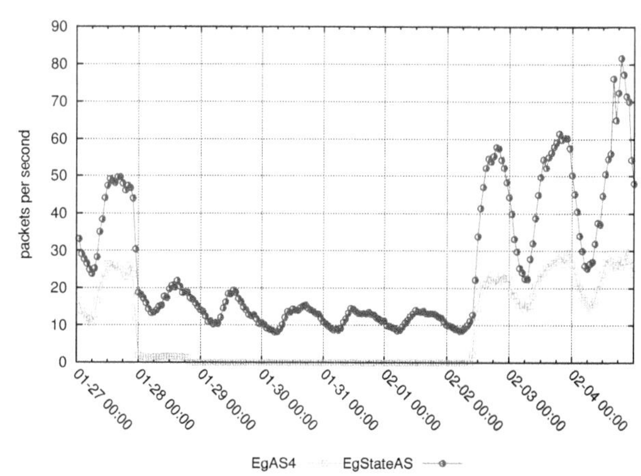

Figure 7: Unsolicited packets from IPs geolocated in Egypt to UCSD network telescope: EgAS4, EgStateAS. Traffic from EgStateAS is still significant during the outage because: (i) some prefixes remain visible; (ii) some networks probably retain outbound connectivity. The decay observable in the first days of the outage matches the progressive withdrawal of further routes.

BGP. Figures 4 and 11 respectively show time-series of BGP announcements in aggregate and for each of the six larger ASes. Figure 11 shows each AS re-injecting sets of previously withdrawn routes, with most of them globally visible within 20 minutes. The process began with a first step at 09:29:31 GMT; by 09:56:11 GMT more than 2500 Egyptian IPv4 prefixes are back in BGP tables around the world. BGP data suggests that the key decisions on the outage were quite synchronized, and produced dramatic globally observable consequences.

5.1.3 *Denial-of-service attacks*

Analysis of the UCSD darknet traffic also allowed us to identify some denial-of-service attacks to institutional sites of the Egyptian government, which because of the timing and victims look strongly

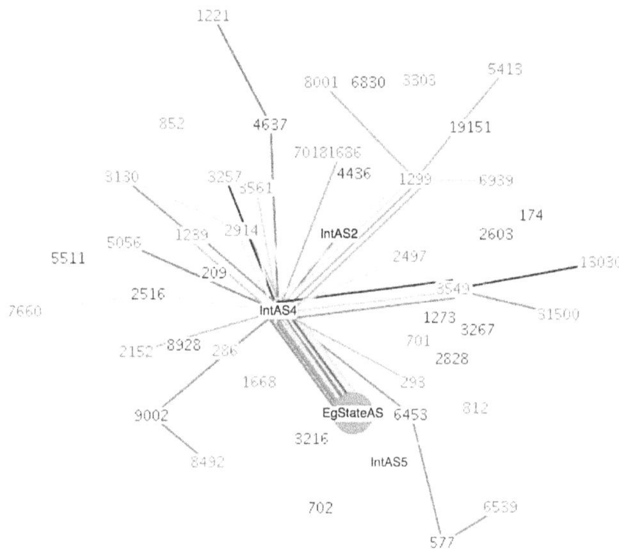

(a)

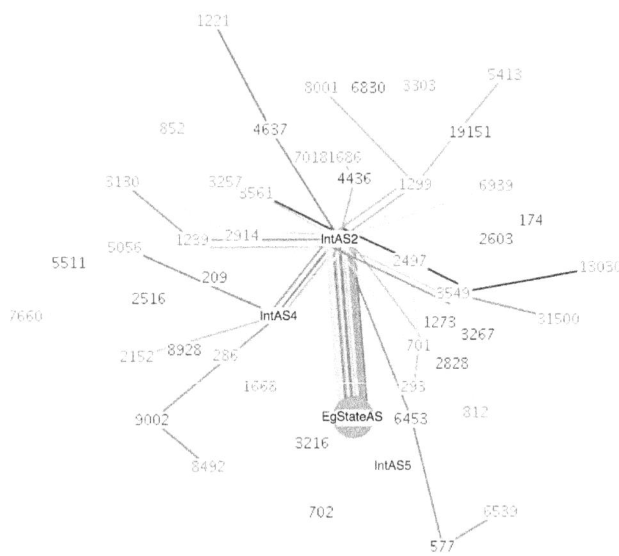

(b)

Figure 8: BGPlay snapshot showing the reachability graph of a prefix owned by EgStateAS before (a) and after (b) the outage on January 27. Each color represents the path used by an AS to reach the target prefix.

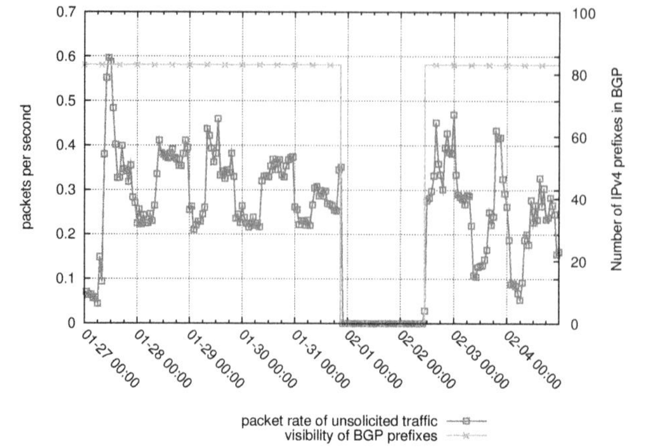

Figure 9: The case of EgAS7: a perfect match across data sources: unsolicited traffic to UCSD's network telescope vs. BGP reachability of its 83 prefixes.

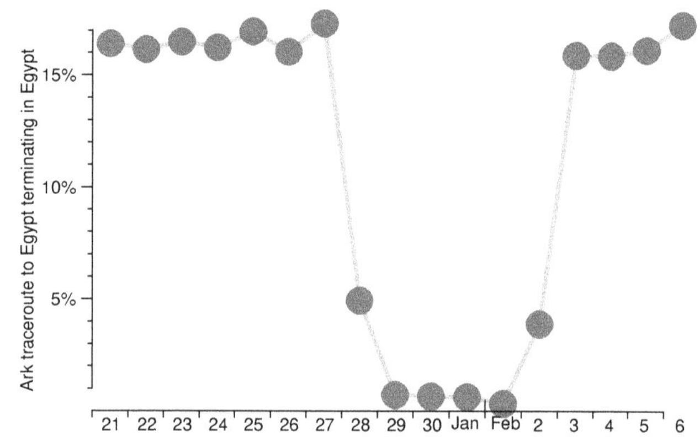

Figure 10: Fraction of Ark traceroutes that terminated (either at the destination or the last reachable hop) in Egypt. The few IP addresses that retained bi-directional connectivity (required for traceroute) throughout the outage were in BGP prefixes that were not withdrawn.

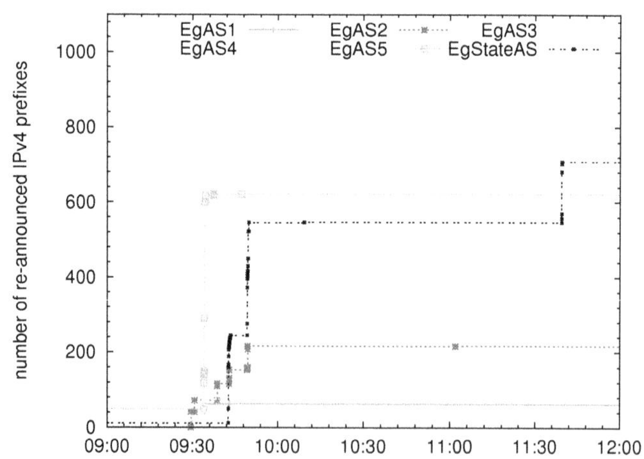

Figure 11: Reconnection of main Egyptian Autonomous Systems via BGP at the end of outage on February 2, based on data from RouteViews and RIPE NCC's RIS. Each AS is plotted independently; as in Figure 4, each line rises at the instant in which a stable BGP announcement from that AS is first observed.

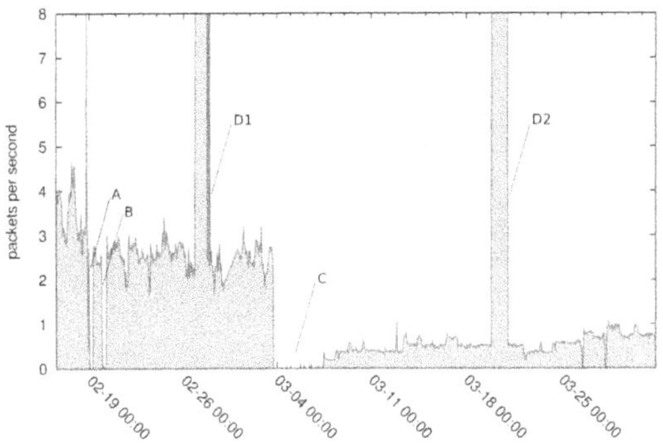

Figure 12: UCSD darknet's traffic coming from Libya. Labels A, B, C indicate the three outages. Spikes labeled D1 and D2 are due to backscatter from two denial-of-service attacks.

related to protests in the country. The web site of the Ministry of Communications (*mcit.gov.eg*) was attacked with a randomly-spoofed DoS attack just before the outage started, on January 26 at different times: 15:47 GMT (for 16 minutes), 16:55 GMT (17 minutes), and 21:09 GMT (53 minutes). Analysis of the *backscatter* traffic to the darknet allows estimation of the intensity of the attack in terms of packet rate, indicating average packet rates between 20k and 50k packets per second.

On February 2 the web site of the Egyptian Ministry of Interior (*www.moiegypt.gov.eg*) was targeted by two DoS attacks just after the end of the censorship from 11:05 to 13:39 GMT and from 15:08 to 17:17 GMT. The same IP address was attacked another time the day after, from 08:06 to 08:42 GMT. In this case the estimated packet rates were smaller, around 7k packets per second.

5.2 Libya

5.2.1 Overview

Libya's Internet infrastructure is even more prone to manipulation then Egypt's, judging from its physical structure. International connectivity is provided by only two submarine cables, both ending in Tripoli [39], and the Internet infrastructure is dominated by a single, state owned, AS. We only found two other ASes having a small presence in Libya, as described in Section 5.2.2.

In Libya three different outages in early 2011 were identified and publicly documented (Figure 1). Figure 12 shows the traffic observed by the UCSD network telescope from Libya throughout an interval encompassing the outages. The points labeled A, B and C indicate three different blackout episodes; points D1 and D2 refer to two denial-of-service attacks discussed in Section 5.2.3. Toward the right of the graph it is difficult to interpret what is really happening in Libya because of the civil war.

5.2.2 Outages in detail

The first two outages happened during two consecutive nights. Figure 13(a) shows a more detailed view of these two outages as observed by the UCSD telescope. Figure 13(b) shows BGP data over the same interval: in both cases, within a few minutes, 12 out of the 13 IPv4 prefixes associated with IP address ranges officially delegated to Libya were withdrawn. These twelve IPv4 prefixes were announced by LyStateAS, the local telecom operator, while the remaining IPv4 prefix was managed by IntAS2. As of May 2011, there were no IPv6 prefixes in AfriNIC's delegated file for Libya. The MaxMind IP geolocation database further puts 12 non-contiguous IP ranges in Libya, all part of an encompassing IPv4 prefix announced by SatAS1, which provides satellite services in the Middle East, Asia and Africa. The covering IPv4 prefix also contained 180 IP ranges in several other countries predominantly in the Middle East. We considered this additional AS because the UCSD darknet generally observed a significant amount of unsolicited traffic coming from IPs in those 12 ranges before the first outage (about 50k packets each day). This level of background traffic indicates a population of customers using PCs likely infected by Conficker or other malware, allowing inference of network conditions. Traffic from this network also provided evidence of what happened to Libyan Internet connections based on satellite systems not managed by the local telecom provider.

Comparing Figures 13(a) and 13(b) reveals a different behavior that conflicts with previous reports [17]: the second outage was not entirely caused by BGP withdrawals. The BGP shutdown began on February 19 around 21:58.55 UTC, exactly matching the sharp decrease of darknet traffic from Libya (and in accordance with reports on Libyan traffic seen by Arbor Networks [31]) but it ended approximately one hour later, at 23:02.52. In contrast, the Internet outage as shown by the telescope data and reported by the news [17] lasted until approximately February 20 at 6:12 UTC. This finding suggests that a different disruption technique – a packet-blocking strategy apparently adopted subsequently in the third outage and recognized by the rest of the world – was already being used dur-

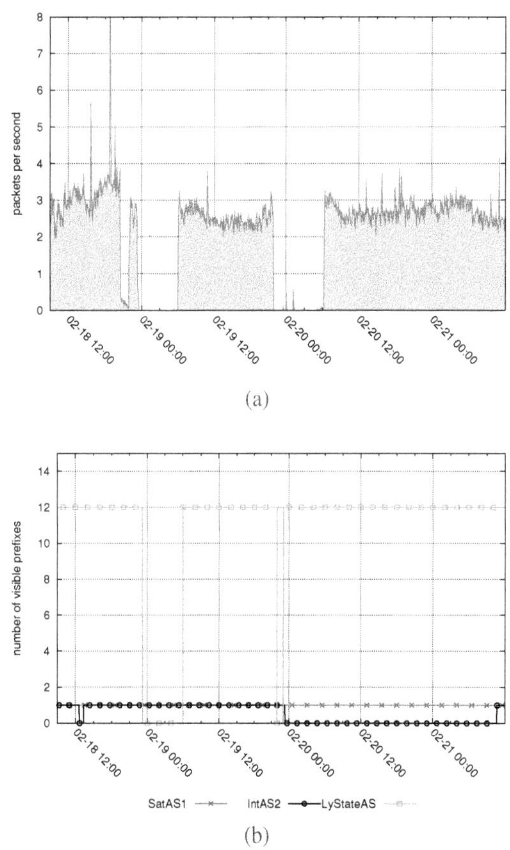

Figure 13: The first two Libyan outages: (a) unsolicited traffic to UCSD darknet coming from Libya; (b) visibility of Libyan IPv4 prefixes in BGP data from RouteViews and RIPE NCC RIS collectors. Note that the control-plane and data-plane observations of connectivity do not match, suggesting that different techniques for censorship were being used during different intervals.

ing this second outage. The firewall configuration may have been set up during the BGP shutdown and the routes were restored once the packet blocking was put in place.

Figure 13(b) shows that the IPv4 prefix managed by SatAS1, the satellite company, was not withdrawn, which seems reasonable considering that this IPv4 prefix was managed by a company outside of Libya. But the darknet traffic from both the local telecom and SatAS1 plummeted when the two outages occurred (see Figure 14). A tiny amount of traffic still reached UCSD's darknet from SatAS1 IPs in Libya, especially during the second outage (Figure 14), suggesting that the government could have used signal jamming to disrupt the satellite service for Internet connectivity, as they did for satellite TV news and mobile communication services [47,54].

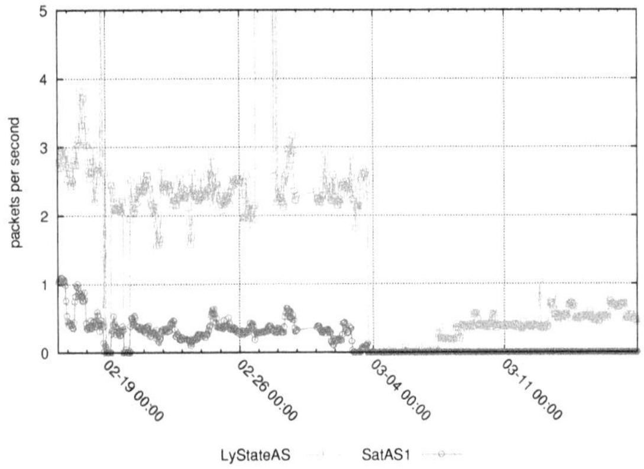

Figure 14: UCSD darknet's traffic coming from Libya: traffic from selected ASes. The connectivity of satellite-based provider SatAS1 was probably disrupted through deliberate jamming of the satellite signal.

As for IntAS2, there was not enough unsolicited traffic reaching the darknet preceding and during the outages to usefully analyze, likely due to lack of end users in this network. However, the only Libyan IPv4 prefix announced by IntAS2 was withdrawn twice: (i) on the same day of the first outage but several hours before it started (for approximately 40 minutes, from 12:38.58 to 12:41.25 UTC); (ii) approximately 10 minutes after the BGP routes of the local telecom were withdrawn in the second outage. The matching times in the latter case suggest a form of coordination or forcing the common loss of BGP connectivity. Figure 13(b) shows that the BGP disruption of the Libyan IPv4 prefix of IntAS2 lasted for about two days (from February 19 23:20.22 UTC to February 21 10:38.15 UTC), far longer than the duration of the second outage.

The third outage in Libya happened several days later. We verified, by analyzing all BGP updates collected by RouteViews and RIPE NCC RIS, that all BGP routes stayed up without interruption. However, Figure 16 shows that the darknet traffic sharply dropped at March 3 16:57:00 UTC. Perhaps not surprisingly given their earlier experimenting with different censorship techniques, the third and longest Libyan outage was not caused by BGP disruption, but by packet filtering, confirmed by other sources [18].

While probing in the Ark data was not frequent enough to see the first two Libyan outages, the third, and longer outage caused a significant drop in the fraction of reachable destinations in IPv4 prefixes geolocated in Libya, as seen in Figure 15. The remaining reachable destinations in Libya were both from wired and satellite-based ASes, showing that bidirectional connectivity for some hosts in both types of networks was possible during this longer outage, although the drop in reachable destinations suggests two-way connectivity was available for significantly fewer hosts.

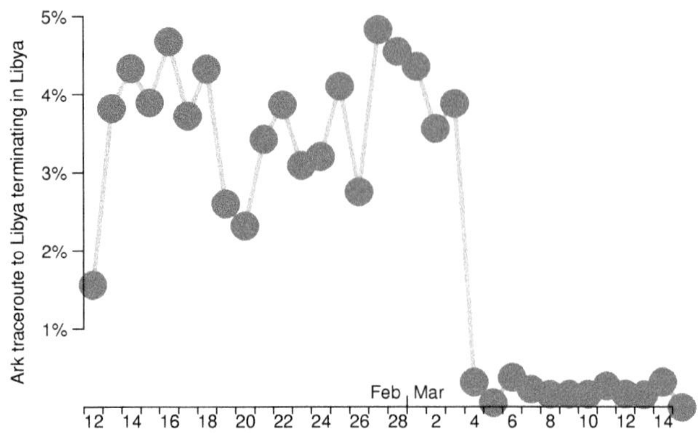

Figure 15: Fraction of Ark traceroutes that terminated (either at the destination or the last reachable hop) in Libya.

Our analysis revealed three discoveries:

- We established the potential of network telescopes to detect country-wide filtering phenomena, even phenomena that cannot be detected by monitoring BGP connectivity. The sharp decrease in traffic shown in Figure 16 suggests that a simple change point detection algorithm would automatically raise an alert in this case, similar to how others used sharp drops in observed BGP announcements.
- We confirmed that packet filtering techniques for censorship were used, because we still had visibility of a few packets from a few subnets, suggesting that perhaps the regime wanted to preserve connectivity for some sites.
- We discovered that packet filtering techniques were also used for previous outages that were reported as BGP-only disruptions. Moreover, we captured a retrospective of what happened, also explaining the short gap (February 18 from 20:24 to 21:57 UTC) in traffic visible on the UCSD network telescope (Figure 13(a)) a few hours before the first outage. This short drop in traffic was also visible in data published by others [31], but was never discussed. We verified (Figure 13(b)) that all the BGP routes were up during this gap in observed traffic, which suggests that Libya was already testing firewall blocking during this interval. The fact that the first two out-

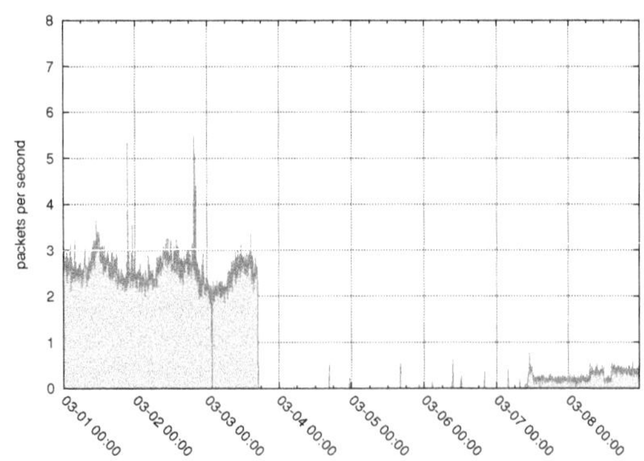

Figure 16: UCSD darknet's traffic coming from Libya: detail of the third outage. The small but visible amount of traffic during the third outage (coming from a small number of /24 networks) is consistent with the use of selective packet filtering, instead of BGP withdrawals, to effect the outage.

ages were BGP-based may indicate that the censors were unsatisfied with the results of these tests, and used BGP-based disruption for the first two outages as an alternative while they further tested packet filtering techniques.

5.2.3 *Denial of service attacks*

In addition to reflecting the outages, our analysis of the UCSD darknet traffic shows two denial-of-service attacks to systems located in Libya. Because these attacks used randomly spoofed source addresses, we do not know if the attackers were inside or outside the country (or both), or how many machines were used to source the attack. The first attack, labeled D1 in Figure 12, started on February 26 at 20:27 UTC, targeted a few IPs in a subnet of the Libyan Telecom (ltt.ly) and lasted approximately 24 hours and 19 minutes. Analysis of the *backscatter* traffic allows us to estimate an average packet rate of 30390 packets per second.

The second attack, labeled D2, started on Saturday March 19 2011 at 20:31 UTC and the victim was a single IP assigned to the Libyan telecom provider. The attack lasted for about 27 hours and 51 minutes with an estimated average packet rate of 30280 packets per second.

6. DISCUSSION AND CONCLUSION

Political events in the Middle East this year, as well as political discussions in the U.S. Congress [55] have inspired popular as well as technical interest in possible mechanisms, impact, circumvention, and detection of Internet filtering at different layers. Our study of Egypt's and Libya's government-ordered Internet outages have revealed a number of challenges and opportunities for the scientific study of Internet filtering and disruption. Given the growing interest and expanding circumstances that will give rise to large-scale Internet filtering behaviors, and the need to inform policy development with the best available empirical data and analysis of such behavior, we believe the topic will necessarily merit its own discipline. This study offers an intitial contribution in this direction.

We used multiple types of large-scale data in this analysis, all from data sets already available to academic researchers. The first type of data – BGP interdomain routing *control plane* data – was already widely analyzed and reported on during the outages. Our analysis of BGP data suggested that key decisions related to the outage were quite synchronized, and produced dramatic, globally observable consequences.

The second type of data – unsolicited *data plane* traffic to unassigned address space (darknet or telescope data) – we have not seen previously used for this purpose, and we were surprised at the range of insights it yielded. Unsolicited and unwanted traffic on the Internet has grown to such significant levels that instrumentation capturing such traffic can illuminate many different types of macroscopic events, including but not limited to broad-scale packet-filtering-based censorship, which is not observable in BGP data. From this unidirectional traffic data we detected what we believe were Libya's attempts to test firewall-based blocking before they executed more aggressive BGP-based disconnection. This data also revealed Libya's use of such packet filtering technology during the second BGP-based connection. Interestingly, the backscatter component of this traffic data enabled us to identify some denial-of-service attacks against Egyptian government web sites before and after the censorship interval.

We also made limited use of active ping and macroscopic traceroute measurements toward address space in these countries during the outages. We used CAIDA's IPv4 topology data set to observe surprising two-way connectivity surviving the outage intervals that span more then a day. Using both *control plane* and *data plane* data sets in combination allowed us to narrow down which form of Internet access disruption was implemented at different times in a given region.

Our methodology required determining which IP address prefixes were in each country using RIR-delegation data and public geolocation database (MaxMind) data, and then mapping those prefixes of interest to origin ASes using publicly available BGP data repositories in the U.S. and Europe. Looking deeper into all sources of data can reveal different filtering approaches, possible satellite jamming, ranges of IPs not filtered by the firewall; different forms of (or lack of) coordination with other authorities. These techniques could also be used to improve the accuracy of geolocation databases, e.g., detecting errors in geolocation databases that map IP addresses to completely censored countries, but such IP addresses still show up in measurements.

We also note that BGP-based and firewall-based traffic control are only two of many layers where connectivity and content censorship may occur. A taxonomy of blocking technologies would include everything from physical layer disconnection, DPI-based content blocking by an ISP, DNS-based blocking or manipulation at multiple granularities, and end-client software blocking in an enterprise or household.

Since IPv6 is not as widely deployed as IPv4, there is a lack of feature parity in IPv4 and IPv6 technologies, including censorship technologies such as deep packet inspection. This disparity means that IPv6 may offer a time-limited opportunity for evasion of layer-3 IP censorship. The fact that all IPv6 prefixes in Egypt were unaffected by the outage, shows that currently data flows using IPv6 are easily overlooked or ignored. Whether it was a willful act of disobedience by the network operators or (more likely) an oversight, the effect is the same: unless or until IPv6 gains considerably more traction, IPv6 data flows may remain "under the radar" (or more accurately, may continue to slip through the firewall).

Additional data sources would deepen the analysis, especially since only a subset of data sources may be available at any time. We used Ark data as supporting evidence for bidirectional layer 3 reachability of prefixes in Egypt and Libya, but the same data also contains forward path information that we have not yet explored. This data should allow us to see path changes at the data plane that happened due to the censorship we described. Comparing path changes observed in the data plane with those observed in the control plane, i.e. BGP, may expose non-BGP routing phenomena, such as use of default routes in the default free zone [13].

The opportunity to observe such a macroscopic event is a historical experience, and would not be possible without public (or at least researcher) access to globally relevant Internet data archives. Indeed, additional sources of data would further improve our ability to characterize the nature, timing, and effects of outages. A real-time hybrid BGP+traceroute+traffic monitoring system with geolocation capability would be able to capture such events in far greater detail. The methodology we developed could be used, augmented, and automated, to detect outages or similar macroscopically disruptive events in other geographic or topological regions. Our next step is to expand our use of CAIDA's macroscopic topology data for this purpose, as well as using Ark's measurement-on-request functionality to trigger higher fidelity measurements to observably affected areas, similar to what the Hubble project does for single-prefix outages [29].

Acknowledgements

We are grateful to the anonymous reviewers for their feedback. We would also like to thank Niels Raijer for assistance in understanding satellite technology. Antonio Pescapé has been partially supported by LINCE project of the FARO programme jointly financed by the Compagnia di San Paolo and by the Polo delle Scienze e delle Tecnologie of the University of Napoli Federico II. Support for the UCSD network telescope operations and data collection, curation, analysis, and sharing is provided by DHS S&T NBCHC070133 and UCSD. The Ark infrastructure operations and data collection, curation, and sharing, as well as Kimberly Claffy's effort on this project, is supported by DHS S&T NBCHC070133, DHS S&T N66001-08-C-2029, and NSF CNS-0958547. Emile Aben was supported by RIPE NCC, although the majority of his contribution was on his own time so as to not interfere with his RIPE-NCC responsibilites. Marco Chiesa and Claudio Squarcella were partially supported by MIUR of Italy under project AlgoDEEP prot. 2008TFBWL4. Part of their research was conducted in the framework of ESF project 10-EuroGIGA-OP-003 GraDR "Graph Drawings and Representations".

7. REFERENCES

[1] AfriNIC: The Registry of Internet Number Resources for Africa. http://www.afrinic.net.

[2] Archipelago Measurement Infrastructure. http://www.caida.org/projects/ark.

[3] Opennet initialive. http://opennet.net.

[4] RIPE NCC: BGPviz. http://www.ris.ripe.net/bgpviz/.

[5] RIPE NCC: REX, Resources EXplained. http://albatross.ripe.net/cgi-bin/rex.pl.

[6] RIPE NCC: Routing Information Service (RIS). http://www.ripe.net/data-tools/stats/ris/routing-information-service.

[7] UCSD Network Telescope, 2010. http://www.caida.org/data/passive/network_telescope.xml.

[8] Freedom on the Net 2011: A Global Assessment of Internet and Digital Media. http://www.freedomhouse.org/images/File/FotN/FOTN2011.pdf, Apr. 2011.

[9] E. Aben. Conficker/Conflicker/Downadup as seen from the UCSD Network Telescope. http://www.caida.org/research/security/ms08-067/conficker.xml, 2008.

[10] E. Aben. Unsolicited Internet Traffic from Libya. http://labs.ripe.net/Members/emileaben/unsolicited-internet-traffic-from-libya, March 2011.

[11] BGPmon. Internet in Egypt offline. http://bgpmon.net/blog/?p=450, January 2011.

[12] J. Burris. Comcast: Internet service restored after regional outage. http://articles.baltimoresun.com/2010-11-29/news/bs-md-comcast-20101128_1_outage-internet-service-disruptions, Nov 29 2010.

[13] R. Bush, O. Maennel, M. Roughan, and S. Uhlig. Internet optometry: assessing the broken glasses in Internet reachability. In *ACM SIGCOMM conference on Internet measurement*, 2009.

[14] R. Clayton, S. Murdoch, and R. Watson. Ignoring the Great Firewall of China. *Privacy Enhancing Technologies workshop 2006*, 4258:20–35, June 2006.

[15] J. Cowie. Strange Changes in Iranian Transit. http://www.renesys.com/blog/2009/06/strange-changes-in-iranian-int.shtml, Jun 14 2009.

[16] J. Cowie. Egypt Leaves the Internet. http://www.renesys.com/blog/2011/01/egypt-leaves-the-internet.shtml, Jan 27 2011.

[17] J. Cowie. Libyan Disconnect. http://www.renesys.com/blog/2011/02/libyan-disconnect-1.shtml, February 2011.

[18] J. Cowie. What Libya Learned from Egypt. http://www.renesys.com/blog/2011/03/what-libya-learned-from-egypt.shtml, March 2011.

[19] J. Cowie, A. Ogielski, B. Premore, E. Smith, and T. Underwood. Impact of the 2003 blackouts on Internet communications. November 2003.

[20] J. Cowie, A. Ogielski, B. Premore, and Y. Yuan. Internet worms and global routing instabilities. In *Proc. of SPIE International symposium on Convergence of IT and Communication*, July 2002.

[21] J. Crandall, D. Zinn, M. Byrd, E. Barr, and R. East. ConceptDoppler: A Weather Tracker for Internet Censorship. In *Proceedings of the 14th ACM conference on Computer and communications security*, pages 352 – 365, 2007.

[22] A. Dainotti, A. Pescapé, and G. Ventre. Worm traffic analysis and characterization. In *IEEE ICC 2007*, June 2007.

[23] S. Deshpande, M. Thottan, T. K. Ho, and B. Sikdar. An Online Mechanism for BGP Instability Detection and Analysis. *IEEE Trans. Comput.*, 58:1470–1484, November 2009.

[24] S. Garret. We can confirm that Twitter was blocked in Egypt around 8am PT today.... http://twitter.com/#!/twitterglobalpr/status/30063209247408128, Jan 25 2011.

[25] Google. Google Transparency Report. http://www.google.com/transparencyreport/traffic/?r=LY&l=YOUTUBE&csd=1296723600000&ced=1299142800000.

[26] Google. Google Transparency Report. http://www.google.com/transparencyreport/traffic/?r=LY&l=EVERYTHING&csd=1296862200000&ced=1299281400000.

[27] B. Huffaker, M. Fomenkov, and kc claffy. Geocompare: a comparison of public and commercial geolocation databases. In *Network Mapping and Measurement Conference (NMMC)*, May 2011. http://www.caida.org/publications/papers/2011/geocompare-tr/.

[28] Y. Hyun, B. Huffaker, D. Andersen, E. Aben, C. Shannon, M. Luckie, and K. C. Claffy. The IPv4 Routed /24 Topology Dataset, 2011. http://www.caida.org/data/active/ipv4_routed_24_topology_dataset.xml.

[29] E. Katz-Bassett, H. V. Madhyastha, J. P. John, A. Krishnamurthy, D. Wetherall, and T. Anderson. Studying Black Holes in the Internet with Hubble. *USENIX Symposium on Networked Systems Design & Implementation (NSDI)*, 2008.

[30] R. Khosla, S. Fahmy, and Y. C. Hu. BGP Molecules: Understanding and Predicting Prefix Failures. In *Proc. IEEE INFOCOM Mini-Conference 2011*, 2011.

[31] C. Labovitz. Libya Firewall Begins to Crumble? http://monkey.org/~labovit/blog//viewpage.php?page=libya_firewall_cracks.

[32] C. Labovitz. Egypt Loses the Internet. http://monkey.org/~labovit/blog/viewpage.php?page=egypt_loses_internet, Jan 28 2011.

[33] C. Labovitz. Egypt returns to the Internet. http://asert.arbornetworks.com/2011/02/egypt-returns-to-the-internet/, February 2011.

[34] C. Labovitz. Middle East Internet Scorecard. http://asert.arbornetworks.com/2011/02/middle-east-internet-scorecard-february-12-%E2%80%93-20/, February 2011.

[35] C. Labovitz, G. R. Malan, and F. Jahanian. Origins of Internet Routing Instability. In *Proc. IEEE INFOCOM*, pages 218–226, 1999.
[36] C. Labovitz, S. Member, G. R. Malan, S. Member, and F. Jahanian. Internet routing instability. In *IEEE/ACM Transactions on Networking*, pages 515–528, 1997.
[37] S. LaPerriere. Taiwan earthquake fiber cuts: a service provider view. *NANOG 39*, February 2007.
[38] J. Li and S. Brooks. I-seismograph: Observing and measuring Internet earthquakes. *Infocom 2011 proceedings*, April 2011.
[39] G. Mahlknecht. Greg's Cable Map. http://www.cablemap.info/, retrieved 12 September 2011.
[40] MaxMind. MaxMind GeoLite Country: Open Source IP Address to Country Database. http://www.maxmind.com/app/geolitecountry.
[41] Ministry of Communications and Information Technology, Arab Republic of Egypt. ICT indicators in brief. http://www.mcit.gov.eg/Upcont/Documents/ICTinBriefFeb2011-E.pdf, Feb 2011.
[42] D. Moore, V. Paxson, S. Savage, C. Shannon, S. Staniford, and N. Weaver. Inside the Slammer Worm. *IEEE Security and Privacy*, 1(4):33–39, July 2003.
[43] D. Moore, C. Shannon, D. J. Brown, G. M. Voelker, and S. Savage. Inferring Internet denial-of-service activity. *ACM Trans. Comput. Syst.*, 24:115–139, May 2006.
[44] S. Nasrawi. Libya Protests: Anti-Government Protesters Killed During Day Of Rage. http://www.huffingtonpost.com/2011/02/17/libya-protests-antigovern_0_n_824826.html, February 2011.
[45] R. Pang, V. Yegneswaran, P. Barford, V. Paxson, and L. Peterson. Characteristics of Internet background radiation. In *Proceedings of the 4th ACM SIGCOMM conference on Internet measurement*, IMC '04, pages 27–40, New York, NY, USA, 2004. ACM.
[46] I. Poese, S. Uhlig, M. A. Kaafar, B. Donnet, and B. Gueye. IP Geolocation Databases: Unreliable? *ACM SIGCOMM Computer Communication Review*, 41(2), April 2011.
[47] Reuters. http://af.reuters.com/article/libyaNews/idAFLDE71N2CU20110224, February 2011.
[48] Reuters. Egypt govt denies disrupting websites – cabinet. http://www.reuters.com/article/2011/01/26/egypt-web-idUSLDE70P28720110126, Jan 26 2011.
[49] Reuters. Facebook says has seen drop in traffic from Egypt. http://www.reuters.com/article/2011/01/27/facebook-egypt-idUSN2727880720110127, Jan 2011.
[50] RIPE. Analysis of Egyptian Internet outage 27th January - 2nd February 2011. http://stat.ripe.net/egypt, 2011.
[51] A. Sahoo, K. Kant, and P. Mohapatra. Characterization of BGP Recovery Time under Large-Scale Failures. In *IEEE International Conference on Communications*, volume 2, 2006.
[52] Y. Shavitt and N. Zilberman. A study of geolocation databases. *Journal on Selected Areas of Communications*, abs/1005.5674, 2011.
[53] M. Skoric, N. Poor, Y. Liao, and S. Tang. Online Organization of an Offline Protest: From Social to Traditional Media and Back. In *System Sciences (HICSS), 2011 44th Hawaii International Conference on*, pages 1 –8, jan. 2011.
[54] T. D. Star. http://www.dailystar.com.lb/News/Politics/Feb/23/Libya-source-of-jamming-of-Lebanese-news-channels-TRA.ashx#axzz1Ev3JP000, February 2011.
[55] J. Swartz. 'Kill Switch' Internet bill alarms privacy experts. http://www.usatoday.com/tech/news/internetprivacy/2011-02-15-kill-switch_N.htm, Feb 15 2011.
[56] S. T. Teoh, S. Ranjan, A. Nucci, and C.-N. Chuah. BGP eye: a new visualization tool for real-time detection and analysis of BGP anomalies. In *Proceedings of the 3rd international workshop on Visualization for computer security*, VizSEC '06, pages 81–90, New York, NY, USA, 2006. ACM.
[57] T. Underwood. Con-Ed Steals the 'Net. http://www.renesys.com/blog/2006/01/coned_steals_the_net.shtml, Jan 22 2006.
[58] R. T. University. BGPlay - graphical visualisation of BGP updates. http://bgplay.routeviews.org/.
[59] University of Oregon. University of Oregon Route Views project. http://www.routeviews.org.
[60] I. van Beijnum. How Egypt did (and your government could) shut down the Internet. http://arstechnica.com/tech-policy/news/2011/01/how-egypt-or-how-your-government-could-shut-down-the-internet.ars, February 2011.
[61] T. Wan and P. van Oorschot. Analysis of BGP prefix origins during Google's May 2005 outage. In *Parallel and Distributed Processing Symposium, 2006. IPDPS 2006. 20th International*, page 8 pp., april 2006.
[62] Wikipedia. Ramses Exchange. http://en.wikipedia.org/wiki/Ramses_Exchange, Sep 12 2011.
[63] B. Woodcock. Overview of the Egyptian Internet Shutdown. http://www.pch.net/resources/misc/Egypt-PCH-Overview.pdf, Feb 2011.
[64] X. Xu, Z. M. Mao, and J. A. Halderman. Internet Censorship in China: Where Does the Filtering Occur? *Proceedings of PAM 2011*, 2011.
[65] H. Yan, R. Oliveira, K. Burnett, D. Matthews, L. Zhang, and D. Massey. BGPmon: A real-time, scalable, extensible monitoring system. In *Proceedings of IEEE Conference on Cybersecurity Applications and Technologies Conference for Homeland Security*, 2009.
[66] E. Zmijewski. Georgia Clings to the 'Net. http://www.renesys.com/blog/2008/08/georgia-clings-to-the-net.shtml, Aug 10 2008.
[67] E. Zmijewski. Mediterranean cable break. http://www.renesys.com/blog/2008/01/mediterranean_cable_break.shtml, Jan 30 2008.
[68] E. Zmijewski. Mediterranean cable break – part ii. http://www.renesys.com/blog/2008/01/mediterranean_cable_break_part_1.shtml, Jan 31 2008.
[69] E. Zmijewski. Mediterranean cable break – part iii. http://www.renesys.com/blog/2008/02/mediterranean_cable_break_part.shtml, Feb 2 2008.

APPENDIX

A. ETHICAL CONSIDERATIONS

We recognize that this paper could possibly expose network operators' disobedience to government orders, with potential harmful consequences to the operators. Therefore we believe it would be ethical to anonymize the ASes that might be at risk for harm. Here we describe and justify the reasoning for our anonymization policy.

Our main concern is that we do not know the nature of the relationships between the operators of these networks to their governments, whether they disobeyed direct orders and what the penalties might be. We assume that the national incumbent telecom operators will follow orders from their respective governments; our research did not reveal behavior that suggests otherwise. Furthermore, the behavior of both incumbent telecom operators has been described in detail elsewhere, e.g., [16]. So in this paper we label these ASes *EgStateAs* and *LyStateAs*. For the remaining ASes we anonymized ASes that were operating nationally in Egypt with an *Eg*-prefix, e.g., *EgAs1*, *EgAs2*, etc. We did not need to do so for Libya, because we didn't find ASes operating at the national level in Libya, except for the state-owned telecom operator.

As the upstreams of networks in Libya and Egypt may have personnel operating in one of these countries, we decided to anonymize these as well, and labeled them *IntAs1*, *IntAs2*, etc. One distinguishing characteristic of censorship activity we observed is whether it occurs via wireless satellite connectivity; depending on who owns the satellite links, disrupting such connectivity may require jamming technology rather than firewall-based filtering. To acknowledge this distinction, which is revealed in the data anyway, we labeled the one international satellite connectivity provider we show data for *SatAs1*. We realize this anonymization policy cannot guarantee to prevent deanonymization by careful examination of publicly available data, but it raises the threshold for doing so without compromising the scientific value of this paper.

Summary Review Documentation for

"Analysis of Country-wide Internet Outages Caused by Censorship"

Authors: A. Dainotti, C. Squarcella, E. Aben, K. Claffy, M. Chiesa, M. Russo, A. Pescapè

Reviewer #1

Strengths: The paper is timely, these events just having happened this year, and with continuing instability in the region, may happen again.

The study uses multiple sets of data, and the authors show a clear understanding of the strengths and weaknesses of each dataset.

Weaknesses: It may be tempting to write this paper off as "yet another" because this topic has received plenty of attention, even at the technical level. However, that would miss the point that it is important to have such studies reported in peer-reviewed literature to serve as an archive for future investigators. Only by such efforts will be improve the Internet, and for that matter, human rights.

Comments to Authors: In Table 1, it would be very useful to see the intersections between NIC and Geomapped IP addresses located to the country. At a qualitative level it would help inform about how consistent they are. At a quantitative level it might even allow a Petersen-like estimate of how many IPs are missing, e.g. see Matthew Roughan, Jonathan Tuke, Olaf Maennel, "Bigfoot, Sasquatch, the Yeti and other missing links: what we don't know about the AS graph", Proc. IMC'08, pp. 325-330, Vouliagmeni, Greece, October 20 - 22, 2008.

Please be more careful about the term "permanently withdrawn". Presumably you mean withdrawn for the life of the event, but for instance, the before and after states from Figures 3 and 4 don't seem to quite match, so maybe some prefixes did go away forever?

Reviewer #2

Strengths: A methodology to combine multiple sources of data to detect Internet outages. The paper provides a very good application of large scale monitoring of the Internet.

Weaknesses: There is not much technical innovation in the paper. Most of the analyses in this paper use standard techniques for analyzing such data.

Comments to Authors: I find the topics of discussion in the paper interesting from historical and political point of view. I also like your careful analyses of the data. However, I find that the technical innovation in the paper is a bit weak for a full IMC paper. Most of the techniques are standard analyses of the data.

The observations on the reachability of IPv6 addresses are interesting as it provides an opportunity for people to by-pass censorship. It would be great if the authors can elaborate on this point and its potential application to censorship elsewhere.

A more effective detection system should use more targeted active probes. Perhaps, these measurements could be triggered by alarms from BGP and darknet data.

The work can have even bigger impact if the authors use the same analysis for other types of outages such as network failures, natural disasters, not just political censorships.

Reviewer #3

Strengths: This very well done paper could be of interest to more than just the measurement community. Also, its completeness has a chance to make it the definitive work on the subject.

Weaknesses: For completeness, I would have liked to better understand the physical topology and the resulting limitations.

Comments to Authors: Great paper - timely, well written, and complete. Not sure what more I can add.

A small story that I feel like should be better emphasized: that the backscatter detectors were actually sensitive enough to track both the censorship of these prefixes, but also the DDoS random src-address spoofing.

The fact that Egypt did not withdraw its Ipv6 prefixes is interesting: do the authors believe this was just an oversight?

I realize that there is a lot of information in this paper, but I feel like its still not the "complete picture" because of the lack of physical topology information: how many external links do these countries have and how many operators run them?

I very much appreciated the note about ethics in Appendix A and believe that more researchers should stop and consider the implications of their work, even if in the end they decide not to anonymize their data.

Reviewer #4

Strengths: Timely analysis. Interesting to see that as a community, we have developed or otherwise have publicly available access to tools with adequate visibility into such events.

Weaknesses: Not a breakthrough on the technical front.
Also, finding what you are looking for is much easier than if you did not know what was happening. In most cases, there are widely published timelines of disruption and reconnection events

and this paper shows those times to be correlated with the feeds they analyzed. However, it is unclear if the same techniques can be used when such public timelines are unavailable.
For example, there could be many events causing similar smaller disruptions (misconfigurations, power outages, religious holidays) and seems that the data has little predictive value besides indicating abnormality.

Comments to Authors: I enjoyed reading the analysis!

Regarding traffic received by the darknet, there are multiple places where the paper seems to worry too much. If you can distinguish which traffic originated from the observed IP ranges and which was due to backscatter from spoofed probes as you seem to be able to, what is the concern?

I am surprised at the synchronization disconnection across multiple ISPs... I was hoping to see some distance between the complying ASes and those trying to circumvent or resisting the censorship.

Could you tell what fraction of the flat periods in Figure 3, when some prefixes have started disappearing but not all, are due to BGP reconvergence?

For both darknet traffic (Figure 2) and BGP visibility (Figure 3), it would be good to show a longer time-frame control graph. That ways, we could figure out the 'natural' variation in these feeds.

The matching from address space to prefixes in 4.1, prefers to find prefixes that are more likely to contain the required set of IPs at the cost of completeness in coverage. It would help to explicitly call that out and use both sets of prefixes: 'accurate but potentially incomplete', and 'complete but potentially inaccurate'.

You seem to have compensated for temporary disappearances of prefixes, but how?

Results are a slight let-down: mostly BGP withdrawals, except for Libya, which perhaps used data-plane filters. Near universal compliance from regional ISPs, some resistance from International providers...

Interesting side-effect to see the DoS attacks.

Reviewer #5

Strengths: The paper is useful in that it sheds light on a relatively new type of event (country-wide, censorship-induced outage). It also presents an interesting and practical idea (to use network telescopes to early-detect such outages).

Weaknesses: Ideally, this should have been a short paper (there is not enough technical content here to warrant 14 pages).

Comments to Authors: My only complaint is that this should have been a short rather than a long paper. The main contribution of the paper lies in the BGP and telescope measurements, and these can certainly fit in 6 pages. Section 4 can be significantly condensed: I believe that most people who would be interested in reading this paper already know about RouteViews and the UCSD telescope, and the way the authors used these sources is straightforward and similar to the way others have used them before (in my opinion, it does not warrant two pages of explanation). Section 6 repeats the conclusions drawn in Section 5. Section 5 itself has a fair amount of redundancy and graphs that are larger than necessary (and Fig. 8, which can be completely omitted). In general, the paper gives the impression that it was written and formatted to use more space than necessary.

A less serious complaint is that, in my opinion, the paper overclaims. I think that the first and third contributions stated in the introduction are the same ("We document a rich view of the disruptions..." "We report previously unknown details of each event..."). Also, I think that the fourth contribution ("We sketch a general methodology...") is not supported by the paper: first, I don't think that the paper presents any novel methodology for collecting or analyzing measurements; second, even if it did, I do not think that *sketching* (as opposed to describing and evaluating) a methodology could count as an IMC-level contribution. However, this is a matter of opinion and presentation, so I did not hold it against the paper.

Minor questions:
- Section 5.1.2 says that "only 176 prefixes remain[ed] visible" after the start of the outage. Is there anything special about these prefixes? Is there any indication as to why they were spared (do they host any particularly important infrastructure)?
- The same section says that "several of the visible ... prefixes were reachable through ... (IntAS2) ... or ... (IntAS3) ..." Does this observation say anything about the outage? Is there any indication that the spared prefixes were spared *because* they were reachable through the particular ASes?
- Later, one reads that "at least three ... prefixes, amongst those ... not withdrawn ... were actually reachable." Is there any indication that the remaining non-withdrawn prefixes were *not* reachable? The text implies that the ad-hoc active measurements targeted only very few prefixes. Was there a particular reason for that? In general, a better description of this ad-hoc measurement process would help.

Response from the Authors

We thank the anonymous reviewers for their insightful comments, which inspired improvements to the camera-ready version of the paper, both in terms of better clarity and additional content.

One of the reviewers observes ``The work can have even bigger impact if the authors use the same analysis for other types of outages such as network failures, natural disasters, not just political censorships''. This paper represents a first step in this direction, however, we focused on these specific events for two reasons: (i) we wanted to provide sufficient detail to demonstrate the power of our analysis methodology, including to reveal aspects of the observed phenomena not previously discussed; (ii) the prevalence of censorship-related Internet blackouts is growing, and there has been little scientific study of the different approaches and their effects. We recognize there are ethical issues, including revealing holes in censorship that could endanger people in the censored country, and we appreciate the reviewer support for our anonymization of operator names.

With regard to the paper being a better short than a long paper, we saw sufficient novel technical content to justify a full-length paper. Even if the tools and methods we used are not new, some of them, e.g., the network telescope, have not been used to study macroscopic Internet outages or censorship. We combined several different methods and granularities to reveal new insight into censorship-induced network behavior. We highlighted their complementarities, and suggested a path toward automation of our methods. Background and analysis of the events, description of the data sources, and the findings we illustrated with the figures, just would not have fit into a small paper. Two reviewers asked us to further elaborate on the reachability of IPv6 addresses. We changed the IPv6 paragraph in the discussion based on these comments, adding two possible causes. Our thoughts on the limitations of current geolocation databases, requested by one of the reviewers, were limited to the focus of the paper; we cite references that provide more specific studies of the topic. Finally, to better contextualize our study, we added information on the physical connections of these countries to the rest of the world.

Pingin' in the Rain

Aaron Schulman and Neil Spring
University of Maryland
{schulman,nspring}@cs.umd.edu

ABSTRACT

Residential Internet connections are susceptible to weather-caused outages: Lightning and wind cause local power failures, direct lightning strikes destroy equipment, and water in the atmosphere degrades satellite links. Outages caused by severe events such as fires and undersea cable cuts are often reported upon by operators and studied by researchers. In contrast, outages cause by ordinary weather are typically limited in scope, and because of their small scale, there has not been comparable effort to understand how weather affects everyday last-mile Internet connectivity.

We design and deploy a measurement tool called *ThunderPing* that measures the connectivity of residential Internet hosts before, during, and after forecast periods of severe weather. ThunderPing uses weather alerts from the US National Weather Service to choose a set of residential host addresses to ping from several vantage points on the Internet. We then process this ping data to determine when hosts lose connectivity, completely or partially, and categorize whether these failures occur during periods of severe weather or when the skies are clear. In our preliminary results, we find that compared to clear weather, failures are *four times* as likely during thunderstorms and *two times* as likely during rain. We also find that the duration of weather induced outages is relatively small for a satellite provider we focused on.

Categories and Subject Descriptors

C.2.5 [**Computer Communications Networks**]: Local and Wide-Area Networks—*Internet*

General Terms

Experimentation, Measurement

Keywords

ThunderPing, Weather, Outage, Ping

1. INTRODUCTION

Last-mile residential Internet links are increasingly relied upon, even for emergency communication. Yet despite their apparent reliability on temperate days, network links are somewhat more prone to failure during times of severe weather. Branches may fall on telephone wires or power lines, and lightning strikes interfere with wireless transmissions and can destroy antenna towers.

Researchers have studied the Internet-wide effects of large scale outages, including undersea cable cuts [1] and terrorist attack [2]. Large-scale failures cause the Internet to fall back to large-scale redundancy: alternate geographic paths that absorb the load. Residential Internet connectivity, in contrast, lacks similar redundancy.

In this paper, we present a preliminary study into the prevalence of weather-related residential Internet outages in the United States. Our broader goal is to understand the factors involved in day-to-day network reliability, including aspects inherent to link type (e.g., wireless or cable), geography (a hurricane zone), or, when possible, the ISP itself. We focus on the US in this work because of the diversity of weather and the availability of a feed of weather alerts and coverage by Internet-accessible weather stations.

We find that compared to clear weather, failures are four times more likely during thunderstorms and two times more likely during rain. We expect that failures during clear weather are a baseline, typically indicating hosts that are powered off by users. We also observed that the failures for a satellite ISP that we studied tend to be shorter during thunderstorms than they are in clear conditions. Our dataset is available on the project website[1].

There are limitations to our study. First, we do not (yet) isolate weather-related power failures from network failures. Although the ISP should not be blamed for the failure, the effect (to us and to the user) is likely the same. Second, we do not (robustly) distinguish between actions of individuals from network failures that affect many hosts: For example, people may turn off their computers (and home routers). Further, they may be more likely to power down if they believe doing so will protect them from unstable power during a lightning storm. Third, we use scalable, but imprecise reports of weather and of host location to find correlations between both. As such, this work is preliminary, but shows promise in understanding the susceptibility of various networks to varied weather events in practice.

This paper is organized as follows. In Section 2, we describe the design of our measurement tool, ThunderPing,

[1] http://www.cs.umd.edu/~schulman/thunderping.html

```
<title>Severe Weather Statement issued May 12 at 4:46PM CDT
 expiring May 12 at 5:15PM CDT by NWS GreenBay
 http://www.crh.noaa.gov/grb/</title>
<summary>...A SEVERE THUNDERSTORM WARNING REMAINS IN EFFECT
 FOR CENTRAL WAUPACA AND NORTHWESTERN OUTAGAMIE COUNTIES
 UNTIL 515 PM CDT... AT 443 PM CDT...NATIONAL WEATHER
 SERVICE DOPPLER RADAR INDICATED A SEVERE THUNDERSTORM
 CAPABLE OF PRODUCING QUARTER SIZE HAIL...AND DAMAGING
 WINDS IN EXCESS OF 60 MPH. THIS STORM WAS LOCATED 7 MILES
 NORTH OF NEW LONDON...OR 20 MILES NORTHEAST OF
 WAUPACA...MOVING</summary>
<cap:effective>2011-05-12T16:46:00-05:00</cap:effective>
<cap:expires>2011-05-12T17:15:00-05:00</cap:expires>
<cap:urgency>Immediate</cap:urgency>
<cap:severity>Severe</cap:severity>
<cap:certainty>Observed</cap:certainty>
<cap:geocode><valueName>FIPS6</valueName>
<value>055087 055135</value></cap:geocode>
```

Figure 1: Example XML entry for a weather alert for two counties in Wisconsin. Some XML entries omitted for brevity.

which collects reachability samples for hosts before, during, and after severe weather events. Section 3 describes our analysis of the data to observe failures. Section 4 presents our preliminary results. We conclude with a discussion of the implications of this work and describe our future work in Section 5.

2. MEASURING THE RESPONSIVENESS OF INTERNET HOSTS DURING WEATHER

We developed ThunderPing to test our hypothesis that weather affects the performance of residential Internet connections, measured by connectivity, loss rate, and latency. In this section, we describe the design of ThunderPing. At a high level, ThunderPing listens for severe weather alerts issued by the US National Weather Service (NWS). When one is issued, ThunderPing finds IP addresses in the area covered by the alert and uses ten geographically distributed PlanetLab hosts to ping those addresses every eleven minutes for up to six hours before, during, and six hours after the alert. Because we are interested in distinguishing network failure from network congestion, ThunderPing retries a lost ping at most ten times, if it has seen a successful ping in a prior interval.

2.1 Finding IP addresses subject to weather

The first problem to address is to find residential network IP addresses in a geographic region that can be matched to a US National Weather Service alert. We select IP addresses by a scan of the reverse DNS space, classify each IP address as residential by DNS suffix (domain), and determine their approximate location by the MaxMind GeoIP database.

The focused scan of reverse DNS records proceeds as follows. First we choose three IP addresses, ending in .1, .44, or .133 from every possible /24 block, and query for the name of each. If any of the three have a name matching a well-known US residential ISP, such as comcast.net or verizon.net, we determine all the names of all the IP addresses in the block and include the addresses with matching names. This approach is comparable to that used to study residential Internet connections in prior work [3, 13]. From this method, we discovered 100,799,297 US residential IP addresses.

The US National Weather Service provides an XML feed of the latest severe weather alerts for regions in the US [7]. An example alert appears in Figure 1. The regions under alert are listed by FIPS code, which is a numeric code for each county in the US. The FIPS code for Los Angeles, for example, is 06037. We consider all weather alerts including "watches," which indicate conditions conducive to severe weather, and "warnings," which indicate that severe weather has been observed.

To link IP addresses to the FIPS codes used in weather alerts requires IP geolocation. We used MaxMind's GeoIP [5] database to determine an estimate of the latitude and longitude of each IP, and the US Census Bureau's county border data file[2] to determine the FIPS county location for any IP address.

We use MaxMind's database because of its availability and the potential to determine the location of every possible residential IP address. Researchers have questioned its accuracy [9], and have developed probing-based methods for positioning Internet hosts [10, 12] that seem impractical for locating 100 million hosts. Clearly, improved IP geolocation methods would yield more precision to the location and might lend more accuracy to our analysis. We expect, however, that precision in geolocation would have limited benefit because weather alerts are provided on the scale of a county and because weather does not respect city or county boundaries.

After an alert comes in, we pick 100 IP addresses from every provider and link type (when embedded in the DNS name) in each FIPS-coded region in the alert. We identify a provider and link type by the DNS name without numbers (e.g., pool----.sangtx.dsl-w.verizon.net).

2.2 Pinging (residential IPs) in the rain

Testing our hypothesis that weather affects the Internet is difficult because weather's effect on the connectivity of Internet hosts may be hidden by congestion, outages at the source, or other network events.

2.2.1 *Ping infrequently*

Internet measurement traffic has a tendency to generate reports of network abuse from recipients of unsolicited traffic. We send typical ICMP echo messages with an identifying payload as infrequently as possible.

We follow the inter-ping interval chosen by Heidemann et al. in their Internet census. [4]. They surveyed the occupancy of IP addresses on the Internet on the scale of tens of minutes. They reported that they could send pings at an interval of 5 minutes without generating any abuse reports. For their surveys they pinged IP addresses for several weeks at an 11 minute interval without generating many abuse reports, so we do the same.

2.2.2 *Omit needless pings*

In addition to sending more probes to determine if a host is down, ThunderPing must cull the set of observed hosts during a weather alert to include only those that respond to pings. Otherwise, the pinger would waste time pinging addresses that either are not assigned to a host or have a host that is not awake for the weather event. We implement a simple timeout: If after an hour (five pings from ten vantage points) a response is not heard from the host, then it is no longer pinged for that weather alert.

[2] http://www.census.gov/geo/cob/bdy/co/co00ascii/co99_d00_ascii.zip

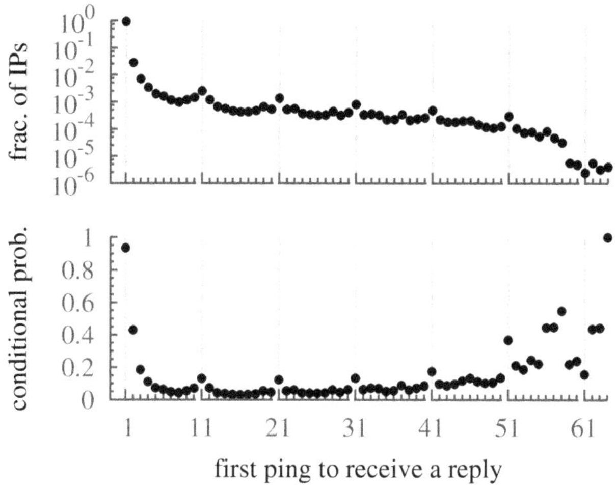

Figure 2: Hosts may not respond to the first ping. The lower graph shows the conditional probability that a host first replies to ping x, given that it does not reply to any of the pings preceding x. The upper graph shows the fraction of hosts (in log scale) that first reply to ping x. The gray lines indicate the ping interval when all ten vantage points are operational.

2.2.3 One vantage point is not enough

ThunderPing distinguishes between faults in the middle and faults at the endpoint, the observed host, by simultaneously pinging from several vantage points. The responsiveness of the host is not determined by any individual vantage point, but by agreement between the vantage points. For the experiment in this paper we used ten PlanetLab machines as vantage points: Ten permitted some to fail occasionally while giving each IP address a good chance of demonstrating availability even during partial outages.

2.2.4 One ping is not enough

Pings can be lost: A single failed ping is not convincing evidence of a host being unavailable. Clearly, then, a failed ping must be followed up to test whether the failure is transient or persistent. ThunderPing vantage points retry a failed ping up to ten times, doubling the interval between each attempt to avoid flooding the host.

The short-term retry of a failed ping is important beyond the simple reaction to background loss: because of a nuance in ARP, at least a second ping is *necessary* to determine whether a host is up. When a packet reaches a router that does not have an ARP table entry for the next hop (in our case, likely the destination) IP address, the ARP RFC [8] states that the router should drop the packet and send an ARP request instead. We confirmed that Cisco's IOS follows this behavior. This means if you only send one ping to an IP, if there are any expired ARP entries along the path, the packet will be dropped. However, we also observed that the default behavior of Cisco IOS is to attempt to refresh an ARP entry as soon as it expires, which mitigates the problem.

In our dataset, if a host does not respond to the first ping, the first reply is most likely to come from the second ping. For the 1,240,114 hosts that reply to pings within one hour of receiving pings, the bottom of Figure 2 shows the conditional probability that a host first replies to ping request x, given that it does not reply to any of the ping requests preceding x. The conditional probability for the second ping is at least 2.3x the conditional probability for all pings preceding ping 41. For the remaining pings (41-64), fewer than 0.5% of the hosts that respond in one hour remain. The expected conditional probability at the right edge of the graph, when there are few hosts remaining, is to increase until the 64th ping where all remaining hosts reply. This is because the graph is constrained to show only those addresses that responded to at least one of the 64 pings.

The hosts that do not reply to the first few pings, but still reply within the first hour, appear to come online at a random time during the hour. The data indicate this because the conditional probability is consistent after the third ping and it peaks every ping interval. When all ten (occasionally 11) vantage points are operational, all ten ping once every 11 minutes: the first vantage point to ping during each epoch is more likely to discover a newly-online host.

The apparent importance of the second ping might be an artifact of our measurement setup. However, we examined the data to filter out hosts that might be biased by the measurement setup. In particular, we noticed that as a source sends a long sequence of pings to various hosts, a suffix of this sequence sometimes receives no responses. Pings in that suffix may fail to be transmitted due to overload at the PlanetLab source, or fail to traverse the network past some buffer. In response, we observe whether the sequence of pings has a failed suffix and filter out hosts pinged in that suffix for this analysis.

2.3 Potential sources of error

A source of error for our probing would be when a host appears to have failed, but in reality, its DHCP lease just ran out and it was given a new address. From correlating Hotmail identities to IP addresses for one month of data, Xie et al. [13] report that for SBC, one of the largest DSL providers in the US, most users retained the same IP for one to three days. For Comcast, one of the largest cable providers in the US, they report that 70% of IP addresses do not change for users within a month-long trace. This stability suggests that the addresses of responsive hosts will not be reassigned in a way that would suggest failure during weather events.

3. ANALYZING THE PINGS

The severe weather forecasts and geolocation to IP addresses derived in the previous section permit ThunderPing to observe residential hosts before, during, and after weather events. There are two remaining tasks, however: first to determine the actual weather during the instrumentation, and second to interpret the ping data to decide whether a host or set of hosts failed. We discuss each in turn.

3.1 The weather at a host during a ping

The NWS and Federal Aviation Administration (FAA) administer approximately 900 Automated Surface Observing System (ASOS)[3] weather stations at airports in the US. These stations provide hourly weather measurements, primarily for pilots, in METAR format. Beyond the basic wind, pressure, and rainfall sensors, ASOS stations include a Light

[3] http://www.weather.gov/asos/

	Cable			DSL						Satellite	Fiber
	Charter	Comcast	Cox	Ameritech	CenturyLink	MegaPath	Speakeasy	Windstream	Verizon DSL	WildBlue	Verizon FiOS
pinged	321,705	746,051	161,756	156,327	167,347	23,076	110,795	370,018	213,737	395,810	86,344
alive	54,277	100,627	31,918	8,553	76,705	3,771	7,869	113,541	47,839	52,979	36,143
UP to DOWN	3,689	6,769	2,552	742	12,746	216	418	8,988	5,376	17,825	805
UP to HOSED	1,227	2,111	644	240	5,385	107	163	3,358	2,565	13,807	211
airports	237	320	130	113	203	129	229	186	189	424	145
Clear	17.5	14.0	57.4	21.3	30.3	51.3	39.8	22.5	20.4	33.3	13.3
Cloudy	10.9	9.9	28.9	15.5	13.7	39.3	30.5	9.4	17.0	17.4	10.1
Fog	1.8	1.5	6.4	1.5	2.0	10.8	5.4	1.9	1.8	2.3	2.8
Rain	1.6	1.6	3.7	2.7	2.2	5.2	3.6	1.6	4.3	3.4	1.2
Thunderstorm	0.7	0.6	1.6	1.0	1.0	1.4	1.4	0.7	1.0	1.1	0.3

Table 1: Summary of a small portion of the data collected by ThunderPing. For a sample of providers, the number of IP addresses pinged, the number that are ever seen alive, as well as the number of IP addresses that transition at least once from UP to DOWN and UP to HOSED. The next row is the number of airports that the alive IPs map to. The final five rows are the average time (in hours) ThunderPing pings an IP address during each weather condition.

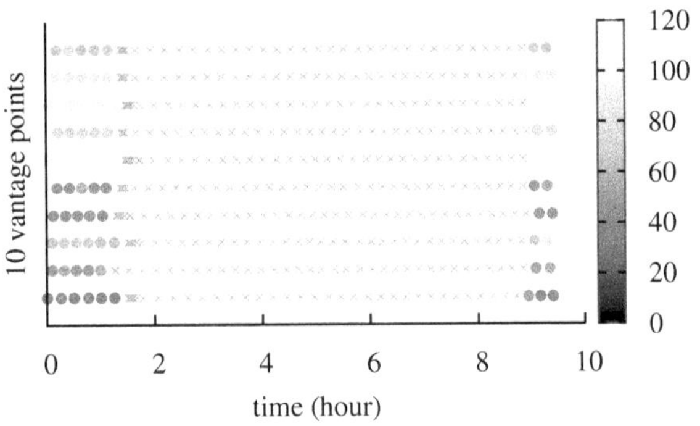

Figure 3: During heavy thunderstorms reported at KTUP airport in Tupelo, Mississippi at 3:16AM on April 27th, 2011, ten vantage points (y-axis) saw Comcast cable customer 75.66.230.135 go down for 7.6 hours. A • represents a ping with a response, a × represents a ping that timed out. At this time, eight other Comcast customers near this airport failed.

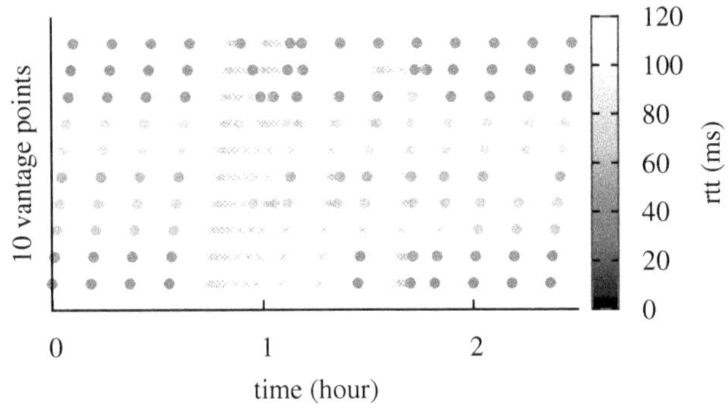

Figure 4: We also observed hosts enter a state of partial responsiveness. In this state, the host intermittently responds to pings. CenturyLink DSL customer 209.206.208.59 goes into a partial responsiveness state for 37 minutes during heavy thunderstorms reported at KSTP in St Paul, Minnesota at 6:30AM on May 9th, 2011.

Emitting Diode Weather Indicator (LEDWI) that measures the type (Rain, Hail, Snow) and density of precipitation. Most stations also have antennas that measure lightning strikes. Weather Underground provides an archive of the hourly METAR readings from many ASOS stations [11]. We do not use the larger network of older AWOS weather stations because some do not have the LEDWI sensor, which provides data we consider important.

We interpret the ping data to classify a host into three states: UP, where most pings receive responses, HOSED where few pings receive responses, and DOWN where none of the pings receive responses. The task is to identify when hosts transition between these states and to correlate those transitions with the current weather conditions for the IP address.

The transition rules are as follows. UP to DOWN occurs as soon as all vantage points report failure (Figure 3). We intend for DOWN to represent a complete lack of responsiveness, and we do not assume a short interval of failed pings represents a failed host. A DOWN to UP transition occurs as soon as all active vantage points agree that the host is up.

These are the simple transitions, but these rules permit an intermediate state. The HOSED state represents a situation in which fewer than half of the pings see responses: The host is not entirely DOWN, but there is *something* going on (Figure 4). To identify these transitions, we slide a window of three pings from every vantage point (30 pings total) across time. To enter HOSED, more than half (but not all) of the pings in the sliding window must fail. To leave HOSED, more than half of the pings must succeed. The sliding window prevents short periods of UP-like responsiveness from splitting an interval of HOSED-state behavior. Because ThunderPing retries pings that fail, the HOSED state will be found quickly: much more quickly than three ping intervals. We have not observed oscillations between UP and HOSED when loss rates are near 50%, perhaps because this is rare.

To handle vantage point failure, we exclude those that fail from the unanimous voting for UP or DOWN. In our experiments, when vantage points fail they are automatically replaced, though we developed the analysis to work despite up to four failures at once.

4. RESULTS

We collected pings with ThunderPing for 66 days, between April 27th, 2011 and August 1st, 2011. Table 1 shows a summary of the observations. ThunderPing pings IP addresses at providers only if a weather alert is issued for an area in which the provider has customers. Because both weather and ISPs are regional, the IP addresses of some providers will spend different amounts of time in each condition.

Although we probed customers of many providers, in this analysis we focus on relatively large providers where the cus-

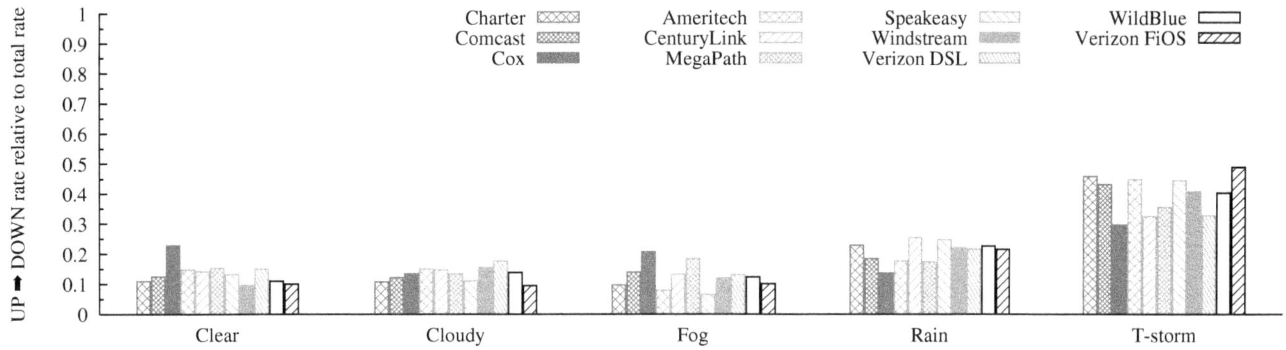

Figure 5: The rate of UP to DOWN failures relative to the total failure rate for each provider. Weather affects the failure rate for all types of links, and for all selected providers.

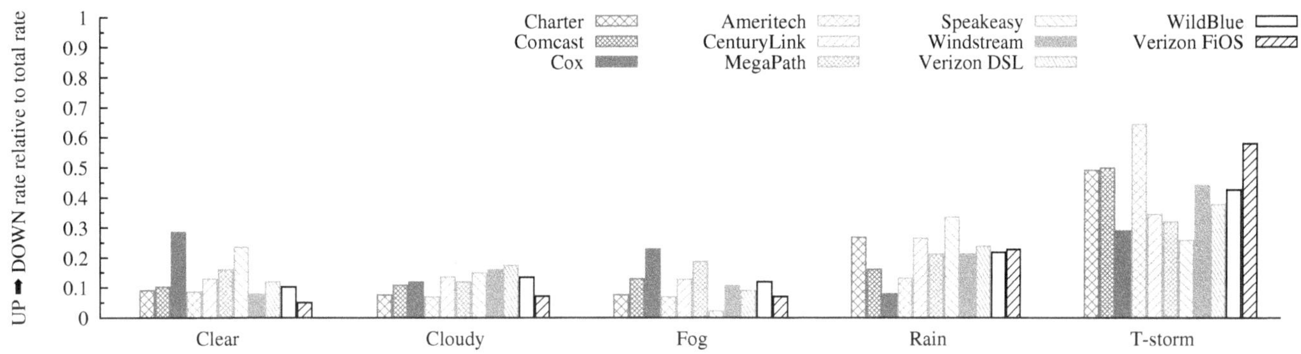

Figure 6: The normalized rate of correlated UP to DOWN failures. Thunderstorms appear to affect the failure rate for all types of links and providers.

tomer's link type is known and easy to identify in their reverse DNS names. We avoid providers that offer various link types but do not include that information in their DNS names. We chose three prominent cable providers: Charter, Comcast, and Cox; six DSL providers: Ameritech, CenturyLink, MegaPath, Speakeasy, Windstream and Verizon DSL; and two uncommon link types: the rural satellite provider WildBlue, and Verizon's fiber optic service.

4.1 Weather affects residential Internet

To understand the effect of weather on the Internet we found the transitions from UP to DOWN for all IP addresses broken down by provider. To isolate failures that are severe (longer than a few minutes) and not caused by human behavior (e.g., turning a computer off for at least 8 hours at night[4]) we plot transitions where the IP address is unresponsive for more than 30 minutes but less than 8 hours. Then, we total up the time that each provider experiences each type of weather. The *failure rate* is the number of UP to DOWN transitions divided by the total time each IP address observed each weather condition.

Figure 5 depicts the failure rate for each weather condition, relative to the total failure rate for that provider. This normalization allows us to observe the effect that weather has on the different providers, and compare the effect across providers. During thunderstorms the failure rate more than doubles compared to clear for most providers across all link types. For example, the failure rate for Comcast (cable) during thunderstorms is 3.58 times the failure rate in clear weather; for the least affected DSL provider the failure rate is 3.21 times higher than clear. As expected, due to rain fade of their Ka band (30 GHz) signal, rain appears to double the failure of the satellite provider WildBlue, but surprisingly an increased failure rate appears across providers. We address the outlying reliability of Cox during thunderstorms in the following section.

In Figure 6, we perform the same analysis for correlated failures. We define a correlated failure as a failure where at least one other host from the same provider, located near the same airport where we measure the weather, 5.5 minutes before and after the failure (one ping interval). Selecting failures that are correlated in time attempts to choose those that are caused by factors beyond the user's control: individual people may turn off their computer independently, but are unlikely to do so simultaneously, while a network outage may affect more than one customer. In this plot, the effect of weather is even more evident than when looking across all failures. During thunderstorms, several providers have about five times the clear correlated failure rate.

4.2 Duration of failures

Failures of the rural satellite provider WildBlue are relatively short compared to the other providers we observed

[4] In our dataset, most UP to DOWN transitions occur at 10 PM local time, with an average DOWN time of 12 hours.

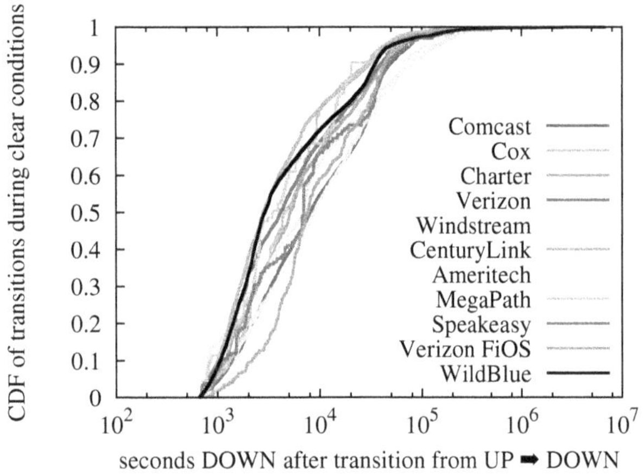

Figure 7: CDF of the time DOWN after transitioning from UP in clear conditions. Some providers stay DOWN longer than others and it does not appear to be related to link type.

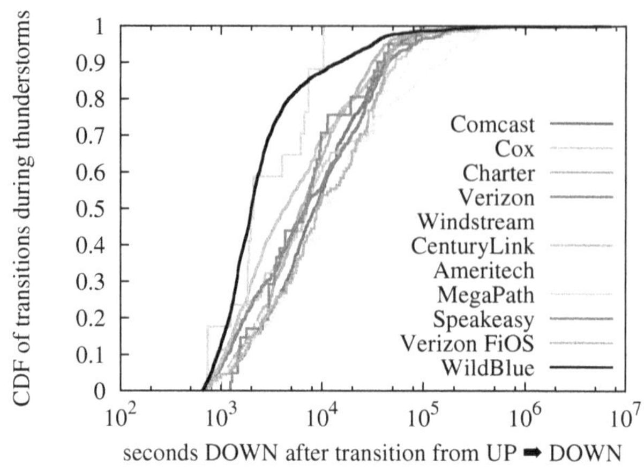

Figure 8: CDF of the time DOWN after transitioning from UP during thunderstorms. Surprisingly, the satellite provider's failures are shorter than in clear conditions.

(Figure 7). A likely explanation for this is that bursty outages caused by weather and atmospheric conditions are a common failure for Ka band satellite networks [6]. Our dataset confirms this hypothesis, WildBlue has the shortest median duration of failures as well as the shortest median time between failures.

As expected, in clear conditions, failures of a satellite provider are bursty, but in a thunderstorm, failures could be much longer. Figure 8 shows the distribution of the time hosts are DOWN after a failure during thunderstorms. Surprisingly, however, the time between failures for WildBlue appear to be shorter in thunderstorms than they are in clear conditions. Long failures also do not occur for a large portion of the WildBlue IPs observed. Of the 2,833 WildBlue IPs that fail at least once in thunderstorms, only 14% fail at least once for at least 3 hours, compared to 54% for the 1,121 Windstream IPs.

In the failure rate plot, Figure 6, Cox has correlated failures that do not seem to be related to weather. Cox has a significant fraction of transitions that last 0.8 hours. We observed a large correlated failure of 68 Cox customers with the reverse name mta*.mm.br.br.cox.net where the numbers appear to be a MAC address. The MAC address manufacturer is Arris equipment, and their E-MTA product is a cable modem and VoIP endpoint. This model of modems has a battery backup to provide voice service even if the power goes out. Considering that all 68 failed at night (12:40AM) at the same time, during clear weather at their closest airport KDTS, this seems likely to be a provider caused outage, possibly a firmware update.

5. DISCUSSION AND FUTURE WORK

We presented a preliminary study of failures during fairly typical weather events. Despite the short measurement duration of 66 days, for the large providers discussed in the results we observed the failures of 65,529 distinct IP addresses (23,957 more went HOSED) and observed significant correlation between severe weather and unreachability, even when looking only for simultaneous failures of nearby hosts. We see this as a promising preliminary analysis into the typical causes of everyday Internet unavailability.

We plan to continue this study by addressing sources of potential inaccuracy. We chose our location database for its ability to quickly position 100 million host IP addresses so that we might determine which to ping, but after data collection, we might need accurate positions of only the 129,631 that showed faults. Such may permit the use of more precise methods after-the-fact. Increased precision in IP positioning would demand increased precision in weather observations. The weather observed at an airport might not be observed just a few miles away. We would like to augment these surface measurements with more precise weather location and precipitation density information from Doppler radar. (Radar images on television that include precipitation type are a similar synthesis of surface observations of the precipitation type and the radar image showing precipitation location, but are not provided by NWS.)

We would also like to identify whether observed failures are indeed in the "last mile" network or are instead in a backhaul network. We expect that intermittent TTL-limited probing may help identify at least some upstream faults, depending on the network technology deployed.

We expect that additional data will enable study of how weather-induced outages depend, not just on the currently active condition, but also on measurable quantities, such as the duration of a storm, the inches of precipitation, or wind speed.

Finally, we would like to expand the study beyond the United States; the key stumbling point is in finding standardized, location-specific forecast data like that provided by NWS and a public network of standardized sensors, comparable to ASOS, that includes the precipitation type sensor.

6. ACKNOWLEDGMENTS

Thanks to Patrick Shoemaker and Dave Levin for helpful discussions. Also thanks to the anonymous reviewers and our shepherd Fabián Bustamante for their comments. This work was supported by NSF-0643443, NSF-0917098 and NSF-0626629.

7. REFERENCES

[1] E. W. W. Chan, X. Luo, W. W. T. Fok, W. Li, , and R. K. C. Chang. Non-cooperative diagnosis of submarine cable faults. In *Passive and Active Measurement Conference (PAM)*, 2011.

[2] Committee on the Internet Under Crisis Conditions: Learning from the Impact of September 11. *The Internet Under Crisis Conditions Learning from September 11.* National Academies Press, 2003.

[3] M. Dischinger, A. Haeberlen, K. P. Gummadi, and S. Saroiu. Characterizing residential broadband networks. In *Proceedings of the ACM Internet Measurement Conference (IMC)*, 2007.

[4] J. Heidemann, Y. Pradkin, R. Govindan, C. Papadopoulos, G. Bartlett, and J. Bannister. Census and survey of the visible Internet. In *Proceedings of the ACM Internet Measurement Conference (IMC)*, 2008.

[5] MaxMind, Inc. GeoIP city database. http://www.maxmind.com/app/city, Jan. 2011.

[6] I. Minei and R. Cohen. High-speed internet access through unidirectional geostationary satellite channels. In *IEEE Journal on Selected Areas in Communications*, 1999.

[7] National Weather Service. NWS public alerts in XML/CAP v1.1 and ATOM formats. http://alerts.weather.gov/.

[8] D. C. Plummer. RFC 826: Ethernet Address Resolution Protocol: Or converting network protocol addresses to 48.bit Ethernet address for transmission on Ethernet hardware, Nov. 1982.

[9] I. Poese, S. Uhlig, M. A. Kaafa, B. Donnet, and B. Gueye. IP geolocation databases: Unreliable? In *ACM SIGCOMM Computer Communication Review (CCR)*, 2011.

[10] Y. Wang, D. Burgener, M. Flores, A. Kuzmanovic, and C. Huang. Towards street-level client-independent IP geolocation. In *USENIX Symposium on Networked Systems Design and Implementation (NSDI)*, 2011.

[11] Weather Underground. Weather history and data archive. http://www.wunderground.com/history/.

[12] B. Wong, I. Stoyanov, and E. G. Sirer. Octant: A comprehensive framework for the geolocalization of Internet hosts. In *USENIX Symposium on Networked Systems Design and Implementation (NSDI)*, 2007.

[13] Y. Xie, F. Yu, K. Achan, E. Gillum, M. Goldszmidt, and T. Wobber. How dynamic are IP addresses? In *Proceedings of the ACM SIGCOMM Conference*, 2007.

Summary Review Documentation for

"Pingin' in the Rain"

Authors: A. Schulman, N. Spring

Reviewer #1

Strengths: Novel, fun idea, interesting results.

Weaknesses: Validation is a little weak.

Comments to Authors: Fun paper. Now I wish I could get that song out of my head...

Clearly a novel idea, and an interesting one at that. Given personal experience of living in different rural areas of the states and dealing with power outages of different lengths during storms, it makes sense that there is some elevation in network outages during bad weather.

I appreciate the discussion of weaknesses and potential sources of error. There are clearly some potential issues there, but it appears that, given the steps taken to mitigate those problems, the measurements are accurate enough to say that there are clearly some network problems correlated with bad weather. Still, coming up with some ways to validate what you are measuring, even for a subset of locations (e.g., select some location(s) in tornado alley, with cooperative ISPs and/or users) would lend much more credence to the work. The couple anecdotes were helpful (Figs 2 and 3), but something a little more systematic would benefit the work.

There was no discussion as to the coverage of the 100k ip addresses. How are these distributed geographically? Are there clumps of addresses in different places, or are they distributed similarly as population? Are all zip codes covered, or what fraction? Put another way, were there weather alerts for which you had few or no addresses to ping?

I wonder whether there are electric grid outage reports that can be correlated with your measurements. It might get to the interesting question you raise regarding whether you are seeing power outages or ISP outages.

It is too bad some measurements were not done in a slightly more intrusive way to try to get more fine grained measurements, especially of outage times.

Reviewer #2

Strengths: Neat, novel idea and pretty good approach.

Weaknesses: Not so many interesting results and relatively poor analysis; quite a few magic numbers (5.5 minutes, 8hrs,...).

Comments to Authors: This is a neat piece, if perhaps a bit premature. The report reads somewhat like a class project, which it probably is, and the analysis is a tad surfacy.

There is a large number of interesting questions unanswered, which perhaps makes sense for this as a short paper.

For instance, how are you going to address the second and third weaknesses in your approach? What is the impact of bad geolocation? How commonly would users turn off their machines during a storm and how could you get rid of those data points?

The definition of a weather event is rather broad, basically independent of the severity of it (wind speed, for instance). Also, I will assume that storm or high-wind prone areas are less susceptible to their common phenomena than other areas.

While I have no problem with the need for more than one ping, the argument is weak - starting from section header like "one ping is not enough" to go down to "2.3% fewer responses than the 2nd ping".

What do you mean by "to instrument" residential hosts (Sec. 3)?

You state - "to isolate failures that are not caused by human behavior we plot transitions where the IP address is unresponsive for more than 30 minutes but less than 8 hours"; I assume you mean to say "to factor out failures caused by human behavior"; it is unclear, however, what this filtering yields and the logic behind the bounds - why 8hrs?

You aggregate failures for a provider *across* all the events of a certain type; I assume this is due to not having enough data points? Treating all T-storms as a single set, for instance, is a bit too simplistic and may hide some interesting results on the impact of more common weather phenomena.

Why 5.5' in your correlation analysis? How sensitive are your results to this?

This is just a few of my main issues, perhaps none of them totally negative.

Reviewer #3

Strengths: An interesting, enticing hypothesis that is novel and requires methodological innovations to prove or disprove.

The authors have made enough headway to show viability.

Weaknesses: All said and done, the evidence in the paper of higher failure rates during bad weather is circumstantial. (But given its a short paper and a first attempt to do such a thing, we should accept this paper.)

Comments to Authors: This is a great short paper! You have taken an interesting hypothesis and tried to prove it. I've always

wondered about the impact of weather on network connectivity, for both residential connectivity as well as wireless (what with moisture absorbing my transmissions).
It was also interesting to see how you've managed to extract some of the needed signal by correlation different data sources. I think others would pick up these information sources.

The weakest part of the paper, and I suspect that you realize it already, is how do you validate such a thing. I am sympathetic here because I realize the difficulty of doing so. But are there other data sources you can pull on?

A couple of things that come to mind: publicly available information sources on failures (e.g., outages list or FCC filings); or private sources (e.g., internal ticket databases) acquired through collaboration with one of the providers.

Also, I hope that some of the issues with evidence can be handled through more sophisticated data analysis, which might require a lot more data. That would eliminate anomalies like Speakeasy and Megapath that you have to explain away. In any case, you should figure out a way to add confidence intervals to these findings, so we can judge which ones are statistically significant. (Your attempts at pulling signal out of highly noisy numbers reminds me of what sociologists and economists do often; consider talking to someone or looking up their methods.)

I wondered if Figure 4 is better plotted by providers (a group of adjacent bars per provider), rather than by weather condition. In the end, your primary goal is to enable us to visually compare the impact of weather within each provider, rather than compare the failure rate for different providers in a given weather condition.

From the introduction, why were you surprised that the median failure time for the satellite ISP was lower? Also, how (statistically) significant is that finding? (You need a lot of failures and, depending on the statistical tools used, some assumptions about the distribution of failure time.)

I did not understand why you could not use the older AWOS stations. What exact information that you need is missing? They perhaps enable a coarser (but more reliable) analysis of more data?

Reviewer #4

Strengths: It is a really fun topic, and, more importantly, it is true as well. My AT&T connection dies regularly during periods of heavy rain.

Weaknesses: There is plenty of room for improvement in the paper, which the authors acknowledge from the start. The biggest problem for me is the uncertainty as to the reason of *why* a host goes offline, which could include powering down for briefer periods. The fact that your best shot at identifying weather-related outage is the fact that bad weather was around and the outage was brief is not that great (again judging from personal experience, where the time to recovery can vary substantially, up to days). The dataset is also too thin to draw conclusions for some ISPs..

Comments to Authors: Very fun topic - I really enjoyed it.

It seems that one approach to distinguish regular machine uptime from bad weather effects would be time of day, as it is less likely that a computer remains powered up during the night but powered down for a few hours during the day.

In Table 1 I cannot distinguish the boundaries of connectivity type. Either add horizontal lines left and right of "Cable", "DSL", etc in order to indicate (preferred), or add vertical lines that separate the categories.

I encourage you to broaden the study to other countries. I personally have multi-year experience of three countries on two continents and can tell you that to me the sensitivity of Internet connectivity during bad weather is a uniquely American problem.

Finally, I thought I would share a weather-related story. A few years ago rain-induced outages were common enough for me that I called my ISP and asked for an engineer to come out. So one did, on a perfectly sunny day, and he promptly found nothing wrong with my DSL connection at all. He suggested I make an appointment with him for a day when the weather forecast is heavy rain... yeah right.

Reviewer #5

Strengths: To my knowledge, this is the first paper to provide quantitative evidence that weather affects residential connectivity.

Weaknesses: I do not think this is a good topic for a short paper..

Comments to Authors: My only negative comment is that this should have been a full paper: It does not introduce any new and/or interesting measurement technique. The conclusion (that weather affects connectivity) is not surprising, hence, I don't quite see the point of publishing preliminary evidence to support it. I think it would have made more sense to publish a full paper with a complete analysis of weather-induced network disruptions, most importantly try to identify the reason behind weather-induced network problems.

That said, what constitutes a good short paper is, admittedly, a subjective issue. I do acknowledge that this is the first paper to look at the impact of weather on residential connectivity, and I am sure it will create interesting discussion at the conference.

Response from the Authors

Comments addressed in the camera ready version of the paper:

We added a geographic distribution statistic for the providers that we focused on. There is a new row in the dataset description table (Table 1) that shows for each provider, the number of airports that customer IPs map to.

We clarified the reasoning behind removing failures shorter than 30 minutes and longer than 8 hours. To justify the 8 hour cutoff we included measurements of the diurnal failure pattern in the dataset.

We added two plots and text to indicate why we were surprised that the median failure time for a satellite ISP was relatively low.

In summary, we expected satellite provider failures would be longer during thunderstorms than in clear weather.

We strengthened the argument for more than one ping by providing a graph of the effectiveness of each ping and several other measurements.

Comments that we do not address in the paper:

Validating the cause of outages is a future goal for the project. Early on we tried to collect all reported power outages. However, we encountered two problems. (1) In the US, only a few power companies publish live power outage information on their website. (2) In the US it is difficult to map a geographic location to the power company that serves that location. In future work we may be monitoring social networks for reports of power outages. We also plan to correlate outages with the outages.org mailing list.

We binned weather conditions broadly because we did not have enough samples of specific conditions. The weather stations do report intensity, for example, the ASOS station reported both "heavy thunderstorms" and "light thunderstorms," for Ameritech customers. However, there were only 205 Ameritech failures observed during all thunderstorm intensities, and only 54 were during heavy thunderstorms.

We did not compute confidence intervals for the failure rate plots because we have not determined the dependence between failure rate samples; failures may be related by network links, geography and time. Although we do not quantify the confidence that failures are four times more likely in thunderstorms and two times more likely in rain, these observations are consistent across providers.

We would like to see how weather affects residential Internet connections outside of the US. We can add countries to the study only if they provide a feed of weather alerts and way to collect measurements from weather stations with precipitation type sensors.

Detecting, Validating and Characterizing Computer Infections in the Wild

Elias Raftopoulos
ETH Zurich
Zurich, Switzerland
rilias@tik.ee.ethz.ch

Xenofontas Dimitropoulos
ETH Zurich
Zurich, Switzerland
fontas@tik.ee.ethz.ch

ABSTRACT

Although network intrusion detection systems (IDSs) have been studied for several years, their operators are still overwhelmed by a large number of false-positive alerts. In this work we study the following problem: from a large archive of intrusion alerts collected in a production network, we want to detect with a small number of false positives hosts within the network that have been infected by malware. Solving this problem is essential not only for reducing the false-positive rate of IDSs, but also for labeling traces collected in the wild with information about validated security incidents. We use a 9-month long dataset of IDS alerts and we first build a novel heuristic to detect infected hosts from the on average 3 million alerts we observe per day. Our heuristic uses a statistical measure to find hosts that exhibit a repeated multi-stage malicious footprint involving specific classes of alerts. A significant part of our work is devoted to the validation of our heuristic. We conduct a complex experiment to assess the security of suspected infected systems in a production environment using data from several independent sources, including intrusion alerts, blacklists, host scanning logs, vulnerability reports, and search engine queries. We find that the false positive rate of our heuristic is 15% and analyze in-depth the root causes of the false positives. Having validated our heuristic, we apply it to our entire trace, and characterize various important properties of 9 thousand infected hosts in total. For example, we find that among the infected hosts, a small number of heavy hitters originate most outbound attacks and that future infections are more likely to occur close to already infected hosts.

Categories and Subject Descriptors

C.2.0 [**Computer-Communication Networks**]: [General Security and Protection]; C.2.3 [**Network Operations**]: [Network Monitoring]

General Terms

Measurement, Security, Verification

Keywords

Network Security, Intrusion Detection, Alert Correlation, Malware, Snort, J-Measure

1. INTRODUCTION

Evaluating and improving network defenses necessitates the use of realistic traces, like IDS alerts, from production networks labeled with information about validated security incidents. Although this is a well-known and long-held problem, presently the community is largely lacking both real-world security data and systematic techniques for evaluating network defenses. Given a database of IDS alerts, it is critical to find and validate security incidents in order to build benchmarks for evaluating network defenses. Motivated by this problem, in this work we introduce a heuristic to detect and propose an approach to validate active infections in our infrastructure. An infection is simply a client or a server with malicious software, which, in our context, leaves a network trace detectable by an IDS sensor. For example, the malware could be a trojan, worm, spyware, backdoor, etc.

The second problem that motivates our work is IDS false-positive reduction in the context of extrusion detection. Modern malware increasingly involve the user in their propagation by leveraging various social engineering techniques that bypass intrusion prevention measures. For this reason, security administrators need tools for detecting hosts within their network, i.e., *extrusion detection*, that are already infected by malware. Detecting extrusions from IDS alerts bears the challenge of reducing the large number of false positives IDSs are known to generate, e.g., figures of 99% false positives have been reported in the literature [33].

Our first contribution is a heuristic for finding infected hosts from IDS alerts. Our heuristic uses an information theoretic measure, called *J-Measure*, to identify statistically significant temporal associations between a selected pool of alerts. In this manner, it finds hosts that exhibit a recurring multi-stage alert trace. To validate that hosts with this footprint are indeed infected, we conduct a complex experiment: over a period of approximately one month we remotely assess a number of live suspected infections on unmanaged hosts within a production environment. Using six independent security-related information sources, namely IDS alerts, blacklists, threat reports, host scanning logs, vulnerability reports and search engine queries, we conclude that our heuristic reduces the amount of false positives to approximately 15%. In addition, we analyze the root causes of the false positives and draw insights for filtering them out.

Then, we apply our heuristic to 832 million alerts collected over a period of 9 months and identify 12,915 different infections on 9,163 out of the of the 91,512 distinct hosts that generated IDS alerts. We characterize the extracted infections and make a number of important observations:

- Out of a total of 91 thousand distinct active hosts we observed during the 9-month period, approximately 9% exhibited signs of infections at least once during their lifetime.
- The probability of infection for a server and a client during a specific day is 0.18% and 0.37%, respectively.
- Infections drastically increase the attractiveness of infected hosts to further inbound attacks.
- A small percentage of hosts are popular sources and targets of attacks. In particular, 5% of the internal hosts account for more than 70% of the total recorded attacks originating from the intranet. In addition, servers are much more preferable targets than clients.
- Healthy hosts closer in terms of IP address distance to infected hosts are much more likely to become infected.
- The infection points exhibit diurnal patterns.
- Our time series analysis shows that server infections are almost independent in time, while client infections are consistently more bursty and this is more evident for aggregation time-scales above two minutes.

In summary, in this work we make the following **contributions**:

1. **Detection**: We introduce a heuristic for detecting infections that uses a statistical correlation measure, namely the *J-Measure*, to find hosts that produce a recurring multi-stage alert footprint involving specific classes of alerts.
2. **Validation**: We introduce a methodolgy and conduct a complex experiment to systematically validate suspected live infections on unmanaged hosts within a production environment. We find that the false positive rate of our heuristic is 15%.
3. **Characterization**: We characterize 9,163 infections over a period of 9 months. To the best of our knowledge, this is the first characterization of a very large number of infections.

The remainder of this paper is structured as follows. In Section 2 we describe the IDS alert traces we used in our experiments. We introduce our heuristic in Section 3 and describe our validation experiments and results in Section 4. Then, we characterize a number of interesting properties of the identified infections in Section 5. Finally, we review related work in Section 6, we discuss our findings in Section 7 and conclude our paper in Section 8.

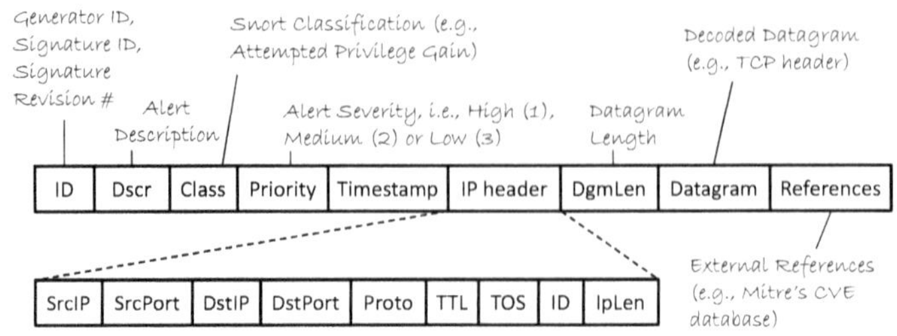

Figure 1: Snort Alert Full Format

2. IDS DATA

Our dataset is comprised of raw IDS alerts triggered in the main campus of ETH Zurich by a Snort [47] sensor, which is placed between the edge router of the campus and the network firewall. The sensor monitors all the upstream and downstream traffic of the campus. It uses the official Snort signature ruleset and the Emerging Threats (ET) ruleset [19], which are the two most commonly-used Snort rulesets. As of April 2011 the two rulesets have a total of 37,388 distinct signatures to detect malicious activities.

The collected alerts have the standard full Snort format shown in Figure 1. For example, the following is an actual high priority alert (with anonymized IP addresses) about a suspected MySQL bot:

```
[**] [1:2001689:7] ET WORM Potential MySQL bot scanning for SQL server [**]
[Classification: A Network Trojan was detected] [Priority: 1]
01/01-22:04:51.319793 aaa.bbb.ccc.ddd:41276 -> xxx.yyy.zzz.hhh:3306
TCP TTL:61 TOS:0x0 ID:14368 IpLen:20 DgmLen:44 DF
******S* Seq: 0xC2A22307  Ack: 0x0  Win: 0x16D0  TcpLen: 24
```

The fields we use are the unique rule identification number, the rule description, the timestamp that denotes when the alert was triggered, the IPs and ports of the communicating hosts, the default rule classification, which indicates the type of suspected malicious activity, and the rule priority, which provides a severity rank. The complete raw alerts as generated by Snort are sent every hour to our collection and archiving infrastructure.

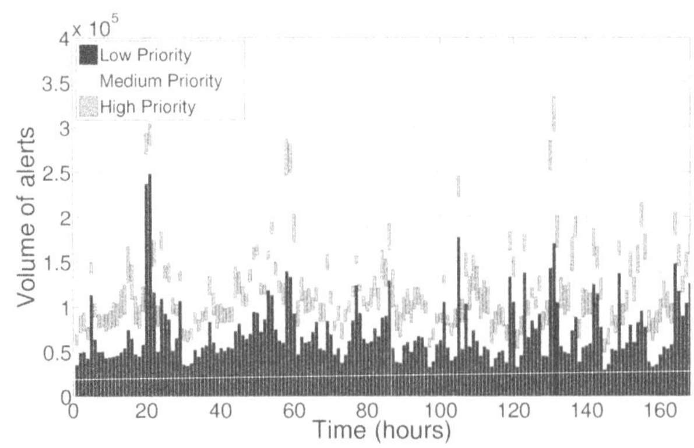

Figure 2: Volume of low, medium, and high priority alerts per hour during a period of a week

The dataset is both large and rich. During the 9 month period we study, spanning from January 1st 2010 to September 22nd 2010, our monitoring ran on a 24/7 basis with only minor interruptions (corresponding to approximately 99% availability), capturing more than 832 million alerts

Table 1: Classtype frequency of rules in `sql.rules`

#	Classification	Description
691	misc-activity	Miscellaneous activity
293	successful-recon-limited	Information leak
52	attempted-admin	Attempted administrator privilege gain
22	attempted-user	Attempted user privilege gain
4	unsuccessful-user	Unsuccessful user privilege gain
3	shellcode-detect	Executable code was detected
2	suspicious-login	An attempted login using a suspicious username was detected
2	misc-attack	Miscellaneous attack

from 91,512 thousand internal IPs. Figure 2 illustrates the amount of alerts that we collect during a regular week. On an hourly basis we record on average more than 130 thousand alerts. The vast majority of these alerts have low priority and usually correspond to policy violations that are not directly related to security incidents. However, a significant portion, approximately 6%, consists of high priority alerts.

To identify unique host infections, we restrict our analysis to hosts with static IP addresses and exclude alerts from dynamic IP address ranges. We distinguish between dynamic and static subnets using a catalog maintained by our network administrators that documents each campus subnet. Additionally, this information enables us to find whether a subnet accommodates server or client machines. The excluded alerts originating from dynamic IP address ranges, correspond to less than 17% of the total active internal IPs in our data. The fact that most hosts use static IP addresses is important as it enables us to track and characterize their behavior over time.

3. METHODOLOGY

3.1 Alert Bundling

The first challenge that we need to deal with is that security events often trigger spurts of very similar alerts. For example, certain types of port scanning targeting a range of destination ports will generate a large number of almost identical alerts that only differ in the destination port and timestamp fields. Besides, malware often change slightly their behavior in order to evade detection. Snort rulesets often include different signatures for each different malware version. When the malicious behavior is manifested, multiple versions of the same signature may be triggered in a very short time window. For example, we observe spurts of the alert "ET DROP Known Bot C&C Server Traffic group (X)" that only differ in the version number X. Such spurts of almost identical alerts are not desirable, since they defuse a single event into multiple segments. Alert bundling groups spurts of very similar alerts into a single aggregate alert. Compared to different forms of alerts aggregation, which have been studied in the literature [51], alert bundling aims at aggregating spurts of almost identical alerts instead of creating groups of much more diverse alerts that correspond to the same aggregate multi-stage incident. Alert bundling is useful as it reduces the amount of alerts that need to be processed and facilitates the statistical analysis of different events.

We perform alert bundling over three fields, source/destination ports and alert ID. We generalize the port fields from a numerical value to {*privileged*,*ephemeral*}, based on whether the port number is below or above 1024, respectively. We also generalize alert IDs that correspond to different flavors of the same malware into a single alert ID by ignoring the version number. We then merge alerts triggered within a short time window into a single generalized alert. We preserve the timestamp of the first alert of the merged sequence. We select an aggregation window of 5 seconds. Our calibration showed that this is sufficient to substantially reduce the number of alerts, while further increasing this window had a negligible effect on the volume of alerts. Alert bundling reduced the total number of alerts in our data by 19%.

3.2 Alert Classification

Our dataset includes alerts triggered from 37,388 thousand unique rules. Snort rules are mainly community-contributed and follow a loose two-level classification scheme. Each rule is part of a ruleset, which groups related rules. For example, the ruleset `imap.rules` groups rules associated with the IMAP protocol. The second level of classification is based on the class field that is contained within each rule. The class field associates each rule with a unique class that provides information regarding the intended goal of an intrusion.

For our purposes, we find the default two-level classification scheme insufficient to extract alerts that relate to attacks and compromised hosts, which are the types of alerts we are interested in. The first shortcoming is that rules are grouped into rulesets based on different criteria. For example, some rulesets, like `imap.rules` and `voip.rules`, group rules based on the protocol or the application that is targeted, while some other rulesets, like `ddos.rules`, groups rules based on the type of the intrusion. A second problem is that rulesets often contain very diverse rules. For example `sql.rules` contains rules that range from accessing a database, which could correspond to benign behavior, to SQL worm propagation, which could indicate an infected host. Moreover, the classes associated with the classtype field are scarcely documented and in some cases ambiguous. In Table 1 we list the classes for alerts in the `sql.rules` file and provide the official documentation for each class. Some classes are quite intuitive, for example *Attempted administrator privilege gain* denotes that a privilege escalation attack took place. However, some other classes, like *Miscellaneous activity*, are quite cryptic and can result in loose classifications.

To address this problem, we use a hierarchical approach to classify the rules included in our data into three classes, namely *Attacks*, *Compromised hosts*, and *Policy violations* (similarly to [30]). In the first step, we manually examined all the rulesets and identified the ones that clearly character-

Table 2: Rulesets and classtypes assigned to the *Compromise* class

Rulesets	Description
attack-responses.rules	Privilege escalation attempts
backdoor.rules	Trojan activity operating as Backdoor
ddos.rules	Bot initiating a DDoS attack
virus.rules	Malicious code attempting to propagate
emerging-botcc.rules	Bot-related trojan activity
emerging-compromised.rules	Attacks from blacklisted IPs
emerging-user_agents.rules	Data stealing malware
emerging-virus.rules	Malicious code attempting to propagate
Classtypes	**Description**
trojan-activity	A network Trojan was detected

ize an attack or a compromised host. With this step we were able to classify 72.5% of the total number of rules. For the remaining set of rules, we used the classtype field and identified 16 classes that can be clearly associated with attacks or compromised host activity. Finally, for the remaining 681 rules, we manually classified them by examining the details of the signature, the assigned default priority level, the exact byte sequence, and when possible we validated our results with information provided in security archives and bulletins [47, 20]. In Table 2 we summarize the rulesets and classtypes we used for our *Compromise* class.

Finally, the alerts that are not classified as attacks or compromised hosts, mostly occur when a user does not comply with a specific policy. Typically these alerts correspond to P2P, VoIP, and chat related rules. We discard these rules since they do not provide any useful information about infections. For the remaining sections, we only work with alerts of the *Attack* and *Compromise* class.

3.3 Identifying Infections

A naive approach in identifying infections of internal hosts is to rely on occurrences of *Attack* and *Compromise* related alerts. However, the excessive amount of false positives, makes it very hard to have any level of confidence that we can infer an actual infection using a single alert.

We build our heuristic to extract infections based on the following design goals.

- **Keep it simple**: We opt to keep our heuristic simple as parsimony provides a number of advantages: 1) inferences are interpretable and easier to trace and validate both for a scientist and an IDS operator; and 2) the heuristic can efficiently analyze large archives of millions of IDS alerts.
- **Reduce false positives**: The number of false positives is involved in a fundamental trade-off with the sensitivity of the detector. Presently, IDSs suffer from a very large number of false positives. In this trade-off, we opt to make our heuristic conservative, i.e., less sensitive, so that the inferences it produces include a small number of false positives. This also means that we may incur some false negatives, which we prefer than triggering a large number of false positives. In order to reduce the number of false positives, we engineer our heuristic to combine multiple evidence.
- **Detect recurring multi-stage behavior**: Pre-sently, malware developers bundle a plethora of features and capabilities to make their product more attractive. For example, malware attempt to redirect users to malicious websites and download additional trojans; they update, receive instructions, share confidential data, and participate in (D)DoS attacks or spamming campaigns; they attempt to propagate by scanning for exposed nodes and by exploiting vulnerabilities, etc. This means that most modern malware exhibit a multi-stage network footprint. Additionally, the multi-stage behavior is typically recurring. For example, a host infected with an SQL worm, will scan for vulnerable machines running an unpatched version of the Microsoft SQL server. Every time a target is found, the infected host will initiate a buffer overflow attack in order to exploit the vulnerability and eventually infect the victim. A Zeus trojan will attempt to inject fake HTML code every time the user visits an online bank page, in order to steal confidential data. The collected details will be then delivered to databases residing in a remote site. Based on these observations, our heuristic attempts to reduce the number of IDS false positives by searching for malware that exhibit a recurring multistage behavior.
- **Focus on extrusion detection**: Our heuristic aims at detecting hosts within an organization that are already infected. It does not try to proactively prevent an infection.

Detection Heuristic: Our approach aims at detecting a recurring multi-stage footprint generated by infected hosts. In the simplest case, a multi-stage footprint resolves into tuples of strongly correlated alerts. Such tuples capture different actions undertaken by an infected host that occur frequently and consistently over time, increasing our certainty that an actual infection has indeed occured. We use an entropy-based information-theoretic criterion to detect significant tuples of alerts.

Our input data is a time series of alerts, where each alert is identified by the following five fields: *<ID; SrcIP; DstIP; SrcPort; DstPort>*. We examine each internal host separately, discretize its sequence of alerts into time windows of length T, and mine for tuples of the type: if alert X occurs, then alert Y occurs within the time window T. We denote the above tuple with $X \Rightarrow Y$. Each tuple is associated with a frequency and a confidence, where the frequency is the normalized number of occurrences of the first alert X and the confidence is the fraction of occurrences that alert X

is followed by alert Y within T. A well-known measure of tuple significance that combines these two basic metrics and enables to rank tuples is the *J-Measure* [46] (for an overview of tuple ranking methods refer to [40]):

$$J\text{-}Measure(Y;X) = P(X)(P(Y|X)log(\frac{P(Y|X)}{P(Y)})+ P(\bar{Y}|X)log(\frac{P(\bar{Y}|X)}{P(\bar{Y})})),$$

where $P(X)$ is the probability that alert X occurs; $P(Y)$ is the probability of at least one Y occurring at a randomly chosen window; $P(Y|X)$ is the probability that alert X is followed by at least one alert Y within T; and $\bar{Y}$ denotes the event that Y does not occur. Intuitively, the first term $P(X)$ captures the frequency of X, while the second term is the well-known cross-entropy and captures the average mutual information between the random variables X and Y. In this way, the *J-Measure* ranks tuples in a way that balances the trade-off between frequency and confidence.

The cross-entropy between X and Y drops when the two events tend to occur together. In particular, there are two cases when the corresponding entropy of Y drops. When X happens, Y always happens, or it doesn't ever happen. Clearly, the first case is of interest to us, since it reflects the probability of the two alerts co-occurring in a specific time window T. The second case is irrelevant since there will always be numerous alerts that do not occur when a specific alert happens, resulting in an inflated *J-Measure* value. Therefore, we only keep the left term of the cross-entropy to evaluate the significance of a tuple.

One desirable characteristic of the *J-Measure* is its limiting properties. Its value ranges from 0, when random variables X and Y are independent, to $\frac{1}{P(Y)}$, when they are completely dependent, which facilitates the process of defining a threshold above which tuples are considered significant. An internal host that produces at least one significant tuple is considered infected. We fine-tune the threshold to $\frac{0.85}{P(Y)}$ as described in Section 4.4 using validated infections from our most reliable source, which is security tickets about infected and remediated systems by our security group. From the set of significant tuples we can easily extract the infection timestamps. For each tuple $X \Rightarrow Y$, if there is no other tuple $Z \Rightarrow W$ involving the same internal host within a time window T_{inf}, then this is a new infection at the timestamp of alert X. Otherwise, this is an ongoing infection and we ignore the corresponding tuple.

In Algorithm 1 we show the pseudo-code of our heuristic. Its complexity is $O(n^2)$, where n is the number of unique alerts triggered by an internal node during T. In our experiments n is quite low and on average equal to 3.1. To run our heuristic on one day of data takes on average 19.3 minutes on a system running Debian Etch with a 2GHz Quad-Core AMD Opteron.

Parameter Tuning: For the window size T we conservatively select one hour, since most alerts related to the same infection in our data occur within minutes. Selecting a larger window has negligible impact on the results. Moreover, we consider that a host is re-infected if the host is active in our dataset, but for a period of T_{inf} it is not detected as infected by our heuristic. We set the T_{inf} threshold to two weeks. We select this value in a conservative way based on two observations. Incidents identified and investigated in the past

Algorithm 1 Pseudo-code of our heuristic for detecting infections

```
Require: Set L of alerts triggered by internal hosts
Ensure: Significant tuples S_i for internal node i
  for all internal nodes i do
    for all hourly timebins T_k do
      for all tuples (A_i, B_i) in L, triggered in T_k, where
      A_i ≠ B_i do
        if A_i ⇒ B_i in candidate tuple set R_i then
          R_i.UpdateTupleStats(A_i ⇒ B_i)
        else
          R_i.AddTuple(A_i ⇒ B_i)
        end if
      end for
    end for
    for all tuples M_i ⇒ N_i in R_i do
      if J-Measure(M_i ⇒ N_i) > J_thresh then
        S_i.AddTuple( M_i ⇒ N_i )
      end if
    end for
  end for
```

in our infrastructure suggest that the worst case delay required by our security group to fix a reported problem is approximately one week. This time frame covers the stages of threat identification, threat assessment, and remediation of the host either by completely removing the malware or by rebuilding the entire system. On the other hand it is known, that some malware infections stay dormant for predefined time periods or wait for an external command to trigger their behavior [4]. In this case, the host will be reported as benign by our heuristic, since no network trace of malicious activity is being generated. However, after the initial stimulus and assuming that the malicious behavior has been manifested, it is highly unlikely that the malware will fall again into idle mode for a time period longer than T_{inf} [44]. Out of the total infections we find in our characterization, 4.9% are re-infections.

4. VALIDATING INFECTIONS

In this section we present the process we follow to validate inferred infections and to assess the false positive rate of our heuristic. Remotely validating several suspected infections on unmanaged hosts within a production infrastructure is a very challenging problem that to the best of our knowledge has not been previously addressed in the literature. A first challenge is that typically no single tool or information source provides sufficient evidence that an actual security incident has occurred. A second challenge is that the types of malicious behaviors we examine are diverse, ranging from multi-stage attacks and worm propagation events to complex trojan and malware communication patterns.

Our validation follows a three step process as shown in Figure 3. Given a suspected infection, we first extract useful information from six security-related independent information sources about the infected host and the remote hosts it communicates. We refer to this information as *evidence*. A collection of evidence about suspected infections is passed in real-time (e.g., within a day of the first time an infection was detected) to a security expert. The expert correlates the expected behavior of the malware with the collected evidence. If all the evidence agree with the expected behavior, then a positive assessment is made about the suspected infection, otherwise it is concluded that the infection could not be validated, i.e., it is unknown if the suspected host is indeed infected or not. We conservatively consider the latter a false positive.

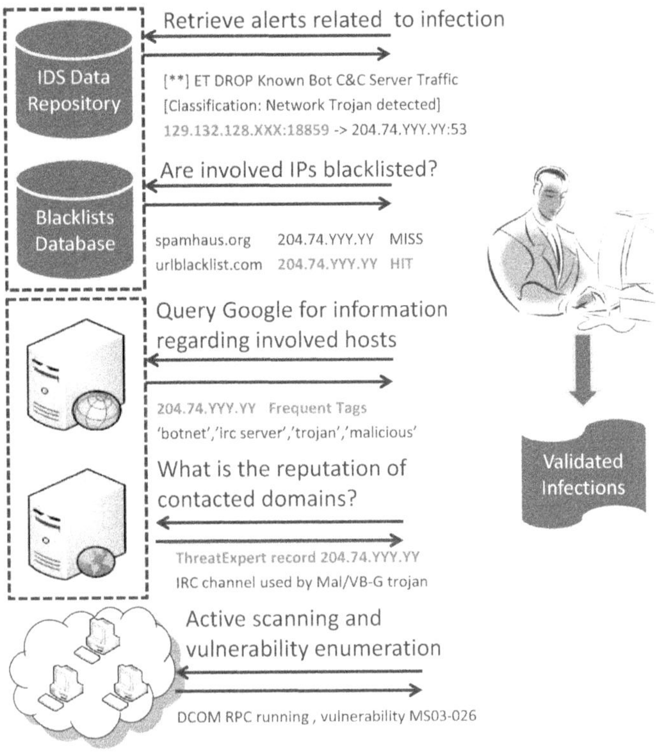

Figure 3: Validation Process

This process is very demanding and time consuming for the analyst, therefore, we limit ourselves to a subset of the reported infections. Specifically, we analyze 200 consecutive incidents that were reported by our heuristic and validate the existence or absence of a variety of malware types. Although, this sample of infections is rather small compared to the total number of infections we report, the analyzed nodes are diverse spanning from servers, to desktop PCs in offices and wireless guests in labs and social areas. Also, the malicious software we investigate is quite diverse and can be categorized based on its goals and propagation methods into the following classes [37]:

- *backdoors/bots* allow an external entity to remotely control an infected machine.
- *trojans* masquerade as benign programs, but clandestinely perform illegal actions, such as information leakage and *url*-redirection.
- *worms* are self-replicating and propagating programs that attach themselves to processes or files making them carriers of a malicious behavior.
- *spyware* are useful pieces of software that are bundled with some hidden fraudulent activity.

4.1 Information Sources

IDS Alerts: For infected nodes we examine the relevant IDS alerts we have collected. We focus on alerts that are triggered in temporal proximity to the infection incident. We evaluate the quality of the alerts based on the following assumption: we consider that oversimplified signatures will tend to generate too many false positives, since it is very likely that they get triggered by benign traffic. On the other hand complex signatures are much more reliable. In order to evaluate the complexity of a signature we check if specific byte sequences within a packet are checked, if the rule specifies the ports, packet size and TCP/IP flags, if previous packets of the same flow are taken into account, and if regular expressions are being used.

Blacklists: We use independent blacklists in order to characterize a suspected host and its communicating remote hosts. We use information provided by five publicly available blacklists [22, 23, 28, 15, 17] and by one commercial blacklist [27]. We then inspect if an internal node is listed in any of these blacklists within the analyzed tracing period, and if we get a hit we tag the node based on the type of blacklist that generated the hit, e.g., spam or botnet list. Note that due to the rather high percentage of false positives [45] in most reputation-based blacklists, a blacklist hit is insufficient evidence to confirm a suspected infection. It is though a useful indicator that needs to be correlated with additional observations. Moreover, we perform the same blacklist search for external hosts that the analyzed internal machine communicated with. For example communication with hosts within the *Russian Business Network*, a network providing hosting services to cyber-criminals, could signify that the user visits some dangerous websites or that he is redirected to these URLs by an active clickbot [11] or spyware.

Threat Reports: Threat reports are publicly available security logs provided by automated systems [14] or security companies [29, 18] that analyze the behavioral patterns and common actions of a wide range of security threats including worms, trojans, and spyware. They provide a security reputation value for domains based on their observed activity during a specific interval. By investigating threat reports we can identify if a suspected host is contacting URLs that correspond to botnet rendez-vous points or malware landing pages to receive instructions, perform updates or share stolen confidential data.

Web-based Host Profiling: Apart from relying on network traces and threat analysis reports to build a security profile for a suspected host, we also use publicly available data residing on the web, which often provide useful information about the role (type of server, etc.) and involvement of hosts in security incidents [50]. This information originates from several diverse sources such as DNS-lists, website access logs, proxy logs, P2P tracker lists, forums, bulletins, banlists, IRC-lists, etc. In order to retrieve this information we query the Google search engine using as input string the IP of the analyzed host and the respective domain name we get using a reverse-DNS lookup. In an semi-automated fashion we search for tags that reveal possible roles or actions of the host such as 'trojan', 'botnet', 'spam','irc server', 'adserver', 'pop3' and 'webserver'.

Reconaissance and Vulnerability Reports: Analyzing network based data provides us with rich information regarding the behavioral patterns exhibited by a monitored host. However, we do not get any information about the running services, the patching level of critical components, and the existence or absence of vulnerabilities. Naturally, this type of information can be used to validate if an investigated node is susceptible to a specific type of infection or if the set of alerts used to infer the infection correspond to false positives, since they are not relevant to the build and operation of the specific node. Our network security assessment process consists of the following steps:

1. Host Enumeration and Basic Reconnaissance. In this step we use basic reconnaissance techniques such as IP sweeps, NIC whois querying, and TCP/UDP port-scanning in order to identify if a host is reachable and exposed to external attacks. In addition, we determine its role within the infrastructure, such as web, mail, or DNS server.

2. Network Scanning and Probing. In this step we perform targeted network scanning using nmap in order to retrieve detailed information regarding the TCP and UDP network services running on suspicious hosts, details about the OS type and version, and information regarding the types of ICMP messages a host responds to, which reveals its filtering policies and firewall effectiveness.

3. Investigation of Vulnerabilities. After having detected the accessible network services, we investigate the corresponding host for known vulnerabilities. We use publicly available sources [16, 24, 21] to identify the existence of exploitable bugs on running services. We augment this assessment with complementary information provided from vulnerability scanners, namely Nessus [25] and OpenVas [26], in order to build a comprehensive profile regarding the vulnerability status of a node.

4.2 Security Assessment

To better understand the security assessment process, in the following, we outline a set of frequent infection cases we established during our validation. For each case, we mapped the collected evidence into the behavior that was manifested by a specific malware. The four cases correspond to the four main types of malware we found in our infrastructure, namely backdoors, spyware, worms, and trojans[1].

Case 1: Backdoor infection. W32/SdBot is a typical family of IRC-controlled trojans with more than 4,000 known variants. It is used by cybercriminals as backdoor in order to gain unauthorized access to a target machine and perform unsolicited actions such as stealing private information or launching active attacks. The typical vulnerabilities we search for when we investigate an SdBot-related infection are the MS-LSASS buffer overflow, the MS-RPC malformed message buffer overflow, and the MS-WebDav vulnerabilities. These are related to the MS network shares services, which are exploited by the trojan to propagate. Regarding its command and control (C&C) activity, an infected host will attempt to use IRC to contact the adversary in order to receive instructions. This communication will typically trigger alerts with ID within the ranges [2500000:2500500] and [9000077:9000113]. The communicated C&C is typically present in our blacklst or/and profiling data. Additionally, the malware might try to propagate to other subnets. In this case we expect to see extensive scanning activity (mostly on port 445). If a vulnerable host is found and exploited successfully, then the trojan will either attempt to download a version of itself or other additional malware (typically W32/Koobface and Trojan.FakeAV) via ftp.

Case 2: Spyware Infection. The Win32/Hotbar type of malware is the most widespread infection in our infrastructure. Most variants appear as a web-browser add-on that provides a seemingly legitimate functionality. However, this malware will clandestinely steal and report user confidential data, like banking information, passwords, browsing habits, etc. For this type of infection, we find IDS alerts with IDs in the range [2003305:2003500]. We trust these alerts as the signatures are quite complex and the malware does not put any effort in disguising. Moreover, the malware operates as clickbot, changing results displayed by search engines and generating pop-ups to redirect the user to potentially malicious websites. These domains are likely to appear in our blacklists or/and web profiling data, usually with tags like 'malware-hosting', 'fraudulent', and 'phishing'.

Case 3: Worm Infection. W32/Palevo is the most common malware type found in the rather short list of worm-related infections detected in our infrastructure. It usually spreads automatically using P2P file sharing or Instant Messaging (IM) spam. When investigating this type of infection we expect to see IDS alerts with IDs in the range [2801347:2801349], which are worm specific, or more generic alerts related to activities complying with a P2P or IM protocol (typically IDs in the ranges [2451:2461], [549:565] and [2008581:2008585]). The worm will attempt to directly contact C&C nodes, without hiding the communication in an IRC channel, using an ephemeral set of port numbers. Commonly, the remote hosts `irc.ekizmedia.com`, `story.dnsentrymx.com`, and `irc.snahosting.net` are contacted. These malicious domains usually appear both in our blacklist data and in our profiling information with tags including 'botnet', 'C&C', 'Rimecud', and 'Mariposa'.

Case 4: Trojan infection. Win32/Monkif is a typical trojan that will attempt to fetch and install malicious software on a victim host. This type of malware is usually bundled with pirated software or is pushed to the victim by using phishing or social engineering attacks. When we investigate this family of infections we expect the host to connect to specific domains (including `www.clicksend.biz` and `stats.woodmedia.biz`) in order to download malicious binaries. These domains are likely to appear in our threat reports as malware hosting and generate tags as 'trojan', 'botnet', 'malware' and 'downloader' in our host profiling results.

The manual security assessment lasted for approximately one month. On a daily basis a security expert was given a list of suspected infections produced by our heuristic for the previous day along with a pool of evidence that were extracted in a semi-automated way. The expert thoroughly investigated in total 200 infections. During the first week of the validation process, two experts assessed indepedently

[1] We note that this is not a unique malware taxonomy. Putting malware into a taxonomy is challenging as most malware today have a complex behavior, usually incorporating multiple components allowing them to propagate, communicate with remote hosts to receive commands, and automatically update or initiate the download of additional malicious software.

the same suspected infections and then compared, discussed and converged on their assessments.

4.3 Validation Results

In Table 3 we summarize the number of suspected and verified infections along with the corresponding false positive rate for the four types of infections. We first note that the overall false positive rate is approximately 15%, which is remarkable. Recall that in our input data, we observe on average 3 million alerts per day, which we believe include a large number of false positives. By reversing our bundling procedure we find that only 0.6% of our input alerts of the class *Attack* and *Compromise* are associated with an infection. Our heuristic helps focus the attention of administrators to a small number of actionable cases that include substantially fewer false positives. The false positive rate for trojans, spyware, worms, and backdoors is 12.3%, 10.6%, 11%, and 35%, respectively.

Table 3: Validated infections for different infection types

	Reported Incidents	Validated Incidents	False Positive Rate (%)
Trojans	97	85	12.3
Spyware	66	59	10.6
Worms	9	8	11.0
Backdoors	28	18	35.0

Moreover, to understand better the strengths and limitations of our heuristic, we investigate the root causes of the observed false positives. The following cases were the source of most false positives.

DNS Servers. First, we find that DNS servers within our infrastructure frequently trigger signatures from the *Compromise* class. The reason is that they often attempt to resolve domains that are considered malicious. These DNS requests trigger signatures that check the destination IP address and compare it against a list of known compromised hosts. An alert will be raised in this case, typically with IDs in the range [2500000:2500941], which corresponds to backdoor related activity. DNS related false positives are mainly responsible for the inflated value regarding backdoors false positive rate shown in Table 3. However, a network administrator should be able to easily identify that these incidents do not constitute actual infections, and filter them out.

Skype Supernodes. Second, Skype supernodes within our network generate alerts with IDs in the ranges [2406000:2406966] and [2500433:2500447]. Skype supernodes connect Skype clients by creating the Skype P2P overlay network. However, if it happens that a remote Skype user connecting to a local supernode is blacklisted, then Snort will trigger an alert identifying this system as malicious. This communication is persistent and frequent since whenever a Skype client attempts to initiate a communication, it will access a distributed database provided by supernodes in order to get the details of the contacted peer.

Antivirus. Third, a specific antivirus program generates IDS alerts of the class *Compromise* while updating. The triggered signatures check for known patterns of malicious activity found on the payload of the transmitted packets. It appears that the updates of this antivirus contain the actual pattern that it attempts to detect in plain format.

Online Games. Finally, we have observed that certain types of online games generate Snort alerts with IDs in the ranges [2003355:2003626] and [2510000:2510447]. In the case of browser-based games the triggered signatures suggest that there is an ongoing spyware-related activity. The reason is that the corresponding websites exhibit a behavior that is very similar to clickbots, attempting to redirect the player to 3rd party, potentially malicious, websites for profit. In the case of standalone gaming applications, we observe that the client will tend to preserve multiple concurrent connections with several other players. Often a small set of these remote IPs originate from domains which are blacklisted, and therefore an alert is raised.

4.4 Fine-tuning the Heuristic

As discussed in Section 3.3 an important parameter of our heuristic is the *J-Measure* threshold that determines if a specific tuple will be tagged as an active infection. In order to adjust this threshold we performed the discussed validation process on an additional small set of nodes in the local subnet of our institute. The duration of this training phase was two weeks and occurred chronologically before the main validation. During this period we run our heuristic using variable *J-Measure* threshold values and evaluated its inference results.

For the local subnet of our institute we were able to use very reliable information sources to validate a small number of detected infections. In particular, for a set of nodes we physically visited their owners and verified an infection either by performing an on the spot assessment of a system or by receiving a confirmation from an owner aware that her system was indeed infected. Secondly, our second very reliable information source for our local subnet is security tickets of our IT team. These are logged events about security incidents that have been detected, assessed, and remediated.

Using information for 28 systems we adjusted the *J-Measure* threshold in a conservative manner, i.e., aiming at keeping the false positives as low as possible, but without increasing the false negatives significantly. Selecting a threshold of $\frac{0.85}{P(Y)}$ achieved a good tradeoff, limiting the false positive rate to below 10% and the false negative rate to below 23%. For threshold values below $\frac{0.80}{P(Y)}$ the corresponding false positive rate increases above 24%, whereas for threshold values above $\frac{0.90}{P(Y)}$ we miss more than 32% of active infections.

5. CHARACTERIZING INFECTIONS

Volume and Types of Infections: The first interesting finding, illustrated in Figure 4, is that on a daily basis from an average of 11,850 active[2] hosts, we detect on average 50 new infections. The vast majority of the infected hosts correspond to client machines. Specifically 97% of the total reported incidents occur in end-host systems whereas we only see on average 10 infections per week on servers. If we normalize these numbers based on the total number of active servers and clients in our infrastructure, we see that *the probability of infection for a server system during a specific day is 0.18%, whereas the corresponding value for clients is 0.37%.*

The relatively small number of server infections can be attributed to two causes. Firstly, these systems are heavily

[2] An active host generates at least one IDS alert during an indicated period

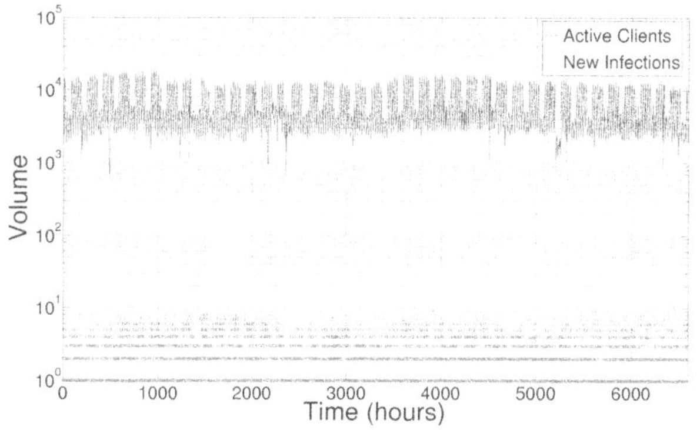

Figure 4: Active clients and new infections time-series

managed, closely monitored, and often have their OS hardened, meaning that unnecessary and potentially vulnerable services are disabled. Secondly, as we saw in Section 4 most of the malware that we observe propagate using indirect methods (e.g. drive-by-downloads, phishing) that involve the user and exploit his negligence, rather than initiating direct attacks, like scanning or buffer overflow attacks.

Moreover, *out of a total of 91 thousand distinct active hosts we observed during the 9-month period, approximately 9% exhibited signs of infections at least once during their lifetime*, whereas the total number of infections (including nodes that were re-infected) was 12,915. The number of nodes exhibiting re-infections was 675, corresponding to less than 1% of the entire active population. The majority of these nodes were connected to highly dynamic subnets in our network, corresponding to student labs and recreation areas, which are not heavily monitored. These are mostly private laptops without administrative restrictions on the installed applications and services. Therefore, the attack vector of these machines is broader, which is reflected on the increased probability of reinfection.

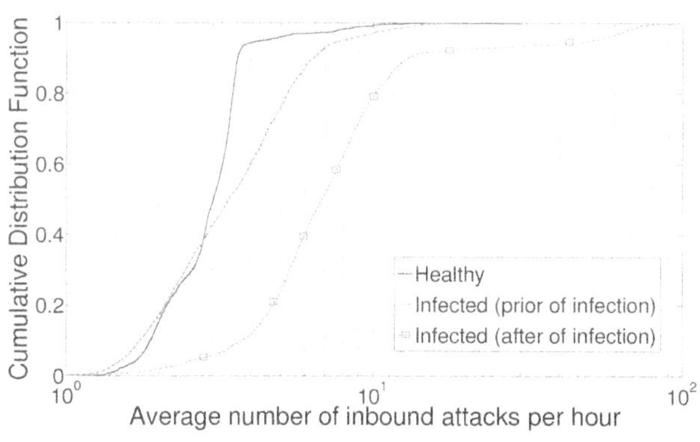

Figure 5: Infection impact on the number of inbound attacks

Infections Impact: Figure 5 illustrates the impact of an infection on the number of monitored inbound attacks. We count the average number of alerts classified as attacks targeting hosts in our intranet in an hourly basis, for all healthy hosts, for infected hosts prior to their infection, and infected hosts after their infection. Note, that based on our heuristic the infection time is estimated only after the actual infection manifests. If a node is infected but the corresponding malware remains dormant, it will not generate a malicious footprint on the network, and thus we cannot detect it. Therefore, in Figure 5, this type of nodes are considered to be in the pre-infection phase.

In the median case, healthy nodes and nodes in the pre-infection phase appear to be targets of approximately 3 attacks per hour on average. These are mostly reconnaissance attacks, such as scanning, that could be precursors of a more serious attack. The corresponding number of inbound attacks in the case of infected hosts is more than double and equal to 7. However, if we observe the tails of the distributions we see a much more sharp change. For the top 5% targets of external attacks we see that in the case of healthy nodes and nodes in the pre-infection phase we record at least 5 and 9 inbound attacks per hour on average respectively. However, in the case of infected hosts this number rises to more than 50 inbound attacks per hour.

We learn that *infections drastically increase the attractiveness of infected hosts to further inbound attacks.* We speculate that this is because most malware also operate as backdoors, allowing the installation of additional malicious code. In this way they increase the attack vector of the infected host making it a much more attractive target. This is especially true for servers, which dominate the tail of the distributions shown in Figure 5.

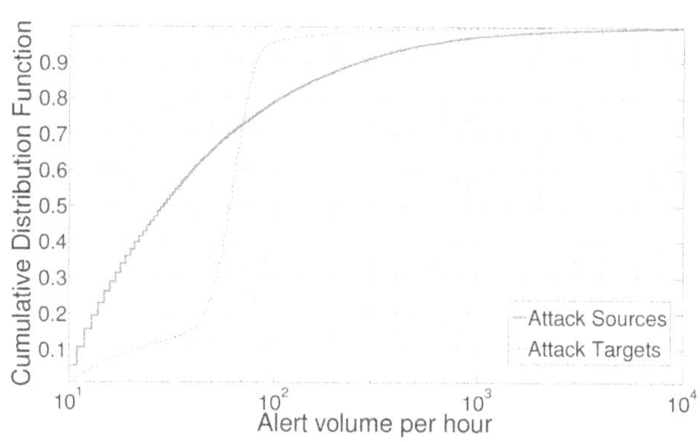

Figure 6: Distribution of alert sources and destinations for outbound traffic

Heavy Hitters: From the large pool of active clients, *a small percentage of hosts are popular sources and targets of attacks*, as shown in Figure 6. Regarding the attack popularity distribution we see that the median number of recorded inbound attacks is equal to 60 per hour. However, this number increases significantly for a small set of internal nodes that are targets to up to 970 attacks per hour. Almost, all the servers in our infrastructure are within this highly exposed set. This indicates that *servers are much more preferable targets than clients.* The reason is that most malicious pieces of self-spreading software have an initial hit-list of possibly vulnerable hosts. These hit-lists are generated using either scanning or by employing web-spiders and DNS-searches [49]. The inclusion of the public servers in our infrastructure in such hit-lists might have increased the volume of inbound attacks.

The same skewed behavior is observed in the case of the attack source distribution. We observe that approximately *5% of the internal hosts account for more than 70% of the total recorded attacks originating from the intranet.* These are highly suspicious nodes that require additional investigation. Blocking or better defending against these systems can significantly reduce the number of recorded extrusions, safeguarding at the same time exposed internal nodes. The outbound attack count could act as a crude indicator of possible malicious activity and combined with our heuristic it can facilitate administrators in focusing their efforts and identifying top offenders within their premises.

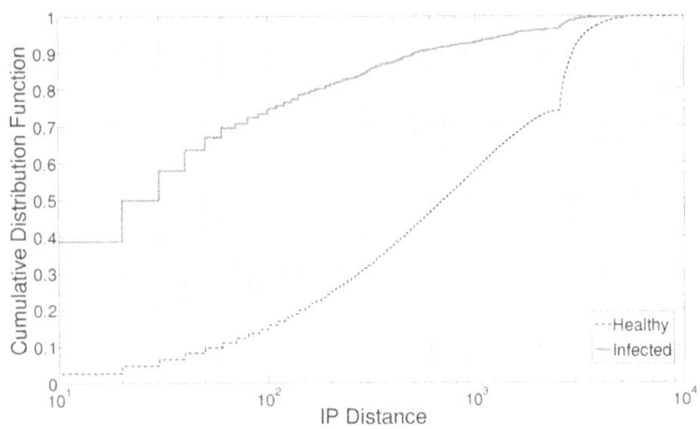

Figure 7: Infections spatial correlation

Spatial Correlations: The infections we observe exhibit strong spatial correlation. We define *IP distance* as the absolute difference between the integer representation of two IP addresses. For each host that remains healthy throughout the tracing period, we measure its *IP distance* to the closest infected host. For each host that becomes infected, we measure its IP distance to the nearest infected host at the time of infection. In Figure 7, we plot the Cumulative Distribution Function (CDF) of the IP distance for healthy and infected hosts. Note that in our infrastructure we use two large blocks of IP addresses, which explains the sharp increase we see for IP distance values above 2,600.

We observe that infected hosts are consistently in very close proximity with other infected hosts. 80% of these hosts have at least one other infected host in an *IP distance* which is less than 200, meaning that they are likely located in the same subnet. The corresponding percentage for healthy hosts considering the same *IP distance* value is significantly lower, equal to 15%.

The presence of strong spatial correlations indicates that certain subnets within a network are weak links. *Hosts close to existing infections are much more likely to become infected in the future.* Observing clusters of infections should guide administrators to review and revise the deployed baseline defenses and security policies.

Correlations Across Time: *The infection points exhibit diurnal patterns* as illustrated in Figure 8 where it is shown that most of the infections occur during working hours. This is due to the fact that client nodes, which dominate the infections set, exhibit strong diurnal patterns. This effect

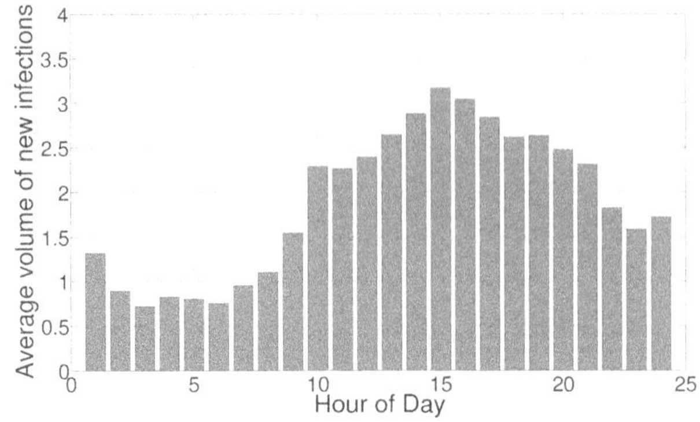

Figure 8: Distribution of infections for different hours of day

related to human behavior is reflected on the infections time series.

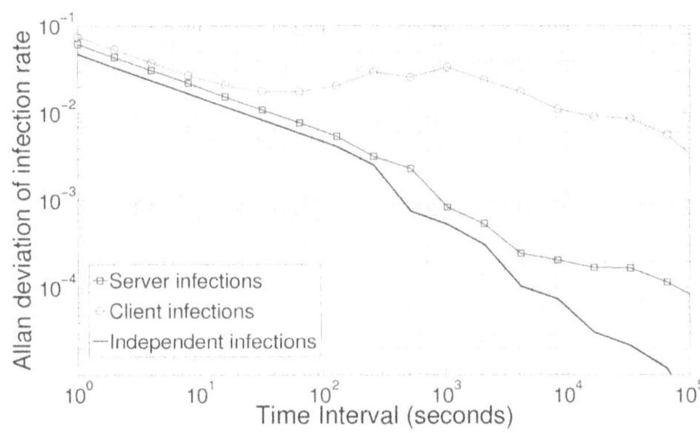

Figure 9: Infections burstiness for clients and servers

Another interesting aspect of the extracted infection time series that we study is burstiness across different time scales. To quantify burstiness, we compute the Allan deviation [2] of the infection time series at different scales. The Allan deviation is given by the following equation:

$$\sigma_x^2(\tau) = \frac{1}{2}\langle(\Delta x)^2\rangle$$

The time series is discretized into time intervals of length τ and each interval yields a sample x_i of the number of infections that occurred within it. The equation measures the difference between successive samples x_i for different interval lengths τ.

In Figure 9, the bold line in the bottom shows the minimum possible deviation which occurs when all infections have independent time arrivals. Intuitively, the Allan deviation should diverge from this reference significantly in time scales where the signal exhibits high burstiness. Figure 9 shows that *server infections in low time-scales are almost independent*, however, this changes if we look at time scales above one hour. This non-burstiness of server infections in low time scales suggests that measuring the infections over hourly intervals can provide a useful long-term average of the expected infections. This observation can be used to build a predictor of near-future infection incidents using simple linear time series models that capture short-range dependences, like ARIMA. On the other hand, *client infections are consistently more bursty and this is more evident for time-scales above two minutes.*

6. RELATED WORK

IDS Evaluation: The DARPA dataset [35] remains today one of the best options, although it dates back to 1999 and has several well-known shortcomings [1, 3]. Another well-known dataset, the DARPA Cyber Panel Correlation Technology Validation [31] was created in 2002 but unfortunately is not anymore available. These datasets were created in testbeds under controlled experiments. A lot of research has focused on generating synthetic traffic. More related to our work, MACE [48] is an environment for generating malicious packets for evaluating IDSs in testbeds. In addition to testbed experiments, in this work we stress the need to use and label and use traces collected in the wild.

Intrusion Measurements: Large traces of intrusion data, like IDS alerts and firewall logs collected by DShield [17], have been analyzed in previous studies. In particular, Yegneswaran *et al.* [52] made a number of observations regarding the distribution, types, and prevalence of intrusions. In addition, they projected the global volume of intrusions and estimated the potential of collaboration in intrusion detection. Kati *et al.* [34] analyzed a large trace of IDS alerts, reported characteristics of correlated attacks, and investigated how to effectively collaborate in intrusion detection. In this work we provide a number of further insights about intrusions focusing specifically on infections, which have not been studied as a separate class in the past.

Besides, a number of previous studies have focused on IDS alert correlation and aggregation. These studies evaluate proposed solutions on a small number of testbed-based benchmarks, like the DARPA dataset, and are tailored for general-purpose alert analysis rather than for extrusion detection. In our work, we highlight the need for using and analyzing measurements from real networks in addition to testbed-based evaluation methods. In particular, related work on alert correlation and aggregation can be classified in three categories.

Statistical/temporal Alert Correlation: A group of studies explores statistical [41, 36] or temporal [42] alert correlations to identify causality relationships between alerts. Statistical correlation methods estimate the association between different alerts by measuring the co-occurrence and frequency of alert pairs within a specific time frame. Qin [41] introduced a Bayesian network to model the causality relationship between alert pairs, while Ren *et al.* [43] proposed an online system to construct attack scenarios based on historic alert information. Temporal-based correlation approaches perform time series analysis on the alert stream to compute the dependence between different alerts. Qun and Lee [42] generate time series variables on the number of recorded alerts per time unit and use the Granger causality test to identify causal relationships. We also use a statistical alert correlation test in our heuristic and show how alert correlation can be useful specifically for extrusion detection.

Scenario- and Rule-based Alert Correlation: On the other hand, a number of studies hardcode details about attack steps into full scenarios [38, 12] or into rules [39, 6, 5], which are used to identify, summarize, and annotate alert groups. Scenario-based correlation approaches try to identify causal relationships between alerts in order to reconstruct high-level multi-stage events. Most approaches rely on attack scenarios specified by human analysts using an attack language [7, 13]. Deriving attack scenarios for all observed attacks requires significant technical expertise, prior knowledge, and time. In order to automate the scenario derivation process, machine learning techniques have been used [8]. Rule-based approaches are based on the observation that attacks can be usually subdivided into stages. These methods attempt to match specific alerts to the prerequisites and consequences of an active attack stage. The idea is to correlate alerts if the precondition of the current alert stream is satisfied by the postcondition of alerts that were analyzed earlier in time. A main limitation of scenario- and rule-based approaches is that the detection effectiveness is limited to attacks known a priori to the analyst or learned during the training phase. Therefore, they are not useful against novel attacks that have not been encountered in the past.

Alert Aggregation: The goal of alert aggregation is to group alerts into meaningful groups based on similarity criteria, making them manageable for a human analyst and amenable for subsequent statistical analysis. Each new alert is compared against all active alert sequences and is associated with the most relevant one. The set of attributes used to compute the corresponding similarity measure are diverse spanning from inherent alert features such as IP addresses, port numbers, and alert signatures, to topological and contextual information about the monitored network, such as the role and operation of nodes that triggered the alert or the deployed operating system and services. The work by Valdes *et al.* [51] represents each alert as a vector of attributes and groups alerts based on the weighted sum of the similarity of different attributes. The weight of an attribute is heuristically computed. Dain *et al.* [10, 9] propose a system that associates incoming alerts to groups in an online fashion. Julisch [32] proposes a clustering technique that aims at grouping alerts sharing the same root-causes, based on attribute-oriented induction. To address the problem that prior knowledge regarding how the alerts should be aggregated might not be available, machine learning techniques have been used. Zhu *et al.* [53] propose a supervised learning approach based on neural networks. Compared to these studies, we also use a simple form of alert aggregation in our heuristic, which we call alert bundling, that groups spurts of almost identical alerts for further statistical analysis rather than potentially diverse alerts based on complex similarity functions.

7. DISCUSSION

False Negatives: We opt to design our heuristic to produce a small number of false positives. This is one of our main goals as the excessive amount of false positives is an important limiting factor for IDSs. This means that in the trade-off between false positives and negatives we prefer to incur more false negatives in order to reduce the amount of false positives. Quantifying the false negative rate in a production environment is not possible. However, to assess false-negative rates one can use synthetic or testbed-based evaluation traces, as discussed in Section 6, where security incidents are known and controlled. Our work is complementary to such approaches and establishes techniques to find and validate security incidents in traces from production environments.

Academic Infrastructure: Our characterization results in Section 5 are based on data from an academic infrastructure and should only be carefully generalized, when possible, to other types of networks. For example, we expect that similar qualitative findings about the impact of infections and the presence of heavy hitters hold in networks of different type. In contrast, we expect that the volume of infections will be lower in more tightly managed environments.

8. CONCLUSIONS

In this paper, we present a novel approach to identify active infections in a large population of hosts, using IDS logs. We tailor our heuristic based on the observation that alerts with high mutual information are very likely to be correlated. Correlated alerts of specific types reveal that an actual infection has occurred. By applying this heuristic to a large dataset of collected alerts, we find infections for a population of more than 91 thousand unique hosts. We perform an extensive validation study in order to assess the effectiveness of our method, and show that it manages to reduce the false-positive rate of the raw IDS alerts to only 15%. Our characterization suggests that infections exhibit high spatial correlations, and that the existing infections open a wide attack vector for inbound attacks. Moreover, we investigate attack heavy hitters and show that client infections are significantly more bursty compared to server infections. We believe that our results are useful in several diverse fields, such as evaluating network defenses, extrusion detection, IDS false positive reduction, and network forensics.

9. ACKNOWLEDGEMENTS

The authors wish to thank Prof. Bernhard Plattner and Dr. Vincent Lenders for their invaluable help and fruitful discussions. Furthermore, we would like to thank Matthias Eggli for helping with the validation of the infection incidents. We would also like to thank Stephan Sheridan and Christian Hallqvist at ETH for their help in the collection and archiving of the data used in this paper. This work was supported by the Armasuisse Secmetrics [2-7841-09] project.

10. REFERENCES

[1] Testing intrusion detection systems: a critique of the 1998 and 1999 darpa intrusion detection system evaluations as performed by lincoln laboratory. *ACM Trans. Inf. Syst. Secur.*, 3:262–294, November 2000.

[2] D. W. Allan. Time and frequency (time domain) characterization, estimation and prediction of precision clocks and oscillators. *IEEE Trans. UFFC*, 34, November 1987.

[3] Carson Brown, Alex Cowperthwaite, Abdulrahman Hijazi, and Anil Somayaji. Analysis of the 1999 darpa/lincoln laboratory ids evaluation data with netadhict. In *Proceedings of the Second IEEE international conference on Computational intelligence for security and defense applications*, CISDA'09, pages 67–73, Piscataway, NJ, USA, 2009. IEEE Press.

[4] David Brumley, Cody Hartwig, Zhenkai Liang, James Newsome, Dawn Song, and Heng Yin. Automatically identifying trigger-based behavior in malware, 2008.

[5] Steven Cheung, Ulf Lindqvist, and Martin W. Fong. Modeling multistep cyber attacks for scenario recognition, 2003.

[6] Frédéric Cuppens and Alexandre Miège. Alert correlation in a cooperative intrusion detection framework. In *Proceedings of the 2002 IEEE Symposium on Security and Privacy*, pages 202–, Washington, DC, USA, 2002. IEEE Computer Society.

[7] Frédéric Cuppens and Rodolphe Ortalo. Lambda: A language to model a database for detection of attacks. In *Proceedings of the Third International Workshop on Recent Advances in Intrusion Detection*, RAID '00, pages 197–216, London, UK, 2000. Springer-Verlag.

[8] D. Curry and H. Debar. Intrusion detection message exchange format: Extensible markup language document type definition, 2003.

[9] Oliver Dain and Robert K. Cunningham. Fusing a heterogeneous alert stream into scenarios. In *In Proceedings of the 2001 ACM workshop on Data Mining for Security Applications*, pages 1–13, 2001.

[10] Oliver M. Dain and Robert K. Cunningham. Building scenarios from a heterogeneous alert stream, 2002.

[11] Neil Daswani, The Google Click Quality, Security Teams, and Google Inc. The anatomy of clickbot.a. In *In USENIX Hotbots'07*, 2007.

[12] Hervé Debar and Andreas Wespi. Aggregation and correlation of intrusion-detection alerts. In *Proceedings of the 4th International Symposium on Recent Advances in Intrusion Detection*, RAID '00, pages 85–103, London, UK, 2001. Springer-Verlag.

[13] Steven Eckmann, Giovanni Vigna, and Richard A. Kemmerer. Statl: An attack language for state-based intrusion detection, 2002.

[14] Advanced automated threat analysis system. `www.threatexpert.com`.

[15] Anonymous postmasters early warning system. `www.apews.org`.

[16] Common Vulnerabilities and Exposures dictionary of known information security vulnerabilities. `cve.mitre.org`.

[17] Cooperative Network Security Community - Internet Security. `www.dshield.org`.

[18] Damballa - Botnet and Advanced Malware Detection and Protection. `www.damballa.com`.

[19] Emerging Threats web page. `http://www.emergingthreats.net`.

[20] Network Security Archive. `http://www.networksecurityarchive.org`.

[21] Packet Storm Full Disclosure Information Security. `packetstormsecurity.org`.

[22] Projecthoneypot web page. `www.projecthoneypot.org`.

[23] Shadowserver Foundation web page. `www.shadowserver.org`.

[24] Symantec SecurityFocus technical community. `www.securityfocus.com`.

[25] The Nessus vulnerability scanner. `www.tenable.com/products/nessus`.

[26] The Open Vulnerability Assessment System. www.openvas.org.

[27] The Spamhaus Project. www.spamhaus.org.

[28] The Urlblacklist web page. www.urlblacklist.org.

[29] TrustedSource Internet Reputation System. www.trustedsource.org.

[30] Loic Etienne and Jean-Yves Le Boudec. Malicious traffic detection in local networks with snort. Technical report, EPFL, 2009.

[31] Joshua Haines, Dorene Kewley Ryder, Laura Tinnel, and Stephen Taylor. Validation of sensor alert correlators. *IEEE Security and Privacy*, 1:46–56, January 2003.

[32] Klaus Julisch. Clustering intrusion detection alarms to support root cause analysis. *ACM Transactions on Information and System Security*, 6:443–471, 2003.

[33] Klaus Julisch and Marc Dacier. Mining intrusion detection alarms for actionable knowledge. In *KDD '02: Proceedings of the eighth ACM SIGKDD international conference on Knowledge discovery and data mining*, pages 366–375, New York, NY, USA, 2002. ACM.

[34] Sachin Katti, Balachander Krishnamurthy, and Dina Katabi. Collaborating against common enemies. In *Proceedings of the 5th ACM SIGCOMM conference on Internet Measurement*, IMC '05, pages 34–34, Berkeley, CA, USA, 2005. USENIX Association.

[35] Richard Lippmann, Joshua W. Haines, David J. Fried, Jonathan Korba, and Kumar Das. The 1999 darpa off-line intrusion detection evaluation. *Computer Networks*, 34:579–595, October 2000.

[36] Federico Maggi and Stefano Zanero. On the use of different statistical tests for alert correlation: short paper. In *Proceedings of the 10th international conference on Recent advances in intrusion detection*, RAID'07, pages 167–177, Berlin, Heidelberg, 2007. Springer-Verlag.

[37] Gary McGraw and Greg Morrisett. Attacking malicious code: A report to the infosec research council. *IEEE Softw.*, 17:33–41, September 2000.

[38] Benjamin Morin and HervÃl' Debar. Correlation of intrusion symptoms: an application of chronicles. In *RAIDâĂŽ03*, pages 94–112, 2003.

[39] Peng Ning, Yun Cui, and Douglas S. Reeves. Constructing attack scenarios through correlation of intrusion alerts. In *In Proceedings of the 9th ACM conference on Computer and communications security*, pages 245–254, 2002.

[40] G. Piatetsky-Shapiro. Discovery, analysis and presentation of strong rules. In G. Piatetsky-Shapiro and W. J. Frawley, editors, *Knowledge Discovery in Databases*, pages 229–248. AAAI Press, 1991.

[41] Xinzhou Qin. *A probabilistic-based framework for infosec alert correlation*. PhD thesis, Atlanta, GA, USA, 2005. AAI3183248.

[42] Xinzhou Qin and Wenke Lee. Statistical causality analysis of infosec alert data. In *RAID 2003*, pages 73–93, 2003.

[43] Hanli Ren, Natalia Stakhanova, and Ali A. Ghorbani. An online adaptive approach to alert correlation. In *Proceedings of the 7th international conference on Detection of intrusions and malware, and vulnerability assessment*, DIMVA'10, pages 153–172, Berlin, Heidelberg, 2010. Springer-Verlag.

[44] Vyas Sekar, Yinglian Xie, Michael K. Reiter, and Hui Zhang. Is host-based anomaly detection + temporal correlation = worm causality?, 2007.

[45] Sushant Sinha, Michael Bailey, and Farnam Jahanian. Shades of grey: On the effectiveness of reputation-based blacklists. In *Proceedings of the 3rd International Conference on Malicious and Unwanted Software (MALWARE '08)*, pages 57–64, Fairfax, Virginia, USA, October 2008.

[46] P. Smyth and R. M. Goodman. An information theoretic approach to rule induction from databases. *IEEE Trans. on Knowl. and Data Eng.*, 4:301–316, August 1992.

[47] A free lightweight network intrusion detection system for UNIX and Windows. http://www.snort.org.

[48] Joel Sommers, Vinod Yegneswaran, and Paul Barford. A framework for malicious workload generation. In *Proceedings of the 4th ACM SIGCOMM conference on Internet measurement*, IMC '04, pages 82–87, New York, NY, USA, 2004. ACM.

[49] Stuart Staniford, Vern Paxson, and Nicholas Weaver. How to own the internet in your spare time. In *Proceedings of the 11th USENIX Security Symposium*, pages 149–167, Berkeley, CA, USA, 2002. USENIX Association.

[50] Ionut Trestian, Supranamaya Ranjan, Aleksandar Kuzmanovi, and Antonio Nucci. Unconstrained endpoint profiling (googling the internet). In *Proceedings of the ACM SIGCOMM 2008 conference on Data communication*, SIGCOMM '08, pages 279–290, New York, NY, USA, 2008. ACM.

[51] Alfonso Valdes and Keith Skinner. Probabilistic alert correlation. In *Recent Advances in Intrusion Detection*, pages 54–68, 2001.

[52] Vinod Yegneswaran, Paul Barford, and Johannes Ullrich. Internet intrusions: global characteristics and prevalence. In *Proceedings of the 2003 ACM SIGMETRICS international conference on Measurement and modeling of computer systems*, SIGMETRICS '03, pages 138–147, New York, NY, USA, 2003. ACM.

[53] Bin Zhu and Ali A. Ghorbani. Abstract alert correlation for extracting attack strategies, 2005.

Summary Review Documentation for

"Detecting, Validating and Characterizing Computer Infections in the Wild"

Authors: E. Raftopoulos, X. Dimitropoulos

Reviewer #1

Strengths: This problem is very important and the authors present a nice solution validated using real ground truth. Well written paper with good evaluation using a lot of real data.

Weaknesses: The paper focuses on a rather narrow set of attacks. System description needs to be clearer.

Comments to Authors: The way I understood the paper is that, the J-measure heuristic first groups together alerts that are correlated somehow. Then it looks at all the alerts that are correlated for a given machine and then uses the composite signature to classify whether the infection is a backdoor infection or spyware or worm or trojan. So far it is clear, but I am not sure how the mapping is done. The whole section 4.2 gives a vague description of the different types of attacks, but does not precisely define how the matching process is done. This is a key piece missing from the paper.

Further, the system descriptions are very vague; how does one use the system in practice. What constitutes the system itself is unclear. There is a lot of manual effort, it seems, in classifying the alert groups and annotating them. There is a lot of vagueness in the description unfortunately for me to understand the exact components of the system. The output of the system is also unclear. Does it output the set of alerts that correspond to XYZ worm, XYZ trojan or it just says worm and trojan. I suspect different worms or trojans have different signatures. So, does one need to build different signatures for each of these separately in advance?

If the only output is broad classes of infection, I am not sure what the advantage of this system is compared to just combining the alerts that are for a given host. Yes, the alert group will be big, but would'nt an expert just look at the types of alerts and quickly figure out what type of an attack is ? What additional advantage one has in using the J-measure.

There is another component of the paper that involves characterizing the attacks observed in their campus trace data. This study is kind of orthogonal to the other parts of the paper. This study is also not easily generalizable to other networks. I did not know what to interpret and take out of those findings.

Reviewer #2

Strengths: Well written and evaluation; quite an important problem, relieving network administrators of the false alert overload would be quite beneficial.

Weaknesses: Its not clear to me what is automated, and what is not. In other words, how much reduction in human effort could one expect by deploying this system.

Comments to Authors: The paper argues that by grouping alerts together for a host or for some other metric, one can identify the likelihood of an infection as well as the type of infection. But how is this final step done. Does the system present these clusters to the administrator and he determines whether there is an infection? I guess I am asking how does this system exactly reduce the large fraction of useless IDS alerts. Is it mainly by grouping similar alerts into one? But if that's the case, wont a simple grouping based on some IDS alert type as well as IP be sufficient? The administrator could then quickly decide what to do from this smaller set of data.

Reviewer #3

Strengths: Important and challenging problem (reducing the false-positive rate of intrusion-detection systems). Interesting idea (to use the cross entropy of alerts to detect recurring multi-stage behavior). Impressive validation effort (to manually validate each reported infection against multiple sources).

Weaknesses: The algorithm is not well defined or explained (I *think* I got it after reading the relevant section three times). It is based on manually set parameters, and it is not clear how these should be set or how they affect accuracy (although, to be fair, I have not heard of any IDS system that does not rely on manual calibration). The evaluation of the algorithm could be (easily) improved.

Comments to Authors: The main weakness of the paper is that it does not clearly describe the proposed algorithm. The second half of Section 3.3 (which is meant to describe the algorithm) is really hard to follow. Here is my understanding of what it says: (i) the ideal goal is to detect recurring multi-stage behavior, i.e., detect sequences of alerts that occur multiple times; (ii) a simplified version of this goal is to detect sequences of 2 alerts that occur multiple times (call these "significant sequences"); (iii) to do that, the algorithm computes the cross-entropy of each sequence of 2 alerts -- low cross-entropy means that the sequence does occur; (iv) each significant sequence that is time-wise separated (by more than some threshold) from the other significant sequences is reported as an infection incident. If this is what the algorithm does, there are two ways to make it clearer: One is to explicitly state steps (i) and (ii), which are currently missing. The other is to *not* use the term "rule" to refer to sequences of alerts. When reading an IDS paper, the term "rule" makes the reader think of an IDS rule, i.e., a criterion applied to a packet to determine whether an alert should be raised. I strongly recommend using some other term -- "alert sequence" or something like that.

Another weakness is the use of manually set parameters (the J-Measure threshold, the time window, and the infection threshold). I am not sure that manual calibration is avoidable in IDS systems. However, the paper could at least provide some evidence that the proposed algorithm is not significantly sensitive to its parameters. In particular, the authors could vary the values of the parameters and show how that affects the false-positive rate of their algorithm.

In Section 4.4, it would be nice to see some discussion on the false negatives -- what kind of incidents were not detected the algorithm? In line with the previous comment, how does the false negative/positive rate of the algorithm (applied on the 28-system dataset) change as a function of the parameters of the algorithm?

Other (minor) things that I did not understand about the algorithm: What is the complexity of the algorithm? Does it compute the cross-entropy of all possible pairs of alerts within each time window? In Section 3.2, I did not get which steps of the classification are manual and which ones are automated (is the second step automated?) Also, how do the first and third steps differ? The first step "manually examined all rulesets and identified groups that clearly characterize an attack or a compromised host." The third step "manually classified [the remaining rules] by examining the details of the signature, ..." They both sound to me like manual examination.

Reviewer #4

Strengths: There is an interesting observation on the locality of infected nodes.

Weaknesses: It is not clear what are the contributions of the paper. The methodology used is a compilation of previously proposed techniques to infer specific attacks. It is not clear how general is the proposed methodology. J-measure that is used has not been formally introduced and motivated. Despite the fact that the authors claim that their methodology is general they only address well known infections. You repeatedly mention that intrusion detection systems generate a large number of false positive rates (99%), but you do not provide any reference on this. It is not clear what is the trade-off between low rate of false positives and false negatives.

Comments to Authors: Section 3.3: The use of the J-Measure is not well motivated. J-Measure is used throughout the paper. You have to provide enough justification on why this is the right metric. As you mentioned there are other metrics have also been proposed in the literature. Thus, you have to evaluate them in your dataset.

Sections 4.2 and 4.3: Despite the fact that you claim that your framework is very general when you dive into the analysis and evaluation you attack only a few cases (some of them are well addressed in the literature). Please elaborate more on the generality and applicability of your method. You should also clearly state your contributions.

You should provide a reference that shows that off-the-shelf intrusion detection tools generate a large number of false positive rates, close to 99% as you mentioned; you have to apply these tools in your traces and then show how your proposed system reduces the false positive rate.

Section 6: The related work is too lengthy (more than two pages) and does not contribute much to the understanding of the related body of work, not it puts your contributions into context.

Your methodology identifies 9000 infected machine in the campus. It is not clear how you validated that all these machines are infected; is there a ground truth that you rely on for your statistics.

You claim that the false positive rate is low. How about the false negative -- is it high in your study? Is there a fundamental trade-off between low false positive and false negative rate?

Reviewer #5

Strengths: A working method deployed at a real-world, large-scale site. I like the balance of methodology, validation, and findings. The paper's dataset is great and I actually find it refreshing to see work that names the actual site at which traces are collected. The paper is nicely executed and structured, and mostly well-written.

Weaknesses: The novelty of this paper is very small. IDS alert aggregation has been studied in depth in the past, and the findings in the paper are mostly confirmations of known effects. The reduction of false positives is good, but the resulting false positives of 16% are still far from great.

Comments to Authors: In the abstract you say you "assess the security of [...] live infections". What is the security of an infection supposed to be?

The idea of malware tending to co-locate in "bad" networks is not novel, see for example Sinha & Bailey's "Improving spam blacklisting through dynamic thresholding and speculative aggregation".

Despite the high number of false positives it seems you make no attempts of tuning your signature set -- why? I can see practical reasons for doing so, including easy of rules updates, but unfortunately even 16% false positives, viewed in isolation, is a lousy result. I personally know of large-scale sites who use other intrusion detection approaches than Snort that fare far, far better.

I struggled with 3.3. You start out saying you want to identify real infections, and then present causality inference rules of the form "if A then B follows in time window T", but you never say *why* you do that. I suspect you mean that the fact that two alerts (can there be more than two kinds?) occurring in sequence increases confidence in a particular attack being present. It would help to be clearer here.

I could have done without 4.2, given how tightly you've packed the paper. Then again, I suspect readers of different backgrounds may find it more valuable to have. 4.3, on the other hand, I found quite informative. In that section, you also say you believe your unaggregated alerts to consist virtually completely of false positives. Can't you put a precise number to it by reversing your bundling procedure?

I can confirm your hypothesis in the "Infections Impact" section. The pay-per-install approach to malware distribution means that initial infections can trigger entire cascades of additional malware ending up on a system. However, I'm not sure I follow how this explains increase in *inbound* attacks on these systems.

It would be nice to see a "step back" section in the paper. For example, given you experience, is signature-based misuse detection the way to go? Would there be point in actively maintaining the signature set instead of accepting the crud that Snort's default ruleset with Emerging Threats spews into your logs?

Response from the Authors

We made several changes to the paper to address the comments of the reviewers. Most reviewers noted that the description of the heuristic in Section 3.3 was not very clear. A major change was that we substantially clarified Section 3.3.

Answers to specific questions (in the beginning we mark the reviewer number):
R1: Our heuristic builds on attacks detectable by snort, which provides a rather rich set of signatures for detecting attacks of various types.
R1, R2: We clarified that our heuristic does not classify the type of a detected infection; it solely detects an infection.
R2: We made more clear what it automated. The detection process of our heuristic is entirely automated. It uses an assignment of snort rules into three classes, which classification we derived manually.
R2: Trivially combining alerts from a host and passing them to an administrator would not work because it results in a prohibitively large number of suspected systems an administrator needs to manually inspect.
R3: Using a set of detection parameters is common in most detection studies. We have used security tickets for re-mediated incidents and have physically visited the owners of infected systems to derive a reliable ground truth for fine-tuning the detection threshold of our heuristic. In addition, we extended Section 4.4 to report how the number of false positives/negatives changes with the detection threshold.
R3: We discuss in detail the root-causes of the main types of false positives in Section 4.3.
R4: We provide a reference for the 99% false-positives figure in the introduction. In addition, we confirmed this figure with our data too based on the suggestion of reviewer 5.
R4: We extended Section 4.4 to report how the false-positive/negative rate changes for different thresholds.
R5: Although alert correlation has been studied extensively in the past, compared to previous studies the main novelty in our work is the characterization of 9 thousand infected hosts in a production network.
R5: The authors agree that the false positive rate could be further reduced. Some hints for improving it are given in the discussion of the root-causes of false positives in Section 4.3. This could be interesting future work.
R5: We liked the suggestion of reversing the bundling process to compute the initial false positive rate. We followed this suggestion and found 99.4% false-positive un-aggregated alerts (excluding policy alerts). This confirms our expectation.

I Know Where You Are and What You Are Sharing:

Exploiting P2P Communications to Invade Users' Privacy

Stevens Le Blond* Chao Zhang† Arnaud Legout‡ Keith Ross† Walid Dabbous‡
* MPI-SWS, Germany † NYU-Poly, USA ‡ INRIA, France

ABSTRACT

In this paper, we show how to exploit real-time communication applications to determine the IP address of a targeted user. We focus our study on Skype, although other real-time communication applications may have similar privacy issues. We first design a scheme that calls an identified-targeted user *inconspicuously* to find his IP address, which can be done even if he is behind a NAT. By calling the user periodically, we can then observe the mobility of the user. We show how to scale the scheme to observe the mobility patterns of tens of thousands of users. We also consider the linkability threat, in which the identified user is linked to his Internet usage. We illustrate this threat by combining Skype and BitTorrent to show that it is possible to determine the filesharing usage of identified users. We devise a scheme based on the identification field of the IP datagrams to verify with high accuracy whether the identified user is participating in specific torrents. We conclude that any Internet user can leverage Skype, and potentially other real-time communication systems, to observe the mobility and filesharing usage of tens of millions of identified users.

Categories and Subject Descriptors

C.2.2 [**Computer Communication Networks**]: Network Protocols

General Terms

Design, Measurement, Security

Keywords

File sharing, Mobility, Privacy, Skype

*The first author contributed to this work while a Ph.D. student at INRIA.

App	# Users	Dir	P2P
Skype	560M	✓	✓
MSN Live	550M	✗	✓
QQ	500M	✓	✓
Google Talk	150M	✗	✓

Table 1: Number of users claimed by Skype [11], MSN Live [9], QQ [10], and Google Talk [8] and for each of these systems, whether it has a directory service and employs P2P communications.

1. INTRODUCTION

The cellular service providers are capable of tracking and logging our whereabouts as long as our cell phones are powered on. Because the web sites we visit see our source IP addresses and cookies, the web sites we frequently visit – such as Google [5] and Facebook [4] – can also track our whereabouts to some extent. Although tracking our whereabouts can be considered a major infringement on our privacy, most people are not terribly concerned, largely because they trust that the cellular and major Internet application providers will not disclose this information. Moreover, these large companies have privacy policies, in which they assure their users that they will not make location history, and other personal information, publicly available.

In this paper, we are not concerned about whether large brand-name companies can track our mobility, but instead about whether smaller less-trustworthy entities can leverage the Internet to *periodically track our whereabouts.* Is it possible, for example, for an ordinary user with modest financial resources, operating from his or her home, to periodically determine the IP address of a targeted and identified Internet user and to link it to this user's Internet activities (e.g., file sharing)? We will show that the answer to this question is yes!

Real-time communication (e.g., VoIP and Video-over-IP) is enormously popular in the Internet today. As shown in Table 1, the applications Skype, QQ, MSN Live, and Google Talk together have more than 1.6 billion registered users.

Real-time communication in the Internet is naturally done peer-to-peer (P2P), i.e., datagrams flow directly between the two conversing users. The P2P nature of such a service, however, exposes the IP addresses of all the participants in a conversation to each other. Specifically, if Alice knows Bob's VoIP ID, she can establish a call with Bob and obtain his current IP address by simply sniffing the datagrams arriving to her computer. She can also use geo-localization services to map Bob's IP address to a location and ISP. If Bob is mobile, she can call him periodically to observe his mobility over, say, a week or month. Furthermore, once she knows Bob's IP address, she can crawl P2P file-sharing systems to see if that IP address is uploading/downloading any files. Thus VoIP can *potentially* be used to collect a targeted user's location. And VoIP can *potentially* be combined with P2P file sharing to determine what a user is uploading/downloading. This would clearly be a serious infringement on privacy.

However, for such a scheme to be effective, there are several technical challenges:

- For a specific targeted individual – such as Bob Smith, 28 years old, living in Kaiserslautern Germany – can Alice determine with certainty his VoIP ID?
- Can Alice determine which packets come from Bob (and thereby obtain his IP address)? Indeed, during call setup, Alice may receive packets from many other peers. In addition, can Alice call Bob inconspicuously, so that Alice can periodically call Bob and get his IP address without Bob knowing it? Finally, can Alice obtain Bob's address, even when Bob configures his VoIP client to block calls from Alice?
- If Bob's IP address, found with VoIP, is the same as an IP address found in a P2P file-sharing system, then we cannot conclude with certainty that Bob is downloading the corresponding file, since Bob may be behind a NAT (with the matching IP address being the public IP address of the NAT). Thus, is it possible to verify that Bob is indeed uploading/downloading the files, given that NATs are widely deployed in the Internet?

In this paper, using Skype, we develop a measurement scheme to meet all the above challenges. (This may be possible with other VoIP systems as well, which we leave for future work.) Our main contributions are the following:

- *We develop a scheme to find a targeted person's Skype ID and to inconspicuously call this person to find his IP address, even if he is behind a NAT.* By carefully studying Skype packet patterns for a Skype caller, we are able to distinguish packets received from the Skype callee from packets received from many other peers. Having identified these packets, we extract the callee's IP address from the headers of the packets. Furthermore, through experimentation, we determine how to obtain the IP address of the callee fully inconspicuously, that is, without ringing or notifying the user. Finally, we show that Skype privacy settings fail to protect against our scheme.
- *We show our scheme can be used periodically to observe the mobility of Skype users.* By scaling our scheme, we demonstrate that Skype does not implement counter measures to hinder such schemes. Although there are several challenges to measure the mobility of a large number of users, we show that it can be done efficiently and effectively.
- *We show that the scheme introduces a linkability threat where the identity of a person can be associated to his Internet usage.* We illustrate this threat by combining Skype and BitTorrent to show that it is possible to determine the file-sharing usage of identified users. One of the challenges here is that a BitTorrent user is often NATed, so that he may share his IP address with many other users. When a common IP address is discovered in both Skype and BitTorrent, we immediately launch a verification procedure in which we simultaneously call the corresponding user and perform a BitTorrent handshake to the IP address, port and infohash (which identifies the file being shared). We then use the identification field of the IP datagrams to verify with high accuracy whether an identified user is participating in specific torrents. To the best of our knowledge, we are the first ones to show that such a scheme can be used in the wild.

In addition to the technical contributions of this paper, another contribution is that we are alerting Internet users (and the Skype company as discussed in the next section) of a major privacy vulnerability, whereby targeted users can have their mobility and Internet usage tracked. As of May 2011 (more than six months after having notified the Skype company), all the schemes presented in this paper are still valid. We provide some relatively simple solutions so that future real-time communication systems can be made less vulnerable to these attacks.

One solution that would go a long way is to design the VoIP system so that the callee's IP address is not revealed until the user accepts the call. With this property, Alice would not be able to inconspicuously call Bob. Moreover, if Alice is a stranger (that is, not on Bob's contact list), and Bob configures his client to not accept calls from strangers, then this design would prevent any stranger from tracking him, conspicuously or otherwise. However, even with this solution in place, any friend of Bob, say Susan, can still call him conspicuously and obtain his IP address. Susan could be Bob's spouse, parent, employer, or employee, for example. It would be hard for Susan to periodically track Bob this way, but Susan could still (i) get Bob's current location, and (ii) check to see if Bob is downloading content from a P2P file-sharing system. Preventing these attacks would require more fundamental changes in the VoIP system (specifically, using relays by default) or more fundamental changes in the underlying Internet protocols.

This paper is organized as follows. We discuss the legal and ethical considerations of this paper in Section 2. In Section 3, we describe our scheme to determine the current IP address of a person using Skype. We then show that this scheme can be used periodically to observe the mobility and file-sharing usage of identified users in Section 4 and 5. Finally, we discuss some simple defenses in Section 6, the related work in Section 7, and we conclude in Section 8.

2. LEGAL AND ETHICAL CONSIDERATIONS

In this measurement study, all testing involving identified users has been performed on a small sample of volunteers who gave us their informed consent to make measurements and publish results. Unfortunately, the informed consent process for privacy, as for fraud [25], may significantly bias user behavior. For example, informed users may stop using Skype or BitTorrent. For this reason, we also needed to consider a larger sample of (anonymized) users in order to accurately assess the amount of personal information that is revealed by a normal usage, e.g., the mobility and file-sharing usage of Skype users. For the sake of privacy, we only stored and processed anonymized mobility and file-sharing information.

Based on these arguments, the INRIA IRB approved this study. In the following, we describe our motivation to run privacy measurements, the tests that we ran with volunteers, and the remaining measurements.

Motivation for Running Privacy Measurements.

Internet users publish a lot of personal information that can be exploited in non-trivial ways to invade their privacy. Indeed, recent research demonstrates that personal information can be correlated in ways that would have been hard to anticipate [32]. One goal of this study is to show that any Internet user can leverage popular real-time communication applications to observe the mobility patterns and file-sharing usage of tens of millions of Internet users. It is important to give public visibility to these privacy issues, as they constitute serious invasions into users' privacy, and can potentially be used for blackmail and phishing attacks.

Volunteers.

In this study, we have relied on two sets of volunteers for which we have obtained informed consent. The first set comprises 14 research faculty in the CSE department at NYU-Poly for which we have attempted to find the Skype IDs.

The second set comprises 20 people spread throughout the world (4 in Asia, 2 in Australia, 7 in Europe, and 7 in USA) in cable and DSL ISPs, with 10 users directly connectable and 10 users behind NAT. We deliberately chose users located in different continents and with different Internet connectivity to observe a large diversity of user and client behaviors. We have relied on the second set of volunteers to (*i*) determine Skype packet patterns between caller and callee, (*ii*) develop and test inconspicuous calling, and (*iii*) evaluate the accuracy of mobility measurements. After manual testing, we called each volunteer 100 times and systematically observed one of the three packet patterns described in Section 3 between caller and callee. We also observed that our inconspicuous calling procedure never notified them about the calls in any way.

Anonymized users.

We relied on two samples of users for which we did not store their personal information in this study. We first used a sample of 10,000 random users to quantify their mobility. We then used a second sample of 100,000 random users that we used to illustrate a linkability threat, where the identity of a person can be associated to his Internet usage (e.g., file sharing).

We always collected the IP addresses of the anonymized users using inconspicuous calls, which we validated on the volunteers. Therefore, *no human contact was ever made with any of the anonymized users*. Moreover, we processed and stored only anonymized information, e.g., we anonymized all localization information, downloaded content, and we did not store the IP addresses. Details of all anonymized information are given in Section 4 and 5.

Other considerations.

In order to conform to the responsible disclosure process, we informed the Skype company of our conclusions in November 2010. In addition, we did not perform any reverse engineering on Skype binaries. Finally, our measurements generated at most 2.7 calls per second and a few kilobytes of bandwidth per second, so the load that we created on the Skype infrastructure was marginal.

3. MAPPING A PERSON TO AN IP ADDRESS

In the following, we first describe how to find a targeted person's Skype ID, that is a unique user ID of a person in Skype. Then, we present our scheme to find, based on a Skype ID, the IP address used by this person. We explain how to make this scheme inconspicuous for the user, and we show that the privacy settings in Skype fail to protect against our scheme.

3.1 Finding a Person's ID

When creating a Skype account, a user needs to provide an e-mail address and Skype ID. The user is also invited to provide personal information, such as birth name, location, gender, age, and/or website. This information is recorded in the Skype directory. Therefore, in attempting to define a person's Skype ID, the obvious first step is to input into the directory's search service the person's e-mail address or birth name.

When searching for a birth name, Skype will often return many results. Along with these results, there is often side information, such as city and country of residence. As we will discuss below, if there is still ambiguity about which Skype ID corresponds to the targeted person, we can, using the methodology described in the following section, inconspicuously call each of the candidate Skype IDs, obtain a current or recent IP address for each of those IDs, and from the IP addresses determine current city and ISP (which might be a University or an employer ISP). Such a procedure often determines a person's Skype ID without ambiguity. We briefly remark that if this search was instead based on a service that doesn't provide a directory (such as MSN Live or Google Talk), one may still be able to determine the ID by scraping homepages, scraping pages from various social networks, or simply by guessing.

To illustrate that one can easily find the Skype IDs for a set of identified individuals, we attempt to find the IDs of the 14 research faculty in the CSE department at NYU-Poly, all of whom gave us their informed consent. By searching the corresponding 14 professional e-mail addresses, we found 2 Skype IDs and by searching the corresponding 14 birth names, we found 7 additional IDs with a single match. Among the 5 people for which we did not find a conclusive Skype ID, there was multiple matching IDs for 4 and no matching Skype ID only for 1. For the professors with multiple candidate IDs, it would have been possible to inconspicuously call each of the candidate IDs (as described below), geo-localize each candidate, and most likely pinpoint the correct ID. In summary, among 14 NYU-Poly faculty members, we found the Skype IDs for nine of them, and we could have very possibly determined the IDs for four more.

3.2 Finding a Person's IP Address

We have seen how to find the Skype ID of a targeted person. We now discuss how, given the person's Skype ID, we can find the IP address of the machine on which that person is currently active. (If the machine is behind a NAT, then we instead obtain the public IP address of the NAT.) The basic idea is to call the Skype ID, receive IP datagrams from the machine on which that ID is currently logged in, and sniff the packets to get the machine's IP address from the IP header. We describe in the following when this IP address is available.

When the caller calls a Skype user who is currently offline, the Skype application will still provide to the caller the user's most recent IP address, as long as the user was running Skype in the past 72 hours. For this reason, we are able to retrieve the IP address of a Skype user that used Skype within the past 72 hours.

By examining traffic patterns to and from a Skype client when our client makes a call to a Skype ID that has been active in the past 72 hours, we have observed that Skype behaves as follows. At the time of the call, the user may be in one of three possible states (*i*) the user is online and not behind a NAT; (*ii*) the user is online and behind a NAT; (*iii*) the user is offline, but was online (with or without a NAT) within the past 72 hours. (There is also the possibility that the user is logged in at more than one address simultaneously. We will discuss that case subsequently.) For case (*i*), when the user (callee) is online and not behind a NAT, the caller will initiate communication with the callee, sending packets directly to the callee (with the callee's IP address in the destination address field of the datagrams). For case (*ii*), when the callee is online but behind a NAT, the callee will be instructed (via the callee's supernode) to initiate communication to the caller. In this case, the callee's public IP address will be in the source address field of the incoming datagrams. For case (*iii*), when the targeted user is offline (but was online in the past 72 hours), the caller's Skype client will still attempt to call the targeted user, using the IP address that was most recently observed by Skype in the past 72 hours. (If the targeted user is behind a NAT, the caller will try to initiate a call, using the public IP address of the NATed user.) In this last case, the callee's most recent (public) IP address can be determined from the IP datagrams. Thus, the callee's IP address (current or most recent) can be extracted from the source and destination fields of IP datagrams.

However, there is a major complication here. In the process of establishing a call, the call triggers communication with tens of IP addresses (supernodes and relays). As supernodes and relays are hosted by Skype users, their IP addresses belong to a multitude of address ranges that we cannot just filter out. So it is complex to determine which Skype datagrams are for direct communication with the callee. As Skype uses a proprietary protocol and encrypts the payloads of its messages, we cannot perform direct packet inspection to find packets originating from the callee. To solve this problem, we designed a scheme that relies solely on the packet patterns between the caller and the various Skype nodes it is communicating with.

To understand Skype's traffic, we placed calls to the second set of volunteers for which we knew the IP addresses of (see Section 2). We observed three identifiable patterns of communication that take place between the caller and callee during the call establishment phase. By exploiting these patterns, we were able to filter out the noise, such as

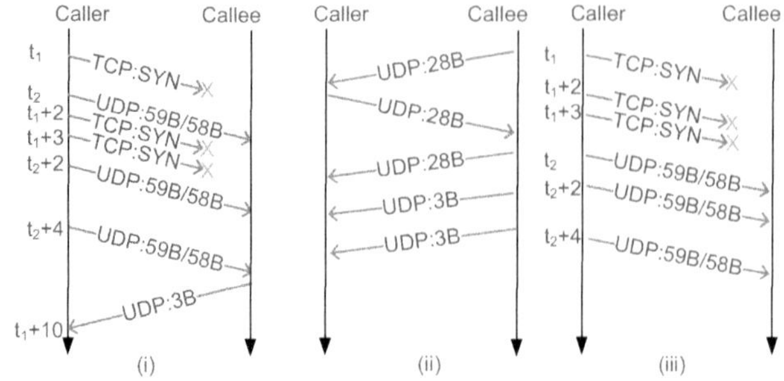

Figure 1: Communication pattern: (i) callee is online and public; (ii) callee online and behind a NAT; (iii) callee is offline. Crosses correspond to SYN packets that we dropped in order to call inconspicuously.

communication with supernodes. Fig. 1 shows these three patterns.

We observe the first pattern when the callee is online and public (case (*i*)). In that case, the caller will try to initiate the TCP connection by sending a SYN packet. We will see in Section 3.3, that we need to drop SYN packets to make inconspicuous calls. When the TCP timeout occurs, the caller retransmits the SYN, making two tries after the initial attempt before giving up. The first timeout interval is 3 seconds and the second is 1 second. In addition to the TCP packets, there are UDP packets between the caller and the callee. We always observe three 59 byte or 58 byte packets from caller to callee, and the intervals between them are 2 seconds and 4 seconds. Thus, between caller and callee there is a specific traffic pattern, which is shown in Fig. 1 (*i*). There is also communication between caller and supernodes; however, the communication with non-callees does not exhibit the pattern in Fig. 1 (*i*). In summary, by identifying the IP address that has packets with the pattern in Fig. 1 (*i*), we identify the IP address of the callee. We remark that the TCP packets and UDP packets don't always appear sequentially. Most of the time, they are mixed.

The second pattern is observed when the callee is online but behind a NAT (case (*ii*)), that is, the caller cannot initiate communication with the callee. In that case, we have observed that the callee will send a 28 byte UDP packet to the caller. The caller replies with the same size UDP packet. Next, the caller and callee will exchange UDP packets of varying sizes. After about 10 seconds, the callee sends 3 byte UDP packets to the caller. We do not observe these 3 byte UDP packets from any other source besides the callee. The pattern is shown in Fig. 1 (*ii*).

The last pattern occurs when the callee is offline but has been online in the past 72 hours. In that case, the caller still attempts to call the user at its last-seen IP address. The pattern is shown in Fig. 1 (*iii*). Note this pattern has the same structure as that of case (*i*) except now there is no response from the callee, since it is offline.

To make things even more complicated, a Skype ID can be simultaneously online at more than one machine. In this case, for each online machine either the pattern in Fig. 1 (*i*) or (*ii*) will occur once for each online machine. We developed a script that searches for the various patterns and identifies the callee's IP address(es).

3.3 Inconspicuous calling

In the following, we define the tracking client as the Skype client we use to exchange packets with a callee. The tracking client is an actual Skype client controlled by a script via the Skype API. Importantly, each of the tracking client is not behind a NAT and, therefore, has a public IP address. Therefore, communication between each tracking client and any user (NATed or not) will always be P2P rather than relayed.

Whenever a Skype call comes in, it is accompanied with a ring and a pop-up window for notification. The callee then chooses to accept, reject, or ignore the call. (We use the terminology "user" and "callee" interchangeably, depending on context.) Since the tracking client actually makes calls to callees, if not designed carefully, it will cause ringing and pop ups on the callees' machines. Not only would this disturb the callee, but it would expose the attacker. We therefore need to design our scheme so the tracking client exchanges packets directly with the callee – *without notifying the callee of the call.*

In our testing, we have observed that during call establishment, both TCP and UDP packets are sent between the tracking client and the callee. We have found that if we prevent TCP connections from being established with the callee, the callee will not be notified about the call. Thus, a possible simple solution is to have the tracking client drop all TCP SYN packets sent to and from the callee. However, at the time when we make the call, we have no clue about the callee's IP address, and we cannot tell whether an observed TCP SYN is going to (or coming from) a Skype infrastructure node, a supernode, a relay node, or the targeted callee.

To solve this problem, during each call, we prevent the establishment of any new TCP connection by dropping all outgoing and incoming SYN packets (to all IP addresses). Note this procedure does not terminate the tracking client's TCP connections that were in progress before making the call (for example, an ongoing connection to a supernode). With this simple mechanism, the callee is never notified, even if the callee is behind a NAT. To check that no pop ups appear, we tested this scheme on the volunteers as described in Section 2.

3.4 Skype Privacy Settings

Skype has two privacy settings to block calls from specific people. The first setting, *allows call from people in my Contact list only*, is a white list. The second setting called *blocked people* is a black list blocking all people whose Skype ID is in this list.

We tested the impact of both settings on our scheme to inconspicuously get the IP address of a callee. For the first setting, the caller was not in the contact list of the callee. For the second setting, the callee explicitly blocked the Skype ID of the caller. In both cases, we were able to inconspicuously retrieve the IP address of the callee. *In summary, we observed that Skype privacy settings fail to protect against our scheme.*

4. MOBILITY OF SKYPE USERS

In the previous section, we presented a scheme to map a person's name to an IP address. We now investigate whether our scheme can be used to periodically observe the mobility patterns of large sets of Internet users.

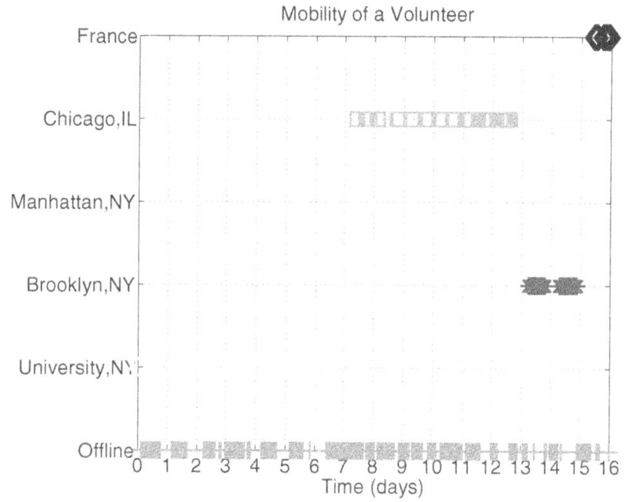

Figure 2: Example of mobility of a volunteer.

4.1 Mobility of a Volunteer

4.1.1 Geo-Localize Skype Users

In the following, we use MaxMind [6] to geo-localize the IP addresses that are obtained from the tracking client, hence providing us with the location of users. MaxMind is a service that, given an IP address, provides a city, country, and AS. To determine city and country, it first aggregates known IP locations from websites that ask their users to provide their geographic location. Then, it uses various heuristics to interpolate the location of other IP addresses. MaxMind claims that it achieves 99.8% accuracy at the country level and 83% on a city level for the US within a radius of 25 miles.

Apart from our set of volunteers, for the sake of user privacy, we anonymized (using a salted hash) all location information. Therefore, we can tell when users change locations at the city, AS or country scale, but not where they actually are.

4.1.2 Example

To give a concrete idea of the kind of mobility that can be observed, we plot in Fig. 2 the mobility of a user in our second set of volunteers. (This volunteer has seen the paper and has given us his consent for all the information about him disclosed.) This person makes publicly available his birth name, gender, date of birth, language, and city of residence in Skype. By searching his birth name and city on Facebook and LinkedIn, we are able to determine his profession and employer.

We now briefly describe the mobility of this user. He confirmed to us that during our measurement period he was first visiting a university in New York; he then took a vacation in Chicago; then returned to university and lodged in Brooklyn; and finally returned to his home in France. Fig. 2 gives an accurate description of the real mobility of this user during the measurement period. The Manhattan location corresponds to an Internet cafe (confirmed by the user).

We remark that if we had followed the mobility of the Facebook friends of this user as well, we likely would have determined who he was visiting and when. In conclusion, mobility combined with information from social networks can provide a vivid picture of the daily activities of a targeted user. It is, in our opinion, a major privacy concern for users of real-time communication systems.

Whereas this volunteer has an active mobility pattern well suited for our illustrative purpose, a legitimate question is whether it is possible to observe mobility for any Skype user. We answer this question in the following.

4.2 Mobility of the Anonymized Users

We now describe how to scale our scheme to measure the availability and mobility of a representative sample of anonymized Skype users. To confirm the frequent mobility of Skype users, these users indeed need to be often running Skype and from several locations. In addition, we are also interested in evaluating the cost of scaling our scheme and in examining whether Skype employs counter measures to hinder it.

For the sake of privacy, we anonymized (as described in section 4.1.1) all location information, and we do not store IP addresses. Therefore, we can only report aggregated statistics, and not detailed user location information.

4.2.1 Obtaining Millions of Skype IDs

In the following, we show that one can easily retrieve a large number of Skype IDs along with the personal information associated with these IDs. To this end, we use the Skype API to collect the IDs. For each ID, we check whether the birth name and other personal information is available. We do not store this information, but instead just note whether it is available in the Skype user's profile.

The Skype public API provides a mechanism for third party applications to control a Skype client. This API operates as follows. After registering with the Skype client, the application can send to the client plain text commands such as *search* and *call*. The Skype client then returns plain text messages to the application. In particular, the Skype API has a *search users* command that takes a search string as a parameter and returns a list of users whose ID, birth name, or e-mail address matches the string. If the search string contains @, the search is performed by e-mail address and has to be an exact match. If the search string is a valid Skype ID, the search is performed on the birth name and ID. Otherwise, the search is made on the birth name only. In addition to the Skype ID of a user, this command will return any other personal information that the user provided at registration, such as birth name, age, gender, homepage, country, language, and other identifying information.

To build our search strings, we use a set of 580K birth names that we collected on Facebook using a similar technique as the one described by Tang et al. [29]. This set is made up of 66K first names and 156K last names. We then combine the birth names, first names, and last names, to obtain 802K unique search strings. For each of these search strings, we send the *search users* command, which typically returns a long list of users, some of whom didn't specify birth names. We then aggregated these lists together and obtained 13M Skype IDs together with which identifying information was available in the profile. For these 13M Skype IDs, 88% provide their birth names and 82% provide either age, gender, homepage, country or language identifying information (we only store a binary information indicating whether a user has provided a given personal information). We note that even though we used Facebook to build our search strings, we could use any database of first and last names.

4.2.2 Parallel Calling

From the Skype IDs obtained in the previous section, we select 100,000 Skype IDs at random. From these 100,000 IDs, we then determine (using the techniques discussed in Section 3) that 10,000 Skype IDs (10%) have been active in the past 72 hours. Finally, we call these 10,000 Skype IDs on an hourly basis. From this result based on a random sample of 100,000 Skype users, we can extrapolate that we can retrieve the IP address of approximately 10% of all Skype users at any time, which represents 56 million of users at any moment in time. We now describe the methodology to call the 10,000 Skype IDs.

We deploy several tracking clients in parallel, each of which calls a subset of the 10,000 Skype IDs. The tracking client calls sequentially all the Skype IDs in its subset, and then repeats the procedure every hour. We determine the IP address of each called Skype ID using the inconspicuous call methodology described in Section 3.3. Based on this IP address we compute the anonymized location of the user as described in section 4.1.1.

Scaling our scheme is challenging. To be able to call 10,000 users on an hourly basis, we need to deploy many tracking clients in parallel, with each one sequentially making one call after another. In order to keep the number of parallel tracking clients to a reasonable level, the time s between two successive calls for a given client should be short.

Indeed, there is an important tradeoff in considering an appropriate value for s. Consider that the tracking client calls one user, waits s seconds, terminates the call, and then repeats the process with another user. If s is large, our tracking client will call users at a relatively low rate. If s is too small, we may terminate the call before the packet pattern is initiated, in which case we may incorrectly assign the IP address of the subsequent Skype ID to the current Skype ID. Thus, special care must be taken to associate the IP addresses with the correct Skype IDs.

The simplest approach is, before making the subsequent call, to wait long enough so that the complete packet pattern elapses. Normally, this takes about 15 seconds from when the first packet is observed until the whole packet pattern occurs. But if we wait 15 seconds between each call, only 4 Skype IDs per minute can be probed.

To increase the calling rate, we performed further tests and observed that (a) once a packet pattern starts, it completes even if the call is terminated before completion; (b) all packet patterns begin within three seconds after making the call. Based on these observations, by waiting three seconds before calling a new Skype ID, we always see the pattern beginning before the end of the three second interval, and also see the pattern complete (extending beyond the 3 seconds). To verify claim (a), we randomly pick 500 users from our Skype ID pool, and call them using two different values of s: 3 seconds and 20 seconds. After comparing the mappings generated from the two approaches, we observe that they are identical for all 500 random Skype users. This implies that the interval of 3 seconds is sufficiently large; we therefore use $s = 3$ seconds in our measurements.

To validate the accuracy of our scalable calling scheme, every 100 calls, we call a random Skype ID among our second set of volunteers (see Section 2). We stress that these volunteers were not in the contact list of the tracking clients, so the patterns generated when calling them are identical to those of the other 10,000 users we are calling. On the 1,368 calls that we made when volunteers were online, we observed only 4 false positives (0.3%) due to patterns that have been reordered during parallel calling. By assigning each IP address to the only Skype user that is the most often designated by the packet patterns, we were able to remove all false positives.

4.2.3 Cost of the Scaling

To call 10,000 users on a hourly basis, we run our tracking clients on 30 physical machines, each one with a different IP address. Each physical machine runs one Skype client and can call 340 IDs per hour. We estimate the costs of running this measurement on a cloud computing platform such as EC2 [1] to be approximately $500 per week.

Preliminary tests suggest that it would have been possible to increase the number of called users by one order of magnitude with virtualization. Indeed, the main issue we faced is that running several tracking clients on a machine makes it harder to isolate packets from each client. One solution we tested but did not use in our scheme, is to run several tracking client per physical machine, each client in a different virtual machine. Because the goal in this paper is to demonstrate the feasibility of our scheme and not to fully optimize it, running a single tracking client per machine is sufficient.

4.2.4 Measurement Results

Whether our scalable calling scheme actually captures the *mobility* of a significant fraction of Skype users depends on three questions that we address in the following.

1) Is it possible to periodically call a large number of Skype users? In Fig. 3 (left), we see that at any given time, we are calling between 2,000 and 3,000 online users among the 10,000 users. The diurnal behavior is due to the heterogeneous distribution of Skype users worldwide. A large fraction of Skype users are from the US and Western Europe. So during the daytime in the US and Western Europe, there are more Skype users online than during night in these geographical areas. We also see in Fig. 3 (left) that after two weeks, we have found at least one current IP address for 9,500 users, which represents 95% of the users we were periodically calling. In summary, it is possible to periodically call a large number of Skype users.

2) How often are Skype users online? We define availability as the fraction of the time a given user is online. In Fig. 3 (middle), we plot the CDF of availability for the 9,500 Skype users that we have seen online at least once. Skype users are surprisingly available with 20% of all users available more than 50% of the time. One explanation for this behavior is that the Skype clients starts automatically at the startup of the system. In summary, Skype users are highly available so one can call them to collect their location most of the time.

3) Can Skype users be found in several locations? Mobility results in a change of IP address geo-localized in a different city, AS, and/or country. For each user that is online at least once, we determine the different locations he visits over the two-week period. This location information is anonymized (see section 4.1.1). In Fig. 3 (right), we see that 40% of the 9,500 Skype users change city, 19% change AS, and 4% change country at least once in two weeks. In summary, Skype users run Skype from several locations so one can observe their mobility. In summary, Skype users often run Skype from different locations, and this mobility can be tracked by our methodology.

Our methodology to measure the number of locations of a user has two limitations. First, in some cases (e.g., dynamic IP address), MaxMind might erroneously associate a same user to different locations. We believe that such errors are very unlikely at the scale of a country or an AS, and only occurs rarely at the scale of cities so that it does not significantly impact our conclusions (see Section 4.1.1). Second, the IP address may not capture the location of users running Skype on their mobile phones [17]. Although this may impact our ability to track Skype users in the future, we believe that relatively few users fall into this category today.

We may observe that significantly more users are mobile among cities than among ASes for two reasons. First, some ISPs have broad geographical coverage, so users located in those ISPs are likely to move within the same ISP, even though they change city. Second, some ISPs provide country-wide free Wifi hotspots to their users. When users of such ISPs change of city, they are likely to use these hotspots, thus connecting from the same AS but a different city.

We note that, as the accuracy of IP geo-localization improves, it will be possible to determine the locations of users with much finer granularity. For instance, a recent paper shows that it is possible to geo-localize IP addresses with a median error distance of 690 meters [30].

5. FILE-SHARING USAGE OF SKYPE USERS

In the previous sections, we established that it is possible to map a person to his IP address in a scalable manner. We are now interested in validating that this scheme introduces a linkability threat where the identity of a person can be associated to his Internet usage. In particular, we focus in this section on finding the identity of file-sharing users. We focus on the BitTorrent application; however, other P2P applications – such as eMule [3] or Xunlei [12] – could instead be used.

One of the challenges here is that many file-sharing users are NATed, that is, they may share their IP address with several users. We present in the following a scheme exploiting the identification field in the IP datagrams to check whether two different applications actually run on the same machine. To the best of our knowledge, we are the first ones to run and validate such a scheme in the wild.

In this section, we anonymized (as described in section 4.1.1) all localization information, we do not store IP addresses after the verification procedure, and we never store any information (including the infohash and the content name) related to the contents downloaded by a given user.

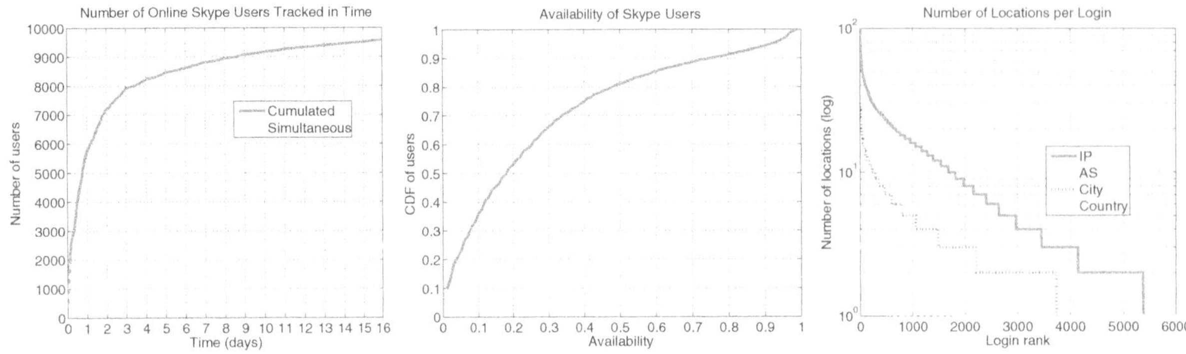

Figure 3: (left) Number of simultaneous and cumulative unique online Skype users (of 10,000) called in two weeks. (middle) CDF of availability of Skype users. (right) Number of locations visited in two weeks by each Skype user, sorted by decreasing number of locations. *Skype users are mobile.*

5.1 Methodology

Our measurement system comprises a *Skype tracker*, an *Infohash crawler*, a *BitTorrent crawler*, and a *Verifier* which communicate through shared storage. We begin by randomly selecting a set of 100,000 identified Skype users. The Skype tracker employs ten tracking clients to daily collect the IP address for the 100,000 users. The Infohash crawler determines the infohashes (file identifiers) of the 50,000 most popular BitTorrent swarms. Operating in parallel with the Skype tracker, the BitTorrent crawler collects the IP addresses participating in the 50,000 most popular swarms, and determines the IP addresses found in both Skype and BitTorrent. Finally, the Verifier attempts to initiate P2P communications with the two applications in order to verify that the same user is indeed running both of them. In the following, we describe in more detail the operation of each component. The operation of the Verifier will be described in Section 5.3.

The Skype Tracker.

We use the methodology developed in Section 3 and Section 4 to find 100,000 active Skype users. In order to daily call 100,000 Skype users, the Skype tracker uses ten tracking clients. Because we are now not interested in fine grain mobility measures but instead in file-sharing usage, we only call each user once per day. We then analyze packet patterns to determine the latest IP address of these users and temporarily save them to a shared storage. (Keep in mind we collect the IP addresses not only of users that are online but also of all users that have logged into the system in the last 72 hours.) These IP addresses are then loaded from the shared storage by the BitTorrent crawler to determine which files are distributed from these IP addresses.

The Infohash Crawler.

We collect file identifiers (infohashes) from the PublicBitTorrent tracker [14], which is the largest BitTorrent tracker at the time of this writing. PublicBitTorrent publishes a file with all the infohashes it tracks on its website. This file is the dump of a request, *scrape-all*, supported by trackers running the OpenTracker software [19]. This request returns all infohashes of files it is tracking and the number of downloaders (leechers) and uploaders (seeds). We download this file every day from the PublicBitTorrent website and extract the infohashes for the 50,000 most popular files.

The BitTorrent Crawler.

In this step, we seek an efficient mechanism to obtain the IP addresses participating in the 50,000 most popular torrents. BitTorrent trackers such as PublicBitTorrent support a request, *announce started*, that returns a list of peers participating in a torrent identified by an infohash. As tracker developers became aware that such requests can be abused they started to limit the number of requests a given peer can send before being blacklisted. Therefore, instead of using the PublicBitTorrent tracker to collect IP addresses, we use a decentralized tracker (DHT).

We collect the IP addresses participating in the top 50,000 torrents from the Mainline DHT every hour for two weeks. This DHT is a decentralized tracker that is primarily used by μTorrent [7] and Mainline BitTorrent [2], the most popular BitTorrent clients. However, we note that other popular P2P file-sharing clients, such as Xunlei, also support it.

When a peer wants to download a new file, it contacts the Mainline DHT to obtain a list of peers distributing that file. This peer first finds the DHT node maintaining the list of peers for that file using the *find_node* request. That request takes an infohash as a parameter, and essentially returns the ID and (IP, port) pair of the DHT node responsible for that infohash. Then, the peer sends a *get_peers* request to that node, which returns a list of (IP, port) pairs belonging to peers distributing the file.

Unlike centralized trackers, we observed that DHT nodes do not implement blacklisting strategies. So we located the nodes responsible for the 50,000 files that we wanted to crawl and then repeatedly sent get_peers requests to collect the peers distributing these files. The whole procedure distributed over 10 machines takes about one hour.

Each of our crawling bots periodically loads the (Skype_ID, IP) pair of active Skype users into memory. If the IP address of an active Skype user is also found in a BitTorrent swarm, the user is possibly downloading the corresponding file (this correlation is performed on-the-fly and we never store the mapping IP address, infohash). *However, we must verify this hypothesis as an IP address may correspond to a NAT shared by several users.* We refer to this problem as the NAT problem. We note that several types

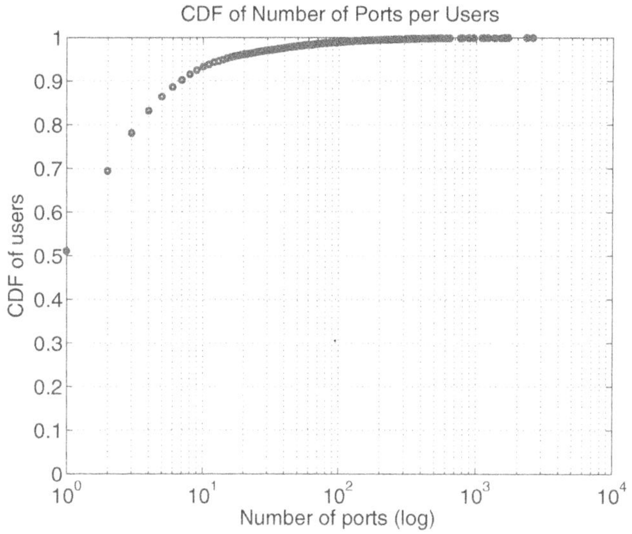

Figure 4: CDF of the users using BitTorrent as a function of BitTorrent ports. ***50% of collected BitTorrent users share their IP address with other BitTorrent users.***

of middleboxes, including NATs and IPv6 routers can use a single public IP address for different users. For the sake of simplicity, we use the term NATs when we refer to the generic notion of middleboxes in the following. (We note that dynamic IP addresses can also be shared by several users, resulting in the same problem.)

5.2 The NAT Problem

Depending on the Internet connectivity of a user, an IP address may correspond to a computer or to a NAT shared by a household, a company, or even an ISP. Because several users can share the same IP address, we may wrongly associate an identified Skype user to the BitTorrent downloads of another user behind the same NAT. To the best of our knowledge, all BitTorrent clients multiplex torrents on a single port. This port is picked at random at the installation of the client, and remains the same in subsequent utilizations. Therefore, we can associate each IP/port pair to a single BitTorrent user [19]. However, this observation alone does not allow us to match a Skype user to a BitTorrent user when the user is behind a NAT, as described below.

We found 15,000 users (out of 100,000) who have IP addresses that were simultaneously found in Skype and BitTorrent during a period of two weeks. Of these 15,000 Skype users using BitTorrent, approximately 7,500 (50%) share their IP address with another BitTorrent user (as indicated by users with more than one port in Fig. 4). In other words, a significant fraction of the 15,000 Skype users are behind a NAT and may therefore not be the ones using BitTorrent (false positives).

5.3 The Verifier

We now describe the operation of our Verifier tool, which is responsible for definitively establishing whether Skype and BitTorrent are run on the same machine. Although more than one person *simultaneously* share the same machine, the granularity of a machine is enough for our purpose. For the sake of simplicity, we assume in the following that each machine is used by a single person.

Given an IP address that participates in both Skype and BitTorrent (matching IP), we now describe how the Verifier makes sure the person identified in Skype is indeed the one using BitTorrent. Consider a scenario where two users, Alice and Bob, are behind the same NAT. Suppose that, by calling Alice on Skype, we have determined that her IP address is in a swarm in BitTorrent, but the IP address is a NATed one. Two scenarios are possible. In the first scenario, Alice is using both Skype and BitTorrent on the same host. In the second scenario, Alice is using Skype on one host and Bob is using BitTorrent on another host. The second scenario corresponds to a false positive because Alice is not the one using BitTorrent.

To detect false positives, we leverage the predictability of the identification field in the IP datagrams (IP-ID) originating from the same machine [18]. As soon as the BitTorrent crawler detects a matching IP address, it signals the Verifier, which immediately calls the corresponding Skype user and, at the same time, initiates a handshake with the BitTorrent client. If the distance between the IP-IDs generated by Skype and those generated by BitTorrent is small, Alice is very likely to be the identified BitTorrent downloader. Otherwise, Alice is likely to be a false positive.

At the end of the verification procedure, IP addresses are anonymized using a salted hash. All subsequent analysis is performed on this anonymized data.

Limitations.

Our verification procedure has two limitations. The first limitation is that we can only initiate communication to public peers or NATed peers that accept incoming communications (e.g., when UPnP is used). This limitation significantly restricts the number of BitTorrent users we can verify. However, for this proof of concept, it is not necessary to verify all the Skype users who are downloading with BitTorrent. An aggressive attacker could easily verify more users by registering the IP address of the Verifier to the Mainline DHT. In this manner he would also receive incoming communication from peers whose NATs refuse incoming communications. Therefore, an attacker could in principle verify NATed peers also.

The second limitation is that we assume that the IP-IDs originating from the same machine are predictable, which depends on two conditions. The first condition is that the IP-IDs originating from the same machine should be predictable (e.g., sequential). Because IP-IDs are attributed by the TCP stack of an Operating System (OS), this first condition highly depends on the fraction of OSes observed in the wild whose attribution is indeed predictable. By testing Windows XP, Vista, and 7, we verified that they all use sequential IP-IDs. As these three versions of Windows alone account for 90% of all OSes found in the wild [13], we conclude that this first condition is largely met. The second condition is that NATs do not modify the IP-IDs as attributed by the TCP stack of the machine. This condition is supported by (*i*) related work in which this behavior was not observed in practice [18] and by (*ii*) the specification of the IPv4 ID field, which specifies that NATs should ignore this field [15].

In conclusion, we expect that our verification procedure based on the predictability of the IP-ID field to be highly

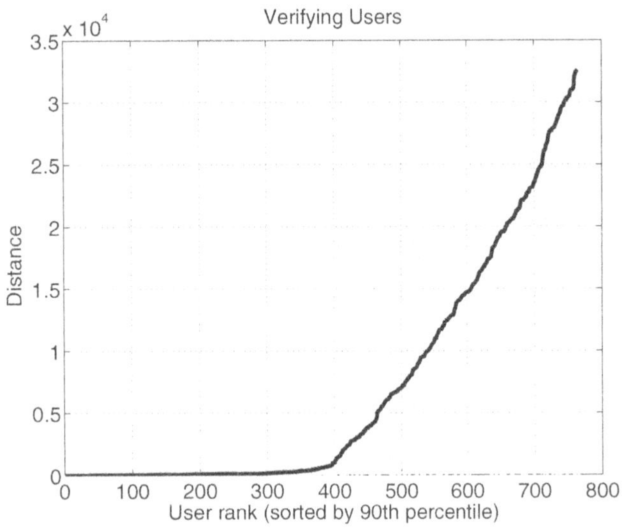

Figure 5: After two weeks, we plot the 90th percentile of the shortest distance between the IP-IDs on a ring of 2^{16} elements of the first Skype and BitTorrent packets received from a verifiable user, sorted by increasing 90th percentile (curve). There is one dot per verification experiment. ***We verify 400 users out of 765 users.***

accurate, that is, with no, or few, false positives (due to similar IP-IDs originating from different machines) and relatively few false negatives (due to OSes with unpredictable IP-IDs attribution or IPv6 routers that re-attribute IP-IDs unpredictably).

5.4 Experimental Results

By running our verification procedure for two weeks, we successfully triggered communication between the Verifier and 765 unique users on both Skype and BitTorrent. We refer to these users as *verifiable*.

We investigate the fraction of verifiable users that we actually fully verified. For the 765 verifiable users, we compute the shortest distance on a ring of 2^{16} elements between the IP-IDs of the first packet received from Skype and from BitTorrent. The smaller the distance, the more likely the identified Skype user is indeed using BitTorrent. In Fig. 5, we see that running this procedure finds 400 unique users for whom the 90th percentile of the distance is less than 1,000. We conclude that approximately 400 users (52% of the 765 verifiable users) are indeed using BitTorrent. We cannot conclude for sure that the remaining 48% of the verifiable users are not BitTorrent users (they might be false negatives). However, as we have seen that at least 90% of the OSes use sequential IP-IDs, we strongly believe that most of them are not using BitTorrent.

In summary, we have determined 400 identified Skype users (from a random set of 100,000) who are definitely using BitTorrent. Table 2 shows the information that is readily available about the top-10 BitTorrent users. When registering with Skype, all of these users provided their last names and all but two users also provided their first names. In addition, all but one of these users provided their cities of residence. However, we remind that we do not store any per-

Rank	# Files	First name	Last name	City	Country
1	23	✓	✓	✓	✓
2	18	✓	✓	✓	✓
3	12	✓	✓	✗	✓
4	11	✓	✓	✓	✓
5	11	✓	✓	✓	✓
6	11	✓	✓	✓	✓
7	9	✗	✓	✓	✓
8	8	✗	✓	✓	✓
9	7	✓	✓	✓	✓
10	6	✓	✓	✓	✓

Table 2: For each of the top10 verified user, we show the number of files shared by that user, whether the user provides in its Skype profile a first or last name, a city, and a country.

sonal information (e.g., name and city) for the purpose of this measurement; instead, we only store a binary information indicating whether a personal information is available or not.

6. DEFENSES

In the previous sections we have seen that it is possible for an attacker to develop and deploy (possibly from a home) a tool that periodically determines the current IP address of a targeted VoIP user. Even if the VoIP user is behind a NAT, the attacker can determine the user's public IP address. Observing the mobility of a targeted individual could be used for many malicious purposes. In this section we briefly discuss defenses for this attack, both at the application level and at the user level.

One measure that can go a long way is for the designers of the VoIP signaling protocol to simply *ensure that the callee's IP address is not revealed to the caller until the callee accepts the call.* That is, before the callee accepts the call, callee's signaling packets are sent to supernodes or infrastructure nodes, and not to the caller; furthermore, the caller is not provided the callee's IP address during call set-up. By only revealing the callee's IP address after the callee accepts the call, then (*i*) it is no longer possible to make an inconspicuous call to the target; and (*ii*) if Alice chooses to block all calls from strangers (i.e., people not on her contact list), then a stranger will no longer be able to determine her IP address and observe her mobility. This solution has a very low overhead as only a few signalling messages are relayed. Thus, we strongly recommend that all VoIP applications adopt this simple mechanism.

However, even with this simple mechanism in place, a friend of Alice (that is, anyone on her contact list, including friends, old boyfriends, family members, employers, and employees) would still be able to determine her IP address (and location) when they call her and she accepts the call. We now outline some measures that defend against this attack.

One blanket defense for these attacks is to have all calls pass through relays. When a datagram passes through a relay, the relay regenerates the datagram with the source IP address of the relay. If the relay can be trusted, then neither party in the call sees the other's IP. In fact, in Skype, if both caller and callee are behind a NAT, then the call is typically relayed through a third skype user (who is not behind a NAT), serving as a relay. The relays must be selected so as not to give away the location of the callee. (For example, the system shouldn't strive to find a relay in same city as the callee.) The main problem with this solution is that it detracts from the efficiencies of P2P communication because (i) relays must now be made available to support the huge bandwidth demands of large-scale real-time voice and video communication systems; and (ii) access ISPs will see an increase of upstream and downstream relay traffic.

In order to not excessively route traffic through relays, the system can be designed so that Alice can specify for which contacts in her address book the calls are to be routed through relays. For example, if Alice is only concerned about her boss observe her mobility, she can configure her client to have calls between her and her boss pass through relays. The client could also be designed to make this decision on a call-by-call basis: whenever, her boss attempts to call her, she is asked whether this should be a P2P or relayed call.

We briefly mention that another approach for providing location privacy is to run the P2P communication application through a third-party anonymizing service such as Tor [22]. However, the delay and throughput performance of Tor and similar services is clearly insufficient for supporting real-time voice and video [21, 24]. In addition to being inefficient, Tor also introduces privacy issues for certain applications (e.g., P2P file sharing) [20].

We conclude this brief discussion on defenses by mentioning that these location attacks actually have their roots in the current Internet architecture, for which all datagrams carry source and destination IP addresses. We are not advocating a total re-design of the Internet, but we mention that this and other Internet privacy problems could be resolved by using alternative underlying network architectures. For example, if the Internet were to use virtual circuits (as with X.25 and ATM), then it would be much more difficult for a stranger or a friend to observe a user's mobility.

7. RELATED WORK

7.1 Mobility

We now describe the related work on observing the mobility of users by using IP addresses and cell phones.

IP Address Mobility.

Guha et al. [23] is the work on IP address mobility that is the closest to ours. The authors show that by periodically retrieving the IP address of dynamic DNS users, an attacker can observe the mobility of these users. Whereas the goal of their attack is similar to ours, there are two major differences between exploiting dynamic DNS and Skype to measure mobility. First, dynamic DNS allows to infer the identify of the user in "some cases" whereas we have showed that 88% of Skype users provide their birth name, and that 82% also provide either age, gender, homepage, country, or language. Second, targeting dynamic DNS users limits the scope of the attack. Whereas there are a few millions users of dynamic DNS in the world, we showed that much more Skype users are susceptible to have their mobility tracked.

Cell Phone Mobility.

The Carmen Sandiego Project [16] recently showed how to use cell phones to observe the mobility of a user. The authors first use the caller ID service to collect persons-to-cell phone numbers mappings. Then, by accessing the Home Location Register (HLR), they show that an attacker can collect the current Mobile Switching Center (MSC) identifier for a given phone number. As MSC identifiers often gives the indication of the location of a user, an attacker can periodically collect that information to observe the mobility of an identified cell phone user. One important weakness of this attack is that there is no convention on how an operator attributes MSC identifiers. So the naming convention for MSCs varies from one operator to the other and it is hard to determine to which location a given identifier corresponds.

Even though it is not our primary purpose, we believe our scheme, and in particular the description of Skype packet patterns between caller and callee, also has the potential to significantly simplify the tracing of Skype calls.

To the best of our knowledge, we are the first to show that it is possible to use real-time applications to map a person to an IP address and to scale that scheme to observe the mobility of a large number of persons. As we have shown it might be possible to observe the mobility of 56 million identified Skype users worldwide at any moment in time, we claim that the scope and the severity of our attack are very severe.

7.2 File-sharing Usage

We now describe the related work on observing file-sharing usage and verifying users. Because we have used BitTorrent in this paper and it is one of the most popular file-sharing system, we focus on BitTorrent in the following. However, we remind that all file-sharing systems are in principle vulnerable to our attack.

In recent works, the scale of BitTorrent measurements has significantly increased [19, 28, 33]. For example, Zhang et al. collected 5 million IP addresses in 12 hours [33], Siganos et al. collected 37 million IPs in 45 days [28], and Le Blond et al. collected 148 million IPs in 103 days [19]. As noted by Le Blond et al. and more recently by Wolchok et al. [31], being able to continuously collect the IP addresses is a serious privacy threat in itself. In this paper though, we have not only collected the IP addresses of a large number of BitTorrent users but we have also identified a significant fraction of these users.

A security threat noted by Piatek et al. consists in injecting the IP address of random Internet users into BitTorrent trackers to falsely implicate them into copyright infringement [27]. We note that the ability to map a targeted person to an IP address significantly worsens this threat because an attacker could also implicate that particular person into copyright infringement.

As far as we know, we are the first to show that it is possible to find the identity of BitTorrent users without requesting that information from an ISP. We believe that this attack introduces a serious potential for blackmail and phishing attacks.

Verification.

We relied on IP-IDs to verify the identity of BitTorrent downloaders. This technique has been used in the context of passively counting the number of machines behind a NAT [18] (on a LAN). As far as we know, it has never been used on the Internet to actively verify that several applications were running on the same machine. Alternatively, we could have used remote physical device fingerprinting [26] but using IP-IDs was simpler and sufficient for our purpose.

8. CONCLUSION

We have shown that it is possible for an attacker, with modest resources, to determine the current IP address of identified and targeted Skype user (if the user is currently active). It may be possible to do this for other real-time communication applications that also send datagrams directly between caller and callee (such as MSN Live, QQ, and Google Talk). In the case of Skype, even if the targeted user is behind a NAT, the attacker can determine the user's public IP address. Such an attack could be used for many malicious purposes, including observing a person's mobility or linking the identity of a person to his Internet usage.

We have further shown that by deploying modest resources, it is possible for an attacker to scale this scheme to not just one user but tens of thousands of users simultaneously. A prankster could use this scalable calling scheme to, for example, create a public web site which provides the mobility and file-sharing history of all active Skype users in a city or a country. Parents, employers, and spouses could then search such a web site to determine the mobility and file-sharing history of arbitrary Skype users.

Acknowledgements. We would like to thank the volunteers for the considerable amount of time they have spent to help us test our scheme. We also would like to thank Justin Cappos, David Choffnes, Paul Francis, Krishna Gummadi, Engin Kirda, and the anonymous reviewers for their constructive comments. This research was partially supported by the NSF grant CNS-0917767.

9. REFERENCES

[1] Amazon EC2. `http://aws.amazon.com/`.

[2] BitTorrent. `http://www.bittorrent.com/`.

[3] eMule. `http://www.emule-project.net`.

[4] FaceBook. `http://www.facebook.com`.

[5] Google. `http://www.google.com`.

[6] MaxMind. `http://www.maxmind.com/`.

[7] μTorrent. `http://www.utorrent.com/`.

[8] Number of Google Talk Users. `http://tinyurl.com/6h4lxbd`.

[9] Number of MSN Live Users. `http://tinyurl.com/6z3mno8`.

[10] Number of QQ Users. `http://tinyurl.com/5w2scvq`.

[11] Number of Skype Users. `http://tinyurl.com/6ce49sv`.

[12] Xunlei. `http://www.xunlei.com`.

[13] OS Market Share, 2010. `http://tinyurl.com/6myem6`.

[14] Public BitTorrent: An Open Tracker Project, 2010. `http://publicbt.com`.

[15] Updated Specification of the IPv4 ID Field, 2010. `http://tools.ietf.org/html/draft-ietf-intarea-ipv4-id-update-01`.

[16] BAILEY, D., AND DEPETRILLO, N. The Carmen Sandiego Project. In *Proc. of BlackHat* (Las Vegas, NV, USA, 2010).

[17] BALAKRISHNAN, M., MOHOMED, I., AND RAMASUBRAMANIAN, V. Where is that Phone?: Geolocating IP Addresses on 3G Network. In *Proc. of IMC* (Chicago, Illinois, USA, 2009).

[18] BELLOVIN, S. M. A Technique for Counting NATed Hosts. In *Proc. of IMW* (Marseille, FR, 2002).

[19] BLOND, S. L., LEGOUT, A., LEFESSANT, F., DABBOUS, W., AND KAAFAR, M. A. Spying the World from Your Laptop - Identifying and Profiling Content Providers and Big Downloaders in BitTorrent. In *Proc. of LEET* (San Jose, CA, USA, 2010).

[20] BLOND, S. L., MANILS, P., CHAABANE, A., KAAFAR, M. A., CASTELLUCCIA, C., LEGOUT, A., AND DABBOUS, W. One Bad Apple Spoils the Bunch: Exploiting P2P Applications to Trace and Profile Tor Users. In *Proc. of LEET* (Boston, MA, USA, 2011).

[21] DHUNGEL, P., STEINER, M., RIMAC, I., HILT, V., AND ROSS, K. W. Waiting for Anonymity. In *Proc. of P2P* (2010).

[22] DINGLEDINE, R., MATHEWSON, N., AND SYVERSON, P. Tor: the Second-generation Onion Router. In *Proc. of USENIX* (Boston, MA, 2004).

[23] GUHA, S., AND FRANCIS, P. Identity Trail: Covert Surveillance Using DNS. In *Proc. of PETS* (Ottawa, Canada, 2007).

[24] ISDAL, T., PIATEK, M., KRISHNAMURTHY, A., AND ANDERSON, T. Privacy-Preserving P2P Data Sharing with OneSwarm. In *Proc. of SIGCOMM* (Bangalore, India, 2010).

[25] JAKOBSSON, M., FINN, P., AND JOHNSON, N. Why and How to Perform Fraud Experiments. *Proc. of IEEE Security & Privacy 6*, 2 (2008), 66–68.

[26] KOHNO, T., BROIDO, A., AND CLAFFY, K. C. Remote Physical Device Fingerprinting. In *Proc. of Security & Privacy* (Oakland, CA, 2005).

[27] PIATEK, M., KOHNO, T., AND KRISHNAMURTHY, A. Challenges and Directions for Monitoring P2P File Sharing Networks or Why My Printer Received a DMCA Takedown Notice. In *Proc. of HotSec* (San Jose, CA, 2010).

[28] SIGANOS, G., PUJOL, J., AND RODRIGUEZ, P. Monitoring the Bittorrent Monitors: A Bird's Eye View. In *Proc. of PAM* (Seoul, South Korea, 2009).

[29] TANG, C., ROSS, K. W., SAXENA, N., AND CHEN, R. What's in a Name: A Study of Names, Gender Inference, and Gender Behavior in Facebook. In *SNSMW* (2011).

[30] WANG, Y., BURGENER, D., FLORES, M., KUZMANOVIC, A., AND HUANG, C. Towards Street-Level Client-Independent IP Geolocalization. In *Proc. of NSDI* (Boston, MA, 2011).

[31] WOLCHOK, S., AND HALDERMAN, J. A. Crawling BitTorrent DHTs for Fun and Profit. In *Proc. of WOOT* (Washington, DC, USA, 2010).

[32] WONDRACEK, G., HOLZ, T., KIRDA, E., AND KRUEGEL, C. A Practical Attack to De-anonymize Social Network Users. In *Proc. of Security & Privacy* (Oakland, CA, USA, 2010).

[33] ZHANG, C., DHUNGEL, P., WU, D., AND ROSS, K. W. Unraveling the BitTorrent Ecosystem. *TPDS* (2010).

Summary Review Documentation for

"I Know Where You Are and What You Are Sharing: Exploiting P2P Communications to Invade Users' Privacy"

Authors: S. Le Blond, C. Zhang, A. Legout, K. Ross, W. Dabbous

Reviewer #1

Strengths: The practical demonstration of an unobtrusive tracking attack that undermines privacy for a popular Internet application (Skype). Unlike most attacks, this one is not exotic. It is straightforward to run at scale and represents a real vulnerability in Skype at least.

Weaknesses: In terms of writing, the paper is a bit thin; it would be better as a tighter 10-pager (or to have a deeper evaluation if it remains at 14 pages) and so other papers may have larger contributions.

Note that the work is a straightforward combination of largely known techniques, but I don't think this is a weakness. Rather, it makes the result more of a vulnerability.

Comments to Authors: Nice job. I particularly like the way you tied all of the pieces together to provide a method of tracking and profiling a user starting with only their name and email.

The title doesn't seem right. You are not exploring limits as best I can tell. The work is more like a practical, scalable technique for tracking the location and activity of Internet users via Skype.

Why not try to find the Skype ID of the other 4 faculty?

Re mobility, it would be better to gather ground truth for all of your consenting users and compare this to inferred location, instead of presenting a single user. This might identify ways that the tracking fails, e.g., remote desktop?

In 5, I would have considered counting users behind NATs to be pretty close to testing whether two applications behind a NAT are the same user -- if they are not then they will count as two users, not one.

The defenses section seems a bit weak. There is a large performance tradeoff in the relaying that you get to. Another, possibly better option might be to change the Skype client so that it would alert users to unobtrusive calls so that tracking can't proceed silently.

Similarly, for IPID, using non-IP networks seems overkill. What about this as a solution: have NATs keep virtual IPID counters per external destination and protocol (or more detailed key). The NAT could add a random offset for each different external destination and protocol, recording the offset in the connection record to rewrite as packets pass through. Seems like a privacy-enhancing NAT. Problem solved? Hosts could directly keep virtual IPID counters for destination IP/port pairs, which would be more effective.

Related work is verbose and doesn't add much value. Note that there are other bodies of work related to VoIP and privacy, e.g., look at the work of Fabian Monrose, including recovering the likely contents of conversations despite encryption.

Reviewer #2

Strengths: This is an interesting work showing a rather surprising attack against skype.

The main contribution of this study is highlighting an important design flaw in a popular application (Skype) that enables an attacker to find the IP address of a Skype ID (even when the attacker is not a friend with or is the blacklist of the victim).

The authors demonstrate how information from BitTorrent and Skype can be linked to find private information about their users.

Weaknesses: The described attack is not a fundamental problem is real-time communication applications, but rather a design flaw that can be rather easily fixed.

Comments to Authors: The main lesson I learned from the paper is that a real-time communication network should not disclose the IP address of a callee before the callee answers an incoming call, which I found interesting.

20 people spread across the world is a rather small sample to claim "a large diversity of user and client behaviors". At some points, I found the authors over-claim a bit.

The authors conclude based on Figure 3 that 40% of Skype users change city. I don't trust this result. Each user is associated with multiple IP addresses over time. Even if one of the IP addresses is geolocalized incorrectly (which is possible and rather likely when the number of IP addresses is large), then the resulting figure (40%) will be artificially inflated.

Skype could obfuscate the patterns the authors observe in Section 3.2 making it hard to identify the callee traffic. It would be nice if the paper discussed this defense as well.

In Section 6, the authors explain that their attack could be avoided by relaying signaling traffic. If a relay is adversarial, what further security holes does this open?

Reviewer #3

Strengths: One of the first works that explores privacy leakage in distributed applications. We need more examples like these before we can start developing principles for systems that are reasonably private. (An analogy here would be to developing secure protocols.)

Despite the weakness mentioned below, we should accept this paper because the results are so telling. This work will likely encourage others to go analyze other systems.

Weaknesses: The whole thing hinges on a Skype oddity which lets me call you inconspicuously. Unlike some of the other privacy holes that this work exploits, this one appears easy to fix, and once fixed the problem goes away. So, the work might be of short-lived value, given that it's hard to see how the methodology generalizes.

Comments to Authors: I love this paper! It's amazing how much information you manage to glean for an individual. I appreciate you treating Skype behavior like a bug and following the best practices that apply to serious bugs. You have any insight into why the report was not taken seriously by Skype? I only have some minor comments on the paper:

1. The title of the paper seems all wrong. What privacy limit has been explored by you?
2. To increase parallelism of tracking, why don't you start close-by calls from different IP addresses (by using multiple IP addresses for your NIC)? That way, you wouldn't have to worry about carefully tunings.
3. Why don't you worry about false positives in IP Id matching? Two machines can accidentally have similar IP Ids. Rocketfuel folks report on running into false positives when using IP Ids for resolving router IP aliases. My guess is that you would run into that as well.

Reviewer #4

Strengths: Nice simple idea that is well studied in the paper. Being able to show that by doing this at a large scale for Skype, one can find the IP addresses, that are mapped to real people, in a separate data set like P2P logs.

Weaknesses: Doesn't cover the case of IP addresses assigned to cellular users. The actual problem to solve is given an IP address, can we find who is the user behind it? You are solving the opposite problem which is much simpler.

Comments to Authors: Nice paper to read. Here are some comments:

1. Intro: you cannot claim 1.6B because of the overlap between users.

2. You should mention in the list of questions in the intro: who owns this IP address? This is really the key question about Internet privacy. While you don't solve that problem, you can say that you show that by collecting a large data sets and a large number of user IDs, you can being to answer that question in some cases. You want to emphasize that point further. It is really the critical question.

3. Section 3.2: somehow the case iii doesn't make sense to me. If the targeted user was online in the past 72 hours but was NATed and is now offline, why would the application try to contact directly the IP? This would automatically fail because of the NAT. Why would the application even try? Am I missing something?

4. Section 3.2 case (i) signature. You don't explain for the first signature, what is similar and what is distinctive about the pattern observed between the callee and other Skype communications. Can you be clearer about what the signature is?

5. It might be interesting to share some stats about the population. For instance, how many users have multiple machines active at the same time.

6. Section 4.1: you talk about Mobility but you don't mention about the case of Skype users on cellular network. Recent work has shown that the IP addresses can be assigned to regions covering hundreds or thousands of miles. You should mention that caveat: IMC 2009: Where's that Phone?: Geolocationg IP Addresses on 3G Networks Mahesh Balakrishnan, Iqbal Mohomed, Venugopalan Ramasubramanian (Microsoft Research) and/or Sigmetrics 2011: Qiang Xu, Junxian Huang, Zhaoguang Wang, Feng Qian, Alexandre Gerber, Zhuoqing Morley Mao: Cellular data network infrastructure characterization and implication on mobile content placement.

7. One major caveat that you missed is in section 5: because you only collect the Skype ID once a day, when the IP address match a Bittorrent IP address. You don't know if you are looking at the same access line. This is not just about NATs. A common scenario is that the ISP will simply reassign the IP address to another access line (this is not about Bob and Jim behind the same NAT box. This is Bob and Jim in 2 different houses.), so you need to rewrite that whole section. Related to that point, you can see that your initial 15,000 matching users goes down to 765 verifiable. I think most of the issue is due to DHCP and dynamic public IPs.

Reviewer #5

Strengths: The techniques are simple and effective. The privacy implication is strong and the large-scale measurement is convincing.

Weaknesses: The proposed techniques have a few assumptions/ weakness, which may not be present in the future. In other words, the attack can be defeated with relative ease.

Comments to Authors: I like the uncovered threat with a major vendor, which allows an attacker to get huge amount of information with relatively small amount of resources.

Despite the findings, there are also two main techniques proposed in the paper: (1) Inconspicuous calling (by reverse-engineering Skype traffic and dropping SYN packet). (2) Application co-location detection (via sequential IPID).

The first technique has an implicit assumption (which is not mentioned in the paper) that the IP address of other users can be obtained/queried continuously. I would assume that the IP address of other users are stored in some directory node (or supernode) which can only be queried when a call is about to be placed. However, a normal user may never query the directory node so frequently (every 3s). I'm actually surprised that Skype does not enforce any kind of rate limiting on this.

As mentioned by the authors, there's an even stronger assumption (which is more like a bug) -- Even though a user chooses to accept calls from only friends, its IP address can still be queried easily by essentially anyone. I doubt there will be many applications allowing this. For example, as far as I know, QQ does not allow a user's IP address to be revealed without being added as a friend of the attacker first.

The second technique relying on sequential IPID made a fair argument that windows machines are the most popular machines, thus the technique is widely applicable. However, if we think about the emerging mobile world (which are mostly iPhone and Android), neither of them uses sequential IPIDs as far as I know. As a result, when mobile users are on Skype through Wifi, there is no way to detect what other applications are running simultaneously (be it BitTorrent or not) through IPID.

A related issue is that the IP-to-location mapping is not going to work in the cellular network, as IPs are assigned from a very large pool that serves millions of users covering a large geographic area.

Despite these limitations, I think the paper is still an interesting one. Fairly easy to read.

Response from the Authors

We made several changes to the paper based on the reviewers' comments. We changed the title (reviewers 1&3). We also mentioned the issues of two users with overlapping IP-IDs behind the same NAT (reviewer 1), and of precisely geolocating mobile users (reviewers 4&5). Finally, we indicated that dynamic IPs can also be a source of false positives at the IP level (reviewer 4). However, we emphasize that the existence of dynamic IPs does not invalidate our verification scheme based on IP-IDs.

Several reviewers commented on the defenses. Reviewer 1: a) We agree that it would go a long way if the callee's IP was not revealed until he accepts the call. However, a spouse, employee or a motivated attacker impersonating the callee's friend, could place a call, and hang up after collecting the callee's IP. While such an attacker would not be able to track the callee's mobility, he may still be able to link the callee's identity to his Internet usage (for example, file sharing), or break into the callee's machine. b) Building NATs that rewrite the IP-IDs would be great but it might significantly increase the manufacturing costs. Also, IP-IDs could still be used to verify users with a public IP.

Reviewer 2: Obfuscating packet patterns is difficult to do when the attacker can call several times and observe overlapping IPs (without proxying the one overlapping IP will be the callee's). Relaying all calls is a potential solution, but would require a significant change in the software, and significantly increase Internet traffic, since many calls today are video calls.

Reviewer 5: It is hard to limit the number of calls per caller if the directory is distributed over users' clients, as it is likely that a different client will be responsible for different callee's IPs.

Analyzing Facebook Privacy Settings: User Expectations vs. Reality

Yabing Liu
Northeastern University
Boston, MA, USA
ybliu@ccs.neu.edu

Krishna P. Gummadi
MPI-SWS
Saarbrücken/Kaiserslautern, Germany
gummadi@mpi-sws.org

Balachander Krishnamurthy
AT&T Labs–Research
Florham Park, NJ, USA
bala@research.att.com

Alan Mislove
Northeastern University
Boston, MA, USA
amislove@ccs.neu.edu

ABSTRACT

The sharing of personal data has emerged as a popular activity over online social networking sites like Facebook. As a result, the issue of online social network privacy has received significant attention in both the research literature and the mainstream media. Our overarching goal is to improve defaults and provide better tools for managing privacy, but we are limited by the fact that the full extent of the privacy problem remains unknown; there is little quantification of the incidence of incorrect privacy settings or the difficulty users face when managing their privacy.

In this paper, we focus on measuring the disparity between the desired and actual privacy settings, quantifying the magnitude of the problem of managing privacy. We deploy a survey, implemented as a Facebook application, to 200 Facebook users recruited via Amazon Mechanical Turk. We find that 36% of content remains shared with the default privacy settings. We also find that, overall, privacy settings match users' expectations only 37% of the time, and when incorrect, almost always expose content to more users than expected. Finally, we explore how our results have potential to assist users in selecting appropriate privacy settings by examining the user-created friend lists. We find that these have significant correlation with the social network, suggesting that information from the social network may be helpful in implementing new tools for managing privacy.

Categories and Subject Descriptors

H.5.m [**Information Interfaces and Presentation**]: Miscellaneous; H.3.5 [**Information Storage and Retrieval**]: Online Information Services—*Web-based services*

General Terms

Measurement, Experimentation

Keywords

Facebook, privacy, measurement, online social networks

1. INTRODUCTION

Nearly half of the users who have access to the Internet are members of some online social network network (OSN) [6], resulting in a fundamental shift in the patterns of context exchange over the Web. The result of this shift is that instead of just being content *consumers*, individual end users are now required to be content *creators* and *managers*. Today, for every single piece of content shared on sites like Facebook—every wall post, photo, status update, and video—the uploader must decide which of his friends, group members, and other Facebook users should be able to access the content. The per-user average of 130 friends and 80 groups and events [21]—compounded with the average 90 pieces of content uploaded per user per month [21]—has turned the task of simply managing access to content into a significant mental burden for many users. As a result, the issue of privacy on sites like Facebook has received significant attention in both the research community [12,25,27,29] and the mainstream media [1–5,8,9].

Our overarching goal is to improve the set of privacy controls and defaults, but we are limited by the fact that there has been no in-depth study of users' privacy settings on sites like Facebook. While significant privacy violations and mismatched user expectations are likely to exist, the extent to which such privacy violations occur has yet to be quantified. In this paper, we take the first steps towards addressing the problem by analyzing the current state of affairs on Facebook. In particular, we center our analysis around two questions:

- What are the *ideal* privacy settings desired by users? How close are these to the actual settings that users have?
- Is there potential to aid users in selecting the *correct* privacy settings for their content? Can we reduce the mental burden on users by automatically grouping others into meaningful groups for expressing privacy settings?

Since we wish to examine whether users' desired privacy settings differ from their existing settings, we need to ask users detailed questions, i.e., survey them. Thus, we design a survey (implemented as a Facebook application) that examines users' current privacy settings and queries users about their desired settings.[1] In order to scale to a significant number of Facebook users, we recruited users to participate in the study using Amazon Mechanical Turk (AMT). We automatically crawled the existing privacy settings of each piece of uploaded content for 200 users, resulting in 116,553 observations of existing privacy settings. Additionally, each of the users answered survey questions about their desired privacy settings for up to 10 of their photos, resulting in a total of 1,675 measurements of desired settings.

In brief, we find that the current Facebook privacy settings match users' expectations only 37% of the time, indicating that current settings are incorrect the majority of the time. More worrisome, when the settings are incorrect, they almost always tend to be *more open* than the users' desired settings, exposing the content to more users than expected. Additionally, we find that even when users have changed their default privacy settings, the modified settings only match expectations 39% of the time, indicating that even the users who are more privacy-aware have difficulty managing and maintaining their privacy settings correctly. Finally, we demonstrate how our results suggest a potential way forward by showing that many user-defined friend lists (similar to the Circles feature on Google+ [10]) have significant correlation with the structure of the social network. This suggests that the membership and maintenance of friend lists may be aided through the use of community detection algorithms [16, 19, 35, 36, 38].

The remainder of this paper is organized as follows: Section 2 provides a brief overview of related work on measuring privacy in OSNs. Section 3 describes our data collection methodology and data set statistics. Section 4 analyzes our survey data, focusing the relationship between the actual and desired privacy settings. Section 5 focuses on potential ways to aid user privacy management and Section 6 provides a concluding discussion.

2. BACKGROUND

In this section, we briefly provide background on Facebook's privacy model before discussing studies of OSNs privacy and studies that recruit users from AMT.

2.1 Facebook's privacy model

At the time we deployed the survey, Facebook allowed users to manage the privacy settings of uploaded content (photos, videos, statuses, links and notes) using five different granularities: Only Me, Specific People, Friends Only, Friends of Friends, and Everyone.[2] Specific People allows users to explicitly choose friends (or pre-created friend lists, discussed below) to share content with. The default or "recommended" privacy setting for all content is Everyone, meaning users share their content with all 750 million Facebook users [7] if they decline to modify their privacy settings.

Facebook allows users to re-use Specific People privacy settings via friend lists. Users create a friend list, add a subset of their friends to it, name it, and can then select the list as a basis for privacy control. Friend lists are private to the user who creates them, unless the user explicitly chooses to display them as part of his profile.

The granularity of privacy settings varies according to content type. Photos are grouped into albums, and privacy settings are specified on an album granularity (i.e., all photos in an album must have the same privacy setting). For the remaining content types, users can specify different privacy settings for each piece of content.

2.2 User privacy

Privacy is an emerging challenge in OSNs, and a number of researchers have examined different aspects of the privacy problem.

Researchers have examined the privacy model of existing OSNs, demonstrating that sites often leak numerous types of privacy information [12, 26, 29]. A number of papers report that users have trouble with existing extensive privacy controls, and are not utilizing them to customize their accessibility [28, 30, 40]. Other work surveys users' awareness, attitudes, and privacy concerns towards profile visibility and show that only a minority of users change the default privacy preferences on Facebook [11, 22]. However, they do not study to what extent the actual selected settings match users' preferences. There is also significant work that explores new approaches that can enhance the content sharing privacy on OSNs [14, 15, 18, 20, 39].

There are several closely related papers which have measured the privacy considerations of different kinds of information, such as News Feed [23], tagged photos [13], basic profile information [32]. All of these papers demonstrate the importance of the ease of information access in alleviating users' privacy concerns. Madejski et al. [32] show that privacy settings for uploaded content are often incorrect, failing to match users' expectations. There are two primary distinctions between their work and ours. First, they rely on text analysis to select content that is potentially privacy-sensitive; doing so locates additional privacy violations but prevents an overall estimate of the fraction of content that has incorrect settings. Second, we directly compare the user survey results to the in-use settings, instead of relying on inferring the existing privacy setting though fake accounts.

2.3 Using Amazon Mechanical Turk

Most prior work uses small-scale surveys of locally recruited users to study user attitudes towards privacy. This approach affords more control over the surveyed population, but also limits the scalability of the survey. In our work, we take a different approach, recruiting users from Amazon Mechanical Turk (AMT), which offers the potential of greater scalability and a lower cost of running experiments [33]. We now give a brief overview of other studies that have recruited users from AMT.

There have been multiple studies showing that the behavior of participants on AMT is comparable to the behavior of laboratory subjects in more traditional economic and psychological experiments [24, 37]. Considering that compensation may affect the quality of survey results, Mason and Watts [34] show that in online peer production systems like AMT, increased financial incentives increase the quantity, but not the quality of work performed by participants. These studies provide evidence that AMT offers a

[1] This study was conducted under Northeastern University Institutional Review Board protocol #10-10-04.

[2] Facebook has since simplified their privacy setting options, presenting only Friends and Everyone by default. The other options are still available via Custom settings.

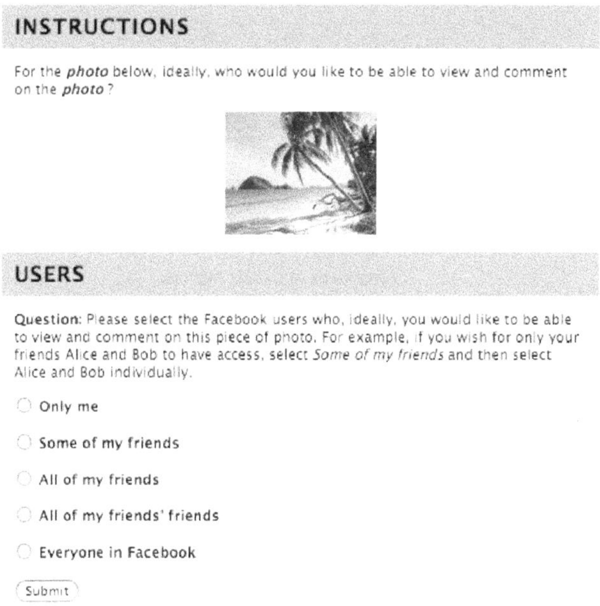

Figure 1: Screenshot of our survey. Each user was asked about 10 different uploaded photos.

potentially attractive way of quickly recruiting significant numbers of survey users.

3. METHODOLOGY

We now describe our approach for collecting data from Facebook users concerning privacy settings. We then detail a few statistics of the collected data set, and examine the demographics of the users who participated in our survey.

3.1 Approach

Our survey was hosted on a web server located at Northeastern University, and is available at `http://socialnetworks.ccs.neu.edu/yabing`. We designed our survey as a Facebook application. By doing so, the application is able to query Facebook to select content to query the user about, as well as to collect the current privacy settings for the user's uploaded content. It is important to note that all data collected is immediately hashed and anonymized; no non-anonymized data is ever written to disk.

When the user begins the survey, he is shown a consent form detailing the purpose and methodology of the experiment and asked to provide optional demographic information (age, gender, income, education level, and U.S. state). Then, the user is asked to answer questions about the ideal privacy settings of some of his uploaded content. Finally, the survey collects information from the user's profile, including the privacy settings for all uploaded content (photos, videos, statuses, links, and notes), any user-created friend lists, and the structure of the user's one-hop social network (i.e., the friendship connections between the user's friends).

The survey selects 10 photos to query the user about. In order to ask the user about both benign and potentially privacy-sensitive photos, the survey first randomly selects up to 5 photos that have non-default privacy settings (i.e., photos where the user has previously modified the privacy settings). Then, the survey chooses the remaining photos randomly from among all photos uploaded, regardless of privacy settings. For each photo, the survey asks the user who, ideally, should be able to view and comment on the photo. The user is presented with a number of options, which approximate the privacy settings currently allowed by Facebook (abbreviations are used in the remainder of the paper):

- **Only Me (Me)** Indicating that the photo should be private the user.
- **Some Friends (SF)** The user is asked which of his friends should be able to access the photo. The user can select friends individually from a list, or can specify users using any friend lists they have created.
- **All Friends (AF)** Indicating that all of the user's friends should be able to access the photo.
- **Friends of Friends (FoF)** Indicating that all of the user's friends, and all of their friends, should be able to access the photo.
- **Everyone (All)** Indicating that all Facebook users should be able to access the photo.

A screenshot of our survey is shown in Figure 1.

One of the benefits of building the survey as a Facebook application is the ability to quickly attract a large number of diverse users. To do so, we recruited users using AMT. We posted a Human Intelligence Task (HIT) describing the application, and offered users $1 to add our application and complete our survey. On average, we found that our survey took users 6 minutes and 30 seconds to complete, implying that completing our survey represented an average hourly wage of $9.23.[3]

There are a few limitations of our methodology that are worth addressing. We focus on photos, as these represent the most commonly uploaded content on Facebook and they have the most diverse privacy settings. Additionally, we only focus on content that is uploaded by the surveyed user; content uploaded by other users (even if it concerns the surveyed user) is not considered. However, Facebook applications are able to access all content uploaded by the user (i.e., the user cannot have a set of more privacy-sensitive photos that are hidden from applications). Finally, we treat each photo equally (in terms of the impact of an incorrect privacy setting), even though certain photos are likely to be more privacy-sensitive than others.

3.2 Data statistics

We now provide a brief overview of the data set that was collected. We deployed our HIT to AMT on May 2nd, 2011, and 200 users completed the survey. These users had an average of 248 friends, and had uploaded an average of 363 photos, 185 status updates, 66 links, 3 notes, and 2 videos. Only 45 users had uploaded fewer than 10 photos (of which 7 users had uploaded none). 81 out of our 200 users had also created at least one friend list, with a total of 233 observed friend lists. Thus, the average user who had created at least one friend list had 3 friend lists.

3.3 User demographics

One potential concern with recruiting users from AMT is the issue of bias; these users are unlikely to be a random

[3]We chose the compensation rate to be in line with recommendations from existing literature, which recommends paying close to the U.S. minimum wage of $7.25 per hour [33].

Type	Count	Me	SF	AF	FoF	Net	All
Photo	65,182	<0.1%	17%	37%	18%	1.3%	26%
Video	428	0.5	5.6	32	11	3.5	48
Status	37,144	0.1	9.7	35	4.5	3.4	47
Link	13,197	<0.1	5.4	36	9.2	2.0	47
Note	602	0.5	6.3	28	5.8	9.8	50
Total	116,553	<0.1%	13%	36%	13%	2.0%	36%

Table 1: Existing privacy settings for all content items. The different content types possess similar privacy setting distributions, and the default (All Facebook users) is selected for the plurality of the items.

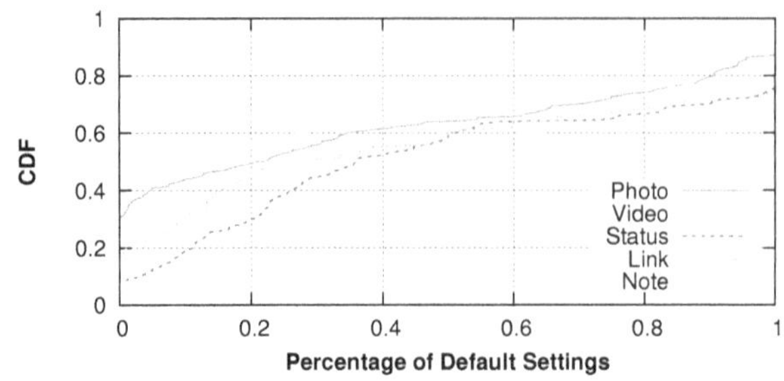

Figure 2: Cumulative distribution of the fraction of each user's content that remains at the default privacy setting, for the five different content types. The distribution differs across the content types; with many users only having changed the settings for a subset of their content.

sample of the Facebook population. We first note that the issue of bias is fundamental in user studies (e.g., psychology studies often use college students, another biased population), and our survey is no different. Nevertheless, we use the self-reported demographics in order to help to understand the nature and distribution of our user population.

In total, 195 (98%) users answered all demographic questions. We restricted our AMT user population to users only in the United States, and we had users from 40 of the 50 U.S. states. The most popular states were California (11%), Florida (11%), and New York (8.2%). We observed a slight male bias, with 54% of our users self-reporting as male; this differs from the overall U.S. Facebook breakdown of 42% male [17]. The self-reported age ranged between 18 and 60, with the median age being 24; this distribution is in-line with the overall U.S. Facebook population [17]. Finally, the self-reported yearly income level ranged from \$0 to more than \$120,000, with the median being \$10,000–\$20,000. These results demonstrate a wide variety of users, and are consistent with prior studies of AMT users [34].

One additional concern with our recruitment methodology is that our AMT users might be a "close-knit" group of friends, and not a more general sample of the user population. To evaluate whether this is the case, we examine how closely related our users are by examining the number of users who are friends on Facebook, and the number of user pairs with at least one common friend. Out of the 19,900 pairs of users [$\binom{200}{2}$], 11 (0.05%) were direct friends and 13 (0.07%) were not direct friends but had at least one friend in common. Thus, our user population is not biased towards one small region of the Facebook social network.

4. ANALYSIS OF PRIVACY SETTINGS

In this section, we begin by investigating the distribution of user-selected privacy settings. We then use our user survey to compare the *desired* privacy settings and *actual* privacy settings, quantifying the frequency of discrepancies. Finally, in the following section, we examine the potential for aiding users in managing privacy by automatically grouping related users.

4.1 Existing privacy settings

We begin our analysis by examining the distribution of existing privacy settings. For each user who completed our survey, we collected the current privacy settings for all of their uploaded content (photos[4], videos, statuses, links, and notes). Table 1 presents an overview of the aggregated privacy settings.[5]

We make two observations. First, out of 116,553 content items, 41,437 (36%) are shared with default privacy settings, meaning they are each visible to over 750 million Facebook users. This fraction is significantly higher than users indicated they desire (20%, discussed below in Table 2), suggesting that the users have not bothered to change the privacy setting from the default. Second, while the various content types show similar distributions, we note that photos have the most privacy-conscious setting: photos have the highest fraction of Some Friends, All Friends, and Friends-of-Friends, and the lowest fraction of Everyone. This suggests that users are more aware of the privacy settings for photos, implying that our survey below (which focuses exclusively on photos) is likely to underestimate the frequency of privacy violations for other types of content (since we observed that other types of content are much more likely to have default settings).

Next, we take a closer look at the per-user settings distribution in order to determine the fraction of users who have changed none, some, or all of their privacy settings from the default. To do so, we calculate the fraction of each user's content that remains at the default setting; Figure 2 presents the cumulative distribution of this fraction across our 200 users. We observe that the fraction of users who have changed either all or none of their privacy settings varies according to content type: for photos, this fraction is 43%, while for notes this fraction is 74% (implying that for photos, for example, 57% of people have some, but not all, of their photos shared with the default privacy setting).

4.2 Desired privacy settings

We now turn to examine the privacy settings that are desired by users, with a focus on comparing the desired settings with the current privacy settings. Recall that to measure the users' desired settings, we survey users concerning up to 10

[4]We do not consider the special album "Profile Pictures", as the user's profile picture is required to be publicly visible. We also disregard a total of 60 additional photo albums containing 7,540 photos for which the Facebook API returned uninterpretable privacy settings.

[5]Note that we also include the legacy **Networks (Net)** setting, indicating that all users in the same network (e.g., university or workplace) should be able to access the photo. This setting can no longer be selected by all users.

Actual setting	Desired setting Me	SF	AF	FoF	All	Total
Me	3	5	2	3	2	15
SF	3	12	28	3	0	46
AF	38	2	184	25	42	291
FoF	16	8	80	15	22	141
All	46	23	171	56	118	414
Total	106	50	465	102	184	907

Table 2: Comparison of the actual privacy settings and desired privacy settings for randomly-selected photos. The shaded cells represent instances where two are the same; this only occurs in 332 (37%, ± 3.14%) photos. When the two are different, they are more often shared with more users than desired (443 photos) than fewer users than desired (132 photos).

Actual setting	Desired setting Me	SF	AF	FoF	All	Total
Me	2	6	4	0	4	16
SF	2	12	29	8	11	62
AF	40	8	237	40	69	394
FoF	39	17	148	45	47	296
All	0	0	0	0	0	0
Total	83	43	418	93	131	768

Table 3: Comparison of the actual privacy settings and desired privacy settings for photos with non-default privacy settings. The shaded cells represent instances where two are the same; this only occurs in 296 (39%, ± 3.45%) photos. When the two are different, they are shared with more users than desired (254 photos) with approximately the same frequency as fewer users than desired (218 photos).

of their uploaded photos. Of our 200 surveyed users, 193 (97%) had at least one photo (and could therefore answer at least one survey question) and 155 (78%) had at least 10 photos (and could therefore answer all 10 survey questions). Additionally, Facebook also offers users the option of sharing photos with Networks [41]. We disregard this feature because many users are not members of networks and are unable to select this setting; this affects approximately 1.3% of photos. In total, our users answered questions concerning 1,675 photos (907 randomly selected photos and 768 random photos with non-default privacy settings).

It is important to note that while we selected photos independent of the albums to which they are assigned, Facebook's privacy settings are *per-photo album* rather than *per-photo*. We now briefly examine how many albums our random photo selection strategy covered. In total, the randomly selected photos came from 578 distinct albums. Our users had a total of 752 albums, meaning that we covered over 76% of all possible albums. Similarly, the non-default-privacy-setting photos came from 449 distinct albums out of 586 total non-default-privacy-setting albums, for a similar coverage of over 76% of all possible albums. Thus, our strategy of randomly selecting photos did not bias our survey towards a minority of the albums.

We divide our analysis into two parts, first focusing on a random selection of photos, and then focusing on photos with non-default privacy settings.

4.2.1 Randomly-selected photos

Table 2 presents the results of our survey for the 907 randomly selected photos, counting the number of photos with each combination of desired setting (columns) and actual setting (rows). First, we observe that for only 332 (37%, ± 3.14%[6]) of photos do the actual and desired settings match; indicating that 63% of the time, current privacy settings do not match users' expectations. Second, we observe that if we focus on the 575 photos that have incorrect privacy settings, 443 (77%, ± 3.44%) of them are shared with more users than desired. Third, and most worrisome, 296 (51%, ± 4.09%) of the 575 photos with incorrect privacy settings are incorrectly shared with all 750 million Facebook users. Taken together, our observations indicate that the problem of privacy management is endemic on Facebook—nearly two out of three of photos have incorrect privacy settings, and over half of these are incorrectly shared will all other Facebook users.

[6]All reported confidence intervals represent 95% confidence intervals.

4.2.2 Photos with non-default privacy settings

One cause of the observations in the previous section are poor defaults: since it is known that users do not always adjust default settings, many of the photos could have incorrect settings because users have not bothered to adjust them. In order to shed light on the frequency of default settings causing privacy violations, we turn to examine only those photos which have non-default privacy settings. Since these photos, by definition, have had their privacy settings adjusted, we can see if the adjusted privacy settings better match users' expectations.

Table 3 presents the survey results for the 768 photos with non-default privacy settings. We observe that the fraction of correct privacy settings (296 photos or 39%, ± 3.45%) is approximately the same as the randomly selected photos. This indicates that even photos where the user has explicitly adjusted privacy settings still do not match the users' expectations the majority of the time. However, we also observe that the fraction of incorrect photos that are shared with more users than expected (54%, ± 4.50%) is much more even, when compared to the same fraction for randomly selected photos (77%, ± 3.44%). This suggests that while poor privacy defaults cause photos to be shared with more users than expected, users who are cognizant enough to modify their settings still have significant difficulty ensuring their privacy settings match their expectations.

4.2.3 Summary

Our analysis reveals that while users are uploading significant amounts of content to Facebook, almost half of the content is shared with the default privacy settings, which expose the content to all Facebook users. Users in our survey reported that this was the desired setting only 20% of the time, suggesting that the default settings are poorly chosen. More worryingly, even for photos for which the privacy settings have been modified by the user, the modified privacy settings match users expectations less than 40% of the time. This strongly suggests that users are having trouble correctly configuring their privacy settings and calls for new tools to manage privacy.

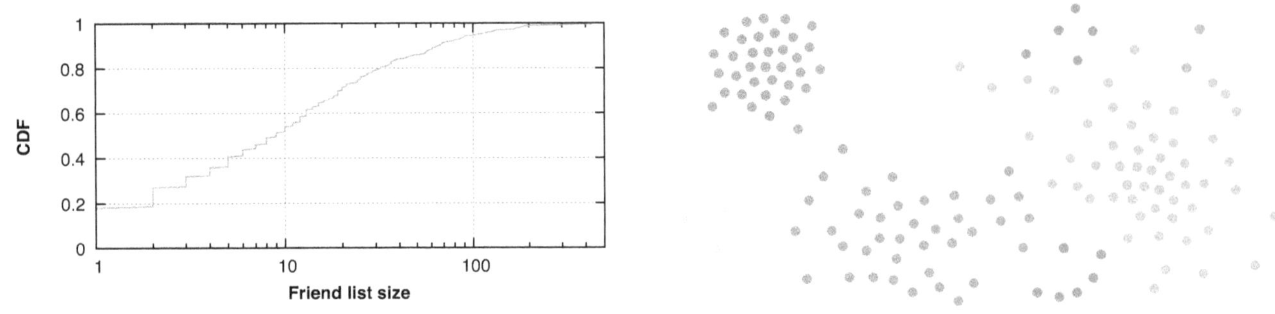

(a) (b)

Figure 3: (a) Cumulative distribution of the sizes of observed friend lists and (b) the 8 automatically detected groups of friends from one of the authors' Facebook social network. Nodes represent the author's friends and links exist between pairs of friends who are also friends. Nodes with the same color are automatically grouped together by the community detection algorithm.

5. IMPROVING PRIVACY TOOLS

As our final point of analysis, we examine the potential for assisting users in managing their privacy. Specifically, we focus on friend lists, a mechanism for users to group their friends that is similar to the Circles feature of Google+. We explore whether the friend lists could be automatically populated using community detection algorithms [16,19,35, 36,38] over the social network.

To do so, we examine the friend lists of our 200 surveyed users using the Facebook API. The cumulative distribution of the sizes of the 233 friend lists we examine is shown in Figure 3(a). More than 50% of friend lists have more than 10 members, while 20% of the lists have more than 30 members, which indicates the potential difficulties with manually generating and maintaining such large lists of friends.

One potential solution to the challenge of privacy management lies in leveraging the social links between the friends of a user to automatically group them into communities, where each community of friends can be used to create a friend list. We illustrate this in Figure 3(b), where we used a community detection algorithm [16] to automatically group the 144 Facebook friends of one of the authors into 8 friend lists.

For this approach to work effectively, users' friend lists need to correspond to tightly-knit communities in the network graph. To verify the extent to which users in friend lists form closely connected communities, we examine the normalized conductance [31] of the existing friend lists, whose value ranges from -1 to 1, with strongly positive values indicating significant community structure. Prior studies of social network graphs have found that normalized conductance values greater than 0.2 correspond to strong communities, that could be detected fairly accurately by community detection algorithms [31]. We analyzed the conductance values for our 233 friend lists and we found a significant positive bias. Over 48% of the friends lists have values larger than 0.2, suggesting that a large fraction of friend lists could be automatically inferred from the social network.

6. CONCLUDING DISCUSSION

We now briefly discuss a few issues brought up in the preceding analysis.

Automatically updating friend lists The results in Section 5 suggest that the social network can be automatically leveraged to aid users in selecting groups of friends to share content with. In ongoing work, we are developing Facebook applications that use the social network to help users generate friend lists conveniently. This is complementary to recent work on privacy "wizards" [18], which uses machine learning algorithms to infer communities. One potential advantage of leveraging the structure of the social network is the potential to easily update the friend lists as the user forms or breaks friendships.

Measuring privacy In general, privacy is a hard thing to measure, especially since it's hard even for users themselves to quantify. For example, photos alone are likely to have wildly varying privacy requirements, depending on who is in the photo, where it was taken, etc. In our survey, we simply treated all privacy violations as being equal, even though this is certainly not true in practice. In future work, we will explore mechanisms for measuring the "importance" of the various privacy violations, potentially by asking the users or using machine learning approaches on content metadata.

Additionally, when measuring the users' ideal privacy settings, we are treating the users' answers as ground truth. This may not always be the absolute ground truth, as the users' answers may vary with time (as social relationships change), or the users' may have not fully thought through the implications of a given setting. However, other user studies [18] are subject to the same limitation.

Reasons for incorrect settings Due to space constraints, we refrain from exploring *why* the privacy settings were incorrect. However, we note that such a study is non-trivial: just a few of the reasons for privacy violations include poor human–computer interaction mechanisms, the static nature of privacy settings, and the significant amount of work forced on the user to maintain the privacy of their content. We leave a full exploration of these to future work.

Acknowledgements

We thank the anonymous reviewers and our shepherd, David Wetherall, for their helpful comments. This research was supported in part by NSF grants IIS-0964465 and CNS-1054233, and by an Amazon Web Services in Education grant.

7. REFERENCES

[1] Facebook Stirs Privacy Concerns Again. *The New York Times*, 2010. http://gadgetwise.blogs.nytimes.com/2010/04/27/facebook-stirs-privacy-concerns-again.

[2] Facebook Executive Answers Reader Questions. *The New York Times*, 2010. http://bits.blogs.nytimes.com/2010/05/11/facebook-executive-answers-reader-questions/.

[3] Is There Life After Facebook? *The New York Times*, 2010. http://bits.blogs.nytimes.com/2010/05/12/is-there-life-after-facebook/.

[4] Price of Facebook Privacy? Start Clicking. *The New York Times*, 2010. http://www.nytimes.com/2010/05/13/technology/personaltech/13basics.html.

[5] Marketers Can Glean Private Data on Facebook. *The New York Times*, 2010. http://www.nytimes.com/2010/10/23/technology/23facebook.html.

[6] Global Publics Embrace Social Networking. *PewResearchCenter*, 2010. http://pewglobal.org/2010/12/15/global-publics-embrace-social-networking/.

[7] Facebook Climbs Toward 700 Million Users Worldwide, with Steady Growth in the US. *Inside Facebook*, 2011. http://www.insidefacebook.com/2011/04/21/facebook-climbs-toward-700-million-users-worldwide-with-steady-growth-in-the-us/.

[8] Facebook Facelifts Its Privacy Policy. *The New York Times*, 2011. http://gadgetwise.blogs.nytimes.com/2011/03/01/facebook-facelifts-its-privacy-policy/.

[9] Social Networks Offer a Way to Narrow the Field of Friends. *The New York Times*, 2011. http://www.nytimes.com/2011/05/10/technology/10social.html.

[10] Organizing My Online Friends. *The New York Times*, 2011. http://bits.blogs.nytimes.com/2011/07/12/organizing-my-online-friends/.

[11] A. Acquisti and R. Gross. Imagined Communities: Awareness, Information Sharing, and Privacy on the Facebook. *PET*, 2006.

[12] S. Ahern, D. Eckles, N. Good, S. King, M. Naaman, and R. Nair. Over-Exposed? Privacy Patterns and Considerations in Online and Mobile Photo Sharing. *CHI*, 2007.

[13] A. Besmer and H. R. Lipford. Moving Beyond Untagging: Photo Privacy in a Tagged World. *CHI*, 2010.

[14] L. Banks and S. F. Wu. All Friends Are Not Created Equal: An Interaction Intensity Based Approach to Privacy in Online Social Networks. *CSE*, 2009.

[15] R. Baden, A. Bender, N. Spring, B. Bhattacharjee, and D. Starin. Persona: an online social network with user-defined privacy. *SIGCOMM*, 2009.

[16] V. D. Blondel, J.-L. Guillaume, R. Lambiotte, and E. Lefebre. Fast unfolding of community hierarchies in large networks. *Journal of Statistical Mechanics: Theory and Experiment*, 10, 2008.

[17] P. Corbett. Facebook Demographics and Statistics Report 2010. 2010. http://www.istrategylabs.com/2010/01/facebook-demographics-and-statistics-report-2010-145-growth-in-1-year.

[18] L. Fang and K. LeFevre. Privacy Wizards for Social Networking Sites. *WWW*, 2010.

[19] S. Fortunato. Community detection in graphs. *Phys. Rep.*, 486, 2010.

[20] P. W. L. Fong, M. Anwar, and Z. Zhao. A privacy preservation model for Facebook-style social network systems. *ESORICS*, 2009.

[21] Facebook Statistics. http://www.facebook.com/press/info.php?statistics.

[22] R. Gross and A. Acquisti. Information Revelation and Privacy in Online Social Networks (The Facebook case). *WPES*, 2005.

[23] C. M. Hoadley, H. Xu, J. J. Lee, and M. B. Rosson. Privacy as Information Access and Illusory Control: The Case of the Facebook News Feed Privacy Outcry. *Electronic Commerce Research and Applications*, 9(1), 2009.

[24] J. J. Horton, D. G. Rand, and R. J. Zeckhauser. The Online Laboratory: Conducting Experiments in a Real Labor Market. *National Bureau of Economic Research*, w15961, 2010.

[25] B. Krishnamurthy and C. E. Wills. Characterizing Privacy in Online Social Networks. *WOSN*, 2008.

[26] B. Krishnamurthy and C. E. Wills. On the Leakage of Personally Identifiable Information Via Online Social Networks. *WOSN*, 2009.

[27] B. Krishnamurthy. I know what you will do next summer. *CCR*, 40(5), 2010.

[28] C. Lampe, N. B. Ellison, and C. Steinfield. Changes in Use and Perception of Facebook. *CSCW*, 2008.

[29] K. Lewis, J. Kaufman, and N. Christakis. The Taste for Privacy: An analysis of College Student Privacy Settings in an Online Social Network. *Computer-Mediated Communication*, 14(1), 2008.

[30] H. R. Lipford, A. Besmer, and J. Watson. Understanding Privacy Settings in Facebook with an Audience View. *UPSEC*, 2008.

[31] A. Mislove, B. Viswanath, K. P. Gummadi, and P. Druschel. You are who you know: Inferring user profiles in Online Social Networks. *WSDM*, 2010.

[32] M. Madejski, M. Johnson, and S. M. Bellovin. The Failure of Online Social Network Privacy Settings. Department of Computer Science, Columbia University, Technical Report CUCS-010-11, 2011.

[33] W. Mason and S. Suri. Conducting Behavioral Research on Amazon's Mechanical Turk. *SSRN*, 2010.

[34] W. Mason and D. J. Watts. Financial Incentives and the Performance of Crowds. *KDD*, 2009.

[35] M. E. J. Newman. Fast algorithm for detecting community structure in networks. *Phys. Rev. E*, 69(6), 2004.

[36] M. E. J. Newman. Modularity and community structure in networks. *PNAS: Proceedings of the National Academy of Sciences of the United States of America*, 103(23), 2006.

[37] G. Paolacci, J. Chandler, and P. G. Ipeirotis. Running experiments on Amazon Mechanical Turk. *Judgment and Decision Making*, 5(5), 2010.

[38] F. Radicchi, C. Castellano, F. Cecconi, V. Loreto, and D. Parisi. Defining and identifying communities in networks. *PNAS: Proceedings of the National Academy of Sciences of the United States of America*, 101(9), 2004.

[39] F. Stutzman and J. Kramer-Duffield. Friends Only: Examining a Privacy-Enhancing Behavior in Facebook. *CHI*, 2010.

[40] K. Strater and H. R. Lipford. Strategies and Struggles with Privacy in an online Social Networking Community. *BCS-HCI*, 2008.

[41] C. Wilson, B. Boe, A. Sala, K. P.N. Puttaswamy, and B. Y. Zhao. User interactions in social networks and their implications. *EuroSys*, 2009.

Summary Review Documentation for

"Analyzing Facebook Privacy Settings: User Expectations vs. Reality"

Authors: Y. Liu, K. Gummadi, B. Krishnamurthy, A. Mislove

Reviewer #1

Strengths: The authors try to understand the privacy setting, which is not researched a lot by others.

Weaknesses: The main weakness for this paper is its methodology. Usually survey is not a good method for computer science research. It is very doubtable about the results. Some of the inferences don't make sense. And it is not clear why the size of friend lists can affect users' privacy settings.

Comments to Authors: The methodology of this paper is doubtable, because survey based research is always hard to prove its objectivity. Usually surveys cannot be a good methodology for computer science research, because it is well known that it is very hard to design an objective survey, and it is very hard to find the representative people to ensure the correctness of result.

There will always be an argument on how many people are enough for a survey, but 200 is definitely a small number. For the content of this survey, it is also doubtable about whether the pictures used by the application are sensitive enough - there should be some limitations on Facebook applications, that the applications should not have the rights to access all user's content. In other words, the photos that this application can access may not be sensitive and random enough.

Some inferences in this paper are also doubtable. For example, using survey time to infer their hourly wage does not make any sense. Section 5 mentions that "even for which the privacy settings have been modified by the user, the modified privacy settings match users expectations less than 40% of the time." It sounds strange, like the users changed their settings, but the settings are still not what they want? It is more likely that the users are making mistakes, than the problems stem from the system.

The paper also shows the distributions of size of friend lists, but it is not clear why this size is related to the privacy settings.

In conclusion, it is hard to convince the readers by the giving methodology and results.

Reviewer #2

Strengths: - The paper conducts an interesting experiment to evaluate the mismatch between real and expected privacy settings.
- The conducted research focuses on Facebook privacy, which is an interesting and timely topic.
- The paper is well written.

Weaknesses: - The main take-away message of this paper about the complexity of managing privacy settings is not something very new or surprising.

- I was not fully convinced about the reported figures (36%, 37%, etc). How representative are these numbers? The paper should ideally compute confidence intervals.

Comments to Authors: The conducted experiment is very interesting, a clever idea, however the take-away lessons were not as exciting, i.e., the paper finds that the default privacy settings of Facebook are too open and that managing the privacy settings for several content items is complex. These findings are somewhat well known.

I wonder how significant are the differences we observe in Fig. 2? Could these differences just be due to sampling noise.

In general, a number of sources add bias to the reported figures, i.e., sampling error (at the user and content level), response error (deliberate or unintentional bias in the given answers), coverage bias (low income Facebook users), etc. For some of these sources it is impossible to do something. However, for the sampling and response error, I suspect the paper could compute confidence intervals and use methods to detect/filter outliers. This would help trusting more the computed numbers.

Reviewer #3

Strengths: Very interesting topic, nicely studied, with careful coverage of potential bias, and interesting, easy to absorb findings.

Weaknesses: It is very incremental. In particular, reference 30 is key: its authors have studied the same topic, likewise via a user survey, in more depth, but focusing on the arguably more relevant and complex privacy settings of the users' profile.

The authors do not comment at all on why the users may be getting the photo privacy settings wrong. Why did you not compare it to the correctness of the profile settings, providing an opportunity to verify the results from the Columbia study?

Comments to Authors: Could you justify why 200 users? Was it all you could recruit, or did you not want more?

It would help if you could be clearer from the outset that you first went to Mechanical Turk to recruit users who then used a Facebook-enabled survey. It's confusing in the beginning.

The whole argument that helping the users construct friend lists is an aid to privacy management feels contrived to me and not fitting well with the theme of the paper. I didn't get the point at all when you mention it in the Intro's bullet point, wondered what is the point later in the Intro, and didn't find its analysis in the Discussion (while by itself nicely done) all that helpful.

Why did you sample photos randomly, and not with awareness of album structure? As you say, the privacy settings apply per-album, so it would help to sample albums first and next inside them.

In Sec. 3.3, the last paragraph is confusing. You present it in terms of user pairs, saying 11 were direct friends. That (i) means user pairs were friends, and (ii) skews the percentage numbers down. Why don't you just say how many users were friends?

Throughout the paper you suggest that the user did not bother to get the privacy settings right. What if they tried and could not figure it out? Did you ask them that?

In Figure 2, is "user content" albums or photos? I hope it is albums, because again, given that the privacy setting applies per-album, counting photos would skew the results depending on the size of every album on which users use unintended privacy settings.

Reviewer #4

Strengths: This is a timely study on the increasingly important topic of privacy, reporting data on how people use different Facebook privacy settings and that the settings often don't match their stated preferences. It is also a bit of a departure from typical IMC fare in that the main method is a user study, where participants are recruited via mechanical Turk and run a Facebook application that involves a survey. This is an important direction for the evolution of IMC, as it is the kind of tool that is needed to study the user-facing aspects of networked applications. The paper is also well done in this respect; user study experts might disagree, but it exceeds user study standards for systems papers.

Weaknesses: The main point of the study, repeated many times, is that people's privacy settings are found to be often "incorrect", but it is unclear if this is meaningful. Perhaps people are not always sure what privacy level they want for a particular image and would give you different answers on different days, or their answers might evolve over time. The methodology does not admit these possibilities. Thus it may be possible for settings to be mostly "incorrect" yet to do a reasonable job in capturing people's desired levels of privacy. While that would be an extreme case, so is the black and white characterization of privacy settings as correct/incorrect that is used in the paper.

Comments to Authors: See the weakness comment above as my main constructive feedback. For example, I am not sure that I could give you a specific privacy level for many images. This is typical of privacy -- there are some things that I care about a great deal, and other things that I just don't care about much and hence do not have a clear preference. Please think about this comment, as it impacts your methodology and survey. An informal, formative study with a small number of users would flush out whether this or similar considerations are issues.

Can you look at when the preferences were last set, or perhaps when the photo was uploaded? This might let you gather data on the most recent images for which preferences were set versus other images. Presumably non-default preferences that are set very recently do indicate actual user preferences. This would give you a way to baseline the study by comparing survey versus recently set non-default user preferences. The two might agree or disagree. Either way you could compare against a null hypothesis, which you currently are not doing.

Why does studying photos imply that you will likely underestimate the fraction of privacy violations? I don't see that it follows.

Reviewer #5

Strengths: The paper focuses on the investigation of privacy in social networking which is a important and also challenging issue.

Weaknesses: - The user set is likely to be biased and the sample size is too small.
- There is a lack of clear, objective definition on the basic concepts (i.e. "ideal privacy setting).
- The proposed user assisting scheme has unclear value.

Comments to Authors: A first concern about this paper is the user sample size and potential bias: 200 Facebook users recruited via Amazon Mechanical Turk, each was asked about their privacy setting for up to 10 pieces of content. First, it seems that a much bigger user sample size would be needed to draw concrete observations. Second, as the paper stated itself, compensation may affect the quality of survey results; each user only took 6 minutes or so to finish the survey reported in this paper.

With the limited data set, the authors seem to have done a pretty thorough job in analysis. However it seems a mismatch between the goal of the authors and the results obtained. The paper started with two interesting questions:
1. What are the ideal privacy settings desired by users? How close are these to the actual settings users have selected?
2. Is there potential to aid users in their role as content managers?

By the end I did not see a convincing answer to either of the questions.

Regarding question 1, it is unclear whether the quantitative conclusion from this study is representative. There was not a precise definition of the "ideal privacy setting"; what the paper did was simply asking each user whether the setting matched what each expected, and the answer was collected from a small user set with unclear representative quality.

The paper spent most effort in addressing question 1; the answer to question 2 was roughly sketched out in less than a page under discussion, to examine whether the friend lists (to share content) could be automatically populated using community detection algorithms that have been proposed in a few recent efforts. The data may suggest a potential for future investigation but seems a bit of stretch for any conclusion.

Response from the Authors

To address concerns over our sampling of random photos instead of random photo albums, we include analysis of the number of photo albums we cover for each user with our strategy (using our collected photo album data from each participant). The results show that our strategy of randomly selecting photos does not bias our survey towards a minority of the albums; in fact, we cover over 76% of all photo albums that our users had. To address concerns over photo albums that the user may have hidden from our application, we note that Facebook does not allow users to mark certain photos as private to certain application. An application either has access to all albums, or none.

We address reviewers' concerns about the representativeness of our user population in three ways. First, we point out that while our sample size (200 users) is not particularly large (especially when compared to the entire Facebook population), when compared with many other Facebook-based user studies, we cover more users. Second, to address any potential bias, we examine some basic user demographics and find that our user population is not biased towards a single region of the U.S. or the Facebook social network. Third, to better quantify the representativeness of the results, we added 95% confidence intervals that demonstrate that our results are statistically significant.

Finally, to address the higher-level issues of measuring privacy and asking users, we note that, in general, privacy is a hard thing to measure (especially since it is hard even for users themselves to quantify). We acknowledge that asking users introduces unique limitations, but note that we know of no other way to quantify the privacy settings that users desire. We also suggest examining ways of measuring the "importance" of each piece of content in future work.

To address the questions over the underlying reasons for incorrect settings, we provide a brief discussion and note that we are exploring the underlying causes in ongoing work. Our purpose in this study is to understand the frequency of unmatched privacy settings and explore new techniques for aiding users; a proper understanding of the myriad of reasons for incorrect privacy settings is beyond the scope of this paper.

An Analysis of Underground Forums

Marti Motoyama, Damon McCoy, Kirill Levchenko, Stefan Savage and Geoffrey M. Voelker
Department of Computer Science and Engineering
University of California, San Diego

ABSTRACT

Underground forums, where participants exchange information on abusive tactics and engage in the sale of illegal goods and services, are a form of online social network (OSN). However, unlike traditional OSNs such as Facebook, in underground forums the pattern of communications does not simply encode pre-existing social relationships, but instead captures the dynamic trust relationships forged between mutually distrustful parties. In this paper, we empirically characterize six different underground forums — BlackHatWorld, Carders, HackSector, HackE1ite, Freehack, and L33tCrew — examining the properties of the social networks formed within, the content of the goods and services being exchanged, and lastly, how individuals gain and lose trust in this setting.

Categories and Subject Descriptors

H.3.5 [**Information Storage and Retrieval**]: Online Information Services; J.4 [**Computer Applications**]: Social and Behavioral Sciences; K.4.4 [**Computers and Society**]: Electronic Commerce

General Terms

Human factors, Measurement, Security

Keywords

Underground forums, Online social networks

1. INTRODUCTION

Online social networks (OSNs) capture, in a concrete form, the character and dynamics of human social relationships. Consequently, the popularity of such services (e.g., Facebook, Twitter, etc.) has been followed closely by researchers using the explicit nature of these networks to characterize social graph properties and how they inform user interaction [6, 11]. While less well explored, there are also a range of *implicit* social networks defined via interaction on other shared interaction sites (e.g., Web forums, blogs, etc.). In this paper, we focus on a particular sub-population of such activities: *underground forums*.

Users of underground forums participate in many activities similar to those found on traditional online social networks: they maintain profiles, add fellow users to buddy lists, and engage in conversations via private messaging. However, the "raison d'etre" for such forums is not simply for social contact, but to support criminal (or at best "grey hat") activities. Thus, users of these forums regularly engage in the buying, selling and trading of abusive services and illegally obtained goods such as credit card numbers, online currencies, compromised accounts and even drugs. However, since underground users frequently *only* know each other online (and via pseudonyms even there), they must develop new means to establish trust among themselves.

In this paper, we examine these implicit social networks and how they are used in the context of six underground forums — BlackHatWorld, Carders, FreeHack, HackEl1te, HackSector, and L33tCrew — for which we have complete activity records. Our analysis is organized into three parts: first, we analyze the structure of the underlying social networks present on the forums, followed by an examination of the commercial aspects of the sites (e.g., what types of products are being sold, who are the most active players in the market, etc.) and finally we look at how different reputational factors impact behavior. We believe our work is the first analysis of this type and provides valuable insight into how online criminal actors create and develop social relationships in support of their goals.

2. BACKGROUND

Online underground markets have existed in various forms for decades. Early markets used Internet Relay Chat (IRC), documented by Thomas *et al.* [10] and Franklin *et al.* [4], to provide a public medium for sharing information about the availability and pricing of goods and services (e.g., stolen credit cards, accounts, botnets, cash out services, etc.). [1] Over time, many of these markets moved to using persistent Web forums and expanded to cover a broader range of information sharing. Zhuge *et al.* first documented the use of such forums in China [12] and contemporary analyses have been published by Holt *et al.* [5], Radianti [7] and Fallmann *et al.* [3]. Over time, some of these forums have specialized and many have moved to "closed" models (i.e., in which new members must be explicitly vouched for by existing members); for example, Stone-Gross *et al.* [9] recently documented the membership and goods on offer on the private Spamdot.biz forum, which specialized in support for email spammers. Ultimately, the goal of all such forums is to expand the knowledge base of the participants (e.g., which registrars will "look the other way", how to best manipulate Google ranking results, etc.) as well as to expand the set of potential trading partners. However, there is little public research that empirically examines the social networks formed in such forums or the mechanisms employed to manage trust. Indeed, such analyses can be difficult since modern forums combine public sections, restricted sections (requiring higher status) and person-to-person private messages (PMs) that may not be externally visible.

[1] For a brief overview of the how this credentials market operates today, see Shilman [8].

IMC'11, November 2–4, 2011, Berlin, Germany.

Forum	Abbrv	Dates Covered	Subforums	Threads	Posts	Pvt Msgs	Users	Lurkers
L33tCrew	LC*	May 07 – Nov 09 (30 mo.)	239	120,560	861,459	501,915	18,834	46.5%
HackSector	HS	Nov 01 – Nov 07 (72 mo.)	147	72,734	724,820	78,777	33,986	55.0%
FreeHack	FH	Jul 04 – Dec 10 (77 mo.)	152	62,972	499,736	112,318	38,377	62.9%
Carders	CC*	Sep 08 – Dec 10 (27 mo.)	121	52,188	373,143	197,067	8,425	35.0%
BlackHatWorld	BH	Oct 05 – Mar 08 (29 mo.)	38	7,270	65,572	20,849	8,718	47.9%
HackeL1te	HL	Mar 10 – Apr 11 (13 mo.)	43	5,501	9,018	541	2,431	66.7%

Table 1: Summary of the data from the six forums, ranked by number of posts (* denotes forums geared toward commerce).

	Buddy				Private Message				Thread			
Forum	Partic.	Links	L/P	WCC	Partic.	Links	L/P	WCC	Partic.	Links	L/P	WCC
LC	2,587	4,448	1.7	214	7,898	170,954	21.6	7	9,124	3,791,330	415.5	1
HS	1,282	1,057	0.8	352	9,562	43,807	4.6	69	13,502	2,582,513	191.3	1
FH	1,921	5,944	3.1	100	10,294	55,945	5.4	21	11,833	1,473,824	124.6	3
CC	1,000	1,834	1.8	154	5,065	63,409	12.5	12	4,593	792,962	172.6	2
BH	199	205	1.0	37	3,438	11,183	3.3	3	2,940	320,028	108.9	2
HL	38	65	1.7	4	174	271	1.6	5	690	10,477	15.2	3

Table 2: Summary of the basic social networking statistics for each forum. *Partic.* means participants, or users who have links of the specified type; *L/P* represents the number of links divided by the number of participants. *WCC* means weakly connected components.

3. DATA OVERVIEW

In this study we have the luxury of "ground truth" — complete records of six underground forums via SQL dumps of their underlying databases. We do not claim that these six are representative of all underground forums, but they provide us with a starting point for understanding the dynamics of underground forums. Each of these datasets has been acquired by unknown outside parties and made public ("leaked") via various methods. Each forum contains a wealth of information: user registration data, private messages exchanged, forum posts, member status changes, banned user logs, etc. For a more comprehensive list of the available data, please refer to the Invision Power Board (for L33tCrew) and vBulletin database schemas [1, 2]. We briefly describe the purpose of each forum.

BlackhatWorld (BH) was founded in approximately 2005 and is primarily English speaking. The main focus of BH is blackhat search engine optimization (SEO), a practice in which users attempt to abusively manipulate search engine algorithms to gain increased page rank. At the time our dataset was obtained, BH did not have a vibrant trading marketplace, as the site was initially oriented towards the discussion of blackhat techniques. Today, however, the site contains over 800 threads in the services-for-sale section and more than 275 threads in the goods-for-sale section.

Carders (CC) is a German-speaking site primarily focused on the monetization of stolen credit card numbers and bank account information. The site is heavily geared towards the exchange of goods and services. The L33tCrew (LC) forum is very similar to CC, both in its content and the types of products exchanged.

Freehack (FH) is another German site, but does not target any one industry. The threads on the forum cover a number of different topics, ranging from crypting (encoding software to make detecting malware more difficult) to video games. Items for sale include Steam (gaming) accounts, automatic account creators, and hacking software. The users typically do not buy or sell stolen credentials. The remaining sites, HackSector (HS) and HackeL1te (HL), are similar although HL is English speaking.

Table 1 summarizes the membership and activity across each of these forums. In total, our analysis covers over 2.5 million posts, 900k private messages, and 100k users. Our dataset also spans a range of time periods, with the FH and HS datasets covering approximately six years, while HL is our shortest at roughly a year. LC is our largest dataset by forum activity, with the largest number of threads (120k), posts (860k), and private messages (500k). The six forums exhibit different properties with regards to the number of posts and private messages exchanged. The forums geared towards commerce, CC and LC, have a much higher number of private messages, since many business transactions occur over private messaging. For example, we observed 23–26 PMs/user for CC and LC, while the other four forums, whose users primarily swap information, exhibit less than 3 PMs/user. Across all forums a fair number of "lurkers", or individuals who simply register an account but take no action, exist on each forum. Over 55% of the users on FH, HS and HL are lurkers. Again, the trading forums have a smaller fraction of lurkers with only 35% in CC and 46% in LC.

4. UNDERGROUND SOCIAL NETWORKS

In this section, we analyze the structural properties of the six different forums. This task is nontrivial in the context of a forum, since the definition of a link between nodes (users) remains ambiguous. To that end, we consider three types of relationships that exist in the forums: buddy, private message, and thread. Table 2 summarizes the basic social networking statistics for each forum.

A buddy link is the most explicit relationship that exists between users, and is a directed link since buddy requests may be accepted, pending, or denied. Thus, accepted requests result in symmetric links, while pending requests produce unidirectional links. However, the number of explicitly declared buddy relationships across the forums is quite small. Less than 10% of all users in each forum issued a friend request to another user, suggesting that underground forum users do not think of their relationships as persistent, or that the members see no utility in friending other users.

Because buddy links do not fully capture the latent relationships present in the forums, we further analyze the social network by including links that result from private messaging. If user u_1 sends a PM to user u_2, we establish a directed link from u_1 to u_2.

Lastly, thread relationships result when two users post in the same sub-forum thread. To establish these links, we order all posts in the same thread by their post times. We then create a link from user u_2 to user u_1 if u_2 posted after u_1, with the reasoning being that u_2 is interacting with all users in the thread prior to his or her post. Unsurprisingly, Table 2 shows that these one-to-many thread relationships produce the most links and fewest weakly connected components. One may use more advanced techniques (e.g., parsing "[QUOTE]" and "@<username>" expressions) to establish finer-grained thread relationships, but we leave this to future work.

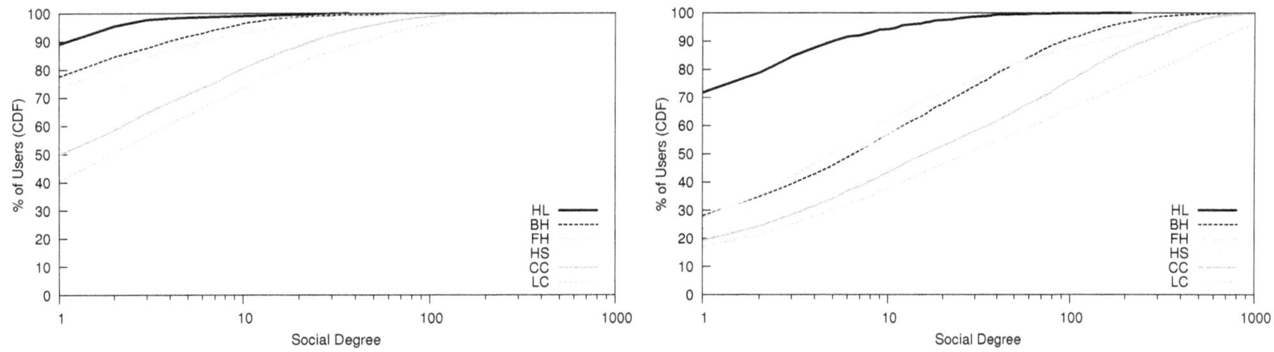

(a) Private Message (b) Thread

Figure 1: Degree distribution for reciprocated links.

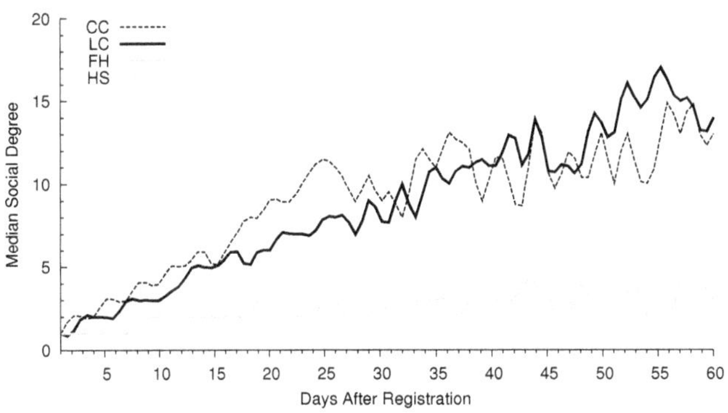

Figure 2: The median social degree for users based on private messages in a 60-day window surrounding their registration dates.

Because so few buddy links exist, we only consider the private message ("PM") and thread ("thread") link types in our analyses.

4.1 Degree Analysis

Figure 1 shows the degree distributions for the six forums. We only consider pairs of nodes with reciprocal links. Figure 1(a) shows that few users exchange private messages on HL, BH, FH and HS, with less than 40% of users involved in more than one private message exchange. Members on CC and LC create more relationships through private messages, with over 50% of their users linked to at least one other forum member, and more than 25% of their users involved in at least 10 conversations. This difference is likely due to users being more actively engaged in commerce, with many transactions taking place over private messages. The users in all forums (except for HL, being relatively new) create a comparable number of links via posting, which makes sense since this is the primary means of communication in forums. CC and LC exhibit more links, with over 50% of their users linked to over 20 other members via public postings (double the amount of other forums).

4.2 Social Network Growth

Figure 2 shows how the median private messaging social degree changes among forum users in the 60 days following their registrations. We only consider reciprocal links when computing the social degree. For each pair of linked users, we looked at the difference between their registration dates and the latest timestamp associated with their first private message exchange. We omit HL and BH due to the noise present in their curves. For the private messaging social graph, there is little change in the median social degree after the first week for users on FH and HS. In contrast, for CC and LC, both sets of users experience growth after the first week, again likely due to the business transactions occurring over PM to a dynamic set of partners. After the first month, the median social degree for the users on LC and CC is approximately nine, versus two for FH and HS. The growth rate for the thread social graph (not shown) follows the same trend across all forums: users undergo the largest growth in the first several weeks. In contrast, however, all forums show members continuing to interact with new users via public postings.

		German (*DE*)			English (*EN*)	
		LC	**FH**	**CC**	**BH**	**HL**
DE	LC	–	13.99	3.16	0.05	0.03
	FH	6.87	–	2.23	0.02	0.08
	CC	7.09	10.19	–	0.02	0.39
EN	BH	0.11	0.10	0.02	–	0.00
	HL	0.25	1.19	1.36	0.00	–

Table 3: Percentage of overlapping email addresses across all pairs of forums. Percentages listed in each row are with respect to the population size of the forum specified in that row. The HS dataset lacked addresses.

		German (*DE*)				English (*EN*)	
		LC	**HS**	**FH**	**CC**	**BH**	**HL**
DE	LC	–	17.34	21.47	6.18	1.57	0.62
	HS	9.61	–	13.13	3.03	1.24	0.44
	FH	10.54	11.63	–	4.43	1.07	0.46
	CC	13.80	12.21	20.19	–	1.86	1.03
EN	BH	3.38	4.82	4.73	1.80	–	0.33
	HL	4.77	6.17	7.20	3.58	1.19	–

Table 4: Percentage of overlapping usernames across all pairs of forums.

4.3 User Overlap

To study the population overlap among forum members, Tables 3 and 4 show the percentage of overlapping email addresses and usernames (respectively) between each pair of forums. Of the six, only HS did not list any email addresses for its registered members. LC and FH share over two thousand email addresses, while LC and CC share 595, roughly 7% of the CC membership. This overlap is unsurprising, since both forums are geared toward the trading of stolen credit cards. However, even the newest English-based forum, HL, shared 6 to 33 email addresses across the German forums. Though email addresses are likely a more reliable metric for establishing population overlap, usernames also provide insight into overlap since users desire unique public identities to maintain their reputations. All forum pairs contained some number of overlapping usernames, with the German forums (CC, FH, HS, LC) sharing an appreciable number of usernames. For example, over 10% of the usernames on CC are present in all three of the other German forums. Likewise, over 17% of the usernames on LC appear in both FH and HS.

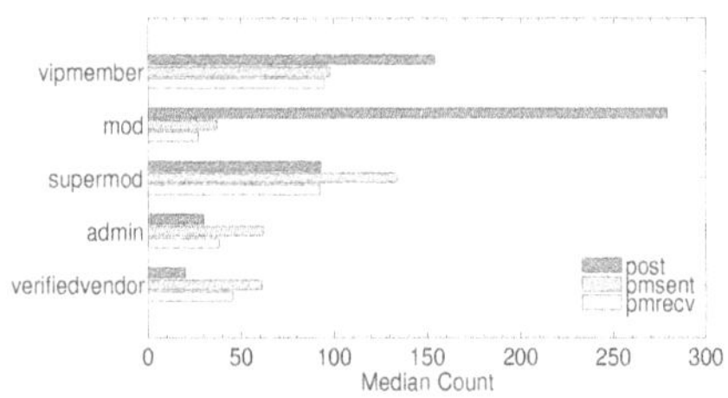

Figure 3: Median activity users engaged in prior to transitioning groups for CC.

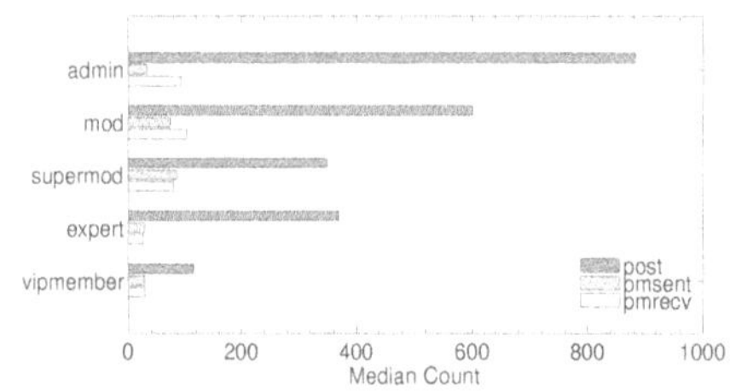

Figure 4: Median activity users engaged in prior to transitioning groups for FH.

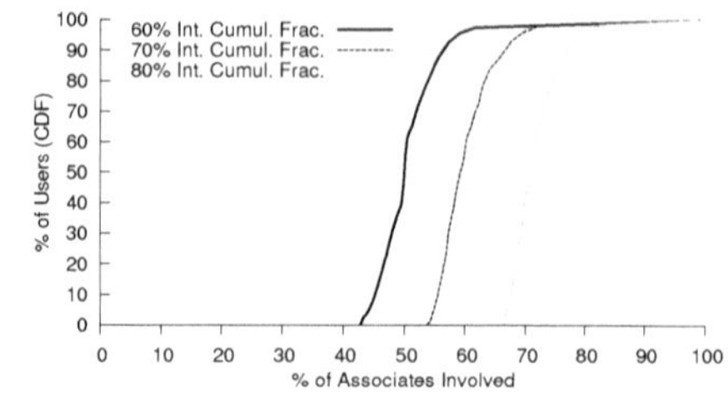

Figure 5: Distribution of users' interactions for PMs on LC.

Category	Threads B	Threads S	Users B	Users S	Top Subcategory
payments	5,294	5,074	1,354	1,281	paysafecard
game-related	935	951	449	459	steam
credit cards	597	798	339	421	unspecified cc
accounts	761	566	382	356	ebay
merchandise	390	518	246	334	iphone
software/keys	355	485	214	296	key/serial
services	155	562	119	384	carder
victim logs	380	334	237	232	viclog
mail/drop srvs	347	292	248	203	packstation
fraud tools	203	343	132	239	socks

Table 5: Top 10 most commonly traded merchandise categories on CC

Category	Threads B	Threads S	Users B	Users S	Top Subcategory
payments	8,507	8,092	1,539	1,409	paysafecard
game-related	2,379	2,584	924	987	steam
accounts	2,119	2,067	850	974	rapidshare
credit cards	996	1160	467	566	unspecified cc
software/keys	729	1410	422	740	key/serial
fraud tools	652	1155	363	601	socks
tutorials/guides	950	537	562	393	tutorials
mail/drop srvs	751	681	407	364	packstation
merchandise	493	721	264	404	ipod
services	266	916	176	555	carder

Table 6: Top 10 most commonly traded merchandise categories on LC.

4.4 Group Elevation

Users that join a forum are assigned a group, which roughly corresponds to their social status on the site. Generally, users start in the pending authorization group, meaning they must perform some action (e.g., respond to email confirmation) or undergo some type of scrutiny before being given access to the forum. Once the user has jumped through the necessary hoops, they begin in the "newbie" group. After some activity, users are generally elevated to a non-newbie group and advance from there. Figures 3 and 4 show the median amount of activity that users engaged in prior to transitioning to higher group levels for CC and FH (BH and HL were similar to FH). All the forums place a large emphasis on public postings versus private messaging, indicating that reputation comes from being publicly active on the forums. Users with greater standing in the CC forum have the most balanced amount of activity, posting and private messaging in roughly equal amounts.

4.5 User Interaction Analysis

Figure 5 shows how private message interactions are distributed among users' "associates" (i.e., fellow members they are linked with) on LC, which has the greatest number of PMs. We looked at these distributions to determine the extent to which users interact with different individuals. For each user, we compute a distribution of private messaging events over the user's associates. We then looked at the 60%,70%, and 80% points in that distribution. Figure 5 suggests that users on LC exchange private messages with a diverse set of individuals, versus users on traditional OSNs, who interact with few of their friends. Wilson *et al.* [11] found that, for users on Facebook, 20% of their friends account for 70% of their interactions. In contrast, for users on LC, approximately 70% of their associates are responsible for 70% of their private messages. The corresponding graph for users linked via threads is similar.

5. MARKETPLACE

In this section we look at the types of goods and services exchanged on LC and CC, the two forums with the most well developed and active trading marketplaces. We first look at what types of goods are traded among these two underground communities, and then analyze how social degree and reputation affect trading.

5.1 Merchandise

To determine what types of items are available on the forums, we extracted thread titles containing the markers "[B]" or "[S]", denoting items that are being traded for and sought after, respectively. We then wrote over 500 regular expressions to bin the items into 18 categories; these hand-defined categories include merchandise, banking information, drugs, mailing and dropping services, and a number of other commonly observed wares/services. We created the categories based on domain knowledge of illicit goods and by randomly sampling trading thread titles. Using our regular expressions, we categorized 87% of the 14,430 CC threads and 77% of 31,923 LC threads. Because users typically list several items for trade in a single thread, a thread may be counted in multiple categories. There is a long tail of merchandise types that we did not cover with our regular expressions; for example, on LC, threads mention such items as "Internet hack N95" or "Proteine - Inko X-TREME Muscle Gainer", while on CC, threads offer up such goods as "Conrad.de Kundenlogins" or "Pall Mall umsonst".

Tables 5 and 6 show the top 10 most commonly traded items on CC and LC (respectively), ordered by the number of total binned threads in the designated category. The thread column shows the number of thread titles containing terms associated with the category, while the user column shows the number of distinct users who created those threads. The "B" and "S" columns denote threads where items were being traded for or sought after, respectively.

The items most commonly traded for are offline/online payments, including PayPal, cash, Ukash, and PaySafeCards (PSC). Over 5% of all threads involve trading for offline/online payments on both forums. Traders in the underground market prefer PSC, a type of prepaid online currency that is widely used in Europe. Gaming accounts, in particular Steam, are the second most commonly traded item; credit cards and accounts make up the next two traded for

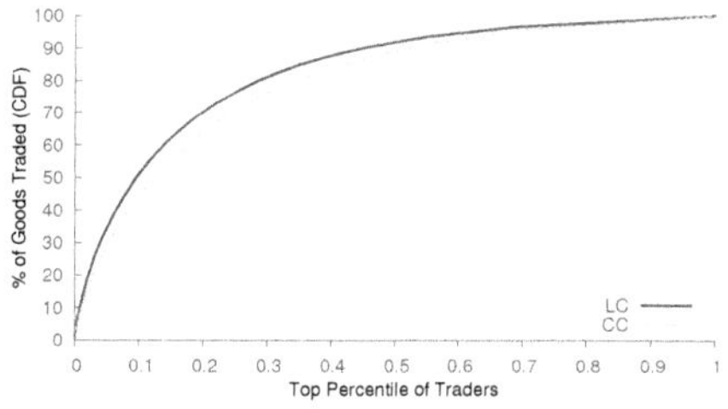

Figure 6: Top percentile of traders vs percentage of goods traded.

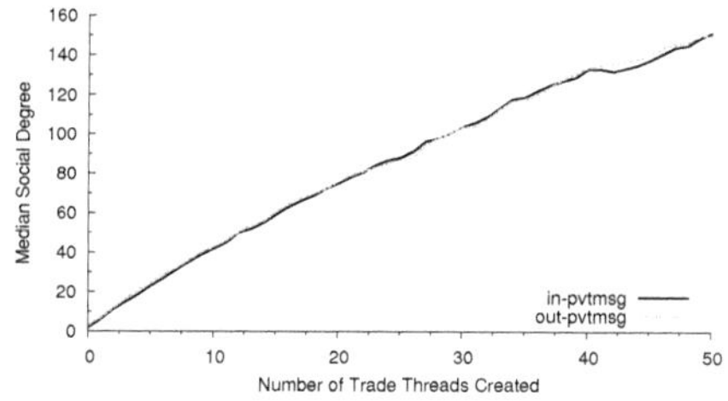

Figure 7: Number of LC trading threads created vs. median social degree.

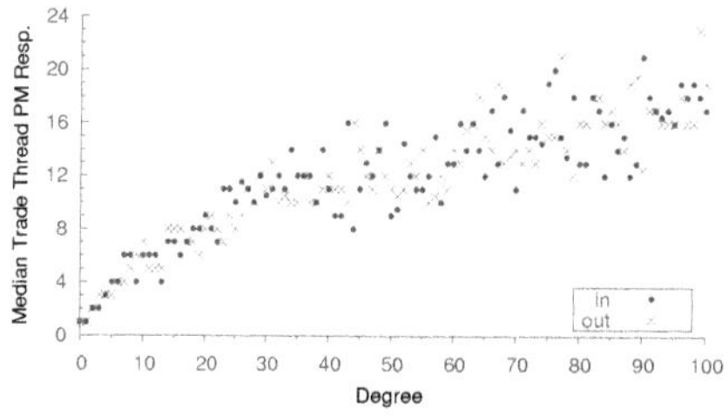

Figure 8: PM social graph degree vs median number of trading thread response PMs for LC.

items. While not shown in the table, drugs also made up a notable number of traded items on CC: over 100 threads listed weed, 25 mentioned Viagra, and 15 specified speed.

Next, we look at the number of trading threads the top merchants are responsible for. Figure 6 shows the relationship between the top percentile of traders on both forums and the percentage of goods traded. For example, the top 10% of the traders on both sites (measured by the number of trading threads created by the user) account for 40–50% of the goods traded. One implication of this trading distribution is that law enforcement can pursue the top tier traders to shut down much of the marketplace activity. The top traders can create multiple accounts to mask their activity levels, but accruing reputation for possibly numerous accounts is nontrivial.

5.2 How Social Degree Affects Trading

Now, we analyze the effect of the social network on trading. Figure 7 shows how the median social degree measured in private message links increases for users after posting trading threads on LC. We order each user's trading threads by time. Subsequently, we compute the user's PM social degree just before he or she creates each thread. We then bin that social degree with respect to the thread's posting order, taking the median over all users. The results suggest that, as users trade more, they continue to interact with increasingly larger numbers of individuals and hence, potential customers. For LC, the median out and in degrees for the PM social graphs increases at a roughly constant rate of four for every trading thread created. The CC graph looks similar; the PM out/in degree increases at a rate between one and two for each thread.

We now investigate how PM in/out degree affects the response to a trading thread. Figure 8 plots the in/out PM degrees for LC users before they post a trading thread against the number of PMs they receive in the following week. In comparison, LC and CC members receive on average 0.07 (standard deviation $\sigma = 0.68$) and 0.11 ($\sigma = 1.19$) private messages per week when issuing no posts prior to that week. The graph suggests that traders with higher PM social graph degrees receive more PMs in the week after they post a trading thread. For CC, the numbers look similar, but become increasingly noisier after an in/out degree of 30.

Lastly, we look at what fraction of private messages are sent by new users to traders in the week following a trading thread post. Figure 9 shows that for approximately 30% of all trading threads, the posters receive only PMs from individuals they have interacted with before. For 50% of the trading threads on LC and CC, 60–75% of the PMs came from prior acquaintances. Finally, for approximately 20–25% of all trading threads, the trader interacted with only new people.

5.3 Effect of Group Status

Figure 10 shows how a user's group affects the responsiveness to a trading thread; we focus on CC because LC does not contain any data regarding user group transitions. We looked at the trading threads posted by users at a certain group level. We then determined how many PMs the users received in the week after posting trading threads. Figure 10 suggests that a user's group status does influence how many PMs the user receives upon posting a trading thread. Verified vendors and VIP members receive between 2–3 times more response PMs than "newbies".

5.4 Effect of Ratings

The only forum with an explicit rating system for trading transactions is CC. The rating system is ternary: traders receive either a positive, negative, or neutral feedback. Surprisingly, most of the reviews are positive: of the 3,157 reviews (20% of discernible trading threads), only 67 were negative and 2 were neutral. Of the 67 negatively rated users, 43 were banned, and the rest were generally rated negatively due to "poor" or "unfriendly" service. We suspect that bad traders are outed publicly in separate thread posts (see Section 6.2) and banned before being rated. Because so few users were rated poorly, we do not differentiate between the rating types.

We now consider the effect of the rating system on the amount of interest a trader receives (either in the form of response posts or private messages) after posting a trading thread. Figure 11 shows the effects of the first 10 ratings on the median number of PMs users receive in the week following a trading thread post. With zero ratings, the median response PM count is one, but with a single rating, the median count rises to 15. The median PM count continues to increase from there, though not in a well-defined manner. While rated traders receive more private messages, they do not experience an increase in the number of response posts; the median response post count remains constant at one. We speculate that the rating system lends more credibility to a trader's threads, and people are not so quick to question the trader's reputation in the public space.

5.5 Activity To First Rating

We now analyze how much activity users must participate in before they earn enough trust such that they engage in a business transaction with another forum member. We measure the number of actions users take (postings, private messaging) before they receive their first ratings. Relying on the rating system is subject to error, since users can conduct business outside of the forum, but it provides us with some idea about how trust is earned. Figure 12 shows that, before approximately 50% of users received their first ratings, they posted around 60 times in 50 different threads, received about 35 private messages from 13 users, and sent around 33 private messages to 13 users.

6. BANNED ANALYSIS

Some users in underground forums behave maliciously towards other members. In this section, we look at the top reasons why users are banned from the forums. We also investigate different properties associated with accusations of fraud in the marketplace.

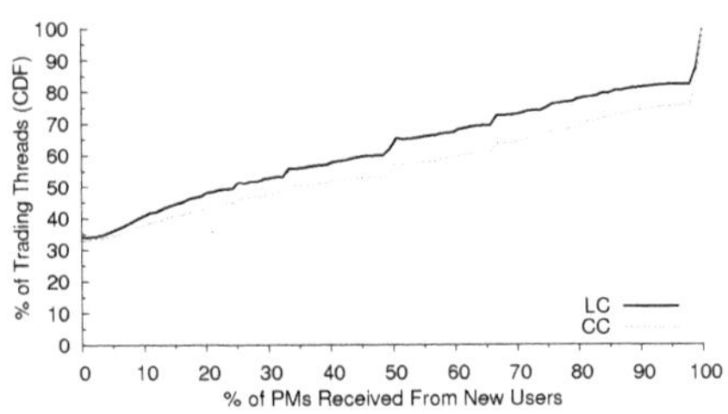

Figure 9: Fraction of PMs received from new users after posting a trading thread.

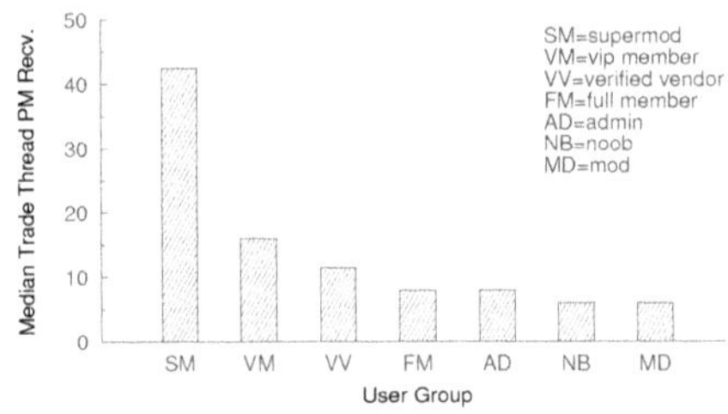

Figure 10: User group vs median number of trading thread response PMs for CC.

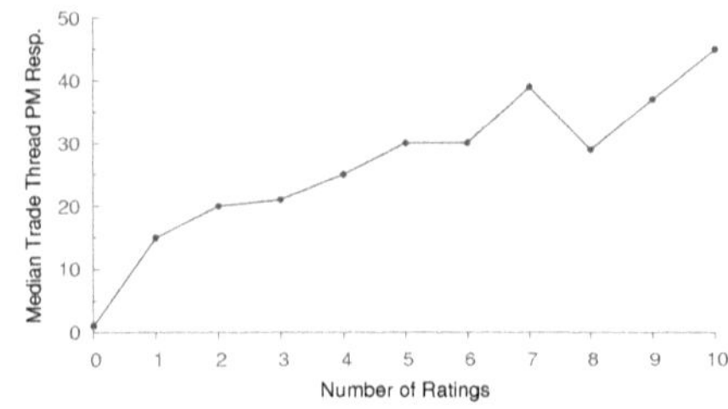

Figure 11: Effect of ratings on response to trading threads.

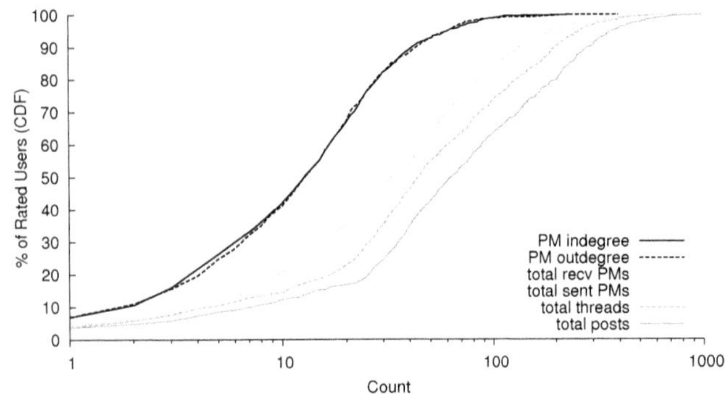

Figure 12: CDF showing the activities a user participated in prior to receiving a first rating.

	Rank 1		Rank 2		Rank 3	
Forum	Reason	%	Reason	%	Reason	%
BW (22)	spammer	40.9	dup. acc	22.7	infl. posts	22.7
CC (1,587)	dup. acc	60.7	ripper	12.1	spammer	7.3
FH (447)	dup. acc	30.6	malware	16.6	spammer	14.1
HS (317)	spammer	24.6	malware	10.7	dup. acc	9.8
HL (75)	infl. posts	52.0	trade-rel.	34.7	spammer	13.3
LC (247)	misuse	37.7	spammer	17.4	ripper	17.0

Table 7: The top three reasons why users are banned on each of the forums.

6.1 Why Users are Banned

The fraction of users that are banned on the forums is non-trivial. For example, the moderators on CC have banned over 20% of the users that appear in their members table. Because the individuals who participate in underground forums generally lack some scruples, this is not surprising. Table 7 shows the top three reasons why users are banned in the forums. To generate the data, we analyzed a specific table in five of the forums (BW, CC, FH, HS, HL) that explicitly holds information regarding user bans. LC did not have such a table, so we analyzed the warnings issued to banned users and assumed that the final warning received by the user resulted in the ban. Next, we created 13 categories for the most commonly appearing banned reasons and wrote 35 regular expressions to bin them. Again, users can be banned for multiple reasons. Also, not every ban is explained (the reason is sometimes left blank), so the percentages shown are with respect to the explained bans (represented by the numbers in parenthesis). These regular expressions covered over 70% of the banned reasons across all five forums.

The most common problem across the forums involves duplicate accounts (dup. acc), which appears in the top three reasons in four of the forums. Users often create duplicate accounts to circumvent a prior ban. Another problem in the forums is, ironically, spamming and malware attacks, with BW and HS particularly inundated with spammers. In the commerce oriented forums (LC and CC), rippers comprise over 10% of the bans. Rippers are individuals who rip off other members, and threads are created to identify these users.

	Banned		**Unbanned**	
Stat Name	Accuser	Accused	Accuser	Accused
Num PMs Sent	243.0	34.5	22.0	73.5
Num PMs Recv	271.0	31.0	24.5	57.5
PM InDegree	101.0	12.0	10.0	21.5
PM OutDegree	104.0	12.0	7.0	22.0
Num Posts	299.5	50.0	72.5	134.0
Thread InDegree	500.5	182.0	180.0	333.0
Thread OutDegree	527.0	183.5	198.0	332.0
Total Pairs	314		62	

Table 8: Statistics for ripper accusers and accusees. The numbers represent the medians across all accuser/accused pairs.

6.2 Accusers vs. Accused

We next investigate the repercussions of accusing one member of being a ripper on the CC forum. To do this, we extracted all the threads where a user accused another member of being a ripper. The titles of these threads often take the form "Ripper <username>". Once we identified both parties, we compared the amount of activity the users engaged in prior to the accusation time. Table 8 shows the median values for several statistics about the accusers and the accused. We see that, in the cases where the accused person was ultimately banned, the accusers were much more active on the CC forum. For example, accusers had more than eight times the number of links in their PM graphs than the banned accused users, and the accusers had roughly twice as many links in their thread graphs. In the cases where the accusation did not result in a ban, the accused exhibited more activity than the accusers. Also, the unbanned accused users had a larger number of links in their PM (e.g., 10 vs. 21 for PM indegree) and thread (e.g., 180 vs. 330 for thread indegree) graphs than their banned counterparts.

7. CONCLUSION

This paper has characterized the social network makeup for six underground forums, how users interact, how baseline reputation is established and how it changes over time. This work is a first step in a larger research agenda to understand the social dynamics of the underground and how they impact e-crime market efficiencies.

Acknowledgments

We thank the reviewers for their valuable suggestions, and Vyas Sekar for his assistance with the accompanied public reviews and comments. This work was supported by NSF grants NSF-0433668 and NSF-0831138, ONR MURI grant N000140911081, and by generous support from Google, Microsoft, Yahoo, Cisco, and the UCSD Center for Networked Systems (CNS). McCoy was supported by a CCC-CRA-NSF Computing Innovation Fellowship.

8. REFERENCES

[1] Ivision Power Board. `http://www.invisionpower.com`.

[2] vBulletin. `http://www.vbulletin.com`.

[3] H. Fallmann, G. Wondracek, and C. Platzer. Covertly Probing Underground Economy Marketplaces. In *Proceedings of DIMVA*, July 2010.

[4] J. Franklin, V. Paxson, A. Perrig, and S. Savage. An Inquiry into the Nature and Causes of the Wealth of Internet Miscreants. In *Proceedings of CCS*, October 2007.

[5] T. J. Holt and E. Lampke. Exploring Stolen Data Markets Online: Products and Market Forces. *Criminal Justice Studies*, 23(1):33–50, 2010.

[6] A. Mislove, M. Marcon, K. P. Gummadi, P. Druschel, and B. Bhattacharjee. Measurement and Analysis of Online Social Networks. In *Proceedings of IMC*, October 2007.

[7] J. Radianti. A Study of a Social Behavior inside the Online Black Markets. In *Proceedings of SECURWARE*, July 2010.

[8] A. Shilman. The Underground Credentials Market. *Computer Fraud and Security*, 2010(3):5–8, 2010.

[9] B. Stone-Gross, T. Holz, G. Stringhini, and G. Vigna. The Underground Economy of Spam: A Botmaster's Perspective of Coordinating Large-Scale Spam Campaigns. In *Proceedings of LEET*, 2011.

[10] R. Thomas and J. Martin. The Underground Economy: Priceless. *;login:*, 31(6):7–16, Dec. 2006.

[11] C. Wilson, B. Boe, A. Sala, K. P. N. Puttaswamy, and B. Y. Zhao. User Interactions in Social Networks and their Implications. In *Proceedings of EuroSys*, April 2009.

[12] J. Zhuge, T. Holz, C. Song, J. Guo, X. Han, and W. Zou. Studying Malicious Websites and the Underground Economy on the Chinese Web. In *Proceedings of WEIS*, June 2008.

Summary Review Documentation for

"An Analysis of Underground Forums"

Authors: M. Motoyama, D. McCoy, K. Levchenko, S. Savage, G. Voelker

Reviewer #1

Strengths: This is a new, interesting direction for research. The dataset is unique and this paper will generate a lot of excitement/discussion.

Weaknesses: The connection of the actual analysis presented to the motivation is slightly weak (e.g., its different from conventional OSNs, reputations, dynamics of graph).

Comments to Authors: I would have liked to see a better analysis of the following: (1) how are these graphs structurally different from regular OSNs? (2) is the temporal dynamics of these graphs different from OSNs -- e.g., are there frequent interactions between a pair of entities or are people constantly finding new friends etc?

You say the dataset is "public" -- Is it public to your group or more broadly??

Why are German forums surprisingly a high fraction of your dataset-- are underground groups more active there?

Section 4: I like how you break down relationships based on buddy/PM/thread. I wonder if the thread category can be more finely divided; e.g., don't the forum posts have some sort of "Reply-To" semantics where user 1 responds to user 2's comments etc?

Section 5.1: you claim that most trading can be shut down -- wouldnt the obvious response then be to create a lot of sybil-like proxies or pseudonyms?

Section 5.4 -- the majority of positive ratings makes me worry about collusion/sybil effects here. Is it possible for you to rule these out?

Section 5.5 -- what fraction of transactions have ratings? Isnt the number of posts to first transaction or the time to first PM/thread response to trading post a more accurate measure of what you are trying to show here?

Reviewer #2

Strengths: This is the first study of the kind i have encountered. Moreover, the 6 datasets have sufficient differences to make the study interesting.

Weaknesses: None of the results actually surprised me or stayed in my mind after I finished reviewing the paper (this is typically a bad sign in my opinion). Second, I do not really see any strong methodological contribution that could be the lesson learnt here. More importantly, the metrics studied as rarely precisely defined or discussed - the paper appears as a series of plots of different metrics.

Comments to Authors: I wish I were more enthusiastic about this work, but I am really not. I think the authors deserve credit for having looked for those data sets and for having analyzed them under the same lens. However, I do not really see anything that exciting coming out of the study itself. Moreover, I do not really see a strong methodological contribution either.

In particular, for a measurement paper, the authors have done a poor job describing the studied metrics. As an example, section 5.2 discusses "the average social degree for a user after posting trading threads". I would like to see the precise definition of this metric.

Second, and given that this is a measurement paper as well, all metrics that present average values should also present confidence intervals. I think extracting conclusions based on the average values alone can be very misleading.

In summary, I do not really feel like I learnt something new from this paper. I would love if the authors had managed to frame the discussion in a more impactful way...

More detailed comments: you talk about using regular expressions to identify specific categories. Those matches tend to lead to non 100% matches. It would be nice to know what the remaining threads contained that did not match the regular expression. Have you looked through them?

Reviewer #3

Strengths: The first strength is the novelty of the paper. The second strength is its impact to the community. It brings knowledge about background economy to the network research community, hopefully will trigger more research in this direction. The background section (although brief -- but this is a short paper) provides pointers to background reading in the area, that I believe majority of network researchers still do not have a comprehensive understanding.

Weaknesses: I wish the paper could go one step deeper to discuss how the results from this paper can be applied to mitigate the underground problems.

Comments to Authors: None.

Reviewer #4

Strengths: Interesting study of underground forums based on complete datasets. Some interesting observations regarding banned accounts and the effect of rating.

Weaknesses: The authors claim that underground forums are quite different than regular ones, but never attempt to quantify or examine this difference. The classification of topics is based on a manual process.

Comments to Authors: This is a well-written paper examining underground forums. Overall, I enjoyed reading the paper, although the analysis could go in more depth describing in more detail some of the findings observed.

What I felt is definitely missing from the paper, is a comparison with regular forums. It is unclear to me whether characteristics are significantly different as the authors argue.

In particular, I would argue that, intuitively, observations in section 4 do hold for most of the online forums at least qualitatively. Quantifying the differences would be interesting here.

In section 5, I found the analysis a bit incomplete. For example, the authors describe the number of PMs after thread response versus the user degree (figure 6). However, it is hard to get any context from this figure without a similar one that is not conditioned on thread response. What is the PMs/week without thread participation? Also the figure presents averages that might be misleading or provide an incomplete picture. Some percentiles would be helpful. This is true for other figures in the same section.

I did not understand at all Section 5.3. Figure 7 shows that there is some correlation between user status and PMs received but the text claims otherwise. Am I missing something here?

I found the analysis in sections 5.5 and 6 interesting and perhaps the authors could devote more space to these observations. Section 5.5 shows that one needs significant activity before a rating is received. Again comparison with regular forums would be interesting here.

Section 6 implies that banning decisions do depend on the activity and social characteristics of users. Providing similar numbers as in Table 5 conditioning on the reason for ban would perhaps be interesting here.

Reviewer #5

Strengths: Interesting topic, good data sets, reasonably good analysis.

Weaknesses: Analysis has limited depth and merely presented basic points, implications of findings are not discussed.

Comments to Authors: I found the topic of this paper interesting and overall like the paper. I found it rather ironic that these forums are called underground and then such a detailed data sets of their transaction is available even through wikileaks. The obtained data sets appear to be database (or log) on the original server. It is hard to get such information (e.g. level of seniority of users in a forum, number of private messages, content of messages, ...) even for forums such as twitter and fb that are not underground. I found it intriguing that such a data is available for several underground forums. It is helpful if authors spell out what information are available in these data sets in section 3. For example, availability of users' level of seniority and destination of private messages (for later analysis in the paper) were surprise to me.

For some of the analysis, authors come up with set of expressions to classify messages. Is there a methodology or known list for such an expression or authors have other ways to define these expressions?

It is useful to have some explanations on how the presented findings can be used to disrupt these venues or defend against their attacks (or other purposes), and some minor explanation on how the observed behavior is different from other forums that are not underground. Of course such a discussion should be limited given the length of this paper.

It is useful if authors provide a link to their data sets on wikileaks so the rest of the research community can examine them.

Response from the Authors

The reviewers inquired about many interesting ways in which the analyses could be extended. We share these reactions. In the spirit (and constraints) of short papers, we view this paper as exploratory work seeding the analysis of the social networking properties of underground forums. We plan to expand on this topic in future, more comprehensive work.

In preparing the camera-ready version, we have further emphasized the differences between the commerce-oriented forums (Carders and L33tCrew) and those focused primarily on the exchange of information. We placed all the reciprocal degree distributions for the underground forums on the same graphs to emphasize the structural differences between the forum types. We point out how the trading forums are much more interconnected among the different link types. Also, we have omitted statements about the differences between underground and regular forums, since we do not make direct comparisons between the two types in this work.

Several reviewers inquired about making the data public; unfortunately, the data is not ours to share. As mentioned in the paper, however, others have leaked the data.

One reviewer asked how we might disrupt the forums. We discuss how 10% of the traders are responsible for 40-50% of the goods traded. Targeting the forum members with the most activity could disrupt, or at least impede, the marketplace. Another reviewer pointed out that traders can mask their activity levels by creating multiple accounts. However, reputation is hard to accrue, and we do not believe creating multiple accounts is a viable option for high volume traders.

We made clarifications where possible, especially regarding the metrics we define. We included a brief description of the information available in the back-end databases, along with pointers about the various packages powering each forum.

Another reviewer commented on the lack of negative ratings. Many users with negative ratings are banned, and the rest are generally accused of providing ``poor'' service. Also, we discuss in Section 6 how ripper accusations are levied against forum members outside the rating system.

Some reviewers commented on our methodology for classifying the merchandise being traded for. We expanded on the methodology in the paper. Briefly, we developed our list of regular expressions using domain knowledge, and by randomly sampling threads to capture the most frequently traded items. Also, we looked at threads we did not classify under our regular expressions; we found a long tail of traded items.

Sharing Graphs Using Differentialy Private Graph Models

Alessandra Sala
Computer Science Dept.
UC Santa Barbara
Santa Barbara, CA 93106
alessandra@cs.ucsb.edu

Xiaohan Zhao
Computer Science Dept.
UC Santa Barbara
Santa Barbara, CA 93106
xiaohanzhao@cs.ucsb.edu

Christo Wilson
Computer Science Dept.
UC Santa Barbara
Santa Barbara, CA 93106
bowlin@cs.ucsb.edu

Haitao Zheng
Computer Science Dept.
UC Santa Barbara
Santa Barbara, CA 93106
htzheng@cs.ucsb.edu

Ben Y. Zhao
Computer Science Dept.
UC Santa Barbara
Santa Barbara, CA 93106
ravenben@cs.ucsb.edu

ABSTRACT

Continuing success of research on social and computer networks requires open access to realistic measurement datasets. While these datasets can be shared, generally in the form of social or Internet graphs, doing so often risks exposing sensitive user data to the public. Unfortunately, current techniques to improve privacy on graphs only target specific attacks, and have been proven to be vulnerable against powerful de-anonymization attacks.

Our work seeks a solution to share meaningful graph datasets while preserving privacy. We observe a clear tension between strength of privacy protection and maintaining structural similarity to the original graph. To navigate the tradeoff, we develop a *differentially-private graph model* we call Pygmalion. Given a graph G and a desired level of ϵ-differential privacy guarantee, Pygmalion extracts a graph's detailed structure into degree correlation statistics, introduces noise into the resulting dataset, and generates a synthetic graph G'. G' maintains as much structural similarity to G as possible, while introducing enough differences to provide the desired privacy guarantee. We show that simply applying differential privacy to graphs results in the addition of significant noise that may disrupt graph structure, making it unsuitable for experimental study. Instead, we introduce a partitioning approach that provides identical privacy guarantees using much less noise. Applied to real graphs, this technique requires an order of magnitude less noise for the same privacy guarantees. Finally, we apply our graph model to Internet, web, and Facebook social graphs, and show that it produces synthetic graphs that closely match the originals in both graph structure metrics and behavior in application-level tests.

Categories and Subject Descriptors

H.3.5 [**Information Storage and Retrieval**]: Online Information Services—*Data sharing*; K.4.1 [**Computers and Society**]: Public Policy Issues—*Privacy*

General Terms

Algorithms, Security

Keywords

Differential Privacy, Graph Models, Online Social Networks

1. INTRODUCTION

Studying structure of real social and computer networks through graph analysis can produce insights on fundamental processes such as information dissemination, viral spread and epidemics, network dynamics and resilience to attacks [4,26,27,38]. The use of real graphs generated from measurement data is invaluable, and can be used to validate theoretical models or realistically predict the effectiveness of applications and protocols [2,12,41,43].

Unfortunately, there is often a direct tension between the need to distribute real network graphs to the research community, and the privacy concerns of users or entities described by the dataset. For example, social graphs from real measurements are used to capture a variety of artifacts in online social networks, including strength of social ties, number and frequency of social interactions, and flow of information. Similarly, detailed topology graphs of enterprise networks or major ISPs contain confidential information about the performance and robustness of these networks. Releasing such sensitive datasets for research has been challenging. Despite the best of intentions, researchers often inadvertently release more data than they originally intended [35,36,47]. Past experience has taught us that traditional anonymization techniques provide limited protection, and often can be overcome by privacy attacks that "de-anonymize" datasets using external or public datasets [5,35,36].

Thus we are left asking the question, *how can researchers safely share realistic graph datasets from measurements without compromising privacy?* One option is to develop and apply stronger anonymization techniques [24,30], many of which modify the graph structure in subtle ways that improve privacy but retain much of the original graph structure. However, these approaches generally only provide resistance against a specific type of attack, and cannot provide protection against newly developed deanonymization techniques. Techniques exist in the context of databases and data mining which provide provable levels of protection [18,19], but are not easily applied to graphs. Still other techniques can protect privacy on graphs, but must significantly change the graph structure in the process [24,39].

Our approach to provide graph privacy and preserve graph structure. We seek a solution to address the above question, by starting with observation that any system for sharing graphs must deal with the tension between two goals: *protecting privacy* and *achieving structural similarity to the original, unmodified graph.* At one extreme, we can distribute graphs that are isomorphic to the original, but vulnerable to basic deanonymization attacks. At the other extreme, we can distribute random graphs that share no structural similarities to the original. These graphs will not yield any meaningful information to privacy attacks, but they are also not useful to researchers, because they share none of the real structures of the original graph.

Ideally, we want a system that can produce graphs that span the entire privacy versus similarity spectrum. In such a system, users can specify a desired level of privacy guarantee, and get back a set of graphs that are similar to the real graph in structure, but have enough differences to provide the requested level of privacy.

The main premise of our work is that we can build such a system, by distilling an original graph G into a statistical representation of graph structure, adding controlled levels of "noise," and then generating a new graph G' using the result statistics. This requires two key components. First, we need a way to accurately capture a graph's structure as a set of structural statistics, along with a generator that converts it back into a graph. For this, we use the *dK-series*, a graph model that is capable of capturing sufficient graph structure at multiple granularities to uniquely identify a graph [13, 31]. We can achieve the desired level of privacy by introducing a specific level of noise into G's degree correlation statistics. Second, we need a way to determine the appropriate noise necessary to guarantee a desired level of privacy. For this, we develop new techniques rooted in the concept of *ϵ-differential privacy*, a technique previously used to quantify privacy in the context of statistical databases.

In this paper, we develop *Pygmalion*, a differentially private graph model for generating synthetic graphs. Pygmalion preserves as much of the original graph structure as possible, while injecting enough structural noise to guarantee a chosen level of privacy against privacy attacks. Initially, we formulate a basic differentially private graph model, which integrates controlled noise into the dK degree distributions of an original graph. We use the dK-2 series, which captures the frequency of adjacent node pairs with different degree combinations as a sequence of frequency values. However, when we derive the necessary conditions required to achieve ϵ-differential privacy, they show that an asymptotical bound for the required noise grows polynomially with the maximum degree in the graph. Given the impact of dK values on graph structure, these large noise values result in synthetic graphs that bear little resemblance to the original graph.

To solve this challenge, we seek a more accurate graph model by significantly reducing the noise required to obtain ϵ-differential privacy. We develop an algorithm to partition the statistical representation of the graph into clusters, and prove that by achieving ϵ-differential privacy in each cluster, we achieve the same property over the entire dataset. Using a degree-based clustering algorithm, we reduce the variance of degree values in each cluster, thereby dramatically reducing the noise necessary for ϵ-differential privacy. Finally, we apply isotonic regression [6] as a final optimization to further reduce the effective error by more evenly distributing the added noise.

We apply our models to a number of Internet and Facebook graphs ranging from 14K nodes to 1.7 million nodes. The results show that for a given level of privacy, our degree-based clustering algorithm reduces the necessary noise level by *one order of magnitude*. Isotonic regression further reduces the observed error in dK values on our graphs by 50%. Finally, we experimentally show that for moderate privacy guarantees, synthetic graphs generated by Pygmalion closely match the original graph in both standard graph metrics and application-level experiments.

Access to realistic graph datasets is critical to continuing research in both social and computer networks. Our work shows that differentially-private graph models are feasible, and Pygmalion is a first step towards graph sharing systems that provide strong privacy protection while preserving graph structures.

2. GRAPHS AND DIFFERENTIAL PRIVACY

In this section, we provide background on graph anonymization techniques, and motivate the basic design of our approach to graph anonymization. First, we discuss prior work, the inherent challenges in performing graph anonymization, and our desired privacy goals. Second, we introduce the main concepts of ϵ-Differential Privacy, and lay out the preconditions and challenges in leveraging this technique to anonymize graphs. Finally, we motivate the selection of the dK-series as the appropriate graph model on which to build our system.

2.1 Data Privacy: Background and Goals

A significant amount of prior work has been done on protecting privacy of datasets. We summarize them here, and clarify our privacy goals in this project.

Private Datasets. Many research efforts have developed privacy mechanisms to secure large datasets. Most of these techniques, including cryptographic approaches [7] and statistical perturbations [19, 37], are designed to protect structured data such as relational databases, and are not applicable to graph datasets. An alternative, probabilistic approach to privacy is k-anonymity [42]. It is designed to secure sensitive entries in a table by modifying the table such that each row has at least $k - 1$ other rows that are identical [18]. Several public datasets have been successfully anonymized with k-anonymity [1, 33] or through clustering-based anonymization strategies [8].

Graph Anonymization. Several graph anonymization techniques have been proposed to enable public release of graphs without compromising user privacy. Generally, these techniques only protect against specific, known attacks. The primary goal of these anonymization techniques is to prevent attackers from identifying a user or a link between users based on the graph structure. Several anonymization techniques [24, 30, 39, 46, 48] leverage the k-anonymity model to create either k identical neighborhoods, or k identical-degree nodes in a target graph. These types of "attack-specific" defenses have two significant limitations. First, recent results have repeatedly demonstrated that researchers or attackers can invent novel, unanticipated de-anonymization attacks that destroy previously established privacy guarantees [5, 35, 36, 45]. Second, many of these defenses require modifications to the protected graph that significantly alter its structure in detectable and meaningful ways [24, 39].

Our Goals: Edge vs. Node Privacy. In the context of privacy for graphs, we can choose to focus on protecting the privacy of either node or edges. As will become clear later in this paper, our approach of using degree correlations (*i.e.* the dK-series), captures graph structure in terms of different subgraph sizes, ranging from 2 nodes connected by a single edge (dK-2) to larger subgraphs of size K.

Our general approach is to produce synthetic graphs by adding controlled perturbations to the graph structure of the original graph.

This approach can provide protection for both node privacy and edge privacy. This choice directly impacts the sensitivity of the graph privacy function, and as a result, how much structural noise must be introduced to obtain a given level of privacy guarantees.

In this paper, we choose to focus on edge privacy as our goal, and apply this assumption in our analysis of our differential privacy system in Section 3. We chose to target edge privacy because our work was originally motivated by privacy concerns in sharing social graphs, where providing edge privacy would address a number of practical privacy attacks.

2.2 Differential Privacy

Our goal is to create a novel system for the generation of anonymized graphs that support two key properties:

1. Provides quantifiable privacy guarantees for graph data that are "future-proof" against novel attacks.
2. Preserves as much original graph structure as possible, to ensure that anonymized data is still useful to researchers.

Differential privacy [14] is a recently developed technique designed to provide and quantify privacy guarantees in the context of statistical databases [15,25]. Others have demonstrated the versatility of this technique by applying differential privacy to distributed systems [40], network trace anonymization [32], data compression techniques [44], and discrete optimization algorithms [22]. Other work focused specifically on applying differential privacy to simple graph structures such as degree distributions [23,25]. In contrast, our work has the potential to inject changes at different granularities of substructures in the graph, instead of focusing on a single graph metric.

One piece of prior work tried to guarantee graph privacy by adding differential privacy to Kronecker graphs [34]. Whereas this approach tries to guarantee privacy by perturbing the Kronecker model parameters, our strategy acts directly on graph structures, which provides tighter control over the perturbation process. Unfortunately, the author asserts there are incorrect results in the paper[1].

Basic Differential Privacy. The core privacy properties in differential privacy are derived from the ability to produce a query output Q from a database D, which could also have been produced from a slightly different database D', referred to as D's neighbor [14].

DEFINITION 1. *Given a database D, its neighbor database D' differs from D in only one element.*

We obtain differential privacy guarantees by injecting a controlled level of statistical noise into D [16]. The injected noise is calibrated based on the sensitivity of the query that is being executed, as well as the statistical properties of the Laplace stochastic process [17]. The *sensitivity* of a query is quantified as the maximum amount of change to the query's output when one database element is modified, added, or removed. Together, query sensitivity and the ϵ value determine the amount of noise that must be injected into the query output in order to provide ϵ-differential privacy.

Differential privacy works best with *insensitive queries*, since higher sensitivity means more noise must be introduced to attain a given desired level of privacy. Thus insensitive queries introduce lower levels of errors, and provide more accurate query results.

[1] See the author's homepage.

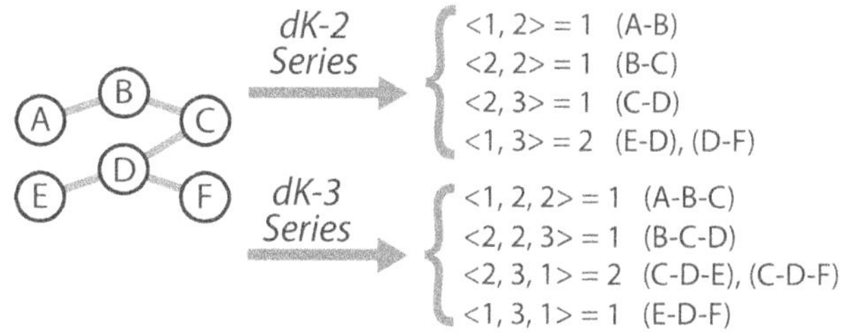

Figure 1: An illustrative example of the dK-series. The dK-2 series captures the number of 2-node subgraphs with a specific combination of node-degrees, and the dK-3 captures the number of 3-node subgraphs with distinct node-degree combinations.

2.3 Differential Privacy on Graphs

We face two key challenges in applying differential privacy concepts to privacy protection on graphs. First, we must determine a "query" function in our context which we can use to apply differential privacy concepts. Second, the sensitivity of this query function must be low enough, so that we can attain privacy guarantees by introducing only low levels of noise, thus allowing us to preserve the accuracy of the results. In our context, this means that we want to generate graphs that retain the structure and salient properties of the original graph. We address the former question in this section by proposing the use of the dK-series as our graph query operation. We address the accuracy question in Sections 3 and 4, after fully explaining the details of our system.

Recall that the problem we seek to address is to anonymize graph datasets so that they can be safely distributed amongst the research community. We leverage a *non-interactive* query model [14], such that the original graph structure is queried only once and the entire budget to enforce privacy is used at this time. dK is used to query the graph and the resulting dK-series is perturbed under the differential privacy framework. Note that only the differentially private dK-series is publicized. Unlike applications of differential privacy in other contexts, we can now generate multiple graphs using this differentially private dK-series without disrupting the level of privacy of the original graph. Therefore, we use a non-interactive query model to safely distributed graph datasets without being constrained to a single dataset.

The dK-Graph Model. We observe that the requirements of this query function can be met by a descriptive graph model that can transform a graph into a set of structural statistics, which are then used to generate a graph with structure similar to the original. Specifically, we propose to use the dK-graph model [31] and its statistical series as our query function. dK captures the structure of a graph at different levels of detail into statistics called dK-series. dK can analyze an original graph to produce a corresponding dK-series, then use a matching generator to output a synthetic graph using the dK-series values as input. The dK-series is the degree distribution of connected components of some size K within a target graph. For example, dK-1 captures the number of nodes with each degree value, *i.e.* the node degree distribution. dK-2 captures the number of 2-node subgraphs with different combinations of node degrees, *i.e.* the joint degree distribution. dK-3 captures the number of 3-node subgraphs with different node degree combinations, *i.e.* an alternative representation of the clustering coefficient distribution. dK-n (where n is the number of nodes in the graph) captures the complete graph structure. We show a detailed example in Figure 1, where we list dK-2 and dK-3 distributions for a graph.

dK is ideal for us because the dK-series is a set of data tuples that provides a natural fit for injecting statistical noise to attain differential privacy. In addition, together with their matching generators, higher levels of dK-series, *i.e.* $n > 3$, could potentially provide us with a bidirectional transformation from a graph to its statistical representation and back.

While larger values of K will capture more structural information and produce higher fidelity synthetic graphs, it comes at the expense of higher computation and storage overheads. Our work focuses on the dK-2 series, because generator algorithms have not yet been discovered for dK-series where $K \geq 3$. While this may limit the accuracy of our current model, our methodology is general, and can be used with higher order dK-series when their generators are discovered.

ϵ-Differential Privacy in Graphs. Given the above, we can now outline how to integrate differential privacy in the context of graphs. An ϵ-differentially private graph system would output a graph that given a statistical description of an input graph, the probability of seeing two similar graphs as the real input graph is close, where closeness between the two probabilities is quantified by ϵ. A larger value of ϵ means it is easier to identify the source of the graph structure, which means a lower level of graph privacy.

Prior work has demonstrated that in many cases, accuracy of query results on differentially private databases can be improved by decomposing complex queries into sequences of "simple counting queries" that happen to have extremely low sensitivity [9, 10, 15]. Unfortunately, this approach will not work in our context, since our goal is to achieve privacy guarantees on whole graph datasets, and not just privacy for simple graph queries such as node degree distributions. In the next section, we start with a basic formulation of a differentially private graph model, and then provide an optimized version. We illustrate the final process, shown as *Pygmalion* in Figure 2.

3. FIRST STEPS

In this section, we perform the analytical steps necessary to integrate ϵ-differential privacy into the dK graph model. Our goal is to derive the amount of noise necessary to achieve a given ϵ-privacy level. The amount of Laplacian noise necessary is a function of both ϵ, the user-specified privacy parameter, and S, the sensitivity of the dK function. First, we formally define the dK-2 series, and derive its sensitivity S_{dK-2}. Next, we describe the dK-perturbation algorithm (dK-PA) for injecting noise into the original dK-2 series, and prove that it provides the desired ϵ-differential privacy. Our analysis shows that the asymptotic bound on noise used in dK-PA grows polynomially with maximum node degree, which means we need to inject relatively large levels of noise to guarantee ϵ-privacy. Finally, as expected, our experiments on real graphs confirm that dK-PA generates synthetic graphs with significant loss in accuracy. This poor result motivates our search for improved techniques in Section 4.

3.1 Sensitivity of dK-2

dK-function. We formally define dK-2 as a function over a graph $G = (V, E)$, where V is the set of nodes and E is the set of edges connecting pair of nodes in V:

$$dK(G) : G^n \rightarrow \Im$$

where G^n is the set of graphs with $n = |V|$ nodes and $\Im$ is the set of unique degree tuples in the dK-2-series with the corresponding count of instances in G. Formally, $\Im$ is a collection of $\{d_x, d_y; k\}$ where each entry represents that the number of connected components of size 2 with degree (d_x, d_y) is k. Let m be the cardinality of $\Im$. Because the maximum number of entries in dK-2 is bounded by the number of possible degree pairs, $\sum_{i=1}^{d_{max}} i$, where d_{max} be the maximum node degree in G, thus $m = O(d_{max}^2)$. Prior studies have demonstrated that in large network graphs d_{max} is upper bounded by $O(\sqrt{n})$ [29, 43], and thus, in those cases, m is upper bounded by $O(n)$.

Sensitivity Analysis. In the context of differential privacy, the sensitivity of a function is defined as the maximum difference in function output when one single element in the function domain is modified. The domain of dK-2 is a graph G. Neighbor graphs of G are all the graphs G' which differ from G by at most a single edge. Changing a single edge in G will result in one or more entries changing in the corresponding dK-2-series. Thus, the sensitivity of dK-2 is computed as the maximum number of changes in the dK-2-series among all of G's neighbor graphs.

LEMMA 1. *The sensitivity of dK-2 on a graph G, S_{dK-2}, is upper bounded by $4 \cdot d_{max} + 1$.*

PROOF. Let e be a new edge added to a graph $G = (V, E)$ between any two nodes $u, v \in V$. Once the edge e is added to G the degrees of u and v increase from d to $(d + 1)$ and from d' to $(d' + 1)$ respectively. This graph transformation produces the following changes in the dK-2 on G: the frequency k of tuple $\{d + 1, d' + 1; k\}$ gets incremented by 1 because of the new edge (u, v). For example, a new edge between A and C in Figure 1 produces an increment of the frequency k of the tuple $\{2, 3; k\}$ from $k = 1$ to $k = 2$. Furthermore, a total of $d + d'$ already present tuples need to be updated with the new degree of u and v, and so the tuples with the old degrees get decremented by a total of $d + d'$ and the tuples reflecting the new degree get incremented for a total of $d + d'$. To summarize, the overall number of changes in the dK-2 -series is $2(d + d') + 1$. In the worst case, when u and v are nodes of maximum degree d_{max}, the total number of changes in the original dK-2-series by adding an edge between u and v is upper bounded by $4 \cdot d_{max} + 1$. □

Lemma 1 derives only the upper bound of the sensitivity because, as in Definition 3 [14], it is the sufficient condition to derive the necessary amount of noise to achieve a given ϵ-privacy level. Lemma 1 shows that the sensitivity of dK-2 is high, since d_{max} has been shown to be $O(\sqrt{n})$ in measured graphs [29, 43]. Note that prior work on differential privacy [9, 10, 15, 23] generally involved functions with a much lower sensitivity, *i.e.* 1. In these cases, the low sensitivity means that the amount of noise required to generate differentially private results is very small. In contrast, the sensitivity of our function indicates that the amount of noise needed to guarantee ϵ-differential privacy in dK-2 will be high. Therefore, the accuracy of synthetic graphs generated using this method will be low. Note that if we use a higher order dK-series, *i.e.* $K \geq 3$, we would have found an even higher sensitivity value, which may further degrade the accuracy of the resulting synthetic graphs.

3.2 The dK-Perturbation Algorithm

We now introduce the dK-perturbation algorithm (dK-PA) that computes the noise to be injected into dK-2 to obtain ϵ-differential privacy [14]. In dK-PA, each element of the dK-2-series is altered based on a stochastic variable drawn from the Laplace distribution, $Lap(\lambda)$. This distribution has density function proportional to $e^{-\frac{|x|}{\lambda}}$, with mean 0 and variance $2\lambda^2$. The following theorem

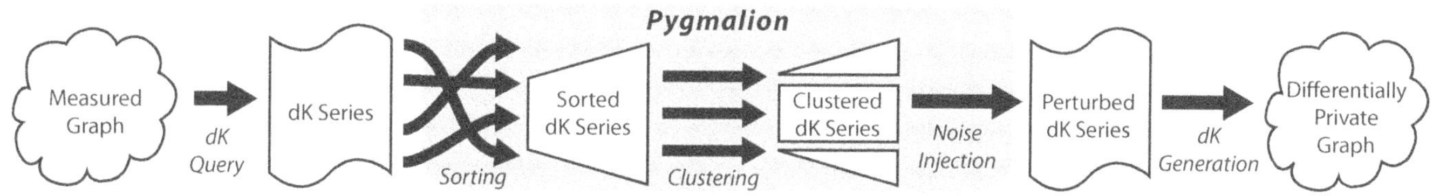

Figure 2: Overview of Pygmalion. ϵ-differential privacy is added to measured graphs after sorting and clustering the dK-2-series.

proves the conditions under which ϵ-differential privacy is guaranteed [17].

THEOREM 1. *Let $\widetilde{DK}$ be the privacy mechanism performed on dK such that $\widetilde{DK}(G) = dK(G) + Lap(\frac{S_{dK-2}}{\epsilon})^m$. For any G and G' differing by at most one edge, $\widetilde{DK}$ provides ϵ-differential privacy if:*

$$\left| \ln \frac{Pr[\widetilde{DK}(G) = s]}{Pr[\widetilde{DK}(G') = s]} \right| \leq \epsilon$$

PROOF. Let $s =< s_1, s_2, ..., s_m >$ be a possible output of $\widetilde{DK}(G)$ and m the number of its entries, and let G' be the graph with at most one different edge from G. Using the conditional probabilities, we have:

$$\frac{Pr[\widetilde{DK}(G) = s]}{Pr[\widetilde{DK}(G') = s]} = \prod_{i=1}^{m} \frac{Pr[\widetilde{DK}(G)_i = s_i | s_1, ...s_{i-1}]}{Pr[\widetilde{DK}(G')_i = s_i | s_1, ...s_{i-1}]},$$

since each item of the product has the first $i-1$ values of dK-2 fixed. Each s_i is the result of applying Laplacian noise calibrated by S_{dK-2}. Note that Lemma 1 has studied the sensitivity of dK-2, S_{dK-2}, under the condition that two graphs differ by at most one edge. Thus, the conditional probability is Laplacian, allowing us to derive the following inequalities:

$$\prod_{i=1}^{m} \frac{Pr[\widetilde{DK}(G)_i = s_i | s_1, ...s_{i-1}]}{Pr[\widetilde{DK}(G')_i = s_i | s_1, ...s_{i-1}]} \leq \prod_{i=1}^{m} e^{\frac{|\widetilde{DK}(G)_i - \widetilde{DK}(G')_i|}{\sigma}}$$

where σ is the scale parameter of the Laplace distribution that is $\frac{4d_{max}+1}{\epsilon}$. Thus,

$$\prod_{i=1}^{m} e^{\frac{|\widetilde{DK}(G)_i - \widetilde{DK}(G')_i|}{\sigma}} = e^{\frac{||\widetilde{DK}(G) - \widetilde{DK}(G')||_1}{\sigma}}$$

where, by definition $\widetilde{DK}(G) = dK(G) + Lap(\frac{S_{dK-2}}{\epsilon})$, and $||DK(G) - DK(G')||_1 \leq S_{dK-2}$ with $S_{dK-2} \leq 4d_{max} + 1$ as proved in Lemma 1. Thus, we have:

$$e^{\frac{||\widetilde{DK}(G) - \widetilde{DK}(G')||_1}{\sigma}} =$$

$$= e^{\frac{||dK(G) + Lap(\frac{S_{dK-2}}{\epsilon}) - dK(G') - Lap(\frac{S_{dK-2}}{\epsilon})||_1}{\sigma}} \leq e^{\frac{4d_{max}+1}{\frac{4d_{max}+1}{\epsilon}}} = e^{\epsilon}$$

and so, by applying the logarithmic function, we have that

$$\left| \ln \frac{Pr[\widetilde{DK}(G) = s]}{Pr[\widetilde{DK}(G') = s]} \right| \leq \epsilon$$

which concludes the proof. □

Type	Graph	Nodes	Edges
Internet	WWW	325,729	1,090,108
	AS	16,573	40,927
Facebook	Monterey Bay	14,260	93,291
	Russia	97,134	289,324
	Mexico	598,140	4,552,493
	LA	603,834	7,676,486

Table 1: Different measurement graphs used for experimental evaluation.

Theorem 1 shows that by adding noise to the dK-2-series using independent Laplace random variables calibrated by S_{dK-2} from Lemma 1, we achieve the desired ϵ-privacy.

Quantifying Accuracy. We apply the *error analysis* proposed by [25] on dK-PA to quantify the accuracy of the synthetic graphs it produces, compared to the original graphs.

DEFINITION 2. *For a perturbed dK-2-series that is generated by the privacy mechanism $\widetilde{DK}$ on a graph G, as defined in Theorem 1, the estimated error on $\widetilde{DK}$ can be computed as the expected randomization in generating $\widetilde{DK}$.*

We now quantify the expected randomization in $\widetilde{DK}$:

$$\sum_{i=1}^{m} E[(\widetilde{DK(G)}_i - dK(G)_i)^2] = mE[Lap(\frac{S_{dK-2}}{\epsilon})^2]$$

Using Lemma 1 and that $m = O(d_{max}^2)$we have:

$$mE[Lap(\frac{S_{dK-2}}{\epsilon})^2] = mVar(Lap(\frac{d_{max}}{\epsilon})) = \frac{2m \cdot d_{max}^2}{\epsilon^2} = O(\frac{d_{max}^4}{\epsilon^2}).$$

This asymptotical bound shows that the noise injected by dK-PA into dK-2 scales with the fourth-degree polynomial of d_{max}. This result implies that synthetic graphs generated by dK-PA will have relatively low accuracy because of the large error introduced by the perturbation process. Furthermore, it implies that even for relatively weak privacy guarantees, dK-PA will introduce large errors that may significantly change the structure of the resulting synthetic graphs from the original.

3.3 Validation on Real Graphs

At this point, we have demonstrated analytically that the impact of adding noise to the dK-2-series using dK-PA will result in synthetic graphs that deviate significantly from the originals. In this section, we empirically evaluate the impact of adding noise to the dK-2-series by executing dK-PA on real graphs.

Methodology. To illustrate that our system is applicable to different types of graphs, we select a group of graphs that include social graphs from Facebook [41,43], a WWW graph [3] and an AS topology graph [38] crawled on Jan 1st, 2004, which have

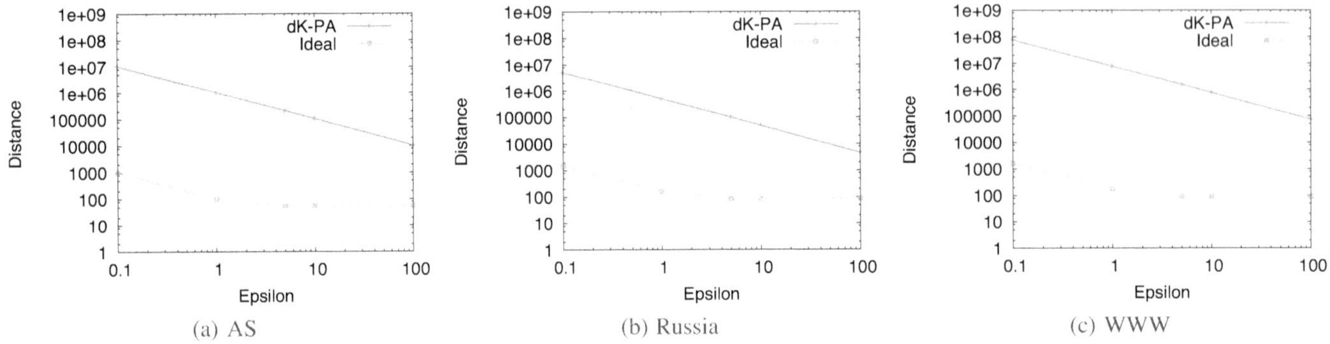

(a) AS (b) Russia (c) WWW

Figure 3: The noise required for different privacy levels quantified as the Euclidean distance between a graph's original and perturbed dK-2 series.

been used in prior graph mining studies [28]. The social graphs were gathered using a snowball crawl of the Facebook regional networks [43], and show graph metrics highly consistent with Facebook graphs generated using unbiased sampling techniques [21]. Table 1 lists the graphs used in our evaluation, which range from 14K nodes to 650K nodes.

We extract the dK-2-series for each graph, introduce noise using the dK-PA strategy, then compute the Euclidean distance between the perturbed dK-2-series and the original as a measure of the level of graph structural error introduced. We computed results for all graphs in Table 1, and they are consistent. For brevity, we limit ourselves to report results only for the AS graph, the WWW graph, and the Russia Facebook graph. We choose Russia to represent our social graphs because its results are representative of the other graphs, and its size does not result in extremely long run time for our experiments.

Results. Figure 3 shows that the dK-PA strategy produces a large error for small values of ϵ (*i.e.* strong privacy guarantees). We compute the error as the Euclidean distance between the original dK-2-series and the perturbed dK-2-series with dK-PA strategy. As we mentioned, the low level of accuracy is due to the large noise dK-PA injects into dK-2, resulting in a perturbed dK-2 that is significantly different from the original. The bright side is that the dK-PA strategy is robust across different datasets, and the error decreases exponentially as ϵ grows, which is shown by the linear correlation in the log-log scale plot of Figure 3.

The high error is largely due to the high sensitivity of our function dK-2. To understand the potential lower-bound on the error, we imagine a scenario where if we had a function with sensitivity of 1, then we could achieve much lower error, plotted in Figure 3 as the *Ideal* line. Note that this line is a hypothetical lower bound that is only meant to demonstrate the impact of the dK function's sensitivity on the final result. Indeed, Figure 3 shows that the loss in accuracy of our model can largely be attributed to the sensitivity of the dK-2 series.

4. PRIVACY VIA PARTITIONING

The results in the previous section demonstrate the loss of accuracy in the perturbed dK-2-series after adding noise to guarantee ϵ-differential privacy. In this section we propose a novel algorithm called Divide Randomize and Conquer (DRC) that enables more granular control over the noise injected into the dK-2-series. This qualifies DRC to support ϵ-differential privacy while also allowing for more accurate results. First, we discuss the design of DRC and prove that it does guarantee ϵ-differential privacy. Next, we investigate the amount of error introduced with this approach, and show that DRC requires significantly less noise than dK-PA to achieve an equal level of privacy. Finally, we propose an optimized version of DRC, called LDRC, and empirically verify the improved accuracy of our algorithms using measured graphs.

4.1 Divide Randomize and Conquer Algorithm

Our goal is to develop an improved privacy mechanism that significantly reduces the amount of noise that must be added to achieve a given level of ϵ-privacy. While we cannot change the fact that the sensitivity of dK-2 scales with d_{max}, our insight is to partition data in the dK-2-series into a set of small sub-series, then apply the perturbation independently to achieve ϵ-privacy within each sub-series.

If we carefully perform the partitioning to group together tuples with similar degree, we effectively reduce the value of d_{max} for each of the vast majority of sub-series. This means we can achieve ϵ-privacy on each sub-series for a fraction of the noise required to achieve ϵ-privacy across the entire series. We will then prove that ϵ-differential privacy holds across the entire dK-2-series if it holds for each of the partitioned sub-series. Thus, we produce an alternative algorithm that achieves the same level of privacy as dK-PA, while introducing significantly less noise.

We instantiate our ideas as the Divide Randomize and Conquer algorithm (DRC). The core steps of DRC are:

1. Partition (*Divide*) the dK-2-series into sub-series with specific properties;
2. Inject noise into each sub-series (*Randomize*);
3. *Conquer* the perturbed sub-series into a single dK-2-series.

In the remainder of this section we discuss the partitioning step of DRC. We first define an ordering function on dK-2 to sort tuples with similar sensitivity. The ordered dK-2 is then partitioned into contiguous and mutually disjoint sub-series. We prove that the properties of these sub-series lead to the definition of a novel sensitivity function and consequently to a novel methodology to add noise. Noise injection, conquering, and the resulting error analysis are discussed in Section 4.2.

∂ **ordering on dK-2.** The dK-2-series is sorted by grouping dK-tuples with numerically close pairs of degrees. In particular, the dK-tuples are sorted in the new dK-2 series, named β-series, by iteratively selecting from the original series all the tuples $\{d_x, d_y; k\}$ with degrees $(d_x \;\&\; d_y) \leq i, \forall\, i \in [1, d_{max}]$. Thus, the β-series is simply the sorted list of dK-tuples that adhere to the above inequality ordering. For example, the tuple $\{1, 2; k\}$ is closer to $\{5,5;k'\}$ than to $\{1,8;k''\}$. We can formally describe this transformation with the following function:

DEFINITION 3. *Let ∂ be the sorting function on dK-2 which is formally expressed as:*

$$\partial(i) = \min_{d_x, d_y \in dK} \{\max(d_x, d_y) \geq \max(d_{x'}, d_{y'}) = \partial(i-1)\}$$

Note that $\{d_x, d_y; k\} \neq$ the first $i-1$ tuples. Thus, the ∂ function is a transformation of dK-2 such that $\partial : \Im \rightarrow \beta$ where β identifies the ordered dK-2.

Partitioning the β-Series. The β-series is partitioned into $\widetilde{m}$ sub-series, with the ith named β_i for $i \in [1, \widetilde{m}]$. The partition of β is based on two properties. First, the ∂ ordering has to be obeyed and thus each partition can only acquire *contiguous* tuples in the β-series. Second, each tuple can appear in *one and only one* sub-series. Given the ∂ ordering and the above two rules we can guarantee *mutually disjoint* and *contiguous* sub-series β_i. These two constraints are fundamental to satisfying the sensitivity properties we prove in the following Lemma 2 and Lemma 3.

Sensitivity of β_i sub-series. The sensitivity of each β_i-series can be studied following the same logic used to find the sensitivity of dK-2, by quantifying the maximum number of changes that may occur in the β_i-series due to an edge change in the graph G. Due to the ∂ ordering imposed in each sub-series, we can show that the maximum degree in each β_i plays a fundamental role in bounding its sensitivity.

LEMMA 2. *The sensitivity S_{β_i} of a sub-series β_i with tuple degrees almost equal to $d_k + 1$ is upper bounded by $4 \cdot d_k + 1$.*

The proof of this lemma is sketched because it follows the logic of Lemma 1. Due to the proposed ∂ ordering, each sub-series i is composed only of tuples where both degrees are less than or equal to a particular integer d. The worst-case (*i.e.* the maximum number of changes to the tuples in the same β_i) occurs when the tuple with degrees $d-1$ are in the same sub-series. Therefore, the maximum number of changes occur when a new edge is added between two nodes (u, v) both with degree $d-1$, after which both nodes u and v have degree d. Adding a new edge between u and v causes $d_k = d-1$ entries in β_i to become invalid. Each invalid entry is replaced with new entry of degree d. Thus, the upper bound on the total number of changes is $2 \cdot d_k$ deletions, $2 \cdot d_k$ additions, and one new edge, with the total being $4 \cdot d_k + 1$.

Given the partitioning approach and the imposed ∂ ordering across sub-series, we are able to exploit further properties on the β_is-series. In particular, the sensitivity of any β_i is independent from the location where the change occurs in the graph. Conversely, the sensitivity of a particular partition is dependent on the tuple with the highest degree values, as proved in Lemma 2. Therefore:

LEMMA 3. *The sensitivity of any β_i is independent by the sensitivity of any other β_j with $i \neq j$.*

PROOF. The proof proceeds by contradiction from the following assumption: *the sensitivity of a β_i is impacted by a change occurring in a β_j with $i \neq j$.* Without loss of generality, assume $i < j$, and $\partial(i')$ is a tuple in β_i and $\partial(j')$ is a tuple in β_j, as from Definition 3. Assume that an edge is formed between a node x with corresponding tuples $< \partial(i'), \partial(i'+1), .. > \in \beta_i$ and a node y with corresponding tuples $< \partial(j'), \partial(j'+1)... > \in \beta_j$. The maximum number of changes that can occur due to this event is bounded by the degree values of x and y. Let d be the new degree of x. The maximum number of tuples that can change in β_i are $d-1$ tuples that get deleted and d that get added, which is $< 2 \cdot d$. Symmetrically, let b be the new degree of y so the maximum number of tuples that can change in β_j is $< 2 \cdot b$. Even if d and b are equal to the maximum degree value d_k within their sub-series, as demanded in Lemma 2, the number of changes involved in each sub-series is $2 \cdot d_k < 4 \cdot d_k + 1$ which means that the sensitivity of both β_i and β_j are not mutually effected, which contradicts the hypothesis. □

4.2 Theoretical Analysis

This section is devoted to the theoretical analysis of the privacy and accuracy properties the DRC approach achieves. First, we prove that ϵ-differential privacy can be applied to each sub-series created during the partitioning phase of DRC. Next, we build on this result to prove that the individual differentially private sub-series' can be reunified into a complete dK-2-series that is also ϵ-differentially private. Lastly, we perform error analysis on DRC and compare the results to dK-PA.

Analyzing ϵ-Privacy in β_is. We now quantify the privacy of each β_i and prove that they satisfy ϵ-differential privacy.

THEOREM 2. *For each cluster β_i with $i = 1, .., \widetilde{m}$, let $\widehat{\beta}_i$ be a novel privacy mechanism on β_i such that $\widehat{\beta}_i = \beta_i + Lap(\frac{S_{\beta_i}}{\epsilon})^{|\beta_i|}$. Then, for all sub-series β_i and β'_i derived from graphs G and G' that differ by at most one edge, $\widehat{\beta}_i$ satisfies ϵ-differential privacy if:*

$$\left| \ln \frac{Pr[\widehat{\beta}_i = s]}{Pr[\widehat{\beta}'_i = s]} \right| \leq \epsilon$$

PROOF. Let m^* be the the cardinality of cluster β_i. Let G' be a graph with at most one edge different from G. Let s_j be the jth item of the $\widehat{\beta}_i$-series, that is $\widehat{\beta}_i[j] = s_j$. Using the conditional probability on s_j we can write:

$$\frac{Pr[\widehat{\beta}_i = s]}{Pr[\widehat{\beta}'_i = s]} = \prod_{j=1}^{m^*} \frac{Pr[\widehat{\beta}_i[j] = s_j | s_1, ...s_{j-1}]}{Pr[\widehat{\beta}'_i[j] = s_j | s_1, ...s_{j-1}]}$$

Each item of the product has the first $j-1$ tuples of the $\widehat{\beta}_i$-series fixed. Each s_j is the result of the Laplace noise that has been calibrated for β_i based on its sensitivity, as calculated using in Lemma 2. The sensitivity of this function is derived under the assumption that the two graphs have, at most, one edge difference. Thus, the conditional probabilities are Laplacians, which allows us to derive the following inequalities:

$$\prod_{j=1}^{m^*} \frac{Pr[\widehat{\beta}_i[j] = s_j | s_1, ...s_{j-1}]}{Pr[\widehat{\beta}'_i[j] = s_j | s_1, ...s_{j-1}]} \leq \prod_{j=1}^{m^*} e^{\frac{|\widehat{\beta}_i[j] - \widehat{\beta}'_i[j]|}{\sigma}}$$

By definition $\widehat{\beta}_i = \beta_i + Lap(\frac{S_{\beta_i}}{\epsilon})^{|\beta_i|}$ and by Lemma 2 $||\beta_i - \beta'_i||_1 \leq S_{\beta_i}$ with $S_{\beta_i} \leq 4d_{k_i} + 1$. Let σ_i be the scale parameter of the Laplacian noise applied in each cluster i, thus:

$$\prod_{j=1}^{m^*} e^{\frac{|\widehat{\beta}_i[j] - \widehat{\beta}'_i[j]|}{\sigma}} = e^{\frac{||\widehat{\beta}_i - \widehat{\beta}'_i||_1}{\sigma}}$$

$$= e^{\frac{||\widehat{\beta}_i + Lap(\frac{S_{\beta_i}}{\epsilon}) - \widehat{\beta}'_i - Lap(\frac{S_{\beta_i}}{\epsilon})||_1}{\sigma}} = e^{\frac{||\beta_i - \beta'_i||_1}{\sigma}} \leq e^{\frac{4d_{m_i}+1}{\frac{4d_{m_i}+1}{\epsilon}}}$$

Finally, by applying the logarithmic function the theorem statement is proved. □

Theorem 2 shows that adding noise does achieve provable ϵ-differential privacy on each cluster. In particular, we prove that by

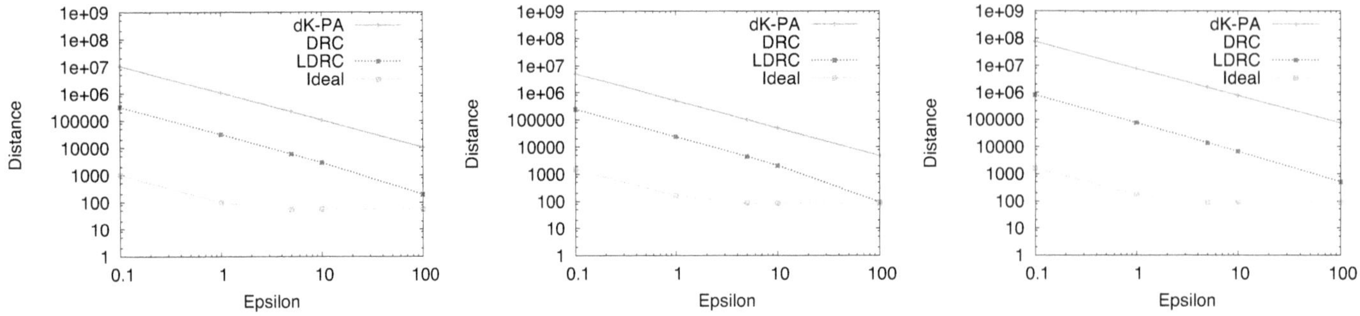

(a) AS (b) Russia (c) WWW

Figure 4: Euclidean distances of the dK-2-series of different ϵ-Differential Privacy strategies on three real graphs.

only leveraging m^* independent Laplace random variables, with parameter $\lambda = (\frac{S_{\beta_i}}{\epsilon})$, it is possible to generate sufficient noise per cluster to satisfy the privacy requirement.

Conquering ϵ-privacy into $\cup_i \widehat{\beta}_i$. Our next task is to leverage the proved ϵ-differential privacy of each independent $\widehat{\beta}_i$ to guarantee privacy on the entire perturbed $\widehat{\beta}$-series$= \cup_i \widehat{\beta}_i$. In order to achieve this goal a further step is required, shown in the following corollary.

COROLLARY 1. *The amount of information an attacker can learn on $\widehat{\beta}_i$ by observing any $\widehat{\beta}_j$ with $i \neq j$ is null.*

This proof considers only two sub-series for simplicity. Given Lemma 3, this proof can be extended to any number of clusters.

PROOF. Let A and B be two sub-series built out of our partition strategy and let $\widehat{A}$ and $\widehat{B}$ be their ϵ-differentially private projection as proved in Theorem 2. Finally, let a and b be events on $\widehat{A}$ and $\widehat{B}$, respectively. Through the Shannon Entropy Theory we quantify the information a sub-series could exploit on another sub-series. In particular, the Mutual Information

$$I(\widehat{A};\widehat{B}) = \sum_{a,b} p(a,b) \log \frac{p(a,b)}{p(a)p(b)}$$

is the amount of information an attacker can infer on $\widehat{A}$ by observing $\widehat{B}$. By construction the sensitivity of the sub-series A is independent from the sensitivity of the sub-series B, as proved in Lemma 3. This means that the sub-series A is perturbed by a Laplace random process with parameter λ_A that is independent from the Laplace random process acting on B, as consequence of Lemma 2. Thus, this independence property directly implies that the Mutual Information $I(\widehat{A},\widehat{B}) = 0$, that is, an attacker gains no information on $\widehat{A}$ by observing $\widehat{B}$, which concludes the proof. □

The properties derived on the different β_is are sufficient to begin the **conquer phase** of our DRC approach. The goal of the conquer phase is to unify the $\widehat{\beta}_i$s such that the union set inherits the ϵ-privacy guarantees from the individual sub-series.

THEOREM 3. *Given $\widetilde{m}$ different sub-series $\widehat{\beta}_i$ with $i = 1, ..., \widetilde{m}$, the result of the DRC conquer strategy $\cup_i \widehat{\beta}_i$ satisfies the ϵ-differential privacy property.*

PROOF. The DRC strategy produces $\widetilde{m}$ ϵ-differentially private sub-series $\widehat{\beta}_i$, as proved in Theorem 2. Each β_i satisfies Lemma 2 and Lemma 3, and any combination of $\widehat{\beta}_i$s satisfies Corollary 1. The privacy independence property, from Corollary 1, implies that $\cup_i \widehat{\beta}_i$ satisfies the ϵ-Differential Privacy property. □

Thus, we have proven that our perturbed dK-2, $\cup_i \widehat{\beta}_i$, satisfies the ϵ-differential privacy requirement. DRC achieves a tighter bound on noise than dk-PA due to the properties from Lemmas 2 and 3.

Error Analysis. We now quantify the error introduced to dK-2 via our DRC strategy. Error analysis on DRC is complicated because our algorithm does not specify the number of clusters to generate during partitioning. Instead, our clustering approach is general, and covers any possible set of cuts on the β-series such that the resulting sub-series differ in cardinality and sensitivity from each other, so long as they respect Lemmas 2 and 3. Therefore, in order to provide an error analysis that covers any possible clustering of the β-series we have to study both the lower and the upper bound of the error injected into those series.

DEFINITION 4. *The error estimation of the union of the $\widehat{\beta}_i$s under the ∂ ordering on dK-2 of a graph G can be computed as the expected randomization in generating $\widehat{\beta} = \cup_i \widehat{\beta}_i$.*

The expected randomization in $\widehat{\beta}$ is quantified as

$$\sum_{i=1}^{\widetilde{m}} E\left(\sum_j (\widehat{\beta}_i[j] - \beta_i[j])^2\right) = \sum_{i=1}^{\widetilde{m}} |\beta_i| E[Lap(\frac{S_{\beta_i}}{\epsilon})^2]$$

The lower bound is found when each S_{β_i} have the same minimum value, which is 1, and thus

$$\sum_{i=1}^{\widetilde{m}} |\beta_i| E[Lap(\frac{S_{\beta_i}}{\epsilon})^2] \geq d_{max}^2 Var(Lap(\frac{1}{\epsilon})) = \Omega(\frac{d_{max}^2}{\epsilon^2})$$

Note that the considered minimum, *i.e.* 1, happens only when a graph of nodes with zero degree is considered, and after adding an edge S_β is 1. The upper bound is found when each S_{β_i} have the maximum value that, as proved in Lemma 2, is $O(d_{max})$, and thus

$$\sum_{i=1}^{\widetilde{m}} |\beta_i| E[Lap(\frac{S_{\beta_i}}{\epsilon})^2] \leq d_{max}^2 Var(Lap(\frac{d_{max}}{\epsilon})) = O(\frac{d_{max}^4}{\epsilon^2})$$

The worst-case error level of DRC is equal to that of dK-PA. However, depending on graph structure, the error level can decrease down to $\Omega(\frac{d_{max}^2}{\epsilon^2})$. As we demonstrate in the next section, real graphs exhibit error rates towards the lower bound. Thus, in practice, DRC performs much better than dK-PA.

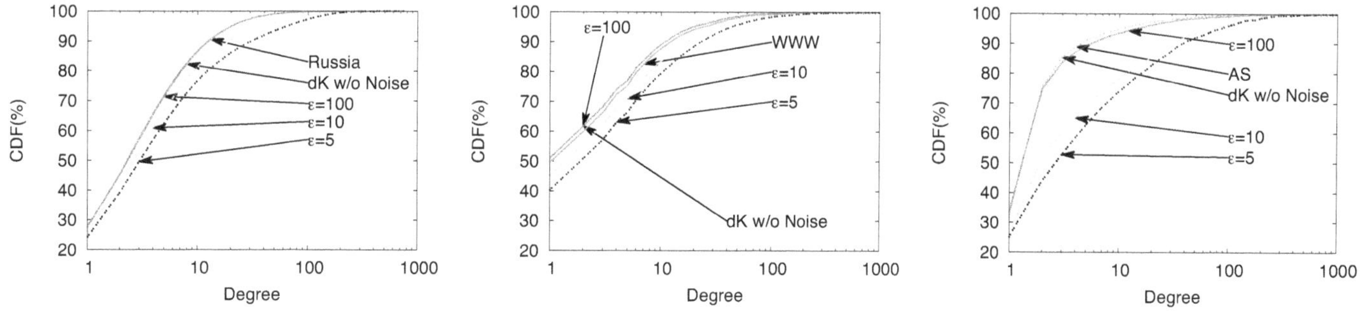

(a) Russia (b) WWW (c) AS

Figure 5: Degree distribution of three real measured graphs, *i.e.* Russia, WWW and AS, each compared to the dK-synthetic graph without noise and Pygmalion synthetic graphs with different ϵ values.

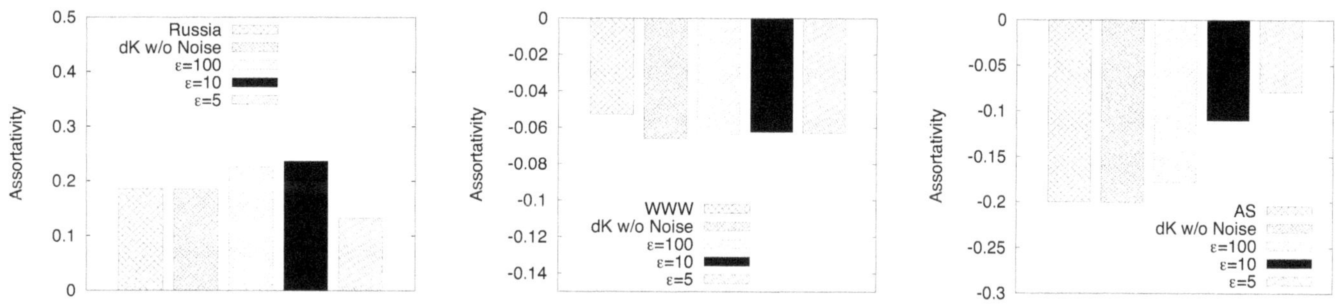

(a) Russia (b) WWW (c) AS

Figure 6: Assortativity of three real measured graphs, *i.e.* Russia, WWW and AS, each compared to the dK-synthetic graph without noise and Pygmalion synthetic graphs with different ϵ values.

4.3 Evaluating and Optimizing DRC

To quantify the improvement DRC achieves over the dK-PA strategy, we compare the results of applying each algorithm on our graphs. As before in Section 3.3, we quantify error using the Euclidean distances between each of their dK-2-series and the dK-2-series of the original graph. As seen in Figure 4, DRC reduces the Euclidean distance by one order of magnitude for different graphs and a range of ϵ values. As is the case for dK-PA, error introduced by DRC decreases exponentially as the value of ϵ increases, which is clear from the linear correlation in the log-log scale plot of Figure 4.

Further Optimization with LDRC. Despite its improvement over dK-PA, DRC is still quite far from the idealized function in terms of error (see Figure 4). We apply a prior result from [25] that proves how to use isotonic regression [6], *i.e.* evenly "smooth" out the introduced noise across tuples, without breaking differential privacy properties. This technique enables a reduction of the error introduced in the dK-2-series by another constant factor.

Formally, given a vector p of length p^*, the goal is to determine a new vector p' of the same length which minimizes the L_2 norm, *i.e.* $||p - p'||_2$. The minimization problem has the following constraints: $p'[i] \leq p'[i+1]$ for $1 \leq i < p^*$. Let $p[i,j]$ be a sub-vector of length $j - i + 1$, that is: $< p[i], ..., p[j] >$. Let define $M[i,j]$ as the mean of this sub-vector, *i.e.* $M[i,j] = \sum_{k=i}^{j} p[k]/(j - i + 1)$.

THEOREM 4. *[6] The minimum L_2 vector, p', is unique and is equal to $p'[k] = \widetilde{M_k}$, with:*

$$\widetilde{M_k} = min_{j \in [k,p^*]} max_{i \in [1,j]} M[i,j]$$

We apply this technique on the set of all tuples produced by DRC. We refer to it as the L_2 minimization Divide Randomize and Conquer algorithm, or LDRC. We include LDRC in our comparison of algorithms in Figure 4, and see that LDRC provides roughly another 50% reduction in error over the DRC algorithm. Since it consistently outperforms our other algorithms, we use LDRC as the algorithm inside the Pygmalion graph model.

Implications. Finally, we note that our DRC partition technique is general, and has potential implications in other contexts where it is desirable to achieve differential privacy with lower levels of injected noise. More specifically, it can serve to reduce the amount of perturbation necessary when the required perturbation is a function of a parameter that varies significantly across values in the dataset.

5. END-TO-END GRAPH SIMILARITY

We have already quantified the level of similarity between real and synthetic graphs by computing the Euclidean distances between their respective dK-series datasets. These values represent the distortion in the statistical representation of a graph, *i.e.* the dK-series, but do not capture the ultimate impact of the added noise on graph structure. In this section, we evaluate how well Pygmalion preserves a graph's structural properties by comparing Pygmalion's differentially private synthetic graphs against the originals in terms of both graph metrics and outcomes in application-level tests. Strong structural similarity in these results would establish the feasibility of using these differentially private synthetic graphs in real research analysis and experiments.

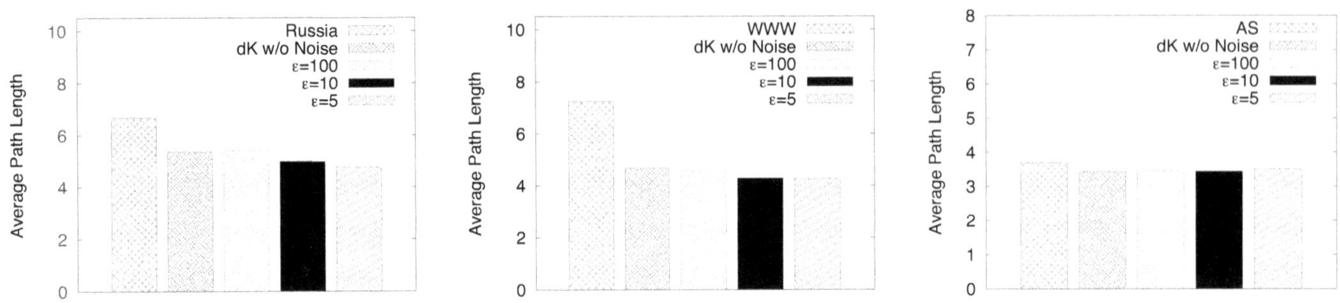

(a) Russia (b) WWW (c) AS

Figure 7: Average path length of three real measured graphs, *i.e.* Russia, WWW and AS, each compared to the dK-synthetic graph without noise and Pygmalion synthetic graphs with different ϵ values.

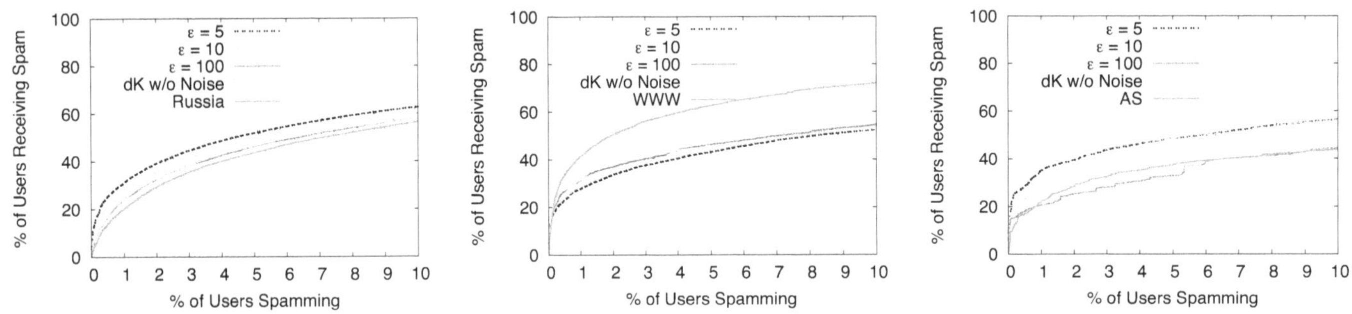

(a) Russia (b) WWW (c) AS

Figure 8: Reliable Email (RE) experiment run on three real measured graphs, *i.e.* Russia, WWW and AS, each compared with the dK-synthetic graph without noise and Pygmalion synthetic graphs with different ϵ values.

5.1 Graph Metrics

Our evaluation includes two classes of graph metrics. One group includes *degree-based metrics* such as: Average Node Degree, Degree Distribution, Joint Degree Distribution and Assortativity. These are basic topological metrics that characterize how degrees are distributed among nodes and how nodes with particular degree connect with each other. The second group includes *node separation metrics* that quantify the interconnectivity and density of the overall graph. This group includes metrics such as Graph Diameter, Radius and Average Path Length.

For our evaluation purposes, we always use our most advanced algorithm, *i.e.* Pygmalion LDRC. We only focus on Pygmalion LDRC, because there are practical problems in generating large graphs from dK values after significant noise has been added. As shown earlier, the dK-PA model introduces the highest noise. In fact, errors introduced by dK-PA are so large that the generator fails when trying to generate large graphs with the resulting noisy dK distributions.

We generate ϵ-private graphs for $\epsilon \in [5, 100]$, and compare the graph metrics of the resulting synthetic graphs against those of the original graph, and a synthetic graph generated by the dK model with no additional noise added. We limit ourselves to ϵ-private graphs with $\epsilon \in [5, 100]$ because of two reasons. First, we aim to find the ϵ value that contributes to a smallest noise such that it is statistically similar to the synthetic dK-2 graph with no privacy enforced. This way, we can indirectly quantify the level of privacy introduced by a pure synthetic graph with no additional steps taken to improve privacy. This by itself is a potentially interesting result. In particular, we obtain this property only when ϵ is equal to 100. Second, the dK-2 distribution is a very sensitive function and it naturally requires a high level of noise to provide strong levels of privacy guarantees. Unfortunately, very small values of ϵ require larger noise values, thus producing synthetic graphs that are extremely different in structure from the original. Finally, for $\epsilon < 1$, the required noise level is so high for larger graphs, that the dK graph generator fails to produce synthetic graphs that match the resulting dK distributions. This is clearly a limitation of the current system, one that we hope will be removed with the discovery of less sensitive models and optimization techniques to further reduce noise required for ϵ-differential privacy.

As we mentioned, our results are highly consistent across our pool of graphs (Table 1), and we only report experimental results on three graphs: the Russia Facebook graph, the AS graph and the WWW graph.

Degree-based Metrics. These metrics are fundamental in understanding the statistical properties of node degrees and how nodes connect to each other to form specific topological structures. Out of the four metrics mentioned above, we report results for Degree-Distribution (which supersedes average node degree) and Assortativity (which is related to joint degree distribution).

Degree Distributions. Figure 5 compares the node degree CDFs. For each of the Russia, WWW, and AS graphs, the degree distributions of both the Pygmalion (ϵ=100) graph and the dK-synthetic graph very closely match the degree distribution of the original graphs. When we increase the strength of the privacy guarantees, *i.e.* smaller ϵ values of 5 and 10, the accuracy of the synthetic degree distribution progressively decreases. For example, both the Russia and WWW graphs show a small deviation from the original distribution even for $\epsilon = 5$. Across all models for these two graphs, the worst-case degree distribution deviation is still within 10% of the original.

The AS graph, on the other hand, shows a slightly different behavior. For small ϵ values, *i.e.* $\epsilon = 5$ and $\epsilon = 10$, the largest error is within 35% from the original graph values. The AS graph shows a different behavior because a small number of high degree nodes connect the majority of other nodes. Thus, when the privacy perturbation hits those high-degree nodes, it can produce structural changes that send ripples through the rest of the graph.

Assortativity. Figure 6 reports the results of the assortative metric computed on both real and synthetic graphs for each of the three graphs (Russia, WWW and AS). The assortativity metric describes the degree with which nodes with similar degree are connected to each other. Positive assortativity value denotes a positive correlation between the degrees of connected nodes, and negative values indicate anti-correlation. Note that both the WWW and AS graphs show negative assortativity (Figure 6(b) and Figure 6(c)).

As with the degree distribution results, for each of our graphs (Russia, WWW, and AS), assortativity results from synthetic graphs for $\epsilon = 100$ and those from the dK-series closely match results from the original graphs. As we increase the level of privacy protection, the results get slightly further from the original values. For example, using $\epsilon = 5$ on Russia produces an error less than 0.05 on the assortativity value. The same ϵ value for the WWW graph produces negligible error on assortativity. Assortativity results on the AS graph are also consistent with degree distribution results. Under high privacy requirements, *i.e.* $\epsilon = 5$, error on assortativity reaches 0.12.

Node Separation Metrics. For brevity, we report only the Average Path Length as a representative of the node separation metrics. Figure 7 shows the Average Path Length (APL) values computed on Russia, WWW and AS compared to the APL values on their synthetic graphs. On Russia and WWW, APL results denote a moderate level of error (higher when compared to results for the earlier graph metrics). We can see that the error is mainly introduced by the impreciseness of the dK-model, since the synthetic graph from the dK-series with no noise shows the same error. In comparison, the error introduced by strengthening privacy (and hence decreasing ϵ) is relatively small. This is encouraging, because we can eliminate the bulk of the error by moving from dK-2 to a more accurate model, *e.g.* dK-3.

As with previous experiments, the AS graph shows a slightly different behavior. In this case, all of our synthetic graphs do a good job of reproducing the average path length value of the AS graph.

Summary. Our experimental analysis shows that synthetic graphs generated by Pygmalion exhibit structural features that provide a good match to those of the original graphs. As expected, increasing the strength of privacy guarantees introduces more noise into the structure of the synthetic graphs, producing graph metrics with higher deviation from the original graphs. These observations are consistent across social, web, and Internet topology graphs.

Overall, these results are very encouraging. They show that we are able to effectively navigate the tradeoff between accuracy and privacy by carefully calibrating the ϵ values. The fact that significant changes in ϵ values do not dramatically change the graph structure means owners of datasets can guarantee reasonable levels of privacy protection and still distribute meaningful graphs that match the original graphs in structure.

5.2 Application Results

For a synthetic graph to be usable in research, ultimately it must produce the same results in application-level experiments as the original graph it is replacing. To quantify the end-to-end impact of trading graph similarity for privacy protection, we compare the results of running two real world applications on both differentially private synthetic graphs and the original graphs. We implement two applications that are highly dependent on graph structure: Reliable Email (RE) [20] and Influence Maximization [11].

Reliable Email. RE [20] is an email spam filter that relies on a user's social network to filter and block spam. One way to evaluate the security of RE is to compute the number of users in a network who can be spammed by a fixed number of compromised friends in the social network. This experiment depends on the structure of the network, and is a useful way to evaluate whether Pygmalion graphs can be true substitutes for measurement graphs in research experiments.

Figure 8 shows the portion of the nodes flooded with spam as we increase the number of malicious spammers, using different graphs as the underlying social network topology. We show results on the usual three graphs, Russia, WWW and AS. On the Russia Facebook graph, all synthetic graphs closely follow the original graph. Even in the case of the strongest privacy setting, *i.e.* $\epsilon = 5$, the difference between the synthetic graph result and those of the original is at most 10%. For both the WWW and AS graphs, all synthetic graphs with and without noise produce results within 20% of the original graphs.

Influence Maximization. The influence maximization problem tries to locate users in the network who can most quickly spread information through the network. This problem is most commonly associated with advertisements and public relations campaigns. Evaluating a solution to this problem includes two steps. First, the solution must identify the nodes who can maximize influence in the network. Second, it must model the spread of influence through the network to quantify how many users the influence has ultimately reached.

For our purposes, we use a recently proposed heuristic for influence maximization that minimizes computation. The heuristic is called the Degree Discount method [11], and is able to find the most influential nodes, called "seeds," on a given graph. Starting from those seed nodes, we run three different influence dissemination models: Linear threshold (LT), Independent Cascade (IC) and Weighted Cascade (WC), to determine the total number of users in the network influenced by the campaign. We use source code we obtained from the authors. However, significant memory overhead in the code meant that we had to limit our experiments to smaller graphs. Therefore, we use the MontereyBay Facebook graph and the AS network topology graph in this experiment.

For both AS and MontereyBay graphs and each of the three influence dissemination models, Figure 9 shows the expected number of influenced nodes when increasing the number of initial seed nodes. While the actual percentage of users influenced varies across dissemination models, there are clear and visible trends. Results on the AS graph in Figures 9(a), 9(b), 9(c) all show that Pygmalion with $\epsilon = 100$ and the dK-synthetic graph without noise are almost identical to the original AS graph under all three dissemination models. Graphs with stronger protection, Pygmalion $\epsilon = 10$ and $\epsilon = 5$, progressively diverge from the results of the AS graph. Results on the MontereyBay graph are shown in Figures 9(d), 9(e), 9(f), and are quite similar to those on the AS graph. They confirm that Pygmalion $\epsilon = 100$ produces near perfect results, but higher

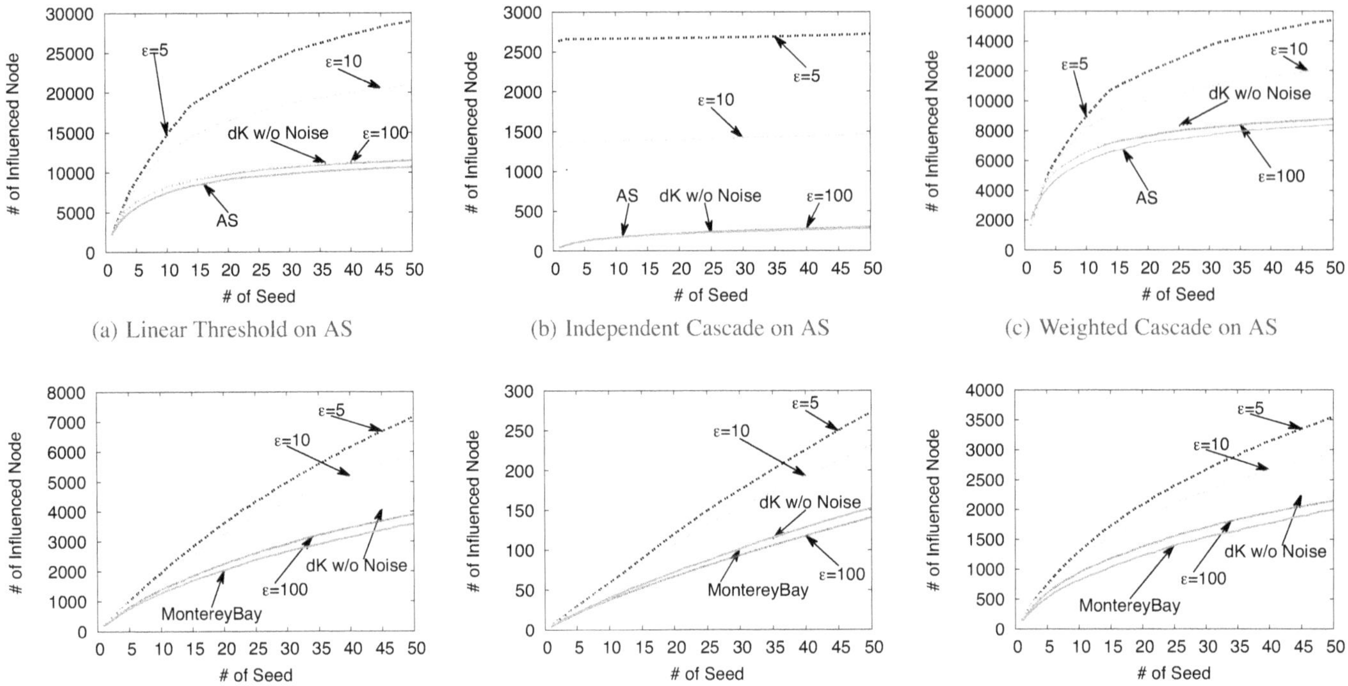

(a) Linear Threshold on AS (b) Independent Cascade on AS (c) Weighted Cascade on AS

(d) Linear Threshold on MontereyBay (e) Independent Cascade on MontereyBay (f) Weighted Cascade on MontereyBay

Figure 9: Results of the Degree Discount Influence Maximization algorithm on the AS and MontereyBay graphs, compared to dK graphs without added noise, and Pygmalion synthetic graphs with different ϵ values.

privacy protection increases the deviations from results on the original MontereyBay graph.

5.3 Summary

We have used both popular graph metrics and application-level tests to evaluate the feasibility of using differentially private synthetic graphs in research. Our tests are not comprehensive, and cannot capture all graph metrics or application-level experiments. However, they are instructive because they show the observable impact on graph structure and research results when we replace real graphs with differentially private Pygmalion graphs.

Our results consistently show that Pygmalion introduces limited impact as a result of adding noise to guarantee privacy. In fact, many of the largest errors can be attributed to limitations of the dK-2 series. Given the significant demand for realistic graphs in the research community, we expect that generator algorithms for more complex dK models will be discovered soon. Moving to those models, *e.g.* dK-3, will eliminate a significant source of error in these results.

6. CONCLUSION

We study the problem of developing a flexible graph privacy mechanism that preserves graph structures while providing user-specified levels of privacy guarantees. We introduce *Pygmalion*, a differentially-private graph model that aims these goals using the dK-series as a graph transformation function. First, we use analysis to show that this function has a high sensitivity, *i.e.* applied naively, it requires addition of high levels of noise to obtain privacy guarantees. We confirm this on both social and Internet graphs. Second, we develop and prove a partitioned privacy technique where differential privacy is achieved as a whole when it is achieved in each data cluster. This effectively reduces the level of noise necessary to attain a given level of privacy.

We evaluate our model on numerous graphs that range in size from 14K nodes to 1.7 million nodes. Our partitioned privacy technique reduces the required noise by an order of magnitude. For moderate to weak levels of privacy guarantees, the resulting synthetic graphs closely match the original graphs in both graph structure and behavior under application-level experiments.

We believe our results represent a promising first step towards enabling open access to realistic graphs with privacy guarantees. The accuracy of our current model is fundamentally limited by both the degree of descriptiveness of dK-2 series, and the high noise necessary to inject privacy properties. There are two ways to improve our results. One way is to use a more descriptive, higher-order dK model, under the assumption that its sensitivity is reasonable low. While generators for higher order dK-models are still unknown, our techniques are general, and can be applied to obtain more accurate models as higher-order dK generators are discovered. Another way to improve is to discover a function (or model) of graph structure with much lower sensitivity. If such a function exists, it can potentially lower the noise required for a given privacy level by orders of magnitude.

7. ACKNOWLEDGMENTS

We thank the anonymous reviewers for their comments. This material is based in part upon work supported by the National Science Foundation under grants IIS-0916307 and IIS-847925. Any opinions, findings, and conclusions or recommendations expressed in this material are those of the authors and do not necessarily reflect the views of the National Science Foundation. This work is also supported in part by South Korea National Research Foundation under the World Class University program.

8. REFERENCES

[1] AGGARWAL, G., FEDER, T., KENTHAPADI, K., MOTWANI, R., PANIGRAHY, R., THOMAS, D., AND ZHU, A. Approximation algorithms for k-anonymity. *Journal of Privacy Technology* (2005).

[2] AHN, Y.-Y., HAN, S., KWAK, H., MOON, S., AND JEONG, H. Analysis of topological characteristics of huge online social networking services. In *Proc. of WWW* (2007).

[3] ALBERT, R., JEONG, H., AND BARABÁSI, A.-L. Internet: Diameter of the World-Wide Web. *Nature 401*, 6749 (1999), 130–131.

[4] ALBERT, R., JEONG, H., AND BARABASI, A.-L. Error and attack tolerance of complex networks. *Nature 406* (July 2000).

[5] BACKSTROM, L., DWORK, C., AND KLEINBERG, J. M. Wherefore art thou r3579x?: anonymized social networks, hidden patterns, and structural steganography. In *Proc. of WWW* (2007), pp. 181–190.

[6] BARLOW, R. E., AND BRUNK, H. D. The isotonic regression problem and its dual. *Journal of the American Statistical Association 67*, 337 (1972), 140–147.

[7] BELLARE, M., BOLDYREVA, A., AND O'NEILL, A. Deterministic and efficiently searchable encryption. In *Proc. of CRYPTO* (2007), vol. 4622, pp. 535–552.

[8] BHAGAT, S., CORMODE, G., KRISHNAMURTHY, B., AND SRIVASTAVA, D. Class-based graph anonymization for social network data. *Proc. VLDB Endow. 2* (August 2009), 766–777.

[9] BLUM, A., DWORK, C., MCSHERRY, F., AND NISSIM, K. Practical privacy: the sulq framework. In *Proc. of PODS* (2005).

[10] BLUM, A., LIGETT, K., AND ROTH, A. A learning theory approach to non-interactive database privacy. In *Proc. of STOC* (2008).

[11] CHEN, W., WANG, Y., AND YANG, S. Efficient influence maximization in social networks. In *Proc. of KDD* (2009).

[12] CHUN, H., KWAK, H., EOM, Y.-H., AHN, Y.-Y., MOON, S., AND JEONG, H. Comparison of online social relations in volume vs interaction: a case study of Cyworld. In *Proc. of IMC* (2008).

[13] DIMITROPOULOS, X., KRIOUKOV, D., VAHDAT, A., AND RILEY, G. Graph annotations in modeling complex network topologies. *ACM Trans. Model. Comput. Simul. 19* (November 2009).

[14] DWORK, C. Differential privacy. In *Proc. of ICALP* (2006).

[15] DWORK, C. Differential privacy: A survey of results. In *Theory and Applications of Models of Computation* (2008).

[16] DWORK, C., KENTHAPADI, K., MCSHERRY, F., MIRONOV, I., AND NAOR, M. Our data, ourselves: Privacy via distributed noise generation. In *Proc. of EUROCRYPT* (2006).

[17] DWORK, C., MCSHERRY, F., NISSIM, K., AND SMITH, A. Calibrating noise to sensitivity in private data analysis. In *Proc. of IACR TCC* (2006).

[18] FRIEDMAN, A., WOLFF, R., AND SCHUSTER, A. Providing k-anonymity in data mining. *The VLDB Journal* (2008).

[19] FU, Y., CHEN, Z., KORU, G., AND GANGOPADHYAY, A. A privacy protection technique for publishing data mining models and research data. *ACM Trans. Manage. Inf. Syst. 1* (December 2010), 7:1–7:20.

[20] GARRISS, S., KAMINSKY, M., FREEDMAN, M. J., KARP, B., MAZIÈRES, D., AND YU, H. Re: Reliable email. In *Proc. of NSDI* (2006).

[21] GJOKA, M., KURANT, M., BUTTS, C. T., AND MARKOPOULOU, A. Walking in Facebook: A case study of unbiased sampling of OSNs. In *Proc. of INFOCOM* (2010).

[22] GUPTA, A., LIGETT, K., MCSHERRY, F., ROTH, A., AND TALWAR, K. Differentially private combinatorial optimization. In *Proc. of SODA* (2010).

[23] HAY, M., LI, C., MIKLAU, G., AND JENSEN, D. Accurate estimation of the degree distribution of private networks. In *Proc. of IEEE ICDM* (2009).

[24] HAY, M., MIKLAU, G., JENSEN, D., TOWSLEY, D., AND WEIS, P. Resisting structural re-identification in anonymized social networks. In *Proc. of VLDB* (2008).

[25] HAY, M., RASTOGI, V., MIKLAU, G., AND SUCIU, D. Boosting the accuracy of differentially private histograms through consistency. In *Proc. of VLDB* (2010).

[26] JIANG, J., WILSON, C., WANG, X., HUANG, P., SHA, W., DAI, Y., AND ZHAO, B. Y. Understanding latent interactions in online social networks. In *Proc. of IMC* (Nov. 2010).

[27] KUMAR, R. A. Structure and evolution of online social networks. In *Proc. of KDD* (2006).

[28] KWAK, H., CHOI, Y., EOM, Y.-H., JEONG, H., AND MOON, S. Mining communities in networks: a solution for consistency and its evaluation. In *Proc. of IMC* (2009).

[29] KWAK, H., LEE, C., PARK, H., AND MOON, S. What is twitter, a social network or a news media? In *Proc. of WWW* (2010).

[30] LIU, K., AND TERZI, E. Towards identity anonymization on graphs. In *Proc. of SIGMOD* (2008).

[31] MAHADEVAN, P., KRIOUKOV, D., FALL, K., , AND VAHDAT, A. Systematic topology analysis and generation using degree correlations. In *Proc. of SIGCOMM* (2006).

[32] MCSHERRY, F., AND MAHAJAN, R. Differentially-private network trace analysis. In *Proc. of SIGCOMM* (October 2010).

[33] MEYERSON, A., AND WILLIAMS, R. On the complexity of optimal k-anonymity. In *Proc. of PODS* (2004).

[34] MIR, D., AND WRIGHT, R. A differentially private graph estimator. In *Proc. of ICDMW '09.* (December 2009), pp. 122 –129.

[35] NARAYANAN, A., AND SHMATIKOV, V. Robust de-anonymization of large sparse datasets. In *Proc. of IEEE S&P* (2008).

[36] NARAYANAN, A., AND SHMATIKOV, V. De-anonymizing social networks. In *Proc. of IEEE S&P* (2009).

[37] NISSIM, K., RASKHODNIKOVA, S., AND SMITH, A. Smooth sensitivity and sampling in private data analysis. In *Proc. of STOC* (2007).

[38] OLIVEIRA, R. V., ZHANG, B., AND ZHANG, L. Observing the evolution of internet as topology. In *Proc. of SIGCOMM* (2007).

[39] PUTTASWAMY, K. P. N., SALA, A., AND ZHAO, B. Y. Starclique: Guaranteeing user privacy in social networks against intersection attacks. In *Proc. of ACM CoNEXT* (2009).

[40] RASTOGI, V., AND NATH, S. Differentially private aggregation of distributed time-series with transformation and encryption. In *Proc. of SIGMOD* (2010).

[41] SALA, A., CAO, L., WILSON, C., ZHENG, H., AND ZHAO, B. Y. Measurement-calibrated graph models for social network experiments. In *Proc. of WWW* (2010).

[42] SWEENEY, L. k-anonymity: A model for protecting privacy. *Int. J. Uncertain. Fuzziness Knowl.-Based Syst. 10* (2002), 557–570.

[43] WILSON, C., BOE, B., SALA, A., PUTTASWAMY, K. P. N., AND ZHAO, B. Y. User interactions in social networks and their implications. In *Proc. of EuroSys* (2009).

[44] XIAO, X., WANG, G., AND GEHRKE, J. Differential privacy via wavelet transforms. *IEEE Trans. on Knowledge and Data Engineering* (2010).

[45] ZHELEVA, E., AND GETOOR, L. Preserving the privacy of sensitive relationships in graph data. In *Proc. of PinKDD* (2008), pp. 153–171.

[46] ZHOU, B., AND PEI, J. Preserving privacy in social networks against neighborhood attacks. In *Proc. of ICDE* (2008).

[47] ZIMMER, M. Facebook data of 1.2 million users from 2005 released: Limited exposure, but very problematic. Blog, February 2011. `http://michaelzimmer.org`.

[48] ZOU, L., CHEN, L., AND OZSU, M. T. K-automorphism: A general framework for privacy preserving network publication. In *Proc. of VLDB* (2009).

Summary Review Documentation for

"Sharing Graphs Using Differentially Private Graph Models"

Authors: A. Sala, X. Zhao, C. Wilson, H. Zheng, B. Zhao

Reviewer #1

Strengths: Focuses on the important and timely problem of privacy-preserving graph anonymization. This is a very general and interesting problem. The paper proposes a novel approach to apply differential-privacy concepts on graphs. It produces anonymized graphs with specific privacy guarantees. The proposed method is thoroughly analyzed and evaluated. The paper is very well written.

Weaknesses: The evaluation results show that proposed method produces accurate graphs mainly for weak privacy guarantees (large \epsilon).

Comments to Authors: Without perturbation, the output of a query is the dk-2 distribution. This hides some information about the original graph, which the presented approach ignores. I wonder how much information it hides? Is it possible to quantify this? and/or take it into account in the anonymization procedure?

I understand that in the context of graph an edge corresponds to a database record. Should edges not be independent? Edges in real graphs are not created independently. The paper is not very clear about this point.

The paper misses perhaps the most related study (X. Dimitropoulos et al, "Graph Annotations in Modeling Complex Network Topologies" ACM Transactions on Modeling and Computer Simulation, vol. 19(4), Sep. 2009). This work distills an original graph to a 2K-series representation, creates empirical models of the 2K-series profile (unlike [30]), generates a new random 2K-series statistical profile from the modeled 2K-distributions (effectively adding noise), and synthesizes a graph. Combining the dk-series framework for graph anonymization makes sense. The original dk-series framework [30] produces synthetic graphs that are too similar to the original graph. This property is useful for privacy-preserving graph publishing.

I found the notation in the product of Theorem 1 somewhat cryptic, could not fully parse it.

The values of \epsilon for which the authors get good results in Section 5 are very high.

It is not clear which query model the paper assumes. Is the interactive query model supported?

Reviewer #2

Strengths: Important problem, and a good, first stab at the problem (where the problem is sharing graphs in a manner that is private and supports arbitrary queries, rather than a few select queries).

Weaknesses: 1. The paper assumes that edges in the graph is what needs to be private and the methods do not work if we wanted information about nodes to be private. This assumption is fundamental to the work and, worse, it is implicit. There is no discussion in the paper why this definition of privacy is an appropriate one.
2. The experiments are not stressing the scheme and should be done differently. Details below.

Comments to Authors: Let me expand on the two complaints above.

1. First, you are (implicitly) assuming that what needs to be hidden is whether an edge is present or absent in the graph. This is a good goal, but not the only (or the most private) one. For instance, another natural goal is to hide the presence/absence/properties of nodes in the graph. Your methods do not protect against attacks on node properties. To protect against node-level attacks, the neighboring graph would be one with an extra node added or deleted. It should be apparent that this change has way more sensitivity than adding or deleting an edge. It would be good to make this point clear in your paper; I believe it to be an important distinction. This does not detract from your paper but makes it more precise; I think what you are doing is a great first step. At the same time, please discuss why you believe edge-level privacy to be an appropriate definition.

2. Second, I thought several aspects of your experiments should be done differently:
- The choices of \epsilon values are strange. What are they motivated by? My understanding is that \epsilon~10 is considered weak, but the lowest you go is 5. It is fine to study higher \epsilon values, but you need to study values for the more private end of the spectrum as well.
- I would like to see results in Sec. 5 for dK-PA as well. Does the poor performance that you show in earlier sections hinder it for the metrics in Sec. 5. After all, per measures in Sec. 3 and 4, even LDRC is orders of magnitude further away from the ideal.
- I disagree with how you summarize your experimental findings in Section 5.3. You basically blame dK-2 series for most of the loss in fidelity that you observe. But it is pretty clear from Figure 9, and to some extent Figure 8, that dK is not the fundamental bottleneck. dK-2 series itself is pretty close, but end-to-end measures come close only with very high \epsilon values (100). It means that it is the perturbation process that is responsible.

That said, I do like the fact that in your experiments you study applications that are not perfect matches for LDRC. You should just draw the right conclusions from them.

How do you compute the sub-series in your scheme? What if there are multiple partitions that satisfy your constraints?

Why do you see a non-monotonic behavior with respect to \epsilon in Fig. 6a? The error from the original is greater for \epsilon=10 than \epsilon=100. If this is entirely due to randomization, you should be conducting multiple experiments and plotting error bars.

Reflecting on DRC at a higher-level, I find it intriguing on two counts. First, the trick of partitioning the data and independently adding noise seems general and might find use in other places. You may consider highlighting this aspect. Second, it is also a bit counter-intuitive to me. I would have thought that considering the entire series would let one add lower noise than adding noise to individual subsets. This was essentially the observation in [39]. But you are going in the opposite direction. The difference perhaps is that you are able to find "natural" partitions of data. But it also suggests to me that better perturbation mechanisms can be designed, which treat the whole series together.

Reviewer #3

Strengths: Interesting idea. Seems fairly complete.

Weaknesses: Impact on end-to-end metrics is not clear. Unclear whether the contributions are only theoretical. Some sloppiness in the techniques. The authors show that repeat queries cannot be handled very well with diffPriv. It is unclear that distributing graphs with noise fits the diffPriv use case, which is more about answering some queries than shipping the dataset.

Comments to Authors: There is a mismatch between what differential privacy provides - the ability to respond to queries without revealing anonymity versus the canonical use case with measurement datasets which involves releasing the dataset. I did not see a way of reconciling that in this paper.

DiffPriv also has a problem dealing with succession of queries. They typically operate with a privacy budget, each answered query uses up part of it. Once budget is depleted, no more queries can be supported on the dataset without leaking information. How does the use case here work around this concern?

I see that theoretically the amount of noise injected is lower O(d_max^4/\epsilon^2) to about O(d_max^3 / \epsilon^2) but I do not see the impact on stats that matter. For example, the results in Section 5 do not compare with dk-PA, the technique that injects noise as per standard diffPriv. For Fig. 4, I cannot really tell why 'distance' is a good metric. Employ something that users may care about, and show how the accuracy of that maps onto 'distance'.

The required amount of privacy parameter, \epsilon, impacts results. \epsilon=100 is great, others not so good. In Fig. 5, the distributions are far even when the X axes is on a log scale. How does a user choose \epsilon? How exactly is an \epsilon = 5 better in terms of privacy than \epsilon = 100? The loss in accuracy is clear but the gains in terms of privacy not.

What about the AS graph makes it much harder to keep accurate? for e.g., at \epsilon=100, the accuracy is quite poor.

dK-Graph model: For network topology aspects, this is a good model. Is there nothing in the social graph that goes beyond topology of the friend graph? Metadata? Group memberships? Activity? (When is she online more often? Does he play farmville?) Correlation in activity?

Theorem 1 seems more of a sufficient than a necessary condition.

\sigma is not E[Lap(...)] which by definition is zero.

Error analysis, the lower bound seems impossible, i.e., the minimum value of 1.

It is unclear if the L2 minimization works across partitions, as it does in the vanilla case.

Sec. 5: it is not clear until the end of Sec. 5.1 that by dK you mean dK-2, which loses a lot of fidelity (Fig. 7). Use dK-3 instead?

Reviewer #4

Strengths: Anonymization is a useful tool. We lack as many datasets in this domain as we would like because commercial interests prevent them being shared.

Weaknesses: The obsession of graph theorists with node degree is really damaging to networking research. It is not clear that node degree sequences really tell us anything we need to know about data networks, or that the node-degree sequence approach really does what it claims to do.

Comments to Authors: A lot of this paper is based on statements in [30]. I never found that that paper convincingly showed that the ensemble of graphs it generated were (i) meaningfully different from the graphs that they came from (two graphs that differ by two edits can easily be homomorphic - are they then usefully different); and (ii) showed that the resulting graphs were similar in any sense except those related to node degree.

It may naively seem that both problems cannot be true, because they are almost the opposite problem. However, the problems can be different for different instantiations. For instance, for either the clique, or graph with no edges, all possible graphs with identical node degree distribution are the same. On the other hand, we know from the work of Willinger et al that graphs with identical degree distributions can be quite different in nature. Adding higher order degree sequences does not fix this. So we could have a mapping that for some graphs just creates what are effectively homomorphisms, and for others, creates a range of graphs that are in no useful sense similar to the original.

What is the worst case for this algorithm in both senses? Does it fail to anonymise for some cases, and fail to produce meaningful information in others? Limiting to dK-2 introduces similar questions. Adding noise complicates the matter further.

The graph datasets lack the types of labels that would make them interesting for many practical problems, e.g., link capacity, policies and so on. Most of the graph datasets have substantial errors. What is the effect of errors in the initial measurements?

As the framework is defined in terms of a particular set of queries, why not just distribute the results of the query on the graph? We do not know that the technique will work for other queries, so we cannot just blindly apply them when we come to another graph. If the dK sequence is so important, why generate alternative graphs at all: just give people the dK sequence and let them work with it.

Reviewer #5

Strengths: - Addresses an important and difficult problem with some novel angle and non-trivial observation.
- combines design with concrete validation that provides more ground (even if it does not close the topic).

Weaknesses: - The reader should be ready to accept semi-proof and lack of complete rigorous formal model and proof, for the sake of exposition of interesting observations.
- Limitations are severe (only releasing k=2 reduces the k series to its single most expression: assortativity). The extension is conceptually interesting but far from being as attainable as the authors say.
- The levels of privacy proposed are not ready for prime time. Most \epsilon-differential privacy work recommends \epsilon at most 0.1 this paper considers the parameter between 5 and 100!

Comments to Authors: I think this is an interesting candidate for publication. The use of dk series seems promising to address the need to manipulate realistic graphs, this paper is making one step for it. This has potential to impact an important problem.

We are far from a contribution solidly written in the marble given the choices made by the authors in terms of high \epsilon and a rather poor exposition of the methods, which seem to follow more high-level intuition than precise first principles. Nevertheless the point that partitioning improves sensitivity and brings guarantee is a good catch, and the paper makes the case serious.

p.1 "We take a different approach to address the above question, by making the observation" the current claim of ownership of this observation is strange. This tension is the very much at the core of much research including k-anonymity, differential privacy.

The limitation of k=2 might appear a bit hard to swallow after such a grand claim. I still think it is an interesting step because that is the way to go. Who knows how sensitivity behave for k=3 and if any partitioning make sense.

"In contrast, our goal is to inject changes into all aspects of the graph topology, instead of focusing on a single graph metric." You do not reproduce all aspects, and you will likely never. You propose to recover what the dk series can obtain, starting with k=2. It does already make your approach original (and promising) but stating it so broadly is a countersense.

"Unfortunately, the author asserts there are incorrect results in the paper 1." This is perhaps unfortunate but it does not explain how your method is intrinsically better. It would much stronger to highlight the difference first and then mention this point.

Lemma 1 is a partial result. You only provide an upper bound, which does not prove that the real sensitivity is necessarily high.

The statement of error measure is very vague. How does random noise alter the actual structure of the graph?

Please clarify what happens between clusters? Are the data lost with some forms of random generation of links between them?

Have you ever seen a single paper advocating \epsilon between 5 and 100? You are essentially saying the users "Do not worry, your chance of being identified by joining the database are only multiplied between 148 and about 10^43". What kind of guarantee is that?

Response from the Authors

We thank the reviewers for their insightful comments. Several comments were results of ambiguous text in the paper, which we have addressed by clarifying our claims and assumptions and providing deeper explanations of our findings. In particular, we explain that the omission of the dK-PA was simply because it generated so much noise that the dK-generator failed to generate matching graphs. Two additional key points stood out in the comments, and we address them in detail below.

First, on the issue of dK-2 as a graph statistical representation, we modified text to more clearly explain the advantages and the limitations of our choice. We explain that we require a statistical representation of a graph that can be converted to and from an unique graph. The dK-series is ideal for this. We use the dK-2 series, because it is the most detailed dK-series that has a corresponding graph generator (e.g. there is currently no known dK-3 series graph generator that works on large graphs). While the choice of dK-2 limits the accuracy of our current model, our methodology is general, and can be used with higher order dK-series when their generators are discovered (e.g. we are currently working on developing a scalable dK-3 generator). It is possible that providing privacy on higher order dK-series may require more severe noise, which could consequently destroy their higher accuracy. Therefore, our conclusion is that higher order dK-series will become a practical solution only if we are able to preserve their accuracy through the perturbation process and when a generator will be invented.

Second, we address via text edits questions on the choice of \epsilon: smaller \epsilon indicates stronger privacy. We use moderate to high values of \epsilon in our tests for two reasons. One, we wanted to find the \epsilon value that contributes to the smallest noise such that it produces a graph statistically similar to the synthetic dK-2 graph with no privacy. Thus we can indirectly quantify the level of privacy inherent in a synthetic graph without additional privacy constraints. We show that this property is achieved when \epsilon is equal to \$100\$. In addition, the dK-2 series is a very sensitive function and naturally requires high level of noise to guarantee strong privacy. Our primary goal was to identify the feasibility of this approach, and leave further optimizations to achieve high fidelity graphs for lower \epsilon values as goals for future work.

Can They Hear Me Now?: A Case for a Client-assisted Approach to Monitoring Wide-area Wireless Networks

Sayandeep Sen*, Jongwon Yoon*, Joshua Hare*, Justin Ormont, Suman Banerjee
University of Wisconsin-Madison
{sdsen, yoonj, hare, ormont, suman}@cs.wisc.edu

ABSTRACT

We present WiScape, a framework for measuring and understanding the behavior of wide-area wireless networks, e.g., city-wide or nation-wide cellular data networks using active participation from clients. The goal of WiScape is to provide a coarse-grained view of a wide-area wireless landscape that allows operators and users to understand broad performance characteristics of the network. In this approach a centralized controller instructs clients to collect measurement samples over time and space in an opportunistic manner. To limit the overheads of this measurement framework, WiScape partitions the world into zones, contiguous areas with relatively similar user experiences, and partitions time into zone-specific epochs over which network statistics are relatively stable. For each epoch in each zone, WiScape takes a minimalistic view — it attempts to collect a small number of measurement samples to adequately characterize the client experience in that zone and epoch, thereby limiting the bandwidth and energy overheads at client devices. For this effort, we have collected ground truth measurements for up to three different commercial cellular wireless networks across (i) an area of more than 155 square kilometer in and around Madison, WI, in the USA, (ii) a road stretch of more than 240 kilometers between Madison and Chicago, and (iii) locations in New Brunswick and Princeton, New Jersey, USA, for a period of more than 1 year. We justify various design choices of WiScape through this data, demonstrate that WiScape can provide an accurate performance characterization of these networks over a wide area (within 4% error for more than 70% of instances) with a low overhead on the clients, and illustrate multiple applications of this framework through a sustained and ongoing measurement study.

*Primary authors.

IMC'11, November 2–4, 2011, Berlin, Germany.

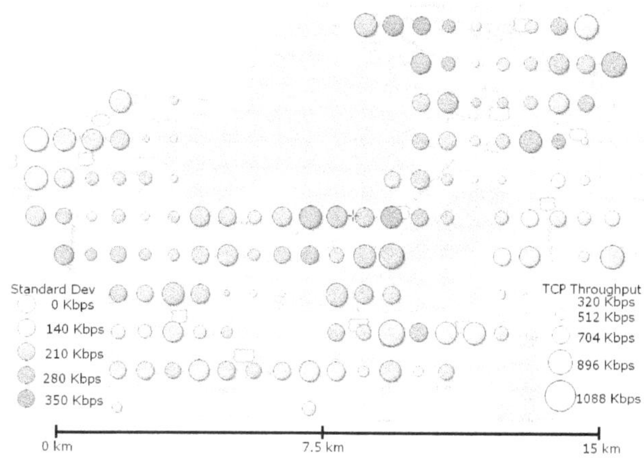

Figure 1: A Snapshot of TCP throughput distribution within our NetB network, covering a 155 sq. kilometer city-wide area. Throughputs are collected based on 1MB downloads, collected using WiScape. Each dot corresponds to a circular area of radius 600 meters.

Categories and Subject Descriptors

C.2.3 [**Network Operations**]: Network Monitoring, Public networks; C.2.1 [**Computer Communication Networks**]: Network Architecture and Design—*Wireless Communication*

General Terms

Documentation, Experimentation, Measurement, Performance, Reliability

Keywords

Cellular Networks, Measurement, Client Assisted

1. INTRODUCTION

The ability to observe an entire network's performance is an important precursor to understanding and predicting its behavior, and in debugging its performance problems. Gathering such detailed observations at a network-scale is challenging for any network, whether wired or wireless.

In wired networks, such as enterprises or ISPs, operators typically deploy multiple monitoring nodes in carefully chosen vantage points within the network to capture and aggregate necessary information [1]. In the context of WLANs, multiple early efforts emulated these wired approaches by deploying similar monitoring nodes in the wired part of the network [2]. However, wired-only observations fail to capture the impact of *location-specific* RF characteristics. Hence, more recent WLAN monitoring efforts, e.g., Jigsaw [3], chose to deploy numerous wireless sniffers across an entire physical space, e.g., a campus building. While deployment of such a widespread wireless monitoring infrastructure is still feasible in building-wide settings, the logistics of densely deploying and managing such infrastructure is impractical when the wireless networks are significantly larger in scale. In particular, it is virtually impossible to densely deploy wireless sniffers to monitor the performance of a *city-scale or a nation-scale* cellular data network. In this paper, we examine a different solution for monitoring and measuring such large-scale wireless networks, one that leverages the potential assistance of a large number of clients. More specifically, we present *WiScape,* a framework to characterize the wireless land*scape*, using data collected from three commercial cellular data networks over more than one year across large regions: (i) more than 155 square kilometers in and around Madison, WI, in the USA, (ii) a road stretch of 240 kilometers between Madison and Chicago, and (iii) targeted regions in the cities of New Brunswick and Princeton in New Jersey, USA. Figure 1 presents a snapshot of some of our measurement data collected from one of the monitored cellular networks across Madison, WI. The figure partitions the entire area into coarse-grained zones (each zone is a 0.2 sq.km.), with only a sampled subset of zones shown, and the size of the circles represent the average values of the TCP download throughputs (the shade of the circle represent the variance of throughput samples).

In this paper, we also demonstrate, via experimentation, how network operators and users (applications) can benefit from data accumulated by the WiScape framework. For instance, in our experiments we found that a network operator can use WiScape to easily identify significant changes in user experiences within their own network, while an application such as MAR [4] (which uses multiple cellular network interfaces to provide aggregated wireless bandwidth into vehicles) can improve its own performance by up to 41% by leveraging WiScape collected data. Finally, an approach such as WiScape can potentially serve as a *performance watchdog* and can provide a neutral view of different commercial wireless networks over time and space.

Client-assisted monitoring in WiScape

Cellular data networks nationwide are placing increasing emphasis on performance, mobility and wide-area coverage. As these networks attempt to provide ubiquitous connectivity to large geographic areas, operators continue to seek better tools to observe network performance at all locations. Each network operator sends out its RF monitoring trucks during initial deployment of cellular towers and periodically after that to various neighborhoods. Occasionally, if the operator receives a large volume of consumer complaints of network performance from a certain area, they would also conduct additional RF surveys at those specific locations [5]. Each such RF survey is quite labor-intensive.

Furthermore, user complaints are unlikely to capture a vast majority of network performance issues that occur. Users often only complain when a problem is particularly serious and persistent, causing major disruptions to the user over a long period of time.

In WiScape we propose to measure the network's performance, *as perceived by the clients and through the help of clients.* More specifically, in this approach diverse mobile clients measures network properties based on instructions from a central controller to map out the performance across the entire network. Since the clients are naturally mobile, they are perfectly positioned to monitor the network performance from various vantage points. If implemented successfully, this approach can mitigate significant costs that operators might otherwise have to incur in order to collect data of the same level of richness and detail. In addition, such an approach provides us with unique data from the client's point of view, which is not available otherwise.

This high-level idea is actually a fairly common one and different variants of it have been referred to as crowd-sourcing, war-driving, and participatory sensing. Such approaches have been used to collect locations of WiFi APs worldwide, and have been proposed in various types of health-related applications (air pollution, audio noise level, and radiation exposure monitoring across a city), as well as social interactions (detecting presence of friends nearby) [6, 7]. In the wireless setting, there are now ongoing efforts that attempt a similar approach to collect performance data of different cellular networks. Examples include RootWireless [8] a company that distributes mobile phone applications that collect measurements from volunteers to generate coverage maps of cellular operators, the 3gtest application from U Michigan [9] and AT&T's "Mark the Spot" iPhone application that allows iPhone users to record the location of where a phone call was dropped.

While the main idea is relatively simple, the core technical challenge in designing an effective, scalable, and useful system lies in its ability to manage the volume of measurements required and the manner in which measurement tasks can be coordinated across multiple clients. We comment on this issue next.

WiScape approach and usage scenarios: In a client-based monitoring system, if all clients are requested to collect performance measurements all the time, the volume of such measurement traffic could prohibit useful activity in the network. Such an effort could also place a significant burden on the client devices leading to quicker depletion of the limited battery power of these devices. Therefore, the key in designing a client-based monitoring infrastructure is to ensure that the volume of data collected is low, yet is adequate to present the operators and users with a broad understanding of network performance. At the same time, since this approach is able to collect measurements only from specific locations clients are available at any given instant, the number of measurement samples available from any arbitrary location and at any desired time is likely to be quite sparse, often zero, and hence not statistically significant. Therefore, in WiScape *we need to aggregate collected measurements from clients, both in time and space* so that it is statistically significant for observations.

Burdened by above considerations, we partition the world into *zones* (around 0.2 sq. kilometer each) and time in each zone into *epochs* (a few tens of minutes). We define zones such that measurements within each zone have relatively low variance most of the time. We define epochs such that statistics across multiple consecutive epochs of the same zone have low variance. (Note that epochs may have smaller durations in zones with rapidly changing performance observed by clients.) In other words, each epoch for each zone is the smallest time-space granularity that WiScape attempts to accurately estimate to provide a stable measure. Based on our models, we require around 100 measurement samples to estimate network layer performance of each epoch of a zone, such as throughput, delay, loss, and jitter. We believe for most zones this measurement volume is easy to obtain, especially for zones in dense urban areas with many users. which often require greater attention from network operators.

The nature of data collection in WiScape also dictates the type of its use. Given our intent of collecting a small amount of data, WiScape will miss many of the short-term and transient variations, e.g., as a result of sudden burst of active users arriving in a given location and then disappearing within a few minutes. However, any persistent network behavior (persistent in the order of an epoch, typically tens of minutes) will be captured by our system quite accurately. We show this through multiple examples in Section 4. An interesting such example was WiScape's detection of 4× increase in latencies in a specific zone of two cellular networks in Madison, encompassing the UW-Madison football stadium, for nearly 3 hours on a football Saturday when nearly 80,000 people packed into the stadium for the game.

In the rest of the paper, we explain how we designed the WiScape framework through detailed measurements and statistical analysis of the data and make the following key contributions:

- We establish the feasibility of client-assisted monitoring of wide area wireless networks by carrying out extensive measurements over a duration of more than 1 year, spanning a geographical area of more than 155 sq.km. across multiple cities, a long road stretch of 240 k.m. and across three 3G cellular networks. Traces used for the paper will be made publicly available through CRAWDAD [10].

- We design and implement WiScape — a monitoring system that bins measurements into epochs and zones and collects a relatively small number of measurements per epoch per zone. We establish appropriate parameters for epochs, zones, and the number of measurement samples through detailed data collection, analysis, and experimentation.

- We demonstrate the benefits of WiScape through multiple simple use cases: (i) to quickly detect somewhat persistent changes to network behavior and alert network operators of need to perform detailed investigations of such changes, (ii) to apply WiScape collected data to improve the performance of multi-network applications like MAR and "multi-sim."

In the next section, we present some details on our measurement and data collection efforts used designing and evaluating different aspects of WiScape. Subsequently, in Section 3, we present the overall design of WiScape including related validation. In Section 4 we demonstrate some uses of data collected by WiScape, and finally discuss related work and present our conclusions in Sections 5 and 6 respectively.

2. PRELIMINARIES

Our measurement setup consists of a measurement coordinator running on a desktop in our university laboratory, with well provisioned connectivity to the Internet, that periodically requests and collects measurements from different client devices (based on Windows and Linux platforms). In our measurements, we have gathered data from three different cellular networks with nation-wide footprints, referred to as NetA , NetB , and NetC [1]. The data collection process has been ongoing in multiple stages for more than one year now (Table 1) and different clients in our measurement setup had different capabilities and characteristics as discussed next.

Data collection process: While we have collected measurement data for both uplink and downlink, in this paper, we focus on the downlink direction. This is motivated by the observation that most of data traffic is downlink. Our data collection has been done using multiple platforms, some of which are mounted on vehicles (public transit buses in Madison, intercity buses, as well as nodes mounted on personal vehicles), while others are static.

Wide-area: The spatially biggest datasets are labeled *Standalone* and *WiRover* . The *Standalone* dataset was collected using up to five public transit buses in Madison, covering an approximate area of 155 sq. kilometer in this city. These public transit buses typically run from 6am to midnight and each particular bus gets randomly assigned to different routes each day. Even in a single month, this set of buses is able to cover a significant fraction of Madison and its neighboring cities. The *WiRover* data collection process is the newer incarnation of the *Standalone* process, in which all of these bus-mounted nodes now are equipped with two network interfaces (NetB and NetC), and provide free WiFi service to bus passengers using the multi-network setup [13]. In addition to the public transit buses of Madison, we also placed additional nodes on two intercity buses between Madison and Chicago, a distance of more than 240 kilometer. Over time, these buses generated multiple measurement values for each location along this path stretch. We did not evaluate if any bias was introduced by the periodic nature of bus routes on the collected data.

Spot: The vehicular setup cannot provide us with long running contiguous measurements from a specific location. To study cellular network performance over a longer timescale, we selected some indoor locations to continuously collect data for up to 5 months. These included multiple locations in Madison, WI, and Princeton and New Brunswick, NJ. We describe our criteria for selecting the specific locations in Section 3.1. These datasets provide a more detailed and fine-grained view than is possible using with the vehicular collection methods of our *Wide-area* data. We apply these datasets to understand network performance over time for a given static location as will be demonstrated in Section 3.2.1.

Region: This consists of multiple datasets: *Proximate-WI*, *Proximate-NJ*, and *Short segment*. The two *Proximate* datasets were collected in neighborhoods close to the previously selected *Spot* locations. All three datasets consist of targeted measurement data to understand the feasibility of

[1]Since our goal for this paper currently is to explore a measurement framework, and *not* to answer which of these networks perform best or worst in different locations, we did not find it useful to reveal the identities of these nation-wide cellular providers.

Networks	NetA	GSM HSPA [11], Uplink ($\leq$1.2Mbps), Downlink ($\leq$ 7.2Mbps)
	NetB	CDMA2000 1xEV-DO Rev.A [12], Uplink ($\leq$ 1.8Mbps), Downlink ($\leq$ 3.1Mbps)
	NetC	CDMA2000 1xEV-DO Rev.A [12], Uplink ($\leq$ 1.8Mbps), Downlink ($\leq$ 3.1Mbps)
Hardware	Server	3 Desktops with well provisioned wired Internet connection
	Client	3 Laptops with 3 cellular data cards & GPS
Measurement params		Transport protocol (TCP/UDP), Transmission duration (10sec$\sim$5min)
		Inter packet delay (1msec$\sim$100msec, adaptively varies base on available capacity)
		Download size (200 and 1200Bytes for UDP, 100Bytes$\sim$2048Bytes for TCP)
Params logged		Packet sequence number, Receive timestamp, GPS coordinates

Table 1: Measurement setup details.

Group	Name	Span	Months	Nets	Location
Spot	*Static-WI*	5 locations	5	A, B, C	Madison, WI
	Static-NJ	2 locations	1	B, C	New Brunswick, Princeton, NJ
Region	*Proximate-WI*	Vicinity of the static locations	5	A, B, C	Madison, WI
	Proximate-NJ	Vicinity of the static locations	1	B, C	New Brunswick, Princeton, NJ
	Short segment	20 km road stretch	3	A, B, C	Madison, WI
Wide-area	*WiRover*	155 sq.km. city-wide area and a 240 kilometer road stretch	6	B, C	Madison, WI and Madison to Chicago
	Standalone	155 sq.km. city-wide area	11	B	Madison, WI

Table 2: Different data sets and details of locations. All measurements used TCP and UDP flows, except *Standalone* which used ICMP pings instead of UDP flows.

composing infrequently collected measurement samples from multiple (and potentially diverse) sources for estimating network performance, as will be seen in Section 3.3. These measurements were collected using client devices placed inside personal automobiles and regularly driven over fixed routes.

All of our measurements reported in this paper were collected using laptops or single-board computers equipped with different models of cellular modems (some were USB-based and others were PCMCIA).

Measurements collected: The *Spot* measurements and *Region* measurements collected a specific set of performance metric over three cellular networks, including TCP and UDP throughput, UDP packet loss rate, application level jitter measured in terms of Instantaneous Packet Delay Variation (IPDV) [14], application level RTT, and ICMP-level RTT (NetB only).

Throughput measurements were not conducted while using the *WiRover* system, as they would had affected the network performance experienced by the clients of the WiRover system. Hence, we only collect latency measurements using UDP pings, roughly 12 pings a minute. Details regarding measurement settings for each dataset are summarized in Table 2 and Table 1.

Effect of vehicular mobility on measurements: In our effort to collect measurements from a vast region over sustained durations, we were forced to utilize vehicles traveling at varying speeds. To understand the effects of the vehicular speeds on our data we analyzed the distribution of RTT latency (UDP ping test) as a function of vehicular speed for the zones in our *WiRover* dataset in Figure 2(a).

As can be seen from the plot, there was very limited correlation (correlation coefficient mostly close to zero) between the latency and the vehicle speed. We also plot the CDF of the correlation coefficients which were measured from each zone in Madison and on the path from Madison to Chicago in Figure 2(b). The plot shows that 95% of zones had little correlation (0.16) between the speed of vehicle and latencies observed, for typical vehicle speeds ranging from 0 km/h to 120 km/h. The absence of a correlation between the speeds at which these measurements were collected assures us that our datasets are representative of cellular network performance, which are independent of (typical) vehicle speeds.

3. DESIGN OF WISCAPE FRAMEWORK

In this section we describe the design of WiScape. Figure 3 summarizes the flow of this section. First, we analyze our *Wide-area* datasets to characterize the performance of cellular networks over a large spatial region to determine if data is aggregatable in space. In Section 3.1 we use these datasets to determine the appropriate size of zones for our measurement framework. In Section 3.2 we use our *Spot* and *Region* datasets comprising of measurements collected at finer time scales to analyze the performance variations of the three cellular networks at fine-grained and coarse-grained time scales at multiple locations. In Section 3.3.1 we determine the number of measurement samples necessary to determine the bandwidth at a zone with certain degree of accuracy. Then in Section 3.2 we determine the frequency with which the measurements should be repeated. Finally, in Section 3.3 we analyze our *Region* dataset to ascertain the feasibility of carrying out client-sourced, coarse grained performance estimation for cellular networks, involving multiple clients.

3.1 Aggregation in space (zones)

As it is not feasible to blanket monitor a entire wide-area wireless network we must aggregate data into spatial zones. We desire zone sizes which are small enough to ensure similar performance at all locations inside the zone but big enough to ensure enough measurement samples can be collected for each zone to properly characterize the network's performance. For this purpose we analyze the variation of TCP bandwidth measurements for NetB collected in *Standalone* dataset across city locations by dividing them into circular zones of radius varying from 50 to 750 meters in steps of 100 meters. We have not experimented with other shapes of zones.

In Figure 4 we plot the CDF of relative standard deviation (standard deviation of samples/mean of samples) for all zones, for which we have at least 200 samples per week over the duration of the measurement study. The left most

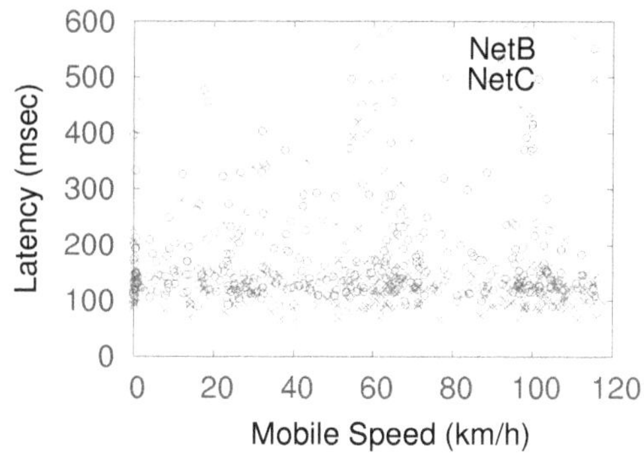

(a) *WiRover: Vehicle Speed (vs) Network latency*

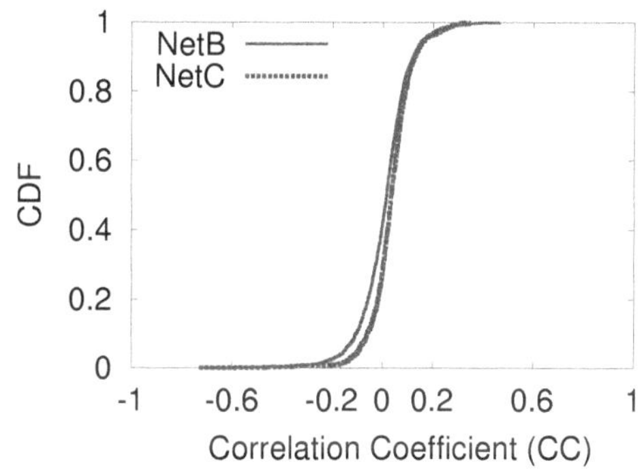

(b) *WiRover: CDF of Correlation Coefficient*

Figure 2: Latency is weakly correlated with typical vehicular speeds. In Figure 2(a), the latencies are mostly around 120 msec, with no observable trend with increasing speeds. In Figure 2(b), the CDF of correlation coefficient between latency and vehicular speed is less than 0.16 in 95% of zones.

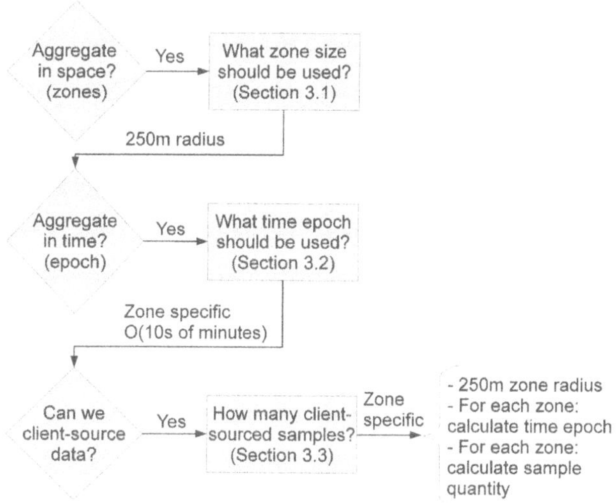

Figure 3: The flow of text in Section 3, describing the design choices made in WiScape.

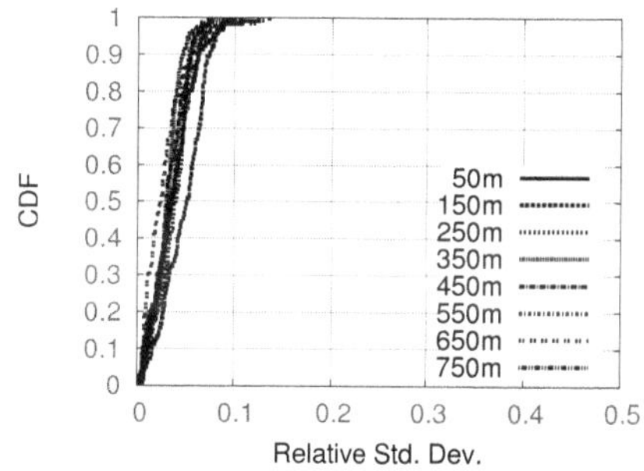

Figure 4: CDF of relative standard deviation of TCP throughput across a cross-section of the city with NetB as a function of increasing zone radius, only zones with more than 200 data-points have been considered.

curve corresponds to zone size of 50 meters while the right most curve corresponds to zone size of 750 meters. Furthermore, the relative standard deviation of for 80% of the zones is around 2.5% for zones with radius of 50 meters and 7% for zones with radius of 750 meters[2]. The increase can be explained by the change in terrain conditions across bigger zones. As can be seen from the plot, despite increasing zone radius the relative standard deviation tends to vary only slightly. We pick a zone radius of 250 meters as 80% of the zones with 250 meter radius have relative standard deviation less than 4% and 97% of zones have a relative standard deviation of 8% or lower. The low relative standard deviation, implies that the characteristics of locations inside the zone are mostly similar.

[2]In Figure 1, some zones have a relative standard deviation greater than 0.3 (mean = 1080 Kbps, dev = 350 Kbs). These zones in Figure 1 correspond to regions with very few samples (less than 200 hundred samples) and hence are not considered while plotting Figure 4.

We find that the TCP throughput does not vary significantly for the cellular network. Specifically, we note that 80% of zones have a relative standard deviation between 2% and 8% regardless of zone size. Moreover, less than 2% of the zones have a standard deviation of 15% or higher. Based on the above observation we selected *representative* zones with overall performance variability for NetB that was between 2% and 8% and zones with TCP throughput variability of the other two networks that was less than 15%. These *representative* zones are used for our *Spot* data collection, as seen in Section 3.2.

We also examined data from WiFi-based networks as reported by others (GoogleWiFi [15], RoofNet [16] and us (MadCity Broadband [17]) in prior work on how throughput measurements for cellular networks might compare to that of such WiFi-based networks. Such prior work report high and sudden variations in achievable throughputs in the WiFi networks, often due to the use of unlicensed spectrum, random access nature, and the characteristic of the spectrum itself. This is contrast to the more coordinated access methods and the licensed nature of the cellular spectrum that provides some performance stability across epochs as defined above. Hence, epochs in WiFi system are likely more difficult to define than compared to these cellular systems. The low degree of variability in cellular performance is the motivation for exploring the feasibility of estimating cellular data network performance using a small number of measurements.

A closer look: To understand the stability of measurements within individual zones, we use the *Static* and *Proximate* datasets. As noted in Section 2, data for our *Proximate* dataset was collected by driving around in a car within a 250 meter radius from corresponding *Static* dataset locations. The *Proximate* dataset, provides us with network performance measurements from multiple locations in close vicinity of the locations in *Static*. The measurements in *Proximate* dataset are, thus, representative of the kind of measurements we can expect to gather for a given zone from a set of clients in a real deployment of WiScape system. The data for *Proximate* dataset was collected for each zone over a span of 5 months in Madison and 1 month in New Brunswick. In the rest of this section, we present results for a single zone from Madison and one in New Brunswick and omit the results for the remaining five static locations. We examine how the average throughput measured from *Static* subset relates to the throughput measurements from the corresponding *Proximate* measurements.

We present the average and standard deviation for the *Static* and corresponding *Proximate* measurements in Table 3. From the table we note that the client sourced measurements form a reasonable approximation of the expected performance at a given location.

We observe that the average UDP throughput of NetB-WI for the ground truth and the client sourced UDP traces are 876 Kbps and 855 Kbps respectively, where the percentage of error is less than 1%. The observation holds true even in case of representative zones from New Brunswick which has higher degree of performance variation compared to zones in Madison.

The jitter values reported in the *Proximate* dataset are also close to 7 msec for NetA-WI which matches the corresponding *Static* dataset jitter value shown in Table 3. Similarly, the jitter for NetB-WI and NetC-WI are around 3 msec in the *Proximate* dataset which again matches the *Static* jitter value of the two networks at the location, as shown in Table 3. We also have noted the same behavior for NetB-NJ and NetC-NJ whose jitter values are 2.8 msec and 1.6 msec respectively. From the above results we find that measurements collected across multiple locations within a zone are close to each other.

Summary: We choose a radius of 250 meters for zones as 97% of such zones in Madison have low (8%) relative standard deviation for TCP throughput for NetB .

3.2 Aggregating in time (zone-specific epochs)

We analyze data from *Spot* dataset to understand the performance of the three cellular networks over different granularities of time. As noted in Table 2, the *Spot* data was collected at five distinct locations in Madison and two locations in New Jersey, for all three networks, to characterize the performance of the cellular networks at a fine granularity. In particular we study coarse (30 minutes) and fine (10 seconds) time scale variations of different performance parameters such as throughput, loss rate etc. and in Section 3.2.2 we explain the mechanism for calculating the epoch duration for the monitored zones.

3.2.1 Performance at different time granularities

We look at *Spot* data measurements to characterize the performance variability of cellular networks. We present data from two representative locations, one in Madison and another in New Brunswick where the relative standard deviation (standard deviation/average) of any of the parameters (TCP and UDP throughput, Jitter, Loss rate) was less than 0.15, for the entire monitored duration. The highest relative standard deviation of 0.15 was observed for TCP throughput at both locations. We observed similar properties for the other four measured locations in Wisconsin and one other location in New Jersey, but do not present them in this paper for the sake of brevity.

Coarse time scale: We present the average throughput, jitter, and error rates, averaged in 30 minute bins collected in Madison and New Brunswick in Figure 5(a,b,c,d) and 5(e,f,g,h) respectively. As can be seen from Figure 5, for the selected location in Madison, the NetA network on an average offers throughput benefit greater than 50% for both TCP and UDP over the worst performing network. We also find that the variance in throughput across all three networks over the entire duration is less than 0.15 of their long term average. Moreover, all three networks have a packet loss rate less than 1% with a very low variation (Figure 5(d)). We find from Figure 5(c) that the jitter is around 3 msec for NetB and NetC networks while it is around 7 msec for the NetA network.

For the location in New Brunswick, looking at Figure 5(e,f), we find that the TCP and UDP throughput for NetB and NetC has higher variability than the location in Madison. Although the overall variation is still lower than 0.15. Akin to the location in Madison, both networks have low jitter (less than 3 msec) and packet loss (less than 1%).

Fine time scale: In Table 4, we present the standard deviation for throughput, jitter, and loss rate calculated for 10 seconds bins and 30 minute bins for all three networks for both locations, to compare and contrast the network characteristics at fine time scales with coarse time scales.As can be seen from the table, the standard deviations over coarse and fine timescales vary significantly. For example, at the location in Madison, the standard deviation of TCP throughput is 211 Kbps at coarse timescales, whereas it is around 377 Kbps at finer timescales, a difference of 159 (377-211) Kbps. Similar observations can be drawn for other metrics across all the networks. This difference in standard deviation is expected as 30 minutes is a large duration of time which can hide large fluctuations in performance. We can make similar observation for the measurements collected at the location in New Brunswick. The high degree of variation at short time scales effectively rules out the use of small and infrequent measurements to estimate performance.

Finally, given the relatively low overall jitter (less than 10 msec) and no losses in the networks, we desist from presenting further jitter and loss performance results for the sake of brevity.

3.2.2 Calculating zone specific epochs

To determine the zone specific epoch duration, we need to determine the granularity of time over which a given met-

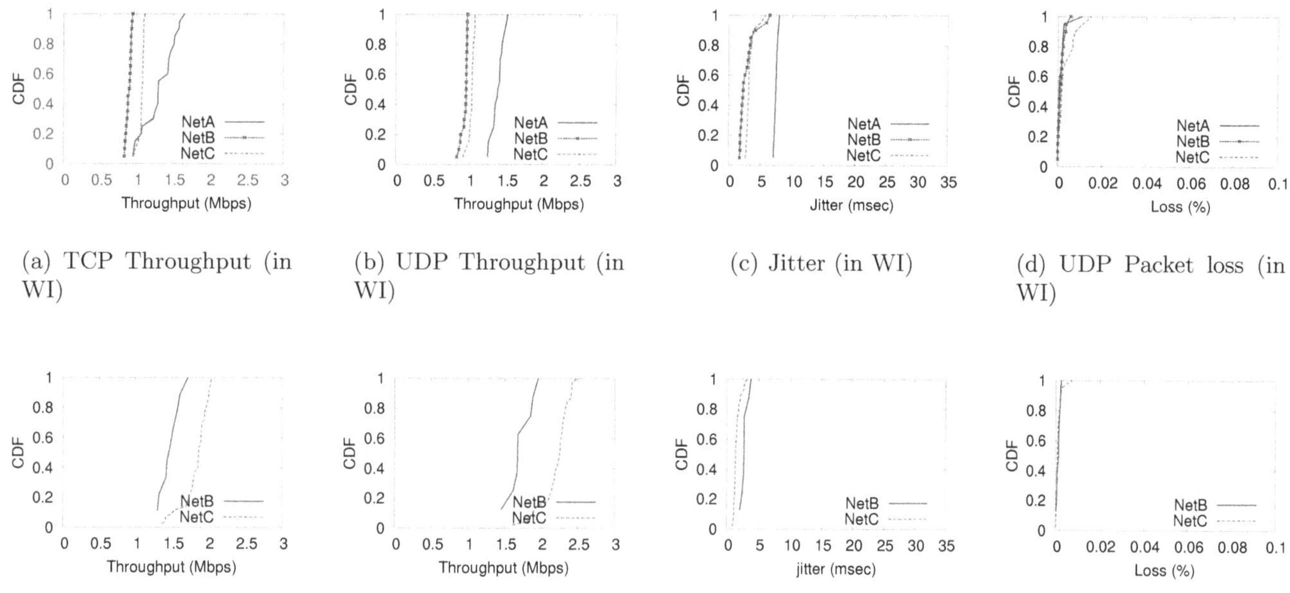

(a) TCP Throughput (in WI) (b) UDP Throughput (in WI) (c) Jitter (in WI) (d) UDP Packet loss (in WI)

(e) TCP Throughput (in NJ) (f) UDP Throughput (in NJ) (g) Jitter (in NJ) (h) UDP Packet loss (in NJ)

Figure 5: CDF of long term (30 min) average data. Plots (a)-(d) correspond to a location in Madison and (e)-(f) correspond to a location in New Brunswick. The variation in throughput across all the networks at two locations is below 15%. Location in New Brunswick shows higher variance in throughput. The average and variation of both jitter and loss are low across all locations.

	NetA-WI		NetB-WI		NetC-WI		NetB-NJ		NetC-NJ	
	Static	Proximate	Static	Proximate	Static	Proximate	Static	Proximate	Static	Proximate
TCP (Kbps)	1242 (196)	1266 (180)	845 (63)	827 (82)	1067 (61)	1005 (78)	1494 (222)	1549 (196)	1850 (201)	1869 (159)
UDP (Kbps)	1241 (101)	1257 (135)	867 (67)	855 (89)	1017 (62)	962 (72)	1690 (290)	1748 (248)	2204 (221)	2245 (166)
Jitter (msec)	7.4 (0.4)	8.5 (0.6)	3 (1.6)	5.4 (1.6)	3.4 (1.2)	5.6 (2.4)	2.8 (1.5)	2.8 (0.9)	1.6 (0.9)	1.5 (0.6)
Loss (%)	∼0	∼0	∼0	∼0	∼0	∼0	∼0	∼0	∼0	∼0

Table 3: Table showing the closeness average and standard deviation (in parentheses) of different nearby locations (*Proximate* dataset) from the same zones for each network.

ric is stable. A metric should be estimated for each epoch independently. We use the Allan deviation measure [18] to determine the epoch for which the metric is stable. The Allan deviation is used to calculate the frequency stability of a variable and is defined as the square root of the Allan variance. Allan variance is then defined as the variance between two measurement values formed by the average of the squared differences between successive values of a regularly measured quantity. The sampling period of the measurement also forms a parameter which determines the time granularity at which the Allan deviation is measured. The difference from standard deviation arises from the usage of immediate measurement values to calculate the difference terms, instead, of using the long term mean.

It is mathematically expressed as,

$$\sigma_y(\tau_0) = \sqrt{\frac{\sum_{i=1}^{N-1}(T_{i+1}-T_i)^2}{2(N-1)}}$$

Where, T_i are the averaged measurement values collected at time instance i and N is the total number of available measurement values. A low Allan deviation implies that the current values do not differ much from the previous values. In contrast, large Allan deviation would signify that the coherence of the measured metric is changing.

We present the Allan deviation of UDP throughput at the two zones for the NetB network using the *Proximate* dataset in Figure 6 as an example. In the figure, the x-axis of the plot represents the periodic burst duration while the y-axis represents the corresponding Allan deviation. We find that, for the zone in Madison, Allan deviation becomes the lowest around a time duration of about 75 minutes. This value is higher (mostly greater than 0.5) at both smaller and larger values. For the zone in New Brunswick we find that Allan deviation is lowest around 15 minutes. We pick this minimum value of the Allan deviation is the epoch duration for the corresponding zone. Epochs for other metrics can similarly be determined using the above method.

In WiScape, we collect measurements from clients to get stable estimates in each epoch for a zone, re-starting this process as we move from one epoch to the next. Hence, for the representative zone from Madison, the measurement

	NetA-WI		NetB-WI		NetC-WI		NetB-NJ		NetC-NJ	
	Long (30m)	Short (10s)	Long (30m)	Short (10s)	Long (30m)	Short (10s)	Long (30m)	Short (10s)	Long (30m)	Short (10s)
TCP (Kbps)	211	370	33	102	36	96	126	408	167	414
UDP (Kbps)	77	241	39	82	38	94	153	429	182	365
Jitter (msec)	0.2	0.7	1.3	2.1	0.7	1.6	0.5	1.6	0.5	1.0
Loss (%)	~0	~0	~0	~0	~0	~0	~0	~0	~0	~0

Table 4: Table showing the standard deviation of long term (30 min) and short term (10 sec) data for each network. The standard deviation of short term data is significantly higher than that of long term data.

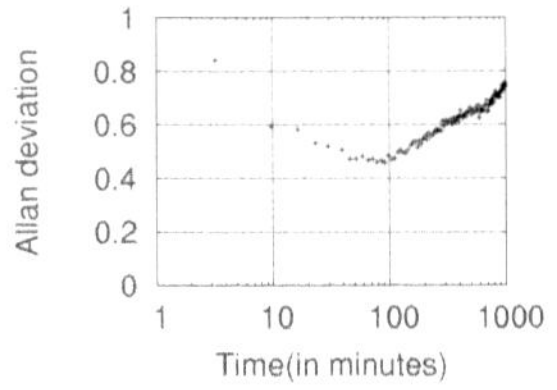

(a) Location in WI

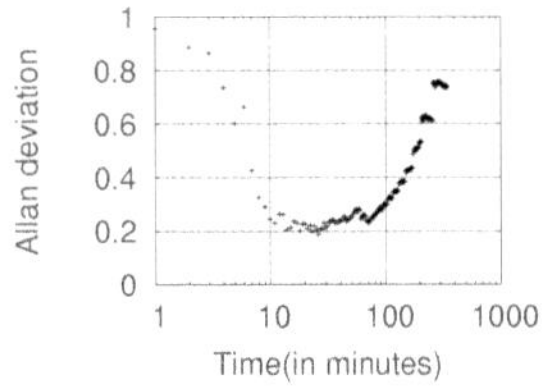

(b) Location in NJ

Figure 6: Allan deviation for UDP throughput measurements at a given zone for NetB using *Proximate subset* traces. For the measured data, the Allan deviation is lowest around 75 minutes, which corresponds to the epoch of the zone.

process repeats every 75 minutes, while for the zone in New Brunswick it repeats every 15 minutes.

Summary: When aggregated at finer time scales (tens of seconds), the network metrics vary significantly more, than when aggregated at a coarser time scale (tens of minutes). Hence, we use the minimum value of the Allan deviation in each zone to determine the epoch of that zone. This value is estimated regularly for each zone.

3.3 Composability of client sourced measurements

We use client sourcing to collect measurements from different client devices, leading to estimation of network properties for each epoch in each zone. Composability of measurements collected from diverse sources would be feasible only when they are similar (to a certain) extent to one another. In our work, we have only used laptop or single-board computer (SBC) based hardware, each equipped with different cellular modems. This section shows that composability across this class of clients is, indeed, possible. However, composability of measurements from a mobile phone and a laptop equipped with a USB modem may not always work well. This is because a mobile phone, among its other characteristics, has a more constrained radio front-end and antenna system, than a USB modem. Potentially data collected from such devices with different capabilities need to go through a normalization or scaling process. We have not addressed such types of composition in this work. Instead we suggest that we group devices into broad categories — mobile phones, laptops or SBCs with USB or PCMCIA modems, etc., and perform client-assisted monitoring for each individual category separately. Given our experimentation was performed using laptops and SBCs equipped with cellular modems (as this was the platform used in our wide-area data collection efforts for various practical and logistical reasons), we demonstrate that composability within its category. Future work would require us to re-create some of these results with the mobile phone category as well as as examining techniques for normalization across categories, a significant effort unto itself.

To demonstrate the closeness of client sourced samples to stationary data, we evaluate a) if the probability distribution of the measurements collected at the *same location* (same GPS coordinates) by *different clients* at *different times* within the time epoch are statistically similar to the overall long-term distribution at that location and b) if the probability distribution of the measurement samples collected by *different clients* at *different locations* (within a bounded distance) during the *same time* epoch are statistically similar to the overall long-term distribution at that location. While (a) measures the temporal variability, (b) measures the spatial variability of the measurement samples inside a zone.

We measure the similarity of two probability distribution functions, using the symmetric Normalized Kullback-Leibler Divergence (NKLD) between the data from the *Static* dataset and the *Proximate* dataset for a given location. The symmetric NKLD is a measure of the dissimilarity between two distributions.

The Kullback Liebler divergence (KLD) quantifies the relative entropy between two probability distributions which are generated from a common event. The KLD is zero for two identical probability distributions. To rectify the asymmetric nature of the metric we use a symmetric and normalized version of the metric as used in [19]. The normalized symmetric Kullback Leibler metric,

$$NKLD(p(x), q(x)) = \frac{1}{2}\left(\frac{D(p(x)||q(x))}{H(p(x))} + \frac{D(q(x)||p(x))}{H(q(x))}\right)$$

where, $p(x)$ and $q(x)$ are the two probability distributions based on a common set χ.
$H(p(x)) = \sum_{x\in\chi} p(x)log(1/p(x))$ is the entropy of the random variable x, with probability distribution $p(x)$, and,

$$D(p(x)||q(x)) = \sum_{x\in\chi} p(x)|log\frac{p(x)}{q(x)}|$$

is the Kullback-Leibler divergence. A small value of NKLD would signify that the two distributions are "close". For our experiments, we take an NKLD value of 0.1 and lower to signify that the distribution of measurements are similar. We plot the KLD distributions for UDP throughput for the NetB network in Figure 7.

Temporal variability of samples: We randomly select two measurement traces of two clients of progressively in-

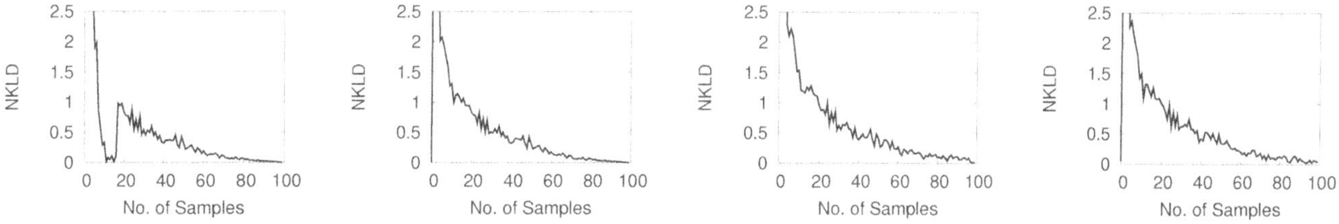

(a) NKLD for samples collected at same location (GPS co-ordinates) at different times in WI.

(b) NKLD for samples collected at different locations (within a zone) at the same time in WI.

(c) NKLD for samples collected at same location (GPS co-ordinates) at different times in NJ.

(d) NKLD for samples collected at different locations (within a zone) at the same time in NJ.

Figure 7: Plot of NKLD for UDP throughput (a) and (c) shows that samples collected at temporally different instances at same location are highly similar, (b) and (d) shows data collected at spatially different locations which are in the same zone are highly similar. Plots (a) and (b) corresponds to location in Madison, Wisconsin, while (c) and (d) corresponds to location in New Brunswick, New Jersey.

creasing time durations with the same GPS coordinates and calculate the divergence of this distribution with the overall distribution consisting of all measurements, this process is repeated across 100 iterations and the average of the NKLD is calculated. We plot the results in Figure 7(a) and Figure 7(c). We find that for the location in Madison, by the time we have accumulated 50 to 60 samples, the NKLD goes down to a 0.1 signifying that the two distributions are similar to each other. For the location in New Brunswick, we find that the NKLD goes below 0.1 once we have accumulated 80 to 90 samples. Furthermore, the two distributions become similar once we have gathered around 120 samples.

We need higher number of samples in New Brunswick, due to the greater degree of variation of its performance compared to the network in Madison.

Spatial variability of samples: We randomly select locations which are 50-250 meters apart from each other and simultaneously start UDP downloads using two clients at both locations for a duration of 2 minutes. The test is repeated at 10 different locations. We plot the divergence of the distribution of throughput values collected from two locations in Figure 7(b) for Madison and Figure 7(d) for New Brunswick. We find that with 80 and 100 measurements in Madison and New Brunswick respectively the NKLD is less than 0.1. This signifies that by the time we have accumulated around 100 samples at two locations the distribution of such samples becomes similar to one another in both the representative locations.

Based on above results, we conclude that client sourced measurements can be used as a estimator of the ground truth for a zone.

3.3.1 Example: client sourced throughput estimation

We intend to determine the minimal amount of measurements necessary to estimate the network's performance at a given location with a certain degree of accuracy. In this section, we use throughput estimation as an example. We note that similar methods can be used for client-sourced estimation of other metrics such as jitter, loss and latencies etc..

A lot of research has focused on estimating the available network bandwidth for wired as well as WiFi based networks [20, 21]. In contrast, few studies have concentrated on characterizing the available bandwidth for the cellular networks. Availability of an accurate and efficient estimation algorithm is vital for client-assisted monitoring.

Network-Location	UDP	TCP
NetA-WI	90	60
NetB-WI	60	40
NetC-WI	40	40
NetB-NJ	120	120
NetC-NJ	70	50

Table 5: Table showing the number of back-to-back measurement packets to be sent to estimate TCP/UDP throughput within an accuracy of 97% of the expected value.

We experimented with two such bandwidth measurement tools: Pathload and WBest [20, 21]. To estimate the accuracy of these tools we take the average of UDP throughput measured over 100 seconds for 10 iterations as the *ground truth* at that location. We then define relative error as $E = \frac{X - G_{UDP}}{G_{UDP}} \times 100\%$, where X is the result from available bandwidth measurement tools (i.e., Pathload or WBest) and G_{UDP} is the ground truth UDP throughput. In our evaluations we found that neither of the two tools give an accurate approximation. WBest consistently under-estimates the actual bandwidth by up to 70% while Pathload under-estimates up to 40%. Similar benchmarking results are also reported in [22]. Hence, we carry out simple UDP downloads over a duration of time to measure the network performance. In the rest of this section, we determine how many such samples should be sent to fairly accurately (~97%) estimate the network throughput at a specific location. We intend to diagnose the reason behind the estimation inaccuracies for the two bandwidth measurement tools as part of our future work.

How many packets necessary? We revisit our TCP and UDP throughput measurements from our *Proximate* datasets to determine the minimum number of packets to be collected for attaining a maximum accuracy in estimating the expected performance of a zone.

We select a given number of client collected packets and calculate their average. We then compare it with the ground truth throughput at that instant (calculated as mentioned above). We repeat this process 100 times for a given packet size. We present the number of packets necessary to attain an accuracy of 97% in Table 5. We find that for the

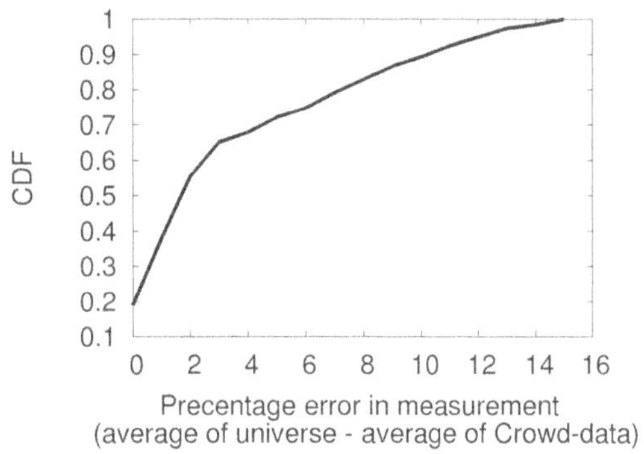

Figure 8: Error of WiScape measurements in comparison to our extensive measurements collected.

zone in Madison, we need 90 TCP packet measurements to obtain an accuracy within 97% of the expected measurement for NetA . From the same table, we can estimate the expected TCP throughput which is within 97% of the expected throughput by collecting as many as 40 back-to-back measurement packets for NetC for both TCP and UDP. The number of packets are marginally higher for NetA as compared to NetB and NetC as the network performance varies more for NetA clients (Figure 5, Table 4).

For the zone in New Brunswick, we find that we need 120 packets for estimating the TCP and UDP performance of NetB network. Whereas, for the NetC network we need to send only 70 UDP and 50 TCP packets back-to-back for a estimation accuracy of 97%. With an expected cellular data-rate in hundreds of Kbps, a client can thus, finish a measurement in less than a second.

Summary: *We validate that network performance estimation using a small number of measurements collected by different clients inside a zone is indeed feasible.* Specifically, we find that for the monitored zone, the distribution of the observed metric becomes almost similar to that of any other client present in the same zone (or from the same client at an earlier time epoch) we have accumulated more than 80 packets.

3.4 Putting it all together

We envision a simple user agent in each client device, e.g., as part of the software in the mobile phones or bundled with drivers of cellular NICs. A measurement coordinator, deployed by the operator or by third-party users, will manage the entire measurement process. Each cellular device periodically reports its coarse-grained zone (based on associated cellular tower) to the measurement coordinator[3]. Based on this zone information, our measurement coordinator periodically provides each mobile device with a measurement task list.

When a mobile device performs a task, it is required to collect more precise zone information at which the task is initiated as well as completed. If the mobile phone has a built-in GPS receiver, it is possible for it to obtain zone information quite easily. However, alternate techniques to obtain zone information include triangulation and fingerprinting based techniques, using the cellular, WiFi, or Bluetooth interfaces [23, 24, 25].

[3]Current cellular systems already collect such zone information from all mobile devices in order to correctly and quickly route calls and traffic to them.

The rate of refreshing the measurements for each zone would depend on the coherence period of that zone as determined by looking at the Allan deviation.

For a given zone, once in every coherence time-period, the measurement coordinator will provide a measurement task to each active mobile client with a probability, chosen such that the number of measurement samples collected over each iteration is sufficient for estimating accurate statistics, as determined by the NKLD algorithm. Once the selected clients report their measurements, the server checks if the measured statistic has changed substantially from its previous update (say by more than twice the standard deviation). In such a situation the server would update its record for the zone with the new value.

Validation: To analyze the accuracy of our WiScape framework, we partitioned our *Standalone* dataset which consists of around 400 zones with 200 or more samples, into two subsets (*Client sourced data* and *Ground truth*). For each zone, we assume that the entire *Ground truth* set provides our expected value (consisting of up to 125,000 packets for various zones). Figure 8 shows the CDF of error in estimation of TCP throughput for the WiScape data from the *Client sourced* dataset and the *Ground truth* data. As can be seen from the plot, WiScape data has less than 4% error in estimating the TCP throughput for more than 70% of the zones. The maximum error in performance measurements is around 15%, which indicates that WiScape is able to determine the necessary measurement parameters for each zone and provide a fairly accurate performance estimate.

Discussion: We note that there is an important trade off between the volume of measurements collected, the ensuing accuracy, and the energy and monetary costs incurred. Our design in WiScape defines one specific design choice in this multi-dimensional space. Many other alternatives are certainly possible and would make for interesting exploration in the future.

4. APPLICATIONS OF WISCAPE

In Section 4.1 we demonstrate how client-assisted monitoring of networks can help discover zones with highly variable network performance. Variability in network performance can be an indicator of possible network problems. Hence, client-assisted monitoring can help network operators short-list zones which need further detailed diagnosis. Finally, in Section 4.2 we characterize the potential performance enhancement for two applications when using coarse grained measurements. Both applications use more than one cellular network.

4.1 Helping operators

To ensure that the network performance at the deployed regions is above a certain quality, the cellular service providers carry out periodic drive-by tests to validate the performance of their network. This involves using a car equipped with network measurement equipment, and then carrying out network performance tests at specific locations. However, such tests are labor intensive and hence not scalable for wide area wireless networks. Client-assisted monitoring can help network operators in this regards by pin-pointing zones with performance characteristics significantly different than neighboring zones.

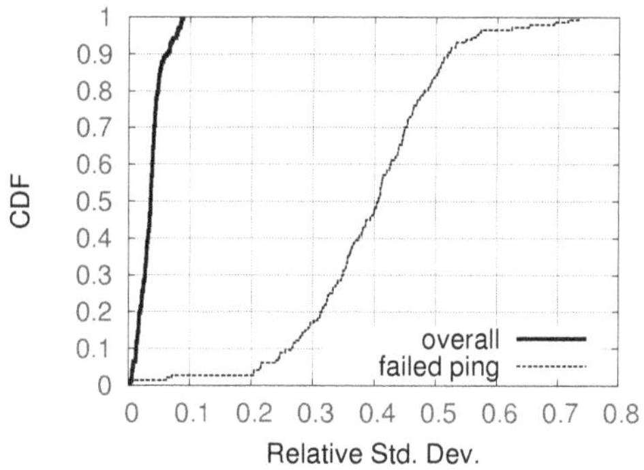

Figure 9: CDF of Relative standard deviation (standard deviation/average) of TCP throughput for all zones (with 250 meter radius) and those with more than 20 days with at least one ping failure.

Identifying locations with variable performance

Let us assume the network operator intends to determine potential locations with highly variable throughput (say relative standard deviation greater than 20%). This information would be difficult to deduce from a relatively low number of client sourced measurements because of the fact that the accuracy of client sourcing depends on low variability in network performance. We note that while small throughput tests conducted infrequently every tens of minutes might miss out on zones with highly variable performance, other infrequently calculated metrics may be used to detect such variability. To highlight such a metric, we revisit our *Standalone* dataset. As mentioned in Section 2, we present data for ICMP ping tests in our *Standalone* dataset. From this dataset, we first determine zones, with radius 250 meters, that have multiple ping test failures. In Figure 9 we present the CDF of relative standard deviation of all the zones with more than 200 measurements and those zones with at least one failed ping tests every day, for a period of 20 consecutive days or more. As can be seen from the plot, zones with 20 or more consecutive days with at least one ping failure have a very high variation in their relative deviation of TCP throughput. For example, 65% of the links have a relative deviation of the order of 40%. We also find that zones with back-to-back ping failures constitute 97% of the zones with relative standard deviation above 20%. This is in contrast with the majority of other zones which have less than 1% relative standard deviation.

Identifying locations for additional provisioning

Coarse grained estimates can also help network operators determine places where additional resources might be needed to satisfy periodic surge in demands. For example, Figure 10, shows the network latency of two cellular networks near a football stadium (80,000 seating capacity) during a football game. The shaded region in the plot represents the scheduled time of the football game. As can be seen from the plot, for the duration of the game the average ping latencies go up from 113msec to 418msec, an increase of the order of 3.7X for NetB. As the duration is in order of 100s of minutes, infrequent periodic monitoring can detect the above event and help operators take corrective measures.

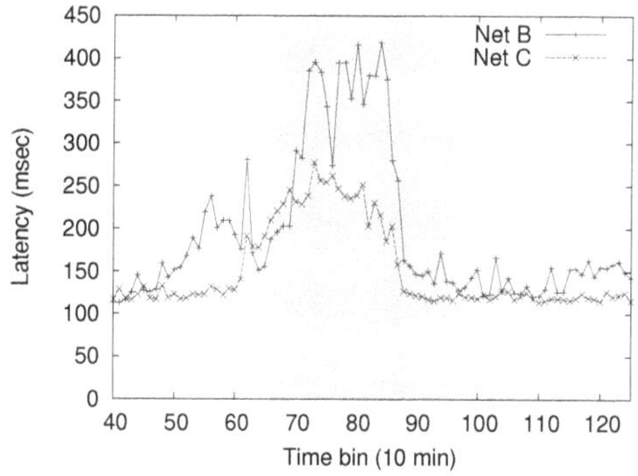

Figure 10: Network latency (averaged over 10 minutes) during a football game. The scheduled time of the game is covered by the shaded region.

4.2 Improving client performance

To show the potential benefits of a WiScape like system for clients, in Section 4.2.1 we show that for a large number of zones the performance of one cellular network is persistently better than other networks over large duration of time, and hence observable using infrequent measurements. In Section 4.2.2 we explain how such information can be utilized by clients with multiple cellular connections to choose the best network of operation for each zone.

4.2.1 Persistent network dominance

We intend to understand if the relative performance characteristics of different cellular networks are persistent over large periods of time (for each zone). For this purpose, we define *persistent network dominance* as follows: when the lower 5 percentile of the best network's metric is better than the upper 95 percentile of other networks in a given zone, we say the zone is *persistently dominated* by the best network. The fact that the lowest 5 percentile of performance of the dominant network is better than the 95 percentile of the other networks implies that the dominance is persistent over time and hence observable using infrequent measurements made by a WiScape like system. In Figure 11, we present the percentage of zones with a persistently dominant network, in terms of RTT latency collected from the *WiRover* dataset, as a function of the zone size. As we see, persistent network dominance is observed in 85% of the zones and across different zone sizes. The consistently better performance of one network at a given zone can be explained by observing that the network performance is dependent on the base-station location, technology, and traffic load on the base-station; a combination which would be expected to vary across different network operators.

We use measurement data from our *Short segment* dataset to further investigate the presence of persistent network dominance. The measurements were collected with our vehicle driving across this stretch of roadway regularly for a period of 5 months, at average speeds of 55 km/h. We show a part (10 km) of the road stretch in Figure 12. Each circle corresponds to a zone of 250 meters radius and the shade on the circle corresponds to the network which performs best in that zone.

We plot average TCP throughput performance of NetA, NetB, and NetC networks for each zone over entire experiment duration in Figure 13. In conformance with our observations of persistent dominance in terms of latencies, we

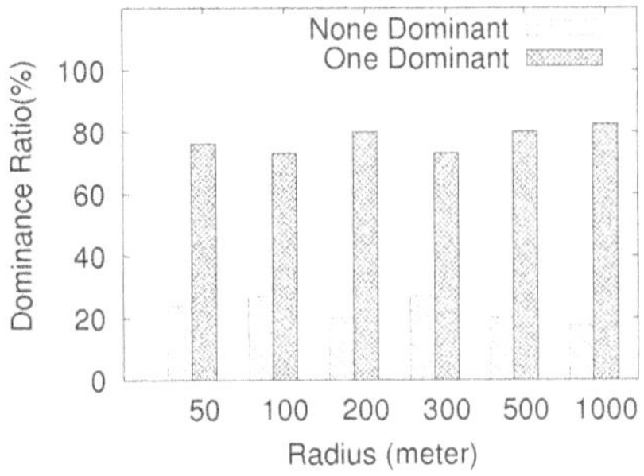

Figure 11: Most of the zones are persistently dominated in terms of network latency, by either NetB or NetC regardless of the zone size.

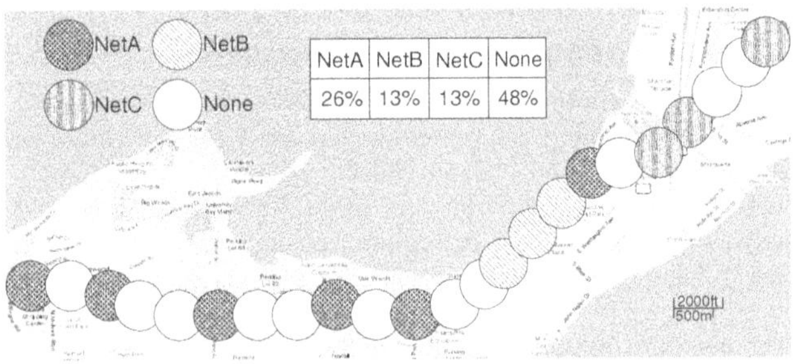

Figure 12: Map depicting the Short segment dataset and the dominant network for each zone. Over all zones we observe that 52% of zones have a dominant network.

find that for a significant number of zones a specific network offers better performance on an average than the other two networks. For example, at zone 20 (as marked in the x-axis) the performance difference between the best network gives 42% higher throughput than the next best network over the entire measurement set. Similarly, the performance at zone 4 of the best network is almost 30% higher than others. We also find that multiple zones exist where none of the networks give clear performance advantage for the entire set of measurements. We identify zones where the lower 5 percentile of the best performing network is better than the upper 95 percentile of other two networks. The inset table in Figure 12 shows the number of zones where one network dominates other networks. From the table we note that there are 52% of zones where one network gives better performance than other consistently over the measurement period. We color the zones in Figure 12 based on which network dominates it. A white color indicates a lack of a persistently dominant network.

4.2.2 *Application performance improvement*

We present two application scenarios which can benefit from approximate network quality estimates for a specific location. The first is a client equipped with a mobile phone that has two or more SIM cards and hence can connect to any *one* of two or more alternate cellular networks at a given point in time. We call this the *multi-sim* application. Such phones are cheaply available in the market today, e.g., Samsung Fizz [26] and Jinpeng S3288 [27], and are gaining in popularity in developing countries like India and China. In

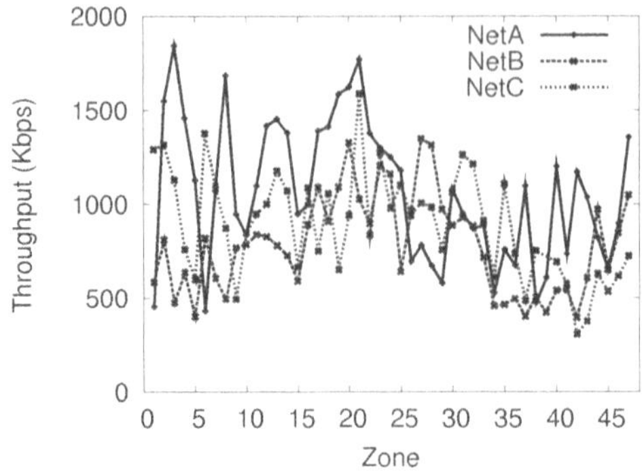

Figure 13: TCP performance on each zone across 20 km stretch of road for three monitored networks.

absence of any knowledge of which network gives the best performance at the current location, the clients with such phones would be forced either to select a network in a random fashion or to carry out measurements to ascertain the network quality for all the networks.

The second application that can benefit from location specific information is a MAR [4] — a multi-network Internet gateway mounted on a vehicle that can aggregate bandwidth from all networks that it simultaneously connects to. The scheduler in MAR stripes traffic flows to different network interfaces. While authors in [4] suggest using location specific network performance information to further optimize performance by intelligently mapping data requests to interfaces based on locality of operation, we highlight the benefits of such a scheme over a simple multi-interface striping algorithm where all currently active requests from different clients are mapped onto different cellular networks in a round robin fashion.

To illustrate the benefits of coarse throughput estimates for the above two applications, we consider the following experiment scenario. A client (either a MAR gateway or a Multi-sim phone) places back-to-back requests for a set of pages from the Internet while driving on a road stretch depicted in Figure 12. In our experiments, the client requested pages from a webserver hosting a pool of 1000 wep pages with sizes between 2.8 KBytes and 3.2 MBytes, generated using SURGE [28]. Akin to [4] we also experiment with popular Web sites by downloading wepages to a depth of 1 from their starting page. For our experiments we run the car on the same road-segment (Table 2) multiple times during the experiment. We compare performance between a system where data is requested in a round robin fashion on each network. The other system with a monitoring agent uses the GPS to determine the location of the vehicle and based on zone information selects the best network to minimize download latency.

Multi-sim Improvements: We present the results in terms of HTTP latency averaged over ten runs in Table 6. As can be seen from the Table 6, we can decrease the HTTP latency by 30% by selecting best performed interface at a given location. We show the HTTP latency for well known Web pages in Figure 14(a). As can be seen from the plot, our scheme gives the maximum improvement for amazon.com webpage (32% improvement) and minimum improvement for microsoft.com webpage (13% improvement).

MAR performance improvements: Here we compare the download latency for the two schemes. We measured

	Avg.(in sec)	Std.(in sec)
WiScape	87.66	8.33
NetA	124.26	14.90
NetB	158.55	33.69
NetC	145.46	14.89
MAR-WiScape	25.72	3.48
MAR-RR	36.8	6.44

Table 6: Average latency and standard deviation for downloading 1000 HTTP files. We can improve HTTP latency by 30% using Multi-sim-WiScape.

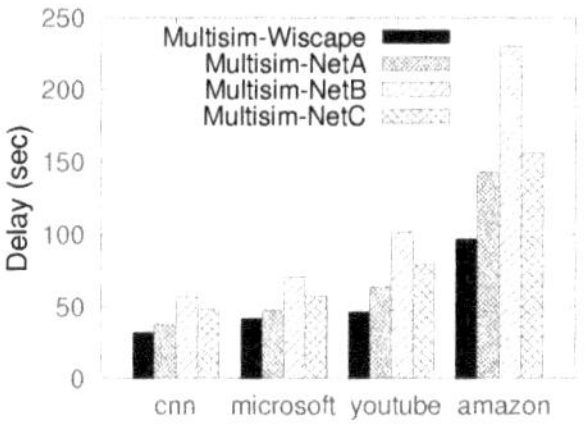

(a) Multi-sim improvement

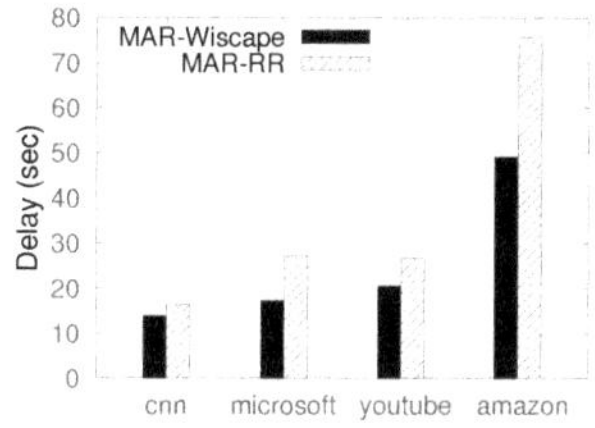

(b) MAR improvement

Figure 14: Multi-sim and MAR latency improvements with well known Web pages over round-robin (MAR).

the HTTP latency by running our car with a MAR client with 3 interfaces on a 2.4 Km segment of road (from zone 10 to 15 from Figure 13). We measure the performance of MAR system using network performance information and while mapping client requests to interfaces in a throughput-weighted Round Robin fashion (MAR-RR). As can be seen from Table 6 (last two columns) by using the information provided by WiScape we can decrease the HTTP latency by 32% compared to MAR-RR.

We have also experimented with well known Web pages as described above. We present results in Figure 14(b). As can be seen from the plot, using a locality aware scheme can improve performance by 37% over a naive round robin scheme.

We note that the applications can also estimate network performance through explicit measurements of its own, which would result in a steady measurement overhead on all the network interfaces. Besides, applications like MAR would also need to stop all client traffic thus potentially hampering performance. In contrast a client-sourcing base approach would gather this data ahead of time and can simply make it available to potential clients, at a low overhead. We would also like to note, that we did not account for multiple system level issues, such as energy efficiency, time to switch between links, or presence of client think time into account while calculating the performance. Accounting for such issues might lead to changes in achievable benefits that we present. However, we believe that independent of the specific metric being optimized (energy or completion time) information about link performance can always be leveraged for better performance.

5. RELATED WORK

We compare and contrast our contributions in WiScape with prior work on two separate fronts.

Prior monitoring research: With the rapid growth of cellular based Internet connectivity, cellular providers and third-party developers have started developing client-based techniques to learn about the properties of these networks. They include the AT&T's "Mark the Spot" [29] application, 3gtest [9], and applications by Root Wireless [8]. Unlike these applications, WiScape focuses on a measurement methodology for client-sourcing that systematically reduces the number of measurements required across time periods and zones based on data already collected while ensuring that collected data is statistically useful.

Other recent work has conducted detailed measurements of specific 3G cellular networks to understand their performance for both static and mobile environments [30, 31]. Lie *et al.* presents the characterization of PHY and MAC layer of 3G network and its impact on TCP performance [30]. Akin to [30] where the authors find the DRC (dependent on SINR) to vary significantly over large time scales, we also found a high variation in RSSI over the period of a day. Similar to [30], we did not find any correlation (0.03) between the expected application level TCP throughput and RSSI. In light of the above observation we discarded RSSI statistics from further consideration.

Similar studies have also been conducted on outdoor WiFi mesh networks [32, 15]. Again, such prior works are primarily measurement studies and do not focus on our focus of a client-sourced measurement framework with goals of minimal data collection from diverse clients.

Related applications: The novelty of our work is that we collected long term city-scale data and built the WiScape framework which harnesses the performance measurement of 3G network to maximize the performance of multi-network applications, e.g., MAR [4]. Many other vehicular networking systems have been designed and deployed in recent years, each with different target applications. Examples include VanLAN [33, 34], a WiFi based Internet service into vehicles [33, 34], PluriBus [35, 36] a WiFi, 3G, and WiMAX based system with similar goals but with different algorithms, DieselNet [37, 38] that mostly focused on delay tolerant networking and opportunistic Internet services. We believe that many of these systems could potentially leverage client-based data collected by WiScape to better optimize their data striping algorithms (analogous to our design of improvements to MAR).

6. CONCLUSION

In this paper we presented the design for a client-assisted network monitoring system. Through extensive measurement over a period of more than one year, in and around Madison and small parts of New Jersey, we have validated the possibility of carrying out client assisted network monitoring. With experimentation we show how client-assisted network monitoring can help cellular network users and operators. We believe this work is merely a starting point in larger scale measurements and network monitoring, spanning multiple cities, state, or across the whole country.

Cellular data traffic volume is set to increase dramatically in near future, placing enormous load on the infrastructure. Moving forward, we intend to expand the spatial and temporal reach of our client-assisted cellular data network monitoring, with the goal of understanding the effects of increased cellular networks on performance.

We hope to organically grow our efforts in the months and years to come. Specifically, we intend to extend our study to bigger cities, where high number of users, would present a more challenging monitoring problem.

To deploy our ideas developed in WiScape, we plan to integrate our proposed sampling techniques into a publicly available cellular network based measurement and monitoring tool called Network Test [39], available for both the Android and iPhone platforms currently. We believe this would further enrich our understanding of the client-sourced network measurement process.

7. ACKNOWLEDGEMENTS

We would like to thank Shan-Hsiang Shen, Lance Hartung, Hoewook Chung for their help in collecting measurements. We thank the Madison Metro Transit and the Van Galder Bus Company, for letting us use their buses to collect measurements. Sayandeep Sen, Jongwon Yoon, Joshua Hare, Justin Ormont, and Suman Banerjee have been supported in part by the US National Science Foundation through awards CNS- 1059306, CNS-0855201, CNS-0747177, CNS-0916955, CNS-1040648, and CNS-1064944.

8. REFERENCES

[1] C. Fraleigh, S. Moon, B. Lyles, C. Cotton, M. Khan, D. Moll, R. Rockell, T. Seely, and C. Diot. Packet-level traffic measurements from the sprint ip backbone. In *IEEE Network*, 2003.

[2] D. Kotz and Essian K. Analysis of a campus-wide wireless network. In *MobiCom*, 2002.

[3] Yu-Chung Cheng, John Bellardo, Péter Benkö, Alex C. Snoeren, Geoffrey M. Voelker, and Stefan Savage. Jigsaw: solving the puzzle of enterprise 802.11 analysis. In *SIGCOMM*, 2006.

[4] P. Rodriguez, R. Chakravorty, J. Chesterfield, I. Pratt, and S. Banerjee. Mar: A commuter router infrastructure for the mobile internet. In *MobiSYS*, 2004.

[5] B. Cankaya, V. Watcon, and Metters D. Wireless cell site finder and customer service system. In *United States Patent 7236767*, 2007.

[6] Aman Kansal, Michel Goraczko, and Feng Zhao. Building a sensor network of mobile phones. In *IPSN*, 2007.

[7] Emiliano Miluzzo, Nicholas D. Lane, Kristóf Fodor, Ronald Peterson, Hong Lu, Mirco Musolesi, Shane B. Eisenman, Xiao Zheng, and Andrew T. Campbell. Sensing meets mobile social networks: the design, implementation and evaluation of the cenceme application. In *SenSys*, 2008.

[8] Root wireless inc. http://www.rootwireless.com.

[9] Smart phone 3g test. http://www.eecs.umich.edu/3gtest/.

[10] Community resource for archiving wireless data at dartmouth. http://crawdad.cs.dartmouth.edu/.

[11] High-speed packet access. http://www.3gamericas.org.

[12] N. Bhushan, C. Lott, P. Black, Attar R., Y. Jou, M. Fan, Ghosh D., and Au J. Cdma2000 1xev-do revision a: A physical layer and mac layer overview. In *IEEE Comm. Magazine, 44(2)*, 2006.

[13] Wirover. http://host.madison.com/wsj/news/local/article_e1a67156-dea9-11df-9332-001cc4c002e0.html.

[14] C. Demichelis and P. Chimento. Ip packet delay variation metric for ip performance metrics (ippm). RFC 3393, IETF.

[15] Mikhail Afanasyev, Tsuwei Chen, Geoffrey M. Voelker, and Alex C. Snoeren. Analysis of a mixed-use urban wifi network: when metropolitan becomes neapolitan. In *IMC '08*.

[16] John Bicket, Daniel Aguayo, Sanjit Biswas, and Robert Morris. Architecture and evaluation of an unplanned 802.11b mesh network. In *ACM Mobicom*, 2005.

[17] Vladimir Brik, Shravan Rayanchu, Sharad Saha, Sayandeep Sen, Vivek Shrivastava, and Suman Banerjee. A measurement study of a commercial-grade urban wifi mesh. In *IMC*, 2008.

[18] D.W. Allan. Time and frequency characterization ,estimation and prediction of precision clocks and oscillators. In *IEEE Transactions*, 1987.

[19] V. Shrivastava, D. Agrawal, A. Mishra, S. Banerjee, and T. Nadeem. Understanding the limitations of transmit power control for indoor wlans. In *IMC*, 2007.

[20] Manish Jain and Constantinos Dovrolis. Pathload: A measurement tool for end-to-end available bandwidth. In *PAM Workshop*, 2002.

[21] Mingzhe Li, Mark Claypool, and Robert E. Kinicki. Wbest: A bandwidth estimation tool for ieee 802.11 wireless networks. In *LCN*, pages 374–381. IEEE, 2008.

[22] D. Koutsonikolas and Y. Charlie Hu. On the feasibility of bandwidth estimation in 1x evdo networks. In *MICNET*, 2009.

[23] P. Bahl and V. N. Padmanabhan. Enhancements to the radar user location and tracking system. In *INFOCOM*, 2000.

[24] Moustafa Youssef and Ashok Agrawala. The horus wlan location determination system. In *MobiSys*, 2005.

[25] A. Haeberlen, Flannery E., Ladd A., A. Rudys, D. Wallach, and L. Kavrakt. Practical robust localization over large-scale 802.11 wireless networks. In *MobiCom*, 2004.

[26] Samsung fizz phone. http://www.gsmarena.com/samsung_c5212-2709.php.

[27] Jinpeng s4100 mobile phone. http://www.chinatronic.com/products.php/S4100.

[28] Paul Barford and Mark Crovella. Generating representative web workloads for network and server performance evaluation. In *ACM SigMetrics*, 1998.

[29] At&t news release. http://www.att.com/gen/press-room?pid=4800&cdvn=news&newsarticleid=30336&mapcode=.

[30] Xin Liu, Ashwin Sridharan, Sridhar Machiraju, Mukund Seshadri, and Hui Zang. Experiences in a 3g network: interplay between the wireless channel and applications. In *MobiCom*, 2008.

[31] Wee Lum Tan, Fung Lam, and Wing Cheong Lau. An empirical study on the capacity and performance of 3g networks. *IEEE Transactions on Mobile Computing*, 7(6):737–750, 2008.

[32] J. Robinson and E.W. Knightly. A performance study of deployment factors in wireless mesh networks. 2007.

[33] Aruna Balasubramanian, Ratul Mahajan, Arun Venkataramani, Brian Neil Levine, and John Zahorjan. Interactive wifi connectivity for moving vehicles. In *SIGCOMM*, 2008.

[34] Ratul Mahajan, John Zahorjan, and Brian Zill. Understanding wifi-based connectivity from moving vehicles. In *IMC*, 2007.

[35] Mahajan, Ratul and Padhye, Jitendra and Agarwal, Sharad and Zil, Brian. E pluribus unum: High performance connectivity on buses. Technical Report MSR-TR-2008-147, Microsoft Research TechReport, 2008.

[36] Aruna Balasubramanian, Ratul Mahajan, and Arun Venkataramani. Augmenting mobile 3g using wifi. In *MobiSys*, 2010.

[37] Aruna Balasubramanian, Brian Neil Levine, and Arun Venkataramani. Enhancing interactive web applications in hybrid networks. In *MobiCom*, 2008.

[38] Xiaolan Zhang, Jim Kurose, Brian Neil Levine, Don Towsley, and Honggang Zhang. Study of a bus-based disruption-tolerant network: mobility modeling and impact on routing. In *MobiCom*, 2007.

[39] Network test. http://networktest.org/.

Summary Review Documentation for

"Can They Hear Me Now?: A Case for a Client-Assisted Approach to Monitoring Wide-Area Wireless Networks"

Authors: S. Sen, J. Yoon, J. Hare, J. Ormont, S. Banerjee

Reviewer #1

Strengths: Lengthy explanation of the choices of the parameters (size of zones, epochs and number of samples).
Large set of measurements over space, time and wireless networks.
Evaluate the benefits of a multi-network strategy for data connectivity.

Weaknesses: The framework idea is expected, so a key contribution is the choice of parameters. However since it is mainly based on data collected in once city, it is not clear how reusable the parameters for over environments like countryside or dense urban areas like NYC.

Comments to Authors: It is great to see such attention spent on choosing the right parameters for your system. I do not have many comments as the paper was well written and the idea was clear.

Since you collect data from buses, I was wondering if it would not introduce some bias in your data set. For instance, data in one location often collected around the same time.

Aggregation in space:

It seems that you have done your study by aggregating over time instead of keeping time constant.
How would the standard deviation look like if you would compare different zones during the same time of the day?
It would be nice to get similar results from other environments like Manhattan or the countryside.
Did you evaluate the incremental benefits of having zones of different sizes or different shapes (e.g., clustering)?
RTT is an important metric for wireless environments. Why is it not part of the zone size evaluation?

I find your last section on multi-Sim, MAR, network dominance interesting. You might want to develop that aspects in future papers.

Reviewer #2

Strengths: The paper has rich data: 3 cellular network performance measured by clients at several different locations. The use of client-side measurements for network monitoring makes a lot of sense.

Weaknesses: The paper mostly focuses on aggregation, but aggregation would miss interesting temporal and spatial dynamics.

Comments to Authors: I enjoy reading your paper. The goal of understanding the effectiveness of using client-side measurement to quantify the wide-area wireless network performance makes a lot of sense. Understanding the level of aggregation both in time and in space is useful. On the other hand, using aggregation to find the time interval and zones to smooth out the data is simple, and the paper should shorten this part, and spend more time on the more interesting and less obvious part on the applications. Moreover, aggregation filters out interesting variation across time and space, which is equally interesting to the aggregation results if not more and is more challenging technically than aggregation. I would like to see some discussion on this part.

The authors promise to publish their datasets, which would be very useful to the community.

Reviewer #3

Strengths: - detailed measurement study which is well thought out
- empirically informed design
- potential impact of the data.

Weaknesses: - tedious to read, though its not this particular paper's fault
- not clear how actionable the results are except for long term network planning and fault detection.

Comments to Authors: My main comment is on how this data can be acted on. For example, it is not clear if a user observed poor performance, how this data can help him improve or even diagnose his performance problems. While it is nice to have a sense of the network performance at long time scales, it is not clear how useful it is to the end user.

Can we isolate uplink and downlink performance? It would be useful since cellular links are notoriously asymmetric.

How are measurements impacted by client parameters such as battery levels etc? I guess since you are using laptops this is not a concern, but with smart phones battery dictates uplink and downlink behavior which would bias your measurements.

Reviewer #4

Strengths: Extensive measurements have been collected, from a variety of situations. The framework has some practical applications. The authors intend to share their measurements.

Weaknesses: The active measurement approach seems less ideal than a passive one for gathering the information for network providers. The presentation needs quite a bit of improvement. In particular, it is often difficult to follow which of the variety of data sets is being used. The paper does not consider smart phones, and in general does not consider the various practical issues for deploying this in practice.

Comments to Authors: A more compelling motivation is needed as to why network operators would want to use this framework. I agree that these operators would like more information on where problems are occurring in their network, for the various reasons that you describe in the paper. What I do not agree with is the need to collect (only) active measurements to get that information. Most of the information shown in this paper could be gathered with passive measurements, which have numerous benefits: no overhead on the wireless infrastructure, they are measurements of actual user traffic, they would not require instrumenting the user devices, etc. Only in cases where the user could not connect to the network might active measurements be useful.

I agree that users could take advantage of this framework, e.g., to compare the performance of multiple network providers in a given location. However, that seems to have limited applicability, at least for cell phone users, the majority of whom will have a contract with one provider (even though some will have multiple SIM cards, as stated in your paper).

Since access to the passive measurements may not be available to you, the active measurements that you have collected could fill in. However, the paper currently does not touch on the issue of the benefits of passive measurements for the provider, which is why my rating is lower than it might otherwise have been.

Minor Comments

Section 2
- In the discussion of the WiRover data set, the throughput tests could affect other users in all of the wireless environments, not just the tests done on buses.
- Please clarify where the various tests were run between (i.e., where is the server(s) that is used in each test located?)

Section 3.1: In "A closer look", please explain the intuition behind "driving around in a car within a 250 meter radius"; i.e., people may sit at a location that is within a short distance of an access point, but not too many will drive around in a circle to stay in range.

Section 3.2: It would help to have some more insight on what test duration will provide a reasonable throughput value with low enough variance for the tasks that a user may care about; e.g., someone trying to decide between using provider A and provider B is not going to run two 30 minute tests; they might run two 30 second tests, if that is sufficiently long to make a confident decision
Section 3.2.2: A time duration of 75 minutes seems rather long for a throughput test that is supposed to have "low overhead"

Section 3.3: In the discussion of UDP downloads (or earlier), clarify how many clients you have at your disposal

Section 3.3.1:
- Can't a provider monitor available bandwidth at each access point, rather than run active tests? (i.e., is there any technical reason they could not do this, even if they are not doing so today?)
- While UDP downloads will obtain useful information, it seems like a heavyweight way to do so. why (generally speaking) can providers not obtain this information passively?
- In "Summary", why would there be any doubt that one could use clients under your direct control to estimate network performance?

Section 3.4: clarify what is meant by "sufficient collect accurate statistics"

Section 4: in the caption of Figure 9, shouldn't "200 meter radius" be "250 meter radius"?

Section 4.1
- Clarify why throughput tests "cannot detect zones with highly variable performance"; it seems quite plausible, depending on how you conduct the tests and measure the results
- Note that passive measurements by the provider could also determine this information.

Section 4.2.1: Clarify which is the "best network's metric"

Section 4.2.2
- While there are certainly users who use multiple SIM cards, it seems like it will be a minority of users, due primarily to cost; thus, I do not find the arguments here particularly compelling
- SURGE uses a synthetic workload, does it not? Are you testing against a Web server running these synthetic pages? (If so, please clarify)

Section 5: if you consider my comments on passive measurements, then there will obviously be a bunch of new material to consider here

Reviewer #5

Strengths: Real data, geographically dispersed, over a year. Data submitted to CRAWDAD.

Weaknesses: Most of the hard systems problems were not confronted, even the stated challenge of scale. It is not clear how typical their data is with respect to line-of-sight problems.

Comments to Authors: There are really two parts to this paper: the measurement collection system and the results of the measurements themselves. The measurement collection system seems to ignore all of the hard parts of the problem - including those brought up and stated by the authors. The measurements themselves may be of independent use for others, particularly because they are being made publicly available via CRAWDAD.

For the system, you state in the intro that the core technical challenges are related to scaling, but no where in your system do you *explicitly* consider scaling. Yes, you spend a lot of time trying to figure out how often to measure something (my concerns for that are below) but you never relate it back to the amount of bandwidth or power consumed at the client (as implied by both the abstract and intro) or how many simultaneous clients your system can support or what infrastructure would be required to monitor, for example, a nationwide cellular deployment. Your measurements have fewer than 20 clients in total and no mention was made as to how many of these were working in parallel. Further, it reads as if all of your measurements were done with laptops instead of handheld devices, so no inference about the power consumption of WiScape can be made either. The lack of these points makes the assertion that client-side monitoring is viable unsupported.

Further, the big challenge that you ignore is deployment: how do you get your measurement infrastructure (be it an app or what have you) deployed on to enough client phones to get decent coverage? In my opinion, this is the hardest part of a client-side measurement system and it's not at all mentioned here.

The fact that WiScape has apparently not been tested on an actual portable handset seems to be a big strike against the viability of this system.

Now, ignoring all of that, there are still problems. Most of the interference in cellular networks is caused by line of sight issues. How typical are your data sources with respect to line of sight? Intuitively, a bus on a road outside does not have significant line of sight issues. Your data description of your spot nodes was not sufficient to determine what line-of-sight issues they had. So, it is not clear how your empirical zone and epoch derivations would change if the client was indoors, for example.

That said, the graphs in Figure 5 seemed very interesting - if this paper is the first to present this level of data (from different regions, over time), please say so.

In Section 3.1, is the assumption that zones are square? If yes, please say so. Any reason not to consider other shapes?

The data in Fig 4. seems to contradict Fig 1. and Fig.9 ; why are all of the relative standard deviations so small in Fig 4 (<0.1), whereas in Fig 1, they seem to be much higher (350 Kbs std dev / 1080 Kbs mean = 0.3 relative std dev) and Fig 9 shows relative stddevs > 0.7: it seems unintuitive that the stddev should be so small in Fig 4 (independent of zone size) when lots of the other Figures show much higher variation.

In Section 3.2, the implicit assumption here is "stable is better", where I am not convinced. Intuitively, operators are not as interested in the average performance as much as the "trouble spots", so by optimizing for inter-epoch stability, are you not just averaging away what the operator wants to know?

The conclusion did not add much to the paper: were there any lessons learned? Are the plans for a WiScape iOS or Android app? What are your concrete next steps?

Response from the Authors

We thank the reviewers for their constructive comments that helped improve the paper. We have fixed the text to address some of the reviewer concerns regarding clarity of description.

Some questions regarding interpolability of our observations in bigger cities, while using various cellular phones, in presence of severe line-of-sight issues etc., can be answered only by increasing the scale of our study to a broader geographical location and by involving more people in the process. We intend to do so in future and have expanded the conclusions section to describe our concrete next steps to this end.

In particular we understand that design, implementation and deployment of client-assisted wide-area wireless network monitoring systems would involve addressing multiple hard challenges, a few of which are described by Reviewer#5. However, designing and deploying the system is not the main focus this paper. Our main contribution is, first, to analyze measurement data for three cellular service providers over the span of an entire city, and at various other locations for a period of two years. Second, we identified characteristics of wide-area cellular networks which help estimate performance efficiently and highlighted how such minimal coarse grained client collected measurements can be leveraged by some applications. We believe that establishing the effectiveness and utility of lightweight coarse grained monitoring is an important first step for designing and implementing a scalable client-assisted monitoring system.

That said, as mentioned in Section 6, we are actively working towards building such a measurement platform for both vehicular communication systems as well as for cellphone users.

We also agree with Reviewer#4 that passive measurement is a potential lightweight alternative for understanding network performance. We are presently in the process of augmenting our measurement mechanisms with such passive estimation techniques. In future we intend to publish our findings on the same.

Finally, we have shown how client assisted in Section 4 can help network service providers and users of multiple cellular cards. We agree with Reviewer#3's concern on the utility of client-assisted measurements for individual users. Client-assisted monitoring in the context of cellular networks is a new technique and we intend explore other aspects of cellular network monitoring that client assisted monitoring can help with.

Specific comments:

Reviewer#3: Test duration of 75 minutes... The measurements for a zone need to be retaken every 75 minutes, the test themselves involve sending 40-120 packets (as noted in Table 5). We have made this clearer in the text.

Reviewer#5: In Section 3.2, ... here is "stable is better", ... We meant "stable is better" in the sense that, we can potentially take less number of measurements to converge to the correct estimate if the network is stable.

Reviewer#5: The data in Fig 4. seems to contradict ... In Figure 1, the zones have a radius of 800 meters, and include locations with less than 200 measurements, hence some zones show high standard deviation. In Figure 9 the higher relative standard deviation is for zones with multiple ping failures, which we took as an indicator of high performance variance. The high standard deviation for such zones, thus, when compared to the small relative standard deviation for the aggregation of all zones (also plotted in same graph) proves our point.

Reviewer#5: Line of sight issue ... All our static measurements were taken in indoor locations and hence were not in line-of-sight from the base station, we have clarified it in the text.

Evaluation of Data Communication Opportunities from Oil Field Locations at Remote Areas

Yang Chen, Jens O. Berg
Schlumberger PPCU
Sugar Land, TX
yangchen, joberg@slb.com

Mostafa Ammar and Ellen Zegura
College of Computing, Georgia Tech
Atlanta, GA
ammar, ewz@cc.gatech.edu

ABSTRACT

Cellular data links are an effective outdoor Internet access solution in urban environments. In this paper, we evaluate cellular data service as a potential data communication solution for oil field crews operating at remote areas in the United States. In our study, we first record the performance of cellular data service at twelve oil field locations. Measurement results show extensive availability of cellular service at those locations making it potentially a data communication solution at field locations. We then design a measurement framework and deploy measurement units to five oil field crews and carry out a side-by-side comparison of two different satellite links and cellular links from two service providers. Analysis of data sets consisting of more than 300 days' measurement shows that the cellular link has comparable or even higher availability than conventional satellite link at many field operations. However, the quality of its coverage is location dependent. This indicates that both cellular and satellite links should be used to provide highly available and cost-effective data communication for such operations.

Categories and Subject Descriptors

C.4 [**Performance of Systems**]: Measurement techniques; C.2.1 [**Network Architecture and Design**]: Wireless Communications

General Terms

Measurement, Experimentation, Performance

Keywords

Cellular, Satellite

1. INTRODUCTION

In today's oilfield operations, data communication at field locations is essential for operation control, equipment monitoring and crew coordination. Data communication is also desirable between oil field locations and applications on the Internet or inside an enterprise network infrastructure. For example, important job parameters during a field job can be sent to a data server where clients are able to view the job progress and provide feedback/comments. After the 2010 Macondo well blowout in the Gulf of Mexico [1], stricter governmental regulations introduced new data communication requirements to field operations. For example, status of oilfield equipment should be reported to a data center regularly. Since most field operations are conducted in remote areas, satellite links have been considered as the only option for a long time. With limited bandwidth provisioning and expensive usage cost, we are evaluating data communication alternatives from field operations to the Internet, in particular, to servers inside our Schlumberger Information Network (SINet).

Recent research evaluated outdoor Internet access from vehicles using 3G cellular service [2–4]. High bandwidth and stable connectivity from 3G data links exist at all those areas. However, all these studies were conducted in urban regions where cellular tower deployment density is high. Performance of cellular data links at remote areas far from cellular towers has not been evaluated in depth.

In this paper, we explore the potential for less costly cellular data usage at remote sites where such usage has not traditionally been contemplated. It is clear that there is significant diversity in availability of cellular and satellite coverage among remote locations. We provide a framework for assessing this availability through systematic measurement and analyze results from this framework at different geographical locations.

We first conducted a series of performance measurements of cellular data links with a field trip covering twelve remote operation locations. Coverage and link characteristics were collected at those locations. Based on analysis of collected information in this trip, we designed the measurement framework and deployed five testing units to field crews to collect performance data of cellular and satellite links over a total time period of more than 300 days. To our knowledge, this is the first side-by-side comparison between cellular data link and satellite links at remote areas.

The rest of the paper is organized as follows. Related work is described in Section 2. We introduce our measurement setup and test scenarios in Section 3 and present analysis of measurement results in Section 4. This paper concludes in Section 5 with summary of findings and plans of future work.

IMC'11, November 2–4, 2011, Berlin, Germany.

2. RELATED WORK

2.1 Wireless Communication at Oil Fields

Modern oil field operations from exploration to production require a significant amount of interactions between software and hardware as well as collaboration among field personnel. Providing data communication at field locations is not only essential but critical. Wireless technology has been widely adopted since most of oil field operations are conducted at locations where a conventional wired network infrastructure is physically or financially impractical. Wireless LAN (WLAN) and two-way radio are common equipment of field crews with high mobility nowadays. And wireless communication technology continues extending its reach at oil field operations [5, 6]. Correlation between transfer delay and TCP packets' size over GPRS link is studied in [7] for a potential application of real-time oil field monitoring.

2.2 Outdoor Internet Access

Studies of outdoor data access mainly focus on connectivity from moving vehicles. This connectivity can be provided via open WiFi APs [8, 9]. Due to the limited communication range of those APs and their uncoordinated coverage, handoffs with predictive methods and using prefetching to download experience were discussed in [10]. Cellular data service is also considered as a good source for outdoor data access because of its better coverage and less frequent service interruptions. Using tools from information theory, the work in [4] shows a certain level of predictability of bandwidth on 3G links in a metro area. Most recently, performance comparisons between WiFi and 3G connectivity is conducted in urban areas. Although these two types of data links have different characteristics, they can be good supplements to each other based on studies in [2, 3].

2.3 Cell and Satellite Links Characterization

Cellular data service providers normally apply sophisticated control/scheduling method in their networks. The configuration can be highly customized from location to location due to quality of service (QoS) and business concerns [11]. Empirical study of transport layer performance over those managed cellular data links are reported in [12–14].

Satellite networks are under strict regulation and management due to the expensive and limited bandwidth over such links. Research on satellite links focuses on measuring TCP's performance over those links and "tuning" the TCP protocol stack to fit link characteristics such as long end-to-end latency [15–17].

3. MEASUREMENT SETUP

The objective of this work is to evaluate new communication opportunities from oil field locations to the Internet provided by rapidly expanding cellular data service across the continental USA. In the first phase of our study, we conducted a series field tests in northern Texas/Louisiana. During these tests, we evaluated cellular data links on their availability and average TCP throughput. With positive results in this study, we deployed test units to five crews and conducted the second phase of the study. We compare cellular data services and satellite links side-by-side at remote field locations. Our measurement studies target an answer to the question of whether we can cost-effectively improve the connectivity from remote oilfield operations to the Internet at certain geographical regions.

3.1 Hardware Platform

During the first phase of the study, we built a mount so that two vertical masts were setup on each back corner of a pick up truck. This allowed us to position antennas at a 4-meter elevation above the ground. This matches the elevation of those antennas in field deployments where they are installed on the roof of trailers.

We use two dual-band flexible omnidirectional antennas. The choice of this type of antenna stems from a specific oilfield operational restriction: The cellular antenna on the roof of trailers must be flexible to prevent damage caused by strong vibrations or impacts from vegetation when field operation are carried out at places with harsh road conditions. This restriction rules out many other choices such as electronically steerable antennas [18]. The gain of this flexible antenna is 5 dB as higher gain antennas are usually longer and associated with a higher probability of breakage during field operations. The AT&T and Verizon 3G modems used in our measurement studies come with one or two (Verizon model) external antenna connectors. Both antenna and cellular data modems installation pass our internal environmental qualification procedure, which involves tests for conditions such as strong vibration and extreme temperature.

A different communication system setup was used in the second phase study. We installed a cellular data modem and a BGAN modem from Inmarsat [19] on trailers of five field crews which used the VSAT modem from iDirect [20] as the data access link to the Internet.

Cellular and satellite data modems are connected to a Dell Latitude™ laptop via Ethernet port or USB/Ethernet converter. Our measurement application is running on the Windows® XP operating system.

3.2 Methodology

In our phase one study, we visited 12 field-operation locations. A commercial Internet speed test server [21] and an internal link speed test server inside SINet were used to measure the upload/download link speed. If data service was available, the average link speed was recorded. Data service coverage and link speed of both service providers were evaluated. Good coverage revealed during this study led us to continue further comparison between cellular and satellite links in field locations.

In our test unit deployed on field crew's trailer, we developed an application to probe for Internet access over each data link every 30 seconds. Furthermore, when the field crew started the field operations, data files with a size of 1 MByte are generated regularly. This is to mimic data generation from a planned application for field service-quality improvement. Our application automatically uploaded those files to a FTP server inside SINet over an available data link. Interrupted uploading was resumed when the connectivity was restored. Each FTP transmission's size and duration was recorded and used to compute average TCP throughput at that time.

Throughout our measurement studies, we used the original TCP stack of the Windows operating system. Our results can serve as the basis for future effort on "tuning" the TCP stack for performance improvement over cellular or satellite links.

End-to-end latency is the link metric which essentially affects TCP stack's performance and determines service quality experienced by many applications. To collect end-to-end latency measurement results, periodical ping's are sent over cellular and satellite links.

3.3 Switching between Network Interfaces

In order to send probe traffic through each network interface, we developed an interface switching mechanism at application layer by manipulating the Windows operating system's local routing table.

Different IP addresses are assigned by DHCP protocols on each of these three interfaces. For example, 192.168.1.100 is the IP address at the interface connected to a satellite data modem which serves as the gateway with the IP address 192.168.1.1. In the meanwhile, 192.168.2.100 is the IP address assigned by a cellular data modem with IP address 192.168.2.1.

Destination	Netmask	Gateway	Interface
10.0.0.1	255.255.255.255	192.168.1.1	192.168.1.100
0.0.0.0	0.0.0.0	192.168.2.1	192.168.2.100

Figure 1: Samples of routing table entry

By setting a routing table entry for all IP addresses, i.e., destination IP is 0.0.0.0 shown in Figure 1, all network traffic is forwarded onto the cellular link. Note that a more specific routing table entry can be created at the same time to specify which interface should be used for the network application with a pre-determined destination IP address. In Figure 1's example, the application with a destination IP address 10.0.0.1 is using the satellite link.

4. MEASUREMENT RESULTS

Results from the Phase 1 study were recorded manually when we visited each field locations. After we deployed measurement units to field crews, measurement results were recorded automatically in a local database on the laptop. We developed scripts to retrieve essential information from database records as log files and upload them to a FTP server from time to time. Logs from both phases are used to present following analysis.

4.1 Phase 1 Study

From March 31, 2010 to April 9, 2010, we visited 12 field locations spread out in an area of more than 35,000 km^2 shown in Figure 2a[1]. Selection of those locations is based on operational scheduling and business concerns other than geographical or service coverage consideration.

Coverage (%)	ATT	VZN	Bandwidth (kbps)	ATT	VZN
3G	0	75	Upload	94	323
non-3G	100	0	Download	106	645

Table 1: Field test summary of cellular links

Field test results are summarized in Table 1. AT&T has EDGE service at all those locations but no high-speed 3G coverage at any of them. On the other hand, Verizon provides 3G EVDO service at nine of the locations and no service in the other three. Therefore, significant differences

[1]Due to business concerns, we cannot disclose those fields' exact locations on this map.

(a) Cellular coverage over field tests area

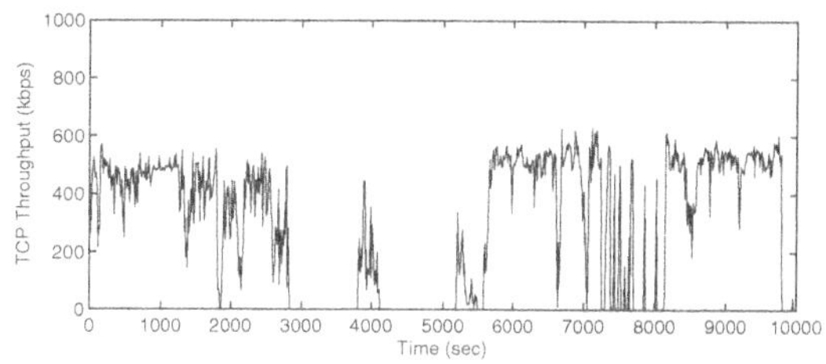

(b) Upload rate on the route

Figure 2: Phase 1 study's locations

in the average upload/download speeds between these two service providers were observed.

During our tests, we found out that the coverage map from service providers can be a good reference but disagreements from actual measurement do occur. We overlaid Verizon's coverage map from [22] on the map of our field tests. The shadows in Figure 2a represent areas without coverage. Among the three field locations where we did not get Verizon data service, two are actually inside those shadows. The one location that "should" have service but does not is outside any shadows. However, its topographic situation is not favorable: the surrounding ground is higher than the field location. We also monitored the TCP throughput in a 3-hours drive from point A on the map (not among the field locations) to a nearby city, point D. During this trip, 600 MByte of data was uploaded continuously. The TCP throughput over time illustrated in Figure 2b generally agrees with coverage along the route with occasional differences.

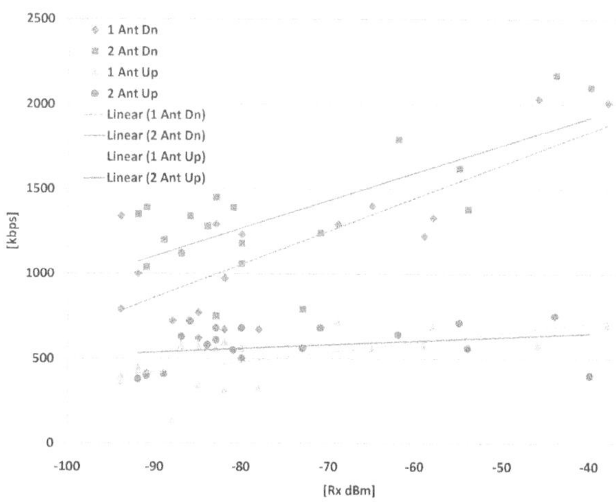

Figure 3: Antenna setup and Verzion's data link speed

We plot download/upload speeds over Verizon's links against

signal strength readings from data modems in Figure 3. Linear fittings indicate that a 1-dB increment on signal strength can lead to an increment of 28.4 kbps in download speed and 7 kbps in upload speed with one antenna. Using two antennas generally increases average signal strength by 1 dB. However, the effect is a 15% download speed increment. We believe this is a result of spatial diversity provided by two antennas. On the other hand, uploading speed is not affected much. Unlike the signal spatial diversity study in [23] where geographic distance between antennas can be up to 500 meters, the distance between antennas in our setting is a few meters. Using two antennas helps on link speed in our field tests but cannot make 3G data service available at locations where a single antenna setup fails.

After we finished this series of field tests, we decided to use a Verizon data modem with the two-antennas setting as the standard 3G data link in our further studies.

4.2 Phase 2 Study

During our phase 2 study, we collected measurement results from four crews stationed at Shreveport, Louisiana. They are named as SLA1 to 4 in this paper. Measurement study was also conducted at one crew stationed at Williston, North Dakota which is named as WIL1 in this paper. Normally, each crew operates within an area of thousands of square kilometer around the city where it is stationed. SLA1 is the pilot crew with which we finalized the hardware and software configuration during the time period from November 2010 to March 2011. Note that the AT&T cellular link was used during that time period. This is because Verizon did not have enterprise-level access to our company's network until early 2011 after certain business procedures were carried out. Therefore, we name the data set from January 26, 2011 to March 20, 2011 as "SLA1 ATT". At the end of March, we replaced SLA1 crew's AT&T link with Verizon service so that it has the same configuration as other four crews. We present analysis of link availability, TCP throughput and end-to-end latency from measurement results collected at those five crews.

4.2.1 *Availability*

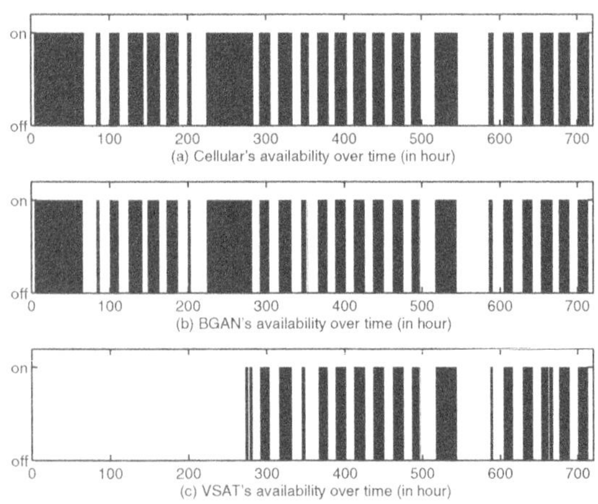

Figure 4: Availability comparison at SLA2 in April 2011

Data link availability via cellular, BGAN and VSAT over time for each crew is the first metric of interest in our measurement study. We find out this metric is affected by the work shift pattern of each crew. Figure 4 shows the link up and down sequences of SLA2 crew in April 2011. This crew is a day crew which stops operation and shuts down all equipment at night. SLA2 and SLA3 belong to this category and thus their link availability is always interrupted by such operation halts. SLA1 and SLA4 are 24-hour crews which operate continuously at field locations. All crews normally move to next field location after working 5 to 10 days at one place. The job location transition may take 1 to 3 days during which all equipment is powered off.

We retrieved Windows OS's native logs containing PC power on/off events from different crews. With this type of information, we reprocessed availability logs of cellular and satellite interfaces so that the probability that a link is available is only calculated when the equipment is powered on. Therefore, we eliminated the effect of job transition/equipment down schedule on availability evaluation of those data links.

Difference on costs associated with usage of satellite data links (USD 5/MByte) and cellular one (USD 100 per month with 2-GByte cap) indicates a potential cost reduction if a cellular link instead of a satellite link is used when data communication happens. Therefore, we not only calculate $P(X)$, probability that link X is available, but also the $P(X|Y)$, conditional probability that link X is available given link Y is available. Higher value of $P(X|Y)$ represents more opportunities of using link X instead of Y.

	$P(C)$	P(B)	P(V)	$P(C\|B)$	$P(C\|V)$
SLA1	98.50%	71.29%	66.42%	98.99%	98.99%
SLA2	97.03%	83.95%	52.86%	99.52%	99.48%
SLA3	93.76%	88.15%	56.99%	98.12%	97.78%
SLA4	89.73%	88.90%	44.79%	91.89%	99.28%
	C: Cellular;	B: BGAN;	V: VSAT		

(a) Measurement results in April

	$P(C)$	P(B)	P(V)	$P(C\|B)$	$P(C\|V)$
SLA1	96.86%	26.96%	87.10%	99.67%	98.31%
SLA2	96.07%	80.40%	75.19%	99.05%	99.07%
SLA3	97.28%	91.21%	63.86%	99.27%	99.02%
SLA4	76.11%	75.68%	50.89%	98.03%	97.79%

(b) Measurement results in May

Table 2: Normalized link availability comparison

Table 2 shows the availability analysis of SLA1 to 4 in April and May 2011. Note that cellular data link has high availability comparable to the BGAN data link at those measurement locations. The drop on BGAN's availability at SLA1 in May is caused by a device mis-configuration which was corrected after a few weeks. Note that the existing data link solution using VSAT is not as reliable as the other two links. One major contributor to the low availability is its bulky and heavy directional antenna (size ranges from 75cm to 1.2m) which fails to track satellite signal from time to time due to reasons such as mechanical parts failure.

High conditional probabilities in Table 2 indicate that a cellular link is always available when satellite links are at locations around Shreveport, an geographical region with good cellular service coverage. The same conclusion might not hold at other regions.

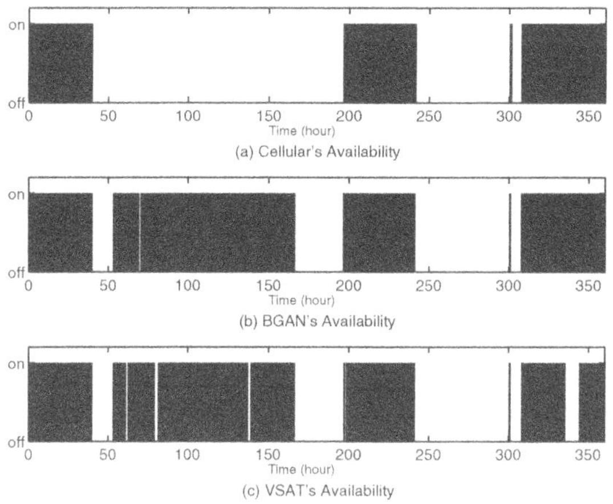

Figure 5: Availability comparison at SLA4 in Aug. 2011

SLA4 crew traveled to southern Texas and operated there for two weeks from Aug. 10 to Aug. 25, 2011. Side-by-side link availability comparison in Figure 5 shows that cellular link was down for a 5 day time period when satellite links were available. Therefore, $P(C|B)$ and $P(C|V)$ are 54.31% and 53.33% in those two weeks. In the meanwhile, P(B) and P(V) are 90.24% and 84.84%.

Measurement results in Table 2 and Figure 5 indicate that no ideal data communication solution can be provided by a single type of data links in our evaluation. A multi-interface system with data link management policy should be developed based on financial consideration and link availability. Implementation on network interface selection can be done via the technique mentioned in Section 3.3.

Both Figure 4 and 5 show regular availability interruptions on those data links. These interruptions may last for hours or even days. There are two reasons for such long interruptions: 1) The crew is working at a field location with no coverage for a few days; 2) The job location transition takes a few days to finish.

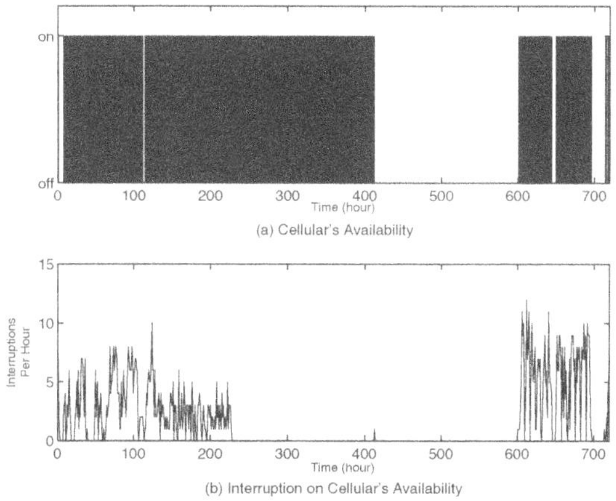

Figure 6: Interruptions on cellular link availability at WIL1

In the meanwhile, interruptions on those wireless links caused by weak signal can be very frequent. We present cellular link's availability from data collected at WIL1 during August in Figure 6. In this month, over 1100 interruptions occurred with a peak rate of more than 10 times per hour.

Overall, data access from field location to the Internet is a delay-tolerant network scenario [24]. Applications running over these data links at field locations should include disruption/delay-tolerance features to handle intermittent link availability as mentioned in [3].

4.2.2 TCP Throughput Profiling

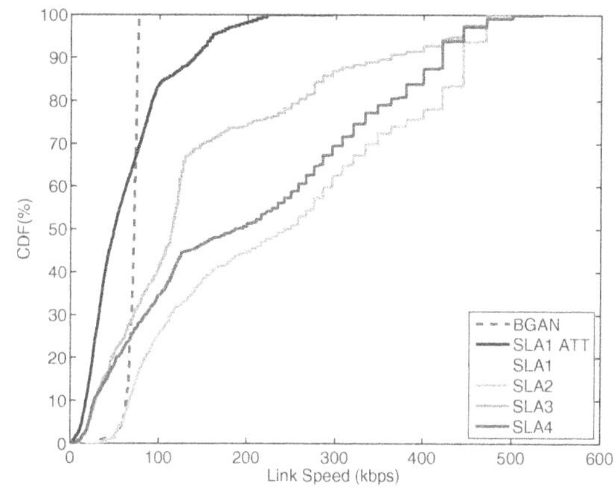

Figure 7: CDF of average TCP throughput

There were 200 to 1000 FTP uploads via Verizon's cellular links in each SLA crew during April 2011. Another 2000 FTP uploads were finished in data set SLA1 ATT. In addition, a BGAN link was used for more than 600 FTP uploads from SLA1 crew from October 2010 to November 2010. No FTP upload was conducted on VSAT link in our measurement study since this link is strictly managed and only business applications with recorded and approved bandwidth consumption profile may access it.

Figure 7 illustrates Cumulative density functions (CDFs) of average TCP throughput in those data sets. We notice the significant variation on average TCP throughput over cellular links. This is caused by fluctuation of signal quality as field locations are normally far from cellular towers or by contentions of spectrum usage, which will be discussed later in this section. Verizon's cellular service provides higher maximum achievable uplink speed (500kbps) than AT&T's (250kbps) but is associated with bigger variations. The average TCP throughput is stable over the BGAN link as it is tightly managed and has less background traffic fluctuation due to limited accesses.

Temporal correlation/predication of TCP throughput over wireless links in small time scales of tens of seconds are investigated in previous work [2,4]. We are interested in average TCP throughput over cellular links and we conduct our study in a much larger time scale.

We show the average TCP throughput of each upload from the SLA1 ATT data set according to the hour when it starts in Figure 8a. Each dot represents one average TCP throughput measured at a certain hour. We also draw the range bounded by 5 percentile and 95 percentile of all values at each hour. Although 5% to 95% ranges are similar across different hours as link quality fluctuates all the time, the 25% to 75% range is narrow which indicates that a significant portion of TCP throughput measurements at each hour are around the median value.

Average TCP throughput is generally low during busy hours of the day and high otherwise. We believe this is re-

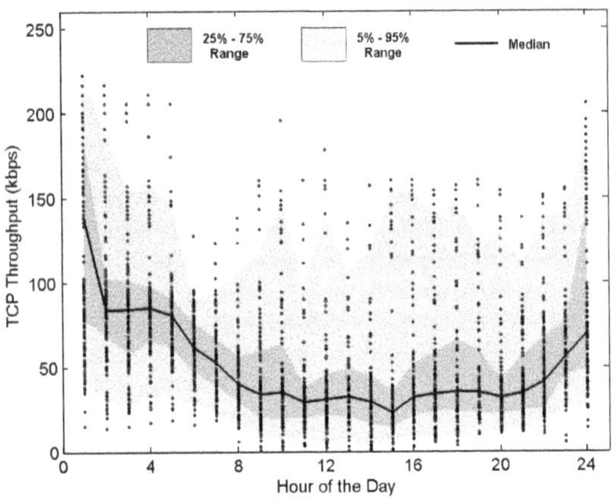

(a) SLA1 ATT data set

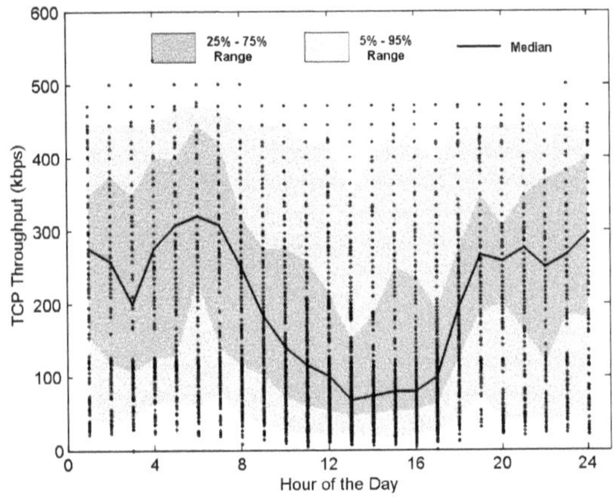

(b) SLA1-4 Verizon data set

Figure 8: TCP throughput at each hour of the day

lated to contention of spectrum usage towards the cellular tower from other cellular devices at the same field location or the diurnal congestion on cellular service providers' backbone. As median values change significantly from hour to hour, collecting statistics for each hour of the day would help TCP throughput predication in the same hour of the day.

Similar hourly-shifted pattern can be found in Figure 8b, which illustrates results from the data set consists of over 6000 TCP throughput measurements over Verizon's service from SLA1 to 4 in April and May, 2011.

4.2.3 End-to-end Latency

End-to-end latency is the link metric which essentially affects TCP stack's performance and determines service quality experienced by many applications. To collect measurement of this metric, ping packets are sent over SLA1-4's cellular link and VSAT link periodically with an interval of 5 minutes and 15 minutes respectively. Ping packets are also sent over SLA4's BGAN link with an interval of 15 minutes.

Figure 9 shows those measurements in August 2011. Note that VSAT link's end-to-end latency is stable around 500 ms. In the meanwhile, the latency on BGAN link is significantly longer with a lower bound of 1000 ms and 80% measurement results are around 2000 ms. Compared with satellite links, cellular links have a better lower bound around 200

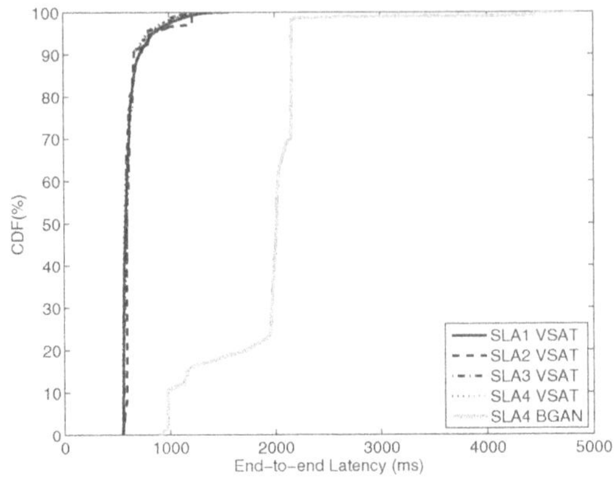

(a) Measurements over satellite links

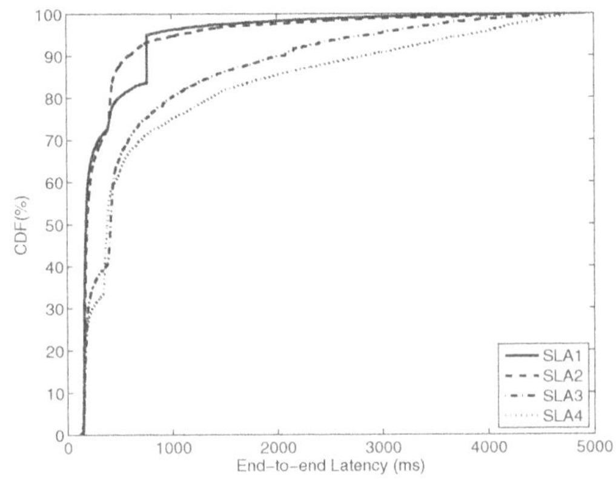

(b) Measurements over cellular links

Figure 9: CDF's of end-to-end latency

ms. However, measurements of latency on cellular links are heavy-tailed which means long end-to-end latency may occur from time to time.

Although BGAN and cellular links may have higher availability than the VSAT link according to previous discussions, they might not be used by applications having a tight latency requirement. On the one hand, this indicates multiple network interfaces should be jointly used to provide effective data communication at remote areas; on the other hand, significant differences on end-to-end latency characteristics could make the link management a challenging task as one more criteria should be evaluated besides the cost and availability mentioned in previous discussion. Furthermore, an application's data communication may switch between different interfaces when availability interruptions occur. Whether we should make TCP stack aware of such latency discrepancy in advance so that a faster rate adjustment can be achieved is being evaluated and will be reported in future study.

5. SUMMARY AND FUTURE WORK

We conducted a coverage evaluation in a certain region of the United States in 2010 to confirm the expanding presence of cellular data services in remote areas. Due to the distance from test locations to cellular towers and possibly unfavorable terrestrial conditions, variations in service coverage and data link speed are high. Spatial diversity using two antennas provides improvements over cellular link's speed, but there was no coverage difference in our study. Encouraged by overall good coverage of cellular service, we conducted comprehensive field tests with five oil field operation crews at the different geographical region in 2011. We evaluated communication opportunities provided by satellite and cellular links in this study of a total over 300 days.

At certain regions, the cellular data link shows comparable availability to satellite links which were once deemed as the only solution for accessing the Internet at remote areas. This indicates a potential operational cost reduction from replacing the satellite link with a more cost-effective cellular data link or developing network policy to manage those data links with financial consideration. We also notice that the operational pattern of the field crew may affect data links' availability over time. Delay-tolerance capability is desirable for potential applications using those links due to intermittent availability at field locations. Average TCP throughput on cellular links shifts according to the hour of the day.

We are selecting crews operating at other districts in the United States to extend our measurement study to other geographical regions. In addition, we will provide more comprehensive characterization on those data links at a finer time granularity. For example, end-to-end latency or jitter performance will be measured so that we are able to evaluate possibilities of introducing more interactive applications such as real-time collaborations between office and field locations. Interaction between TCP/UDP stack and link characteristics will be investigated for potential "tuning" of the transport layer for performance improvements over those links.

6. REFERENCES

[1] BP Deepwater Horizon Explosion. [Online]. Available: http://en.wikipedia.org/wiki/Deepwater_Horizon_explosion

[2] P. Deshpande, X. Hou, and S. R. Das, "Performance Comparison of 3G and Metro-Scale WiFi for Vehicular Network Access," in *Proc. of Conference on Internet Measurement*, 2010, pp. 301–307.

[3] A. Balasubramanian, R. Mahajan, and A. Venkataramani, "Augmenting Mobile 3G Using WiFi," in *Proc. of ACM MobiSys*, 2010, pp. 209–222.

[4] J. Yao, S. S. Kanhere, and M. Hassan, "An Empirical Study of Bandwidth Predictability in Mobile Computing," in *Proc. of ACM WiNTECH*, 2008, pp. 11–18.

[5] S. Petersen, B. Myhre, S. Carlsen, J. H. Linden, B. Myhre, M. Sansom, A. Skavhaug, E. Mikkelsen, and D. Sjong, "A Survey of Wireless Technology for the Oil and Gas Industry," *SPE Projects, Facilities and Construction*, vol. 3, no. 4, pp. 1–8, 2008.

[6] S. Savazzi and U. Spagnolin, "Synchronous Ultra-Wide Band Wireless Sensors Networks for Oil and Gas Exploration," in *Proc. of IEEE Symposium on Computers and Communications*, 2009.

[7] W. Yin-wen and H. Min-xian, "Remote Monitoring System For Oil Wells Based On GPRS Technology," in *Proc. of International Conference on Computer Engineering and Technology (ICCET)*, vol. 7, 2010.

[8] A. Balasubramanian, Y. Zhou, W. Croft, B. Levine, and A. Venkataramani, "Web Search From a Bus," in *Proc. ACM workshop on Challenged Networks*, 2007, pp. 59–66.

[9] V. Bychkovsky, B. Hull, A. Miu, H. Balakrishnan, and S. Madden, "A Measurement Study of Vehicular Internet Access using In Situ Wi-Fi Networks," in *Proc. of ACM Mobicom*, 2006, pp. 50–61.

[10] P. Deshpande, A. Kashyap, C. Sung, and S. R. Das, "Predictive methods for improved vehicular WiFi access," in *Proc. of Mobisys*, ser. MobiSys '09, 2009, pp. 263–276.

[11] W. L. Tan, F. Lam, and W. C. Lau, "An Empirical Study on the Capacity and Performance of 3G Networks," *IEEE Transactions on Mobile Computing*, vol. 7, no. 6, pp. 737–750, 2008.

[12] Y. Lee, "Measured TCP Performance in CDMA 1xEV-DO Network," in *Proc. of PAM conference*, 2006.

[13] K. Mattar, A. Sridharan, H. Zang, I. Matta, and A. Bestavros, "TCP over CDMA2000 Networks: A Cross-Layer Measurement Study," in *Proc. of PAM conference*, 2007.

[14] J. Prokkola, P. Perala, M. Hanski, and E. Piri, "3G/HSPA Performance in Live Networks from the End User Perspective," in *Proc. of IEEE ICC*, 2009, pp. 1–6.

[15] K. Zbynek, N. Marek, and B. Leos, "Optimization of TCP Satellite Communication in Inmarsat Network," in *Proc. of IEEE ICWMC*, 2010, pp. 544–548.

[16] Y. Chotikapong, H. Cruickshank, and Z. Sun, "Evaluation of TCP and Internet traffic via Low Earth Orbit Satellites," *IEEE Personal Communications*, vol. 8, no. 3, pp. 28–34, 2001.

[17] I.F.Akyildiz, G. Morabito, and S. Palazzo, "TCP-Peach: a new congestion control scheme for satellite IP networks," *IEEE/ACM Transactions on Networking*, vol. 9, no. 3, pp. 307–321, 2001.

[18] V. Navda, A. P. Subramanian, K. Dhanasekaran, A. Timm-Giel, and S. Das, "Mobisteer: Using steerable beam directional antenna for vehicular network access," in *Proc. of Mobisys*, 2007, pp. 192–205.

[19] Broadband Global Area Network (BGAN). [Online]. Available: http://www.inmarsat.com/Services/Land/Services/High_speed_data/default.aspx

[20] Very Small Aperture Terminal (VSAT). [Online]. Available: http://www.idirect.net/Products.aspx

[21] Speakeasy Speed Test. [Online]. Available: http://www.speakeasy.net/speedtest/

[22] Verizon Coverage Locator. [Online]. Available: http://www.verizonwireless.com/b2c/CoverageLocatorController

[23] F. P. Tso, L. Cui, L. Zhang, W. Jia, D. Yao, J. Teng, and D. Xuan, "DragonNet: A Robust Mobile Internet Service System for Long Distance Trains," in *Proc. of IEEE INFOCOMM*, 2011.

[24] K. Fall, "A Delay-Tolerant Network Architecture for Challenged Internets," in *Proc. of ACM SIGCOMM*, 2003, pp. 27–34.

Summary Review Documentation for

"Evaluation of Data Communication Opportunities from Oil Field Locations at Remote Areas"

Authors: Y. Chen, J. Berg, M. Ammar, E. Zegura

Reviewer #1

Strengths: Novel measurement study that compares satellite and cellular links at remote places. Well written paper and interesting to read.

Weaknesses: Cannot generalize these results as the study is too specific to those particular locations in the southwest US.

Comments to Authors: The paper is an interesting study of cellular and satellite network connectivity at oil field locations. It is of course hard to generalize the results to other locations, but sheds light on the general trends of expanding cellular infrastructure that might prove to be a more compelling alternative to more expensive satellite links. I like this general thesis of the paper.

I have only one major comment regarding the experimentation. It might be good to use the job transition and equipment down schedules from the crews to weed out periods of planned unavailability. Right now, the paper reads a bit speculative. For instance, the reasons for the longer tail in Figure 4 are vaguely attributed to these causes. It might be good to separate them out so that results are more reflective of actual availability of the links. Of course it might be a bit harder since somebody has to collect those logs!

P3: I don't understand how the author's results can serve as the basis for future effort on "tuning" TCP stack. It would be good clarify.

Table 1 needs units for upload and download bandwidths. Are the coverage results based on actual measurements or coverage maps from ATT and Verizon ?

P3: 1dB gain in signal strength translates to 28.4 Kbps in download speed and 7kbps in upload speed. 1dB gain due to multiple antennas is 15% download speed increment. It's not easy to see the comparison between absolute and relative increments. Please standardize.

Reviewer #2

Strengths: Understanding network access in remote/non urban areas sounds like a new emerging area.

Weaknesses: I am not sure any of the findings have much generality or application to other networking problems. The results or techniques are not particularly surprising or interesting.

Comments to Authors: I am all in favor of emerging problem areas and you seem to have the potential to do so with your setup. Unfortunately, there is not much interesting networking in this paper. It would be nice if you can use your measurements to develop new insights or implications for networking -- e.g., how can you use a hybrid cellular-satellite combination or how can DTN help or how should a TCP stack be optimized etc. Sadly, this is missing here.

You mention "high availability" of cellular, but that seems likely biased by the coverage/workload for the providers and what their economic and business considerations are. I am not sure how we can generalize this to other settings or deployments

Reviewer #3

Strengths: One step in a new environment: how to build communication network at lower cost for remote areas and operational deployment of oil company. The need for information in this system needs to be on the rise. Big deployment effort. Four teams are covered with different schedules, and different providers and satellite are used for completion. Points to need for better accommodation of delay in application, and the role of different factors.

Weaknesses: Apart from the obvious benefit for the operational cost of the oil company, the depth of the problem is not made very precise. In particular, since satellite already have longer delay and more sporadic availability, it seems that switching to cellular is not going much more into the DTN area. The cellular network seems to underperform the satellite in terms of raw bandwidth (through is generally below 70kbps). It is a little frustrating that unavailability due to hardware switched off (or non operation of the team) is not factored out from the experience altogether.

Comments to Authors: I think this paper is a good fit for a short communication at IMC since it deals with measuring availability in a new context (operational team of oil field) and brings several insights on a potential new area of applications for wireless system. This work seems in an early phase, as the result are somewhat limited (old technology from satellite are shown to be more expensive but more predictable). The main surprising message is that availability of cellular networks is higher than satellite.

I think the work can benefit from clarifying a few issues, in particular with regard to its conclusion for future research. This could potentially be included in the paper with a little time.

What are the factors to include in the satellite availability? Is that mostly a hardware and deployment issue (directional antenna and failure) or a fundamental limitation (moving satellites that are not always present). Distinguishing these factors (even roughly) to tell what's counted and what is not would help.

Similarly, as a sanity check it would be important to at least say a word about unavailability due to non-work. Are the trucks left in a place with coverage (in that case, we should see that at night for SLA2). Is that guaranteed that both satellite and cellular are off then?

The time where the power is off, it seems to indicate that the radio is also off. Hence it should be able to find that in the data itself and factor it out.

Can you specify your related improvement w.r.t. [5] and [7]. It seems that [7] already proposed to use cellular network for oil field, so it would be important to contrast your finding or system.

Can you elaborate on the impact of unavailability. Apparently, satellite links are more sporadic (but more predictable when available) than cellular link. That seems to indicate that they would already benefit from DTN. Maybe the cellular network is not making a strong case then. Unless the variability of available throughput is making DTN a must.

For these reasons, the unavailability duration of satellite should be discussed along with Fig.4. while Fig.2 seems not to be critical and left to a tech report.

Clearly the impact of cellular coverage is huge here. If it is modified by 20% then the result of availability will be strongly modified. Can you at least have a quick back of the envelope calculation to prove that other locations considered for oil fields (mentioned in introduction) are not much less exposed to cellular service? That would help making the result representative.

The fact that the entropy reduces as a significant parameter like the time of the day is used seems trivial. This section seems not to add much to the paper at this time (although the general problem of prediction could be important).

Since cellular is better for coverage but less for instantaneous throughput, a total comparison of the volume that can be transported would be useful.

Reviewer #4

Strengths: This is the first paper I am aware of that compares satellite and cellular network performance in remote rural settings. The paper topic is of interest, as it provides insights into a new aspect of Internet use.

Weaknesses: The presentation needs significant copy editing (normally I provide a list of specific issues to correct, but in this case it needs a native English speaker to work directly with the authors (actually, at least one of the authors appears to fit this description, and thus should be able to do this). The analyses are perhaps less rigorous than is typically expected of IMC papers, but given the challenges in obtaining the measurements, are likely acceptable for a short paper.

Comments to Authors: The most glaring issue with the paper is the need for copy editing. There are many, many minor language issues that need to be corrected. Fixing these will make the paper much more enjoyable for a wider audience. There is also quite a bit of repetition in the paper (e.g., about conducting a study with 12 sites, then a follow-up study with four sites).

Please provide more insights on how the initial 12 sites were selected, and then how the final four were selected.

In Section 3.1, please explain in more detail the benefits of an additional 5db from the flexible antenna. Keep in mind that not everyone who reads this paper may understand signal strength measurements.

In Section 3.2, is ftp really used in operations? that is an insecure protocol. if you meant sftp or something similar, please be specific.

It would be helpful to have a table that summarizes the data sets; e.g., how many flows are in each.

The cost information is very interesting; it serves as a good motivation. Thus, you may want to mention this in Section 1.

Figure 6(b) is very interesting. Please make it at least column width. This graph suggests that some changes to business practices/policies may be required; e.g., leaving the IT equipment on at night to take advantage of the increased data rates.

Please clarify what value the entropy analysis provides over the straightforward graph in Figure 6(b).

As future work, I think passive measurement techniques should be explored, since this is clearly a bandwidth constrained environment. Obviously, it would require the network to be in use for business purposes, and then that traffic would be passively monitored.

Reviewer #5

Strengths: The practical nature of this work makes it interesting. It is nice to see work aimed at solving a real problem (data connectivity on oilfields).

Weaknesses: The paper lacks real insight, and it is just too poorly written to really merit attention in IMC.

Comments to Authors: Apart from very frequent problems in English, it is hard from the start to understand exactly what the problem being solved here.

If it is connectivity in remote locations, then how is AT&T or any other service provider relevant. At really remote locations, e.g., and oil rig at sea, such as in the motivating citation to the BP disaster, then clearly a commercial data service is unlikely to be a viable option.

If the question is how well does 3G and related data services work near the edge of their range, then the paper doesn't really answer that because we don't know the positions of cell centers relative to measurements.

Are you proposing that cellular data be installed at remote locations for oil field operators? Even so, the data would have to be backhauled by some technology, e.g., satellite.

These questions aside, a large part of the performance which is diurnal is probably dominated by usage of the cell by other users. That hardly seems relevant to any of the problems above.

Response from the Authors

(1) Generality of contributions (Reviewers 1, 2, 3 and 5): The paper's contribution is in exploring the potential for less costly

cellular data usage at remote sites where such usage has not traditionally been contemplated. It is clear that there is significant diversity in availability of cellular and satellite coverage among remote locations. Our goal in this paper is to provide a framework for assessing this availability through systematic measurement and evaluation and analyzing instances of this framework at different geographical locations.

(2) Filtering data based on job transition and equipment downtimes (Reviewers 1 and 3): We retrieved Windows OS's native logs containing PC power on/off events from different crews. With this type of information, we reprocessed availability logs of cellular and satellite interfaces and eliminated the effect of job transition/equipment down schedule on availability comparison.

(3) About optimizing the TCP stack (Reviewers 1 and 2): Although optimization of TCP performance is outside the scope of this paper, we added end-to-end latency measurements in the final paper, which shows high variation across different interfaces. This indicates a specially designed TCP stack which adapts to high latency variation might have better performance over the default TCP stack of Windows OS in such a multi-interface system.

(4) Discussion on entropy analysis (Reviewers 3 and 4): We removed the discussion on entropy analysis about bandwidth prediction as the information presented in this analysis can be found in other parts of the paper as reviewers pointed out.

(5) Writing and presentation (Reviewers 4 and 5): Several rounds of editing were applied to the final version of this paper to improve the English and presentation.

(6) Clarification of Table 1 (Reviewer 1): Clarification of coverage results in Table 1 is provided and the unit of measurement is also added.

(7) Hybrid cellular and satellite usage (Reviewer 2): The methodology we developed in this measurement study is actually used to provide a simple link management scheme. Therefore, an application can select among interfaces based on their availability and a pre-determined preference.

(8) Measurement location/crew selection (Reviewer 4): We've added a discussion on the criteria and process of location/crew selection.

(9) Cellular link's availability is questionable at certain locations (Reviewer 5): Our objective is not replacing satellite links with cellular links or vice versa. On the contrary, our measurement framework shows that highly-available and cost-effective data communication may be achieved via a multi-interface system.

Over the Top Video: The Gorilla in Cellular Networks

Jeffrey Erman, Alexandre Gerber, K.K. Ramakrishnan, Subhabrata Sen, Oliver Spatscheck
AT&T Labs - Research, New Jersey, USA
{erman,gerber,kkrama,sen,spatsch}@research.att.com

ABSTRACT

Cellular networks have witnessed tremendous traffic growth recently, fueled by smartphones, tablets and new high speed broadband cellular access technologies. A key application driving that growth is video streaming. Yet very little is known about the characteristics of this traffic class. In this paper, we examine video traffic generated by three million users across one of the world's largest 3G cellular networks. This first deep dive into cellular video streaming shows that HLS, an adaptive bitrate streaming protocol, accounts for one third of the streaming video traffic and that it is common to see changes in encoding bitrates within a session. We also observe that most of the content is streamed at less than 255 Kbps and that only 40% of the videos are fully downloaded. Another key finding is that there exists significant potential for caching to deliver this content.

Categories and Subject Descriptors

D.4.8 [**Performance**]: Measurements—*web caching*

General Terms

Networking Optimization

1. INTRODUCTION

Thanks to the emergence of user-friendly smartphones and tablets, cellular networks have recently experienced a phenomenal rise in data traffic. One US cellular operator observed a growth of 8000% over the last 4 years [4]. According to a network equipment manufacturer [5], strong growth will continue at a rate of 92% per year over the next 5 years, driven primarily by video traffic. Indeed, they estimate that video traffic accounts for half of the cellular traffic today and that this share will increase to two thirds of the traffic by 2015. Given such predictions, it becomes crucial for network providers to understand and then determine how to optimize delivery of video traffic for cellular networks. This traffic type is often referred to as Over The Top (OTT) video, as the content doesn't typically come from the cellular carrier, but from third party providers that leverage the Internet connectivity of cellular customers.

Unfortunately, little is known about the characteristics of cellular video traffic. For example, today there does not even exist a study on the popularity of the actual video streaming protocols used on cellular networks: previous studies have either looked at general cellular traffic usage or just focused on WiFi [10, 11, 13–16, 18, 19]. In cellular networks, the most constrained and expensive resource is the wireless spectrum in the Radio Access Network (RAN) and it is critical that the video delivery is optimized for this environment. A key step in that direction is developing a deep understanding of the video content. In particular, the frame size, encoding rate and other video parameters are important factors to better undstand, to evaluate how much optimization opportunity exists, identify the appropriate optimization techniques and where (content provider, cellular provider, user equipment) to implement them. For instance, the knowledge of the current encoding rates and video abandonment probabilities (how much of a video is likely to be watched) could suggest the need techniques such as video pacing or transcoding at the source servers or at in the network middleboxes.

While not as expensive, and, therefore less critical, backbone resources upstream of the RAN can also be optimized based on the characteristics of video traffic. Indeed, on the wireline Internet, [12, 17] have highlighted that 80% of multimedia streaming traffic was delivered over HTTP, and in this paper, we will show that the rate for cellular network is even higher with 98%. Hence, proxy caching based techniques which have been proposed for wired video distribution over HTTP might also be applicable to cellular networks and should be investigated.

This paper is the first study to provide answers to these types of questions about video traffic on a large cellular network. It is based on a data set collected early in 2011 covering approximately three million smartphones and tablets in the US over 48 hours. Some of the key takeaways of our analysis are as follows:

Protocol mix: Video traffic accounts for 30% of the downstream cellular traffic during the busy hour and a couple of streaming protocols running over HTTP dominate. HTTP Live Streaming (HLS) [2, 7] accounts for 36% of the video traffic, while progressive downloads (defined in Section 2) account for 60%.

Content Providers: 77% of the traffic is concentrated in just the top 10 content providers.

Bitrate Encoding: 80% of the video objects are encoded at low rates, at or below 255 kbps.

Video Abandonment: Most videos are downloaded partially. Only 40% of the video objects are completely downloaded.

Cacheability: There exists substantial potential for caching. 24% of the bytes for progressive downloads requests can be served from cache.

IMC'11, November 2–4, 2011, Berlin, Germany.

Table 1: Data set overview

Data Set	Location	Start time	Duration	Objects	Traffic (TB)
NE	US N/E	2/16/2011 15:00 GMT	24 hours	4.8M	8.09 TBytes
WEST	US West coast	2/16/2011 15:00 GMT	48 hours	5.0M	9.05 TBytes

2. METHODOLOGY

We categorize the videos downloaded over HTTP into three classes based on the streaming method used:

Progressive Download (PD): A single video is downloaded with a single HTTP request for the entire object from the client. The client can access the partially downloaded data before the download is complete.

PD with Byte-Range Requests (PD-byterange): A single video download involves multiple HTTP byte-range requests to get different portions of the content.

HTTP Live Streaming (HLS): This belongs to a broad class of protocols called Adaptive Bit Rate Video streaming [3]. The HLS protocol is a proposal to the IETF from Apple [2, 7]. In HLS, a video is downloaded in a series of chunks that are encoded using the MPEG4 H.264 Transport Stream. These chunks are typically around 3 to 10 seconds of video. They allow the stream to adapt to the changes in the network condition and also other factors, such as the device CPU load - by increasing or decreasing the bit rate and resolution of the video in real time when it requests the next chunk. This protocol is used generally by content providers that have long duration video content, such as Netflix or Hulu. Other examples of Adaptive Bit Rate Videos include HTTP Smooth Streaming advocated by Microsoft with Silverlight and HTTP Dynamic Streaming advocated by Adobe [9].

For Android-based devices, we found usage of both PD and PD-byterange based approaches in our analysis. The usage is dependent on the type of video subsystem used on each device model. In iOS-based devices, for most short-videos (less than 10 minutes) PD-byterange is used; however, for some videos Apple's developer guidelines require the use of HLS [8]. We did not find any examples of the HTTP Smooth Streaming or HTTP Dynamic Streaming from Adobe in the traffic from the devices we studied but this may be biased based on the subset of devices in the network studied.

In addition non-HTTP based protocols do not account for a significant amount of traffic as we show in Section 3, and therefore we do not investigate them further.

2.1 Data Sets

The data for this study was collected in two national data centers of a large US based wireless provider. More specifically, the traffic is analyzed on the Gn interface between the Gateway GPRS Support Nodes (GGSN) and Serving GPRS Support Nodes (SGSN). Table 1 shows the details of the two data sets. They were collected at the same time and were covering a fraction of the traffic in each data center which mainly contains traffic of smartphones and tablet type devices. In total, the data sets represent usage from approximately 3 million subscribers between the two data sets. While this is a large data set, the results may not be representative of other networks or countries, depending on the combination of wireless devices, the types of content providers and the behavior of users. The collection was limited to 8-9TB of data traffic in each dataset due to 3TB of storage available to each data collector to store flow records. As the traffic volumes observed by each data collector differed between data centers, each data set was collected for different durations.

To perform our analysis we collected flow records, HTTP headers and the first 20KB of each video flow. Video flows were identified using real-time signatures. They include in particular all HTTP objects with a "video" or "FLV" mime type as well as RTMP (Real Time Messaging Protocol) and RTSP (Real Time Streaming Protocol) traffic. Limiting our collection to the first 20KB of each video represents a compromise motivated by the fact that most video formats contain sufficient information in the first 20KB of a video stream to infer encoding rates and other video parameters necessary for our analysis, and that collecting the entire video would have severely limited our study period or the number of subscribers in our study. The privacy of the subscribers was preserved, since the flow data was not mapped to individual devices and the study focused on the aggregate statistics across all the devices in the data set. All the video content analysis was complete on the data collector using automated tools and no content was exported off the data collector.

2.2 Data Preprocessing

After the data was collected it was preprocessed in multiple ways to support our analysis.

* The HTTP requests and responses were correlated and the actual amount of user layer data was calculated using the flow records and also the TCP sequence number differences for pipelined requests, as in many cases the byte volumes in the HTTP headers were unreliable (see Section 2.3). The device type is also determined from information set in the User-Agents of the request.

* Progressive video downloads (PDs) with multiple byte ranges requests were combined to represent one video object based on the URL used for the byte range requests.

* The multiple video chunks downloaded by HLS for a video are combined into a single video object (i.e. session as a video that is paused and later resumed in split into two seperate objects in our analysis). As there is no generally agreed method on how to combine HLS traffic, for each content provider we needed to develop seperate hueristics based on the request patterns to combine the HLS chunks to sessions. We only combined them for the major content providers which utilize HLS in our trace. In combination our heuristics allowed us to associate over 95% of all HLS traffic volume with their video object.

* To compute such video characteristics as video duration, codec, screen resolution and bitrate, the first 20KBytes of each video object was reassembled and replayed into the popular ffmpeg [6] tool, which provides such meta information to the user in clear text after analyzing the video headers. This allowed for 45% of the video objects to be analyzed by ffmpeg and have their video characteristics extracted. Unfortunately, not all videos contain enough information in the first 20KB or else place the meta data at the end of the video which does not allow ffmpeg to work on our data. In addition, some HLS content providers use DRM to encrypt their video objects which also limited ffmpeg's ability to extract these characteristics. Overall, ffmpeg was able to extract the full set of additional characteristcs from 45% of the video objects.

2.3 Sample Video Behaviours

In the rest of the paper much of the results focus on the complete video objects and HLS sessions. Figure 1 and 2 show two illustrative examples of the more interesting detailed behaviours observed.

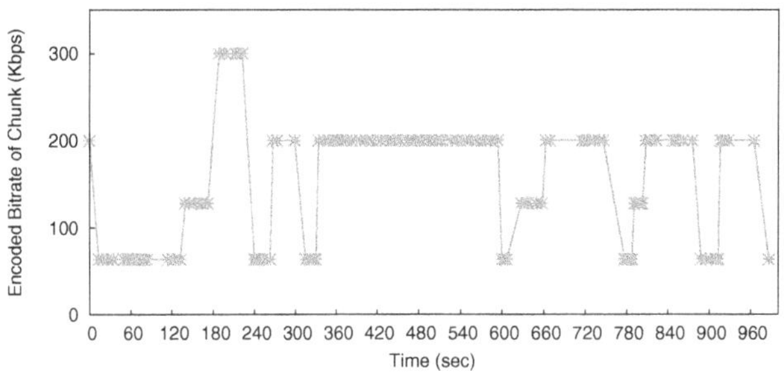

Figure 1: Adaptive Bit Rate: Hulu example

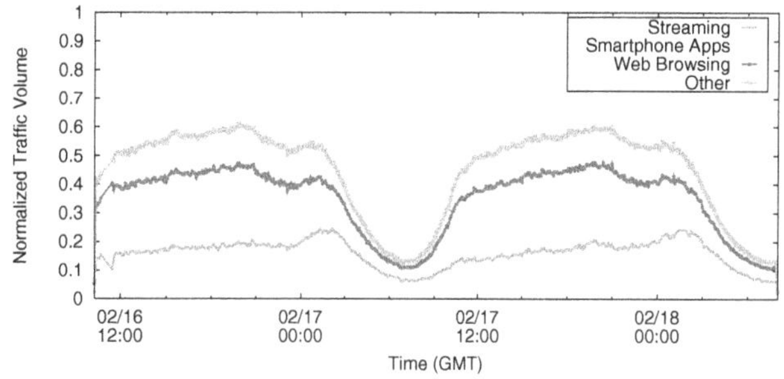

Figure 3: Application Mix of Overall Traffic using a stacked line chart.

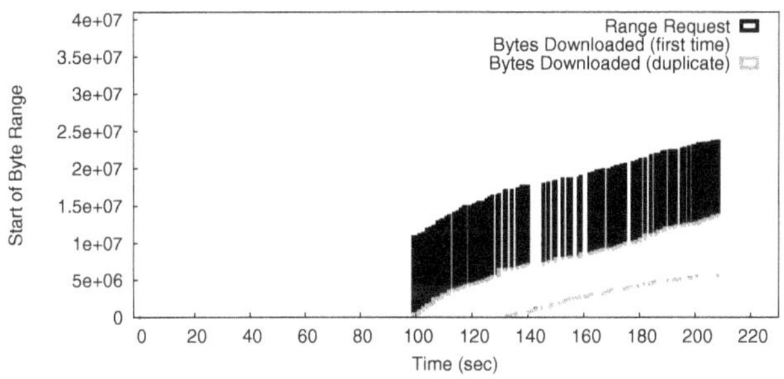

Figure 2: Malfunctioning Byte-Range Example

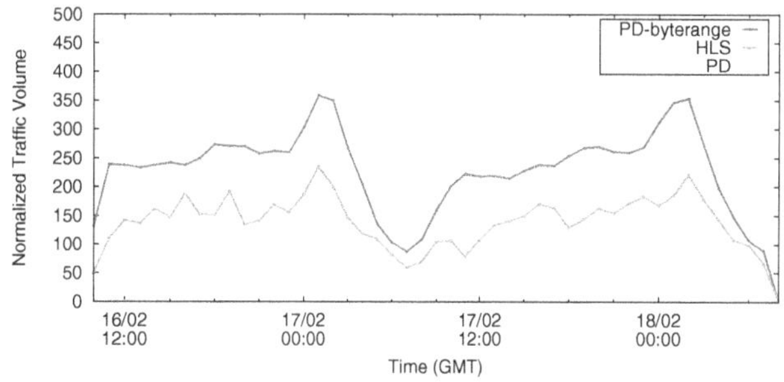

Figure 4: Type of Video Traffic

An example of an HLS video session is shown in Figure 1. This was a Hulu video session where the adaptive protocol can be seen changing between 64, 128, 200, and 300 Kbps encoding rates quite frequently during the session. The interarrival times between chunks is approximately 10 seconds in this example. On average, we measure HLS flows changing bitrates 0.2 times per minute in the video session for content provider which we could determine the bitrate of the chunks. This highlights that available bandwidth in cellular networks can change several times during the course of a TV show or movie session and also that HLS protocols are actively adaptiving their bitrates to these flucutations.

The second example is of an observed PD-byterange download (Figure 2). The black bars show the range of the actual data downloaded and the green bars the byte-range requests size. The red bars show data downloaded of the video that was already previously downloaded. As seen in the graph, the byte-ranges are much larger than the actual content downloaded before the device closes the HTTP connection and starts another. We also observe that for longer videos a large initial download is typically followed by a sequence of smaller downloads for the same byterange. Further lab testing showed that the behavior was reproducible. For instance, after some larger videos were fully downloaded, and until the user had finished watching the video, additional duplicate downloads would occur. This case was observed frequently and generated a significant amount of unnecessary duplicate video content in the trace.

3. TRAFFIC CHARACTERIZATION

In this section, we show highlights of the video traffic we studied. While our analysis was completed on both the NE and WEST data sets, many of the results are quantitatively similar, therefore, we have chosen for more clarity to provide the WEST data set results only unless noted otherwise.

Overall, video streaming traffic accounts for 36% of the traffic in the data studied. This is shown in Figure 3 in a stacked line chart. During the busy hour the video streaming share is actually 30% but peaks at 50% during the off peak hours.

The streaming video traffic is primarily delivered using HTTP-based methods. The use of HTTP-based method is true across multiple smartphone OS's as well. Traditional multimedia protocols like RTSP and RTMP account for only 1.3 % and 0.4 % of the traffic respectively. A more in depth analysis actually shows that the use of RTSP and RTMP on smartphones and tablets is much lower than reported as nearly all such traffic originates from either a laptop with a cellular card or a laptop tethered to a smartphone.

The number of video objects and the data volume in each category of the HTTP-based methods is shown in Table 2. One surprising category of video content was being generated by one advertising company (labeled separately as Advertisement Objects in the table). Interestingly, the number of objects of this category is rather large accounting for 44.5% of the objects in the NE data set and 44.8% in the WEST data set, even if by volume this type of traffic accounts for less than 0.1% of all video traffic. On closer examination we discovered that even though this content is marked as video content in the mime header, it actually contains just text-based user tracking information and no video content at all. As this study is focused on understanding video content in cellular networks, we excluded this data from the analysis presented in the remainder of this paper.

Table 3 shows the video characteristics per content provider and have been obfuscated to hide marketshare. The % objects fields after the "Top" columns shows the share the top category account for, and the UGC label refers to User Generated Content. In this table,

Table 2: Video Object Types

Data Set	HLS Objects	PD Objects	PD byterange Objects	Adv. Objects	HLS TBytes	PD TBytes	PD byterange TBytes	Adv. TBytes
NE	0.2 (5.4%)	0.8M (15.2%)	1.9M (34.9%)	2.1M (44.5%)	2.6 (29.5%)	0.4 (4.6%)	5.9 (65.7%)	< 0.1 (.1%)
WEST	0.2 (4.8%)	0.7 (15.3%)	1.7M (35.1%)	2.1M (44.8%)	2.9 (36.3%)	0.3 (4.2%)	4.8 (59.4%)	< 0.1 (.1%)

Table 3: Content Provider Breakdown

Content Providers	Objects	Bytes	HLS	PD-BR	PD	Top Type	Objects	Top Screen Size	Objects	Avg Bitrate	Avg Dur.	Median Dur.
Video Stream 1	2.8%	33.2%	100%	0%	0%	HLS	100%	Unknown	100%	613.59	10.8	9.5
UGC 1	37.4%	19.2%	0%	99.53%	0.47%	video/3gpp	92%	176x144	3%	161.59	4.09	3.5
Adult 1	2.8%	6.1%	0%	99.66%	0.34%	video/mp4	100%	240x176	6%	955.8	4.82	7.0
Adult 2	1.5%	4.1%	0%	99.45%	0.55%	video/mp4	98%	240x176	2%	1057.63	4.84	10.0
UGC 2	4.2%	4.0%	0%	94.25%	5.75%	video/3gpp	58%	640x360	4%	334.44	3.95	3.4
Adult 3	2.1%	3.5%	0%	99.45%	0.55%	video/mp4	100%	320x240	2%	498.71	5.98	3.5
Music 1	6.0%	2.3%	0%	15.43%	84.57%	video/mp4	100%	480x270	63%	1146.51	0.26	0.3
Video Stream 2	0.3%	2.0%	99.21%	0%	0.79%	HLS	99%	Unknown	99%	435.05	9.16	4.8
Music 2	0.8%	1.4%	98.37%	1.45%	0.18%	HLS	98%	Unknown	98%	1339.04	0.96	0.6
Adult 4	0.6%	1.3%	0%	99.57%	0.43%	video/3gpp	100%	640x480	0%	389	0.72	2.0
Social Network 1	2.8%	1.3%	0%	99.68%	0.32%	video/mp4	100%	400x300	2%	364.4	0.85	0.6
Social Network 2	1.7%	1.0%	99.98%	0.01%	0.01%	HLS	100%	Unknown	100%	319.72	1.06	1.5
Adult 5	0.9%	0.7%	0%	99.68%	0.32%	video/mp4	100%	320x240	5%	474.97	2.33	2.0
Adult 6	0.2%	0.6%	0%	99.78%	0.22%	video/mp4	100%	320x240	3%	549.54	3.42	3.6

it can be seen that video content delivered is dominated by a few top content providers: the top 10 account for 77% of the video streaming. We also observe that each content provider is using mainly a single method to deliver the videos. While some of the previous distributions had some distortions due to some smaller content providers, comparing only the top 2 content providers, which are also the top HLS and top PD-byterange providers, a clearer picture emerges. HLS has longer duration video sessions and a higher average bitrate.

Table 4 is a similar table to the previous but shows the video characteristics by device type. The most common container and screen size resolutions of the videos with the % objects columns after the "Top" columns showing the share the top value accounted for in the data.

Figure 5 shows the average bitrate encoding for the HLS and PD byte-range videos. The PD videos can be seen to be encoded at 3 main rates of 87 Kbps, 255 Kbps, and 1150 Kbps. For the HLS streams, the average bit rates are relatively stable with an average delivered bit rate around 500-600 Kbps. The similarity is not surprising as HLS is an adaptive bit rate protocol that adapts to the available bandwidth and resources on the device. Many of the content providers using HLS have a variety of bitrates that are available. For example, *Video Stream 2* in Table 3 has 64, 128, 200, 300, 400, 650, 1000, 1500 Kbps, as encoded rates of the chunks we saw delivered. Several other content providers using the same CDN encode their video chunks at: 110, 200, 450 and 800 Kbps. Unfortunately for *Video Stream 1*, this content provider encrypts its traffic, so we do not know the exact encoding rate levels used the individual chunks for this provider.

Figure 6 shows the object size distribution of the individual "chunks" of the PD-byterange and HLS videos, as well as the stitched total videos object sizes. As pointed out in Section 2.3 the chunk sizes of byte range requests for one device are rather odd. In fact, 70% of all requests in our data set are for small chunks which follow the large initial chunk.

The average HLS chunk is 362 KB with most ranging between 100-300 KB in size. The interarrival times between chunk requests are clustered around 3 and 10 second intervals, with a small number of sessions at 20 and 30 second intervals as well. We were able to verify the 10 second chunk encoding using the video durations extracted on many of the video chunks decoded by ffmpeg.

Surprisingly, when comparing the HLS object sizes and durations to the PD-byterange results in Figure 6 and Figure 7, the HLS durations are shorter than the PD-byte-ranges durations. This is the result of HLS being influenced by a small number of content providers. The video duration of one HLS content provider is always between 1 to 1.5 minutes long. While other content providers have much longer session durations such as *Video Stream 1* and *Video Stream 2*. It is also interesting to note that, for these streaming providers, few sessions last the entire movie or TV show length. For many cases, sessions are interrupted and are then later seen to be resumed. On average, for these content providers each video is resumed 0.19 times.

Another interesting observation is that for HLS video the video containers of the videos are already in an optimized state for mobile video. For PD and PD-byterange video objects, we were expecting to see more variety initially with different formats supported and used on different types of devices. However, we found that not to be the case, and that most videos were already in optimized containers for 3GPP video. They were encoded using H.264 and are in either "video/mp4" or "video/3gpp" containers for 80.7% of the objects and 95.2% of bytes. Only 1.1% of objects and 0.8% of bytes were in FLV format in the WEST data set and 2.1% and 1.2% of bytes were in FLV format in the NE data set. This is also consistent across different devices type that FLV is not a popular format as observed in Table 4.

Finally, we studied how many videos were fully downloaded. Fortunately for PD videos we were able to measure the total amount of data actually downloaded before abandonment (Figure 8) and compare it to the video size reported. Some videos are observed to download more than 100% of video. This is a combination of the issue observed in Section 2.3 and also from fastforwardng and rewinding when a video is not fully cached. What can be observed is that only 40% of videos are completely downloaded, and for 50% of videos only 60% of the video was downloaded. While this does not show how much was watched, due to buffering, it gives a glimpse into the amount of video that is abandoned before being fully watched.

4. VIDEO POPULARITY AND CACHING

Having observed that streaming video accounts for a dominant part of the cellular broadband traffic and that the lion's share of this traffic is carried over HTTP, a natural question is what are effec-

Table 4: Devices Breakdown

Device	Top Content Type	% Objects	Top Screen Size	% Objects	Average Bitrate	Median Duration
Smartphone 1	video/mp4	58%	480x270	3%	278.9	2.85
Tablet 1	video/mp4	55%	320x240	2%	315.5	2.78
Laptop 1	video/x-ms-wmv	46%	640x360	7%	689.5	0.50
Smartphone 2	video/mp4	76%	320x240	2%	169.8	3.55

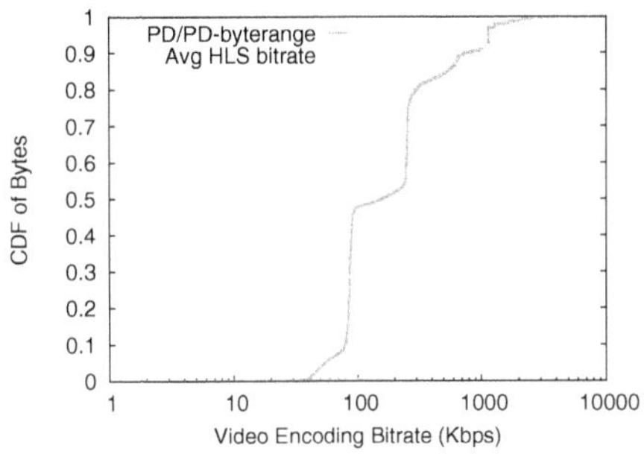

Figure 5: Distribution of Encoded Video Bitrates for PD,PD-byterange

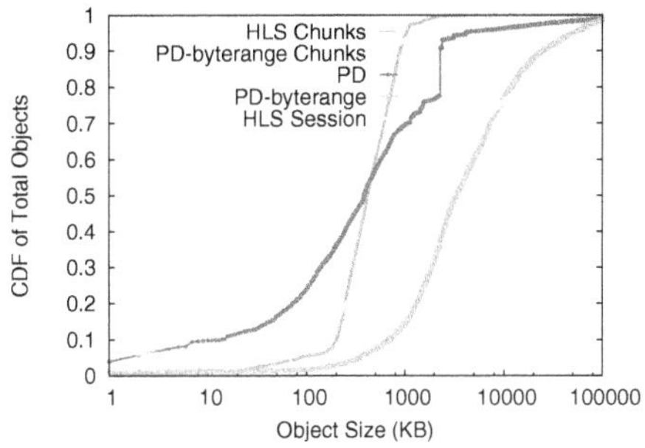

Figure 6: Object Size Distribution of Video Objects

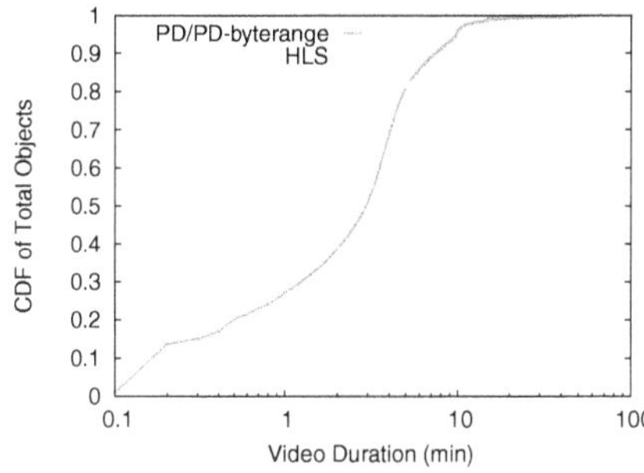

Figure 7: Distribution of Video Durations

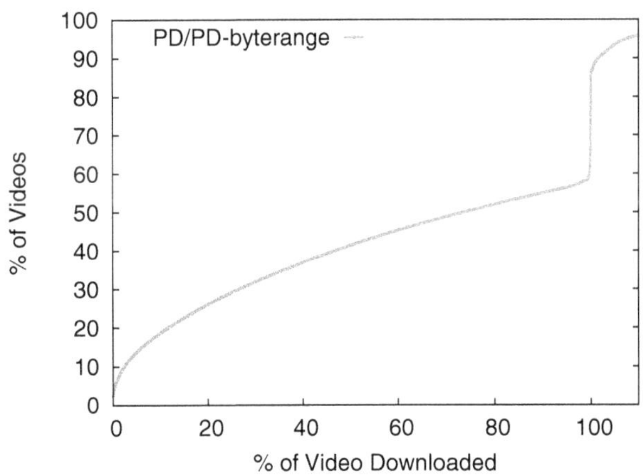

Figure 8: Percentage of each Video Object Downloaded

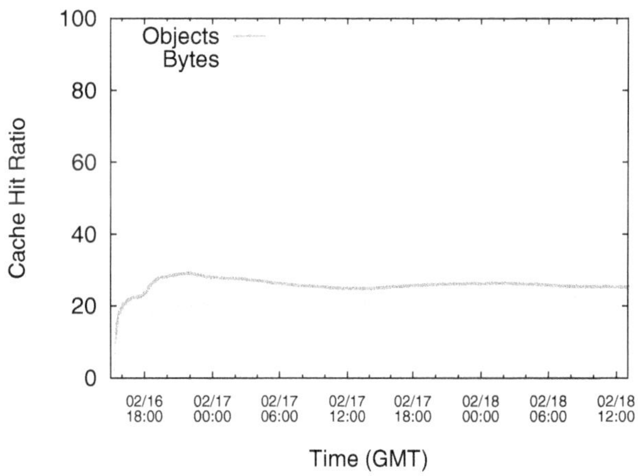

Figure 9: Cache Hit Ratio of Video and Cache Size

tive ways to deliver this content. Even though the impact of video caching on the RAN is limited, as highlighted in the Introduction, the growth of video traffic in cellular network still warrants a close study of the topic to understand the possible bandwidth savings in the backkhaul networks and the potential to improve end-user experience by reducing delay. To answer how much potential exists one must in particular consider multiple aspects of the traffic characteristics: whether content providers allow their video objects to be cached, the spatio-temporal popularity characteristics of the requested video objects, and whether the content is encrypted, etc.

We first examine the requested objects based purely on the cache control directives in the HTTP request response messages. These enable specification of *Cacheability* : the server can specify whether a requested object can be cached, and then can indicate if a particular request can be served from cache or needs to be fetched from the server. *Freshness* : the duration for which a downloaded copy of a cacheable resource is valid for serving a request.

Combining the relevant information bits from the request-response pairs for a video object, we can categorize all the requests in terms of *Cacheability* as:

uncacheable: the request can not be cached;

cacheable-local: the requested object is cacheable and the request can be served from the cache without contacting the server as long as it is fresh;

cacheable-validate: the requested object is cacheable, but the cache needs to check with the server that its local copy is valid every time the object is served to a client.

We find that for PD-all (both PD and PD-byterange) traffic, 8.0% of all the requested data are uncacheable, 63.2% are cacheable-local and 28.8% are cacheable-validate. For HLS traffic the corresponding percentages are 78%, 11% and 11%, respectively. An upper bound on the proportion of requests (by bytes) that can be potentially served from the cache (assuming that the content is fresh for cacheable-local cases and that the copy is still valid for the cacheable-validate cases) is a very large 92.0% of all the requested traffic for PD-all and only 22% for HLS.

We next consider the distribution of the freshness for object requested with a server-specified freshness duration > 0. Across all

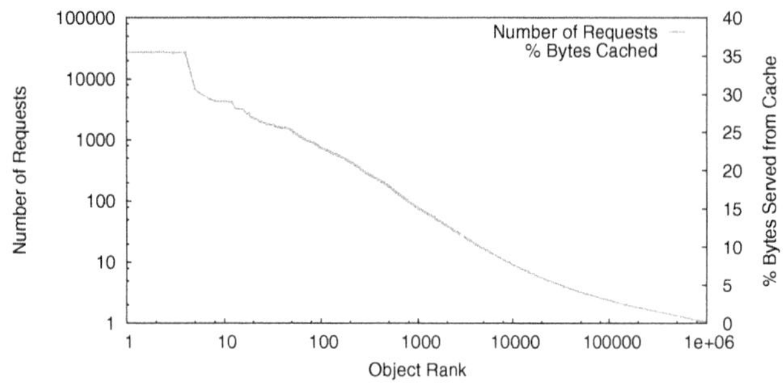

Figure 10: Object Popularity of PD-all Videos

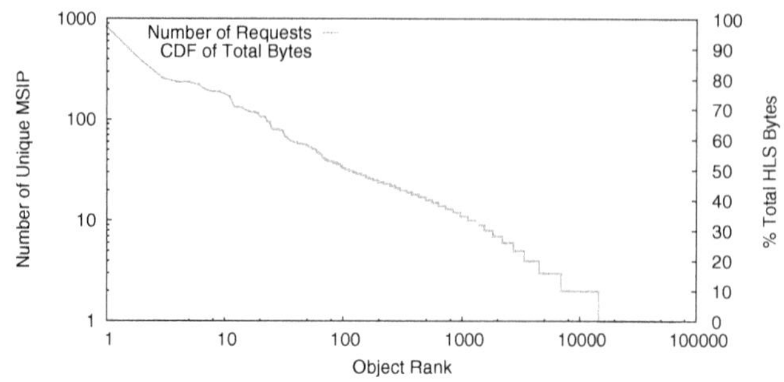

Figure 11: Object Popularity of HLS Videos

the video types, we find that overall freshness duration is $< 1hour$ for 9.4% of the requested traffic, and exceeds 1 day for 32.3% of the requested traffic. There are 2 concentrations: 14.5% of the traffic has freshness duration of 1 hour and 43.8% of the traffic have freshness duration of 1 day. The results show that substantial fraction of the traffic seems to have very short freshness durations set. Given that video objects normally do not change at short timescales, and that increasing the freshness duration would increase the likelihood of serving more requests from cache, content providers should examine whether longer freshness durations (eg. a day) would meet their application needs.

4.1 Caching Simulation

In addition to the HTTP caching directives, the cache size and the spatio-temporal pattern of request arrivals also determine the extent to which requests can be served from the cache. To understand the maximum obtainable benefits and to focus on the impact of the spatio-temporal pattern of request arrivals, we consider an unlimited cache size and simulate HTTP forward caching for the entire traffic data for PD-all. Conceptually the result achieves the spatio-temporal caching benefits of a cache located at the National Data Center (NDC), which hosts the GGSNs through which all the measured traffic flows. Our simulator is implemented to follow the HTTP caching standard in [1].

Figure 9 depicts, for a given time instant t, the fraction of all traffic that was served from the cache from the beginning of the simulation until time t. At the end of the 48 hour trace, we see that around 23.5% of all the requested traffic (in terms of bytes) was served from the cache. Recall that 92.0% of the PD-all traffic was cacheable based on caching directives, therefore 25.5% of the cacheable PD-all traffic was actually served from cache. The remaining 74.5% of the cacheable traffic had to be sourced from the server - either because they accounted for the first download of an object, or because the cached object was stale when requested.

Figure 10 shows the ranked list (red curve) of all the PD-all videos requested, in decreasing order of popularity and their cumulative contributions to the proportion of total traffic that was served using cached content (green curve). There is significant skew in popularity. The top-100 and top-1000 most popular objects account for 11.3% and 19.2% of all the requests respectively. The caching simulation reveals that the traffic served from cache that was associated with the top 100 and top 1000 objects is 4.5% and 7.7% of the total requested traffic respectively. Recalling that overall, 23.5% of all the requested traffic (in terms of bytes) was served from the cache, a policy that caches just the top-1000 objects of the total 1.2 million unique PD-all videos would already realize a third of the overall caching benefits. Detailed examination showed that the top 5 objects were the same video being served from different servers of a content provider and that most of the top 200 objects were advertising videos. Another interesting point is that the popularity distribution has a long tail which potentially limits the overall caching that can be achieved: 50% of all requests for cacheable objects, were for objects that were requested once.

Recall that unlike PD-all videos, a relatively small proportion of HLS traffic is cacheable because the HTTP cache control directives set by the content provider do now allow it to be cached. In addition, we also found that much of the HLS objects were encrypted - this adds complexity to using HTTP cache-based delivery for such objects, as clients would also need appropriate keys to decrypt the objects. While the combination of wide-spread non-caching directives and encryption are negatives from a caching viewpoint , it is still interesting to examine the popularity characteristics of content being transmitted using HLS. Specifically, assuming HTTP directives were more permissive and it were possible to address the encryption-induced challenges, would it make sense to use caching for this content ? As a first step to answering this question, in Figure 11 we plot the ranked list (red curve) of all the HLS videos requested, in decreasing order of popularity and their cumulative contributions to the proportion of total traffic (green curve). Of the total 66000 unique HLS objects, the top 1000 and the top 2800 account for 27.4% and 50% of all the HLS traffic respectively. This popularity skew suggests that caching even a small fraction of the popular HLS videos can lead to substantial caching gains.

5. CONCLUSION

This paper is the first large scale fine grain analysis of video traffic generated by 3 million devices on a cellular network. Some of the findings include the fact that one third of the cellular traffic comes from Over The Top video traffic, that one third of that traffic is HLS and that, in practice, adaptive bitrate encoding seems to be effective as frequent bitrate adaptations are observed to sustain the video stream (0.2 bitrate changes per minute). Moreover, we also observed that only 40% of the videos are completely downloaded and that 80% of the videos are encoded at or below 255kbps. Finally, we studied the cacheability of that video content. These results will help guide future video modeling and optimization work.

6. REFERENCES

[1] Hypertext Transfer Protocol – HTTP/1.1 . `http://www.w3.org/Protocols/rfc2616/rfc2616.html`, 1999.

[2] iOS Technical Note TN2224. `http://developer.apple.com/library/ios/#technotes/tn2224/_index.html`, April 2010.

[3] Adaptive Bitrate Protocols. http://en.wikipedia.org/wiki/Adaptive_bit_rate, 2011.

[4] AT&T SXSW Press Release. www.att.com/Common/docs/SXSW_Network%20Fact_Sheet.doc, March 2011.

[5] Cisco Visual Networking Index: Global Mobile Data Traffic Forecast Update, 2010Ű2015. http://www.cisco.com/en/US/solutions/collateral/ns341/ns525/ns537/ns705/ns827/white_paper_c11-520862.html, February 2011.

[6] FFmpeg. http://www.ffmpeg.org/, 2011.

[7] HTTP Live Streaming. http://tools.ietf.org/html/draft-pantos-http-live-streaming-06, 2011.

[8] iOS Developer Library. http://developer.apple.com/library/ios/#documenation/networkinginternet/conceptual/streamingmediaguide/UsingHTTPLiveStreaming/UsingHTTPLiveStreaming.html, 2011.

[9] S. Akhshabi, A. Begen, and C. Dovrolis. An Experimental Evaluation of Rate-Adaptation Algorithms in Adaptive Streaming over HTTP. In *MMSys'11*, San Jose, USA, 2011.

[10] J. Chesterfield, R. Charkravorty, J. Crowcroft, P. Radriguez, and S. Banerjee. Experiences with multimedia streaming over 2.5G and 3G Network. In *BroadNets'04*, Chicago, USA, 2004.

[11] J. Erman, A. Gerber, M. T. Hajiaghayi, D. Pei, S. Sen, and O. Spatscheck. To Cache or not to Cache: The 3G case. In *IEEE Internet Computing*, 2011.

[12] J. Erman, A. Gerber, M. T. Hajiaghayi, D. Pei, and O. Spatscheck. Network-Aware Forward Caching. In *WWW'09*, Madrid, Spain, 2009.

[13] H. Falaki, D. Lymberopoulos, R. Mahajan, S. Kandula, and D. Estrin. A first look at traffic on smartphones. In *Proc. IMC*, 2010.

[14] H. Falaki, R. Mahajan, S. Kandula, D. Lymberopoulos, R. Govindan, and D. Estrin. Diversity in Smartphone Usage. In *MobiSys'10*, San Francisco, USA, 2010.

[15] A. Gember, A. Anand, and A. Akella. A Comparative Study of Handheld and Non-Handheld Traffic in Campus WiFi Networks. In *Proc. Passive and Active Measurement*, 2011.

[16] J. Huang, Q. Xu, B. Tiwana, Z. M. Mao, M. Zhang, and P. Bahl. Anatomizing Application Performance Differences on Smartphones. In *MobiSys '10*, pages 165–178, New York, NY, USA, 2010. ACM.

[17] G. Maier, A. Feldmann, V. Paxson, and M. Allman. On Dominant Characteristics of Residential Broadband Internet Traffic. In *IMC'09*, Chicago, USA, 2009.

[18] G. Maier, F. Schneider, and A. Feldmann. A First Look at Mobile Hand-held Device Traffic. In *PAM'10*, pages 161–170, Berlin, Heidelberg, 2010. Springer-Verlag.

[19] Y. J. Won, B.-C. Park, S.-C. Hong, K. B. Jung, H.-T. Ju, and J. W. Hong. Measurement Analysis of Mobile Data Networks. In *PAM'07*, pages 223–227, Berlin, Heidelberg, 2007. Springer-Verlag.

Summary Review Documentation for

"Over the Top Video: The Gorilla in Cellular Networks"

Authors: J. Erman, A. Gerber, K. Ramakrishnan, S. Sen, O. Spatscheck

Reviewer #1

Strengths: The authors collect data from the link connecting the SGSN and GGSN nodes in a large cellular network, and on two different locations. They analyze it to identify the videos, the protocol they are relayed on, the resolution, as well as cacheability. Very nice study.

Weaknesses: The paper seems to be rushed at times. One figure is repeated the same in two places (5 and 8), the authors never introduce the content providers and make mention to them without and explanation. But these could be fixed in the final version.

Comments to Authors: This is a very nice short paper. The authors use a new source of data, carefully collected for 24 and 48 hours in two different locations in a large cellular network. They collect flow information and packet information (the first 20KB), thus being able to also look into the streaming bit rate of the video, the type of video, its resolution, information that is not easily accessible. Moreover, they are able to see the protocol that carries the video in question and study its properties.

Interesting findings are:
- majority of video is carried over HLS
- the transmission of the video is done over varying bit rates that can be observed through the trace, indicating the actual need for streaming rate adaptation to wireless conditions
- most content today is streamed at rather low streaming rates
- 40% of the videos never complete
- given that the majority of video traffic is transported over HTTP, the question of cacheability is asked and the authors simulate the actual gains one could expect from such a solution by replaying the collected traces.

One question I had is whether the authors know if there are any content acceleration middleboxes in the path observed. That would be essential to understand since then your infrastructure monitors the behavior of the middlebox and not the origin video server.

More detailed comments:
- Section 2.1: I assume that the capacity for data collection is 9 TB and not 3 (otherwise text disagrees with Table1)
- Figure 3 says that it displays normalized volume, but in that case I would expect the x-axis to be between 0 and 1 or 0 and 100%. In your final version, you need to describe the metrics displayed in the figures more carefully.
- The paragraph below Figure 5 points to Figure 4, but that figure does not contain the information discussed.
- Video providers are discussed in page 4 without any prior reference and only appear in the next page. You need to reorganize the paper for better exposition.
- I was actually surprised that the top resolution covers only 3% of the videos. How many resolutions do you see being used in total?

All in all, I think this is a very decent attempt for this first study of its kind. The writing is rushed but I think the content is there and it's interesting. I would be in favor of acceptance.

Reviewer #2

Strengths: The paper presents characteristics of a large volume of video traffic on a cellular network. There are some interesting data points, e.g., the distribution of different types of video streaming methods.

Weaknesses: The data seems not well analyzed, even for a short paper and some of the results are too anecdotal. The paper is poorly written in parts.

Comments to Authors: Video streaming over cellular networks is definitely a growing part of traffic, and this analysis from a large cellular network is certainly of great interest. However, I found the paper to have inadequately analyzed, what certainly is a very rich dataset.

As an example, Figure 2 shows an anecdotal download using the PD-byterange method. The results are strange and unexplained in the paper. Does this kind of download happen a lot, or is it just a rare occurrence?

Fig 5 and Fig 8 appear to be identical.

Some of the results presented in the paper, i.e., choice of video adaptation rates used by different applications, are not really actionable. The only part of the paper that I personally found particularly useful was the cacheability discussion.

Overall, this seems like a large dataset that requires more interesting analysis and the authors probably have barely scratched the surface with this work.

Reviewer #3

Strengths: Important topic.

Weaknesses: This reader is somewhat concerned with the representativeness of the results from this study, due to various indications shown in the paper. For example, Section 2.3 stated that video objects were replayed into the popular ffmpeg tool to extract out the needed information, and "In our data set ffmpeg was able to parse 45% of the video objects".

Another concern is the rather different ratio of uncacheable data between PD and HLS (8% vs 78%), which was stated but not clearly explained. The paper explained this is largely due to encryption of HLP. But how should one view this result together with the Section 2.3 statement in the above ("was able to parse 45% of the video objects")?

Section 4 stated that " the impact of video caching on the RAN is limited". Is this referring to the above result, or something else?

Comments to Authors: None.

Reviewer #4

Strengths: This is a classic network measurement paper. The measurements are strong, interesting, and provide some new insights.

Weaknesses: The paper tends, at times, to feel like a data dump.

At times some of the underlying issues of data quality seem a little brushed under the carpet. For instance, how do the authors account for a possible bias caused by some brands of devices more represented than others in their dataset, in comparison to other wireless networks?

Comments to Authors: The paper seems to be along the same lines as "P2P, the Gorilla in the Cable (2003)" by some of the same authors. Although the topic is actually different, the similarity of titles leads one to want to know the relationship between the two papers.

There are a few statements that are just a little off. For instance, the two datasets were collected at the same time, but one is longer than the other. I guess it is just the same start time? The data collector had 3 TB storage, but the traces where both over 8 TB? Please clarify.

There is a general statement about the number of subscribers covered in the study, but it isn't made clear if this is a total of which we see a sample (in each area), or if this is the number sampled.

Why does Figure 9 go above 100%?

There are quite a few small bugs and typos in the paper.

Reviewer #5

Strengths: - Novelty: new aspect of mobile cellular network usage captured for the first time, with some important new insights (on the amount of incomplete videos, and the relative spread of their popularity).
- Level of detail: practitioners and people working on detailed protocols of video encoding could find interesting bits.
that there are a couple of anecdotal evidences it is nice to monitor how YouTube works in a systematic fashion.

Weaknesses: - Not much, some limitations could be mentioned a bit more clearly, and naturally it would be awesome to understand spatial property as well, but there is so much one can do in 6 pages.
- The authors could have contrasted their findings with wire networks to emphasize the new characteristics found in this context.

Comments to Authors: This paper is I think a no-brainer accept. It is not revolutionary but it provides detailed insights into video traffic on cellular network, by using collected measurements and presenting a very clear set of numbers. Among them one that stands out particularly is that a large part of the videos are not completed (although it is only seen on a part of the data set), and that caching is not going to reduce the traffic much, although it will be effective for the most popular videos.

This is well done and contains quite clear description of video encoding characteristics. Seems a great match for a short paper.

A few points to improve:

1. I think that it is important to put some of the results in perspective of your limitation. In particular, the fact that only PD videos are examined from the completion standpoint is (1) only establishing this result on a part of the data set, (2) may be biased (some of these videos may take more time to load as they retrieve from multiple sources and needs reassembling, and hence may create too much impatience in the users). This point ought to be clarified.

2. When you mentioned caching, it could also be the case that caching improves delay, which seems to be an important thing given the relative fraction of uncompleted download indicating that users are affected by delay. It would be nice to see that point discussed.

3. I am surprised not to see any discussion of previous findings of videos on other networks. I imagine that the rate could be quite different (although it depends on which year we consider). But would the popularity be the same? Would the amount of abandons and video lengths be different?

4. The restriction to remove ad-video seems appropriate, but it seems also a bit incomplete (you mention you remove another domain, but isnt there more like these ones)? Could you provide some numbers (based on duration) to justify that no more are present?

This seems in particular important as you indicate later that the most popular videos are ads.

Response from the Authors

We thank the reviewers for their constructive comments.

We have addressed all the minor issues in the paper and made the appropriate adjustments (e.g. we have removed the duplicate figure pointed out in the review).

While we have done a careful example of the sample video behaviors in Section 2, this was more to illustrate the behavior than to come to our conclusions based on them. For example, we have observed that HLS sessions, in general, show their ability to adapt to changing conditions. Figure 1 is an example to illustrate this more carefully. The issue of duplicate downloads, as highlighted in Figure 2 is not an exception, but a common behavior across multiple applications that we have observed on multiple platforms (device OSs). We have explained this anomalous behavior better in Section 2, and also described how the behavior can be reproduced. To further establish that this is not just based on the observation of a few example situations, Figure 8 shows that for a significant percentage of videos more than 100% of the content is downloaded by the end-point. We believe that this adequately addresses the issue brought up by the fourth reviewer.

In addition to providing a novel characterization of video traffic on 3G networks, we also make useful observations about how a carrier can appropriately handle this class of traffic. This study is also important for application developers to understand their impact on the network and to more optimally use the cellular network.

This study and observations are based on traffic generated by millions of users in a large tier-1 network. The large footprint of the data set gives us a lot of confidence about the generality of our main findings. While there may be some idiosyncrasies e.g., the device mix studied, we have looked at other platforms with different devices and OS mixes and many of these conclusions still hold. Finally, we have also reminded readers that the results naturally may not be completely representative of the video traffic in every cellular network, since the combination of wireless devices, the types of content providers and the behavior of users might be different.

We leave the comparison of our results on cellular networks with video characteristics on wireline network for future work. Thanks for the suggestion

Airshark: Detecting Non-WiFi RF Devices using Commodity WiFi Hardware

Shravan Rayanchu, Ashish Patro, Suman Banerjee
{shravan, patro, suman}@cs.wisc.edu
University of Wisconsin, Madison, USA

ABSTRACT

In this paper, we propose Airshark—a system that detects multiple non-WiFi RF devices in *real-time and using only commodity WiFi hardware*. To motivate the need for systems like Airshark, we start with measurement study that characterizes the usage and prevalence of non-WiFi devices across many locations. We then present the design and implementation of Airshark. Airshark extracts unique features using the functionality provided by a WiFi card to detect multiple non-WiFi devices including fixed frequency devices (e.g., ZigBee, analog cordless phone), frequency hoppers (e.g., Bluetooth, game controllers like Xbox), and broadband interferers (e.g., microwave ovens). Airshark has an average detection accuracy of 91–96%, even in the presence of multiple simultaneously active RF devices operating at a wide range of signal strengths (−80 to −30 dBm), while maintaining a low false positive rate. Through a deployment in two production WLANs, we show that Airshark can be a useful tool to the WLAN administrators in understanding non-WiFi interference.

Categories and Subject Descriptors

C.2.1 [**Network Architecture and Design**]: Wireless Communication

General Terms

Design, Experimentation, Measurement, Performance

Keywords

WiFi, 802.11, Spectrum, Non-WiFi, RF Device Detection, Interference, Wireless Network Monitoring

1. INTRODUCTION

The unlicensed wireless spectrum continues to be home for a large range of devices. Examples include cordless phones, Bluetooth headsets, various types of audio and video transmitters (security cameras and baby monitors), wireless game controllers (Xbox and Wii), various ZigBee devices (e.g., for lighting and HVAC controls), even microwave ovens, and the widely deployed WiFi Access Points (APs) and clients. Numerous anecdotal studies have demonstrated that links using WiFi, which is a dominant communication technology in this spectrum, are often affected by interference from all of these different transmitters in the environment. In Figure 1, we present results from our own experiments where a single, good quality WiFi link was interfered by different non-WiFi devices—an analog phone, a Bluetooth device, a videocam, an Xbox controller, an audio transmitter, a frequency hopping cordless phone, a microwave, and a ZigBee transmitter—when placed at different distances from the WiFi link.

The figure shows the normalized UDP throughput under interference, relative to the un-interfered WiFi link, as a function of the interfering signal strength from these different devices. While all of these devices impede WiFi performance to a certain degree, some of these devices, e.g., the videocam and the analog phone, *can totally disrupt WiFi communication* when they are close enough ($\geq$ 80% degradation at RSSI ≥ -70 dBm, and throughput drops to *zero* in some cases).

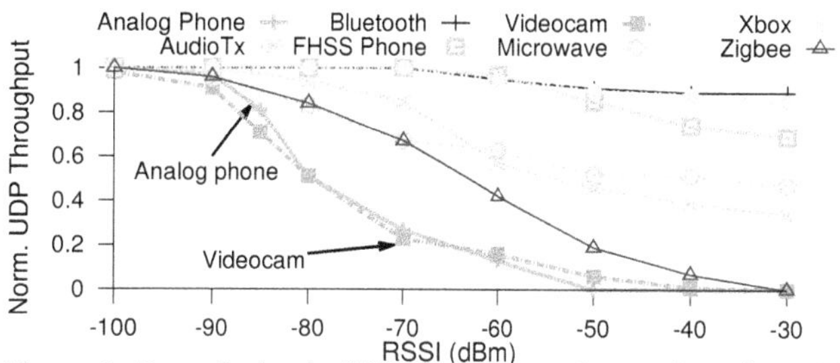

Figure 1: Degradation in UDP throughput of a good quality WiFi link (WiFi transmitter and receiver were placed 1m apart) in the presence of non-WiFi devices operating at different signal strengths.

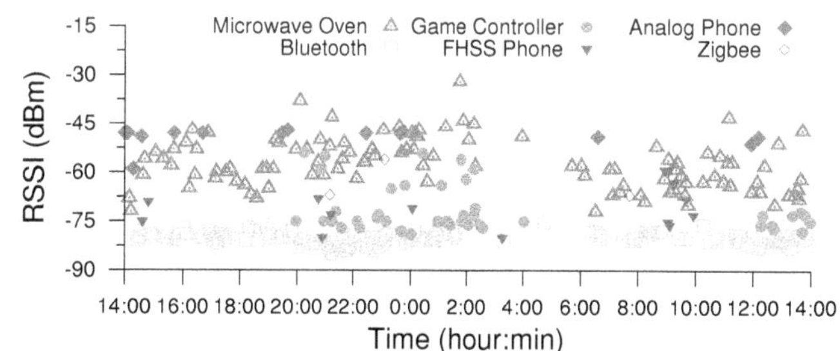

Figure 2: Average RSSI from different non-WiFi RF device instances shown against the device start times. Measurements were taken at a dorm-style apartment (location L16, dataset §2) for a 24 hour period.

IMC'11, November 2–4, 2011, Berlin, Germany.

Furthermore, our measurements across diverse home, office, and public environments, and over many weeks, show that many of these devices are routinely visible at all times of the day often at significantly high signal levels to be disruptive to WiFi links. Figure 2 shows an example of non-WiFi RF activity in a dorm-style apartment building, where some respite is observable only in the wee hours of the night.

Non-WiFi RF device detection: Traditional WiFi systems (Access Points or clients) utilize various mechanisms in the 802.11 MAC to detect and avoid interference from other WiFi sources, and are largely *oblivious* to non WiFi sources. However, with the continued growth of non-WiFi activity in this shared unlicensed band and the consequent impact on WiFi performance, hardware vendors and network administrators are increasingly exploring techniques to better detect non-WiFi sources of interference. Among commercial systems, Spectrum XT [2], AirMaestro [3], and CleanAir [4] are examples of custom hardware systems that integrate unique spectrum analyzer functionality to facilitate non-WiFi device detection. In the research community, work by Hong et. al. [17] utilizes a modified channel sounder and associated cyclostationary signal analysis to detect non-WiFi devices. RFDump [21] uses USRP GNU Radios and phase/timing analysis along with protocol specific demodulators to achieve similar goals. In this paper, we focus on techniques to detect non-WiFi RF devices but using commodity WiFi hardware instead of more sophisticated capabilities available in dedicated spectrum analyzers, expensive software radios, or any additional specialized hardware.

Using commodity WiFi hardware for non-WiFi RF device detection: Commercial spectrum analyzers or software radio platforms have specialized capability of providing "raw signal samples" for large chunks of spectrum (e.g., 80–100 MHz) at a fine-grained sampling resolution in both time domain ($O(10^5)$ to $O(10^6)$ samples per second) and frequency domain (as low as 1 kHz bandwidth). In contrast, commodity WiFi hardware, can provide similar information albeit at a much coarser granularity. For instance, Atheros 9280 AGN cards, as available to us, can only provide RSSI measurements for an individual WiFi channel (e.g., a 20 MHz channel) at a resolution bandwidth of OFDM sub-carrier spacing (e.g., 312.5 kHz), and at a relatively coarse timescale ($O(10^3)$ to $O(10^4)$ samples per second). This capability is part of the regular 802.11 frame decoding functionality. If we can design efficient non-WiFi device detection using signal measurement samples drawn from commodity WiFi hardware, then it would be easy to embed these functionalities in all WiFi APs and clients. By doing so, each such WiFi AP and client can implement appropriate mitigation mechanisms that can quickly react to presence of significant non-WiFi interference. The following are some examples.

1) A microwave oven, which typically emits high RF energy in 2.45-2.47 GHz frequencies, turns on in the neighborhood of an AP (operating on channel 11) significantly disrupting the throughput to its clients. The AP detects this microwave, infers its disruptive properties, and decides to switch to a different channel (say, 1).

2) An AP-client link experiences short term interference from an analog cordless phone in a narrowband (< 1 MHz). The AP detects the analog phone and its characteristics, and hence decides to use channel width adaptation functions to operate on a narrower, non-overlapping 10 MHz channel instead of the usual 20 MHz channel.

Summarizing, if non-WiFi device detection is implemented using only commodity WiFi hardware, both these examples are possible natively within the AP and the client without requiring any additional spectrum analyzer hardware (either as add-on boards or chipsets) to be installed in them.

Our proposed approach — Airshark

Motivated by the above examples, we propose Airshark, a system that detects non-WiFi RF devices, *using only the functionality provided by commodity WiFi hardware.* Airshark, therefore, is a software-only solution which addresses multiple goals and challenges described next.

1) Multiple, simultaneously active, RF device detection: While Airshark can most accurately detect individual non-WiFi RF devices, it is also designed to effectively discern a small number of *simultaneously operating* non-WiFi devices, while keeping false positives low.

2) Real-time and extensible detection framework: Airshark operates in real-time allowing the WiFi node to take immediate remedial steps to mitigate interference from non-WiFi devices. In addition, its detection framework is extensible—adding hitherto unknown RF device profiles requires a one-time overhead, analogous to commercial systems based on spectrum analyzers [3].

3) Operation under limited view of spectrum: Being implemented using commodity WiFi hardware, Airshark assumes that typically only 20 MHz spectrum snapshots (equal to the width of a single WiFi channel) are available for its use in each channel measurement attempt. This limitation implies that Airshark cannot continuously observe the entire behavior of many non-WiFi frequency hoppers (e.g., Bluetooth). Further, the resolution of these samples are at least 2 orders of magnitude lower than what is available from more sophisticated spectrum analyzers [1] and channel sounders [17]. In addition to this low sampling resolution, we also observed infrequent occurances of missing samples. Finally, various signal characteristics that are available through spectrum analyzer hardware (e.g., phase and modulation properties) are not available from the commodity WiFi hardware. Therefore, Airshark needed to operate purely based on the limited energy samples available from the WiFi cards, and maintain high detection accuracy and low false positives despite these constraints.

Overview of Airshark: Airshark overcomes these challenges using several mechansisms. It uses a *dwell-sample-switch* approach to collect samples across the spectrum (§3.1). It operates using only energy samples from the WiFi card to extract a diverse set of features (§3.3) that capture the spectral and temporal properties of wireless signals. These features are robust to changes in the wireless environment and are used by Airshark's light-weight decision tree classifiers to perform device detection in real-time (§3.4). We systematically evaluate Airshark's performance in a variety of scenarios, and find its performance comparable to a state-of-the-art signal analyzer [3] that employs custom hardware.

Key contributions

In this work, we make the following contributions:

- *Characterizing prevalance of non-WiFi RF devices.* To motivate the need for systems such as Airshark, we first

RF Device Category	Device Models (set up)	Airshark's Accuracy (low RSSI — high RSSI)
High duty, fixed frequency devices — spectral signature, duty, center frequency, bandwidth		
Analog Cordless Phones	Uniden EXP4540 Compact Cordless Phone (phone call)	97.73%—100%
Wireless Video Cameras	Pyrus Electronics Surveillance Camera (video streaming)	92.7%—99.82%
Frequency hoppers — pulse signature, timing signature, pulse spread		
Bluetooth devices (ACL/SCO)	Bluetooth-enabled devices: (i) iPhone, (ii) iPod touch, (iii) Microsoft notebook mouse 5000, (iv) Jabra bluetooth headset (data transfer/audio streaming)	91.63%—99.46%
FHSS Cordless Base/Phones	Panasonic 2.4 KX-TG2343 Cordless Base/Phones (phone call)	96.47%—100%
Wireless Audio Transmitter	GOGroove PurePlay 2.4 GHz Wireless headphones (audio streaming)	91.23%—99.37%
Wireless Game Contollers	(i) Microsoft Xbox, (ii) Nintendo Wii, (iii) Sony Playstation 3 (gaming)	91.75%—99%
Broadband interferers — timing signature, sweep detection		
Microwave Ovens (residential)	(i) Whirlpool MT4110, (ii) Daewoo KOR-630A, (iii) Sunbeam SBM7500W (heating water/food)	93.16%—99.56%
Variable duty, fixed frequency devices — spectral signature, pulse signature		
ZigBee Devices	Jennic JN5121/JN513x based devices (bulk data transfer)	96.23%—99.12%

Table 1: Devices tested with the current implementation of Airshark. Features used to detect the devices include: Pulse signature (duration, bandwidth, center frequency), Spectral signature, Timing signature, Duty cycle, Pulse spread and device specific features (e.g., Sweep detection for Microwave Ovens). Accurac y tests were done in presence of multiple active RF devices and RSSI values range from -80 dBm (low) to -30 dBm (high).

performed a detailed measurement study to characterize the prevalence of non-WiFi RF devices in typical environments — homes, offices, and various public spaces. This study was conducted for more than 600 hours over several weeks across numerous representative locations using signal analyzers [3] that establish the ground truth.

- *Design and implementation of* Airshark *to detect non-WiFi RF devices.* Airshark extracts a unique set of features using the functionality provided by a WiFi card, and accurately detects multiple RF devices (across multiple models listed in Table 1) while maintaining a low false positive rate (§4). Across multiple RF environments, and in the presence of multiple RF devices operating simultaneously, average detection accuracy was 96% at moderate to high signal strengths (≥ -60 dBm). At low signal strengths (-80 dBm), accuracy was 91%. Further, Airshark's performance is comparable to commercial signal analyzers (§4.1.6).
- *Example uses of* Airshark. Through a deployment in two production WLANs, we demonstrate Airshark's potential in monitoring the RF activity, and understanding performance issues that arise due to non-WiFi interference.

To the best of our knowledge, Airshark is the first system that provides a generic, scalable framework to detect non-WiFi RF devices using only commodity WiFi cards and enables non-WiFi interference detection in today's WLANs.

2. CHARACTERIZING PREVALENCE OF NON-WIFI RF DEVICES

In this section, we aim to characterize the prevalence and usage of non-WiFi RF devices in real world networks. First, we describe our measurement equipment, and data sets.

Hardware. We use AirMaestro RF signal analyzer [3] to determine the ground truth about the prevalence of RF devices. This device uses a specialized hardware (BSP2500 RF signal analyzer IC), which generates spectral samples (FFTs) at a very high resolution (every 6 μs, with a resolution bandwidth of 156 kHz) and performs signal processing to detect and classify RF interferers accurately.

— *"Ground truth" validation.* Before using AirMaestro to understand the ground truth about the prevalence of non-WiFi devices, we benchmarked its performance in terms of (i) device detection accuracy and (ii) false positives. We activated different combinations of RF devices (up to 8 devices, listed in Table 1) by placing them at random locations and measuring the accuracy at different signal strengths (up to -100 dBm). Measurements were done during late nights to avoid any external non-WiFi interference. Our results indicate an overall detection accuracy of 98.7% with no false positives. The few cases where AirMaestro failed to detect the devices occurred when the devices were operating at very low signal strengths (≤ -90 dBm).

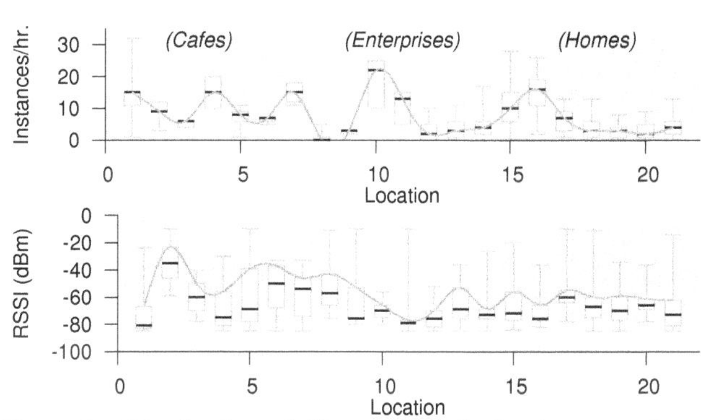

Figure 3: Distribution of (i) non-WiFi device instances/hour at different locations (top), and (ii) RSSI of non-WiFi devices at these locations (bottom). Min, Max, 25th, 50th and 75th percentiles are shown.

Data sets. We collected the RF device usage measurements using the signal analyzer at 21 locations for a total of 640 hours. We broadly categorize these locations into three categories: (i) *cafes (L1-L7)*: these included coffee shops, malls, book-stores (ii) *enterprises (L8-L14)*: offices, university departments, libraries and (iii) *homes (L15-L21)*: these included apartments and independent houses. Measurements were taken over a period of 5 weeks. At some locations, we could collect data for more than 24 hours (e.g., enterprises, homes) but for others we could collect measurements only during the day times (e.g., coffee shops, malls). We now summarize our observations from this data.

Non-WiFi devices are prevalent across locations and often appear with fairly high signal strengths.

Figure 3 (top) shows the distribution of non-WiFi device instances observed per hour in different wireless environments.

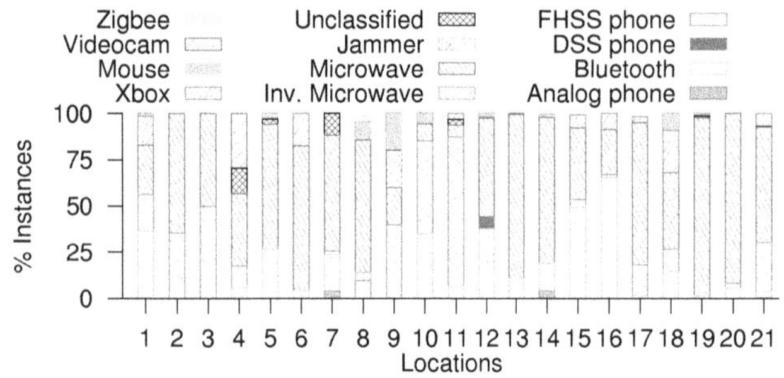

Figure 4: Distribution of non-WiFi device instances at various locations.

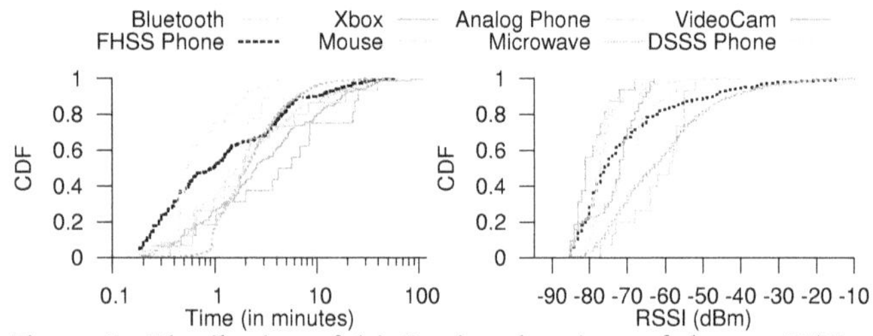

Figure 5: Distribution of (a) Session durations of the non-WiFi device instances (X-axis in log-scale) and (b) RSSIs of the non-WiFi device instances aggregated across all locations.

We observe that device instances/hr. varied across locations, with some locations showing very high device activity (e.g., a median of 22, 16 instances/hr. at locations L10 (an office), L16 (dormitory) respectively). Figure 3 (bottom) shows the distribution of non-WiFi device RSSI at these locations[1]. We observe that the median RSSI varied from -80 to -35 dBm. Further, for around 62% locations, we observe that 75th percentile of RSSI was greater than -60 dBm (shown using a gray line) suggesting strong non-WiFi interference.

Popularity of devices varied with locations, although few devices are popular across many locations.

Figure 4 shows the distribution of non-WiFi instances at different locations. Microwaves, FHSS cordless phones, Bluetooth devices and game controllers were the most popular. However, some other devices appeared frequently at specific locations e.g., video cameras accounted for 29% of instances at location L4 (cafe).

Session durations for non-WiFi devices varied from a few seconds to over 100 minutes.

Figure 5 (left) shows the CDF of the session times for each class of non-WiFi devices. Many devices appear in our traces for a short duration (≤ 2 minutes). These included (i) devices like microwaves that are activated for short durations and (ii) device instances with low signal strengths (≤ -75 dBm) that appeared intermittently at the locations where the signal analyzer was placed. However, for 25% of the cases, the devices were active for more than 5 minutes and in some traces, devices like game controllers (e.g., Xbox) were active for durations of up to 1.8 hours.

[1]Observed RSSI is dependent on the exact location where the measurement node was placed. While we tried to be unbiased, node placement in reality was influenced by few factors like availability of power connection.

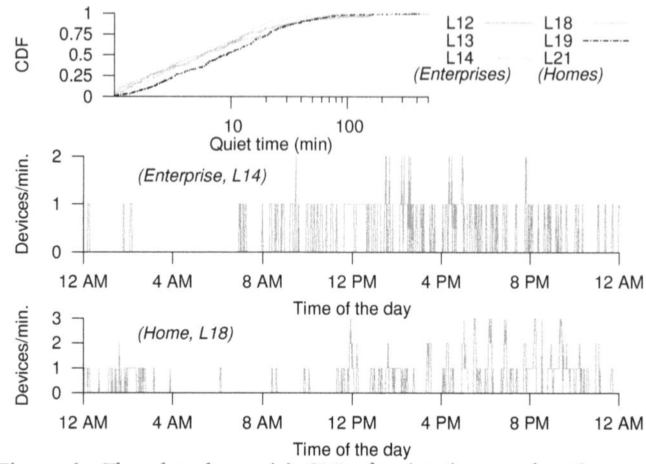

Figure 6: The plot shows (a) CDF of quiet times at locations where 48 hours of trace data was collected (enterprise and home locations). Time-series of non-WiFi device instances per minute at (b) an enterprise (location L14) and (c) and home (location L18) for a 24 hour period shows increased quiet times during late nights.

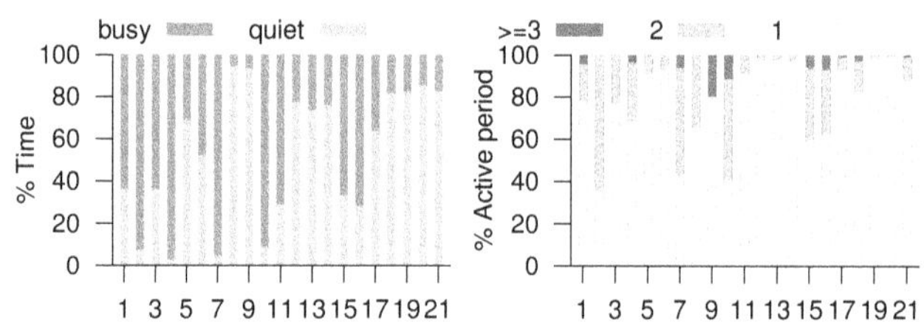

Figure 7: Distribution of (a) quiet and busy periods (b) simultaneously-active devices during the busy periods across different locations

Some of the devices operate at high signal strengths indicating potential interference.

Microwave ovens, video cameras, and analog phones were the most dominant in terms of RSSI (Figure 5 (right)). For e.g., RSSI was ≥ -55 dBm for more than 35% of the observed microwave oven instances, indicating potential interference to nearby WiFi links. Wireless game controllers and Bluetooth devices on the other hand, mostly occurred at low to moderate RSSI of -80 to -65 dBm.

More than 50% of the periods with no non-WiFi device activity were less than 10 minutes.

We define a *quiet period* as a duration in which no non-WiFi devices were active. Figure 6 (top) shows the CDF of the quiet periods for locations (homes, enterprises) at which we collected data for 48 hours. The figure shows that non-WiFi devices appeared quite frequently—more than 50% of the quiet periods were less than 10 minutes, and maximum quiet period in our trace was 8 hours at L12 (office). Figure 6 (middle, bottom) shows a 24 hour time-series of the number of active non-WiFi devices/min. at L14 (enterprise) and L18 (home) respectively. We observe that the longer quiet periods occurred during late nights to early mornings (3 am to 8 am), and most of the non-WiFi device activity was during the daytime, when WiFi utilization is also typically significant.

At most locations, only 1 or 2 non-WiFi devices were active simultaneously for more than 95% of the busy times.

Figure 7 (left) shows that the aggregate quiet times (percentage time with no non-WiFi activity) vary at different locations. In many locations, the aggregate quiet times were around 70−80% *i.e.*, non-WiFi devices were visible for 20−30% of the time. Quiet times were much lesser for cafes (e.g., only 3% at L4) as the traces did not include the measurements during the night times and there was frequent microwave oven and cordless phone activity when we collected the traces (during the day time). Figure 7 (right) shows the distribution of the number of active non-WiFi devices per minute, during the busy times (periods with non-WiFi activity). We find that only a single device was active for 35% (L2, cafe) to 99% (L20, home) of the time, and more than 2 devices were active simultaneously for at most 20% of the time (L9, office).

3. Airshark: DEVICE DETECTION

Prior work has developed device detection mechanisms using commercial signal analyzers [3], channel sounders [17] or software radios [21] which offer fine-grained, very high resolution signal samples, typically collected using a wide-band radio. We focus on designing such a system *using commodity WiFi cards*. WiFi cards are capable of providing similar spectrum data, albeit with limited signal information, and 2 orders of magnitude lesser resolution compared to signal analyzers. Traditionally, WiFi cards have not exposed this functionality, but emerging commodity WiFi cards provide an API through which we can access *spectral samples*— information about the signal power received in each of the sub-carriers of an 802.11 channel, which opens up the possibility of detecting non-WiFi devices. Designing such a detection system using WiFi cards, however, imposes several challenges as discussed below.

Why is it hard to detect devices using WiFi cards?

- *Limited spectrum view.* Unlike sophisticated signal analyzers [1,17] that can sample a wideband of 80−100 MHz (e.g., the entire 2.4 GHz band), current WiFi cards are designed to operate in a narrowband (e.g., 20 MHz).
- *Limited signal information.* Current WiFi cards provide limited signal information (e.g., the received power per sub-carrier) compared to software radios that provide raw signal samples. Thus traditional device detection approaches like cyclostationary analysis [17], phase analysis or use of protocol specific decoders [21] are not feasible.
- *Reduced sampling resolution.* WiFi cards have a resolution bandwidth of 312.5 kHz (equal to sub-carrier spacing) compared to signal analyzers [1] that offer resolution bandwidths as low as 1 kHz. Further, WiFi cards also have a lower sampling rate—our current implementation uses ∼2.5k samples/sec, as opposed to that used by commercial signal analyzers [3] (160k samples/sec) or prior work [21] employing software radios (8 million samples/sec).
- *Other challenges.* Coupled with the above constraints, the presence of regular WiFi packet transmissions in the spectrum further increase the "noise" in the spectral samples, making it more challenging to detect devices.

Overview. We wish to detect the presence of multiple (simultaneously operating) non-WiFi devices in real-time. The above challenges imply that Airshark is constrained to use the *limited signal information* (spectral samples) provided by a WiFi card and must employ *light-weight* detection mechanisms that are *robust to missing samples*. We now present an overview of Airshark's device detection pipeline. Figure 8 illustrates the four steps listed below.

Delay	minimum	25th pc.	median	75th pc	maximum
Inter-sample time	116μs	116μs	122μs	147μs	4.94 ms
Sub-band switching	12.2 ms	14.5 ms	19.7 ms	31 ms	163 ms

Table 2: Time between valid consecutive spectral samples and time taken to switch sub-bands in our current implementation.

1. Spectral samples from the WiFi card are generated using a scanning procedure (§3.1). This procedure divides the entire spectrum into a number of *sub-bands* and generates spectral samples for each sub-band. Samples that comprise only WiFi transmissions are "purged" and remaining samples are passed to the next stage.
2. Next, spectral samples are processed to detect signal *pulses*—time-frequency blocks that contain potential signals of interest, and collect some aggregate statistics based on received power values (§3.2).
3. In this stage, we extract a set of *light-weight* and unique features from the pulses and statistics (§3.3)—derived using only received power values—that capture the spectral and temporal properties of signals. Example features include: *spectral signatures* that characterize the shape of the signal's power distribution across its frequency band, *inter-pulse timing signatures* that measure the time difference between the pulses, and device specific features like *sweep detection* (used to detect microwave ovens).
4. In the final stage of the pipeline, the above features are used by different device analyzers that employ decision tree models (§3.4) trained to detect their target device.

We now explain the above detection procedure in detail.

3.1 Spectral Sampling

We start by explaining the details of sampling procedure employed in our current implementation.

Spectral samples. We implement Airshark using an Atheros AR9280 AGN wireless card. We use the card in 802.11n 20 MHz HT mode, where a 20 MHz channel is divided into 64 sub-carriers, spaced 312.5 KHz apart and the signal data is transmitted on 56 of these sub-carriers. Each spectral sample (FFT) generated by the wireless card comprises the power received in 56 sub-carriers (FFT bins) and corresponds to a 17.5 MHz (56×0.3125 MHz) chunk of spectrum, which we refer to as a *sub-band*. Additionally, the wireless card also provides the timestamp t (in μs) at which the sample was taken, and the noise floor at that instant.

Purging WiFi spectral samples. We efficiently filter the spectral samples that comprise only WiFi transmissions as follows: all the samples for which Airshark's radio is able to successfully decode a WiFi packet are marked as potential candidates for purging. Airshark then reports a spectral sample for further processing only if it detects non Wi-Fi energy in that sample. To be more precise, if the radio is receiving a packet, Airshark will not report the sample unless the interference signal is stronger than the 802.11 signal being received. One downside to this approach is that Airshark will also report spectral samples corresponding to weak 802.11 signals that fail carrier detection. However, as we show in §3.3, this is not a problem as Airshark can filter out the

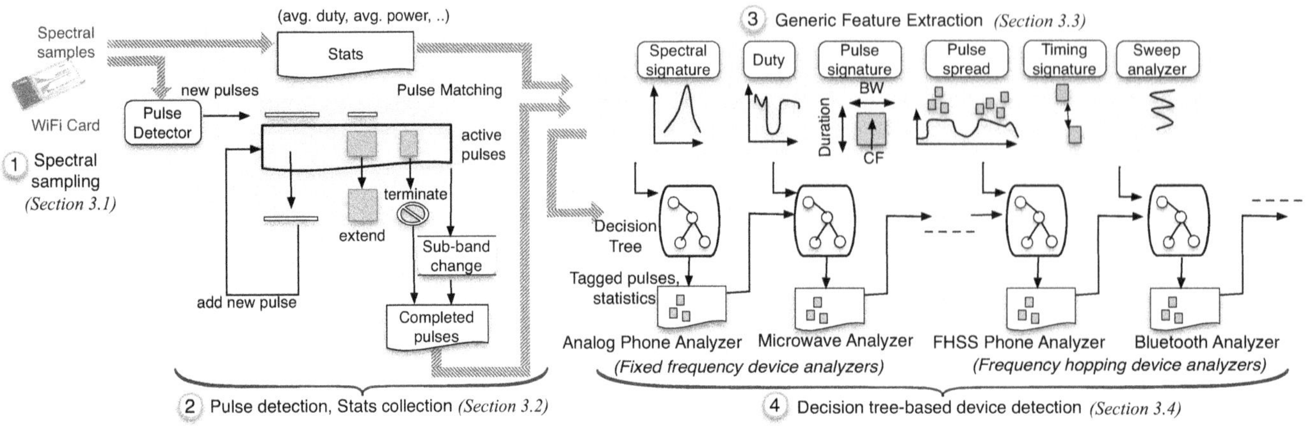

Figure 8: (a) Illustration of Airshark's detection pipeline. Spectral samples from the WiFi card are generated using a scanning procedure (§3.1). These samples are processed to detect signal *pulses*, and collect some aggregate statistics based on the received power values (§3.2). In the next stage, various features capturing the spectral and temporal properties of the signals are extracted (§3.3), and are used by different device analyzers that employ decision tree models (§3.4) trained to detect their target RF devices.

samples relevant to non-WiFi transmissions by employing device detection mechanisms. We term the samples reported by Airshark after this purging step as *valid* spectral samples.

Scanning procedure. Airshark divides the entire spectrum (e.g., 80 MHz) into several (possibly overlapping) sub-bands, and samples one sub-band at a time. Our current implementation uses 7 sub-bands with center frequencies corresponding to the WiFi channels 1, 3, 6, 9, 11, 13 and 14. Table 2 shows (i) inter-sample time: the time between two consecutive valid spectral samples (within a sub-band) and (ii) time taken to switch the sub-bands. Increased gap in the inter-sample time for a few samples ($\geq 150\mu s$) is due to the nature of the wireless environment—in the absence of strong non-WiFi devices transmissions, intermittent interference from WiFi transmissions causes gaps due to purged spectral samples. Sampling gaps are also caused when switching sub-bands (~ 20 ms on an average, and 163 ms in the worst case).

To amoritize the cost of switching sub-bands, Airshark employs a *dwell-sample-switch* approach to sampling: Airshark dwells for 100 ms in each sub-band, captures the spectral samples and then switches to the next sub-band. As we show later, in spite of the increased gap for few samples, we find the sampling resolution of current WiFi cards to be adequate in detecting devices (across different wireless environments) with a reasonable accuracy (§4). In §4, we demonstrate the adversarial case where strong WiFi interference coupled with weak non-WiFi signal transmissions can affect Airshark's detection capabilities.

3.2 Extracting signal data

We now explain the next stage in the detection pipeline that operates on the spectral samples to generate signal *pulses*, along with some aggregate statistics.

"Pulse" Detection. Each spectral sample is processed to identify the signal "peaks". Several complex mechanisms have been proposed for peak detection [11, 16]. To keep our implementation efficient, we use a simple and a fairly standard algorithm [12, 14]—peaks are identified by searching for "local maximas" that are above a minimum energy threshold γ_s. For each peak, the pulse detector generates a *pulse* as a set

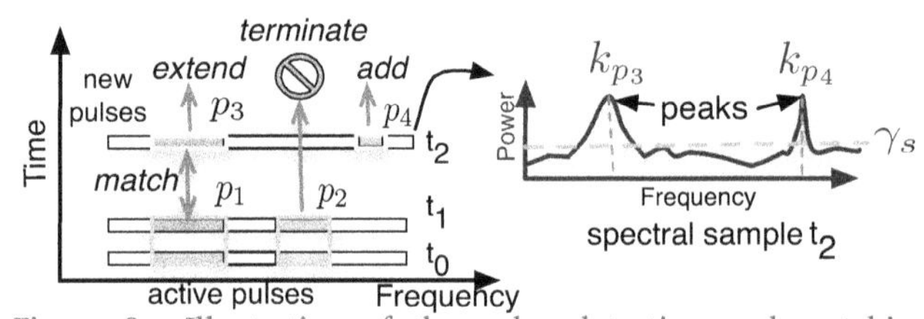

Figure 9: Illustration of the pulse detection and matching procedure. Pulse detector processes the spectral sample at time t_2 to output two new pulses p_3 and p_4. New pulse p_3 matches with the active pulse p_1, and results in extending p_1. Active pulse p_2 is terminated as there is no matching new pulse, and new pulse p_4 is added to the active pulse list.

of contiguous FFT bins that surround this peak. A pulse corresponds to a signal of interest, and its start and end frequencies are computed as explained below.

— *frequency and bandwidth estimation:* Let k_p denote the peak bin and $p(k_p)$ denote the power received in this bin. We first find the set of contiguous FFT bins $[k'_s, k'_e]$ such that $k'_s \leq k_p \leq k'_e$ and power received in each bin is (i) above the energy threshold, γ_s and (ii) within δ_B of the peak power $p(k_p)$ *i.e.*, $p(k) \geq \gamma_s \bigwedge p(k_p) - p(k) < \delta_B \forall k \in [k'_s, k'_e]$. The center frequency (CF) and the bandwidth (BW) of a pulse corresponding to this peak bin can be characterized by considering its mean localization and dispersion in the frequency domain:

$$k_c = \frac{1}{\sum_k p(k)} \sum_k k \cdot p(k), \;\; k'_s \leq k \leq k'_e$$

$$B = 2\sqrt{\frac{1}{\sum_k p(k)} \sum_k (k - k_c)^2 \cdot p(k)}, \;\; k'_s \leq k \leq k'_e$$

The center frequency bin k_c is computed as the center point of the power distribution, and the frequency spread around this center point is defined as the bandwidth B of the pulse. For each peak, we restrict the bandwidth of interest to comprise bins whose power values are more than γ_s and are within δ_B of the peak power $p(k_p)$. We use this mechanism as it is simple to compute and it provides reasonable estimates as we show in §4. Based on the computed bandwidth, the start bin (k_s) and the end bin (k_e) are determined. The pulse detector

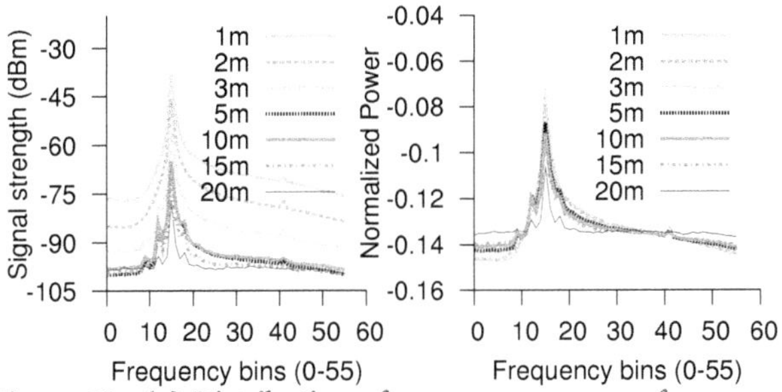

Figure 10: (a) Distribution of average power vs. frequency for an analog cordless phone at different distances. (b) Spectral signatures for the analog cordless phone are not affected for RSSI values of ≥ -80 dBm.

can potentially output multiple pulses for a spectral sample. Each pulse in a spectral sample observed at time t can be represented using the tuple $[t, k_s, k_c, k_e, [p(k_s) \ldots p(k_e)]]$

Pulse Matching. Airshark maintains a list of *active pulses* for the current sub-band. This active pulse list is empty at the start of the sub-band, and the first set of pulses (obtained after processing a spectral sample in the sub-band) are added to this list as active pulses. For the rest of the samples in the sub-band, a pulse matching procedure is employed: the pulse detector outputs a set of *new pulses* after processing the sample. These new pulses are compared against the list of active pulses to determine a match. In our current implementation, we use a strict criteria to determine a match between a new pulse and an active pulse: the CFs and BWs of the new pulse and the active pulse must be equal, and their peak power values must be within 3 dB (to accommodate signal strength variations). Once a match is determined, the new pulse is merged with the active pulse to *extend* it *i.e.*, the duration of the active pulse is increased to accommodate this new pulse, and the power values of the active pulse are updated by taking a weighted average of power values of the new and the active pulse.

After the pulse matching procedure, any left over new pulses in the current spectral sample are added to the active pulse list. The active pulses that did not find a matching new pulse in the current sample are terminated. Active pulses are also terminated if Airshark encounters more than one missing spectral sample (*i.e.*, inter-sample time ≥ 150 μs). Once an active pulse is terminated, it is moved to the current sub-band's list of *completed pulses*. It is possible that some of the active pulses are prematurely terminated due to the strict match and termination criteria. However, doing so helps Airshark maintain a low false positive rate as it only operates on well-formed pulses that satisfy this strict criteria (§4). Figure 9 illustrates this pulse detection procedure.

Stats Module. The stats module operates independently of the above pulse logic. It processes all the spectral samples of a sub-band to generate the following statistics: (i) *average power*: this is the average power in each FFT bin for the duration of the sub-band, (ii) *average duty*: this is the average duty cycle for each bin in the sub-band. The duty cycle of an FFT bin k is computed as 1 if $p(k) \geq \gamma_s$, otherwise it is 0. (iii) *high duty zones*: After processing a sub-band, a mechanism similar to peak detection, followed by CF and BW estimation procedure is applied on the "average power" statistic to identify the high duty zones in the sub-band. These are used to quickly detect the presence of high duty devices.

Before switching to the next sub-band, all the active pulses for the current sub-band are terminated and pushed to the list of the sub-band's completed pulses. The list of completed pulses along with the aggregate statistics are then passed on to the next stage of the pipeline to perform feature extraction.

3.3 Feature Extraction

Using the completed pulses list and statistics, we extract a set of *generic features* that capture the spectral and temporal properties of different non-WiFi device transmissions. These features—frequency, bandwidth, spectral signature, duty cycle, pulse signature, inter-pulse timing signature, pulse spread and device specific features like sweep detection—form the building blocks of Airshark's decision tree-based device detection mechanisms. We now explain these features.

(F1) Frequency and Bandwidth. Most RF devices operate using pre-defined center frequencies, and their waveforms occupy a specific bandwidth. For e.g, a ZigBee device operates on one of the pre-defined 16 channels [22], and occupies a bandwidth of 2 MHz. The center frequency and bandwidth of the pulses (and sub-band's high duty zones) are used as features in Airshark's decision tree models.

(F2) Spectral signatures. Many RF devices also exhibit certain power versus frequency characteristics. We capture this using a *spectral signature*: given a set of frequency bins $[k_s \ldots k_e]$ and corresponding power values $[p(k_s) \ldots p(k_e)]$, if we treat the frequency bins as a set of orthogonal axes, we can construct a vector $\vec{s} = p(k_s)\hat{k_s} + \ldots + p(k_e)\hat{k_e}$ that represents the power received in each of the bins. We then normalize this vector to derive a unit vector representing the spectral signature: $\hat{s} = \frac{\vec{s}}{|s|}$. Given a reference spectral signature $\hat{s}_r$ and a measured spectral signature $\hat{s}_m$, we compute the similarity between the spectral signatures as the *angular difference* (θ): $\cos^{-1}(\hat{s}_r \cdot \hat{s}_m)$. The angular difference captures the degree of alignment between the vectors, and is close to $0°$ when the relative composition of the vectors is similar.

Spectral signatures can be computed on the average power values of the pulses (e.g., ZigBee pulse) or on the high duty zones (e.g., for high duty devices like analog phones) to aid in device detection. Figure 10 shows the power distribution of an analog cordless phone at different distances, and the corresponding spectral signatures computed at each distance. The figure shows that normalization aids in making the signatures robust to the changes in the signal strengths of the RF devices. However, at very low signal strengths (≤ -90 dBm), the spectral signatures tend to deviate and result in an increased theta, leading to false negatives (§4).

(F3) Duty cycle. The duty cycle $\mathcal{D}$ of a device is the fraction of time the device spends in "active" state. This can be used to identify high duty devices, e.g., analog phones and wireless video cameras have $\mathcal{D}$=1, or identify devices with characteristic duty cycles e.g., microwave ovens have $\mathcal{D}$=0.5. In reality, due to the presence of multiple devices, it is possible for the duty cycle of the bandwidth (FFT bins) used by a device to be more than its expected duty cycle. We therefore use the notion of *minimum* duty cycle $\mathcal{D}_{min}$ for devices ($\mathcal{D}_{min}$=0.5 for a microwave oven) as one of the features.

Protocol/Device	Bandwidth	Duration	Frequency usage
WDCT Cordless Phone	0.892 KHz	700 μs	FHSS, 90 channels
Bluetooth	1 MHz	366 μs - 3 ms	FHSS, 79 channels
ZigBee	2 MHz	< 5 ms	Static, 16 channels
Game controller	500 KHz	235 μs	FHSS, 40 channels

Table 3: Pulse signatures for different RF devices.

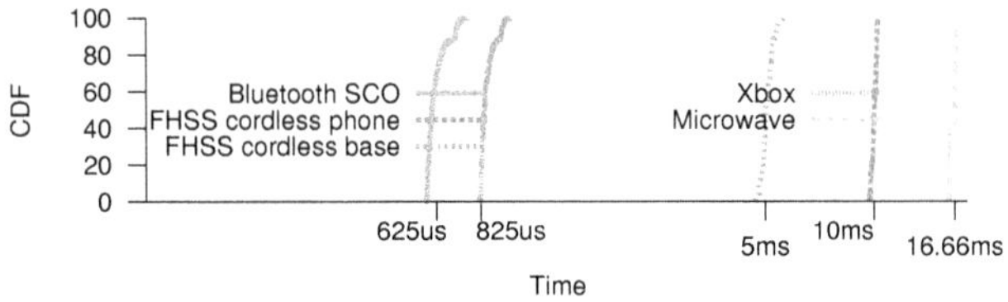

Figure 11: Inter-pulse timing signature for different devices.

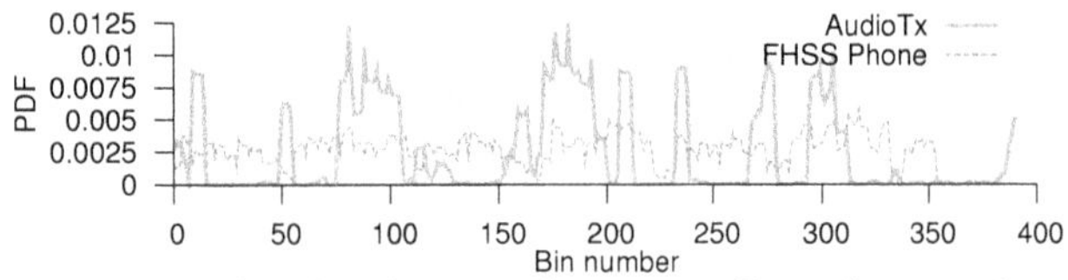

Figure 12: Pulse distribution of FHSS cordless phone and an audio transmitter as captured by Airshark.

(F4) Pulse signatures. Along with CF and BW, the transmission durations of many devices conform to their protocol standards. For e.g., in Bluetooth, the duration of a transmission slot is 625 μs, out of which 366 μs is spent in active transmission. Similarly, WDCT cordless phones (FHSS phones) have a pulse duration of 700 μs. Table 3 shows these properties (frequency, bandwidth, and duration of the pulses) for different devices. Airshark combines these three properties together to define *pulse signatures* for devices that communicate using pulses (e.g., ZigBee, Bluetooth) and uses them as features in the detection process.

(F5) Inter-pulse timing signatures. Timing between the transmissions of many devices also exhibit certain properties. In Bluetooth SCO, for example, examining the spectrum will reveal sets of two consecutive pulses that satisfy the Bluetooth pulse signature (Table 3) and are separated by a time difference of 625 μs. WDCT cordless phones and game controllers (e.g., Wii) exhibit similar properties with time difference between consecutive pulses (occuring at the same center frequency) in a set being 5 ms and 825 μs respectively. Similarly, microwaves exhibit an ON-OFF cycle with a period of 16.6 ms. Figure 11 illustrates these timing properties.

Since Airshark can only sample a particular sub-band at a time, it cannot capture all the pulses of a device. This is especially true for frequency hopping devices. Due to the nature of sampling, we cannot expect every captured pulse to exhibit the above timing property. Airshark's device analyzers therefore use a relaxed constraint—number of pulse sets that satisfy a particular timing property is used as one of the features in the decision tree models (§3.4).

(F6) Pulse spread. Airshark accumulates the pulses for a number of sub-bands, and extracts features from pulses belonging to a particular pulse signature to detect the presence of frequency hopping devices. Together, these features represent the *pulse spread* across different sub-bands.

1. *Pulses-per-band (mean and variance).* We use the average number of pulses per sub-band, and the corresponding variance as one of the measures to characterize the pulse spread. For frequency hoppers, we can expect the average number of pulses in each sub-band to be higher (and the variance lower) compared to fixed frequency devices.

2. *Pulse distribution.* Pulses of many frequency hopping devices tend to conform to a particular distribution. For example, FHSS cordless phone pulses are spread uniformly across the entire 80 MHz band, whereas, the pulse distribution for other frequency hoppers like audio transmitters may tend to be concentrated on certain frequencies of sub-bands, as shown in Figure 12. The X-axis shows the bin number b for each of the seven sub-bands ($b_{max} = 56 \times 7 = 392$), and Y-axis shows the fraction of the pulses that fall into each bin.[2]

Airshark checks whether the distribution of pulses across the sub-bands conforms to an expected pulse distribution using Normalized Kullback-Leibler Divergence (NKLD) [20], a well known metric in information theory. NKLD is simple to compute and can be used to quantify the 'distance' or the relative entropy between two probability distributions. NKLD is zero when the two distributions are identical, and a higher value of NKLD implies increased distance between the two distributions. The definition of NKLD is assymetric, therefore we use a symmetric version of NKLD [20] to compare two distributions. Let $r(b)$ be the reference pulse distribution over all the bins ($b \in \mathcal{B} = [0, b_{max}]$), computed over a large period of time. Let $m(b)$ be the measured pulse distribution over a smaller time period t_m. The symmetric NKLD for two distributions $r(b)$ and $m(b)$ can be defined as:

$$\text{NKLD}(m(b), r(b)) = \frac{1}{2}\Big(\frac{D(m(b)\|r(b))}{H(m(b))} + \frac{D(r(b)\|m(b))}{H(r(b))}\Big)$$

where, $D(m(b)\|r(b))$ quantifies the divergence and is computed as $\sum_{b \in \mathcal{B}} m(b) \left|\log \frac{m(b)}{r(b)}\right|$, and $H(m(b))$ is the entropy of the random variable b with distribution $m(b)$ *i.e.*, $H(m(b)) = -\sum_{b \in \mathcal{B}} m(b) \log_2 m(b)$.

While Airshark can measure the pulse distribution $m(b)$ over a large time scale, and check if it conforms to $r(b)$, this will increase the time to detect the device. This leads to the question, "what is the minimum time scale t_m at which the pulse distribution can be measured?" We chose this time scale by empirically measuring how the NKLD values converge with the increase in the number of samples under different conditions. For the devices that we tested, we observed around 15000 samples (around 6 scans of the entire 80 MHz band, amounting to 6−7 seconds) was sufficient. We show how the number of samples affect the NKLD values in §4.2.3. We note that not all devices conform to a particular pulse distribution e.g., in our experiments, we found variable pulse distributions for Bluetooth as it employs adaptive hopping mechanisms.

(F7) Device specific features. Detection accuracy can be improved by using features unique to the target device. We illustrate this using a feature specific to microwave ovens.
— *Sweep detector.* The heating source in a residential

[2]Instead of measuring the actual pulse distribution over the 80 MHz band, we stitch the sub-bands together (ignoring the overlaps) and measuring the pulse distribution over the stitched sub-bands.

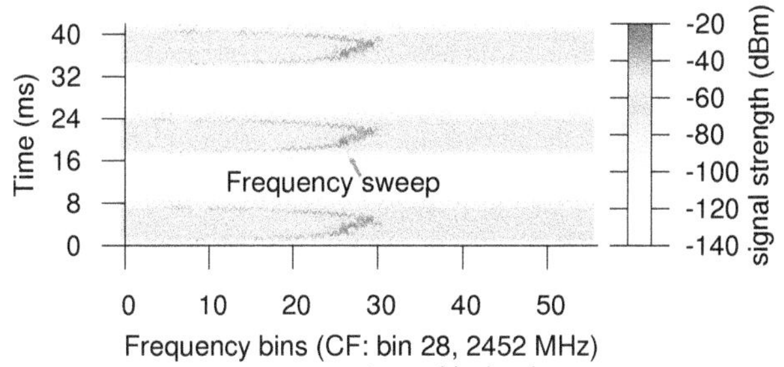

Figure 13: Spectral samples from Airshark capturing the activity of a residential microwave. The plot shows (i) the ON-OFF cycle for is around 16.6 ms and (ii) "frequency sweeps" during the ON periods.

microwave oven is based on a single magnetron tube that generates high power electromagnetic waves whenever the input voltage is above some threshold. This results in an ON-OFF pattern, typically periodic with a frequency of 60 Hz (frequency of the AC supply line). Although there might be differences between the emissions from ovens of different manufacturers, the peak operational power is mostly around 2.45-2.47 GHz and during the ON periods, the radiated signal exhibits a *frequency sweep* of around 4–6 MHz [19, 27].

Figure 13 shows the resulting 16.66 ms periodic ON-OFF pattern and the frequency sweeps during the ON periods of a microwave oven as captured by Airshark. In the current prototype of Airshark, the microwave oven analyzer includes sweep detection, along with timing signature analysis. We tested 6 microwaves (from different manufacturers), and Airshark was able to detect all of them using these features.

3.4 Device Detection

Airshark uses decision tree [24] based classifiers in order to detect the presence of RF devices. A decision tree is a mapping from observations about an item (feature set) to conclusions about its target value (class). It employs a supervised learning model where a small set of labeled data, referred to as training data, is first used to build the tree and is later used to classify unlabeled data. In Airshark, we use the popular C4.5 algorithm [24] to construct the decision trees. For further details about mechanisms to build decision trees and the classification process, we refer the readers to [24].

Airshark employs a separate analyzer for each class of devices. These device analyzers operate on a subset of features described previously, and make use of decision tree classifiers trained to detect their corresponding RF devices. The advantages of using per-device classifiers are three-fold: (i) each classifier can use a separate feature subset, (ii) classifiers can operate at different time granularities e.g., fixed frequency device analyzers (e.g., analog phone) can carry out the classification when Airshark finishes processing a sub-band, whereas for frequency hopping device analyzers like (e.g., Bluetooth, game controllers) the classification decision can only take place after enough samples have been processed (§3.3), (iii) classification process is more efficient when multiple devices are simultaneously active—each classifier outputs either label 1 (indicating the presence of the device), or label 0 (indicating the absence of the device). The alternative approach of using a single classifier is cumbersome as it requires training the classifier for all possible device combinations (each with a separate label).

Training. Before Airshark can identify a new RF device, its features have to be recorded for training. To do this, features relevant to this device are identified, and then extracted from spectral samples for the cases when the device is *active in isolation* (label 1), and when the device is inactive (label 0). For example, when adding the analog phone analyzer, we collected the spectral samples when the phone was activated in isolation and when the phone was inactive. We then instantiated analog phone's device analyzer to extract these features: bandwidth, spectral signature and duty cycle (measured from the recorded spectral samples) and the list of possible CFs the phone can operate on. It is worth pointing out that identifying the relevant feature set for a device and training the corresponding device analyzer is a *one time overhead before adding a new RF device* to Airshark. Table 1 lists the feature set employed by device analyzers in our current implementation.

Classification. We now summarize Airshark's detection pipeline. Each sample is processed by the first stage of the pipeline, and results in updating the completed pulse list and aggregate statistics. Device analyzers are invoked when Airshark finishes processing a sub-band:

1. Each device analyzer operates on the completed pulses and aggregate statistics, to derive its features. The features may include: CF, BW, angular difference (corresponding to its spectral signature), duty cycle, number and the spread of the pulses satisfying its pulse signature and timing signature.
2. The device analyzer's decision tree is invoked to output either label 1 or 0.
3. In case the decision tree outputs label 1, Airshark invokes a module that tags the selected pulses (satisfying the pulse signature and timing signature) as "owned" by this RF device.

An additional check is performed for frequency hopping device analyzers: if there are not enough accumulated samples to perform the classification, the classification decision is deferred to the next sub-band.

Dealing with multiple RF devices and overlapping signals. When multiple RF devices are simultaneously active, the spectrum may be occupied by a large number of transmissions (signal pulses). If the transmissions from multiple devices do not overlap in time or in frequency (either because of the diversity in the device transmission times, or because the devices operate in a non-overlapping spectrum bands), Airshark's device analyzers can proceed as is. Further, for certain combinations of devices, transmissions may overlap in both time and frequency, but not always. For example, this is the case when frequency hopping devices and fixed-frequency, low duty devices are present. In our benchmarks for these combinations, Airshark could always find enough pulses that do not overlap, and therefore was able to correctly detect the devices.

Transmissions from multiple devices that *always* overlap in time and frequency, however, can decrease the detection accuracy if the above techniques are used as is. For example, if the transmissions from a fixed-frequency, always-on device (e.g., analog phone) overlap in frequency with another fixed-frequency device (e.g., ZigBee device), features like spectral signatures will not perform well. This is because overlapping signals change the "shape" of the power distribution and increase the angular difference as shown in Figure 14(a). One

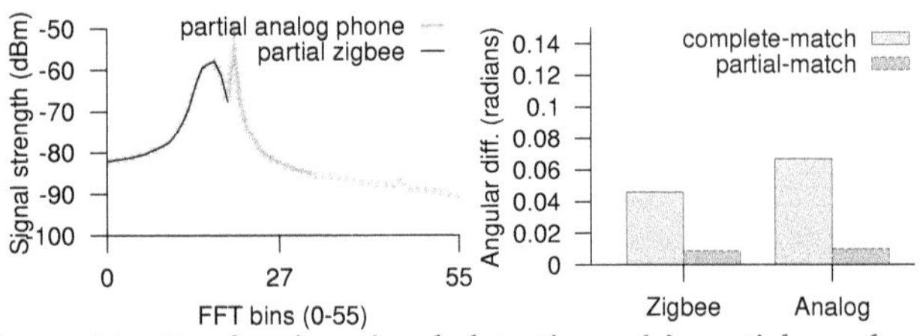

Figure 14: Overlapping signal detection. (a) partial overlap between ZigBee and analog signals (b) using partial matches between spectral signatures reduces the angular difference in overlapping cases.

approach to resolve such overlaps, is to use cyclostationary analysis [17] on raw signal samples. Such rich signal information (very high resolution, raw signal samples), however, is not available through WiFi cards. We extend the basic approach used in Airshark to handle these cases as follows: device analyzers first identify the potential peaks that match their CFs. For each peak, instead of a complete match on the signal's bandwidth BW, a *partial match* of the spectral signatures is performed. The bandwidth BW_{par} for the partial match is decided by the bandwidth detection algorithm, and is required to be above a minimum bandwidth BW_{min} in order to control the false positives (*i.e.*, $BW_{min} \leq BW_{par} \leq BW$). In our benchmarks, setting BW_{min} to $0.6\times BW$ improved the accuracy without increasing the false positives (§4). Figure 14(b) shows the reduction in angular difference when using a partial match.

Alternative classifiers. We also built another classifier based on support vector machines (SVM) [5]. In our experiments, we found that in most cases, Airshark's SVM-based and decision tree based classifiers had similar detection accuracies. In some scenarios involving multiple devices, SVM-based classifier performed slightly better (§4.1.5). However, we elected to use a decision tree based classifier, as it has very low memory and processing requirements, thus making it feasible to embed non-WiFi device detection functionality in commodity wireless APs and clients.

4. EXPERIMENTAL RESULTS

In this section, we evaluate Airshark's performance under a variety of scenarios, and present real-world applications of Airshark through a small scale deployment. We start by presenting the details of our implementation and testbed set up, followed by the metrics used for evaluation.

Implementation. Our implementation of Airshark consists of few hundred lines of C code that sets up the FFT sampling from the Atheros AR9280 AGN based wireless card, and about 4500 lines of Python scripts that implement the detection pipeline. We used an off-the-shelf implementation of the C4.5 decision tree algorithm [6] for training and classification. For the alternative SVM-based classifier, we used an SVM implementation [5] employing a radial basis function kernel with default parameter setting. We focus on detecting devices in 2.4 GHz spectrum, and our current prototype has been tested with 8 classes of devices (across multiple device models) mentioned in Table 1.

Evaluation set up. We performed all our experiments in a university building (except those in §4.1.4). Our training data was taken during the late evenings and night times to minimize the impact of external non-WiFi interference. Our

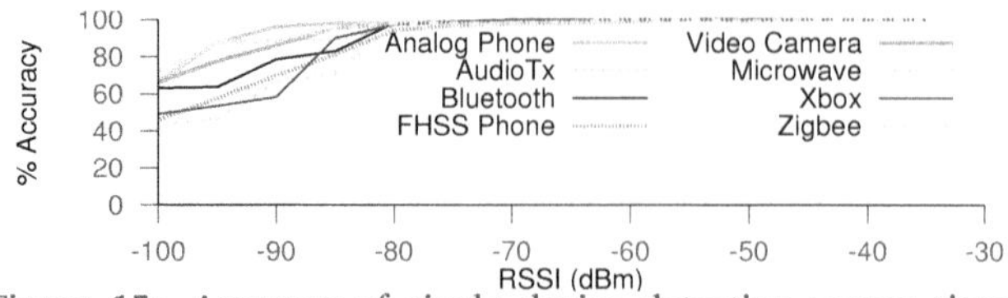

Figure 15: Accuracy of single device detection across signal strengths for different RF devices.

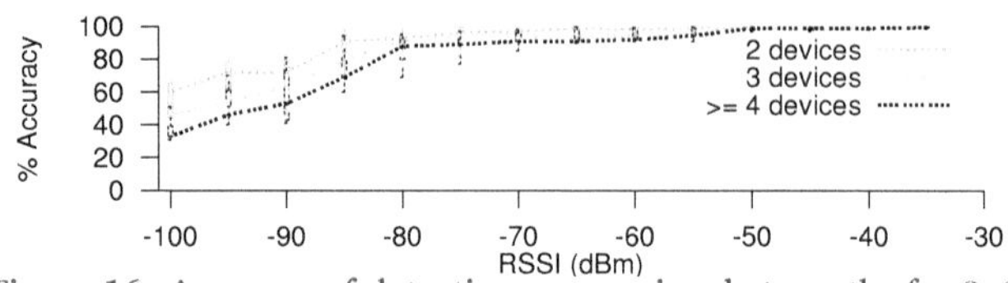

Figure 16: Accuracy of detection across signal strengths for 2, 3, and ≥ 4 device combinations.

evaluation experiments, however, were performed over a period of one week that included both busy hours and night times. We also used the AirMaestro signal analyzer [3] in order to determine the "ground truth" about the presence of any external non-WiFi RF devices during our experiments.

Evaluation Metrics. We use the following metrics to evaluate the performance of Airshark:
1. *Detection accuracy:* This is the fraction of correctly identified RF device instances. This estimates the probability that Airshark accurately detects the presence of an RF device.
2. *False positive rate (FPR):* This is defined as the fraction of false positives. This estimates the probability that Airshark incorrectly determines the presence of an RF device.

We will first evaluate Airshark's performance in various scenarios, and then comment on the parameters we chose. We set the energy threshold γ_s to -95 dBm, δ_B to 10 dB, and for computing NKLD we use 15000 samples. The RF devices tested and the features used are listed in Table 1.

4.1 Performance evaluation

We start by evaluating Airshark using controlled experiments with different RF devices.

4.1.1 *Single device detection accuracy*

Method. We measured the accuracy of device detection when only one of the RF devices mentioned in Table 1 was activated. The methodology used to activate the devices is also listed in Table 1. We placed the devices at random locations to generate the samples at different RSSI values, and then computed the average detection accuracy at each RSSI.

Results. Figure 15 shows the detection accuracy as a function of RSSI for different RF devices. We observe that Airshark achieves an accuracy of 98% for RSSI values as low as -80 dBm. For RSSI values ≤ -80 dBm, the accuracy drops down due to the reduced number of pulses detected at such low signal strengths. Further, the drop is sharper for frequency hopping devices, compared to fixed frequency, high duty devices like analog phones and video cameras.

4.1.2 *Multiple device detection accuracy*

Method. For each run, we chose $2 \leq n \leq 8$ random devices from our device set, placed them at random locations and activated them simultaneously to generate samples at different RSSI values. We then computed the average detection

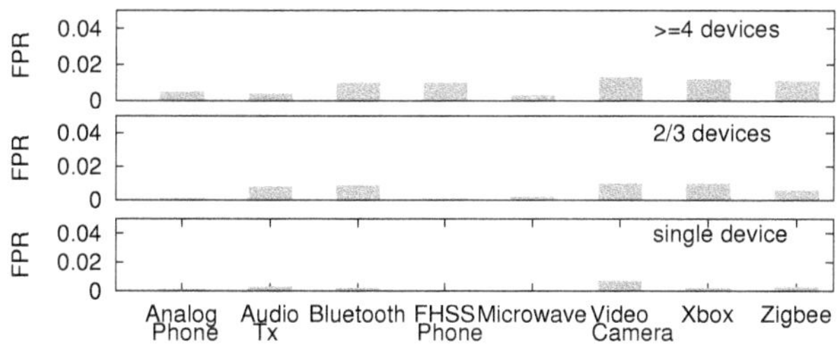

Figure 17: False positive rate for different devices.

Location/environment	Accuracy	False +ves
Indoor offices (floor-to-ceiling walls)	98.47%	0.029%
Lab environment (cubicle-style offices)	94.3%	0.067%
Apartments (dormitory-style)	96.21%	0.043%

Table 4: Airshark's performance in different environments.

accuracy at each RSSI. We repeat the experiments for different combinations of devices and locations. We note that our experiments include the "overlapping signal" cases (§3.4).

Results. Figure 16 shows the detection accuracy for 2, 3, and ≥ 4 device combinations. We observe that even when ≥ 4 devices are activated simultaneously, the average detection accuracy is more than 91% for RSSI values as low as −80 dBm. For higher RSSI values (≥ -60 dBm), the detection accuracy was 96%. For lower RSSI values, in the presence of multiple RF devices, we observed that features like spectral signatures, duty cycles do not perform well, and hence result in reduced accuracy (§4.2.1). Overall, we find that Airshark is reasonably accurate, and as we show in §4.1.6, its performance is close to that of signal analyzers [3] using custom hardware.

4.1.3 False positives

Method. When performing the above experiments for single and multiple device detection, we also recorded the false positives. Figure 17 shows the distribution of false positive rate across different RF devices.

Results. We observe that Airshark has a particularly low false positive rate — even when using ≥ 4 RF devices, operating under a wide range of signal strengths, the average FPR was 0.39% (maximum observed FPR was 1.3%). Further, for RSSI values ≥ -80 dBm, the average FPR was $\leq 0.068\%$.

Overall performance summary. For a total of 8 classes of RF devices used in our evaluation, across multiple runs and in presence of simultaneous activity from multiple RF devices at different signal strengths, Airshark exhibits detection accuracy of $\geq 91\%$ even for very low signal strengths of −80 dBm. The average false positive rate was 0.39%. At higher signal strengths (≥ -60 dBm) the accuracy was $\geq 96\%$.

In a typical enterprise deployment with multiple APs running Airshark, performance at low RSSI might not be a concern as we can expect at least one AP to capture the non-WiFi device signals with RSSI $\geq$−80 dBm. Below, we benchmark the performance under the cases with RSSI ≥ -80 dBm. We revisit the performance at lower RSSI in §4.2.1.

4.1.4 Location insensitivity

Method. To understand whether the peformance of our decision tree models was affected by the location and the nature of the wireless environment, we repeated the controlled experiments in three different environments. In each case, we activated the RF devices at different signal strengths and measured Airshark's performance.

Results. Table 4 shows that Airshark performs reasonably well under all the three environments with an average detection accuracy of 94.3%−98.4% and an average FPR of 0.029%−0.067%. This shows that our decision tree models are general, and are applicable in different environments.

4.1.5 Performance of SVM-based classifier

Method. We compared the performance of SVM-based implementation of Airshark with the decision tree based version. Both SVM and decision tree implementations were trained using the same data. Similar to the previous experiments, we placed the RF devices at random locations to evaluate the performance at different signal strengths.

Results. Table 5 shows that the performance of SVM and decision tree for different RF devices. We observe that while SVM based implementation performs slightly better in terms of the detection accuracy (an improvement of up to 4%), the number false positives also increase. We elected to use the decision tree approach as it was much faster and has comparable performance.

4.1.6 Comparison with specialized signal analyzers

Method. We compared the accuracy of Airshark with the AirMaestro RF signal analyzer [3] by employing following methodology: we performed experiments by activating a

RF device	Airshark-SVM (%) Accuracy/FPR	Airshark-DTree (%)Accuracy/FPR
Analog cordless phone	98.31% / 0.037%	97.73% / 0.012%
Bluetooth (ACL/SCO)	92.03% / 0.094%	91.63% / 0.076%
FHSS cordless phone	98.44% / 0.052%	96.47% / 0.037%
Microwave oven	94.02% / 0.012%	93.16% / 0.06%
ZigBee device	97.49% / 0.048%	96.23% / 0.036%
Video camera	94.24% / 0.08%	92.70% / 0.072%
Audio tx/headphones	92.27% / 0.016%	91.23% / 0.014%
Game controller (Xbox/Wii)	90.32% / 0.064%	91.75% / 0.046%

Table 5: Comparison of SVM and decision tree based approaches. Table shows per-device accuracy in the presence of multiple RF devices. The RSSI of the devices were ≥ -80 dBm.

Detection device	Online tests	Accuracy	False +ves
AirMaestro [3]	1827	1803 (98.7%)	NA
Airshark	1827	1761 (96.3%)	12 (0.07%)

Table 6: Comparison of Airshark and a detection device that uses a specialized hardware (AirMaestro RF signal analyzer).

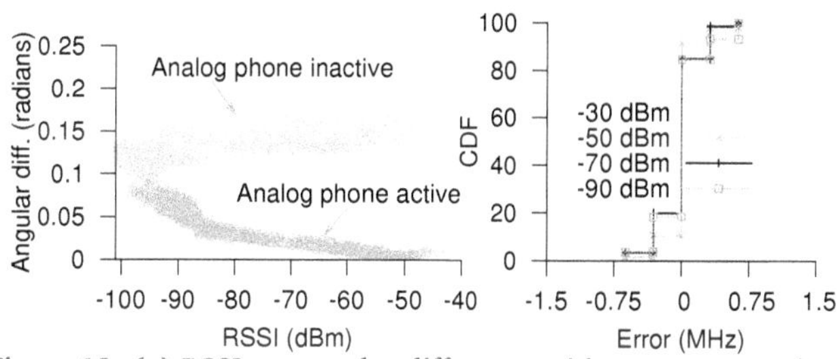

Figure 18: (a) RSSI vs. angular difference with respect to analog phone's spectral signature when the device is switched on and off (b) CDF of bandwidth estimation error at different signal strengths.

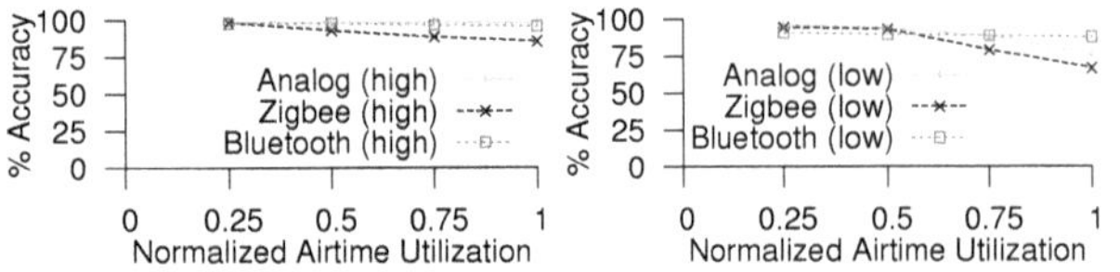

Figure 19: Stress testing Airshark with extreme WiFi interference. Detection accuracy is reduced for pulsed transmission devices (e.g., ZigBee), whereas accuracy for frequency hoppers is minimally affected.

combination of RF devices at different signal strengths and collected traces from both Airshark and the AirMaestro device simultaneously. Table 6 shows the results.

Results. We observe that out of 1827 device instances, AirMaestro was correctly able to detect 1803 (98.7%), whereas Airshark detected 1761 (96.3%) instances. Further, out of 66 instances where Airshark failed to identify the device, 48 instances had RSSI values of less than −80 dBm and the rest involved frequency hopping devices with multiple other RF devices operating simultaneously. We observed a total of 12 (0.07%) false positives and these instances occured when operating multiple RF devices at low signal strengths.

4.2 Microbenchmarks

Airshark's detection accuracy is affected by low signal strengths and increased WiFi interference. Below we investigate these scenarios.

4.2.1 *Performance under low signal strengths*

We now highlight some of the reasons for reduced accuracy at low signal strengths by examining two of the features.

— *Spectral signatures.* Consider a particular center frequency and associated bandwidth where we can expect an analog phone to operate. We wish to compute the spectral signature on this band (based on the received power in the FFT bins) and then measure the angular difference w.r.t. analog phone's spectral signature for (i) when the analog phone is active at this center frequency, (ii) when the phone is inactive. For Airshark to clearly distinguish between these two cases, there must be a clear separation between the angular differences *i.e.*, angular difference must be low when the phone is active, and higher when it is inactive. To understand the worst case performance, we also activate multiple other RF devices by placing them at random locations. Figure 18(a) shows that even in the presence of multiple devices, the angular difference is very low when the phone is operating at higher RSSI. However, when the phone is operating at lower signal strengths, the angular difference increases, thereby reducing Airshark's detection accuracy.

—*Bandwidth estimation.* In each run we activate a random RF device at a random location and let Airshark compute the bandwidth of the signal. Figure 18(b) shows the error in computed bandwidth at different RSSI values. We observe that Airshark performs very well at high RSSI values, but the bandwidth estimation error increases at low signal strengths, thereby affecting the detection accuracy.

4.2.2 *Performance under extreme interference*

We performed stress tests on Airshark by introducing additional WiFi interference traffic. We placed a WiFi transmitter close to the Airshark node (distance of 1m) and let it broadcast packets on the same channel as the fixed frequency RF devices. We changed the WiFi traffic load resulting in different airtime utilizations. We tested the detection

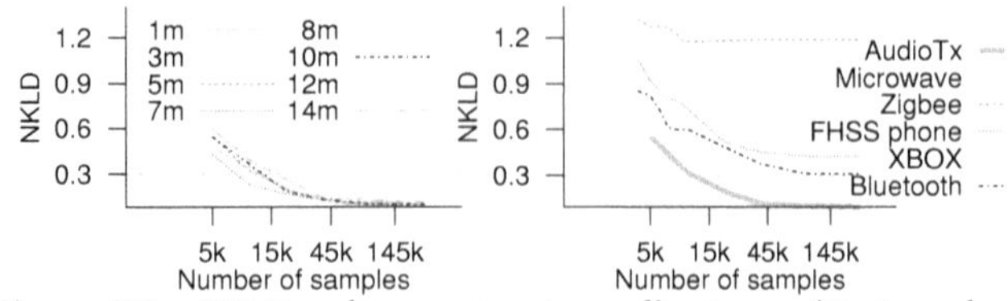

Figure 20: NKLD values wrt. to audio transmitter's pulse distribution for (a) audio transmitter at different distances (b) different RF devices

Choice of γ_s	−105 dBm	−95 dBm	−85 dBm
Accuracy (FPR)	97.3% (4.7%)	92.13% (0.041%)	89.24% (0.023%)

Table 7: Effect of different thresholds on Airshark's performance.

Deployment	Proportion of RF device instances				
	Microwave	Bluetooth	FHSS Phone	Videocam	Xbox
WLAN1	37.16%	52.34%	9.87%	-	0.6%
WLAN2	81.65%	17.43%	-	0.917%	-

Table 8: Proportion of non-WiFi RF device instances in 2 production WLANs. We collected data using Airshark for a duration of 48 hours.

accuracy of RF devices at HIGH and LOW signal strengths (−50 dBm and −80 dBm respectively). Figure 19 shows the effect on Airshark's detection accuracy w.r.t. normalized air time utilization (air time utilization is maximum, when the transmitter broadcasts packets at full throughput). Accuracy of high duty devices (analog phone) is affected only in the LOW case, when normalized airtime utilization is close to 1. For devices like ZigBee (fixed frequency, pulsed transmissions), the effect is more severe in the LOW case under increased airtime utilization. Frequency hopping devices like Bluetooth, however, are not affected because Airshark is able to collect enough pulses from other sub-bands. It is worth pointing out that all the previous experiments were performed in the presence of regular WiFi traffic and in different wireless environments. We therefore believe that Airshark performs reasonably well under realistic WiFi workloads.

4.2.3 *Parameter tuning*

We now discuss the empirically established parameters of our system. Table 7 shows the effect of using different energy thresholds. The set up for the experiments was similar to that in §4.1.2. We observe that while it is possible to improve Airshark's accuracy at lower RSSI values by lowering the threshold, this comes at the cost of increased false positives. Increasing the threshold reduces the number of peaks (and hence pulses) detected and reduces the detection accuracy.

We now show the effect of number of samples on the NKLD values. Figure 20 (left) shows how the NKLD values converge for an audio transmitter device (placed at different distances) with the total number of samples processed by Airshark. We find that around 15000 samples, the NKLD values converge to 0.3. Figure 20 (right) compares the NKLD of different RF devices when using the pulse distribution of the audio transmitter device as reference. We find that 15000 samples are sufficient, as NKLD values of ≤ 0.3 can be used to indicate the pulse distribution of the audio transmitter.

4.3 Example uses of Airshark

We now demonstrate Airshark's potential through example applications. We monitored the RF activity on a single floor of two production WLANs using regular wireless laptops that ran

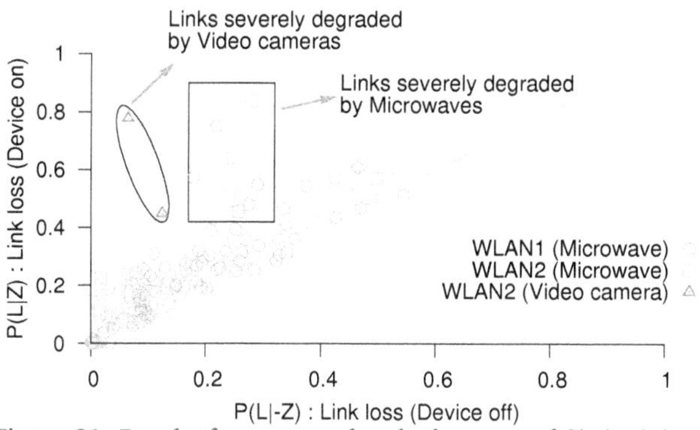

Figure 21: Results from a two day deployment of Airshark in two production WLANs. Each point in the scatter plot denotes the loss rate for a link in the absence ($p(L|\neg Z)$) and the loss rate in the presence ($p(L|Z)$) of (i) microwave ovens, (ii) video cameras, for a total of 224 links (168 links in WLAN1 and 56 links in WLAN2).

Airshark Trace		Loss rate	Airshark Trace		Loss rate
Duration	Microwave	Link L1	Duration	Microwave	Link L2
14:35:19–14:55:18	OFF	10.52%	16:50:36–16:53:19	OFF	16.66%
14:55:18–14:55:46	ON	86.20%	16:53:19–16:53:52	ON	79.61%
14:55:46–15:00:22	OFF	10.91%	16:53:52–17:13:22	OFF	15.78%
15:00:22–15:02:40	ON	45.88%	17:13:22–17:15:19	ON	48.78%
15:02:40–15:04:45	OFF	7.63%	17:15:19–17:33:20	OFF	15.00%

Table 9: Airshark traces for the time periods relevant to links L1 and L2 (WLAN1) showing increased losses due to microwave oven activity.

Airshark and also captured packets using *tcpdump*. WLAN1 used 7 APs and WLAN2 employed 3 APs on the monitored floor. We collected the data for 48 hours at each location. To provide confidence in our statistical estimates, we restrict our analysis to a total of 224 links (168 links in WLAN1, 56 links in WLAN2) that exchange at least 150 packets in our packet traces. Airshark can help WLAN administrators answer the following questions about RF device activity in their networks:

Question. "Which non-WiFi RF devices were visible in the WLANs? How long were the devices active, and which devices appeared more frequently?"

Analysis. Using traces from Airshark, we found that non-WiFi devices were active for 22.6% (10.48 hrs) and 13.92% (6.68 hrs) of the trace duration in WLAN1 and WLAN2 respectively. Table 8 shows the proportion of non-WiFi RF device instances in the two WLANs—microwave ovens (37.16% and 81.65%) and Bluetooth devices (52.34% and 17.43%) occurred most frequently in WLAN1 and WLAN2. FHSS cordless phones accounted for 9.87% of the instances in WLAN1. Game controllers and video cameras were also visible, albeit for very short durations.

Question. "Did any of the links in the WLAN suffer from interference due to non-WiFi devices? Which non-WiFi devices caused the most interference?"

Analysis. Airshark can help identify the interference-prone links as follows: Let L denote the event of a packet loss on a wireless link. We note that L might include losses due to non-WiFi interference as well as those due to "background losses" (e.g., due to weak signal)[3]. Let Z be the event that a non-WiFi device z is active. We compute the probability of a packet loss given the device is active, $p(L|Z)$, and the probability of a packet loss given the device is inactive, $p(L|\neg Z)$ as follows:

1. Using Airshark, we identify the periods when the device z was active (t_{on}), and when the device z was inactive (t_{off}).
2. For each link, we compute the total number of packets transmitted on the link during t_{on}, and the corresponding number of packets lost, to measure $p(L|Z)$. Similarly, we compute $p(L|\neg Z)$ by measuring the loss rate during t_{off}.
3. For the links severely interfered by device z, we can expect $p(L|Z) \gg p(L|\neg Z)$.

We make the following observations:

— *Microwave Ovens:* Figure 21 shows the impact of microwave oven activity using a scatter plot of $p(L|Z)$ and $p(L|\neg Z)$. We observe increased losses for a few links (70–80%). We found that around 20% links in WLAN1 and 10% links in WLAN2 had more than 20% increase in loss rates. Further, for around 5% of the links, the loss rates increased by more than 40%. Table 9 shows snapshots of Airshark traces and loss rates for two links L1 and L2 that experienced interference from microwave ovens.

— *Video camera:* The camera was active only for around 3 minutes in the WLAN2 trace, but it had a severe impact on two of the links as shown in Figure 21. Losses for the two links increased from 6.47% to 77.67%, and 12.47% to 44.85% during the period the camera was on.

— *Bluetooth/Xbox/FHSS phones:* In both the traces, we did not find any impact of these devices on the link loss rates.

5. RELATED WORK

There is a large body of literature on signal classification that includes work on cyclostationary signal analysis [28], blind signal detection [23], and other spectrum sensing techniques [8]. In our work, we only focus on signal detection methods that can be implemented on top of the functionality exposed by commercial WiFi cards. Present day solutions that detect RF devices include entry-level products like AirMedic [2], Wi-Spy [7] that use extra hardware to display spectrum occupancy, but cannot detect RF devices automatically. More expensive solutions like Cisco Spectrum Expert/CleanAir [4], AirMagnet Spectrum XT [2], and Bandspeed AirMaestro [3] use specialized hardware (signal analyzer ICs) to perform high resolution spectral sampling and detect RF devices. Airshark offers a similar performance, is more cost effective as it operates using commodity WiFi cards, and requires only a software upgrade to be readily integrated in existing WLAN deployments.

Recent research work [17, 21] also leverages specialized hardware to detect non-WiFi devices. Hong et. al [17] use a modified channel sounder to sample a wideband (100 MHz), and present novel cyclostationary signal analysis to accurately detect non-WiFi devices. RFDump uses GNURadio and employs timing/phase analysis along with protocol specific demodulators to detect devices. Airshark builds such functionality under the constraints of using commodity WiFi hardware.

Using controlled measurements, prior work [9,13,15,22,25] has studied the impact of non-WiFi devices on WiFi links. Many of them have focused on targeted interference scenarios, e.g., between Bluetooth-WiFi [13] or ZigBee-WiFi [22, 25], and

[3]We note that intermittent losses may also occur due to potential hidden terminals in the network. We used PIE [26], a system that can detect hidden conflicts, to discard such cases from the traces.

proposed mechanisms for co-existence [10, 18]. Similar to [9, 15], we consider the general problem of non-WiFi interference, but specifically, we focus on the problem of making existing WiFi links better aware of non-WiFi RF devices, thereby paving the way for corrective actions that can be implemented in today's networks. Further, our mechanism is complementary to the above solutions, and can be used in conjunction to more effectively tackle non-WiFi interference.

6. CONCLUSION

In this work, we first motivated the need to detect non-WiFi RF devices by characterizing their prevalence in typical environments. We then presented Airshark, a system that can detect the non-WiFi devices using only the functionality provided by commodity WiFi cards. Airshark extracts unique features using energy samples from a WiFi card and presents a generic, and extensible framework to accurately detect multiple non-WiFi devices, while maintaining a low false positive rate. We also found its performance to be comparable to a commercial signal analyzer. Through a deployment in two production WLANs, we demonstrated Airshark's potential in understanding non-WiFi interference issues.

We envision embedding Airshark in commodity wireless APs that opens up numerous other possibilities. WLAN administrators can monitor RF device activity across the network without deploying additional hardware. APs can also employ real-time, non-WiFi interference mitigation mechanisms based on the input from Airshark (e.g., device RSSI/channel). Another application is to physically locate the RF interferer. Localization can be done by correlating the device transmissions across samples from multiple Airshark nodes and then using triangulation methods.

Acknowledgements

We thank Vishnu Katreddy for help with some of the measurements carried out in this paper. We would also like to thank the anonymous reviewers, whose comments helped bring the paper into its final form. Shravan Rayanchu, Ashish Patro, and Suman Banerjee have been supported in part by the US National Science Foundation through awards CNS-1059306, CNS-0855201, CNS-0747177, CNS-0916955, CNS-1040648, and CNS-1064944.

7. REFERENCES

[1] Agilent spectrum analyzers (signal analyzers). http://www.agilent.com/.

[2] AirMagnet AirMedic and Spectrum XT. www.airmagnet.net/products.

[3] Bandspeed AirMaestro spectrum analysis solution. http://www.bandspeed.com/.

[4] Cisco Spectrum Expert. http://www.cisco.com/en/US/products/ps9393/index.html.

[5] LIBSVM: A Library for Support Vector Machines. http://www.csie.ntu.edu.tw/ cjlin/libsvm/.

[6] The WEKA data mining software: an update. ACM SIGKDD Explorations Newsletter.

[7] Wi-Spy spectrum analyzer. www.metageek.net.

[8] I. F. Akyildiz, W.-Y. Lee, M. C. Vuran, and S. Mohanty. Next generation/dynamic spectrum access/cognitive radio wireless networks: a survey. *Comput. Netw.*, 2006.

[9] A. Baid, S. Mathur, I. Seskar, T. Singh, S. Jain, D. Raychaudhuri, S. Paul, and A. Das. Spectrum MRI: Towards diagnosis of multi-radio interference in the unlicensed band. In *IEEE WCNC 2011*.

[10] M. C.-H. Chek and Y.-K. Kwok. Design and evaluation of practical coexistence management schemes for Bluetooth and IEEE 802.11b systems. In *Computer Networks,'07*.

[11] P. Du, W. A. Kibbe, and S. M. Lin. Improved peak detection in mass spectrum by incorporating continuous wavelet transform-based pattern matching. In *Bioinformatics'06*.

[12] G. Palshikar. Simple algorithms for peak detection in time-series, trddc technical report'09. In *Technical Report, TRDDC*.

[13] N. Golmie, N. Chevrollier, and O. Rebala. Bluetooth and WLAN coexistence: Challenges and solutions. *IEEE Wireless Communications Magazine'03*.

[14] R. C. Gonzalez and R. E. Woods. Digital image processing, 3rd ed. 2006.

[15] R. Gummadi, D. Wetherall, B. Greenstein, and S. Seshan. Understanding and mitigating the impact of RF interference on 802.11 networks. In *SIGCOMM '07*.

[16] K. Harmer, G. Howells, W. Sheng, M. Fairhurst, and F. Deravi. A peak-trough detection algorithm based on momentum. In *CISP'08*.

[17] S. Hong and S. Katti. Wispy: Knowing your RF neighborhood. In *ACM SIGCOMM 2011*.

[18] X. Jing, S. Anandaraman, M. Ergin, I. Seskar, and D. Raychaudhuri. Distributed coordination schemes for multi-radio co-existence in dense spectrum environments. In *IEEE DySpan '08*.

[19] A. Kamerman and N. Erkogevi. Microwave oven interference on wireless Lans operating in the 2.4 GHz ISM band. In *PIMRC'97*.

[20] Kullback, S. Information theory and statistics, 1959.

[21] K. Lakshminarayanan, S. Sapra, S. Seshan, and P. Steenkiste. RFDump: an architecture for monitoring the wireless ether. In *CoNext'09*.

[22] C.-J. M. Liang, N. B. Priyantha, J. Liu, and A. Terzis. Surviving Wi-Fi interference in low power zigbee networks. In *ACM SenSys'10*.

[23] O. Zakaria. Blind signal detection and identification over the 2.4 GHz ISM band for cognitive radio. In *MS Thesis USF'09*.

[24] J. R. Quinlan. *C4.5: programs for machine learning*. Morgan Kaufmann Publishers Inc., 1993.

[25] S. Y. Shin, J. S. Kang, and H. S. Park. Packet error rate analysis of zigbee under wlan and bluetooth interferences. In *IEEE Trans. Wireless Comm.'06*.

[26] V. Shrivastava, S. Rayanchu, S. Banerjee, and K. Papagiannaki. PIE in the Sky: online passive interference estimation for enterprise WLANs. In *NSDI'11*.

[27] T. M. Taher, A. Z. Al-Banna, D. R. Ucci, and J. L. LoCicero. Characterization of an unintentional Wi-Fi interference device-the residential microwave oven. In *Milcom'06*.

[28] W. Gardner. Exploitation of spectral redundancy in cyclostationary signals. In *IEEE Signal Processing Magazine'91*.

Summary Review Documentation for

"Airshark: Detecting Non-WiFi RF Devices Using Commodity WiFi Hardware"

Authors: S. Rayanchu, A. Patro, S. Banerjee

Reviewer #1

Strengths: Though overstated repeatedly, the use of typical hardware is a strength. The study of 20 locations and the interfering objects in each is a bit of a contribution as a spot check (not as contribution #1).

Weaknesses: The writing is poor, redundant, and compressed at a low level, making it difficult to extract the key scientific contributions: why this work was technically difficult and what novel method emerged to address that problem. The practical implication is not quite apparent: if performance is poor, perhaps the remedy is the same no matter what the issue is.

Comments to Authors: Should APs simply change channels whenever performance is poor to find another? Does it matter whether the channel is simply oversubscribed by someone streaming video over 802.11 or is someone talking on a phone? I suspect not. This leaves much of your work an oversell: it's great that you can do this, and I think it may have implications for backoff parameters and rate selection, and maybe even pop-ups for the user, but it doesn't mean much for channel selection.

Wouldn't it be easier to tell people, "hey, this radio uses 2.4 GHz: don't use a cordless phone on the same frequency."? I suspect this problem will resolve itself.

Contributions 1 and 3 seem effectively the same. I'd rate this paper higher if the tool were made available as a contribution for proper validation and use.

Why is there a line on figure 3?

What is the source of error? Why is airshark ever wrong? Is airshark only wrong when it doesn't matter (the interference is not strong?) Or just wrong 8% of the time for no good reason?

The microwave comparison is pretty obvious given prior work that detected microwaves using commodity hardware. Since that work was published some time ago, the repeated assertion about using "commodity" hardware was not as impressive to me, especially given that you're using what amounts to a baby spectrum-analysis feature in the hardware that you've only shown is present in one card from one manufacturer. Was that functionality included for this purpose? or for some other? If for some other, then you've done something interesting. If for this purpose, and atheros just hasn't gotten around to making a useful tool on it, good for you, but the "commodity" tag has less value.

Reviewer #2

Strengths: Works with off the shelf wifi cards Extensive evaluation well motivated with an empirical evaluation.

Weaknesses: Faulty comparisons with prior work; could be written better; it's never clear why the features picked were the right ones; it's hard to understand performance wrt SNR, results presented in a card specific RSSI measure, but no noise figure is given, so hard to tell how robust the scheme is to low.

Comments to Authors: I don't quite understand what you mean by coarse resolution in time. Even though the Wifi card may be exposing energy averaged over small time windows, in the radio itself it is computing FFTs over digital samples whose rate is at least the Nyquist rate, if not more. What you are getting is essentially FFTs over windows of samples, which is exacty what prior work like Wispy (Sigcomm 11) is using. So that statement isn't correct

Similarly I am confused by the resolution in frequency argument, isn't it the same as computing FFT of a certain resolution? Maybe the Wifi card smoothens it a bit, but it's not significantly different than a standard FFT resolution

Prior work such as RFdump and Wispy did much more than device detection, RFdump also detects bandwidth occupancy of non-Wifi signals, while WiSpy does both bandwidth occupancy as well as angles of arrival. So while Airshark's ability to work with commodity cards is nice, you do give up something in return. The paper should make that clearer.

Reviewer #3

Strengths: Valiant attempt to use commodity devices. Fairly intuitive techniques. Results comparable to commercial detectors.

Weaknesses: Comparable to commercial != advancing the state of the art. In particular, the technique seems sensitive to overlap in signals, whether from >1 non-wifi devices or between wifi and non-wifi interferer as would happen during a busy wifi period.

It isn't entirely clear from the suggested applications why knowing which non-wifi device is causing the source of interference is terribly important. Yes, for diagnosis and troubleshooting; but to be able to shift to greener pastures upon interference does not require knowing who is causing the interference.

Comments to Authors: I liked this paper.

It is interesting that the characteristics of the non-wifi RF devices are stark enough to be discovered with the coarse lens of a commodity card (freq of samples is low, range of frequencies observable at the same time is small, very little info besides received signal strength etc.)

I would have liked further insight... Which of the several features that you mention were more accurate, more discriminative? How close were the devices in terms of signatures to each other? Can you tell apart different types of micro-waves?

At the end of the day, modulo troubleshooting and curiosity concerns, how does precise knowledge of the interferer help with system design? Changing channels for e.g., doesn't require this.

I found the end of 3.4, dealing with overlapping channels somewhat un-inspired. I realize the problem is harder, but there is a fair bit that can still be done; for example, Fig 14 clearly _looks_ like the composition of two signals. Can you not derive decision tree classifiers for frequently co-occurring compositions of signals? I know this space is larger, but as you conclude that only certain types of signals are likely to co-occur repeatedly, it might improve analysis to look for those.

How many training samples do you end up using? (is this same as the # of samples for NKLD)

Feature F4 (pulse signatures, i.e., freq, bandwidth, duration) is very similar to feature F1 (freq, bandwidth)

Can hack to improve switching times between bands to a few ms from the 20ms if needed. (3.1)

Techniques are fairly straightforward.

F2 is quite cool, looking for spread. I can't tell how much discriminative power there is in it though; how often are these spectral signatures different. Normalizing for power also gets you to look at different center frequencies, e.g., hoppers.

In 3.4, creation of training data, using the "list of possible CFs" is key. Because, it is unlikely that you will be able to create training data that mimics all possible configurations of a certain device. I suspect for other devices you'd have to incorporate more meta-data beyond just the possible CFs.

Can these techniques apply to non RF devices? The front-ends of the card can typically operate in a wider band than just RF. Not sure if other parts of the pipeline are specific to RF though.

Reviewer #4

Strengths: The proposed system has high detection accuracy The evaluation was solid and comprehensive. The paper was well structured.

Weaknesses: The technical contribution is not clearly described The characterization part is a bit weak See comments below for details.

Comments to Authors: This is a solid piece of work, in terms of both characterization and system evaluation. I also like Section 4.3 that presents example users of Airshark. There are however two concerns about the paper.

First, the technical contribution is not clear. Section 3 of the paper is really long and boring. It exposes too many details without clearly justifying how authors address the four challenges mentioned at the beginning of Section 3. In other words, the authors employ standard technique for each building block of Airshark while it remains unclear how these building blocks are magically assembled to a novel system that achieves qualitatively similar accuracy on commodity WiFi devices compared to those on sophisticated spectrum analyzers. A more clear high-level picture is critical in Section 3. I suggest that the authors expand the overview part and shorten the remaining part.

Second, Section 2 measures the prevalence of non-WiFi RF devices in terms of device popularity, session duration, signal strengths, and concurrency at different locations. One critical question remains unanswered is: in such real environments, how do these non-WiFi devices affect WiFi performance? You can measure this by establishing long-lived data transfer sessions using WiFi and monitoring the performance.

Reviewer #5

Strengths: Sound techiques and good experimental results.

Weaknesses: The techniques are a little incremental and may not work as well as cyclo-stationary analysis.

Comments to Authors: This is a strong wireless network measurement paper. Unlike existing work on measuring non-WiFi devices, this paper adds an interesting twist that the detection done on WiFi devices. This new twist makes the problem more challenging. On the other hand, does not come for free because WiFi devices cannot receive signals at arbitrary SNR or arbitrary channel width. As future work, it'd very interesting to directly compare the results with those obtained from using more powerful spectrum analyzers (e.g., "DOF: A Local Wireless Information Plane").

Identifying a single interference is relatively easy since the types of signatures associated with Zigbee, Microwaves, and cordless phones are known. The challenge lies in how to classify signals when multiple interference are present. To this problem, the solution in this paper are not robust and may under-perform some existing approaches, like cyclo-stationary analysis. In fact, the paper claims that cyclo-stationary analysis is not applicable to this context. Why? Please elaborate.

The paper could also be strengthened by giving some applications of the classification. After knowing the type of interference, how can we use this information to improve WiFi performance?

Response from the Authors

We would like to thank the reviewers for the constructive comments that helped improve the paper. We have fixed the text in the paper to address some of the reviewer concerns and expanded some portions to make the technical contributions more clear. Some of the reviewer comments seemed to have stemmed because of confusion regarding understanding some of the aspects of our work and how Airshark's design was driven by the constraints imposed by commodity WiFi cards. Below, we address these concerns:

Sources of error (Reviewer 1): Airshark can make an error in detection under when the signal strength of non-WiFi device is low (< -80 dBm) or under extreme WiFi interference (specifically explained in Sections 4.2.1 and 4.2.2).

Prior work on detecting Microwave ovens (Reviewer 1): We are not aware of any prior work which detects microwave oven activity using a systematic approach that works only using commodity WiFi hardware, and the reviewer does not specify a reference. Jigsaw work (Sigcomm'07)/Shaman (UCSD Tech. report) seems to the only work that indirectly "speculates" that a microwave oven might be active by looking into physical errors experienced by links --- the scheme requires "enough" packets to be in error, and will fail to detect the microwave oven in presence of interference from other non-WiFi devices (e.g., an analog phone or a high duty video camera).

Confusion regarding prior work on device detection (Reviewer 2,5): Prior work like Wispy/DOF (Sigcomm '11) requires "raw digital samples" (not exposed by WiFi cards) to apply cyclostationary analysis and detect angles of arrival. Such analysis is not possible with commodity WiFi cards as they only expose the receiver power samples. Compared to RFDump, Airshark does (and needs to) estimate the bandwidth of the wireless signals to detect them (see Section 3.2).

Concerns regarding motivation behind our work (Reviewer 1,3): Comments from Reviewer 1 seems to suggest some confusion regarding understanding the motivation behind device detection. Changing channels/widths was only included as an example reaction on behalf of APs to tackle a specific type of interference. We believe that the remedial action would depend on the type of device causing interference and may definitely include adjusting other operational wireless parameters like backoff/bit-rate/transmit power. We agree with Reviewer 3 that knowing what devices are in the air definitely provides the WLAN administrator with a better picture for troubleshooting concerns.

Overlapping signal detection (Reviewer 3): We agree that the overlapping signal detection can be improved by adding more functionality to the decision tree classifier. We will certainly incorporate the suggested ideas and benchmark this case further in our future work.

Impact of non-WiFi devices on real WiFi networks (Reviewer 4): We agree with the reviewer's concern that it is important to be able to detect the impact of non-WiFi devices on WiFi links in real environments. While Section 4.3 does provide some evidence in this regard, there is a need for a solution that answers these questions more systematically. We believe Airshark is only a first step toward effectively managing non-WiFi interference. Our current efforts are indeed focused on developing a system that can answer these questions.

Proportional Rate Reduction for TCP

Nandita Dukkipati, Matt Mathis, Yuchung Cheng, Monia Ghobadi
Google, Inc.
Mountain View
California, U.S.A
{nanditad, mattmathis, ycheng}@google.com, monia@cs.toronto.edu

ABSTRACT

Packet losses increase latency for Web users. Fast recovery is a key mechanism for TCP to recover from packet losses. In this paper, we explore some of the weaknesses of the standard algorithm described in RFC 3517 and the non-standard algorithms implemented in Linux. We find that these algorithms deviate from their intended behavior in the real world due to the combined effect of short flows, application stalls, burst losses, acknowledgment (ACK) loss and reordering, and stretch ACKs. Linux suffers from excessive congestion window reductions while RFC 3517 transmits large bursts under high losses, both of which harm the rest of the flow and increase Web latency.

Our primary contribution is a new design to control transmission in fast recovery called proportional rate reduction (PRR). PRR recovers from losses quickly, smoothly and accurately by pacing out retransmissions across received ACKs. In addition to PRR, we evaluate the TCP early retransmit (ER) algorithm which lowers the duplicate acknowledgment threshold for short transfers, and show that delaying early retransmissions for a short interval is effective in avoiding spurious retransmissions in the presence of a small degree of reordering. PRR and ER reduce the TCP latency of connections experiencing losses by 3-10% depending on the response size. Based on our instrumentation on Google Web and YouTube servers in U.S. and India, we also present key statistics on the nature of TCP retransmissions.

Categories and Subject Descriptors

C.2 [COMPUTER-COMMUNICATION NETWORKS]: Network Protocols

General Terms

Algorithms, Design, Experimentation, Measurement, Performance.

IMC'11, November 2–4, 2011, Berlin, Germany.

Keywords

TCP, fast recovery, proportional rate reduction, early retransmit, retransmission statistics.

1. INTRODUCTION

Web latency plays a key role in producing responsive Web applications, making information more accessible and helping to advance new cloud-based applications. There are many factors that contribute to Web latency including content that is not optimized for speed, inefficient Web servers, slow browsers, limited network bandwidth, excess losses and suboptimal network protocols. In this paper, we focus on reducing latency for TCP connections experiencing packet losses. Measurements show that over 6% of HTTP responses served from Google.com experience losses and that these losses impact user experience. We investigate some of these loss statistics and revisit TCP's loss recovery mechanisms with the goal of reducing Web latency for users.

To get a sense for how much packet losses increase Web latency, we compare the TCP latency of HTTP responses experiencing losses to their ideal achievable latency. Figure 1 (top plot) shows the average TCP latency for responses with sizes ranging between 4kB and 8kB broken down in 200ms round-trip time (RTT) buckets, measured from billions of user TCP connections to Google Web servers world-wide. The TCP latency of a HTTP response is measured from when the server sends the first byte until it receives the acknowledgment (ACK) for the last byte. We define the ideal response time to be the fixed portion of the network delay, which we approximate to be the minimum measured RTT for any given HTTP response. The approximation works well because the 4-8kB responses fit well within TCP's initial congestion window of 10 segments used on Google servers. Responses experiencing losses last 7-10 times longer than the ideal, while those with no losses are very close to the ideal. The CDF in Figure 1 (bottom plot) shows that the latency spread for responses with losses is 200 RTTs - about 10x greater than those without losses. Several independent factors, including slow user network bandwidths, long queuing delays, and TCP's mechanisms must be addressed for latency to approach the ideal.

TCP has two primary means of detecting and recovering from losses. First is fast retransmit, where TCP performs a retransmission of the missing segment after receiving a certain number of duplicate acknowledgments (dupacks) [4]. As a fall back, whenever fast retransmission is unsuccessful or when a sender does not receive enough duplicate ACKs, TCP uses a second slower but more robust mechanism where

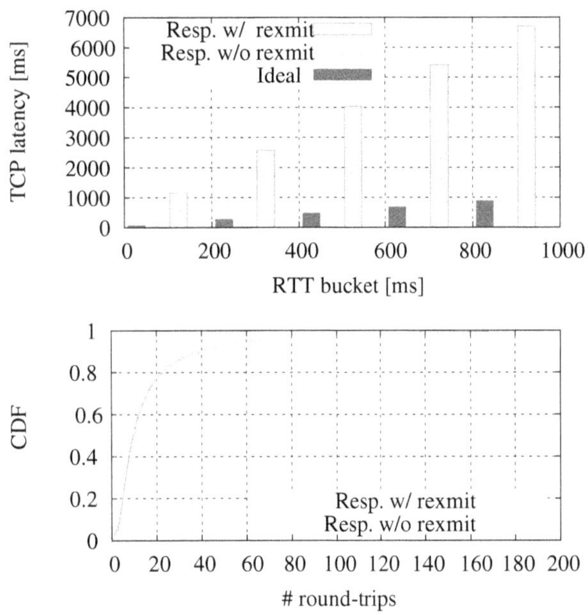

Figure 1: Top plot shows the average TCP latency of Google HTTP responses in different round-trip time buckets for response sizes between 4kB and 8kB. Bottom plot shows CDF of the number of RTTs taken by responses of all sizes with and without retransmissions.

it waits for a duration of retransmission timeout (RTO) before deducing that a segment is lost.

Our measurements show that fast recovery accounts for about 25% of all retransmissions in short flows served from Google Web servers and over 50% of retransmissions in bulk video traffic. There are two widely deployed algorithms used to adjust the congestion window (*cwnd*) during fast recovery, RFC 3517 [8] and rate halving [17], implemented in Linux. After extensive analysis of these algorithms on Google servers, we find that in practice both can be either too conservative or too aggressive resulting in a long recovery time or in excessive retransmissions.

The three main contributions of this paper are as follows:

1. **Proportional rate reduction:** We designed a new fast recovery algorithm, proportional rate reduction (PRR), which is inspired by the rate halving algorithm [17]. PRR recovers from losses both *quickly* and *smoothly* by using Van Jacobson's packet conservation principle to pace out retransmissions across received ACKs. Specifically, PRR improves upon the existing (non-standard) Linux fast recovery and RFC specified standard fast recovery under a number of conditions including: a) burst losses where the losses implicitly reduce the amount of outstanding data (*pipe*) below the slow start threshold value selected by the congestion control algorithm and, b) losses near the end of short flows where application runs out of data to send. PRR also performs accurate *cwnd* adjustments even under stretch ACKs or ACK loss and reordering. Furthermore, PRR is designed to work with the diverse set of congestion control algorithms present in today's Internet [28]: when the recovery finishes, TCP completes the window adjustment as intended by the congestion control algorithm.

   PRR has been approved to become the default Linux fast recovery algorithm for Linux 3.x.

2. **Experiments with Early Retransmit (ER):** We address the question of how to trigger fast retransmit for short flows. This question is important because short HTTP transactions frequently do not receive the three dupacks necessary to trigger conventional fast recovery. We evaluate the TCP early retransmit (ER) algorithm [2] that lowers duplicate acknowledgment threshold (*dupthresh*) for short transfers. Google Web server experiments show that the Internet has enough reordering to cause naive ER to exhibit excessive spurious retransmissions. We show that delaying early retransmissions for a short interval is effective at mitigating the spurious retransmissions.

3. **Retransmission statistics of Google Web servers:** We analyse TCP data from Google Web and video servers and present key statistics on the nature of retransmissions.

The rest of the paper is organized as follows: Section 2 describes TCP measurements of Google's user traffic. Section 3 reviews state-of-the-art fast recovery as described in the standards and the non-standard Linux variant. In Section 4, we present the design and properties of proportional rate reduction. Section 5 evaluates PRR's performance on Google Web and YouTube servers. In Section 6, we describe the experimental results of early retransmit. Section 7 summarizes related work. Section 8 concludes the paper along with a discussion on future work.

2. GOOGLE MEASUREMENTS

We sampled TCP statistics on unmodified Google Web servers world-wide for one week in May 2011. The servers use a recent version of Linux 2.6 with settings listed in Table 4. The servers do not include the changes proposed in this paper. The global statistics for interactive Web services are summarized in Table 1. Among the billions of connections sampled, 96% of the connections negotiated SACK but only 12% of the connections negotiated Timestamps. The majority of clients are Microsoft Windows which by default do not use TCP Timestamps.

Although over 94% of connections use HTTP/1.1 and the Google Web Servers keep idle TCP connections up to 4 minutes, there were on average only 3.1 HTTP requests per connection. The average HTTP response size from Google.com was 7.5KB, which is similar to the average Web object size of 7.2KB measured for billions of Web sites in 2010 [21]. The average user network bandwidth as observed from Google is 1.9Mbps and is in agreement with another study in 2010 [1]. While the average per segment TCP retransmission rate is 2.8%, 6.1% of the HTTP responses have TCP retransmissions.

2.1 Detailed retransmission statistics

We examine the existing[1] Linux loss recovery mechanisms as measured from the Google Web servers. We measure the

[1]Note PRR is already slated to be released in upstream kernels.

TCP	
Total connections	Billions
Connections support SACK	96%
Connections support Timestamp	12%
HTTP/1.1 connections	94%
Average requests per connection	3.1
Average retransmissions rate	2.8%
HTTP	
Average response size	7.5kB
Responses with TCP retransmissions	6.1%

Table 1: Summary of Google TCP and HTTP statistics sampled for one week in May 2011. The data include both port 80 and 443 but exclude YouTube videos and bulk downloads.

	DC1	DC2
Fast retransmits	24%	54%
Timeout retransmits	43%	17%
Timeout in Open	30%	8%
Timeout in Disorder	2%	3%
Timeout in Recovery	1%	2%
Timeout Exp. Backoff	10%	4%
Slow start retransmits	17%	29%
Failed retransmits	15%	0%

Table 2: A breakdown of retransmissions on Google Web servers in two data centers. All percentages are with reference to the total number of retransmissions.

types of retransmissions from a large U.S. data center, DC1, which primarily serves users from the U.S. east coast and South America. We selected this data center because it has a good mix of different RTTs, user bandwidths and loss rates. We also measured another data-center, DC2, which is in India and exclusively serves YouTube videos. For ease of comparison analysis, we also use the same data centers to experiment with our own changes to fast recovery described in later sections.

We collect the Linux TCP SNMP statistics from Google Web servers for 72 hours at DC1 in April 2011 and DC2 in August 2011. Observations described here are consistent across several such sample sizes taken in different weeks and months. The average (server) retransmission rates are 2.5% in DC1 and 5.6% in DC2. DC2 has a higher retransmission rate because the network in India has lower capacity and higher congestion.

Table 2 shows the breakdown of TCP retransmission types. It shows that fast recovery is a key mechanism to recover losses in both bulk download (video) and short flows (Web pages). In DC2, the retransmissions sent during fast recovery, labeled as *fast retransmits*, comprise 54% of all retransmissions. In DC1, fast recovery still recovers nearly a quarter (24%) of losses. This difference between DC1 and DC2 is because the long video flows of DC2 have a greater chance of entering fast recovery compared to the shorter Web traffic of DC1. The first retransmission upon a timeout, labeled as *timeout retransmits*, constitute 43% of the retransmissions in DC1. This is mainly caused by the Web

	DC1	DC2
Fast retransmits/FR	3.15	2.93
DSACKs/FR	12%	4%
DSACKs/retransmit	3.8%	1.4%
Lost (fast) retransmits/FR	6%	9%
Lost retransmits/retransmit	1.9%	3.1%

Table 3: Fast recovery related statistics on Google Web servers. All numbers are with respect to the total number of fast recovery events or fast retransmits as indicated.

objects that are too small to trigger fast recovery. Moreover, the highest query volume in DC1 turns out to be from statistics collection applications such as Google Analytics. Typically their HTTP responses are tiny and fit entirely into one segment. As a result losses can not cause any dupacks so the only available recovery mechanism is a timeout. Interestingly, DC1 and DC2 shows very different distribution of timeouts in various TCP recovery states. In DC1, the majority of timeouts happen in the open state, i.e., without any preceding dupacks or other indication of losses.[2] However in DC2, more timeouts occur in non-Open states.

In DC1 and DC2, 17% and 29% of total retransmissions occur in the slow start phase after the timeout retransmission has successfully advanced *snd.una*. These are called *slow start retransmissions* because typically the sender has reset *cwnd* to one after a timeout and it is operating in slow start phase. DC2 has more timeout retransmissions than DC1 because the timeout happens when outstanding data are typically much larger for video download. The three types of retransmissions, fast retransmits, timeout retransmits, and slow start retransmits, successfully recover the losses and constitute 85% and 100% of the total retransmissions in data centers DC1 and DC2 respectively.

For the remaining 15% retransmissions in DC1 termed *failed retransmits*, TCP failed to make any forward progress because no further TCP acknowledgments were received from the client and the server eventually aborts the connection. This difference is partially due to differing maximum timeout setting on the servers in DC1 and DC2, however we suspect that there may be other contributing factors.

Table 3 shows some additional statistics on how well fast recovery is performing.

Both data centers exhibit about three fast retransmits per fast recovery event. This suggests that loss is highly correlated (a property of the network) and provides a sense of how much the network around each data center exercises TCP's loss recovery machinery. This metric should be mostly insensitive to changes in recovery algorithms, although there may be some higher order effects.

Duplicate segments at the TCP receiver normally trigger DSACKs [9]. The DSACK statistics provide a measure of network resources that were wasted by overly aggressive retransmits of nearly all types, except segments with no pay-

[2]This statistic is particularly odd, because a timeout from the open state implies that an entire window of data or ACKs was lost in a single RTT. Although the high volume of tiny transactions contribute to timeouts from open, they can not explain numbers this large. Some other mechanism must be present.

load. In DC1, we see an average of 12% fast-recoveries causing DSACKS, implying at least a 3.8% spurious retransmission rate. In DC2 the spurious retransmission rate is at least 1.4%. Note that since some Web clients don't generate DSACKS, these are lower bounds of the actual spurious retransmissions.

Linux also detects lost retransmissions as described in section 3.2. Since the retransmissions are delivered in a new round trip, they provide some indication of how quickly congestion subsides following the initial packet losses. With lost retransmission detection, lost retransmissions cause additional RTTs in recovery. Without it, they cause timeouts. In DC1 and DC2, about 2% and 3% fast-retransmits are lost.

The data shown here is for the Linux baseline, however these metrics are important for comparing any recovery algorithms, and are used elsewhere.

3. STATE-OF-THE-ART FAST RECOVERY

Our work is based on the Linux TCP implementation, which includes several non-standard algorithms and experimental RFCs. The goal of this section is two-fold: first, we highlight the differences between standard TCP recovery algorithms [4, 8] and the design of widely deployed Linux recovery. Second, we discuss the drawbacks of each design, specifically in the context of short Web transactions.

3.1 Fast recovery in RFC standards

Standard congestion control in RFC 5681 [4] requires that TCP reduce the congestion window in response to losses. Fast recovery, described in the same document, is the reference algorithm for making this adjustment. Its stated goal is to recover TCP's self clock by relying on returning dupacks during recovery to clock more data into the network. Depending on the pattern of losses, we find that the standard can be either too aggressive or too conservative.

Algorithm 1: RFC 3517 fast recovery

On entering recovery:

```
// cwnd used during and after recovery.
```
$cwnd = ssthresh = FlightSize/2$

```
// Retransmit first missing segment.
```
$fast\_retransmit()$

```
// Transmit more if cwnd allows.
```
$Transmit\ MAX(0, cwnd - pipe)$

For every ACK during recovery:

$update\_scoreboard()$ $pipe =$ (RFC 3517 pipe algorithm)

$Transmit\ MAX(0, cwnd - pipe)$

Algorithm 1 briefly presents the standard RFC design for recovery. A TCP sender enters fast recovery upon receiving *dupthresh* number of dupacks (typically three). On entering recovery, the sender performs the following: 1) sets *cwnd* and *ssthresh* to half of the data outstanding in the network and, 2) *fast retransmit* the first unacknowledged segment, and further transmits more segments if allowed by *cwnd*.

On subsequent ACKs during recovery, the sender recomputes the *pipe* variable using the procedure specified in RFC 3517. *pipe* is an estimate of the number of total segments in the network based on the SACK scoreboard. It is only an estimate because it relies on heuristics that determine if a segment can be marked as lost. The algorithm then transmits up to $cwnd - pipe$ segments. Fast recovery ends when all data that was outstanding before entering recovery is cumulatively acknowledged or when a timeout occurs.

Features	RFC	Linux	Default
Initial cwnd	3390	p	10
Cong. control (NewReno)	5681	+	CUBIC
SACK	2018	+	on
D-SACK	3708	+	on
Rate-Halving [17]		+	always on
FACK [16]		+	on
Limited-transmit	3042	+	always on
Dynamic *dupthresh*		+	always on
RTO	2988	p	min=200ms
F-RTO	5682	+	on
Cwnd undo (Eifel)	3522	p	always on
TCP segmentation offload		+	determined by NIC

+ indicates the feature is fully implemented.
p indicates a partially implemented feature.

Table 4: Loss recovery related features in Linux. Non-standard features are those without RFC numbers.

There are two main problems exhibited by the standard:

1. *Half RTT silence*: The algorithm waits for half of the received ACKs to pass by before transmitting anything after the first fast rertansmit. This is because *cwnd* is brought down to *ssthresh* in one step, so it takes *cwnd-ssthresh* ACKs for *pipe* to go below *cwnd*, creating a silent period for half of an RTT. This design wastes precious opportunities to transmit which sometimes results in nothing being sent during recovery. This in turn increases the chances of timeouts.

2. *Aggressive and bursty retransmissions*: The standard can transmit large bursts on a single received ACK. This is because $pipe - cwnd$ can be arbitrary large under burst losses or inaccurate estimation of losses. Furthermore, the more losses there are, the larger the bursts transmitted by the standard.

Note that both problems occur in the context of *heavy* losses, wherein greater than or equal to half of the *cwnd* is lost. We will see in Section 5 that such heavy losses are surprisingly common for both Web and YouTube.

3.2 Fast recovery in Linux

Linux implements a rich set of standard and non-standard loss recovery algorithms [23]. Table 4 lists the main algorithms related to loss recovery and their default settings.

Linux keeps a SACK scoreboard as described in RFC 2018 [18] and computes *pipe*, the estimate of the number of segments in the network, per RFC 3517. Our detailed analysis of TCP retransmissions is based on the following four recovery states in the Linux TCP code base:

- Open: There is no missing data and the sender is receiving in-sequence ACKs.
- Disorder: The sender has received dupacks indicating that there is data missing, but has not yet retransmitted anything.

- Recovery: There has been a fast retransmit.
- Loss: There has been a timeout and resetting of *cwnd* to one to recover TCP's self clock.

There are three key differences between Linux and RFC 3517.

Linux is more aggressive in marking segments lost because it implements several algorithms from FACK [16] in addition to the standard loss detection described in RFC 3517. FACK was developed at an earlier time when network reordering was relatively rare, so it makes some simplifying assumptions. Specifically, fast retransmit can be triggered immediately by the very first SACK if it indicates that more than dupthresh segments are missing (so called threshold retransmission). Furthermore, once in fast recovery, all holes below the highest SACK block are assumed to be lost and marked for retransmission. Linux also includes a slightly later algorithm for detecting lost retransmissions. If any new data sent after a retransmission is later SACKed, the retransmission is deemed to have been lost [17]. If any reordering is detected then FACK and some of the related algorithms are disabled, the loss detection falls back to use conventional *dupthresh*.

Linux implements the rate halving algorithm [17, 19] in recovery. When *cwnd* is reduced, Linux sends data in response to alternate ACKs during recovery, instead of waiting for *cwnd*/2 dupacks to pass as specified in the standard. A minor problem with rate *halving* is that it is based on the original Reno TCP that always halved the *cwnd* during fast recovery. Several modern congestion control algorithms, such as CUBIC [10], reduce the window by less than 50% so unconditionally *halving* the rate is no longer appropriate.

While in recovery, Linux prevents bursts by reducing *cwnd* to *pipe* + 1 on every ACK that reduces *pipe* for some reason. This implies that if there is insufficient new data available (e.g., because the application temporarily stalls), *cwnd* can be become one by the end of recovery. If this happens, then after recovery the sender will slow start from a very small *cwnd* even though only one segment was lost and there was no timeout!

The main drawbacks of the fast recovery in Linux are its excessive window reductions and conservative retransmissions, which occur for the following reasons:

1. *Slow start after recovery* : Even for a single loss event, a connection carrying short Web responses can complete recovery with a very small *cwnd*, such that subsequent responses using the same connection will slow start even when not otherwise required.
2. *Conservative retransmissions* : There are at least two scenarios where retransmissions in Linux are overly conservative. In the presence of heavy losses, when *pipe* falls below *ssthresh*, Linux (re)transmits at most one packet per ACK during the rest of recovery. As a result, recovery is either prolonged or it enters an RTO.

   A second scenario is that rate halving assumes every ACK represents one data packet delivered. However, lost ACKs will cause Linux to retransmit less than half of the congestion window.

4. PROPORTIONAL RATE REDUCTION

Proportional Rate Reduction is designed to overcome all four problems mentioned in the previous section.

The PRR algorithm determines the number of segments to be sent per ACK during recovery to balance two goals: 1) a speedy and smooth recovery from losses, and 2) end recovery at a congestion window close to *ssthresh*. The foundation of the algorithm is Van Jacobson's packet conservation principle: segments delivered to the receiver are used as the clock to trigger sending additional segments into the network.

PRR has two main parts. The first part, the proportional part is active when the number of outstanding segments (*pipe*) is larger than *ssthresh*, which is typically true early during the recovery and under light losses. It gradually reduces the congestion window clocked by the incoming acknowledgments. The algorithm is patterned after rate halving, but uses a fraction that is appropriate for the target window chosen by the congestion control algorithm. For example, when operating with CUBIC congestion control, the proportional part achieves the 30% window reduction by spacing out seven new segments for every ten incoming ACKs (more precisely, for ACKs reflecting 10 segments arriving at the receiver).

If *pipe* becomes smaller than *ssthresh* (such as due to excess losses or application stalls during recovery), the second part of the algorithm attempts to inhibit any further congestion window reductions. Instead it performs slow start to build the *pipe* back up to *ssthresh* subject to the availability of new data to send.[3]

Note that both parts of the PRR algorithm are independent of the congestion control algorithm (CUBIC, New Reno, GAIMD [29] etc.) used to determine the new value of *ssthresh*.

We also introduced a complete description of PRR into the IETF as a possible future RFC [15].

4.1 Examples

We present TCP time-sequence graphs of packet traces to illustrate and compare the three fast recovery algorithms. The traces are produced by our Linux kernel implementation and an internally developed TCP testing tool. The measurement setup is a simple network with a 100ms RTT and 1.2Mbps link and a 1000 byte MSS. The server application writes 20kB at time 0 and 10kB at time 500ms. TCP use traditional Reno congestion control, which sets *ssthresh* to half of the *cwnd* at the beginning of recovery.

The first example is shown in Figure 2. Vertical double ended arrows represent transmitted data segments that carry a range of bytes at a particular time. Retransmitted data is red. The green staircase represents advancing *snd.una* carried by the ACKs returning to the sender, and the vertical purple lines represent SACK blocks, indicating data that has arrived at the receiver, but is above *snd.una*.

In this example, the first 4 segments are dropped. Since TCP uses FACK, in all three traces TCP enters fast recovery after receiving first dupack and sets *ssthresh* to 10 (half of *cwnd*). In the PRR trace (top), the proportion part of

[3]We considered several alternative reduction bound algorithms, as described in [15], and this variant provides the best combination of features. This combined algorithm should more properly be called Proportional Rate Reduction with Slow-Start Reduction Bound (PRR-SSRB), but we shortened it to PRR.

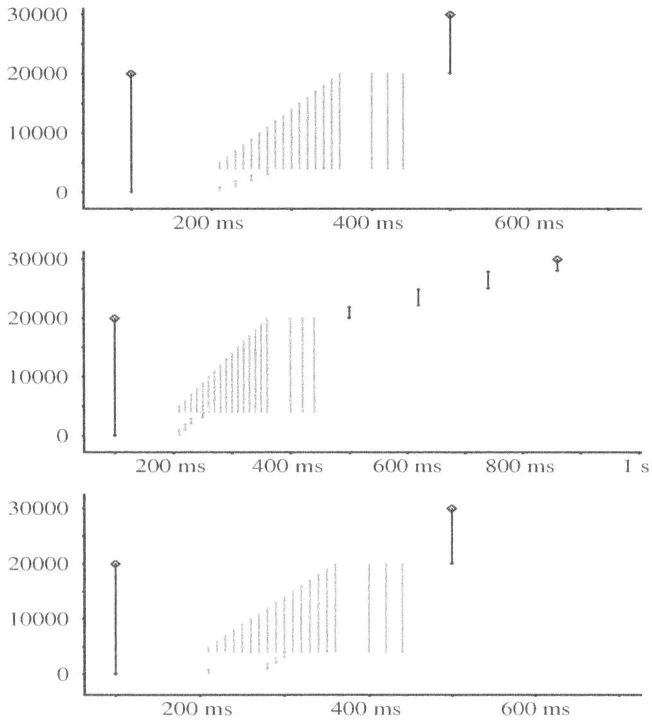

Figure 2: A comparison of PRR (top), Linux recovery (middle), and RFC 3517 (bottom). Legend for the plot: Original data transmissions (Black), retransmissions (Red), snd.una (Green), duplicate ACKs with SACK blocks (Purple).

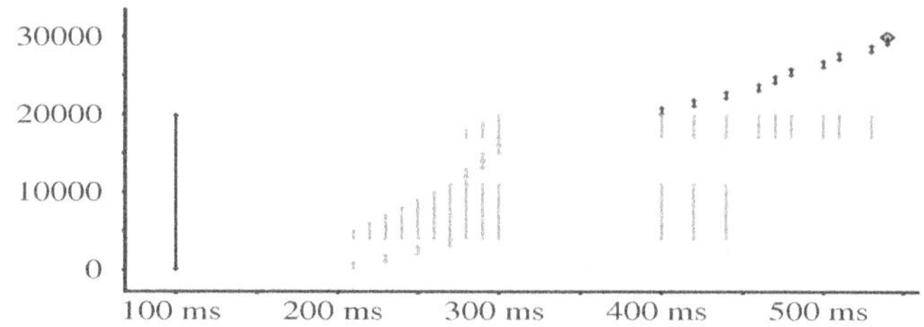

Figure 3: PRR algorithm under heavy losses.

PRR retransmits one segment every other ACK. At time 460ms, the sender completes the recovery and sets the *cwnd* to *ssthresh* (10). When the application writes 10 segments into the socket at time 500ms, the segments are sent in one RTT. The Linux trace (middle) highlights the first problem in Section 3.2. The retransmission timings are similar to the PRR trace because Linux does rate-halving. But the key difference is that *cwnd* remains $pipe + 1$ when fast recovery completes, *pipe* is 1 right before recovery completes. Therefore it takes 4 RTTs to deliver the next 10 segments in slow-start. The RFC trace (bottom) highlights the first problem in Section 3.1: the 2nd retransmission happens after about half of the *cwnd* of ACKs are received resulting, in the half RTT silence.

Figure 3 illustrates how PRR reacts to heavy losses. We use the same setup but drop segments 1 to 4 and 11 to 16. After first cluster of drops and *pipe* is larger than *ssthresh*, the proportional part of the algorithm is active transmitting on alternate received ACKs. However, after the second cluster of losses when *pipe* falls below *ssthresh*, PRR operates in slow start part and transmits two segments for every ACK.

4.2 Pseudo code for PRR

Algorithm 2 shows how PRR determines the number of bytes that should be sent in response to each ACK in recovery. The algorithm relies on three new state variables:

Algorithm 2: Proportional Rate Reduction (PRR)

Initialization on entering recovery:

`// Target cwnd after recovery.`
$ssthresh = CongCtrlAlg()$

`// Total bytes delivered during recovery.`
$prr\_delivered = 0$

`// Total bytes sent during recovery.` $prr\_out = 0$

`// FlightSize at the start of recovery.`
$RecoverFS = snd.nxt - snd.una$

On every ACK during recovery compute:

`// DeliveredData is number of new bytes that the current acknowledgment indicates have been delivered to the receiver.`
$DeliveredData = delta(snd.una) + delta(SACKd)$
$prr\_delivered += DeliveredData$
$pipe =$ (RFC 3517 pipe algorithm)

if $pipe > ssthresh$ **then**
  `// Proportional Rate Reduction`
  $sndcnt = CEIL(prr\_delivered * ssthresh / RecoverFS) - prr\_out$
else
  `// Slow start`
  $ss\_limit = MAX(prr\_delivered - prr\_out, DeliveredData) + 1$
  $sndcnt = MIN(ssthresh - pipe, ss\_limit)$

$sndcnt = MAX(sndcnt, 0)$ `// positive`
$cwnd = pipe + sndcnt$

On any data transmission or retransmission:
$prr\_out += data\_sent$

At the end of recovery:
$cwnd = ssthresh$

1. *prr_delivered* is the total number of unique bytes delivered to the receiver since the start of recovery accounted through cumulative ACKs or through SACKs.

2. *prr_out* is the total bytes transmitted during recovery.

3. *RecoverFS* is the FlightSize (defined as *snd.nxt* − *snd.una* in RFC 3517 [8]) at the start of recovery.

In addition to these, PRR maintains two local variables:

1. *DeliveredData* is the number of new bytes that the current acknowledgment indicates have been delivered to the receiver.

2. *sndcnt* determines how many bytes to send in response to each ACK. Note that the decision of which data to send (e.g., retransmit lost data or send additional new data) is independent of PRR.

Algorithm 2 shows how PRR updates *sndcnt* on every ACK. When *pipe* is larger than *ssthresh*, the proportional part of the algorithm spreads the the window reductions across a full round-trip time, such that at the end of recovery, *prr_delivered* approaches *RecoverFS* and *prr_out* approaches *ssthresh*. If there are excess losses that bring *pipe* below *ssthresh*, the algorithm tries to build the *pipe* close to *ssthresh*. It achieves this by first undoing the past congestion window reductions performed by the PRR part, reflected in the difference *prr_delivered* − *prr_out*. Second, it grows the congestion window just like TCP does in slow start algorithm. We note that this part of the algorithm increases the number of segments in flight during recovery, however it does so more smoothly compared to RFC 3517 which would send *ssthresh-pipe* segments in a single burst.

A key part of Algorithm 2 is its reliance on the newly delivered data per acknowledgment, referred above as *DeliveredData*. This is a stark difference from the existing standard and widely implemented TCP algorithms which make their congestion window adjustments based on the number of ACKs received as opposed to the actual data delivered. The use of *DeliveredData* is especially robust during recovery. The consequence of missing ACKs is that later ones will show a larger *DeliveredData*. Furthermore, for any TCP connection, the sum of *DeliveredData* must agree with the forward progress over the same time interval. In addition, for TCP using SACK, *DeliveredData* is an invariant that can be precisely computed anywhere in the network just by inspecting the returning ACKs.

4.3 Properties of PRR

In this section we discuss a few key properties of PRR that follow from its design. For each property, we also discuss the corresponding behavior for RFC 3517 and Linux fast recovery.

1. **Maintains ACK clocking:** PRR maintains ACK clocking even for large burst segment losses, primarily due to the slow start part of the algorithm. This property is not true for the existing RFC 3517 standard which under heavy losses, can send an arbitrarily large burst of size (*ssthresh* − *pipe*), as mentioned in the RFC problem of bursty retransmissions (Section 3.1). Linux fast recovery maintains the ACK clocking property, however it does so by bringing the congestion window down to *pipe* + 1.

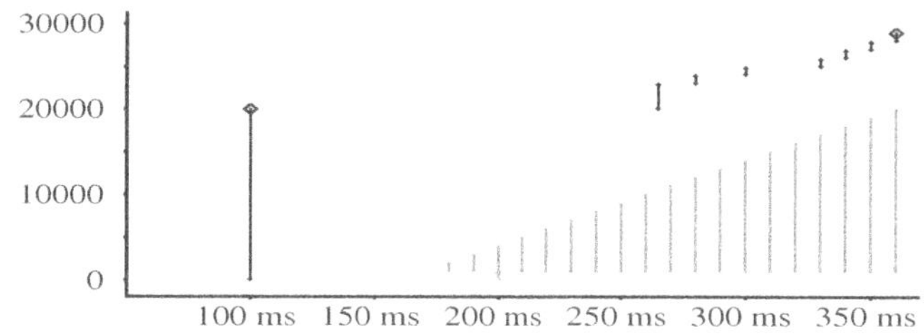

Figure 4: Example illustrating that PRR banks sending opportunities during recovery. Application first has 20 segments to send of which 1 segment is lost. In the middle of recovery, application has 10 more segments to transmit. RTT=100ms. Legend for the plot: Original data transmissions (Black), retransmissions (Red), duplicate ACKs with SACK blocks (Purple), snd.una (Green).

2. **Convergence to ssthresh:** For small number of losses (losses ≤ *RecoverFS* − *ssthresh*), PRR converges to exactly the target window chosen by the congestion control algorithm, *ssthresh*. The algorithm for the most part operates in the proportional mode which decrements the congestion window until *pipe* reaches *ssthresh* at which point the second part of the algorithm maintains the *pipe* at the *ssthresh* value. We note that for very heavy losses, the property will not always hold true because there may not be sufficient ACKs to raise *pipe* all the way back to *ssthresh*.

   If there is sufficient new data and at least a few segments delivered near the end of the lossy round trip, RFC 3517 achieves this property regardless of the amount of loss, because it transmits a large burst. Linux fast recovery does not achieve this property when losses are heavy or when the application temporarily runs out of data to send. In both of these cases, *pipe* becomes too small and does not grow until after the recovery ends.

3. **Banks sending opportunities during application stalls:** If an application stalls during recovery, e.g., when the sending application does not queue data for transmission quickly enough or the receiver stops advancing *rwnd*, PRR stores these missed opportunities for transmission. During application stalls, *prr_out* falls behind *prr_delivered*, causing their difference *prr_delivered* − *prr_out* to be positive. If the application catches up while TCP is still in recovery, TCP will send a burst that is bounded by *prr_delivered* − *prr_out* + 1.[4] Note that this property holds true for both parts of the PRR algorithm.

   Figure 4 shows an example of the banking property where after an idle period, the application has new data to transmit half way through the recovery process. Note that the algorithm in the PRR mode allows

[4]Although this burst might be viewed as being hard on the network, this is exactly what happens every time there is a partial RTT application stall while not in recovery. We have made the response to partial RTT stalls uniform in all states.

a burst of up to *ratio* × (*prr_delivered* − *prr_out*) which in this example is three segments (ratio is 0.5 for New Reno). Thereafter PRR continues spreading the new segments among incoming ACKs.

RFC 3517 also banks missed sending opportunities through the difference *ssthresh* − *pipe*. However, these banked opportunities are subject to the inaccuracies of the *pipe* variable. As discussed below, *pipe* is only an estimate of the outstanding data that can be inaccurate in certain situations, e.g., when reordered segments are incorrectly marked as lost. Linux does not achieve this property since its congestion window tracks *pipe* closely, thereby losing any history of missed sending opportunities.

4. **Robustness of DeliveredData:** An integral part of PRR is its reliance on the newly delivered data per acknowledgment or *DeliveredData*, as opposed to RFC 3517 and Linux recovery which make their congestion window adjustments based on the number of ACKs received and the *pipe* size. With SACK, *DeliveredData* allows a TCP sender to learn of the precise number of segments that arrived at the receiver. The properties below follow from the robustness of *DeliveredData*.

   Decouples data transmission from loss estimation/marking: PRR is less sensitive to errors in the *pipe* estimator compared to RFC 3517 as well as Linux fast recovery. In recovery, *pipe* is an estimator, using incomplete information to continually guess if segments that are not SACKed yet are actually lost or out-of-order in the network. *pipe* can have significant errors for some conditions, e.g., when a burst of reordered data is presumed to be lost and is retransmitted, but then the original data arrives before the retransmission. Both RFC 3517 and Linux recovery use *pipe* directly to regulate transmission rate in recovery. Errors and discontinuities in the *pipe* estimator can cause significant errors in the amount of data sent.

   On the other hand, PRR regulates the transmission rate based on the actual amount of data delivered at the receiver, *DeliveredData*. It only uses *pipe* to determine which of the two algorithm modes, proportional reduction or slow start, should compute the number of segments to send per ACK. Since both parts of the algorithm progressively converge to the same target congestion window, transient errors in the *pipe* estimator have much less impact on the final outcome.

   Precision in the number of transmitted segments: PRR retains its precision in the number of transmitted segments even in the presence of ACK loss, ACK reordering, and stretch ACKs such as those caused by Large Receive Offload (LRO) and Generic Receive Offload (GRO). The rate halving algorithm in Linux is not robust under these same scenarios as it relies heavily on the *number* of ACKs received, e.g., Linux transmits one segment on receipt of every two ACKs during rate halving, and fails to transmit the right number of segments when receiving stretch ACKs. Similarly when *pipe* estimation is incorrect in any of the above scenarios, RFC 3517 also doesn't achieve transmission of a precise number of segments.

   Data transmitted during recovery is in proportion to that delivered: For PRR the following expression holds true for the amount of data sent during recovery:

$$prr\_out \leq 2 \times prr\_delivered$$

   The relation holds true for both parts of the PRR algorithm. Transmitted data in RFC 3517 and Linux do not have such a relation to data delivered due to their reliance on *pipe* estimate. In fact under heavy losses, the transmission rate in RFC 3517 is directly proportional to the extent of losses because of the correspondingly small value of *pipe* value.

5. EXPERIMENT RESULTS

In this section, we evaluate the effectiveness and performance of PRR in comparison to RFC 3517 and the widely deployed Linux fast recovery. We ran several 3-way experiments with PRR, RFC 3517, and Linux fast recovery on Google Web servers for five days in May 2011 and on YouTube servers in India for four days during September 2011. For fair comparisons, all three recovery algorithms use FACK loss marking. Furthermore they all use CUBIC congestion control. These newer algorithms have the effect of making RFC 3517 slightly more aggressive than envisioned by its original authors.

There are three metrics of interest when evaluating the fast recovery schemes: length of time spent in loss recovery, number of timeouts experienced, and TCP latency for HTTP responses. The recovery time is the interval from when a connection enters recovery to when it re-enters Open state. A connection may have multiple recovery events, in which case the recovery time for each of the events is logged.

We first describe our experiments on Google Web servers and then go on to describe the YouTube experiments in India.

5.1 Experiment setup on Google Web servers

All of our Web server PRR experiments were performed in a production data center (DC1 described in Section 2.1) which serves traffic for a diverse set of Google applications. The Web servers run Linux 2.6 with the default settings shown in Table 4 except that ECN is disabled. The servers terminate user TCP connections and are load balanced by steering new connections to randomly selected Web servers based on the server and client IP addresses and ports.

Calibration measurements over 24-hour time periods show that the SNMP and HTTP latency statistics agree within 0.5% between individual servers. This property permits us to run N-way experiments concurrently by changing TCP configurations on groups of servers. If we run a 4-way experiment, then 5% of current connections are served by an experimental Web server while the remaining 80% connections are served by unmodified production Web servers.

The transactions are sampled such that the aggregate rate for the experiment is roughly one million samples per day.

Note that multiple simultaneous connections opened by a single client are likely to be served by different Web servers in different experiment bins. Since we are not looking at interactions between TCP connections this does not compromise the results presented here.

pipe < *ssthresh* [slow start]	32%
pipe == *ssthresh*	13%
pipe > *ssthresh* [PRR]	45%
pipe − *ssthresh*	
Min	-338
1%	-10
50%	+1
99%	+11
Max	+144

Table 5: Statistics of *pipe* − *ssthresh* at the start of recovery.

Quantiles for *cwnd* − *ssthresh* (segments).								
Quantile:	5	10	25	50	75	90	95	99
PRR:	-8	-3	0	0	0	0	0	0

Table 6: Values for *cwnd* − *ssthresh* just prior to exiting recovery.

5.2 PRR in practice

We measured the percentage of recovery events that PRR begins operation in the proportional versus the slow start modes. Measurements, summarized in Table 5, show that approximately 45% of the fast recovery events start with operating in the proportional part of the algorithm (*pipe* > *ssthresh*), 32% of the events start in the slow start part (*pipe* < *ssthresh*) and 13% of the events start with *pipe* == *ssthresh*. Table 6 shows that in approximately 90% of the recovery events, the congestion window in PRR converges to *ssthresh* by the end of recovery. In the rest of the recoveries, the segment losses were too heavy for slow start to complete building the *pipe* value to *ssthresh*.

5.3 Performance of PRR vs RFC 3517 and Linux

We first compare the recovery times, followed by retransmission statistics and impact on TCP latency for HTTP responses.

Figure 5 shows that PRR reduces the time spent in recovery as compared to both RFC 3517 and Linux fast recovery. PRR has a shorter recovery time primarily due to its smaller number of timeouts during recovery, as we will see shortly.

Table 7 shows the value of *cwnd* on exiting recovery. PRR sets *cwnd* to *ssthresh* on exiting recovery, and therefore has a similar *cwnd* distribution to that of RFC 3517. Note that the slightly larger values of *cwnd* for PRR compared to RFC 3517 are because of the reduced number of timeouts in the recovery phase. As described in Section 3.2, Linux pulls the *cwnd* value down to at most *pipe* + 1 in recovery. A consequence of this is that for short HTTP responses which have limited new data to transmit, over 50% of recovery events in Linux end with *cwnd* smaller than three segments.

Table 8 compares the retransmission statistics. The main point is that PRR reduces the number of timeouts in recovery by 5% compared with Linux and by 2.6% compared with RFC 3517. Furthermore, PRR reduces the number of retransmissions by 3% compared to RFC 3517. We also note that RFC 3517 incurs greater lost retransmissions as compared to PRR. This is due to the fact that when *pipe* falls far below *ssthresh*, RFC 3517 sends most of the retransmissions as a single large burst, thereby increasing the likelihood of drops in retransmissions. About 32% of the fast recovery events start of with *pipe* strictly lower than *ssthresh*. In these cases, RFC 3517 has the possibility of transmitting large bursts, with the largest burst size up to 338 segments, and about 1% of the recovery events might generate bursts greater than ten segments (Table 5).

We picked two representative Google services, search and page ads, to evaluate the latency differences. Table 9 shows the quantiles for TCP latency measured. Compared to Linux fast recovery, PRR and RFC 3517 reduce the average latency of the responses with retransmissions by 3-10%, and the overall latency (including responses without losses) by 3-5%. PRR achieves similar latency as compared to RFC 3517, however, it does so without sending large bursts.

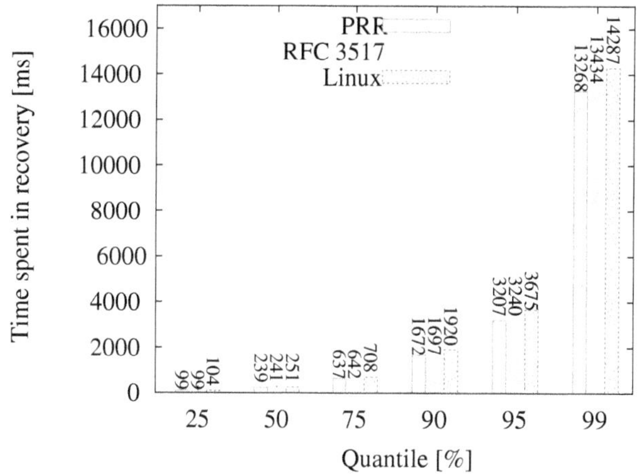

Figure 5: A comparison of time spent in recovery for PRR, RFC 3517 and Linux.

Quantiles for *cwnd* after recovery (segments).							
Quantile:	10	25	50	75	90	95	99
PRR:	2	3	6	9	15	21	35
RFC 3517:	2	3	5	8	14	19	31
Linux:	1	2	3	5	9	12	19

Table 7: A comparison of PRR, RFC 3517 and Linux recovery.

5.4 YouTube in India

We evaluated the three algorithms in our India YouTube video servers, to observe how they performed with long-running TCP transfers. The YouTube service is built on progressive HTTP which normally uses one TCP connection to deliver an entire video. The server sends the first couple tens of seconds of video as fast as possible, then it rate-limits the transfer based on the video encoding rate to minimize wasted network capacity if a user cancels the rest of the video. However, for most video downloaded in India, there is little or no difference between the throttled and un-throttled data rates because there is little or no surplus network capacity above the video encoding rate. In this case

Retransmissions measured in 1000's of segments.			
Retransmission type	Linux baseline	RFC 3517 diff. [%]	PRR diff [%]
Total Retransmission	85016	+3119 [+3.7%]	+2147 [+2.5%]
Fast Retransmission	18976	+3193 [+17%]	+2456 [+13%]
TimeoutOnRecovery	649	-16 [-2.5%]	-32 [-5.0%]
Lost Retransmission	393	+777 [+198%]	+439 [+117%]

Table 8: A comparison of retransmission statistics and timeouts of PRR, RFC 3517 and Linux recovery.

	Google Search			Page Ads		
Quantile	Linux	RFC 3517	PRR	Linux	RFC 3517	PRR
25	487	-39 [-8%]	-34 [-7%]	464	-34 [-7.3%]	-24 [-5.2%]
50	852	-50 [-5.8%]	-48 [-5.6%]	1059	-83 [-7.8%]	-100 [-9.4%]
90	4338	-108 [-2.4%]	-88 [-2%]	4956	-461 [-9.3%]	-481 [-9.7%]
99	31581	-1644 [-5.2%]	-1775 [-5.6%]	24640	-2544 [-10%]	-2887 [-11.7%]
Mean	2410	-89 [-3.7%]	-85 [-3.5%]	2441	-220 [-9%]	-239 [-9.8%]

Table 9: A comparison of TCP latency (ms) for PRR, RFC 3517 and Linux recovery. Quantiles are shown for responses that have at least one retransmission.

TCP is busy most of the time and there are long stretches where the data rate is determined entirely by TCP congestion control and the network, i.e., TCP is effectively in bulk transfer mode.

We sampled roughly 0.8 million connections in 96 hours and list key statistics in Table 10. Video downloads served with different fast recovery algorithms have almost identical sample size and average transfer size (2.3MB per connection).

The *network transmit time* measures the total time per connection when there is unacknowledged data in the TCP write queue, i.e., when TCP is actively transmitting data. Similarly, the *network recovery time* is that part of the network transmit time when the sender is in either fast recovery or timeout-recovery. Overall, RFC 3517 has the best performance since on average it delivered video in 4.7% less network transmit time than the Linux baseline. PRR is about 3% faster than the baseline.

The video downloads in India spent 43% to 46% of the network transmit time recovering from losses. While RFC 3517 spent more time and sent more retransmission in recovery than PRR and Linux baseline did, it also delivers more data during fast recovery: 5% more bytes compared to Linux baseline. This is because the network losses are clustered such that in fast recovery, *pipe* drops below *ssthresh* for about 40% of the events (not shown in table), causing RFC 3517 to send as much data necessary to keep the *pipe* at *ssthresh*. This aggressive transmission, described as Problem 2 in Section 3.1, causes 16.4% of the RFC 3517 fast-retransmits to drop, while Linux and PRR both lose less than 5% of the fast-retransmits. Furthermore after recovery, Linux transitions directly into slow-start 56% of the time. Both PRR and RFC 3517 end with *cwnd* at or close to *sshtresh* and do not need to perform this extra slow-start.

In summary, RFC performs the best but it retransmits too aggressively and has much higher (retransmission) drop rate. PRR achieves good performance with a slight increase of retransmission rate.

6. EARLY RETRANSMIT

As observed in section 2.1, the average Google HTTP response is only 7.5kB or about 5-6 segments. Early retransmit (ER) [2] is designed to overcome the well known limitation with fast retransmit: if a loss occurs too close to the end of a stream, there will not be enough dupacks to trigger a fast retransmission. ER lowers the *dupthresh* to 1 or 2 when the outstanding data drops to 2 or 3 segments respectively.

Clearly, any reordering can falsely trigger early retransmit. If this happens near the end of one HTTP response, the sender will falsely enter fast recovery which lowers the *cwnd* and slows the next HTTP response over the same connection. To make ER more robust in the presence of reordering, RFC 5827 describes three mitigation algorithms:

1. Disabling early retransmit if the connection has detected past reordering.
2. Adding a small delay to early retransmit so it might be canceled if the missing segment arrives slightly late.
3. Throttling the total early retransmission rate.

We implemented the first two algorithms. The first one is straightforward because Linux already detects reordering based on SACK. For the second algorithm, we use the RTO timer to delay the early retransmission for a configurable short interval. The sender cancels early retransmit if it receives an ACK during this interval. We do not implement the last mitigation because it only makes sense for servers facing a homogeneous user pool.

6.1 Results

We used the experimental framework described in Section 5.1 to run a 4-way experiment for 72 hours in April 2011. We compared: the baseline (original kernel), the naive ER without any mitigation, ER with first mitigation, and ER with both mitigations.

The statistics show that naive early retransmit causes a significant increase, 31%, in the number of fast retransmits for a 2% reduction in the number of timeouts relative to unmodified Linux TCP. These come at a substantial cost: a

	Linux baseline	RFC 3517	PRR
Network Transmit Time (s)	87.4	83.3	84.8
% Time in Loss Recovery	42.7%	46.3%	44.9%
Retransmission Rate %	5.0%	6.6%	5.6%
% Bytes Sent in FR	7%	12%	10%
% Fast-retransmit Lost	2.4%	16.4%	4.8%
Slow-start after FR	56%	1%	0%

Table 10: India YouTube video transfers loss recovery statistics. The average transfer size is 2.3MB and average RTT is 860ms.

Quantile	Linux	ER
5	282	258 [-8.5%]
10	319	301 [-5.6%]
50	1084	997 [-8.0%]
90	4223	4084 [-3.3%]
99	26027	25861 [-0.6%]

Table 11: A comparison of TCP latency (ms) for Linux baseline and ER with both mitigations.

27% increase in the number of "undo" events where it was determined that the retransmission was spurious, and the *cwnd* change is reversed. We were surprised by the amount of small reordering in the network. After we inspected the TCP traces with Google network operators, we confirmed that the reordering happens outside of Google networks, i.e., in the Internet.[5]

The first mitigation is not as effective because most HTTP connections are short. Although Linux also implements RFC 2140 [27] which caches the reordering history of past connections of the same IP, the cache hit rate is very low due to the server load-balancing and the size of web server farm.

The second mitigation, using a short timer to slightly delay the early retransmit, provides a substantial improvement, because it gives time for the ACKs from out-of-order segments to arrive and cancel the pending early retransmission. For the timer, we used 1/4 of the smoothed RTT bound to the range of 25ms to 500ms. One of the things that we noticed when we were tinkering with the timer design was that it does not affect the results much. This insensitivity to timer details is interesting, because it gives some hints about typical reordering distance, but we chose not to investigate it at this point and picked a reasonable compromise design.

ER with both mitigations can reduce 34% of the timeouts in Disorder state with 6% of early retransmits identified as spurious retransmissions via DSACKs. Some losses in ER with mitigation are now repaired by fast recovery instead of by timeout, therefore the total number of retransmissions remain almost the same as the baseline (1% increase). We compare the TCP latencies in ER with both mitigations and the original Linux in Table 11. Responses that do not experience losses or fit entirely into one segment are excluded because ER can not repair these responses. For the remaining responses, ER with both mitigations reduces latencies up to 8.5% and is most effective for short transactions. However, the overall latency reduction by ER is significantly limited in Google Web servers. Since the number of timeouts in disorder is very small compared to timeouts occurring in the open state.

We end the section with a note on the combined experiments with PRR and early retransmit. The main observation is that the two mechanisms are independent features of TCP fast recovery, wherein the early retransmit algorithm determines when a connection should enter recovery, while PRR improves the recovery process itself.

[5]The traces also reveal that such reorderings are likely due to router load-balancing on the forward paths where the last sub-MSS segment is SACKed before the prior full MSS segment. Clearly, the mitigations in ER are needed [6].

7. RELATED WORK

Several researchers have investigated the performance of TCP loss recovery in TCP traces of real user traffic [12, 5, 22, 26]. In data from 1995 it was observed that 85% of timeouts were due to receiving insufficient duplicate acknowledgments to trigger Fast Retransmit [12]. Interestingly, Google still shows 46% to 60% retransmissions happen during timeout recovery. In a study of the 1996 Olympic Web servers it was estimated that SACK might only save 4% of the timeouts [5]. The authors invented limited transmit which was standardized [3] and widely deployed. An analysis of the Coral CDN service identified loss recovery as one of the major performance bottlenecks [26]. The idea of progressively reducing the window, rather than a half RTT silence, has been explored before [11], including prior work by Mathis [19].

Improving the robustness and performance of TCP loss recovery has been a recurrent theme in the literature. TCP recovery improvements fall into several broad categories: better strategies for managing the window during recovery [11, 16, 5]; detecting and compensating for spurious retransmissions triggered by reordering [7, 13, 14]; disambiguating loss and reordering at the end of a stream [24]; improvements to the retransmission timer and its estimator.

The Early Retransmit algorithm shares many similarities with thin stream support for TCP [20], which is designed to help applications such as interactive games and telephony that persistently send small messages over TCP.

8. CONCLUSION

Proportional rate reduction improves fast recovery under practical network conditions. PRR operates smoothly even when losses are heavy, is quick in recovery for short flows, and accurate even when acknowledgments are stretched, lost or reordered. In live experiments, PRR was able to reduce the latency of short Web transfers by 3-10% compared to Linux recovery and proved to be a smoother recovery for video traffic compared to the standard RFC3517. While these seem like small improvements, we would like to emphasize that even delays as small as 100ms in page load times have been shown to impact user satisfaction in several independent experiments [25]. Based on its promise in live experiments, PRR was accepted to be in the mainline Linux as the default fast recovery algorithm, and is proposed as an experimental RFC in the IETF [15].

Going forward, we will revisit the effectiveness of the RTO mechanisms in practice. Measurements show that timeouts (and any subsequent exponential backoffs) in short flows constitute over 60% of the retransmissions. Most of these occur when flows are in the Open state and receive no duplicate acknowledgments. Our research will address if and how timeouts can be improved in practice, especially for short flows.

9. ACKNOWLEDGMENTS

We would like to thank Ankur Jain, Bernhard Beck, Tayeb Karim, John Reese for facilitating our experiments on live traffic. The following people greatly helped to improve the paper itself: Larry Brakmo, Neal Cardwell, Jerry Chu, Ilpo Järvinen, Sivasankar Radhakrishnan, Neil Spring, Mukarram Bin Tariq, and our anonymous reviewers.

10. REFERENCES

[1] State of the internet, 2010. http://www.akamai.com/stateoftheinternet/.

[2] Allman, M., Avrachenkov, K., Ayesta, U., Blanton, J., and Hurtig, P. Early retransmit for TCP and SCTP, May 2010. RFC 5827.

[3] Allman, M., Balakrishnan, H., and Floyd, S. Enhancing TCP's loss recovery using limited transmit, January 2001. RFC 3042.

[4] Allman, M., Paxson, V., and Blanton, E. TCP congestion control, September 2009. RFC 5681.

[5] Balakrishnan, H., Padmanabhan, V. N., Seshan, S., Stemm, M., and Katz, R. H. TCP behavior of a busy internet server: Analysis and improvements. *In Proc. of INFOCOMM* (1998).

[6] Bennet, J. C., Patridge, C., and Shectman, N. Packet reordering is not pathological network behavior. *IEEE/ACM Trans. on Networking* (December 1999).

[7] Blanton, E., and Allman, M. Using TCP DSACKs and SCTP duplicate TSNs to detect spurious retransmissions, February 2004. RFC 3708.

[8] Blanton, E., Allman, M., Fall, K., and Wang, L. A conservative SACK-based loss recovery algorithm for TCP, 2003. RFC 3517.

[9] Floyd, S., Mahdavi, J., Mathis, M., and Podolsky, M. An extension to the SACK option for TCP, July 2000. RFC 2883.

[10] Ha, S., Rhee, I., and Xu, L. CUBIC: a new TCP-friendly high-speed TCP variant. *SIGOPS Oper. Syst. Rev. 42* (July 2008), 64–74.

[11] Hoe, J. Improving the start-up behavior of a congestion control scheme for TCP. *SIGCOMM Comput. Commun. Rev.* (August 1996).

[12] Lin, D., and Kung, H. TCP fast recovery strategies: Analysis and improvements. *In Proc. of INFOCOMM* (1998).

[13] Ludwig, R., and Katz, R. H. The eifel algorithm: Making TCP robust against spurious retransmissions. *(ACM) Computer Communication Review 30* (January 2000).

[14] Ludwig, R., and Meyer, M. The eifel detection algorithm for TCP, April 2003. RFC 3522.

[15] Mathis, M., Dukkipati, N., and Cheng, Y. Proportional rate reduction for TCP, March 2011. Work in progress, draft-mathis-tcpm-proportional-rate-reduction-00.txt.

[16] Mathis, M., and Mahdavi, J. Forward acknowledgment: refining TCP congestion control. *SIGCOMM Comput. Commun. Rev. 26* (August 1996), 281–291.

[17] Mathis, M., and Mahdavi, J. TCP rate-halving with bounding parameters, December 1997. http://www.psc.edu/networking/papers/FACKnotes/current/.

[18] Mathis, M., Mahdavi, J., Floyd, S., and Romanow, A. TCP selective acknowledgement options, October 1996. RFC 2018.

[19] Mathis, M., Semke, J., Mahdavi, J., and Lahey, K. The rate-halving algorithm for TCP congestion control, June 1999. draft-mathis-tcp-ratehalving-00.txt, http://www.psc.edu/networking/ftp/papers/draft-ratehalving.txt.

[20] Petlund, A., Evensen, K., Griwodz, C., and Halvorsen, P. TCP enhancements for interactive thin-stream applications. In *NOSSDAV* (2008).

[21] Ramachandran, S. Web metrics: Size and number of resources. http://code.google.com/speed/articles/web-metrics.html.

[22] Rewaskar, S., Kaur, J., and Smith, F. D. A performance study of loss detection/recovery in real-world TCP implementations. *In Proc. of ICNP* (2007).

[23] Sarolahti, P., and Kuznetsov, A. Congestion control in linux tcp. In *Proceedings of USENIX* (2002), Springer, pp. 49–62.

[24] Scheffenegger, R. Improving SACK-based loss recovery for TCP, November 2010. Work in progress, draft-scheffenegger-tcpm-sack-loss-recovery-00.txt.

[25] Schurman, E., and Brutlag, J. The user and business impact of server delays, additional bytes, and HTTP chunking in web search. http://velocityconf.com/velocity2009/public/schedule/detail/8523.

[26] Sun, P., Yu, M., Freedman, M. J., and Rexford, J. Identifying performance bottlenecks in CDNs through TCP-level monitoring. In *SIGCOMM Workshop on Measurements Up the Stack* (August 2011).

[27] Touch, J. TCP control block interdependence, April 1997. RFC 2140.

[28] Yang, P., Luo, W., Xu, L., Deogun, J., and Lu, Y. TCP congestion avoidance algorithm identification. In *Proc. of ICDCS* (June 2011).

[29] Yang, Y., and Lam, S. General aimd congestion control. *Proc. International Conference on Network Protocols.* (November 2000).

Summary Review Documentation for

"Proportional Rate Reduction for TCP"

Authors: N. Dukkipati, M. Mathis, Y. Cheng, M. Ghobadi

Reviewer #1

Strengths: The A/B testing at scale that gathers a wealth of data from production Web systems. It tells us something about Web latency in practice and that the TCP refinements lead to a modest reduction in loss for some of the cases. The TCP refinements themselves are small contributions, given that they are close to Early Retransmit guidelines and Rate-Halving, but they are useful.

Weaknesses: It's a bit hard to piece together from the way the data is presented in the paper, but there is a *substantial* penalty for any loss/retransmissions, say 7-10X?, and your TCP refinements are barely reducing it -- by 3-10%. I think this calls for looking at the data and problem in a different way (see below).

Comments to Authors: You have so much great data here, but you are barely presenting any of it! Fig 1 is tantalizing, but I would really like to see more. For example, some CDFs would show the variation of latency (you can put the averages in a table!), and for different sizes would help to show us where connections with retransmissions really break out in terms of latency. Also, can you present any data on how many packets are lost from these connections? That would be great.

The main question I would have then is what the causes are for the outliers. Timeout in Open looks like a big one, while Timeout in Disorder looks like a very small one, so why not tackle the big one first? For example, how often is a timeout in Open caused by the last packets of an HTTP response being lost? Or the entire window? Or what else is going on? You have tackled the small cause, I think, so it helps the big picture by a very small amount.

BTW, I would hope to see some kind of picture like Fig 1 for after you apply your techniques to see how much better the situation has gotten. Right now my guess is that they would look very similar as the 7X case has gotten 10% better. Another way to get at this would be if you can tell us how much better it makes the latency when the new mechanisms make a difference. That is, in the cases where they "fire" can you estimate how much lower the latency is? Hopefully it is *much* lower ...

I did not understand how HTTP1.1 and persistent connections fit in here. The emphasis of the analysis is all on the average HTTP response size. Why are persistent connections not helping more?

Your definition of latency excludes TCP connection setup. Normally it would make sense to include this because it is a component of page load time. Perhaps you are excluding it because you can't measure it easily? Please tell us.

Reviewer #2

Strengths: The proposed modifications to TCP are thoroughly evaluated with large numbers of real flows terminating in Google servers. The scale of evaluation of the proposed system is fairly detailed.

Weaknesses: The gains appear to be fairly small. While this work is likely to have significant impact, especially since it is being deployed into Google servers, the authors do not convince us this is better than some alternate published work. The proportional rate reduction part reminds me of the different GAIMD techniques designed as extensions to TCP about a decade back. How do they compare to this proposal?

Comments to Authors: The most impressive part of the work is that the proposed ideas are evaluated using a large volume of real flows that terminate in Google servers. This work is clearly likely to have significant impact just because it might affect a lot of flows through such a deployment. The authors are also proposing this effort as a IETF draft and this work detailed evaluation of this proposal.

However, it is not clear if the impact of the proposal is quite significant. First, the overall performance of the proposal does not improve TCP performance (latency of downloading short flows) by more than 7-8%, often it is much smaller. Second, there is a large body of prior work in this domain over the last decade, which have similarity to aspects of the modifications proposed. For instance, there are the GAIMD and Binomial congestion control proposals that alter TCP's congestion control behavior that appear similar to the proportional rate reduction method. The authors could have considered using such schemes or could have compared their proposal to such older schemes.

Also, RFC 3517 modifications proposed before, also seem to perform quite well relative to what is being proposed in this paper. Why not simply use RFC 3517 alone. What are the additional gains of this work relative to RFC 3517?

The modification to early retransmit proposed in this work is what was proposed in RFC 5827. This work takes 2 of the 3 methods in RFC 5827, and evaluates it thoroughly through their experimental setup.

I liked the way the experiments and comparisons were conducted.

Overall, a nice and thorough piece of work but the ideas are small and incremental, much of which seem to be available from prior literature. The gains are not very significant.

Reviewer #3

Strengths: Clear writing, unique evaluation, important (well known) problem, useful solution, authoritative description of linux.

Weaknesses: Yet another TCP paper. I didn't like figure 1 very much. Weaknesses do not seem severe.

Comments to Authors: It's not clear to me what "The performance of connections experiencing losses is significantly slower than those with no losses" means in practice, since links that are crummy are likely to have losses and have poor performance. (i.e., correlation does not imply causation.) I didn't see that your experiment would control for that, so I don't really appreciate the figure as motivation.

Linux P2 didn't seem like too much of a problem... isn't there a rule where quiet connections, after losing the ack clock, have to restart from slow start anyway, regardless of retransmission events earlier?

I liked this paper a lot, and would likely encourage students to read it, particularly when linux seems to adopt tcp features without much study.

Is there a sense for how this fix would likely improve perceived browser performance? Will the user see fewer spinning wheels or does the browser already collect partial flows well enough to hide any performance trouble in TCP.

I appreciated that the paper was as long as necessary and not longer.

Reviewer #4

Strengths: Problem identification. Careful experimentation.

Weaknesses: Substantial gap between how worse the problem is and how much improvement the suggested modifications achieve. For e.g., the best variant PRR-* performs comparably to RFC3517 (table 8), but with fewer retransmissions (table 7).Impact of these modifications on large transfers, video streams? Slice losses by connection type? Not all losses require the same types of reaction, e.g., wireless losses. Unclear if understanding sources of losses would get more benefit.

Comments to Authors: The first parts of the paper were more interesting than the proposed modifications.

When presenting the problem, is there a way to figure out what an ideal retransmission mechanism could achieve?

What are the causes of losses, you allude later on about shifting to lower capacity paths, burst retransmissions having higher likelihood of being lost... It is important because, at the core, the ideal retransmission strategy depends crucially on the causes.

Is there reason to believe that the losses are mostly due to congestion or buffer overflow?

Do losses happen in large bursts? (fraction of lost packets among those that constitute a web response)

Would end-to-end coding, to guard against 1 or 2 packet losses in a web download end up faring significantly better?

Table 2, nothing in the paper seems to help with timeouts in open. PRR helps do fast retransmits better and reduces need for timeouts. ER helps deal with disorder scenarios.

I was surprised that ER ended up being as useful given the small number of Timeouts that happen in Disorder.

Parts of 3.1 and 3.2 do not seem to be needed, since once you present the mechanisms, there isn't much there that depends on the reader knowing this background. The background info is useful, but not essential.

Figure 2, ER does not seem to help much the latencies of connections on the tail, so what causes the longest retransmissions (long RTT flows taking multiple RTTs to recover?), and how can that be improved?

Reviewer #5

Strengths: Some real data on TCP performance in the wild against highly popular servers. Nice exposition of existing fast recovery mechanisms and their weaknesses.

Weaknesses: The problem does not strike me as very important, especially given the low gains achieved in the end. Only ~6% of the connections suffer retransmissions, and the proposes mechanism cut down their latency by 10%.

Comments to Authors: I don't quite appreciate the motivation for your work. It's only 6% of the responses, and you help them by only 10% or so. Is it worth it? It might be from a business perspective if this reduction matters, but you don't really make the case.

The real value for me in this paper was not your solution but the data on TCP retransmissions and the exposition of TCP recovery mechanisms. Even if the current paper does not go above the bar for me, those aspects of the paper are valuable and should get out. So, if the paper is not accepted, consider sending it to something like the CCR.

On the data front, the India data center, which you allude to would be valuable addition to the paper.

What experiments are being talked about in 6.5, when you mention PRR-RB being too conservative and PRR-UB being too aggressive?

Your paper did make me wonder about one thing: How much room for improvement there is really to improve fast recovery? Based on your traces, can you construct a fast recovery oracle, which knew what would happen next, and acted accordingly. How much reduction in latency would such an oracle bring to the table?

Response from the Authors

Summary of changes applied to the original submission "Improving TCP Loss Recovery"

- Major changes:

We included both retransmission statistics as well as experiments with our changes in a India data-center serving Youtube traffic.

The main thread of the paper is PRR as also reflected in the paper title, unlike the original paper that had three distinct loosely connected items - PRR, ER, and Google measurements.

We rewrote the introduction to provide a clear motivation - our goal is to reduce TCP latency by improving fast recovery, which as per the retransmission statistics is the key mechanism for loss recovery.

We illustrated the PRR algorithm and its properties through carefully chosen examples.

- Other changes and comments on reviews:

1. Concern: there is a substantial penalty (7-10X) for any losses/retransmissions (Fig. 1 of Introduction) and the TCP refinements described in the paper are barely reducing it by 3-10%.

The intent of showing Fig. 1 comparing response latency with ideal is to provide context on the latency disparity that exists. Not all of this can be addressed by improving TCP's loss recovery since the latency also includes effects of slow user bandwidths and queueing delays, as noted in the camera-ready version. We do not have a breakdown of latency attributed to different factors, nor have a way to compare an ideal retransmission scheme without further insights into the bottleneck network conditions.

As requested by reviewer #1, we included a CDF to show the variation of latencies between responses with/without retransmissions and the ideal latency of 1 RTT.

2. Comparison with alternate published work such as GAIMD techniques and Binomial congestion control.

GAIMD and Binomial are congestion control algorithms orthogonal to current work. PRR is designed to work in conjunction with any congestion control algorithm including GAIMD and Binomial.

3. What are the additional gains of this work relative to RFC 3517?

Addressed in the camera-ready paper - RFC 3517 is overly aggressive in the presence of heavy losses wherein it can transmit large bursts of retransmissions which then incur further losses.

4. What causes the losses? Do losses happen in bursts?

These are interesting questions, however, ones that we did not investigate as part of our current work.

5. Nothing in the paper seems to help with timeouts in open state.

Timeout in open state has to be addressed as an independent problem in itself and not the focus of current work on fast recovery.

6. Only ~6% of the connections suffer retransmissions, and the proposed mechanisms cut down their latency by 10%.

The paper includes a pointer to several independent studies that show even latency changes as small as 100ms impact user experience. Even small changes such as in the paper are crucial in ultimately bringing the latency of a Web page as close to ideal as possible, where ideal is close to one round-trip time.

Measuring the State of ECN Readiness in Servers, Clients, and Routers

Steven Bauer
MIT CSAIL
bauer@mit.edu

Robert Beverly
Naval Postgraduate School
rbeverly@nps.edu

Arthur Berger
MIT CSAIL / Akamai
awberger@csail.mit.edu

ABSTRACT

Better exposing congestion can improve traffic management in the wide-area, at peering points, among residential broadband connections, and in the data center. TCP's network utilization and efficiency depends on congestion information, while recent research proposes economic and policy models based on congestion. Such motivations have driven widespread support of Explicit Congestion Notification (ECN) in modern operating systems. We reappraise the Internet's ECN readiness, updating and extending previous measurements. Across large and diverse server populations, we find a three-fold increase in ECN support over prior studies. Using new methods, we characterize ECN within mobile infrastructure and at the client-side, populations previously unmeasured. Via large-scale path measurements, we find the ECN feedback loop failing in the core of the network 40% of the time, typically at AS boundaries. Finally, we discover new examples of infrastructure violating ECN Internet standards, and discuss remaining impediments to running ECN while suggesting mechanisms to aid adoption.

Categories and Subject Descriptors

C.2.3 [**Computer Communication Networks**]: Network Operations—*network monitoring*; C.2.1 [**Computer Communication Networks**]: Network Architecture and Design

General Terms

ECN, Measurement, Experimentation

Keywords

Explicit Congestion Notification, Router-Assisted Congestion Control

1. INTRODUCTION

The Internet's traditional end-to-end approach to congestion control, TCP, attempts to simultaneously optimize efficiency and fairness between traffic flows[14]. Cooperating end host TCPs must *infer* congestion via packet loss. As a distributed control problem, on the whole, TCP works remarkably well and has scaled through orders of magnitude speed increases. However, a large body of prior work recognizes several shortcomings.

First, the TCP rate equation biases against particular flows, particularly those that are short-lived or with high delay. Second, given the ubiquity of wireless devices, loss may be an inappropriate congestion signal. Third, the TCP feedback control loop necessarily results in under-utilization and oscillatory behavior (the TCP "sawtooth"). Finally, large bandwidth-delay flows are unable to fully utilize available bandwidth as the bandwidth-probing is conservative [14].

A well-studied approach to congestion is active queue management. Routers along a path know precisely their buffer occupancy and may signal an end host to slow its sending rate in the face of incipient congestion, i.e. without inducing packet loss. Explicit Congestion Notification (ECN) is a standardized TCP addition providing such feedback [24].

The benefits of ECN are only realized when end-hosts and routers support ECN. Today, equipment vendors largely support ECN and all major operating systems (Windows, Linux, OSX) support ECN. After more than a decade, much of the Internet has the capability to leverage ECN. However, few networks employ ECN and few devices at the edge initiate ECN connections.

The adoption of ECN may change given a renewed interest in managing congestion (e.g. [12]). Recent work illustrates how ECN may be leveraged to provide new Internet primitives and semantics. In addition to IETF standards leveraging ECN [10, 23], the IETF congestion exposure (conex) group is developing experimental standards that expose the source and location of congestion along a path potentially enabling new economic and billing models [7]. Among service providers, congestion, rather than traffic volume, is a potential alternative basis for interconnection and peering agreements [8]. Similar arguments apply to using induced congestion to bill and monitor residential broadband connections rather than adopting volume caps [4].

Finally, managing congestion is increasingly important within data centers and cloud providers. The common practice of partitioning a problem (e.g. web query) and aggregating the results must be performed within stringent latency requirements. Long-lived heavy bandwidth flows hamper this ability by inducing large queues. Recent proposals based on an analysis of real-world data center traffic rely on ECN to better handle such workloads [2].

In light of recent system and infrastructure adoption of ECN and the growing realization that ECN provides poten-

IMC'11, November 2–4, 2011, Berlin, Germany.
Copyright 2011 ACM 978-1-4503-1013-0/11/11 ...$10.00.

tial benefits to managing congestion [15], we perform large-scale measurements to reappraise the Internet's ability to properly support ECN. Our primary contributions include:

1. An examination of ECN support among various server populations, including updated measurements of a previously surveyed population [17, 22].
2. Analysis of millions of Internet paths to identify where ECN fails or is mis-marked, and the implications for congestion safety.
3. Case studies of infrastructure ECN misbehavior; implications on deployment and protocol design.
4. A novel measurement of client-side, e.g. eyeball, ECN support.

2. BACKGROUND

Explicit Congestion Notification (ECN) [24, 26, 6] defines an enhancement to TCP/IP that provides router-assisted congestion control in the Internet. The fundamental idea is to allow routers along a path, devices with explicit knowledge of their output queue occupancy, to *mark* packets of a TCP flow. This mark is *echoed* back to the source TCP. The source TCP thus receives notification of incipient congestion, allowing it to reduce congestion *before* loss occurs.

Mechanically, ECN adds two additional bits in the flags portion of the TCP header: ECN Echo (ECE) and Congestion Window Reduced (CWR), and changes the original semantics of the 8-bit type-of-service (ToS) field in the IP header. Instead of a byte of ToS, six bits are used for the Differentiated Service Code Point while two remaining bits encode three possible ECN states: no-ECN '00', ECN Capable Transport (ECT) '10' or '01', and Congestion Experienced (CE) '11'. As shown in §4, legacy handling of these bits as the old ToS field is a frequent cause of ECN failure.

ECN capability is *negotiated* between TCP end-points by setting the ECE and CWR flags in the SYN and the ECE flag in the SYN/ACK of TCP's three-way handshake. If negotiated, TCP sets ECT in the IP header of data segments. Routers along the path may, in response to congestion, set CE on packets marked as ECN capable with ECT. Upon receiving a segment with CE, a TCP sets ECE on all acknowledgments until the source reduces its congestion window and sets CWR.

ECN requires both TCPs and routers along an end-to-end path of a flow to support ECN. There are several points of potential failure or misbehavior. In this paper, we examine all of these points. In particular, we ask several questions:

1. What fraction of hosts successfully negotiate ECN?
2. When TCP negotiates ECN, is the connection marked as ECN capable at the IP layer?
3. Do routers and/or middleboxes erroneously clear or set congestion marks?
4. If a synthetic IP congestion signal (CE) is introduced, is a corresponding TCP ECE observed?
5. If a synthetic TCP ECE is sent, is the corresponding TCP CWR observed?

Previous measurement efforts [17, 22] found little support for ECN: on the order of 2% of servers or less, and an even smaller percentage of flows with ECN apparently enabled [19]. These results were not surprising as ECN was turned off by default on most operating systems due to an ECN blackhole problem. Of servers tested [22] in 2008, TCP SYN packets with ECN set were silently dropped 0.56% of the time. However, the recent widespread adoption of, and support for, ECN in operating systems suggests that a reappraisal of previous studies is warranted. For instance, server-mode ECN was introduced into the Linux kernel (2.6.29) in 2009, and enables ECN for incoming TCP connections that indicate ECN capability. Thus, while ECN is finally part of all major operating system TCP/IP stacks, it is being deployed conservatively – clients must be explicitly configured to initiate ECN for outgoing TCP connections, presenting a challenge we address in §3.3.

Given the potential network impact of these widespread changes, we reexamine and extend previous studies of ECN. In addition to enhanced testing of all the ECN messages two hosts can exchange, we also sought to test other parts of the network for ECN readiness, not just popular web servers. These include client-side (e.g. eyeball) networks such as residential broadband networks and tests that provide insight into the use of ECN by mobile devices. Mobile infrastructure is of interest not only because of the particular utility of ECN in wireless environments, but also because operators often control both the handset and network proxies.

3. METHODOLOGY

3.1 Server Testing

We measure three web server populations: 1) the top one million web servers [1] as ranked by Alexa; 2) a collection of approximately 7500 university and college web servers identified by [11]; and 3) web servers that handle requests from mobile devices (which we discuss separately below).

For each domain, we retrieve the complete web page (HTML and all page resources hosted by the same domain) using a client configured to initiate outgoing ECN connections. We use the native TCP stack of the measurement host's Linux operating system to retrieve the resources. Using Linux's iptables firewall connection tracking and mangling rules we artificially introduce all ECN signals.[1] We simulate congestion along the outgoing path by setting CE on all data packets sent by the measurement host and we simulate congestion along the incoming data path by reporting ECE to the remote sender. Our implementation guarantees that all data packets, including retransmissions, sent by our client have CE set until ECE is heard. Similarly it guarantees ECE is sent in response to all incoming data packets until CWR is heard. If a server fails to respond to SYNs with ECN, we retry the server with a non-ECN enabled SYN to identify possible ECN blackholes. A benefit of our implementation is that we can easily test any application or service which relies upon TCP – a feature we leverage to test additional populations described below.

We capture all packets that occur during the exchange and analyze the resulting trace. The analysis of whether or not ECN is negotiated on a particular connection is straightforward – does the response SYN/ACK from the server have the ECE flag set. Next, we examine whether the ECN capable transport code point (ECT) is set in the IP header of data packets for those flows which negotiate ECN. Note, re-transmitted packets and packets without data do not set ECT. However, if no data packets are marked with ECT,

[1] See `http://ecn.csail.mit.edu` for full details.

Table 1: Server population results; "-" indicates no data available

Year/Population	2004	2008	Alexa	University	Mobile
Hosts classified	80,498 (100%)	1,349,711 (100%)	541,885 (100%)	7563 (100%)	3,591 (100%)
ECN-capable	1,765 (2.2%)	14,407 (1.1%)	93,232 (17.2%)	1061 (14.0%)	559 (15.6%)
Not ECN-capable	78,733 (97.8%)	1,335,304 (98.9%)	448,653 (82.8%)	6,502 (86.0%)	3032 (84.4%)
Possible ECN blackhole	814 (1.0%)	7,627 (0.6%)	3293 (0.6%)	37 (0.5%)	5 (0.1%)
ECT in non-ECN flow	-	-	698 (0.15%)	13 (0.2%)	9 (0.3%)
no ECT in ECN flow	758 (42%)	-	5,598 (6.0%)	302 (28.5%)	63 (11.3%)
no ECE for CE	1,302 (1.6%)	-	3,995 (4.3%)	267 (25.2%)	21 (3.8%)
no CWR for ECE	-	-	55 (0.05%)	0 (0.0%)	1 (0.2%)

we show with our traceroute measurements that something along the path likely is improperly clearing the ECN bits. (We discuss some of the causes for this misbehavior in later sections.) We believe that all major operating systems implement ECN functionality correctly

Since we set CE on the client's packet that contained the HTTP request (and all potential retransmissions), we expect to see a ECE in all traces where the web server responded with a HTTP status message. The analysis of CWR however is dependent upon the number of data packets we receive from the server since some data packets will already be in flight by the time the server receives the first ECE message (which we only send in response to data packets from the server). We attempt to maximize the number of packets a server sends by setting the TCP's maximum segment size option to 300. We also turn off all segmentation and receive offload features in Linux.

We report on full ECN functionality tests from a single vantage point at MIT, but have conducted limited testing from other vantage points, in particular from non-Internet2 connected networks. We describe the ECN tests of paths that we run from > 125 PlanetLab [25] locations below.

3.2 Mobile Infrastructure

ECN can be particularly beneficial in wireless environments where loss does not necessarily indicate congestion. We therefore seek to characterize the ECN capabilities and behavior of web server side wireless-specific infrastructure by obtaining a population of servers dedicated to hosting content for wireless mobile devices, e.g. cellular smartphones.

We note that the content provided from a web server to a client is often tailored to the properties of the client device, especially for mobile devices. Additionally, mobile devices are frequently redirected to a different, dedicated server for mobile content. We leverage this common practice to obtain a population of servers dedicated to serving mobile content for subsequent ECN analysis.

For all domains in the Alexa 1M population, we issue five different HTTP GET queries, each with a distinct "User-Agent" HTTP header string. The user agent string mimics a desktop, and four different mobile phones. If the queried web server returns an HTTP 3xx redirect to a location different than the desktop query for any of the phone queries, we record the location. For example, a query from a desktop to `www.bloomberg.com` is not redirected, while a query from a phone user agent is redirected to `mobile.bloomberg.com`; these hostnames correspond to different IP addresses.

Using this technique, we find ~82,000 sites performing HTTP redirection on the basis of the user agent. Of those, 7,422 redirect to distinct mobile infrastructure, i.e. redirect to a URL that resolves to a different IP address. We use the later population for analysis of mobile web sites.

3.3 Client Testing

Understanding client-side ECN support is important for several reasons, notably since clients represent "eyeballs" in the network, i.e. humans sensitive to congestion. However, while prior work (§2) investigates the prevalence of server-side ECN, client-side support has received little attention.

Maier et al. observe a negligible number of hosts initiating ECN capable TCP in a large residential broadband network [19]. The lack of ECN in Maier's study is unsurprising as operating systems that support ECN, with typical default settings, did not and still do not negotiate ECN for outgoing connections. Because passive measurements provide only a limited view into client-side ECN capabilities, we develop a new hybrid passive/active method.

Our technique measures a large section of two peer-to-peer (P2P) networks – where nodes act as both clients and servers – to capture the ECN behavior of a population of Internet *clients*. We build BitTorrent and Gnutella crawlers on an ECN-enabled measurement host under our control. Our BitTorrent [9] crawler discovers torrents via aggregated RSS feeds, connects to the torrent's tracker(s), and obtains a list of torrent peer IP addresses. The crawler attempts a BitTorrent handshake with each peer, thereby initiating ECN and sending data segments without transferring content. Simultaneously, we capture all packets for analysis. For Gnutella, we use an existing crawler [27].

Our crawlers negotiate ECN for all connections to remote nodes in the P2P network, the majority of which reside in residential networks. By observing the behavior of the negotiation, and subsequent response to synthetic ECN signals introduced using the aforementioned iptables rules (§3.1), we gain insight on the prevalence of ECN on an end-to-end basis in the Internet.

3.4 End-to-End ECN Path Testing

If a router does not have any features turned on that leverage the ECN field, it should not modify the ECN field in any way. From conversations with network operators, none reported turning on ECN markings. However, we leverage traceroute to identify links where the ECN bits in the IP header are being modified. ICMP TTL-exceeded messages include the first 28B of the packet that expired, the so-called ICMP "quotation." This quotation provides path-level visibility into the ECN field. We make use of this feature by setting the ECT code point in a series of tests from our PlanetLab nodes to the web server populations described above.

While most ICMP quotations are reliable and accurate, like [20] we find some small evidence of quotation error.

Filtering differences raise the question of which type of probe (ICMP, UDP, TCP-SYN, TCP-ACK) should test a path. We did not find any apparent differences in how routers responded to packets with the ECN field set in a comparison of probe types to a 10,000 node sample set. Therefore we used Scamper's [18] ICMP-paris traceroute mode [3] (even though ICMP packets would not normally be ECN marked) since it was likely to discover more hops.

4. RESULTS

4.1 Server results

Table 1 provides our results of ECN testing to the web server populations in September of 2011. Where applicable, we include results from previous studies in 2004 [21] and 2008 [17] for comparison purposes. The number of servers which negotiated ECN rose to between 14% to 17% in all web server populations. A possible ECN SYN blackhole existed in less than 0.6% of tests. But we caution that this may over-estimate the percentage as false positives could occur both in our methodology and the previous studies if a lossy link happened to drop the ECN enabled SYN packets but not the subsequent SYN packets without ECN. Definitively identifying ECN blackholes would require repeated probing of the same server with both ECN and non-ECN SYNs.

The rest of the table rows report various ways in which the ECN congestion feedback loop can be broken. We conservatively report on not receiving a CWR in response to ECE only if we receive more than 10 data packets from the server i.e. we receive a subsequent flight of packets after the server must have received ECE notifications. The variation across different populations is striking – the ECN field in the IP header on flows to and from university networks is being cleared 25.2% and 28.5% of the time respectively.[2] This is far higher than the comparable percentages of paths to Alexa web hosts – 3.8% outbound and 11.3% inbound.

In limited testing from different vantage points, the percentages of ECN capable servers across target populations remained consistent. The results characterizing the broken ECN feedback loop showed more variation. This is expected given that these results depend upon the network path between our measurement vantage points and the target servers. Our traceroute measurements below shed additional light on these variations.

4.2 Client-side results

Table 2 shows that fewer clients negotiated ECN on incoming connections; 4.2% to less than 0.1% depending on population. To better understand this discrepancy, we employ stack fingerprinting to the TCP SYN/ACK packets [5] to infer the operating system of the client. Table 3 shows a striking difference between the ECN capable and non-ECN capable populations: the vast majority of ECN capable hosts are Linux (88.4%).

4.3 End-to-End ECN Paths

We collected two sets traces to determine *where* on the path the ECT codepoint was cleared, and related aspects. The first trace set includes one randomly-chosen destination

[2]When there is no ECE for a CE, either the outbound CE could be being cleared or the inbound ECE.

Table 2: Client Population Data

Population	Gnutella	BitTorrent
Hosts classified	126,984 (100%)	16,602 (100%)
ECN-capable	106 (0.1%)	701 (4.2%)
Not ECN-capable	126,878 (99.9%)	15,901 (95.8%)
ECT in non-ECN flow	2,153 (1.7%)	452 (2.8%)
no ECT in ECN flow	44 (42%)	117 (17%)
no ECE for CE	10 (9%)	167 (24%)
no CWR for ECE	0 (0.0%)	0 (0.0%)

Table 3: Inferred O/S of Client Populations

O/S	Gnutella (All)	Gnutella (ECN)	BT (All)	BT (ECN)
Windows	29.9%	0.0%	24.6%	0.0%
Mac/BSD	3.9%	29.5%	8.9%	4.4%
Linux	1.1%	46.6%	7.0%	88.4%
Other	65.1%	23.9%	59.5%	7.14%

from each of the globally routable BGP prefixes ($\simeq$ 367,000) in order to touch all origin AS's and be broadly representative of Internet paths. The second trace set represents "popular" destinations, and thus used the 542,000 unique addresses from the Alexa top 1 million [1]. For the prefix-traces, we used 127 PlanetLab nodes, from 29 countries and 5 continents, to initiate the traces. And for the website-traces, we were able to use some additional nodes for a total of 140. Each PlanetLab node executed a trace to each of the destinations, for a total of 117 million traces collected.

Percent of Traces which passed the ECT codepoint

The location of any devices that modify the ECT codepoint relative to our tracing vantage points is important. At one extreme, ECT is cleared on 100% of the traces originating from particular PlanetLab nodes due to all traces passing through a misbehaving device at the first or second hop. Traces from these nodes are not reflective of the whole Internet, but are relevant for the clients at that location.

ICMP filtering behavior impacts our macro analysis as well. For a few vantage points, the vast majority of their traces are blocked after a few hops, and for the hops that did respond, the ECT codepoint remained set; thus these traces could be grouped with those that preserved the codepoint, though in reality farther along the path the codepoint might have been cleared.

Across all traces, the ECT codepoint is unmodified for 83% and 82% of the popular website and prefix traces respectively. Restricting the analysis to those traces where all hops respond, including the destinations, does not qualitatively affect our results, yielding 84% and 80% respectively. To remove the impact of nodes where the ECT codepoint is cleared on almost all of the traces, if we omit the 20% of nodes that had the fewest traces where the ECT remained set, then for each of remaining nodes, the ECT codepoint remained set on 94% to 98% of the website-traces and 90% to 99% of the prefix-traces.

Location on the path where the ECT codepoint is cleared

When the ECT codepoint is modified, we wish to attribute such misbehavior to an interface hop on the path. However, there is ambiguity in identifying the responsible device. For example, while sending probes with ECT set, suppose interface hops 1-4 respond with ICMP TTL exceeded quotations

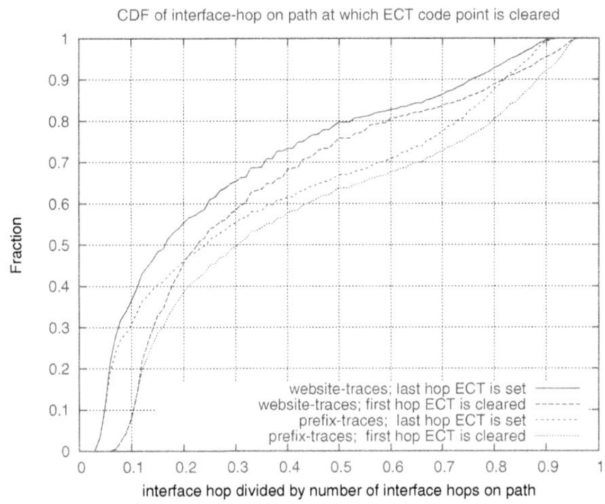

Figure 1: CDF of interface-hop on path at which ECT codepoint is cleared

that preserve ECT, while the fifth hop's quotation shows ECT cleared. The responsible device could be the router at the fifth hop, the router at the fourth hop, or some middlebox (e.g. a firewall, switch, or load balancer) between the two that does not decrement TTL. The case of the prior router being responsible occurs when routers decrement TTLs and expire packets before performing other processing on the incoming packet. As mentioned in Section 3.4, there is also the possibility of ICMP misquotations.

To resolve this ambiguity, we collect into a set "A" the interfaces that did not clear ECT, i.e. interfaces where, on any trace, the response from the next hop preserved ECT. Assuming that an interface/router is consistent as to whether it clears or preserves ECT, then for all the traces, the interfaces in "A" should not clear ECT. We find cases where: (1) the interface first reporting ECT cleared is in "A," and (2) the prior interface is in "A." In our traces, one case does not dominate the other. More interestingly, we discover a third case where both interfaces are in "A," which suggests the action of middleboxes, and/or casts into doubt the assumption of consistency. In the following we do not assume which box cleared the codepoint, but report the two bounding possibilities (given that the returned value is accurate).

For traces where all interface hops respond, and where ECT is cleared, we record the hop number of the last router interface that preserves ECT, and of the interface that first reported the cleared codepoint. By normalizing by the number of interface hops on the path, Figure 1 shows the CDF of the relative position of ECT misbehavior along probed paths. Examining at the bottom curve, "prefix-traces; first hop ECT is cleared," for 40% of the traces the interface hop which first reports ECT cleared is at 20% or less along the path. At the upper end of the CDF, for 20% of the traces, the hop which first reports ECT cleared is in within the last 20% of the path. Thus 40% of the traces fall in-between. All four CDF's show that there is a substantial portion of the mass in the middle range of the path – suggesting that there is significant misbehavior within the core of the network. (For both the website and prefix traces, the median number of interface hops was 16 and only 4% of the paths had 10 or fewer hops.) Since the last hop where the ECT is set always comes before the first hop where ECT is cleared, the CDF of the former lies above that of the latter. Figure 1 shows that, overall, the ECT is cleared earlier on paths to the popular websites.

AS's where the ECT codepoint is cleared

Attributing cleared ECT to an AS introduces a well-known ambiguity: router interfaces between AS's may be assigned addresses from either peer AS, or even use outside or private addresses. We perform a basic disambiguation by scanning across all traces and looking for instances where the subsequent hop's interface address is from the address space originated by the same AS as the address of current hop. With this requirement, many interface hops are not resolved to an AS, and are simply labeled as "unknown." With this determination, we then scan through the traces a second time, looking for where the ECT codepoint is cleared. In the future, we will perform a more thorough procedure to determine border routers [13].

In analogy to Figure 1, we would like to estimate where on the AS path the ECT codepoint is first cleared. For the set of prefix-traces where all hops responded, we revisit the subset on which the ECT codepoint was cleared, and the pair of router-interface hops between which this first occurred. Using our restricted inference technique, frequently one, or both, of these router interfaces can not be associated with certainty to an AS. This is expected since some providers still clear the legacy ToS byte at their network ingress, i.e. between AS's. We find that 55% these pairs of router-interface hops have one of the AS's classified as "unknown," and 11% have both so classified, and thus 34% have both hops associated with an AS. When the two AS's are known, for 99% of the traces, the two AS's are the same; and for these, 32% are the same as the source AS, 17% are the same as the destination AS, and the remainder, 51%, are distinct from the source and destination AS. Thus we do see cases where the ECT codepoint is cleared interior to an AS (that is not the source AS).

Of all the AS's seen on the prefix-traces, only about 1% were detected to have cleared the ECT codepoint. In particular, of the over 37,000 AS's seen on the prefix-traces, only 177 AS's were detected to have definitely cleared the codepoint (the two AS's that bound the clearing of the codepoint are the same); and only an additional 343 AS's might have cleared the codepoint. Though, if the codepoint had not been cleared at the given interface, it possibly would have been cleared at a subsequent interface/AS that was not detected by our experiment.

In order to proceed with the estimation, we assume an interface whose AS has been classified as "unknown" is actually in the nearest, previous AS that was known on the path. Since we know the AS of the source, this assumption allows us to assign an AS number to every interface on the path. Note that this assumption biases the location at which the ECT codepoint is cleared towards earlier on the AS path.

The results are presented in Table 4 (This is analogous to the plot "prefix-traces; first hop ECT is cleared" in Figure 1.) We restrict the table to AS-paths lengths that accounted for at least 1% of the traces. For a given AS-path length (a given row in the table) and for each AS hop on the path, we report the percent of traces at which the ECT codepoints is first observed to be cleared. For paths of length 4, the most popular length, the ECT codepoint was cleared at an intermediate AS on 30% of the traces, and for paths of length

Table 4: AS hop at which ECT is cleared

Number of AS hops on path	Percent of traces with given number of AS's	For each AS hop on path, precent of traces in which ECT codepoint is first cleared
2	1	58 42
3	19	60 25 15
4	40	58 11 19 12
5	28	44 16 12 19 9
6	10	37 8 28 11 12 4
7	1	37 4 35 6 11 6 1

5, the percentage is 47%. If the calculation is repeated where we no longer require that all interfaces on the path respond, but only that the destination responds, the percents in Table 4 are roughly the same.

Note that since our assumption of assigning "unknown" AS's to the previous known AS on the path introduces a bias towards earlier on the path, the percents in Table 4 underestimate how far along the path the ECT codepoint is cleared. Also recall that Table 4, and Figure 1, report the location where the ECT codepoint is *first* cleared; and thus if the codepoint had not been cleared at the given interface, it possibly would have been cleared at a subsequent one. Thus, the percents in Table 4 should be viewed as approximations. However, the implication from Table 4, consistent with Figure 1, is that the ECT codepoint is not only being cleared in the origin (and destination AS), but also at intermediate AS's.

Other notable behaviors

For 99% of the website and prefix traces, the quoted ECN field from probe responses had either ECT set for all hops or had ECT cleared at some hop and the field remained cleared. For the remaining 1% of the traces, we observe a variety of behaviors. On some traces, the reported ECT codepoint changes several times between set and cleared; a few traces had as many as 14 switches in value. We also find instances where the Congestion Experienced (CE) codepoint is set. Across the two trace sets, there were 98 unique hop pairs for which the ECN field switched to CE. For these pairs, the CE codepoint is often set in conjunction with the diffserv codepoint having a non-zero value, thus in all likelihood the network is making use of the legacy ToS field.

5. MITIGATION OPTIONS

While ECN nonce[26] is often seen as a mechanism to ensure that a receiver correctly reflects the congestion signal carried in the ECN bits of the IP header, it can also serve as a mechanism for ensuring correct ECN behavior along a path (see section in 6.2 [26]). Network devices that mangle the ECN bits destroy the ability of the receiver to correctly calculate the ECN nonce sum. How a sender responds to incorrect nonce sums is a matter of policy, but ceasing to set ECT in outgoing segments would be one obvious response. Across all of our data sets, we see no instances of ECN nonce support. Manual inspection of arriving packets with ECT1 set reveals that these flows always set ECT1, even when ECN is not negotiated by TCP. (Thus, TCP continues to rely on cooperative and friendly behavior.)

One other mitigation strategy for dealing with paths that mangle the ECN bits in the IP header is to check upon receipt of an ECN enabled SYN packet that the ECN field is zero and refusing to enable ECN if it is not. While RFC 5562 suggests adding ECN capabilities to SYN/ACK packets (thus allowing a non-zero ECN field), TCP SYN packets should never be ECN marked [16]. While this approach does not help on paths that clear the ECN field, which is the common error, it does address some particularly problematic manglings of the ECN field like always setting CE (i.e. signaling constant congestion.)

6. CONCLUSION

While some impediments to wider use of ECN appear to be diminished (i.e. servers have increasingly enabled it), an important finding of this paper is the presence of a non-trivial number of paths that mangle the ECN field in the IP header. This problem compromises a carefully designed congestion feedback loop and potentially raises concerns about the congestion safety or fairness of using ECN if senders do not receive the signal to slow their rate. Eventually a sender would overflow the bottleneck queue and then back off, but other flows that share partial paths would be disadvantaged.

Similar concerns exist in the case of congestion echo (ECE) not making it to the sender. While the possibility of such behavior is mentioned in [24], repeated tests to servers demonstrate this is not just a random event but rather can be a persistent problem along a path. If the CWR is being cleared on the other hand, the problem is instead that the sender receives a constant stream of ECE flagged messages and therefore never opens its congestion window – resulting in very low throughput.

While the existence of these problems is potentially discouraging we have found that the problems can often be rapidly fixed. We identified problems on both our lab and our residential broadband network. Both networks were quickly fixed when we supplied packet captures and traceroutes illustrating the problem. In the case of our lab, the intent had been to copy the 802.1p field from Ethernet to DSCP but an Ethernet switch instead ended up overwriting all eight bits of the ToS field. In the case of the broadband provider, the intent had been to clear the diffserv field but instead the entire old ToS field was being set to zero. We suspect that many of the problems we found have similar origins. Other potential sources of error include NATs and home routers, load balancers, tunnels, and other types of middle-boxes. Our tools and methodology will hopefully aid in quickly finding and fixing these problems.

Acknowledgments

We thank Jim Gettys and all the anonymous reviewers for their feedback and insights. R. Beverly was partially supported by a Cisco Research Grant. Views and conclusions are those of the authors and should not be interpreted as representing the official policies, either expressed or implied, of the U.S. government.

7. REFERENCES

[1] Alexa. Top 1,000,000 sites, 2011. http://www.alexa.com/topsites.

[2] M. Alizadeh, A. Greenberg, D. A. Maltz, J. Padhye, P. Patel, B. Prabhakar, S. Sengupta, and M. Sridharan. Data center tcp (dctcp). In *Proceedings of ACM SIGCOMM*, 2010.

[3] B. Augustin, X. Cuvellier, B. Orgogozo, F. Viger, T. Friedman, M. Latapy, C. Magnien, and R. Teixeira. Avoiding traceroute anomalies with paris traceroute. In *Proceedings of the 6th ACM IMC*, 2006.

[4] S. Bauer, D. Clark, and B. Lehr. The evolution of internet congestion. In *Proceedings of the 37th TPRC*, 2009.

[5] R. Beverly. A robust classifier for passive tcp/ip fingerprinting. In *Proceedings of the 5th Passive and active network measurement conference*, pages 158–167, 2004.

[6] B. Briscoe. Tunnelling of Explicit Congestion Notification. RFC 6040 (Proposed Standard), Nov. 2010.

[7] B. Briscoe, A. Jacquet, C. Di Cairano-Gilfedder, A. Salvatori, A. Soppera, and M. Koyabe. Policing congestion response in an internetwork using re-feedback. In *Proceedings of ACM SIGCOMM*, 2005.

[8] B. Briscoe and S. Rudkin. Commercial models for ip quality of service interconnect. *BT Technology Journal*, 23:171–195, April 2005.

[9] B. Cohen. Incentives build robustness in bittorrent, 2003.

[10] P. Eardley. Metering and Marking Behaviour of PCN-Nodes. RFC 5670 (Proposed Standard), Nov. 2009.

[11] K. Forster. Universities worldwide, 2011. http://univ.cc/.

[12] J. Gettys. Bufferbloat, 2011. http://www.bufferbloat.net/.

[13] B. Huffaker, A. Dhamdhere, M. Fomenkov, and K. Claffy. Toward topology dualism: improving the accuracy of as annotations for routers. In *Proceedings of the 11th Passive and active measurement conference*, 2010.

[14] D. Katabi, M. Handley, and C. Rohrs. Congestion control for high bandwidth-delay product networks. *SIGCOMM Comput. Commun. Rev.*, 32, August 2002.

[15] A. Kuzmanovic. The power of explicit congestion notification. In *Proceedings of ACM SIGCOMM*, 2005.

[16] A. Kuzmanovic, A. Mondal, S. Floyd, and K. Ramakrishnan. Adding Explicit Congestion Notification (ECN) Capability to TCP's SYN/ACK Packets. RFC 5562 (Experimental), June 2009.

[17] A. Langley. Probing the viability of tcp extensions, 2008. http://www.imperialviolet.org/binary/ecntest.pdf.

[18] M. Luckie. Scamper: a scalable and extensible packet prober for active measurement of the internet. In *Proceedings of the 10th ACM IMC*, IMC '10, 2010.

[19] G. Maier, A. Feldmann, V. Paxson, and M. Allman. On dominant characteristics of residential broadband internet traffic. In *Proceedings of the 9th ACM IMC*, 2009.

[20] D. Malone and M. Luckie. Analysis of icmp quotations. In *Proceedings of the 8th Passive and active network measurement conference*, 2007.

[21] A. Medina, M. Allman, and S. Floyd. Measuring interactions between transport protocols and middleboxes. In *Proceedings of the 4th ACM IMC*, 2004.

[22] A. Medina, M. Allman, and S. Floyd. Measuring the evolution of transport protocols in the internet. *SIGCOMM Comput. Commun. Rev.*, 35, April 2005.

[23] T. Moncaster, B. Briscoe, and M. Menth. Baseline Encoding and Transport of Pre-Congestion Information. RFC 5696 (Proposed Standard), Nov. 2009.

[24] K. Ramakrishnan, S. Floyd, and D. Black. The Addition of Explicit Congestion Notification (ECN) to IP. RFC 3168, Sept. 2001.

[25] N. Spring, L. Peterson, A. Bavier, and V. Pai. Using planetlab for network research: myths, realities, and best practices. *SIGOPS Oper. Syst. Rev.*, 40, January 2006.

[26] N. Spring, D. Wetherall, and D. Ely. Robust Explicit Congestion Notification (ECN) Signaling with Nonces. RFC 3540, June 2003.

[27] D. Stutzbach, R. Rejaie, N. Duffield, S. Sen, and W. Willinger. On unbiased sampling for unstructured peer-to-peer networks. *IEEE Trans. Netw.*, 17, April 2009.

Summary Review Documentation for

"Measuring the State of ECN Readiness in Servers, Clients, and Routers"

Authors: S. Bauer, R. Beverly, A. Berger

Reviewer #1

Strengths: The results: hard, new datapoints on ECN readiness over much Internet infrastructure (still a good way to go but starting to build) and data on various pathologies that is useful to work out how to best improve ECN readiness (such as knowing that the core is clearing ECT relatively often). A well-executed measurement study in a very readable paper that looks at an impressive number of Internet paths over a variety of sub-populations.

Weaknesses: Well, you could say that the paper is small in scope, just giving better datapoints on one TCP/IP mechanism, and unimportant, given that the mechanism is not much used in practice. But I think this would be a bit unfair.

Comments to Authors: These comments are intended to help you improve your paper further. (1) What I liked most was your division of Internet devices into different sub-populations and the exploration of "what went wrong". Both help to move us beyond a simple but unhelpful statistic ("we find that the Internet is 15% ECN ready"). Where you could go further is with ways to improve the status quo based on your findings. Are there simple tests that TCP/IP implementations should perform to avoid being adversely affected by the pathologies (detect and turn off?) or do they not matter much? Note that the ECN nonce can potentially help here by serving as a robust testing mechanism for correct implementations along a path -- if used properly it will detect middleboxes interfering with the ECN bits as well as "cheating hosts". (2) Also, the material in looking for the location of problems along the path did feel rather speculative, since you cannot come to firm conclusions, but I appreciated it nonetheless.

Reviewer #2

Strengths: Repetition of old results with new outcomes. ECN deployment is still underway, but there are new challenges. Comprehensive testing for a short paper.

Weaknesses: None.

Comments to Authors: Nice short paper. Good coverage of a moderately interesting topic. Most of the interest is in the fact that there is a positive trend, but it's disheartening to see how slow the positive trend is.

The information in S4.2 would have been much more interesting if divided by AS instead of by hop-count. Once the network is blocking ECN, IMHO it's more important who is doing it rather than where.
It would have been useful to correlate the BitTorrent implementations types (by bittorrent id) or the Gnutella implemenations (by user-agent) to the ECN-capable nodes to better understand which types of nodes are ECN-capable.

Reviewer #3

Strengths: Fairly broad study of ECN. Results are interesting. Good positioning of results and contribution into the historical context.

Weaknesses: Methodology is confusing; esp description in 2 and the state machine in Figure 1 seem to not match later text. While results are interesting, their significance can be improved, for example, by listing out the top fewcauses of ECN misbehavior today.

Comments to Authors: Writing is mostly good, though another pass would help. Results are interesting. A more precise breakdown of the types of idiosyncracies that are happening, their potential causes, and fixes would be very useful. In the sense that, they would prescribe how ECN can be better supported. (The examples at the of Sections 4 and 5 are steps along the right path.)
State machine in Figure 1 is cryptic. What you really mean to do, is to use iptables rules to mimic a congestion event along the path as a router would have otherwise done (mark CE on packets). However some of the transitions are based on packets coming in from different directions; ECE would come from the local client, CWR would come from the remote host. Also, I can't tell what the left path of the tree is doing.
OSes have ECN support but don't turn it on by default, i.e., if the other end does not request ECN they wouldn't use it. Is this accurate? Can you quantify how many clients/ OSes are like this?
There seems to also be a fair bit of re-use of the ToS field, some of which doesn't seem to interact correctly with ECN. It would help to be more concrete about these anomalies.
In 3.4, wouldn't using TCP @port 80 get you better pass through rates from proxies?
From Table 1, it isn't clear that mobile servers are doing any better on ECN.Neither are the more popular servers or university clients. Is there bias in the experiments, with the measuring host, or the first few links on the path to the measurement host(s) dominating the results here?
In 4, Is 'hop' an IP hop, as visible from ICMP? That would be vulnerable to not seeing mpls segments or other circuits.
The ambiguity, when ECT is cleared, whether it is cleared on the outgoing part of the previous hop or the incoming part on the next hop doesn't seem to be worth chasing down. Localizing it to that pair would be helpful in itself. You might even get away by looking at multiple pairs that share an endpoint to get a better handle on which of those two end points may be clearing that bits.

Using p2p traffic to measure client eyeballs is cool, but probably not a big deal.

Reviewer #4

Strengths: Keeping track of the ECN capabilities of Internet devices is important to improve TCP's behavior across the Internet.

Weaknesses: Given that lack of ECN capabilities of the measured end-hosts, I do not see a point in this paper. The methodology for the mobile infrastructure is weak, while this is the environment where ECN is likely to matter more.

Comments to Authors: To understand mobile devices' ECN, the authors can't simply go to the mobile version of websites, but also need to conduct measurements from mobile devices themselves or use NAT devices as used by mobile operators.
Why exactly are passive measurements not a reliable indicator of the prevalence of client-side ECN support? Is it the number of observed end-hosts? I don't quite understand. Why would a P2P-biased view be better? If the authors want to make claims a bout some bias, then please argue.
From table 2, given that most hosts are not ECN-capable, why should we care about what routers do? If end-hosts were ECN capable and impeded by routers on the way, I would understand. But given the current deployment of ECN, the paper is weak.
What is the relationship between the paths that you are probing and the original end-hosts for which you wanted to check the ECN capabilities?
Adding to Figure 2 the absolute hop count and AS hops where ECT is cleared would help. The discussion on figure 2 is too short. The authors spend much time in the paper on discussions and methodological considerations, while not really giving a take-home message. I would see this as a CCR paper, not so much a research paper

Reviewer #5

Strengths: This paper presents a thorough study of the current support for ECN. It measures all three parts: servers (including servers for mobile clients), clients, and network paths. Nice technique to measure client support by crawling Bittorrent and Gnutella networks.

Weaknesses: Having updated numbers is interesting, but the results are not that surprising. The paper lacks more analysis of the causes for the small ECN support and the reasons for network elements to mistakenly clear ECN bits.

Comments to Authors: This paper presents a nice update on ECN support. It is important to study servers, clients, and network paths to fully understand the potential for ECN utilization. At the end the results and the analysis are not very novel.
The paper does present a separate characterization of web servers for mobile devices, but the results are similar to other websites and there is no further discussion about this point.
The technique to crawl p2p clients to study client support for ECN is nice. In general, it is hard to measure the client side. The results are not very telling, because the paper presents no characteristics of these clients. Is there a way to find out the operating system and other configuration details of these clients? It would be interesting to complete these tests with hosts where you know the OS, so that you can study of different OSes for ECN.
Sec. 3.4 says that it uses ICMP traceroute probes, because the use of ECN doesn't change depending on the protocol. It would be nice to have at least a short description of this experiment.
In Sec. 4.2 paragraph 6, is it true that routers are consistent in the way they treat the ECN bits? In this section, it would be nice to have a discussion of why routers sometimes clear the ECN bits. Maybe bringing the last paragraph of the discussion to this section would help the readers understand this point.
The results in Fig. 2 are biased because after a router clears the ECN bits, if another router in the path also clears these bits, you cannot detect it. So, it is expected that this curve is shifted to the left. The paper should at least discuss this bias or even change the presentation of this result. It makes more sense to discuss the ASes or pair of ASes where ECN bits are cleared. The analysis in terms of fraction of the total number of hops is confusing.
Also in Sec. 4.2, last paragraph under "AS's where the ECT codepoint is cleared," why use the restricted inference technique? What is the fraction that is not labeled? Instead of trying to pinpoint an AS, you could characterize pairs of ASes.

Response from the Authors

We valued and addressed the feedback from all reviewers. The most valuable contribution came from Reviewer 1 who points out the fact that an ECN nonce (RFC 3540) can serve as a robust testing mechanism for correct ECN behavior along a path not just correct ECN behavior by receivers. This is noted in RFC 3540 but we had overlooked it.
A number of the reviews noted confusion on how we implemented the server testing using the iptables functionality of Linux. There are a number of details to the implementation that are subtle particular if one is not familiar with iptables rules and capabilities or the exact protocol details of ECN. We updated the description of our methodology to hopefully make it more clear but perhaps more importantly we have all our configuration scripts and testing tools available for any reader wishing to replicate our measurements. A benefit of our implementation is that one can easily test any application or service that relies upon TCP -- a feature we leverage to test both web servers and hosts running p2p software without needing any additional implementation effort.
Some of the reviews noted a general lack of interest in our ECN measurements. Our interests simply differ. When we started this research we intended it as an email to the IETF Conex WG. The discovery of the devices along the path mangling the ECN bits both at our home and lab networks suggested there was a more interesting phenomenon worthy of investigation. We were encouraged by a number of individuals to conduct a careful study. Even if one is not interesting in ECN in particular, there are interesting lessons in regards to the challenges associated with reusing fields (ToS to diffserv/ECN) or using previously reserved bits (TCP's CWR and ECE flags). Also our traceroute technique of diagnosing ECN problems can be used for other purposes, one of which is a survey of diffserv code points being set by each AS (a study we are currently conducting.)

Is it Still Possible to Extend TCP?

Michio Honda*, Yoshifumi Nishida*, Costin Raiciu†, Adam Greenhalgh‡, Mark Handley‡, Hideyuki Tokuda*

Keio University*, Universitatea Politehnica Bucuresti†, University College London‡

{micchie,nishida}@sfc.wide.ad.jp, costin.raiciu@cs.pub.ro

{a.greenhalgh,m.handley}@cs.ucl.ac.uk, hxt@ht.sfc.keio.ac.jp

ABSTRACT

We've known for a while that the Internet has ossified as a result of the race to optimize existing applications or enhance security. NATs, performance-enhancing-proxies, firewalls and traffic normalizers are only a few of the middleboxes that are deployed in the network and look beyond the IP header to do their job. IP itself can't be extended because "IP options are not an option" [10]. Is the same true for TCP?

In this paper we develop a measurement methodology for evaluating middlebox behavior relating to TCP extensions and present the results of measurements conducted from multiple vantage points. The short answer is that we can still extend TCP, but extensions' design is very constrained as it needs to take into account prevalent middlebox behaviors. For instance, absolute sequence numbers cannot be embedded in options, as middleboxes can rewrite ISN and preserve undefined options. Sequence numbering also must be consistent for a TCP connection, because many middleboxes only allow through contiguous flows.

We used these findings to analyze three proposed extensions to TCP. We find that MPTCP is likely to work correctly in the Internet or fallback to regular TCP. TcpCrypt seems ready to be deployed, however it is fragile if resegmentation does happen—for instance with hardware offload. Finally, TCP extended options in its current form is not safe to deploy.

Categories and Subject Descriptors

C.2.2 [**Computer-communication Networks**]: Network Protocols; C.2.6 [**Computer-communication Networks**]: Internetworking

General Terms

Measurement, Design, Experimentation, Standardization

Keywords

Middleboxes, Measurements, TCP, Protocol design

IMC'11, November 2–4, 2011, Berlin, Germany.

1. INTRODUCTION

The Internet was designed to be extensible; routers only care about IP headers, not what the packets contain, and protocols such as IP and TCP were designed with options fields that could be used to add additional functionality. The great virtue of the Internet was always that it was *stupid*; it did no task especially well, but it was extremely flexible and general, allowing a proliferation of protocols and applications that the original designers could never have foreseen.

Unfortunately the Internet, as it is deployed, is no longer the Internet as it was designed. IP options have been unusable for twenty years[10] as they cause routers to process packets on their slow path. Above IP, the Internet has benefited (or suffered, depending on your viewpoint) from decades of optimizations and security enhancements. To improve performance [2, 7, 18, 3], reduce security exposure [15, 29], enhance control, and work around address space shortages [22], the Internet has experienced an invasion of middleboxes that *do* care about what the packets contain, and perform processing at layer 4 or higher *within* the network.

The problem now faced by designers of new protocols is that there is no longer a well defined or understood way to extend network functionality, short of implementing everything over HTTP[25]. Recently we have been working on adding both multipath support[11] and native encryption[5] to TCP. The obvious way to do this, in both cases, is to use TCP options. In the case of multipath, we would also like to stripe data across more than one path. At the end systems, the protocol design issues were mostly conventional. However, it became increasingly clear that no one, not the IETF, not the network operators, and not the OS vendors, knew what will and what will not pass through all the middleboxes as they are currently deployed and configured. Will TCP options pass unchanged? If the sequence space has holes, what happens? If a retransmission has different data than the original, which arrives? Are TCP segments coalesced or split? These and many more questions are crucial to answer if protocol designers are to extend TCP in a deployable way. Or have we already lost the ability to extend TCP, just like we did two decades ago for IP?

In this paper we present the results from a measurement study conducted from 142 networks in 24 countries, including cellular, WiFi and wired networks, public and private networks, residential, commercial and academic networks. We actively probe the network to elicit middlebox responses that violate the end-to-end transparency of the original Internet architecture. We focus on TCP, not only because it is by far the most widely used transport protocol, but also because while it is known that many middleboxes modify TCP behavior [6], it is not known how prevalent such middleboxes are, nor precisely what the *emergent behavior* is with TCP extensions that were unforeseen by the middlebox designers.

We make three main contributions. The first is a snapshot of the Internet, as of early 2011, in terms of its transparency to extensions to the TCP protocol. We examine the effects of middleboxes on TCP options, sequency numbering, data acknowledgment, retransmission and segmentation.

The second contribution is our measurement methodology and tools that allow us to infer what middleboxes are doing to traffic. Some of these tests are simple and obvious; for example, whether a TCP option arrives or is removed is easy to measure, so long as the raw packet data is monitored at both ends. However, some tests are more subtle; to test if a middlebox coalesces segments it is not sufficient to just send many segments—unless the middlebox has a reason to queue segments it will likely pass them on soon as they arrive, even if it has the capability to coalesce. We need to force it to have the opportunity to coalesce.

Finally we examine the implications of our measurement study for protocol designers that wish to extend TCP's functionality. In particular, we look at proposals for Multipath TCP[11], TcpCrypt[5], and TCP Extended Option Space[9], and consider what our findings mean for the design of these protocols and their deployability.

The remainder of this paper is organized as follows: Sec. 2 describes related work; in Sec. 3 we describe our methodology and introduce the TCPExposure tool, our tool to inspect middlebox behavior; in Sec. 4 we examine middlebox behavior on each protocol component in more detail, show how to detect this behavior, then present our measurement results from running TCPExposure in 142 networks; in Sec. 5 we examine the impact on TCP extensions as case-study. We summarize our conclusions in Sec. 6.

2. RELATED WORK

There exists a large body of work related to the measurement, analysis and identification of different deployed TCP implementations, but none of it has specifically focused on analyzing TCP middlebox behavior.

Padhye and Floyd perform a client-side analysis of numerous public web servers to test their congestion control behavior and ECN and SACK capabilities [23]. The client-only methodology leverages existing public web servers to give great coverage, allowing the authors to examine the behavior of many different TCP implementations.

The study focuses on remote TCP implementations rather than middlebox interactions; the same methodology is not applicable for this middlebox study for three reasons. First, most users access the Internet through home and cellular networks, yet few public servers exist in these networks that could be used for tests. Further, it is not possible to test qualitative middlebox behavior without co-ordination of both end systems. Finally, the Padhye and Floyd techniques cannot distinguish the effects due to middleboxes from the particularities of remote TCP implementations and remote hardware (such as segmentation offload).

Medina *et al.* measure in their 2005 study the impact of network middleboxes on path MTU discovery transparency, sequence number shifting, as well as their effect on IP and TCP options [21]. This study undertakes similar client-only measurements as in [23], and suffers from the same limitations.

Allman [1] and Hätönen *et al.* [16] both examine the quantitative application-level performance of various middleboxes in testbeds where the box being tested is known and under their control. Allman measures transaction delay, throughput and connection persistence over the middleboxes he evaluated. Hätönen *et al.* measure NAT binding timeouts, queueing delays, throughput and support of new transport protocols over their testbed which includes a large number of home-gateway devices. We adopt the end-to-end methodology of these papers and extend it further to examine the qualitative middlebox behavior in the wild that we are interested in.

Paxson measures end-to-end packet dynamics such as out-of-order delivery, packet corruption and retransmission on TCP bulk transfers [24]. The author operates both end systems of each end-to-end measurement by remote login; this limits the applicability of the study to networks where the authors have (or are given temporary) direct access to hosts. This poses two challenges: first, obtaining shell access to users' machines to run privileged commands is really difficult; second, even if permitted, accessing NATed boxes is not possible unless users specifically open up NAT ports. To avoid these issues we adopted the alternative approach of asking contributors to run a single, self-contained, shell script and to post the results.

Ford *et al.* [13] test hole punching availability of NAT boxes for TCP and UDP. Tests are performed with a portable client tool running behind NATs and two public servers that accompany test traffic. This work does not measure middlebox behavior that we are interested in. However, its methodology is similar to our work in terms of real Internet path measurement, study of qualitative middlebox behavior, and control of both ends of measuring paths with distributing a tool to contributors.

3. METHODOLOGY AND DATASETS

We use regular end-hosts to actively measure paths in the Internet. Our aim is to test relevant properties that could impact yet-to-be-deployed TCP extensions. We have resorted to active measurement for a number of reasons:

- We need to generate traffic that mimics new TCP extensions.
- We generate artificial traffic patterns such as contiguous small segments or gaps in the sequence space. It is difficult to use passive measurements for this purpose.
- Packets need to be inspected at both sender and receiver for tests detecting TCP option removal, sequence number shifting, re-segmentation, etc.
- We need to test different destination ports including ports not normally in use, as middlebox behavior depends on the destination port.

3.1 Testing Tool

Our middlebox inspection tool is called **TCPExposure** and consists of a client and a server tool. The client acts as an initiator of a TCP connection (the end that sends the SYN), and the server acts as a responder. These are a 3000-line program and a 500-line program both written in Python. The initiator and the responder run tests aiming to trigger on-path middlebox actions. The tools send and receive TCP segments in user space via a raw IP socket or using the Pcap library similarly to Sting [26].

The client tool was built to be easy to use, as most of our tests are run by contributors. To maximize reach, the client tool is cross-platform running on Mac OS, Linux and FreeBSD. It is self-contained and only requires Python and libpcap on the host; these come pre-installed on most systems. The client is straightforward to run: all users need to do is to download it, launch a single shell script and post the results.

The responder tool runs on Linux. It does not maintain state for the TCP connections it is emulating; its replies depend solely on the received TCP segments. For example, the responding segment contains SYN/ACK if the responder has received SYN, acknowledges the end of the sequence number, and has the sequence number based on the received acknowledgement (ACK) number. This

Table 1: Default TCP Parameters

Parameter	Initiator	Responder
Initial Sequence Num (ISN)	252001	11259375
Window Size	8064	32768
MSS	512	512
Window Scale	-	6
SACKOK	-	1
Timestamp (TS_val)	-	12345678

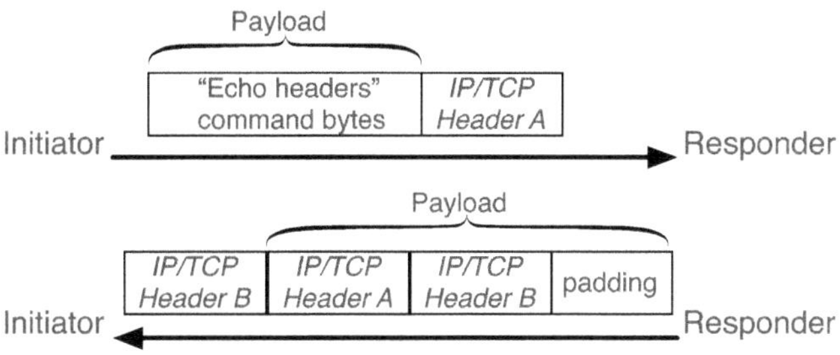

Figure 1: Echo Headers Command

stateless behavior makes it relatively easy to reason about observed behavior because there is no hidden server state.

3.2 Common Procedures

Table 1 lists the fixed TCP parameters at the initiator and the responder. These values are used in all our measurements unless stated otherwise.

We use a 512 byte MSS at both ends, less than what most TCP implementations advertise. This value is smaller than the MTU of most Internet paths, and was chosen to avoid unexpected fragmentation during tests.

We expect middleboxes to behave differently depending on the application type, and so our responder emulates TCP servers on ports 80, 443, and 34343. Ports 80 and 443 are assigned by IANA for http and https traffic; port 34343 is unassigned. The client port is randomly chosen at connection setup.

Segments sent from the initiator include commands to operate the responder. The default command is "just ack", and the responder sends back a pure ACK (no data). Another command is "echo headers". Fig. 1 illustrates how this command works.

The initiator transmits a crafted segment that includes bytes indicating this command in its payload. The responder replies with a segment that contains in its payload both the received headers and the headers of the reply. The client then compares the sent and received headers for both segments to detect middlebox interference. The last command is "don't advance ack". The responder does not advance the ACK number when it receives this command; instead it sends back an ACK with the first sequence number of the receiving segment. This command is used in only the retransmission test in Sec. 4.5.

3.3 Measurement Data

Our measurements target access networks, where ISPs deploy middleboxes to optimize various applications with the goal of improving the experience of the majority their customers. The core is mostly just doing "dumb" packet forwarding. Many contributors and we ran the TCPExposure client in a variety of access networks detailed below. Contributors are mainly from IETF community, related research projects, and our labs. We ran the server tool (the responder) in *sfc.wide.ad.jp*, a middlebox-free network that we operate.

Table 2: Experiment Venues

Country	*Home*	*Hotspot*	*Cellular*	*Univ*	*Ent*	*Hosting*	Total
Australia	0	2	0	0	0	1	3
Austria	0	0	0	0	1	0	1
Belgium	4	0	0	1	0	0	5
Canada	1	0	1	0	1	0	3
Chile	0	0	0	0	1	0	1
China	0	7	0	0	0	0	7
Czech	0	2	0	0	0	0	2
Denmark	0	2	0	0	0	0	2
Finland	1	0	0	3	2	0	6
Germany	3	1	3	4	1	0	12
Greece	2	0	1	0	0	0	3
Indonesia	0	0	0	3	0	0	3
Ireland	0	0	0	0	0	1	1
Italy	1	0	0	0	1	0	2
Japan	19	10	7	3	2	0	41
Romania	1	0	0	0	0	0	1
Russia	0	1	0	0	0	0	1
Spain	0	1	0	1	0	0	2
Sweden	1	0	0	0	0	0	1
Switzerland	2	0	0	0	0	0	2
Thailand	0	0	0	0	2	0	2
U.K.	10	4	4	2	1	1	22
U.S.	3	4	4	0	4	2	17
Vietnam	1	0	0	0	1	0	2
Total	49	34	20	17	17	5	142

From 25th September 2010 to 30th April 2011, we measured 142 access networks in 24 countries. Table 2 shows the venues and the network types of the experiments.

Access networks are categorized in six types by human annotation. Home networks consisting of a consumer ISP and a home-gateway are labeled as *Home*. Public hotspots for example in cafes, airports, hotels, and conference halls are labeled as *Hotspot*. Mobile broadband networks such as 3G and WiMAX are labeled as *Cellular*. Networks in universities are labeled as *Univ*. We count two different networks (e.g., the lecture and the residence segments) in the same university as two university networks. Enterprise networks (also including small offices) are labeled as *Ent*. Networks in hosting services are labeled as *Hosting*.

4. TESTS AND RESULTS

4.1 TCP Option Tests

TCP Options are the intended mechanism by which TCP can be extended. Standardized and widely implemented options include Maximum Segment Size (MSS), defined in 1981; Window Scale, defined in 1988; Timestamp, defined in 1992; and Selective Acknowledgment (SACK), defined in 1996. IANA also lists TCP options defined since 1996, but SACK is the most recently defined option in common use, and predates almost all of today's middleboxes. The question we wish to answer is whether it is still possible to rapidly deploy new TCP functionality using TCP options by upgrades purely at the end systems.

Unknown TCP options are ignored by the receiving host. A TCP extension typically adds a new option to the SYN to request the new behavior. If the SYN/ACK carries the corresponding new option in the response, the new functionality is enabled. Middleboxes have the potential to disrupt this process in many ways, preventing or at least delaying the deployment of new functionality.

If a middlebox simply removes an unknown option from the SYN, this should be benign—the new functionality fails to negotiate, but otherwise all is well. However, removing an unknown option from the SYN/ACK may be less benign—the server may think the functionality is negotiated, whereas the client may not. Removing unknown options from data packets, but not removing them from the SYN or SYN/ACK would be extremely problematic: both endpoints would believe the negotiation to use new functionality succeeded, but it would then fail. Finally, any middlebox that crashes, fails to progress the connection, or explicitly resets it would cause significant problems.

To distinguish possibly problematic behaviors, we performed the following tests:

1. **Unknown option in SYN.** The SYN and SYN/ACK segments include an unregistered option.
2. **Unknown option in Data segment**. The test includes unknown options in data segments sent by client and server.
3. **Known option in Data segment.** The test includes a well-known option in data segments sent by client and server.

All three tests are performed using separate connections. We do not use the unknown option in SYN for test 2 and 3. Test 3 is included to allow us to determine whether it is the unknown nature of the option that causes a behavior, or just any option. We use an MP_CAPABLE option for test 1 and an MP_DATA option for test 2; both options are defined in a draft version of MPTCP [12] and neither is currently registered with IANA, and no known middlebox yet supports them. On receipt of a SYN with MP_CAPABLE, our responder returns a SYN/ACK also containing MP_CAPABLE, and on receipt of a data segment with MP_DATA, it returns an ack packet containing an MP_ACK option, mimicking an MPTCP implementation.*

For test 3, we used the TIMESTAMP option [17], which is not essential to TCP's functionality, but which is commonly seen in TCP data segments. This option elicits a response from the remote endpoint; a stateful middlebox may also respond, allowing us to identify such middleboxes.

In the *unknown option in SYN test*, our code tests for the following possible middlebox behaviors:

- SYN is passed unmodified.
- SYN containing the option is dropped.
- SYN is received, but option was removed.
- Connection is reset by the middlebox.

In the *unknown* and the *known option in data* tests, we test for the same behaviors as in the SYN test. After a normal handshake, the initiator transmits a full-sized TCP segment including MP_DATA or TIMESTAMP, using the "echo headers" command described in Sec. 3.2 to identify what the responder received. With this method we can identify which outbound or inbound option is interfered and whether the option is modified or zeroed. We also look for middleboxes that split the connection, processing the TIMESTAMP at the middlebox on either the inbound or outbound leg.

Middlebox Behavior on TCP Options

Tables 3 – 5 summarize the results of the options tests. 142 paths were tested in total; for ports 80 (http) and 443 (https), we obtained results from all paths for all tests. However seven paths did not pass the unregistered port 34343, even with regular TCP SYN segments. These paths appear to run strict firewall rules allowing only very basic services.

*We use March 2010 draft version of these options' formats; MP_CAPABLE is 12 byte length, MP_DATA is 16 byte length, and MP_ACK is 10 byte length. Option numbers are 30, 31 and 32, respectively.

Table 3: Unknown Option in Syn

Observed	TCP Port		
Behavior	34343	80	443
Passed	129 (96%)	122 (86%)	133(94%)
Removed	6 (4%)	20 (14%)	9 (6%)
Changed	0 (0%)	0 (0%)	0 (0%)
Error	0 (0%)	0 (0%)	0 (0%)
Total	135 (100%)	142 (100%)	142 (100%)

Table 4: Known Option in Data

Observed	TCP Port		
Behavior	34343	80	443
Passed	129 (96%)	122 (86%)	133 (94%)
Removed	6 (4%)	9 (6%)	6 (4%)
Changed	0 (0%)	4 (3%)	3 (2%)
Error	0 (0%)	7 (5%)	0 (0%)
Total	135 (100%)	142 (100%)	142 (100%)

Table 5: Unknown Option in Data

Observed	TCP Port		
Behavior	34343	80	443
Passed	129 (96%)	122 (86%)	133(94%)
Removed	6 (4%)	13 (9%)	9 (6%)
Changed	0 (0%)	0 (0%)	0 (0%)
Error	0 (0%)	7 (5%)	0 (0%)
Total	135 (100%)	142 (100%)	142 (100%)

Most of the paths we tested passed both known and unknown TCP options without interference, both on SYN and data packets. The results are port-specific though; 96% of paths passed options on port 34343, whereas only 80% of paths passed options on port 80. This agrees with anecdotal evidence that http-specific middleboxes are relatively common.

All the paths which passed unknown options in the SYN also passed both known and unknown options in data segments. In the tables, the "*Removed*" rows indicate that packets on that path arrive with the option removed from the packet. For the unknown options in the SYN packet, this was the only anomaly we found; no path failed to deliver the packet due to its presence. In addition, all the paths which passed the unknown option in the SYN also passed unknown options in data segments. This bodes well for deployability of new TCP options—testing in the SYN and SYN/ACK is sufficient to determine that new options are safe to use throughout the connection.

Our test did not distinguish between middleboxes that stripped options from SYNs and those that stripped options from SYN/ACKs. With hindsight, this was an unfortunate limitation of our methodology that uses a stateless responder. However it is clear that any extension using TCP options to negotiate functionality should be robust to stripped unknown options in SYN/ACK packets, even if they are passed in SYNs. If it is crucial that the server knows whether or not the client received the option in the SYN/ACK, the protocol must take this into account. For example, TcpCrypt requires that the first non-SYN packet from the client contains the INIT1 option - if this is missing, TcpCrypt moves to the disabled state and falls back to regular TCP behavior.

Table 6: Types of removal behavior (SYN)

Path Type	Other Observed Effects	TCP Port 34343	80	443
Elim.	None	5	4	5
Proxy	Proxy SYN-ACK	1	16	4
Total		6	20	9

For port 34343 and 443, the only behaviors seen were passing or removing options. The story is more complicated for port 80 (http). There were seven paths that did not permit our testing methodology on port 80. In data packets our stateless server relies on instructions embedded in the data to determine its response. These seven paths appear to be application-level HTTP proxies, and we were foiled by the lack of a proper HTTP request in our data packets. They are labeled *Error* in the tables. We were able to go back and manually verify two of these paths were in fact HTTP proxies; we did not get a second chance to verify the other five. All seven were in the set that removed options from SYN packets, which is to be expected if they are full proxies. Two HTTP proxies that we manually verified removed options from data packets and resegmented TCP packets as well as proxies that are not HTTP-level ones.

There were no other unexpected results with unknown options, but we did observe some interesting results with the TIMESTAMP "known option in data" test. Four paths on port 80 and three paths on port 443 passed on a TIMESTAMP option to the responder, but it was not the one sent by the initiator. In these cases, although the responder sent TIMESTAMP in response, this was not returned to the initiator. This implies that the middlebox is independently negotiating and using timestamp with the server. These paths are labeled "*Changed*" in the tables. Paths in the *Removed* row in Table 5 correspond to those in the *Removed* or the *Changed* rows in Table 4 for all three ports. This implies that option removal on data segments is not the unknown nature of the option.

Returning to the middleboxes that remove unknown options from the SYN, we can use the results of additional tests to classify these into two distinct categories. In the first category, the SYN/ACK received is essentially that sent by the responder, whereas in the second the SYN/ACK appears to have been generated by the middlebox. In Sec. 4.4 we explain how fingerprints in the SYN/ACK let us distinguish the two. Paths in the first category appear to actively eliminate options (we label them "*Elim*" in Table 6), whereas a middlebox in the second category is acting as a proxy, and unknown options are removed as a side effect of this proxy behavior (these are labeled "*Proxy*").

These two categories (*Elim* and *Proxy*) also hold when we look at data segments (see Table 7). Paths that eliminate SYN options also eliminate data options, whereas paths that show proxy behavior on SYNs also exhibit proxy behavior for data. In particular, the proxy symptoms we see are Proxy Data Acks (Ack by the middlebox, see Sec. 4.4), segment caching (the middlebox caches and retransmit segments, see Sec. 4.5), and re-segmentation (splitting and coalescing of segments, see Sec. 4.6). These proxy middleboxes show symptoms of implementing most of the functionality of a full TCP stack, rather than just being a packet-level relay.

Before we ran this study, anecdotal evidence had suggested that cellular networks would be much more restrictive than other types of network. The results partially support this, as shown in Table 8. For port 80, eight out of 20 cellular networks that we tested remove options; six of the eight proxy the connection. WiFi hotspots are also relatively likely to remove options or proxy connections, especially for http. Overall though, the majority of paths do still pass new TCP options.

Table 7: Types of removal behavior (Data)

Path Type	Other observed effects	TCP Port 34343	80	443
Elim.	None	5	4	5
Proxy	Proxy Data ACK, Segment Caching, Re-segmentation	1	9	4
Total		6	13	9

Table 8: Option removal by Network Type

Network Type	Remove option (Proxy conn) port 34343	port 80	port 443
Cellular (out of 20)	4 (1)	8 (6)	4 (1)
Hotspot (out of 34)	1 (0)	6 (5)	4 (3)
Univ (out of 17)	0 (0)	3 (3)	0 (0)
Ent (out of 17)	1 (0)	3 (2)	1 (0)
Total	6	20	9

We conclude that it is still possible to extend TCP using TCP options, so long as the use of new options is negotiated in the SYN exchange, and so long as fallback to regular TCP behavior is acceptable. However, if we want ubiquitous deployment of a new feature, the story is more complicated. Especially for http, there are a significant number of middleboxes that proxy TCP sessions. For middleboxes that eliminate options, it seems likely that very simple updates or reconfiguration would allow a new standardized option to pass, assuming it were not considered a security risk. But for transparent proxies, the middlebox would not only need to pass the option, but also understand its semantics. Such paths are likely to be more difficult to upgrade.

4.2 Sequence Number Modification

TCP Selective Acknowledgement (SACK) [20] is an example of a TCP extension that uses TCP options that quote sequence numbers, in this case to indicate precisely which segments arrived at the receiver. How might middleboxes affect such extensions?

In our sequence number modification test, we examine both the outgoing and incoming initial sequence number (ISN) to see whether middleboxes modify the sequence numbers sent by the end systems. Table 9 shows the result. Paths where neither the outbound nor inbound sequence number is modified are labeled as *Unchanged*. Paths where the outbound or inbound sequence number is modified are labeled as *Mod. outbound* and *Mod. inbound*, respectively.

Table 9: Sequence Number Modification Test

Behavior	TCP Port 34343	80	443
Unchanged	126 (93%)	116 (82%)	128 (90%)
Mod. outbound	5 (4%)	5 (4%)	6 (4%)
Mod. inbound	0 (0%)	1 (1%)	1 (1%)
Mod. both	4 (3%)	13 (9%)	7 (5%)
Proxy (probably mod. both)	0 (0%)	7 (5%)	0 (0%)
Total	135 (100%)	142 (100%)	142 (100%)

Paths where both the outbound and inbound sequence numbers are modified are labeled as *Mod. both*.

Sequence numbers on at least 80% of paths arrive unchanged. However 7% of paths modify sequence numbers in at least one direction for port 34343 and 18% modify at least one direction for port 80. For port 80, the same seven paths identified earlier as having application-level HTTP proxies cannot be tested outbound, but do modify inbound sequence numbers and almost certainly modify both directions.

One might reasonably expect that middleboxes that proxy a connection would split a TCP connection into two sections, each with its own sequence space, but that other packet-level middleboxes would have no reason to modify TCP sequence numbers. If this were the case, then TCP extensions could refer to TCP sequence numbers in TCP options, safe in the knowledge that either the option would be removed in the SYN at a proxy, or sequence numbers would arrive unmodified. Unfortunately the story is not so simple.

At a TCP receiver, one use of sequence numbers is to verify the validity of a received segment. If an adversary can predict the TCP ports a connection will use, only the randomness of the initial sequence number prevents a spoofed packet from being injected into the connection. Unfortunately TCP stacks have a long history of generating predictable ISNs, so a number of firewall products try to help out by choosing a new more random ISN, and then rewriting all subsequent packets and acknowledgments to maintain consistency [15, 29].

We compared those paths that pass unknown options in the SYN with those that modify sequence numbers in at least one direction. On port 34343, 5 out of 9 allow unknown options and still modify the sequence numbers. For port 80, 7 out of 26 pass unknown options, and for port 443 it is 7 out of 14. The numbers are the same for unknown options in data packets.

We conclude that it is *unsafe* for TCP extensions to embed sequence numbers in TCP options (or anywhere else), even if the extension negotiates use via a new option in the SYN exchange.[†]

4.3 Sequence Space Holes

TCP is a reliable protocol; its cumulative Ack does not move forwards unless all preceding segments have been received. What would happen if from the vantage point of a middlebox, a TCP implementation violated these rules? Perhaps it wished to implement partial reliability analogous to PR-SCTP [28], or perhaps it simply stripes segments across more than one path in a similar manner to Multipath TCP?

We can distinguish two ways a middlebox might observe such a hole:

- **Data-First:** it sees segments before and after a hole, but does not see the segment from the hole. If the middlebox passes the segment after the hole, it sees it cumulatively acked by the recipient, despite the middlebox never seeing the data from the hole.
- **Ack-First:** It sees a segment of data, then an ack indicates the receiver has seen data not yet seen by the middlebox. If the middlebox passes the Ack, the next segment seen continues from the point acked, leaving a hole in the data seen by the middlebox.

These form the basis of our tests shown in Fig. 2. The left side is the initiator's time-line in both tests.

[†]SACK does embed sequence numbers in options, but it predates the existence of almost all middleboxes. We hope that these middleboxes are aware of SACK and either rewrite the options or explicitly remove SACK negotiation from the SYN exchange.

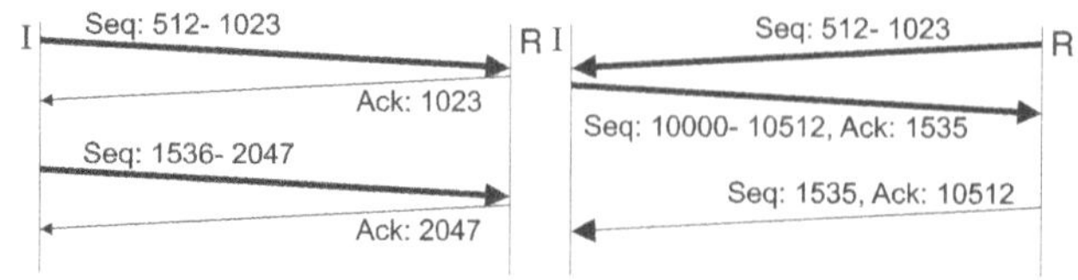

Figure 2: Sequence Hole Tests: data first (left) and ack first (right)

Table 10: Data-First Sequence Hole Test

Behavior	TCP Port 34343	80	443
Passed	131 (97%)	120 (85%)	135 (95%)
No response	2 (1%)	6 (4%)	2 (1%)
Duplicate Ack	1 (1%)	9 (6%)	5 (4%)
Test Error	1 (1%)	7 (5%)	0 (0%)
Total	135 (100%)	142 (100%)	142 (100%)

Table 10 shows the result of the data-first sequence hole test. Paths where the second Ack was correctly received are labeled *Passed*, and clearly have no middlebox that requires TCP flow reassembly. As before, on port 80 there are seven paths with http proxies we cannot fully test; these are labeled *Test Error*. The one path using port 34343 labeled *Test Error* was due to high packet loss during the experiment rather than middlebox interference.

The remaining cases are the most interesting. We observed two distinct middlebox behaviors:

- *No response* was received to the second data packet.
- A *Duplicate Ack* was received, indicating receipt of the first data packet and by implication, signaling loss of the packet in the hole.

A middlebox implementing a full TCP stack would be expected to break the path into two sections, separately acking packets from the initiator before sending the data to the responder. This would give the *Duplicate Ack* behavior. As expected, we see more such middleboxes on port 80.

A middlebox that does not respond to the second packet is clearly maintaining TCP state (or it would pass the second Ack), but it is not independently acking data. Its reasons for doing so are unclear—perhaps it is attempting to analyze the stream contents and is unwilling to pass an ack for data it has not seen? Whatever the reason, we still see more such middleboxes on port 80.

In the ack-first sequence hole test (Fig. 2, right), the initiator acks a segment beyond that which is received (i.e., proactive ack). The responder skips the data acked and sends an ack packet the sequence number of which follows on from the point that was acked. To receive a response packet from the responder, the segment from the initiator to the responder also contains data, but what we are interested in is whether the proactive ack is received, and subsequently whether the packet following the hole is received. Table 11 shows the results.

The results of this test were a surprise—even on port 34343, middleboxes interfered with end-to-end behavior 24% of the time. As before, seven paths on port 80 could not be tested. Of those that could be tested, we saw three distinct behaviors:

- On around 20% of paths we saw *no response* to the proactive ack. Either the proactive ack was dropped or the packet

Table 11: Ack-first Sequence Hole Test

Behavior	TCP Port 34343	80	443
Passed	102 (76%)	95 (67%)	105 (74%)
No response	28 (21%)	28 (20%)	29 (20%)
Ack fixed	4 (3%)	5 (4%)	3 (2%)
Retransmitted	1 (1%)	7 (5%)	5 (4%)
Test Error	0 (0%)	7 (5%)	0 (0%)
Total	135 (100%)	142 (100%)	142 (100%)

above the hole was dropped, but the lack of a response does not allow us to distinguish.

- On quite a few paths (labeled *Ack fixed*), an ack packet is received, but the sequence number of which follows the last packet sent by the responder as if we sent an ack without a hole. Perhaps the proactive ack was re-written by the outgoing middlebox to indicate the highest data cumulatively seen by the middlebox.

- On some paths, the middlebox itself actually *retransmitted* the last data packet sent by the responder from before the hole. These paths also sent back ack packets observed on *Ack fixed* paths, except for one path on port 80 and 443.

It is clear from these results that TCP extensions relying on sequence number holes are *unsafe*. Although some of the results can be explained by proxy behavior at middleboxes, some paths that did not exhibit clear proxy behavior (by performing separate acknowledgment) do affect both sequence holes and proactive acking. Perhaps some firewalls attempt to protect the initiator from potentially malicious proactive acks? [27].

One interesting observation is that around 10% of home networks give *no response* in the ack-first sequence hole test. This is striking because none of the home networks strip unknown options.

4.4 Proxy Acknowledgments

In Tables 6 and 7 we observed that a subset of the paths that remove TCP options appear to show TCP proxy behavior. We now elaborate on the tests we used to elicit this information.

A hypothetical TCP proxy[2] would likely split the TCP connection into two sections; one from the client to the proxy and one from the proxy to the server. Each section would effectively run its own TCP session, with only payload data passed between the two sections. Are the proxies we observed of this form, which is fairly easy to reason about, or is their behavior more complex?

One symptom of a TCP proxy would be that acknowledgments for data are locally generated by the middlebox. We performed two tests examining this behavior:

- **Proxy SYN-ACK:** Is the SYN/ACK locally generated by the proxy? In its SYN/ACKs, our responder generates quite characteristic values for the initial sequence number, advertised receive window, maximum segment size, and Window Scale options. It is improbable that a proxy would generate these values. We simply check the value of these fields in the SYN/ACK received by the initiator—if they differ then this is symptomatic of a proxy that crafts its own SYN/ACKs.

- **Proxy Data Ack:** Is data acknowledged by the proxy before delivering it to the destination? Our initiator sends a data packet to the responder, requesting the ack is sent on a packet that includes data. If the ack received does not include data, it is extremely likely it was generated by the proxy rather than the responder.

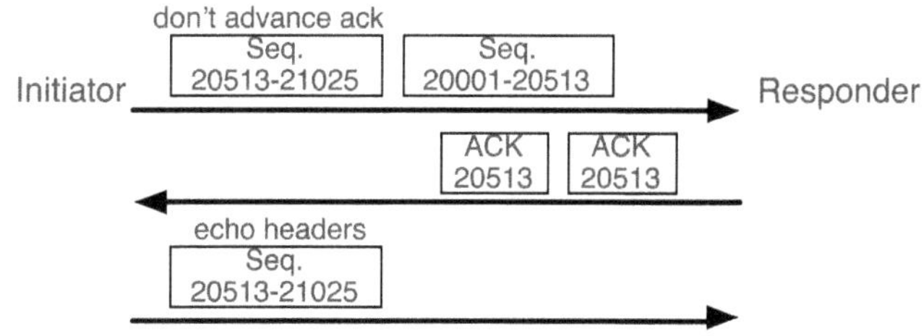

Figure 3: Retransmission Test

Neither test is conclusive by itself, but taken together they give a good picture of proxy behavior. As before, there are seven paths which have HTTP-level proxies; on port 80, all seven sent proxy SYN/ACKs, but could not be tested for proxy data acks. Tables 6 and 7 show the number of proxies identified. The set of paths showing Proxy SYN/ACK behavior is precisely the same as those showing either Proxy Data Ack or HTTP proxy behavior. Taken together, these tests provide good evidence for proxies of the form described above.

4.5 Inconsistent Retransmission

If a TCP sender retransmits a packet, but includes different data than the original in the retransmission, what happens? This might seem like a strange thing to do, but it might be advantageous for extensions that do not need stale data (such as VoIP over TCP). Given that we know sequence holes are a bad idea (see Sec. 4.3), it might make sense to fill the sequence hole with previously unsent data.

Such inconsistent retransmissions would be explicitly "corrected" by a traffic normalizer[15], as its role is to ensure that any downstream intrusion detection system sees a consistent picture. Equally, depending on their implementation, TCP proxies might reassert the original data. We set out to test what happens in reality.

Fig. 3 shows our retransmission test. The initiator sends two consecutive segments, but we request that the responder sends a cumulative ack only for the first segment, then a duplicate Ack. Any stateful middlebox will infer that the second segment has not been received by the responder, and depending on its implementation, it may retain the unacked segment. We then send a "retransmission" of the second packet, but with a different payload (one that requests the responder echo the packet headers so we can see what is received).

We also repeat the test, but with the "retransmitted" packet being either 16 bytes smaller or 16 bytes longer than the original packet.

From the responses, we can distinguish four distinct middlebox behaviors, as listed in Table 12:

- Most paths *passed* the inconsistent retransmission to the responder unmodified. In the case of port 34343, only one path did not do this.

- On some paths the initiator observes that the cumulative *Ack advanced*, but the headers were not echoed. This implies that the middlebox cached the original segment and resent it. Most of these paths were ones that we had previously identified as TCP proxies, but one on port 80 was not—it caches segments but does not separately ack data. We cannot know for sure, but this would be symptomatic of a traffic

Table 12: Results of Retransmission Test

Observed Behavior	34343 same	34343 smaller	34343 larger	80 same	80 smaller	80 larger	443 same	443 smaller	443 larger
	TCP Port / Retransmitting size								
Passed	134 (99%)	134 (99%)	132 (98%)	124 (87%)	124 (87%)	123 (87%)	138 (97%)	138 (97%)	136 (96%)
No response	0 (0%)	0 (0%)	1 (1%)	0 (0%)	0 (0%)	1 (1%)	0 (0%)	0 (0%)	1 (1%)
Ack adv'ced	1 (1%)	1 (1%)	1 (1%)	10 (7%)	10 (7%)	10 (7%)	4 (3%)	4 (3%)	4 (3%)
Reset conn	0 (%)	0 (0%)	0 (0%)	1 (1%)	1 (1%)	1 (1%)	0 (0%)	0 (0%)	0 (0%)
Error	0 (0%)	0 (0%)	1 (1%)	7 (5%)	7 (5%)	7 (5%)	0 (0%)	0 (0%)	1 (1%)
Total	135 (100%)			142 (100%)			142 (100%)		

normalizer or a snoop [3]. For port 443, one path in fact echoed headers after the separate cumulative ack packet for the retransmission of the 16 byte longer packet. However, what the responder received is a 16 byte piece that does not overlap with the original—the other part is probably cached by the middlebox.

- One path returned *no response* at all when the inconsistent retransmit was larger than the original, and did so for all ports. There is no obvious reason for such behavior, so we speculate it might be a minor bug in a middlebox implementation.

- One path on port 80 *reset the connection*. This seems to be a fairly draconian response.

The usual seven paths with HTTP proxies could not be tested. One path on port 34343 and one on port 443 also failed to complete the test due to high packet loss.

Overall, any extension that wished to use inconsistent retransmissions would encounter few problems, so long as it did not matter greatly whether the original or the retransmission actually arrives. The one path that resets connections might however give the designers of extensions cause for concern.

We note that the proposal for TCP extended options might result in retransmissions that appear inconsistent to legacy middleboxes, even if the payload is consistent. This might occur if the value of an extended option such as a selective acknowledgment changes between the original and the retransmission.

4.6 Re-segmentation

TCP provides a reliable bytestream abstraction to applications, and makes no promises that message boundaries are preserved. Some TCP extensions such as TcpCrypt wish to associate a new option with a particular data segment—in the case of TcpCrypt to carry a MAC for the data. How will such extensions be affected by middleboxes?

We expect that TCP proxies will coalesce small segments if a queue builds in the proxy, and might split segments if the proxy negotiates a larger MSS with the client than that negotiated by the server. However, our results show such proxies remove unknown options from the SYN exchange, so any adverse interaction (beyond falling back to regular TCP) is unlikely. Our concern therefore is whether there are middleboxes that are not proxies that re-segment packets. In particular, any middlebox that passes new options *and* also re-segments data might be problematic.

To test segment splitting, we simply send a full-sized segment. Our responder advertises a relatively small 512 byte MSS. Any middlebox advertising a more normal (larger) MSS will be forced to resegment larger data packets into smaller ones. In fact, MSS advertised by 16 SYN proxies we observed at port 80 varied between 1372 – 1460 bytes. We perform the test without option, that with

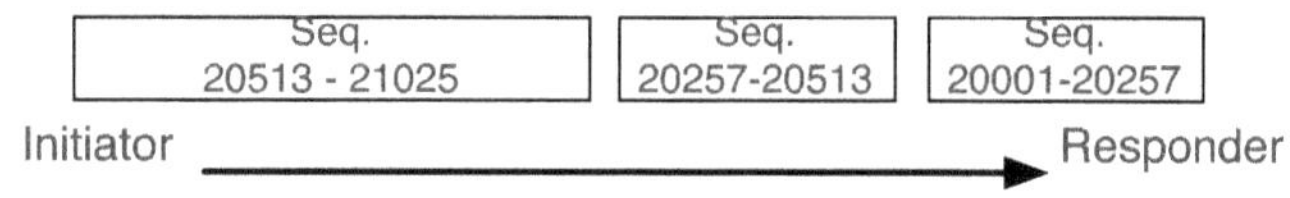

Figure 4: In-order Segment Coalescing Test

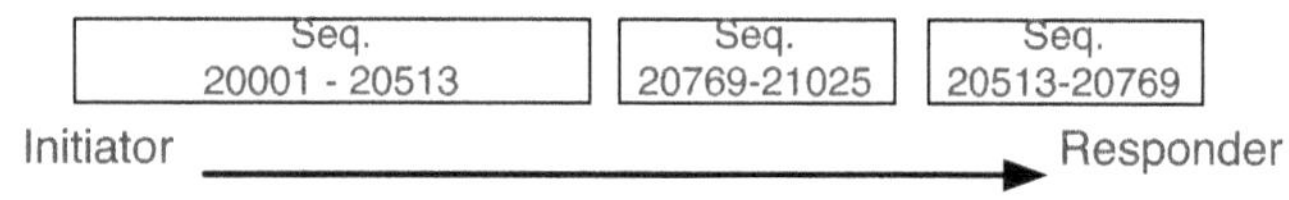

Figure 5: Queued Segment Coalescing Test

the known option (TIMESTAMP) and that with the unknown option (MP_DATA) to see if options are copied to the split segments.

We found that 1 path on port 34343, 9 paths on port 80 and 4 paths on port 443 split segments in this way. These are the same paths identified as proxies in Table 7. None passed options to the split segments.

The opposite of segment splitting is segment coalescing, where a middlebox combines two or more segments into a larger segment. To test for this, we must send two consecutive small segments and observe whether a single larger segment arrives. However, a middlebox that has the ability to coalesce might still not do so unless it is forced to queue the segments. We therefore perform two versions of the test, as shown in Figures 4 and 5.

- We test if segments are coalesced if the two small segments arrive in order (Fig. 4).

- We reorder the segments so that the small segments arrive after a gap in the sequence space, creating an opportunity for middleboxes to queue them (Fig. 5). We then send the segment which fills the sequence hole. If a middlebox queued the small segments, this will release them, potentially allowing coalescing to occur.

As before, we repeat the tests without options and with both known and unknown options.

Table 13 shows the results. Most middleboxes running TCP proxies coalesced segments in both in-order and queued cases (labeled *Coal. both*), and the other proxies did so in only the queued case (labeled *Coal. queued*). No middlebox copies either known or unknown options to the coalesced segments. One non-proxy path did coalesce segments in the in-order test on ports 80 and 34343 (labeled *Coal. ordered*), but passed all the other tests. Interestingly, it only coalesced when options were not present.

As before, on port 80 seven HTTP proxy paths could not be tested. Three other cases gave unexpected results. One path on port 34343 failed in the queued test that does not contain options,

Table 13: Results of Segment Coalescing Test

Observed Behavior	TCP Port 34343	80	443
Passed	132 (98%)	123 (87%)	138 (97%)
Coal. ordered	1 (1%)	1 (1%)	0 (0%)
Coal. queued	1 (1%)	3 (2%)	1 (1%)
Coal. both	0 (0%)	6 (4%)	3 (2%)
Error	1 (0%)	9 (6%)	0 (0%)
Total	135 (100%)	142 (100%)	142 (100%)

but did not coalesce in the other tests. One path on port 80 acked only the third segment in the queued test—returned no payload; other tests show this path does not show proxy behavior and does pass TCP options, but gives no reply to the data-first sequence hole. Likely it is also ignoring out of order segments in this test too. The other path on port 80 showed similar behavior except that it does not return payload even in the in-order test and does cache segments. We do not know what form of middleboxes these are, but their behavior seems fragile.

Among those paths that coalesced, we saw quite a variety of behavior. The two small segments we sent were of 244 bytes. When coalescing occurred, depending on the path, the first coalesced segment received could be of 256, 488, 500 or 512 bytes in the in-order test and 256, 476 or 488 bytes in the queued test. We have no idea what motivates these particular segment sizes.

Overall, the story is quite good for TCP extensions. Although middleboxes do split and coalesce segments, none did so while passing unknown options (indeed one changed its behavior when options were present). Thus it seems relatively safe to assume that if an option is passed, it arrives with the segment on which it was sent.

4.7 Intelligent NICs

Most of the experiments in this paper probe the network behavior, but with the rise of "intelligent" Network Interface Cards, even the NIC can have embedded TCP knowledge. Thus the NIC itself might fight with new TCP extensions.

We are concerned in particular with TCP Segmentation Offload (TSO), where the host OS sends large segments and relies on the NIC to resegment to match the MTU or the receiver's MSS. In Linux, the TCP implementation chooses the split segment size to allow all the TCP options to be copied to all the split segments while still fitting within the MTU. But what do NICs actually do—do they really copy the options to all the split segments?

We tested twelve TSO NICs from four different vendors; Intel (82546, 82541GI, 82566MM, 82577LM, 82567V, 82598EB), Nvidia (MCP55), Broadcom (BCM95723, BCM5755) and Marvell (88E8053, 88E8056, 88E8059). For this, our initiator tool consists of a user application and a custom Linux kernel, and we reused the responder tool from the earlier middlebox tests. The key points about the experiment are:

- Our application calls write() to send five MSS of data to the socket layer at one time.
- The OS TCP stack composes one TCP segment that includes all the data and passes it to the TSO layer. This large segment also includes the TIMESTAMP or MP_DATA TCP option.
- The NIC performs TSO, splitting the large segment into multiple segments and transmits them.
- Our responder receives these segments and responds with a segment echoing the headers in its payload so we can see what was received.

All the NICs we tested correctly copied the options to all the split segments. TSO is now sufficiently commonplace so that designers of extensions to TCP should assume it. The implication is that TCP options must be designed so that when they are duplicated on consecutive segments, this does not adversely affect correctness or performance.

We also tested Large Receive Offload (LRO) behavior with the Intel 82598EB ten gigabit ethernet NIC to see how TCP options are treated. First, we receive bulk TCP traffic with the NIC; all packets in the traffic include an MP_DATA option with the same values. Second, we receive similar traffic, but change the values of the MP_DATA between packets. We also conducted the same tests with a TIMESTAMP option instead of the MP_DATA. For both option kinds, packets were coalesced only when their option values are same. The coalesced segment has one of the options on the original segments. This behavior seems sane: on this particular NIC, LRO simply tries to undo what TSO did by duplicating options. If options are different, no coalescing happens.

Both TSO and LRO seem to forbid TCP extensions to reliably use the counts of sent and received options for signaling. Instead, TCP extensions experiencing offload should be prepared to handle both duplicate and "merged" options. Disabling offload altogether at endpoints is possible, but will result in a performance penalty.

5. PROTOCOL DESIGN IMPLICATIONS

5.1 Multipath TCP

As more and more mobile devices come equipped with multiple network interfaces such as 3G and WiFi, single path transport is fundamentally unable to utilize the aggregate capacity and robustness of the separate links. Multipath TCP (MPTCP) [11, 12, 30] enables each TCP connection to be striped across multiple paths, while offering the same reliable, in-order, byte-oriented transport service to unmodified applications.

At first sight, MPTCP seems straightforward to implement, but the design has been evolving for a couple of years now, with most changes aimed at accommodating the middleboxes deployed today in the Internet. The measurement results in this paper have guided the design, now undergoing standardization at the IETF.

To negotiate MPTCP, the endpoints use the MP_CAPABLE TCP option on SYN packets; they fall back to regular TCP if either endpoint does not support MPTCP or middleboxes along the path remove the new option. Our results indicate that if the option handshake goes through, MPTCP options will also be allowed on data segments. To be on the safe side though, MPTCP reverts to regular TCP if its options do not get through on any of the data segments sent during the first RTT of the connection.

Sequence numbers are fundamental to the MPTCP design. It would be easiest to reuse the TCP sequence numbers by striping segments coming from the TCP stack across different paths (e.g., by selecting different addresses for the same endpoint). A shortcoming of this approach is that, on each path, MPTCP subflows will look like TCP flows with holes in their sequence space. Our results show that 2 – 10 % of paths do not allow sequence holes by data segments and around 25 % of paths do not allow those by Ack segments to pass, and so MPTCP *had to* use one sequence space per subflow to pass through middleboxes. This in turn implies the need to add an additional data-level sequence number to allow the receiver to put segments back in order before passing them to the application.

How should the sender signal the data sequence numbers to the receiver? There are two possibilities: use TCP options or embed them in the TCP payload. Sending control information in the payload implies some form of payload chunking, similar to TLS-style TLV encoding. This would cause the inconsistent retransmission that is risky (see Sec. 4.5). This approach also would make it difficult for future middleboxes to work with MPTCP, as they would be forced to parse the payload. From these reasons it is cleaner to encode data sequence numbers as TCP options.

The simplest solution is use a TCP option to add a data sequence number (DSN) to each segment. Although we observed no middlebox that both passed options and resegmented data, NICs performing TCP Segmentation Offload (TSO) would replicate the data sequence number onto multiple segments. Multiple segments would then have the same DSN—not what is desired.

Such a failure is a consequence of an *implicit* mapping of subflow sequence numbers (in the TCP headers) to data sequence numbers (in the options). The solution adopted by MPTCP is to make this mapping explicit: a data sequence mapping option carries the starting data sequence number, the starting subflow sequence number and the length of the mapping. This allows MPTCP to support both TSO as well as LRO if coalescing happens only for segments with duplicate options.

To complicate things more, we have seen that subflow sequence numbers may be rewritten by middleboxes. To avoid this problem, MPTCP signals subflow sequence numbers relative to the initial subflow sequence number.

Finally there is one form of application-level gateway we did not test for—a NAT with knowledge of FTP or SIP that rewrites IP addresses in the TCP payload. Such rewriting can change the payload length and would be really bad for MPTCP: Reordering at the receiver might result in arbitrary-ordered data being passed to the application. MPTCP includes a checksum in the DSN mapping option to guard against such payload changes, and falls back to single path TCP if required.

There are many more design decisions in MPTCP that were dictated by verified, anecdotal or just possible middlebox behaviors. We quickly list two here:

- Retransmitting data: to avoid the problems we observed with sequence holes, MPTCP always sends the original data on retransmission, even though that same data may already have been received by the receiver via a different subflow.

- Proactive ACKing middleboxes might fail before sending data to the receiver; this would halt MPTCP if data-level ACKs were inferred from subflow ACKs. Although we observed no pro-actively acking middlebox that would pass MPTCP options, MPTCP includes a data-level acknowledgement, sent as a TCP option, to guard against such failures.

MPTCP was designed from ground up to co-exist with current middleboxes and to play nicely with future ones. Our tests conducted in this paper have provided a solid basis for MPTCP's design choices.

5.2 TcpCrypt

TcpCrypt is a proposed extension to TCP that opportunistically encrypts all TCP traffic [4, 5]. TcpCrypt endpoints share a public key on the wire and use that to derive a session key. After the initial handshake TcpCrypt connections are secure against eavesdropping, segment insertion or modification and replay attacks. During the initial handshake, connections are susceptible to man-in-the-middle or downgrade attacks, but TcpCrypt also provides hooks to allow application-level authentication of the encrypted connection.

TcpCrypt was motivated by the observation that server computing power is the performance bottleneck. To make ubiquitous encryption possible, highly asymmetric public key operations are arranged so that the expensive work is performed by the client which does not need to handle high connection setup rates. This is in contrast to SSL/TLS where the server does more work. This reversal of roles together with ever increasing computing power makes it feasible to have "always on" protection [5].

Use of TcpCrypt is negotiated with new CRYPT options in SYN segments, and keying material is included in INIT messages that are sent in both directions in the TCP payload before application data is sent. The INIT exchange also probes the path support for new options on data segments, thus coping with any middleboxes that allow new options on SYNs but not on data. After the initial negotiation, TcpCrypt can be either in the *encrypting* or *disabled* states. In the *disabled* state TcpCrypt behaves exactly like regular TCP. No further transitions are allowed once the connection reaches one of these two states [4]. This is because applications can query the TcpCrypt connection state and use it to make authentication decisions.

In the *encrypting* phase TcpCrypt encrypts the TCP payload with the shared session key and also adds a TCP MAC option to each segment that is validated at the receiver. The keyed MAC covers the encrypted payload as well as parts of the TCP header: the sequence numbers, the TCP options, and the length, as well the acknowledgement sequence number. The MAC covers neither the TCP ports nor the IP header to allow network address translation.

TcpCrypt only accepts segments whose MAC is correct; when the TCP MAC option is missing or incorrect the segment is silently dropped. Hence, each segment will have a unique MAC, which also will prevent segments from being coalesced by LRO.

Middleboxes that resegment TCP packets would cause TcpCrypt's MAC to fail validation, causing the connection to stall. Unlike MPTCP, fallback to vanilla TCP behavior after entering the *encrypting* state is not viable. Fortunately we have not observed any paths that both pass new TCP options and resegment data. TSO would also cause TcpCrypt to fail, but the OS can disable this—the performance penalty is negligible compared to the cost of encryption.

To guard against segment injection and replay attacks the MAC needs to cover the TCP sequence numbers. This would fail when middleboxes rewrite the ISN, so TcpCrypt includes the number of bytes since the start of the connection in the pseudo-header covered by the MAC rather than the absolute sequence number.

The MAC also covers acknowledgement sequence numbers. Any proactive ACKs sent by middleboxes will just be dropped. If no ACKs are passed end-to-end the connection will fail. Fortunately, this problem is unlikely as such boxes are proxies (see Sec. 4.4), and so would prevent TcpCrypt negotiation in the initial handshake by removing the SYN options. Finally, HTTP-level proxies require a valid HTTP header, which TcpCrypt would hide. However, such proxies also prevent the initial handshake.

A key difference between TcpCrypt and MPTCP is the distinction between disabled and enabled; when TcpCrypt is enabled it gives extra security to applications, which then rely on the protection provided. Once enabled it is unacceptable from a security point of view to revert to TCP. MPTCP, on the other hand, provides the same reliable, in-order, byte-stream service to applications, and can detect problems and revert to TCP at almost any time during a connection's lifetime.

5.3 Extending TCP Option Space

Extending TCP option space has been a discussion topic on IETF mailing lists on many occasions, starting as early as 2004. The main reason that no solution was standardized is because people felt there was no pressing need for more option space. MPTCP uses a relatively large option space, as does TcpCrypt; this usage, combined with existing options in use, leaves very little TCP option space remaining. With MPTCP approaching standardization, extending the TCP option space has now gained enough support to happen in practice.

Option space is scarce on both SYN and regular data packets. Extending the option space on the first SYN (active open) is difficult because of the need to be backward compatible: if one adds more options to the SYN, a legacy host might treat the extra options as application data, corrupting the connection [19].

Extending the option space in regular segments seems straightforward at first sight; the sending host simply needs to "extend" the data offset field in the TCP header. This is what the Long Option (LO) draft [9] suggests: add a new LO option that a 16 bit-wide value of the data offset. As with the other extensions we have discussed, resegmentation would be problematic here, but we did not observe any middlebox that passes options and resegments. Still, it would be good if the use of long options did not preclude TSO, and this solution would—every split segment would appear to carry a long option when in fact only the first would.

To allow TSO, the sender must be explicit about the placement of extended options, and solutions will resemble MPTCP's data sequence mapping. The receiver will be told the start of extended options and their length[‡].

The same constraints apply as in the case of MPTCP signaling: the ISN may be rewritten, thus the sequence number must be relative to the beginning of the flow. If middleboxes change payload length (for instance by rewriting IP addresses for FTP/SIP), the extended option sequence numbers will be inaccurate; a checksum covering the extra options is needed to cover such cases.

Another problem with extending TCP option space is the interaction between middleboxes that understand deployed TCP options, such as SACK. A middlebox might modify sequence numbers in both the header and SACK blocks, but not understand the LO option. However, if the sender places a SACK block in the extended option space, such middleboxes will not see it, and so cannot correct the selective acknowledgment numbers. We observed a significant number of middleboxes that modify sequence numbers and pass the unknown TCP options, so this problem does not seem hypothetical.

Segment caching middleboxes can also affect the LO option. If the options in the payload differ between the original and the retransmitted segments, the middlebox will consider them as different application data. We observed such segments could induce connection failures.

Work arounds are possible—SACK blocks would have to be placed in the regular options space, and no option in the extended option space would be allowed to change on a retransmission. But such workarounds rather limit the usefulness of extended options and increase both the complexity of implementations and the potential for subtle bugs.

6. CONCLUSION

Our goal in this paper has been to determine whether it is still possible to extend TCP. In particular, what limitations are imposed on TCP extensions by middleboxes and by "intelligent" NIC hardware? To answer these questions necessitated building novel measurement tools and recruiting volunteers from all over the world to run them on a wide range of networks.

[‡]This is very much the functionality provided by the urgent pointer, but this is known not to go well through middleboxes[14]

From our results we conclude that the middleboxes implementing layer 4 functionality are very common—at least 25% of paths interfered with TCP in some way beyond basic firewalling. We also conclude that it is still possible to extend TCP using its intended extension mechanism—TCP options—but that there are some caveats. Here are some guidelines:

- Negotiate new features on the SYN exchange before use.
- Be robust if an option is removed from the SYN/ACK—just because the server agrees to use a feature does not mean the client sees that agreement.
- Assume segments will be split (by TSO) and options duplicated on those segments.
- Assume segments will be coalesced by LRO and some of duplicated options eliminated.

There are also some warning stories, regarding behavior that is not safe to assume:

- Do not assume sequence numbers arrive unmodified—if you have to quote them, quote bytes from the start of the connection rather than absolute sequence numbers.
- Do not leave gaps in the sequence space—middleboxes need to see all the packets.
- Retransmitting inconsistent information is risky.
- Proxies are common, especially on port 80, and will strip TCP options.
- If options are removed, don't assume message boundaries will be preserved.
- Some middleboxes are surprisingly fragile to out of order packets.

Based on this information, we looked at whether three extensions to TCP had made sensible choices. We found that for the most part they had; in fact they were rather tightly constrained by middlebox behaviors to the solutions they had chosen. Of the three extensions we considered, TCP Long Option presents the greatest cause for concern. In particular, it becomes quite easy with long options to produce behavior that looks to a middlebox like inconsistent retransmission due to the contents of extended options changing. Such inconsistent retransmission is demonstrably unsafe. If TCP Long Option were to be deployed, it would require additional constraints to avoid this problem.

Here are some guidelines for middlebox designers:

- Do not drop packets including new options: this makes deploying new options very difficult as it impacts performance. Remove new options instead, if new functionality is not be allowed.
- Resegmentation should only be enabled if new options are not allowed to pass. Otherwise, TCP extensions wishing the option to be strictly bound to the original segment will fail to be deployed.
- Be consistent in the treatment of segments with new options: if new options are allowed on the SYN, they should be allowed both on the SYN/ACK and the data segments.
- Inconsistent retransmissions might happen for good reasons: they should be allowed through whenever possible.

Middleboxes currently deployed in the wild are relatively benign from our measurements; all paths conformed to our first three recommendations. For example, none of them dropped segments including new options. Resegmentation was only observed for full TCP proxies that prohibit new extensions from being negotiated, or on segments that do not contain options. Finally, when new options got through in the initial exchange, they were also allowed in the data segments.

In general, we note that it is tricky to implement stateful processing of TCP segments in middleboxes that do not behave like full proxies. For instance, some middleboxes gave no response when they saw holes in the sequence number space, and one middlebox reset the connection when they saw inconsistent retransmissions.

We urge middlebox designers to consider explicitly whether they want to allow new TCP extensions when implementing certain functionality. It is much better to stop new negotiation of new extensions than to allow it through only to fail unexpectedly later. Failure to do so seriously complicates the seemingly easy task of extending TCP; we have experienced this in our long running quest to standardize MPTCP.

We continue our work to extend its coverage in both tests run and networks examined. Long-term continuous measurements are necessary to study the evolution of middleboxes and their effects on the Internet; this paper only presents a snapshot. Recent work has advocated using HTTP as the narrow waist of the future Internet [25]. It would be interesting to conduct measurements to test whether HTTP is allowed to evolve, or has itself already ossified.

7. ACKNOWLEDGMENTS

We especially want to thank the volunteers from all over the world who ran our test code; without their help, we would have been unable to gather these results. Data traces and tools used in this paper are publicly available [8]. We also thank the anonymous reviewers for their helpful feedback. Michio Honda was funded by JSPS KAKENHI (21-5729). Costin Raiciu, Adam Greenhalgh and Mark Handley were partially supported by the CHANGE project funded by the European Commission in its Seventh Framework programme.

8. REFERENCES

[1] M. Allman. On the Performance of Middleboxes. *ACM IMC*, 35(2):307–312, 2003.

[2] A. Bakre and B. Badrinath. I-TCP: Indirect TCP for Mobile Hosts. In *Proc. IEEE ICDCS*, pages 136–143, 1995.

[3] H. Balakrishnan, S. Seshan, E. Amir, and R. Katz. Improving TCP/IP Performance over Wireless Networks. In *Proc. ACM MOBICOM*, pages 2–11, 1995.

[4] A. Bittau, D. Boneh, M. Hamburg, M. Handley, D. Mazieres, and Q. Slack. Cryptographic protection of TCP Streams (tcpcrypt). *draft-bittau-tcp-crypt-00.txt*, July 2010.

[5] A. Bittau, M. Hamburg, M. Handley, D. Mazieres, and D. Boneh. The case for ubiquitous transport-level encryption. In *Proc. USENIX Security Symposium*, Aug 2010.

[6] B. Carpenter and S. Brim. Middleboxes: Taxonomy and Issues. *RFC 3234*, Feb. 2002.

[7] R. Chakravorty, S. Katti, J. Crowcroft, and I. Pratt. Flow Aggregation for Enhanced TCP over Wide-Area Wireless. In *Proc. IEEE INFOCOM*, pages 1754–1764, 2003.

[8] Dataset for Middlebox Measurement. URL `http://web.sfc.wide.ad.jp/~micchie/mbox-dataset.html`.

[9] W. Eddy and A. Langley. Extending the Space Available for TCP Options. *Internet Draft*, Jul. 2008.

[10] R. Fonseca, G. Porter, R. Katz, S. Shenker, and I. Stoica. IP options are not an option. *Tech. Rep. UCB/EECS- 2005-24*, 2005.

[11] A. Ford, C. Raiciu, M. Handley, S. Barre, and J. Iyengar. Architectural guidelines for multipath TCP development. *RFC 6182*, Mar. 2011.

[12] A. Ford, C. Raiciu, M. Handley, and O. Bonaventure. TCP Extensions for Multipath Operation with Multiple Addresses. *Internet Draft*, July. 2011.

[13] B. Ford, P. Srisuresh, and D. Kegel. Peer-to-Peer Communication Across Network Address Translators. *USENIX ATC*, 2005.

[14] F. Gont and A. Yourtchenko. On the Implementation of the TCP Urgent Mechanism. *RFC 6093*, Jan. 2011.

[15] M. Handley, V. Paxson, and C. Kreibich. Network intrusion detection: evasion, traffic normalization, and end-to-end protocol semantics. In *Proc. USENIX Security Symposium*, 2001.

[16] S. Hätönen, A. Nyrhinen, L. Eggert, S. Strowes, P. Sarolahti, and M. Kojo. An Experimental Study of Home Gateway. *ACM IMC*, pages 260–266, 2010.

[17] V. Jacobson, R. Braden, and D. Borman. TCP Extensions for High Performance. *RFC 1323*, May. 1992.

[18] J.Border, M. Kojo, J. Griner, G. Montenegro, and Z. Shelby. Performance Enhancing Proxies Intended to Mitigate Link-Related Degradations. *RFC 3135*, Jun. 2001.

[19] Re: [tcpm] Extending the TCP option space - yet another approach. http://www.ietf.org/mail-archive/web/tcpm/current/msg06481.html.

[20] M. Mathis, J. Mahdavi, S. Floyd, and A. Romanow. TCP Selective Acknowledgment Options. *RFC 2018*, Oct. 1996.

[21] A. Medina, M. Allman, and S. Floyd. Measuring the Evolution of Transport Protocols in the Internet. *ACM CCR*, 35(2):37–52, 2005.

[22] P. Srisuresh and M. Holdrege. IP Network Address Translator (NAT) Terminology and Considerations. *RFC 2663*, Aug. 1999.

[23] J. Padhye and S. Floyd. On Inferring TCP Behavior. In *ACM SIGCOMM*, pages 287–298, Oct. 2001.

[24] V. Paxson. End-to-End Internet Packet Dynamics. In *Proc. ACM SIGCOMM*, pages 139–152, 1997.

[25] L. Popa, A. Ghodsi, and I. Stoica. HTTP as the Narrow Waist of the Future Internet. In *Proc. ACM Hotnets*, 2010.

[26] S. Savage. Sting: a TCP-based Network Measurement Tool. In *USENIX USITS*, 1999.

[27] S. Savage, N. Cardwell, D. Wetherall, and T. Anderson. TCP Congestion Control with a Misbehaving Receiver. *ACM CCR*, 29(5):71–78, 1999.

[28] R. Stewart, M. Ramalho, and et al. Stream Control Transmission Protocol (SCTP) Partial Reliability Extension. *RFC 3758*, May. 2004.

[29] D. Watson, M. Smart, G. R. Malan, and F. Jahanian. Protocol Scrubbing: Network Security Through Transparent Flow Modification. *IEEE/ACM ToN*, 12(2):261–273, 2004.

[30] D. Wischik, C. Raiciu, A. Greenhalgh, and M. Handley. Design, implementation and evaluation of congestion control for multipath TCP. In *Proc. USENIX NSDI*, 2011.

Summary Review Documentation for

"Is it Still Possible to Extend TCP?"

Authors: M. Honda, Y. Nishida, C. Raiciu, A. Greenhalgh, M. Handley, H. Tokuda

Reviewer #1

Strengths: Interesting, timely problem. Pretty thorough and extensive measurement setup and analysis. Good tie-in to actual system/application implications!

Weaknesses: Maybe a bit dry. I would like to see some more details/insights on the measurement setup/process.

Comments to Authors: I dont have anything seriously against this paper. This is a relevant and timely problem, and a pretty thorough study with a set of good implications for protocol designers.

I found the abstract a bit jarring -- understanding how tcp extensions would work in the wild is a valid and interesting study in of itself! I worry that you may throw readers off with the needless rant about Internet ossifications etc; I don't see why you need a philsophical stance here.

In Section 3.3, can you also comment about the diversity in ISPs in your dataset rather than just "access network"; from the discussion you seem to count each "cafe" as an access network when in theory it's the upstream ISP that could potentially be the cause of trouble. On a related note, it might also be interesting to see if the pathological cases you see (e.g., the 7 http proxies) have something in common w.r.t ISP?

I would also like to hear about how you gathered volunteers for running the tool -- just friends, released on a website and the profile of people who are willing to try this (e.g., did they need to be proficient in python?)

Also, it might be useful to create a high-level taxonomy of the testing tool; right now it comes across as a series of corner cases you came up with for the specific protocols you tested. That is perfectly fine, I am curious if there was a systematic way in which you created these test cases?

Reviewer #2

Strengths: To my knowledge this is the first paper that reports a large scale systematic measurement study on the impact of middleboxes on TCP options. Very clearly defined objective, systematic study, clear results, that others know how to use.

Weaknesses: I do not have a specific concern, but a general feeling that I wish the paper could have gone a bit deeper. for example, besides the specific conclusion that "We conclude that it is still possible to extend TCP using TCP options, so long as the use of new options is negotiated in the SYN exchange, and so long as fallback to regular TCP behavior is acceptable", can we also learn something more general from this study?

Comments to Authors: None.

Reviewer #3

Strengths: Careful experiments. Solid writing. Good discussion on implications.

Weaknesses: Too few paths, 135 to be precise. To draw the level of conclusions that this paper does, it needs at least two orders of magnitude more paths. For e.g., if middlebox will do something bad it would also strip out TCP options is a key insight that is used multiple times. It is unclear if this is universally true.

Several of the implications and the tests are specific to multi-path TCP or TCP Crypt, rather than to all possible TCP extensions. It is OK to have some editorial bias and the more general insights are called out fairly well. However, this paper isn't really about all possible extensions to TCP, so some care in articulation would help.

Comments to Authors: In many places you talk about how HTTP proxies hindering probing, but I don't think you spell out the reason why anywhere... Is this a fundamental problem (guess not) or something that the current tool wasn't geared to circumvent. For example, it could carry the signaling between the initiator and responder as HTTP payload. I thnk the lack of properly formatted HTTP may be what is crimping the test here...

There is also some confusion as to which way connection initiations are happening. Does the remote script primarily serve as a client? I can't see how it can easily act as a server due to NATs and firewalls...

You certainly need measurements from a lot more paths, one to two orders of magnitude more.

Since only a few paths have middleboxes, it is highly likely that you results are due to just a handful of middleboxes discovered along the observed paths; it is dangerous to generalize from such a small sample...

The tests are all very simple; nothing wrong with that; but the contribution is primarily in terms of what the tests reveal and the implications to future design.

3.1, the tool need admin privs to use raw sockets... Not as simple as you make it out to be...

3.3, core is "mostly dumb"... net neutrality violations mostly result in throttles but not any rewritition/ policing?

It would be interesting if you can figure out _where_ along the network path these middleboxes were found.

3.3, how did you classify clients; as HotSpot/Cellular/Univ? Human annotation or ISP names?

Table 2, too few samples, esp: the interesting ones that have middleboxes.

3.3, middlebox behavior, you blame inability to detect SYN/ACK option stripping on to the statelessness of your tool, but that doesn't seem to be accurate.

4.3, "We hope that these middleboxes are aware of SACK"... are they or are they not? Hoping doesn't do...

4.7, the main trouble is that simply duplicating options onto all segments, as TSO does isn't enough in many cases...

Reviewer #4

Strengths: Detailed catalog of behavior "in-the-wild". Relatively well thought out experiments, and some unexpected findings.

Weaknesses: Writing is repetitive. A number of 'problems' were due to mis/aggresively configured HTTP proxies and do not reflect behavior of other TCP flows.

Comments to Authors: Is there a reason for the distribution of the 142 networks in the paper? They are not representative of Internet traffic volume, and it is not clear that they are representative of middlebox behavior.

The related work should refer to the TCP Sidecar paper (IMC 2006) which describes how active measurements can go through middleboxes.

For the most part, the results are not surprising. Application layer gateways try to parse data and fail if they don't see everything. Proxies/middleboxes that regenerate sequence numbers don't preserve options that refer to literal sequence numbers (much like FTP PORT command and NAT interaction). However, the paper is valuable in that it provides a systematic catalog of anecdotal behavior.

The paper is repetitive, and the writing verbose. The information here can be fit into a very good seven page paper, as opposed to the loose fourteen pager that is presented. Section 4.5+ adds very litle that has not already been stated or could be put inline with the other results. The entire issue with the seven HTTP proxies is a red herring and could be mentioned once in a footnote.

The paper is also very difficult to follow since the tables are scattered all over, making it difficult to refer to them while reading the text.

Reviewer #5

Strengths: An extensive study. I particularly like that the test traffic is controlled at both ends of the path (by having clients voluntarily download and run a test program) as it is much less limiting than client or server only approaches. Useful results that are not otherwise known. Anyone seriously looking to extend TCP will want to read this paper.

Weaknesses: The paper is a bit ad hoc. The questions that are asked about how middleboxes handle TCP are mostly driven by efforts to deploy a multipath TCP, which is both good (they are relevant questions!) and bad (as it causes them to focus heavily on sequence numbers and is unclear that they will cover the needs of other extensions that may come). The paper would benefit from being a bit more systematic in its exploration of the space.

Comments to Authors: Thanks for an interesting paper; I have relatively few comments.

I think your paper will benefit from stepping back a bit to separate it from MTCP. What other aspects of middlebox behavior might be important for extensions? For example, are there games with flow control? What about the window scale, MSS, and authentication options, etc., as they at least seem worth some study? One exercise you might attempt is to go through all known extensions and make a a table with the TCP header fields or other properties/invariants on which they depend for correct behavior.

People are likely to read your paper to get guidance on what is safe/unsafe. Thus you might provide an easily accessible and complete summary of the takeaways (that is more comprehensive and standalone than in the conclusion).

I'd also be interested in recommendations to middlebox developers for what to do or not to do wrt unsupported options to maximize the ability for future extensions, i.e., how can we make the future better. Is this already done?

Section 5 seems misnamed. It is really a set of three case studies of how TCP extensions should work with TCP options. The bit that I found odd here is that the extensions have been designed in light of what was known about middlebox behavior by the authors. The presentation makes it sound like there are these new protocols that are to be assessed to see how they will interact with middleboxes -- and they are found to be mostly compatible.

Response from the Authors

First, we made the description on our dataset clearer; for example, how we collect data, and how we identified the venue.
Second, we added a few paragraphs guiding middlebox design that will work together future TCP extensions.
Third, we added a sentence describing how HTTP proxies behave on manually verified two paths.
In addition to these update, we've polished the entire document to provide more precise and explicit information. Also, we added results of tests for Large Receive Offload (LRO) as supplemental information.

Q-score: Proactive Service Quality Assessment in a Large IPTV System

Han Hee Song[§], Zihui Ge[‡], Ajay Mahimkar[‡], Jia Wang[‡], Jennifer Yates[‡], Yin Zhang[§], Andrea Basso[‡], Min Chen[‡]

The University of Texas at Austin[§]
Austin, TX, USA

AT&T Labs – Research [‡]
Florham Park, NJ, USA

{hhsong,yzhang}@cs.utexas.edu {gezihui,mahimkar,jiawang,jyates,basso,mc4381}@research.att.com

Abstract — In large-scale IPTV systems, it is essential to maintain high service quality while providing a wider variety of service features than typical traditional TV. Thus service quality assessment systems are of paramount importance as they monitor the user-perceived service quality and alert when issues occurs. For IPTV systems, however, there is no simple metric to represent user-perceived service quality and Quality of Experience (QoE). Moreover, there is only limited user feedback, often in the form of noisy and delayed customer calls. Therefore, we aim to approximate the QoE through a selected set of performance indicators in a proactive (*i.e.*, detect issues before customers reports to call centers) and scalable fashion.

In this paper, we present a service quality assessment framework, Q-score, which accurately learns a small set of performance indicators most relevant to user-perceived service quality, and proactively infers service quality in a single score. We evaluate Q-score using network data collected from a commercial IPTV service provider and show that Q-score is able to predict 60% of the service problems that are reported by customers with 0.1% false positives. Through Q-score, we have (i) gained insight into various types of service problems causing user dissatisfaction, including why users tend to react promptly to sound issues while late to video issues; (ii) identified and quantified the opportunity to proactively detect the service quality degradation of individual customers before severe performance impact occurs; and (iii) observed possibility to allocate customer care workforce to potentially troubling service areas before issues break out.

Categories and Subject Descriptors

C.4 [**Computer-Performance of Systems**]: Reliability, availableity, and serviceability

General Terms

Management, Reliability

Keywords

IPTV, Service, Quality, QoE, Assessment, Analysis, Video

1. INTRODUCTION

IPTV technologies are transforming the global television industry, enabling new operators to provide TV services whilst also enabling a wealth of innovative new IP-based services integrated with more traditional TV. However, there is a pressing need to ensure that the IPTV services being deployed deliver a Quality of Experience (QoE) that is equal to or better than traditional TV services.

The traditional approach to assessing quality of experience (QoE) has been through subjective evaluation in controlled laboratory environments. Unfortunately, subjective evaluation is expensive, error-prone and unreliable. A complementary approach is through user feedback. It is, in general, collected by the call centers and it provides a direct measure of the service performance problems experienced by the users. However, user feedback is not always complete (not all users report service quality issues) and delayed (users have already been negatively affected by the time they call customer care center to report their service quality issues).

What operators lack today is a proactive approach to obtaining comprehensive views of user's quality of experience. Such views are critical to proactively detecting service issues that matter to customers, so that operators can rapidly respond to them to ensure a high-quality customer experience. Without such visibility, operators risk being unaware of service degradations - instead they learn about issues only when customers reach frustration points and report to customer care call centers. Thus, proactive assessment of quality of experience is crucial to providing operators with insights into the ultimate metric - what customers are experiencing - so that they can effectively manage their service offerings and detect and ideally respond to issues *before customers report issues*. Proactive assessment of quality of experience can also help operators to effectively dimension the customer care workforce in anticipation of the large volume of user calls and customer-impacting conditions can be avoided.

Although there is extensive monitoring of network elements in place today and operators rapidly react to issues which are reported by the network elements - there is no technology which can directly measure *customer perception* of TV service quality. Video monitoring technologies exist, but it is still non-trivial to relate such measurements to customer perception. Deploying video monitoring to millions of customers is also prohibitively expensive, and service providers are typically constrained by the technology available within the Set-Top Boxes.

In the absence of direct measurements, we instead focus on using network measurements to infer customer service experience. However, such an approach is still challenging, due to (i) incomplete knowledge about the relationship between user-perceived issues and network performance metrics, and (ii) user feedback about quality of experience is biased towards the negative (i.e., customer calls on reporting issues) and is often delayed, noisy and limited.

In this paper, we propose a new framework, which we refer to as *Q-score*, for proactive assessment of user perceived quality of experience. Q-score constructs a single quality of experience score using performance metrics collected from the network. Q-score consists of two key components: (i) offline learning of the association between the service quality of experience and the network performance metrics collected from the servers, routers and in-home equipment, and (ii) online computation of the score for individual users or groups of users. Q-score captures the quality of experience by users in a timely fashion and can provide operators with rapid notification of service issues, often giving them a lead time of several hours before the user reports to the call center.

Q-score Design Challenges. Due to the interwoven server and network system, as well as the sophisticated hardware and software composition of home network devices, assessing service quality of experience is a sophisticated task. The proposed Q-score approach uses customer reports (e.g., tickets) to provide feedback regarding issues that customers are concerned about. Designing Q-score required us to address the following key challenges:

1. **Associating QoE with network performance.** Because of the inherent difference between network-level performance indicators and user-perceived quality of service, associating the two does not occur naturally. Even for domain experts, since there is no objective video quality metric, it is not trivial to identify key performance indicators that are closely related to quality of experience. Even if the metric were available, it would require more finely grained monitoring of network indicators, which in turn might introduce scalability issues.

2. **Lack of timely, high-quality user feedback.** User feedback is inherently noisy, incomplete and delayed. Depending on situations such as the individual viewer's living schedule, the severity of the issue, there are large variances between the beginning of service quality issues and reporting times. Some users issue a report immediately after they observe a service quality degradation; others may wait hours before calling customer service centers. Similarly, different users have different tolerance levels to service quality issues - one user may report incessantly regarding issues that another user may barely notice. This all makes it inherently challenging to use such feedback to associate service quality of experience with network performance.

3. **Large volume of diverse performance measurements.** From a network perspective, service providers typically collect fine-grained measurements from the routers and servers (*e.g.*, real-time syslogs, and regular polls of SNMP performance counters such as CPU, memory, packet counts, and losses). Some performance measurements inside the home may be fine-grained (*e.g.*, residential gateway events), whereas others may be coarse-grained (*e.g.*, hourly or daily summaries of Set-Top Box events). Set-Top Box (STB) data collection is intentionally not fine-grained to minimize the potential of service disruption due to measurements and due to the massive scale of the measurement infrastructure that would be required. The diversity in the granularity of performance measurements poses interesting technical challenges in inferring the quality of experience.

Our Contributions.

1. We design and implement a prototype Q-score system for proactively assessing quality of experience for IPTV users. Q-score uses a multi-scale spatio-temporal statistical mining technique for computing a single score capturing the quality of experience. By performing spatio-temporal aggregation and multi-scale association of the user feedback with network performance metrics, it identifies the right set of metrics useful for accurately quantifying the quality of experience.

2. We evaluate Q-score using data collected from a large commercial IPTV service provider and show that Q-score is able to predict 60% of customer service calls with 0.1% of false positives.

3. We create three applications above Q-score. (i) *Identifying important Key Performance Indicators (KPIs)* that are statistically associated with the quality of experience , (ii) *Predicting bad quality of experience* to users and generating alerts to the Operations team, and (iii) *Effective dimensioning of the customer care workforce* to dynamically allocate repair personnel to service regions as they experience issues for conducting root-cause diagnosis and rapid repair.

Organization. The remainder of the paper is organized as follows. In Section 2, we provide background information regarding the IPTV network architecture and its data. We describe the design of Q-score in Section 3, with details on its offline learning component and online monitoring component. We present performance evaluation results in Section 4. In Section 5, we explore three important applications of Q-score. We review related work in Section 6 and offer conclusions in Section 7.

2. BACKGROUND

In this section, we give an overview of the IPTV service architecture followed by a detailed description of the data sets used in the paper.

2.1 IPTV Service Architecture

Figure 1 provides a schematic overview of an IPTV system. The service network exhibits a hierarchical structure where video content is delivered via IP multicast from servers in the provider's core network to millions of Set-Top Boxes (STBs) within home networks. Specifically, either the Super Head-end Office (SHO) which serves as the primary source of national content or Video Head-end Offices (VHOs) which governs local content at each metropolitan area encodes, packetizes and sends the content towards end users. Depending on the service provider, the video content goes through several routers and switches in Intermediate Offices (IOs), Central Offices (COs), a Digital Subscriber Line Access Multiplexer (DSLAM), and a Residential Gateway (RG) before reaching STB where the packetized content gets decoded and displayed on the TV. All of the network entities comprising the IPTV service logs Key Performance Indicators (KPIs) such as delivery status of data and health diagnostics.

2.2 Data Sets

In the paper, we use data collected from a large commercial IPTV service provider in the United States, which has customers spread throughout four different time-zones. Our data set consists of (i) network performance indicators, (ii) user behaviors and activities, and (ii) user feedback in the form of customer trouble tickets

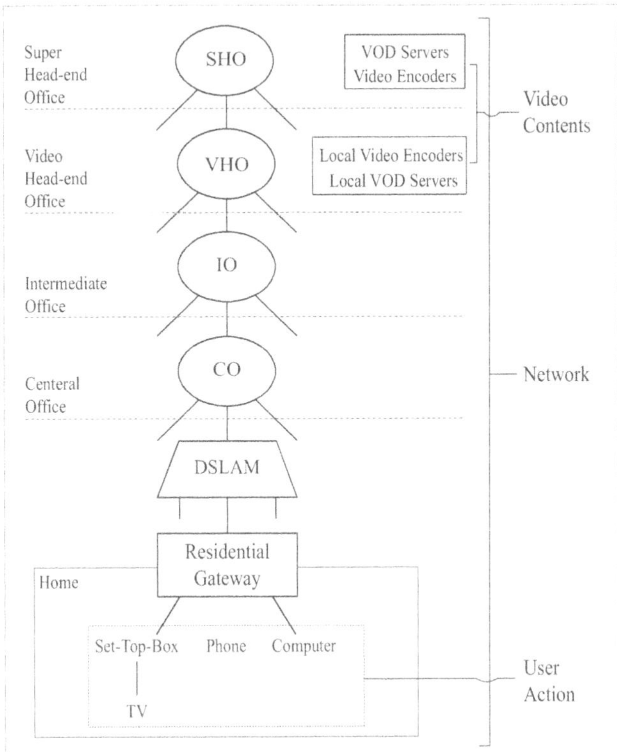

Figure 1: IPTV service architecture

Data Set Type	Spatial Level	Description
Network Performance Indicators	STB	STB audio quality indicators
		STB video quality indicators
		STB syslog
		STB resets
		STB crashes
	RG	RG Reboots
	IO & CO	SNMP MIBs of routers & switches
	SHO & VHO	SNMP MIBs of routers & switches
User Activity Indicators	User	STB power on/off log
		STB Channel change log
		STB Stream control log
User Feedback	User	Customer trouble tickets

Table 1: Summary of data sets

as summarized in Table 1. We normalize timestamps in all data sets to GMT to accurately and effectively associate the user feedback with performance metrics and user behaviors. The data has been collected for 45 days from August 1st to September 15th, 2010. Note that all the information related to the users are anonymized to preserve their previcy.

Network Performance Indicators. Network performance indicators are categorized into two types: (i) provider network performance indicators, which are collected from routers and switches in SHO, VHO, IO, CO of the IPTV service provider as shown in Figure 1 and (ii) home network performance indicators, which are collected from components inside user's homes (i.e., RG and STB). For the provider network performance data, we collected SNMP MIBs from every router and switch in SHO, VHO, IO, and CO. The SNMP MIBs report five minute average performance statistics of CPU utilization and fifteen minute average summaries for packet count, packet delivery errors and discards.

From the home network side, we first collected data relevant to each STB and RG. Each STB records audio and video streaming-related information including video throughput, receiver transport stream errors, codec errors, DRM errors, and viewing duration of TV channels. The video streaming-related information is reset when the TV tuner clears its buffer by switching channels. While each STB logs all the TV viewing information at all times, polling servers only take a subset of the STBs' statistics at each polling interval (due to the high volume of audio and video log and traffic overhead during data delivery). As a result, only a sampled set of STBs (i.e., 2% of all STBs) are used in our study. Secondly, we collected STB syslog information that contains a wide variety of hardware and software information, such as hard disk usage and memory usage, data delivery status such as packet error rate and buffer usage. The diagnostic information are collected in the same way as the STB audio and video log, *i.e.*, sampled data were polled by collection server in round robin fashion. Thirdly, we collected crash and reset events log from each STB. The crash events log refers to unexpected rebooting of STBs due to software malfunctions and the reset refers to intentional and scheduled reboots commanded by network operators due to, for instance, software updates. The crash and reset log are periodically collected from all STBs with millisecond scale time stamps. Last performance indicator taken from home network is the reboot log of RGs that are commanded by operators remotely. RG reboot logs are collected in the same way as STB reboot logs. The crash and reboot logs are collected from the entire seven million STBs.

User Activity Indicators. Because IPTV networks are highly user-interactive systems, certain user activity patterns or habits can create overload conditions on the STB and cause a service issue (*e.g.*, a user changing channels too frequently may cause its upstream device such as a DSLAM to be overwhelmed, leading to an inability to handle all of the remaining STBs that it serves). Hence, user activities are another important factor to be considered. Similar to conventional TV users, IPTV users use a vendor/provider-customized remote controller to control the STB. For this paper, we collected logs from every STB that captures four types of user activities performed: (i) power on/off: this is the result of the user pressing the power button to turn on or off the STB; (ii) channel switch: this can be the result of one of the three actions: target switching by directly inputting the channel number, sequential scanning by pressing the Up/Down button, or pre-configured favorite channel list; (iii) video stream control: this includes actions such as fast forward, rewind, pause and play that are performed on either live TV streams, VoD, or DVR; and (iv) on-screen menu invocation: this log saves the user action of pulling up the STB menu displayed on TV screen that lets the users to access the features provided by the IPTV system.

User Feedback. For user feedback, we used calls made to the customer care center of an IPTV service. Customer care cases are records of user interactions at call centers. A customer call can be related to service provisioning, billing and accounting, or service disruption. Since the focus of our paper is on quality of experience (QoE), we specifically examined users' reports on service disruptions that later involved technical support as our user feedback. Each customer call related to service disruption includes the anonymized user ID, report date and time, brief description of the problem, and resolution of the issue.

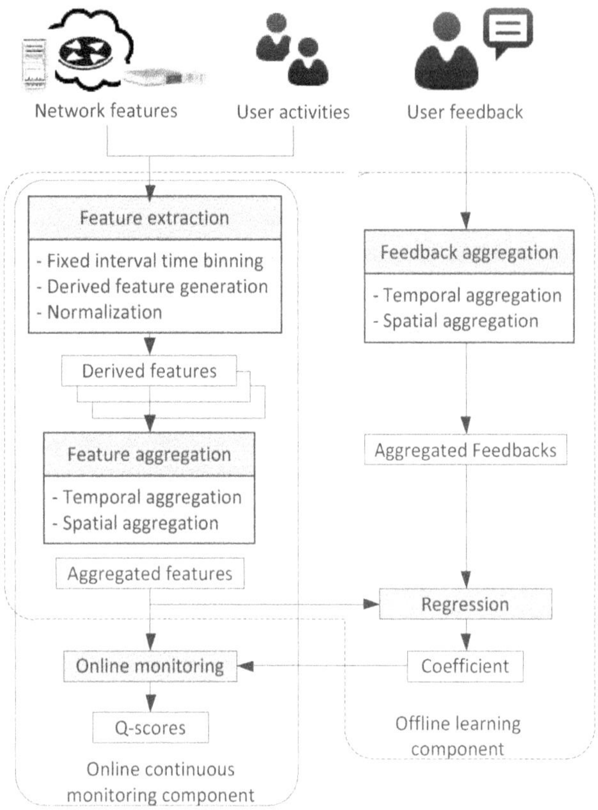

Figure 2: Overview of Q-score design

3. Q-SCORE DESIGN

In this section, we introduce our proposed scheme, Q-score. The high level idea is to extract a useful association between the noisy, incomplete, and indeterminately-delayed user feedback and the various network (including the servers, transport and in-home devices) performance indicators through an offline learning process, and then transform the knowledge into an online monitoring system that estimates/predicts user-perceived service quality based on the available network KPIs. We start by giving an overview of the Q-score system architecture and then dive into details of each component.

3.1 Overview

Figure 2 presents the system architecture of Q-score. As shown in the figure, Q-score takes input from network (including servers, transport and in-home devices) performance indicators, which we refer to as *features*, the user control activities, and the user feedback in the form of customer call service records. The output is a series of Q-scores, one for each user of the service, quantifying the received service quality. At a high level, our system is composed of two components: (i) an offline learning component and (ii) an online continuous monitoring component. The overall dataflow in Q-score system begins with the offline relationship learning between user feedback on service quality and the measurements from the network features and user activities. Ideally, if there had been any accurate and fine-grained user-level service quality measure, we would use it to train a model for network feature selection. However, as stated earlier, the best available method for discovering user-level service quality issue is through the lossy, noisy and indeterminately-delayed calls to customer care centers. Consequently, we need to carefully design the appropriate temporal and spatial aggregations to remedy the inherent loss, noise and delay with user feedback. Furthermore, by applying statistical regression over a large quantity of historical data between various network KPIs and the user feedback, we obtain a set of regression coefficients which quantitatively capture their relationship. These regression coefficients are fed into the online monitoring component.

With the regression coefficients, we can turn the up-to-date network KPI measurements into a single numerical score for each user or groups of them within a given spatial region. The numerical score, which we refer to as the *Q-score*, captures the likelihood of any on-going service quality problem. Tracking the Q-score over time enables many service management applications, as will be described in Section 5.

3.2 Spatio-Temporal Feature Extraction

In order to discover possible correlation between user's quality of experience and IPTV system events, we apply a comprehensive set of performance indicators ranging from provider network performance indicators to home network component status logs, and to user interaction logs with IPTV. On each of the network performance indicators and user interaction indicators described in Section 2.2, we apply the following series of transformations to obtain a measurement matrix.

3.2.1 *Transformations of Measurement Readings*

Conversion to Fixed-Interval Time Bins. Network measurement data collected from different sources and devices are bound to different time periods, posing challenge in correlating them. Some data sets, such as CPU level of routers in SNMP MIBs, contain periodically collected measurement data, and the value represents the average or total over the measurement interval. Some other data sets, such as user activities to STB and STB crash logs, contain events that take place at a single point of time, hence are intermittent and have zero duration. Data sets such as STB audio and video quality indicators contain data polled either on demand or at irregular intervals and represent the cumulative counters over a variable time interval (e.g., due to channel switches clearing the diagnostic counter entries).

To unify the data representation, we define a data point $d(m, l, s, e) = v$ as composed in a four dimensional specification: (i) metric $m \in M$ where M is a set of metrics such as CPU level of routers and count of video decoding errors at STBs. (ii) location $l \in L$ where L is a set of spatial location identifiers such as a set of users, DSLAMs, or COs. (iii) beginning time for the data binding interval $s \in T$, where T is the total time window, and (iv) ending time of the data binding interval $e \in T$. v is the measurement value that d contains. Note that for measurement data pertaining to a single time point, $s = e$.

The above representation is comprehensive in capturing various cases of periodic/intermittent or fixed/variable duration measurements. However, it requires a moderate amount of computation to determine the overlaps among the time intervals, which becomes prohibitively expensive for a large data set as in our case. To reduce the complexity, we convert all $d(m, l, s, e)$ into a fixed-size time interval data representation $b(m, l, s, \delta)$ as follows:

$$b(m, l, s, \delta) = \{v \mid v = d(m, \bar{l}, \bar{s}, \bar{e}), \text{ where } l = \bar{l} \text{ and } [\bar{s}, \bar{e}] \text{ overlaps with } [s, s + \delta]\} \quad (1)$$

where δ is length of the feature time interval. Note that if there exist two or more ds with matching measurement time to $[s, s+\delta]$, there could also be multiple identical values for b – making b not well defined. We need to introduce the aggregation functions as below.

Conversion to Derived Features. To deal with multiple ds colliding into the same b (either due to time bin or spatial aggregation), we define three types of aggregate data points, which we refer to as the *derived features*. They contain (i) the minimum, (ii) the maximum, and (iii) the average of all the values for b respectively. Formally,

$$f_m(m,l,s,\delta) = \min_{l \in child(\bar{l})} (\cup(b(m,\bar{l},s,\delta))).$$

$$f_M(m,l,s,\delta) = \max_{l \in child(\bar{l})} (\cup(b(m,\bar{l},s,\delta))). \quad (2)$$

$$f_a(m,l,s,\delta) = \operatorname{avg}_{l \in child(\bar{l})} (\cup(b(m,\bar{l},s,\delta))). \quad (3)$$

In this way we can limit the number of derived features to be three regardless of the number of actual readings in b. Unless specified otherwise, all features referred in the rest of the paper are the derived features.

Feature Normalization. To identify a small set of network features most relevant to customer feedback, we need to fairly compare each network feature to others. However, the network features we consider typically take numerical values, potentially having different signs and across large range of scales. This makes it difficult to assess the significance of their associated coefficient under regression.

To deal with the diverse data values, we further normalize features to be binary-valued by comparing to a threshold, which is determined depending on the metric and location.

Consider a vector of features of the same metric and location over different time and interval combinations:

$$\vec{f_a}(m,l) = \langle f_a(\bar{m},\bar{l},s,\delta) \text{ where } m=\bar{m}, l=\bar{l} \rangle \quad (4)$$

We need to identify a threshold value τ for $\vec{f_a}$. To do so, we bring in the user feedback in the form of user call logs. We consider the conditional distribution function of the metric value of interest when (1) there is one or more entries of the user call log being associated with the location l and when (2) there is no such entry. Ideally, a threshold τ can separate the instances between cases 1 and 2. When threshold τ is low, the chance of having instances in case 1 passing the threshold increases, and when the threshold is high, the chance of having instances in case 2 failing the threshold increases. So, we set the threshold τ such that the two factors balance out. Using empirical CDFs of the case 1 (F_1) and case 2 (F_2), we can define τ to be the intersecting point of F_1 and $1-F_2$ such that

$$F_1(\tau) = 1 - F_2(\tau). \quad (5)$$

Once τ is determined, we can normalize of f_a as follows.

$$f_a(m,l,s,\delta) = \begin{cases} 1 & \text{if } f_a(m,l,s,\delta) >= \tau \\ 0 & \text{otherwise.} \end{cases} \quad (6)$$

Features f_m and f_M can be normalized in the same way.

3.2.2 *Constructing Measurement Matrix*

In order to support multi-scale analysis that accounts for the indeterminate delay in user feedback, we construct the regression input matrix $\mathbf{X}$ over all measurement metrics, location, and time parameters as below.

$$\mathbf{X} = \begin{bmatrix} \begin{bmatrix} f_m(m_1,l_1,s_1,\delta) f_M f_a \\ f_m(m_1,l_1,s_2,\delta) f_M f_a \\ \vdots \quad \vdots \; \vdots \\ f_m(m_1,l_1,s_t,\delta) f_M f_a \\ f_m(m_1,l_2,s_1,\delta) f_M f_a \\ f_m(m_1,l_2,s_2,\delta) f_M f_a \\ \vdots \quad \vdots \; \vdots \\ f_m(m_1,l_2,s_t,\delta) f_M f_a \\ \vdots \quad \vdots \; \vdots \end{bmatrix} \begin{bmatrix} f_m(m_2,l_1,s_1,\delta) f_M f_a \\ f_m(m_2,l_1,s_2,\delta) f_M f_a \\ \vdots \quad \vdots \; \vdots \\ f_m(m_2,l_1,s_t,\delta) f_M f_a \\ f_m(m_2,l_2,s_1,\delta) f_M f_a \\ f_m(m_2,l_2,s_2,\delta) f_M f_a \\ \vdots \quad \vdots \; \vdots \\ f_m(m_2,l_2,s_t,\delta) f_M f_a \\ \vdots \quad \vdots \; \vdots \end{bmatrix} \cdots \end{bmatrix} \quad (7)$$

The columns of $\mathbf{X}$ represent different metrics of derived features. Thus, each column has f with a unique m_i, where i is an instance of time bins. The rows of $\mathbf{X}$ represent all feature values during a specific time (s_i, δ) at a specific location l_j. Assuming there are n locations, t different time bins, and k different KPI metrics and feature aggregations, the number of rows in $\mathbf{X}$ is $n \times t$ and the number of columns is k.

3.2.3 *Multi-scale Temporal Level Aggregations*

The time-window parameter δ plays an important role in capturing the extend of cause-effect delays. Large δ would include cause-effect relationship with long delay. However, large δ would make it insensitive to dense measurements with short cause-effect delay, as the aggregation weakens the significance of correlation. Since different δ values have advantages over others, we adopt a multi-scale analysis approach by including multiple time window parameters into our consideration. Our matrix representation in Eq (7) is flexible enough to enable this – we append in columns the $\mathbf{X}(\delta_i)$s with different time-intervals (δ_i).

$$\mathbf{X}_{\mathbf{Temp.Comb.}} = [\mathbf{X}(\delta_1) \cdots \mathbf{X}(\delta_\mathbf{v})] \quad (8)$$

where v is the number of different values of the time window parameter.

3.2.4 *Multi-scale Spatial Level Aggregation*

Similarly to the temporal aggregation captured by the time window parameter, there can be multiple spatial aggregation levels with an IPTV system architecture. Based on the hierarchical structure in Figure 1, we consider three different spatial aggregation levels in Q-score, namely user, DSLAM, and CO levels.

Single-Scale Spatial Level Aggregation. We set the baseline spatial aggregation level to per-user aggregation. This is because the customer service report logs are associated with a household, which we loosely refer to as a user. Matching the network features to the household/user level, one of the following process is necessary: (i) for features at finer grained spatial level than user (such as STB related features since one household may have multiple STBs), we take the maximum among different feature values for the more specific locations as the representation for f_M, the minimum for f_m, and the average for f_a, at the user level; (ii) for features with coarser grained spatial level than user (such as DSLAM and CO), we replicate the coarser grained feature values for each associated user within the hierarchy. In this way, we preserve the number of samples to be $n \times t$ in each row of $\mathbf{X}_{\mathbf{user}}$. The same spatial level aggregation is applied for the DSLAM level and the CO level to obtain $\mathbf{X}_{\mathbf{DSLAM}}$ and $\mathbf{X}_{\mathbf{CO}}$ respectively.

Multi-Scale Spatial Level Aggregation. In parallel with the multi-scale analysis with respect to time window parameter, different spatial aggregation levels can be fed into regression altogether. The idea is that the most prominent feature would be at a suitable spatial aggregation level and would dominate the same features aggregated at other spatial levels. We append in column the feature matrices for different spatial levels to get the $\mathbf{X}_{\mathbf{Spat.Comb.}}$:

$$\mathbf{X}_{\mathbf{Spat.Comb.}} = [\mathbf{X}_{\mathbf{userID}}\ \mathbf{X}_{\mathbf{DSLAM}}\ \mathbf{X}_{\mathbf{CO}}]. \tag{9}$$

3.3 Feedback Aggregation

As outlined in Section 2.2, we use the customer service call logs as the user feedback regarding service quality. This feedback is inherently unreliable. It is incomplete as not all service quality problems (e.g., video glitches) would be noticed and reported by users. And there is an indeterminate delay ranging from minutes to hours to even days between the service problem and the trouble ticket log entry (*i.e.*, entries of customer reporting issues to call centers). All of these require some denoise processing for such user feedback to be useful even in statistical sense.

We adopt the same principle applied in the spatio-temporal aggregation with respect to network features. Let c be the predicate of the presence of a matching entry in the feedback log (B):

$$c(l, u, \gamma) = \begin{cases} 1 & \text{if } \exists\, b \in B \text{ during } [u, u+\gamma]; \\ 0 & \text{otherwise.} \end{cases} \tag{10}$$

where u is the beginning time for a feedback binding interval and γ is the length of feedback time interval. Once $c(l, u, \gamma)$ is defined, we can use the same spatio-temporal aggregation method for the network features on c.

A network event or user activity is always a cause of user feedback but cannot be an effect. Thus we set $u = s + \delta$ so that when we correlate c_i to b_i, we take account of the causal sequence between network (or user activity) events and user feedback. Let y be a vector of feedback for different users over time

$$\mathbf{y} = [c(l_1, u_1, \gamma), ..., c(l_1, u_t, \gamma), c(l_2, u_1, \gamma), ..., c(l_2, u_t, \gamma), ...]^T.$$

The length of the vector $\mathbf{y}$ is determined by the number of locations n and the number of time bins t, making it to be $n \times t$ which is the same as the row count of $\mathbf{X}$.

3.4 Regression

Given the measurements of network indicators $\mathbf{X}$ and user feedback $\mathbf{y}$, we now aim to find a coefficient vector β that provides a compressed representation of the relationship between $\mathbf{X}$ and $\mathbf{y}$. Note that, in the event of measurement or data collection error which results in parts of $\mathbf{X}$ or $\mathbf{y}$ to have no values, we remove the affected rows of $\mathbf{X}$ and $\mathbf{y}$ from consideration to eliminate possible false correlation.

Such an optimization can be performed using *regression*. A baseline regression model of linear regression [9], however, cannot provide the optimal solution as our system of equation $\mathbf{X}\beta = \mathbf{y}$ is over-constrained (*i.e.*, the equation has far smaller number of unknowns than the number of equations ($k \ll (m * n)$)). To prevent β from over-fitting due to high variance, we apply Ridge regression [11] that imposes a penalty λ on the complexity of model by minimizing a penalized residual sum of squares $\mathcal{RSS}$ as follows

$$\min_{\beta} \mathcal{RSS}(\mathcal{D}, \beta) \ s.t. \sum_{i=1}^{n} \beta^2 \le s. \tag{11}$$

where $\mathcal{D}$ is the set of observed data points $\mathcal{D} = x_n, y_n$.

We can state this optimization problem in Ridge regression as

$$\hat{\beta} = arg \min_{\beta} \sum_{i} (y_i - \beta_0 - \sum_{j=1}^{p} x_{ij}\beta_j)^2 + \lambda \sum_{j=1}^{p} \beta_j^2. \tag{12}$$

The Ridge coefficient $\hat{\beta}$ becomes

$$\hat{\beta} = (\mathbf{X}^{\mathsf{T}}\mathbf{X} + \lambda\mathbf{I})^{-1}\mathbf{X}^{\mathsf{T}}\mathbf{y}. \tag{13}$$

where $\mathbf{I}$ is the identity matrix.

There are other regression methods we have explored including l_1-norm minimization and logistic regression. However, as our system of equation has tens of thousands of equations and thousands of unknowns, l_1-norm minimization and logistic regression either took excessive amounts of time in computation or failed to converge to an answer. The complexity and scale of our system make these other techniques infeasible.

Finding Significant KPI Weights. From the β coefficients, we can identify key performance indicators (KPIs) that are more closely related to user feedback. This involves sorting the regression coefficients by their absolute value and identifying the top N KPIs associated with them. Furthermore, by analyzing the commonality and difference of the same metric across different temporal and spatial aggregation configuration, we can gain insight on how each of these KPIs impact the users' quality of experience specific to the most significant spatio-temporal aggregation. The analytical results on the most significant KPIs in IPTV are presented in Section 5.1.

3.5 Compute Q-score in Runtime

Once the offline learning of β completes, we can compute from the available key performance indicators the Q-scores either for individual users or groups of users aggregated spatially depending on the feedback aggregation scheme used.

Detecting Significant Q-score Changes. We apply β from the offline learning to the current network measurement data $\mathbf{X}$ and obtain Q-score that estimates per-user level service quality. Running continuously as network KPI data streaming into Q-score, we track the series of Q-scores over time. Since Q-scores are real-valued numbers, we need to identify the thresholds for alarming on the Q-scores to the operations. The alarms can be proactively used to predict customer calls. We apply simple threshold-based change detection on the time-series of Q-scores to generate the alarms.

False alarm rate of Q-score. As a prediction mechanism of possible outbreaks, it is very important to have a low false alarm rate in a service quality assessment. In Q-score, a multitude of components prevent a single user, one end-user device, or a network device from raising false alarms for a large population of users. The feature normalization described in Section 3.2.1 regulates feature values, an exceptional feature value for an individual cannot affect much to the entire population. The multi-scale aggregations (Section 3.2.3, 3.2.4) further reduces the possibility of falsely emphasizing rare events. In the case of spatial aggregation, because Q-score considers both individual users and spatial groups of users, the score is stable even when an individual's feature value is high. Similarly, temporal aggregation prevents the chance of false alarms due to highly transient feature value changes. Additionally, in practice, we carefully set the threshold of Q-scores to focus on minimizing false positives, even with slight sacrifice to coverage (recall).

4. EVALUATION

In this section, we present the performance evaluation results of Q-score and show that the regression results are accurate and robust, and the multi-scale aggregation of spatio-temporal features has benefit over single scale, non aggregated cases.

4.1 Evaluation Methodology

Metrics. We compare the number of predicted customer trouble tickets and that of received customer trouble tickets and measure the accuracy of prediction of service quality issues by false negative rate (FNR) and false positive rate (FPR). The FNR and FPR are computed per user basis.

$$FNR = \frac{\#\text{of time bins that Q-score fails to predicts a trouble ticket}}{\#\text{of time bins that have received trouble tickets}}$$
$$FPR = \frac{\#\text{of time bins that Q-score incorrectly predicts a ticket}}{\#\text{of time bins that do not have any trouble tickets}}$$

Note that due to the sparsity in the occurrence of user feedback (i.e., trouble tickets), the number of time bins without any user feedback is orders of magnitude higher than the number of time bins with user feedback.

Training and Testing Sets. In our evaluation of the Q-score system, we use data sets collected from a commercial IPTV network provider in US over two months time period from August 1st, 2010 to September 30th, 2010. Unless otherwise mentioned, we use 15 days of data collected from August 15th, 2010 to August 29th, 2010 as the training data set for β and the subsequent 15 days of data collected from September 1st, 2010 to September 15th, 2010 as the testing data set. In addition, we use multi-scale temporal aggregation of $X_{Temp.Comb.}$ combining δ of 3-24 hours and multi-scale spatial aggregation of $X_{Spat.Comb.}$ combining spatial levels of user, DSLAM, CO, and VHO as the default setting. Lastly, we set the default feedback time bin γ to be $\gamma = 24$ hours.

We assign λ a small positive value within $(0, 0.05]$. While different λ exhibit small differences in accuracy, the optimal λ varied from data set to data set. Since the selection of λ is specific to data set in each test, we present the results with the best λ while omitting to show its actual value.

4.2 Results

4.2.1 *Accuracy Analysis*

We begin our evaluation by assessing how well Q-score follows the ground truth of user-perceived service quality. In our evaluation, we use user feedback as an approximation of the ground truth of user-perceived service quality issues in training and testing Q-score system. Recall that the user feedback is incomplete in reflecting user perceived service quality. In fact, the user feedback captures a subset of user perceived service quality issues and thus underestimates the actual occurrences of service performance degradations. Fortunately, major and/or long lasting service performance degradations are likely to be captured by the user feedback [24]. Hence, it is likely that the computed Q-score underestimates the actual user perceived performance issues, but expected to capture major outages and performance degradations.

While Q-score does not perfectly match with the user perceived service quality at the individual user level, the changes or trends in the distribution of Q-score are expected to follow closely with that of the actual service quality degradation at certain spatial aggregation levels. In our evaluation, we choose CO as the aggregation level[1]. By summing up individual users' feedback within each CO into a single value, we obtain an aggregation vector $\mathbf{S_{actual}}$ of user feedback. Since $\mathbf{S_{actual}}$ is a spatio-temporal aggregation of user feedback, its element now signifies the level of user-perceived service quality issues. Similarly, by summing up the individual users' Q-score inside each CO into a single value, we can obtain an aggregation vector of Q-scores $\mathbf{S_{estim}}$ that signifies our estimated level of user-perceived service quality.

Aggregation method	P value in F-test	Correlation coefficient $\mathcal{R}$
CO	0.00	0.6826
Random	2.21e-31	0.7165

Table 2: Accuracy analysis results of Q-score

To evaluate the significance of the relation between the actual ($\mathbf{S_{actual}}$) and estimated ($\mathbf{S_{estim}}$) user perceived service quality level, we run an F-test between them. Let the null hypothesis $H_0 : r = 0$ where $\mathbf{S_{actual}} = r * \mathbf{S_{estim}}$. We find that for the significance level of 0.1, the hypothesis test is rejected, implying that the relation between the two vectors does exist. A Pearson's correlation test also shows relatively high correlation coefficient $\mathcal{R}$ between $\mathbf{S_{actual}}$ and $\mathbf{S_{estim}}$, proving that the relationship between the two is linear. In other words, Q-score does follow the user-perceived service quality.

Because CO level aggregation represents spatial proximity of user geographical locations, user feedback rates can be different across COs. To evaluate if CO aggregation introduce any bias on the results, we also conduct the same evaluation using a random grouping with the same number of groups as the number of COs and compute aggregation vectors. Table 2 summarizes the F-test and Pearson's correlation tests results for both CO level aggregation and random grouping based aggregation. The random grouping based aggregation generally shows the same results as the CO level aggregation, supporting that Q-score indeed follows user feedback regardless of how we aggregate users in Q-score computation.

4.2.2 *Multi-scale Temporal Aggregation*

In this section, we evaluate the impact of different time-bin size (δ) on network indicators (single-scale temporal level aggregation). Then we show the performance benefits by using multi-scale temporal aggregation on network performance indicators (multi-scale temporal level aggregation).

Figure 3 shows the Q-score on FPR-FNR trade-off curves using various δs ranging from 3 hours to 24 hours (*i.e.*, each curve corresponds to an $\mathbf{X}$ with a given δ). Note that FPR shown on the x-axis is in log-scale and FNR shown on the y-axis is in normal scale. The figure shows that the prediction accuracy gets generally better as we shorten δ (i.e., the curve gets closer to the lower left corner of the plot). However, comparing $\delta = 3hours$ and $\delta = 6hours$, their FNR overlaps over different range of FPR, indicating that there is no single optimal δ to be chosen.

Figure 4 shows the results of $\mathbf{X_{Temp.Comb.}}$ by applying multi-scale temporal aggregation on network performance indicators. There are three curves obtained by combining (i) shorter time bins of 3-12 hours, (ii) longer time bins of 15-24 hours, and (iii) the entire range of 3-24 hours. We observe that (iii) provides the best performance among them. At the same time, (iii) is also strictly

[1]We considered various levels of spatial granularity in the IPTV hierarchy including DSLAM, CO, and VHO levels. Among them, CO level aggregation is most adequate for the accuracy analysis because it yields a statistically sound number of user IDs in each CO and enough number of COs to make meaningful comparisons between aggregation vector Ses.

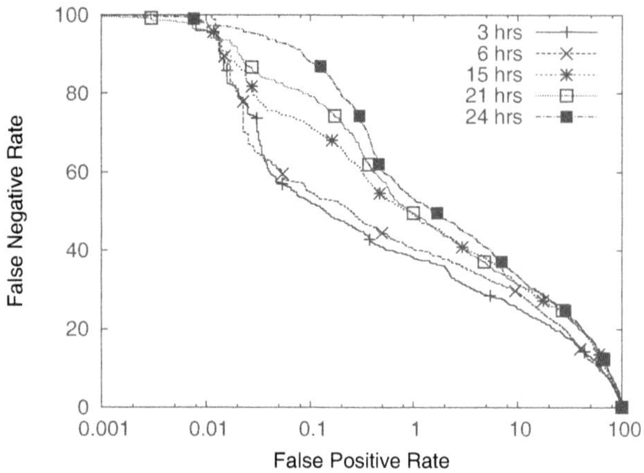

Figure 3: Comparison of various δs on features (performance indicators)

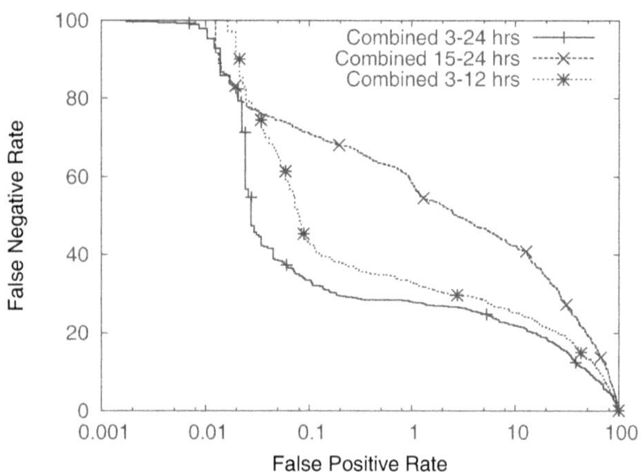

Figure 4: Comparison of multi-scale temporal aggregations on features (performance indicators)

better than any curves in Figure 3, proving that simultaneously regressing on multiple scales of temporal aggregations on network performance indicators does improve the accuracy of Q-score prediction on service quality issues.

4.2.3 *Multi-scale Spatial Aggregation*

We now evaluate the impact of various levels of spacial aggregation on network performance indicators and the benefit of using multi-scale spatial aggregation in Q-score.

Figure 5 shows the trade-off curves of $\mathbf{X}$ with various single-scale spatial aggregation ranging from user ID ($\mathbf{X}_{\mathbf{userID}}$), to DSLAM ($\mathbf{X}_{\mathbf{DSLAM}}$), to CO ($\mathbf{X}_{\mathbf{CO}}$), and to VHO ($\mathbf{X}_{\mathbf{VHO}}$) level. As the spatial aggregation level changes from user ID to DSLAM (*i.e.*, smaller-sized region to larger-sized region), we observe that the FNR increases from 35% to 100% when FPR is at 0.1%. A possible explanation to this is that if the service quality issues reported by users are more related to a home network problem rather than a provider network problem, spatial aggregation of network performance indicators can attenuate signals relevant to the end-user devices at home. As we will show in Section 5.1, by analyzing significant KPIs, we are able to confirm that the significant KPIs are mostly related to STB and RG (*i.e.*, home network devices) while backbone network appeared to be well provisioned.

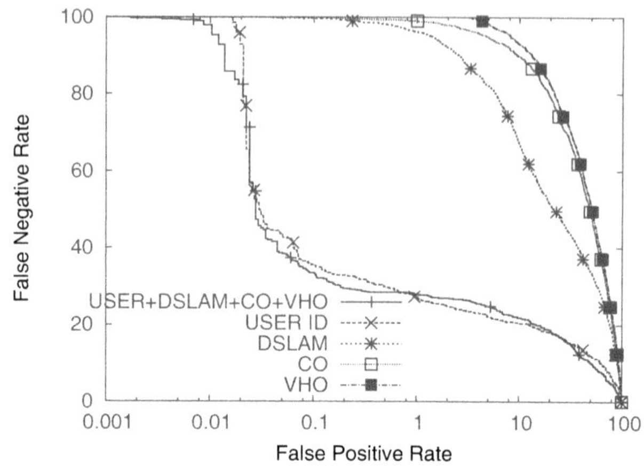

Figure 5: Comparison of various spatial aggregation levels on features (performance indicators)

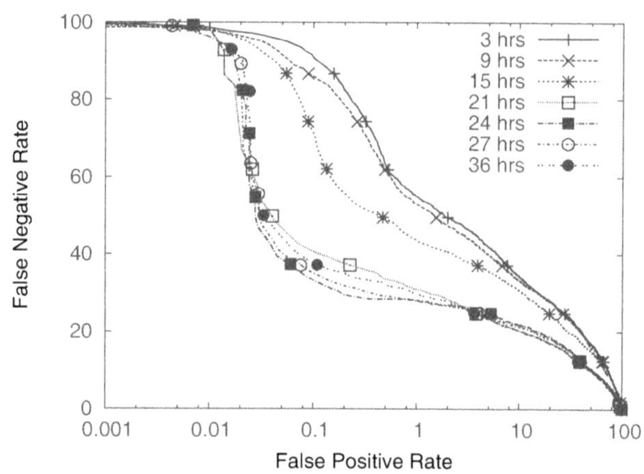

Figure 6: Comparison of various time bin size γ on user feedback

In addition to the single-scale spatial aggregation, the first plot of Figure 5 (denoted as 'USER + DSLAM + CO + VHO') shows multi-scale spatial aggregation (with measurement matrix $\mathbf{X}_{\mathbf{Spat.Comb.}}$). We observe that the multi-scale spatial aggregation outperforms any single-scale aggregation in terms of overall prediction accuracy, proving that the regression algorithm makes the most accurate selection of spatial level of features.

4.2.4 *Feedback Aggregation*

To show the effect of user feedback duration being aggregated together, Figure 6 compares various lengths of γ. We observe that as γ gets longer, the regression performance gets better. An explanation for this is, as mentioned in Section 3.3, there is a significant delay between the occurrence of a problem and the filing of user feedback. Due to the elongated delay, time-bins with short γs may fail to contain feedback correlated with significant network indicator values.

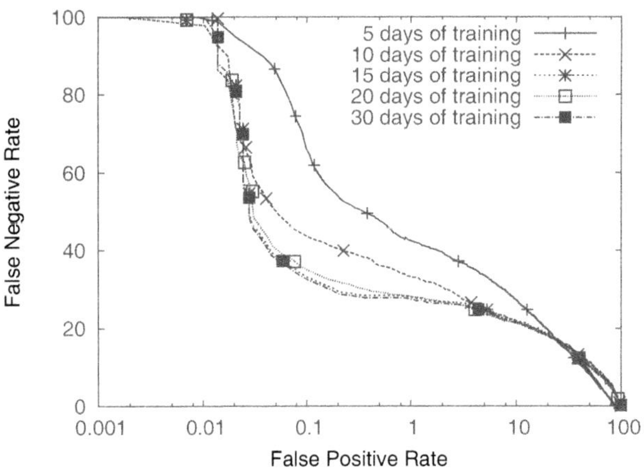

Figure 7: Comparison of accuracy with various training durations

4.2.5 *Sensitivity to Training Duration*

Finally, we evaluate the sensitivity of testing accuracy on the duration of training. In this experiment, we fix the testing duration and assess how accuracy changes by varying the training duration. Table 3 shows the dates of training and testing periods used in our evaluation. Figure 7 shows the accuracy trade-off curves of using different training durations. We observe that in general, the testing accuracy improves as we increase the training duration. However, the gain becomes marginal once the training duration is longer than 15 days. This result suggests that using 15 days as training period is a good choice.

A closer examination of the curves corresponding to the use of 15 and 20 days of training duration reveals that the accuracy of using 15 days training duration is marginally better. A possible reason for this is that in the month of August, there was a network-wide STB firmware upgrade. The upgrade that took place between 08/10/2010 and 08/14/2010 could have obstructed measurement of STB logs (*i.e.*, STB audio and video quality measurement logs, syslog, reset and crash logs) and caused learning of β to be affected. Since this kind of glitches occurs in real data, we take small amount of noise as granted. In all, we observe that 15 days of training is enough to learn β.

Summary. In this section, we evaluate the accuracy and robustness of Q-score. Q-score, combined with multi-scale temporal aggregation and multi-scale spatial aggregation, successfully predicts 60% of service problems reported by customers with only 0.1% misclassification (*i.e.*, false positive rate). While an in-depth analysis is in order, our preliminary test shows that a portion of the remaining 40% of unpredicted issues are either (i) unrelated to any of the network KPIs we measure (*e.g.*, remote controller malfunction, wiring issues between STB and TV inside home) or (ii) fallacies that our regression does not capture (*e.g.*, gradual and long term changes in network KPIs). For (i), as feedback is reported and logged by humans in plain text, it is difficult to completely rule out trouble tickets unassociated to our KPIs. Thus, we account a small portion of misclassification to inherent noise of feedback. For (ii), we address with our previous works Giza [18] and Mercury [19] as they are specifically designed to detect and mitigate recurring and persistent events in application service networks. In a future work, we plan to conduct an extensive analysis on the false negatives to determine the proportions of the issues in each of the categories and further improve the success rate.

	Duration	Dates
Testing duration	15 days	09/01/2010 - 09/15/2010
Training durations	5 days	08/25/2010 - 08/29/2010
	10 days	08/20/2010 - 08/29/2010
	15 days	08/15/2010 - 08/29/2010
	20 days	08/10/2010 - 08/29/2010
	30 days	08/01/2010 - 08/30/2010

Table 3: Training and testing durations

5. APPLICATION

In this section, we demonstrate the utility of Q-score by presenting three applications on it. First, we present a set of network KPIs that are closely related to user-perceived service quality. Second, we illustrate how much Q-score can predict user calls. Third, we show the possibility of intelligently dimensioning the call center workforce. In all applications, we successfully identify interesting results through online analysis of Q-score.

5.1 Identification of Significant KPIs

Today's commercial IPTV services support up to millions of user devices. If for every single device, few KPIs are monitored continuously, the measurement space can easily reach to the order of billions. In addition, time-lapse analysis in the diagnosis (as many diagnosis schemes employs) is required to be conducted on multiple data snapshots in short periods of time. Thus, in service assurance of a large-scale IPTV system, it is infeasible to blindly measure, collect, and analyze such large volume of diverse KPIs from the entire network. In this application, we discuss our experience on identification of a small number of significant KPIs with respect to user-perceived quality of experience.

Significant KPIs. In the generation of Q-score, we relate the network KPIs and user feedback by means of the factor β. β measures the relevance of significant KPIs by its magnitude. The analysis of the magnitude of β for different temporal aggregation levels indicates how KPIs correlate with user feedback. Tables 4 and 5 list top ten significant KPIs for relatively long history hours (15-24 hours) and short history hours (3-9 hours), respectively. Being regressed with individual users' feedback, the significant KPIs exhibit some commonality (shown in bold) as well as differences.

From the KPIs relevant to network delivery statistics, we observe that "tuner fill", "hole without session packets", "hole too large", "bytes processed per sec" are particularly interesting KPIs. "Tuner fill" logs the number of packets lost by STBs before they are requested for TCP retransmission. The lost packets are supposed to be retransmitted by content distribution servers. Tuner fill counts can be related with video quality in that they indicate the condition of the delivery network and gives a sense of the average packet loss that would occur without any packet recovery scheme. A 'hole' represents a time interval greater than a given threshold (assumed to affect video quality) in which no video packets have been received. 'Hole without session packets' counts the number of such holes occurred during a STB's viewing session (since the user's last channel change). And 'hole too large' error is triggered when the hole size is larger than the maximum end-to-end delay of $150ms$ recommended by [2].

On the audio and video related KPIs, "decoder error" logs are general types of errors that occurred during the decoding of audio data. Decoder errors can occur due to various situations including, but not limited to, out-of-order data packet reception, audio buffer underrun or overrun, and packet loss. 'DRM errors' and 'crypto error' indicates errors caused by the video DRM decoder . This error can occur when encoder packets containing DRM keys are

KPI Type	KPI Label	β Coef.
Network delivery	RTP payload error	0.68
	Tuner fill	0.63
	Hole Too Large	0.61
	Decoder stall	0.42
	Bytes processed per sec	-0.32
Audio	**Audio decoder errors**	0.84
Video	**Video DRM errors**	0.73
	Video decoder errors	0.53
	Video frames decoded	-0.49
	Video data throughput	-0.49

Table 4: Significant KPIs for large δ (15-24 hrs)

KPI Type	KPI Label	β Coef.
Network delivery	Hole without session packets	0.60
	Tuner fill	0.57
	Bytes processed per sec	-0.34
	ECM parse errors	0.32
Audio	**Audio decoder errors**	1.03
	Audio samples dropped	0.84
	Audio crypto error	0.64
	Audio data dropped	0.55
	Audio DRM errors	0.34
Video	**Video DRM errors**	0.63

Table 5: Significant KPIs for small δ (3-9 hrs)

KPI Type	KPI Label	β Coef.
Network delivery	**Tuner fill**	0.67
	Src unavailable received	0.5
	Hole without session packets	0.52
	ECM parse errors	0.35
	Bytes processed per sec	-0.33
Audio	**Audio decoder errors**	0.74
	Audio data dropped	0.57
	Audio crypto error	0.44
Video	**Video DRM errors**	0.68
	Video frames dropped	0.65

Table 6: Significant KPIs for multi-scale temporal aggregation (0-24 hrs)

lost. In IPTV, every video program is encoded with DRM, and inability of decoding DRM blocks viewing of the programs. Thus, the occurrence of this error blocks TV viewing until new encoder keys are received regardless of receipt of the data packets. Lastly, the 'video frames dropped' error represents the number of video frames drops (below the normal frame rate of 29.97 frames per second) due to packet loss or decoder errors. When large frame drop occurs, viewers can notice choppy or skippy motions.

Observations. We observe an interesting finding by comparing significant KPIs of long-term event durations (*i.e.*, large δ) and short-term event durations (*i.e.*, small δ). The finding is that the former tend to have more video related KPIs as the most significant ones, whereas the latter has more KPIs related to audio. This relates with the relevance that audio has with respect to video in the user experience. Audio data is more susceptible to losses and errors than the video data. The reason is because the total volume of the data in audio is much less than that of the video, thus the impact of lost or delayed audio data is relatively greater than that of video data. Naturally, the viewers of the programs have less tolerance to audio issues than to video issues, and report about audio issues much earlier than video issues. The contrasting finding between long and short history hours has uncovered that, depending on the characteristics of the issues (*i.e.*, whether the issue is about audio or video), there are differences in urgency.

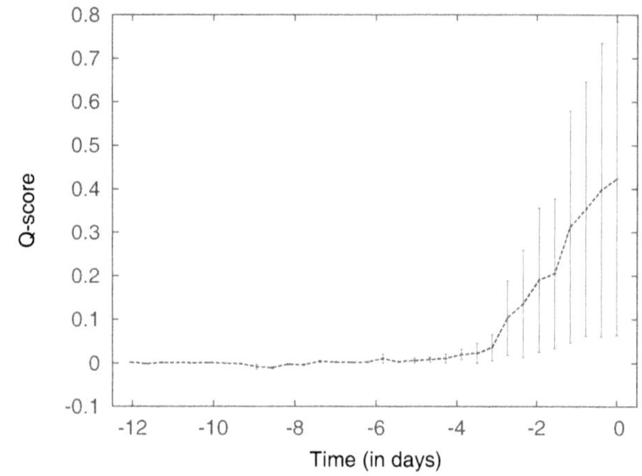

Figure 8: Growth pattern of Q-score

Another finding from the KPI analysis is drawn from multi-scale temporal aggregation. As shown in Table 6, by combining long-term and short-term event duration δ in regression, we observe both video and audio related issues appear as the most significant KPIs. This further confirms the effectiveness of letting the regression algorithm to choose important KPIs among multiple temporal aggregations.

Noticing that different KPIs have different degrees of relevancy to user feedback, we aim to guide monitoring of network KPIs by enlisting a small number of significant KPIs to user-perceived service quality. This way, forthcoming fine-grained network diagnosis can focus on the significant KPIs rather than analyzing excessive amount of KPIs.

5.2 Predicting Bad Quality of Experience

In order for Q-score to be useful for alerting services, it should have the capability to provide triggers well before users start to call. Thus, there is a need to study how much into the future we can infer customer calls using Q-score. To understand the feasible level of proactiveness in Q-score, we evaluated two characteristics: (i) the growth pattern of Q-score over time and (ii) stability of Q-score with a time gap between network events and user feedback.

Growth of Q-score Over Time. Figure 8 shows the growth pattern of Q-score for individual user IDs who filed trouble tickets. In the figure, we align the time by the trouble ticket filing time ($time = 0$) and observe how Q-score grows. The solid line represents the average value of the scores and the upper and lower tips of error bars represent one standard deviation plus and minus the average. From the graph, we observe that the increase of average Q-score is close to linear when it is greater than 0.05. The monotonic and gradual increase of Q-score suggests a possibility of using Q-score as a proactive trigger for alerting because (i) it keeps increasing once it becomes non-negligible level and (ii) its growth is not too abrupt. However, due to great variance among different users' Q-scores, we cannot use Q-score of 0.05 as the significant value triggering forthcoming actions. Instead, we seek a more realistic lead time by conducting a further study on the stability of Q-score.

Feasible Level of Proactiveness. As aforementioned in Section 3.3, user feedback has indeterminate delay from the occurrences of network events. Here, we test the amount of lead time Q-score can provide before customer calls by measuring the accuracy loss as we increase the time gap between the occurrence times of network

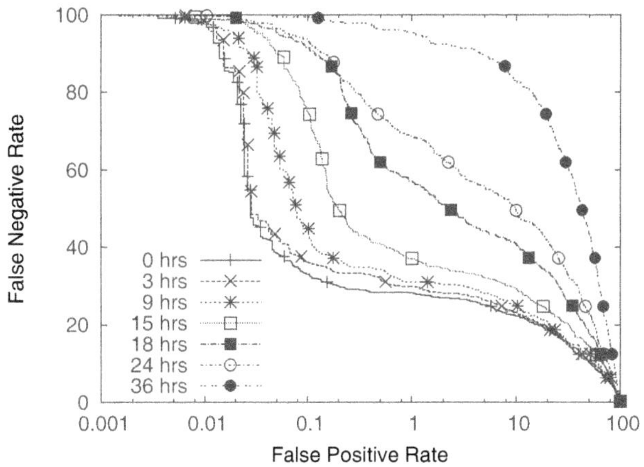

Figure 9: Comparison of accuracy of Q-scores with different skip intervals Δ

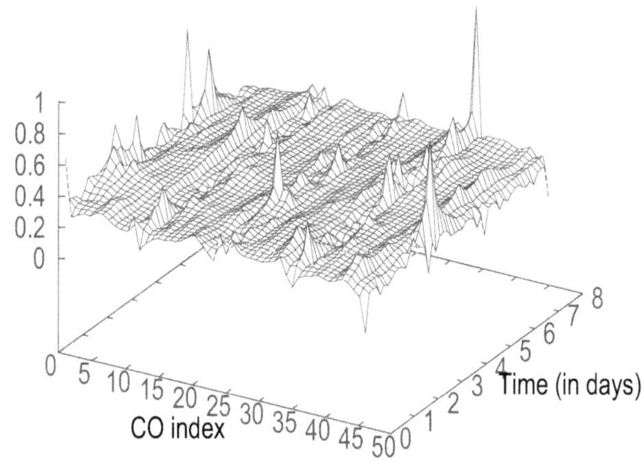

Figure 10: Normalized amount of users with customer reports over different spatial locations (COs) and times.

events b_i and user feedback c_i. The default time gap (or skipping interval) between $s_i+\delta$ and u_i is 0 hour because we set $u_i = s_i+\delta$ in Section 3.3. In this test, we add the skipping time gap Δ to the equation $u_i = s_i + \delta + \Delta$. By increasing Δ in the online monitoring step of Q-score generation, we test the regression for larger delays between b_i and c_i, in other words, we test for the stability of Q-score in proactive, early warning.

With various Δ ranging from 0 hours to 36 hours, Figure 9 exhibits FPR-FNR of learned β with different skipping times. As we increase Δ, the regression gets to rely on the user feedback of longer time after the occurrences of network events. And we observe that the FPR-FNR trade off gets worse as results. While the choice of lead time should mainly be left to the discretion of network administrators, we find 9 hours of lead time is at the feasible level, as observing 9 hours of skip interval preserves 0.1% of FPR only sacrificing 10% of FNR (*i.e.*, FNR is 30% when skip interval is 0 hours and 40% when skip interval is 9 hours).

5.3 Dimensioning Customer Care Workforce

If network problems occur locally to regional service areas rather than globally, an efficient management of field operators (*e.g.*, customer care representatives and repair men at customer premises) and servicing resources (*e.g.*, devices for fine-grained monitoring of network) would be to dynamically allocate them to challenging service regions than assigning static work areas. Thus, predicting the volume of forecoming issues to a service region at a given time is beneficial in adaptively allocating workforce across service regions. In this application, we assess the possibility of pre-allocating a customer care workforce to potentially troubling service areas using Q-score. To begin, we first assess the volume of service quality issues per different spatial regions and see if the issues are contained locally or spread out globally.

Spatial Distribution of User Feedback. Figure 10 shows the spatial distribution of user feedback across different COs. The x-axis shows indexes of different COs, the z-axis shows temporal trend. The y-axis shows the amount of customer calls normalized by the peak value (*e.g.*, a value of 1 represents that the corresponding CO and time has the highest amount of calls shown in the figure) [1]. At a given time, we observe that high user feedback is local to each CO. And over time, the areas of high user feedback changes from one CO to another. From the fact that high feedback values generally being uncorrelated across time and CO (or space), we can affirm that the issues are temporal rather than permanent and local to an area rather than being global.

Leveraging Q-score for Dimensioning Workforce. Now that we have seen the possibility of dynamic resource allocation over different COs, we evaluate how closely Q-score follows user feedback in its magnitude when aggregated across individuals within each COs. Note that, to focus on its similarity to user feedback rate, we ignored the lead time of Q-score in this test. Figure 11 shows the trend of Q-score and user feedback aggregated per-CO. In doing so, Q-scores of individual user ID are first computed, and the scores corresponding to individuals within each CO are aggregated together to form per-CO Q-score. To compare three subfigures under the same scale factor, the plots are normalized by the peak customer call rate appearing in Figure 11(a), 22 hour time. Figure 11(a) shows the trend of per-CO Q-score and user feedback for a CO with relatively high customer feedback (*i.e.*, customer report rates). Over the course of 24 days, the percentage of users call the support center on the y-axis gets as high as 11%. Despite that there are some overestimations, the general trend of per-CO Q-score closely follows that of user feedback with Pearson's correlation coefficient $\mathcal{R} = 0.8797$. Figure 11(b) shows per-CO Q-score and user feedback for COs with moderately high customer feedback. We again see that the Q-score follows feedback whenever feedback increases over 2%. Here, $\mathcal{R} = 0.7478$ Figure 11(c) shows the same for a CO with few customer calls. Because there are only a small increase (2% of users calling) in the user feedback, Q-score remains at low level of 0.17% on average with $\mathcal{R} = 0.5011$. From the observations from three different COs with high, medium, and low level of feedback, we confirmed that Q-score, when aggregated across individuals within each CO, closely follows the trend of per-CO user feedback. Since Q-score is confirmed to have several hours of lead time before users begin to report, we can leverage Q-score in dimensioning the workforce and prioritizing resources to areas with more upcoming issues ahead of time.

6. RELATED WORK

In this section, we introduce related works on the two important components of networked service assurance: quality of experience assessment and network diagnosis.

[1]To protect proprietary information, we normalize some information in the results to the extent that the normalization does not obstruct interpretation of results

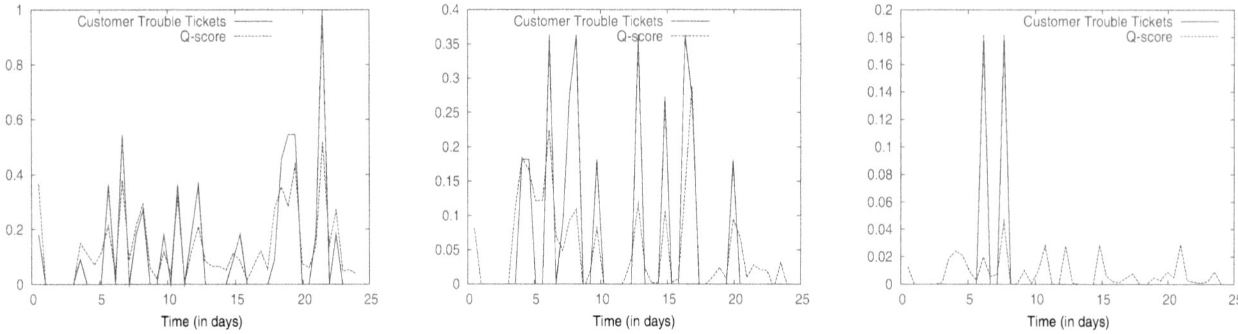

(a) CO with high customer report rates (b) CO with moderate customer report rates (c) CO with low customer report rates

Figure 11: Trend of customer trouble tickets and Q-score per CO.

6.1 Quality of Experience Assessment

Controlled Performance Assessment. A traditional approach in the performance assessment of network devices is to use controlled lab environments. The code analysis, protocol analysis, testbed tests, and debugging done in such controlled environments serve to localize faults to each individual component of the system. [5,6] apply principles of automated software fault diagnosis and model-based approaches. [21] outlines the methods of software and hardware verification using formal logic theorem provers. While theorem prover-based service assessment can be extensive and correct, the process of converting system operation to mathematical logic and inventing theorems thereafter restrict its application to a few specialized software and hardware systems such as that of the CPU and its microcodes. For validating network protocols, there have been several proposals [8, 12] based on simulation and system modeling using finite state machine, traffic modeling, and queuing theory.

Controlled testing has been extremely successful in detecting and preventing critical software bugs and hardware failures. Despite their best efforts, however, they are simply unable to replicate the immense scale and complexity of large operational systems and networks. Thus, there is always the risk of issues creeping into operational settings when they are missed in controlled environments. In this paper, we focus on a data-oriented mining approach that analyzes the data collected from an operational network. We believe a combination of data mining, lab reproduction, and software/hardware analysis is required to correctly identify anomalous service quality.

Video Quality Assessment. Subjective evaluation is the most reliable way of assessing the quality of an image or video, as humans are the final judges of the video quality in great part of the video related applications. The mean opinion score (MOS) [1] is a subjective quality measurement used in subjective tests which has been regarded as the most reliable assessment for video. However, subjective video assessment method is very inconvenient, expensive and slow. Thus there is a field of research dedicated to the design and development of objective quality metrics. Ongoing studies are both on standardizing the subjective measurement of video quality [23] and on developing objective video quality metrics that model and approximate the quality [3].

There are also video quality measurement studies in the context of networked systems [4]. The work includes discussions on the metrics of video quality measurable from various parts of a network. [17] studies the viewers' perception of video quality under packet loss-induced video impairments. [27, 28] proposes a loss-distortion model based PSNR metric applied to video quality monitoring. Recently, ITU and other standardizing organizations began to roll out video quality measures such as [22]. Besides the lack of consensus in arriving at a single formula, video quality metrics may not be readily usable in the context of network service quality assessment as they require fine-grained measurements of per flow network traffic which current services dismiss due to the costs of measurement and data collection. While our method uses the customer trouble ticket as a proxy for user feedback, the concept of our methodology is open to employing a variety of video quality metrics as the measure of user experience.

6.2 Reactive Performance Diagnosis

Bayesian network and graph analysis are among the most widely used techniques in the diagnosis of network performance issues and troubleshooting [7, 10, 14, 16, 26, 29]. Kompella *et al.* [16] model the fault diagnosis problem using a bipartite graph and uses risk modeling to map high-level failure notifications into lower-layer root causes. WISE [29] presents a what-if analysis tool to estimate the effects of network configuration changes on service response times. Recent systems [15, 25] have used information available to the OS to identify service quality issues using the dependency structure between components.

[18–20] have shown the importance of focusing on recurring and persistent events and enabling the detection and troubleshooting of network behavior modes that have been previously flown under the operations radar. NICE [20] focuses on detecting and troubleshooting undesirable chronic network conditions using statistical correlations. Giza [18] applies multi-resolution techniques to localize regions in IPTV network with significant problems and l_1-norm minimization to discover causality between event-series. Mercury [19] focuses on detecting the long-term, persistent impact of network upgrades on key performance metrics via statistical mining. A work on proactive prediction of service issues on access network [13] focuses on capturing changes over long-term (*e.g.*, weeks and months) and conduct prediction. The main difference between the above methods and ours is in the proactiveness of assessing service quality of experience (QoE). The reactive performance diagnosis works mostly focus on network problems but not on service quality of experience. We believe, Q-score is the first work in using the network performance indicators to proactively construct the quality of experience scores for large services. By capturing the quality of experience for users in a timely and scalable fashion, Q-score offers the operators with rapid notification of user-perceived issues and a lead time of several hours before customer reports.

7. CONCLUSION

In this paper, we develop Q-score, a novel framework for proactive assessment of user perceived service quality in a large operational IPTV network. By associating coarse-grained network KPIs with imperfect user feedback, Q-score generates a single score that represents user-perceived quality of experience (QoE). Accuracy analysis of Q-score reveals that it is able to predict 60% of service problems reported by customers with only 0.1% of false positive rate. Applying Q-score to various application scenarios, we have: (i) identified a set of KPIs most relevant to user-perceived quality of experience; (ii) quantified how early it can alert bad quality of experience; (iii) observed the possibility to pre-allocate the customer care workforce to potentially affected service areas.

As an improvement of our work, we consider the following two methods aimed at increasing the successful prediction rate. First, to filter out more noise from user feedback, we plan to investigate the trouble tickets that fell into false negatives. Collaborating with video experts, we will conduct simulation based controlled test-bed experiments in conjunction with our current operational data-driven approach. Second, to make Q-score to be more resilient to incompleteness of user feedback, we will further improve user grouping methods. In doing so, we plan on applying end-user clustering techniques in relation to user-perceived QoE.

There are many other network services that are sensitive to service quality that lack objective measures of user-perceived quality of experience. Our future work includes applying the proactive service quality assessment beyond the specific context of IPTV networks. For example, we plan to apply Q-score to VoIP and mobile networks so that operation teams can predict call drops and voice quality degradation without having to wait for customers to report them.

8. REFERENCES

[1] Methods for subjective determination of transmission quality. *ITU-T Rec. P.800*, 1998.

[2] One-way transmission time. *ITU-T Rec. G.114*, 2003.

[3] Objective perceptual multimedia video quality measurement in the presence of a full reference. *ITU-T Rec. J.247*, 2008.

[4] Perceptual audiovisual quality measurement techniques for multimedia services over digital cable television networks in the presence of a reduced bandwidth reference. *ITU-T Rec. J.246*, 2008.

[5] R. Abreu, A. G. 0002, P. Zoeteweij, and A. J. C. van Gemund. Automatic software fault localization using generic program invariants. In *SAC*, 2008.

[6] R. Abreu, P. Zoeteweij, and A. J. C. van Gemund. Spectrum-based multiple fault localization. In *ASE*, 2009.

[7] P. Bahl, R. Chandra, A. Greenberg, S. Kandula, D. A. Maltz, and M. Zhang. Towards highly reliable enterprise network services via inference of multi-level dependencies. In *Sigcomm*, 2007.

[8] L. Breslau, D. Estrin, K. Fall, S. Floyd, J. Heidemann, A. Helmy, P. Huang, S. McCanne, K. Varadhan, Y. Xu, and H. Yu. Advances in network simulation. *IEEE Computer*, 33(5), 2000.

[9] S. Chatterjee and A. S. Hadi. Influential observations, high leverage points, and outliers in linear regression. *Statistical Science*, Vol. 1:379–416, 1986.

[10] I. Cohen, J. S. Chase, M. Goldszmidt, T. Kelly, and J. Symons. Correlating instrumentation data to system states: A building block for automated diagnosis and control. In *OSDI*, 2004.

[11] A. E. Hoerl and R. W. Kennard. Ridge regression: Biased estimation for nonorthogonal problems. *Technometrics*, Vol. 12, No. 1:55–67, 1970.

[12] G. Holzmann. *Design and Validation of Computer Protocols*. Prentice-Hall, 1991.

[13] Y. Jin, N. G. Duffield, A. Gerber, P. Haffner, S. Sen, and Z.-L. Zhang. Nevermind, the problem is already fixed: proactively detecting and troubleshooting customer dsl problems. In *CoNEXT*, page 7, 2010.

[14] S. Kandula, D. Katabi, and J.-P. Vasseur. Shrink: A tool for failure diagnosis in IP networks. In *MineNet*, 2005.

[15] S. Kandula, R. Mahajan, P. Verkaik, S. Agarwal, J. Padhye, and P. Bahl. Detailed diagnosis in enterprise networks. In *ACM SIGCOMM*, 2009.

[16] R. R. Kompella, J. Yates, A. Greenberg, and A. C. Snoeren. IP fault localization via risk modeling. In *NSDI*, 2005.

[17] T.-L. Lin, S. Kanumuri, Y. Zhi, D. Poole, P. Cosman, and A. R. Reibman. A versatile model for packet loss visibility and its application in packet prioritization. *IEEE Transactions on Image Processing, to appear*, 2010.

[18] A. Mahimkar, Z. Ge, A. Shaikh, J. Wang, J. Yates, Y. Zhang, and Q. Zhao. Towards automated performance diagnosis in a large IPTV network. In *ACM SIGCOMM*, 2009.

[19] A. Mahimkar, H. H. Song, Z. Ge, A. Shaikh, J. Wang, J. Yates, Y. Zhang, and J. Emmons. Detecting the performance impact of upgrades in large operational networks. In *ACM SIGCOMM*, 2010.

[20] A. Mahimkar, J. Yates, Y. Zhang, A. Shaikh, J. Wang, Z. Ge, and C. T. Ee. Troubleshooting chronic conditions in large IP networks. In *ACM CoNEXT*, 2008.

[21] J. S. Moore and M. Kaufmann. Some key research problems in automated theorem proving for hardware and software verification. In *RACSAM*, 2004.

[22] Perceptual evaluation of video quality. 2011. `http://www.pevq.org`.

[23] M. Pinson and S. Wolf. Comparing subjective video quality testing methodologies. In *SPIE Video Communications and Image Processing Conference*, pages 8–11, 2003.

[24] T. Qiu, J. Feng, Z. Ge, J. Wang, J. Xu, and J. Yates. Listen to me if you can: Tracking user experience of mobile network on social media. In *IMC*, 2010.

[25] K. Shen, C. Stewart, C. Li, and X. Li. Reference-driven performance anomaly identification. In *SIGMETRICS*, 2009.

[26] M. Steinder and A. Sethi. Increasing robustness of fault localization through analysis of lost, spurious, and positive symptoms. In *Infocom*, 2002.

[27] S. Tao, J. Apostolopoulos, and R. Guérin. Real-time monitoring of video quality in ip networks. In *Proceedings of the international workshop on Network and operating systems support for digital audio and video*, NOSSDAV '05, pages 129–134, New York, NY, USA, 2005. ACM.

[28] S. Tao, J. Apostolopoulos, and R. Guérin. Real-time monitoring of video quality in ip networks. *IEEE/ACM Trans. Netw.*, 16:1052–1065, October 2008.

[29] M. Tariq, A. Zeitoun, V. Valancius, N. Feamster, and M. Ammar. Answering what-if deployment and configuration questions with WISE. In *SIGCOMM*, 2008.

Summary Review Documentation for

"Q-score: Proactive Service Quality Assessment in a Large IPTV System"

Authors: H. Song, Z. Ge, A. Mahimkar, J. Wang, J. Yates, Y. Zhang, A. Basso, M. Chen

Note: The authors of this paper opted out of this year's reviewing experiment. As a result, the final version of this paper is not accompanied by the reviews that the paper received during the reviewing process.

Measurement and Analysis of a Large Scale Commercial Mobile Internet TV System

Yuheng Li
Tsinghua University
Beijing, China
liyuheng07@mails.tsinghua.edu.cn

Yiping Zhang
Shandong Technology
Beijing, China
jumping@dopool.com

Ruixi Yuan
Tsinghua University
Beijing, China
ryuan@tsinghua.edu.cn

ABSTRACT

Large scale, Internet based mobile TV deployment presents both tremendous opportunities and challenges for mobile operators and technology providers. This paper presents a measurement based study on a large scale mobile TV service offering in China. Within the one month measurement period, our dataset captured over 1 million unique mobile devices and more than 49 million video sessions. Analysis showed that mobile viewing patterns are different from that of landline based IPTV and VoD systems. In particular, the average viewing time is significantly shorter, and the channel popularity distribution is more skewed towards top ranked channels than that of landline based systems. For the channel sojourn time, the distribution follows a piecewise model, which combines lognormal and pareto distribution. The lognormal part, which fits the majority of video sessions, more closely resembles the mobile phone call holding time, rather than the power law distribution in the landline IPTV case. In comparing the 3G and WiFi access methods, we found that users exhibit different behaviors when accessing from different networks. In 3G networks, where users are subject to data charge, users tend to have shorter channel sojourn time and prefer lower bit-rate channels. The parameters of the distributions are also different. Understanding these user behaviors and their implications on network traffic are critical for the success of future mobile TV industry.

Categories and Subject Descriptors

C.2.4 [**Distributed Systems**]: Distributed applications; C.4 [**Performance of Systems**]: Measurement techniques

General Terms

Measurement, Performance, Human Factors

Keywords

Mobile Video, Human Behavior, Sojourn Time, Distribution

1. INTRODUCTION

The rapid growth of Internet video applications and the proliferation of mobile smart phones have made it possible to provide live streaming TV content to mobile users. Mobile TV, an emerging application over mobile networks has seen initial deployments around the world.

Both digital broadcasting technologies (e.g. DMB, CMMB, MediaFLO) and wireless Internet data (e.g. 3G) based technologies can be used to support mobile TV deployments. While one-way broadcast offers the closest resemblance to traditional broadcast TV reception, the broadcast based mobile TV services offered mixed commercial results. In the United States, the MediaFLO based FLO TV was discontinued in March 2011 due to its failure to attract enough viewers. In South Korea, the T-DMB based service achieved considerable market penetration, reaching over 25 million devices sold in the third quarter of 2009.

Video streaming service based on mobile Internet connections, on the other hand, offers a greater flexibility and interactivity through the two-way Internet connection. The proliferation of mobile applications with video streaming capabilities means that mobile video traffic is rapidly becoming the dominant form in the mobile networks. In a recent released study, Cisco systems reported that mobile video was 49.8 percent of total mobile traffic in 2010, and will exceed 50 percent in 2011 [1].

The realization of mobile TV will significantly change the landscape of mobile communication and television industries, two important industries of the global society. How will the factors of mobility, screen size and other consumption factors affect user behaviors and traffic characteristics? Is the mobile network infrastructure adequate to support mobile TV services? How should the content be adapted for mobile TV consumption? These are pressing questions need to be answered for the emerging market of mobile TV.

From the Internet measurement point of view, mobile TV services using wireless Internet connections (e.g. 3G, WiFi networks) offer a great opportunity to collect traffic data and analyze user behaviors. In conjunction with the large mobile TV service deployment from "CNLive", we are able to collect a large amount of data from both the video streaming servers and the mobile device clients. To the best of our knowledge, this measurement represents the first large scale mobile TV measurement effort.

In this paper, we present an in-depth analysis of the mobile TV measurement data. The data spans over a month of measurement period, contained approximately 49 million TV viewing sessions, which included 840 million video segment downloads. We evaluate users' viewing qualities and characterize the aggregated channel population dynamics and dwelling time. Our analysis focus on the issues of user behaviors and the impact on network traffic and design. The highlights of our contributions can be summarized as follows:

- We observed that both 3G networks and WiFi networks have adequately supported the video viewing experience. Greater than 95% of video playback is continuous and the vast majority of startup delays are within 10 seconds.

- Although the user population evolution is similar to that of the landline based IPTV, with a strong night-time peak and a smaller peak during the lunch break, the exact time of peaks are different.

- Biased preferences on contents are observed on mobile TV. The channel popularity is highly skewed and follows a Pareto distribution, with a dropped tail.

- The channel sojourn (dwell) time distribution can be best fitted by two piecewise distributions. The distribution for the shorter sojourn times ($\leq$ 10 minutes) follows a lognormal distribution, which resembles the call holding time distribution in cellular telephony. The distribution for the longer sojourn time ($>$ 10 minutes) follows a generalized Pareto distribution, which resembles the traditional channel dwell time in landline based IPTV but with a dropped tail.

- There are slight quantitative differences when users accessing the content via data charging 3G networks and WiFi networks. Users tend to stay longer in the free of charge WiFi networks, and 3G users tend to have a traffic-saving habit due to the traffic volume charging effect of 3G mobile networks.

Our analysis, based on the large volume measured data, has several important implications for the future mobile TV deployment. First, it is both feasible and practical to deploy large scale mobile TV service through the 3G mobile and WiFi networks. Second, the highly skewed channel popularity distribution meant that effective content distribution network (CDN) can be engineered for the highly popular channels. Third, the lognormal distribution of channel sojourn time in the short duration period indicates that users are conscious of the traffic volume charges, and television contents need to be adapted to the mobile networks, both in terms of the device display size, as well as the shorter viewing times.

The rest of this paper is organized as follows: Section 2 reviews related works. In section 3, we provide an overview of "CNLive" mobile TV system, our measurement methodology and describe our dataset in detail. Section 4 provides an analysis on the traffic characteristics, and infers user viewing quality. Section 5 focuses on channel popularity and sojourn time, where we develop distributions that best fit the empirical data. We also investigate the quantitative difference in user behavior through 3G and WiFi accesses. Finally, we conclude and summarize implications in Section 6.

2. RELATED WORKS

In the last decade, video streaming over the Internet has attracted much research interests. There are many measurement studies of VoD and live TV streaming networks [3, 4, 6, 7, 24, 27, 29]. In [29], it is found that streaming realvideo content across of the Internet with either TCP or UDP protocols offer reasonable viewing experiences. In [6, 7, 24], Web viewing of user-generated content (such as YouTube) and their distribution patterns were studied, it was found that a Zipf-like waist with truncated tail could describe the video popularity ranks, and caching popular videos can significantly reduce the server load. Arlitt et. al studied the web server load characteristics for 1998 World Cup site [3], and found that the server load exhibits bursty behaviors. Yin et. al studied the large scale VoD deployment from the 2008 Olympics [34] and found that 80% of the viewing session time was below 600 seconds, and there were flash crowd phenomena during popular events.

There are also many measurement based studies on P2P based video streaming systems. The measurement methods included traffic capture from network sniffing tools [9, 25, 26, 28], active network crawling [11, 12, 30], and streaming server logs [14,15,31] . These studies were mainly focused on peer population dynamics, user playback qualities, peer to peer overlay topologies and chunk selection algorithms. For example, studies of the CoolStreaming system [14, 15, 31] , one of the earliest large scale P2P video streaming systems, found that pure P2P systems suffer from long start-up delays and peer failures during flash crowd periods, and suggested a hybrid system with assistance from geographical distributed video servers.

Several studies from the measurement of infrastructure based IPTV service were published recently [8, 21, 22]. In [21,22] Measurements from over 2 million STBs from a large scale IPTV deployment in the U.S. were analyzed. Models were developed for user behaviors and channel popularities. In [8], STBs from over 250,000 households in South Korea were monitored for over six months and the data analyzed to study the viewing session behaviors, channel popularity. It was found that the channel holding time follows a power law distribution and the channel popularity ranking follows a Zipf-like distribution with fast decay for non-popular channels.

There are several studies of hand-held mobile TV and mobile TV on cellphone based on surveys. Miyauchi et al. [19] adopted a qualitative study on the usage of live mobile TV that reveal the different attitudes concerning usage of live mobile TV in different scenarios. Cui, Chipchase and Jung [10] carried out a qualitative study of mobile TV usage, and point out that the typical usage situations were killing time while commuting, personal use at home, secret use at school and macro breaks. Buchinger et al. [5] compared different user studies on mobile TV, and summarized different aspects that affect user behaviors and interests on mobile TV. These studies gave the usage scenarios of mobile TV, which is quite different from Internet TV. From a human computer interaction perspective, Xu et al. [32] argued that the user attention constraint of the mobile media platform can significantly influences user experience and behaviors.

Recently, mobile video delivery begin to attract attention. [17] summarizes HTTP-based mobile video delivery protocols and shows how segment-based delivery enables HTTP-

Figure 1: Client Software user interface

based live streaming with increased scalability through the use of existing CDN infrastructure at the same time.

To the best of our knowledge, there is no analysis of user behaviors and network traffic based on measurements from large scale mobile TV service deployment. In this paper, we present a measurement based study of video streaming traffic of a nationwide mobile TV system deployed in China. Using similar analysis methods from those used in landline based video streaming systems, our study revealed similarities and differences between landline based and mobile TV services, both will have important implications for future mobile TV deployments.

3. MEASUREMENT METHODOLOGY

3.1 System Overview

CNLive is a leading mobile TV service provider in China (The platform is provided by Shandong Technology, Beijing). It provides a mobile content distribution platform for TV and radio stations to broadcast programs to smart phones and other mobile devices (e.g. iPad). The media streaming is in the format of Quicktime with a resolution of 320×240 with a bitrate of approximately 256kpbs. The system currently supports live video streaming on more than 120 TV channels as well as audio streaming on 16 radio channels at 32kbps. These channels are from various content providers, including satellite channels in most provinces in China and many other specialized channels. Users access media streams from a client software running on mobile device, which displays a hierarchical list of channels and leads users to channels they interested as shown in Figure 1.

HTTP Live Streaming [20] was chosen as the technology to stream contents to user clients because of its support for cellular networks and the ease of firewall traversal for the HTTP protocol. The basic idea of HTTP Live Streaming is to transfer video data in segments at maximized speed and minimized time rather than on constant rate stream to adapt to the wireless network environment. Although HTTP Live Streaming supports adaptive bitrate on transferring video data, the system uses a constant bitrate to encode and transfer multimedia contents.

As shown in Figure 2, encoding servers divide live TV signals into segments of 10 seconds and encapsulate segmented video data in MPEG2 transport streams. Playlists are generated for different channels containing a list of segments to be played in order. End servers distributed in different

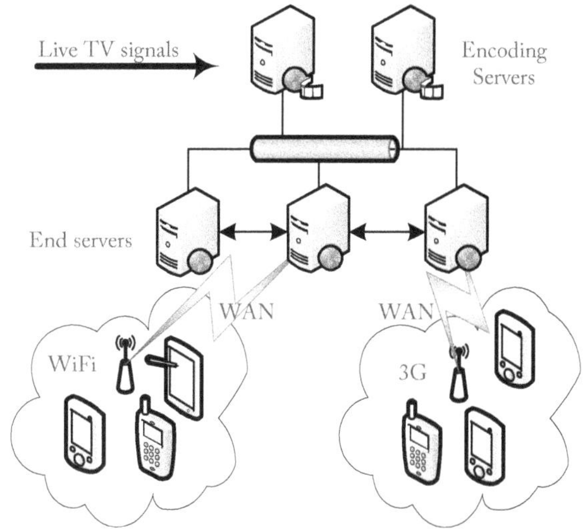

Figure 2: System structure

ISPs are responsible for data distribution between encoding servers and clients. Requests from clients are dispatched to different end servers comprising a DNS-based load balance strategy.

On the mobile device, the client software first requests for the playlist and downloads an initial buffer (3 to 8 segments depending on the device OS and client software version) to guarantee playback quality. The client starts to play when the buffer is filled with the first segment. The buffering process runs in the background until the buffer is full. The client updates the playlist and downloads a new video segment every 10 seconds.

The network used to access mobile TV can be WiFi or 3G network. WiFi networks are generally accessible indoors only, whereas 3G networks cover most areas indoors and outdoors. Mobile operators in China provide several plans for 3G network usage. Most of them have a flat rate with a fixed cap, and the data amount over the cap being charged proportionally to the actual usage. For example, a popular China Unicom's 3G bundle plan for iPhone is 286RMB/month with a data cap at 1.1GB, which amounts to 0.26RMB/MB. However, typically, the overuse rate is only slightly more expensive than the average rate under the cap. In the China Unicom case, the overuse rate is 0.30RMB/MB. Considering the living standard in China, the 3G data usage fee is not cheap for many ordinary Chinese.

Our measurement system collects log data from both HTTP Live Streaming servers and the mobile clients. Server-side log helps us track download of every video segment, while client-side log provides more detailed information on client devices and user behaviors.

3.2 Server-side Logs

The server-side log system deployed on HTTP end servers is designed to log and collect all the user requests (including playlist and video segment requests) from all the clients. A log collector is deployed at a centralized collection server to gather all the client access logs from video servers. The clock at each of the video servers are synchronized using the

Field	Description
Timestamp	The time server received the request
Requesting Time	Time length of the request processing
Client IP and Port	IP address and port of HTTP connection
Node	Name of the server
Connection number	A unique and consistent identifier of the TCP connection
Channel	The channel selected by user
HTTP Code	HTTP status code
File size	The size of requested resource

Table 1: Description of fields in segment log entries

NTP protocol, hence the timestamps in the log entries are comparable with each other.

The log gathered on the collection server is called the *access log*. A single access log entry contains fields such as timestamp of the request, client IP and port, a sequence number of the connection, URL of requested content, HTTP status, bytes transmitted, and time spent on data transmission. The access log can be further divided into *playlist log* and *segment log* by logged request content. Accesses of different channels can be identified from URL of requested playlist and video segment. In this paper, our study is mainly based on segment logs. The fields in a single segment log entry is described in Table 1.

To adopt an in-depth study of traffic and user behavior, we need to further find internal relations among the segment downloads. A *video session* is defined as the whole process of video streaming playback, from user clicking play to stop playing. Recalling the progressive downloading mechanism of HTTP Live Streaming, a video session typically includes multiple video segment log entries. Mobile TV clients use persistent HTTP connections to transfer video data, that is, if the video session continues, server will have consecutive segment access log entries in the same connection. Therefore, video sessions can be identified by server name and the connection number corresponding to every TCP connection in segment log.

3.3 Client-side Logs

We also embedded an analytic module to collect data from user devices and directly report to the server in new versions of mobile TV clients. The info collected from the client side is at three levels. The first level is device information, such as device type, manufacturer, OS, and screen size. On the second level, we call a single run of client software as an *application session*. Application session information includes: network type (WiFi/3G), and the time the software starts and ends. The third level is *video session* information. We log the channel, the video playback start and end time, and the time spent on buffering in the video session. We designed unique identifiers for devices, application sessions, and video sessions. However, only clients in new versions contain the analytic module. In other words, the new versions only covered part of the client population. Logs collected from client side can only be considered as complementary to the server-side logs.

As described in Table 1, we do not have the knowledge of network type from server-side logs directly. However, such information can be inferred from the IP address of the client. In China, the ISP's IP address assignment blocks are fixed (e.g. after a C-block address pool is assigned to a WiFi service, it will not be used for a 3G service). Therefore, the client-side logs provide us a detailed address map that separate the 3G accesses from the WiFi accesses. This map is then applied to the server-side logs to infer the access network types.

3.4 Overview of datasets

Our analysis in this paper is mainly based on two datasets collected from March 1, 2011 to March 31, 2011. Dataset 1 is server-side log collected from March 01 to March 31, 2011. It contains 140 channels, 840,671,888 segment downloads, and 49,746,882 video sessions.

Dataset 2 is the client-side logs collected from the same period. It logged information from 1,134,364 different devices, 6,228,188 application sessions, and 10,011,897 video sessions. Because multiple versions of the client-side software exist in the field, and only new versions have the client-side logging capability, the number of video sessions from the client-side logs is considerably smaller than that of the server-side logs.

4. TRAFFIC ANALYSIS

The HTTP Live Streaming protocol uses a different manner on video data transmission compared with traditional video streaming protocols. In this section, we measure the traffic of mobile TV on WiFi and 3G networks as well as evaluate the actual service quality of mobile TV.

4.1 Understanding Traffic Patterns

HTTP Live Streaming protocol with a 10 second segment size is implemented for the mobile TV service. On average, a video segment is around 350KB whereas a playlist is less than 1KB. The protocol itself has little overhead. Intuitively, when downloading the video segments, the link bandwidth would be nearly 100% occupied. During the intervals between successive segment downloads, the link would most likely be idle. To discover the actual mobile TV traffic pattern, we run TCPDUMP on a controlled Apple iPhone to capture traffic generated by a mobile TV client on both 3G and WiFi connections.

Figure 3 gives an example of client traffic of mobile TV on both high-speed WiFi connection and 3G (WCDMA) connection. The playback begins at 0s, and only the first 120 seconds of playback is illustrated in the figure. It can be seen that network traffic is pulse-shaped as the client updates playlist and downloads video data periodically in Figure 3(a). The buffering period of 3 segments at first 6 seconds can be identified as well. We refer the time between two consecutive updates of playlist as a *cycle*. In each cycle, the HTTP Live Streaming protocol downloads at the maximum speed, and then sleep after finishing the video segment until next cycle, whereas other streaming protocols such as RTSP tend to download video streams at a constant rate. However, due to delay in data transmission and the quality of connection in real circumstances, measured length of cycles and width of pulses in Figure 3(b) are not exactly equal as described in [20].

The speed and quality of the network connection have a great effect on the playback quality. Under a good network condition in 3(a), data traffic can be easily identified as described in [20]. On the contrary, a poor connection quality

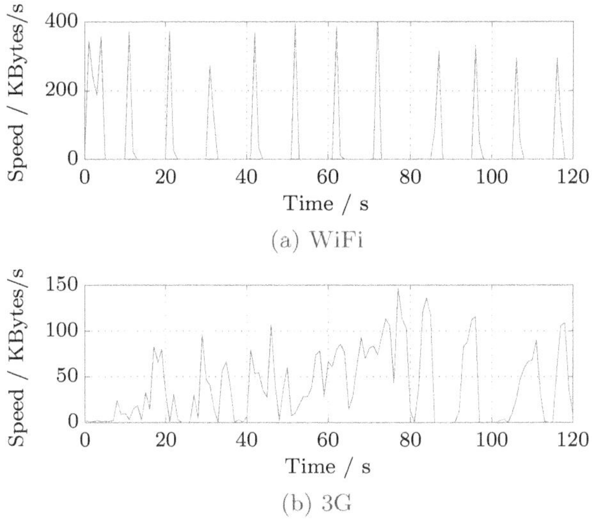

Figure 3: Mobile TV client data throughput

may result in overlapping of data downloading in consecutive cycles. If it takes too long to download a segment that the buffer gets empty, the video will freeze. Connection quality also influences playback start-up time, as it needs more time to fill up the buffer as well.

Generally speaking, 3G networks are usually less stable than WiFi connections. As shown in Figure 3(b), the protocol is quite flexible in adapting to the instability of network connection.

4.2 Viewing Quality Estimation

A frequent consideration for the deployment of Internet based mobile TV is the quality of video viewing derived from unreliable wireless connections. While the viewing quality on the smart phone screen cannot be directly monitored, the video continuity can be inferred from the segment requesting timestamps in server-side logs.

We define the video segment transmission delay as the time passed from when the server received the request of a video segment to the time the segment is successfully delivered (the data is delivered via HTTP, hence every byte of the data is being acknowledged). The complementary cumulative distribution function (CCDF) of the transmission delay of all video segment requests in dataset 1 is plotted in Figure 4. Because users may connect via either WiFi or 3G connections, we have taken into account of the different connection types. The curve drops quickly when $x < 5$s. Overall 90.0% of the video segments were successfully delivered within 5 seconds, and 97.5% within 10 seconds. We can see that the distribution of the serving time over WiFi and 3G connections are quite close. The ratios of segments delivered within 10 seconds are 97.8% and 97.2% via WiFi and 3G connections, respectively. Because each video segment has a 10 second-long playing time, requests that take more than 10 seconds may lead to a downgraded viewing experience.

However, buffering may prevent playbacks from stuttering even if some segments do not arrive in time. To assess the QoS of video playback, we further emulate the process of data downloading and video playing based on the knowledge of the moment and transmission time consumption of

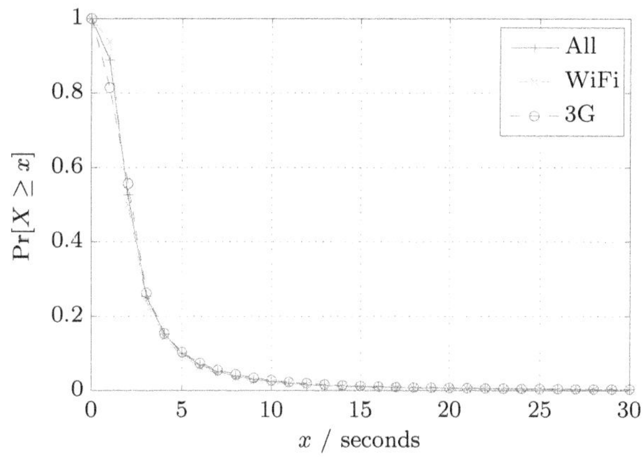

Figure 4: CCDF of segment transmission delay

every segment in dataset 1. We denote the time point that segment k of the video session is downloaded as t_k, where $k = 1, 2, 3, \cdots$. Given that the length of each segment is 10 seconds, the downloaded video data can be played for $D(k) = 10k$ seconds at t_k. On the other hand, as the image starts to show on screen after the first segment is downloaded, the viewer is supposed to have already watched the channel for $P(k) = t_k - t_1$ seconds at t_k if the playback never gets stuck. By comparing downloaded video length $D(k)$ and expected playback length $P(k)$, we can obtain the length of video data in the buffer at t_k:

$$B(k) = D(k) - P(k) = 10k - t_k + t_1 \qquad (1)$$

Obviously, zero is the critical value of $B(k)$. If $B(k) > 0$, there are downloaded video data remaining in buffer that the playback will be continuous. If $B(k) < 0$, the buffer is already empty that the playback gets stuck and the viewer have to wait the player to buffer sufficient data to play. In the emulation, we check $B(k)$ of the k-th segment of each video session in dataset 1, marking sessions with $B(k) < 0$ as "stuttered session".

Overall, 4.5% of all sessions have stuttered while playing. The stutter ratio of WiFi and 3G sessions are 4.7% and 4.3% respectively. In other words, over 95% of video sessions enjoy uninterrupted playback. We note that the timeout ratio for a single segment on 3G connection is higher than WiFi, but the stutter ratio of video sessions on 3G connections is a little lower than that seen with WiFi. This is due to the fact that the length distribution of WiFi and 3G connections are different. Longer duration of video sessions leads to a larger possibility of stuttering. By emulation, we also find that only around 47% of segment download timeouts finally lead to a stutter thanks to buffering on both WiFi and 3G connections.

We also measured the start-up time, namely the time between when the viewer presses the play button to when the video appears on the screen. This start-up time is logged in dataset 2 and its CCDF is shown in Figure 5. Around 40% of video playbacks start within 5 seconds, 80% of video playbacks start within 10 seconds, and 90% of video playbacks start within 15 seconds. While the playback time is considerably longer than the traditional cable TV switching time of less than 1 second, it is comparable to the state of

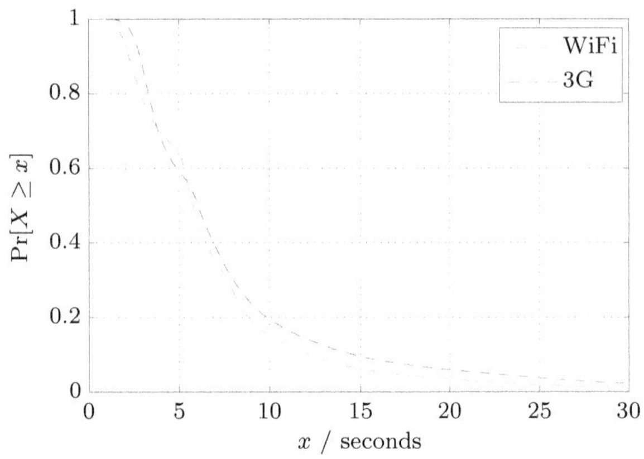

Figure 5: CCDF of start-up time

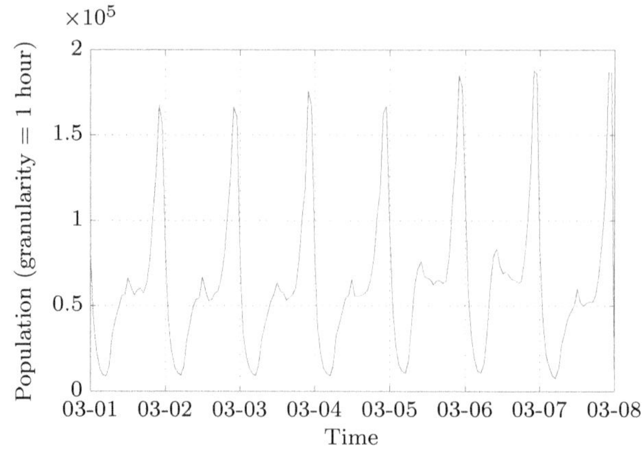

Figure 6: Population from March 1 to March 7

art P2P based Internet TV buffering time of 5 to 15 seconds [11]. Generally speaking, the 3G users and WiFi users have similar start-up time profiles, with 3G users experiencing a slightly longer start-up time than WiFi users on average.

From the measurement and analysis of mobile TV traffic, we find that mobile TV based on HTTP Live Streaming can provide fairly continuous playbacks and have a relatively short start-up time.

5. UNDERSTANDING USER BEHAVIORS

Handheld devices and wireless networks provide mobile TV viewers a high degree of mobility, which is a very different experience than that offered by traditional TV sets and IPTV systems. We are interested in investigating user behaviors in the mobile environment, and how the handheld device and mobility can influence users' viewing habits. In addition, users may connect through either WiFi or 3G networks. In 3G networks, users have to pay for the data traffic generated by the video streaming. As video streaming is very data intensive, the charge is generally not trivial. Hence it is possible for the data charge to influence user behaviors.

We will present a thorough analysis of user behaviors in this section.

5.1 User Access Patterns

To make it easier to illustrate, we picked one representative week data (March 1 to March 7) from dataset 1. March 5 and 6 are a Saturday and Sunday respectively. Figure 6 shows time variation of population in the system (time granularity is set to 1 hour in the figure). It can be easily seen that there is a strong diurnal pattern of population, with a daily peak at around 11PM, followed by a sharp decrease in number which reaches the daily nadir at around 5AM, and then ramps up in the morning to the first peak during the day. The population drops only slightly in the afternoon, and then rises quickly after 6PM to the second peak at night. The population is highly dynamic, as the number at the peak in the night is around 16 times of the value at the nadir every day.

At the same time, we observed that the access pattern in weekends (March 5 and 6 in Figure 6) differs slightly from weekdays. The first peak is reached around 10AM during weekends, earlier than the 12PM during the weekdays. In addition, users tend to watch more mobile TV during the day on the weekend than on weekdays.

We note that the daily access pattern of mobile TV exhibits both similarity and differences from those of the observed in landline based Internet TV services. For example, in the Korean IPTV study [8], a similar diurnal pattern was observed. However, the first peak in the IPTV study occurred at 3PM, while the peak in our dataset occurred at 12PM. We believe that the IPTV study probably captured the home TV viewers, and the mobile TV study probably captured the lunch time crowds.

We illustrate time variation of population of 3G and WiFi users of the same representative week from dataset 1 with the same time granularity and time range in Figure 7. Generally, WiFi users and 3G users have similar diurnal access patterns. At the same time, the ratio of population via WiFi/3G evolves over time. The WiFi population is smaller than 3G during the day, and surpasses 3G population in the evenings. There are almost the same number of WiFi and 3G users from the midnight to the morning. The difference between WiFi and 3G population appears to be smaller in the daytime during the weekends (March 5 and 6) than that of the weekdays. We believe this results from the fact that people tend to connect via 3G outside and via WiFi in home.

5.2 User Geographical Distribution

Geographical information of users is extracted from IP addresses by querying the public GeoIP database [13], which has a better accuracy on Chinese IP range than the well known free Maxmind GeoIP database [18]. Figure 8 shows the distribution of user accesses in dataset 1. The fractions in the figure are calculated by total segment downloads from the corresponding province. We only plotted the top 20 provinces in China, and put other provinces together.

Because all the programs broadcast on mobile TV are in Chinese, the vast majority of the viewers are from China, and only 4.31% accesses come from overseas. We observed an unbalanced distribution of mobile TV users in China as well. The developed provinces along the seacoast account for a large fraction of total accesses. This indicates that the acceptance of mobile TV in different areas of the country is quite different. The distribution of accesses gives useful information on server deployment as well.

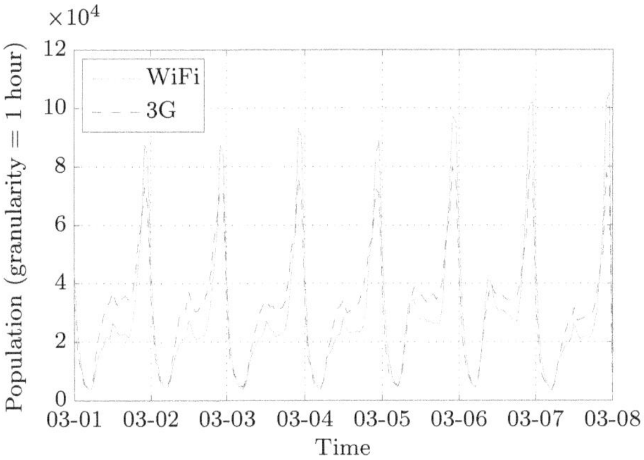

Figure 7: 3G/WiFi population comparison in a week

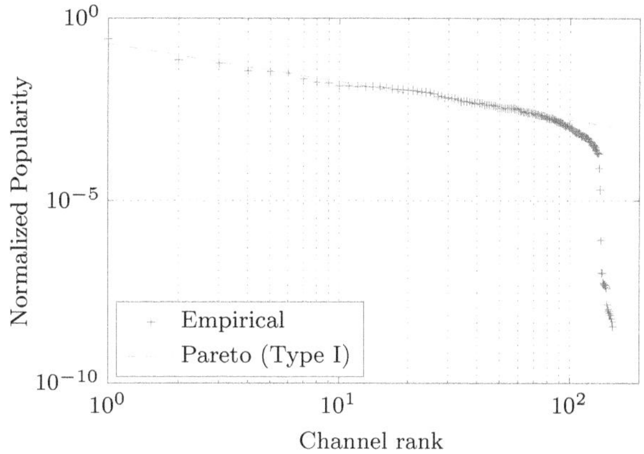

Figure 9: Channel popularity in dataset 1

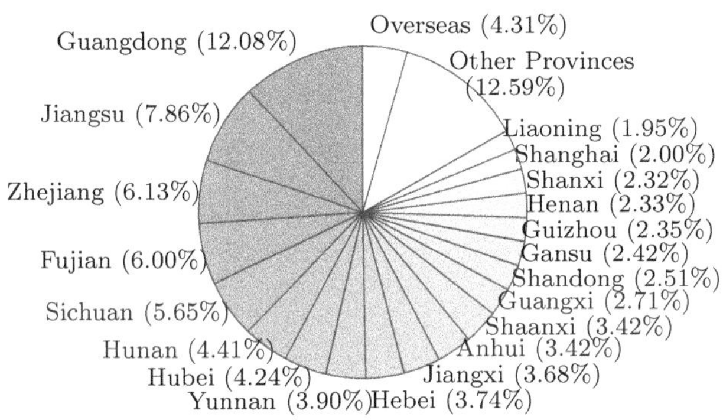

Figure 8: Geographical distribution of user accesses

5.3 Channel Popularity

In this subsection, we investigate the channel popularity distribution of mobile TV. First, we need to define a proper metric for channel popularity. Channel popularity is mainly reflected on two aspects: one is the ability to attract viewers, and the other is the ability to hold viewers on the channel. Correspondingly, there are two candidate metrics: the access frequency and the total playback length.

To account for the variation due to the change in online population over time, we use probability (normalized among all channels) instead of absolute values of the metrics to measure channel popularity. We compared the two metrics, namely access frequency and total segment downloads of channels, by computing the Spearsman's rank correlation coefficient between ranks under the two metrics, which is given by

$$\rho = 1 - \frac{6\sum d_i^2}{n(n^2-1)} \qquad (2)$$

where d_i is the distance between the ranking from the two metrics of channel i.

We have $\rho = 0.985$ between the rank of access frequency and total segment downloads, indicating the strong correlation between the two ranking metrics in dataset 1. We believe that the relative wider range of access frequency compared to average segment downloaded in single session account for the high correlation. In the rest of this paper, we use total segment downloaded of a channel as the metric of channel popularity.

Figure 9 shows the popularity distribution in dataset 1. Channels are ranked by total segment downloads. We can see that the popularity of channels is highly skewed in that the top one channel attracts more than 25% of viewing time. We use Pareto distribution Type I to capture the characteristics of channel popularity. Channel popularity is expressed as $p(i) = C/i^{1-\alpha}$, where C is normalization constant and α is the shape parameter. The model in Figure 9 with $\alpha = 0.047$ fits empirical data quite well on more than 100 channels which account for 99% accesses. The result is quite useful for some application such as server capacity allocation and advertising.

However, we cannot tell whether the distribution is stable and how it evolves over time from Figure 9. For some application (i.e. predicting and caching incoming requests on servers), the stationary distribution of channel popularity is insufficient. To discover the time variation of channel popularity, we need to observe the differences of channel popularity across multiple time intervals. We chose 1 hour as granularity, which is comparable to most TV programs. Let $c_j(i)$ be the aggregate number of video segment downloads of channel j in time slot i. Then the popularity of channel j in time slot i, $p_j(i)$ is given by:

$$p_j(i) = \frac{c_j(i)}{\sum_j c_j(i)} \qquad (3)$$

Obviously, $\sum_j p_j(i) = 1$. $T_k(i)$, the normalized popularity of top k channels in time slot i, is defined as the proportion of segments downloaded from the top k channels among all channels. That is, $T_k(i) = \sum_{j \in M_k(i)} p_j(i)$, where $M_k(i)$ is the set of the top k channels sorted by total video segments downloaded in time slot i. $T_k(i)$ can also be regard as the total viewing time of top-k channel in interval i.

We observed a diurnal pattern of the top-k channel popularity. Figure 10 gives the time variation of $T_k(i)$ during a day. Values on the plot are averaged over a week. The top-k channel popularity rises on prime time, and the peak of the day is at 0AM. Near the peak, the fraction of time spent on

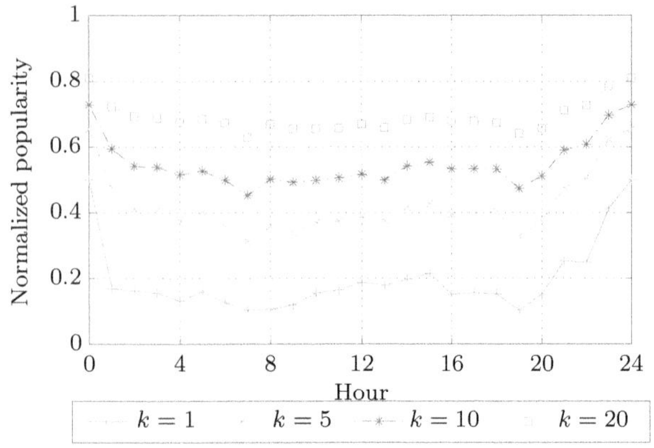

Figure 10: Normalized popularity of top k channels

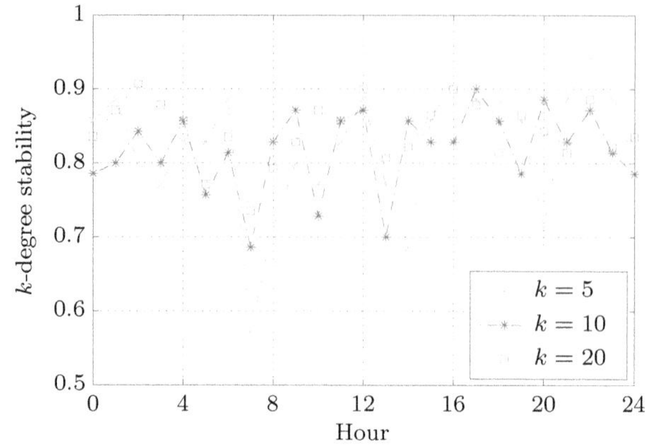

Figure 11: k-degree stability of popularity

top 20 channels is as high as 80%, where the fraction of top 1 channel surpasses 40%. Outside of evening times, $T_1(i)$ is mostly in range 0.1 to 0.2, $T_5(i)$ in range 0.3 to 0.4, $T_{10}(i)$ in range around 0.5, and $T_{20}(i)$ in range 0.6 to 0.7. Recall that the peak of population occurs at 10PM to 11PM every day as shown in Figure 6. This result implies that viewers concentrate on some hot channels near the population peak. A large portion of viewers in the evening focus on top channels rather than aimlessly browsing around all channels. The skewness of viewer interests is stronger than other time of the day.

The top-k channel popularity can only tell the popularity evolution regardless of the change of top channels. To find out the dynamics of top channels, we define k-degree stability of channel popularity as the proportion of same top k channels between two sequent intervals:

$$S_k(i) = \frac{\left|M_k(i) \cap M_k(i-1)\right|}{k} \tag{4}$$

We plot the average k-degree stability of channel popularity $S_k(i)$ during a day over a week in Figure 11, where $k = 5, 10, 20$. A relatively large value of $S_k(i)$ means stable popularity at the interval, and vice versa. There is a time-of-day effect of channel popularity. The channel popularity changes most around 7AM to 8AM in the morning, when $S_k(i)$ gets the minimum during a day. During other times of the day, the popularity remains moderately stable with $S_k(i)$ around 80%. Viewers' top-5 interests also switch to TV series on 8PM, but the top-10 and top-20 channels remains stable.

We also examine the size of union of all $M_k(i)$, namely the total number of channels that have ranked at top k. We have $\left|\bigcup_i M_5(i)\right| = 21$, that is, in the period of the dataset, 21 channels have ranked at top 5. In addition, 4 of them have ranked at top 5 for more than 100 out of 168 intervals in a week. This suggests that from a long term perspective, viewer interests are quite stable in the trace.

The connection type may influence user interests as well. We rank channels by total segment downloaded via WiFi and 3G connections in dataset 1 separately. Then we compare the channel rank under different types of connections. Figure 12 shows the channel rank under the two connection types. Each point on the figure represents a channel. The x and y axes are channel rank under WiFi and 3G respectively. Points near $y = x$ (dashed line) imply that the channels have almost equal ranks between WiFi and 3G users. The dotted lines in the figure are $y = x \pm 20$. We refer the area between these two dotted lines as normal area, in which the popularity rank difference is not significant (< 20). Channels in the normal zone are considered to be equally attractive to WiFi and 3G users. Points in the zone above the normal area mean WiFi users are more interested on the channel, whereas points below the normal area represent channels preferred by 3G users.

From Figure 12, we see a large fraction of points distribute in the normal area. For points outside the normal area, we find that financial channels and movie channels constitute a large proportion in the upper area. On the other hand, more than 60% of channels in the lower area are radio channels. From these observations, we know that: 1) WiFi and 3G users have almost even interests on most channels. 2) WiFi users are more likely to watch financial and movie channels. 3) 3G users are more interested in radio channels than WiFi users.

To verify the third point, we counted the fraction of sessions and segments transmitted (also regarded as the aggregate sojourn time) over WiFi and 3G networks, as shown in Table 2. Overall, 51.52% of all sessions were 3G sessions, but 58.40% of the audio sessions were from 3G networks. This meant that 3G users had a higher probability of choosing audio channels. In addition, the 58.40% audio sessions from 3G users only consumed 48.34% of the audio sojourn time. Similarly, 3G users provided 47.60% of the video sessions, but only 38.04% of the video sojourn time. This data indicated that 3G users are more conscious about the data rate and the channel dwell time. We believe that the cost of 3G data usage is one factor influencing the user behaviors.

5.4 Channel Sojourn Time

User sojourn time is another important characteristic of user access. In traditional television services, channel dwelling time is considered as one of the most important metrics in advertisement placement. Measurement from the landline IPTV system has observed that the dwell time in a channel follows a power law distribution [8]. On the other hand, it is known that in cellular telephony, the channel holding time follows a lognormal distribution [33]. Web

	All		Audio		Video	
	Soj. Time	Session	Soj. Time	Session	Soj. Time	Session
WiFi	58.05%	48.48%	51.66%	41.60%	61.97%	52.35%
3G	41.92%	51.52%	48.34%	58.40%	38.03%	47.65%

Table 2: User interests on audio/video channels over WiFi/3G connection

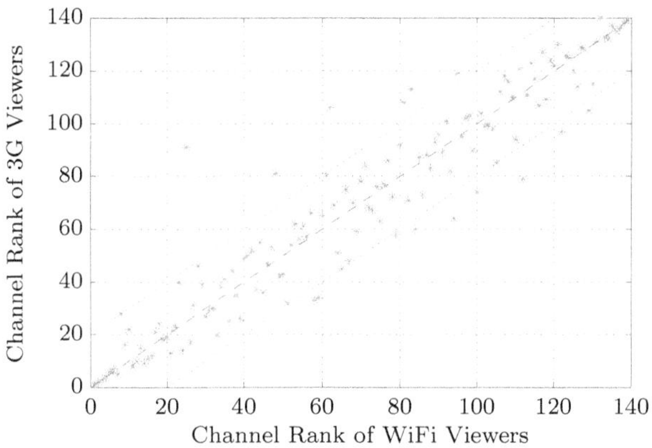

Figure 12: Channel rank comparison of WiFi and 3G users

page dwell time analysis showed a range of complex behaviors depending on the page features [16]. Understanding the sojourn time of mobile TV viewing behavior will be important for both the content distribution network design and the business model of mobile TV in the future.

As described in section 3, we identify video sessions from segment access log entries by HTTP connection number. However, the moment server transmitted the last segment of a video session is not the exact time the user stopped viewing in dataset 1. As HTTP Live Streaming is a discretized video streaming protocol, we estimate user sojourn time by total segment downloaded within a video session (or session segment count, SSC for short). The average of SSC is 16.93, the skewness is 10.69, and the median is 6. This indicates viewer sojourn in sessions for only around 170 seconds on average. The SSC distribution is highly skewed as shown in Figure 13(a). Short viewing sessions constitute a high proportion of all playbacks.

There is a large fraction of short sessions observed in IPTV systems, which usually attribute to the surfing behavior of users [8]. In IPTV systems, users can surf through channels easily by pressing the "Program Up/Down" button on the remote. However, surfing is not that easy in mobile TV due to two factors. Users can only choose desired channels from a list. At the same time, users have to wait several seconds to buffer the video data. In addition, EPG information is provided along with the channel list on mobile TV that users do not need to surf through channels to see what content is on. Thus, we believe that the short sojourn time in mobile TV reflects a different type of channel browsing behavior rather than the traditional channel surfing in landline TV.

To capture characteristics of the empirical trace, we first compare candidate models including Pareto (Type I), generalized Pareto (GP) and lognormal. The PDF of the candidate distributions are given in Equation 5, 6, and 7, respectively. Note we only give the PDF of GP under $k \neq 0$ condition. GP distribution is equivalent to exponential distribution when $k = 0$.

Pareto	$\alpha = 1.5470, x_{\min} = 1$
Gen. Pareto	$k = 1.0259, \sigma = 4.0102, \mu = 1$
Lognormal	$\sigma = 1.3450, \mu = 1.8370$

Table 3: Parameter of candidate distributions

$$f(x; x_{\min}, \alpha) = \frac{\alpha - 1}{x_{\min}} \left(\frac{x}{x_{\min}} \right)^{-\alpha} \quad (5)$$

$$f(x; k, \sigma, \mu) = \frac{1}{\sigma} \left(1 + k\frac{x - \mu}{\sigma} \right)^{-1-\frac{1}{k}}, k \neq 0 \quad (6)$$

$$f(x; \mu, \sigma) = \frac{1}{x\sigma\sqrt{2\pi}} e^{-\frac{(\ln x - \mu)^2}{2\sigma^2}}, x > 0 \quad (7)$$

Parameters estimated by MLE are shown in Table 3, and estimated distribution against empirical data is shown in Figure 13(a).

We first examine the four distributions by visual test: Generalized Pareto distribution fits empirical data when X is not large. The shape of lognormal distribution is quite close to empirical data on the entire range, but decays a little faster than empirical data when X gets large. We use the Kolmogorov-Smirnov Goodness-of-fit Test (KS-test) to determine whether the empirical data fits the model. All of the four distributions are tested against empirical data under KS-test, and none of them have a p-value larger than 0.05, which means none of them have a significance level larger than 0.05.

We find that the lognormal distribution captures the characteristics of empirical data while $X \leq 60$ (which covers around 95% of data), while generalized Pareto distribution fits the tail well. MLE of model parameters and respective p-value of KS-test are given on the first line in Table 4.

The piecewise model against empirical trace is shown in Figure 13(b). We can see that the model fits the empirical data very well. The tail drops from fitted model when $X >$ 1200, but it accounts for only around 0.01% of all playbacks.

In [8], the user sojourn time in IPTV system is found to obey Pareto distribution (Type I). Traditionally, the telephone call duration [23] and fixed wireless access [2] followed exponential distributions. However, a large fraction of mobile TV user sojourn times is quite close to the lognormal distribution, which is found in most cellular call holding time [33]. The tail of user sojourn time distribution fits generalized Pareto distribution which is used to describe survival time. We believe that there are several factors lead to this interesting result. The wireless network might contribute to the lognormal distribution of 95% playbacks, and the limitation of device, such as battery capacity, may account for the dropped tail of the distribution.

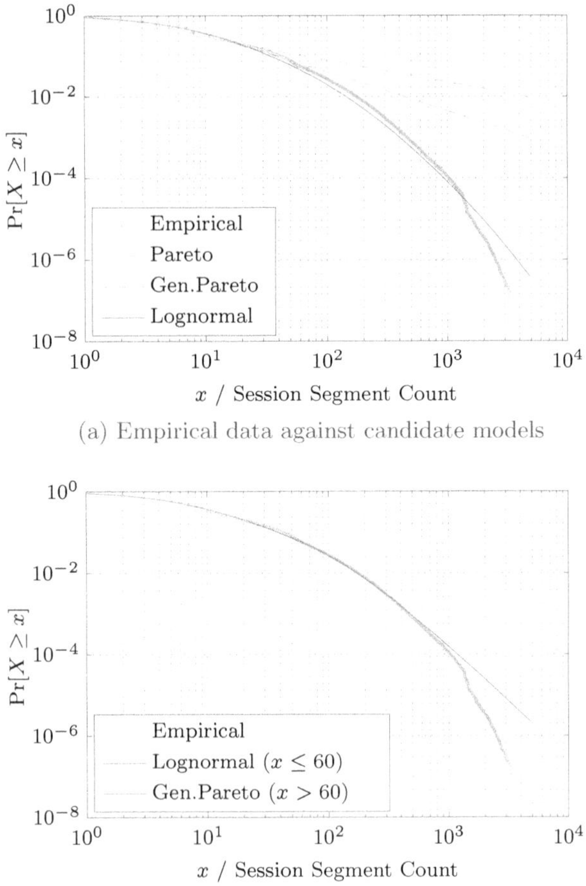

(a) Empirical data against candidate models

(b) Piecewise fitted model

Figure 13: Modeling the SSC distribution

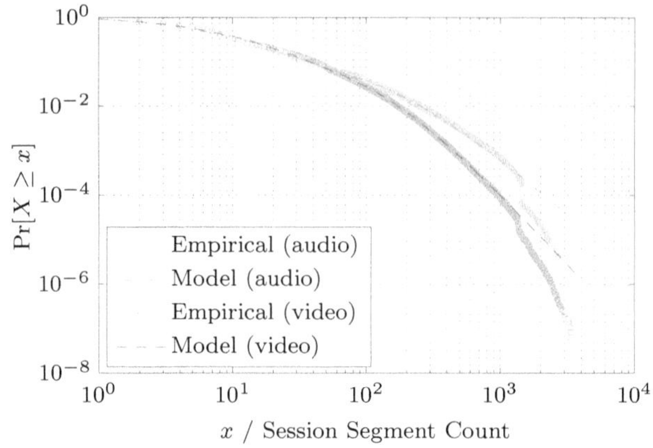

Figure 14: Comparison of SSC distribution on audio and video channels

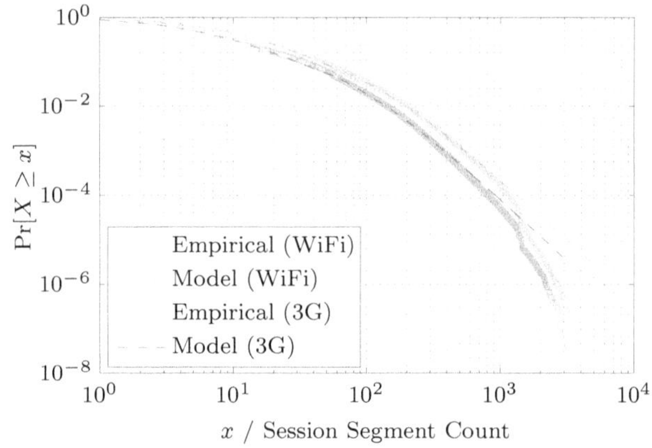

Figure 15: CCDF and fitted model of SSC over WiFi/3G connection

	Mean	Median	Skewness
WiFi	16.3933	6	12.1946
3G	13.5146	5	10.9549

Table 5: Descriptive statistics of WiFi/3G empirical data

We compare SSC distribution of audio channels and video channels in Figure 14. And the estimated model parameters are shown on the second and third line in Table 4. However, the model does not fit the empirical data when $x \leq 60$ due to the influence of buffering. The mean of SSC on audio and video channels is 18.6592 and 16.8673 respectively. This means that users generally stay longer on audio channels. We observed a larger fraction of long-time users on audio channels than that of video channels in the figure.

We count total segments downloaded (SSC) in 3G/WiFi video sessions separately. The descriptive statistics are shown in Table 5. We note that the average SSC in WiFi video sessions is larger than 3G video sessions, indicating viewers sojourn 30 seconds longer on average over WiFi connection. However, the SSC distribution of WiFi connections is more skewed than that of 3G connections.

The CCDF in Figure 15 depicts the empirical data and corresponding piecewise model. Model parameters and p-values of KS-test are given in the fourth and fifth line in Table 4. We find the model fits both WiFi and 3G data. Larger p-values of WiFi data imply that the model can better capture the characteristics of WiFi sessions.

Figure 16 shows the SSC distribution of different periods in a day. Each period covers 6 hours. We have the following observations from the figure: 1) distributions in the three period other than 0AM-6AM are quite similar. 2) users tend to stay longer in the time period between 0AM-6AM. Upon further examination, we found that only a few movie channels are still broadcasting during that time period. This implies the distribution of user sojourn time is related to channel content.

5.5 Observations

We highlight the following key observations of mobile TV user behaviors:

- User accesses of mobile TV have a diurnal pattern. In weekdays, the peak of population happens in lunch hour and in the night (near 11PM). During the week-

	Lognormal ($x \leq 60$)	p-value	Gen.Pareto ($x > 60$)	p-value
All	$\sigma = 1.3450, \mu = 1.8370$	0.1736	$k = 0.3591, \sigma = 45.7754, \mu = 60$	0.2628
Audio	$\sigma = 1.3391, \mu = 1.7547$	0.0381	$k = 0.3797, \sigma = 75.2293, \mu = 60$	0.1882
Video	$\sigma = 1.3454, \mu = 1.8400$	0.1817	$k = 0.3006, \sigma = 49.1292, \mu = 60$	0.2073
WiFi	$\sigma = 1.2997, \mu = 2.0738$	0.5736	$k = 0.3562, \sigma = 48.8771, \mu = 60$	0.3192
3G	$\sigma = 1.3429, \mu = 1.5808$	0.0884	$k = 0.3487, \sigma = 40.8420, \mu = 60$	0.3113

Table 4: SSC Model parameters

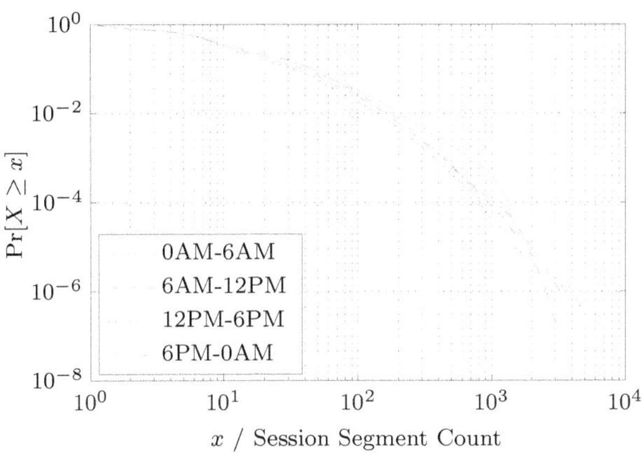

Figure 16: Time variation of SSC distribution

ends, the first peak occurs earlier in the morning, and there are more mobile TV consumers than weekdays.

- Channel popularity of mobile TV follows a Pareto distribution with a dropped tail. The interests of viewers are more biased towards top channels during the second population peak in the night. The popularity remains moderately stable during the rest of the day.

- The average playback length of mobile TV sessions is quite short compared to that of landline IPTV sessions. The channel sojourn time distribution can be best fitted by two piecewise distributions. The shorter sojourn times fit the lognormal distribution (which accounts for more than 90% of the sessions), whereas the longer sojourn times follows a generalized Pareto distribution with a dropped tail.

In comparing user access patterns of WiFi and 3G connections, our observations include:

- During the daytime, there are more 3G users than WiFi users. In the evening and nighttime, there are more WiFi users than 3G users.

- The sojourn time of 3G users are generally shorter than that of WiFi users. For example, 58.40% of the audio sessions are from 3G connections, but they only consume 48.34% of the audio sojourn time.

- Although the majority of channels have similar access patterns for both 3G and WiFi users, there are several channels that exhibited differences. In particular, several movie and financial channels had disproportionate majority of sessions from WiFi users.

The main factors accounting for these observations include network accessibility, connection quality and cost associated with network usage. First, 3G connections provide almost ubiquitous access, while WiFi networks are usually accessible indoors only. This can lead to different access patterns of WiFi and 3G users. Second, the data charge of 3G networks could be the main factor for the traffic-saving viewing habits of 3G users such as shorter sojourn time and preference for lower bitrate audio channels. Third, although a number of factors may contribute to the difference of sojourn time length between 3G and WiFi users, such as the difference in viewing time, we note that from Figure 16, the distribution of sojourn time is quite similar throughout the day, with the exception of time period between 0AM and 6AM. Since the viewer population during 0AM to 6AM is quite small when compared to the daytime (as shown in Figure 6), we believe that the different viewing time is not the main factor.

The results provide useful insights on mobile TV system design and deployment.

1. The unbalanced geographical access and highly skewed channel popularity suggests that content distribution network (CDN) should be deployed near large user groups and adjusted for the more popular contents. Placing edge servers near gateways of mobile operators can provide better quality of delivery between mobile operators and contents although it does not affect the wireless spectrum resource utilization. The unbalanced access also challenges mobile operators to optimize mobile carrier networks.

2. Video at different bitrates should be considered to improve the video quality for WiFi users and the traffic efficiency for 3G users at the same time. We believe that an adaptive bitrate would provide a better quality of video broadcasting service.

3. The short channel sojourn time indicates that users' interests may not last for a long time on mobile TV. The viewing quality of some programs on mobile TV is not satisfactory. Short and specialized video clips might be more attractive on mobile devices.

4. As users may abandon video watching session during playbacks, data that was downloaded but not played would be wasted. This is particularly important since mobile TV users' sojourn time is short and the 3G bandwidth is valuable. Therefore, the buffering strategy should be carefully designed to balance the viewing quality and the traffic efficiency.

6. SUMMARY AND FUTURE WORKS

Video streaming over the mobile network is an emerging application that may drastically change the landscape of future mobile networks and television industries. In this paper, we present a measurement based study on a large scale nationwide mobile TV system for the first time. The traffic characteristics from the HTTP Live Streaming protocol indicated that both 3G mobile networks and WiFi networks can adequately support continuous video playback. Although both user access patterns and the channel popularity distribution are found to be similar to that of the landline based Internet TV services, the average channel sojourn time is found to be shorter than that of the traditional TV services, with the average viewing session time being 135 seconds for 3G connections and 164 seconds for WiFi connections. The distribution of the viewing time follows the lognormal distribution in the shorter time scale, which is similar to the call holding time in cellular telephony. In the longer time scale, the distribution follows a generalized Pareto distribution similar to the traditional television channel dwell time.

Our measurement and analysis on the large scale mobile TV service enable us to gain in-depth understanding of user behaviors and traffic characteristics of the emerging mobile TV system, provide guidance for the design of mobile TV content distribution networks, and can be the basis for modeling and simulating mobile TV systems. Our future work includes the deeper understanding of user behaviors, simulation of server loads of mobile TV systems and traffic characteristics, optimizing buffering strategies, and the design of mobile content distribution networks based on the channel popularity model.

7. ACKNOWLEDGMENTS

This research work was supported in part by NSFC (Project 60721003, 60736027). The authors would like to thank the anonymous reviewers for their valuable comments and feedbacks.

8. REFERENCES

[1] Cisco Visual Networking Index: Global Mobile Data Traffic Forecast Update, 2010-2015. Technical report, Cisco, 2011.

[2] H. Anderson. *Fixed broadband wireless system design.* Wiley, 2003.

[3] M. Arlitt and T. Jin. A workload characterization study of the 1998 world cup web site. *Network, IEEE*, 14(3):30–37, 2000.

[4] M. Arlitt and C. Williamson. Internet web servers: workload characterization and performance implications. *Networking, IEEE/ACM Transactions on*, 5(5):631–645, 1997.

[5] S. Buchinger, S. Kriglstein, and H. Hlavacs. A comprehensive view on user studies: survey and open issues for mobile TV. In *Proceedings of the seventh european conference on European interactive television conference*, pages 179–188, Leuven, Belgium, 2009. ACM.

[6] M. Cha, H. Kwak, P. Rodriguez, Y. Ahn, and S. Moon. I tube, you tube, everybody tubes: analyzing the world's largest user generated content video system. In *Proceedings of the 7th ACM SIGCOMM conference on Internet measurement*, IMC '07, page 1–14, New York, NY, USA, 2007. ACM. ACM ID: 1298309.

[7] M. Cha, H. Kwak, P. Rodriguez, Y. Ahn, and S. Moon. Analyzing the video popularity characteristics of Large-Scale user generated content systems. *Networking, IEEE/ACM Transactions on*, 17(5):1357–1370, 2009.

[8] M. Cha, P. Rodriguez, J. Crowcroft, S. Moon, and X. Amatriain. Watching television over an IP network. *IMC '08: Proceedings of the 8th ACM SIGCOMM conference on Internet measurement*, pages 71–84, 2008.

[9] D. Ciullo, M. Mellia, M. Meo, and E. Leonardi. Understanding P2P-TV systems through real measurements. In *Global Telecommunications Conference, 2008. IEEE GLOBECOM 2008. IEEE*, pages 1–6, 2008.

[10] Y. Cui, J. Chipchase, and Y. Jung. Personal TV: A qualitative study of mobile TV users. *Interactive TV: A shared experience*, pages 195–204, 2007.

[11] X. Hei, C. Liang, J. Liang, Y. Liu, and K. Ross. A measurement study of a Large-Scale P2P IPTV system. *Multimedia, IEEE Transactions on*, 9(8):1672–1687, 2007.

[12] X. Hei, Y. Liu, and K. Ross. Inferring Network-Wide quality in P2P live streaming systems. *Selected Areas in Communications, IEEE Journal on*, 25(9):1640–1654, 2007.

[13] JinHu software Inc. CHUNZHEN QQ IP database.

[14] B. Li, S. Xie, G. Keung, J. Liu, I. Stoica, H. Zhang, and X. Zhang. An empirical study of the CoolStreaming+ system. *Selected Areas in Communications, IEEE Journal on*, 25(9):1627–1639, 2007.

[15] B. Li, S. Xie, Y. Qu, G. Keung, C. Lin, J. Liu, and X. Zhang. Inside the new coolstreaming: Principles, measurements and performance implications. In *INFOCOM 2008. The 27th Conference on Computer Communications. IEEE*, pages 1031–1039, 2008.

[16] C. Liu, R. W. White, and S. Dumais. Understanding web browsing behaviors through weibull analysis of dwell time. *Proceeding of the 33rd international ACM SIGIR conference on Research and development in information retrieval*, page 379ÍC386, 2010. ACM ID: 1835513.

[17] K. Ma, R. Bartos, S. Bhatia, and R. Nair. Mobile video delivery with HTTP. *Communications Magazine, IEEE*, 49(4):166–175, 2011.

[18] MaxMind, LLC. GeoIP, 2011.

[19] K. Miyauchi, T. Sugahara, and H. Oda. Relax or study? a qualitative user study on the usage of live mobile TV and mobile video. *Comput. Entertain.*, 7(3):1–20, 2009.

[20] R. Pantos. HTTP Live Streaming. http://tools.ietf.org/html/draft-pantos-http-live-streaming-01, 2009.

[21] T. Qiu, Z. Ge, S. Lee, J. Wang, J. Xu, and Q. Zhao. Modeling user activities in a large iptv system. In *Proceedings of the 9th ACM SIGCOMM conference on Internet measurement conference*, pages 430–441, New York, NY, USA, 2009. ACM.

[22] T. Qiu, Z. Ge, S. Lee, J. Wang, Q. Zhao, and J. Xu. Modeling channel popularity dynamics in a large iptv

system. In *Proceedings of the eleventh international joint conference on Measurement and modeling of computer systems*, pages 275–286, New York, NY, USA, 2009. ACM.

[23] P. Reynolds. Call center staffing. *The Call Center School Press, Lebanon, Tennessee*, 2003.

[24] M. Saxena, U. Sharan, and S. Fahmy. Analyzing video services in web 2.0: a global perspective. In *Proceedings of the 18th International Workshop on Network and Operating Systems Support for Digital Audio and Video*, NOSSDAV '08, page 39–44, New York, NY, USA, 2008. ACM. ACM ID: 1496056.

[25] T. Silverston and O. Fourmaux. Measuring P2P IPTV systems. In *Proc. of ACM NOSSDAV*, 2007.

[26] T. Silverston, O. Fourmaux, K. Salamatian, and K. Cho. Measuring P2P IPTV traffic on both sides of the world. In *Proceedings of the 2007 ACM CoNEXT conference*, pages 1–2, New York, New York, 2007. ACM.

[27] K. Sripanidkulchai, B. Maggs, and H. Zhang. An analysis of live streaming workloads on the internet. In *Proceedings of the 4th ACM SIGCOMM conference on Internet measurement*, IMC '04, page 41–54, New York, NY, USA, 2004. ACM. ACM ID: 1028795.

[28] X. Su and L. Chang. A measurement study of PPStream. In *Communications and Networking in China, 2008. ChinaCom 2008. Third International Conference on*, pages 1162–1166, 2008.

[29] Y. Wang, M. Claypool, and Z. Zuo. An empirical study of realvideo performance across the internet. In *Proceedings of the 1st ACM SIGCOMM Workshop on Internet Measurement*, IMW '01, page 295–309, New York, NY, USA, 2001. ACM. ACM ID: 505239.

[30] C. Wu, B. Li, and S. Zhao. Exploring Large-Scale Peer-to-Peer live streaming topologies. *ACM Trans. Multimedia Comput. Commun. Appl.*, 4(3):1–23, 2008.

[31] S. Xie, G. Keung, and B. Li. A measurement of a Large-Scale Peer-to-Peer live video streaming system. In *Parallel Processing Workshops, 2007. ICPPW 2007. International Conference on*, page 57, 2007.

[32] X. Xu, W. W. K. Ma, and E. W. K. See-To. Will mobile video become the killer application for 3G mobile internet? a model of media convergence acceptance. *Information Systems Frontiers*, 12(3):311–322, 2008.

[33] E. Yavuz and V. Leung. Modeling channel occupancy times for voice traffic in cellular networks. In *Communications, 2007. ICC '07. IEEE International Conference on*, pages 332–337, 2007.

[34] H. Yin, X. Liu, F. Qiu, N. Xia, C. Lin, H. Zhang, V. Sekar, and G. Min. Inside the bird's nest: measurements of large-scale live VoD from the 2008 olympics. In *Proceedings of the 9th ACM SIGCOMM conference on Internet measurement conference*, pages 442–455, Chicago, Illinois, USA, 2009. ACM.

Summary Review Documentation for

"Measurement and Analysis of a Large Scale Commercial Mobile Internet TV System"

Authors: Y. Li, Y. Zhang, R. Yuan

Reviewer #1

Strengths: Impressive data set: not only do the authors have the logs from the streaming server, but they also have data from a client application that can give them additional information on the waiting time before playback and the means of access (3G vs. WiFi). The analysis is carefully done and the authors do not limit themselves to reporting the numbers but clearly discuss their implications. They further contrast their findings with reported results on wireline IPTV services and cellular calls.

Weaknesses: The only weakness I could list has to do with the evaluation of the quality of user experience in Section 4.2 - given that the authors have complete knowledge of the inner-workings of the client they could have done better here (suggestions later). Second, the language of the manuscript could certainly be improved. I would encourage the authors to have their manuscript proofread by a native English speaker.

Comments to Authors: This is a really nice measurement paper. It relies on a very large data set of an operational mobile Internet TV system, covering 1 million unique devices and 49 million video sessions. The authors have managed to gather the logs from the streaming server and information from a subset of all devices (using a client application), that covers approximately 20% of all devices seen in the complete server log. The authors have explicit knowledge of the inner workings of the mobile Internet TV client. They know that it uses HLS, that it downloads 350KB segments every 10 seconds and that it download 8 segments at the beginning, while starting playing the video after the first segment is fully received.

Based on the information collected the authors are able to provide statistics about channel dwell time, preference of users in terms of audio or video, popularity of specific channels, the quality of the user experience. They further contrast all this with a prior study on wireline IPTV and with typical statistics for cellular phone calls. The analysis is carefully done and the results always accompanied by implications for the service provider.

Given the existence of the second data set, the authors are further able to differentiate user behavior according to access technology, i.e. 3G and WiFi.

On the technical side, the one point that I would really like the authors to have done a better job is in the assessment of the quality of experience of users (Section 4.2). Right now, the only statistic they provide is the distribution of transmission delay of the different segments. Based on that they report that only 2.5% of the segments may have been downloaded past their 10 second potential deadline. However, the authors also know that the phone client starts by downloading 8 segments, they know the timestamp for client requests for the next segment and they know the streaming rate of video consumption. Therefore, they could easily emulate what each client would do in practice. The client starts playback when reported in data set 2, and then requests future segments while having a number N of segments in its buffer. Try to go along the timeline and identify any point in time when the client needs to play a segment but has no segments in its buffer. This is how you would assess the actual quality, and this exercise is perfectly doable given all the information you have.

Second, the authors make a statement on the possibility for a CDN to be very effective in the studied deployment. That would certainly help with wireline resource optimization but would it help with spectrum resource optimization too? I think it would be useful for the authors to comment on this.

Dataset 2 gives you information on the interface used to connect to the mobile Internet TV service. It would be interesting to describe the pricing plans for 3G in China. The authors mention that the main deterrent for users to use that mobile Internet TV service on 3G is the cost. However, if the data plan has a flat fee, then this is not the case, and what the authors observe is less use of the service over 3G because of potentially worse performance.

I would like to see Figure 3(a) with explicit mention of buffering and segment downloads. The beginning of Figure 3(a) has approximately 6 seconds of downloads at 350 KB/sec. Given that you download 8 segments of 350 KB plus 1 KB for the playlist, that time should probably be close to 8 seconds. Please verify...

In all the results reporting use according to 3G and WiFi, I assume that you correlate data set 1 with data set 2, therefore reducing the number of data points to 20% of the actual server log population, right? You should make that explicit. Then the results are not based on data set 1, as stated in the paper, but on the information of data set 1 for all devices in data set 2.

In Section 5.3, the authors conclude that "Noting that audio date is less data intensive, we believe the data charge is the main factor of this phenomena". I think this conclusion is premature. Users may be using audio only, because they work at the same time, because they do not like watching TV on a small screen, because the quality is not that great. You need to first exclude those factors before you can make such a statement. I would remove this sentence from this section.

All in all, I found that this paper contains a number of interesting findings that will be interesting to the community. It is based on an authoritative data source, and careful analysis. I hope the above suggestions help the authors improve the paper even further.

Reviewer #2

Strengths: As the first measurement study on large-scale mobile Internet TV, the work is very timely. The measurement dataset is significant. The findings are very interesting. The paper is also mostly well written.

Weaknesses: Nothing major.

Comments to Authors: I think the paper has all the ingredients of a very good measurement paper: The study is timely, the dataset is substantial, the analysis is thorough and insightful, the findings are interesting and potentially valuable for future mobile TV system design and deployment, and the paper is mostly well written.

Section 4.2 mentions that "requests taking more than 10 seconds could lead to a downgraded viewing experience". It is worth pointing out that the buffer can absorb some of the delay variation. E.g., with a 4-piece buffer, as long as a piece arrives within 40 seconds, it can still be played in time. So the continuous playing percentage is indeed higher than 97.5%.

The paper can benefit from a more careful proofread.

Reviewer #3

Strengths: - The measurement data set is significant.
- The timing of the work is very good.
- This study comprehensively compares the user behaviors of 3G vs. WiFi.

Weaknesses: - The impact of user mobility is not completely characterized.
- It could be better if the study could conduct a more in-depth analysis.

Comments to Authors: Two fundamental differences between cellular and WiFi are performance and user mobility behaviors. Regarding the performance, this study proposes a very comprehensive comparison between 3G and WiFi. However, regarding the impact of user mobility behavior, I expect the study could do better. I was captured by the title of Section 5 at the first look expecting some analysis of the impact of user mobility patterns. In Section 3.3, this paper describes the client-side logs. If the client-side logs captured the GPS location of smartphone devices, they could evaluation user behaviors (such as channel sojourn time) under different mobility degree.

Reviewer #4

Strengths: - This paper is based on a great data set: large number of measurements and comparison between Wifi and 3G.
- New results are extracted from the data set and compared to previous results from other environments like IPTV.

Weaknesses: - Only based on one content provider, so results are not necessarily reflecting the experience and behavior across all video content, and maybe dependent on the content provided.
- Impact of using HLS, which is adaptive bitrate encoding, not covered in the paper. This can potentially completely change your results.
- No section on video abandonment rate.
- Some explanations are not always convincing (audio vs. video, Wifi vs. 3G).

Comments to Authors: While this is a nice paper to read, I have some comments/concerns:

- The service studied is based on HLS, which is an adaptive bitrate encoding approach. What is the implication for your study? If there is network congestion, the video stream will adapt itself and lower the bitrate to make sure that the video can be streamed continuously. Your results show that the startup delay is less than 10 seconds and that the video playback is continuous, but did the encoding rate change? Did the content provider have to lower the bitrate to continue to keep up with the content consumption? To answer these questions, you should study how often the bitrate changes and how often could the video be encoded at the highest quality. Without these answers, it is not clear, what the takeaway is.

- What GeoIP database did you use? Please add a reference.

- In Section 5.4, you mention the session length and short sessions. You should elaborate, study and quantify the impact of abandonment rates on the content transmitted that is wasted due to buffering and abandonment.

- In Section 5.4, you hypothesize that video sessions are shorter than audio sessions because more content is downloaded for video and that users are sensitive to the amount of traffic downloaded on 3G networks. I think a more likely explanation is that audio content can be consumed while multi tasking, while video content requires the end user attention. Therefore you would expect audio sessions to be longer.

- In Section 5.5, you write that users on Wifi watch videos for longer periods on time than users on cellular networks, and then you say that it is because of network quality and usage based billing. However, there might be other reasons. For instance, Wifi users and 3G users don't always watch the same content and they do not watch it at the same time of the day. In particular, if the Wifi usage is at night and the 3G usage is during the day. It seems that a simpler explanation is that people watch content for longer periods of time on Wifi because at night they have more spare time and might be at home in a more comfortable environment to consume content.

- You mention several times the impact of usage-based billing. You should explain to the reader what some of the typical plans are in China (proportional to usage for every byte, flat rate until 2 Gb/month etc.)

Reviewer #5

Strengths: - Mobile Internet TV has reached a momentum is some parts of the world, eg Korea, Japan and Hong Kong. It is a timely problem and the traces analyzed in the paper are new.
- The scale of the data is also high; 50 millions sessions and 1 million devices.

Weaknesses: - There is a contradiction between the claims in the abstract and the major contributions mentioned in the introduction.
- There is no novelty in analyzing the data. The techniques that are used have also been used in previous studies on Internet video services.

Comments to Authors: In the abstract/introduction, please clarify if the behavior of the users is different in the mobile TV service and the landline service; there is a lot of confusion. In the summary you repeat that the pattern in the mobile TV and the landline TV is similar.

It would be nice if you could comment on the reasons why there is some initial delay in the beginning of the session. Is this due to protocol, the state of the server, or the power-up of the received mobile device.

It would be also nice to comment on the effect of the device and the access technology used by then end-users.

It would be nice to comment if there are any failures in receiving data or if there any restrictions in accessing channels.

Figure 1 does not add anything in the understanding of the system.

Response from the Authors

We thank all the reviewers for their valuable comments and feedbacks. These comments are tremendously helpful and improve our work.

In the following, we outline the revisions and additions in our paper that address the reviewers' comments:
1. As suggested by several reviewers, a brief description of typical 3G data pricing plans in China is added in section 3.1
2. As suggested by reviewer 1, we went through all the data traces, and emulated all the video sessions. The detailed video quality assessment results are added in section 4.2 in the revised paper.
3. When comparing user accesses to audio and video sessions, the reviewers are right that multiple reasons may account for the longer session length for audio. We have thus removed the mention on the "main factor", and now simply present a detailed analysis of the data.
4. We have clarified in section 3.3 how the 3G/Wifi information from dataset 2 is utilized to identify the access network type in dataset 1.
5. Regarding the comment by reviewer5, we have revised the introduction to emphasize the differences between landline IPTV and mobile TV systems.
6. We clarified in section 3.1 that the CNLive service offered more than 120 different TV channels and 16 different audio channels. Each video channel has a constant bitrate of 256kbps and each audio channel has a constant bitrate of 32kbps.
7. As suggested by reviewer4, there might be other reasons for the session length difference between WiFi and 3G. We have added more discussion in section 5.5 regarding this issue.
8. As suggested by reviewer 4, the transmitted but not viewed content wastes valuable bandwidth. This issue is important in the design of buffering scheme and content delivery network. We felt that more detailed analysis on this issue is warranted and could be left as future works, and have added a brief discussion in Sec. 6.
9. Specific comments regarding Fig. 3(a), initial buffering, GeoIP database references, correlation between dataset 1 and 2, CDN's effect on wireless spectrum usage, are addressed accordingly in the revised text.
We did not address the comment by reviewer3 regarding user mobility. This is because the client software did not collect user location from the GPS, thus we did not have detailed mobility information.
Finally, as suggested by multiple reviewers, we have asked a native English speaker to proofread the paper.

Understanding Couch Potatoes: Measurement and Modeling of Interactive Usage of IPTV at large scale

Vijay Gopalakrishnan, Rittwik Jana, K. K. Ramakrishnan,
Deborah F. Swayne, Vinay A. Vaishampayan
AT&T Labs Research, 180 Park Ave, Florham Park, NJ, 07932
{gvijay,rjana,kkrama,dfs,vinay}@research.att.com

ABSTRACT

We investigate how consumers view content using Video on Demand (VoD) in the context of an IP-based video distribution environment. Users today can use interactive stream control functions such as skip, replay, fast-forward, pause, and rewind to control their viewing. The use of these functions can place additional demands on the distribution infrastructure (servers, network, and set top boxes) and can be challenging to manage with a large subscriber base. A model of user interaction provides insight into the impact of stream control on server and bandwidth requirements, client responsiveness, etc.

We capture the activity users in a natural setting, viewing video at home. We first develop a model for the arrival process of requests for content. We then develop two stream control models that accurately capture user interaction. We show that stream control events can be characterized by a finite state machine and a sojourn time model, parametrized for major periods of usage (weekend and weekday). Our semi-Markov (SM) model for the sojourn time in each stream control state uses a novel technique based on a polynomial fit to the logarithm of the Inverse CDF. A second constrained model (CM) uses a stick-breaking approach familiar in machine learning to model the individual state sojourn time distributions. The SM model seeks to preserve the sojourn time distribution for each state while the CM model puts a greater emphasis on preserving the overall session duration distribution. Using traces across a period of 2 years from a large-scale operational IPTV environment, we validate the proposed model and show that we are able to faithfully predict the workload presented to a video server. We also provide a synthetic trace developed from the model enabling researchers to also study other problems of interest. We also use the techniques to model consumer viewing of video content recorded on their personal Digital Video Recorder (DVR).

IMC'11, November 2–4, 2011, Berlin, Germany.

Categories and Subject Descriptors

H.5.1 [**Multimedia Information Systems**]: Video

General Terms

Measurement, Performance

Keywords

Video-on-Demand, IPTV, Data Mining

1. INTRODUCTION

Viewers are increasingly watching stored video, delivered over IP networks, in preference to broadcast television. The new modes of viewing content offer greater interactive control; at the same time, they place additional demands on the distribution infrastructure (servers, network, and set top boxes), which can be challenging to manage with a large subscriber base. In addition to video quality, a consumer's viewing experience is determined by the system's responsiveness to stream control operations (e.g., pause, fast-forward, rewind). A poorly engineered and unresponsive system leads to confusion for the user about whether a stream control event was registered by the system, generates unnecessary additional requests, and ultimately leads to decreased user satisfaction. A provider's infrastructure must be able to provide a minimum level of responsiveness despite the demands that user interactions place on the set-top box, the network, and the server.

Knowing how consumers use stream control features allows the provider to optimize the delivery system and make it responsive. This includes provisioning the system with the requisite number of servers, network bandwidth, and set-top box processing, identifying the right delivery mechanisms (unicast, multicast or P2P), choosing the right method for serving functions such as fast-forward and rewind, and fine-tuning timers and buffering. In order to correctly engineer the servers and network to support such interaction, providers need to have a good understanding of users' interactive behavior.

This paper provides a comprehensive model of a large population of consumers downloading and interactively viewing Video-on-Demand (VoD) content. Our overall model consists of two main components: an arrival process model and a stream control usage model. We model the arrival process for VoD requests, with the objective of capturing the distinctive diurnal pattern and having a traffic intensity that can be scaled as a function of the number of users provisioned in a VoD system. Our model for stream control usage enables us to get a better understanding of the usage of these functions than ever before.

Previous studies of user interactivity have either been based on a small set of users under laboratory conditions [3] or with P2P users [22]. With the former, users are not in their natural environment and are aware of being monitored. With the latter, responsiveness can be dramatically affected by peer bandwidth and latency and users tend to adapt their behavior to the system's responsiveness. As a result, inference based on these approaches can lead to biased results.

In contrast, to develop our model, we use comprehensive data collected over a long period of time from a nationally deployed IPTV service. Our data includes users requesting VoD content and all the stream control requests generated. The data is obtained from a large population of users viewing television programs and videos over a long period in a natural setting – in their own homes. Our data spans a period of two years, capturing two representative weeks from each of the four different seasons. We used this large data set to understand the variability in VoD viewing that may be influenced by seasonal patterns in television programming and human behavior. We also use this data to characterize the user's interaction with their DVR for viewing recorded content.

To characterize the arrival process of user requests for VoD content, we have examined a total of 120 days of data collected from nine metropolitan areas, all of which has been used for characterizing the arrival process. The average number of set-top boxes provisioned was approximately 3 million over this period.

We characterize a user's stream control interactions for both VoD and DVR based on analyzing detailed traces of *all* interactions generated by a more limited population of about 300K users over a period of 9 days from 10 metropolitan areas (to capture both weekend and weekday behavior), while viewing either videos from the provider's VoD library or recordings on their in-home DVR. Even though the stream control modeling work reported here is based on traces covering the 9 day period, we have verified the validity of our model structure using the traces from the longer 2-week periods spanning the 2 year interval.

As a preview of one of the main results in the paper, we show the state transitions that model the stream control operations performed by a typical user (our typical couch potato) in Fig. 1. As an example of the information the figure conveys, note that while viewing VoD (and thus in the PLAY state), the most common action a viewer initiates is FASTFORWARD (FF), followed by PAUSE and REWIND. We provide the details of the model, its derivation and the sojourn times in each state later in this paper. As will be evident, our typical couch potato is an active participant in interactive viewing of on-demand content. This has implications on the system design, especially as on-demand viewing grows.

The contributions of this paper are as follows.

1. *Arrival Process model:* We develop a VoD request arrival process model based on data from two years. The arrival process is parametrized by a set of K Fast Fourier Transform coefficients which can be inverted to generate arrival counts by the second for a given weekday or weekend. This enables us to generate an aggregate stream control arrival process at a VoD server.

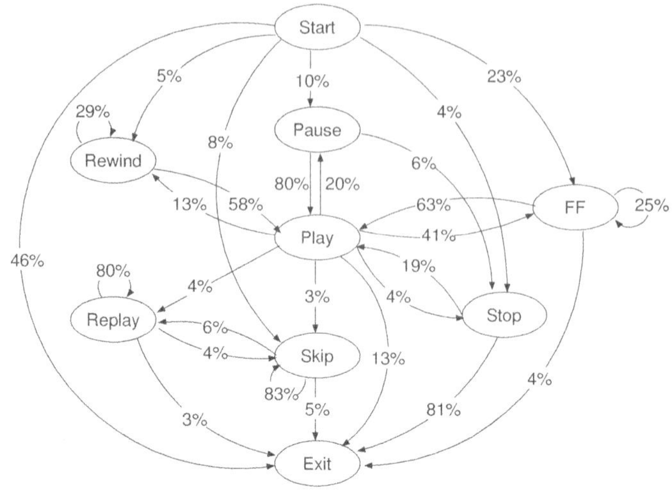

Figure 1: The weekend version of our synthetic couch potato for VoD.

Each arrival of a request translates to a session that contains multiple stream control events.

2. *Stream control model:* We develop two stream control models. Each model uses a common finite state machine (FSM) in order to model the sequence of stream control events in a given session. A state in the FSM is a particular type of stream control event (e.g. REWIND or PLAY). The models differ in the methods by which the state sojourn times are generated. In the first model, state sojourn times are assumed to be independent and are fitted using a polynomial function of the CDF on a logarithmic scale. This sojourn-time model is referred to as the independent sojourn time model (IS). Thus, the first model is a conventional semi-Markov model (SM = FSM + IS) and will be referred to as such. In our second model, we constrain the state sojourn times in order to preserve the aggregate session duration distribution. The approach follows the well-known stick-breaking (SB) paradigm, as it is commonly referred to in the statistical literature [14]. We call the second model the *constrained model* (CM = FSM + SB). We use these techniques to also model stream control events for a user viewing recorded content on the in-home DVR.

3. *Validation:* We provide extensive validation of our model by using a simulator to compare the server load and interruptions to the user viewing the content (because of the under-run of the client playout buffer) from a purely synthetically generated workload with that of a real trace, and showing a good match on other significant statistics as well.

4. *Public data:* We provide synthetic traces of stream control events that researchers can use to validate other algorithms [9].

The main body of the paper is devoted to describing the modeling process. Although we recognize that it would be ideal to provide a real trace (or traces) to readers so as to enable them to arrive at their own models as well as use it to study other problems of interest, we are limited by privacy agreements and legal constraints. However, we provide the 'next best' thing, a synthetic trace for a weekday and weekend day that we believe would serve the same purpose. In addition, we believe the complete model parameters that we provide in [9] will enable readers to generate their own synthetic trace for a given population of users.

2. RELATED WORK

Modeling interactive behavior is important in designing any networked system which offers interactive usage, such as Web browser navigation and IPTV systems, and a variety of data mining techniques have been used to analyze such data (e.g., click stream modeling [1, 17]). User behavior is typically modeled using Markov processes [3]. Such modeling work often focuses on predicting individual user behavior in order to provide personalized services, but our interest is in global behavior so that we can characterize the workload of a centralized VoD server.

Branch et al. [3] report on the statistics of user behavior for a VoD based system of 63 viewing sessions conducted in a controlled setting. They report that lognormal sojourn time distributions are good approximations for all the states of the Markov state machine. In addition to the potential limitations of characterizing user behavior in a controlled setting, we find that a lognormal distribution does not adequately capture the complete statistics (mean, variance, third moment and median). Furthermore, this study also lacked stream control functions for discontinuous viewing, such as "skip" and "replay".

Mongy et al. [18] investigate user behavior by clustering video sessions to measure similarity between session groups. From the standpoint of clustering user behavior, we identified that weekday and weekend sessions are sufficiently different in their VoD server requirements that they must be modeled separately.

There have also been several studies on modeling access patterns for Web-based streaming video systems. Cha et al. [4] have investigated how users access videos in YouTube. Guo et al. [11] compared access patterns for live streaming, Web, P2P and VoD. They do not specifically model the individual stream control operations. We believe that stream control operations have a significant impact on the server load and it is therefore important to understand and model these operations.

Several other studies have sought to characterize P2P-TV and P2P-VoD traffic on the Internet [13]. [15] and [21] describe designs for peer-assisted VoD solutions that offer capabilities such as fast forward and seek to random play points. Our work on a system to cooperatively use peer assists and multicast [8] also seeks to provide a complete suite of stream control operations for VoD usage in a large-scale IPTV distribution environment. Such designs could benefit from a comprehensive model for stream control operations that a typical VoD user would generate. We believe our proposed model can guide the design of such P2P-VoD systems.

More recently, Qiu et al. [20] and Cha et al. [5] have investigated modeling the user activities for an IPTV system but have primarily focused on LiveTV sessions. Their model captured events related to channel switching and STB power on/off events. A synthetic workload generator is proposed to estimate the load on a server due to channel change events, taking as input the arrival process of an aggregate set of users. We believe that for VoD it is equally important to model the individual stream control events as these have a direct impact on the VoD server. Yin et al. [23] present a data characterization study of a live Internet VoD system for the Beijing Olympics. They study how presentation models (e.g., instant messaging and advertising) impact user behavior. To the best of our knowledge, ours is the first study of user stream control operations based on a commercially deployed IPTV system at national scale.

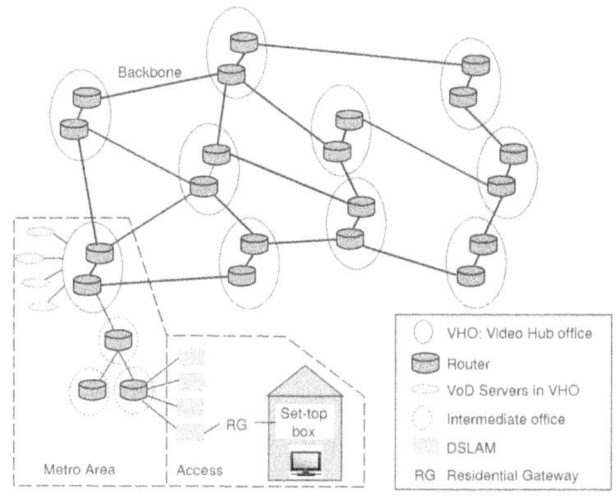

Figure 2: Architecture of a typical IPTV network

3. VOD USAGE

In this section, we describe a typical IPTV network, describe the data we use in this paper, and finally present the characteristics of stream control events.

3.1 System Architecture

Fig. 2 shows the typical architecture used for IPTV delivery. These networks consist of a set of interconnected Video Hub Offices (VHO), each of which serves one or more metro areas. All the customers in a metro area connect to a Video Hub Office (VHO) and receive content from the VoD servers in that VHO using unicast [8]. When a customer watching a video performs a stream control event that can not be satisfied using the local buffer, a request is transferred to the server to execute the appropriate action. DVR use, on the other hand, does not place that sort of demand on the server. The broadcast content recorded on the customer's DVR is delivered using IP-multicast, after which every action performed as part of DVR viewing is local to the customer. In both cases, stream control events, like all other events performed using the remote control, are logged and the logs are uploaded to the VHO. Understanding these events would help in the design of VoD delivery, as well as DVR solutions, as they evolve.

3.2 Data used

Table 1 shows the different snapshots of data that we have used throughout the paper. We have used multiple data sets spanning over two years and covering a large subscriber footprint. DS1 is used for the modeling of the arrival process, DS2 for the stream control finite state machine characterization, and DS3 for characterizing the evolution of video popularity.

We briefly describe the different stream control operations that are available to users; from those operations, we construct the finite state machine (FSM) shown in Fig. 1 and

Data set	Duration (days)	# of VHOs	# of STBs	Time 2009/2010
DS1	120 days	9	3M	Jan/Apr/July/Nov
DS2	9 days	10	300K	Jan
DS3	60 days	10	300K	Jan/Feb

Table 1: Data description

develop it further in subsequent sections. When users select a video, they enter the START state. The video begins playing (equivalent to being in the PLAY state). At that point there is a set of stream control operations that a VoD user has access to: PLAY, FASTFORWARD, REWIND, SKIP, REPLAY, PAUSE, and STOP. Users who do not use any stream control operations in a session transition directly from START to EXIT (users EXIT when they watch the video until the end or explicitly exit before the end).

While most of these operations are self-explanatory, it is important to distinguish between START and PLAY. Users enter the START state when they first start the video; they enter PLAY when they resume playing the video after another stream control operation (e.g., PAUSE or FASTFORWARD). Finally, when they end the session, users enter the EXIT state.

3.3 Stream Control Usage Characterization

Understanding the intensity of stream control operations and their breakdown, as well as the influence of the length of the video, is useful and motivates our modeling work. We briefly describe relevant VoD usage characteristics and refer the reader to a short paper [10] for further details. We have observed that the number of stream control events per session is higher during weekdays than weekends.

For this study, we used the nine days of trace data collected at *ten* VHOs. The data was anonymized to protect the identity of the users. It contained over two million requests for videos from ~300K users. The data included information about the videos requested by the users, the set of stream control operations performed, and when they were performed. The library contains a large number of videos of different genres and lengths.

Video length (in min)	Weekend Mean	Weekend 95%	Weekday Mean	Weekday 95%
0-10	4.8	13	4.8	13
10-30	8.9	32	8.9	32
30-60	13.2	46	15.2	54
60-120	9.7	39	13.3	54
120-	8.8	33	10.7	41

Table 2: Statistics of the number of events per viewing session by video length.

We first look at the the statistics for stream control events based on the content length (referred to as *video length*). The statistics are provided for five ranges of video lengths in Table 2. We notice that the mean and 95th percentile attain peak values for video lengths in the range 30–60 mins. This indicates that there is a correlation between the number of stream control events and the length of the video, which is expected. We also looked at the the number of stream control events based on video genre, and cost (i.e., paid vs. free videos). We *did not* find significant differences in the average number of stream control events in either of the two cases.

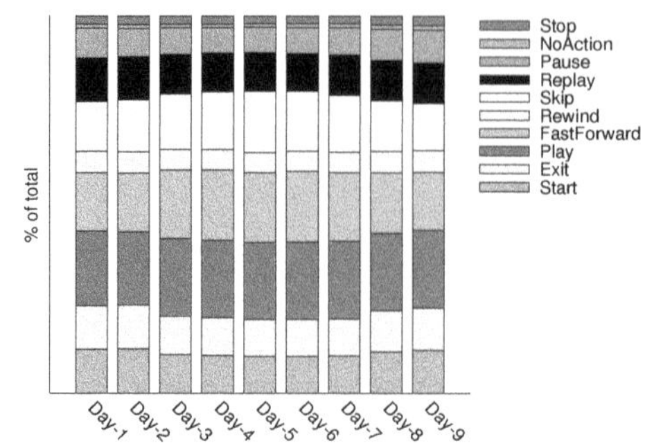

Figure 3: Breakup of VoD stream control events

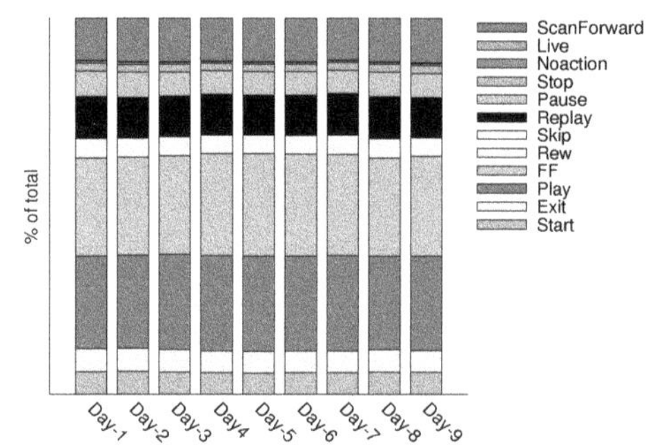

Figure 4: Breakup of DVR stream control events

Fig. 4 and Fig. 3 show the relative proportion of the various stream control operations. The sum of FASTFORWARD (FF), PLAY, and REPLAY comprise 45% of the total. SKIP is also frequent; FASTFORWARD is very common in DVR viewing (presumably to skip over commercials).

3.4 VoD Content Length and Popularity

We next look at the distribution of the video lengths. Figure 5 shows the video length distributions. We observe that a significant fraction are short videos, and there are about 5 clusters of video lengths.

We also characterize the popularity-rank distribution of the VoD library. Fig. 6 shows the logarithm of video popularity (number of times each video was requested) against the logarithm of the video's rank for one representative day; the dotted reference line has a slope of -1, characteristic of

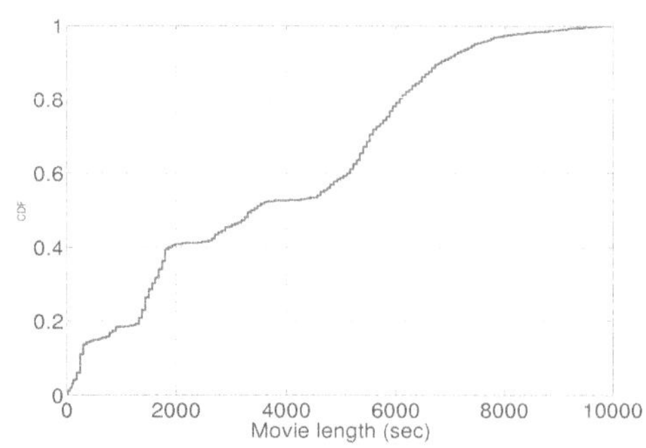

Figure 5: Video length distribution

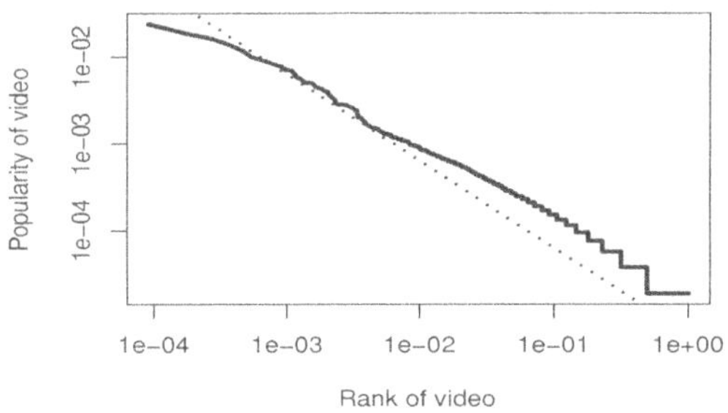

Figure 6: VoD popularity distribution

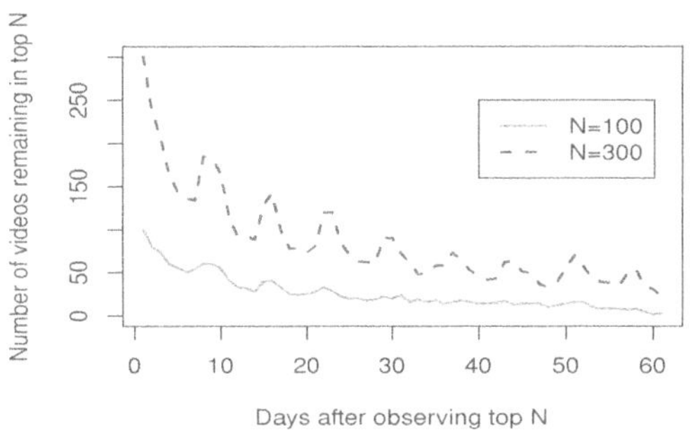

Figure 7: Evolution of VoD popularity

the Zipf distribution, similar to observations made by others (e.g., [4]). This plot is based on all the videos requested by all subscribers over one 24-hour period; we chose a day that falls within our primary 9 day study period. We observe that this popularity distribution is similar to what has been reported in other studies.

In addition to the popularity, we believe it is also useful to understand the evolution over time of the popularity of a particular video. Figure 7 starts on that same day as in the previous plot, and we chose the 300 (or 100) most popular videos as an initial list. For the next 60 days, we counted how many of those popular videos remained among the top 300 (or 100) most popular. We chose a window of 60 days because some videos in the library get aged out and are replaced by new content. We note the rapid drop-off in the popularity of both the top 100 as well as the top 300 videos. Furthermore, there is a periodicity associated with this change, indicating that some videos are more popular during the week and others on weekends. This has implications for several system design issues, such as managing the VoD library, caching, etc.

We utilize the characterization of the video length in our synthetic trace generation. We could potentially use the video popularity in the synthetic trace generation as well.

3.5 Quantifying the Impact of Stream Control

To motivate our study of stream control operations, we examined the impact of these operations using a discrete event simulator that faithfully emulates the interactions between clients and the video server in the IPTV environment. Our primary metric for evaluation is the peak server bandwidth, as it serves up the video requests and processes all the stream control operations of the corresponding video.

Figure 8 shows the peak server bandwidth required over a particular 24-hour day based on the actual trace, first accounting only for the video requests (and ignoring all the stream control operations). Second, for the same trace, all

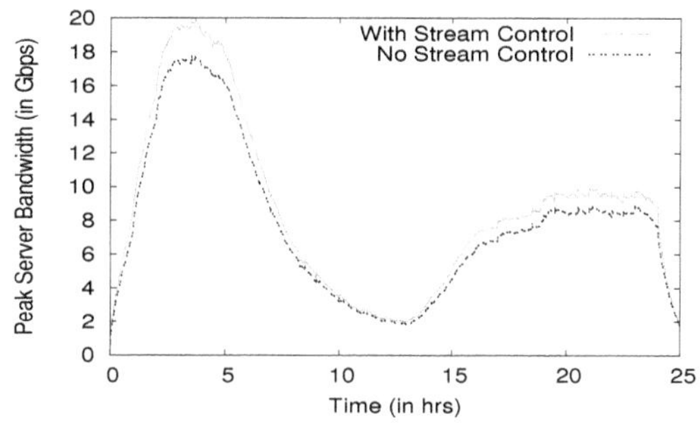

Figure 8: Impact of Stream Control Operations

the stream control operations are also properly accounted for. We observe that server bandwidth increases from about 17 Gbps to about 20 Gbps at the peak when stream control operations are accounted for, a reasonably significant increase. We use this to motivate the need to both model the stream control operations and understand their impact.

4. MODELING ARRIVAL AND STREAM CONTROL PROCESSES

Our objective is to construct a statistical model for the video request arrival process and for a sequence of stream control requests, as seen by a server complex of a large IPTV VOD system. The instantaneous load on a server at a given time, especially for video stream delivery, is determined by the number of concurrent sessions at that time. We define concurrent sessions as all those sessions whose state lies between START and EXIT at a given time. The number of concurrent sessions is determined by the instantaneous arrival rate and instantaneous session duration. Our overall model is thus made up of two components, an arrival (or session-start) process model that mimics the arrivals of new sessions into the system and a stream control model. The stream control model consists of a finite state machine (FSM) that models the detailed stream-control characteristics of a typical customer (the hop sequence from individual state to state), and a model for the sojourn times for each state of the FSM. The arrival process is described in Sec. 4.1, the finite state model in Sec. 4.2 and the sojourn time models in Sec. 4.3. Fig. 9 depicts the overall modeling and validation process. We first generate a sequence of session starts, hereafter referred to as arrivals. Each arrival results in a selection of a video according to the video length distribution described in Sec. 3.4, and spawns a separate state machine which generates a sequence of stream control events. The server sees the aggregate of the arrivals and their stream-control requests generated by each state machine. Our model thus requires that we characterize the arrival process and the state machine with sufficient accuracy.

4.1 Arrival Process Modeling

We first model the arrival process for VoD traffic. Our objective is to retain the shape of the daily profiles (diurnal pattern). The intensity of the profile is however scaled as a function of the number of users provisioned in the system. We noticed that there is a marked increase in the number of arrivals for the weekends compared to the weekdays. For modeling the arrival process, we look at the traces from the

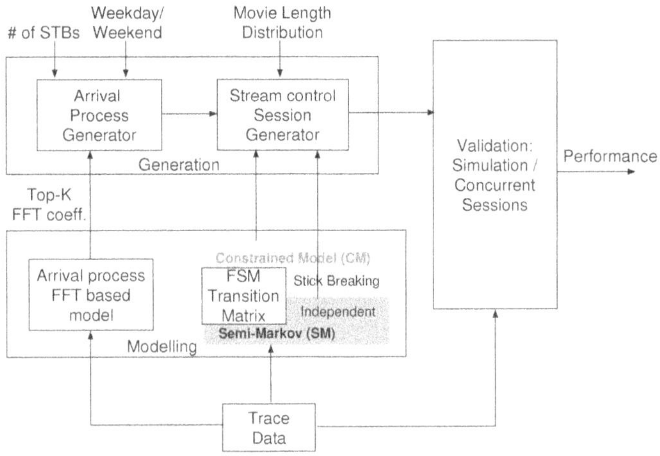

Figure 9: Modeling and validation approach

150 days across 2 years, which includes all 4 seasons of the TV programming cycle.

The arrival process is characterized by the arrival time t_n of the nth customer and the inter-arrival time $\tau_n = t_n - t_{n-1}$ between the nth and $n-1$th customer. If all inter-arrival times are i.i.d random variables with cumulative distribution function (CDF) $F_A(t)$, then $P(\tau_n \leq t) = F_A(t)$. We associate a counting process $N(t), t \geq 0$ to the arrival process $t_n, t \geq 0$ by the equivalence of $N(t) \geq n \iff t_n \leq t$. Thus $N(t)$ is a renewal process with inter-arrival time CDF $F_A(t)$.

Algorithm 1 Arrival process estimation for each day

Require: Input: t_n, D days, $S = \#$ of provisioned STBs; Output: FFT coefficients, F_{dk}.
1: **for** $d \in D$ **do**
2: /* Binning each second and normalize counts */ N_d = histogram(t_n,86400)/S
3: **end for**
4: /* Average N_d over all days */ $\bar{N_d} = N_d/D$
5: /* Perform FFT for average day */ $F_d = \text{FFT}(\bar{N_d})$
6: /* Save top K FFT coefficients */ $F_{dk} = F_d(topK)$
7: /* Regenerate arrival counts with inverse FFT */ $\hat{N_d} = \text{IFFT}(F_{dk})$

For each day of the week we provide parameters that can be used to regenerate a representative synthetic arrival process. To model a particular day of the week (e.g. Saturday) we pooled data for 16 Saturdays over a two year period at different times of the year (January, April, July, and December). The following procedure was then used in Algorithm 1. Arrivals were binned by the second and then normalized by the total number of STBs. This was necessary since the number of subscribers was increasing over the two years. We then computed the average daily profile and its Fast Fourier Transform (FFT). The top-K FFT coefficients were then stored. Through experimentation, we determined that only the top 10 coefficients are required to to regenerate the arrival process with a reasonable accuracy. The mean squared error (MSE) is shown in Table 3 which indicates that the error decreases as the number of FFT coefficients increases. Figures 10, 11, and 12 also show the regenerated arrival process for a varying number of FFT coefficients. Note that the regenerated process matches the diurnal pattern of the trace. In addition, we are also faithful in reproducing the spikes that occur every 30 minutes. These spikes probably occur as a result of users tuning into the VoD catalog after watching a broadcast program.

# of Coeff.	50	25	10
MSE	0.011065	0.011357	0.011549

Table 3: MSE for different FFT coefficients

4.2 Finite State Machine for Stream Control Events

For the purpose of modeling the stream control events, we initially investigated a discrete-time first-order finite state Markov process. A first-order Markov chain is entirely defined by the transition probabilities and an initial state distribution. Comparison with a real trace revealed a poor fit especially in terms of the session durations. To be specific, the session durations (sojourn times) for a Markov chain are geometrically distributed [16], whereas session durations in our traces are not. We first address the state transition probability estimation. The sojourn time estimation is then addressed in Section 4.3. The state transition probability matrix (P) is determined by counting the number of transition events from each state (e.g., PLAY to FASTFORWARD or PLAY to EXIT). We found that a single transition probability matrix does not adequately cover all scenarios. An examination of the state transition probabilities for weekdays and weekends found them to be sufficiently different to warrant separate transition probability matrices. We also examined transition probabilities for specific time-of-day effects (e.g., the busiest viewing period, typically called "prime time," is between 7 P.M. and 10 P.M.) but found that the variation was not large enough to warrant the additional complexity. We have thus chosen, in the interests of simplicity, to retain here only weekday and weekend models.

We observed that the primary determinant was the traffic intensity, rather than the transition probabilities for the stream control events over the busy hour. Although we could consider the effects of content genre and other environmental dependencies, we believe these have a second-order impact on the model.

An example of the estimated Markov chain is shown in Fig. 1. When users begin a VoD session by selecting a VoD video, the video starts to play automatically, initiating the START state. From this state, users may move to the other stream control states. For example, in Fig. 1, the user may go to FASTFORWARD with a probability of 0.23 or to PAUSE with a probability of 0.10. When they resume playing the video, they enter PLAY. While the state transition diagram has transitions from every one of the eight primary states to every other state, we only show the transitions with transition probability of 3% or more in Fig. 1. We refer the reader to the tables in [9] for the transition probability matrices for all the eight states obtained for both weekdays and weekends.

4.3 Modeling Sojourn Time Distributions

We consider two approaches for modeling sojourn time distributions. The first approach (SM), using a semi-Markov model, assumes that the event sojourn times are independent and focuses on fitting the sojourn time distributions for

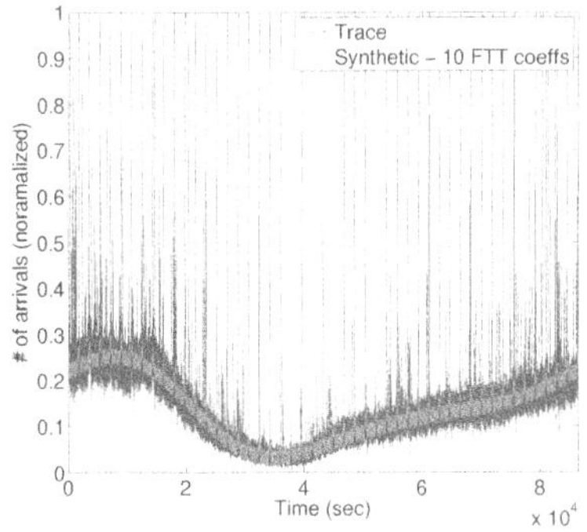

Figure 10: 10 coefficients

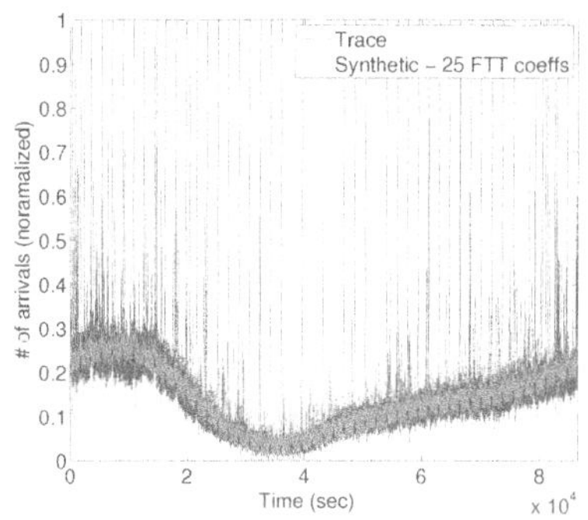

Figure 11: 25 coefficients

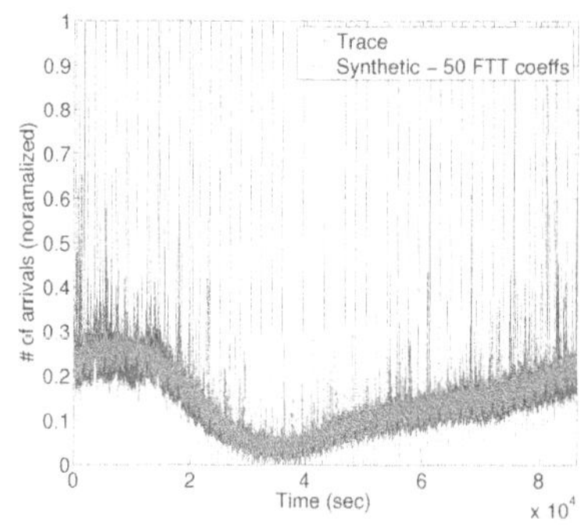

Figure 12: 50 coefficients

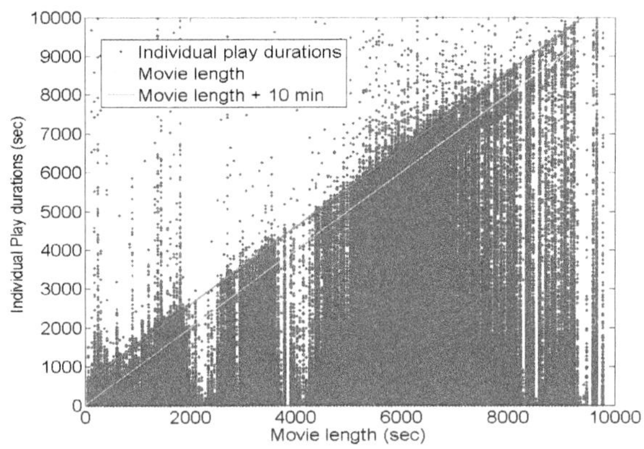

Figure 13: Play duration vs video length

each state of the FSM. In practice since the actual state sojourn times may not be independent, it may not match the distribution of the session durations. The second approach (CM) is a constrained model, the stick-breaking approach, and it imposes the session duration constraint.

4.3.1 Independent Sojourn Time Models (SM)

As motivated in the previous subsection we investigate the use of a semi-Markov model, where the sojourn time distributions can be freely chosen [6]. A semi-Markov model consists of an embedded discrete parameter Markov chain with a corresponding transition probability matrix and a set of conditional sojourn time distribution functions. In its most general form, the sojourn time distributions in state s are dependent on the next state to be visited. We begin with a restricted semi-Markov model, where the sojourn time distributions depend on the current state alone. After some experimentation (taking into account time of day and video length), we opted to normalize sojourn times with respect to video length and to create two separate models; one each for a typical weekend and weekday. Fig. 13 plots PLAY duration against video length. There are some PLAY events that persist longer than the video length (shown by the red line). This is an artifact of the IPTV system, which generates an automatic time-out after ten minutes when a viewer fails to exit after the video has ended, thus releasing this user from the VoD server and conserving resources. From Fig. 13 we observe that the PLAY duration (the dominant event) is seen to be proportional to the length of the video. This justifies normalization of the PLAY duration by the video length. For the sake of simplicity, we chose to normalize the sojourn times in the other states by the video length as well.We found that after normalization by the video length, the sojourn time in each state exhibited a weak day-of-week effect, adding further justification of our choice to normalize by the video length. (see Figure 14).

	Weekend		Weekday	
Operation	Mean	Variance	Mean	Variance
SKIP	53.56	1.48e5	39.29	9.53e4
FASTFORWARD	8.08	113.18	8.53	121.68
PLAY	305.22	8.37e5	195.32	4.92e5
REPLAY	66.61	1.53e5	54.80	1.147e5
REWIND	5.39	52.43	5.62	46.10
STOP	28.44	7.47e3	23.24	6.01e3
PAUSE	55.03	1.44e4	40.27	1.09e4
START	763.19	2.70e6	610.97	2.06e6

Table 4: Statistics of stream control durations (in seconds), for VoD.

We now examine the day-of-week effect on sojourn time. The mean values of the states PLAY and START are far greater than those of any other state; this is where viewers spend most of their time. Most of other states have much smaller means, indicating that users tend to switch out of them quickly. Table 4 shows the mean duration for each state. Note that the mean PLAY duration is smaller on weekdays than weekends (a 32% reduction). A smaller reduction of 19% is seen between weekend days and weekdays for the normalized PLAY durations. See Figure 14).

Thus, we have now reduced the problem to that of modeling the CDFs of the normalized sojourn times. Let $\{T_s(n), n = 0, 1, 2 \ldots\}$ be the sequence of sojourn times in state s for a given user and let random variable T_s denote a generic sojourn time duration. Our objective is to model the CDF $F_s(\tau) := \Pr(T_s \leq \tau)$.

Two commonly used models for characterizing heavy tailed distributions (HTDs) are the generalized Pareto and Weibull distributions. The maximum likelihood parameters for the Generalized Pareto function for shape and scale are $a = 2.174$ and $b = 0.0012$ respectively. Similarly, for the Weibull function they are $a = 0.0108$ and $b = 0.3391$. Fig. 14 and Fig. 15 shows that these standard HTDs are not a very close fit to the observed data.

To investigate further, we examine empirical CDFs (i.e., CDFs computed from data) for different states s in Fig. 16. In this figure, $\log(\tau)$ is plotted against $F(\tau)$ for each state F_s

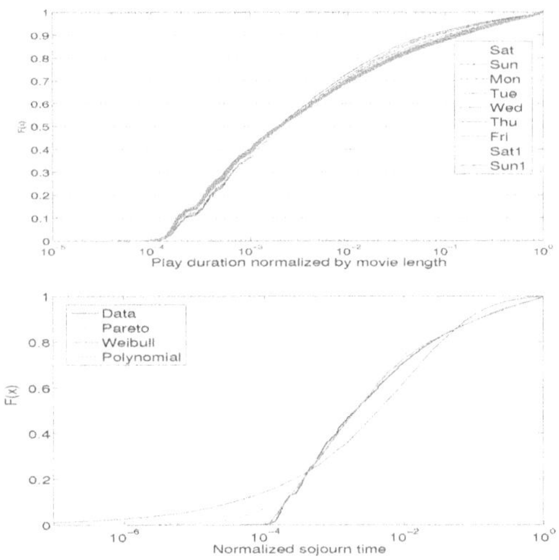

Figure 14: CDF of normalized play durations for VoD, different days and different distribution fits

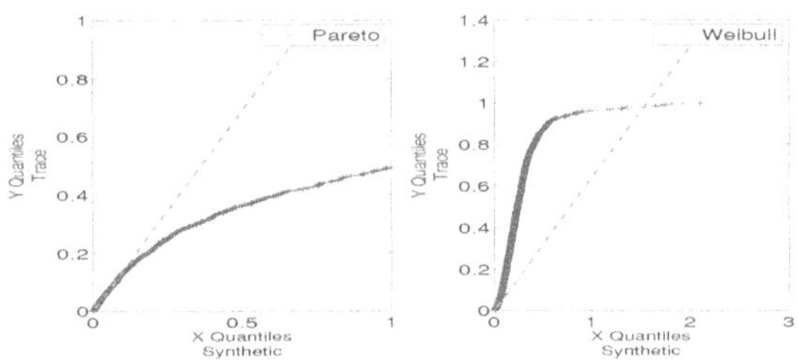

Figure 15: QQ plots for Pareto and Weibull generated synthetic traces

(in other words, this figure shows G_s, the inverse of the CDF on a logarithmic scale).[1] Fig. 16 suggests that we should try to represent $\log G_s(p)$ as a polynomial function of p.

We thus assume that the inverse CDF can be modeled by the $m+1$-term polynomial $\log \hat{G}(p) = \sum_{i=0}^{m} a_i p^{n_i}$ for given n_i, $i = 0, 1, \ldots, m$. For a given set of n_i's, we choose the parameter vector $\bar{a} = (a_0, a_1, \ldots, a_m)^t$ so as to minimize the $(N+1)$-point sum squared error (SSE)

$$SSE(N) = \sum_{p_i} (\log G(p_i) - \log \hat{G}(p_i))^2,$$

where $p_i = i/N$, $i = 0, 1, \ldots, N$ is a uniformly spaced set of points in the interval $[0, 1]$ at which the empirical inverse CDF is sampled. From linear estimation theory, the vector parameter $\bar{a}$ that minimizes the SSE is given by

$$\bar{a} = (U^t U)^{-1} U^t g, \tag{1}$$

where U is a $(N+1) \times (m+1)$ matrix, whose ith column is $(p_0^{n_i}, p_1^{n_i}, p_2^{n_i}, \ldots, p_N^{n_i})^t$, $i = 0, 1, 2, \ldots, m$, and g is the column vector $(\log G(p_0), \log G(p_1), \ldots, \log G(p_N))^t$, which is obtained from the data.

We experimented with several choices for the basis functions and used the quantile-quantile (QQ) plot as a guide to the quality of the fit. Our search over $n_i = i^k$, $k = 1, 2, \ldots, 6$ revealed that $k = 3$ is optimal, and we provide some evidence to support this in the QQ plots shown in Fig. 18 and Fig. 19.

[1]To work around the problem that F_s will not have an inverse when the underlying distribution has nonzero mass at a point, we define $G_s(p) = \arg\min_x \{F_s(x) \geq p\}$.

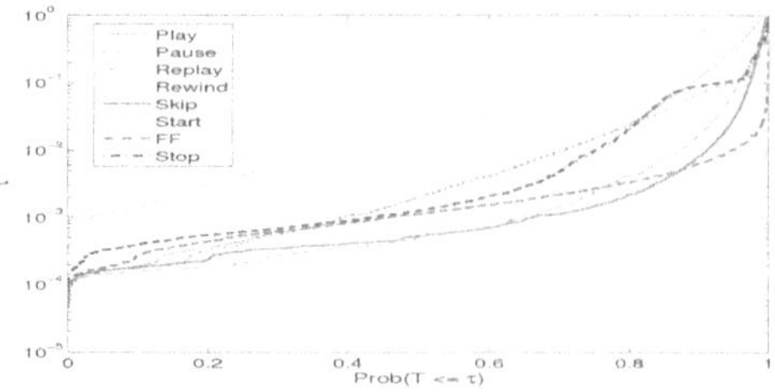

Figure 16: Sojourn time inverse CDFs

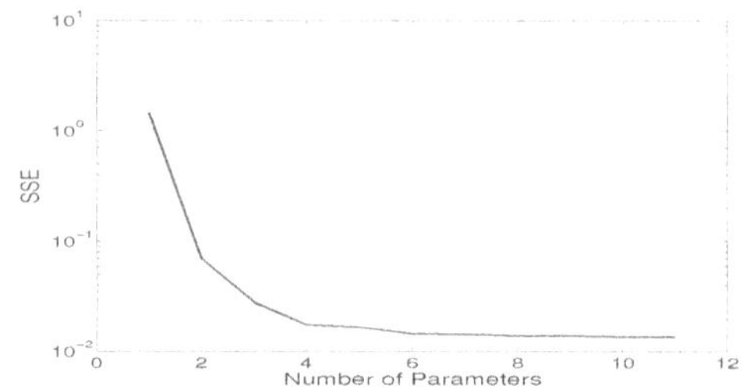

Figure 17: SSE as a function of number of parameters, m, for the Fast-Forward duration CDF.

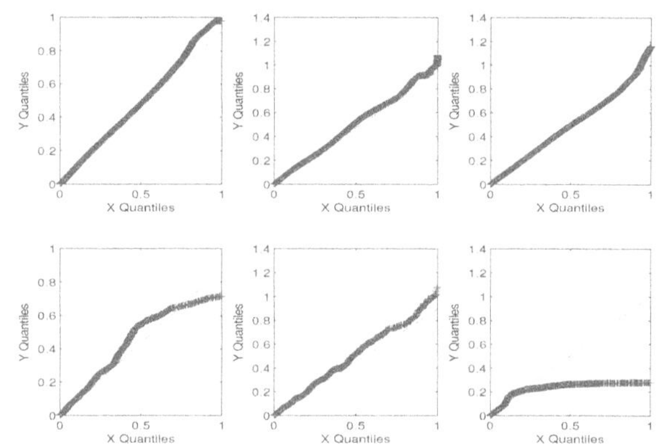

Figure 18: Various QQ plots. Horiz. axis: actual data. Vert. axis: synthetic data. Top row: play; bottom row: Pause. Left to right $(m, k) = (6, 3), (11, 3), (6, 1)$, respectively.

For $n_i = i^3$, the SSE is plotted as a function of m in Fig. 17. Even though this plot suggests that $m = 6$ parameters are sufficient, the QQ plot suggests that the fit is not sufficiently linear until $m = 11$.

We also examined the correlation structure of the collected data. The first-order correlation coefficient, i.e., the correlation coefficient of successive sojourn times, is shown in Table 5. The correlation coefficients are seen to be small, though not insignificant, especially in the PLAY state. While we could choose to model the sequence of sojourn times as a correlated autoregressive process, we would have to give up control over the marginal CDF of the generated process. Given the small correlation coefficients, we opted for simplicity and chose an independent identically distributed process.

Finally, we remark that constructing a fit for the inverse CDF, rather than the CDF, has an added advantage that a random variable T with the desired distribution can be

Play	Pause	Replay	Rew	Skip	Start	FF
0.21	0.21	0.05	0.10	0.16	0.14	0.09

Table 5: First-order corr. coeff. for the sojourn time of each state.

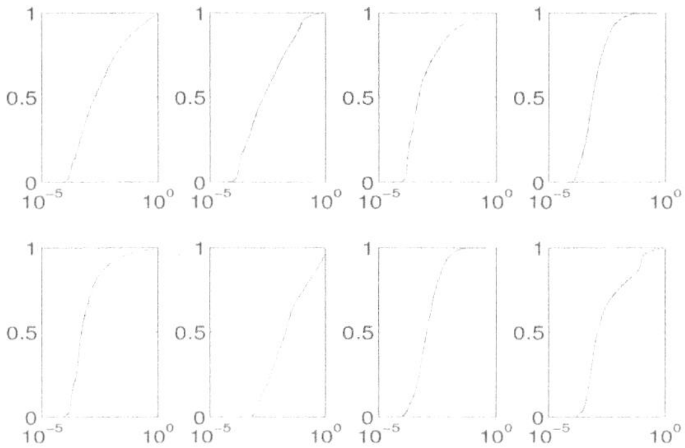

Figure 19: Fitted Distributions, $m = 11$ parameters. Top, left to right: play, Pause, Replay, Rewind. Bottom, left to right: Skip, start, FastForward, stop.

obtained by warping U a random variable uniformly distributed on $[0, 1]$ using the formula $T = \exp(\sum_{i=0}^{m} a_i U^{n_i})$.

We computed the mean, variance, third moment, and median of all state distributions to compare the accuracy of the various fits. As seen in Table 6, the family of polynomial exponential fitting functions performs better than the standard HTDs considered here with respect to these metrics. Table 6 shows that the polynomial fitted distributions fit the third moment and the median of the data set better, unlike the generalized Pareto and Weibull functions. The polynomial distribution has the closest fit and has an accuracy for all metrics to within 1% of the data. Additionally, Fig. 14 shows the closeness of the polynomial fit when compared to the real trace's normalized CDF.

	Trace	Pareto	Weibull	Polynomial
E[X]	0.0499	0.0269	0.0324	0.0498
Var[X]	0.0220	0.0090	0.0068	0.0224
$E[X^3]$	0.0137	0.0051	0.0030	0.0143
Median	0.0019	0.0018	0.0043	0.0019

Table 6: Comparison of statistics of trace data and fitted distributions for play state.

The state transition matrices and polynomial coefficients are tabulated in [9]. Fig. 20 shows the Q-Q plots for the synthetically generated data and the normalized trace data for the sojourn times for each of the VoD stream control states. All the state durations are close to the reference line, indicating a good match between the observed and the modeled data.

4.3.2 Stick-Breaking Sojourn-Time Models (CM)

The modeling approach in Sec. 4.3.1 assumes independent sojourn times for each stream control event. In reality, event sojourn times are not independent—e.g., a REWIND event cannot have a duration that exceeds the total sum of the preceding PLAY events. A problem with the independence assumption is that the session duration distribution for the synthetic trace would be a sum of independent ran-

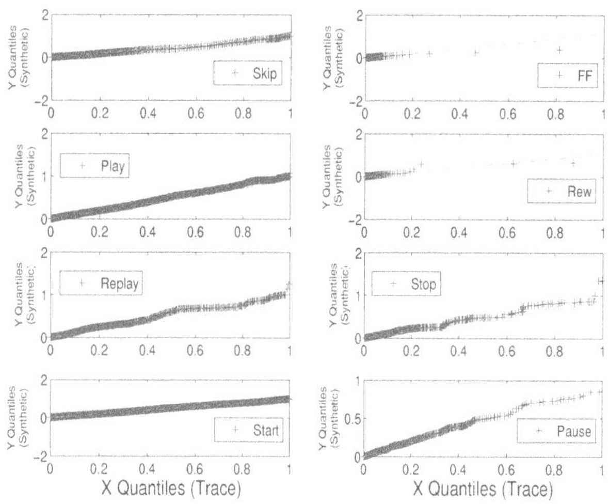

Figure 20: Q-Q plots, weekend (normalized)

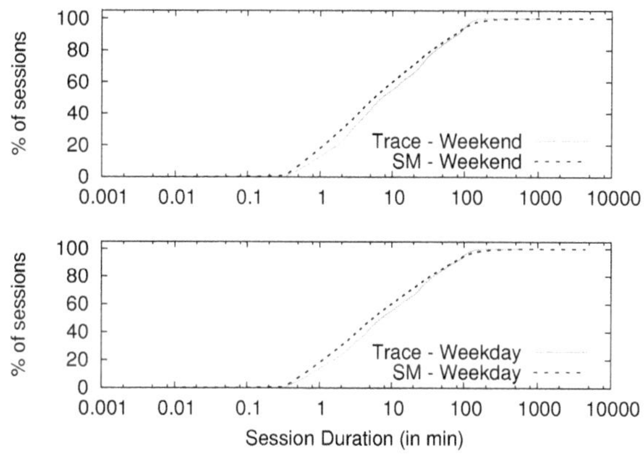

Figure 21: CDF of session duration for real- and SM-based trace on a weekday and weekend.

dom variables and this is in general different from the actual session duration distribution. We show in Fig. 21 the cumulative distribution of session durations observed on a weekday and a weekend in real traces and through the approaches in Sec. 4.3.1. It is clear from the figure that the FSM approach generates a considerable number of short sessions and compensates by generating a few very long sessions.

To rectify this situation, we present an approach that preserves the overall session duration distribution. The main idea is to model the fraction of the session duration taken up by the sojourn time in each state, as well as the overall session duration. Since the state sojourn times must add up to the overall session duration they cannot be independent, so this model does capture some of the subtle dependencies between the state sojourn times. Later in this section, we address the issue of joining together the FSM and state sojourn time models.

Models for non-negative random variables with a specified sum have been studied in the probability theory literature [14] and more recently have found application in machine learning and pattern recognition. If the sum of the random variables is unity, then a probabilistic model for the random variables is equivalent to constructing a measure on the space of probability distributions. In the machine learning literature, the reason for the interest in such random measures comes from a desire to determine a maximum likelihood estimate of the prior distribution given a set of observations, see e.g., [2] for an estimation problem related to Gaussian mixture models.

The approach that we take here is to model the fraction of the residual session duration that is occupied by each state. This approach, referred to as the stick-breaking approach [14], goes back at least as far back as [12]. Let T_s denote the random session duration, and let T_i denote the random duration of the ith event, $i = 1, 2, \ldots, K$ ($K = 7$ in this case). Thus $T_s = T_1 + T_2 + \ldots + T_K$, where K is the number of distinct types of stream control events. We model the distributions of the random variables $X_1 = T_1/T_s$, $X_2 = T_2/(T_s - T_1)$, and in general $X_i = T_i/(T_s - \sum_{j=1}^{i-1} T_i)$, $i = 1, 2, \ldots, K$. Thus X_i is the fraction of the 'remaining' session duration occupied by the ith event, and $X_K = 1$. We also model the distribution of T_s. Let p_i be the modeled pdf of X_i and let p_s be the modeled pdf for T_s. An individual session is then generated by picking the fraction X_i independently and according to p_i, $i = 1, 2, \ldots, K - 1$, $X_K = 1 - \sum_{i=1}^{K-1} X_i$ and T_s according to p_s. The individual session durations are then given by $T_1 = X_1 T_s$, $T_2 = X_2(T_s - T_1)$, and in general $T_i = X_1(T_s - \sum_{j=1}^{i-1} T_j)$. This approach preserves both the total session duration as well as the fraction of a residual session occupied by each event.

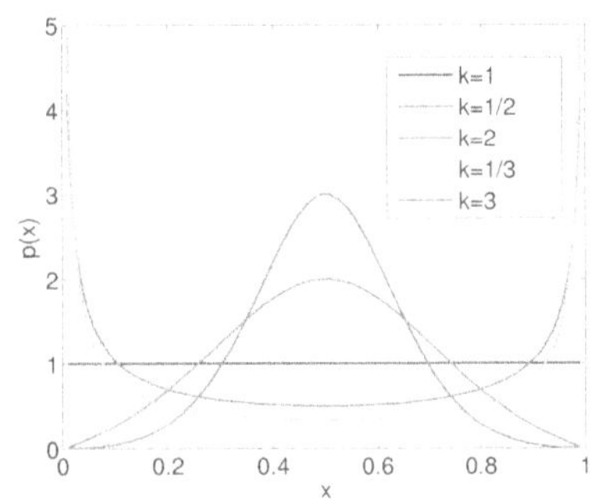

Figure 22: The pdf of X_i for different values of the shape parameter for the underlying Weibull distribution. Heavy tails lead to cup shaped distributions.

We have thus reduced the problem of modeling the state sojourn durations to that of modeling the fractions X_i, $i = 1, 2, \ldots, K$. In most machine learning applications, the observed data comes from a Bernoulli process or Bernoulli scheme, and the estimation problem is to determine the most likely prior probability distribution, given the observed data. The beta distribution is a natural class of prior distributions in this setting [14]. The beta distribution is a parametric family of distributions on the open unit interval given by

$$p(x) = \frac{\Gamma(a+b)}{\Gamma(a)\Gamma(b)} x^{a-1}(1-x)^{b-1}. \quad (2)$$

which are well suited to modeling the X_i's. The mean and variance of the beta distribution is given by $a/(a+b)$ and $ab/(a+b)^2(a+b+1)$, respectively, and the distributions are cup-shaped for a, b in the interval $(0, 1)$.

Compared to the standard machine learning setting, our fractions X_i arise from competing sojourn times and it is not obvious that beta random variables will be useful. Some insight into the modeling of the random variables X_i can be obtained from the following toy example. Consider a pair (T_1, T_2), of independent identically distributed sojourn times with the Weibull distribution,

$$p(x) = \frac{k}{\lambda}\left(\frac{x}{\lambda}\right)^{k-1} e^{-(x/\lambda)^k} U(x) \quad (3)$$

where $U(x)$ is the unit step function. Let $X_1 = T_1/(T_1+T_2)$. The pdf of X_1 is plotted in Fig. 22 for different values of the shape parameter k. It is surprising that the observed pdf's are close in distribution to beta distributions. More interesting is the fact that heavy tails for the Weibull distribution, $k < 1$, lead to cup shaped distributions for the X_i's. In other words, *heavy tails lead to extreme ratios.*

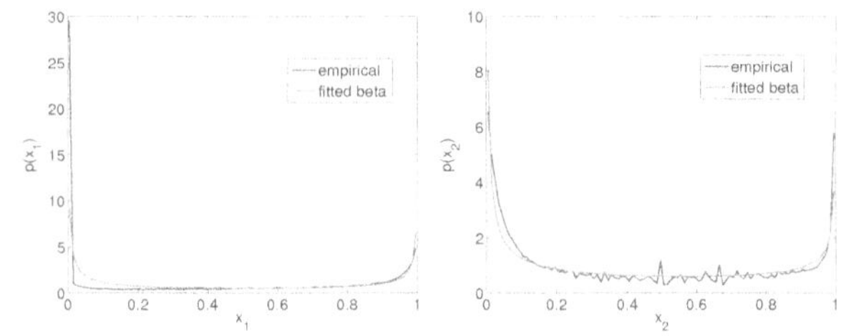

Figure 23: Empirical and fitted beta distributions for X_1 (left) and X_2 (right).

While the above toy example was based on the Weibull distribution for state sojourn durations, it is seen in Fig. 23 that the X_i's obtained from the trace data are also well modeled by the beta distribution, and in fact have the distinctive cup shape that we observed when the Weibull distribution has heavy tails. We also show in Fig. 23 the fitted beta distributions in which the parameters a and b are estimated so as to match the empirical mean and variance of X_1, $i = 1, 2, \ldots, K - 1$. Thus, estimated parameters $\hat{a}$ and $\hat{b}$ are given by $\hat{a} = \mu\gamma$, $\hat{b} = (1-\mu)\gamma$, with $\gamma = \frac{\mu(1-\mu)}{\sigma^2} - 1$. The matching between the empirical and fitted distributions is seen to be quite good.

We now address the problem of joining the stick-breaking sojourn times with the FSM model. There are two issues to be addressed: (i) the FSM might visit a state several times, while the stick-model produces a single number for the aggregate time spent in that state, and (ii) a sample path through the FSM might exclude some states for which the stick-breaking model generates a positive fraction X_i. Setting this X_i to zero will perturb the resulting session duration distribution.

To address (i) the fraction X_i is divided equally by the number times the FSM visits state i. To address (ii) we generate a number of FSM sample paths, as well as a number of sample fractions using the stick breaking model. A matching algorithm is then used to match FSM sample paths and the stick-breaking outcomes, to yield the CM model.

4.4 DVR Model: Highlights

Much of the DVR modeling issues are similar to those encountered while modeling VoD. For example, the DVR arrival process is quite similar to the VoD arrival process – a superposition of a bursty and a smooth component with a well-defined diurnal variation. Hence, we only emphasize the key differences in this section. Figs. 24 and 25 show the normalized sojourn time for VoD and DVR respectively for a weekend day. The estimated state transition matrix for the DVR state machine revealed a few important differences compared to the VoD state machine. The transition probabilities from the START to EXIT states are 46% and

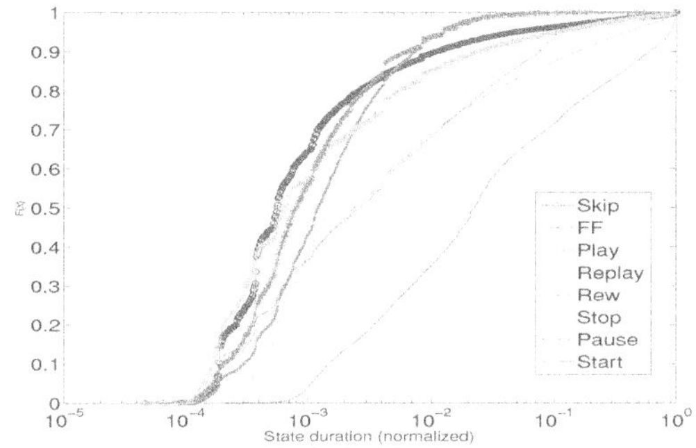

Figure 24: All stream control CDFs, weekend (normalized) for VoD

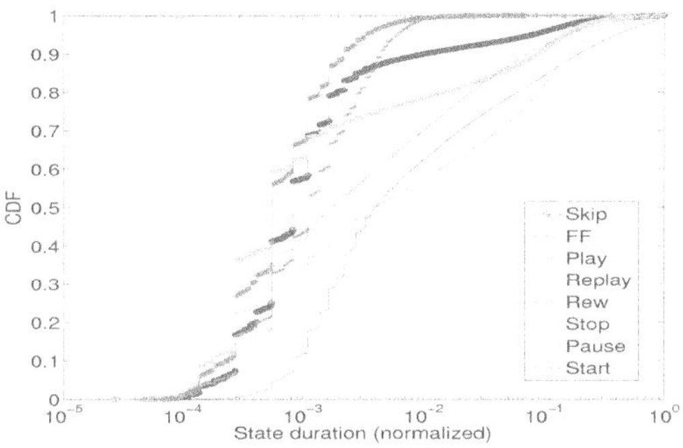

Figure 25: All stream control CDFs, weekend (normalized) for DVR

17% for VoD and DVR respectively, indicating less use of stream control during VoD viewing. Second, the transition probabilities from PLAY to FASTFORWARD are 41% and 55% for VoD and DVR respectively. The higher probablility of FASTFORWARD in the DVR model is probably explained by the efforts of viewers to avoid the advertising that forms such a large part of broadcast television programming. Similarly, SKIP has a higher probability in the DVR model, presumably also due to users' efforts to avoid ads.

We have also developed DVR stream control models for both the weekend and weekday. We refer the reader to our technical report for the detailed model parameters [9].

5. EXPERIMENTAL RESULTS

One of the goals of our work is provide the ability to generate synthetic traces that effectively capture users' behavior in a large-scale VoD system. In this section we validate the accuracy of our models by generating completely synthetic traces and comparing it to real traces using a custom event-driven simulator. Stream control events affect how much of a video is watched. This directly translates into how much load each session places on the server. As a result, we use server load as our primary metric of comparison. We use the simulator to accurately capture the effects of stream control events on server load. However, we also examine the generated traces for other attributes and show that our models are able to successfully capture the important aspects of users' VoD viewing sessions.

5.1 Synthetic Trace Generation

We used our models to generate completely synthetic traces for a given subscriber population. The process starts with the generation of a stream of session start requests. There is variability in the number of arrivals, both on week days and weekends, even for the same number of subscribers over the 2 year period. This may be due to a variety of societal factors (seasonal viewing patterns, TV programming and new content generation cycles etc.) As a result, we compute the mean of all traces (normalized by their respective number of subscribers for those days). We use the process described in Section 4.1 to generate a synthetic trace, and scale our modeled arrival process for a given subscriber population.

Once we have the arrivals, we then model the session behavior using either the SM or the CM model. In the case of SM, for each session, we used the stream control model to generate a sequence of stream control events and their sojourn times. Since each FSM produces events whose lengths are normalized by movie length, the individual state sojourn time durations generated by each FSM are then scaled by the movie length. The movie length is drawn from a distribution fitted (using the Kaplan-Meier technique) to the empirical movie length distribution shown in Figure 5.

In the case of CM, given a realization of X_i, the fraction of the remaining session duration occupied by the ith event, we generate independent sequences of stream control events by using the FSM. The output of the FSM gives us a sequence of events in a particular order from the START state to the EXIT state. We divide the X_i's equally by the number of events for state i to allocate the individual time spent per state. Finally, for a randomly chosen session duration (obtained from an appropriate session duration distribution), the X_i's are rescaled by the session duration. This allows us to retrofit the session durations from the stick-breaking model to the sojourn times with the FSM.

5.2 Experiment Setup

We validated the accuracy of our models, by running the synthetic and actual traces through the simulator. Our simulator faithfully models the message exchanges between a client (i.e., set top box) and a video server with an abstract model of the network between the client and the server.

Modeling Videos. We model videos as consisting of a sequence of 2-second chunks. In the absence of stream control events, these chunks are requested and played out in sequence. This is similar to the techniques used in many P2P systems [8, 15] and in some centralized approaches (e.g., HTTP Live Streaming [19]). With stream control, clients jump to different parts of the video depending on the event, and then request the chunks sequentially from that point on. We assume that FASTFORWARD and REWIND are implemented using "trick streams". Trick streams essentially are alternate video files that encode only certain key frames of the video and provide the impression that the video is being played faster.

Client modeling. Clients initiate requests for videos based on the input file. On receiving a PLAY request, the client sequentially requests one chunk at a time until it executes a stream control event. We assume that a SKIP takes the viewer 30 seconds into the video, while a REPLAY results in a 7-second jump backwards. When clients execute one of these operations, the existing transfer is aborted and a request is sent out to the server for the new chunk or a trick stream.

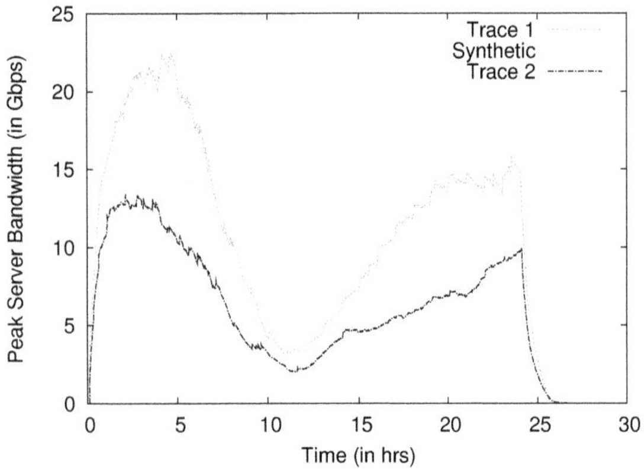

Figure 26: Peak server load generated by two different real traces and the pure synthetic trace, for a commensurate number of subscribers.

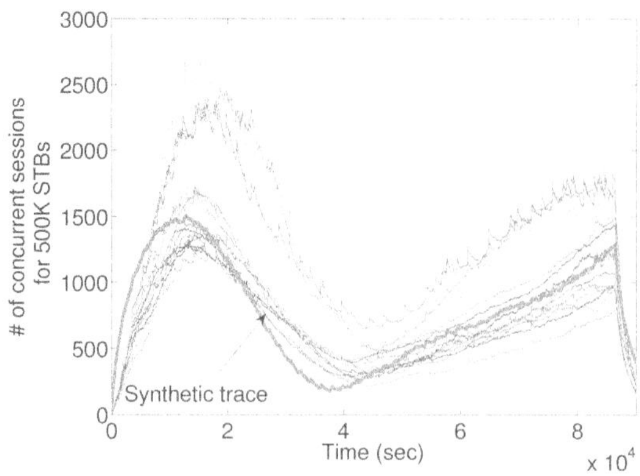

Figure 27: # of concurrent sessions (all Tuesday traces and synthetic trace) scaled for a population of 500K

Each client is assumed to have a local disk which it uses to store the data being transferred by the server for the duration of the video (after which it is deleted). The client waits for four seconds of data in its playout buffer before starting to play the video. Thus, when a client performs a SKIP or a REPLAY, the client waits until sufficient data is buffered before continuing to play. Finally, the client tries to follow the state transitions faithfully and ignores events that it encounters in the trace that cannot be executed in its current state.

Server Modeling. The server in our simulator responds to requests for chunks and trick streams by delivering them as a unicast stream. The server keeps track of the existing transfer for each client. Note that the server only gets chunk requests and is oblivious to the specific stream control operation performed. This behavior is not very different from what many commercial VoD systems implement [7]. If it receives a request for a new chunk or trick stream before the end of an existing transfer, the server aborts the existing transfer, and starts serving the new request. We assume that all video streams and trick streams are encoded at 2 Mbps and that the server transfers the video 10% faster (2.1 Mbps) than the playout rate to accommodate for transient network conditions.

5.3 Server Load: Synthetic vs. Real Traces

For our main result, we compare the load at the server due to real and synthetic traces. Nominally, we generated a synthetic trace for a weekday using a subscriber base of ~3 million. We compare this to the server load due to real traces with a commensurate number of subscribers.

We present the result in Figure 26. The plot shows the peak server bandwidth (measured every minute) over time for the two real traces and the purely synthetic trace. There are a few observations we make. First, the synthetic trace nicely captures the diurnal changes in load and resembles the pattern observed in the real traces. Next, for the same number of subscribers and on the same day of the week, the real traces can actually generate significantly different load. This is because the number of *concurrently active* users is different at these different times. Finally, we see that the load due to the synthetic trace falls between the two real traces. This is not unexpected because we model the session arrivals to be an average of the arrivals across the different days (refer Section 5.1). We validate this next.

5.4 Accuracy of Session Arrival Model

In the first result, we attributed the difference in server load between the synthetic trace and real traces to the variability in load even in the real traces. To validate this, we plot the number of concurrent sessions for all the 16 Tuesdays (spanning 2 years, with varying number of subscribers) in our DS1 data set. To remove the inherent scaling issues with a growing subscriber base, we rescaled each trace individually to a population of 500K subscribers. We show the number of concurrent sessions for the 16 Tuesdays in Figure 27.

The peak number of concurrent sessions varies widely from 1200 to 2700 during the busy hour. We did not observe any distinctive correlation (e.g., based on seasons) between the different Tuesdays. We also plot the concurrent sessions for the purely synthetic trace in the plot using the thick red line. The synthetic trace matches the diurnal variation of the empirical traces. We also observe that the synthetic trace falls within the upper and lower bounds of the number of concurrent sessions. This is important: given the variability, we cannot exactly match the session arrivals, but this result shows that model is able to generate a representative set of session arrivals. In addition to the number of provisioned subscribers, we also examined the variability if we normalize by just the number of *active* subscribers (i.e., makes at least one request on a given day). Our results (not shown) indicate very similar variability across the 16 days.

5.5 Comparison of Stream Control Models

In this experiment we study the accuracy of the two stream control models we have proposed. We generate a semi-synthetic traces using each of the two stream control model approaches (SM, CM), for both a weekday and a weekend and compare them against the representative real traces. In order to eliminate any effects of the session arrival generation process, we use the arrivals from the real traces, but only generate the stream control events and their durations using the stream control models (this is the reason we say these are a semi-synthetic traces). We present the results both for a weekday and a weekend day in Figures 28 and 29 respectively.

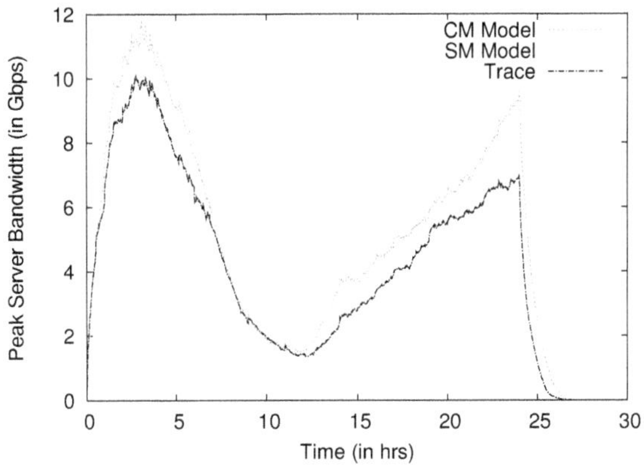

Figure 28: Peak server load on Friday generated by real and synthetic (SM and CM) traces.

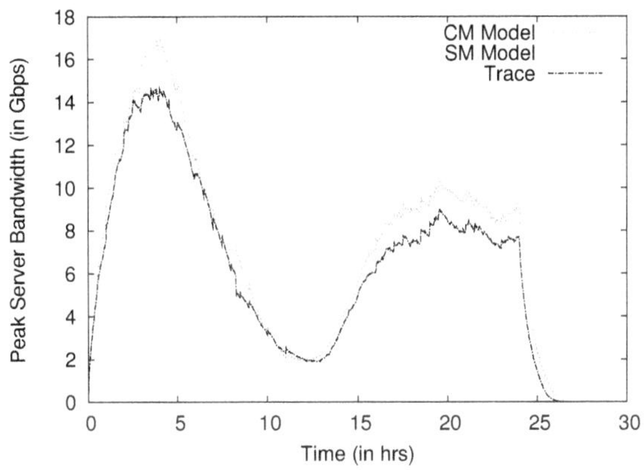

Figure 29: Peak server load on Saturday generated by real and synthetic traces (SM and CM).

The plots shows that our modeling of stream control functions accurately captures the load at the server. In particular the plots show that the SM-based model almost matches the load at the server at all times indicating that it is able to accurately capture the effects of stream control. The stick breaking (CM-model) approach, while performing well, overestimates the load at the server. This result goes to show that it is not only important to generate accurate session durations; it is also important to get the number and sequence of stream control events correct.

5.6 Stream Control Events in a Session

We then compare the number of stream control events observed in the real trace to that generated in the synthetic traces. Specifically we compare the average number and average duration of stream control events per session for both a weekend day and weekday. We report the results in Table 7.

The SM-based approach, on average, generates a similar number of stream control events and durations compared to the CM approach. In particular, we see that the CM approach overestimates the REWIND and FASTFORWARD durations, which adds load to the server. On the other hand, it underestimates the PAUSE duration which reduces load on the server. This explains the difference in the peak server bandwidth observed in Figures 28 and 29 between the SM and CM approaches. The reason for the inaccuracies in event durations generated by the CM model is because of error accumulation in the regenaration process, where beta random variables are successively subtracted off to generate the time intervals associated with each event. For this reason, we believe it is better to estimate the beta random variables in an increasing order of the mean value of the event durations and then reconstruct the sojourn times for each of the states from these generated beta random variables.

It is observed that the SM approach results in very high variability in the session durations, while the trace using CM does not. For example, consider the total time spent by the user in the play state. The real trace had a standard deviation of 1856.46 for the weekday and 1940.22 on the weekend day. The SM model had 2928.95 and 2892.78 for the weekday and weekend respectively. But, the CM model had 1744.70 and 1748.08 for the weekday and weekend, matching the real trace more closely. Thus, while the SM model captures the average durations nicely, CM captures the variability better.

5.7 Client Session Interruptions

As clients perform stream control operations, they may experience interruptions in their viewing of the video until enough data is buffered in the play-out buffer. In this experiment we characterize the interruptions experienced by clients in the real trace in comparison to the synthetic trace. Note that the exact number of interruptions and their duration depends on the specific client implementation, the chunk size used, etc. Our goal here is to compare the viewer experience with the real trace and the synthetic traces with one example implementation.

For each stream control operation, we identify if that portion of the video needed is locally available in the client buffer. If not, we request for that portion from the server. We assume that a minimum of 4 seconds of video has to be buffered before the video can be displayed. If the desired portion is not available, we count it as an interruption and measure the time that the viewer has to wait before the video starts playing again.

Data	% of interr. sessions	Avg. interr. per session	Avg. Duration of interr.
Syn. CM	41.31	3.17	4.98
Syn. SM	38.11	2.51	4.76
Real Trace	37.45	3.47	5.17

Table 8: Session interruption statistics

Table 8 presents the statistics related to interrupted sessions for the real trace as well as the synthetic traces generated using the two alternate models (the CM model and the SM model). The results show that the fraction of sessions experiencing interruptions with the synthetic traces is comparable to that with the real trace, with the SM model doing slightly better than the CM model. However, among the interrupted sessions, the CM model more accurately captures the average number of interruptions per session (3.17 for CM model vs. 3.47 for the real trace) than the SM model (2.51 interruptions per session). The CM model also captures the average duration of interruptions better than the SM model. However, the differences between the two models, for this metric, are not statistically significant enough to advocate one model over the other.

	Weekend						Weekday					
	Avg. Count			Avg.Duration			Avg.Count			Avg.Duration		
State	Real	SM	CM	Real	SM	CM	Real	SM	CM	Real	SM	CM
Play	3.13	3.62	4.73	1163.24	1108.06	1120.03	2.89	3.31	4.61	1232.31	1178.51	1120.75
FastForward	1.93	2.31	3.02	15.78	38.98	90.48	1.55	1.80	2.60	12.38	34.78	89.16
Rewind	0.49	0.63	1.17	2.56	9.89	68.42	0.50	0.64	1.20	2.56	9.89	68.42
Pause	0.71	0.89	1.27	63.44	84.65	37.92	0.70	0.90	1.38	61.16	94.21	37.42
Skip	1.61	1.90	2.82	76.21	138.90	37.38	1.32	1.49	2.50	69.60	129.28	38.47
Replay	1.06	1.39	2.28	62.63	128.92	17.31	0.95	1.19	2.20	62.07	126.68	17.69

Table 7: Breakup of stream control events on weekdays and weekends.

6. CONCLUSIONS

We set out to understand and model interactive user behavior in an IPTV environment, particularly its impact on system resources. We modeled user interactivity based on traces of user actions captured from a nationally deployed, operational system. We developed a video request arrival process model and two comprehensive stream control models. The frequency domain (FFT) based arrival process model faithfully captures the diurnal pattern while also preserving the periodic bursty nature of the traffic with only a few parameters. The stream control model consists of a finite state machine and two alternative models for determining the state sojourn times. The first alternative (SM model) seeks to preserve the sojourn time distribution for each state. The second alternative (CM model) puts a greater emphasis on preserving the overall session duration distribution.

To establish the validity of our overall models for user interaction, we generated completely synthetic traces of user interactions and fed both the synthetic trace and the real trace to a simulator of the IPTV VoD system. We compared the resulting bandwidth requirement on the VoD server and showed that the synthetic load from our model achieves a very good match to the load imposed by the real traces.

When a comparison is made based on the peak server bandwidth, the SM model provides a closer match to the empirically observed peak server bandwidth as compared to the CM model. However, the CM model captures the standard deviation of the session durations more accurately. We feel that while both alternatives are valid the SM model gives us a better estimate for provisioning capacity, a task of interest to providers.

7. REFERENCES

[1] A. Banerjee and J. Ghosh. Clickstream clustering using weighted longest common subsequences. In *Web Mining Workshop*, pages 33–40, April 2001.

[2] D. Blei, T. Griffiths, M. Jordan, and J. Tenenbaum. *Hierarchical Topic Models and the Nested Chinese Restaurant Process*, volume 16 of *Advances in Neural Information Processing Systems*. MIT Press, 2004.

[3] P. Branch, G. Egan, and B. Tonkin. Modeling interactive behavior of a video based multimedia system. In *Proceedings of IEEE ICC*, pages 978–982, 1999.

[4] M. Cha, H. Kwak, P. Rodriguez, Y. Ahn, and S. Moon. I Tube, You Tube, Everybody Tubes: Analyzing the Worlds Largest User Generated Content Video System. In *Proceedings of ACM IMC*, 2007.

[5] M. Cha, P. Rodriguez, J. Crowcroft, S. Moon, and X. Amatrianin. Watching Television Over an IP Network. In *Proceedings of ACM IMC*, 2008.

[6] A. Csenki. Dependability for systems with a partitioned state space. *Springer-Verlag*, 1994.

[7] P. Diminico, V. Gopalakrishnan, R. Jana, K. Ramakrishnan, D. Swayne, and V. Vaishampayan. Capacity Requirements for On-Demand IPTV Services. In *Proceedings of COMSNETS*, January 2011.

[8] V. Gopalakrishnan, B. Bhattacharjee, K. K. Ramakrishnan, R. Jana, and D. Srivastava. CPM: Adaptive Video-on-Demand with Cooperative Peer Assists and Multicast. In *Proceedings of IEEE Infocom*, April 2009.

[9] V. Gopalakrishnan, R. Jana, K. Ramakrishnan, D. Swayne, and V. Vaishampayan. Understanding Couch Potatoes: Modeling Interactive Usage of IPTV at Large-Scale. Technical report, AT&T Labs Research, May 2011. www.research.att.com/~kkrama/papers/stream-control.pdf.

[10] V. Gopalakrishnan, R. Jana, K. K. Ramakrishnan, D. F. Swayne, and V. A. Vaishampayan. Characterizing Interactive Behavior in a Large-Scale Operational IPTV Environment. In *IEEE Infocom (mini-conference)*, March 2010.

[11] L. Guo, E. Tan, S. Chen, Z. Xiao, and X. Zhang. The stretched exponential distribution of internet media access patterns. In *Proceedings of PODC*, 2008.

[12] P. Halmos. Random Alms. *The Annals of Mathematical Statistics*, 15:182–189, 1944.

[13] X. Hei, C. Liang, J. Liang, Y. Liu, and K. Ross. A measurement study of a large-scale P2P IPTV system. *IEEE Transactions on Multimedia*, 9(8):1672–1687, Dec 2007.

[14] H. Ishwaran and L. F. James. Gibbs sampling methods for stick-breaking priors. *Journal of the Americal Statistical Association*, 96:161–173, March 2001.

[15] V. Janardhan and H. Schulzrinne. Peer assisted VoD for set-top box based IP network. In *SIGCOMM workshop on P2P-TV*, Aug 2007.

[16] L. Kleinrock. *Queueing Systems, Volume 1: Theory*. John Wiley & Sons, 1975.

[17] E. Manavoglu, D. Pavlov, and C. L. Giles. Probabilistic user behavior models. In *Proceedings of IEEE ICDM*, Nov 2003.

[18] S. Mongy, C. Djeraba, and D. Simovici. On clustering users' behaviors in video sessions. In *Proceedings of ICDM*, 2007.

[19] R. Pantos and W. May. HTTP Live Streaming. http://tools.ietf.org/html/draft-pantos-http-live-streaming-06.

[20] T. Qiu, Z. Ge, S. Lee, J. Wang, J. Xu, and Q.Zhao. Modeling user activities in a large IPTV system. In *Proceedings of ACM IMC*, 2009.

[21] N. Vratonjic, P. Gupta, N. Knezevic, D.Kostic, and A. Rowstron. Enabling DVD-like Features in P2P Video-on-demand Systems. In *Sigcomm workshop P2P-TV*, Aug 2007.

[22] D. Wu, Y. Liu, and K. Ross. Queuing Network Models for Multi-Channel P2P Live Streaming Systems. In *Proceedings of IEEE Infocom*, 2009.

[23] H. Yin, X. Liu, F. Qiu, N. Xia, C. Lin, H. Zhang, V. Sekar, and G. Min. Inside the Bird's Nest: Measurements of Large-Scale Live VoD from the 2008 Olympics. In *Proceedings of ACM IMC*, 2009.

Summary Review Documentation for

"Understanding Couch Potatoes: Modeling Interactive Usage of IPTV at Large Scale"

Authors: V. Gopalakrishnan, R. Jana, K. Ramakrishnan, D. Swayne, V. Vaishampayan

Reviewer #1

Strengths: The paper is based on a significant data set. The authors have developed one model for the arrival process and two models for the user interaction. They discuss the pros and cons of each of the user interaction models in re-generating interesting properties of the original data set. The results show that the derived models are able to approximate the workload imposed on the server in terms of bandwidth.

Weaknesses: I really appreciate the effort that the authors have put in clearly describing the objectives and analyzing the collected data sets. However, I was left wanting more in terms of validation of the synthetic trace. I may be wrong but I would expect that the interesting aspects of interactivity on the service itself are not restricted to bandwidth alone. I would love to have seen some more complex metrics, such as computational overhead on the server, the number of sessions that are aborted, the number of times a client would need to rebuffer or the delays that the user would experience based on the trace and the model - these metrics are more meaningful when it comes to designing a well performing service - not bandwidth.

Comments to Authors: This is a very complete paper. Based on an authoritative dataset the authors are able to study the interactions of users with an IPTV service. They can derive the different states that a user consuming IPTV may be found at, and derive the associated state and transition probabilities. They can further model the request arrival process. The intellectual exercise then is focused on identifying how to model the sojourn and transition probabilities of the Markov model. The authors make the case that we would need to derive two sets, one for the weekdays and one for the weekend. They then come up with two proposals, one that is able to faithfully replay the transitions from one state to the other, and the second which aims to result in an accurate distribution of the overall session duration.

My main concern with this work is that the final validation of the model leaves me wanting more. When one targets the efficient design of an IPTV system the metric of interest is not really server bandwidth. And the authors test the accuracy of their modeling contrasting the server bandwidth from the trace to that of the model. They further provide an evaluation of the stream control events in Table 6, but frankly the results there are far from conclusive. The errors made by both SM and CM are actually non-negligible.

More importantly, I would claim that there are other evaluation metrics that would be more meaningful. What is the computational overhead on the server, what are the delays faced by the user due to seek times on the server seeking for the appropriate content to stream, how many times did clients have to rebuffer? These would be more meaningful in the study of a system and should be able to be captured by a synthetic model. I do not see that in this paper. Therefore, its potential uses are restricted in my mind.

More detailed comments:

- It is so hard to understand what data the authors actually use. In Section 1 it appears we are talking about 16 weeks but those weeks are never mentioned. Later there is a mention to 150 days (Section 4.1). In Section 3.2 the authors talk about processing the next 60 days!!! How can this be the same dataset? Please be precise.
- There is an assumption that control events create server overhead but this is never proven.
- Table 5 is nice
- In Section 5.2 you talk about clients not following the state transitions faithfully. Why is this the case? What causes those?
- It is not clear which model is used for Figures 23 and 24. Is it the combined model?

Reviewer #2

Strengths: This is a thorough modeling paper, it takes into account various parameters concerning the sojourn time, transition probabilities, request arrival process, etc. It also uses an impressive data set to validate the model and the results show that the model can faithfully regenerate realistic loads.

Weaknesses: The main problem I have with this paper is the very fact that it is a modeling paper since I am not sure what will be its real applicability to inferring the real end2end user experience. The paper models a small part of the whole IPTV ecosystem, e.g. the arrival rate of users and its bandwidth. While this can be useful to model single components of the system, e.g. the server capacity, it still misses other important factors such as STB buffer sizes, routing policies, or other intermediate nodes in the network such as CDN nodes, transcoders in the injection points, etc.

Assuming that one would ignore all those other factors and just focus on those modeled in the paper, the authors do not show either why such a model is better suited than a much simpler one to dimension the system, e.g. a model that uses the mean and the peak capacity. Or for that matter what factors benefit the most by the complexity of this model.

All in all, it is a nice modeling paper but lacks enough results to show that it will have a significant impact in capturing the fundamentals of a real IPTV VoD system.

Comments to Authors: None.

Reviewer #3

Strengths: The problem addressed is an important one. The authors used (large amount) real data to develop and validate their results.

Weaknesses: I would like to better understand the independence, or lack of it, between the data used in model derivation and the trace data used for validation.

After deriving the models, the paper stated that "Nominally, we generated a synthetic trace for a weekday using a subscriber base of ~3 million.", but has this same data been used as real traces in the experiment evaluation? A clear explanation would be helpful.

Comments to Authors: none.

Reviewer #4

Strengths: The model developed in this paper can be useful for other research related to IPTV system. The derivation of the model is done carefully and systematically. The results from the model validation seem promising.

Weaknesses: The presentation of the paper needs more clarification.

Comments to Authors: The paper is well written and interesting to read. The derivation of the model is well supported by the data and analysis. Although there is room for improvement in terms of the accuracy, the results from the validation seem to be promising. Some specific comments for improvements are provided below.

Section 3.1: Is there any explanation/hypothesis why the number of events in the longer videos is smaller than in the 30-60 minute ones?

Section 3.2: What are the 5 clusters? Are those the same as in Table 1?

Section 3.3: How do you do the simulation? Is it the same simulation as in Section 5.2?

Section 4.3.1:
- Logically some events, e.g., skip or stop, might not need to be normalized. This could be determined by looking at the correlation similar to what has been done with the PLAY duration. Have those correlations been considered?
- Paragraph 2, it was mentioned that PLAY, START, and PAUSE are longer than other events, but from Table 3, REPLAY is longer than PAUSE.
- Could you explain why the time for SKIP is quite long? It is quite surprising because I think SKIP is simply a short jump to some specific point of the content and then immediately go back to PLAY state. It might also be a good idea to give a little more detail about each operation in Section 3.

Section 5.2: In the client modeling part, what are the differences between the "SKIP" and "REPLAY" operations you assume and the real ones?

Section 5.6:
- For comparison, it would be interesting to see the standard deviations as well.
- The results show that the average values for some states are still quite different from the real traces. This might be further improved in future work.

Reviewer #5

Strengths: - Understanding and modeling content requests and user interaction in IPTV is a timely issue. This paper can be a good reference. A large dataset in an operational network was used to derive the model.
- Solid analysis and modeling for both the arrival process and the stream control model. They also take into account the user behavior during weekdays and weekends.
- The authors also provide an appendix of results that researchers can use to validate their protocols.
- The paper is well written.

Weaknesses: I am a little bit puzzled with the second to last paragraph in page 2 where the authors describe what is the input data to derive and validate the model.

Comments to Authors: - The authors should elaborate more on the input data they use. Initially they claim that the data is a two-year long trace of IPTV in a large provider. Then they mention that they use a 9-days trace from 10 metropolitan areas, and then that they validate their model in a 2-weeks period. They have to elaborate more on their assumptions as well as the input data for the analysis and the validation. It is also important to verify that the 2-weeks validation period does not overlap with the 9 days they use to train the model.
- The mention that they use a 9-days trace from 10 metropolitan areas. Are all the metropolitan areas in the same time zone? Are there of the same population level? Does time zone or population have any effect on the model?

Response from the Authors

We would like to thank the reviewers for their insightful comments. We have taken careful consideration of all their comments. One reviewer has raised the point that more complex metrics, in addition to the VoD server bandwidth for a complete understanding of user behavior modeling. The computational overhead at the server is proportional to the number of stream control operations. To this end, we have provided in a companion paper [1], where a we did a careful micro- benchmarking of a VoD server by loading it with requests performing various stream control operations. We found that while the overheads are somewhat dependent on the type of operation, for the most part it is important to characterize correctly the number of operations, which we have done in this paper. With regards to aborted sessions and client interruption/rebuffering, our simulator faithfully captures the number of sessions that are aborted and the metric of client starvation. We note that this is very dependent on client implementation. We have added a plot on client starvation in the revised paper to address this comment.

Another suggestion from reviewers was to clarify the various data sets that we have used. We have used multiple data sets spanning over two years and a very large subscriber footprint. Specifically, our data sets include: 1) Data Set 1 (DS1) – for 120 days, from 9

VHOs, 3 Million STBs, from Jan/Apr/July/Nov 2009-2010, which we have used for the arrival process modeling; 2) Data Set 2 (DS2) – over 9 days, from 10 VHOs, 300K users, Jan. 9-17, 2010 used for characterization of the stream control FSM; 3) Data Set 3 (DS3) – for 60 days, from 10 VHOs, 300K users, in 2009, for studying the evolution of popularity. We have included a table in the paper to make this clear.

Finally, in response to the reviewer's request to better understand the independence between the training data and validation data, we note that in all cases the training and validation data were separate and independent. For modeling the arrival process of a particular day (e.g., Saturday), we pooled data from 16 Saturdays across a 2 year period (DS1) and validation is based on a randomly chosen weekday and weekend day from DS2. The DS1 and DS2 datasets are also from different days. Similarly, the finite state machine model was also trained and validated using different data sets.

[1] Pat Diminico, Vijay Gopalakrishnan, Rittwik Jana, Kadangode Ramakrishnan, Deborah Swayne, Vinay Vaishampayan, "Capacity Requirements for On-Demand IPTV Services", in Proc. of the third International Conference on COMmunication Systems and NETworkS (COMSNETS 2011), Bangalore, 2011.

Suspended Accounts in Retrospect: An Analysis of Twitter Spam

Kurt Thomas[†] Chris Grier[†*] Vern Paxson[†*] Dawn Song[†]
[†]University of California, Berkeley [*]International Computer Science Institute
{kthomas, grier, vern, dawnsong}@cs.berkeley.edu

ABSTRACT

In this study, we examine the abuse of online social networks at the hands of spammers through the lens of the tools, techniques, and support infrastructure they rely upon. To perform our analysis, we identify over 1.1 million accounts suspended by Twitter for disruptive activities over the course of seven months. In the process, we collect a dataset of 1.8 billion tweets, 80 million of which belong to spam accounts. We use our dataset to characterize the behavior and lifetime of spam accounts, the campaigns they execute, and the wide-spread abuse of legitimate web services such as URL shorteners and free web hosting. We also identify an emerging marketplace of illegitimate programs operated by spammers that include Twitter account sellers, ad-based URL shorteners, and spam affiliate programs that help enable underground market diversification.

Our results show that 77% of spam accounts identified by Twitter are suspended within on day of their first tweet. Because of these pressures, less than 9% of accounts form social relationships with regular Twitter users. Instead, 17% of accounts rely on hijacking trends, while 52% of accounts use unsolicited mentions to reach an audience. In spite of daily account attrition, we show how five spam campaigns controlling 145 thousand accounts combined are able to persist for months at a time, with each campaign enacting a unique spamming strategy. Surprisingly, three of these campaigns send spam directing visitors to reputable store fronts, blurring the line regarding what constitutes spam on social networks.

Categories and Subject Descriptors

K.4.1 [**Computers and Society**]: Public Policy Issues—*Abuse and Crime Involving Computers*

General Terms

Security, Measurement

Keywords

Social Networks, Spam, Account Abuse

1. INTRODUCTION

As Twitter continues to grow in popularity, a spam marketplace has emerged that includes services selling fraudulent accounts, affiliate programs that facilitate distributing Twitter spam, as well as a cadre of spammers who execute large-scale spam campaigns despite Twitter's efforts to thwart their operations. While social network spam has garnered a great deal of attention in the past year from researchers, most of the interest has involved developing tools to detect spam. These approaches rely on URL blacklists [5, 20], passive social networking spam traps [12, 19], and even manual classification [2] to generate datasets of Twitter spam for developing a classifier that characterizes abusive behavior. These spam detection approaches however have not yet been used to analyze the tools and techniques of spammers, leaving the underground marketplace that capitalizes on Twitter largely obscure.

In this paper we characterize the illicit activities of Twitter accounts controlled by spammers and evaluate the tools and techniques that underlie the social network spam distribution chain. This infrastructure includes automatically generated accounts created for the explicit purpose of soliciting spam; the emergence of *spam-as-a-service* programs that connect Twitter account controllers to marketers selling products; and finally the techniques required to maintain large-scale spam campaigns despite Twitter's counter-efforts. To perform the study, we aggregate over 1.8 billion messages on Twitter sent by 32.9 million accounts during a seven month period from August 17, 2010 to March 4, 2011. Within this period, we identify accounts suspended by Twitter for abusive behavior, including spam, aggressive friending, and other non-spam related offenses. Manual analysis indicates that an estimated 93% of suspended accounts were in fact spammers, with the remaining 7% suspended for mimicking news services and aggressive marketing. In total, our dataset consists of over 1.1 million suspended accounts that we show to be spammers, and 80 million spam tweets from these accounts. In contrast to previous studies [5, 6], only 8% of the URLs we examine were ever caught by blacklists, and the accounts within our dataset are largely fraudulent, as opposed to compromised users. This enables us to provide a unique perspective on a subset of Twitter spammers not previously examined.

At the heart of the of the Twitter spam craft is access to hundreds of accounts capable of reaching a wide audience. We find that 77% of accounts employed by spammers are suspended within a day of their first post, and 92% of accounts within three days. The countermeasures imposed by Twitter's suspension algorithm preclude the possibility of attempting to form meaningful relationships with legitimate users, with 89% of spam accounts having fewer than 10 followers. In place of distributing messages over the social graph, we find that 52% of spam accounts turn to *unsolicited mentions*, whereby a personalized message is sent to another account despite the absence of a social relationship. Another 17% of accounts rely on embedding *hashtags* in their messages, allowing spam to garner an audience from users who view popular Twitter discussions via search and *trending topics*.

Beyond the characteristics of spam accounts, we explore five of the largest Twitter spam campaigns that range from days to months in duration, weaving together fraudulent accounts, diverse spam URLs, distinct distribution techniques, and a multitude of monetization approaches. Together, these campaigns control 145 thousand account that generate 22% of spam on Twitter. Surprisingly, three of the largest campaigns direct users to legitimate products appearing on *amazon.com* via affiliate links that generate income on a purchase, blurring the line regarding what constitutes spam. Indeed, only one of the five campaigns we analyze advertises content generally found in email spam [13], revealing a diverse group of miscreants in the underground space that go beyond email spammers.

Finally, within the amalgam of spam on Twitter, we identify an emerging market of *spam-as-a-service*. This marketplace includes affiliate programs that operate as middlemen between spammers seeking to disseminate URLs and affiliates who control hundreds of Twitter accounts. The most prominent affiliate program, called Clickbank, appeared in over 3.1 million tweets sent from 203 affiliates participating in the program. Other services include ad-based URL shorteners as well as account arbiters who sell the ability to tweet from thousands of accounts under a single service's control. Each of these services enables a diversification in the social network spam marketplace, allowing spammers to specialize exclusively in hosting content or acquiring Twitter accounts.

In summary, we frame our contributions as followers:

- We characterize the spamming tools and techniques of 1.1 million suspended Twitter accounts that sent 80 million tweets.
- We examine a number of properties pertaining to fraudulent accounts, including the formation of social relationships, account duration, and dormancy periods.
- We evaluate the wide-spread abuse of URLs, shortening services, free web hosting, and public Twitter clients by spammers.
- We provide an in-depth analysis of five of the largest spam campaigns targeting Twitter, revealing a diverse set of strategies for reaching audiences and sustaining campaigns in Twitter's hostile environment.
- We identify an emerging marketplace of social network *spam-as-a-service* and analyze its underlying infrastructure.

2. BACKGROUND

In this section, we discuss previous studies of underground markets as well as provide an overview of how spammers abuse the Twitter platform, previous approaches for detecting and measuring social network spam, and Twitter's own detection mechanism, which we rely on as a source of ground truth.

2.1 Twitter Spam

Twitter spam is a systemic problem. Unsolicited content appears throughout personal feeds, search query results, and trending topics. This content is distributed by fraudulent accounts explicitly created by spammers, compromised accounts, malicious Twitter applications, and even legitimate users posting syndicated content. We describe each of these components and how they tie into the Twitter platform.

2.1.1 Exposure to Spam

User Timeline: Users receive content in the form of a *user timeline* that includes tweets broadcast by each of a user's friends as well as posts that *@mention*, or tag, a timeline's owner. Spammers can inject content into this stream by either enticing a user into *following* the spammer (forming a directed social relationship), or by mentioning the user in a post. Mentions require no prior relationship to exist between a spammer and a user.

Trending Topics: Rather than forming relationships with users or targeting single users, spammers can post tweets that contain popular keywords from *trending topics*. Trends result from spontaneous coordination between Twitter users as well as from breaking news stories. Users that explore these trends will receive a feed of legitimate tweets interspersed with spam.

Search: Twitter provides a tool for searching public tweets beyond popular topics. Spammers can embed popular search terms into their tweets, similar to hijacking trends and search engine optimization. However, as there are no public signals to determine what spam tweets were accessed due to search queries, search spam is beyond the scope of this study.

Direct Messages: Direct messages are private tweets sent between two users, effectively duplicating the functionality of email. Spammers can send unsolicited direct messages to users they *follow*; users do not need to reciprocate the relationship in order to receive spam content. As direct messages are private, they are beyond the scope of this study.

2.1.2 Distributing Spam

All interaction with Twitter occurs through authenticated accounts. We distinguish between accounts that are *fraudulent* and explicitly created for spamming versus *compromised* accounts, which belong to legitimate users whose credentials have been stolen. Account compromise can occur due to password guessing, phishing, or mistakenly granting a malicious application privileged access to an account (via OAuth [24] credentials or revealing an account's password). A final approach to distributing spam on Twitter relies on legitimate accounts that post untrusted syndicated content. As we will discuss in Section 5, a number of services have appeared that pay users to post arbitrary content to their profile.

2.2 Detecting Social Network Spam

The diverse array of social network spam and its evasive nature makes it difficult to obtain a comprehensive source of ground truth for measurement. Previous approaches include using blacklists to identify URLs on both Facebook and Twitter directing to spam content [5, 6], deploying passive social networking accounts to act as spam traps [12, 19], and manually identifying spam tweets in trending topics [2]. Each of these approaches introduce a unique bias and error in the type of spam identified. For instance, blacklists preclude URLs that were not reported by users or that failed to appear in email spam traps. Our previous study of Twitter identified that 8% of unique URLs were blacklisted [6], but manual analysis of the same dataset identified 26% of unique URLs directed to spam, indicating blacklists missed a large portion of spam. False positives and negatives also remain a flaw of social spam traps. Stringhini et al. found that passive accounts acting as spam traps received a surprising volume of legitimate traffic, with only 4.5% of friend requests on Facebook originating from spammers, compared to 90% on Twitter [19]. Equally problematic, samples generated from friend requests will omit spam from compromised accounts in addition to spammers who do not form social connections. While manual analysis by experts reduces the potential for error, it is prohibitively expensive for acquiring a large data sample. Our approach of using Twitter's detection algorithm is not without its own bias, which we show in Section 3. As such, we remain cautious of drawing conclusions for *all* spam on Twitter.

2.3 Twitter's Detection Algorithm

Our dataset hinges on Twitter's algorithm for suspending accounts that participate in multiple forms of abusive behavior. While the exact implementation of Twitter's suspension algorithm is not public, many of the parameters are documented in their guidelines and best practices [21]. Accounts will be suspended for frequent requests to befriend users in a short period, reposting duplicate content across multiple accounts, sending unsolicited mentions, posting only URLs, and posting irrelevant or misleading content to trending topics. Other behaviors not clearly related to spam that will result in account suspension include copyright infringement, harassment, and inappropriate content. Given the multiple reasons beyond spam as a grounds for suspension, we validate our dataset in Section 3.1 to confirm the vast majority of suspensions are rooted in spamming behaviors.

2.4 Spam Marketplaces

Within recent years a great deal of effort has been spent on studying the activities of underground economies, and in particular, the spam marketplace. Previous research has examined the hosting infrastructure of scams [1, 7], the organization of email spam campaigns [11], and the economic incentives of spam and malware [9, 18]. Most recently, Levchenko et al. performed an analysis of the infrastructure employed by criminals to monetize email spam, starting from the delivery of an email message and ending with order fulfillment and payment processing [13]. They found that as spammers have become more sophisticated, specialized roles have appeared that separate the marketing of spam products from their actual sale. Organizations with access to pharmaceuticals and replica goods generate affiliate programs, outsourcing the distribution of spam emails to affiliates. As we show in Section 5, a similar diversification of activities is beginning to appear on Twitter, a sign that the Twitter spam market place is maturing.

3. METHODOLOGY

In order to characterize the tools and services that Twitter spammers rely on, we aggregate a dataset of nearly 1.8 billion tweets sent by 32.9 million Twitter accounts over a 7 month period. Of these, we identify 1.1 million accounts suspended by Twitter for abusive behavior. Combined, these accounts sent over 80 million tweets containing 37 million distinct URLs. We manually verify a sample of suspended accounts and find the vast majority were suspended for spamming, providing us with a rich source of ground truth for measuring spam. In addition to our Twitter dataset, we resolve the first redirect of 15 million URLs to deobfuscate a layer of shortening. Finally, for 10 million URLs shortened by *bit.ly*, we download multiple statistics provided by *bit.ly* including clickthrough and, when available, the *bit.ly* account that shortened the URL. A summary of our dataset can be found in Table 1.

3.1 Twitter Dataset

Our Twitter dataset consists of over 1.8 billion tweets collected from Twitter's streaming API [22] during a seven month period from August 17, 2010 to March 4, 2011. We access Twitter's API

Data Source	Sample Size
Tweets	1,795,184,477
Accounts	32,852,752
Distinct URLs	1,073,215,755
Tweets from Suspended Accounts	80,054,991
Suspended Accounts	1,111,776
Distinct URLs from Suspended Accounts	37,652,300
Resolved URLs	15,189,365
Bit.ly URLs	10,092,013
Bit.ly Accounts	23,317

Table 1: Summary of data collected from Twitter, Bit.ly, and from resolving the first redirect of URLs

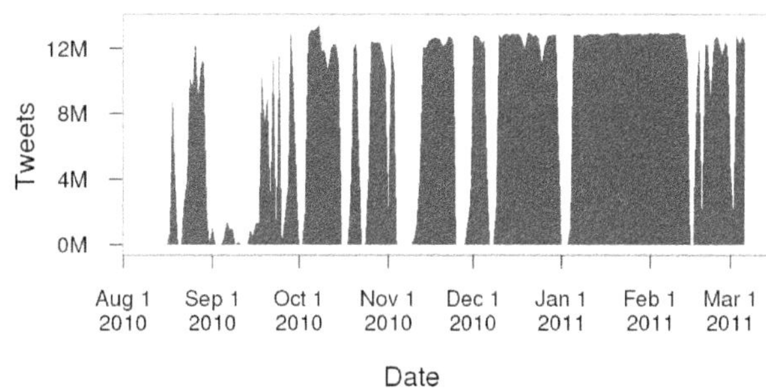

Figure 1: Tweets containing URLs received per day. On average, we receive 12 million tweets per day, with a ceiling imposed by Twitter.

through a privileged account, granting both increased API requests per hour and a larger sample than would be conferred to a default account. We rely on the `statuses/filter` method to collect a sample of public tweets conditioned to contain URLs. For each tweet, we have the associated text of the tweet, the API client used to post the tweet (e.g. web, third-party client), as well as statistics tied to the account who posted the tweet including the account's number of friends, followers, and previous posts. On average, we receive 12 million tweets per day, with a ceiling imposed by Twitter capping our collection at 150 tweets per second. We lack data for some days due to network outages, updates to Twitter's API, and instability of our collection infrastructure. A summary of tweets collected each day and outage periods is shown in Figure 1.

In order to label spam within our dataset, we first identify accounts suspended by Twitter for abusive behavior. This includes spam, aggressive friending, and other non-spam related offenses, as discussed in Section 2.3. Upon suspension, all of an accounts tweets and profile data become restricted and relationships disappear from the social graph. While this provides a clear signal to identify suspended accounts, it also eliminates any possibility of simply downloading an account's history upon suspension. Nevertheless, we are able to reconstruct a composite of a suspended account's activities from all of the tweets in our sample set.

Due to delays in Twitter's account suspension algorithm, we wait two weeks from the last day of data collection before we determine which accounts were suspended by Twitter. This process consists of a bulk query to Twitter's API to identify accounts that no longer have records, either due to deletion or suspension, followed by a request to access each missing account's Twitter profile via the web to identify requests that redirect to *http://twitter.com/suspended*. Of 32.9 million accounts appearing in our sample, 1.1 million were

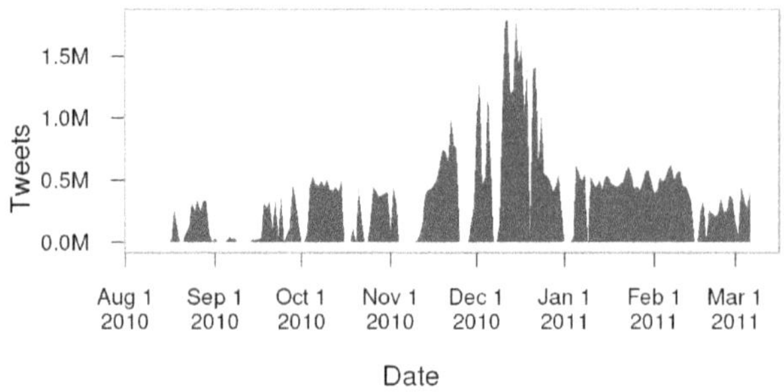

Figure 2: Daily tweet activity of suspended users. Peak activity preceded the holiday season in December.

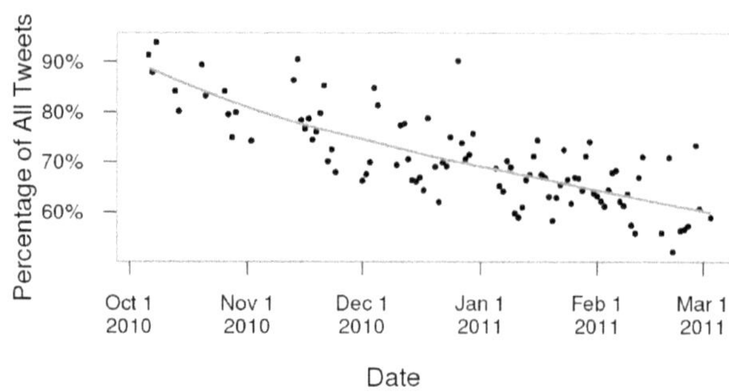

Figure 3: Estimated percentage of all tweets containing URLs we receive per day. Due to Twitter's cap of 12 million tweets per day, we receive a smaller sample size as Twitter grows.

subsequently suspended by Twitter, roughly 3.3% of accounts. These accounts posted over 80 million tweets, with their daily activity shown in Figure 2. We sample a portion of these accounts and manually verify that the vast majority are suspended for spam behavior. Furthermore, we provide an estimate for what fraction of each spam account's tweets appear in our sample, as well as provide an estimate for how many spam accounts go uncaught by Twitter and are thus unlabeled in our data set.

Validating Suspended Accounts are Spammers: When we identify a suspended account, we retroactively label all of the account's tweets in our sample as spam. In doing so, we make an assumption that suspended accounts are predominantly controlled by spammers and are not valid accounts performing unrelated abusive behaviors. To validate this assumption, we draw a random sample of 100 suspended accounts and aggregate every tweet posted by the account appearing in our dataset. We then analyze the content of each tweet to identify common spam keywords, frequent duplicate tweets, and tweet content that appears across multiple accounts. Additionally, we examine the landing page of each tweet's URL, if the URL is still accessible, and the overall posting behavior of each account to identify automation.

Of the 100 accounts, 93 were suspended for posting scams and unsolicited product advertisements; 3 accounts were suspended for exclusively retweeting content from major news accounts, and the remaining 4 accounts were suspended for aggressive marketing and duplicate posts. None of the accounts appeared to be legitimate users who were wrongfully suspended. Presumably, any such false positives would later be resolved by the user requesting their account be unsuspended. From these results, we can discern that the majority of accounts we examine are *fraudulent* accounts created by spammers, though the URLs posted by some of these accounts may direct to legitimate content. We provide further evidence that the accounts in our dataset are created explicitly for spamming rather than compromised or legitimate when we examine the relationships and duration of suspended accounts in Section 4.1. From here on out, we refer to suspended accounts as spam accounts interchangeably.

Validating Active Accounts are Non-spammers: False negatives from Twitter's detection algorithm result in omitting a portion of spam accounts from our analysis. To measure what fraction of spam accounts are missed by Twitter, we randomly sample 200 active accounts and evaluate each account's tweet history using the same criteria we applied to validate spam accounts. Of the 200 accounts, 12 were clearly spammers, from which we can estimate that 6% of active accounts are in fact spammers, with an error bound of ±3.3% at 95% confidence. Consequently, many of our measurements may underestimate the total volume of spam on Twitter and the number of accounts colluding in spam campaigns. For the accounts we manually identified as overlooked spammers, we found no significant distinction between their behavior and that of suspended accounts, leading us to believe they fall below some classification or heuristic threshold that bounds false positives.

Estimating the Likelihood Spammers are Caught: Using our estimates of the number of false positives and false negatives that result from Twitter's spam detection algorithm, we can approximate the algorithm's sensitivity, or the likelihood that a spam account posting URLs will be caught. Of the 31 million accounts that were not suspended, 6% are false negatives, amounting to roughly 1.9 million spam accounts that are overlooked. Another 1 million spam accounts were correctly identified by Twitter's algorithm. Applying the metric for sensitivity:

$$sensitivity = \frac{true\ positives}{true\ positives + false\ negative}$$

we find that only 37% of spam accounts posting URLs on Twitter are caught by the suspension algorithm during the period of our measurement. We note that this estimate is sensitive to the error bound of the false negative rate. Despite the potential for omitting a class of spam from our analysis, we show in Section 3.2 that alternative approaches such as using blacklists to identify spam accounts net an entirely different class of spammers. As such, while our sample may be biased, our analysis provides insights into a large population of spam accounts that have previously been uncharacterized.

Sample Rate: As a final validation step, we measure the fraction of URLs posted to Twitter that we receive in our sample. Our daily sample remains roughly constant at 12 million tweets even though Twitter reports exponential growth [23]. After October 12, 2010, Twitter began to impose a rate limit of 150 tweets per second regardless the actual rate they receive tweets. To measure how this impacts our sample, we take a random sample of 1,600 non-suspended accounts that appear in our dataset and download the entirety of their account history. Of these accounts, 1,245 were still publicly accessible, providing a sample of 798,762 tweets. We then filter out tweets that appear during an outage in our collection or that do not contain URLs, leaving a sample of 32,142 tweets, with roughly 465 samples per day. The daily fraction of these tweets that appear in our sample can be seen in Figure 3 along with a fit curve. At our peak collection, we received 90% tweets containing URLs posted to Twitter. The sample rate has since decreased to nearly 60%.

3.2 Spam URL Dataset

From the 80 million tweets we label as spam, we extract 37.7 million distinct URLs pointing to 155,008 full domains (e.g. *an.example.com*) and 121,171 registered domains (e.g. *example.com*). Given the multitude of shorteners that obfuscate landing pages and no public listing, we attempt to fetch each URL and evaluate whether the HTTP response includes a server-side redirect to a new URL. We only resolve the first such redirect, making no attempt at subsequent requests. In total, we are able to resolve 15.2 million URLs, the remainder of which were shortened by services that have since been deactivated, or were inaccessible due to rate limiting performed by the shortening service.

Blacklist Overlap: In prior work, we examined millions of URLs posted to Twitter that appeared in blacklists [6]. To determine whether the spam we identify from suspended accounts differs significantly from spam detected by blacklists, we examine the overlap of our spam URL dataset with blacklists. We take a sample of 100,000 URLs appearing in tweets regardless of whether they are shortened and a second sample of 100,000 unshortened URLs. We consult three blacklist families: SURBL and all its affiliated lists (e.g. SpamCop, Joewein); Google Safebrowsing, both malware and phishing; and URIBL. If a URL was flagged at any any point in the history of these blacklists from August, 2010 till May, 2011, we consider the URL to be blacklisted. We find only 8% of spam tweet URLs appeared in blacklists and only 5% of unshortened URLs. As such, we believe we present an entirely unexplored subset of spam on social networks from both the perspective of fraudulent accounts as well as non-blacklisted spam.

3.3 Bit.ly URL and Account Dataset

Of the URLs associated with spam tweets in our dataset, over 10 million direct to *bit.ly*, a popular shortening service, or one of its multiple affiliated services (e.g. *j.mp*, *amzn.to*). From *bit.ly*'s public API [22] we are able to download clickthrough statistics for a subset of these URLs found in prominent spam campaigns, and when available, the registered *bit.ly* account that shortened the URL. Roughly 47% of *bit.ly* URLs in our dataset had an associated *bit.ly* account, of which 23,317 were unique.

4. TOOLS OF THE TRADE

Within the amalgam of spam activities on Twitter, we identify a diverse set of tools and strategies that build upon access to hundreds of fraudulent accounts, an array of spam URLs and domains, and automation tools for interacting with Twitter. We explore each of these areas in depth and present challenges facing both spammers and Twitter in the arms race of social network spam.

4.1 Accounts

At the heart of the Twitter spam craft are thousands of fraudulent accounts created for the explicit purposes of soliciting products. 77% of these accounts are banned within a day of their first post, and 89% acquire less than 10 followers at the height of their existence. Yet, within Twitter's hostile suspension environment, spammers are still capable of reaching millions of users through the use of unsolicited mentions and trending topics. We examine a range of properties surrounding spam accounts, including the length of their activity, the rate they send tweets, the social relationships they form, and the stockpiling of accounts.

4.1.1 Active Duration

Spam accounts are regularly suspended by Twitter, but it takes time for Twitter to build up a history of mis-activity before taking action. We measure this window of activity for a sample of 100,000 spam accounts created after our measurement began. We omit accounts that were created during one of our outage periods to reduce bias, though an account appearing at the cusp of an outage period will have its activity window underestimated. For each of these accounts, we calculate the difference between the timestamp of an account's first tweet and last tweet within our dataset, after which we assume the account was immediately suspended. Figure 4 shows a CDF of account activity. 77% of accounts were suspended within a day of their first tweet, with 92% of accounts surviving only three days. The longest lasting account was active for 178 days before finally being suspended. While a minority of accounts are able to persist, we show that rapid suspension impacts both the volume of tweets spammers can disseminate and the relationships they can form.

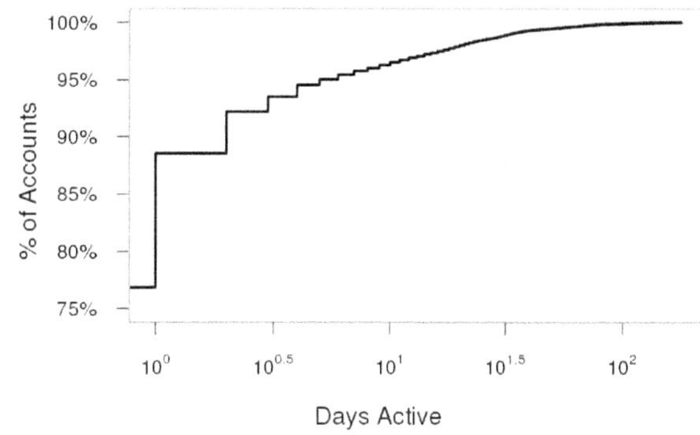

Figure 4: Duration of account activity. 77% of accounts are suspended within a day of their first tweet and 92% within three days.

4.1.2 Tweet Rates

Given the threat of account suspension, we examine whether the rate that spammers send tweets impacts when they are suspended. In order to calculate the total number of tweets sent by an account, we rely on a statistical summary embedded by Twitter in each tweet that includes the *total* number posts made by an account (independent of our sampling). Using a sample of 100,000 accounts, we calculate the maximum tweet count embedded for each account by Twitter and compare it against the account's active duration.

The results of our calculation are shown in Figure 5 along with a fit curve. We identify three clusters in the figure, outlined in ovals, that represent two distinct spamming strategies. The first strategy **(I)** relies on short-lived accounts that flood as many tweets as possible prior to being suspended, representing 34% of our sample. These accounts last a median of 3 days and send 98 tweets. In contrast, a second strategy **(II)** relies on longer lasting accounts that tweet at a modest rate, representing 10% of our sample. While these accounts last a median of 7 days, in the end, they send a nearly equal volume of tweets; a median of 97 tweets per account. The final cluster **(III)** consists of 56% of accounts that are suspended within a median of 1 day and send 5 tweets on average. The reason behind these accounts' suspension is unclear, but it is likely tied to rules beyond tweet count, such as sending URLs duplicated from previously suspended accounts or sharing an email address or IP address with other suspended accounts. While an individual account sending 100 tweets will not reach a large audience, we show in Section 6 that actual spam campaigns coordinate thousands of accounts yielding hundreds of thousands of tweets.

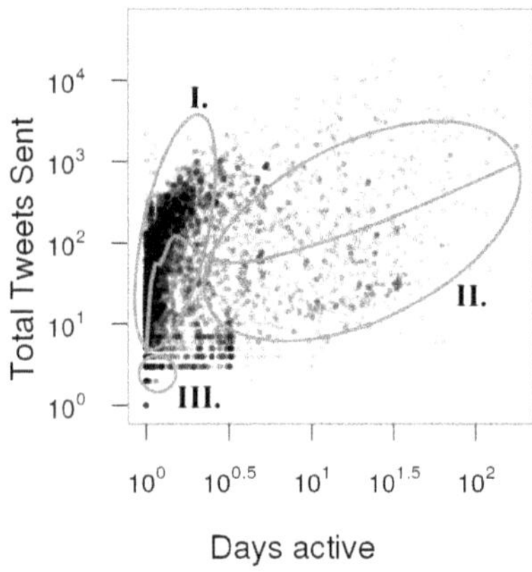

Figure 5: Active duration vs. tweets sent for spam accounts. Two strategies appear: **(I)** burst accounts and **(II)** long-lived, low-daily volume accounts

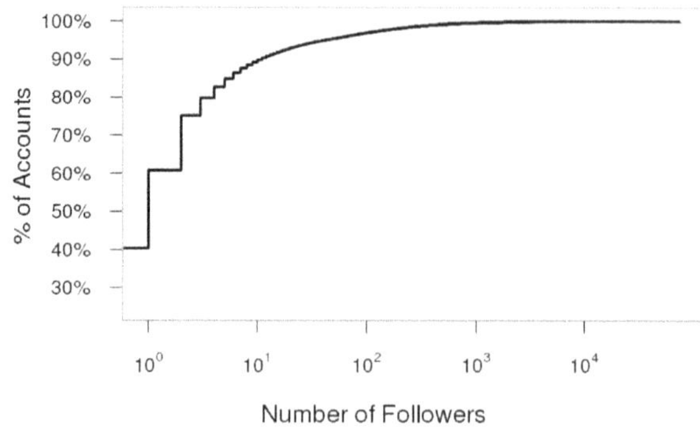

Figure 6: Users following spam accounts. 89% of accounts have fewer than 10 followers; 40% have no followers.

4.1.3 Relationships

The social graph is the focus of regular user interaction on Twitter, yet we find that most spammers fail to form social connections and instead leverage other social networking features to reach an audience. Due to the disappearance of spam accounts from the social graph upon suspension, we are unable to retroactively perform a detailed analysis of the accounts spammers befriended (or whether spammers befriend one another). Nevertheless, each tweet in our dataset includes a snapshot of the number of friends and followers an account held at the time of the tweet. For clarity, we define a *friend* as a second user that an account receives content from, while a *follower* is a second user that receives an account's content. With respect to distributing spam URLs, only followers are important, though spammers will acquire friends in the hope that the relationship will be reciprocated.

To compare relationships formed by both spam and non-spam accounts, we aggregate friend and follower data points for a sample of 100,000 active and suspended users. Figure 6 shows a CDF of the maximum number of followers a spam account acquires prior to suspension. Surprisingly, 40% of spam accounts acquire no followers, while 89% of accounts have fewer than 10 followers. We believe this is due both to the difficulty of forming relationships with legitimate users, as well as a result of the hostile environment imposed by Twitter, where the effort and time required to acquire followers is outpaced by the rate of suspension.

With no followers, spam accounts are unable to distribute their content along social connections. Instead, we find that 52% of accounts with fewer than 10 followers send unsolicited mentions, whereby a personally tailored message is sent to an unsuspecting account that shares no relation with the spammer. Another 17% of accounts rely on embedding hashtags in their spam tweets, allowing spam content to appear in the stream of popular Twitter discussions and through search queries. We examine the success of each of these approaches in Section 6 for a subset of spam campaigns.

For those spam accounts that do form social relationships, their relationships are heavily skewed towards friends rather than followers, indicating a lack of reciprocated relationships. Figure 7 shows the number of friends and followers for spam accounts as well as active accounts presumed to be non-spammers. An identity line in both plots marks equal friends and followers, while a trend line marks the areas of highest density in the scatter plot. Relationships of non-spam accounts center around the identity, while spam

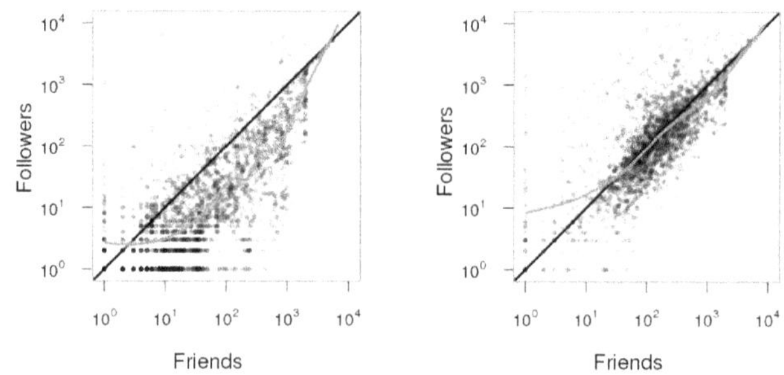

(a) Spam Accounts **(b)** Non-spam Accounts

Figure 7: Friends vs. followers for spam and non-spam accounts. Spammers are skewed towards forming relationships that are never reciprocated.

accounts are shifted right of the identity due to the lack of reciprocated relationships. The modality in both graphs at 2,000 friends results from Twitter imposing a limit on the number of friends possible, after which an account must have more followers than friends to grow their social graph. While 11% of spam accounts attempt to befriend users, either for the purpose of acquiring followers or for obtaining the privilege to direct messages, it is clear that legitimate Twitter users rarely respond in kind.

4.1.4 Dormancy

Long dormancy periods where a spam account is registered but never used until a later date hint at the possibility of stockpiling accounts. To measure account dormancy, we select a sample of 100,000 accounts created during one our active collection periods and measure the difference between the account's creation date (reported in each tweet) versus the account's first post in our sample. The results in Figure 8 show that, unsurprisingly, 56% of accounts are activated within a day of their registration. This indicates most spammers create accounts and immediately add them to the pool under their control. However, 12% of spam accounts remain inactive for over a week and 5% for over one month. We highlight this phenomenon further in Section 6 when we present a number of campaigns that stockpile accounts and activate them simultaneously to generate hundreds of thousands of tweets.

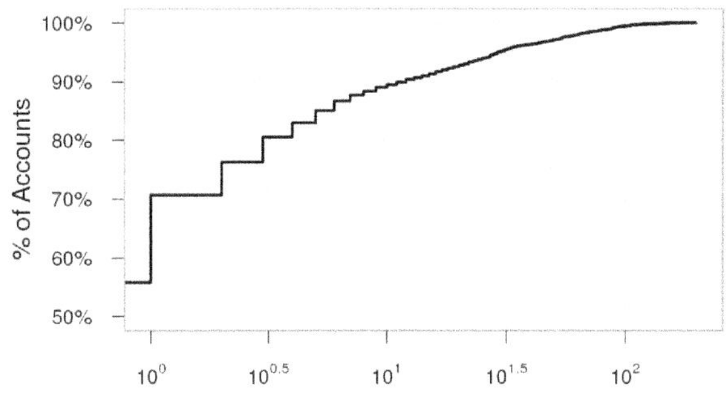

Figure 8: Dormancy duration of accounts. 56% of accounts begin tweeting within the same day the account is created, while 12% lay dormant for over one week, allowing for account stockpiling.

4.2 URLs and Domains

Beyond the necessity of multiple accounts to interact with social networks, spammers also require a diverse set of URLs to advertise. We find that individual spam accounts readily post thousands of unique URLs and domains, simultaneously abusing URL shorteners, free domain registrars, and free web hosting to support their endeavors. Of the 37.7 million spam URLs in our dataset, 89.4% were tweeted *once*. These unique URLs account for 40.5% of spam tweets, while the remaining 10.6% of URLs are massively popular and account for the 59.5% of spam tweets. To understand how spammers are generating URLs, we examine a breadth of properties from the abuse of free services, the diversity of domains, and the overlap of spam URLs with those posted by non-suspended Twitter accounts.

4.2.1 Abusing Shorteners

We find that URL shortening services, such as *bit.ly*, are frequently abused by spammers despite their use of blacklists and spam detection algorithms [3]. In general, URL shorteners simplify the process of generating a variety of unique URLs without incurring a cost to the spammer. URL shorteners also obfuscate the destination of a URL that might otherwise look suspicious to visitors and decrease clickthrough.

Given that any domain can operate a shortening service, we develop a heuristic to identify shorteners used by spammers. Using the first-hop resolution data for 15 million URLs, we identify domains that respond with a server-side redirect (HTTP status code 30x). If a single domain redirects to at least five distinct registered domains, that domain is considered to be a shortening service. Using this criteria, we identify *317 services* that are used in *60% of spam tweets*.

The most popular shorteners abused by spammers are shown in Table 2; 35% of spam tweets are shortened by *bit.ly*, followed in popularity by *tinyurl.com* and a variety of other shorteners with low spam volumes that make up a long tail. For each shortener we compute the bias spammers have towards using the service compared to regular users. First, we calculate $p_1 = p(shortener|spam)$, the probability a spam tweet uses the shortener, and $p_2 = p(shortener \mid nonspam)$, the probability a non-spam tweet uses the shortener. We then compute the likelihood ratio p_1/p_2. This result is strictly a lower bound as our non-spam dataset contains uncaught spam.

As Table 2 shows, all of the top ten shortening services are preferred by spammers, with *3.ly* over 65 times more likely to be used by spammers. The likelihood ratio of a shortener does *not* indicate that more spam URLs are shortened than non-spam URLs. Instead, a likelihood ratio greater than one simply indicates that given the choice of domains available to both spammers and regular Twitter users, spammers are more likely to choose shorteners. Even if popular URL shortening services deployed stronger spam filtering, the presence of hundreds of alternative shorteners and the ease with which they are created makes it simple for spammers to obfuscate their URLs.

Service Name	% of Tweets	Likelihood Ratio
bit.ly	34.86%	1.41
tinyurl.com	6.88%	2.61
is.gd	2.45%	3.01
goo.gl	2.45%	1.14
ow.ly	2.32%	1.40
dlvr.it	1.99%	1.66
tiny.cc	1.38%	12.36
tiny.ly	1.34%	5.23
3.ly	1.14%	65.55
dld.bz	1.10%	3.71

Table 2: Top 10 public shortening services abused by spammers. Likelihood ratio indicates the likelihood a spammer will use the service over a regular user.

4.2.2 Domain Names

Spammers who host their own content require access to hundreds of domains in order to counteract attrition resulting from takedown and blacklisting. Where traditional domain registration carries a cost, we find that Twitter spammers cleverly obtain free hosting and subdomains through the abuse of public services.

Figure 9 visualizes the number of subdomains and the number of registered domains tweeted by each of the 1.1 million spam accounts in our dataset, along with a fit curve showing the densest regions. If an account exclusively posts unique registered domains (e.g. *greatpills.com*), it will appear along the identity line, while accounts that rely on multiple subdomains (e.g. *greatpills.com, my.greatpills.com*) will appear below the identity line. Three distinct approaches to spamming are apparent, outlined in ovals.

The first approach **(I)** consists of 0.13% of spam accounts that abuse free subdomain registration services and blog hosting. These accounts post over 10 subdomains tied to fewer than 10 registered domains, with 0.04% of spam accounts tweeting over 250 subdomains. A second spamming strategy **(II)** consists of using multiple unique domains; we find 1.4% of users tweet over 10 unique registered domains with no additional subdomains, represented by the points scattered along the identify line. The remaining 98.56% of accounts, labeled as **(III)**, tweet fewer than 10 domains in their entire lifetime, appearing as a dense cluster near the origin. Of these clusters, we explore the abuse of free domain registrars and hosting services.

Subdomains:: We identify a number of spammers that rely on free subdomains to avoid registration costs. Services including *co.cc*, *co.tv*, *uni.cc*, and *dot.tk* all allow anyone to register a subdomain that directs to an arbitrary IP address. In total, we find over 350,000 spam URLs directing to these services. The majority of these URLs belong to accounts shown in Figure 9 that post over 250 subdomains.

One particular group of 376 spam accounts advertised over 1,087 subdomains located at *co.cc* with another 1,409 accounts advertising a smaller subset of the same domains. With no limits on subdo-

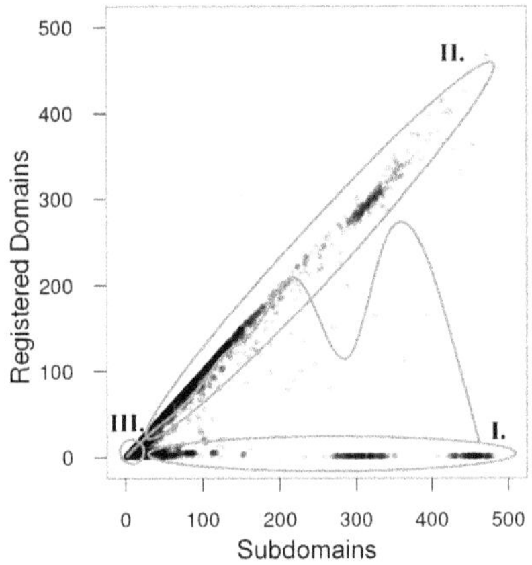

Figure 9: The number of subdomains versus the number of registered domains that URLs posted by a spam account resolve to. Each point corresponds to a single account.

Blog Program	Subdomains	Unique URLs
Blogspot	18,364	249,589
LiveJournal	15,327	54,375
Wordpress	4,290	58,727

Table 3: Top three free blog hosting sites, the number of blogs registered, and the number of unique URLs pointing to the blogs.

main registration services, this *co.cc* campaign displays how spammers can easily circumvent the requirement of domain registration.

Blog Hosting: Free blog pages from Blogspot, LiveJournal, and Wordpress account for nearly 363,000 URLs; roughly 0.1% of the URLs that appear in our dataset after shortening is resolved. While this may seem minute, Blogspot is the third most popular domain for shortened URLs, highlighting the huge variety of domains used by spammers.

To understand how many blog accounts spammers register, we extract the blog subdomain from each URL and calculate the total number of unique account names that appear, shown in Table 3. Over 18,000 accounts were registered on Blogspot and another 15,000 on LiveJournal. As a whole, we identified 7,500 Twitter spam accounts that advertised one of the three blog platforms, indicating a small collection of spammers who abuse both Twitter and blogging services.

4.2.3 *URL and Domain Reputation*

Many of the URLs and domains used by spammers also appear in tweets published by non-suspended users. For instance, of the 121,171 registered domains that appear in spam tweets, 63% also appear in tweets posted by active accounts. To understand whether this overlap is the result of a single retweet of a popular URL or a regular occurrence, we calculate a reputation score for each domain and URL in our dataset. Using all 1.8 billion tweets, we calculate the frequency that a domain or URL appears in spam tweets, and repeat this process for all tweets. The fraction of these two values offers a reputation score in the range $(0, 1)$. A reputation of one indicates a domain or URL appears exclusively in spam, while a reputation near zero indicates the domain or URL was rarely found in spam tweets. We note that due to some spam accounts going unsuspended, our reputation scores underestimate how frequently some domains are used by spammers.

Figure 10 shows the reputation scores for both domains and

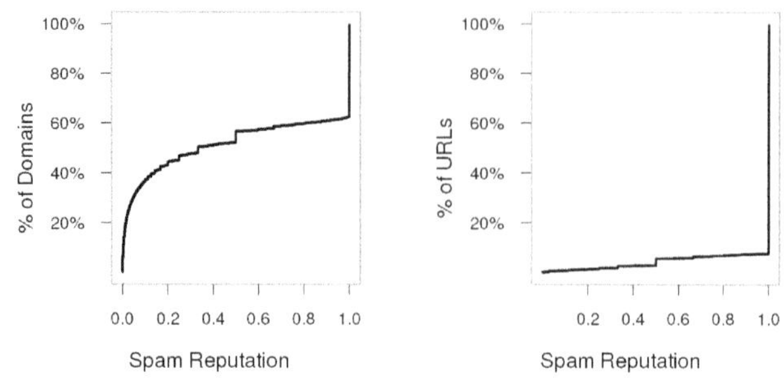

(a) Domain Reputation **(b)** URL Reputation

Figure 10: Reputation of spam URLs and domains. 53% of domains appear more frequently in non-spam tweets than spam tweets, though only 2.8% of URLs.

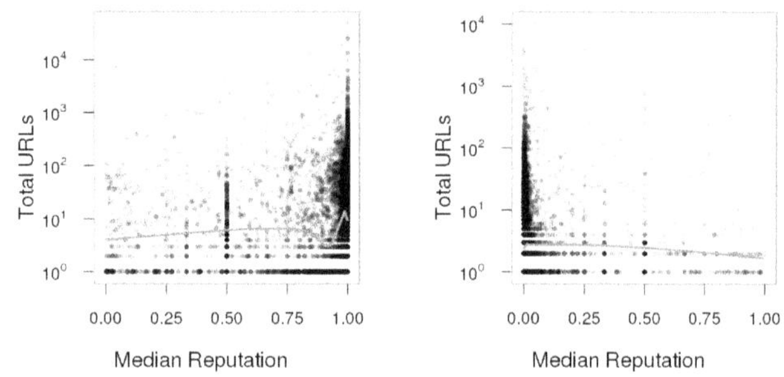

(a) Spam Accounts **(b)** Non-spam Accounts

Figure 11: Comparison of URL reputation and the total spam URLs posted by spam and non-spam accounts, where each point represents a distinct account.

URLs. We find 53% of domains appear more frequently in non-spam tweets than spam, compared to 2.8% of URLs. This indicates that attempting to build a domain blacklist from URLs appearing in spam tweets would be highly ineffective, and more so, attempting to detect unsuspended accounts based on their posting a duplicate spam URLs requires explicit knowledge the URL, not the account posting it, was spam. In fact, 11,573,273 active accounts posted at least one URL also posted by spammers.

To break down this phenomenon further, we examine both the reputation of URLs as well as the frequency that both spam accounts and non-spam accounts post them. Figure 11 shows the median spam reputation of all the URLs posted by an account as well as the number URLs that an account shares in common with spammers. A trend line marks the clusters with the highest density. Spammers are clearly identified by their rarely duplicated, high-spam reputation scores compared to non-spam accounts that post low-spam reputation URLs, though in low frequency. As such, both account behavior as well as the URLs posted would be required to deploy blacklists.

4.3 API Clients

Along with accounts and URLs, spammers require a client to interact with Twitter's API or their web portal. The overall application usage of spam is shown in Table 4. We find 64% of spam

API Name	% of Tweets	Likelihood Ratio
web	58.30%	2.98
twitterfeed	12.39%	1.06
Mobile Web	5.40%	6.07
dlvr.it	2.95%	2.01
hellotxt.com	1.14%	7.89
twittbot.net	1.05%	1.50
EasyBotter	0.98%	4.86
Google	0.83%	0.30
API	0.73%	1.32
www.movatwi.jp	0.72%	1.29
HootSuite	0.71%	0.41

Table 4: Top 10 Twitter clients used by spammers.

originates from the web and mobile web interface, while the remainder of spam is sent from over 10,544 public and custom API clients. We find spammers are nearly three times more likely to use the web interface compared to regular users, and six times more likely to use the mobile web interface. The remaining top 10 applications are automation frameworks that allow scheduled tweets and connecting blog posts to Twitter. Of the API clients we identify, we find over 6,200 are used *exclusively* to send spam, indicating a number of spammers are readily developing custom clients to access their accounts.

5. SPAM-AS-A-SERVICE

We find evidence of an emerging spam-as-a-service market that capitalizes on Twitter, including affiliate programs, ad-based shortening services, and account sellers. Each of these services allow spammers to specialize their efforts, decoupling the process of distributing spam, registering domains and hosting content, and if necessary, product fulfillment. Each of the services we identify reveals a targeted approach to monetizing social networks.

5.1 Affiliate Programs

One aspect of diversification we identify within the underground marketplace is the adoption of affiliate programs, both legitimate and otherwise. From the 15 million URLs we unshortened, we identify two prominent affiliate programs used by spammers: *clickbank.com* and *amazon.com*. Clickbank acts as a middleman, connecting vendors seeking to distribute URLs with affiliates willing to advertise the URLs. Clickbank affiliates are paid based on click-through, while vendors are charged a fee. In contrast, Amazon's affiliate program offers up to a 15% commission on purchases made after visitors click on an affiliate's URL. The use of Amazon's affiliate program by spammers blurs the line between what constitutes legitimate advertisement and abuse.

Table 5 shows that over 3.1 million spam tweets directed to Clickbank and nearly 1.2 million to Amazon. While the total number of accounts involved in both affiliate programs is a small fraction of the spam accounts we identify, the abuse of these services hint at an emerging spam-as-a-service market that allows Twitter spammers to exclusively spend their effort on generating accounts and tweets, leaving the task of domain registration and content generation to other parties.

Affiliate programs provide a unique opportunity to explore how individuals are earning a profit by sending spam on Twitter. Assuming each affiliate ID uniquely maps to one spammer, we can group an affiliate's Twitter accounts and the tweets the account's send based on the affiliate ID embedded in each tweet's URL. The results, shown in Table 6, offer a glimpse at the spam infrastructure each affiliate controls. Our analysis reveals a heavily biased environment where a small number of affiliates account for the vast majority of spam. We repeat this same experiment using the 47% of *bit.ly* URLs that contain an associated *bit.ly* account ID. We find that 50% of the 23,317 *bit.ly* accounts control only two or fewer Twitter accounts. Yet, one *bit.ly* account acquired over 5,000 Twitter accounts and sent over 550,000 tweets, revealing again the same biased marketplace that contains thousands of small actors alongside a few major players.

Service	Twitter Accounts	Tweets	Type
Clickbank	16,309	3,128,167	Affiliate
Amazon	8,129	1,173,446	Affiliate
Eca.sh	343	352,882	Shortener
Vur.me	72	9,339	Shortener
Spn.tw	905	87,757	Account
Assetize	815	120,421	Account

Table 5: Programs enabling spam-as-a-service. These include affiliate programs that connect vendors to affiliate advertisers, shorteners that embed ads, as well as account arbitration services that sell access to accounts.

		Tweets		Tw. Accts	
Service	Affiliates	Med	Max	Med	Max
Clickbank	203	565	217,686	2	151
Amazon	919	2	324,613	1	848
Bit.ly	23,317	2	551,200	1	5318

Table 6: Affiliates identified for Clickbank and Amazon along with Twitter accounts they control and the volume of spam they send. Bit.ly accounts reveal a similar result. Both show a biased environment where a small number of spammers account for the vast majority of spam.

5.2 Ad-Based Shorteners

A second form of monetization we identify is the use of syndicated ads from existing ad networks. Ad-based shortening services such as *eca.sh* and *vur.me* provide public URL shortening services, but in return, embed the destination page for shortened URLs in an `IFrame` and display advertisements alongside the original content. Anyone can register an account with the service and will receive a portion of the revenue generated by the additional advertisements. For ad-based URL shorteners, spammers need not control the content they shorten; any major news outlet or popular URL can be shortened, requiring the spammer only handle distribution on Twitter. Within our set of spam, there are over 362,000 tweets sent by 415 accounts using ad-based shorteners, a breakdown of which is provided in Table 5.

5.3 Account Sellers and Arbiters

The final monetization technique we find in our spam dataset are services that sell *control* of accounts as well as sell *access* to accounts. One particular service, called Assetize (since disabled), allowed Twitter users to sell access to their accounts. Assetize drew in over 815 accounts, in turn composing tweets and sending them on each account's behalf. In return, the account's owner would be paid. A similar service called Sponsored Tweets (*http://spn.tw*) is currently in existence and allows anyone to register to have advertisements posted to their account, with 905 such accounts appearing in our spam dataset.

Campaign	Tweets	Accounts	URLs	Hashtags	Mentions	Med. Followers	Med. Tweets
Afraid	14,524,958	124,244	14,528,613	-	11,658,859	2	130
Clickbank	3,128,167	16,309	1,432,680	3,585	542,923	9	108
Yuklumdegga	130,652	2,242	24	11	-	3	83
Amazon	129,602	848	1	-	118,157	22	123
Speedling	118,349	1,947	89,526	4674	870	95	190

Table 7: Summary of major spam campaigns on Twitter. This includes the number of tweets, accounts, unique URLs, unique hashtags, and unique mentions. In addition, we include the median number of followers and tweets for accounts in the campaign.

A second form of spam-as-a-service includes programs that specialize in the sale of Twitter accounts, violating Twitter's Terms of Service [25]. A number sites including *xgcmedia.com* and *backlinksvault.com* purport to register accounts with unique email addresses and create accounts with custom profile images and descriptions. While we cannot directly measure the popularity or impact of these services on Twitter, previous work has examined advertisements for these programs and their associated costs [14]. Both account arbiters and sellers reveal a fledgling market where spammers with content to advertise can obtain access to Twitter accounts without requiring CAPTCHA solvers or other tools to enable automated account creation.

6. SPAM CAMPAIGNS

In this section, we explore five major spam campaigns executed on Twitter that highlight the breadth of tools employed by spammers and the ingenuity of their approaches. Some campaigns are executed by centralized controllers orchestrating thousands of accounts, while others exhibit a decentralized spamming infrastructure enabled by spam-as-a-service programs. Only one of the five campaigns advertises content also found in major email spam campaigns [13], leading us to believe some of the actors in the Twitter spam market are separate from the email marketplace dominated by botnets. A summary of each campaign can be found in Table 7. Due to the multitude of obfuscation techniques used by spammers, there is no simple mechanism to cluster tweets and accounts into campaigns. As such, we describe our methodology for generating campaigns on a per-campaign basis.

6.1 Afraid

The largest campaign in our dataset consists of *over 14 million tweets and 124,000 accounts*. During a period in December when we first identified the campaign, accounts were distributing Amazon affiliate URLs linking to a variety of products. All the URLs distributed by the campaign directed to custom shorteners that have since disappeared, making further analysis impossible. The sheer volume of spam directing to Amazon underscores the blurred line between what constitutes legitimate content compared to traditional email pharmaceuticals and replica goods. As we will show with two other campaigns, spammers are readily capitalizing on the ability to send unsolicited tweets to large audiences on Twitters to push legitimate goods for their own profit.

Despite regular account suspensions, the campaign sustained itself over a 6 month period, relying on unsolicited mentions to reach out to over 11.7 million distinct Twitter users. As Table 7 shows, accounts in the campaign completely ignore the social graph, acquiring a median of two followers throughout their lifetime. Figure 12a shows the creation time, activation time, and suspension time for each of the accounts in the campaign. Most dates for activation and suspension overlap due to the short-lived nature of accounts. Accounts are clearly registered in bulk (as indicated by the vertical lines resulting from duplicate registration dates), sometimes *months* in advance of their final activation, leading us to believe accounts were controlled in a centralized fashion.

Every tweet of the campaign included at least one unique URL along with a random amalgamation of tweet content stolen from other users' tweets, making text-based clustering difficult. We identify tweets that belong to the campaign based on two criteria: a regular expression that captures a textual artifact appearing in the campaign's tweets, and a second expression that captures the re-use of domains across multiple tweets. A more in-depth treatment of our methodology can be found in Appendix A.1. In total, we find over 178 unique domains used exclusively by the campaign, 140 of which rely on *afraid.org* for nameservers. Those domains still being hosted can be resolved, but do not forward traffic to the original campaign landing page.

6.2 Clickbank

Clickbank is one of the highest volume spam-as-a-service programs we identify within our dataset, consisting of over 16,000 Twitter accounts each operating in a decentralized fashion controlled by over 200 affiliates. Nearly 13% of *bit.ly* URLs redirect to Clickbank, making Clickbank the most frequent spam domain directed to by the shortener. Figure 12b shows the prevalence of accounts tweeting Clickbank throughout time. Clickbank URLs appear consistently from the onset of our collection window to its completion, despite accounts being suspended at regular intervals.

Due to the multiple actors within the campaign, a variety of spamming approaches appear, including the use of unsolicited mentions as well as popular trends. To understand the effectiveness of Clickbank spammers, we take a sample of 20,000 *bit.ly* URLs that direct to the affiliate program and examine their clickthrough. Over 90% of URLs received no clicks at all, though a total of 4,351 clicks were generated for all 20,000 URLs.

We identify tweets belonging to Clickbank participants based on whether the URLs advertised direct to *cbfeed.com* or *clickbank.com*, which serve as intermediate hops for all URLs associated with the service. Our criteria matches both the raw URL appearing in a tweet as well as resolved URLs, provided first-hop data is available.

6.3 Yuklemdegga

The Yuklumdegga campaign consists of over 2,200 accounts that pushed pharmacy goods from one of the largest email spam affiliate programs called Eva Pharmacy [10]. Each of the URLs in the campaign resolved to *yuklumdegga.com*, where we identified the HTML store front associated with the Eva Pharmacy program, previously documented by Levchenko et al. [13]. The presence of well-known pharmacy scams on Twitter indicates that some email spam programs are being carried over to Twitter, though we still identify a variety of Twitter spam that does not have a prominent email equivalent.

The Yuklumdegga campaign relies exclusively on hijacking trending topics to reach an audience with its tweets, embedding one

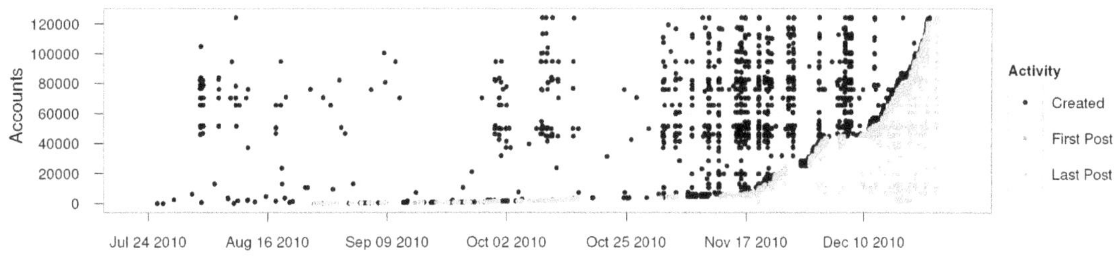

(a) Afraid Campaign

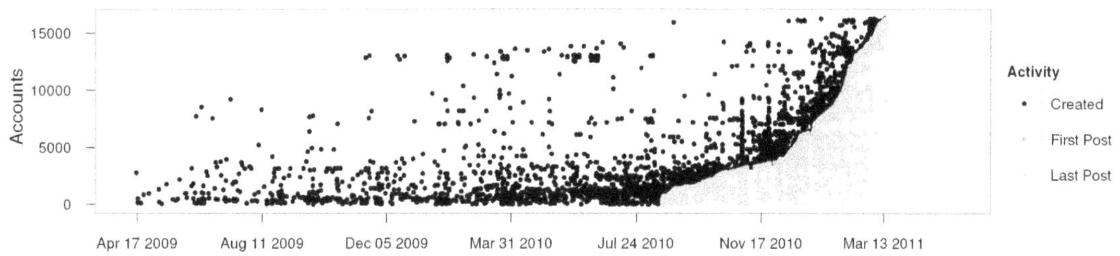

(b) Clickbank Campaign

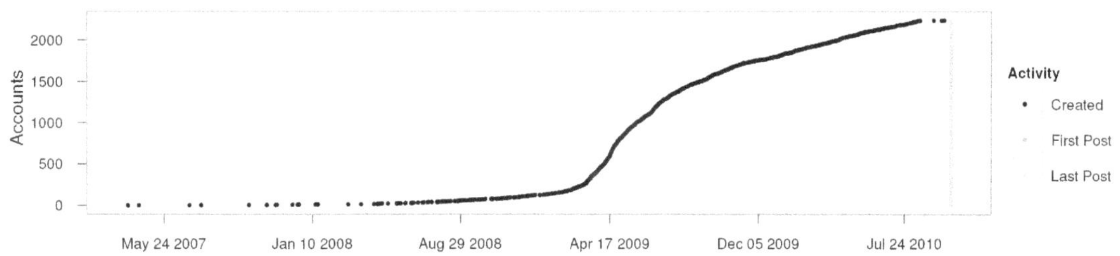

(c) Yuklumdegga Campaign

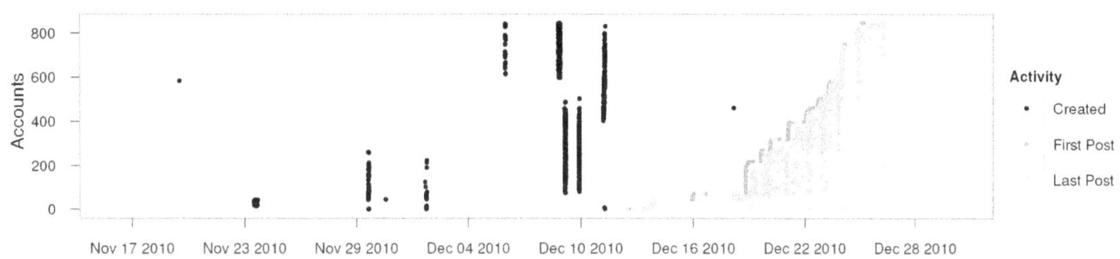

(d) Amazon Campaign

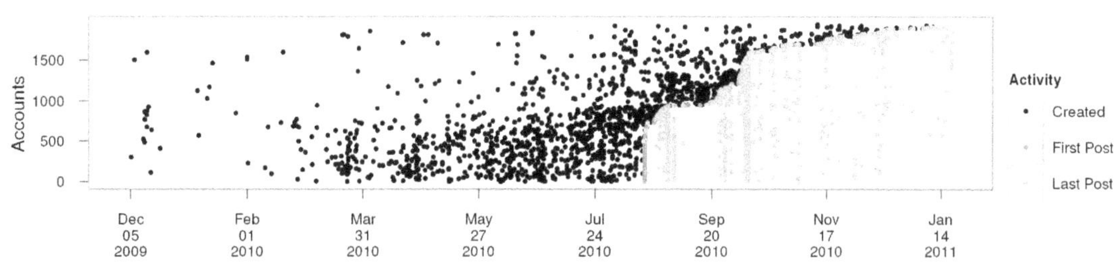

(e) Speedling Campaign

Figure 12: Prominent spam campaigns on Twitter

of eleven trends that existed on the single day of the campaign's operation. We find 6 of the campaigns 24 URLs directed to *bit.ly*, with an aggregate clickthrough of 1,982 visitors. Assuming the number of visitors was identical for all 24 URLs of the campaign, we can estimate a total of 8,000 users accessed the pharmacy site, all from reading popular trends.

The preparation of the Yuklumdegga campaign provides a stark comparison to other Twitter campaigns. Figure 12c shows the creation times of the campaigns' accounts, with activation and suspension times overlapped for the single day of the campaign's existence. The bulk of accounts were created *nearly a year* in advance of the campaign's onset. This can result either from the campaign purchasing accounts from a service, or simply creating accounts in a serial fashion until their final activation.

Given that many of the campaign's accounts were created prior to our collection window, we may incorrectly estimate when an account was activated. We determine this is in fact not the case. We calculate the number of posts sent prior to an account's first tweet in our dataset using statistics embedded in each tweet (described in Section 4.1). We find accounts posted a median of 4 posts prior to the campaign's onset, indicating thousands of accounts were stockpiled and then used to send hundreds of tweets.

6.4 Amazon

Like the Afraid campaign, a second Amazon affiliate spam campaign appeared simultaneously during the holiday season. With only 848 accounts, the campaign relied on unsolicited mentions to reach out to over 118,000 Twitter users, each pushing a single URL shortened by *bit.ly*. *Bit.ly* reports the URL received an astounding *107,380 clicks* during the course of the URL's existence. Using our estimate of our sample size for that day (derived in Section 3.1), we can generate an estimate for how many unsolicited mentions result in a visit. Given we received 70% of URLs posted to Twitter in December, roughly 185,000 tweets would have been sent by the campaign. This would indicate over 58% of users clicked on their unsolicited mention, assuming that no other channels advertised the URL and the absence of automated crawlers visiting the URL.

With respect to the accounts participating in the campaign, Figure 12d shows the majority of accounts were created in bulk prior to the holiday and activated in rolling fashion around December 18th. As Twitter banned the active accounts, dormant accounts were then deployed to keep the total accounts active at any point roughly constant. This technique highlights how stockpiled accounts can sustain a campaign through a high-value period.

6.5 Speedling

Speedling (*http://www.speedlings.com/*) is a software program used to generate thousands of blogs that embed advertisements as well as Amazon affiliate URLs generated from a product theme such as cookbooks, games, or any arbitrary keyword. We identify Speedling participants by the API client they use to access Twitter (Speedling, Go Speedling) as well as the format of Speedling's URLs. Further details can be found in Appendix A.2. In total, we find over 89,526 URLs directing to 1,971 domains, all registered to *speedeenames.com*.

As with Clickbank, Speedling represents a decentralized spam campaign consisting of multiple users of the Speedling software. Figure 12e shows the creation and activation time of accounts within the campaign. The vertical lines of final posts indicate mass suspensions on the part of Twitter, yet new accounts are registered, sustaining Speedling's presence on Twitter from the start of our collection period till mid-January.

The monetization approach of Speedling is one of the most interesting compared to the other Twitter campaigns we examine. Visitors are directed to template blog pages listing thousands of Amazon products catering to a specific interest, in addition to a live stream of recommendations from Twitter users that are in fact Twitter accounts controlled by the Speedling operator. Visitors that click on an ad or purchase an Amazon product directly translate into profit, allowing Speedling participants to operate purely through legitimate advertisements. As with the other Amazon affiliate spam we identified, this approach highlights the semi-legitimate nature of some spam campaigns on Twitter, where the distribution approach rather than the landing page or products sold are what distinguish spam from legitimate advertisements.

7. DISCUSSION

In this section, we discuss the implications of our analysis and how our results compare to previous work on social network spam. We also present potential directions for new spam defenses based on our results, describing both in-network solutions as well as addressing the services that facilitate spamming.

Compromised vs. Fraudulent Accounts: Earlier studies of social networks found that 97% of accounts sending spam on Facebook were compromised [5], compared to 84% of accounts on Twitter [6]. In contrast, we find a majority of suspended accounts in our dataset were fraudulent and created for the explicit purpose of spamming. We believe this disparity results from how the datasets for each study were generated. As we showed in Section 3.2, only 8% of the URLs posted by fraudulent accounts appeared in blacklists. These same blacklists served as the source of identifying social network spam in the previous studies, with an apparent bias towards compromised accounts. Our results should thus be viewed in conjunction with these previous studies, offering a wider perspective of the multitude of spamming strategies in social networks.

Blacklists and Spam Traps: With Twitter catching an estimated 37% of spam accounts, a number of studies have examined how to improve this accuracy. These approaches include account heuristics that identify newly created accounts and the lack of social relationships; the identification of unsolicited mentions based on the social graph; and real-time classification of URLs posted to Twitter [2, 12, 17, 19, 20]. Each of these approaches hinges on access to accurate training data, which in practice is often difficult to acquire.

One potential solution for aggregating training data and improving spam detection is to develop Twitter-specific blacklists and spam traps. As previous research has shown, existing blacklists are too slow at identifying threats appearing on social networks, as well as often inaccurate with respect to both false positives and negatives [6, 15, 16]. Even though only 10.6% of URLs in our dataset appear in multiple spam tweets, they account for 59.5% of spam. To capture this re-use, as soon as an account is suspended, the URLs it posted and their associated final landing pages could be added to a blacklist along with the frequency they appeared. If Twitter consulted this blacklist prior to posting a URL, services such as Clickbank would be taken offline, while campaigns that persist despite account suspension would be forced to diversify the URLs they post.

Additionally, rather than suspended accounts outright, Twitter could quarantine tweets from known spam accounts, obtaining access to a steady stream of spam URLs for both classification and blacklisting. While such quarantine is standard practice for email, Twitter has the added difficulty that spammers can easily observe the system to confirm the delivery of their tweets. They can do so by either forming relationships between their accounts to monitor tweet delivery (though this risks Sybil detection [4, 26]), or, alternatively, polling the search API confirm whether their spam tweets were indexed. These approaches however incur an additional burden to operating fraudulent accounts.

Beyond Social Networks: The Twitter spam marketplace relies on a multitude of services that include popular URL shorteners, free web hosting, legitimate affiliate programs like Amazon, and illegitimate programs such as Clickbank, Assetiz, and account sellers. While the vast majority of research efforts have targeted spam as it appears on social networks, solutions that disincentivize the abuse of these individual programs would be equally viable. Shortening services, including *bit.ly* and HootSuite, already employ blacklists before URLs are shortened [3, 8]. By monitoring which services underpin the spam ecosystem on Twitter as we do in this study, we can deploy customized countermeasures for each service, reducing the support infrastructure available to spammers.

8. CONCLUSION

This paper presents a unique look at the behaviors of spammers on Twitter by analyzing the tweets sent by suspended users in retrospect. We found that the current marketplace for Twitter spam uses a diverse set of spamming techniques, including a variety of strategies for creating Twitter accounts, generating spam URLs, and distributing spam. We highlighted how these features are woven together to form five of the largest spam campaigns on Twitter accounting for nearly 20% of the spam in our dataset. Furthermore, we found an emerging *spam-as-a-service* market that includes reputable and not-so-reputable affiliate programs, ad-based shorteners, and Twitter account sellers.

In particular, we found that 89% of fraudulent accounts created by spammers forgo participation in the social graph, instead relying on unsolicited mentions and trending topics to attract clicks. Surprisingly, 77% of accounts belonging to spammers were suspended within one day, yet despite this attrition rate, new fraudulent accounts are created to take their place, sustaining Twitter spam throughout the course of our seven month measurement. By examining the accounts controlled by individual spammers as revealed by affiliate programs, we find a handful of actors controlling thousands of Twitter accounts, each pushing a diverse strategy for monetizing Twitter. As a whole, our measurements expose a thriving spam ecosystem on Twitter that is unperturbed by current defenses. Our findings highlight the necessity of better spam controls targeting both abusive accounts as well as the services that support the spam marketplace.

9. ACKNOWLEDGMENTS

This material is based upon work supported by the National Science Foundation under Grant No. 0433702, 0905631, 0842694, 0842695, and 0831501. Any opinions, findings, and conclusions or recommendations expressed in this material are those of the authors and do not necessarily reflect the views of the National Science Foundation. This work is partially supported by the Office of Naval Research under MURI Grant No. N000140911081.

10. REFERENCES

[1] D. Anderson, C. Fleizach, S. Savage, and G. Voelker. Spamscatter: Characterizing internet scam hosting infrastructure. In *USENIX Security*, 2007.

[2] F. Benevenuto, G. Magno, T. Rodrigues, and V. Almeida. Detecting Spammers on Twitter. In *Proceedings of the Conference on Email and Anti-Spam (CEAS)*, 2010.

[3] bit.ly. Spam and Malware Protection. 2009. `http://blog.bit.ly/post/138381844/spam-and-malware-protection`.

[4] G. Danezis and P. Mittal. Sybilinfer: Detecting sybil nodes using social networks. In *Proceedings of the Network and Distributed System Security Symposium (NDSS)*, 2009.

[5] H. Gao, J. Hu, C. Wilson, Z. Li, Y. Chen, and B. Zhao. Detecting and characterizing social spam campaigns. In *Proceedings of the Internet Measurement Conference (IMC)*, 2010.

[6] C. Grier, K. Thomas, V. Paxson, and M. Zhang. @spam: the underground on 140 characters or less. In *Proceedings of the ACM Conference on Computer and Communications Security (CCS)*, 2010.

[7] T. Holz, C. Gorecki, F. Freiling, and K. Rieck. Detection and mitigation of fast-flux service networks. In *Proceedings of the 15th Annual Network and Distributed System Security Symposium (NDSS)*, 2008.

[8] HootSuite. Kapow! HootSuite Fights the Evils of Phishing, Malware, and Spam. 2010. `http://blog.hootsuite.com/hootsuite-fights-malware-phishing/`.

[9] C. Kanich, C. Kreibich, K. Levchenko, B. Enright, G. Voelker, V. Paxson, and S. Savage. Spamalytics: An empirical analysis of spam marketing conversion. In *Proceedings of the 15th ACM Conference on Computer and Communications Security*, 2008.

[10] B. Krebs. Battling the zombie web site armies. `https://krebsonsecurity.com/2011/01/battling-the-zombie-web-site-armies/#more-7522`, 2011.

[11] C. Kreibich, C. Kanich, K. Levchenko, B. Enright, G. Voelker, V. Paxson, and S. Savage. Spamcraft: An inside look at spam campaign orchestration. In *USENIX Workshop on Large-Scale Exploits and Emergent Threats (LEET)*, 2009.

[12] K. Lee, J. Caverlee, and S. Webb. Uncovering social spammers: social honeypots+ machine learning. In *Proceeding of the International ACM SIGIR Conference on Research and Development in Information Retrieval*, 2010.

[13] K. Levchenko, A. Pitsillidis, N. Chachra, B. Enright, M. Felegyhazi, C. Grier, T. Halvorson, C. Kanich, C. Kreibich, H. Liu, D. McCoy, N. Weaver, V. Paxson, G. M. Voelker, and S. Savage. Click Trajectories: End-to-End Analysis of the Spam Value Chain. In *Proceedings of the IEEE Symposium on Security and Privacy*, May 2011.

[14] M. Motoyama, D. McCoy, K. Levchenko, S. Savage, and G. M. Voelker. Dirty jobs: The role of freelance labor in web service abuse. In *Proceedings of the 20th USENIX Security Symposium*, 2011.

[15] A. Ramachandran, N. Feamster, and S. Vempala. Filtering spam with behavioral blacklisting. In *Proceedings of the 14th ACM Conference on Computer and Communications Security*, 2007.

[16] S. Sinha, M. Bailey, and F. Jahanian. Shades of grey: On the effectiveness of reputation-based blacklists. In *3rd International Conference on Malicious and Unwanted Software*, 2008.

[17] J. Song, S. Lee, and J. Kim. Spam filtering in twitter using sender-receiver relationship. In *Proceedings of International Symposium on Recent Advances in Intrusion Detection (RAID)*, 2011.

[18] B. Stone-Gross, R. Abman, R. Kemmerer, C. Kruegel,

D. Steigerwald, and G. Vigna. The Underground Economy of Fake Antivirus Software. In *Proceedings of the Workshop on Economics of Information Security (WEIS)*, 2011.

[19] G. Stringhini, C. Kruegel, and G. Vigna. Detecting Spammers on Social Networks. In *Proceedings of the Annual Computer Security Applications Conference (ACSAC)*, 2010.

[20] K. Thomas, C. Grier, J. Ma, V. Paxson, and D. Song. Design and Evaluation of a Real-time URL Spam Filtering Service. In *Proceedings of the 32nd IEEE Symposium on Security and Privacy*, 2011.

[21] Twitter. The Twitter Rules. http://support.twitter.com/entries/18311-the-twitter-rules, 2010.

[22] Twitter. Twitter API wiki. http://dev.twitter.com/doc, 2010.

[23] Twitter. Numbers. http://blog.twitter.com/2011/03/numbers.html, March 2011.

[24] Twitter. OAuth FAQ. https://dev.twitter.com/docs/auth/oauth/faq, 2011.

[25] Twitter. Terms of service, May 2011. http://twitter.com/tos.

[26] H. Yu, M. Kaminsky, P. Gibbons, and A. Flaxman. Sybilguard: defending against sybil attacks via social networks. *ACM SIGCOMM Computer Communication Review*, 2006.

APPENDIX

A. IDENTIFYING CAMPAIGNS

This appendix includes a detailed analysis, when applicable, of the clustering criteria used to identify the campaigns discussed in Section 6. The process of finding spam campaigns is a mixture of manual exploration and automated clustering. We begin by independently clustering all spam tweets based on text, URLs and domains, resolved URLs and domains, and the application used to interact with Twitter. After manually identifying the largest and most interesting clusters across the different approaches, we tune our clustering technique on a per-campaign basis to merge related clusters.

A.1 Afraid

Tweets belonging to the Afraid campaign share no textual similarity other than a rare artifact that multiple retweets are included in a single tweet, violating the definition and functionality of a retweet (i.e. exposing a tweet to an account's audience while maintaining attribution). Additionally, many tweets share the same full domain, though domains alone are not enough to capture all tweets belonging to the campaign. We employ a regular expression to identify tweets with numerous embedded retweets and then group them by the domain advertised. Domain clusters with fewer than tens of thousands of tweets are omitted. The subclusters are finally merged, revealing the full scope of the Afraid campaign. A sample of the campaign's tweets are provided below, with emphasis on our labeling criteria.

@Aguirre_5030 Haha yes for u **RT** nikivic i love him and i care lol **RT** dhegracia: I don't love you
http://ciqf.t6h.ru/HENGK

@mahi58 **RT** PoiintGod11: Didn't you just tweet about bad english? Lol **RT** ashLeyGaneshx3: I didnt get no text **http://boo.lol.vc**/3GbPH

A.2 Speedling

Due to the decentralized nature of the Speedling product, where anyone can purchase the software program, multiple approaches to spamming appear. As a result, text-based clustering is impossible. Nevertheless, many Speedling participants rely on a Twitter application provided by the software that is uniquely identified through the Twitter API in the source field as **Go Speedling** or **Speedlings** depending the software version. Other participants do not rely on these APIs, but instead use a shortener that only appears in our spam dataset from Speedling participants. Tweets that satisfy any of these criteria are included in the cluster. We note that this provides a strict lower bound on the presence of Speedling spam as some tweets may not match any of these criteria. A more sophisticated approach would be to cluster based on the HTML template of Speedling-generated blogs. However, as we lack HTML due to the retroactive nature of our analysis and link rot, this is impossible in the context of our current study.

Summary Review Documentation for

"Suspended Accounts in Retrospect: An Analysis of Twitter Spam"

Authors: K. Thomas, C. Grier, V. Paxson, D. Song

Reviewer #1

Strengths: Large data set that relies on Twitter identifying malicious accounts instead of simply using blacklists.Well written paper that provides the right amount of details in each area covered and highlights some of the caveats.

Weaknesses: Relies on Twitter to identify suspended accounts. We can infer from the paper that this only covers 35% of the accounts that should have been suspended (sensitivity ratio).

Comments to Authors: Nice paper! In the intro, you mention Amazon and ask yourself what the definition of a spam is. I know where you are coming from. But the content or product promoted by the spam should not influence what should be considered a spam.

About the twitter data set: Are you saying that you only collected tweets that contain URLs? Why limiting yourself to spams that point to URLs. It would be interesting to comment on what you see in spams without URLs.

Giving your characterization of suspended accounts, you could go one step further and see if you would have been able to identify automatically faster and more accounts that should have also been suspended. This is probably future work.

It's great that you think of validating the suspended accounts but also the accounts that are not suspended. But let's do the maths here: 32M accounts, 1M suspended accounts and no false positives, 31M active accounts 6% of the 31M accounts are false negatives = 1.86M.

So sensitivity: TP/ (TP+FN) = 1/2.86 = 35%.I think you need to highlights this in your paper directly. It's a weakness of this paper, but you should not shy away from it. The next question is whether your data set is then significantly biased when you characterize it? It would have been interesting to see some comments about the characterization of the false negatives to see if there are some obvious differences.

You should then better highlight again that caveat and mention your sensitivity ration in your domain reputation section.

Sections 5 and 6 are great additions to the paper.

Reviewer #2

Strengths: A very interesting, insightful analysis of spammer behavior.

Weaknesses: The analysis does not shed much light directly on how the spam can be reduced.

Comments to Authors: I like this paper and I learnt a lot from it about Twitter spam.

My one complaint was that you didn't take the natural next step of telling us, based on your experience, how we (or, Twitter) can deal with this problem more effectively. I am of course assuming that this is a problem that needs to be dealt with (I am not a Twitter user, and so I cannot tell if the spam has reached an annoying level for an average user).

It wasn't clear to me how you actually pulled out the spam campaigns from your tweets. Was it all manual, ad hoc investigation? Did you have any out-of-band information? Or, did you just look at what the affiliates were doing?

I was also surprised to see that you didn't find much overlap between Twitter spam and email spam. Are the players different? Or, maybe I am misinterpreting your statements.

You should do a better job at explaining Figures 5 and 9. Based on the graphs, I do not really see the modes you talk about and had difficulty mapping the text to points in the graph, especially for Figure 9. Perhaps highlight the relevant regions in the graph, instead of the fitted curve line which is not adding any value for me.

While expanding URLs, why did you stop at the first redirect and why didn't you try to counter rate limiting by querying at a slower rate? If scale (too many URLs) was an issue, you could try to expand a subset to see if that improves coverage.

I find it interesting that you found evidence of deactivated shortening services. I've always thought of their use as odd in some contexts, such as in paper bibliographies.

In 2.1, what is an OAuth permission?

Reviewer #3

Strengths: Good datasets, detailed and interesting set of analysis.

Weaknesses: No discussion on how to deal with spam.

Comments to Authors: This is a solid study of spam in Twitter based on a large dataset and detailed analysis. My comments are relatively minor.

The paper characterizes the market place behind using spam in Twitter but ironically does not offer any discussion on how these findings may be used to prevent such an abuse. It seems that a paper deserve a discussion section that elaborates on how to use the findings.

Authors seem to have a few papers related to spam in Twitter, it is useful to clarify how these papers complement each other.

Given the rate of data collection, it appears that authors have used white listed accounts which should be stated.

Reviewer #4

Strengths: The paper did a good job in demonstrating how spamming works on Twitter. Each step in the analysis is well justified and done carefully.

Weaknesses: It is not so clear how the findings in the paper could be used to improve spam detection. Although this point is not sufficient to reject the paper.

Comments to Authors: This is an interesting paper to read. It provides an insight into how spamming works on Twitter. The authors also carefully take into account the false positives/false negatives and sample rates in the dataset. However, as mentioned previously, it is not so clear how these findings can be used to improve the spam detection. The authors might want to provide more discussion relating to this.

There are a few places that are a little hard to follow or could have been improved, listed as follows:

It would be nice if the authors provide a related work section so that the contributions of the papers in relative to the previous work are clearer.

Section 2.1.2 you might want to give a reference for OAuth for readers who may not be familiar with it.

Section 2.3 should refer to Section 3.1, which gives the details of how the confirmation that suspended accounts are mostly spammers is performed.

Section 3.1 Subsection Validating Suspended Accounts are Spammers. When you analyze the content of the tweets, what are the templates mentioned in the "tweets that follow a template"?

Section 4.1.3 How do you determine the accounts that rely on trending topicsto spread spams?

Section 4.2.2 Figure 9 What are the registered domains and full domains?

Section 6.5 Paragraph 3 What does "freeing Speedling participants from fulfilling orders" mean?

Reviewer #5

Strengths: Well written paper that provides a comprehensive description of Spammers and their strategies in Twitter.

Weaknesses: Some assumptions (which the authors admit) on what consists a Spammer and a manual process to verify Spamming activities. These are not significant problems with the paper, since as the authors correctly point out the line of what is spam on twitter is blurred.

Comments to author: I enjoyed reading the paper which I believe nicely describes spammer characteristics and their strategies in Twitter. I particularly liked the analysis of the likelihood ratios and the reputation scores for spam and non-spam accounts. Some minor problems with the paper include:

The phrasing that "manual analysis … of 1.1 million accounts reveals" or "We manually verify that the vast majority of these - 1.1 million accounts –" is a bit weird. You are of course referring to verifying a small sample of those but the phrasing is a bit exaggerated.

As you mention the lines between spam messages are blurred, so a bit more detail on your manual verification process is needed. How do you analyze the content, and what content is deemed spam?

Similarly, when identifying the spam campaigns, it was not clear to me how all the different accounts were grouped together in a campaign? I guess using the particular keywords in each case, but how do you know that this is one and not many campaigns? What if you apply some automated content clustering technique in the spam tweets? Can you identify these or other campaigns?

Finally, I guess an interesting next step would be to design an anti-spam mechanism using the characteristics you discuss in the paper.

Response from the Authors

Reviews of our paper were largely positive, so the changes we made targeted clarifications of how campaigns were identified; the sensitivity of Twitter's suspension algorithm and its impact on our results; and improving explanations on a number of our figures. Additionally, we expanded our discussion of how our work compares to previous studies of social network spam and the separate conclusions we draw.

Overwhelmingly, reviewers requested a discussion on how to move forward on Twitter spam based on our results. Given that there is already a great deal of research on how to improve spam detection in social networks (which we provide an overview of), we instead discuss alternative approaches for combating spam. This includes Twitter-specific blacklisting, spam traps, and removing or preventing the abuse of services that spammers rely upon. Our discussion is informal, simply highlighting a number of potential directions and the impact they would have on reducing spam based on our results and experience studying Twitter.

Uncovering Social Network Sybils in the Wild

Zhi Yang
Computer Science Dept.
Peking University
Beijing, China P. R.
yangzhi@net.pku.edu.cn

Christo Wilson
Computer Science Dept.
UC Santa Barbara
Santa Barbara, CA 93106
bowlin@cs.ucsb.edu

Xiao Wang
Computer Science Dept.
Peking University
Beijing, China P. R.
wangxiao@net.pku.edu.cn

Tingting Gao
Renren Inc.
Beijing, China P. R.
tingting.gao@renren-inc.com

Ben Y. Zhao
Computer Science Dept.
UC Santa Barbara
Santa Barbara, CA 93106
ravenben@cs.ucsb.edu

Yafei Dai
Computer Science Dept.
Peking University
Beijing, China P. R.
dyf@net.pku.edu.cn

ABSTRACT

Sybil accounts are fake identities created to unfairly increase the power or resources of a single user. Researchers have long known about the existence of Sybil accounts in online communities such as file-sharing systems, but have not been able to perform large scale measurements to detect them or measure their activities. In this paper, we describe our efforts to detect, characterize and understand Sybil account activity in the Renren online social network (OSN). We use ground truth provided by Renren Inc. to build measurement based Sybil account detectors, and deploy them on Renren to detect over 100,000 Sybil accounts. We study these Sybil accounts, as well as an additional 560,000 Sybil accounts caught by Renren, and analyze their link creation behavior. Most interestingly, we find that contrary to prior conjecture, Sybil accounts in OSNs do not form tight-knit communities. Instead, they integrate into the social graph just like normal users. Using link creation timestamps, we verify that the large majority of links between Sybil accounts are created accidentally, unbeknownst to the attacker. Overall, only a very small portion of Sybil accounts are connected to other Sybils with social links. Our study shows that existing Sybil defenses are unlikely to succeed in today's OSNs, and we must design new techniques to effectively detect and defend against Sybil attacks.

Categories and Subject Descriptors

C.2 [**General**]: Security and protection (e.g., firewalls); J.4 [**Computer Applications**]: Social and behavioral sciences

General Terms

Measurement, Security

Keywords

Sybil Accounts, Online Social Networks

IMC'11, November 2–4, 2011, Berlin, Germany.

1. INTRODUCTION

Sybil attacks [4] are one of the most prevalent and practical attacks against distributed systems. In this attack, a user creates multiple fake identities, known as Sybils, to unfairly increase their power and influence within a target community. Distributed systems are ill-equipped to defend against this attack, since determining a tight mapping between real users and online identities is an open problem. To date, researchers have demonstrated the efficacy of Sybil attacks against P2P systems [10], anonymous communication networks [1], and sensor networks [14].

Recently, online social networks (OSNs) have also come under attack from Sybils. Researchers have observed Sybils forwarding spam and malware on Facebook [5] and Twitter [6], as well as infiltrating social games [13]. Looking forward, Sybil attacks on OSNs are poised to become increasingly widespread and dangerous as more people come to rely on OSNs for basic online communication [9, 12] and as replacements for news outlets [8].

To address the problem of Sybils on OSNs, researchers have developed algorithms such as SybilGuard [24], SybilLimit [23], SybilInfer [3], and SumUp [17] to perform decentralized detection of Sybils on social graphs. These systems detect Sybils by identifying tightly connected communities of Sybil nodes [18].

Recent work showed that one of the key assumptions of community-based Sybil detectors, fast mixing time, does not hold on social graphs where edges correspond to strong real-world trust (*e.g.*, DBLP, Physics co-authorship, Epinions, *etc.*) [11]. Thus, community-based Sybil detectors do not perform well on "trusted" social graphs. To date, however, no large scale studies have been performed to validate the assumptions of community-based Sybil detectors on *untrusted* social networks such as Facebook and Twitter.

In this paper, we describe our efforts to detect, characterize and understand Sybil account activity in Renren, the largest OSN in China. In Section 2, we use ground truth data on Sybils provided by Renren Inc. to characterize Sybil behavior. We identify several behavioral attributes that are unique to Sybils, and leverage them to build a measurement based, real-time Sybil detector. Our detector is currently deployed on Renren's production systems, and between August 2010 and February 2011 it led to the identification and banning of over 100,000 Sybil accounts.

In Section 3 we analyze the graph structural properties of Sybils on Renren, based on the 100,000 Sybils identified by our detector, as well as 560,000 more identified by Renren using prior techniques. Most interestingly, we find that contrary to prior conjecture, Sybil accounts in Renren do not form tight-knit communities:

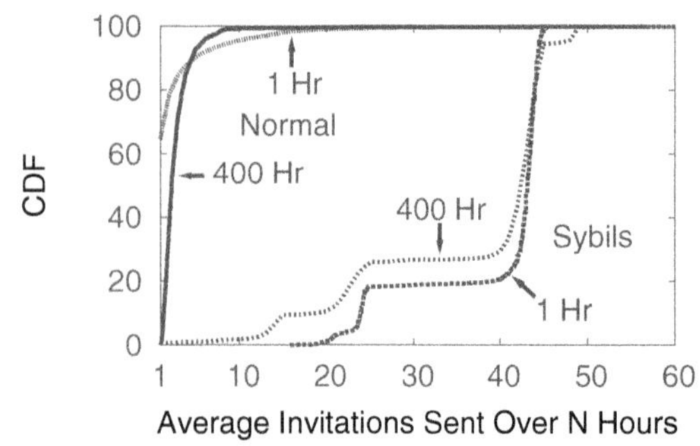

Figure 1: Average friend invitation frequency for Sybil and normal users, over two time scales.

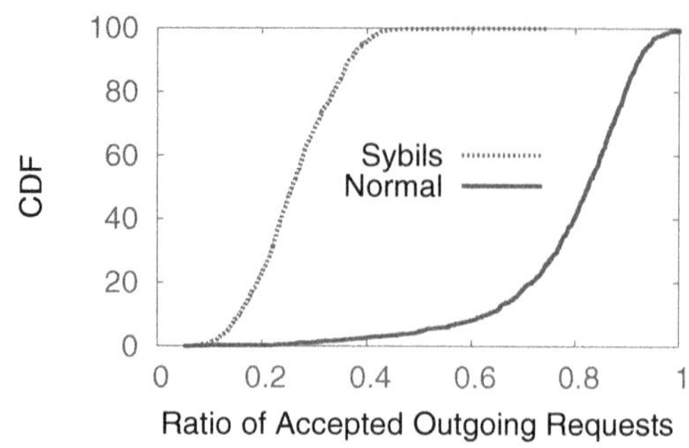

Figure 2: Ratio of accepted *outgoing* friend requests.

>70% of Sybils do not have *any* edges to other Sybils at all. Instead, attackers use snowball sampling to identify and send friend requests to popular users, since these users are more likely to accept requests from strangers. This strategy allows Sybil accounts to integrate seamlessly into the social graph.

We analyze the remaining 30% of Sybils that are friends with other Sybils, and discover that 69% (65,000 accounts) form a single connected component. By analyzing the creation timestamps of these edges, we determine that this component formed accidentally, and not due to coordinated efforts by attackers. We briefly survey several popular Sybil management tools, and show that large Sybil components can form naturally due to bias in the snowball sampling techniques these tools use to locate targets for friending.

Our analysis of Sybil behavior and characteristics demonstrates that existing Sybil defenses are unlikely to succeed on today's untrusted OSNs. This opens the door for the development of new techniques to effectively detect and defend against Sybil attacks.

2. DETECTING SYBILS

In this section, we set the backdrop for our data analysis. First, we briefly introduce the Renren OSN and describe the role of Sybil accounts in Renren. Second, we describe experiments characterizing Sybil accounts on a verified ground-truth dataset provided by Renren. Finally, we describe and build a real-time Sybil account detector deployed on Renren, and show how it led to the large Sybil dataset we analyze in the remainder of the paper.

2.1 The Renren Network and Sybil Accounts

With 120 million users, Renren[1] is the largest and oldest OSN in China, and provides functionality and features similar to Facebook. Like Facebook, Renren started in 2005 as a social network for college students in China, then saw its user population grow exponentially once it opened its doors to non-students. Renren users maintain personal profiles, upload photos, write diary entries (blogs), and establish bidirectional social links with friends. The most popular type of user activity is sharing blog entries, which can be forwarded across social hops like "retweets" on Twitter.

As its user population has grown, Renren has become an attractive venue for companies to disseminate information about their products. This has created opportunities for Sybil accounts to spam advertisements for companies, a growing trend observed by the analytics team at Renren. The increased prevalence of spam on Renren mirrors similar findings from Facebook [5] and Twitter [6].

To effectively attract friends and disseminate advertisements, most Sybil accounts on Renren blend in extremely well with normal users. They tend to have completely filled user profiles with realistic background information, coupled with attractive profile photos of young women or men, making their detection quite challenging.

Prior to this project, Renren had already deployed a suite of orthogonal techniques to detect Sybil accounts, including: using thresholds to detect spamming, scanning content for suspect keywords and blacklisted URLs, and providing Renren users with the ability to flag accounts and content as abusive. However, these techniques are generally ad-hoc, require significant human effort, and are effective only after spam content has been posted. To improve security for their users, Renren began a collaboration with our research team in December 2010 to augment their detection systems with a systematic, real-time solution. To support the project, Renren provided full access to user data and operational logs on their servers, as well as allowing us to test and deploy research prototypes of Sybil detectors on their operational network.

Defining Sybils. In this study, as in prior work [3, 17, 23, 24], we are interested in detecting and deterring the use of mass Sybil identities by malicious users. We broadly define Sybils as fake accounts created for the purpose of performing spam or privacy attacks against normal users. We observe that the main goal of Sybils is to increase the power of the attacker by amassing friend links to normal users, thus integrating themselves into the social graph. Attackers create many Sybils to increase their coverage of the graph, as well as to combat attrition from Sybils getting banned. Although penetrating the graph is simply a precursor for other malicious activity, our work is agnostic to these secondary goals, as well as the specific methods and tools used to create and manage the Sybils.

Our definition of Sybils *does not* include fake accounts generated by users for benign purposes, such as preserving privacy and anonymity, acting on behalf of young children, separating work and personal identities, *etc.* These "benign Sybils" act just like normal accounts, and therefor do not fall under our definition of malicious Sybils. As discussed in Section 2.3, benign Sybils are unlikely to be flagged by the techniques proposed in this work.

2.2 Characterizing Sybil Accounts

Our approach to building a real-time Sybil detector begins by first identifying features that distinguish Sybil accounts from normal users. To help, Renren provided us with two sets of user accounts, containing 1000 Sybil accounts and 1000 non-Sybil accounts, respectively. The Sybil accounts were previously identified using existing mechanisms. A volunteer team carefully scrutinized all accounts in both sets to confirm they were correctly classified by looking over detailed profile data, including uploaded photos, messages sent and received, email addresses, and shared content (blogs and web links).

[1] `http://www.renren.com`

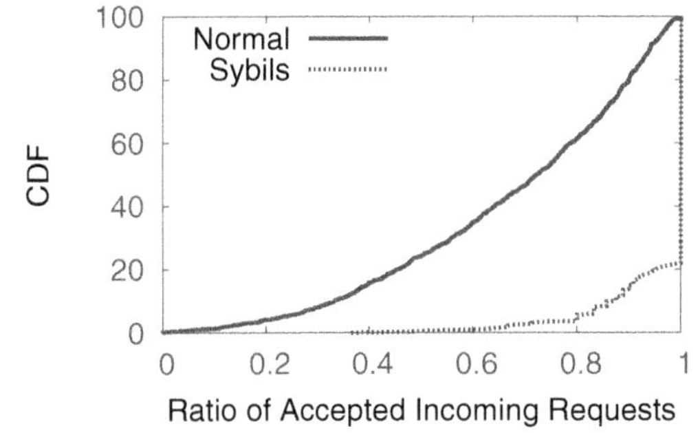

Figure 3: Ratio of accepted *incoming* friend requests.

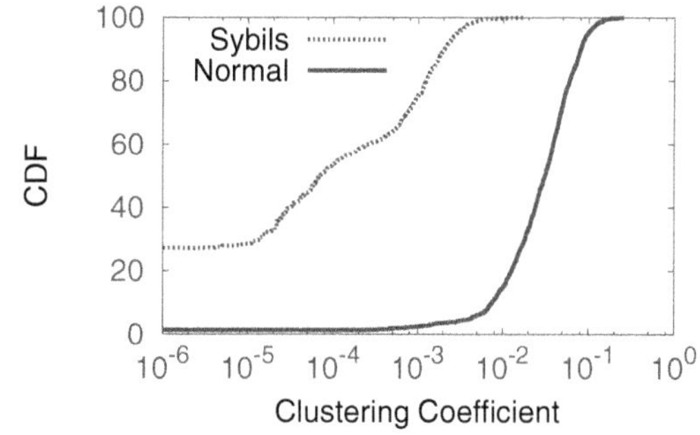

Figure 4: Clustering coefficient for users' 50 first friends.

Using this dataset as our ground truth, we searched for behavioral attributes that may serve to identify Sybil accounts. After examining a wide range of attributes, we found four potential identifiers. We describe them each in turn, and illustrate how they characterize accounts in our ground truth dataset.

Invitation Frequency. Invitation frequency is the number of friend requests a user has sent within a fixed time period (*e.g.,* an hour). Figure 1 shows the friend invitation frequency of our dataset, averaged over long term (400 hour) and short term (1 hour) time scales. Since adding friends is a goal for all Sybil accounts, they are much more aggressive in sending requests than normal users. There is a clear separation: accounts sending more than 20 invites per time interval are Sybils. This result holds true at both long and short time scales, meaning that invitation frequency can be used to detect Sybils without significant delays. For example, a threshold of 40 requests/hour can identify $\approx$70% of Sybils with no false positives. Prior to our work, Renren deployed a threshold based detector that forces users to solve a captcha if they send $\geq$50 requests in a day, which explains the apparent upper limit on friend requests.

Outgoing Requests Accepted. A second distinguishing feature is the fraction of outgoing friend requests confirmed by the recipient. The CDF shown in Figure 2 shows a distinct difference between Sybils and normal users. In general, non-Sybil users generally have high accepted ratios with an average of 79%. On average, however, only 26% of all friend requests sent by Sybil accounts are accepted. This is unsurprising, since normal users typically send invites to people with whom they have prior relationships, whereas Sybils target strangers.

Despite prior studies that show users accept requests indiscriminately [15, 16], our results show that most users can still effectively identify and decline invitations from Sybils. The fact that some users still accept requests from Sybils is explained by two factors. First, most Sybils target members of the opposite sex by using photos of attractive young men and women in their profiles. While women make up 46.5% of the overall Renren user population, they make up 77.3% of the Sybils in our dataset. Second, Sybils typically target popular, high degree users who are more likely to be careless about accepting friend requests from strangers. We further explore this point in Section 3.4.

Incoming Requests Accepted. Figure 3 plots a CDF of users by the fraction of incoming friend requests they accept. The incoming requests accepted by non-Sybil users are spread across the board. In contrast, Sybil accounts are nearly uniform in that they accept all incoming friend requests, *e.g.,* 80% of Sybils accepted all friend requests. In fact, many of the Sybils with <100% accept rate fall into this category because Renren banned them before they could respond to all outstanding requests. However, since Sybil accounts receive few friend requests, this mechanism can incur a significant delay before detecting Sybils.

		SVM Predicted		Threshold Predicted	
		Sybil	Non-Sybil	Sybil	Non-Sybil
True	Sybil	98.99%	1.01%	98.68%	1.32%
	Non-Sybil	0.66%	99.34%	0.5%	99.5%

Table 1: Performance of SVM and threshold classifiers.

Clustering Coefficient. Clustering coefficient (cc) is a graph metric that measures the mutual connectivity of a user's friends. Since normal users tend to have a small number of well-connected social cliques, we expect them to have much higher cc values than Sybil accounts, which are likely to befriend users with no mutual friendships. Figure 4 plots the CDF of cc values for each user's first 50 friends (sorted by time). As expected, non-Sybil users have cc values orders of magnitude larger than Sybil users (average cc values of 0.0386 and 0.0006 respectively). Since cc can be computed based on invitations only (*i.e.,* user responses are not required) it can potentially perform well as a real-time Sybil detection metric.

2.3 Building and Running a Sybil Detector

Our analysis results seem to indicate that a threshold based scheme can effectively detect most Sybil accounts. Our next step is to verify this assertion by comparing the efficacy of a simple threshold detection approach against a more complex learning algorithm.

We apply a support vector machine (SVM) classifier to our ground truth dataset of 1000 normal users and 1000 Sybils. We randomly partition the original sample into 5 sub-samples, 4 of which are used for training the classifier, and the last used to test the classifier. The results in Table 1 show that the classifier is very accurate, correctly identifying 99% of both Sybil and non-Sybil accounts. We compare these results to those of a threshold-based detector: *outgoing requests accepted ratio* $< 0.5 \wedge$ *frequency* $> 20 \wedge$ *cc* < 0.01. Our results show that a properly tuned threshold-based detector can achieve performance similar to the computationally expensive SVM.

Real-time Sybil Detection. Our analytical results using the ground-truth dataset led to the design of an adaptive, threshold-based Sybil detector that identifies Sybil accounts in near real-time. The detector monitors all accounts using a combination of friend-request frequency, outgoing request acceptance rates, and clustering coefficient. It uses an adaptive feedback scheme to dynamically tune threshold parameters on the fly[2]. Tuning the thresholds minimizes the likelihood of false positive classifications of normal accounts as Sybils. Because our system works by detecting abnor-

[2]We omit details of the adaptive scheme for Renren's security and confidentiality.

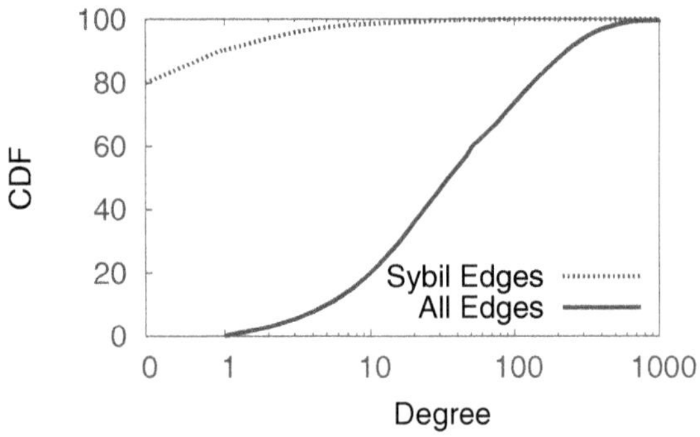

Figure 5: The degree of Sybil accounts.

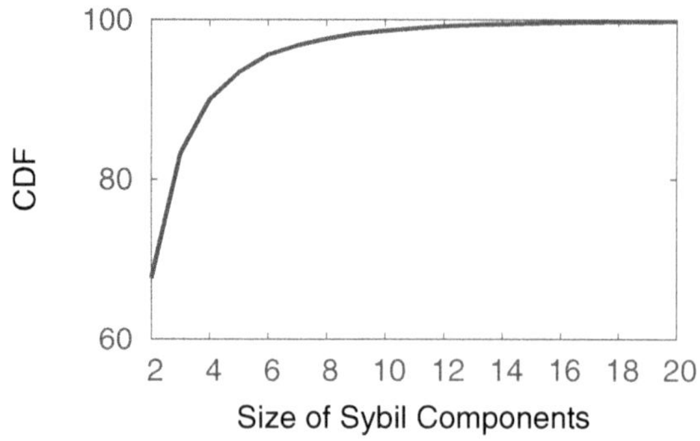

Figure 6: The size of connected Sybil components.

mal behavior in friending or content dissemination, it is unlikely to detect benign Sybils that behave like normal users.

After offline testing, Renren deployed our Sybil detection mechanism in late August 2010, and it has been in continuous operation ever since. From August 2010 to February 2011, Renren administrators used our mechanism to detect and subsequently ban ~100,000 Sybil accounts in Renren. In addition to these accounts, Renren provided us with data on ~560,000 accounts that were detected and banned using prior techniques from 2008 to February 2011. For the remainder of this paper, we will use all of these Sybil accounts (660,000 in all) to study the behavior of Sybil accounts.

Sybil Account Behavior. We confirmed that the Sybil accounts identified by our detector are actually malicious by analyzing the content generated by these accounts. Offline analysis confirmed that 67% of content generated by Sybils trips Renren's spam detectors (*e.g.*, suspicious keyword filter, blacklisted URLs, *etc.*). Of the remaining accounts, the vast majority were banned before they had a chance to generate any content. Analysis of spam keywords and campaign clusters produces results that are consistent with prior work on OSN spam [5, 6], and we omit the results for brevity.

False Positives. To assess false positives, we examine feedback to Renren's customer support department. Renren operates a telephone number and e-mail address where customers whose accounts have been banned for abuse can attempt to get the account reinstated. Complaints are evaluated by a human operator, who determines if the account was banned erroneously.

We use the complaint rate, measured as the number of complaints per-day divided by the number of accounts banned per-day, as an upper-bound on false positives. During the two week period between Dec. 13-26, 2010, Renren received ~50 complaints per-day, with the complaint rate being ~0.015, which is extremely low. Of these complaints, manual inspection confirms that 48% of the accounts are Sybils, meaning that attackers attempted to recover Sybils by abusing the account recovery process. The majority of the remaining complaints can be attributed to compromised accounts. Thus, the true false positive rate is even less than the daily complaint rate.

3. SYBIL TOPOLOGY

In this section we analyze the graph topological characteristics of Sybils on Renren. In particular, we are interested in analyzing whether Sybils in the wild are vulnerable to identification using the community-based Sybil detectors that have been proposed by researchers. Our results show that Sybils on Renren do not conform to the assumptions of existing work. Analysis of the degree distribution of Sybil accounts demonstrates that, contrary to expectations, the vast majority of Sybils do not form social links with other Sybils. Furthermore, temporal analysis of social links between Sybils indicates that these connections are often formed randomly by accident, rather than intentionally by attacker.

3.1 Sybil Community Detectors

SybilGuard [24], SybilLimit [23], SybilInfer [3], and SumUp [17] are all algorithms for performing decentralized detection of Sybil nodes on social graphs. At their core, all of these algorithms are based on two assumptions of Sybil and normal user behavior:

1. Attackers can create unlimited Sybils and form edges between them. Edges between Sybils are beneficial since they make Sybils appear more legitimate to normal users.
2. The number of edges between Sybils and normal users will be limited, since normal users are unlikely to accept friend requests from unknown strangers.

Under these assumptions, Sybils tend to form tight knit clusters, since the number of edges between Sybils is greater than the number of edges connecting to normal users. We refer to edges between Sybils as *Sybil edges*, while edges connecting Sybils and normal users are called *attack edges*.

Sybil detection algorithms identify Sybil clusters by locating the small number of edge cuts that separate the Sybil region from the social graph. SybilGuard, SybilLimit, and SybilInfer all leverage specially engineered random walks for this purpose, while SumUp uses a max-flow approach. Although all of these algorithms are implemented differently, it has been shown that they all generalize to the problem of detecting communities of Sybil nodes [18].

Although these four algorithms have been shown to work on synthetic graphs (*i.e.*, real social graphs with Sybil communities artificially injected), to date no studies have demonstrated their efficacy at detecting Sybils in the wild. In the following sections, we examine the characteristics of Sybils on Renren in order to ascertain whether they are amenable to identification by community-based Sybil detectors.

3.2 Sybil Edges

We begin our analysis of Sybil topology by examining the degree distribution of Sybil accounts on Renren. Our goal is to test the most basic assumption of community-based Sybil detectors: do Sybils in the wild form tight-knit communities? In order for Sybils to cluster, they must have at least one edge connecting to another Sybil, otherwise they will be disconnected.

Figure 5 shows the degree distribution of all 667,723 Sybil accounts. When all edges are considered, the degree distribution is unremarkable: it follows the same general trend that has been observed on numerous other OSNs [21].

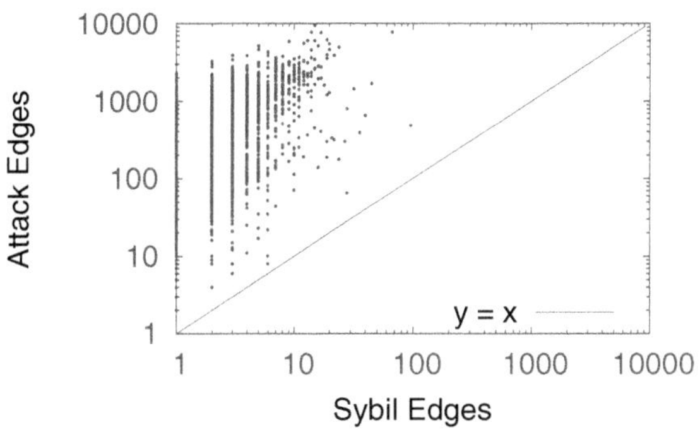

Figure 7: Scatter plot of Sybil edges vs. attack edges for Sybil components on Renren.

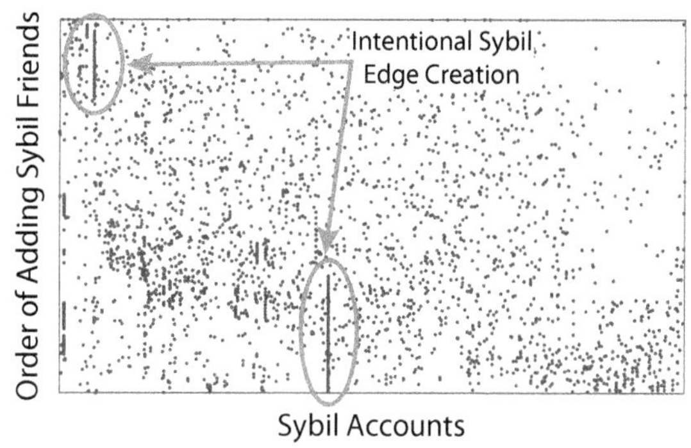

Figure 8: The order of adding Sybil friends for 1,000 Sybils. Each column represents an individual Sybil.

Sybils	Sybil Edges	Attack Edges	Audience
63,541	134,941	9,848,881	6,497,179
631	1153	104,074	21,014
68	67	7,761	7,702
51	50	15,349	15,179
37	40	14,431	13,886

Table 2: Statistics for the five largest Sybil components.

However, when we restrict the distribution to only edges between Sybils, we discover an unexpected result: only 20% of Sybils are friends with one or more other Sybils. This indicates that the vast majority of Sybils do not demonstrate any sort of clustering behavior with other Sybils. Rather, most Sybils only form attack edges, and thus totally integrate into the normal social graph.

3.3 Sybil Communities

We now shift our focus to the minority of Sybils that do connect to other Sybils. Although we can conclude from Figure 5 that most Sybils in the wild do not obey the key assumption of community-based Sybil detectors, it is still possible that the connected minority are vulnerable to community detection. Thus, we now seek to answer the following questions: what are the characteristics of Sybil communities on Renren, and would community-based Sybil detectors be able to identify them?

To bootstrap our analysis, we construct a graph consisting solely of Sybils with at least one edge to another Sybil. The resulting graph is highly fragmented: it consists of 7,094 separate connected components. Figure 6 shows the size distribution of these Sybil components. The distribution is heavy tailed: although 98% of Sybil components have less than 10 members, the vast majority of Sybil accounts belong to a single, large connected component. Table 2 lists the details for the five largest Sybil components.

In order for Sybil communities to be identifiable by existing algorithms, they must form tight knit communities. Put another way, the number of Sybil edges inside the community must be greater than the number of attack edges that connect to the normal population. However, as shown in Table 2, this assumption does not hold for the largest Sybil components on Renren.

Figure 7 shows a scatter plot comparing the number of Sybil edges and attack edges in each Sybil component on Renren. All components are above the 45° line, meaning that they have more attack edges than Sybil edges. Thus, no components meet the requirements for detection using existing community-based Sybil identification algorithms.

3.4 Sybil Edge Formation

We now examine the processes driving the formation of Sybil edges on Renren. In particular, we seek to determine if edges between Sybil nodes are intentionally created by attackers. If they are, then this means that community detection may still be a viable approach to detecting Sybils on OSNs. However, if Sybil edges are not created intentionally, then this raises a new question: what process drives the accidental creation of Sybil edges?

Temporal Characteristics. One simple litmus test for identifying intentional Sybil edge creation is examining the order in which edges were established. If Sybil edges are formed intentionally by attackers, then we would expect to see them created sequentially, before friend requests are sent out to normal users. This behavior maximizes the utility of Sybil edges by giving Sybils the appearance of "normal" friend relations, thus (potentially) deceiving normal users into accepting friend requests from Sybils.

Figure 8 shows the order in which edges were created for 1,000 random Sybils drawn from the largest Sybil component on Renren (containing 63,541 Sybils). For each Sybil i with n edges, we construct the sequence $\langle f_1, f_2, \ldots, f_n \rangle$, where f_i is an edge, and the sequence is sorted chronologically by creation time. Each column of the figure shows the sequence of edge creations for a particular Sybil, with black dots representing Sybil edges.

As shown in Figure 8, the order of Sybil edge creation is almost uniformly random. This indicates that the vast majority of Sybil edges in the large component were formed accidentally: attackers had no intention to link Sybils together and form a connected component. Intentionally created connections between Sybils appear as solid vertical lines in the figure. We highlight two examples in Figure 8 by circling them. It is unclear why a tiny minority of Sybils exhibit correlated behavior; we are currently studying this behavior as part of our ongoing work.

Sybil Degree. In order to reinforce the idea that the vast majority of Sybil edges in the large component are not intentionally created, we plot the degree distribution of the large component in Figure 9. 34.5% of Sybils only connect to 1 other Sybil, and 93.7% connect to ≤ 10. It is unlikely that an attacker would expend the effort to link Sybils in such a loose way, since these edge counts are not high enough to make Sybils appear legitimate to normal users.

Snowball Sampling. At this point we have established that attackers do not create the vast majority of Sybil edges intentionally; instead, they appear to occur randomly by accident. To understand how this happens, we conducted a brief survey of three software tools used to manage Sybil accounts on Renren. The details for

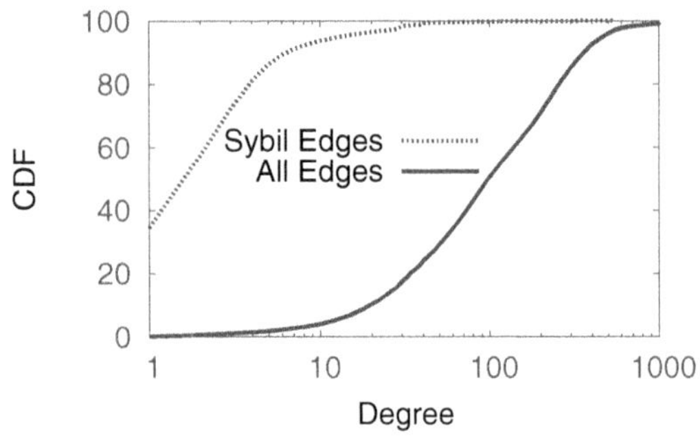

Figure 9: Degree distribution of the largest Sybil component.

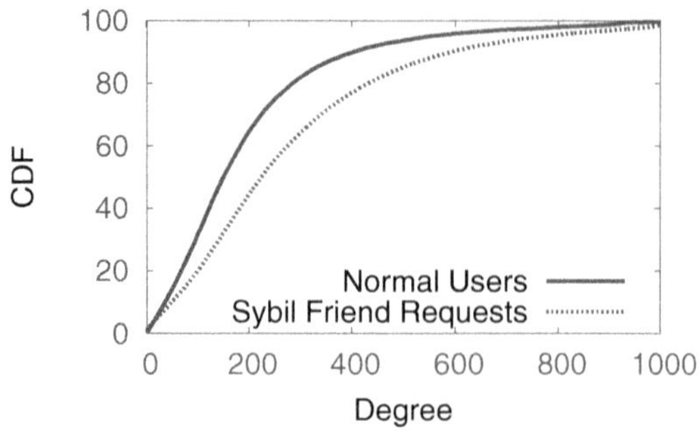

Figure 10: Degree distribution of normal users (from [7]) and targets of friend requests from Sybils.

Tool Name & URL	Platform	Cost
Renren Marketing Assistant V1.0 http://www.duote.com/soft/30348.html	Windows	$37
Renren Super Node Collector V1.0 http://www.snstools.com/snstool/86.html	Windows	Contact Author
Renren Almighty Assistant V5.8 http://www.sns78.com/	Windows	Contact Author

Table 3: Popular Sybil creation and management tools.

each tool are given in Table 3. The purpose of these tools is to automate the process of creating Renren accounts, forming edges between the Sybils and other users, and posting content en-mass.

The documentation for the tools in Table 3 state that they select targets for friending by performing snowball sampling on the social graph to locate popular users. Although we cannot be certain whether the Sybils in our dataset were created using the tools in Table 3, we can show that Sybils on Renren do bias friend requests towards high degree nodes. Figure 10 shows the degree distribution for all users that received friend requests from Sybils, and illustrates that it is skewed towards high degrees when compared to the actual degree distribution of the Renren population [7].

Based on the advertised functionality of these tools, and the results in Figure 10, we can surmise that Sybil edges are created accidentally due to two factors. First, the goal of Sybils is to accrue many friends by sending out numerous friend requests. If a Sybil is successful, it becomes popular by virtue of its large social degree. Second, the snowball sampling performed by Sybil management tools is intentionally biased towards locating popular users. Thus, it is likely that these tools will, unbeknownst to the attacker, occasionally select Sybil nodes to send friend requests to. As shown in Figure 3, Sybils almost always accept incoming friend requests, hence when this situation arises a Sybil edge is likely to be created.

4. RELATED WORK

OSN Spam. Recent studies have characterized the growing OSN spam problem on Facebook [5] and Twitter [6]. These studies rely on offline heuristics to identify spam content in status updates/tweets, as well as aberrant behavior that is indicative of spamming. The authors locate millions of spam messages on each OSN, and use them to analyze the large scale, coordinated spam campaigns. In contrast, our study is focused on the graph topological characteristics of malicious accounts, rather than spam content.

OSN Spam Detection. Various techniques borrowed from e-mail spam detection have been applied to OSN spam. Webb et al. use honeypot accounts on MySpace to trap spammers who attempt to friend them [20]. Our results indicate that unless social honeypots are engineered to appear popular, they are unlikely to be targeted by spammers.

Other studies have leveraged Bayesian filters and SVMs to identify spammers on Twitter [2,19,22] and Facebook [16]. These techniques work well on Twitter, since Sybil friending behavior can be identified using publicly available following and followed information. However, detection on OSNs like Facebook and Renren is less successful, since only existing friendships are publicly viewable, while invitation frequency is hidden. Our Sybil detector overcomes this issue by leveraging friend invitation information that is only accessible from within Renren.

5. CONCLUSION

In this paper we make two contributions to the area of Sybil detection on OSNs. First, we use ground-truth data about the behavior of Sybils in the wild to create a measurement-based, real-time Sybil detector. We show that a computationally efficient, threshold-based classifier is sufficient to catch 99% of Sybils, with low false positive and negative rates. We have deployed our detector on Renren's production systems, and to date it has led to the identification and banning of over 100,000 Sybil accounts.

Our second contribution is a first-of-its-kind characterization of Sybil graph topology on a major online social network. Using edge creation information for over 660,000 Sybil accounts on Renren, we show that Sybils on Renren do not obey behavioral assumptions that underlie previous work on decentralized Sybil detectors. 80% of Sybils do not connect socially to other Sybils, but instead focus on building friendships with normal users. Even in rare cases where Sybils do form connected components, these clusters are loose, rather than tightly knit. Temporal analysis indicates that these Sybil edges are formed accidentally by attackers, rather than intentionally.

Although we cannot be sure that our results generalize to all OSNs, our findings for a traditional, *i.e.*, untrusted, OSN, coupled with results from prior work on trusted OSNs [11], suggest that we should explore new approaches to perform decentralized detection of Sybil accounts on OSNs.

Acknowledgments

We thank the anonymous reviewers for their comments. This material is based in part upon work supported by the National Science Foundation under grants IIS-0916307 and IIS-847925. Any opinions, findings, and conclusions or recommendations expressed in this material are those of the authors and do not necessarily reflect the views of the National Science Foundation. This work is also supported in part by South Korea National Research Foundation under the World Class University program, and the National Basic Research Program of China (Grant No.2011CB302305).

6. REFERENCES

[1] BAUER, K., MCCOY, D., GRUNWALD, D., KOHNO, T., AND SICKER, D. Low-resource routing attacks against tor. In *Proc. of Workshop on Privacy in Electronic Society* (Alexandria, VA, 2007).

[2] BENEVENUTO, F., MAGNO, G., RODRIGUES, T., AND ALMEIDA, V. Detecting spammers on twitter. In *Proc. of CEAS* (Redmond, WA, July 2010).

[3] DANEZIS, G., AND MITTAL, P. Sybilinfer: Detecting sybil nodes using social networks. In *Proc of NDSS* (2009).

[4] DOUCEUR, J. R. The Sybil attack. In *Proc. of IPTPS* (March 2002).

[5] GAO, H., HU, J., WILSON, C., LI, Z., CHEN, Y., AND ZHAO, B. Y. Detecting and characterizing social spam campaigns. In *Proc. of IMC* (2010).

[6] GRIER, C., THOMAS, K., PAXSON, V., AND ZHANG, M. @spam: the underground on 140 characters or less. In *Proc. of CCS* (2010).

[7] JIANG, J., WILSON, C., WANG, X., HUANG, P., SHA, W., DAI, Y., AND ZHAO, B. Y. Understanding latent interactions in online social networks. In *Proc. of IMC* (2010).

[8] KWAK, H., LEE, C., PARK, H., AND MOON, S. B. What is twitter, a social network or a news media? In *Proc. of World Wide Web Conference* (Raleigh, NC, April 2010).

[9] LENHART, A., PURCELL, K., SMITH, A., AND ZICKUHR, K. Social media and young adults. Pew Research Center, February 2010.

[10] LIAN, Q., ZHANG, Z., YANG, M., ZHAO, B. Y., DAI, Y., AND LI, X. An empirical study of collusion behavior in the maze p2p file-sharing system. In *Proc. of ICDCS* (June 2007).

[11] MOHAISEN, A., YUN, A., AND KIM, Y. Measuring the Mixing Time of Social Graphs. In *Proc. of IMC* (2010).

[12] MURPHY, S. Teens ditch e-mail for texting and facebook. MSNBC.com, Aug 2010.

[13] NAZIR, A., RAZA, S., CHUAH, C.-N., AND SCHIPPER, B. Ghostbusting facebook: Detecting and characterizing phantom profiles in online social gaming applications. In *Proc. of SIGCOMM WOSN* (June 2010).

[14] NEWSOME, J., SHI, E., SONG, D., AND PERRIG, A. The sybil attack in sensor networks: Analysis & defenses. In *Proc. of IPSN* (Berkeley, CA, 2004).

[15] SOPHOS. Sophos Facebook ID probe shows 41% of users happy to reveal all to potential identity thieves. `http://www.sophos.com/pressoffice/news/articles/2007/08/facebook.html`, 2007.

[16] STRINGHINI, G., KRUEGEL, C., AND VIGNA, G. Detecting spammers on social networks. In *Proc. of ACSAC* (Austin, TX, December 2010).

[17] TRAN, N., MIN, B., LI, J., AND SUBRAMANIAN, L. Sybil-resilient online content voting. In *Proc. of NSDI* (2009).

[18] VISWANATH, B., POST, A., GUMMADI, K. P., AND MISLOVE, A. An analysis of social network-based sybil defenses. In *Proc. of SIGCOMM* (2010).

[19] WANG, A. H. Don't follow me: Spam detection on twitter. In *Proc. of SECRYPT* (Athens, Greece, July 2010).

[20] WEBB, S., CAVERLEE, J., AND PU, C. Social honeypots: Making friends with a spammer near you. In *Proc of CEAS* (Mountain View, CA, August 2008).

[21] WILSON, C., BOE, B., SALA, A., PUTTASWAMY, K. P. N., AND ZHAO, B. Y. User interactions in social networks and their implications. In *Proc. of EuroSys* (April 2009).

[22] YARDI, S., ROMERO, D., SCHOENEBECK, G., AND BOYD, D. Detecting spam in a twitter network. *First Monday 15*, 1 (2010).

[23] YU, H., GIBBONS, P. B., KAMINSKY, M., AND XIAO, F. Sybillimit: A near-optimal social network defense against sybil attacks. In *Proc. of IEEE S&P* (2008).

[24] YU, H., KAMINSKY, M., GIBBONS, P. B., AND FLAXMAN, A. Sybilguard: defending against sybil attacks via social networks. In *Proc. of SIGCOMM* (2006).

Summary Review Documentation for

"Uncovering Social Network Sybils in the Wild"

Authors: Z. Yang, C. Wilson, X. Wang, T. Gao, B. Zhao, Y. Dai

Reviewer #1

Strengths: The data set is particularly interesting; merely having the ground truth about Sybils is remarkable, and the authors use it well to infer the behavior of Sybil-generators. The results are exceptionally important for social networking research.

Weaknesses: Sybils in Renren have little utility in forming tightly-knit Sybil communities, unlike other social networks such as recommendation systems. It is unclear that the results on Renren sufficiently invalidate the usefulness of Sybil detection algorithms that rely on the assumption of few attack edges for other social networks.

Sybils are presumably being created for a specific reason, to launch a specific attack; there is no need for Sybil-to-Sybil links to launch such attacks (spamming and/or privacy violation attacks) on Renren, but since there is a use for Sybil-to-Sybil links on something like eBay or Amazon (recommendation poisoning attacks), a similar analysis of the social networks on those sites may have very different results.

Comments to Authors: This is a fantastic paper, and the main complaint is the one about the structure of Sybils being different in different networks. It would be good to see this mentioned in the paper as a limitation of the study, though as presented, this work is incredibly valuable and a significant contribution to the field.

One concern that I have that is perhaps out of the scope of this paper is that the metrics used to characterize Sybil accounts can all be, to some extent, controlled by the Sybil generators through a combination of rate limiting and the addition of more Sybils. A clever attacker who is aware of these detection algorithms could thwart it. Though having such an algorithm may limit the speed with which the attacker can generate Sybil identities, it's not clear that they can't simply create more Sybil identities to compensate. This is not really a criticism: this is a typical result of the ongoing battle against spam, where attackers have the advantage because the defenders generally have to reveal what they're doing to some extent.

Finally, and again this is outside of the scope of the paper, it would be interesting to consider impersonation-style Sybils as well. Perhaps such Sybils are less common or harder to detect, so it may be very difficult to repeat your study on these Sybils. However, that these Sybils are radically different from the more random, optimistic attachment Sybils, both in terms of your detection metrics and in terms of their internal clustering.

Minor notes: It is not clear if existing algorithms missed the 100,000 Sybils that were detected using the techniques in this paper. Also, how were the 560,000 Sybils previously found verified to be Sybils?

Reviewer #2

Strengths: The paper involves a very unique data set. The authors' work is being used in practice.

Weaknesses: A very loose definition of Sybil is used. There is a lack of evidence provided that demonstrates all of the users labeled as Sybils are actually malicious (i.e., the paper fails to demonstrate that Hanlon's razor is not applicable).

Comments to Authors: My primary concerns with the paper start with the definition of what a sybil account is. I agree with the first part: "Sybil accounts are fake identities"; I could even agree with the remainder of the definition ("created to unfairly increase the power or resources of a single malicious user"), if "malicious" were properly defined. However, no definition is provided; it simply lumps all users with multiple online identities together, whether they are hackers intending to steal identities, content or other resources, miscreants attempting to propagate spam in OSNs, or simply teenagers having fun. While the latter activities may be considered malicious for some definitions of the word, it is usually harmless fun. Since the paper does not appear to discriminate between different reasons for having multiple online personalities, the results are not that compelling in my opinion; dealing with hackers and spammers is an important matter, addressing users expressions of their individuality is something completely different.

Stated differently, Hanlon's razor reads "Never attribute to malice that which is adequately explained by stupidity." The latter is certainly responsible for at least some of the fake identities on OSNs. As a result, the authors need to provide evidence of malice, to distinguish the detrimental cases from the seemingly harmless ones. The paper fails to do this, which is why I cannot rate it higher. I do think that the topic is an important one, so the authors should continue their work on it.

Section 1: (i) Clarify what is meant by "infiltrating social games"? If no financial gain is possible, is creating numerous players for one's self really malicious? (ii) I agree that certain attacks need to be curtailed to prevent the general public from losing confidence in OSNs; however, I don't see that eliminating all instances of "multiple personalities" is going to solve this issue. (iii) What evidence do you have that each of the 100,000 "Sybil users" attempted any sort of malicious activity?

Section 2: (i) If "Renren provided full access to user data and operational logs", then where is the evidence that the users you labeled as "Sybil" conducted malicious acts? (ii) What evidence is there that the Sybil accounts provided as ground truth were malicious? Did Renren use the same broad definition of malicious? (iii) The last sentence assumes that there are no "stealth" sybils in the "other" population; you have no proof of this.

Section 3: (i) Were any of these Sybils reported for malicious activity, such as sending spam? The paper provides no validation of the claims being made. (ii)- The discussion of Figure 8 assumes that you have positively identified all Sybils, of which there is no proof. (iii) Why would you expect Sybil edges to be created sequentially?

Section 4: While your study may not involve characterizing "spam content", it should involve finding evidence to support your claims that the users labeled as Sybils have actually done at least one malicious activity.

Section 5: The results section did not demonstrate that 99% of Sybils in the data set were identified "with low false positive and negative rates"; this is a key shortcoming of the paper.

Reviewer #3

Strengths: Access to a unique dataset (ground truth for sybil account), reasonable analysis.

Weaknesses: Important details about verifying sybil account (ground truth) and the proposed detection techniques are missing.

Comments to Authors: This clearly written paper benefits from the provided dataset and close collaborations with Renren OSN in China to characterize sybil accounts, uses these characterizations to devise a detection technique. Also using detected sybil accounts to examine their topological properties that appears to debunk the common assumptions about their tight connectivity. Most of the description in the paper seems reasonable. There are a few issues that deserve further clarifications by authors.

1. The key break that enables this study is the availability of confirmed sybil account that are used to bootstrap the identification process. Authors rely on identified sybil account by RenRen based on examination of many attributes (as stated in subsection 2.2). One of the main difficulties is to make sure that an account is indeed a sybil account. This leads to an important question that what tests were conducted on these accounts to ensure that they are indeed sybil? If the identification of sybil accounts are based on the attributes that are presented in subsection 2.3, there is no surprise here. Renren filtered these account based on the four attributes and authors showed that these attributes are different for sybil account. The paper should elaborate on this issue.
2. Authors present only 4 attributes for distinguishing sybil account from many they have examined. It is useful if authors at least briefly mention what other attributes were examined and to what extent they separated sybil from non-sybil accounts, and possibly describe why.
3. Authors suggest that threshold based sybil detection technique works (in subsec 2.3) without providing any information on its success rate. Ironically, the proposed adaptive version of threshold based detection is not described at all!
4. It is not clear to me what the sybil creation and management tools are and how authors got access to them to determine sampling technique used by sybil users. If such tools are available, why are they used to determine many other behaviors of sybil users?
5. One other lingering question is whether all the sybil accounts are related to each other or more likely they belong to different groups. How can this be examined from the connectivity among these accounts?

Reviewer #4

Strengths: The dataset is unique, and the measurements extracted well presented.

Weaknesses: The paper is imprecise: does not define Sybil, does not describe false positives or negatives, does not claim to detect Sybils other than those generated by commercial tools, oversells its contribution and overstates its conclusions.

Comments to Authors: Great problem domain, great dataset. However, I found this paper frustrating.

First problem (no Sybil definition): The goal of being a Sybil in Renren isn't well described. Why do it? Is it the same reason why one would create Sybils in eBay? Or Twitter? Or for Facebook games? No. At this point, you're dealing with what might be a different type of Sybil than researchers often look at, and in turn, your general statements about sybils aren't well-founded. The only passage present is (too late) on page 6 "the goal of Sybils is to accrue many friends by sending out numerous friend requests." This doesn't seem to be the real goal: popularity for its own sake doesn't make money.

First problem, part 2 (Biased Sybil detection): Are *all* types of Sybils discovered by the tool or just the type that are generated by the tools described on page 6? Are there false users for other reasons present in the data set? Are the Sybils in the known-to-be-Sybil set representative? Or are they just the type of Sybils that Renren administrators find to be the most annoying? How were they found? Was a random set of users chosen to provide truly identifying information to renew their accounts? I find an unbiased Sybil detection scheme unlikely, and no details are provided for how known-Sybils are found.

Second problem (Unfounded generalization): What if the Sybils you deal with are selfish and not that bright while the Sybils researchers have dealt with in the past are clever and evil? Vern Paxson published a lovely paper (How to 0wn the Internet...) that suggested what havoc could be wrought by clever, evil Internet worms, and such a paper states a case for defending against the worst case, rather than the typical case. The expectation in section 3, "contrary to expectations, the vast majority do not form social links with other Sybil accounts" and the conclusion in section 5 is then wildly overstated, "Sybils in the wild do not obey behavioral assumptions that underlie previous work on decentralized Sybil detectors". Is it the case that the Sybils to be detected are those bent on manipulating reputation metrics in other networks while the Sybils here are just spammers? Should the "Sybil" name apply for this? Do there need to be many of them for the attacks in your paper?

Third problem (explanation): WHY do sybils behave in the way discovered? Is it for getting better penetration? Or is it for avoiding detection? Such explanation of what you observe would be easy if the goal of a Sybil in Renren (or the goal of Renren in protecting its network) were better described.

It appears that the main mismatch you've encountered is research literature designed to protect against worst case attacks, while Renren is manipulated for different purposes to by different means.

That said, it's good data, and a reasonable contribution for a short paper. The paper just could have been written to rely on the data and the dataset, as well as to present the measurement methodology well and analyze the measurement errors properly, without the unnecessary generalization to all Sybils in all social networks.

Reviewer #5

Strengths: The real-world data set used in the paper is impressive. The analysis on Sybil identities in section 3 is thorough. And it is interesting to see that the finding from the real dataset contradicts the baseline assumption of many previous works on Sybil attack defense.

Weaknesses: The paper does not suggest any significant methodology for the detection of Sybil attacks in general setup. While there are some evidence that sybil edges are created intentionally, the paper omits discussion on it.

Comments to Authors: This is a well-written paper. The flow of the paper is smooth and the level of detail is adequate (except for Section 2.3). My concerns about the paper are the following:

1. While the paper points out the flawed assumptions in previously suggested Sybil detection schemes, it does not suggest any new methodologies on its own. To me, the methodology outlined in Section 2.3. is not directly applicable outside Renren OSN for the following two reasons: First, for each OSN the tool is applied to, it may require a significant amount of man-hour to hand-pick Sybil and non-Sybil identity data in order to train SVM classifier. Second, its classifier requires prior knowledge on a set of good thresholds on <outgoing requests acceptance ratio, frequency, and cc>.
2. In the introduction and at the beginning of section 3, the paper claims that the links between Sybils are formed by accident. However, in Figure 8, there are evidences that there are edges created intentionally by Sybil accounts. I am curious to see why there are few but obvious attempts from some Sybil accounts to connect among them. Can they be the only real Sybil accounts by any chance?

Response from the Authors

We thank all the anonymous reviewers for their time and comments. The camera-ready version of this paper includes several changes and additions in order to address the reviewer's comments.

First, the language of the paper has been adjusted to make it clear that we are focused on analyzing Sybils on untrusted social networks like Facebook and Renren. We acknowledge that our results may not generalize to trusted OSNs like DBLP or Epinions, where edges correspond to real-world trust between users.

Second, additional text has been added in Section 2.1 to clearly define what we consider to be a Sybil account. Our definition is generic, in agreement with definitions from prior work, and not dependent on particular features of Renren or specific tools used by attackers. We note that benign Sybils created by normal users (e.g. to protect individual privacy) are not included in our Sybil definition, and the new text explains why they unlikely to be caught by the techniques proposed in the paper.

Third, in Section 2.3 we address the question "what are Sybil accounts on Renren used for?" We briefly examine the malicious behaviors of Sybil accounts on Renren, and confirm that the majority are used to disseminate spam. Analysis of the generated spam confirms that it exhibits the same salient properties as prior studies on OSN spam.

Fourth, also in Section 2.3, we have added new paragraphs on the false positives of our Sybil detection methodology. We use the complaint rate to Renren's customer service department as the signal to examine how many accounts are erroneously classified and banned as Sybils. Our results show that the false positive detection rate of our techniques is very low.

Fifth, additional text has been added to Section 3.4 discussing Sybil management tools. We acknowledge that the tools listed in the paper are only a small subset of possible tools, and we have no way of confirming whether the Sybils we identified were created using them. However, we have added a new Figure 10 demonstrating that Sybils do exhibit bias towards high degree nodes when selecting targets to friend, which accords with our understanding of the features of popular Sybil management tools.

Lastly, new details on Renren's Sybil detection methods, prior to the deployment of our tool, have been added to Sections 2.1 and 2.2. These existing measures help to explain artifacts in Figure 1.

Monitoring the Initial DNS Behavior of Malicious Domains

Shuang Hao
Georgia Tech
Atlanta, GA, USA
shao@cc.gatech.edu

Nick Feamster
Georgia Tech
Atlanta, GA, USA
feamster@cc.gatech.edu

Ramakant Pandrangi
Verisign, Inc.
Dulles, VA, USA
rpandrangi@verisign.com

ABSTRACT

Attackers often use URLs to advertise scams or propagate malware. Because the reputation of a domain can be used to identify malicious behavior, miscreants often register these domains "just in time" before an attack. This paper explores the DNS behavior of attack domains, as identified by appearance in a spam trap, shortly after the domains were registered. We explore the behavioral properties of these domains from two perspectives: (1) the *DNS infrastructure* associated with the domain, as is observable from the resource records; and (2) the *DNS lookup patterns* from networks who are looking up the domains initially. Our analysis yields many findings that may ultimately be useful for early detection of malicious domains. By monitoring the infrastructure for these malicious domains, we find that about 55% of scam domains occur in attacks at least one day after registration, suggesting the potential for early discovery of malicious domains, solely based on properties of the DNS infrastructure that resolves those domains. We also find that there are a few regions of IP address space that host name servers and other types of servers for only malicious domains. Malicious domains have resource records that are distributed more widely across IP address space, and they are more quickly looked up by a variety of different networks. We also identify a set of "tainted" ASes that are used heavily by bad domains to host resource records. The features we observe are often evident before any attack even takes place; ultimately, they might serve as the basis for a DNS-based early warning system for attacks.

Categories and Subject Descriptors

C.2.3 [**Computer-Communication Networks**]: Network Operations—*Network monitoring*; K.6.5 [**Management of Computing and Information Systems**]: Security and Protection

General Terms

Measurement, Security

Keywords

DNS, Domain Registration, Spam, Malicious Domain

IMC'11, November 2–4, 2011, Berlin, Germany.

1. INTRODUCTION

The Domain Name System (DNS), the Internet's lookup service for mapping names to IP addresses, provides a critical service for Internet applications; unfortunately, it also allows attackers to direct victims to Web sites that host scams, malware, and other malicious content. To mitigate these threats, network operators try to derive a reputation for each domain that reflects the likelihood that the domain is associated with a particular type of attack (e.g., scam, phishing, malware hosting). The rate at which new domains appear makes quickly developing a reputation for these domains particularly challenging: in our analysis, we find that over tens of thousands of new domains are registered every day. Existing DNS reputation systems use the characteristics of DNS lookups from resolvers that look up a domain to distinguish legitimate from malicious domains [1, 2]. Unfortunately, these systems must observe a significant volume of DNS lookups before determining the reputation for a domain, which only occurs *after* compromise has taken place.

Towards facilitating pre-attack detection of malicious domains, we study the initial DNS activity for each domain and characterize how the observable behavior for a malicious domain differs from that of legitimate domains. We study two aspects of initial DNS behavior associated with domains: (1) the *DNS infrastructure* used to resolve the domains to IP addresses; and (2) the *DNS lookup patterns* from the networks that perform initial lookups to the domain. Certain characteristics of the DNS infrastructure may be unique to malicious domains, such as the IP address ranges and ASes that host either the authoritative name servers for the sites, or the sites themselves. Identifying infrastructure that is common across malicious domains may provide hints for identifying malicious domains before the attacks themselves are mounted. Characteristics of early DNS lookups can help network operators discover valuable information about the nature of the domains that are being looked up. Notably, we find that domains that are registered for malicious purposes are initially queried from a much more diverse set of subnets than legitimate domains.

Our study of DNS behavior early in a domain's life cycle is motivated by our ultimate desire to perform early detection of malicious domains. We use domains collected at several large spam traps as a source of domains associated with spam campaigns. To characterize the resource record behavior of each domain, we perform periodic iterative queries of newly registered domains in March 2011. To characterize DNS lookup patterns across networks, we use information about DNS lookups collected from the Verisign top-level domain servers, coupled with registration information about these domains.

We focus exclusively on the early DNS behavior of a domain, which is enabled by two important pieces of information. First, registration records alert us when a domain is registered, and allow us to begin querying it immediately, before attacks. Second, we study a global view of early DNS lookup patterns across the entire Internet for `.com` and `.net` domains. Our study reveals the following findings:

- *Domain registration and resource record establishment happens before attacks take place.* As many as 55% of spam campaigns may occur at least one day after the domain referenced in the spam messages were registered, offering the potential for early discovery of malicious domains based on initial DNS behavior.
- *DNS infrastructure for malicious domains is located in different address space regions and autonomous systems than the infrastructure for legitimate domains.* A few autonomous systems and IP address regions host infrastructure only for domains that are associated with malicious activity. Identifying these at domain registration time can potentially enable early detection.
- *Early lookup patterns for a newly registered malicious domains differ significantly from the patterns for a legitimate domain.* Domains associated with spam campaigns are initially looked up by a more diverse set of network address regions than legitimate domains. Especially, the newly registered spam domains become "popular" more quickly.

These features may ultimately be used to develop unique fingerprints for distinguishing legitimate domains from those that are associated with Internet attacks.

The rest of this paper is organized as follows. Section 2 surveys the problem context and related work. Section 3 describes the data sets that we use for our analysis. Section 4 studies the characteristics of resource records for newly registered legitimate and malicious domains. Section 5 studies the lookup characteristics for different types of domains, and Section 6 concludes.

2. CONTEXT AND RELATED WORK

We provide a brief overview of DNS records and lookups, as well as an overview of recent DNS studies.

2.1 DNS Resource Records and Lookups

When an entity registers a DNS domain, domain name registries insert several basic entries into the zone files to refer to the services for the domain. NS records point to the authoritative name servers for the zone, MX records point to the domain's mail servers, and A records point to the hosts. The NS and MX records can be further resolved to IP addresses. A single domain is typically assigned multiple server records for redundancy, but the number of IP addresses associated with the records is typically much less than the number of the domains being registered.

In March 2011, three million second-level domains under `.com` and `.net` were newly registered with NS records, but the number of distinct IPs mapped from NS records was just 150 thousand; A records and MX records have similar statistics. This observation indicates that the same server has been repeatedly used by many different domains to host DNS infrastructure (e.g., the most "heavily" used IP addresses carry NS records for around 300 scam domains).

Recursive DNS servers relay the users' queries to the zone's authoritative servers to acquire resource records, which reduces DNS traffic in the wide area. Recursive servers commonly respond to the hosts' requests within their respective networks, so the set of recursive servers querying for a domain can be a reasonable approximation for the networks that have attempted to reach the domain. The top-level domain (TLD) name servers thus provide a natural vantage point for monitoring the lookups directed to the second-level domains (the direct sub-domains below a TLD). Although DNS caching prevents us from determining the volume of lookups to a domain, the distribution of the recursive servers contains rich information about which networks have issued lookups for a domain; this statistic is particularly useful during the early part of a domain's life cycle, when it is initially registered and no caching has yet taken place.

2.2 Related Work

Monitoring and analysis on zones' resource records Previous studies have used the mechanism of querying the DNS servers to check the zones' resource records. Holz *et al.* investigated the diversity of the A records returned in the lookups to identify fast-flux service networks [10]. Konte *et al.* studied the changing rates of the IP address in the DNS records of scam domains [12]. Our work, on the other hand, tracks DNS records of newly registered domains to infer spatial and temporal characteristics. Anax scanned the recursive servers to find out anomaly in the cached records and detect poisoning attacks [1]. In contrast, we monitor the records in the zones' authoritative servers to discover the characteristics in the malicious domains' registration.

DNS lookup patterns The first studies of DNS lookup behavior at a local resolver were performed by Danzig *et al.* [8] and Jung *et al.* [11]; both of these studies examined lookup behavior from the vantage point of lookups to a single local resolver, and did not attempt to characterize how these lookup patterns differed for malicious domains. Notos [2] and EXPOSURE [4] studied DNS lookup behavior within a local domain below the DNS resolvers to build the domains' reputation. Such a view of DNS lookup behavior is valuable, but this vantage point cannot reveal coordinated behavior across multiple networks, and it relies first on an attack to take place or hosts being compromised before it can detect any malicious domains. Antonakakis *et al.* also monitored the DNS traffic from authoritative servers or top-level domain servers to detect malware domains [3], but the zones' dynamics were still reconstructed from DNS request and response messages; they did not focus on the behavioral analysis of newly registered domains. Other work has examined DNS lookup behavior at a DNS root server [5–7]. The focus of these studies was different from this paper. Castro *et al.* [7] and Brownlee *et al.* [6] attempted to characterize how much DNS traffic at the DNS root server was illegitimate. Broido *et al.* identified misconfigured hosts using spectrography to identify machines that were mistakenly issuing automatically configured DNS queries [5]. In contrast, we study DNS lookup patterns from the perspective of a top-level domain, and examines the behavior of lookups as seen from recursive resolvers, as opposed to lookups from individual hosts.

Domain registration inference Recently, a number of research efforts have studied domain registration patterns. Kreibich *et al.* [13] investigated the time from a domain's registration to its use in spam. Spring *et al.* examined the delay between registration of a malware domain and the first successfully resolved response in DNS traffic [17]. We make a similar observation, but on a much larger set of domains under `.com` and `.net`; further, we explore the DNS characteristics in domains' early life cycle. Felegyhazi *et al.* [9] proposed to automatically identify malicious domains based on `WHOIS` and name server information. In contrast, we actively collect different types of resource records to track the changes, and monitor the networks querying the domains. Some of the charac-

type	*example*
DNZA entry	add-new example.com NS ns1.example.com
Query record	example.com 111.111.111.0 , 22.22.22.0

Table 1: Data format examples.

teristics that we observe about malicious domains could be used to build efficient dynamic reputation systems.

3. DATA COLLECTION

We describe our data and the process of probing for resource records and correlating with spam messages.

DNS data The top-level domain servers are responsible for maintaining the zone information (more specific, second-level domains) and answer the queries for the registered domains. Verisign, Inc. operates the generic top-level domains (gTLDs) for `.com` and `.net`, which account for over 45% of registered domain names on the Internet [16]. The servers maintain two kinds of dynamics about the second-level domains. The first type of information is the *Domain Name Zone Alert (DNZA)*. This information includes changes about the zone, such as whether a domain name was newly registered or a name server's IP address was modified. The DNZA files keep track of these changes.

The second type of information concerns the *DNS queries* issued by the recursive servers. After the recursive servers sent queries to the TLD name servers for resolving the second-level domains names, Verisign's systems aggregated the source IP addresses into /24 subnets for logging and the TLD name servers recorded the querying subnets each day. The query records show the relationship between the domain names and the queriers. Verisign deploys multiple TLD name servers to resolve second-level domain names, and we collected the logs of querying /24s from all servers for analysis. Table 1 shows the example format of each type of data. The DNZA entry indicates that an "add-new" command created a new domain `example.com` and the NS record was `ns1.example.com`; The query record means that there were queries from /24s of "111.111.111.0" and "22.22.22.0" for the domain. The DNZA files and the query data were collected at Verisign's `.com` and `.net` TLD name servers during the period of March 2011. On average, about 80 million domains were queried each day.

Resource records The DNZA entries with "add-new" commands show what domains are newly registered. To get the new zone's resource records, we must perform active queries to their authority servers, since the second-level domains' records are not available within the TLD name servers. After a second-level domain under `.com` or `.net` is registered, we probe the domain once a day to discover the resource records and the resolved IPs. As mentioned in Section 2, we collect NS, MX and A records. We performed the probing procedure during March 2011. For example, 190 thousand domains were created on March 1, 2011; we continually queried those domains over the next 30 days. At the end of March 2011, we accumulated 4 million domains for monitoring. We use the PlanetLab platform [14] to make it feasible to query a large set of domains. Each PlanetLab node is responsible to query a subset of domains, and deliver the collected information back to the central monitor. Eventually, we deployed around 150 PlanetLab nodes to perform the probing procedure throughout the month. Though the daily querying does not capture all the changes in the resource records, it continually tracks the "snapshots" of DNS infrastructure and implies the change trends.

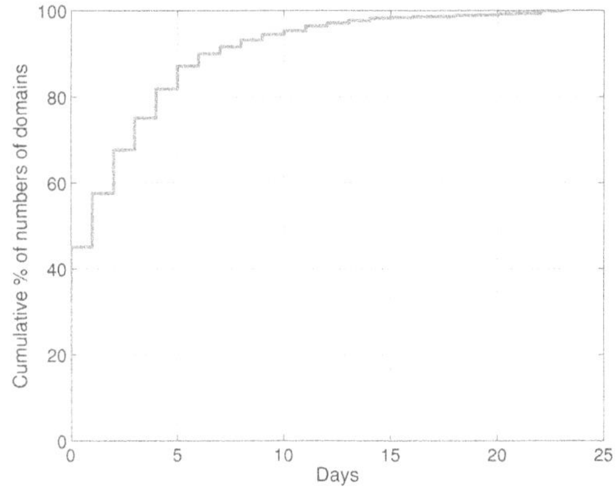

Figure 1: Days between a malicious domain's registration (in March 2011) and the time when the domain showed up in spam.

Spamming Scam domains appearing in spam messages are the major targets in our study, since timestamps in each email help explicitly identify when the spamming activities occurred, and spam is related to many different attacks, such as phishing. We used spam trap to capture emails sent from spammers during March 2011. Because the domains for the spam trap have no legitimate email addresses, emails received at the mail server were all spam. The second-level domains appearing in the messages' URLs were extracted as being involved in spamming activities (overall, 40% of unique second-level domains were found under `.com` and `.net`). In the context of this paper, we use "scam domains" and "malicious domains" interchangeably to refer to the second-level domains identified being associated with spam. From spam traps, we identified $2,045$ scam domains as newly registered during March 2011. We also checked the domains with Spamhaus [15], and identified $4,587$ blacklisted second-level domains. The union of these two sets yielded a total of $5,988$ `.com` and `.net` second-level domains that we considered spamming-related.

To obtain a representative set of legitimate domains for comparison, we sampled $6,000$ domains registered during March 2011 that have not yet appeared in any blacklist.

4. REGISTRATION & RESOURCE RECORDS

We first check the time between the registration of a domain and the subsequent attack to investigate the potential for early detection. Then, we explore how DNS behavior associated with infrastructure—where a domain's resolvers initially reside—can be an early signal for malicious domains.

4.1 Time Between Registration and Attack

We hypothesize that there may be some time between when spammers register new domains and when they send spam. We examine the extent of the delay between the time when a domain is initially registered and when it is ultimately used in an attack. If such a delay exists, it might allow blacklist operators to list the malicious domains, possibly before the spam campaign occurs.

How much time occurs between the domain registration and attack? Figure 1 shows the distribution between the time when we start to observe records about the malicious domains registered in March 2011, and the earliest time when the domains appeared in the spam messages. We take the timestamps in our spam traps, as well as emails received at the Yahoo! mail servers. Yahoo! Inc. provides the received time of all email messages and the URLs contained in the messages. The Yahoo! email gives a broader coverage of monitoring around the world. We take the earliest time points when seeing a "bad" domain in email messages (either in Yahoo! data or in spam trap) as the estimated start of the spamming attack about that domain. The x-axis represents the delay between when a domain was registered and when we first witnessed the domain associated with a spam campaign, and the y-axis is the percentage of the malicious domains registered in March 2011.

Finding 4.1 (Delay until attack) *More than 55% of the malicious domains appeared in spam campaigns more than one day after they were registered.*

We define the first five days after domain registration as *pre-attack period*. About 20% of domains might not be used in attacks during this period, and the time windows for other domains being explored in spamming are also limited. In the rest of the paper, we will analyze the characteristics of DNS infrastructure for malicious domains both throughout their lifetime (i.e., after the domains' registration) and within the pre-attack period. In Section 5, we further investigate the lookup behavior during the early stage.

4.2 Location of DNS Infrastructure

When determining the IP address that maps to each DNS record, we find that the assigned records for spam domains across IP space are far from uniform.

How is the DNS infrastructure that hosts a domain initially distributed across IP address space? The initial distribution of domain records across IP address space may provide clues as to a domain's reputation. Figure 2 shows how the IPs associated with NS, MX, and A records from malicious and legitimate domains are distributed across IP address space. The x-axis represents IPv4 space. If an IP maps to multiple records from different domains, we count it only once in the figure. The y-axis indicates the percentage of addresses less than or equal to the IP value on the x-axis. The solid blue curves plot the distribution of legitimate sample domains, the red dashed curves show the outcome of malicious domains, and the green dash-dot curves represent observed records for the malicious domains during pre-attack period. Interestingly, we observe that the DNS records associated with malicious domains are distributed differently than the records associated with legitimate ones.

Finding 4.2 (Distribution across IP address space) *The IP addresses used by malicious domains in the NS, MX and A records are distributed densely in a small fraction of IP address space.*

The IP addresses associated with DNS resource records are not distributed evenly across the IP address space. Some network range has more IPs pointed from NS, MX or A records; while the record IPs in other fraction of address space are distributed sparsely. Particularly two network blocks carried records from malicious domains, 96.45.0.0/16 and 216.162.0.0/16. The prefix 173.213.0.0/16 has many IPs in spamming domains, but the same range hosts legitimate domains, too. This observation indicates that if IPs corresponding to different domains' records reside close to each other in a network block, those domains may appear in spam in the future.

Is the DNS infrastructure for malicious domains located in particular ASes? Of course, the IP addresses of the records are not sufficient to confirm that a domain is scam-related. We examined the distribution of the resource records across ASes and compared the distribution of legitimate and malicious domains. Table 2 shows the top three ASes ranked by the percentage of domains ever having records being resolved into ASes.

(a) Legitimate domains

Type	*AS*	*domain ratio*	*AS Name*	*Country*
NS	8560	15.9%	1&1 Internet AG	Germany
	26496	10.9%	GoDaddy.com, Inc.	U.S.
	4134	10.1%	Chinanet Backbone	China
MX	26496	30.5%	GoDaddy.com, Inc.	U.S.
	15169	7.3%	Google Inc.	U.S.
	21844	7.0%	ThePlanet.com	U.S.
A	26496	31.8%	GoDaddy.com, Inc.	U.S.
	8560	4.3%	1&1 Internet AG	Germany
	21844	4.1%	ThePlanet.com	U.S.

(b) Malicious domains

Type	*AS*	*domain ratio*	*AS Name*	*Country*
NS	4134	33.6%	Chinanet Backbone	China
	28753	17.0%	Leaseweb De	Germany
	31365	16.3%	SGSTelekom	Turkey
MX	197088	23.9%	Colohost LLC	Latvija
	3292	19.3%	TDC Data Networks	U.S.
	5632	12.3%	3dgwebhosting.com Inc	U.S.
A	4134	19.3%	Chinanet Backbone	China
	197088	14.3%	Colohost LLC	Latvia
	30890	13.8%	Evolva Telecom	Romania

(c) Malicious domains in pre-attack period

Type	*AS*	*domain ratio*	*AS Name*	*Country*
NS	4134	37.8%	Chinanet Backbone	China
	28753	20.4%	Leaseweb De	Germany
	27699	11.3%	Tel. De Sao Paulo S.A.	Brazil
MX	197088	14.3%	Colohost LLC	Latvija
	3292	21.8%	TDC Data Networks	U.S.
	5632	12.3%	3dgwebhosting.com Inc	U.S.
A	4134	19.7%	Chinanet Backbone	China
	197088	15.0%	Colohost LLC	Latvia
	28753	11.6%	Leaseweb De	Germany

Table 2: Top three ASes containing domains' records.

Finding 4.3 (Distribution across ASes) *More than 30% of the malicious domains have at least one record resolving to one or two particular ASes, which are different from those ASes mostly used by legitimate domains.*

We observe that many of the new legitimate domains have larger registrars like GoDaddy operate their DNS, and host their service infrastructure with well-known provider, like Google. On the other hand, spamming domains' records are scattered across multiple ASes and countries. Spammers appear to prefer certain specific ASes to host their DNS infrastructure.

Are there "bad" ASes that host DNS infrastructure exclusively for malicious domains? We define an AS as "tainted" once the number of malicious domains whose DNS records are resolved within the AS exceeds a threshold. The set of tainted ASes represent the networks that attackers most heavily use, as indicated by the malicious domains' registration. After a domain's registration, attackers create DNS entries for the domain, and the records resolve to different IP addresses. We then check whether the resulting IPs belong to the tainted ASes. If a domain accumulates many records that resolve to tainted ASes, we suspect that the domain is related to the observed attacks.

Finding 4.4 (Domains hosted by "bad" ASes) *Most legitimate domains have A, MX, and NS records that are hosted*

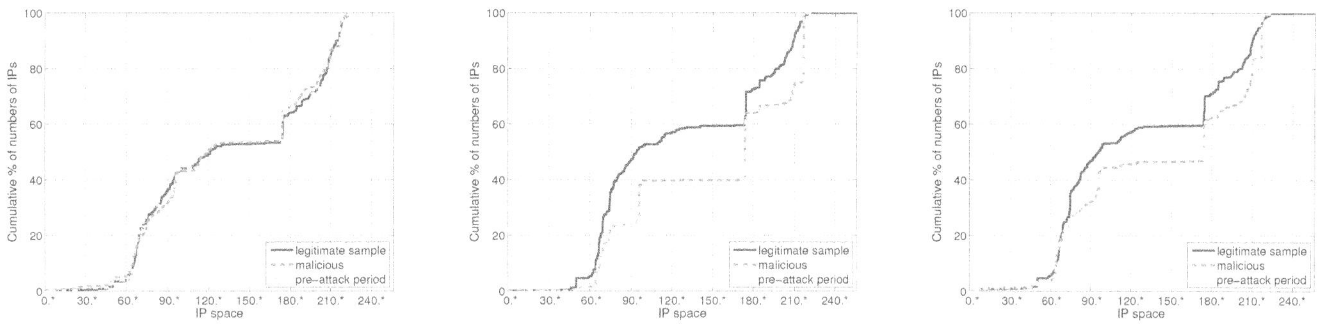

(a) NS records (b) MX records (c) A records

Figure 2: Fraction of IP addresses associated with malicious domains and comparison with legitimate domains.

almost entirely in untainted ASes. On the other hand, the majority of spam domains have records hosted in tainted ASes, even during the pre-attack period.

We derive the tainted AS set by including an AS that has hosted records for more than 100 spam domains. Figure 3 shows the ratio of the tainted record number to the number of all records for the domain. More than 90% of legitimate new domains have zero records belonging to the tainted AS set.

5. EARLY LOOKUP BEHAVIOR

The recursive DNS resolvers initially query the TLD name servers to get referrals to second-level domains. In this section, we explore the characteristics in the lookup networks to different types of domains. Queries to a malicious domain may signal the onset of attack, and the abnormal pattern in the global DNS traffic could help to detect the attack campaign in its infancy.

5.1 Network-Wide Patterns

We first investigate the querying patterns across different domains, to see whether similar sets of networks were looking up different domains. Our intuition is that domains that are used for malicious purposes may be looked up by similar groups of networks as well. For example, a user clicking on a URL in spam might click on other spam URLs. If two domains are queried by the same set of recursive DNS servers, they may be the same type of domain.

Are the networks querying different domains distributed similarly? We measure the similarity using an average pairwise similarity of querying /24 network blocks over n days. Suppose two domains A and B who have sequences of querying /24 set $\{a_1, a_2, \ldots, a_n\}$ and $\{b_1, b_2, \ldots, b_n\}$ over n days. The similarity between domains A and B is

$$S(A, B) = \frac{\sum_{i=1}^{n} J(a_i, b_i)}{n}, \text{ where } J(a_i, b_i) = \frac{|a_i \cap b_i|}{|a_i \cup b_i|}$$

where $J(a_i, b_i)$ is the Jaccard index of set a_i and b_i: the size of the set intersection divided by the size of union. Based on this pairwise similarity, we aggregate the domains into different groups using single-linkage clustering, a simple and efficient clustering method [18]. We considered a 5-day time period from March 1–5, 2011, during which there were 804 malicious domains and $1,104$ sampled legitimate domains registered. We terminate the clustering after $50,000$ comparisons, which places $1,631$ domains into

total	*malicious*	*legitimate*	*% malicious*
1404	463	941	33.0%
157	156	1	99.4%
16	16	0	100.0%
10	10	0	100.0%
10	10	0	100.0%

Table 3: Five largest clusters based on lookup networks.

17 clusters that have more than a single domain. We expect domains to fall into distinct clusters. Tables 3 shows the statistics for the five largest clusters. The first three columns show the domain counts in each cluster. The last column means the percentage of the malicious domains in the cluster.

Finding 5.1 (Similarity in lookups) *Different malicious domains are looked up by similar group of network blocks, which may indicate that they are part of the same spamming campaign.*

The results show that clustering often works well: many of the clusters contain either only all good or all bad domains. The legitimate domains contained in the large cluster are only queried by a small number of networks, which a detection system could easily filter. These results suggest that domains of certain types do share similar network-wide spatial lookup patterns that may ultimately be used as input to a blacklist.

5.2 Evolution of Lookup Traffic

The numbers of distinct networks querying the TLD servers for the second-level domains approximate how widely around the world the users try to connect to these domains. Although there might be multiple connection attempts behind one recursive server, counting all querying recursive servers is a good indicator for the domain's initial "popularity". Our intuition is that once deployed, malicious domains may receive a lot of traffic in a short time, but visits to legitimate domains will increase relatively more slowly.

How quickly do the newly registered domains become popular? Figure 4 shows the average lookup volume from /24s for domains in different categories over time. The x-axis shows the number of days after a domains' registration. The y-axis shows the average number of querying /24s over the domains with error bars (i.e., standard error). The solid blue curve shows lookups for legitimate domains; the y-axis values are multiplied by 10 to make the figure more readable. The dashed red curve shows the patterns of malicious domains.

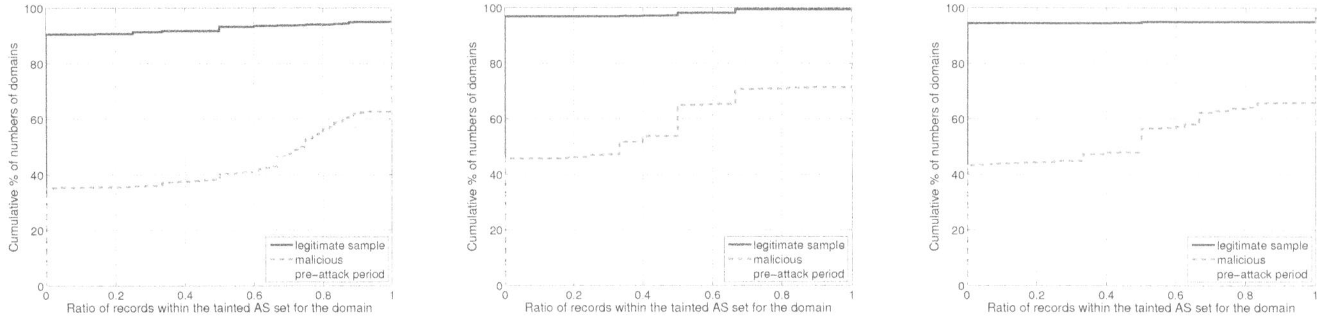

(a) NS records (b) MX records (c) A records

Figure 3: The distribution for the ratio of domains' records falling in the "tainted" AS set.

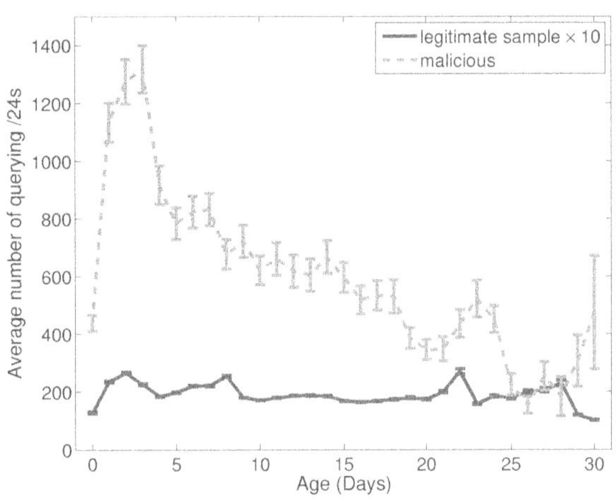

Figure 4: Number of querying /24s after domains' registration.

Finding 5.2 (Initial lookup trends) *Queries to the malicious domains increased quickly after the domains were registered, and usually reached the peak in the first 3–4 days.*

On the other hand, /24s querying for domains not reported as malicious increased slowly and stayed relatively low over the 30-day period. The markedly different lookup patterns of likely legitimate domains and those involved in spamming activities might ultimately help blacklist operators quickly detect bad domains, by watching for newly registered domains that suddenly become popular. The changes to malicious domains also indicate that the initial five-day period may contain valuable information, since these attack domains are heavily queried at the beginning, but lookups quickly trail off after that.

6. CONCLUSION AND FUTURE WORK

We have monitored DNS resource records for second-level domains newly registered in March 2011 and examined the lookup traffic to large authoritative top-level domain servers. We show the DNS characteristics observed at TLD name servers and extracted from zones' resource records for malicious domains are different than those for legitimate domains. Resource records of malicious domains tend to resolve to specific IP address range and ASes. Once we identify a set of "tainted" autonomous systems that host many scam domains, the legitimate domains rarely have resource records within the tainted AS set. We also discover that miscreant domains exhibit distinct clusters, in terms of the networks that look up these domains. Finally, we find that these domains become widely popular considerably more quickly after their initial registration time.

The distinct DNS characteristics and their tendency on different types of domains suggest that it may ultimately be possible to fingerprint domains based on their resource records and lookup traffic close to TLD name servers before an attack ever takes place. Although a single pattern in DNS might have limited power to identify malicious domains, the combination of our findings may ultimately guide the design of future "early warning" systems for DNS.

Acknowledgments

We thank Yahoo! Inc. for providing the received time of the email messages and the contained URLs. We also thank our shepherd, Christian Kreibich, as well as David Dagon and Anirudh Ramachandran for helpful comments on the paper. This work was funded by NSF CAREER Award CNS-0643974 and NSF Awards CNS-0716278 and CNS-0721581.

REFERENCES

[1] M. Antonakakis, D. Dagon, X. Luo, R. Perdisci, W. Lee, and J. Bellmor. A Centralized Monitoring Infrastructure for Improving DNS Security. In *Proc. 13th International Symposium on Recent Advances in Intrusion Detection (RAID)*, Ottawa, Ontario, Canada, Sept. 2010.

[2] M. Antonakakis, R. Perdisci, D. Dagon, W. Lee, and N. Feamster. Building a Dynamic Reputation System for DNS. In *Proc. 19th USENIX Security Symposium*, Washington, DC, Aug. 2010.

[3] M. Antonakakis, R. Perdisci, W. Lee, N. V. II, and D. Dagon. Detecting Malware Domains at the Upper DNS Hierarchy. In *Proc. 20th USENIX Security Symposium*, San Francisco, CA, Aug. 2011.

[4] L. Bilge, E. Kirda, C. Kruegel, and M. Balduzzi. EXPOSURE: Finding Malicious Domains Using Passive DNS Analysis. In *Proc. 18th Annual Network and Distributed System Security Symposium (NDSS)*, San Diego, CA, Feb. 2011.

[5] A. Broido, E. Nemeth, and K. Claffy. Spectroscopy of DNS Update Traffic. *ACM SIGMETRICS Performance Evaluation Review*, 31(1):321, June 2003.

[6] N. Brownlee, K. Claffy, and E. Nemeth. DNS Measurements at a Root Server. In *Proc. IEEE Conference on Global Communications (GlobeCom)*, San Antonio, TX, Nov. 2001.

[7] S. Castro, D. Wessels, M. Fomenkov, and K. Claffy. A Day at the Root of the Internet. *ACM SIGCOMM Computer Communication Review*, 38(5):41–46, Oct. 2008.

[8] P. Danzig, K. Obraczka, and A. Kumar. An Analysis of Wide-Area Name Server Traffic: A Study of the Internet Domain Name System. *ACM SIGCOMM Computer Communication Review*, 22(4):292, Oct. 1992.

[9] M. Felegyhazi, C. Kreibich, and V. Paxson. On the Potential of Proactive Domain Blacklisting. In *Proc. 3rd USENIX Workshop on Large-Scale Exploits and Emergent Threats (LEET)*, San Jose, CA, Apr. 2010.

[10] T. Holz, C. Gorecki, K. Rieck, and F. C. Freiling. Measuring and Detecting Fast-Flux Service Networks. In *Proc. 16th Annual Network and Distributed System Security Symposium (NDSS)*, San Diego, CA, Feb. 2008.

[11] J. Jung, E. Sit, H. Balakrishnan, and R. Morris. DNS Performance and the Effectiveness of Caching. In *Proc. ACM SIGCOMM Internet Measurement Workshop*, San Fransisco, CA, Nov. 2001.

[12] M. Konte, N. Feamster, and J. Jung. Dynamics of Online Scam Hosting Infrastructure. In *Proc. Passive and Active Measurement (PAM)*, Seoul, South Korea, Apr. 2009.

[13] C. Kreibich, C. Kanich, K. Levchenko, B. Enright, G. M. Voelker, V. Paxson, and S. Savage. Spamcraft: An Inside Look At Spam Campaign Orchestration. In *Proc. 2nd USENIX Workshop on Large-Scale Exploits and Emergent Threats (LEET)*, Boston, MA, Apr. 2009.

[14] PlanetLab. `http://www.planet-lab.org/`.

[15] Spamhaus. `http://www.spamhaus.org/`.

[16] Domain Name Industry Brief. `http://www.verisigninc.com/DNIB`, 2011.

[17] J. M. Spring, L. B. Metcalf, and E. Stoner. Correlating Domain Registrations and DNS First Activity in General and for Malware. In *Proc. Securing and Trusting Internet Names (SATIN)*, Teddington, United Kingdom, Apr. 2011.

[18] J. Zupan. *Clustering of Large Data Sets*. John Wiley and Sons, Ltd., 1982.

Summary Review Documentation for

"Monitoring the Initial DNS Behavior of Malicious Domains"

Authors: S. Hao, N. Feamster, R. Pandrangi

Reviewer #1

Strengths: Unique dataset coupled with thorough analysis. The conclusions about tainted address blocks is interesting.

Weaknesses: Paper does not develop/evaluate a (new) technique for predicting whether a new domain is spam or not, but to be fair, that is probably out of scope for a short paper.

Comments to Authors: This is well-written paper based on a relatively unique data set. There are no real "surprises", but the data is analyzed and presented well. It is not clear how useful the observations about spam domains are: for instance, knowing that most spam domains are not immediately used (Figure 1), and that the distribution for MX/A/NS records of spam versus legitimate domains is different (Figure 2) is interesting but does not lead to a "test" for whether a single new domain is legitimate or not. Perhaps there is a method or perhaps a legitimate-use probability can be associated with a domain based on its initial behavior, but such a technique was not developed or evaluated in this paper.

In this short paper, we investigated the potential for using DNS lookup patterns for detection, since the paper is mainly to measure different features and leaves the detection system as future work. To address this comment, we added a paragraph in the conclusion section to discuss future work on detecting malicious versus legitimate domains.

In the absence of such a method, the paper does a competent job of presenting the data cleanly and drawing initial conclusions.

Reviewer #2

Strengths: The topic of the paper is still a cool topic, and I like the combination of datasets and features the authors study.

Weaknesses: The piece is quite rushed and in parts unpleasant to read. The authors miss relevant related work, and each of the three features they use has been touched in previous work.

Comments to Authors: The first finding is not novel. Check the LEET 2009 Spamcraft paper for a plot documenting delays from registration time to time of use.

We have added this paper to the references, although our findings and conclusions are different from those from the Spamcraft paper. The previous work sees similar delays between registration and first lookup for a single campaign, but we focus on the time delay between registration and attack for .com and .net domains to investigate the possibility of early detection before the attack occurs.

Your second finding isn't particularly novel either. The proactive domain blacklisting paper from LEET 2010 is clearly related, as its authors tried to predict malicious domain use from the patterns of registration and the infrastructure touched by a domain's hosting. I'm surprised you don't cite it. You should also cite Spamhaus' DBL, as it too is a predictive spam blacklist.

We have added the paper "On the potential of proactive domain blacklisting" from LEET 2010 to the references. We have already referred to Spamhaus in Section 3, so there is no need to refer to it again.

The third finding is interesting but it too has been covered in previous work, see Spring et al.'s paper at the SATIN workshop.

We have added the paper "Correlating Domain Registrations and DNS First Activity in General and for Malware" (Securing and Trusting Internet Names 2011) to the references. This paper reports some findings that are similar to ours. They examined the delay between registration of a malware domain and the first successfully resolved response in DNS traffic.

Given that all three features are promising I would suggest you actually try to build a predictor for malicious domains so you can report on its accuracy - it would be interesting (particularly its real-time aspects), and I am pretty sure it would work quite well.

Specific comments:

- Sec. 2.1: "When a DNS domain is registered, several basic entries are inserted to refer to the services for the domain." Please make the writing more active -- registered by whom, inserted where?

We changed this sentence to "When an entity registers a DNS domain, domain name registries insert several basic entries into the zone files to refer to the services for the domain."

- Sec 3: again passive voice: "the source IP addresses were aggregated into /24 subnets and the TLD name servers recorded the number of queries for each domain". Is this something you did, or do Verisign's systems provide that?

Verisign provided the information. We changed this sentence to "Verisign's systems aggregated the source IP addresses into /24 subnets for logging and the TLD name servers recorded querying subnets each day."

- How do the query record entries scale? It seems that the number of /24s must be huge for popular domains...

Since we recorded the querying /24s (not the individual queries), the data for each domain has an upper limit (at most the number of all /24s). Our work focuses on the newly registered domains, so fewer domains would get huge queries in a short time.

- Did you build your own PlanetLab experiment or did you use CoDNS?

We designed and built our own experimental platform. We must collect different types of records, including A, NS, and MX records, so we have built and deployed our own system to perform the tasks of resolving the domain names.

- Why would spammers care about their domains' MX records?

We did not make any changes to the paper, but we will briefly clarify this question here. MX records could exhibit certain patterns:

- *When considering email spam, attackers don't hope if someone replies the email, the message gets bounced back. The MX-type could be setup anyway.*
- *If spammers don't care about the MX records, that could be a pattern itself, since the legitimate domains do care to configure correct MX records.*

- I can't make out in Sec 4.2 whether the NS record alone would suffice in detecting malice-related patterns. Per the above papers and my reading of Table 2(b), I am virtually certain they do.) If so, you do npt need to conduct A-record lookups as the NSs are in the zone file, which obviously simplifies the process.

We did not make any changes to the paper, but there are two reasons why we probed for NS-type and A-type records:

- *The NS records in domains' authority name servers might be different from glue NS records in TLD name servers.*
- *The overhead to fetch other types of records (like A-type or MX-type) is marginal. Since we didn't actually evaluate the detection performance (this is a measurement paper), it is still not clear which feature could work well. We hope to show all analysis results.*

Reviewer #3

Strengths: Interesting measurements and conclusions. The proposal to use these conclusions to detect malicious domains early seems promising.

Weaknesses: I do not think that the conclusions are new. The proposal (of how to use these conclusions) is not clear.

Comments to Authors: My main concern is that, despite being useful and interesting, the conclusions are not new. For instance, it is known that machines that participate in malicious activities tend to be clustered ("Observed structure of addresses in IP traffic", IEEE/ACM Trans. on Networking, Dec. 2006).

We did not make any changes to the paper, since the paper "Observed structure of addresses in IP traffic" is not actually that related to our work:
1) The paper did not focus on DNS analysis
2)The traffic monitoring did not occur anywhere near the root DNS resolvers.

Section 5 is confusing to the non-expert, in the following way. The paper is supposed to be looking at the characteristics of malicious domains *before* they are involved in malicious activity. But then, what does "early lookup behavior" refer to? Are malicious domains looked up before they are involved in malicious activity, i.e., before they appear in spam messages? This is what I thought at first, but then the following comment confused me: In Section 5.1, it says that the reason why malicious domains are looked up by the same resolvers is that a user clicking on one spam URL is likely to click on another and/or malicious domains may be participating in the same spamming campaigns. This comment implies that we are talking about lookups resulting from spam, i.e., a point in time after the malicious domains have started demonstrating malicious behavior. Hence, it is not clear how this lookup-clustering characteristic could be used to detect malicious domains *early*. I recommend that the authors clarify this issue.

We have added more explanation in Section 5: "Queries to a malicious domain may signal the onset of attack, and the abnormal pattern in the global DNS traffic could help to detect the attack campaign in its infancy."

Section 4 is clearer in this respect, i.e., it says that malicious domains tend to be served by infrastructure that uses specific address blocks and few "tainted" ASes, which are rarely used by legitimate domains -- implying that an early detection system could investigate domains that are served by these few tainted ASes. This makes sense. However, the numbers in Table 3 (on which this conclusion is based) are confusing: Apparently, the AS mostly used by malicious domains is the Chinanet Backbone AS. My understanding is that this AS hosts a large fraction of the Chinese Internet infrastructure. Hence, if we consider this AS "tainted", a large fraction of legitimate Chinese domains will have to be investigated as suspect of malicious behavior. This does not sound right.

We didn't try to build a detection system and evaluate its performance in this paper. Regarding the "Chinanet backbone" case, if an AS has a large mixture of good and bad domains, that AS should be handled as a special case, since obviously blocking the entire AS is not feasible. In such cases, using other auxiliary patterns to distinguish malicious from legitimate domains (e.g., lookup patterns) may be necessary. Even if a detection method simply suspected all domains involved in "Chinanet backbone", based on our findings in Table 2(a), it saves effort to investigate 10% of legitimate domains compared to all domains.

Reviewer #4

Strengths: - Problem is important and the paper presents some interesting new insights about the DNS dynamics of malware sites.
- Unique datasets from the TLD servers.

Weaknesses: - Not sure how unbiased the data set is.

Comments to Authors: I think the problem is important and the authors do a good job in the paper showing evidence that often there is not much lag between a domain getting registered and beginning to send spam. I like the paper overall.

I have only some minor comments.

The authors mention the use of Yahoo mail servers for collecting timestamps. It might be good to elaborate what exact data they had for this purpose.

We added the following clarification: "Yahoo! Inc. provides the received time of the email messages and the URLs contained in the messages."

Finding 4.1 is not intuitive. I think you may want to say the contrapositive, that 45% of malicious domains appeared within a day, if you want this finding to be reflective of the early detectability. The sentences following this finding also need to be rephrased properly; right now they are confusing.

We made no changes to the paper. We stated that "55% of the malicious domains appeared in spam campaigns more than one day after they were registered", because the intention is to check what is the buffer time people have to detect a bad domain before it is used in malicious activity.

I would use benign as an opposite of malicious. Legitimate is not accurate since all domains are legitimate since they have been registered with the registrar (and not hijacked, which is yet another study).

We do not agree with this suggestion and have not made the change in the paper. It is much clearer to use "legitimate", since this corresponds with standard parlance in the literature (cf. "legitimate" email vs. spam).

Isn't the non-uniform distribution of IP addresses across the NS, MX and A records an artifact of the data you have. Presumably if you have only a partial dataset, you would potentially see only some attack IPs.

We arguably have the most representative dataset possible; it is one of the most expansive datasets that it is possible to obtain: .com (and .net) is a good representative of TLD, and the data have big coverage already. It is true the particular IP blocks will be different for domains under different TLDs, but they will have similar patterns as we see in .com (and .net).
We added some statistics in Section 3, e.g. ".com and .net accounts for over 45% registered domain names on the Internet".

I think 2(a) is not in line with the finding 4.3 and it is not clearly explained. I see very little difference between the benign and malicious domains. MX/A records, I can see some difference, but not so much in 2(a).

The MX and A records of malicious domains are still relatively concentrated in one or two particular ASes (about 30% of the records reside in these ASes). Although the reviewer is correct that some ASes appear in both sets, we are not suggesting that this feature alone would be sufficient to detect bad domains. In some cases, ASes predominantly appear in one list or the other, and this information will be useful for establishing a prior.

I am not sure if the query data collected using recursive queries at the TLD server is unbiased between malicious and benign domains.

This comment does not make sense. We have already emphasized in Section 3: "Verisign deploys multiple TLD name servers to resolve second-level domain names, and we collected the logs of querying /24s from all servers for analysis."

Reviewer #5

Strengths: Interesting insights from a great data set (top level domain DNS request volume).

Weaknesses: - Interesting observation, but can this be turned into some practical policies to blacklist malicious domains?
- Data set only available to the owner of top level domain managers-
- Observation only based on .com and .net. Is this representative?

Comments to Authors: I enjoyed reading the paper. Let me focus on some of the weaknesses:

- The main weakness is that it is not clear how to turn your findings into some practical policies to blacklist domains? You clearly show differences between legitimate and malicious domains, but can you use this information in practice? Would it be easy for domains to avoid the new blacklisting rules identified? I understand this is a short paper and I am hoping that you will cover this in future work.

- Your work is based on .com and .net data. How representative is this? Could you comment on some statistics to say X% of spams or blacklisted domains are .com or .net? Is it 90% or 2%?

Based on analysis of our spam trap data, we see that around 40% of unique second-level domains reside under .com and .net. These figures are derived from all second-level domains in the spamtrap email.

- Your analysis of /24 reminded me of a work that you did not reference: S. Venkataram, A. Blum, D. Song. S. Sen, and O. Spatscheck,"Tracking dynamic sources of malicious activity at Internet-scale", in Proc. NIPS, 2009.

This paper might be a useful clustering method if we were designing a detection scheme, but since our work is not mainly to develop a new clustering algorithm, we do not think this paper is particularly related to our work.

- Regarding Figure 1, do you have finer grain data to show what happens during the first couple of hours for the other 45% of the domains?

Because the active resource-record probing and the lookup data are aggregated on a daily basis, analyzing the data on a more fine-grained basis is not possible.

- Could you add a candle chart on Figure 4 to show the distribution of legitimate traffic to see how practical a policy based on this metric would work? e.g. do a lot of legitimate domain exhibit that same pattern as the malicious domains? You just show the differences between the means.

We included standard error in the figure for both malicious and legitimate domains. Because the value for legitimate domains is comparatively small, these values might be difficult to see in the figure.

Response from the Authors

The review comments fall into three categories.

1) *Some related work is not included, and the differences from our paper are not described carefully.* To correct this concern, we added most of the related papers pointed out by the reviewers, including "On the potential of proactive domain blacklisting" from LEET 2010 and "Correlating Domain Registrations and DNS First Activity in General and for Malware" from the SATIN 2011 workshop. There are three major differences of our work from earlier studies: we focus on newly registered second-level domains, the DNS records are actively probed instead of from passively monitoring, and we observe the lookup pattern at the TLD name servers (with a global view from *all* /24 networks across the Internet). We did not include several of the papers that reviewers mentioned that do not appear to be related to our paper.

2) *It is unclear whether the DNS patterns could be eventually developed into a detection system.* Since the intention of our work is to reveal DNS characteristics that could shed light on identifying different patterns for malicious and legitimate domains, the paper does not actually design a detection system based on the features (which is our next step). We changed text to make the claim clear, e.g. adding a paragraph in the conclusion section to state detection algorithms as future work.

3) *Some details of the data and the findings need more clarification.* To present the Verisign data more clearly, we checked the representativeness of the .com and .net domains and added more details to the paper about the collection process. We also added extra explanation explaining how we correlate second-level domains appearing in spamtrap URLs with those that appear in a Yahoo! email trace.

Understanding Fraudulent Activities in Online Ad Exchanges

Brett Stone-Gross, Ryan Stevens, Richard Kemmerer, Christopher Kruegel, Giovanni Vigna
Department of Computer Science
University of California, Santa Barbara
bstone,rstevens,kemm,chris,vigna@cs.ucsb.edu

Apostolis Zarras
Institute of Computer Science
Foundation for Research and Technology, Hellas
zarras@ics.forth.gr

ABSTRACT

Online advertisements (ads) provide a powerful mechanism for advertisers to effectively target Web users. Ads can be customized based on a user's browsing behavior, geographic location, and personal interests. There is currently a multi-billion dollar market for online advertising, which generates the primary revenue for some of the most popular websites on the Internet. In order to meet the immense market demand, and to manage the complex relationships between advertisers and publishers (i.e., the websites hosting the ads), marketplaces known as "ad exchanges" are employed. These exchanges allow publishers (sellers of ad space) and advertisers (buyers of this ad space) to dynamically broker traffic through ad networks to efficiently maximize profits for all parties. Unfortunately, the complexities of these systems invite a considerable amount of abuse from cybercriminals, who profit at the expense of the advertisers.

In this paper, we present a detailed view of how one of the largest ad exchanges operates and the associated security issues from the vantage point of a member ad network. More specifically, we analyzed a dataset containing transactions for ingress and egress ad traffic from this ad network. In addition, we examined information collected from a command-and-control server used to operate a botnet that is leveraged to perpetrate ad fraud against the same ad exchange.

Categories and Subject Descriptors

K.4.4 [**Computers and Society**]: Electronic Commerce, Security; C.2.0 [**Computer-Communication Networks**]: General

General Terms

Experimentation, Measurement, Security

Keywords

Ad fraud, Ad networks, Online advertising

IMC'11, November 2–4, 2011, Berlin, Germany.

1. INTRODUCTION

Online advertising has developed into a massive economy and is now the main source of revenue for some of the most popular online businesses and search engines (e.g., Google and Yahoo! [5]). In its simplest form, online advertising is a buyer/seller relationship between those who want to show ads (advertisers, who buy space on Web pages) and those who get paid to display ads for others for a fee (publishers, or sellers, who own the Web pages). The process becomes more complicated as more advertisers and publishers are added to the system. To facilitate these endeavors, an intermediary entity called an ad network (or ad commissioner [20]) keeps track of the publishers and advertisers within its domain. It is the ad network's job to take the publishers' ad requests, which are generated when users load a publisher's website, and pair them with the advertisers willing to pay the most for the publishers' niche market. In turn, the network takes a percentage of all revenue that is exchanged in transactions that it oversees. Thus, in the network model of advertising, handling ad requests becomes a broker process that seeks to maximize revenue for all involved parties.

Ad exchanges, such as Google's DoubleClick or Yahoo!'s RightMedia, operate similar to an ad network, where the entities that buy or sell ads are ad networks. This allows one ad network to sell its publishers' ad space to another network or buy ad space for its advertisers, so that advertisers are able to reach a much larger audience than they could if they were part of a single ad network. Unlike an ad network, an ad exchange is not fully connected, and networks in the exchange cannot buy and sell each other's ads freely until they have established a contractual agreement describing how traffic will be bought and sold between them. This allows the ad exchange to handle the distribution of ads from a centralized ad server, which has a public API allowing ad networks to configure and monitor their accounts.

While ad exchanges provide a powerful mechanism for advertisers, ad networks, and publishers to efficiently manage their ad traffic, they have also become a lucrative target for cybercriminals. In particular, miscreants have developed malware that is used to remotely control compromised computers, known as *bots*, and network them into a single *botnet*. A botnet can be instructed to view and click ads, simulating user traffic. As a result, botnet operators can generate revenue simply by creating a website, signing up as a publisher, and directing their bots to view and click on the advertisements contained on their own website.

In this paper, we collaborated with a large ad network that is a member of Yahoo!'s RightMedia, one of the largest ad exchanges. This enabled us to obtain a direct view of how a large real-world ad network operates in the context of an ad exchange, and to analyze the security threats and fraudulent activities that pose the greatest risks. Due to the sensitive nature of the subject, we will refer to this ad network throughout the paper as NETWORKX. Our goal in this project was to study and understand how an ad exchange operates from the perspective of an individual ad network. Moreover, we applied a number of models to the ad network's data to explore methods that might be able to identify suspicious click traffic in the context of an ad exchange. In addition, we obtained access to a command-and-control (C&C) server that was used to control a botnet that engaged in ad fraud targeted towards the RightMedia exchange. Because of our access to the botnet C&C server, our models were geared more towards fraud that was perpetrated by a botnet; however, we also discuss a number of additional fraud techniques we observed. To the best of our knowledge, this is the first large-scale study of fraudulent activities in online ad exchanges from these vantage points.

2. BACKGROUND

In this section, we introduce online advertising and describe how ad exchanges operate to serve ads on the Internet. We then review types of fraud that are known to exist in online advertising, and we describe which techniques are used to prevent this fraud from occurring. Finally, we describe the ad fraud botnet C&C server that was used to perpetrate fraud on RightMedia.

2.1 Terminology

Below are definitions of the various advertising terms we use in this paper. Note that some of the terms below are defined in the context of Yahoo!'s RightMedia. For a more general definition of the terms, refer to the Internet Advertising Bureau's online glossary [3].

- *Publishers* (or *Sellers*) make money through the exchange by hosting websites with advertisements. Each visitor to their sites generates revenue for the publisher depending on the niche market that describes their websites. In general, the more visitors publishers attract to their websites the more money they earn.

- *Advertisers* (or *Buyers*) pay the ad network to have their ads displayed on publishers' websites. Whenever their ads are shown, they have to pay the ad network, and a percentage is paid to the publisher.

- *Ad Networks* are entities in the exchange that manage publishers and advertisers. They are able to buy and sell ad traffic (in the form of ad requests) internally as well as through other ad networks. Ad networks that can buy and sell traffic between each other are called *linked partners*, and each ad network maintains its own list of trusted partner networks.

- Instead of having static ads that display the same content, publishers load ads dynamically by putting *sections* (also called *zones* or *regions*) on their pages. A section simply refers to a block of space on the page that is able to make a request for an ad dynamically when the page is loaded. In practice, this is often implemented by embedding an iframe that loads some JavaScript in the page, which, in turn, detects if the browser has Adobe Flash and whether browser cookies are enabled. This information is sent to an ad server so that an ad can be served to the user's browser, in a process called an *ad request*.

- A *creative* refers to the content of the actual advertisement, which is what the visitor sees on the page after the ad is served. The ad normally consists of an image or an Adobe Flash animation and an anchor tag that points to the advertiser's website, called a *click-through*.

- The *auction process* refers to how a section is populated by a creative. It involves matching up each ad request with the most profitable advertiser bid for the request. Before any ads are served, publishers and advertisers outline a number of ad serving requirements such as budget, when ads should be shown, and targeting information. These requirements are used to match requests and bids autonomously in the exchange in a way that maximizes profit for the publisher. A single successful auction in the exchange is called an *impression*.

- A *click* event is generated when a user clicks on an ad, and it usually brings more revenue to the publisher than an impression alone. Clicks and impressions are handled separately in the exchange, so a user loading a page and clicking on an ad actually generates two events, an impression and a click. The ratio of clicks and impressions is the ad's *Click Through Rate* (CTR). Publishers' CTRs are also recorded for use in fraud detection.

- *Ad campaigns* are the way in which advertisers specify how much they pay when their ads are shown. There are many different types of campaigns, but the most common type is based on *Cost per Mille* (CPM) impressions, which is simply how much one thousand impressions are worth to an advertiser. In this scheme, an advertiser pays an amount to the publisher for each ad that gets served to the site.

- Additional ad campaign types are *Cost per Click* (CPC) and *Cost per Action* (CPA). CPC deals pay the publisher only when a user clicks the ad that is served; CPA deals only pay the publisher when a user clicks the ad and continues on to perform some action on the site (known as a *conversion*), usually filling in a landing page form. Because the amount of revenue associated with CPC and CPA deals depends on a user clicking the ad, the server estimates how much the ad will pay by calculating the *effective Cost Per Mille* (eCPM) impressions. The formula for this is: eCPM = ((Payout per impression) + (Historical CTR) * (Payout per click) + (Historical actions to impressions) * (Payout per action)) * 1000.

- In addition to the auction process, there is a practice called *arbitrage* that ad networks can use to increase their revenue. Arbitrage is done by ad networks buying impressions from publishers as if they were a real advertiser, and starting a new auction for the ad slot as if they were a real publisher. As we will discuss later, this has a number of implications that have to be accounted for when analyzing the data stream from NETWORKX.

2.2 Structure of an Ad Exchange

An ad exchange is structured as a graph where each node is an ad network, which owns its own set of unique publishers and advertisers. Publishers are only able to request ads (sell traffic), and advertisers can only bid on requests (buy traffic). However, ad networks are able to both buy and sell traffic, allowing them to act as brokers between different parts of the exchange that would not be connected otherwise. Thus, publishers and advertisers are edge nodes, and ad networks form the backbone of the exchange, as shown in Figure 1.

As previously mentioned, the exchange is not fully connected and traffic cannot be bought and sold freely across the exchange. This is because an ad network can only interact with another ad network if they are linked partners. Partnerships define an edge in the graph; when two entities become affiliates they decide on the specific parameters that will define their relationship in the exchange, which is usually a revenue share deal. For example, NETWORKX may take 50% of all publisher revenue for a particular partner who targets traffic from users interested in German news, and 60% of

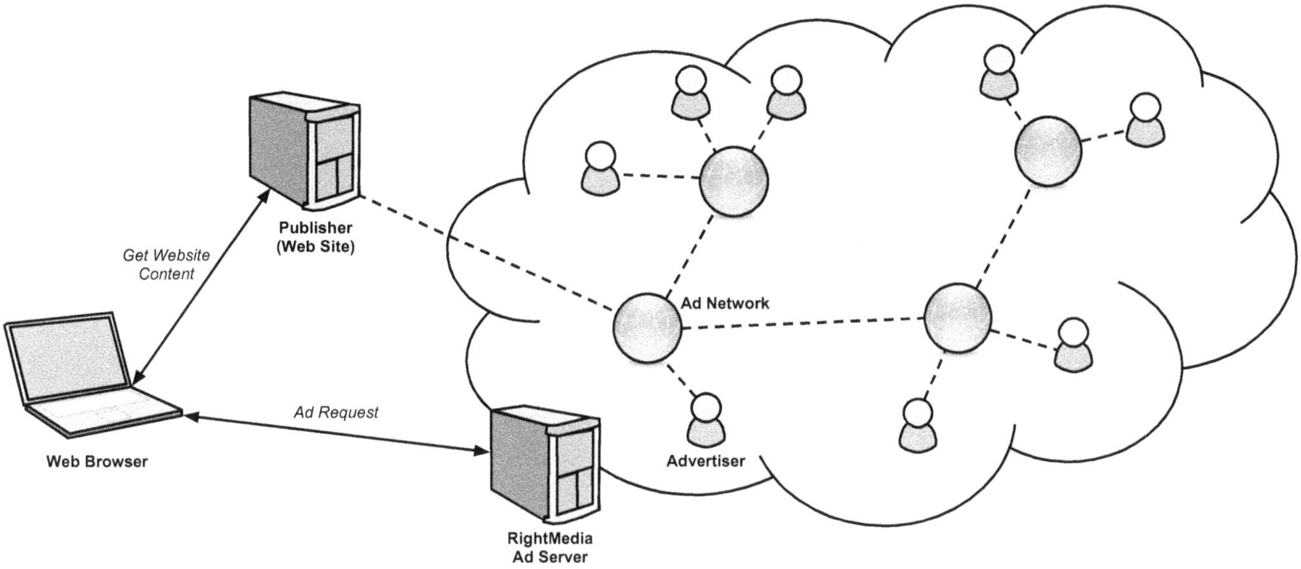

Figure 1: An overview of an online ad exchange.

publisher revenue with another partner that targets American sports traffic.

2.3 How the Auction Process Works

In the ad network model of online ad serving, one advertising network has access to its own advertisers and publishers, and the network searches the list of advertisers for each ad request to determine which would be the most profitable for the publisher and thus the network. The process is similar in an ad exchange, except that the pool of advertisers also includes advertisers who are part of the network's linked partners (and those partners' linked partners, and so on). The process starts when a user loads a Web page that contains a RightMedia HTML iframe or JavaScript popup that initiates a request for an advertisement of a specific size. A unique identifier, known as a *section ID*, enables an ad network to track impressions, clicks, and conversions from a particular publisher. Note that the section ID is the only information that an ad network uses to determine the publisher that should be credited. As we will discuss later, this makes verifying the legitimacy of a single ad request very difficult.

When the ad request is received by the ad exchange's ad server, the ad server is able to lookup which publisher the section ID belongs to. This ad request is then associated with the publisher's ad serving requirements, and it is matched with viable bids, based on the targeting criteria of the advertisers. Each advertiser specifies a maximum bid, but the actual bid amount is determined automatically by the exchange based on the advertiser's Return on Investment (ROI) goals and the number of other advertisers who are able to bid. The bids are always in the form of the effective cost per mille impressions (eCPM), regardless of the types of affiliations between intermediary ad networks. The final amount the bid is worth to the publisher is affected by how many intermediary ad networks are brokering the transaction. For example, consider a publisher and an advertiser who are part of an ad network. The advertiser's campaign with the network is a $1 CPM deal, while the publisher has a 50% revenue share deal. Therefore, the advertiser's bids will only be worth $0.50 to the publisher, because the network is taking half of the revenue. In reality, the ad exchange would take a cut as well. When the value of all available bids has been computed, the exchange simply picks the bid with the highest eCPM for the publisher, and then the ad is served.

2.4 How Arbitrage Works

Arbitrage occurs after the auction process. In order to initiate arbitrage, the network must buy the publisher's ad traffic itself and then resell the traffic in a completely new, independent auction. This is done by serving a new ad tag to the user after the initial auction, instead of an ad. The new ad tag contains a new section ID that is owned by the ad network and not by an actual publisher (note that the ad network could choose to return a non-RightMedia ad tag as well). Whatever revenue is generated in the new auction goes to the ad network that won the first auction, in the hopes that the second auction will make a profit larger than the ad request cost. Since the network must buy the traffic before reselling it, unsold arbitrage traffic is a direct loss for the ad network. Arbitrage can be repeated a number of times across different ad networks until an actual ad is served; this process is called *daisy chaining*. The longer the chain of arbitrage, the longer it takes to load the ad that is finally displayed in the user's browser that first made the ad request.

2.5 Known Types of Fraud

Fraud (or *Ad Fraud*) in the context of an ad exchange is a means by which a member or members in the exchange try to increase their profits at the cost of other members in the exchange. A *fraudster* is simply a member of the exchange who is perpetrating fraud of some kind. The fraudster may be a publisher in the exchange who is attempting to make more money than it deserves, or an advertiser who is targeting other advertisers to reduce ad competition.

The simplest kind of fraud is called *impression spam*, and it involves fabricating HTTP requests to either the publisher's page, or the ad server directly, to artificially inflate the actual amount of traffic. This type of fraud targets CPM deals, but may be mixed in with other types of fraud to remain stealthy [6]. One such kind of fraud that is usually more profitable than impression spam alone is *click spam*, which is done by generating HTTP requests to advertisement click URLs, usually after an ad is served. There are two kinds of click spam fraud. *Click inflation* is the practice of publishers making more money than they deserve through inflating CPC deals, or increasing their CTR and thus their eCPM. *Competitor clicking* is the practice of advertisers making false clicks against competitor's ads to deplete their advertising budget. The last type of traffic inflation is called *conversion (action) spam*, and is like click spam but requires certain GET or POST parameters, requests a file for download, or follows a specific order of pages to generate a conversion against that advertiser. Like click spam, this can be perpetrated by either publishers or advertisers. This type of fraud only works if the action does not require spending money directly, such as purchasing an item from the website.

Lastly, *misrepresentation* is the practice of a publisher breaking some rule of the network or exchange by lying about their website contents or about what pages ads are actually being shown on (e.g., by spoofing the referring URL). The publisher normally does this to get higher value ads on their pages than they would be able to get if they did not lie about their website contents, or because their website contents are illegal and would not be allowed in the network otherwise.

2.6 Known Types of Attacks

Below are the known types of attacks that either have been performed or could be performed in the context of an ad exchange:

• *Hired Clickers*: This type of attack involves someone sitting in front of a computer and constantly reloading a page and clicking on ads.

• *Keyword Stuffing*: A type of misrepresentation fraud that increases the value of ads that are shown on the fraudster's pages. This is done by including a certain amount of "invisible" content that contains many high-value advertising keywords. The invisible content is either in hidden HTML tags, text that is the same color as the background, or very small text. When the network crawls the fraudster's page to classify the content, the page will be classified as being more valuable or targeted than it really is. This drives higher value ads to the fraudster's page,

• *Impression Stuffing*: The practice of fraudster's putting excessive numbers of banners on their pages so that they get a large number of impressions for each page view. This also includes "stacking" ads on top of each other so that background ads cannot be seen [8].

• *Coercion*: This attack is perpetrated by fraudsters who convince users to click on their ads for reasons other than the ad content itself. This includes an administrator simply asking users to click on their ads, but also includes obfuscating ads with actual site content to trick a user into clicking on ads (e.g., making all valid links on the page look like ads as well).

• *Custom Clickbots*: These are custom software components developed by fraudsters that perpetrates a particular kind of fraud against certain publishers or advertisers. These clickbots normally sit on one or more static machines and issue HTTP requests to certain URLs to simulate impressions, clicks, or conversions [6].

• *For-sale Clickbots*: These are bots that are available for download or purchase and perform click fraud. The bots can be configured to perform many types of fraud and can be given lists of publishers' pages to visit, ads to click on, and proxies to use to diversify the bot's IP addresses [6].

• *Botnet Clickbots*: Botnets are the most difficult type of fraud to detect from an ad exchange's perspective, and it is the most common source of fraudulent Internet ad traffic [21]. Botnets are unique in that the software required to perpetrate fraud is located on many benign users' machines. The malicious software usually comes in one of two flavors: those that run behind the scenes and act as normal clickbots, and those that attempt to coerce the user of the machine to perform some of the ad fraud actions.

• *Forced Browser Clicks*: An attack that forces the user's browser to follow the click URL of an ad by including some client-side script, normally JavaScript. This type of attack can be avoided by putting all ads in an iframe with the source attribute set to an ad tag located on the ad network's website. By using this technique, the content of the iframe is not accessible to any script that did not come from the same domain as the iframe's source. However, recent research suggests that there are still ways of getting click URLs out of iframes [9].

2.7 Detection and Prevention Methods

Below are the known defenses against ad fraud in the context of an ad exchange.

• *Signature-based Detection*: This type of detection uses static rules to decide which ad traffic should be considered valid and which discarded as invalid. One example of a common rule is that the second of any duplicate clicks (caused from a user double-clicking an ad) is considered invalid. This type of detection is beneficial in finding known attacks by looking for known malicious patterns, but it does not work on attacks whose patterns are not known or do not follow static rules [17].

• *Anomaly-based Detection*: This approach uses historical information about publishers to find sudden changes in ad traffic patterns. This may involve looking for a sudden increase in the number of impressions from a publisher, the CTR of the publisher, or the classification/quality of traffic the publisher is generating (e.g., a search engine that suddenly only queries for high-value ad keywords). This type of detection is useful for identifying publishers who are misbehaving or for when fraudsters change or update the type of attack that they are perpetrating.

• *Reverse Spidering (Auditing)*: The practice of ad networks, ad exchanges, or advertisers crawling the HTTP `Referer` of incoming impressions to ensure that the referring sites have the content they claim to have. The reverse spiders look at keywords in HTML content, JavaScript, and iframes of the pages to look for any potentially illegitimate content. To avoid this kind of detection, fraudsters assign a unique ID to the referring URL each time a fraudulent click or impression is generated. Then, when the audit program crawls the referrer, the website will recognize that the ID has already been used, and will not serve any malicious content to the spider [9].

• *Bluff Ads*: These are ads that an ad network serves to a publisher to detect fraudulent activity. These ads are served in response to a random percentage of all requests that come from the publisher and are unique in that they are purposefully uninviting (meaning they contain little more than a picture with no text that does not try to attract the user's attention or get them to click on it). If the click-through rate and conversion rate of these bluff ads is not much lower than ads normally displayed, this would indicate fraud from the publisher [11].

• *Web Site Popularity and Page Rankings*: The number of impressions a publisher is generating for their Web page can be checked against known, trusted website rankings such as Alexa or Compete. If the publisher has much more traffic than their page ranking would suggest, this would be indicative of fraudulent activity [2].

• *Performance-based Pricing*: Performance based pricing is simply a name for publisher payment schemes that do not pay on impressions but instead on how much return on investment (ROI) an advertiser gets from a publisher. The simplest performance-based pricing model is CPC, but CPA deals fall into this category too. This type of pricing reduces impression fraud by requiring publishers to provide a certain level of measurable benefit to the advertisers to make money. This also reduces cost to advertisers as networks with more fraud will have a lower ROI for their advertisers, meaning that advertisers will have to pay less to get their ads shown. In this way, performance-based pricing mitigates the effect of fraud on the advertisers without actively avoiding it [12].

2.8 Botnet-Related Ad Fraud: A Case Study

In this section, we describe the process that allowed us to obtain access to a command-and-control (C&C) server that controlled a botnet used to commit ad fraud, and the data that we collected. The bot malware first came to our attention in February 2010, when we were investigating botnets in the wild. By analyzing the network connections generated by the malware sample, we were able to identify the location of the C&C server that was in control of the botnet. We then contacted the hosting provider whose server was being used by the fraudsters and provided them with detailed evidence of the abuse. The hosting provider suspended the criminal account in March 2010 and provided us with access to the information stored on the server.

By studying the behavior of a bot sample and the source code of the botnet C&C, we were able to get a complete view of how the entire operation functioned. There were two primary methods the botmasters used to earn money: impression/click fraud and affiliate programs that paid a commission based on conversions (e.g., registration, sales, etc). The mode of operation for the impression/click fraud was managed by a configuration file received from the C&C server. The configuration contained various parameters for controlling the patterns of impressions and clicks, iframes to load within a Web browser, and a list of domains that were used to spoof the source of the impression/click through the HTTP `Referer` field. The iframes are directly loaded by the malware in the background of a running Internet Explorer instance through a browser-helper object extension, and they are invisible to the user of the infected system. When the malware loads an iframe, it generates an ad request to RightMedia using a section ID of the fraudsters and a spoofed `Referer` that was set by the configuration file. By loading the iframe directly from each bot, the malware does not need to visit an actual website to emulate impression and clicks.

Interestingly, we found that the domains that were used to spoof the `Referer` field of the fraudulent ad requests contained legitimate RightMedia ads. We will discuss the practice of spoofing the referrer later in Section 5.2, but we believe that the fraudsters use such legitimate sites to remain stealthier. There were also a small number of domains (and websites) in the configuration file that were set up by the fraudsters and used to register multiple publisher accounts. At first these sites seemed legitimate, but on closer examination we identified that the content on these pages was actually stolen from other sites. We will describe these fake websites in more detail in the next section.

Periodically, an infected computer connects back to the C&C server to report its status and to receive a new list of instructions. We also found that the C&C server had the ability to push arbitrary binary executables to the bots; this was regularly used to upgrade the click-fraud malware to newer versions, but could have been used to push more intrusive spyware or adware onto the victims' machines. The bot malware also used browser hijacking to redirect users from a target site (e.g., freecreditreport.com) to an affiliate site (e.g., incentaclick.com and adsmarket.com). Depending on the referring site, the affiliate site would redirect a user's browser to a similar website (e.g., gofreecredit.com). Based on the records maintained by the botnet controllers, their malware redirected users 3,425,030 times from mid-February to May 2010. However, the number of conversions was not stored on the C&C server, so we cannot determine how many users fell for the scam.

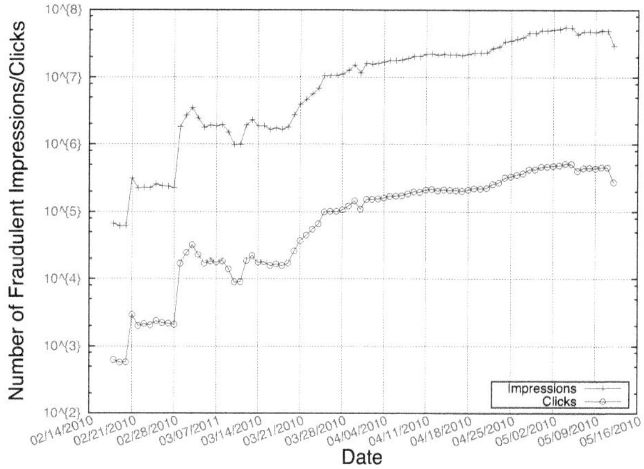

Figure 2: Number of fraudulent impressions and clicks from a click-fraud botnet.

The database for this particular botnet contained records for 530,985 bot installations, with 1,479,036,685 impressions and 14,060,716 clicks (an average click through rate of 0.95%) from mid-February to May 2010. The daily number of impressions and clicks is shown in Figure 2. Interestingly, the ratio of impressions to clicks followed each other almost exactly over time. In Section 4, we will use this behavior as a method for detecting which IP addresses are potentially clickbots. As we will discuss in Section 3.1, the average CPM for impressions and cost-per-click were $0.084 and $0.017, respectively. In other words, the cybercriminals behind the botnet may have netted approximately $124,000 for impressions and another $255,000 for clicks during this 2.5 month period.

We would also like to point out that this botnet malware operates based on an affiliate program out of Eastern Europe (commonly referred to as a *partnerka*) similar to other online criminal operations such as fake antivirus ventures [23]. More specifically, attackers are paid to compromise as many computers as possible and infect them with malware. It should be noted that this botnet has been operational for more than a year, and is still active, at the time of writing.

2.9 Fake Web Sites

The information from the botnet C&C server revealed a number of cases in which the fraudsters used fake websites with seemingly legitimate domain names to register as publishers with different ad networks. At first glance, these websites appeared to contain useful content for Web visitors. However, upon further (manual) inspection, we found that there were common patterns shared by many of these sites. The format of these sites was identical, namely a Wordpress blog template with posts only by an "admin" user, no comments, and a large number of ads (from several different ad exchanges) embedded throughout each of the pages. All of them were based on the same HTML template and, most importantly, contained content that was stolen from other websites. In addition, the sites appeared to be hastily set up with parts of the templates displaying default text (e.g., "text goes here"). Furthermore, we analyzed the WHOIS information for these website domain names and found very similar registration information (name, phone number, address) across many of these domains.

The fraudsters behind the botnet C&C server created a number of these fake websites in order to register as a publisher with several ad networks. After receiving section IDs, the malware spoofed the HTTP `Referer` field and directly loaded the HTML iframe that contained the ads that would normally be found on one of these fake websites. In other words, the malware did not need to visit the fake websites to load advertisements, but rather could bypass the fake websites to reduce the amount of bandwidth and hosting costs.

3. DATA COLLECTION

In this section, we describe the dataset that we utilized to study the RightMedia ad exchange. We also discuss how we manually established a ground truth dataset of good and bad publishers, which we then used to evaluate different models that could be used for fraud detection.

3.1 Data Feed

We obtain a feed of real-world ad data from NETWORKX, which is an ad network that is part of the RightMedia exchange. Every 30 minutes, we receive a batch of the traffic that this ad network has seen in the previous time period.

The traffic can be split into three distinct flows based on the different types of transactions that are allowed in RightMedia. These flows are local publisher traffic, arbitrage traffic, and auction traffic; depending on which flow we were analyzing, different amounts of data were available to us. Local publisher traffic is any traffic that originated from an ad request from one of NETWORKX's own publishers. Of all the flows, local traffic provided us with the most detailed information per impression, both because all the fields in the ad request were populated with meaningful information and because we could look up additional information about the publishers' accounts from NETWORKX's database. Auction traffic is any traffic that NETWORKX made money on through linked partnership as a middleman but that NETWORKX did not buy or sell directly. A number of fields for auction traffic records are suppressed to protect linked partners from being able to learn too much about each other's traffic. Arbitrage traffic is traffic that was either purchased by or sold by NETWORKX itself (see Section 2.4); this was the most difficult type of traffic to analyze. Arbitrage traffic comes in pairs, with one impression representing the purchase of the ad traffic and a corresponding impression for reselling the ad traffic. Unfortunately, there was no way to reliably pair bought impressions with sold ones.

To study the data feed, we implemented an automated system to periodically retrieve NETWORKX's data records and extract relevant information. The data itself was in the form of RightMedia's *Custom Data Feed* format, which contains a log of each impression, click, and conversion that was received by NETWORKX. Each file represented 30 minutes of traffic, was about 200 Megabytes unpacked, and contained, on average, details for approximately 750,000 impressions. The feed had 51 individual fields that were conditionally populated. We found the following fields to be most useful for identifying potential fraud:

- *IP Address*: Right Media only provides an ad network with the first three bytes of the IPv4 address, to preserve users' privacy. However, we were able to estimate how many different users were in each 24 prefix based on how many unique cookie IDs we identified per IP address.
- *Cookie ID*: Unique token given to each browser instance that views an ad; it is stored as a cookie on the local machine and sent with every ad request. Note that this ID is a hash of the actual cookie value.
- *Creative ID*: Unique ID given to each creative to track which specific ad was shown.
- *Section ID*: Unique ID for the particular ad space where the ad was shown. For sold arbitrage traffic, this corresponds to a section ID that NETWORKX owns, and for local traffic, it corresponds to a section ID that a local publisher owns. This field is not populated for auction traffic or purchased arbitrage traffic.
- *Referrer*: Website URL of the referring website for local publisher traffic, or a subdomain of NETWORKX for sold arbitrage traffic. Not populated for auction or purchased arbitrage traffic.
- *Impression/Click/Conversion*: Whether it was an impression, a click, or conversion.
- *Advertiser Cost/Publisher Revenue*: How much the publisher got paid for the ad and how much the advertiser paid out. The difference between the advertiser cost and publisher revenue is how much the intermediary ad networks earned for the ad.
- *Buyer ID*: Unique ID given to each advertiser, or a network-owned buyer ID for bought arbitrage traffic. For auction traffic, this field is populated with the ID of a trusted partner network.
- *Seller ID*: Unique ID given to each publisher, or a network-owned seller ID for sold arbitrage traffic. For auction traffic, this field is populated with the ID of a trusted partner network and not a publisher.
- *User Agent ID*: Identifies the user-agent field that was specified in the HTTP headers. RightMedia currently enumerates 40 different types of browsers and versions.
- *Region ID*: Identifies local geographical areas (state, province, or city) via IP-address-based geo-location services.

Because we were working closely with NETWORKX, we had access to advertiser and publisher accounts that the network owned and managed, which allowed us to glean additional information from the data feed for local traffic. In particular, we could see the domain(s) that publishers used to sign up, how long they have been active, and their traffic statistics. This allowed us to compare our results with RightMedia's software (which was running on NETWORKX's server). With auction and arbitrage traffic, we were not able to relate IDs to real publisher accounts in RightMedia, which limited our analysis on this traffic. Therefore, most of our analysis focused on local traffic.

We investigated in depth ten days worth of data collected from NETWORKX. More precisely, we analyzed the data collected between April 20 and April 30, 2011, which was 513,644,248 total impressions across all the data flows. Overall statistics for each traffic flow are outlined in Table 1. We chose to perform our analysis on the local publisher traffic, because it contained the most information for each impression. Out of NETWORKX's 1,600 publishers, only about 300 are active and generating ad requests. Of these 300, the most popular 1% are responsible for roughly 40% of the local traffic, and the top 10% are responsible for 92% of the local traffic. We observed the impressions, clicks, and conversions,

Traffic Flow	Traffic (%)	Impressions (per hour)	CTR	Conversion Rate
Auction	37.7%	305,318	0.16%	-
Publishers	2.0%	15,794	0.56%	0.01%
Arbitrage	60.3%	489,184	0.12%	0.007%

Table 1: Statistics for each traffic flow.

and we measured a click-through-rate (CTR) of 0.56%, with conversions being 2.22%. In addition, we measured an average CPM of $0.084, an average cost-per-click (CPC) of $0.017, and an average cost-per-action (CPA) of $0.055. We found that there are about 1.5 unique cookie IDs per IP address in an hour, which are responsible for 2.4 impressions.

3.2 Establishing Ground Truth

To determine how well analysis and detection models can identify fraudulent behavior, we require ground truth about known bad and known good publishers. NETWORKX's traffic was coming from relatively few publishers, and the remaining publishers had so little traffic that they could not cause noticeable harm to NETWORKX's advertisers. Therefore, we only had to analyze the top 100 publishers. We chose to manually analyze each of the publishers by visiting the referrer URLs of their ad requests. Since it is not trivial to determine what sites are good and bad, we used the following heuristics (many of these were established from observing the fake fraud websites outlined in Section 2.9):

- The site does not serve content, or the content that it serves does not render.
- The site contains entirely ad content or significantly more ad content than actual user content.
- The site is hosting illegal content or content against the terms of use of RightMedia.
- The content on the site is stolen or contains leftovers from an HTML template.

The following heuristics were used for establishing which sites were not perpetrating fraud:

- The site is well-designed, good looking, and usable.
- The site has a very good Alexa ranking, especially compared to their amount of NETWORKX traffic.
- The site is full of legitimate content that has user support, such as comments or "likes" from various social networks.

For a site to be flagged as either good or bad, it had to conform to more than one of the above heuristics in one category and none of the heuristics in the other. Of the 100 publishers analyzed, 11 were picked out as owning sites that likely perpetrated fraud and 20 were picked out as likely not participating in fraud. The finalized ground truth list was brought to the attention of the development team and the CEO of NETWORKX, who verified our work. They also terminated the malicious publishers' accounts as a result of what they found. None of the publishers whose accounts were terminated attempted to contact NETWORKX for outstanding payments or account renewal.

4. IDENTIFYING SUSPICIOUS TRAFFIC

In this section, we present techniques that could be used for detecting fraudulent ad traffic. In particular, we discuss two main approaches: First, we introduce a detector based on checking the referring web page for signs that indicate fraud. Then, we discuss techniques based on statistical properties of various fields in ad requests.

4.1 Reverse Spidering

To detect the malware described in Section 2.8, we developed a reverse auditing system that crawled the referrers of each impression in our data feed. We deployed 50 virtual machines that utilized the SELENIUM [1] software-testing framework for web applications, which has the ability to programmatically control a real Web browser. The primary benefit that Selenium provided was the ability to interpret JavaScript code. For each audit, we collected the raw traffic, and then we extracted the section ID fields on the web page that is responsible for generating revenue for the publisher. Next, we compared the section ID values from NETWORKX's data feed with the observed section ID values found on that referrer's site. Our intuition was that if the referring page did not contain the section ID that initiated the request, then the request must have been hijacked.

Unfortunately, this detection method was not effective in the real world. After several months (August 2010 - April 2011) of running our reverse spidering system, we noticed that 79.2% of the referred pages in NETWORKX's data feed contained no section IDs when examined. Clearly, this high percentage of traffic could not be fraudulent, so we manually analyzed some of the sites that did not contain section IDs. We found that many sites used IP-address-based geo-location to serve specific ads to particular regions. In addition, some of the sites used ad delivery optimization services, such as Casale Media, that dynamically choose different ad exchanges to maximize conversions. In other words, a visitor may have received a RightMedia ad based on his location, but our crawlers, which are based in the U.S., were delivered ads from DoubleClick's ad exchange. Even if we had found RightMedia ad tags with different section IDs than what we would expect, this would not indicate fraud, as one publisher may have many legitimate RightMedia accounts. As a result, we conclude that reverse spidering for the purpose of fraud detection suffers from significant limitations.

4.2 Modeling Ad Requests

We introduce a number of features that model properties of ad traffic. Similar to traditional intrusion detection systems, we use these features to establish models of normal, expected traffic. When certain requests or sets of requests violate a previously-built model, we consider these requests to be suspicious. We use the fraction of suspicious traffic per publisher to detect fraud. More specifically, when a certain publisher produces a high percentage of requests that are suspicious, this publisher is more likely to be involved in malicious activity.

In the next paragraphs, we discuss our approach for building models. Then, we describe the effectiveness of individual features.

4.2.1 Building Models

Features. We considered a number of simple features for detecting anomalous ad traffic:

- *Impressions Per Cookie*: The number of impressions each cookie generated. Our motivation was that, since each cookie ID represents a unique browser instance, any cookies generating a very large amount of traffic would be fraudulent.

• *CTR Per Cookie*: The click-through-rate for each cookie. On average, CTRs are rarely above 2%, so any cookies generating very high click-through-rates would be suspicious.

• *Publisher Revenue Per Cookie*: How much revenue each cookie generated for a publisher. Our motivation was that for fraud to be effective, fraudulent traffic would have to be generating revenue in addition to just impressions.

• *Unique IP Addresses Per Cookie*: The number of unique IP addresses a cookie is generating requests from. Since cookies are assigned per browser instance, we would not expect one cookie ID to come from many 24 IP subnets within a short period of time.

• *Impressions Per IP Address*: The number of impressions that each IP address generates. Our motivation for this feature is that a naive clickbot might remain at one static IP address and generate many requests.

• *CTR Per IP Address*: The CTR of each IP address. Most users do not click on an ad more than 2% of the time, thus, a very high CTR from a single IP address indicates fraud.

• *Publisher Revenue Per IP Address*: How much revenue each IP address generated for a publisher. Unusually high values are suspicious.

• *Deviation of CTR Per IP Address*: This feature is slightly different than the others because it cannot be computed for traffic in a single time interval. Instead, we compute the standard deviation of the CTR values for a number of consecutive time slots. Malware that commits click fraud often exhibits characteristic behavior in that its click through rates over time are very consistent, even when the number of impressions generated changes. Thus, a low feature value is suspicious.

A number of traditional detection features could not be applied to our dataset due to lack of data in certain fields, especially the IP address field. For example, because we only had the first three octets of the IP address, we could not detect sites that had an unusually high amount of traffic from IP addresses that belong to known Internet proxy services, a behavior that would indicate the presence of static IP address clickbots.

Thresholds. We use a dynamic threshold to determine which features are considered suspicious. Each feature threshold is applied to the feature value computed for a time window of one hour. After that, the threshold is recomputed, based on historical (previously-seen) data. More precisely, a threshold is determined by first computing the mean and variance for a particular feature over all previous time windows. Then, we set the threshold equal to the mean plus N standard deviations. The value of N can be used to tune the sensitivity for each "detector." We empirically determined good values for N based on a subset of the traffic dataset. The concrete values are shown in Table 2.

The threshold for the *CTR standard deviation feature* is computed slightly differently. In particular, suspicious values for the standard deviation are not those values that *exceed* a normal baseline. Instead, a small standard deviation is suspicious, since it indicates a high regularity typically associated with automated (bot) traffic. We empirically found that a value of 0.02 (2%) produces good results.

Anomaly Detection Algorithm	Threshold (Standard Deviation)
Impressions Per Cookie	3
CTR Per Cookie	3
Publisher Revenue Per Cookie	2
Unique IP Addresses Per Cookie	2
Impressions Per IP Address	4
CTR Per IP Address	4
Publisher Revenue Per Cookie	3

Table 2: Detector thresholds.

Classifying publishers. For each time window of analysis (one hour), the detectors produce those cookies and IP addresses that violate at least one of the feature thresholds. Using this information, we identify all requests (impressions) that originate from a suspicious IP or that contain a suspicious cookie. In the next step, we determine the publishers that are associated with these requests (based on the publisher ID in the request). Using this, we can determine the number of suspicious and the number of total requests for each publisher and each time window.

Using the number of suspicious and total requests, we can easily compute a publisher's *fraction* of requests that are suspicious (both for individual time intervals and for an entire observation period). We consider this fraction as an anomaly score for the publisher. The anomaly score can be compared to an anomaly threshold; when the threshold is exceeded, we consider the publisher to perform fraudulent activity in the time period under analysis.

4.2.2 Evaluating Models

We wanted to explore the ability of different detectors to identify fraudulent traffic. To this end, we applied the models described in the previous section to our data set (ten days worth of traffic, as described in Section 3.1). We then computed, for each model, an anomaly score for every publisher. Finally, we compared these anomaly scores to varying thresholds (ranging from 0 to 1, in increments of 0.001). This yielded different sets of publishers that would be classified as suspicious or legitimate.

In the next step, we leveraged our ground truth (see Section 3.2) of good and bad publishers. More precisely, for each model and each threshold value, we could determine the fraction of known, malicious publishers that the models would have correctly identified. Also, we could see the fraction of honest publishers that were incorrectly attributed as suspicious.

Discussion. In this paragraph, we discuss the performance of the individual detection features. Overall, we found that no single model would work as a reliable detector. For example, the best detection features with good threshold settings yielded detection rates between 60% and 80%. However, with these settings, a detector would also incorrectly blame 10% of the legitimate publishers. This indicates that there is a significant variety in the ad traffic, and simple, statistical measures are not sufficient to precisely distinguish between malicious and legitimate players. Nevertheless, the simple models are useful to guide a human analyst (employed by ad networks) to focus on those publishers that produce the largest fraction of suspicious traffic and, hence, are most likely to participate in fraudulent activities.

Impressions per cookie/IP features: The number of impressions per cookie and the number of impressions per IP address were the best indicators for fraudulent activity (and cookies perform better than IP addresses). The good performance of the impressions-per-cookie detector is likely a result of cookie replay attacks, where one cookie ID is used over a long period of time to generate many impressions (see Section 5.1).

CTR per cookie/IP features: Interestingly, the CTR (click through rate) features, both per cookie and per IP, perform very badly for fraud detection. This is most likely because CTRs are closely monitored in the ad industry, and having publishers or users with very high CTRs is one of the simplest indicators of fraud. Thus, fraudsters who want to survive in the exchange need to keep their CTR low to remain undetected.

Revenue per cookie/IP features: Because the number of impressions and the publisher's revenue are related, one would expect that the two feature sets perform fairly similarly. Interestingly, however, publisher revenue models perform much worse. This could be the result of RightMedia's performance-based pricing model, which devalues impressions from publishers who do not exhibit measurable gain to advertisers (in the form of purchases or conversions). Thus, it is significantly easier for fraudsters to generate impressions rather than actual revenue without a sophisticated system or human user to issue conversions. As we will show in Section 5.4, we found a malicious publisher that was generating a very large amount of traffic, but that had an eCPM of only $0.02. Because the eCPM of fraudulent publishers tends to be lower, they are less likely to have unusually high publisher revenue from a single cookie or IP address.

Unique IP Addresses per cookie feature: When studying the ad fraud botnet, we observed that the same cookie was reused by multiple different machines. Thus, one would expect the number of unique IP addresses per cookie to be effective at detecting fraud (in particular cookie replay attacks that are perpetrated across a number of machines). However, we found that this feature produces many incorrect detections. In particular, we found that there are several sites (mostly forums) where users login with the same cookie ID from many different networks (which is also due to networks that frequently assign new IP addresses to its clients). These sites also increased the false positive rate of our impression-based feature because users would remain or revisit the site with the same cookie or IP address over and over again, thus generating many ad requests with that cookie/IP address. The presence of such sites is one of the reasons why gleaning reliable fraud data from an impression stream is difficult for an individual ad network.

Deviation of CTR feature: This model successfully detected a number of malicious publishers that seemed to have used automated tools to convert impressions into clicks. However, since not all malicious publishers were using simple, automated tools to commit fraud, the overall detection capability of this feature was modest.

Note that our models operate under the assumption that each cookie ID and IP address belongs to a unique user, and they report fraud when a cookie or IP exhibits behavior inconsistent with the behavior of a single user. However, as mentioned previously, RightMedia only provides the first three octets of an IP address to an ad network, and, in addition, network address translation (NAT) might hide many users behind a single IP address. As a result, a single IP address value could encompass a large number of individual users. Thus, cookie-based detection techniques typically produce more consistent results than IP-based techniques.

5. OBSERVATIONS

In this section, we examine anomalies that our results indicate as fraudulent activities in the RightMedia ad exchange. In particular, based on our study of ten days of ad traffic, we observed a number of patterns that are associated with fraudulent activity. We looked for similar patterns in our entire data set, which contains traffic for a much longer period of time (specifically, four months from February 2011 until April 2011). This section presents some of our interesting findings.

5.1 Cookie Replay Attacks

As a result of cookie impression analysis on the data feed, we were able to find a number of instances of cookies that had many hundreds or thousands of impressions spread over a week or more. In particular, there was one cookie ID that was consistently generating traffic during the entire time period we analyzed (up to September 2011), and was active before the start of 2011. We observed this cookie's behavior in NETWORKX's local traffic, arbitrage traffic, and auction traffic. Normally, a cookie is associated with a single browser instance, and thus a single unique IP address, browser, and geographic region. However, the data for the suspect cookie indicated that the cookie was coming from 28 different types of browsers, 746 global regions on 666,429 different 24-bit IP subnets, and using 28 browser languages. We also observed this cookie coming from 236 unique local publisher accounts. The cookie's conversion rate is 18 times greater in Table 3 than for the overall traffic in Table 1. Because of the large amount and uncharacteristic nature of this cookie's traffic, we consider it and other cases of cookies with very large amounts of traffic a type of fraud we call *cookie replay attacks*.

The reason why an attacker would randomize the browser version, language, and other fields, but not refresh the cookie value is that cookies set by RightMedia are encrypted with a server-side key, and a Hash-based Message Authentication Code (HMAC) is used to verify its integrity. Thus, generating new values to populate the cookie field of the HTTP header of an ad request is not trivial. To set the cookie properly, the browser must execute some client-side JavaScript embedded within the ad tag that is able to generate the encrypted cookie. Of course, this is possible to automate (our reverse auditing system used Selenium to do it), but this limits potential fraud, both in processing resources and because the IP address field cannot be spoofed when querying the servers for the cookie ID.

From the local publisher traffic flow, which constituted 7% of all NETWORKX's traffic, we calculated that the cookie was generating $32 in revenue for the fraudster per month, and costing advertisers $56 per month. Since these values were collected from only the local traffic flow, the real amount of fraud across the entire exchange would be much larger than this. To get an idea of how much the fraud scales across the exchange, we looked at how much revenue the cookie was generating across all the traffic passing through NETWORKX, and found that the cookie was generating $235 in revenue and $409 in cost every day. However, it is important to highlight the fact that NETWORKX is just one of several hundred ad networks in the RightMedia exchange, so the potential loss due to fraud from this type of operation is likely far greater. Despite the loss from these attacks, it appears that the current fraud systems that are in place are not yet effective enough to detect this type of activity.

Traffic Flow	Impressions (per hour)	CTR	Conversion Rate
Auction	6,103	0.3%	-
Publishers	248	0.6%	0.185%
Arbitrage	13,962	0.6%	0.114%

Table 3: Suspicious cookie statistics for each traffic flow.

5.1.1 *Clicks from the Cloud*

Interestingly, we identified traffic that originated from Amazon's Elastic Compute Cloud (EC2) and that was being used to perpetrate a portion of these cookie replay attacks. While ad traffic from the cloud is not by itself suspicious (Web users may proxy browser traffic through the cloud), we observed the cookie ID discussed previously being used in a large number of requests that originated from the cloud from April 10, 2011 to April 13, 2011. Thus, we believe that this is a strong indication that attackers are using Amazon's cloud (possibly the free tier that allows for 30GB of transfer per month) to generate fraudulent ad impressions and clicks.

5.2 Spoofing the Referrer

Referrer spoofing is performed by clickbots that want to hide their fraudulent traffic across multiple referrers, so that large numbers of impressions do not come from referring domains that are not very popular or well-known. The bots rotate through a list of referrers while performing the fraud, but they always use a section ID that the fraudster owns. We observed this type of fraud on the click fraud botnet command and control server that we had access to. In February and March of 2010, we observed the command-and-control server issuing large numbers of referrers to the bots that included both the fraudster's sites and popular sites that they could not have owned, such as citibank.com. A year later, in April 2011, we observed the command-and-control server issuing only a few possible referring URLs, which only included the fraudster's fake sites. We suspect that this change in behavior was caused by the fact that RightMedia realized that their traffic was coming from a wide variety of referrers that did not match their registered publisher websites. According to RightMedia's online user guide, "If the [referer] report shows a long list of unfamiliar domains for a publisher, it is likely that the publisher has provided their tags to adware or spyware companies for their own profit" [4]. To avoid being caught by this kind of simplistic detection scheme, a malicious publisher would simply include a less varied list of domains in the `Referer` field of their fabricated HTTP request. In the following section, we analyze other publishers that exhibit similar behavior.

5.3 Unrecognized Referrers

During our manual analysis phase we became interested in looking at unrecognized referrers and why they would be generating impressions for a particular section. We define an *Unrecognized Referrer* as any referring site that did not register the section ID that they are using to generate ad traffic. In RightMedia, section IDs are allowed to be placed on sites other than the site that the publisher had originally registered with, so simply observing that a section is getting impressions from unrecognized referrers is not enough to classify the impressions as fraud. Thus, we were not able to develop an automated way to detect fraudulent activity based on the `Referer` field (which can be spoofed anyway, as we saw in the previous section), but we did unearth a number of attacks that can be perpetrated as a result of this policy. Because local publisher traffic is the only traffic with the `Referer` field set, we could only perform this analysis on local traffic, and we found that unknown referrers made up 43.2% of the traffic. The results of our analysis for April 2011 are outlined in Table 4. We looked both at publishers that had a large number of impressions from unknown referrers and those that used a large variety of unknown referrers. From this, we were able to observe a number of sites whose registered domains were no longer active but were still generating impressions through other domains, which we will discuss in the next section. In addition, this analysis allowed us to identify a malicious publisher who was generating impressions across hundreds of unique referring domains.

Publisher	Unknown Referrers	Impressions
PUBLISHERA	300	3,624,162
PUBLISHERB	46	2,720,146
PUBLISHERC	63	1,640,597
PUBLISHERD	1	1,153,357
PUBLISHERE	55	702,209
PUBLISHERF	19	511,066
PUBLISHERG	6	319,442
PUBLISHERH	22	200,334
PUBLISHERI	6	157,033
PUBLISHERJ	1	155,809

Table 4: Top publishers with unknown referrers (April 2011)

5.3.1 *Missing-In-Action Sites*

It was interesting to see that many publishers had homepages that were down, yet they were still generating impressions from other referring sites. We call such sites Missing-In-Action (*MIA*) sites. We calculated that out of NETWORKX's 1,600 publishers, 10% had unreachable domains and 5% were 404 errors, which did not include publishers whose domains were now parking pages. While looking at these sites, we observed a specific instance of a local NETWORKX publisher who was performing a kind of misrepresentation fraud with his MIA site. This allowed the publisher to host ads on a page that had illegal content that violated RightMedia's terms of use. First, the fraudster registered as a benign publisher, in this case PUBLISHERC's site, and received a number of section IDs to use on the site from NETWORKX, who did not find anything wrong with the site's content. Instead of placing the ad tags on the benign site, the fraudster placed them on a site that contains illegal content, in this case something like *full-free-games.com*. Because there is no check to ensure the referrer matches the page, impressions generated from *full-free-games.com* still made money for the fraudster.

5.4 Malicious Publishers

By analyzing cookie replay attacks and unknown referrers, we were able to identify a particularly malicious publisher who was the source of a large amount of fraudulent traffic for NETWORKX. This publisher, which we call PUBLISHERA, had three section IDs that had already been shut down by RightMedia for generating fraudulent traffic, but he was still perpetrating fraud with one section ID that had not been flagged. We first investigated this publisher because it had by far the most unknown referring domains and impressions from these domains, as shown in Table 4. Because many of the impressions were coming from seemingly random sites, there was evidence of an ongoing referrer spoofing attack. In addition, we computed that this publisher was generating 20% of the suspicious cookie traffic but accounted for only 0.2% percent of all of NETWORKX's local publisher traffic. After being notified of our results, those in charge at NETWORKX decided to take action and ban PUBLISHERA from their network.

PUBLISHERA's historical data provides us with insight into the amount of money a fraudulent publisher can make through a single ad network. PUBLISHERA was part of NETWORKX from July 2010 to May 2011, and over that period earned approximately $6,700 on 277,043,885 impressions. This means his eCPM was only $0.02. The fact that he had such a low eCPM is evidence of RightMedia's performance-based pricing, which results in the drop of a publisher's CPM if these publisher's impressions do not bring measurable revenue to advertisers.

6. FRAUD IN AD EXCHANGES

Although the RightMedia exchange contains a number of features to monitor the legitimacy of traffic and provide historical reporting to each ad network, we know from analyzing the data feed that a large amount of fraud goes unnoticed. The nature of online ad serving and ad exchanges is such that there is not a strong sense of accountability between entities in the exchange. This is done to protect the privacy of these entities, but it also keeps the ad networks from being able to do adequate checks on the validity of their own traffic.

6.1 Suppression of Data Fields

The lack of accountability in the exchange is likely done to protect each ad network's private ad serving data, but it also makes it very difficult for an ad network to verify the legitimacy of ad requests from partner ad networks, leaving their advertisers open to fraud. In particular, the suppression of the last octet of each IP address is very limiting when trying to find machines exhibiting a particular kind of behavioral pattern. In addition, all brokered auction traffic does not have a referrer or section ID field, and conversions are not reported on the brokered traffic, even if it was sold to a locally-owned advertiser. The suppression of these fields allows a fraudster to register with a malicious or naive network and perpetrate fraud across many networks that may be more vigilant.

6.2 Consistency vs. Flexibility

As we discussed earlier, RightMedia does not verify or enforce the basic premise that the referrer must match the publisher's registered site's domain and assigned sections. The primary reason for this appears to be that RightMedia wants their service to be user-friendly, and it would be inconvenient if a publisher had to re-register and get new section IDs if they change their domain. We were able to identify one instance of a benign MIA site, where the publisher chose to relocate his site to a new domain and keep his old section IDs. Our analysis tools flagged them as suspicious because their original site *benign-golf-site1.com* (obfuscated) gave us a 404 error, but there were a large number of impressions coming from the referrer *benign-golf-site2.com* (obfuscated). Manual inspection verified that the site had legitimate content, and the change of domain most likely came from the owner wanting a more lucrative domain. Finally, we suspect RightMedia does not verify whether the referrer matches the section ID. This might be because RightMedia considers the ad networks to be responsible for monitoring the validity of their traffic and to filter any potentially fraudulent instances.

6.3 Hiding Fraud in the Exchange

The distributed nature of an ad exchange makes it a platform to commit fraud. Except for Yahoo! and the exchange itself, no entity has a full picture of what is going on, and fraudsters use this to appear far less malicious than they are in reality. For example, in Section 5.1, we showed a case where a malicious cookie was generating 300 times more revenue in NETWORKX's auction traffic than in their local traffic alone. However, NETWORKX only sees a small portion of all auctioned traffic in the exchange, thus knowing how much total fraudulent traffic involving this cookie is impossible with our limited view. Moreover, every fraudulent site that we identified, whether it was a fake site (as discussed in Section 2.9) or one of our manually-identified bad publishers (from Section 3.2), had a large number of ads from many ad networks and ad exchanges. So, the total cost of the fraud gets distributed among many independent and often competing entities (DoubleClick and RightMedia, for example), which makes the fraud harder to identify.

6.4 What RightMedia Does Right

RightMedia does not ignore the problem of fraud. Their user interface provides many tools for ad network administrators to identify the most blatant cases of fraud and shut down any malicious accounts or suspicious partnerships. In addition, especially in our experience with NETWORKX, it seems that the general attitude of ad networks is to stay actively involved in their ad serving process to ensure that their advertisers are protected from the worst cases of fraud. RightMedia's built-in malicious behavior detection system is called SCOUR, and it was able to identify the severe case of fraud outlined in Section 5.4 and take steps to limit (but not stop) the fraud. According to the RightMedia online user guide, SCOUR "searches for patterns exhibited by desktop software and flags sections that exhibit what, in our opinion, may be malicious traffic patterns" [4]. Based on the description, it appears that the system focuses on finding bot signatures and flagging publishers who have large amounts of traffic coming from machines with these bot signatures. With a full view of the exchange, a modified version of this system should be able to detect some of the more sophisticated types of fraud outlined in the paper.

7. RELATED WORK

Previous work focused on various aspects of detecting click-fraud. Majumdar *et al.* proposed a content delivery system to verify broker honesty under standard security assumptions [18]. Efficient algorithms for detecting duplicate clicks were proposed by Metwally *et al.* in [19] and Zhang *et al.* in [26]. Studies also have shown how malware can exploit ad networks [7, 10].

Juels *et al.* proposed a cryptographic approach for replacing the pay-per-click model with one where pay-per-action can attract premium rates and unsuccessful clicks are discarded [14]. Immorlica *et al.* studied fraudulent clicks and presented a click-fraud resistant method for learning the click through rate of advertisements [13]. In contrast, Kintana *et al.* created a system designed to penetrate click-fraud filters to discover detection vulnerabilities [16].

Recent work has examined botnets and researchers have infiltrated or seized control of parts of the botnet infrastructure to gain more insight into their inner-workings [15, 22, 24, 25]. Note that these botnets were targeted at sending spam email and engaging in acts of financial theft.

In contrast to previous work, our analysis is the first that uses near real-time data to investigate the problem of ad fraud from inside an ad exchange and from the vantage point of a botnet controller. This offers us a unique opportunity to study the ad exchange structure in depth and to discover its weaknesses. Unfortunately, many ad networks are still reluctant to provide researchers with access to their data streams. As a result, the effectiveness of the proposed method in preventing fraud and even determining the amount of fraud that occurs in actual ad exchanges is not clear.

8. CONCLUSIONS

In this paper, we described how online ad exchanges work and focused in particular on Yahoo!'s RightMedia. We found that the complexity of the ad exchange provides criminals with an opportunity to generate revenue by developing malware that impersonates legitimate user activities. Regrettably, there is a trade-off between the security of the exchange and the flexibility offered to publishers and ad networks to maximize their profits.

Acknowledgements

This work was supported by the Office of Naval Research (ONR) under Grant N000140911042, by the U.S. Army Research Laboratory and the U.S. Army Research Office under MURI grant No. W911NF-09-1-0553, and by the National Science Foundation (NSF) under grants CNS-0845559 and CNS-0905537.

9. REFERENCES

[1] SeleniumHQ. Web Application Testing System. http://seleniumhq.org/.

[2] Secure Accounting and Auditing on the Web. volume 30, pages 541 – 550, 1998.

[3] IAB Interactive Advertising Glossary. http://www.iab.net/wiki/index.php/Category:Glossary, 2011.

[4] RightMedia Exchange Knowledge Base. https://kb.yieldmanager.com/, 2011.

[5] C. Borgs, J. Chayes, O. Etesami, N. Immorlica, K. Jain, and M. Mahdian. Dynamics of Bid Optimization in Online Advertisement Auctions. In *Proceedings of the International Conference on World Wide Web*, 2007.

[6] N. Daswani, C. Mysen, V. Rao, S. Weis, and S. G. K. Gharachorloo. Online Advertising Fraud. In *Proceedings of Crimeware*, 2008.

[7] N. Daswani and M. Stoppelman. The Anatomy of Clickbot.A. In *Proceedings of the USENIX Workshop on Hot Topics in Understanding Botnet*, 2007.

[8] B. Edelman. Securing Online Advertising: Rustlers and Sheriffs in the New Wild West. In *Harvard Business School NOM Working Paper No. 09-039*, 2008.

[9] M. Gandhi, M. Jakobsson, and J. Ratkiewicz. Badvertisements: Stealthy Click-Fraud with Unwitting Accessories. In *Journal of Digital Forensic Practice*, 2011.

[10] F. Hacquebor. Making a Million: Criminal Gangs, the Rogue Traffic Broker, and Stolen Clicks. http://blog.trendmicro.com/making-a-million%E2%80%94criminal-gangs-the-rogue-traffic-broker-and-stolen-clicks/, 2010.

[11] H. Haddadi. Fighting Online Click-fraud Using Bluff Ads. volume 40, April 2010.

[12] Y. Hu. Performance-based pricing models in online advertising. Number March, 2004.

[13] N. Immorlica, K. Jain, M. Mahdian, and K. Talwar. Click Fraud Resistant Methods for Learning Click-Through Rates. *Internet and Network Economics*, pages 34–45, 2005.

[14] A. Juels, S. Stamm, and M. Jakobsson. Combatting Click Fraud via Premium Clicks. In *Proceedings of the USENIX Security Symposium*, 2007.

[15] C. Kanich, C. Kreibich, K. Levchenko, B. Enright, G. Voelker, V. Paxson, and S. Savage. Spamalytics: An Empirical Analysis of Spam Marketing Conversion. In *Proceedings of the ACM Conference on Computer and Communications Security*, 2008.

[16] C. Kintana, D. Turner, J. Pan, A. Metwally, N. Daswani, E. Chin, and A. Bortz. The goals and challenges of click fraud penetration testing systems. In *In Proceedings of the International Symposium on Software Reliability Engineering*, 2009.

[17] N. Kshetri. The Economics of Click Fraud. volume 8, pages 45 –53, May-June 2010.

[18] S. Majumdar, D. Kulkarni, and C. Ravishankar. Addressing Click Fraud in Content Delivery Systems. In *Proceedings of the IEEE Conference on Computer Communications*, 2007.

[19] A. Metwally, D. Agrawal, and A. Abbadi. Duplicate Detection in Click Streams. In *Proceedings of the International Conference on World Wide Web*, 2005.

[20] A. Metwally, D. Agrawal, and A. E. Abbadi. DETECTIVES: DETEcting Coalition hiT InïňĆation attacks in adVertising nEtworks Streams. In *Proceedings of the International Conference on World Wide Web*, 2007.

[21] L. Rodriguez. http://www.washingtonpost.com/wp-srv/technology/documents/yahoo_may2006.pdf, 2006.

[22] B. Stock, J. Gobel, M. Engelberth, F. Freiling, and T. Holz. Walowdac âĂŞ Analysis of a Peer-to-Peer Botnet. In *Proceedings of European Conference on Computer Network Defense*, 2009.

[23] B. Stone-Gross, R. Abman, R. Kemmerer, C. Kruegel, D. Steigerwald, and G. Vigna. The Underground Economy of Fake Antivirus Software. In *Proceedings of the Workshop on Economics of Information Security*, 2011.

[24] B. Stone-Gross, M. Cova, L. Cavallaro, B. Gilbert, M. Szydlowski, R. Kemmerer, C. Kruegel, and G. Vigna. Your Botnet is My Botnet: Analysis of a Botnet Takeover. In *Proceedings of the ACM Conference on Computer and Communications Security*, 2009.

[25] B. Stone-Gross, T. Holz, G. Stringhini, and G. Vigna. The Underground Economy of Spam: A Botmaster's Perspective of Coordinating Large-Scale Spam Campaigns. In *Proceedings of the USENIX Workshop on Large-Scale Exploits and Emergent Threats*, 2011.

[26] L. Zhang and Y. Guan. Detecting Click Fraud in Pay-Per-Click Streams of Online Advertising Networks. In *Proceedings of the IEEE Conference on Distributed Computing Systems*, 2008.

Summary Review Documentation for

"Understanding Fraudulent Activities in Online Ad Exchanges"

Authors: B. Stone-Gross, R. Stevens, A. Zarras, C. Kruegel, R. Kemmerer, G. Vigna

Reviewer #1

Strengths: The paper takes a fascinating look at an area of Internet activity that is usually hidden. I am not aware of other quantitative, trace-based analysis of online ad fraud, and if that is correct (is it?) then it makes a good case for accepting this paper.

Weaknesses: The paper feels very anecdotal. It is a mix of different tidbits and there is no ground truth on which to assess how well the fraud detection classifiers work. (I do not doubt that they turn up fraud in the worst cases, but have little sense for whether they tag legitimate activity or miss lots of fraud.) Being a bit more systematic in the analysis would help, including precise descriptions of the trace and graphs/stats for the range of presumed normal ad-serving behavior.

Comments to Authors: I enjoyed reading your paper, as much for finding out how ad exchanges work as for learning about fraud, and I have relatively few comments.

Can you put fraud in perspective? For example, do you have an estimate (perhaps from your classifier) as to what percentage of the revenue is lost to fraud? Maybe this is small, but it could be compared to other systems such as credit cards.

Explaining the mechanisms as a figure with a numbered sequence of steps would be helpful. The free-form prose is difficult to put into an overall picture.

Say somewhere that CPM is the cost per 1000 impressions.

Generally, your descriptions are often unsatisfying where they could be more informative! For example, you say the data is in RighMedia's custom format and you use the following 10 fields. Well, I'd like to know basic information about the overall trace. How big is it, in MB and records? XML or something else? How many records are there of what type? Are the fields you look at most of a record, or are there many more fields? etc. Maybe all of this information isn't necessary, but it would help me grasp what you are working with.

Say somewhere that classifier warnings are what you interpret as fraud and they occur when the thresholds you gave earlier are exceeded. Seems obvious, but you never come out and say it.

I did not understand the cookie fraud. The cookie is set by the ad system. Why can't the host simply clear ad system cookies and appear to be a fresh, new client?

Reviewer #2

Strengths: The paper presents a real and challenging problem. It would be useful to publish, both because it explains complex types of fraud that are not well/widely understood by the network community, and because it provides evidence based on real measurements that such fraud occurs in practice.

Weaknesses: The methodology used by the authors to estimate the number of fraud incidents is not convincing (it relies on thresholds that are not justified, hence seem arbitrary). The types of fraud that are described have already been identified by prior work.

Comments to Authors: One weakness of the paper is that the types of fraud that it describes have already been identified by prior work. To me, the paper was fascinating, because I do not know the area and I found it extremely useful to read such a detailed overview of how online ad exchanges work and what opportunities for abuse they offer. However, I think that the paper would be less useful to an expert.

My main complaint has to do with the methodology used to estimate the number of fraud incidents. As the paper describes it, it seems to consist of setting a bunch of thresholds and counting how many times they were violated. For example, the click-through-rate (CTR) threshold for a single IP subnet is set to 0.2%, while the CTR threshold for a single cookie is set to 0.3%. Why the difference? I am sure that the authors had good reasons for picking these thresholds, but they should explain them.

A less important complaint has to do with presentation. The paper targets a general networking audience, not just the experts (otherwise it would not be describing how online add exchanges work nor explaining attacks that were the topic of prior work). Yet it does not clearly explain the most confusing aspects of the story. For example:
- In Section 4.1, I recommend that the authors clearly state how an ad network sets and uses cookies, and what the attacker does with them (I presume that the attacker obtains one valid cookie and sends it to multiple bots).
- The whole story about spoofing the referrer's site: It is mentioned in 2.8 and 3.4 without being explained, then sort-of-explained in 4.2. I got it in the end, but only after going back and forth several times.
- In Section 4.3, the paragraph on "Spoofing Section IDs": At first it talks about fraudsters spoofing the referrer but using their own section IDs. Then it talks about obfuscating fraud by mixing benign with fraudulent section IDs (which, if I understand correctly, is different -- the fraudster sometimes points the

browser to a good site, as opposed to one of her own fraudulent sites). I recommend separating these two scenarios.

Another minor complaint has to do with the proposed countermeasures. In Section 5.1, it says that the main problem with ad exchanges is that they trust the information passed by the browser. This is not what I concluded from reading the paper up to this point; I concluded that the main problem is the fact that there is no practical way to tell whether an impression/click is initiated by an interested customer or a bot. I recommend that the authors explain exactly which of the attacks that they describe could be solved through digital signatures.

Reviewer #3

Strengths: Analysis of data from the real entities gives an interesting view of what kind of attack techniques are being used in real world and reveals that current systems still have weaknesses.

Weaknesses: The paper is read more like a survey paper. Background material takes half of the paper, spanning 7 pages. The measurement and analytical contribution is not deep. Considering this is an early paper on understanding ad exchange, this might not be a show-stopper.

Comments to Authors: This is a well written paper, giving an overview of ad exchange system. Having said this, I would still suggest to shrink the background section somewhat by giving proper citation. This will leave more space to explore technical results.

Section 2.8, how do you compute the net revenues from impressions and clicks?
They do not seems to agree with the number of impressions and clicks & CPMs given in the same paragraph. Also, why the CPM for the impression is higher than the cost-per-clicks?

Section 3.2, IP threshold values seem to be arbitrary. Can you explain how you determine these thresholds?

Section 3.3, it is unclear how the authors determined the cookies/IPs that 'consistently' violated the thresholds. In addition, in Table 3, what does incident and incident > 1 day mean? An incident seems to be different from a warning because the number of incidents does not agree with the percentage of warnings, but it is not clear what it actually is.

Section 4.3, the authors said that the referrer information was suppressed by RightMedia. Since some of the referrer information was present, does this mean only some of the referrers were suppressed? Is there any explanation for this selective suppression?

Reviewer #4

Strengths: - Novel data from real ad network.
- Comprehensive background on ad. networks.

Weaknesses: - Sloppy writing. Not clear what the take home messages are.
- Paper can probably be shrunk to 7 pages without losing significant content.

Comments to Authors: The dataset analyzed here is interesting, but the paper is so poorly written that it is very difficult to follow the many different contexts and subplots. There are seemingly disjointed pieces that are very difficult to piece together into a coherent story. The writing is verbose at parts: going into excruciating detail about different components, and confusing elsewhere: making it impossible to follow different examples.

As presented, the paper is not ready to be accepted. The presentation problems make it difficult to assess the actual contribution. A lot of the 'analysis' is tabulation of the data from 'NetworkX'. There is one 'significant' result in that PublisherA was found to be fraudulent and banned. It is not clear that there is enough meat in the analysis to merit acceptance even if the presentation was fixed.

Detailed comments:

Introduction: Ad exchange is not well defined. Is it a single entity through which networks can exchange ad space, or is it a set of (connected?) entities?

Advertiser: whom do they pay? Ad network or exchange? How does an advertiser create a relationship with an exchange?

Ad network definition: What is traffic in this context? What does it mean to buy and sell traffic?

Arbitrage definition: What does buying 'impressions' mean?

Ad Exchange: What does 'publisher revenue' mean?

The Introduction implies that the authors could control a botnet. It should be clarified that the authors had access to the logs from a botnet C&C server.

Section 2.1: eCPM "formula" is a heuristic/an estimate/expected return, not an exact formula.

Figure 2 shows no Section ID

Section 2.3: "Seller line item cascades through the exchange": what does this mean? The example in the rest of the section is simply unparsable. It is not clear what the process is, how the auction is carried out, how bids are evaluated... What is the exchange? Is it a real or virtual entity? Is it a single server? Are there messages sent between different entities? A specific illustrated example should be part of the complete rewrite of this section.

Section 2.4: Requires specific example. The description of ad fraud /attacks is good, though verbose. Impression, Click, and Action spam can all be described in one paragraph, as can all the 'different' types of clickbots. It is not clear that all of that terminology is required for the rest of the paper and analysis.

Section 2.7: Rule and classifier based detectors don't need separate paragraphs.
Auditing: How does a referrer claim to have content?

Section 2.8: What 'roles' do botnet owners play? Are they advertisers? Are they publishers? The attack(s) are entirely unclear: did the infected user's browser show 'infected' advertisements? Was the user machine used to generate clicks without the user involvement?

The last paragraph on page 6 has to be rewritten. As is, it does not contain sufficient information to understand what (if anything) the bots are doing. The last line implies that the fraudsters are publishers and the infected machines emulate clicks to these pages. Is this true?

First line of page 7: ...third party domains used to spoof origin. What does this mean? What traffic?
The entire discussion of the bot anatomy lacks structure. There are disjointed sections with vague forward pointers. It is not clear why the reader is being given this information or why they should be interested.

Section 3.1 What is "our system"? What was applied to the data feed?

Cookie ID: is NOT assigned to a person. Perhaps to a browser instance.

Section 3.2: CPM costs is per 1000 impressions? Or are clicks cheaper than impressions?

Section 3.3: How many publishers are part of the data? Last sentence does not parse. What is the motivation for botnets to provide third-party referrer URLs with their own section ID? To avoid detection?

Section 4.1: 7% of Network X's traffic is fraudulent due to a single cookie?! This seems extremely negligent on part of the ad. network.

Experiment in 4.3 does not make sense: the tcpdump shows that the referrer field WAS properly set. In the data feed, the referrer feed was NOT set. Why would it be fraudulent for publisher D to have set the referrer field for the impressions that were generated?

Section 4.5 Where did the botnet host its fake sites? Were the websites created only once when the section IDs were generated?

Section 5: The countermeasures are not described well. Who, should sign what, and what types of fraud such signatures would counter: all these points are not clear.

From the text, it is not clear when site names are changed to protect the innocent (guilty) versus not, e.g. is benign-golf-site a real site? If not, why is the name in terminal font, same as pizzahut.com and googleusercontent.com?

Reviewer #5

Strengths: The tutorial nature of presentation should make the material understandable to a wide audience. The paper provides numerous interesting empirical examples of misuse of the Internet advertising market. Given the importance of advertising to the sustainability of the Internet, familiarizing the community with the problems could lead to better solutions.

Weaknesses: The authors have published quite a few papers on the topic already; thus, the novelty of this work is unclear. The paper lacks details about how they infiltrated the command and control server of the botnet they used to collect data, and how they collected the measurements. A number of the methods for identifying malicious activity seem rather ad hoc. The clarity of presentation needs improvement (e.g., there are lots of figures and tables, but often little descriptive text to go with them). The paper cites little recent work besides their own.

Comments to Authors: I enjoyed reading the paper, as it provides sufficient background information for a reader to learn about the Internet advertising market, and then explains the different categories of fraudulent activity in an intuitive manner, complete with examples. I think it could be significantly improved through revisions to the presentation. As mentioned in the "Weaknesses", the paper needs to clarify what is novel about this work over the numerous other papers you have published (and are cited in the references). Even though you have other papers that provide details about how the command and control server was taken over, and how the measurements were collected, some amount of that information needs to be in this paper. In general, the numerous figures and tables in the paper are not described in sufficient detail. You need to explicitly tell the reader about one or two of the key insights that are revealed in each (and how to see them). Lastly, the number of self-references is quite high compared to the references to other work. For example, the security group at UCSD has done a lot of related work, but I only see one of their papers cited (I am not associated with that group/institute, I am only providing them as an example).

Addressing the above issues would make the paper much stronger in my opinion. Here are some additional minor comments.

Section 2.3: Please clarify how in practice an advertiser "trusts the publisher"; is there a technical element to it, or does it just come down to making a judgment call based on brand recognition/price/etc.?

Section 2.7: In reverse spidering, it seems like there is potential for "crowdsourcing" to assist

Section 2.8: Please clarify what happened to the botnet after the command and control server that you controlled was taken offline; the fact that the botnet continues to exist seems like another challenge to describe (in the last paragraph of the section)

Section 2.9: Discuss the "arms race" that exists; i.e., if you deploy a barrier against miscreants, they will look for a way around it.

Section 3.1: Clarify the period of time that the data was collected and who is assigning the cookies, and whether a single user can have more than one.

Section 3.2: For the IP thresholds, please clarify if the impressions are to a single ad, or to multiple ads from the same provider, or something else

Section 4.1: The discussion of "clicks from the Cloud" is interesting; one comment I have is that if someone is willing to commit fraud, I would expect they could use stolen credit cards to "pay" for resources, and not be limited to the "free" tier.

Section 4.2: The discussion of the change in the behavior seems very speculative.

Section 4.3: A "404" error means the requested object (i.e., file) was not found, but a server of some sort was running. (my point is you need to clarify what you observed, many readers may not know what a "404" means). Please elaborate on the key insights from the tables. In the discussion of pizzahut.com, say it appeared in "21" different sections rather than "over 20"; also, is misconfiguration a possible explanation for this behavior, rather than malice? i.e., an unintentional error rather than intentional misuse?
In Table 7, why are some domain names obscured but not all?
The investigation described in the last paragraph seems rather ad hoc; to address miscreants effectively, systematic and scalable solutions are needed

Section 4.4. If PublisherA had been caught before, why wasn't it banned earlier?

Section 4.5. How did you determine that the templates were stolen from other sites?
please briefly explain how Alexa determines its ranking

Section 5. This section needs to anticipate how miscreants will react to these countermeasures, and thus how the countermeasures need to evolve over time. How difficult will the proposed countermeasures be to circumvent?

Section 5.1. Please clarify why would signing requests would require extra bandwidth. Also, if a client is compromised, what difference will extra CPU or bandwidth make to the miscreant (other than they may need to find a few extra bots)?

Section 5.2. Rather than speculate what RightMedia does, why not ask them?

Section 6. As previously mentioned, there is a lot of other research out there; e.g., UCSD has infiltrated a C&C server for a spam botnet. Check out this and other papers from Stefan Savage's group.

Response from the Authors

The three prevailing comments from the reviewers were that our detection methodology was not well defined enough to be convincing, that our proposed countermeasures were limited, and that our figures were not well integrated into the paper. Of these, the primary cause of concern from the reviewers had to do with our detection methodology, both in how it is presented and executed. To address concerns with the presentation, we chose to dedicate a larger portion of the paper to the detection methods and chose to introduce them less abruptly than in our submission. We first introduce our detection techniques (in Section 3), then evaluate the effectiveness of each technique (Section 4), and lastly we have observations about various types of fraud that were unearthed as a result of using the detection system (Section 5). Organizing it like this fixes any confusion that came as a result of mixing our descriptions and results. In addition, we had enough time to evaluate each detection algorithm in detail and produce receiver operator characteristic (ROC) curves to compare the effectiveness of each algorithm. From the curves, we were able to tune our detection system, evaluate new detection algorithms, and better justify our decisions to use a proposed detection technique. Then, we used our improved detection system to measure how much fraud we detect in the exchange and how much revenue is being lost, as suggested by one of the reviewers. Many of the reviewers also suggested changes in our "Proposed Countermeasures" section. Instead of expanding this section, we chose to replace it with a section that focused on what properties of RightMedia (and ad exchanges in general) make it conducive to fraud. We look at some of the problems that an individual ad network in the exchange runs into when they want to verify the legitimacy of their traffic. We also look at what RightMedia does correctly to deter fraudsters. Lastly, a few reviewers suggested changes to some of the figures, for example Figure 1, which was replaced by a clearer diagram of how the ad exchange worked. Figures 4 and 5 were also changed to fix the interval on the X axis to be in weeks. Most importantly, we were sure to reference and describe each figure that we included in the paper so that there was no confusion as to their meaning or purpose.

Towards Understanding Modern Web Traffic

Sunghwan Ihm[†]
Department of Computer Science
Princeton University
sihm@cs.princeton.edu

Vivek S. Pai
Department of Computer Science
Princeton University
vivek@cs.princeton.edu

ABSTRACT

As Web sites move from relatively static displays of simple pages to rich media applications with heavy client-side interaction, the nature of the resulting Web traffic changes as well. Understanding this change is necessary in order to improve response time, evaluate caching effectiveness, and design intermediary systems, such as firewalls, security analyzers, and reporting/management systems. Unfortunately, we have little understanding of the underlying nature of today's Web traffic.

In this paper, we analyze five years (2006-2010) of real Web traffic from a globally-distributed proxy system, which captures the browsing behavior of over 70,000 daily users from 187 countries. Using this data set, we examine major changes in Web traffic characteristics that occurred during this period. We also present a new Web page analysis algorithm that is better suited for modern Web page interactions by grouping requests into streams and exploiting the structure of the pages. Using this algorithm, we analyze various aspects of page-level changes, and characterize modern Web pages. Finally, we investigate the redundancy of this traffic, using both traditional object-level caching as well as content-based approaches.

Categories and Subject Descriptors

C.2.m [**Computer-Communication Networks**]: Miscellaneous

General Terms

Measurement, Design, Performance

Keywords

Web Traffic Analysis, Web Caching, Content-based Caching

1. INTRODUCTION

The World Wide Web is one of the most popular Internet applications, and its traffic volume is increasing and evolving due to the popularity of social networking, file hosting, and video streaming sites [29]. These changes and growth of Web traffic are expected to continue, not only as the Web becomes a *de facto* front-end for many emerging cloud-based services [47], but also as applications get migrated to the Web [34].

Understanding these changes is important for overall system design. For example, analyzing end-user browsing behavior can lead to a Web traffic model, which in turn can be used to generate a synthetic workload for benchmarking or simulation. In addition, analyzing the redundancy and effectiveness of caching could shape the design of Web servers, proxies, and browsers to improve response times. In particular, since content-based caching approaches [28, 49, 50] are a promising alternative to traditional HTTP object-based caching, understanding their implications for Web traffic and resource requirements (*e.g.*, cache storage size) could help reduce bandwidth and improve user experience.

While much research activity occurred a decade ago aimed at better understanding the nature of Web traffic [9, 11, 35, 56, 63], it subsided just as the Web changed significantly, and we must therefore update our understanding of today's Web traffic. However, there are several challenges. First, examining changes over time requires large-scale data sets spanning a multi-year period, collected under the same conditions. Second, earlier Web page analysis techniques developed for static pages are not suitable for modern Web traffic that involves dynamic client-side interactions (*e.g.*, Ajax [18]). Third, understanding the effectiveness of content-based caching approaches requires full content data rather than just access logs.

In this paper, we analyze five years (2006-2010) of real Web traffic from a globally-distributed proxy system, which captures the browsing behavior of over 70,000 daily users from 187 countries. Using this data set, we examine major changes in Web traffic characteristics that occurred during this period. We also present a new Web page analysis algorithm that is better suited for modern Web page interactions by grouping requests into streams and exploiting the structure of the pages. Using this algorithm, we analyze various aspects of page-level changes, and characterize modern Web pages. Finally, we investigate the redundancy of this traffic, using both traditional object-level caching as well as content-based approaches.

Our contributions and key findings are the following:

High-Level Characteristics The rise of Ajax and video content has impacted a number of different traffic measures. Ajax has caused in increase in the sizes of JavaScript and CSS [19] objects, and browsers have increased their simultaneous connection limit to better support it, resulting in burstier traffic but also improved client latency. Flash video (FLV) has grown to dominate video traffic, pushing the share of other video formats lower, and also in-

[†]Current affiliation: Google Inc.

IMC'11, November 2–4, 2011, Berlin, Germany.

creasing bandwidth consumption. Ajax and JavaScript are heavily used in user tracking and we find that analytics sites are reaching an ever-widening fraction of Web users, with some sites being able to track as much as 65% of our client population, which may have privacy implications. In addition, we observe clear regional differences in client bandwidth, browser popularity, and dominant content types that need to be considered when designing and deploying systems. Finally, we observe an increase in the number of computers per household over the years in Network Address Translation (NAT) [59] usage, which is likely related to the scarcity of IPv4 addresses.

Page-Level Characteristics We have developed a new Web page analysis algorithm called StreamStructure, and demonstrate that it is more accurate than previous approaches. Using this algorithm, we find that almost half the traffic now occurs not as a result of initial page loads, but as a result of client-side interactions after the initial page load. Also, the pages have become increasingly complex in that both the size and number of embedded objects have increased. Despite this increase, the page loading latency dropped in 2009 and 2010 due to the increased number of simultaneous connections in browsers and improved caching behavior of Web sites. Furthermore, we quantify the potential reduction of page loading latency from various tuning approaches, such as increasing the number of concurrent connections, and prefetching/caching, via simulations. Finally, we present a simple characterization of modern Web pages.

Redundancy and Caching We find two interesting trends in URL popularity: 1) the popular URLs get more popular, and therefore potentially improves caching, but 2) the long tail of the content is also growing, and therefore potentially hurts caching. Also, we find that content-based caching yields 1.8-2.5x larger byte hit rates than object-based caching, and much larger caches can be effectively exploited using intelligent content-based caching to yield nearly ideal byte hit rates. Most of the additional savings of content-based caching are due to partial content overlap – the redundancy across different versions of an object as well as redundancy across different objects. Finally, a small number of aborted requests (1.8-3.1%), mostly video, can negatively impact object-based caching performance because of its huge volume (12.4-30.8%). Worse, their volume would comprise a significant portion of all traffic (69.9-88.8%) if they were fully downloaded.

The rest of this paper is organized as follows: in Section 2, we describe the details of our data set. Section 3 examines the major changes in high-level characteristics of Web traffic. Section 4 presents the detailed page-level analysis with our new Web page analysis technique, and Section 5 analyzes redundancy and caching. Finally, we discuss related work in Section 6, and conclude in Section 7.

2. DATA SET

Data Collection We use traffic from the CoDeeN content distribution network (CDN) [62], a semi-open globally distributed proxy that has been running since 2003, and serves over 30 million requests per day from more than 500 PlanetLab [45] nodes. The term "semi-open" means that while anyone can use CoDeeN by configuring his or her browser, it only allows GET requests from the general public, and limits other methods such as CONNECT, PUT, or POST to only university-based users. When needed, the system redirects user requests to other proxy nodes based on the load and latency. Some requests are cache misses or uncacheable, and need to be retrieved from the origin Web servers. CoDeeN also deploys an automatic robot detection mechanism and has rejected accesses from malicious robots since 2006 [44].

Country		Year				
		2006	2007	2008	2009	2010
USA	Requests (M)	33.5	40.3	24.5	23.2	14.4
	Volume (GB)	391.2	627.2	338.2	316.2	261.5
	# IPs (K)	19.1	21.8	13.6	13.3	12.9
	# Users (K)	23.3	27.0	17.6	16.9	16.7
China	Requests (M)	22.5	88.8	29.9	38.1	22.9
	Volume (GB)	394.5	1,177.8	405.0	409.6	278.4
	# IPs (K)	49.3	94.9	38.8	43.2	33.4
	# Users (K)	53.9	109.7	45.1	51.8	41.9
France	Requests (M)	2.2	3.9	3.3	3.6	3.3
	Volume (GB)	21.6	45.8	33.6	42.9	50.5
	# IPs (K)	3.6	5.1	3.2	3.7	5.1
	# Users (K)	3.9	5.5	3.5	4.3	6.0
Brazil	Requests (M)	1.5	4.5	2.0	3.9	7.1
	Volume (GB)	16.2	54.8	22.8	44.1	100.2
	# IPs (K)	1.4	8.6	3.3	3.1	9.5
	# Users (K)	1.6	10.0	3.8	3.6	10.9
Total	Requests (M)	59.6	137.5	59.7	68.8	47.7
	Volume (GB)	823.5	1,905.6	799.6	812.8	690.6
	# IPs (K)	73.5	130.4	58.9	63.3	61.0
	# Users (K)	82.8	152.2	70.0	76.7	75.5

Table 1: Summary statistics for captured access logs, sampled one month (April) per year.

Our data set consists of two parts. First, CoDeeN records all requests not served from the client's browser cache in an extended W3C log format with timestamp, service time, request URL, method, user agent, content type, referer, response code, and response size. We use these access logs for examining any longitudinal changes in Section 3, 4, and 5. In addition, we capture the full content of the cache-miss traffic between the CoDeeN nodes and the origin Web servers. Using this full content data, we evaluate both object-based and content-based caching approaches, and analyze aborted transfers in Section 5.

For this study, we consider the data from the five-year period from 2006 to 2010. Due to the large volume of requests, we sample one month (April) of data per year. We only capture the full traffic content in April 2010, and use only traffic logs in all other years. After discarding non-human traffic, the total traffic volume ranges from 3.3 to 6.6 TB per month, and it consists of about 280-460 million requests from 240-360 thousand unique client IPs. The number of users (unique client IP and browser user-agent string pairs) ranges from 280 to 430 thousand, slightly larger than the number of client IPs. The clients IPs originate from 168-187 countries and regions as determined using the MaxMind database [38], and cover 40-60% of /8 networks, and 7-24% of /16 networks. The total number of unique origin servers ranges from 820 thousand to 1.2 million.

We focus on the traffic of users from four countries from different continents – the United States (US), Brazil (BR), China (CN), and France (FR). This essentially generates multiple data sets from different client organizations, and analyzing geographically dispersed client organizations enables us to discover common characteristics of Web traffic across different regions as well as region-specific characteristics. Table 1 shows summary statistics for these countries. In general, the United States and China have larger data sets than France and Brazil, mainly due to their larger client population. The yearly fluctuation of traffic volume is due to the variation of the number of available proxy nodes. Overall, our analysis of four countries covers 48-138 million requests, 691-1906 GB traffic, and 70-152 thousand users per month.

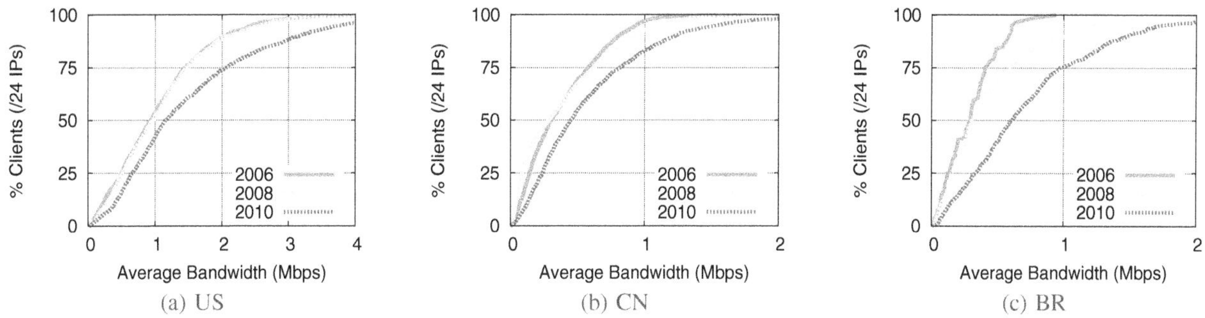

Figure 1: Average client bandwidth: Client bandwidth gets improved over time.

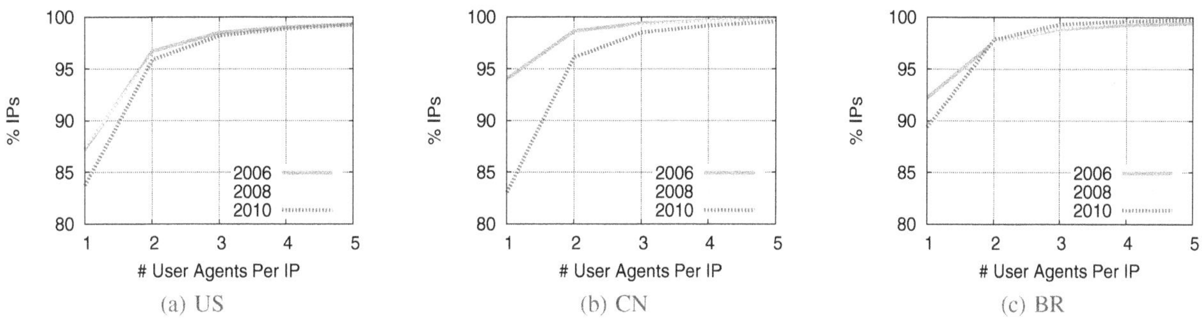

Figure 2: NAT usage: Most (83-94%) client IPs have only one user agent. The number gets slightly bigger over time due to an increase in the number of computers per household.

Users and Content Our large-scale data set spanning many years is much larger than the sets used in previous Web traffic research, and has broader coverage than much previous work, which has typically been restricted to users from a particular university or company [6, 63]. While some self-selection is unavoidable since we are measuring users of our own system, we have found that our user population is quite diverse, covering people who want faster Web access, unfiltered content, better routing, better privacy, and other reasons.

As a high-level check on representativeness, we examine the users of CoDeeN by looking at the `User-Agent` field in the access log, and find that our global trends and regional variations in browser and operating system usage are consistent with other studies [60, 61]. Overall, Firefox and Microsoft Internet Explorer (MSIE) account for more than 86% of the browsers in use over the course of five years in all of the four countries, and more than 83% of the users' operating systems are Windows. In some countries, we see a slightly higher share of Firefox than reported in other studies, which we attribute to the existence of many Firefox Web proxy addons that can use CoDeeN [23]. In most countries, we also observe a decreasing share of MSIE due to the increasing share of other browsers, such as Firefox and Chrome, with the exception of China, which continues to show higher usage of MSIE and Windows.

In addition, we investigate content that the users of CoDeeN browse by examining the top sites in terms of the number of requests. The results also correspond to other studies [5]. We observe that globally-popular Web sites, such as Google, YouTube, Yahoo, and Facebook, are commonly ranked high in all of the four countries. Furthermore, locally-popular Web sites also appear high in the ranking. For example, these sites include `craigslist.org`, `go.com`, and `espn.com` in the United States, `baidu.com`, `qq.com`, and `sina.com.cn` in China, `lequipe.fr`, `free.fr`, and `over-blog.com` in France, and `globo.com`, `uol.com.br`, and `orkut.com` in Brazil.

3. HIGH-LEVEL CHARACTERISTICS

In this section, we analyze high-level characteristics of our Web traffic data, looking at the properties of clients, objects, and Web sites.

Connection Speed We estimate the client bandwidth by observing the download time for objects – from the time when CoDeeN proxy node receives the request from a client to the time when the proxy finishes sending the object to the client. To minimize the effect of link latency, we consider only those objects that are larger than 1 MB. Figure 1 shows CDFs of average client bandwidth per aggregated /24 IP address, but similar patterns exist when using the 95th percentile of download time. Overall, we observe that the client bandwidth is consistently increasing over time, despite no significant change in PlanetLab's own connectivity in that period. Geographically, the speed of the United States and France is faster than Brazil and China. This scarcity of bandwidth is particularly apparent in 2006, when we did not see any clients in Brazil and China with download speeds exceeding 2 Mbps. Interestingly, there still exist many slow clients with less than 256 Kbps, even in the developed countries.

NAT Usage We analyze the use of Network Address Translation (NAT) in Figure 2 where we present CDFs of the number of different user agents per client IP address. The result shows that while most (83-94%) client IPs have just one user agent, the number gets slightly bigger over time. We attribute this increase to an increase in the number of computers per household over the years, which implies the scarcity of IPv4 addresses. The maximum number of user agents per IP we observe is 69 in the United States, 500 in China and 36 in Brazil. Our estimated number of NATs that have two or more distinct hosts (6-17%) is lower than the numbers from other studies that use client-side measurements or IP TTLs [15, 33, 37], possibly due to methodology differences or from only some of the hosts behind a NAT using the CoDeeN system.

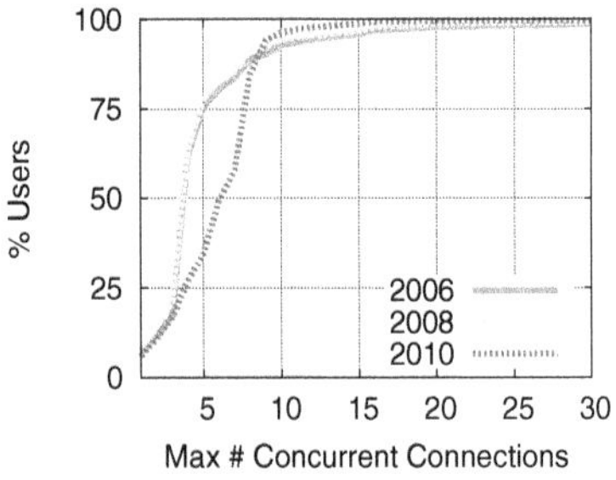

(a) US

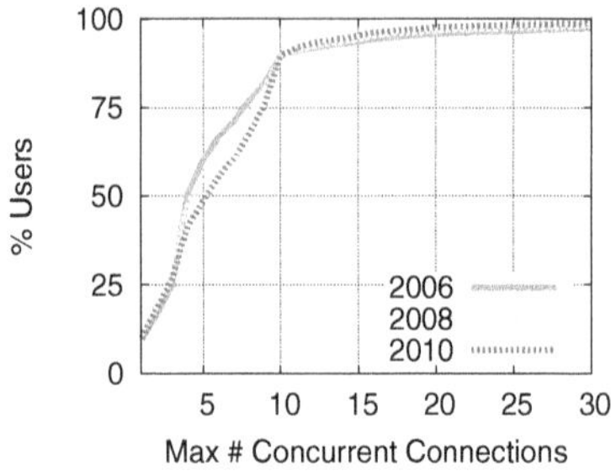

(b) CN

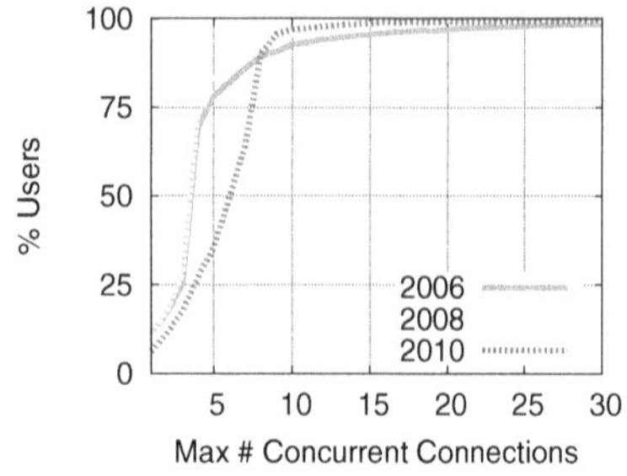

(c) BR

Figure 3: Maximum number of concurrent connections per user: We observe quite a big increase in 2010 due to the browsers increasing the number of connections.

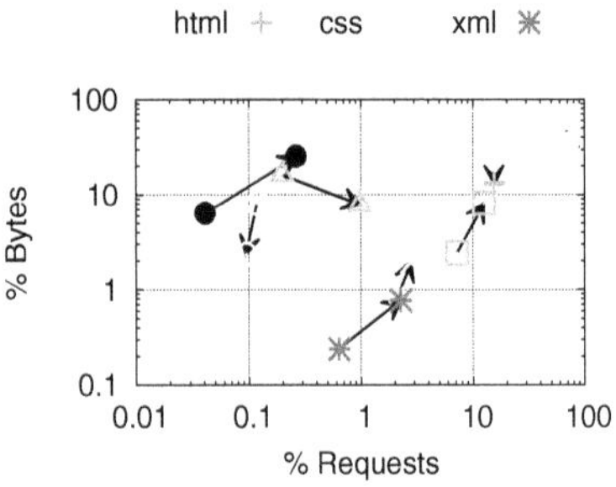

(a) US

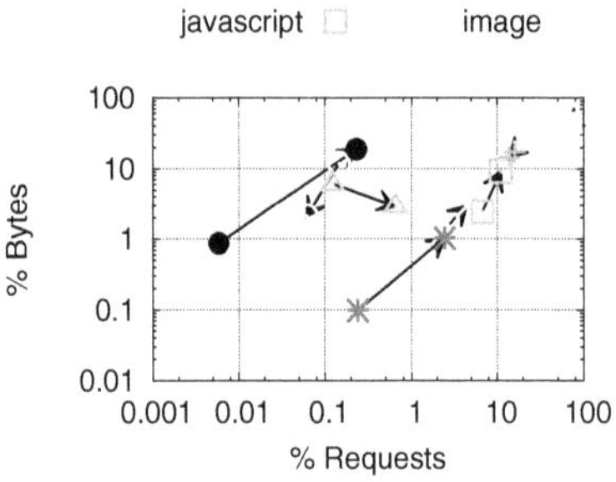

(b) FR

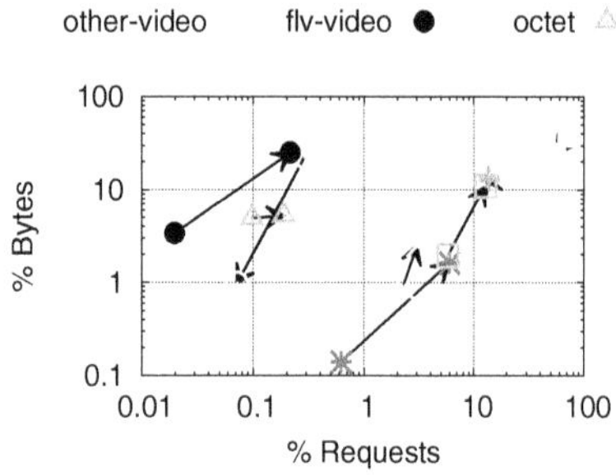

(c) BR

Figure 4: Content type distribution changes from 2006 to 2010: We observe growth of Flash video, JavaScript, CSS, and XML. Images are still dominating request traffic.

Maximum Concurrent Connections Figure 3 shows CDFs of the maximum number of concurrent connections per user agent. We observe quite a big increase in 2010 – the median number grows from 4-5 in 2006 and 2008 to 6-7 in 2010. This increase is mainly because the browsers change the default number of maximum simultaneous connections per server from 4 to 6 in starting in 2008 [4, 51], largely to accommodate Ajax which usually requires many simultaneous connections to reduce latency. In fact, the default number specified in HTTP/1.1 is only 2 [22].

Content Type We observe a shift from static image-oriented Web pages to dynamic rich media Web pages in Figure 4. It presents the content type distribution changes from 2006 to 2010, connected by arrows. The X axis is the percentage of requests, and the Y axis is the percentage of bytes, both in log-scale.

First, we observe a sharp increase of JavaScript, CSS, and XML, primarily due to the popular use of Ajax. We also find a sharp increase of Flash video (FLV) traffic, taking about 25% of total traffic both in the United States and Brazil in 2010, as it eats into the share of other video formats. In addition, while the byte percentage of octet-stream traffic sees a general decrease, its percentage of requests actually increases. This may be related to the custom use of HTTP as a transport protocol for exchanging binary data in many applications. Still, image traffic, including all of its subtypes, consumes the most bandwidth.

Despite the growth of embedded images in Web pages, we do not see a corresponding surge in their numbers in the traffic patterns. We believe that this is due to the improved caching behavior of many Web sites that separate the cacheable parts of their content on different servers and use long expiration dates. As a result, most of these images are served from the browser cache after the initial visit to the Web site.

Object Size We find that the size of JavaScript and CSS to be increasing steadily over time. As an example, Figure 5 (a) presents CDFs of JavaScript sizes in France, and we show CDFs of CSS sizes in China in Figure 5 (b), from 2006 to 2010. We omit the similar results of other countries due to space constraints. The increased code size of JavaScript and advanced CSS is likely related to the increasing popularity of Ajax. In general, other content types do not show consistent size changes over time.

While there seems to be no significant size changes over time in video objects, we observe FLV objects are bigger than other video in general. Figure 5 (c) compares the object size (CDF) of different video types in the United States for 2010. Some video objects (*e.g.*, ASF) are very small in size and they are container objects that do not contain actual video content. Once users fetch this kind of container object, they contact media streaming servers that use non-HTTP protocols such as RTSP [55] or RTP [54] for fetching the content. The median size of such container objects is typically less than 1 KB, while that of FLV, WMV, and MPEG is 1743 KB, 265 KB, and 802 KB, respectively.

Finally, while new video streaming technologies that split a large video file into multiple smaller files for cacheability and performance started gaining popularity in late 2009 and 2010 [1, 8, 41], we do not see its wide deployment in our data set yet. With these new technologies, we expect to observe a decrease in size of video objects with an increasing number of requests. We plan to analyze this case with more recent data set in the future.

Traffic Share of Web Sites We examine the traffic share of 1) video sites [1], and 2) advertising networks and analytics sites [2] in Figure 6. We consider the top 50 sites that dominate these kinds of traffic. In Figure 6 (a), we observe that the advertising network traffic takes 1-12% of the total requests, and it consistently increases over time as the market grows [31]. In addition, we find the volume of video site traffic is consistently increasing as

[1] *e.g.*, youtube.com

[2] *e.g.*, doubleclick.com and google-analytics.com

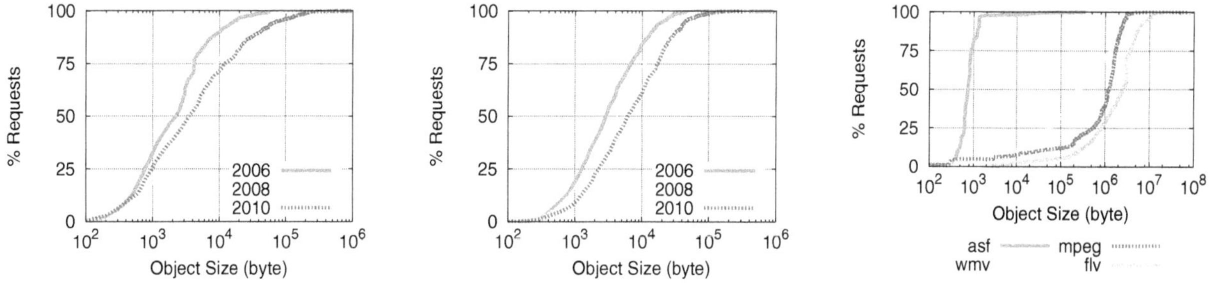

(a) FR: JavaScript (b) CN: CSS (c) US, 2010: video

Figure 5: Object size: The object size of JavaScript and CSS becomes larger. Flash video is bigger than other video.

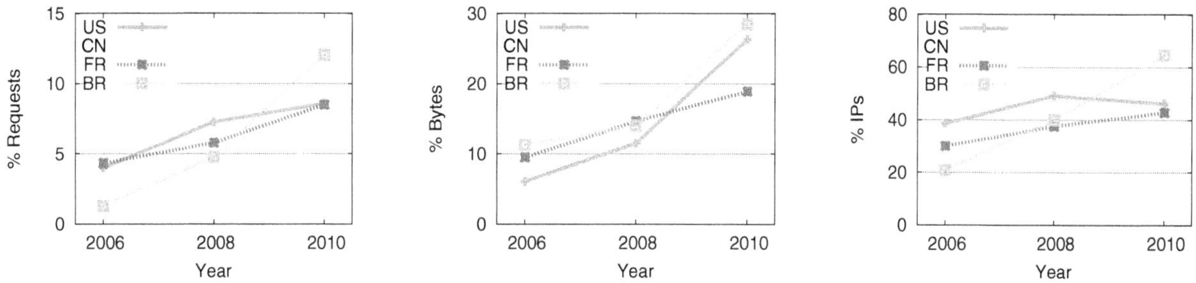

(a) Ads network traffic by requests (b) Video site traffic by bytes (c) Single top site % IPs

Figure 6: Top sites: Ads/video site traffic is increasing. A single top site tracks up to 65% of the user population.

shown in Figure 6 (b), taking up to 28% in Brazil for 2010. China, with lower bandwidth, sees more still image traffic than video. Finally, we see that the single top site reaches a growing fraction of all users over time in Figure 6 (c). All of the single top sites by the number of client IPs during a five-year period are either a search engine (`google.com` or `baidu.com`), or analytics site (`google-analytics.com`), reaching as high as 65% in Brazil for 2010, which may have implications for user tracking and privacy.

4. PAGE-LEVEL CHARACTERISTICS

In this section, we analyze our data with Web page-level details. We first provide background on page detection algorithms and explain the problems with previous approaches in Section 4.1. In Section 4.2, we present a new page detection algorithm called StreamStructure that is better suited for modern Web traffic analysis, and also demonstrate it is more accurate than previous approaches. Using this algorithm, Section 4.3 examines the initial page characteristics, analyzes page loading latency via simulations, and presents a simple characterization of modern Web pages.

4.1 Previous Page Detection Algorithms

A common approach for empirically modeling Web traffic is to reconstruct end-user browsing behavior from the access log data, in which users repeatedly request Web pages. Once Web pages (or main objects) are identified, we can derive relevant model parameters such as the number of embedded objects, total page size, total page time, and inter-arrival time. Thus, detecting Web page boundaries is crucial to the model accuracy.

Previous approaches for detecting page boundaries fall into two categories. The first approach (time-based) is to use the idle time between requests [9, 35, 56]. If the idle time is short enough (less than a predefined threshold), the request is assumed to be generated automatically by the browser, and it becomes an embedded object of the previous Web page. Otherwise, the request is assumed to be generated manually by the user's click, and it becomes the main object of a new Web page. The second approach (type-based) is to use the content type of the object [17]. This approach simply regards every HTML object as a main object, and any non-HTML object as an embedded object of the previous main object.

Unfortunately, the complex and dynamic nature of the current Web traffic blurs the traditional notion of Web pages, and the previous approaches do not work well. For example, client-side interactions (*e.g.*, Ajax) that usually have longer idle time would be misclassified as separate Web pages by the time-based approach. On the other hand, the type-based approach would misclassify frames in a single Web page as separate independent Web pages. As a result, these approaches would generate inaccurate traffic models if applied to modern Web traffic. Worse, they have already been used in hundreds of studies without validation.

4.2 StreamStructure Algorithm

To overcome the limitations of the previous approaches, we develop a new page detection algorithm called StreamStructure, that exploits the stream and structure information of Web pages. Our algorithm consists of three steps – grouping streams, detecting main objects, and identifying initial pages. Figure 7 depicts the definition of streams, Web pages, initial pages, main/embedded objects, and client-side interactions in our algorithm.

Step 1. Grouping Streams Instead of treating all the requests in a flat manner, we first group them into multiple independent streams by exploiting the `Referer` field. The referer of a request reveals the address of an object from which the request came from – a dependency between two objects. For example, if an HTML object includes two embedded objects in it, the referer of those two embedded objects would be the HTML object. Also, if a user clicks a link to move to a new Web page, the first request of the new Web page would have the referer field of an object in the previous Web page.

At a high level, each stream is a transitive closure of the referer relation on the set of requests. Whenever the referer of a request is empty, the request becomes the start (or root) of a new stream. If the

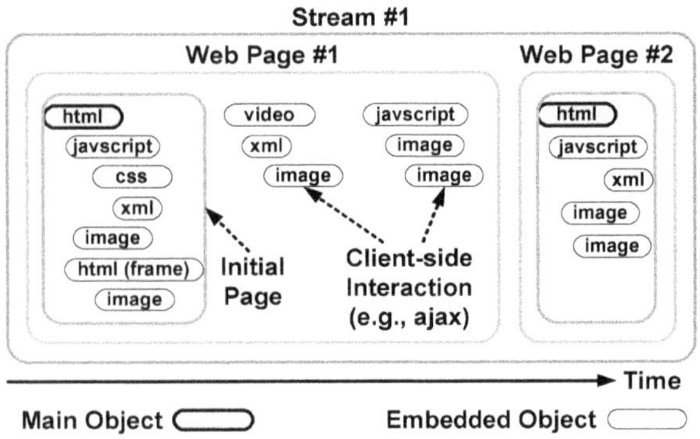

Figure 7: Streams, Web pages, initial pages, client-side interactions, and main/embedded objects.

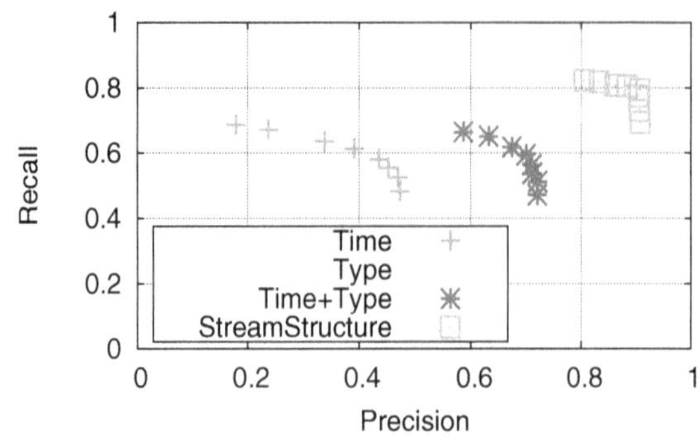

Figure 8: Precision and recall: StreamStructure outperforms previous page detection algorithms, simultaneously achieving high precision and recall. It is also robust to the idle time parameter selection.

referer of the subsequent request matches with any of the requests in the streams, we associate the request with the matched stream. In case there is more than one matched stream, we choose the latest one. If not found, we also create a new stream with the request – this happens because its referer request could be a browser cache-hit thus not present in the log.

Grouping requests with the referer relation allows isolating logs from multiple browser instances or tabs, since they belong to different streams. It also helps identifying frames and client-side interactions, since all the frames from the same Web page and all the client-side interactions to the same Web page belong to the same stream.

Even though the referer field is optional, we can safely rely on this information because most current browsers (Firefox and MSIE) enable it by default. In fact, Firefox and MSIE together account for more than 86% of our client population as discussed in Section 2. When present, we use the referer field to group requests into streams.

Step 2. Detecting Main Objects Once we finish grouping streams, we detect a main object for each stream. We first generate main object candidates by applying the type-based approach. This would find HTML frame objects as main object candidates, but non-HTML interactions would be ignored. Among those main object candidates, we discard those with no embedded object. This is based on the observation that current Web pages are typically complex, consisting of many embedded objects. We detect this by looking at the referer of the next request. If it is not the preceding main object candidate, we remove the preceding object from consideration.

Next, we apply the time-based approach to finalize the main object selection. If the idle time is less than a given threshold, it is likely that they belong to the same Web page – overlapping HTML frame objects with a short idle time would be eliminated from the selection. It is noteworthy that we consider the idle time only among the main object (HTML) candidates. This is because the interactions in a Web page happen at an arbitrary point, and it biases the idle time calculation if included. Now all the remaining objects between two main objects become the embedded objects of its preceding main object. This way, we could include all the interactions in a Web page as its embedded objects.

Step 3. Identifying Initial Pages The final task of our algorithm is to identify the initial pages, as the previous grouping still includes client-side interactions in the Web pages. The basic idea is to apply the time-based approach. However, simply checking the idle time is inaccurate because the DNS lookup [2] or browser processing time can vary significantly, especially while processing the main object before the page is fully loaded.

To this end, we exploit the popular use of Google Analytics in the pages. It is a piece of JavaScript code that collects various client-side information and reports to the analytics server when the `DOMContentLoaded` event fires. Thus, once we see this beacon in the access logs, we can safely assume that the Web page is successfully loaded at that point, and start applying the time-based approach to identify the initial page. Note that our algorithm can also use other ways than the Google Analytics beacon to detect the page loading event. For example, one could utilize beacons from other analytics services, or even instrument Web pages with custom JavaScript at the proxy.

Validation We validate the accuracy of StreamStructure and the existing approaches on the manually collected data set by visiting (via CoDeeN) the top 100 sites of Alexa's list [5] with MSIE. We not only visit the top-level pages, but also follow approximately ten links from those top-level pages for each site, resulting 1,197 Web pages in total. [3] We also record the URLs of those visited Web pages (or main objects), and compare them with the URLs of the Web pages found by each approach. Note that this data collection is different from actual browsing patterns, but we believe that it is sufficient to capture the structure of representative Web pages and thus useful for validation.

Figure 8 shows the precision and recall of various approaches. Precision is defined as the number of correct Web pages found divided by the total number of Web pages found, and recall is defined as the number of correct Web pages found divided by the total number of correct Web pages. For comparison, we also try a simple combination of time-based and type-based approaches (Time+Type) that does not exploit the stream and structure information. Multiple data points represent the results of various idle time (0.1, 0.2, 0.5, and 1–5 seconds) parameters.

The time-based approach performs in general very poorly, and the best result achieves only a precision of 0.45 and a recall of 0.55. Also, the performance is very sensitive to the idle time selection. The type-based approach shows the highest recall above 0.88, which implies that the main objects of most Web pages are HTML. However, the precision is very low, only about 0.27. StreamStructure outperforms all of the previous approaches, achieving high precision and recall above 0.8 simultaneously. Furthermore, it is quite robust to the idle time parameter selection. The time+type approach is less accurate, proving the importance of exploiting the stream and structure information.

Finally, we investigate the sensitivity of the idle time parameter

[3] Some sites have many Web pages while others do not.

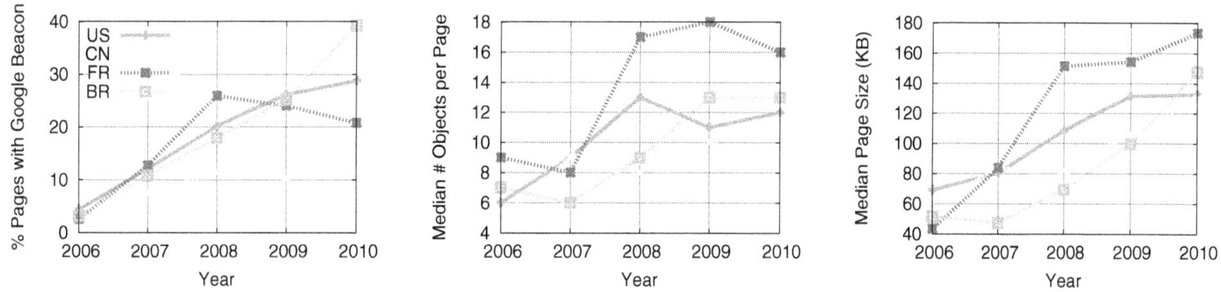

(a) % pages with Google Analytics beacon (b) Median # of objects per page (c) Median page size

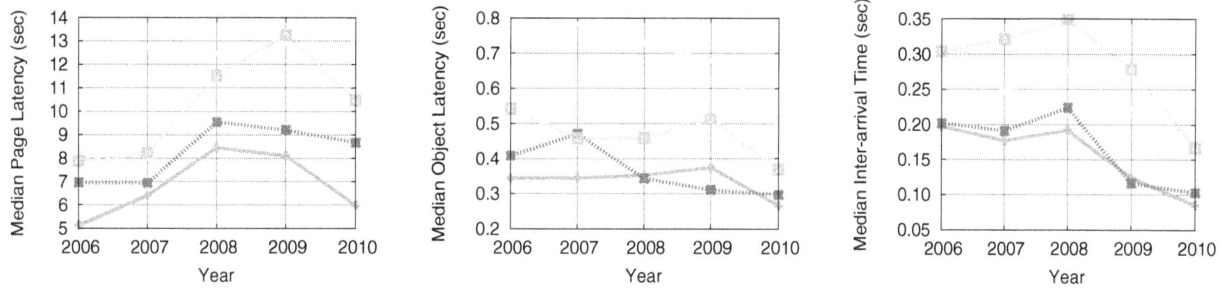

(d) Median page loading latency (e) Median object latency (f) Median object inter-arrival time

Figure 9: Initial page characteristics: The Google Analytics beacon gets increasingly popular, and pages get bigger both in terms of the size and number of objects. On the other hand, the page loading latency has dropped in 2009 and 2010 because of the increased number of concurrent connections and reduced object latency.

for identifying initial pages by comparing CDFs of the page loading time, number of objects, and size of the initial pages with different idle time thresholds. Overall, 23.9% of pages have Google Analytics beacons in our manually collected Alexa data set. We observe that an idle time of 0.1 seconds is too short and 5 seconds is too long, distorting the distribution significantly. On the other hand, an idle time between 0.5 and 2 seconds generates quite stable and similar results.

4.3 Analysis Results

We apply the StreamStructure algorithm to our CoDeeN access log data set, and analyze the derived Web pages in various aspects. We choose the idle time of one second both for identifying Web pages out of streams, and for identifying initial pages out of Web pages. Among all the users, we ignore those who are active for less than 30 minutes to reduce potential bias. We first examine the characteristics of initial pages, and analyze the page loading latency in detail via simulations. Finally, we provide a simple characterization of modern Web pages including client-side interactions.

Initial Page Characteristics We first show the fraction of Web pages that have a Google Analytics beacon in our data set in Figure 9 (a). It is less than 5% in 2006, but it has become increasingly popular and accounts for about 40% in 2010. While there is a little variation over time, the volume of the initial page traffic roughly accounts for about 40-60% of the entire Web traffic in terms of both requests and bytes. The rest of the traffic is client-side interactions, which is quite a significant amount.

In Figure 9 (b)-(f), we examine the changes in the number of objects, size, and latency of the initial pages, and the latency and inter-arrival time of each individual object in the initial pages. We compare the median values rather than the mean, since our page detection algorithm is not perfect and the mean is more susceptible to outliers/errors.

First of all, the pages have become increasingly complex where we observe a consistent increase of the number of objects and the total size in Figure 9 (b) and (c). For example, the median number of objects per page in the United States sees an increase from 6 objects in 2006 to 12 objects in 2010, and the median page size gets bigger from 69 KB in 2006 to 133 KB in 2010. This increase is likely related to the popular use of advertisement/analytics, and the object size increase of JavaScript and CSS in Figure 5 (a) and (b).

While the page loading latency also sees a general increase in Figure 9 (d) until 2008, instead we see it decrease in 2009 and 2010. For example in the United States, the median latency increases from 5.13 seconds in 2006 to 8.45 seconds in 2008, but it decreases to 5.98 seconds in 2010. [4] This decrease likely stems from the increased number of concurrent connections in Figure 3. Another decreasing factor is the reduced latency of fetching an object in Figure 9 (e), and it also makes the object inter-arrival rate burstier in Figure 9 (f). As the object size does not get smaller over time, the decrease of the object latency is likely related to the improved client bandwidth in Figure 1, as well as the improved caching behavior of many Web sites.

Page Loading Latency Simulation As the page loading latency is determined by many factors including the number of concurrent connections per server, object latency, and dependency among objects, we examine the impact of these factors via simulations. Each object is fetched from a central FIFO queue, and we use the measured object latency in the access logs for the simulated object latency. The object dependency is extracted from the referer relations. Since the purpose of this simulation is to assess which factors affect the page loading latency rather than to predict the actual latency, we simplify the simulation as follows. First, we ignore network latency and browser parsing/processing time – there is no net-

[4]The actual user-perceived latency is smaller than our measured latency because users recognize pages to be loaded before all of the embedded objects are completely downloaded.

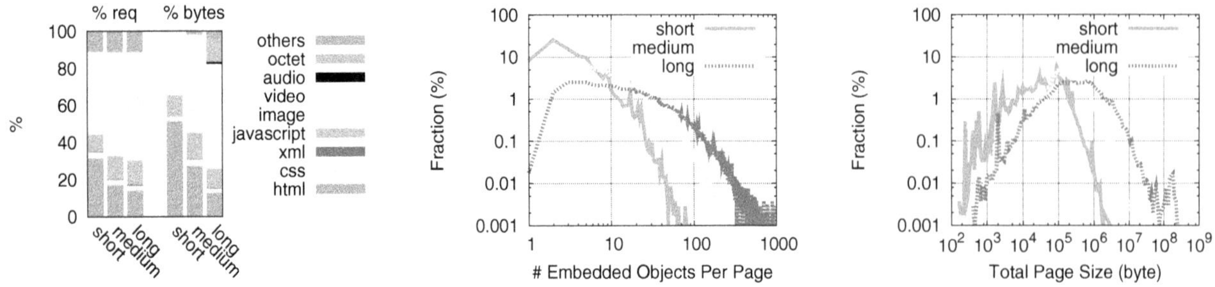

(a) Page content type composition (b) # of objects (c) Total size

Figure 11: Characterization of entire Web pages from the United States in 2010: We define short (0-25th percentile), medium (25-75th), and long (75-100th) pages by total time. Short pages are bursty and HTML-oriented while long pages are video/binary-oriented and involve heavy client side interactions.

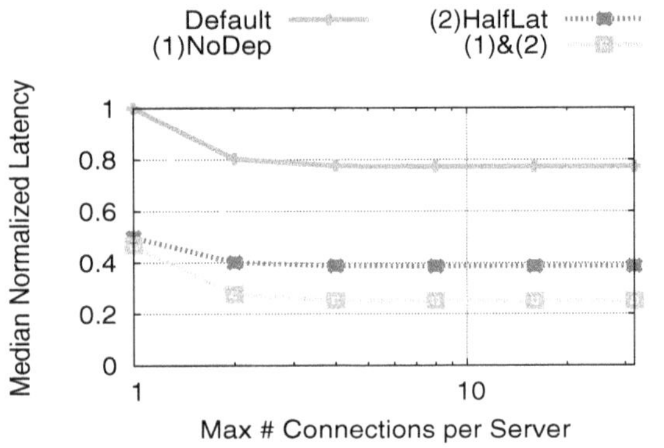

Figure 10: Page loading latency simulation (US, 2010): Increasing the number of simultaneous connections could further reduce page load latency by 23%. Removing dependencies between objects (NoDep) would yield at most a 50% reduction. Reducing per-object latency by 50% (HalfLat) would actually reduce page-load latency by 67% because of the simultaneous connections. Together, page loading latency can be reduced by up to 75%.

work idle time during the page loading process. Second, any dependent object is not fetched before its parent object is finished, which is less aggressive than current practice, where a browser typically starts fetching embedded objects as soon as it finds their URLs.

Figure 10 presents the median simulated latency from the United States in 2010, as a function of the maximum number of concurrent connections per server. We omit the results of other countries that are very similar to that of the United States. We simulate four different scenarios, and the latency is normalized by the default latency with one concurrent connection per server. First, we observe that increasing the number of concurrent connections per server would reduce the latency by up to 23% at 8 connections, beyond which we see no benefit. Second, we simulate the ideal case where there is no object dependency (`NoDep`) – all of the object URLs are known in advance, and it reduces the latency by up to 50%. Given this latency reduction, it is worth exploring ways to relieve/eliminate the object dependency. Third, if per-object latency is reduced by half (`HalfLat`) via better caching/prefetching approaches, it could actually reduce the page loading latency by up to 61% due to the simultaneous connections. All together, we observe that page loading latency could be reduced by up to 75%.

Entire Page Characteristics For a simple characterization of modern Web pages, we divide all of the Web pages including client-side interactions into three groups based on the total page time – short (0-25th percentile), medium (25-75th), and long (75-100th) pages. We then characterize these pages in terms of the number of embedded objects, page size, object inter-arrival time, and content type distribution. Figure 11 presents an example characterization of Web pages from the United States in 2010.

Overall, long pages consume about 55% of total requests, and medium pages take about 40%. In terms of bytes, long pages take even more than 60%. Short pages account for only about 5% in terms of both requests and bytes. The content type distribution in Figure 11 (a) reveals the characteristics of the pages more clearly. Short pages are mainly HTML-oriented, and search activities could be typical examples. On the other hand, long pages show a higher percentage of video and octet-stream bytes than others, meaning these are mainly video watching activities and large file downloads. Medium pages lie in between, and typical examples would be browsing news or blogs.

In terms of the number of embedded objects, short pages mostly have less than 10 objects, and medium and long pages have a larger number of embedded objects, as in Figure 11 (b) where we show PDFs. The median is 4, 12, and 30 for short, medium, and long pages, respectively. Especially, we observe heavy client-side interactions in long pages. Note that medium pages will often specify dozens of embedded images in their HTML but as Web sites improve their cacheability best practices, most of these are cached at the browser, and we observe only a median of 12 fetches for the updated portions of their content. This in part also explains why page loading latency is improving despite the increase in page complexity.

In addition, Figure 11 (c) shows PDFs of the total page sizes, and we observe that the median difference is about 3x between short (40 KB) and medium pages (122 KB), and more than 2x between medium and long pages (286 KB). Note that long pages have a very long tail reaching up to 370 MB, while the largest page size is only about 5 MB for short pages and 13 MB for medium pages. Finally, we observe that short and medium pages are burstier than long pages as it does not usually involve client-side interactions. The median object inter-arrival time is 90, 89, and 114 ms for short, medium, and long pages, respectively.

5. REDUNDANCY AND CACHING

The last part of our study is to analyze the redundancy in Web traffic and the impact of caching. For this study, we analyze the full content of traffic as well as the access logs. Table 2 shows the summary of our content data set from April, 2010. We capture cache misses only to account for simple improvements like using a local proxy cache. Throughout this section, our analysis is based

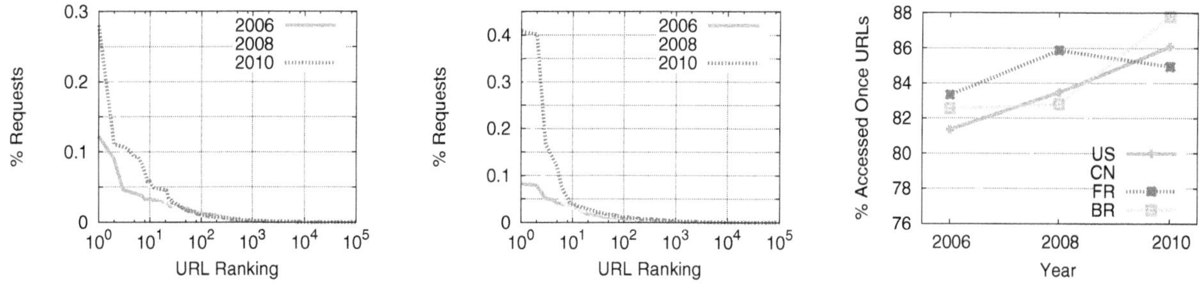

(a) US: Top 100K URLs by % requests (b) CN: Top 100K URLs by % requests (c) % accessed once URLs (tail)

Figure 12: URL popularity: The popular URLs grow, but the long tail of the content is also growing.

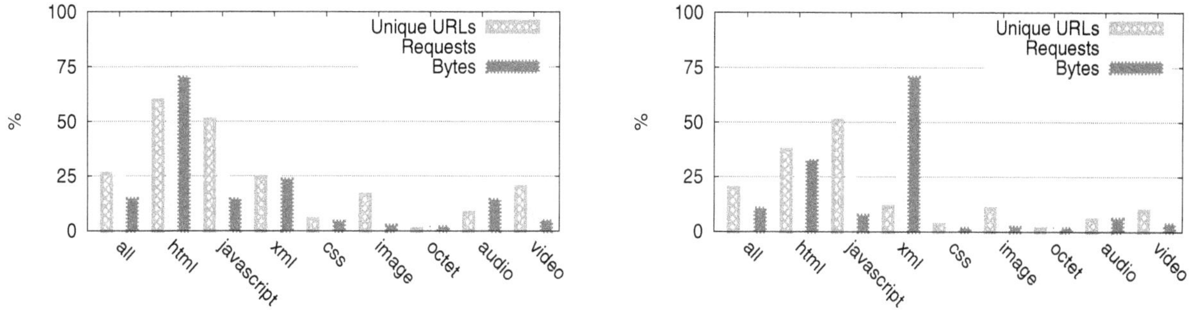

(a) US (b) CN

Figure 13: Uncacheable objects by content types: Overall, 19.8-32.2% of unique URLs, 21.5-28.3% of total requests, and 10.5-14.8% of total bytes are uncacheable. HTML and JavaScript are dynamically generated and thus less cacheable.

	USA	China	France	Brazil
# Requests (K)	8,611	12,036	2,129	4,018
Volume (GB)	198	218	42	79

Table 2: Summary of captured full content data (cache-misses only)

on logically centralized but physically distributed proxy systems, just like CoDeeN.

We first provide the details of content-based caching in Section 5.1. Using the access log data, we examine the changes in URL popularity during the five-year period in Section 5.2. Using the full content data, we directly compare the effectiveness of object-based caching and content-based caching in Section 5.3, and quantify the origins of redundancy in Section 5.4. We also calculate the actual byte hit rates with practical cache storage sizes in Section 5.5. Finally, we analyze the characteristics of aborted transfers, and discuss its caching implications in Section 5.6.

5.1 Content-based Caching

At a high level, content-based caching works by splitting an object or file into many smaller chunks, and caching those chunks instead of an entire object. The chunk boundaries are determined based on the content, commonly with Rabin fingerprinting [48] – if the fingerprinting value over a sliding window of data matches with low order n bits of a predefined constant K, this region of data constitutes a chunk boundary. The expected average chunk size is 2^n byte assuming a uniform distribution of content values. To prevent chunks from being too small or large in a pathological case, we specify the minimum and maximum size of chunks as well. Unlike fixed-size chunking (e.g., every 1 KB), content-based chunking is robust to any insertion/deletion/modification to the content since it only affects nearby chunks.

Once chunk boundaries are detected, chunks are named based on the content, often with SHA-1 hash. The next time the system sees the same chunk, it can pass only a reference instead of the original content. This way, content-based caching could find the same content within an object and across different objects, yielding much higher cache hit rates than object-based caching. Furthermore, it is protocol independent and effective for uncacheable content as well.

5.2 URL Popularity

We investigate the underlying changes in URL popularity during the five-year period with our access log data set, which directly influences the caching effectiveness. We find two interesting trends. First, we observe that the popular URLs are getting more popular as in Figure 12 (a) and (b) where we present the request percentage of the top 100,000 URLs in the United States and China. The request traffic to most popular URL increases from 0.08-0.12% in 2006 to 0.28-0.41% in 2010, and this concentration would increase the cache hit rate. The most popular URL in the United States for 2010 is a dynamically generated beacon object from `google.com`, which is uncacheable, though. At the same time, we also find that the percentage of URLs that are accessed only once is consistently increasing as in Figure 12 (c). We see its increase from 76.9-83.3% in 2006 to 84.6-87.8% in 2010. Overall, they account for a significant amount of traffic – 30.0-48.8% of total requests and 27.3-63.9% of total bytes. These least popular URLs are all cache-misses and would decrease the cache hit rate.

While these two trends in URL popularity could affect cache hit rate both positively and negatively, we do not observe any consistent changes in resulting cache hit rate during the five-year period. This is because they cancel out each other, and cache hit rate is also determined by other factors such as user population. In order to get an upper bound on object-based cache hit rate with our access log data set, we assume every object is cacheable, and two objects are identical (cache hit) once their URLs and content lengths

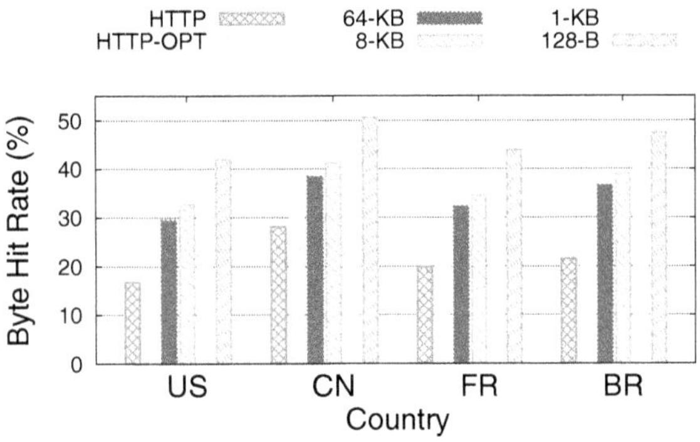

Figure 14: Ideal cache hit rate with infinite cache storage: Content-based caching with 128-bytes chunks achieves almost 2x larger byte hit rate than object-based HTTP caching.

match. The estimated cache hit rate we observe ranges from 35.6% to 54.5%, and the byte hit rate ranges from 15.1% to 49.3%. The byte hit rate is smaller than the cache hit rate because cache hits are biased towards relatively smaller objects. In fact, we observe that the mean object size of those URLs that are accessed only once is always larger than the mean object size of those URLs that are accessed more than once over the five years.

5.3 Caching Effectiveness

In this section, we first investigate HTTP cacheability of the traffic, and calculate the ideal cache hit rate. We then compare the effectiveness of object-based and content-based caching on our full content data, and further examine the impact of content types.

HTTP Cacheability We examine HTTP cacheability of objects with our full content data from 2010. We decide if an object is cacheable or not by looking at its `Cache-Control` and `Pragma` fields in the response header. Figure 13 shows the percentage of uncacheable objects in terms of the number of unique URLs, total requests, and total bytes. Overall, 19.8-32.2% of unique URLs are uncacheable, and it accounts for 21.5-28.3% of total requests and 10.5-14.8% of total bytes. Among different content types, HTML and JavaScript are less cacheable than other content types, implying that they are dynamically generated and updated frequently. Even though the low fraction of uncacheable traffic implies substantial potential for caching, the actual cache hit rates would be severely limited due to the growing fraction of URLs that are accessed only once.

We also observe a few other interesting points. First, a significant portion of XML traffic (over 70%) in China is uncacheable, and it turns out to be due to the popular use of Really Simple Syndication (RSS) [52] feeds – two RSS URLs are responsible for 90.8% of total uncacheable bytes and 64.8% of total uncacheable requests. Second, Brazil (not shown) shows a higher fraction of uncacheable XML and audio traffic than other countries. This is due to the popular use of real time update of sports games and live streaming of audio.

Ideal Byte Hit Rate We calculate the ideal bandwidth savings achievable with a centralized proxy cache having infinite cache storage by the traditional object-level HTTP caching and content-based caching. For object-level caching, we decide if an object is cacheable by respecting cache-control headers. If cacheable, we check if the URLs and content lengths match as in Section 5.2. We also calculate a slightly optimistic behavior of object-based caching by discarding query strings from URLs in order to accommodate the case where two URLs with different metadata actually belong to the same object. For content-based caching, we vary the average chunk size from 128 bytes, 1 KB, 8 KB, to 64 KB. Note that we apply content-based caching on compressed content without decompressing it, because the volume of compressed content such as `gzip` or `deflate` is less than 1% in our data set.

In Figure 14, we observe that content-based caching with any chunk size outperforms object-based caching. The cache hit rate of object-level caching ranges from 27.0-37.1% (not shown in the figure), but the actual byte hit rate is only 16.8-28.1%, which is lower than the byte hit rates from a decade ago, but similar to that in more recent studies [3, 13, 24, 30, 40, 63]. The hit rate of the optimistic version (`HTTP-OPT`) is only slightly larger. On the other hand, the lowest byte hit rate of content-based caching is 29.4-38.4% with 64 KB chunks, and the highest byte hit rate is 42.0-50.6% with 128 byte chunks, 1.8-2.5x larger than object-level caching's byte hit rate. The small chunk size performs better than the large chunk sizes because of its finer granularity. For example, 128 bytes chunks can detect redundancy at the sentence-level, but 64 KB can do only at the document-level.

Impact of Content Types Among many different content types, we find that text resources such as HTML, JavaScript, XML, and CSS have much higher redundancy than binary resources such as image, audio, video, and octet-stream. Figure 15 shows the ideal redundancy by content type. In particular, JavaScript shows over 90% of redundancy with the smallest chunk size of 128 bytes. On the other hand, video exhibits much lower redundancy of 20%, illustrating the impact of long-tailed popularity in video content. Object-based caching performs very poorly, and its redundancy elimination for XML is one-eighth that of the gains with 128 byte chunks in China.

We also find that content-based caching works well regardless of the content types, while the object-based caching is mainly effective for JavaScript and image traffic only. Figure 16 depicts the contribution of byte savings, basically showing which caching scheme works best for which content type. In object-based caching, the contribution of JavaScript and image is relatively larger than that of other content types. It should be noted that the contribution of binary resources such as video, audio, and octet-stream is extremely low, implying that object-based caching is not suitable for them. On the other hand, content-based caching provides more uniform benefits.

5.4 Origins of Redundancy

In order to understand how content-based caching approaches provide more than double the byte hit rate than the object-based caching approach, we quantify the contribution of redundancy from different sources in Figure 17. We use the average chunk size of 128-bytes for this analysis.

Overall, we observe that about 40.3-58.6% of the total redundancy is due to identical objects with the same URLs, which is essentially the upper bound of the object-based caching approach's byte hit rate (`object-hit`). The other half of the total redundancy is purely from the content-based caching approaches, and we further break it into the following three sources. First, there exists redundancy across the content changes of an object (`intra-URL`), and it accounts for about 21.8-32.5% of the total redundancy. Second, some objects with different URLs actually have identical content [32] (`aliasing`), and it represents 6.7-9.8% of the total redundancy. Finally, the rest is due to the redundancy across different objects that have different URLs and non-identical content (`inter-URL`), and it represents 12.8-20.0% of the total redundancy. This analysis result implies that most of the additional savings from the content-based caching approaches come from its abil-

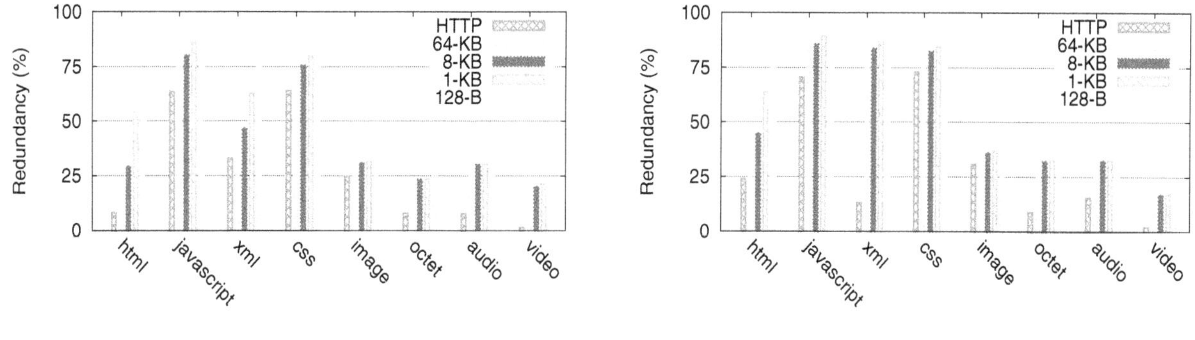

(a) US (b) CN

Figure 15: Ideal redundancy by content types: Text resources have higher redundancy than binary.

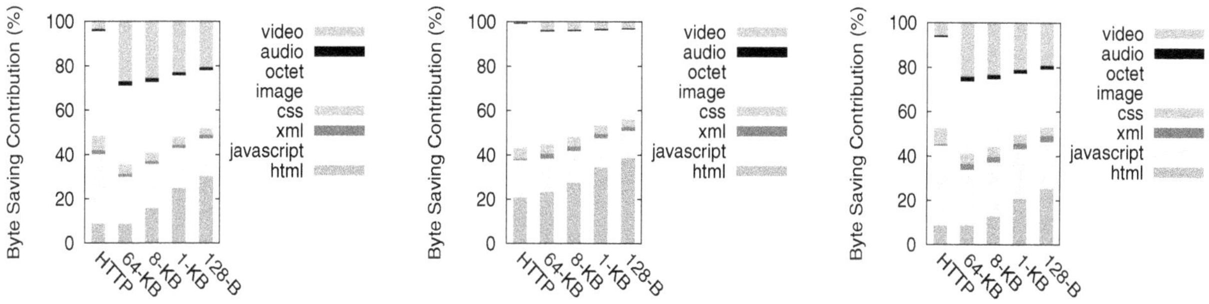

(a) US (b) CN (c) BR

Figure 16: Byte saving contribution by content types: Content-based caching is effective for any content type, but object-based caching works well only for JavaScript and image.

ity to detect and eliminate the redundancy in the content changes of an object as well as redundancy across different objects.

In terms of content types, we find that HTML and XML generally show relatively higher intra-URL redundancy than other content types. It implies that they are frequently updated but their content changes slowly. Also, aliasing in general accounts for a small amount of the total redundancy, but we observe a significant amount of aliasing in XML and audio content types in Brazil. This is again because of the popular use of the real time updates of sports games (XML) and live streaming of audio in Brazil. These objects have identical content but with different URLs. Finally, we see that most of the redundancy in binary resources, especially video, come from partial content overlaps (intra-URL + inter-URL) rather than complete object matches (object-hit + aliasing). This is partly because they are aborted before they are fully downloaded. We examine the aborted transfers in more detail in Section 5.6.

5.5 Cache Storage Size

We simulate cache behavior with different cache storage sizes to determine the required cache storage size for achieving close to the ideal byte hit rate, but also include the metadata overhead (20 bytes per chunk) of content-based caching in the byte hit rate calculation. We use a simple LRU cache replacement policy as a first step, and leave for future work investigating more sophisticated policies [46].

In addition to object-based and content-based caching, we also simulate multi-resolution chunking (MRC), a recently-developed strategy that simultaneously exploits multiple chunk sizes [28] and is well-suited for large storage sizes. MRC always favors large chunks over small ones, and uses small chunks only when large chunks are cache misses. It also caches all different chunk sizes for the same content redundantly for the future reference. This way, MRC minimizes the metadata overhead, disk accesses, and memory pressure at the cost of more disk space.

Figure 18 shows our simulation results in the United States and China, which shows that content-based caching always outperforms object-based caching regardless of cache storage size. However, due to the significant metadata overhead for fixed 128 bytes chunks, the actual byte hit rate of 128 byte chunks is similar to that of 1 KB chunks. The saturation point of cache size is similar across the different caching approaches except for MRC. For example, beyond 100 GB of cache storage, the byte hit rate no longer increases in the United States and China. The saturation point essentially indicates the working set size of the traffic, so increasing the cache size beyond it gives no further benefits. On the other hand, while MRC performs relatively poorly when cache storage is small, it continues to increase the byte hit rate beyond the saturation point, as the multiple chunk sizes reduce metadata overhead. The simulation has a few missing data points because of the limitation of main memory we have (16 GB) during the simulation. Also, the byte hit rate of MRC with infinite cache size is estimated from the ideal byte hit rate of 128 byte chunks minus 1% overhead.

While increasing cache storage size gives diminishing returns for object-based caching, using large cache storage with MRC is highly beneficial as it doubles the byte hit rate compared to object-based caching. This option would be especially attractive in developing regions where the bandwidth is much more expensive than disk storage [27]. Since a TB-sized disk costs less than $100, it makes sense to allocate much more cache storage than was used 10 years ago, when disk sizes were in the tens of GB.

In our data set, we need about 800 GB for the United States and China, 200 GB for France, and 400 GB for Brazil to achieve close to the ideal byte hit rate with MRC. It is roughly four times of the total traffic size because MRC uses four different chunk sizes in

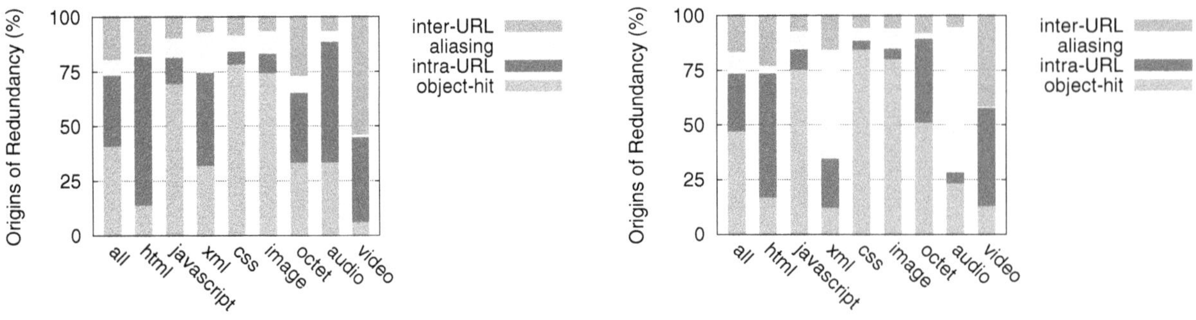

(a) US

(b) BR

Figure 17: Origins of redundancy with 128-bytes chunks: Most of the additional savings from the content-based caching approaches come from partial content overlap – the redundancy across different versions of an object as well as redundancy across different objects.

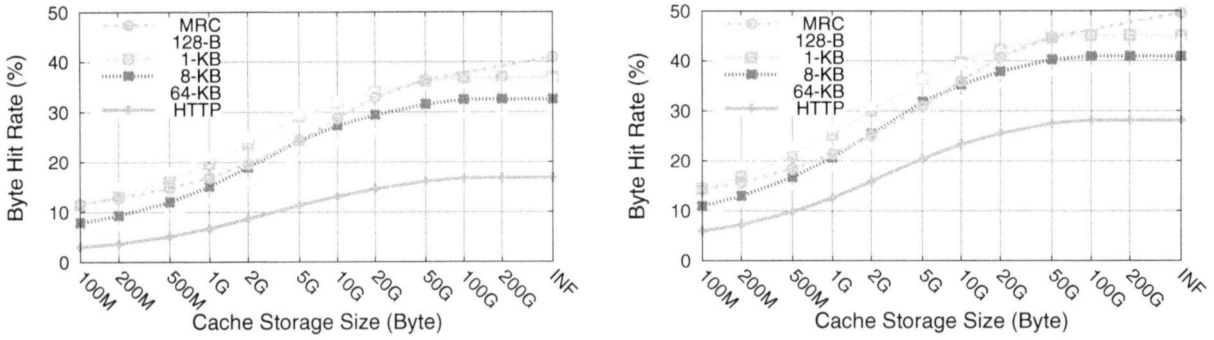

(a) US

(b) CN

Figure 18: Cache size vs. byte hit rate: A large cache with MRC provides 2x the byte hit rate than the object-based caching.

	Request (K)	Byte (GB)	GB if fully downloaded
US	265 (3.1%)	61 (30.8%)	712 (83.8%)
CN	377 (3.1%)	27 (12.4%)	444 (69.9%)
FR	38 (1.8%)	10 (23.6%)	258 (88.8%)
BR	85 (2.1%)	22 (28.3%)	216 (79.3%)

Table 3: Aborted transfers

our simulation. Note that one might want to reduce the storage requirement by storing only unique content and metadata such as offset for different chunk sizes. However, it complicates the cache index management and increases memory pressure, as pointed out by Ihm *et al.* [28].

5.6 Aborted Transfers

In Table 3, we find a small number of requests (1.8-3.1%) are aborted before they are fully downloaded, but their volume is quite significant. These events occur when users cancel ongoing transfers by clicking the stop button of the browser, or move to another Web page. We detect the aborted transfer if the downloaded length is less than the given content-length in the response header. The total volume of the downloaded bytes until aborted is 12.4-30.8%. If they were fully downloaded, it would take 69.9-88.8% of the entire traffic. The investigation of the content type distribution of these transfers reveals that most of the bytes are from the video transfers, presumably previewing the first part of the video clips. In particular, Flash video comprises roughly 40-70% of all aborted transfers, and we also observe users canceling file downloads.

The large volume of aborted transfers could negatively impact the performance of object-based caching proxies. Such systems have roughly four options to deal with the aborted transfers. The first option is to discard and do not cache them, but it just wastes the bandwidth and reduces cache hit rate. The second option is to fully download and cache them (of course, for those cacheable objects only), but it consumes significant bandwidth for downloading objects that might not be referenced in the future. The third option lies in between the first and second, and decides whether to discard or fully download depending on the number of bytes remaining [58]. The final option is to cache the downloaded portion and do a range request on a cache hit, but it is effective only for cacheable objects.

In comparison, content-based caching could cache data from only the downloaded content without any configuration, thus any data received over network, even uncacheable, is useful. As evidence, content-based caching's byte hit rate of video traffic is much higher than object- based caching's byte hit rate in Figure 15.

6. RELATED WORK

Our work is related to previous work in the areas of Internet monitoring, traffic characterization, and caching behavior. We describe our relation to this previous work below.

Internet Monitoring There is a great deal of previous work analyzing traffic behavior. For example, Akamai analyzes data gathered from its global server network, and reports the Internet penetration rate and connection speeds for each country [10]. Also, ipoque examines traffic from its customer ISPs and universities [29], and they find the increase of Web traffic as well as the decrease of P2P traffic due to the popularity of file hosting, social networking, and video streaming sites. Several other studies commonly observe the same trend of increasing Web and video traffic [21, 34, 36].

While all of these previous studies primarily focus on the analysis of overall usage of Internet traffic, our focus is to investigate various aspects of Web traffic changes in great detail. A few other studies also have conducted long-term characterizations of Web traffic [14, 26], but their analyses on the data set from specific organizations, such as universities or research institutes, are tied to their host institutes. Instead, our large-scale data set spanning a multi-year period covers a world-wide user population.

Web Traffic Characterization A very widely used Web traffic model was first proposed by Mah, in which he introduces the idle time based page detection algorithm [35]. Since then, this model has been widely adopted by many researchers for characterizing Web traffic [9, 56]. Later, Choi and Limb developed a method that simply regards every HTML object as a Web page [17]. More recently, several studies have investigated a small number of popular Ajax Web applications such as maps and Web mails, and streaming services [16, 53].

However, all of the previous studies have limitations in that they either assume the simple/static Web pages ignoring client-side interactions, or rely on application/site-specific knowledge. Instead, our page detection algorithm is able to identify initial pages and client-side interactions, and also does not require application/site-specific knowledge. Furthermore, we demonstrate that our algorithm is more accurate than the previous approaches via careful validation.

A contemporary work by Butkiewicz *et al.* [12] investigates the complexity of Web sites with browser-based active measurements from four vantage points. While their use of HTTP archive record (HAR) format [25] allows a precise detection of page load events, their data set consists of only the top-level pages of randomly chosen 2,000 Web sites, also ignoring client-side interactions. Analyzing real users' browsing behaviors with detailed HAR logs would be an interesting future work.

Redundancy and Caching Traditional object-level Web caching works by storing previously seen objects and serving them locally for future requests. However, the benefit of object-based caching is limited only to the cacheable objects such as static text and image files – the typical cache hit rates reported in the previous work range from 35% to 50% in much earlier work, and have dropped over time [3, 13, 24, 30, 40, 63]. The byte hit rate is even worse as a cache hit is biased towards smaller popular objects. Most recently, Ager *et al.* examined potential for HTTP caching in various scenarios by controlling the strictness of object cacheability [3]. More advanced object-based caching techniques include delta-encoding that reduces traffic for object updates [39], and duplicate transfer detection (DTD) that avoids downloading of aliased objects [40].

Spring and Wetherall further extend object-based caching to sub-packet granularity, and develop a protocol independent content-based caching technique [57]. Since then, it has been adapted in many applications – network file systems [7, 42], WAN acceleration [28, 50], Web caching [43, 49], and storage systems [20]. Recently, Anand *et al.* analyzed university and enterprise network traces, and show that 15-60% of the entire traffic is redundant, while the redundancy of Web traffic is only 16-32% [6].

While both the object-based and content-based caching schemes have been studied heavily, the focus of our work is to perform a head-to-head comparison between them on real Web traffic. Our analysis result shows that content-based caching achieves byte hit rates of 42-51%, almost twice that of object-based caching's byte hit rates. Furthermore, we evaluate the effectiveness of MRC [28], and find increasing cache storage size is highly beneficial. Indeed, the redundancy we find (42-51%) is much higher than what Anand *et al.* report (16-32%), and it is partly because we assume a large disk-based cache while they use in-memory cache only.

7. CONCLUSIONS

For a better understanding of modern Web traffic, we analyze five years of real Web traffic from a globally distributed proxy system that captures the browsing behavior of over 70,000 daily users from 187 countries. Among our major findings is that Flash video and Ajax traffic is consistently increasing, and search engine/analytics sites are tracking an increasingly large fraction of users. Our StreamStructure algorithm reveals that almost half the traffic now occurs not as a result of initial page loads, but as a result of client-side interactions after the initial load. Also, while pages have grown in terms of both the number of objects and size, page loading latency has dropped due to the increased number of concurrent connections and improved caching behavior. Finally, multi-resolution chunking (MRC) with large cache storage provides almost twice the byte hit rate of traditional object-based caching, and it is also effective for aborted transfers. Most of the additional savings of content-based caching are due to the partial content overlaps.

8. ACKNOWLEDGMENTS

We would like to thank our shepherd, Steve Uhlig, as well as the anonymous IMC reviewers. We are grateful to KyoungSoo Park for keeping CoDeeN running all these years and for providing us with the logs. We also thank Eric Keller, Wonho Kim, and Siddhartha Sen for their helpful comments on an earlier version of this paper. This research was partially supported by the NSF Awards CNS-0615237 and CNS-0916204.

References

[1] Adobe HTTP Dynamic Streaming. http://www.adobe.com/products/httpdynamicstreaming/.

[2] B. Ager, W. Mühlbauer, G. Smaragdakis, and S. Uhlig. Comparing DNS resolvers in the wild. In *Proc. Internet Measurement Conference*, Melbourne, Australia, Nov. 2010.

[3] B. Ager, F. Schneider, J. Kim, and A. Feldmann. Revisiting cacheability in times of user generated content. In *Proc. 13th IEEE Global Internet Symposium*, San Diego, CA, Mar. 2010.

[4] AJAX - Connectivity Enhancements in Internet Explorer 8. http://msdn.microsoft.com/en-us/library/cc304129(v=vs.85).aspx.

[5] Alexa the Web Information Company. http://www.alexa.com/.

[6] A. Anand, C. Muthukrishnan, A. Akella, and R. Ramjee. Redundancy in network traffic: Findings and implications. In *Proc. ACM SIGMETRICS*, Seattle, WA, June 2009.

[7] S. Annapureddy, M. J. Freedman, and D. Mazières. Shark: Scaling file servers via cooperative caching. In *Proc. 2nd USENIX NSDI*, Boston, MA, May 2005.

[8] Apple HTTP Live Streaming. http://developer.apple.com/resources/http-streaming/.

[9] P. Barford and M. Crovella. Generating Representative Web Workloads for Network and Server Performance Evaluation. In *Proc. ACM SIGMETRICS*, Madison, WI, June 1998.

[10] D. Belson. Akamai state of the Internet report, q4 2009. *SIGOPS Oper. Syst. Rev.*, 44(3):27–37, 2010.

[11] L. Breslau, P. Cao, L. Fan, G. Phillips, and S. Shenker. Web caching and zipf-like distributions: Evidence and implications. In *Proc. IEEE INFOCOM*, New York, NY, Mar. 1999.

[12] M. Butkiewicz, H. V. Madhyastha, and V. Sekar. Understanding website complexity: Measurements, metrics, and implications. In *Proc. Internet Measurement Conference*, Berlin, Germany, Nov. 2011.

[13] R. Cáceres, F. Douglis, A. Feldmann, G. Glass, and M. Rabinovich. Web proxy caching: the devil is in the details. In *Proc. 1st ACM Workshop on Internet Server Performance*, Madison, WI, June 1998.

[14] T. Callahan, M. Allman, and V. Paxson. A longitudinal view of HTTP traffic. In *Passive & Active Measurement (PAM)*, Zurich, Switzerland, Apr. 2010.

[15] M. Casado and M. J. Freedman. Peering through the shroud: the effect of edge opacity on IP-based client identification. In *Proc. 4th USENIX NSDI*, Cambridge, MA, Apr. 2007.

[16] M. Cha, H. Kwak, P. Rodriguez, Y.-Y. Ahn, and S. Moon. I Tube, You Tube, Everybody Tubes: Analyzing the World's Largest User Generated Content Video System. In *Proc. ACM SIGCOMM Internet Measurement Conference*, San Diego, CA, USA, Oct. 2007.

[17] H.-K. Choi and J. O. Limb. A behavioral model of Web traffic. In *IEEE International Conference on Network Protocols (ICNP)*, Toronto, Canada, Oct. 1999.

[18] D. Crane, E. Pascarello, and D. James. *Ajax in Action*. Manning Publications Co., Greenwich, CT, USA, 2005.

[19] Cascading Style Sheets Level 2 Revision 1 (CSS 2.1) Specification. http://www.w3.org/TR/CSS2/.

[20] Data Domain. http://www.datadomain.com/.

[21] J. Erman, A. Gerber, M. T. Hajiaghayi, D. Pei, and O. Spatscheck. Network-aware forward caching. In *Proc. 18th International World Wide Web Conference*, Madrid, Spain, May 2009.

[22] R. Fielding, J. Gettys, J. Mogul, H. Frystyk, L. Masinter, P. Leach, and T. Berners-Lee. *Hyptertext Transfer Protocol – HTTP/1.1*. Internet Engineering Task Force, June 1999. RFC 2616.

[23] Top 7 Firefox Proxy Addons. http://www.techiezine.com/top-7-firefox-proxy-addons/.

[24] S. Gribble and E. Brewer. System Design Issues for Internet Middleware Services: Deductions from a Large Client Trace. In *Proc. 1st USENIX Symposium on Internet Technologies and Systems (USITS)*, Monterey, CA, Dec. 1997.

[25] HTTP Archive Specification. http://groups.google.com/group/http-archive-specification/web/har-1-2-spec.

[26] F. Hernandez-Campos, K. Jeffay, and F. Smith. Tracking the evolution of Web traffic: 1995-2003. In *Proc. IEEE/ACM MASCOTS*, Oct. 2003.

[27] S. Ihm, K. Park, and V. S. Pai. Towards Understanding Developing World Traffic. In *Proc. 4th ACM Workshop on Networked Systems for Developing Regions (NSDR)*, San Francisco, CA, June 2010.

[28] S. Ihm, K. Park, and V. S. Pai. Wide-area Network Acceleration for the Developing World. In *Proc. USENIX Annual Technical Conference*, Boston, MA, June 2010.

[29] ipoque. Internet Study 2008/2009. http://www.ipoque.com/resources/internet-studies/internet-study-2008_2009.

[30] D. L. Johnson, E. M. Belding, K. Almeroth, and G. van Stam. Internet usage and performance analysis of a rural wireless network in Macha, Zambia. In *Proc. 4th ACM Workshop on Networked Systems for Developing Regions (NSDR)*, San Francisco, CA, June 2010.

[31] JPMorgan Chase & Company. The Rise of Ad Networks. http://www.mediamath.com/docs/JPMorgan.pdf.

[32] T. Kelly and J. Mogul. Aliasing on the World Wide Web: prevalence and performance implications. In *Proc. Eleventh International World Wide Web Conference*, Honolulu, Hawaii, USA, May 2002.

[33] C. Kreibich, N. Weaver, B. Nechaev, and V. Paxson. Netalyzr: illuminating the edge network. In *Proc. Internet Measurement Conference*, Melbourne, Australia, Nov. 2010.

[34] C. Labovitz, S. Iekel-Johnson, D. McPherson, J. Oberheide, and F. Jahanian. Internet inter-domain traffic. In *Proc. ACM SIGCOMM*, New Delhi, India, Aug. 2010.

[35] B. A. Mah. An Empirical Model of HTTP Network Traffic. In *Proc. IEEE INFOCOM*, Kobe, Japan, Apr. 1997.

[36] G. Maier, A. Feldmann, V. Paxson, and M. Allman. On dominant characteristics of residential broadband Internet traffic. In *Proc. Internet Measurement Conference*, Chicago, Illinois, Nov. 2009.

[37] G. Maier, F. Schneider, and A. Feldmann. NAT usage in residential broadband networks. In *Passive & Active Measurement (PAM)*, Atlanta, GA, Mar. 2011.

[38] MaxMind. http://www.maxmind.com/.

[39] J. Mogul, B. Krishnamurthy, F. Douglis, A. Feldmann, Y. Goland, A. van Hoff, and D. Hellerstein. *Delta encoding in HTTP*, January 2002. RFC 3229.

[40] J. C. Mogul, Y. M. Chan, and T. Kelly. Design, implementation, and evaluation of duplicate transfer detection in HTTP. In *Proc. 1st USENIX NSDI*, San Francisco, CA, Mar. 2004.

[41] Microsoft Smooth Streaming. http://www.iis.net/download/SmoothStreaming/.

[42] A. Muthitacharoen, B. Chen, and D. Mazieres. A low-bandwidth network file system. In *Proc. 18th ACM Symposium on Operating Systems Principles (SOSP)*, Banff, Canada, Oct. 2001.

[43] K. Park, S. Ihm, M. Bowman, and V. S. Pai. Supporting practical content-addressable caching with CZIP compression. In *Proc. USENIX Annual Technical Conference*, Santa Clara, CA, June 2007.

[44] K. Park, V. S. Pai, K.-W. Lee, and S. Calo. Securing Web service by automatic robot detection. In *Proc. USENIX Annual Technical Conference*, Boston, MA, June 2006.

[45] PlanetLab. http://www.planet-lab.org/, 2008.

[46] S. Podlipnig and L. Böszörmenyi. A survey of Web cache replacement strategies. *ACM Computing Surveys*, 35, Dec. 2003.

[47] L. Popa, A. Ghodsi, and I. Stoica. HTTP as the Narrow Waist of the Future Internet. In *Proc. 9th ACM Workshop on Hot Topics in Networks (Hotnets-IX)*, Monterey, CA, Oct. 2010.

[48] M. O. Rabin. Fingerprinting by random polynomials. Technical Report TR-15-81, Center for Research in Computing Technology, Harvard University, 1981.

[49] S. C. Rhea, K. Liang, and E. Brewer. Value-based Web caching. In *Proc. Twelfth International World Wide Web Conference*, Budapest, Hungary, May 2003.

[50] Riverbed Technologies, Inc. http://www.riverbed.com/.

[51] Roundup on Parallel Connections. http://www.stevesouders.com/blog/2008/03/20/roundup-on-parallel-connections/.

[52] RSS 2.0 Specification. http://www.rssboard.org/rss-specification.

[53] F. Schneider, S. Agarwal, T. Alpcan, and A. Feldmann. The new Web: Characterizing Ajax traffic. In *Passive & Active Measurement (PAM)*, Cleveland, OH, Apr. 2008.

[54] H. Schulzrinne, S. Casner, R. Frederick, and V. Jacobson. *RTP: A Transport Protocol for Real-Time Applications*. Internet Engineering Task Force, Jan. 1996. RFC 1889.

[55] H. Schulzrinne, A. Rao, and R. Lanphier. *Real Time Streaming Protocol (RTSP)*. Internet Engineering Task Force, Apr. 1998. RFC 2326.

[56] F. D. Smith, F. H. Campos, K. Jeffay, and D. Ott. What TCP/IP protocol headers can tell us about the Web. In *Proc. ACM SIGMETRICS*, Cambridge, MA, June 2001.

[57] N. Spring and D. Wetherall. A protocol-independent technique for eliminating redundant network traffic. In *Proc. ACM SIGCOMM*, Stockholm, Sweden, Sep. 2000.

[58] Squid Configuration Directive. http://www.squid-cache.org/Doc/config/quick_abort_min/.

[59] P. Srisuresh and K. Egevang. *Traditional IP Network Address Translator (Traditional NAT)*. United States, 2001. RFC 3022.

[60] StatCounter. http://statcounter.com/.

[61] W3Counter. http://www.w3counter.com/.

[62] L. Wang, K. Park, R. Pang, V. S. Pai, and L. Peterson. Reliability and security in the CoDeeN content distribution network. In *Proc. USENIX Annual Technical Conference*, Boston, MA, June 2004.

[63] A. Wolman, G. M. Voelker, N. Sharma, N. Cardwell, A. Karlin, and H. M. Levy. On the scale and performance of cooperative Web proxy caching. In *Proc. 17th ACM Symposium on Operating Systems Principles (SOSP)*, Kiawah Island, SC, Dec. 1999.

Summary Review Documentation for

"Towards Understanding Modern Web Traffic"

Authors: S. Ihm, V. Pai

Reviewer #1

Strengths: Nice dataset. The analysis confirms the expected increase in complexity of webpages.

Weaknesses: The data covers US and China mostly, which would lead to an interesting comparison if it had been made. The authors throw numbers without giving as much high-level insight, making the observations hard to retain for the reader. Without much information about how representative this dataset is in terms of content, the CDNs from which the content is obtained, the impact of PlanetLab on the CDN answers, it is hard to judge the validity of the observations.

Comments to Authors: The dataset is interesting. However, the number of plots and the writing style make it boring to read. There are way too many numbers for which the authors do not have an explanation. Instead of digging into the data so much, the message of the paper would be more clear if more high-level insights were provided instead of numbers.

I would have preferred to see a more extensive comparison of USA and China rather than having the paper filled with the caching section which is questionable in its applicability. Knowing more about the CDNs that deliver the content and the impact of PlanetLab on wherefrom you get content from CDNs is important while missing.

Detailed comments:

If they want to discuss caching, the authors should discuss more than the proxy-level cacheability but also the network-level one, for example as studied by: - B. Ager et al. Revisiting Cacheability in Times of User Generated Content. IEEE Global Internet Symposium, 2010.

Regarding NAT usage, the authors should cite the recent work by Kreibich et al.: - Netalyzr: Illuminating The Edge Network, IMC 2010.

The high-level description of section 5 in the introduction sounds conflicting: popular URLs grow which improves caching (potentially!) while the long tail also grows which hurts caching (again potentially). The authors should rephrase this. Stating it in the current way is nice as it raises the attention of the reader, but if the reader does not get it he will be frustrated.

Your dataset is great, in principle. However, does it provide realistic latencies as well as representative DNS answers by CDNs? Relying on the PlanetLab infrastructure is a bias from the viewpoint of the DNS answers that CDNs return, which is most of the content in the Internet. Please tone down the claims about the greatness of your dataset. A great dataset does not require overdoing the marketing. The fourth paragraph of section 2 is too strong.

The authors have to reduce the number in terms of the number of countries the dataset really has. USA and China make most of the content of the dataset, so claiming that the dataset spans 187 countries is misleading.

In section 3.1, the authors mention that they provide the results of US, China and Brazil due to space limitations. Those 3 countries represent most of the dataset anyway, only France seems to be important enough and is omitted. This sounds misleading again, as the 187 countries mentioned before. The results of this section should be compared to the results of Kreibich et al.

Figures 3-4 omit years 2007 and 2009. Are the trends for 2006-2008-2010 consistent with them?

How many embedded images do you observe? Embedded content is important nowadays as it pervades a lot of webpages, e.g., advertisement. This part might deserve more attention.

The authors do not observe video streaming that split files into chunks. This may point to a bias of the dataset.

One thing I was curious and was not analyzed by the authors is the properties of the dataset on a per CDN basis. Do the trends show up consistently across all content delivery platforms or is the observed behavior an artefact of the specific content that CoDEEN users are accessing?

For a recent analysis of DNS in the wild, the authors may cite: - B. Ager et al. Comparing DNS resolvers in the wild. IMC 2010.

When the authors mention the increase in Google analytics beacons in the manually collected dataset, what is the message? Is that good, bad, neutral? All mentions of google analytics leave a feeling of "so what?".

From section 4.3, the authors do not discuss changes in RTT and bandwidth that may affect the observations. The placement of CDN servers or their connectivity is likely to have an impact here. It is simplistic to discuss loading latency while completely ignoring the content delivery side.

How much is 'somewhat'? How much do the authors expect to actually under-estimate the loading latency? Did they carry out some tests to check this?

Given the actual lifetime of objects, what is the actual cacheability of web objects? It's not clear from the paper how much of the caching can really be achieved in practice.

Section 5 should be another paper. As it is now it is not strong enough to be comparable to previous work and does not add much to the content of the paper, while bringing issues.

Where is caching assumed to be done? At the browser, the proxy, inside the network? What information is used to assess the cacheability of a specific object? This section should be compared with the following work: - B. Ager et al. Revisiting Cacheability in Times of User Generated Content. IEEE Global Internet Symposium, 2010.

In 5.3, it seems that the authors assume a centralized cache inside a country that would serve all content. This is clearly not feasible, as this would affect the latency to obtain content. The problem of caching is more complex than presented in section 5. That leaves a negative impression on the whole paper.

Reviewer #2

Strengths: The authors have a nice dataset in their disposal, and this alone makes the paper interesting. There is an interesting study on caching and the trends looking at object sizes.

Weaknesses: There are several limitations in the paper. The authors never really describe their dataset and the precise methodology in their analysis, which makes it hard in some cases to follow the paper. Unclear how representative the data is (could easily have been checked). No web model is presented contrary to author claims in the intro and abstract.

Comments to Authors: I was really intrigued by the paper's abstract since historical studies of web traffic are rare due to lack of datasets. However, despite the unique data, the paper fell short of my expectations in many respects.

First, the authors attempt to pack many different things in one paper (trends, web model, caching, etc), with the result of not examining any of them in detail but rather providing initial observations. Also, to do this, the dataset is sampled (trimmed) in many respects (one month per year, only some countries etc) without much justification.

Second, the authors never really describe their data and the information included in them. What fields do the logs include? What type of users are we looking at? Is it mostly academics since this is planetlab? The reader has to infer this information from the analysis (for example, the paper looks at object inter-arrival times, so there must be some sufficient timing information in the logs).

Third, related to the above, how representative the data examined are. For example, the browser popularity appears quite peculiar with firefox reflecting 60-75% of the users in some cases. Comparing this with any public statistic out there (and there are many), the numbers look sufficiently different. Do the data mainly reflect academic users, and as such present a specific community? A way to check this would be to compare the most popular requested URLs with statistics from Alexa for example. Similarly, NAT usage also appears low IMHO.

Fourth, there is no web model presented, but rather statistics and distributions for various web traffic characteristics (e.g., number and size of objects, inter-arrival times etc).

Instead, I believe that the section on caching is interesting and one of the contributions of the paper.

Other detailed comments:
Section 2: Table 1: There seems to be a drop in the number of requests after 2007. Why is this? Also, how is it possible that the number of IPs/Agents in most of the countries is larger than the number of requests? How do you separate non-human traffic? How do you know the number of users?
Section 3 You attribute the increase of javascript and CSS in the use of AJAX. How is this justified? Simply, this could be an effect of more code and advanced style-sheets out there. The paragraph "Domains" is hard to understand, and I was not able to follow it.
Section 4: Is it true that step 3 can be performed only for 23.9% of the pages? If so, the methodology is not very effective. You visit the top-100 sample sites from Alexa. If not mistaken, most of these are simple pages (e.g., search or other simple home pages). It is thus unclear whether the validation of your streamstructure algorithm is sufficient. How do you know the latencies? What type of information do you have in the logs?
Section 5: You need to formally define what you mean by redundancy. You examine the most popular URLs. Which year is your reference for this? For URLs that were examined only once, is that for the whole trace? Since the content-based caching is so important for your discussion, a more complete description of how it works would make the understanding of your results easier.

Reviewer #3

Strengths: This paper represents a great effort in understanding the long term trend of network traffic. The measurement results are of great interest to network community such as IETF.

Weaknesses: 2 comments on the weakness. First, from reading this paper alone I did not fully understand how the data is collected, exactly what is the relation between CoDeeN and PlanetLab, and who are the users.

Second, the authors seem running out of space (e.g. the last paragraph of introduction apparently suffered from over-cut, leaving the sentences incomplete), while at the same time repeated their major results several times word by word; perhaps also running out of time to do a good proof reading.

Comments to Authors: None.

Reviewer #4

Strengths: The combination of a detailed look at many aspects of Web traffic and a fabulous dataset. It's rare that we see this, and the datapoints in the paper are great documentation about how the Web has changed over the past five years, even if they are not always surprising. I don't know of any comparable study for this period, as other notable efforts like Arbor's Internet Atlas/Observatory are more broad but much less detailed wrt Web traffic.
The new page clustering algorithm is also useful, and will help other researchers.

Weaknesses: The paper covers broad ground and thus is a bit thin in places, particularly wrt experimental method. There are a bunch of places where I wanted to object a bit (e.g., Why is the average download time for objects >1MB a good estimator for client bandwidth?) or wanted better validation (e.g., on the page clustering technique). I think this can be handled by being careful in the writing about what the paper has and has not shown.

Comments to Authors: Very nice -- thanks for a good read. You have a fabulous dataset and some nice results. I particularly liked the stat that the majority of requests are now due to page interaction rather than traditional page fetches.

What kind of users browse the Web via CoDeen? You likely have some bias and evolution here (usage drops off over time) that is worth stating.
I can't read your graphs, starting with Fig 1!
It comes across as a bit arbitrary the way you pick US, China, BR, and FR and then jump between them for different results. It would be better to be more consistent and to explain your selection. Related to this comment, consider that a paper is *not* the best way to present your results. You might provide a web page or technical report that does not have space limitations and can show the full set of graphs for a larger set of countries. The paper would then be a representative subset, as you have targeted, but researchers would be able to consult the more complete results as needed.
Why is average download time for objects >1MB a good estimator for client bandwidth? It can fail due to slow servers or points of congestion within the Internet (between US and BR for instance). My guess is that a better measure is the 95% (fastest) download time. Either way, some validation would be really help.
Similarly, I am unsure whether your results indicate that NAT usage is growing or not. They could easily be explained by an increase in the number of computers per (already NATed) household over the years. Can you compare with an independent datapoint, as your claim is presently unvalidated?
Fig 6 felt like an odd extraction of different pieces for different countries.
I do not understand how your page clustering algorithm works for pages that lack Google Analytics. Do you just skip them? If so it is bit of a fragile method! I also encourage you to perform a better validation of the technique; I would not call what you have done "careful validation". This is because visiting 10 pages per top site may be markedly different than task-based Web browsing (doing mail, looking at a stock portfolio). I think that you can validate it fairly easily. Just create a browser extension that spits out a log of the pages visited over time, use it for real surfing, and see how it compares with your inference.
Re the simple model of web traffic: it reads as a rough characterization, not a complete model. It would be better to either specify a complete model (that other researchers could use to generate synthetic traffic) or just keep it as a characterization.
In the text, the median page load latency in 2010 is given as 5.98 seconds. This is really long per my usage! Perhaps there is substantial variation in the median for different countries and access bandwidths that is making the overall median statistic of questionable utility?
Is your use of "page load time" is different than the normal definition of page load time as seen within the browser and indicated by the onLoad() handler firing? I was a bit confused on this.
At the end of 4.3: I really have no idea if the predictions from the simulation are likely to be accurate. There is no validation of any simulated points, and I don't see how you can easily validate. This is a bit troubling and deserves some mention in your text.
In Fig 12(f), the medians look substantially the same, but you describe them as different.
Re caching figures: can you compare with earlier results to put the numbers you give in perspective.
Re aborted transfers: the 12-31% figure seems the right one to use, but you use the higher one (for the full size of the aborted loads) elsewhere in the paper. Even so, I'm surprised that there is so much volume in a small number of aborted transfers -- they may deserve more attention and a look at their distribution.

Reviewer #5

Strengths: The paper is a straightforward, nicely executed analysis of a great longitudinal dataset. It provides helpful numbers and contains a few cute tricks.

Weaknesses: In parts I find the paper repetitive and plot-heavy. I believe the authors could free up a bunch of room by avoiding repeat mentioning of findings and leaving out some plots, making room for additional analysis.

Comments to author: In the introduction when you recap Section 5, I did not understand "the popular URLs grow, and therefore improves caching". It becomes clear later in Section 5.

Table 1 is poorly designed. Show the years only once. Sort the rows alphabetically by country, or make the current sorting criterion clear. Say 33,457 instead of 33457, and use less lines. What are "agents"?
The beginning of Section 3 overlaps the findings summary in the intro a lot. Cut it, and make your figures larger instead, as virtually all are too small.
In 3.1, when you describe connection speed, how does that account for CoDeeN's architecture? Are you measuring the download speed for objects stored on a CoDeeN server to the client, or ... ? Regarding NAT use, I would suspect not so much increase of it, rather than proliferation of browser-enabled devices behind existing NATs.
In Figures 5 and 6 the placement of the legend destroys comparability for the right-hand plot. Fold the legend out horizontally and place it under all three graphs.
I like the trick in 4.1 of relying on observing the activity of entities known to trigger only at specific page load events, in order to delineate initial pages.
In 4.3, what do you mean by "stay less than 30 minutes" -- stay where?
12a and 12f could go, as they add little over the text and would allow you to make the other ones larger.
I like your caching analysis. In "Ideal Byte Hit Rate", you say you optimistically removed query strings from the URLs. A well-designed site should make cacheability of such content explicit, say via ETags. How often is that the case? Also, it would have been interesting to read more about the clients' correct support for HTTP content caching. For example, how often do clients re-request content they should cache locally, etc. Finally, you don't say how your content-based caching relates to cacheability information conveyed in the entities' headers. Are your byte hit rates optimal in the sense that they match content signatures across unrelated downloads and regardless of cacheability, or ...?

Response from the Authors

(1) Data set: We provide a more detailed description of CoDeeN and PlanetLab to help understand our data set. In addition, we compare the users of CoDeeN and the content they browse with other studies. Finally, we describe the limitations of our data set, and explain the origins of potential bias.
(2) High-level analysis: We agree that the average download time of objects might not be the best estimate of client bandwidth because bandwidth estimation itself is a challenging problem. However, we believe our estimates are good enough to show yearly improvements and the existence of many slow clients. In

fact, the same conclusions hold for the 95th percentile of download time. Regarding NAT usage, we agree that the increased number of browser-enabled devices per household is a better explanation, and changed our text accordingly.
(3) Page-level analysis: First, one of the contributions of StreamStructure is to delineate initial page loads by catching any kind of page load event, and we exploit Google Analytics simply because of its popularity. One can easily utilize beacons from other analytics services to increase coverage. Second, regarding our manually collected Alexa data set, we visit not only the top-level pages but also other pages linked from those top-level pages. Of course, our data collection is different from actual browsing patterns, but we believe that it is sufficient for validation as it captures the structure of representative Web pages. Third, we clarify that the purpose of our page loading latency simulation is to raise issues about which factors affect the latency rather than to predict the actual latency.
(4) Caching analysis: We mention that our analysis is based on logically centralized but physically distributed proxy systems, just like CoDeeN. Thus the result should read as potential bandwidth reduction when replacing conventional caching proxies with content-based caching proxies. Also, we add two more results that further analyze uncacheable content and the origins of redundancy.
(5) Miscellaneous: We acknowledge prior work on NAT usage, DNS performance, and caching analysis. We also address all of the presentation issues, cleaning up tables and figures. Finally, a comparison of US and China is a non-goal of this paper. Instead, we encourage interested readers to read our workshop paper: S. Ihm et al. ``Towards Understanding Developing World Traffic'' in NSDR'10, which includes more detailed analysis of aborted transfers including object size distributions, which we omitted due to space limitations.

Understanding Website Complexity: Measurements, Metrics, and Implications

Michael Butkiewicz
UC Riverside
butkiewm@cs.ucr.edu

Harsha V. Madhyastha
UC Riverside
harsha@cs.ucr.edu

Vyas Sekar
Intel Labs
vyas.sekar@intel.com

ABSTRACT

Over the years, the web has evolved from simple text content from one server to a complex ecosystem with different types of content from servers spread across several administrative domains. There is anecdotal evidence of users being frustrated with high page load times or when obscure scripts cause their browser windows to freeze. Because page load times are known to directly impact user satisfaction, providers would like to understand if and how the complexity of their websites affects the user experience.

While there is an extensive literature on measuring web graphs, website popularity, and the nature of web traffic, there has been little work in understanding how complex individual websites are, and how this complexity impacts the clients' experience. This paper is a first step to address this gap. To this end, we identify a set of metrics to characterize the complexity of websites both at a content-level (e.g., number and size of images) and service-level (e.g., number of servers/origins).

We find that the distributions of these metrics are largely independent of a website's popularity rank. However, some categories (e.g., *News*) are more complex than others. More than 60% of websites have content from at least 5 non-origin sources and these contribute more than 35% of the bytes downloaded. In addition, we analyze which metrics are most critical for predicting page render and load times and find that the number of objects requested is the most important factor. With respect to variability in load times, however, we find that the number of servers is the best indicator.

Categories and Subject Descriptors

D.2.8 [**Metrics**]: [Complexity measures]; D.4.8 [**Performance**]: [Modeling and prediction]

General Terms

Measurement, Human Factors, Performance

Keywords

Web page complexity, Page load times

IMC'11, November 2–4, 2011, Berlin, Germany.

1. INTRODUCTION

Over the last decade, web pages have become significantly more complex. Originally used to host text and images, web pages now include several content types, ranging from videos to scripts executed on the client's device to "rich" media such as Flash and Silverlight. Further, a website today fetches content not only from servers hosted by its providers but also from a range of third party services such as advertising agencies, content distribution networks (CDNs), and analytics services. In combination, rendering a single web page today involves fetching several objects with varying characteristics from multiple servers under different administrative domains.

On the other hand, the ill-effects of slow websites are well-documented. Recent surveys suggest two thirds of users encounter slow websites every week [15] and that 49% of users will abandon a site or switch to a competitor after experiencing performance issues [9]. While there is plenty of anecdotal evidence that the increase in web page complexity is a key factor in slowing down websites, formal studies on this topic have been limited. Most prior work on web measurement focuses on characterizing the Web graph [19, 16], analyzing the network footprint of Web traffic [34, 35, 41, 39, 42, 30], or studying the rate of change of content on the Web [29]. While these have contributed to a better understanding of web usage, they do not analyze the websites themselves.

In this paper, we present a comprehensive measurement-driven study of the complexity of web pages today and its impact on performance. We measure roughly 1700 websites from four geographically distributed locations over a 7 week period. These websites are spread across both a wide range of popularity ranks and genre of website categories. In analyzing website complexity, we focus on a *client-side* view of the landing pages of these sites and not on the dependencies in the back-end server infrastructure—an interesting topic complementary to our efforts.

Understanding the complexity of web pages and its implications is vital on several fronts. With the increasing diversity of client platforms for accessing the Web, it is important for browser developers to identify the aspects of web page complexity that impact user-perceived performance. On the other hand, as website providers increasingly incorporate third-party services such as advertising, analytics, and CDNs into their webpages, they need tools and techniques to evaluate the impact of these services on users. Furthermore, beyond the perspective of any given user or web provider, understanding website complexity is a first step toward solutions for automatically customizing web pages for varying client platforms to achieve the right balance between performance, usability, and business interests.

Our study focuses on two broad questions. First, we quantify the complexity of a web page with a broad spectrum of metrics.

We characterize a web page by the content fetched in rendering it—the number of objects fetched, the sizes of these objects, and the types of content. While these features remain largely the same across different rank ranges of websites, we see a marked difference across different website categories. For example, *News* websites load a significantly higher number of objects than others, whereas *Kids and Teens* websites host a higher fraction of Flash content.

In addition to characterizing this content-level complexity, we study the complexity of web pages with respect to the services they build upon. We find that non-origin content accounts for a significant fraction of the number of objects and number of bytes fetched, an observation that holds even on low ranked websites. However, the impact on download time of non-origin content is low—the median contribution to download time is only 15%. Though the most popular third-party services are unsurprisingly analytics and advertising providers, emerging services such as social networking plugins and programming frameworks also appear on a sizeable fraction of websites. A significant difference that we observe in the types of content served from non-origins in comparison to that from website providers themselves is that Javascripts account for a much higher fraction of non-origin objects.

The second focus of our study is to identify the critical complexity metrics that have the most impact on the time to download and render a web page. We find that rather than the total number of bytes fetched to render a website, the number of objects fetched is the most dominant indicator of client-perceived load times. We corroborate this with a linear regression model that predicts page load times with a normalized mean squared error less than 0.1. We also determine that, in contrast to actual load times, variability in load times is better correlated with the number of servers from which content is fetched.

2. RELATED WORK

There have been many efforts to analyze different aspects of the Web ecosystem. This includes work to understand web structure, tools to improve web performance, and measurements of emerging web applications. We describe these next. Note that most of these efforts focus either on *web traffic* or *web protocols*. There has been surprisingly little work on quantifying and understanding *website complexity*.

Structure and evolution: The literature on modeling the Web graph and its evolution focus on the interconnecting links between websites [19, 16] rather than the structure and content of individual websites. Related efforts have studied how the content of individual web pages evolves over time [29]. Recent efforts have also tried to "map" the hosting sites from which content is served [20].

Performance and optimization: As the usage scenarios for the Web have changed, researchers have analyzed inefficiencies in web protocols and suggested improvements [38, 21, 11]. In parallel, there are efforts toward developing better browsers [37], tools to optimize webpages [2, 1, 13], benchmarking tools [27, 12, 24], services for customizing web pages for different platforms [40, 10, 8], and techniques to diagnose performance bottlenecks in backend infrastructures [43] and to debug client performance in the wild [32].

Web traffic measurement: This includes work on measuring CDNs [34], understanding emerging Web 2.0 and AJAX-based applications [35, 41], measuring the network impact of social network applications [39, 42], and characterizing end-user behavior within enterprises [30], and longitudinal studies [31] among many others. These focus on web traffic as observed at the network-level, and not on understanding the structure and performance of individual websites.

Impact of load time on users: Several user experience studies evaluate how page load times impact user satisfaction [18, 26]. There are also commercial services that measure page load times in the wild [5]. These highlight the importance of optimizing page load times. However, there have been few attempts to understand how different aspects of website complexity impact the time to load web pages.

Privacy leakage: Krishnamurthy et al. [33] report the proliferation of third-party services. Our measurement setup is similar to theirs and we quantify the use of third-party services as well. However, our end goals are very different. In particular, they focus on the privacy implications and observe that a small number of administrative entities (e.g., Google, Microsoft) have broad insights into web access patterns. Our focus, instead is on using the presence of third-party services as a metric to characterize website complexity and on studying their impact on page load times.

Complexity metrics in other domains: Other efforts present metrics to quantify the complexity of network protocols [25], network management [22], and systems more broadly [23]. In a Web context, Zhang et al. [44] present metrics to capture ease of web page navigation and Levering et al. [36] analyze the document layout structure of web pages. The high-level motivation in these efforts is the need for quantitative metrics to measure system complexity and understand its impact on performance and usability. Our study follows in the spirit of these prior efforts to quantify website complexity to understand its impact on page load times.

Characterizing webpages: The closest related work appears in recent industry efforts: HTTP Archive [3] and at Google [6]. While the data collection steps are similar, we extend their analysis in two significant ways. First, we consider a more comprehensive set of complexity metrics and present a breakdown across different rank ranges and categories. Second, and more importantly, we go a step further and construct models for correlating and predicting performance and variability in performance with respect to the measured complexity metrics. Furthermore, we view the presence and timing of these parallel industry efforts as further confirmation that there is a *key gap* in understanding website complexity and its performance implications. Our work is a step toward addressing this gap.

3. MEASUREMENT SETUP

We begin by describing the measurements we gathered that serve as input for all of our analysis. All our datasets can be downloaded at `http://www.cs.ucr.edu/~harsha/web_complexity/`. We start with around 2000 websites at random from the top-20000 sites in Quantcast's list of most popular websites.[1] We annotate these sites with content categories obtained from Alexa.[2]

To faithfully replicate the actions of a web browser when a user visits a website, we use a browser (`Firefox`) based measurement infrastructure. We use a "clean" Firefox instance (version 3.6.15) without any ad or pop-up blockers. (We install suitable plugins such as the Adobe Flash player to ensure that websites render properly.) We use the `Firebug` extension (version 1.7X.0b1) with the `Net:Export` (version 0.8b10) and `Firestarter` (version 0.1.a5) add-ons to automatically export a log of all the requests and responses involved in rendering a web page. This extension generates a report in the HTTP archive record (HAR) format [4] that provides a detailed record of the actions performed by the browser in loading the page.

[1] `http://www.quantcast.com/top-sites`
[2] `http://www.alexa.com/topsites/category`

```
"log":{
  "version":"1.1",
  "browser":{
    "name":"Firefox",
    "version":"3.6.11"
  },
  "pages":[{
     "startedDateTime":"18:12:59.702-04:00",
     "title":"Wired News",
       "pageTimings":{
         "onContentLoad":2130,
         "onLoad":4630}]
  "entries":[{
       "startedDateTime":"18:12:59.702-04:00",
       "time":9,
       "request":{
         ...
  "headers":[{
             "name":"Host",
             "value":"www.wired.com" },
         ...}
        "response":{
         ...
         "content":{
           "size":186013,
           "mimeType":"text/html",}},
       }]
       ]
```

Figure 1: Example snippet showing the different fields in a HAR file. From this report, we can reconstruct the exact sequence of requests and responses, the number and size of requests for objects of different content types, and identify the server/origin for each request.

Rank range	Number of websites
1-400	277
400-1000	298
2000-2500	330
5000-10000	443
10000-20000	400
All	*1748*

Table 1: Summary of spread across rank ranges of websites in our measurement dataset.

Figure 1 shows a snippet of a HAR report. It reports two page load metrics—`onContentLoad`, which is the time taken to start rendering content (we call this RenderStart), and `onLoad`, the time to completely render all components of the page (we call this RenderEnd).[3] Our main field of interest is the array of request-response entries. Each entry provides a timestamp of when the request was initiated, the time it took to complete the request, the host to which the request was sent, and the size and content type of the response.

We gathered measurements from four geographically distributed vantage points. Three of these vantage points were Amazon EC2 Micro instances running Ubuntu Linux (version 11.04) located in the US-East, Europe, and Asia Pacific regions of EC2. To discount any effects specific to EC2, our last vantage point is a personal desktop at UC Riverside. We choose multiple vantage points to ensure that our choice of measurement site does not introduce any bias.

[3]There is discussion in the web community on good load time metrics; suggestions include "above-the-fold" time, time to first "paint", time-to-first-byte, etc. [7]. Using a full spectrum of render metrics is outside the scope of our analysis. We pick the two standard metrics reported by the browser itself.

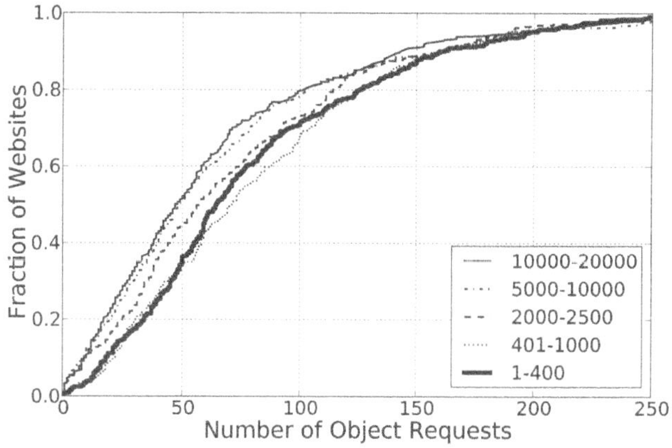

(a) By rank

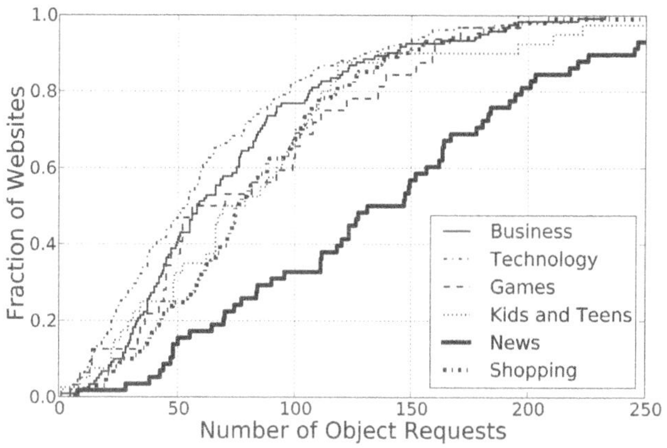

(b) By category

Figure 2: Total number of objects loaded on the base web page of websites across rank ranges and categories.

At each vantage point, we run a measurement agent that periodically (every 60 seconds) selects a website at random from the list of 2000 sites, launches a Firefox instance that loads the base URL (i.e., `www.foo.com`) for the website, generates the log report in the HAR format, and subsequently terminates the Firefox process. We repeat this for a period of 9 weeks (between May and August 2011) and gather roughly 30 measurements per website on average. Our primary focus is on the root or landing pages of these sites; we present a preliminary study of non-landing pages in Section 6.

We perform the following pre-processing on our data. We discard individual HAR files if they have recorded the number of bytes fetched or the page load time as zero, specify the HTTP status code as not 200, or are malformed. We discard measurements from all websites for which we observe consecutive HAR files spaced less than 60 seconds apart. These correspond to corner cases where the Firebug add-on to Firefox had trouble exporting a HAR file for the web page it loaded. These steps for cleaning the dataset leave us with measurements from 1748 websites. Table 1 summarizes the spread of the websites that remain across five rank-ranges.

For each website, we compute the median value for various features, such as number of objects loaded or number of servers contacted, across multiple measurements of the website. We use these median values of features for most of our analysis, though we do

Complexity metric	Key result(s)
Content complexity	
No. of objects	Across all rank ranges, median web page requests over 40 objects and 20% request over 100 objects *News* websites load a significantly greater number of objects than others
MIME type	Contribution of various content types is similar across rank ranges Images dominate in fraction of objects, but to a lesser extent with respect to fraction of bytes *Kids and Teens* websites have a significantly greater fraction of Flash content than others
Service complexity	
No. of servers	25–55% of websites load content from at least 10 servers *News* websites fetch content from significantly more servers than others
Non-origin contribution	60% of websites fetch content from more than 5 non-origins Non-origins make significant contributions to content—30% of objects and 35% of bytes in the median case Contribution of non-origins to page load time is low (80th percentile is 35%) due to browser optimizations Images dominant object type served from origins, but Javascript accounts for sizeable fraction of non-origin objects Advertising and analytics services account for most non-origin objects, but CDNs account for most bytes

Table 2: Summary of key takeaways from our analysis with respect to various web page complexity metrics.

consider variation across samples when studying how complexity impacts variability in page load times.

4. CHARACTERIZING COMPLEXITY

Our analysis of our measurement dataset is two-pronged. First, in this section, we analyze web pages with respect to various complexity metrics. Next, in Section 5, we analyze the impact of these metrics on performance. Note that our focus is on capturing the complexity of web pages as visible to browsers on client devices; we do not intend to capture the complexity of server-side infrastructure of websites [43].

We consider two high-level notions of web page complexity. *Content complexity* metrics capture the number and size of objects fetched to load the web page and also the different MIME types (e.g., image, javascript, CSS, text) across which these objects are spread. Now, loading `www.foo.com` may require fetching content not only from other internal servers such as `images.foo.com` and `news.foo.com`, but also involve third-party services such as CDNs (e.g., Akamai), analytics providers (e.g., Google analytics), and social network plugins (e.g., Facebook). *Service complexity* metrics capture the number and contributions of the various servers and administrative origins involved in loading a web page.

We begin with the content-level metrics before moving on to service-level metrics. In each case, we present a breakdown of the metrics across different popularity rank ranges (e.g., top 1–1000 vs. 10000–20000) and across different categories of websites (e.g., *Shopping* vs. *News*). Here, we only show results for one of the vantage points as the results are (expectedly) similar across vantage points. Table 2 summarizes our key findings for the various complexity metrics.

4.1 Content complexity

Number of objects: We begin by looking, in Figure 2, at the total number of object requests required, i.e., number of HTTP GETs issued, to load a web page. Across all the rank ranges in Figure 2(a), loading the base web page requires more than 40 objects to be fetched in the median case. We also see that a non-trivial fraction (20%) of websites request more than 100–125 objects on their landing web page, across the rank ranges. While the top 1–400 sites load more objects, the distributions for the different rank ranges are qualitatively and quantitatively similar; even the lower rank websites have a large number of requests.

Next, we divide the sites by their Alexa categories. For clarity, we only focus on the top-two-level categories from Alexa. To ensure that our results are statistically meaningful, we consider only

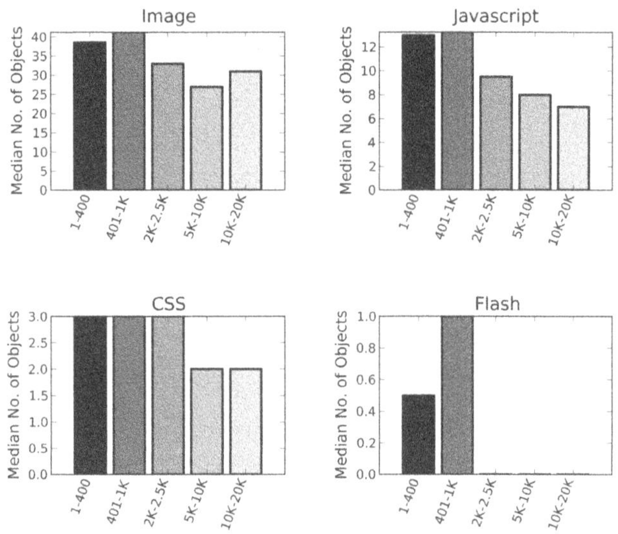

Figure 3: Median number of requests for objects of different MIME-types across different rank ranges.

the categories that have at least 50 websites in our dataset. The breakdown across the categories in Figure 2(b) shows a pronounced difference between categories; the median number of objects requested on *News* sites is nearly 3× the median for *Business* sites. We suspect that this is an artifact of *News* sites tending to cram in more content on their landing pages compared to other sites to give readers quick snippets of information across different news topics.

Types of objects: Having considered the total number of object requests, we next consider their breakdown by content MIME types. For brevity, Figure 3 shows only the median number of requests for the four most popular content types across websites of different rank ranges. The first order observation again is that the different rank ranges are qualitatively similar in their distribution, with higher ranked websites having only slightly more objects of each type.

However, we find several interesting patterns in the prevalence of different types of content. While it should not come as a surprise that many websites use these different content types, the magnitude of these fractions is surprising. For example, we see that, across all rank ranges, more than 50% of sites fetch at least 6 Javascript ob-

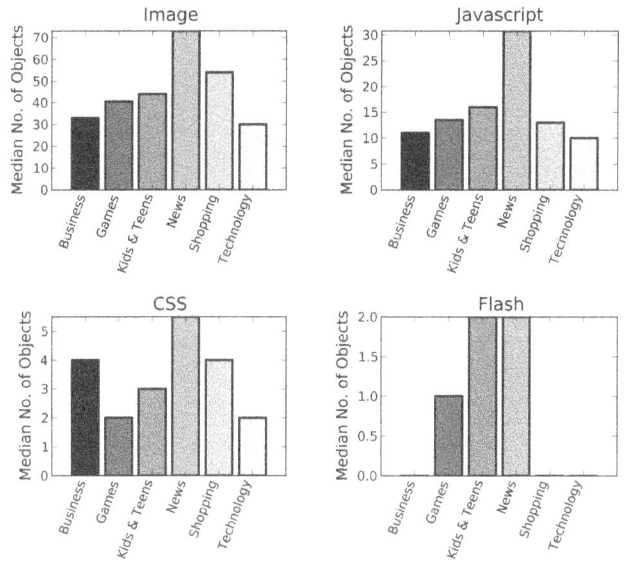

Figure 4: Median number of requests for objects of different MIME-types for different categories.

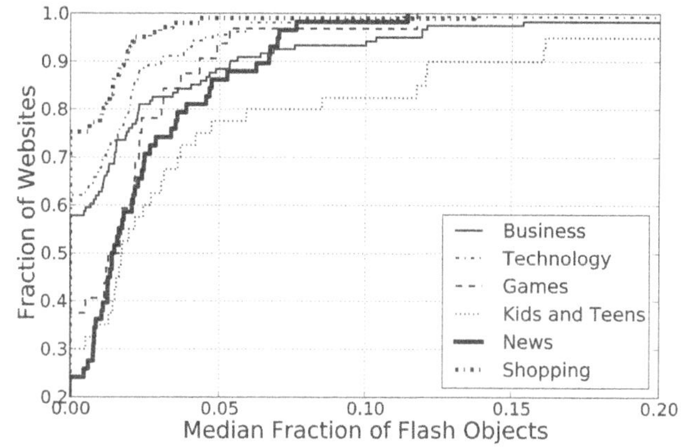

Figure 5: Fraction of objects accounted for by Flash objects, normalized per category.

jects. Similarly, more than 50% of the sites have at least 2 CSS objects. The median value for Flash is small; many websites keep their landing pages simple and avoid rich Flash content. These results are roughly consistent with recent independent measurements [31].

Figure 4 shows the corresponding breakdown for the number of objects requested of various content types across different categories of websites. Again, we see the *News* category being dominant across different content types. As previously seen in Figure 2(b), *News* sites load a larger number of objects overall compared to other site categories. Hence, a natural follow-up question is whether *News* sites issue requests for a proportionately higher number of objects across all content types. Therefore, for each website, we normalize the number of objects of each content type by the total number of objects for that site. The distribution of the median values of the normalized fraction of objects of various content types (not shown) presents a slightly different picture than that seen with absolute counts. Most categories have a very similar normalized contribution from all content types in terms of the median value. The only significant difference we observe is in the case of Flash objects. Figure 5 shows that *Kids and Teens* sites have a significantly greater fraction of Flash objects than sites in other categories.

Bytes downloaded: The above results show the number of objects requested across different content types, but do not tell us the contribution of these content types to the total number of bytes downloaded. Again, for brevity, we summarize the full distribution with the median values for different website categories in Figure 6. Surprisingly, we find that Javascript objects contribute a sizeable fraction of the total number of bytes downloaded (the median fraction of bytes is over 25% across all categories). Less surprising is that images contribute a similar fraction as well. For websites in the *Kids and Teens* category, like in the case of number of objects, the contribution of Flash is significantly greater than in other categories. As in the case of the number of objects, we see no significant difference across different rank ranges.

4.2 Service complexity

Anecdotal evidence suggests that the seemingly simple task of loading a webpage today requires the client-side browser to connect to multiple servers distributed across several administrative domains. However, there is no systematic understanding of how many different services are involved and what they contribute to the overall task. To this end, we introduce several *service complexity* metrics.

Number of distinct servers: Figure 7 shows the distribution across websites of the number of distinct webservers that a client contacts to render the base web page of each website. We identify a server by its fully qualified domain name, e.g., `bar.foo.com`. Across all five rank ranges, close to 25–55% of the websites require a client to contact at least 10 distinct servers. Thus, even loading simple content like the base page of websites requires a client to open multiple HTTP/TCP connections to many distinct servers. Also, Figure 7(b) mirrors the earlier result from Figure 2(b); *News* sites have the most number of distinct servers as well.

Number of non-origin services: Not all the servers contacted in loading a web page may be under the web page provider's control. For example, a typical website today uses content distribution networks (e.g., Akamai, Limelight) to distribute static content, analytics services (e.g., google-analytics) to track user activity, and advertisement services (e.g., doubleclick) to monetize visits.

Identifying non-origins, however, is slightly tricky. The subtle issue at hand is that some providers use multiple origins to serve content. For example, `yahoo.com` also owns `yimg.com` and uses both domains to serve content. Even though their top-level domains are different, we do not want to count `yimg.com` as a non-origin for `yahoo.com` because they are owned by the same entity. To this end, we use the following heuristic. We start by using the two-level domain identifier to identify an origin; e.g., `x.foo.com` and `y.foo.com` are clustered to the same logical origin `foo.com`. Next, we consider all two-level domains involved in loading the base page of `www.foo.com`, and identify all potential non-origin domains (i.e., two-level domain not equal to `foo.com`). We then do an additional check and mark domains as belonging to different origins only if the authoritative name servers of the two domains do not match [33]. Because `yimg.com` and `yahoo.com` share the same authoritative name servers, we avoid classifying `yimg.com` as having a different origin from `yahoo.com`.

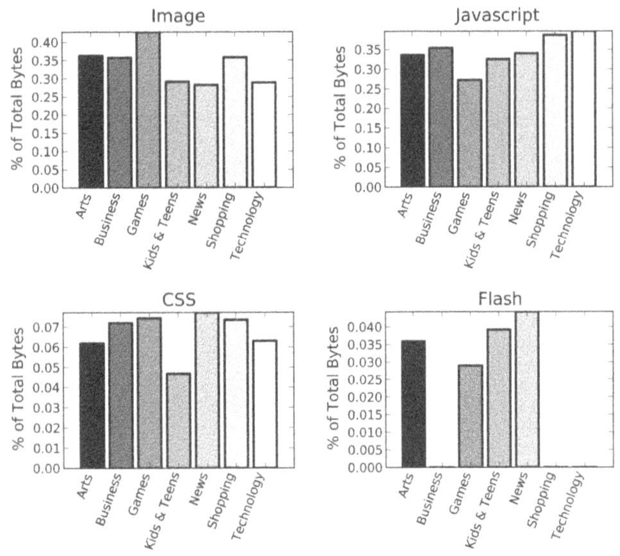

Figure 6: Median normalized contribution of different MIME types to total bytes downloaded.

Figure 8 shows that across the different rank ranges and categories, clients need to contact servers in at least 10 different origins for 20–40% of websites. The presence of non-origin content is even more pronounced on *News* sites; more than 40% of *News* sites serve content from over 20 non-origin providers. On further inspection, we find that because the landing pages of *News* sites have to provide content that spans multiple user interests (e.g., sports, weather) they provide links to non-origin affiliates that serve such content as well.

Contribution of non-origin services: The previous result simply counts the number of distinct domains contacted. Next, we quantify the *contribution* of the non-origin domains along three dimensions: fraction of objects, fraction of bytes, and fractional contribution to total page load time.

Figure 9 shows that, in the median case, over 30% of the total number of objects and over 35% of the total number of bytes downloaded are from non-origin services. At the same time, we see that the distribution is pretty heavy-tailed; for 20% of websites, non-origin services account for roughly 80% of the objects and total bytes.

The total number of objects or bytes may, however, not directly translate into download time because modern browsers can parallelize requests to multiple servers. Now, parallelization also makes it inherently difficult to exactly determine the time contribution of non-origins. In light of this, we use three alternative ways to measure the non-origin contribution to total page load time: (1) the "wall-clock" time where the browser is retrieving content from at least one non-origin (labeled "Time: At Least 1 Non-Origin"), (2) the ratio of the sum of all time spent in downloading non-origin content to the total time spent downloading all content (labeled "Time: Total Cycle Contribution"), and (3) emulating the act of loading the page by disabling all non-origin content using custom Adblock filters (labeled "Time: Block Non-Origin"). We see in Figure 9 that in the median case, content from non-origins contributes to only 15% of the page load time in terms of the *At Least 1 Non-Origin* and around 25% for the *Total Cycle Contribution*. These results suggest that though non-origin services play a significant part of the web ecosystem in terms of the fraction of content they contribute, browser optimizations (e.g., pipelining and parallelizing requests to distinct servers) lower their impact on page load times.

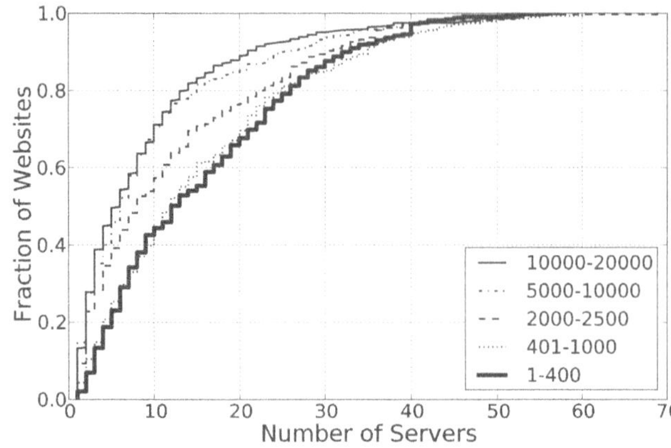

(a) By rank

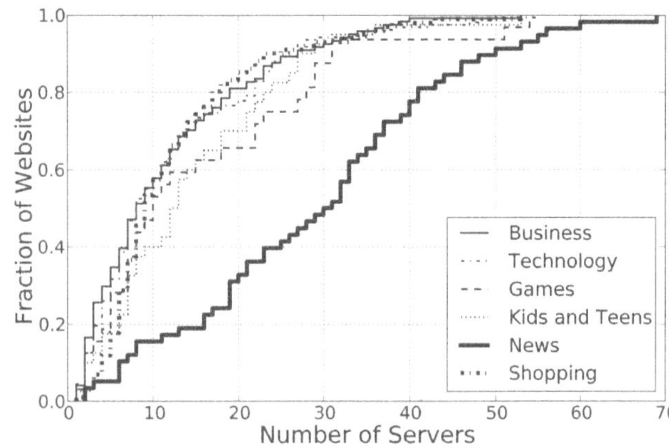

(b) By category

Figure 7: Number of distinct servers contacted to load the base webpage for websites across different rank ranges and categories.

4.3 What do non-origins offer?

A natural question is what types of content and services do non-origins provide. Beyond a basic curiosity of what non-origin content includes, this also has important performance implications. For example, if most non-origin objects constitute content essential for the user experience, then it might be difficult for website providers to directly optimize their delivery or client-side blocking of non-origin content would adversely affect user experience. But, if most non-origin objects are from services for displaying ads or tracking users, they could potentially be consolidated or optimized. Therefore, in this section, we do a more in-depth analysis of the MIME-types of objects served by non-origins, how they differ from objects served from origins, and also identify the class of services that these non-origins provide.

Content type breakdown: As a first step, we want to understand what *types of content* are served by non-origins across different websites. Figure 10 shows the breakdown of the different content types served by non-origins, both in terms of the number of objects and their size in bytes. This breakdown is shown for the median

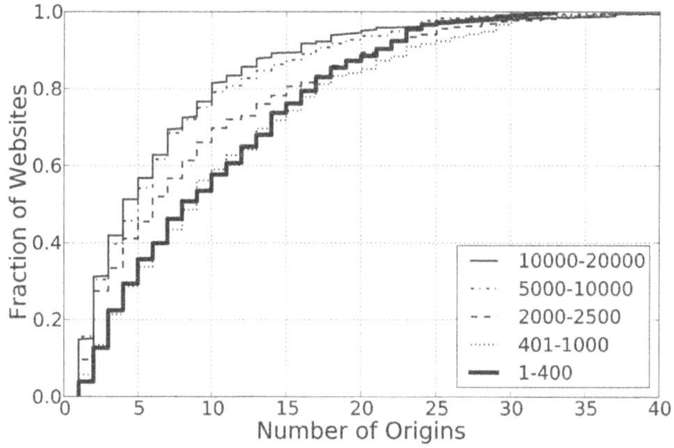

(a) By rank

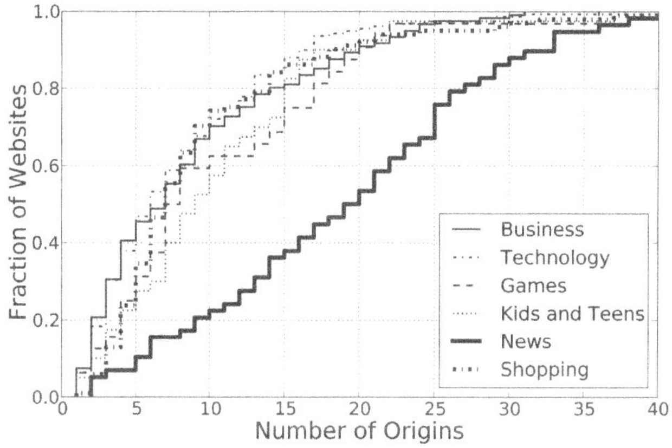

(b) By category

Figure 8: Number of distinct origins needed to load the base web page for websites across different rank ranges and categories.

website, i.e., the website that loads the median number of objects (or median number of bytes) for each content type. Interestingly, we find that while the vast fraction of the number of objects served by non-origins are images, the relative fraction in terms of number of bytes served is much lower. This is at odds with the normal expectation that the contribution of images to bytes fetched will be larger than their contribution to the number of objects, since images are typically larger than Javascript and CSS objects. Investigating this further, we find that this discrepancy is an artifact of the use of small *gifs* fetched from non-origins for analytics services [14]. We illustrate this point in Figure 11, which shows the distribution of the number of objects and object size for each MIME-type. We see that though images are the most common type of content, the median size of an image is less than 2 KB—more than an order of magnitude smaller than the median size of a Flash object.

Origin vs. non-origin content: Next, we proceed to analyze if the content served by non-origins differs significantly from that served by the origin sites themselves. Figure 12 shows the contribution of different MIME-types to the number of objects fetched from origins and non-origins on the median website. The most noticeable difference is that non-origins serve a much higher fraction of Javascript objects while origins serve a greater fraction of images than non-origins.

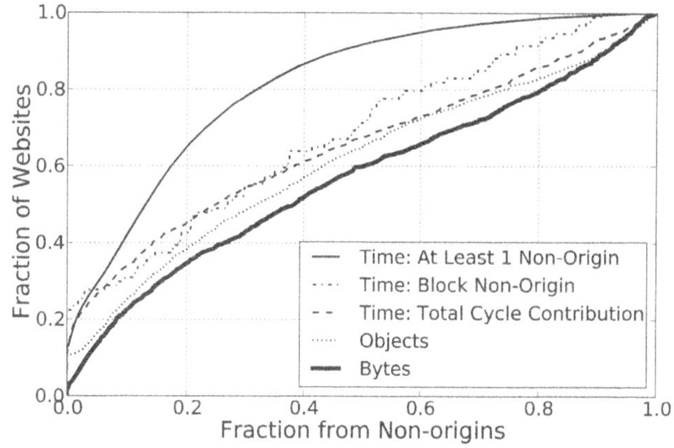

Figure 9: Contribution of non-origin services with respect to number of objects, number of bytes, and download time.

Classifying non-origins: Beyond types of content, we analyze the types of services offered by non-origins. For this study, we rank non-origin domains based on the number of websites in which they occur. Then, for the 200 most popular non-origins, we identify the services they offer by combining three sources of information. First, we lookup each non-origin domain in Alexa's categorization of web domains. Second, we use information from CrunchBase[4] to identify the type of company that runs the non-origin service. Last, we manually classify the remaining non-origins based on information gleaned from their website or keyword-based heuristics on the objects being fetched from them.

Table 3 presents a breakdown of the types of services these top 200 non-origins offer and the number of origins in which each category appears. Here, we only consider the 669 origins, in which all the non-origin objects belong to one of these top 200 non-origins. Unsurprisingly, the top two categories of non-origin services are *Analytics* (e.g., google-analytics and quantserve) and *Advertising* (e.g., doubleclick and googleadservices). However, even beyond these two service types, we see that each of the non-origin service types are seen on a significant fraction of the 669 origins.

To give an example of the types of non-origin services we encounter, Table 4 shows the top 10 non-origins with the type of service they provide and the fraction of sites on which they appear. While many of these are very recognizable ad and analytics providers, we were surprised by some of the less recognized names appearing in a significant fraction of websites. For example, among the top 20, we found other lesser known services like bluekai.com, invitemedia.com, and imrworldwide.com, that each appeared in more than 5% of the websites (not shown).

Finally, we examine the contribution of these non-origin service types on a typical web page. For this analysis, we only consider the 669 websites where all non-origins on their base web page belong to the top 200 non-origins. On each of these 669 websites, we compute the fraction of the number of objects and bytes fetched from non-origins that are attributable to each service type. Figure 10(b) plots these fractions for the median website. In keeping with the relative popularity of non-origin services of different types in the top 200 non-origins, Analytics and Advertising account for most non-origin objects. However, content fetched from CDNs dominate with respect to the number of bytes.

[4] `http://www.crunchbase.com`

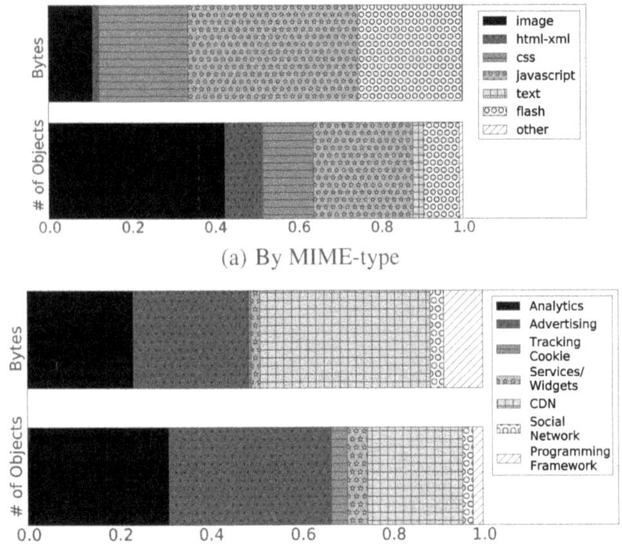

(a) By MIME-type

(b) By service type

Figure 10: Normalized contribution of objects from non-origin services in the median case.

Type of service	Number	Found in no. of origins
Analytics	65	593
Advertising	64	233
Tracking Cookies	23	137
Services/Widgets	21	142
CDN	18	218
Social Networking	5	98
Programming API	4	96
Total	**200**	**669**

Table 3: Breakdown of the types of services provided by top 200 non-origins.

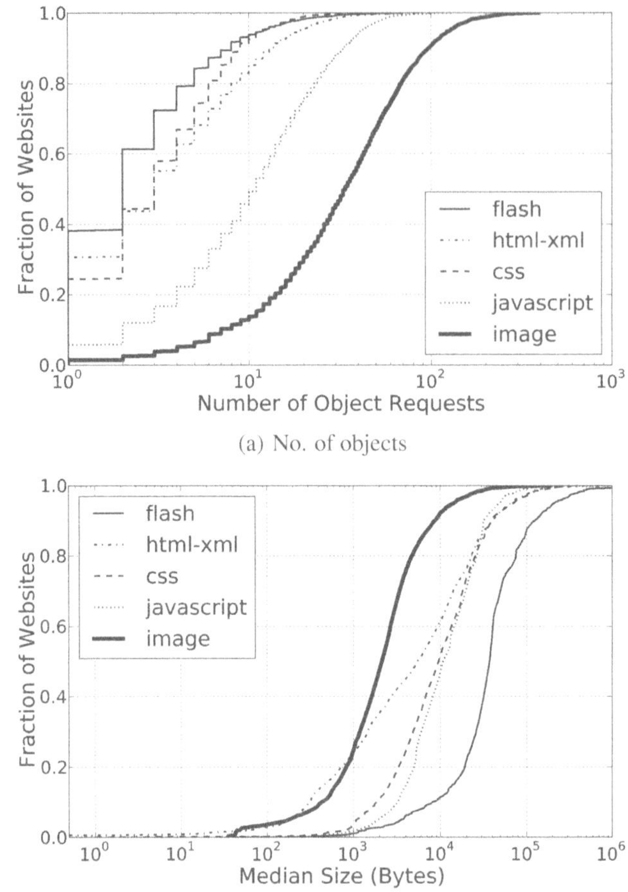

(a) No. of objects

(b) Object size

Figure 11: Distributions across content types of the number of objects and median object size from non-origins.

4.4 Summary of main observations

In summary, our main observations in this section are as follows:

- A website's rank is not a significant indicator of the content complexity, at least within the top 20K websites.
- However, a website's category does matter; *News* sites load significantly more content than others from a lot more servers and origins, while *Kids and Teens* sites have significantly more Flash content than others.
- Most websites load a surprisingly large number of CSS and Javascript objects.
- Content from non-origins represents a significant fraction of objects and bytes on most web pages, but their impact on download time is relatively low.

5. IMPACT ON CLIENT PERFORMANCE

In the previous section, we measured a range of content-complexity and service-complexity metrics. In this section, we tackle the natural follow-up question: which of these metrics have the most impact on *performance*.

We consider two performance measures to characterize page load times. RenderStart measures the time at which the browser has completed parsing the HTML and has fetched sufficient content to begin rendering the page, while RenderEnd measures the total time to fetch and render all content on the web page. For each measure, we are interested in both the *typical* load time for each website and the *variability* in load time across different samples.

To put our analysis in perspective, Figure 13 shows the distribution of the median and 90th percentile of the RenderEnd values for each site across several measurements from one of our vantage points. Rather surprisingly, more than 50% of sites have a median RenderEnd higher than 2 seconds. (We also validated these seemingly high page load times from independent measurements from the HTTP Archive project [3].) User studies and industry surveys show that users are likely to be frustrated beyond this two second threshold [28]. Thus, it is critical to systematically understand what are the key factors affecting page load times.

We use correlation and regression based analysis to identify the key complexity metrics that are the best indicators of page load times and the variability in them. In this analysis, we use a range of complexity metrics from the previous section—the {absolute value or fraction} of {objects, bytes, servers, origins, non-origins} characterized by {content MIME-type, service type}, and whether loaded from {origin, non-origin, either}. We also use other aggre-

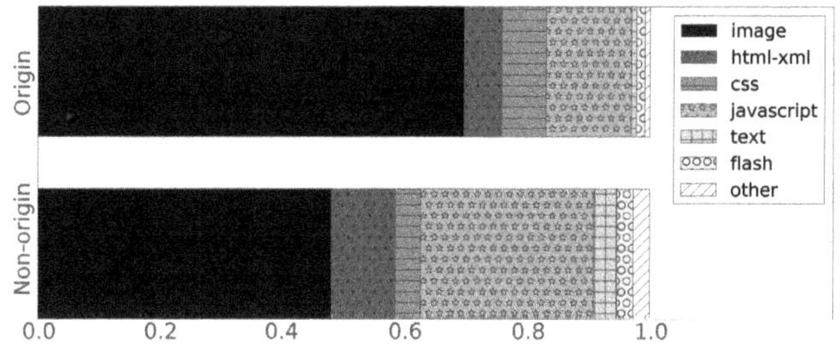

Figure 12: Comparison of types of content served from origin and non-origin servers on the median website.

Rank	Name	Fraction of sites	Type
1	google-analytics.com	0.58	Analytics
2	doubleclick.net	0.45	Ads
3	quantserve.com	0.30	Analytics
4	scorecardresearch.com	0.27	Analytics
5	2mdn.net	0.24	Ads
6	googleadservices.com	0.18	Ads
7	facebook.com	0.17	Social net
8	yieldmanager.com	0.16	Ads
9	atdmt.com	0.14	Analytics
10	googleapis.com	0.12	Prog. API

Table 4: Classification of the services provided by the top-10 non-origin service providers.

gate metrics such as the size of the maximum object fetched. For brevity, we only present results for metrics that turned out to be the most dominant indicators of either absolute load times or their variability.

5.1 Load times

Correlation: First, we analyze the correlation between RenderEnd (RenderStart) and various complexity metrics. For this analysis, we compute for each website the median values of RenderEnd (RenderStart) across multiple measurements of that website and the median value of various complexity metrics. Then, across all websites in our dataset, we compute the Pearson and Spearman rank correlation coefficients between the two load time measures and various complexity metrics. Since the results are similar for RenderStart and RenderEnd, we present only the results for RenderEnd. Also, the results are similar for both Pearson and Spearman correlations; hence, for brevity, we only show the Spearman values. To ensure that the correlations we observe are not artifacts of a particular measurement site, we consider each of the 4 vantage points separately. Figure 14 shows the Spearman correlation coefficients with respect to various complexity metrics in decreasing order of the median value across the different measurement sites. Across all 4 measurement sites, we see that the five most correlated metrics are the total number of objects loaded, the number of these objects that are Javascripts, the total webpage size, the number of servers, and the number of origins contacted in loading the page.

Figure 15 further visually confirms the strong correlation between RenderEnd and the number of objects requested. Here, we bin websites based on the number of objects on their base web page. Then, for each bin, we construct a box-and-whiskers plot showing the median, 25th percentile, and 75th percentile plot in the "box" and the min/max values for the whiskers. Further, tying

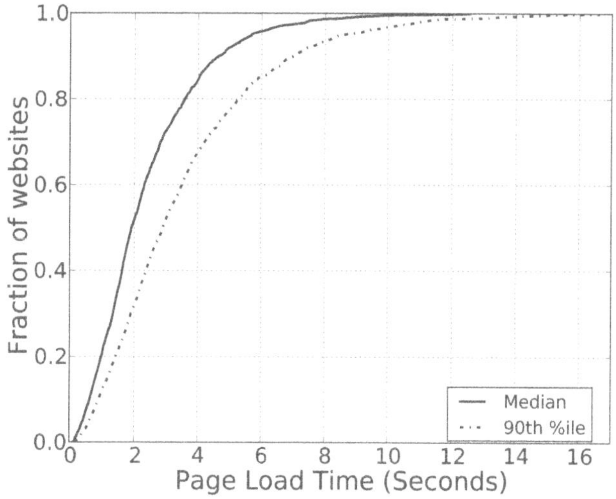

Figure 13: Distribution of RenderEnd times across all websites.

the fact that number of object requests is the most dominant indicator of load times with our observation from Section 4 that *News* sites fetch a significantly larger number of objects than other sites, Figure 16 shows that the page load times for *News* sites are indeed much higher than for other sites.

Regression: The correlation analysis tells us which metrics are good indicators of page load times. Next, we attempt to identify a minimal set of metrics to estimate load times. For this, we augment the above correlation analysis by building a linear regression model using the LASSO technique [17]. Each *feature* in this model represents one of the various complexity metrics presented in the previous section. We use LASSO instead of simple linear regression because it produces a *sparser* model; thus, models with LASSO are more robust. To further avoid overfitting, we use a $k \times 2$ cross validation technique. Here, in each run, we partition the set of websites into two halves—a training set and a testing set. For each run, we run the LASSO procedure and record the coefficients for each feature. Then, we build an aggregate model using the average values of the individual coefficients across all runs.

Figure 17 shows the normalized root mean-squared error (NRMSE),[5] as a function of the top k selected features. In this figure, we sort the features based on the magnitude of their weights in the model after the cross-validation procedure described above.[6] Then, we emulate the effects of using a model that uses only the top k features. As a point of comparison, we also considered a naive estimator that simply predicts the mean value of RenderStart and RenderEnd; its NRMSE was around 50% worse than the LASSO estimate (not shown).

We see two key results here. First, the set of top k features roughly mirrors the correlation result we saw earlier. One notable exception is that the total size is relegated down the list. We spec-

[5] If $\hat{X}$ is a vector representing estimates of page load times, and X contains the true values, then NRMSE = $\frac{\sqrt{E[(\hat{X}-X)^2]}}{\max(X)-\min(X)}$

[6] One obvious concern is whether the magnitude of the weights are meaningful if the different features and the load time are in different "scales". A pre-processing step in LASSO re-scales all features to have zero mean/unit variance and also normalizes the load metric to have zero mean. Thus, the magnitude measures the relative importance of the metric and avoids these scale-related concerns.

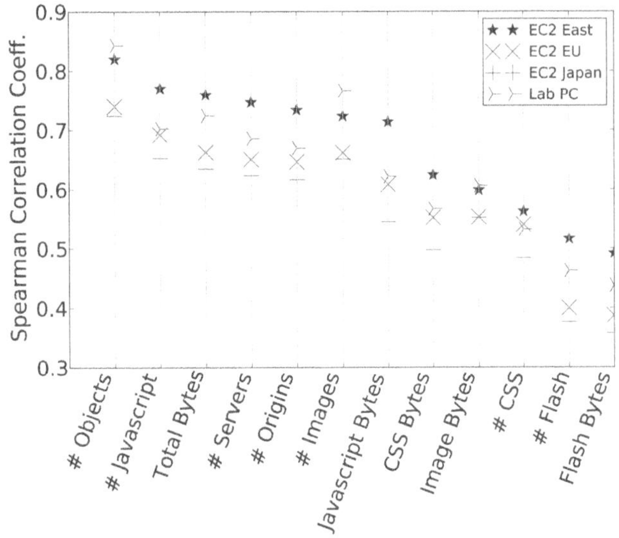

Figure 14: Correlation between RenderEnd and various complexity metrics.

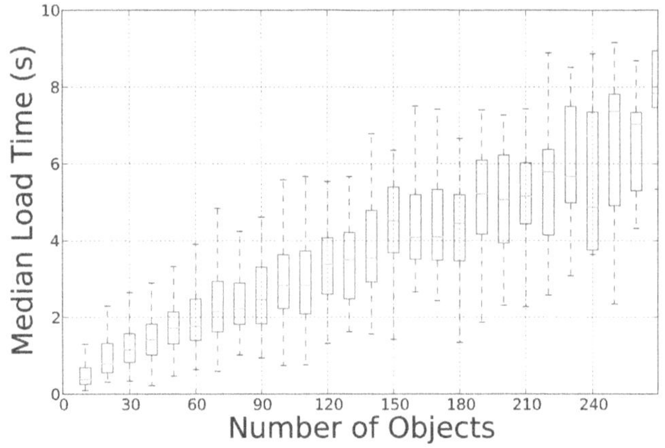

Figure 15: Box-and-whiskers plot confirming the correlation between RenderEnd and number of objects.

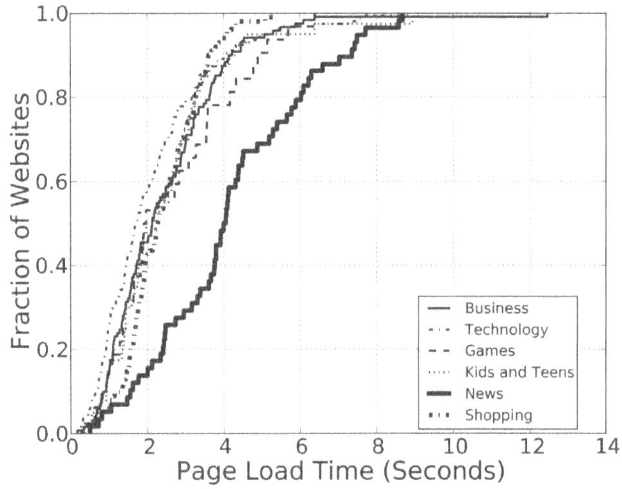

Figure 16: Page load times for websites of different categories.

ulate that because the base web pages of websites are typically not that large, page load times are dominated by the number of RTTs rather than the number of bytes transferred. Thus, having chosen the number of requests and number of scripts as the top 2 features, the marginal contribution of total size is low. Second, we find that the prediction error flattens after the first 4-5 features are selected. In other words, we see a natural diminishing returns effect of adding other features. Identifying a small, but predictive set of features is a critical result for both website designers and performance optimization tools.

Figure 18 visually confirms the goodness-of-fit. The X-axis represents the actual page load time (RenderEnd), and the Y-axis represents the load time predicted by the regression model. One interesting artifact is a *horizontal* cluster near the origin, where the model predicts the same value of RenderEnd for around 30 sites. On further investigation, we discovered that these websites have very sparse landing pages that have little to no content. Thus, the values of the top 5 metrics were zero and the prediction model outputs a constant value.

Having determined the top k complexity metrics for the entire population of websites in our study, we next analyze if there is a significant difference across website categories. We repeat the regression analysis for each category separately. Table 5 shows the top 2 metrics identified by the regression for each category. It also shows the cardinality of the set intersection between the top 5 metrics for each category and the top 5 metrics from the aggregate regression model across all websites (from Figure 17).

First, we see that the top 2 metrics are quite diverse across the different categories. For example, the number of images and requests are most critical for `News` sites, but the total size of Javascript objects and the number of servers are most critical for `Games` sites. Second, there is a significant overlap in the top 5 metrics between the per-category models and the overall model. In fact, for most categories, the metrics in the intersection are the number of objects, the number of servers, and the number of Javascript objects, which are the top 3 metrics in Figure 17. This suggests that while there is some value in customizing the prediction model to identify the critical metrics, the aggregate model is a very useful starting point in itself.

We also experimented with an enhanced regression model where we added nonlinear terms, e.g., $\log(X)$ and X^2, for each feature X. Adding these nonlinear terms does not improve the prediction error and does not change the stability of the top k feature set. We do not present these results given space limitations.

5.2 Variability in load times

So far, we studied the impact of various complexity metrics on median page load times. Next, we analyze if the same set of factors impact how load times *vary*, or if a different set of metrics are critical for predicting variability. Here, we restrict our analysis to only focus on websites where the complexity metrics such as page size and number of object requests do not change significantly across measurements. That is, the variability in RenderEnd cannot be attributed simply to a change in the content of the page across our measurements.

As a starting point, we measure variability in load times for any particular website as the difference between the 75th and 25th per-

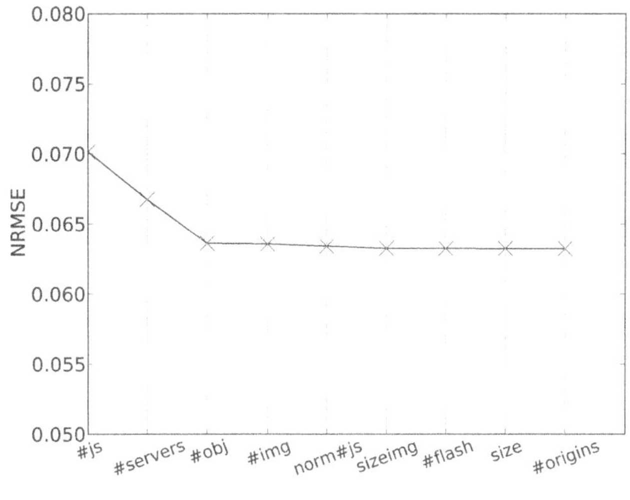

Figure 17: Normalized mean-squared error as a function of top k coefficients.

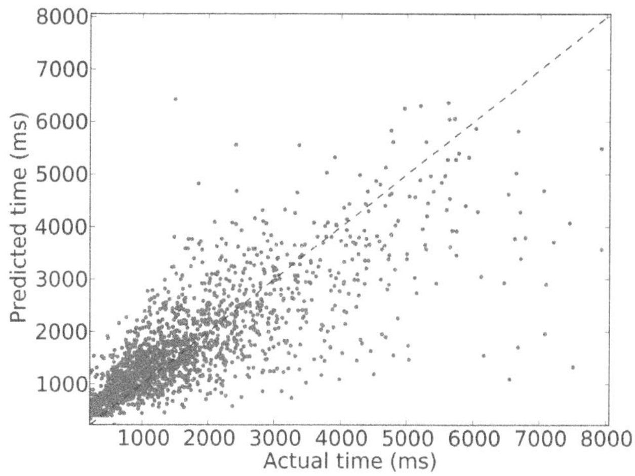

Figure 18: Scatter plot of page load times predicted by the regression model that uses the top 5 features versus the actual page load times.

Category	Top 2	Top 5 Intersection
Business	# objects, # images	3
Technology	# js, # origins	3
Games	# servers, size js	3
Kids and Teens	# js, # objects	3
News	# images, # objects	3
Shopping	size css, # js	3

Table 5: Highest-impact complexity metrics in the regression model for different website categories, and their intersection with aggregate regression model.

centile values of RenderEnd across different measurements for that website; we consider the difference between the 75th and 25th percentiles instead of between the maximum and minimum values to discount for any client-side effects. Then, we correlate the absolute and normalized (by the median) value of this variability versus the various complexity metrics. As seen in Figure 19, in comparison to the earlier correlation result, we find two differences. First, the correlations are weaker in general (e.g., the highest value is 0.65). Second, the number of servers is the most dominant factor in this case, instead of the number of objects, which was the dominant indicator of absolute load times.

5.3 Summary of main observations

The key takeaways from our analysis of load times are:

- The top five complexity metrics that determine RenderStart and RenderEnd are the total number of objects loaded, the number of these objects that are Javascripts, the total webpage size, and the number of servers and origins contacted in loading objects on the page.
- We can build a sparse model for predicting page load times with a normalized mean squared error less than 0.1.
- Variability of load times is less correlated with our complexity metrics, but number of servers is its most dominant indicator rather than the number of objects.

6. DISCUSSION

The previous sections provide a good first-order understanding of how website complexity affects the user experience. We acknowledge that there are likely to be a much wider range of factors that can affect a user's web experience: "deeper" non-landing pages, diversity in client-side platforms, use of client and provider tools for customizing websites, and other forms of personalization (e.g., services that require a login). In this section, we present a preliminary discussion of such factors.

Landing vs. non-landing pages: Our study focused on the landing pages of websites. As a preliminary study to evaluate how "deeper" non-landing pages might differ, we consider a random sample of 100 sites. For each such site, we follow other links to pages within the same domain (e.g., `www.foo.com` has a link to `www.foo.com/bar` or `x.foo.com/bar`) and compute the various complexity metrics for each such non-landing page. For each site and metric, we then look at the difference between the base site and the median across these landing pages, and normalize this difference by the value for the base site. Figure 20 shows the distribution across sites of these normalized differences for five key metrics: number of requests, number of servers, fraction of non-origin objects, page size, and download time. We see that other than from the perspective of the fraction of non-origin objects metric, websites on which non-landing pages are less complex than the base site far outweigh the sites on which the opposite is true. We do, however, see a long negative tail with the non-landing pages of some sites being up to $2\times$ more complex than the base site.

Choice of browser: The choice of browser does not affect our complexity analysis in Section 4. However, browsers may vary in the specific strategies in how they parallelize requests, optimize scripts and so on; this could affect the load time analysis in Section 5. One additional concern when comparing load time results across browsers is that the semantics of `onLoad` might vary [7]. (This is not a concern for our paper because all our measurements use the same version of Firefox.) We leave for future work the task of understanding these effects.

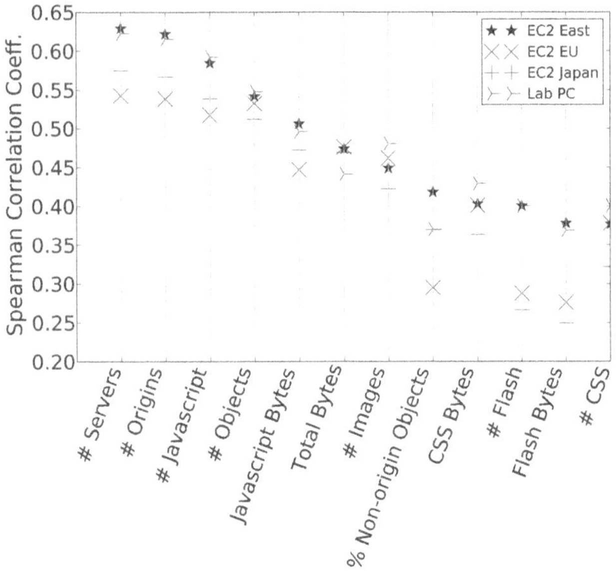

Figure 19: Correlation coefficients between the different metrics and the variability in RenderEnd.

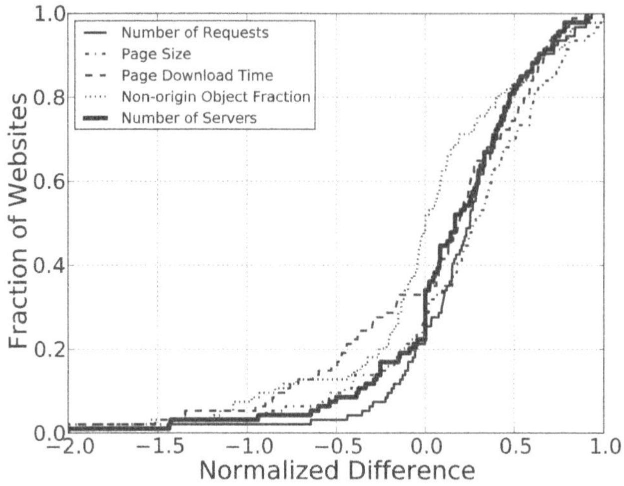

Figure 20: Preliminary result showing that non-landing pages are less complex than landing pages for most sites.

Personalized web services: Some services present different landing pages to users who have subscribed or logged in. For example, `facebook.com` and `igoogle.com` have content that is personalized to the specific user logged in. The key to understanding these effects is to emulate user profiles that are representative of a broad spectrum of browsing habits (e.g., casual vs. expert users). While this is relevant to our broader theme, it is outside the scope of this paper.

Interaction with client-side plugins: Users today deploy a wide range of client-side browser extensions to customize their own web browsing experience. For example, two popular Firefox extensions block advertisements (`Adblock`) and scripts (`NoScript`). We conducted a preliminary study spanning 120 randomly chosen websites from our overall list on how these extensions impact the complexity metrics. We avoid page load time here because these extensions alter the user experience (i.e., it is not showing the same content) and it is unfair to compare the time in this case.

Figure 21 compares two separate browser instances—one with the extension enabled, and the other with the browser instance from our previous measurements. Here, we install each extension with its default configuration. We only show the complexity metrics that were dominant indicators of page load time and variability in load time: number of objects and number of servers. The median number of objects requested reduces from 60 on the vanilla browser to 45 with Adblock and 35 with NoScript. The reduction in the number of servers is even more marked—the median value drops from 8 to 4 with Adblock and to 3 with NoScript. `NoScript`'s effect is more pronounced than that of `Adblock` because disabling scripts can in turn filter out objects that would have been fetched as a consequence of the script's execution.

It is unclear though if the reduction in complexity caused by these client-side controls is entirely good, even though it likely improves page load times. We do not know how this affects the user experience that the website provider intended for the user (e.g., is some useful content being blocked?) and how these may affect the provider's business interests (e.g., ad click/conversion rates).

Customization for client platform: In parallel to the evolution of web pages, the diversity of client platforms (e.g., mobile phones, tablet computers, and even televisions) used for web access has also increased. These platforms vary in their connectivity, display attributes, and user interface. Consequently, providers are interested in customizing the web experience for these platforms.

We considered 120 randomly chosen websites that offer customized web pages for mobile phones. We visited these sites once with the default browser setting and once with the browser instrumented to emulate an iPhone (by spoofing the UserAgent string). Figure 22 shows that the phone-specific customization dramatically reduces the number of objects fetched and the number of servers contacted. Again, we focus only on complexity metrics and not the page load time because it does not represent a reasonable comparison (e.g., time on actual mobile phones would be different than on a spoofing browser). However, as in the case of client-side controls, it is not clear if this customization affects the user experience compared to a desktop-based experience (e.g., was some content dropped).

Optimizations for improving performance: Many tools like PageSpeed from Google [2] suggest optimizations such as compressing images, combining requests for small images and CSS files, and "minify-ing" Javascript objects to improve website performance. Based on some sample websites, we found that *minify js* appears as a "high priority" suggestion for several websites.[7]

To analyze how this optimization would help websites in the wild, we emulate the effect of running it on each website in our dataset. Figure 23 shows the savings this optimization could provide in terms of the fraction of total bytes of Javascript and the fraction of the total size of the web page downloaded. We see that for the vast majority of websites, the potential savings is quite small. While this result is preliminary and does not explore all possible optimizations, it does hint that optimizations that are broadly perceived as high-priority may not yield high gains for all websites. Thus, we need to explore more systematic tools and new avenues to improve page load times.

[7]This is a code compacting tool that removes unnecessary white spaces, and comment lines to reduce the size of Javascript objects.

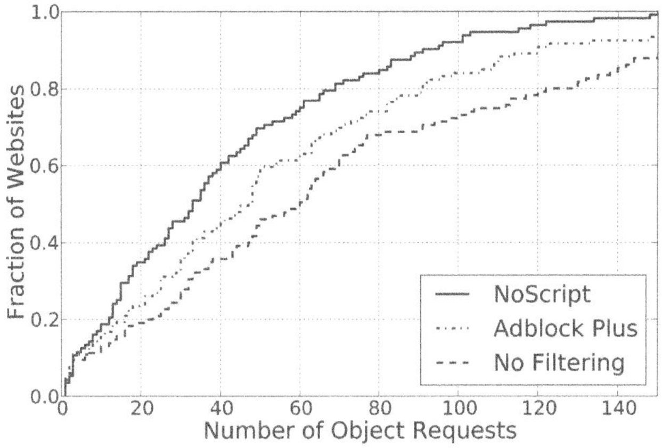

(a) No. of objects

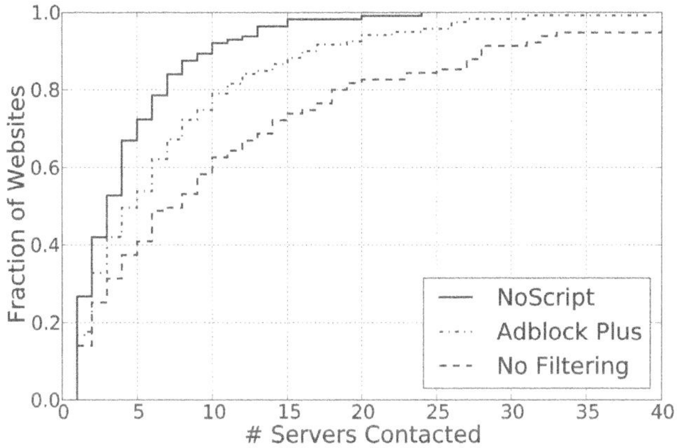

(b) Total no. of servers contacted

Figure 21: Reduction in number of objects and servers contacted with client-side filtering.

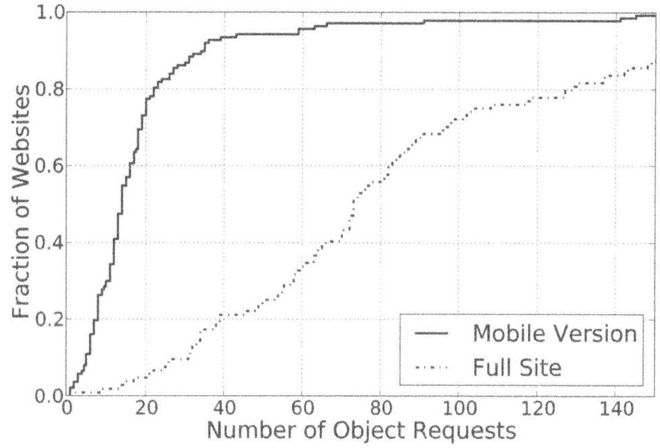

(a) No. of objects

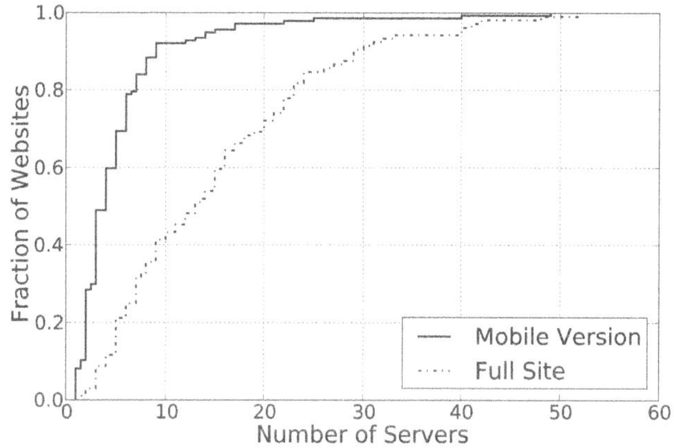

(b) No. of servers

Figure 22: Reduction in number of objects and servers with phone-specific customization.

7. CONCLUSIONS AND FUTURE WORK

The increasing complexity of web pages and its impact on performance has been anecdotally well-recognized, but there have been no rigorous studies of the same. In this paper, we presented a first attempt at characterizing web page complexity and quantifying its implications. We characterized the complexity of web pages both based on the content they include and the services they offer. We find that a website's popularity is a poor indicator of its complexity, whereas its category does matter. For example, *News* sites load significantly more objects from many more servers and origins than other categories. Also, we found that though a significant fraction of objects and bytes are fetched from non-origins on most websites, the contribution of non-origins to page load time is minimal in comparison. Our correlation- and regression-based analysis showed that number of objects and number of servers are the dominant indicators of page load time and variability in page load times, respectively.

Our preliminary results also show that reducing this complexity and improving client performance is not straightforward. Though client-side filtering of particular content types may reduce page load times, it can adversely impact user experience and compromise revenue for web providers. On the other hand, website providers need to understand the impact that non-origin content on their web pages has on their users in order to customize for different client platforms.

As future work, we are continuing our efforts in several directions—deeper analyses of non-landing pages, studying the dependency between the various objects on a page, finding better indicators of performance and variability by focusing on websites within certain rank ranges and certain categories, and designing strategies to systematically balance the tradeoff between performance, user experience, and the provider's business interests.

8. REFERENCES

[1] Firebug. `http://getfirebug.com/`.

[2] Google Page Speed. `http://code.google.com/speed/page-speed/`.

[3] HTTP archive beta. `http://httparchive.org/`.

[4] HTTP archive specification. `http://groups.google.com/group/http-archive-specification/web/har-1-1-s%pec?hl=en`.

[5] Keynote systems. `http://www.keynote.com`.

[6] Let's make the web faster. `http://code.google.com/speed/articles/web-metrics.html`.

[7] Measuring the mobile web is hard. `http://matt-welsh.blogspot.com/2011/08/measuring-mobile-web-is-hard.htm%l`.

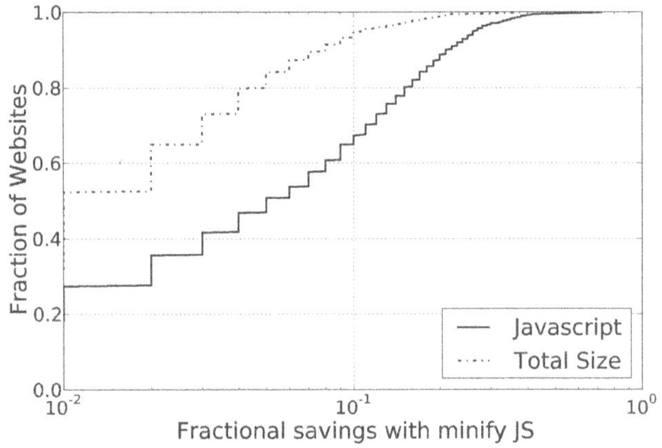

Figure 23: Bytes saved using *minify js*, one optimization from Google's Page Speed for reducing page load times.

[8] Mobify. http://mobify.me.

[9] The need for speed. http://www.technologyreview.com/files/54902/GoogleSpeed_charts.pdf.

[10] Opera Mini & Opera Mobile browsers. http://www.opera.com/mobile/.

[11] SPDY: An experimental protocol for a faster web. http://www.chromium.org/spdy/spdy-whitepaper.

[12] Spec web benchmarks. http://www.spec.org/web2005/.

[13] Strangeloop: Speed up your website. http://www.strangeloopnetworks.com.

[14] Web bug. http://en.wikipedia.org/wiki/Web_bug.

[15] When seconds count. http://www.gomez.com/wp-content/downloads/GomezWebSpeedSurvey.pdf.

[16] J. M. Kleinberg, S. R. Kumar, P. Raghavan, S. Rajagopalan, and A. Tomkins. The web as a graph: Measurements, models and methods. In *Proc. COCOON*, 1999.

[17] R. Tibshirani. Regression shrinkage and selection via the lasso. *Journal of Royal Statistical Society of Britain*, 1996.

[18] A. Bouch, A. Kuchinsky, and N. Bhatti. Quality is in the Eye of the Beholder: Meeting Users' Requirements for Internet Quality of Service. In *Proc. CHI*, 2000.

[19] A. Broder et al. Graph structure in the web. *Computer Networks*, 33(1), June 2000.

[20] B. Ager, W. MÃijhlbauer, G. Smaragdakis, and S. Uhlig. Web content cartography. In *Proc. IMC*, 2011.

[21] H. Balakrishnan, V. N. Padmanabhan, S. Seshan, M. Stemm, and R. H. Katz. TCP behavior of a busy Internet server: Analysis and improvements. In *Proc. IEEE Infocom*, 1998.

[22] T. Benson, A. Akella, and D. Maltz. Unraveling the Complexity of Network Management. In *Proc. NSDI*, 2009.

[23] G. Candea. Toward Quantifying System Manageability. In *Proc. HotDep*, 2008.

[24] J. Cao, W. S. Cleveland, Y. Gao, K. Jeffay, F. D. Smith, and M. C. Weigle. Stochastic Models for Generating Synthetic HTTP Source Traffic. In *Proc. INFOCOM*, 2004.

[25] B.-G. Chun, S. Ratnasamy, and E. Kohler. NetComplex: A Complexity Metric for Networked System Designs. In *Proc. NSDI*, 2008.

[26] D. Galletta, R. Henry, S. McCoy, and P. Polak. Web Site Delays: How Tolerant are Users? *Journal of the Association for Information Systems*, 2004.

[27] D. Mosberger and T. Jin. httperf: A Tool for Measuring Web Server Performance. *SIGMETRICS Performance Evaluation Review*, 26(3), 1998.

[28] F. Nah. A study on tolerable waiting time: How long are Web users willing to wait? *Behaviour & Information Technology*, 23(3), May 2004.

[29] D. Fetterly, M. Manasse, M. Najork, and J. Wiener. A large-scale study of the evolution of web pages. In *Proc. WWW*, 2003.

[30] P. Gill, M. Arlitt, N. Carlsson, A. Mahanti, and C. Williamson. Characterizing Organizational Use of Web-based Services: Methodology, Challenges, Observations, and Insights. *ACM TWEB*, 2011.

[31] S. Ihm and V. S. Pai. Towards understanding modern web traffic. In *Proc. IMC*, 2011.

[32] E. Kiciman and B. Livshits. AjaxScope: A Platform for Remotely Monitoring the Client-Side Behavior of Web 2.0 Applications. In *Proc. SOSP*, 2007.

[33] B. Krishnamurthy and C. E. Willis. Privacy diffusion on the web: A longitudinal perspective. In *Proc. WWW*, 2009.

[34] B. Krishnamurthy, C. E. Willis, and Y. Zhang. On the use and performance of content distribution networks. In *Proc. IMW*, 2001.

[35] M. Lee, R. R. Kompella, and S. Singh. Active measurement system for high-fidelity characterization of modern cloud applications. In *Proc. USENIX Conference on Web Applications*, 2010.

[36] R. Levering and M. Cutler. The portrait of a common HTML web page. In *Proc. ACM Symposium on Document Engineering*, 2006.

[37] L. Meyerovich and R. Bodik. Fast and parallel web page layout. In *Proc. WWW*, 2010.

[38] J. C. Mogul. The case for persistent-connection HTTP. In *Proc. SIGCOMM*, 1995.

[39] A. Nazir, S. Raza, D. Gupta, C.-N. Chuah, and B. Krishnamurthy. Network level footprints of Facebook applications. In *Proc. IMC*, 2009.

[40] S. Gribble et al. The Ninja architecture for robust Internet-scale systems and services. *Computer Networks*, 35(4), Mar. 2001.

[41] F. Schneider, S. Agarwal, T. Alpcan, and A. Feldmann. The new Web: Characterizing AJAX traffic. In *Proc. PAM*, 2008.

[42] F. Schneider, A. Feldmann, B. Krishnamurthy, and W. Willinger. Understanding online social network usage from a network perspective. In *Proc. IMC*, 2009.

[43] Z. Li et al. WebProphet: Automating performance prediction for web services. In *Proc. NSDI*, 2010.

[44] Y. Zhang, H. Zhu, and S. Greenwood. Website complexity metrics for measuring navigability. In *International Conference on Quality Software*, 2004.

Summary Review Documentation for

"Understanding Website Complexity: Measurements, Metrics, and Implications"

Authors: M. Butkiewicz, H. Madhyastha, V. Sekar

Reviewer #1

Strengths: The analysis of the website complexity is pretty complete and the observations are interesting.

Weaknesses: The measurements are limited to 4 vantage points, which may not uncover the whole diversity in performance for site latency, especially given CDN deployment and widespread use.

Comments to Authors: Overall, I think this is a nice study of website complexity. Good job.

Are there 3 or 4 vantage points? The abstract says 3, while the rest of the paper 4.

The authors mention that Web traffic is dominant, in what sense? Please provide references.

How important is the set of websites that were selected for the study? Did the authors check how they were hosted (CDNs)?

Do the 4 vantage points provide enough geographic diversity to the study? If sites are delivered by CDNs this is likely to be a problem.

In Section 4.3, the authors claim that if non-origin objects constitute content essential for the user experience, these cannot be optimized by CDNs? Why is that? It is not clear in what sense they cannot be optimized.

How does the CDF corresponding to Figure 16 look like? Take x-axis as it is but y-axis showing the mass of traffic for webpages with a given loadtime. Where are most websites?

Figure 17 shows the correlation, not what is important or not to explain variability of RenderEnd? What does a PCA analysis say about what matters most to explain variations?

Reviewer #2

Strengths: This is a classic measurement study. It does have limitations, but the details are mostly well explained. The data is being made public. They show a clear relationship between their metrics and performance, using statistically valid techniques.

Weaknesses: The one weakness here is that I was hoping to see some deeper insight into "complexity". In this end, this is just a series of metrics and performance associations. I would have liked to understand complexity either at the computational level, or perhaps the information theoretic level. Either would have given us a deeper insight into the problem. This is really just an issue with the title of the paper, and the results do seem useful.

Comments to Authors: One of the problems with a paper like this is that there are so many details to nail down. For instance in Section 3,
- which version exactly of Firefox is used?
- over exactly what dates was the data collected?
- why choose around 2100 sites (not a round number) and exactly how many were chosen?

I guess some of these details appear in the data, but the paper should be precise as well.

Reviewer #3

Strengths: The paper provides a very nice analysis of contributing factors for download times of different websites. The analysis is detailed and results are very interesting.

Weaknesses: Nothing significant.

Comments to Authors: I thought this was a wonderful paper that had a very detailed analysis of website download performance. I liked the way the authors systematically built the performance model based on more then 20K sites.

It is interesting to see that total bytes corresponding to a website is less of a factor than number of javascript objects and number of servers contacted.

It was also interesting that different site types (News vs Kids sites) have somewhat different characteristics, and one could intuitively explain it.

I also thought that some of the topics covered in the discussion section (AdBlocks, impact of Minify) to be very interesting. Congratulations on a nice and thorough evaluation!

In counting the number of non-origin servers, I could not tell if the proposed method counts yahoo.com and yimg.com as separate domains/servers.

I am not sure if counting the non-origin server contribution in download time is accurate, since the time is overlapped with other downloads.

Should you not be looking at download times that are exclusive to download from non-origin servers?

Reviewer #4

Strengths: - A first attempt at quantifying the complexity of web site, and the paper includes several interesting findings.
- Well-written and presented paper.

Weaknesses: The analysis is somewhat superficial in that it studies the obvious metrics and no deep insights about Web complexity are uncovered.

Comments to Authors: I like this paper and what you are studying. As you note, I indeed find it surprising that a study like this has not been done before. I only have minor comments below.

The landing pages of many sites these days are personalized, which may be impacting your results. www.facebook.com is a very different page with and without the user being logged in, and same holds for even google.com (for folks who use iGoogle). Can you verify that this is not significantly biasing your results?

Why 2100 sites, and not, say, 2000?

Why get the top sites from quantcast but genre from Alexa? What is wrong with Alexa site rankings?

If Figure 3 is plotting median number of objects, why are there fractional values? Are you plotting average of medians? (Then, say so.)

For the experiment in Figure 18, why are you not studying load times?

Are you aware of this work: E. Kiciman and B. Livshits, "AjaxScope: A Platform for Remotely Monitoring the Client-Side Behavior of Web 2.0 Applications", Proc. SOSP'07, October 2007. It presents a method for Web site designers to learn about the performance of their sites in the wild through javascript instrumentation.

Reviewer #5

Strengths: Well written paper that provides a comprehensive examination of several complexity metrics and their impact across websites.

Weaknesses: The study is exclusively based on a Firefox extension, and thus misses any performance dependencies on the client browser that might have an effect on load and render times. Only the root page of websites is examined, which could be significantly simpler than other website pages.

Comments to Authors: Given the increase of web traffic and website complexity, I believe the paper provides a nice description of the basic characteristics of modern web sites. The paper is well written and easy to follow and I only have two main issues with the paper:

- The analysis is solely based on Firefox. This perhaps may not have a significant impact on the first part of the paper where the authors examine the number and type of objects, but it certainly has an effect on the performance as observed in the client. For example, javascript engines are quite different across browsers and this may affect the download times. Further, browsers vary in other things, such as the number of simultaneous TCP connections, object prioritization etc. Some discussion on this, I feel, is needed.

- Second, only the root page is examined. This may have quite an effect in cases of websites such as Google.com or Facebook.com. It would be interesting to examine whether performance dependencies vary if one looks beyond the root page.

Finally, I found the small discussion on mobile clients quite interesting, and I would encourage the authors to look more into this.

Response from the Authors

We thank the reviewers for their positive feedback and their insightful suggestions. The final version addresses most of the reviewers' comments and has helped to improve our paper significantly. First, the paper is more precise about various details of our measurements, such as the number of vantage points, the period over which the data was gathered, and the version of Firefox used to gather measurements. Second, we acknowledge the inherent difficulty of accounting for the contribution of non-origins to download times because requests are parallelized. To address this concern, we provide three different ways to measure this contribution in Section 4.2. Third, since our measurements are focused on the landing pages of websites, we have added a preliminary comparison between the complexity of landing and non-landing pages. Finally, we also present the distribution of our measured page load times.

There are a few reviewer comments that we do not address. We do not perform a PCA analysis of load times vs. complexity metrics since PCA maps the measurement space to dimensions that cannot be tied back to one of our metrics.
Our regression-based analysis provides an intuitive way to distill the most important complexity metrics for explaining load times. Two other suggestions from reviewers, while relevant to the broader theme, are outside the scope of this paper and we leave this for future work: (1) websites where web pages are significantly different when the user is logged in, e.g., facebook.com, igoogle.com and (2) differences across web browsers.

Identifying Diverse Usage Behaviors of Smartphone Apps

Qiang Xu
University of Michigan
Ann Arbor, MI
qiangxu@umich.edu

Jeffrey Erman
AT&T Labs Research
Florham Park, NJ
erman@research.att.com

Alexandre Gerber
AT&T Labs Research
Florham Park, NJ
gerber@research.att.com

Z. Morley Mao
University of Michigan
Ann Arbor, MI
zmao@umich.edu

Jeffrey Pang
AT&T Labs Research
Florham Park, NJ
jeffpang@research.att.com

Shobha Venkataraman
AT&T Labs Research
Florham Park, NJ
shvenk@research.att.com

ABSTRACT

Smartphone users are increasingly shifting to using apps as "gateways" to Internet services rather than traditional web browsers. App marketplaces for iOS, Android, and Windows Phone platforms have made it attractive for developers to deploy apps and easy for users to discover and start using many network-enabled apps quickly. For example, it was recently reported that the iOS AppStore has more than 350K apps and more than 10 billion downloads. Furthermore, the appearance of tablets and mobile devices with other form factors, which also use these marketplaces, has increased the diversity in apps and their user population. Despite the increasing importance of apps as gateways to network services, we have a much sparser understanding of how, where, and when they are used compared to traditional web services, particularly at scale. This paper takes a first step in addressing this knowledge gap by presenting results on app usage at a national level using anonymized network measurements from a tier-1 cellular carrier in the U.S. We identify traffic from distinct marketplace apps based on HTTP signatures and present aggregate results on their spatial and temporal prevalence, locality, and correlation.

Categories and Subject Descriptors

C.2.3 [**Computer-Communication Networks**]: Network Operations - Network monitoring; C.4 [**Performance of Systems**]: Measurement techniques

General Terms

Measurement

Keywords

Smartphone Apps, App Usage Behaviors

1. INTRODUCTION

The number and popularity of mobile apps is rising dramatically due to the accelerating rate of adoption of smartphones. For example, Android has 150K apps and 350K daily activations [12]. Preinstalled with marketplace portals such as the AppStore on iOS, Market on Android, and MarketPlace on Windows Mobile, popular smartphone platforms have made it easy for users to discover and start using many network-enabled apps quickly. By Jan 22, 2011, more than 350K apps are available on the AppStore with downloads of more than 10 billion [1]. Furthermore, the appearance of tablets and mobile devices with other form factors, which also use these marketplaces, has increased the diversity in apps and their user population. The existence of marketplaces and platform APIs have also made it more attractive for some developers to implement apps rather than complete web-based services. Despite the increasing importance of apps as gateways to network services, we have a much sparser understanding of how, where, and when they are used compared to traditional web services, particularly at scale. This paper takes a first step in addressing this knowledge gap.

A previous study found evidence that there is substantial diversity in the way that different people use smartphone apps [7]. However, because the study relied on volunteers using instrumented phones, it was limited to two platforms and less than three hundred users in a few geographic areas. Other studies of mobile application/app usage [11, 18, 22] have been similarly limited in scope. Thus, it is difficult to extrapolate these results to make representative conclusions about spatial locality, temporal variation, and correlation of apps at scale. For example, "where are apps more popular?", "How is their usage distributed across a country?", "How does their usage vary throughout the day?". While there have been studies of smartphone performance at larger scales [14, 2, 10], which use volunteer measurements or network data to obtain measurements at scale, measuring the usage of different apps from these data sources is more challenging. Volunteer measurements are typically obtained by deploying a measurement tool via an app marketplace, but many popular platform APIs do not permit the measurement of other apps in the background, so it is difficult to write an app that captures this information. Network data may contain information that can identify app behaviors, but this information is not typically part of standard traces. To make representative conclusions about apps, we require a network data set that identifies apps in network traffic and contains a significant number of measurements covering a representative number of devices, users, locations, and times.

In this study, we address the limitations by collecting anonymized IP-level networking traces in a large tier-1 cellular network in the

U.S. for one week in August 2010. In contrast to previous work, we use signatures based on HTTP headers (included in the IP-level trace) to distinguish the traffic from different apps. Due to the format of `User-Agent` in HTTP headers when mobile apps use standard platform APIs, this technique gives us the ability to gather statistics about each individual app in a marketplace, not just categories of network traffic characterized by port number. Moreover, our work examines the spatial and temporal prevalence, locality, and correlation of apps at a national scale, not just in one area or over a small population of users.

To our best knowledge, our study is the first to investigate the diverse usage behaviors of individual mobile apps at scale. In this study, we make the following five contributions:

- The data set that we use to study mobile apps is significantly more diverse geographically and in user base than previous studies. It covers hundreds of thousands of smartphones throughout the U.S. in a tier-1 cellular network. This allows us to make more generalizable conclusions about smartphone usage patterns.

- We find that a considerable number of popular apps (20%) are *local*, in particular, radio and news apps. In terms of traffic volume, these apps are accountable for 2% of the traffic in the **smartphone apps** category (*i.e.*, all the marketplace apps that can be identified by `User-Agent`) – that is, their user base is limited to a few U.S. states. This suggests significant potential for content optimization in such access networks as LTE and WiFi where content can be placed on servers closer to clients. Furthermore, it suggests that network operators need to understand the impact of different app mixes in different geographical areas to best optimize their network for user experience.

- Despite this diversity in locality, we also find that there are similarities across apps in terms of geographic coverage, diurnal usage patterns, *etc.* For example, we find that some apps have a high likelihood of *co-occurrence* on smartphones – that is, when a user uses one app, he or she is also likely to use another one. Users also use several alternatives for the same type of app (*e.g.*, multiple news apps). These findings suggest that some apps can be treated as a "bundle" when trying to optimize for their user experience and that there may be opportunities for integration.

- We also find that the diurnal patterns of different genres of apps can be remarkably different. For example, news apps are much more frequently used in the early morning, sports apps are more frequently used in the evening, while other apps have diurnal patterns less visible and their usage is more flat during a day. These findings suggest that cloud platforms that host mobile application servers can leverage distinct usage patterns in classes of apps to maximize the utilization of their resources. Furthermore, network operators may be able to leverage these results by optimizing their network for different apps during different times of the day.

- Mobility patterns can be inferred from network access patterns. Some apps are more frequently used when users are moving around; some of them are used more often when users are stationary. Mobility affects connectivity and performance, so bandwidth sensitive apps that are mobile may need to consider techniques to compensate for bandwidth variability. We find that there is a significant degree of diversity in the mobility of apps.

The rest of this paper is organized as follows: Related work is discussed in §2, §3 describes our data set, §4 presents our measurement results, §5 outlines some implications, and we conclude our study in §6.

2. RELATED WORK

A plethora of studies focus on understanding smartphone apps from different perspectives. Among them, studies of smartphone usage have yielded insights into different entities in the mobile computing community, *e.g.*, content providers, network providers, OS vendors, mobile app designers, *etc.* Accordingly, understanding the usage of mobile apps is critical for content providers to generate, optimize, and deliver content, for network providers to allocate radio resources, for OS vendors to support on-device apps, for app designers to implement efficient programs, *etc.* Overall, our study is the first that attempts to address the lack of sufficient knowledge about how, where, and when mobile apps are used at a national scale.

A group of studies attempted to improve the performance of mobile apps via OS infrastructure support [5, 13, 10, 6], *e.g.*, offloading resource intensive computation to cloud [5], providing clean intermediate interface for apps by the OS [13], and signaling mobile devices by network providers via notification channel to save resource [10]. Our study is complementary to these, as it focuses on profiling the usage patterns of mobile apps; we note that the design of supportive infrastructure would also benefit from the knowledge of mobile app usage patterns.

Also related are studies that proposed measurement tools for smartphone devices characterizing either the device performance or the performance of certain apps [14, 30, 21], *e.g.*, 3GTest [14] measures the network performance of popular smartphone platforms, PowerTutor [30] profiles energy consumption of running apps on Android, ARO [21] characterizes the radio resource usage of mobile apps, *etc.* Compared to these studies, we focus on usage patterns of mobile apps rather than their performance, but our work also has implications on resource consumption.

Studies have also proposed creative mobile apps to enhance user experience under mobility [17, 4, 3, 16], *e.g.*, xShare [17] enabling friendly, efficient, and secure phone sharing on existing mobile phones, Escort [4] leading a user to the vicinity of a desired person in a public place, *etc.* Although mobile apps are fixed in our study, our work provides app designers with measurements and directions that can help them improve design decisions.

Besides app usage, app selection has been explored as well in context-aware mobile apps recommendation systems [26, 29]. A key requirement for an app recommendation system is to identify the users who share certain similar app interests so that it can predict apps of interest. Understanding patterns in user interests is also part of our study.

On a large scale, there have been studies characterizing the mobile traffic [11, 18, 8, 15] and user interactive behaviors with smartphones [7, 22, 23]. Compared to these studies, our study (1) relies on a data set that can represent the majority of smartphone users across the U.S.; (2) covers the impact of more than one factor, *e.g.*, location, time, device, user, *etc.*; (3) places more emphasis on the usage of smartphones rather than traffic flows, content type, and WiFi usage.

We believe that our study makes an important step in addressing the lack of knowledge of usage behaviors of mobile apps.

top X apps	right (%)	wrong (%)	unknown (%)
10	8 (80%)	0 (0%)	2 (20%)
20	17 (85%)	1 (5%)	2 (10%)
50	46 (92%)	2 (4%)	2 (4%)
100	91 (91%)	4 (4%)	5 (5%)
200	176 (88%)	5 (3%)	19 (10%)
500	427 (85%)	14 (3%)	69 (14%)

Table 1: accuracy of using `User-Agent` to categorize apps (via manual comparison to app names in the app marketplace).

3. OVERVIEW OF DATA SET

3.1 Data Set

In this paper, we use an anonymized data set from a tier-1 cellular network provider in the U.S. It is collected during the week of August 24th, 2010 – August 30th, 2010. The data set contains flow-level information about IP flows carried in PDP Context tunnels (*i.e.*, all data traffic sent to and from cellular devices). This data set is collected from all links between SGSNs and GGSNs in tier-1 network's UMTS core network. Hence, we have a nationwide view of cellular data traffic. Due to volume constraints, only traffic from a uniform random sample of devices is collected. For a random sample of devices, the data contains the following information for each IP flow per minute: the start and the end timestamps, per-flow traffic volume in terms of both the bytes and the number of packets, the device identifier, and the app identifier. All device and subscriber identifiers (*e.g.*, IMSI, IMEI) are anonymized to protect privacy without affecting the usefulness of our analysis. Furthermore, the data sets do not permit reversing the anonymization or re-identification of subscribers.

App identifiers include information about application protocol (*e.g.*, HTTP, DNS, and SIP) and class (*e.g.*, streaming audio, streaming video, web, email). Moreover, given that these popular smartphone platforms include the app's name in the `User-Agent` field when the app uses the standard API to access URL network resources, the marketplace apps can be identified by the `User-Agent` field in HTTP headers. We focus on these apps in this paper and we classify them into the **smartphone apps** category. Note that the browser and YouTube are not included in smartphone apps since they come with the smartphone OS and are not present in the marketplace.

We further categorize smartphone apps by the genre that it is listed under in its platform's marketplace. To find the category, we use the API provided by each smartphone platform's market to search for the app name presented in the HTTP `User-Agent`. While the API typically returns multiple results that match the query (by treating it as a wild card), we manually validated the top apps whether the top first result is correct. Table 1 shows the corresponding validation results of the querying. Upon the response of each query, we have three attitudes: *right*, *wrong*, and *unknown*. We consider a response as right or wrong only if we are confident on the correctness. For example, we believe that a `User-Agent` containing `Pandora` is a music app and another `User-Agent` including `Facebook` is not a sport app. There are some apps that are very hard to tell by us according to their `User-Agent` fields such as `WSDU 4`, which we label as unknown. Additionally, those queries whose responses are empty are labeled as unknown. According to Table 1, we are confident on the correctness of the top first result for the majority of the smartphone apps.

In this paper, we are concerned about four main features per app: **traffic volume**, **access time**, **unique subscribers**, and **locations**. We estimate traffic volume as the sum of the flow byte counts, access time as the sum of the flow durations (with a precision of seconds), and the number of unique subscribers as the number of distinct anonymous device identifiers. There is only one anonymized identifier per distinct device. To determine the location of each device at the time a flow is in progress, we use the cell sector identified in the PDP context used to tunnel the flow. This cell sector is typically recorded when the PDP context begins, when a device moves far enough that the SGSN its traffic routes through changes, switches from 2G to 3G (or vice versa), or switches from 3G to WiFi. While this sector may be slightly stale, previous work [27] showed that they are still almost always accurate to within 40 kilometers. Thus, they suffice for most of our results that only look at U.S. states as distinct regions. For other results we present on sector changes, we may underestimate the number of changes due to this limitation.

In total, the sample data set includes approximately 600K distinct subscribers and approximately 22K distinct smartphone apps.

3.2 Limitation

Our approach to identifying apps using the HTTP `User-Agent` field may miss traffic that does not use the standard platform URL API. However, in Section 3.3 we show that this approach captures a large fraction of traffic that is not email, web browsing, streaming, or a marketplace download (which we identify separately based on other well known heuristics). Obviously, our data set will not capture app usage except when there are network flows. This is acceptable for our study, since we are primarily interested in apps that are gateways to Internet services, not apps that do not use the network.

Another limitation is the time difference when we use these August `User-Agent` fields generated from the trace during the week of August 24th, 2010 – August 30th, 2010, and query them on the current marketplace. Because developers may change the `User-Agent` field in updating their apps, this may result inaccuracy of smartphone app identification. However, according to Table 1, this effect should be small.

3.3 Traffic Summary

Figure 1 shows a summary of all traffic in our data set. Devices 1, 2, 3, and 4 are four major device types in this tier-1 network. Figure 1(a) shows the distribution of traffic volume. We observe that the volume of known smartphone apps traffic is comparable with the traffic volume of web browsing and other HTTP traffic, which is a major motivation for our study. Moreover, the market category also contributes to considerable traffic, which indicates a high demand for smartphone apps from subscribers.

Figure 1(b) shows the distribution of access time of app categories. It is interesting to note that the streaming category is only accountable for a small fraction of the total network access time of all smartphone apps. The gaming, p2p, and voip categories include mostly port and header-identified traffic for common desktop apps. We see that they have a small fraction of both traffic volume and access time, which means that these apps are not common on devices on this cellular network. Figure 1(c) shows the distribution of number of unique subscribers. In this figure, the misc category includes DNS requests, so the misc category roughly has the same number of subscribers as total number of subscribers that we observed in the data set. The smartphone apps and web browsing categories cover almost all the subscribers.

For the remainder of this paper, we only examine traffic in the smartphone apps category.

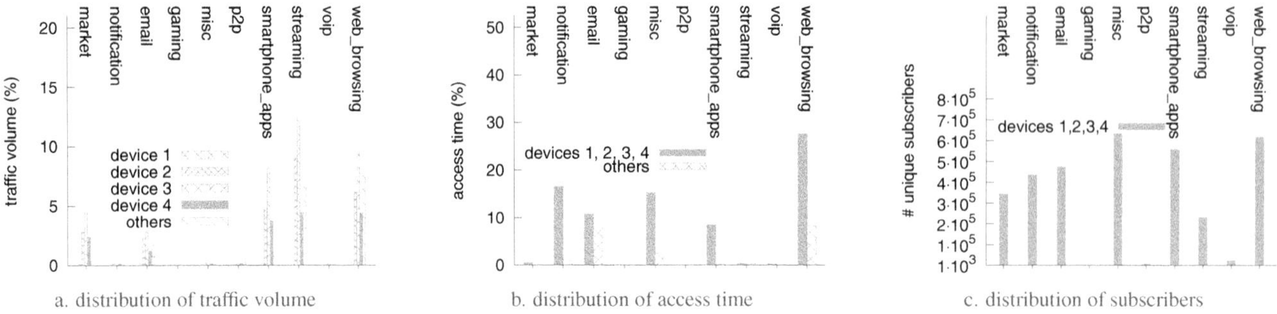

Figure 1: distribution of traffic volume, access time, and subscribers across categories of apps.

4. USAGE PATTERNS OF SMARTPHONE APPS

In this section, we investigate how, where, and when smartphone apps are used from spatial, temporal, and user perspectives. We first choose appropriate metrics to evaluate smartphone apps, and then attempt to understand the impact of location, time, user, and app interest accordingly.

4.1 Characterizing Usage with Different Metrics

We begin our analysis by presenting some broad characteristics of smartphone app usage. For our analysis, we choose a number of different natural metrics that profile network activity. We use the following three metrics for each app through most of our analysis: (a) **traffic volume**, defined as the number of bytes consumed by all subscribers using the app; (b) **number of subscribers**, defined as the number of unique subscribers using this app throughout our week-long data set; (c) **network access time**, defined as the total duration summed across all the IP flows generated by the app over our week-long data set.

Figure 2 shows CDFs of these metrics for the apps. For each metric, we aggregate together all the users of a particular app. The long tail of these CDFs directly shows the huge diversity in smartphone apps and their network characteristics. The top app in Figure 2(a) is a "personalized Internet radio app", and is responsible for more than 3TB data in one week, while the majority of smartphone apps generate only 1 – 10 MB over the same time period. Note that this top app is by itself responsible for generating over 50% of the total traffic volume in the smartphone apps category. This dramatic variation in the traffic volume is due to many factors, *e.g.,* app genres, popularity of apps, device types, preferences of the user base, content of apps, *etc.* For example, both news apps and radio apps may provide users with the latest news, but news apps typically deliver most of their content via text while radio apps deliver content via streaming audio; thus, users of these two apps would receive news on their smartphones with a substantial difference in the volume of traffic generated.

We observe a similar variation in Figure 2(b). The top app here is a "social utility connecting people", with a total network access time exceeding 100 years (aggregated across all its users). This app alone contributes to 86% of the total network access time of the smartphone apps category, but the majority of the smartphone apps are seen accessing the network for only about 1 minute - 1 hour. This "social utility" app also has the largest number of unique subscribers, 540,230 according to Figure 2(c). The total number of unique subscribers in our data set is 633,892 by examining the number of unique subscribers with DNS requests in Figure 1. Thus, we may estimate that 6 in every 7 subscribers use this "social utility" app on their smartphones. Recall that this data set contains only a random sample of subscribers, so the numbers here do not reflect the total number of subscribers in the cellular network. Around 60% smartphone apps have no more than 10 unique users in our data set, thus illustrating the long tail of smartphone apps on the market. Because of this long tail, we filter out the smaller apps for some of our analysis as they do not have enough measurements. We discuss this further in §4.2.

Figure 2(d) shows the correlation between the traffic volume and the number of unique subscribers, and between the access time and the number of unique subscribers. We aggregate the apps with the same $10^{\lfloor \lg N \rfloor}$ (N is the number of unique subscribers) and present the minimum, 25th percentile, median, 75th percentile, and maximum in each aggregation point accordingly. Both the traffic volume and the network access time roughly increase linearly with the number of unique subscribers, but the high variation still exists in the correlation. Due to the high variation, it is difficult to estimate the an app's traffic volume and network access time based only on its number of users. However, given a certain large number of apps together, their traffic volume and access time may be predictable. Accordingly, cellular providers may be able to estimate the radio resource consumption and allocate radio resources.

Figure 3 shows the CDFs of the apps' traffic volume and access time, now normalized by the number of subscribers that use the app. We see a similar variation across apps in these CDFs as well. For example, in Figure 3(a), the app with the largest traffic volume per subscriber consumes 5GB in one week, but the majority of apps consume less than 1MB data per subscriber in the week. Likewise, in Figure 3(b), the app with the longest access time per subscriber lasts for 2 days in one week, while the majority of apps access the network for only 10 seconds - 1 hour per subscriber in the week. From Figure 2 and Figure 3, we also observe apps with very marginal usage in the long tail, *e.g.,* the app consuming only less than 1KB, the app accessing the network less than 10 sec, and the app with only one user. These numbers indicate why we need to filter out these tiny apps for our analysis.

4.2 Popular Smartphone Apps

Figure 2 shows that there are a substantial number of smartphone apps with only 1 subscriber and that 60% of the smartphone apps have no more than 10 unique subscribers. Thus, these apps do not provide enough data for analysis, and, in this section, we explore how to decide systematically which apps can be considered popular and how we can eliminate the effect of apps with marginal usage on our analysis.

In effect, we want to identify the popular smartphone apps based on the numbers of their unique subscribers, but at the same time,

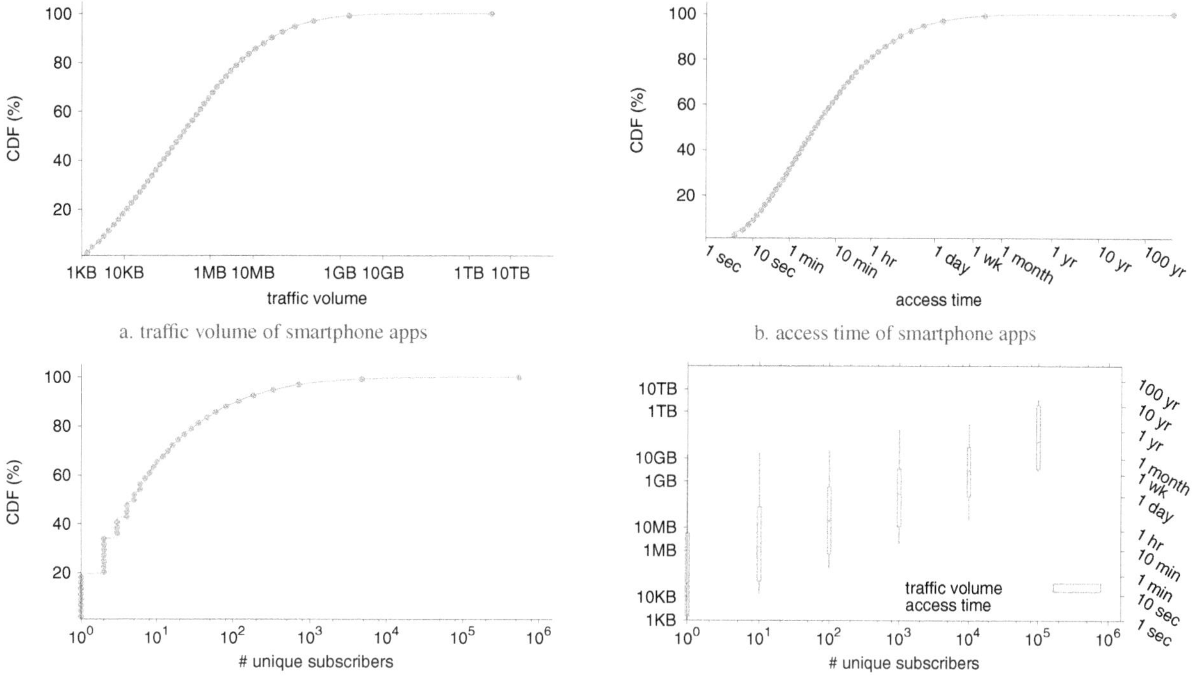

a. traffic volume of smartphone apps

b. access time of smartphone apps

c. # unique subscribers of smartphone apps

d. correlation between metrics of smartphone apps

Figure 2: (a)-(c) CDF of volume, access time, and users, with one data point per smartphone app, aggregating users together in one week.

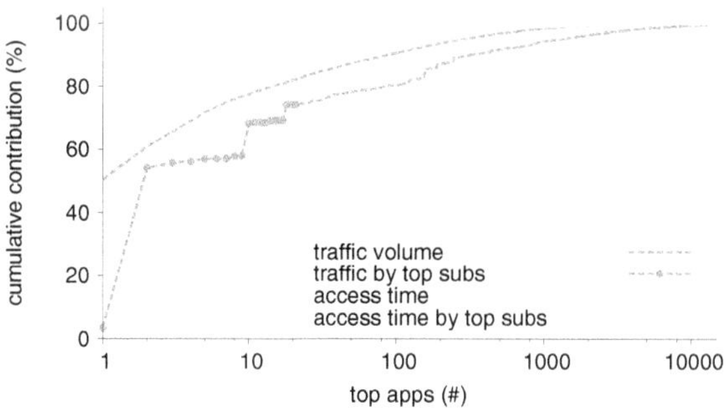

Figure 4: is the number of unique subscribers a good metric for filtering? Contributions of the top X apps to total volume and access time respectively

we do not want to discriminate against apps with few subscribers that have a significant impact on the network, *i.e.*, generate a lot of traffic or access the network for long time periods. So, we have two questions to answer: (1) is the number of unique subscribers a good metric for filtering? (2) if so, what is a reasonable threshold on the number of unique subscribers?

Intuitively, if the number of unique subscribers is a good metric for filtering, the top X apps based on the number of unique subscribers should contribute similar amounts of traffic volume and access times as the top X apps based on the traffic volume or access time. We first compare the contribution of the top X apps based on different metrics. Figure 4 compares the contribution of the top X apps based on the number of unique subscribers against the top X apps based on the traffic volume and based on the network access time. We can observe that the cumulative contributions of the top X apps based on access time and the top X apps based on number of unique subscribers are quite close, by comparing the "access time" and the "access time by top subs". Likewise, the contributions of the top X apps based on traffic volume and number of unique subscribers are also close, although a little difference does exist. We note that over 90% of the total volume and access time is accounted for by the top 1000 apps based on the number of unique subscribers.

Thus, Figure 4 indicates that somewhere above 1000 would be a reasonable boundary to distinguish popular apps from apps in the tail given the 90% coverage. We further explore the marginal nature of the apps ranking above 1000 in Figure 5. Figure 5(a) shows that each app in top 1000 have more than 471 unique subscribers. Figure 5(b) shows the network access time and the traffic volume per user for apps ranking in 1000 – 4000. For both traffic volume and access time, we aggregate every 100 apps into one errorbar that shows the minimum, median, and maximum of every 100 apps. The app accessing network the most consumes only 250 seconds per user in a week, and the app transferring the most data generates only 500 KB per user in a week. Because of these small traffic volumes and short access times, we do not consider these apps to be sufficiently active for our analysis.

Our discussion suggests that a natural threshold would be the top 1000 apps ranked by the number of unique subscribers. Table 2 shows the number of apps in each genre, both for the top 1000 apps as well as all the 22K apps. In the remainder of the paper, we will refer to these top 1000 apps as **popular apps**.

4.3 Spatial Patterns: Distribution of the Geographic Usage of Smartphone Apps

Next, we investigate the diversity of smartphone apps being used by subscribers in different geographic locations. Understanding the spatial usage patterns of smartphone apps suggests ways to improve user experience and performance from many aspects, such as con-

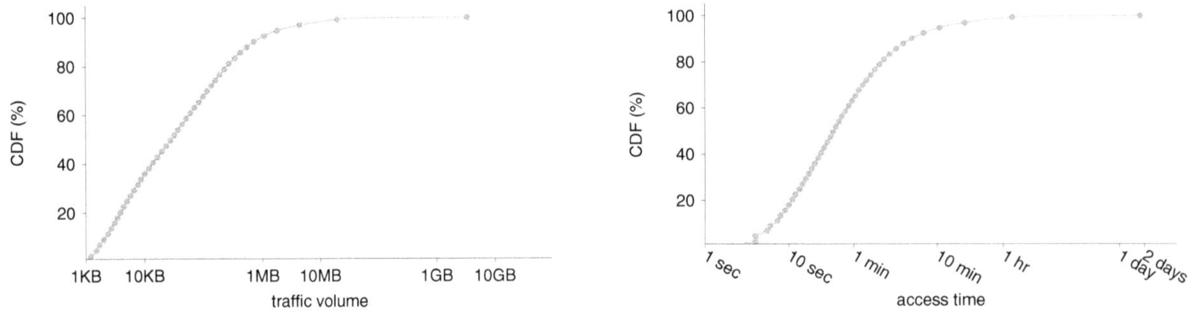

a. traffic volume of smartphone apps per subscriber

b. access time of smartphone apps per subscriber

Figure 3: metrics of smartphone apps (ii) – averaged based on users.

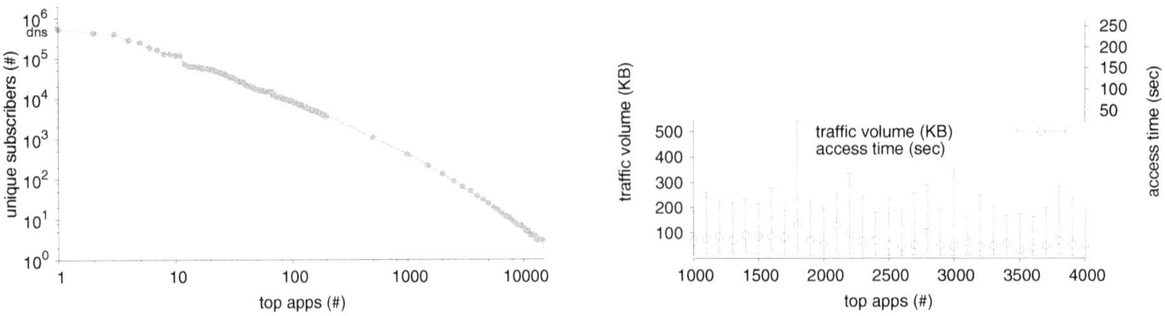

Figure 5: where is the reasonable threshold on the number of unique subscribers?

tent placement, context-aware applications, and mobile advertisement system. Taking content placement as an example, if content providers know that some of their apps are most used at certain locations, they may choose to place content close to those locations so that users experience better performance.

4.3.1 Local Smartphone Apps

We first examine whether any apps are **local apps**, *i.e.*, whether the majority of an app's traffic comes from a region. We perform the following analysis: for each app, we divide its traffic by (U.S.) state of the user, and compute the top 1, 3 and 5 state(s) that contribute the most traffic volume or the longest network access times. We expect that if an app's usage is truly localized, most of its traffic or access time (*e.g.*, 90%) will originate from a small number of states.

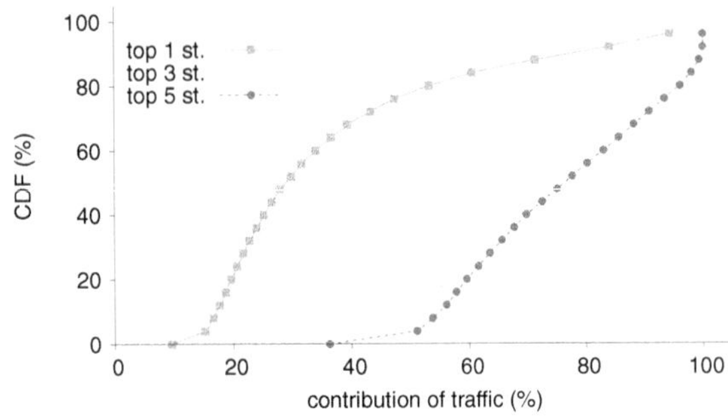

Figure 6: contribution of volume from top X states.

Figure 6 shows the CDF of the fraction of the traffic volume from top 1, 3, and 5 states for top 1000 apps that we have chosen in §4.2. According to Figure 6, 20% of the popular apps have more than 90% of their traffic volume originating from 3 states, 5.8% of the popular apps have 90% of the traffic originating from only 1 state, and 1.7% of the popular apps have all their traffic from 1 state. These 20% apps, which have more than 90% of their traffic volume originating from 3 states, account for 2% traffic in the smartphone apps category. The distribution of the contribution of access time of popular apps are very close to the one of traffic volume. Thus, we see that a significant number of the popular apps are local.

To explore what these local apps are and where they are localized, we examine in more detail the 100 most local apps based on the contribution of the top 3 states; for each of these apps, the top 3 states contribute at least 97% of their total traffic volume. Figure 7 shows the distribution of the top 3 states of the 100 most local apps; we differentiate the rank of the top 3 states for these 100 local apps as well so that we know, for example, California is the state that originated the most traffic for 19 apps, the state originated the second most traffic for 15 apps, and the state originated the third most traffic for 12 apps. As expected, California, Texas, and New York are the states with most local apps – these are the states with large populations of smartphone users. However, there are many states with much smaller populations such as Louisiana, Wyoming, and Kentucky that also have some local apps; upon further analysis, this turn out to be because content from some apps is tailored specifically for users from some regions, *e.g.*, local TV programs, news, radio, weather apps, *etc.* As an example for validation, we show the local apps for Louisiana in Table 3; we see that the six apps that have most of their traffic originating from Louisiana provide TV, news, radio and weather specifically for Louisiana residents.

We also explore the genre-wise breakdown of the local apps, as the genre of an app reflects the content and service type of a smart-

genre	books	business	education	entertainment	finance	games	healthcare	lifestyle	medical	music	navigation	news	photography	productivity	reference	social net.	sports	travel	utilities	weather	unknown
total apps	351	418	643	1827	283	3108	368	1298	205	1296	450	1126	475	527	515	721	787	590	1079	236	5865
popular apps	7	8	13	95	13	199	23	71	4	34	23	89	17	23	26	58	33	29	49	16	170

Table 2: distribution of the genre of apps.

app	description on Google
WWLTV	New Orleans News, Breaking News, Weather ...
KATC	News Coverage at Acadiana-Lafayette, Louisiana ...
KSLANews12	News, Weather and Sports at Shreveport, Louisiana ...
KPLC 7 News	Lake Charles, Louisiana – kplctv.com ...
WBRZ	TV Channel 2 Baton Rouge, LA ...
GoWAFB	Local news, weather ... at Baton Rouge, LA ...

Table 3: local apps from Louisiana.

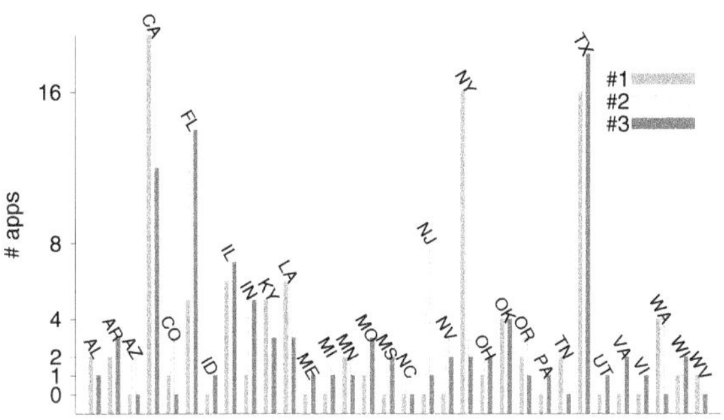

Figure 7: fraction of traffic size in top X states for each smartphone app.

phone app to a great degree. Table 4 shows the distribution of the genres of the 100 most local apps in Table 7. According to Table 4, these apps are mostly news, weather, and entertainment apps, likely due to the local nature of their content, *i.e.*, local weather, local news, local TV, *etc.* In music, the local apps are usually online local radio stations. The local education apps are typically created by universities, and mostly used by the local student populations.

4.3.2 National Smartphone Apps

Next, we examine the spatial patterns of smartphone app usage nation-wide. For this analysis, we remove the 100 apps identified as local in the previous analysis (Section 4.3.1), and examine the nation-wide usage of the remaining apps' traffic. We term these remaining apps as **national apps**. Our analysis explores whether certain genres are more popular (or have heavier usage) in some areas than in other areas; in general, we do not expect users to prefer using apps of a specific genre as a function of their geographic location, but our results show that this does happen under certain conditions.

genre	education	entertainment	games	lifestyle	music	navigation	news	photography	productivity	sports	travel	utilities	weather	unknown
# apps	4	5	2	2	7	3	45	1	1	2	3	3	6	16

Table 4: genres of local apps.

For ease of reference, we term **geographic usage distribution** of a quantity X to be the the empirical probability distribution function (PDF) of X by U.S. state. First, we compute the geographic usage distribution of the unique subscribers and of the aggregate traffic volume generated by all national smartphone apps. We then use them to compute the geographic usage of traffic volume normalized by the number of unique subscribers in the state. Figure 8(a) is the PDF of the geographic usage of the aggregate traffic of all national apps together, while Figure 8(b) is the PDF of the geographic usage of the normalized traffic of all national apps. As expected, California, Texas, New York, Florida, and Illinois are the states that have the highest aggregate traffic from the national apps in Figure 8(a). However, after normalizing the volume to account for the number of subscribers, the distribution looks flatter in Figure 8(b). We perform the rest of our analysis (Figure 8(c-f)) on the normalized traffic, since it makes differences across states be easier identified.

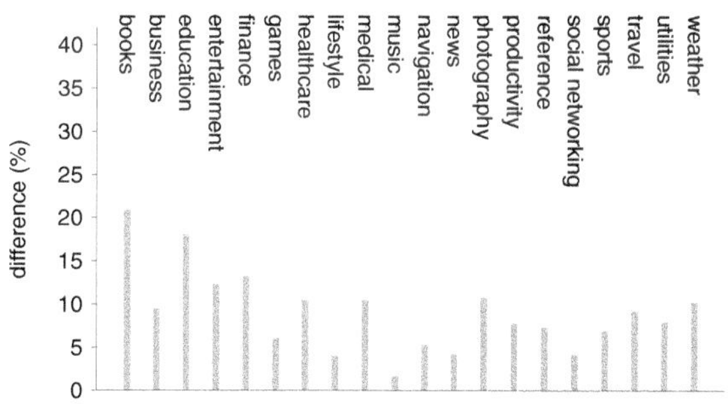

Figure 9: difference in the geographic usage of different app genres

Figure 8(c-f) illustrates the geographic usage of some representative genres (all genres are listed in Table 2). Figure 8(a) demonstrates the PDF of traffic volume from each state of all nation-wide apps. Lifestyle, music, news, and social networking genres have very similar patterns of geographic usage as the aggregate traffic. As an example, we show the social networking apps in Figure 8(c), which is is most similar to the aggregate traffic in Figure 8(b). Education apps in Figure 8(d) appear to be extremely popular in Texas; further analysis revealed that this is because some apps produced by universities (*e.g.*, TAMU) generate a significant fraction of traffic among the education apps. Likewise, Figure 8(f) shows that weather apps seem to be highly used in the south-eastern U.S. This may perhaps have happened because the time periods of our data coincide with the peak hurricane season in those areas [9, 19] – such variable and dangerous weather conditions may cause users to check weather forecasts more frequently.

Next, we measure how far the geographic usage of different genres are from the aggregate geographic usage of the apps. We use the Euclidean distance to measure the distance between a pair of geographic usage distributions. The Euclidean distance between

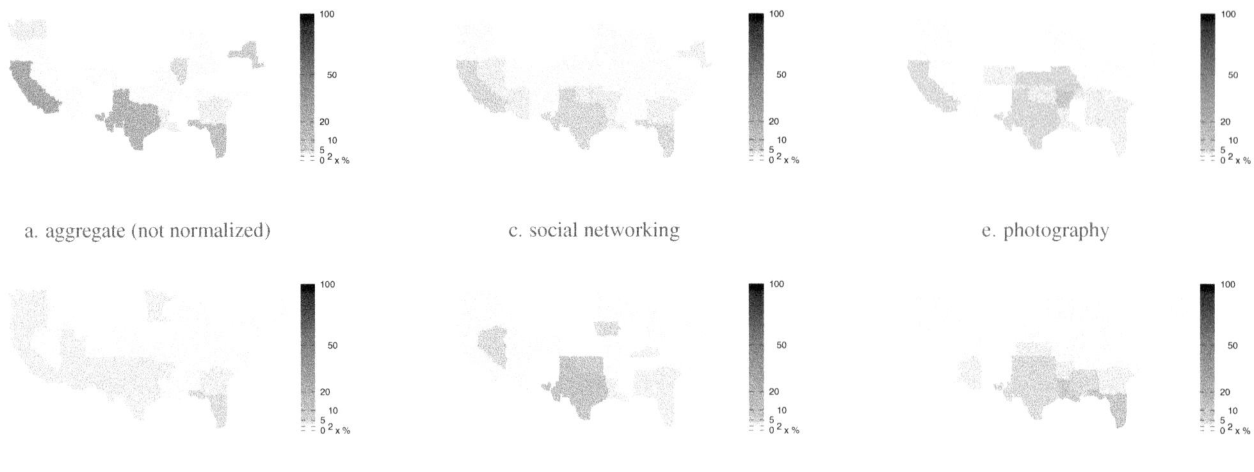

a. aggregate (not normalized) c. social networking e. photography

b. aggregate normalized d. education f. weather

Figure 8: distribution of the geographic usage of apps in different genres.

a pair of distributions $[x_1, x_2, \cdots, x_n]$ and $[y_1, y_2, \cdots, y_n]$ is defined as $\sqrt{\sum_{i=1}^{n}(x_i - y_i)^2}$. Figure 9 shows the distance between each genre's geographic usage distribution and the distribution of aggregate national apps. We note that some genres, such as books and education, are disproportionately used in some states, while others, such as social networking apps generate traffic more proportionate to the total traffic generated by that state.

The distribution of geographic usage of different apps *within* the same genre may also differ. Figure 10 shows the geographic usage distribution of a number of smartphone apps in the news genre. For this analysis, we select the apps of a few newspapers that are well-known across the entire U.S., and cover news relating to any part of the world. The location of each news app in Figure 10 only reflects where the newspaper headquarter is located. However, some of them have a location indicated in their names (marked with [2] in Figure 10). Although all these apps are used nation-wide, we note that apps whose names have a location indicated seem to be disproportionally preferred at those respective locations. In addition, the Washington D.C. news app seems to be highly preferred in Washington state as well, thus suggesting users look for apps that appear to be local to their region.

4.3.3 *Travel Area of Smartphone Apps*

Our final analysis of the spatial patterns of app usage examines whether individual users use some apps across larger geographic areas than others, *e.g.,* whether Internet radio apps, which users may listen to during their commute, are used across a larger area than books. Such an analysis can help understand what kinds of apps need to be more robust to variations in network quality.

For this analysis, we define the **travel-area** as a smartphone's geographic coverage per individual subscriber over short time, *e.g.,* 6 hours. We use the number of sectors to estimate the geographic coverage, since we do not have access to the device's exact locations. As noted in Section 3, the number of sectors observed in our data set is an underestimate of the actual number of sectors that the device passes through, but our results still give an idea of the relative travel-area of different apps. Specifically, for each app, we compute the average number of unique sectors used by active subscribers in each 6 hour time interval.

Figure 11 shows the distribution of the average travel-area of the

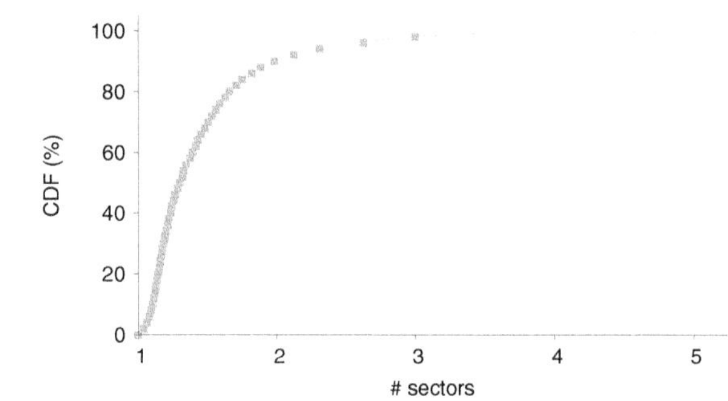

Figure 11: travel-area of apps.

genre	books	business	finance	games	healthcare	lifestyle	music	news	productivity	reference	social net.	sports	travel	unknown
# apps	2	1	4	19	3	5	6	1	3	1	31	2	1	18

Table 5: genres of high travel-area smartphone apps.

top 1000 popular apps. It shows that 10% apps access the network from more than two sectors. Thus, our results indicate that a significant fraction of the apps are used when users move around, creating another issue for content caching and delivery techniques. Base stations in future cellular network designs (*e.g.,* LTE) have been considered potential locations for content caching and optimization (since they would be the first IP hop), so significant amount user movement could make it more difficult to cache content appropriately. Table 5 shows that the majority of these apps are games or social networking apps, but there are also a few music and news apps.

4.4 User Patterns: Impact of User Interests on Smartphone Apps Usage

The needs and interests of individual users are the primary factors that inform their usage of apps. Because of user interests, the usage of different apps tends to be correlated. In this section, we an-

a. aggregate news apps b. headquartered in ATLANTA[1] c. headquartered in NEW YORK[2]

d. headquartered in WASHINGTON, D.C.[2] e. headquartered in CHICAGO[2] f. headquartered in VIRGINIA[1]

[1]: names of these apps do not have any location indicated.
[2]: names of these apps include locations.

Figure 10: distribution of the geographic usage of apps in the same genre.

alyze the extent to which user apps are correlated. Our analysis has many motivations: knowing what sets of apps are correlated would be helpful for both app developers as well as OS vendors, as they can factor this correlation into their designs and help the apps work better with each other. From a network perspective, such knowledge could help optimize performance or user experience for a set of apps as a bundle, and may also enhance troubleshooting. In addition, app markets can leverage this information for recommending new apps to users.

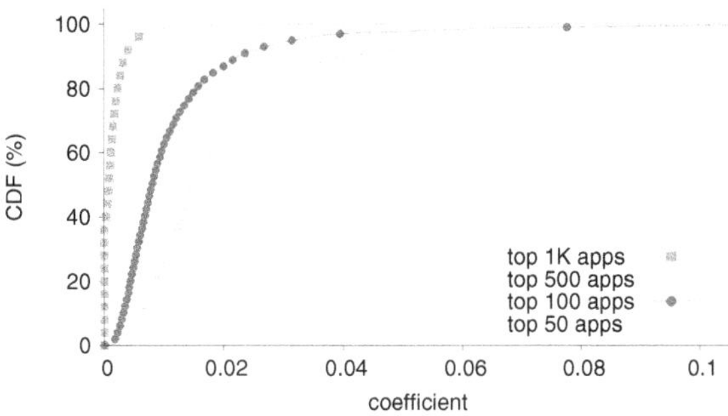

Figure 12: distribution of the Jaccard Similarity Coefficient of the popular apps.

We use the **Jaccard Similarity Coefficient** to quantify the overlap between a pair of apps a and b: we count the number of unique subscribers who have used both a and b, *i.e.*, $joint(a,b)$, and the number of unique subscribers who have used either a or b, *i.e.*, $union(a,b)$. We can obtain $\frac{joint(a,b)}{union(a,b)}$ for all pairs of apps in the popular 1000 apps.

Figure 12 shows the distribution of the Jaccard Similarity Coefficient between the top 1000, 500, 100, and 50 apps. We observe that there is a small fraction of app pairs that have a very high Jaccard Similarity Coefficient. For example, consider a pair of apps a, b whose $\frac{joint(a,b)}{union(a,b)} = 0.05$, and assume that a and b have 2000 unique subscribers together (we know from Figure 5(a) that each of the top 50 most popular apps have over 2000 unique subscribers). Then at this value of the Jaccard Similarity Coefficient, a and b share 100 unique subscribers. Given that there are more than 600,000 unique subscribers in our data set, the overlap of 100 subscribers is unlikely to be due to random chance, indicating that users of app a have a tendency to also use app b. We also note that as we increase the number of popular apps from 50-1000, there is a smaller fraction of app pairs that have a significant overlap in subscribers. This is expected, since an app is more likely to have subscribers overlap with other apps when gets used by more and more subscribers.

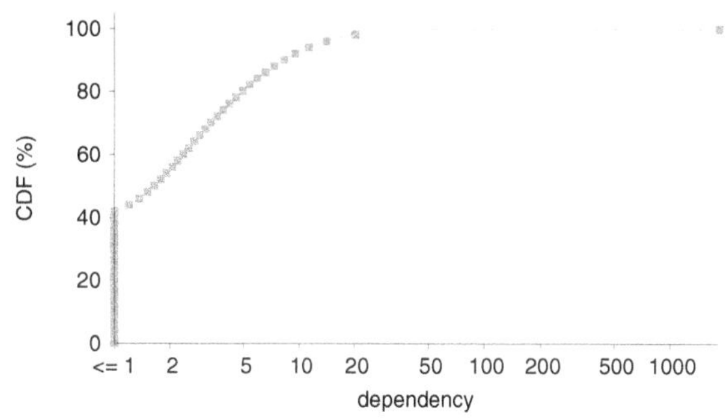

Figure 13: distribution of the dependency between popular apps.

Next, we analyze how likely it is for a pair of apps to have a substantial overlap in their users. Our analysis compares the empirical probabilities of a subscriber using each app individually to the empirical probability of a subscriber using both apps together. More precisely, let a, b denote apps, and $Pr[a], Pr[b]$ denote the empirical probabilities of a subscriber using app a, b respectively. Let $Pr[ab]$ denote the empirical probability of a subscriber using both apps a and b. If the subscribers for each app are selected at random from the total population, then we would expect that $Pr[ab]$ to be somewhat close to the product $Pr[a]Pr[b]$. Figure 13 shows the distribution of the ratio $\frac{Pr[ab]}{Pr[a][b]}$ (we term this quantity the **dependency**

ratio for ease of reference). It shows that nearly 10% of the app pairs have a dependency ratio that exceeds 10, and 254 pairs have a ratio exceeding 100.

Table 6 shows the frequency distribution of the genres of these 254 pairs (*i.e.*, pairs with dependency-ratio exceeding 100). We can make two immediate observations from this table. First, apps in the same genre are much more likely have correlated usage. For example, 110 pairs of two games apps that have high dependency-ratio, but games apps are part of a only 230 pairs in total. Second, apps in similar genres are more likely to have high dependence-ratio, *e.g.*, entertainment and games, news and entertainment, entertainment and social networking, travel and navigation, weather and news, social networking and news, *etc*.

There are many reasons that pairs of apps have highly correlated usage. First, many different apps often provide the same type of content in different forms *e.g.*, there may be multiple local news or Internet radio stations targeting the same location, and users often are interested in trying them all out. Or, there may multiple apps that allow users to access the same social networking sites with different user interfaces. A second reason may be that a pair of apps serve similar purpose, but neither may provide complete service on its own *e.g.*, users may have accounts with multiple banks, and need to use each bank's specific app in order to keep track of all their accounts. Yet another reason may be that different apps target similar user interests, and users may try them all out to identify their favorites, *e.g.*, crossword puzzle apps or sudoku apps.

4.5 Temporal Patterns: Distribution of the Traffic over time of Smartphone Apps

Understanding the diurnal patterns of apps is important for several reasons. For example, differences in when certain apps are used can help inform cloud providers on how to best multiplex resources and operators on what to optimize the network for at different times. In this analysis, we compare the traffic volumes and access times consumed by smartphone apps at different hours of the day, both in aggregate as well as for different genres. Our results show that there are diurnal patterns of app usage both in aggregate, as well as by genre, but that the patterns of different genres are noticeably different.

We first investigate the diurnal patterns by aggregating all the popular apps together. For this analysis, we map each flow to the local time of the device's geo-location (based on the sector where the device is connected to the cellular network). Figure 14(a) shows clear diurnal patterns of traffic volume and network access time. Around 1AM – 2AM, the total traffic volume and access time are at their minimum; they start increasing around 4AM, reach the peak usage around noon, start decreasing after 3PM and drop dramatically after 8PM.

In general, apps have more activity during the daytime than at night. However, this may not apply to every popular app. Figure 14(b) shows the distribution of the traffic contribution during late night for popular apps. According to Figure 14(a), in terms of both traffic volume or access time, the time period 1:00 AM – 3:59 AM contributes 4.2% traffic. Even if an app generates uniform traffic every hour of the day, it should generate 12.5% traffic from 1:00 AM to 3:59AM. So, Figure 14(b) indicates that there are some apps that are quite active late at night. We manually investigate these top 66 *late night* apps according to Figure 14(b) that contribute more than 12.5% traffic late at night. Table 7 summarizes the results. It appears that several entertainment and radio apps are used more frequently than expected at night.

Finally, we analyze diurnal patterns across different genres; we expect that different genres of apps to have different usage patterns, since they appeal to different interests. As we did in earlier analysis, we aggregate together the popular apps in the same genre, and compute the distribution of traffic volumes by genre at hourly intervals (again, using the local time of the flow). Figure 15 shows the normalized traffic volume across the day; it clearly shows how different genres do have very different diurnal patterns. In particular, we see that social network apps have almost exactly the same pattern as the aggregate, but weather and news apps are most frequently used at early morning. Sports apps, on the other hand, peak in the early evening, perhaps because users may watch matches or check scores frequently during those hours. Games apps also peak after standard work hours as we would expect, since that is probably the typical recreation time for most subscribers.

category	# apps	description
entertainment	20	small games, video channels, *etc.*
radio	28	music radio channels, news radio channels, *etc.*
healthcare	12	sleep aid utilities, *etc.*
books	6	bible, references, *etc.*

Table 7: description of late night apps.

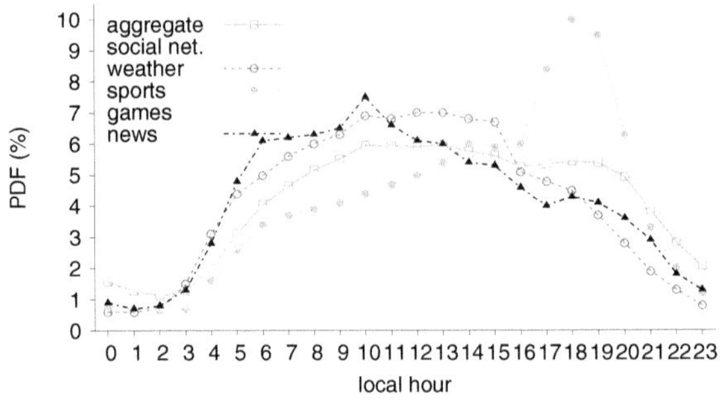

Figure 15: diurnal patterns across different genres.

4.6 Device Patterns: Differences Across Platforms

Finally, we compare smartphone app usage across different kinds of devices. We expect that faster devices allow for longer sessions, faster downloads, and more interactivity, thus enhancing the end-user experience. Power users, who use their devices more, may also gravitate to newer and faster devices. We focus on three different devices from the same device family, as we expect device operating system to also affect overall usage patterns. We compare three devices in the same device family but of different generations – we term these device 2, device 3, and device 4 in Figure 1. Device 2 is a HSDPA category 6 device (capable of 3.6Mbps downlink rate), and device 3 and device 4 are in HSDPA category 8 (capable of 7.2Mbps downlink) [24]. Device 2 and device 3 are not HSUPA enabled while device 4 is HSUPA category 6 (capable of 5.76Mbps uplink) [25].

For this analysis, we use slightly different metrics than we have used in the rest of the paper, since our goal is to measure how long a user interacts with the device, and compare these measurements across different devices. For this, we define **individual access time** and the **individual traffic volume** to be the network access time and the traffic volume per flow respectively. We use these metrics for our analysis as we expect the individual access time to provide a measure of how long a user spends with an app, and the individual traffic volume to reflect how much data is transferred each time a user interacts with an app. Obviously not every flow will be

	books	business	education	entertainment	finance	games	healthcare	lifestyle	medical	music	navigation	news	photography	productivity	reference	social net.	sports	travel	utilities	weather
books	0	0	0	2	0	3	0	1	0	0	0	1	0	0	0	0	0	1	0	0
business	0	0	0	0	0	0	0	4	0	0	0	2	0	0	0	0	0	0	1	0
education	0	0	5	2	0	2	0	0	0	0	2	3	0	0	0	1	0	0	0	0
entertainment	2	0	2	26	0	26	1	16	0	5	1	16	4	3	3	8	4	4	7	0
finance	0	0	0	0	2	0	1	0	0	0	0	4	0	0	0	0	0	1	1	0
games	3	0	2	26	0	110	2	19	1	5	1	3	2	1	13	5	8	12	1	1
healthcare	0	0	0	1	1	2	1	2	1	0	1	8	1	0	0	1	0	0	0	0
lifestyle	1	4	0	16	0	19	2	30	0	5	0	12	0	1	7	6	4	10	6	0
medical	0	0	0	0	0	1	1	0	0	0	0	1	0	0	0	0	0	0	0	0
music	0	0	0	5	0	5	0	5	0	6	0	5	0	1	1	11	3	0	3	0
navigation	0	0	2	1	0	1	1	0	0	0	2	1	0	1	0	1	0	4	0	1
news	1	2	3	16	4	3	8	12	1	5	1	77	1	3	2	12	8	7	4	4
photography	0	0	0	4	0	2	1	0	0	0	0	1	1	1	0	0	0	0	1	0
productivity	0	0	0	3	0	1	0	1	0	1	1	3	1	0	0	9	1	0	0	0
reference	0	0	0	3	0	13	0	7	0	1	0	2	0	0	1	0	1	2	0	1
social networking	0	0	1	8	0	5	1	6	0	11	1	12	0	9	0	32	4	0	3	0
sports	0	0	0	4	0	8	0	4	0	3	0	8	0	1	1	4	13	1	0	1
travel	1	0	0	4	1	12	0	10	0	0	4	7	0	0	2	0	1	9	2	0
utilities	0	1	0	7	1	1	0	6	0	3	0	4	1	0	0	3	0	2	2	0
weather	0	0	0	0	0	1	0	0	0	0	1	4	0	0	1	0	1	0	0	1

Table 6: measuring the dependency between genres: apps with high dependency-ratio.

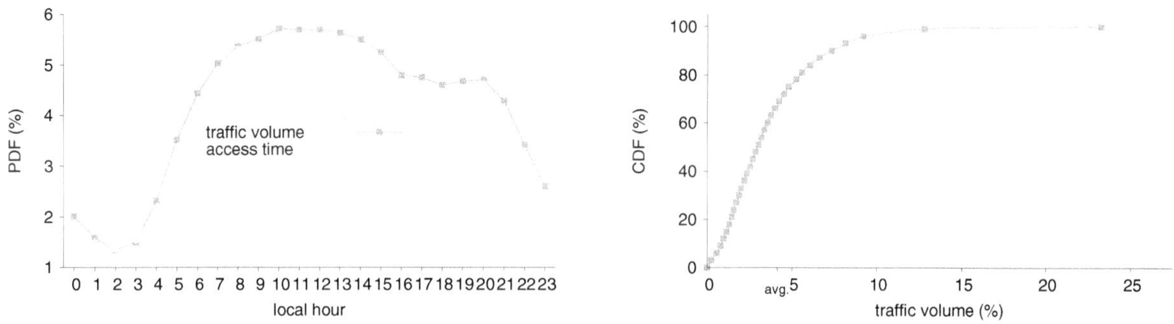

a. diurnal patterns of traffic volume & access time

b. traffic contribution by late night (1:00 – 3:59 AM)

Figure 14: diurnal patterns.

larger or longer, but we expect that a device that allows for better interaction will have on average more large flows and longer flows.

In Figure 16, we compare the individual traffic volume and individual access time between device 2 and device 4, and between device 3 and device 4. For our analysis, we aggregate all the popular apps to first compute directly the individual access time and individual traffic volume for these three platforms, and then compute the relative differences by comparing device 2 against device 4, and device 3 against device 4. According to Figure 16(a), the individual access time for device 2 and device 4 are very close, *i.e.*, the median relative difference is 0. However, individual traffic volume for device 2 is much smaller. The median difference of the individual traffic volume is −30%. Such a big difference indicates that the user experience is substantially different between these two device categories; users of device 4 consume much more data, typically through video. Figure 16(b) shows the comparison between device 3 and device 4; these two device categories are much closer than device 2 and device 4. There may be two explanations. First, a faster device tends to give users better overload experience and encourages them to download more content from the network. Second, power user are more likely upgrade to the latest smartphone, while users not as active may be more likely to keep using their older devices.

5. IMPLICATIONS

In previous sections, we investigate the usage patterns of smartphone apps from spatial, temporal, user, and device perspectives. We believe that our previous observations have important implications for the smartphone community. In this section, we discuss these implications following our previous observations.

5.1 Content Providers

In the analysis of spatial patterns of smartphone usages, we observe a considerable number of local apps (20%) which contribute 2% of the traffic volume in the smartphone apps category. The content provided by these local apps are very deterministic, *e.g.*, news apps, regional radio online services, weather forecast apps, *etc.* Given both the customers and locations for these apps are very closely clustered, content placement and delivery can be further optimized accordingly. It is therefore beneficial to place the content close to GGSNs in the cellular networks [28] for cellular users and place the content close to the geographic location of WiFi users. Besides local apps, for national apps, the distribution of geographic

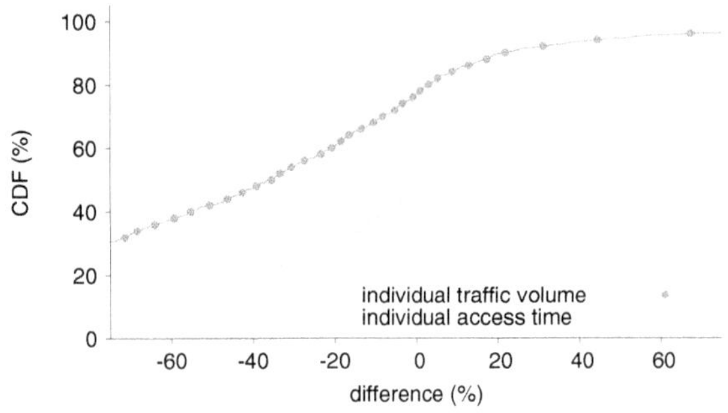

a. device 2 vs. device 4

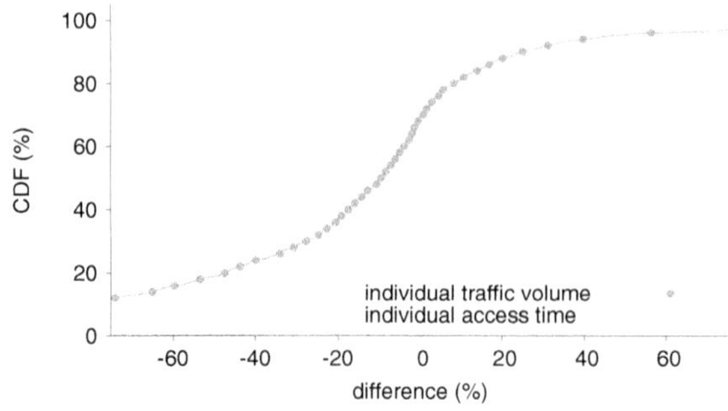

b. device 3 vs. device 4

Figure 16: impact of devices used.

coverage is still very dependent on the genre (*e.g.*, weather apps are highly used in the south-eastern U.S.), even the app's name (*e.g.*, the news app headquartered in CHICAGO), *etc.* Therefore, content placement according to the geographic coverage is advisable for both national and local apps.

5.2 Context-Aware Applications

Despite very diverse usage usage patterns across different smartphone apps, they still have some common traits. According to our observations, first, apps in the same genre share similar geographic coverage. Second, some apps share a large set of common users due to the similarity of content and interests, *e.g.*, social networking apps strongly correlate with entertainment apps, music apps, news apps, *etc.* Third, some apps share similar diurnal patterns due to content characteristics, *e.g.*, the peak hours of news apps and weather apps come at early morning.

Context-aware applications can take advantage of the existing similarity/correlation across smartphone apps. Take smartphone apps recommendation systems as an example. Unlike normal PC users, smartphone users depend on apps far more than browsers. Since a smartphone apps recommendation system is the first approach for users to explore various smartphone apps that meet their interests, these systems can be quite important. As the bridge between app marketplace and app customers, if apps recommendation systems can learn user interests and dependency across apps, they can identify more appropriate apps for users, *e.g.*, suggesting gaming fans more entertainment apps and social networking apps.

Another example of context-aware application is advertisement systems, which upon learning user's interests in apps, can deliver more relevant ads to users. Camera or camcorder advertisements may target more smartphone users that use more entertainment and game apps because photography apps are more correlated with entertainment and game apps.

5.3 Network Providers

Besides content providers, cellular network providers also play an important role in content delivery and customization. By understanding the access patterns of smartphone apps, network providers can benefit in allocating radio resource, setting caching policy, compression policy, *etc.*

If a large number of smartphone apps are targeted, their traffic volume and access time roughly have linear correlation with their number of unique subscribers. Accordingly, cellular providers can estimate and allocate radio resources.

We observe that the several few top apps contribute the majority traffic. For example, the app with the largest traffic volume is accountable for 50% of the total traffic volume of the smartphone apps category, and the app with the longest network access time takes 86% of the total network access time of the smartphone apps category. Understanding the usage patterns of these apps, network providers may do certain optimizations case by case.

The temporal patterns of smartphone apps help network providers allocate radio resource. For example, the access time per IP flow helps network providers decide the timers in state promotion [20].

We observe that some smartphone apps have large usage radius, *i.e.*, users of certain social networking apps and games apps are more likely to move around across several base stations. In future, LTE networks will push the first IP hop forward to base stations, which increases the flexibility of content placement and optimization. However, if users frequently move around, the corresponding mobility may increase the complexity to decide where to cache content and what content to cache.

5.4 OS Vendors and Apps Designers

Since smartphones have limited resources, the OS is accountable for resource management, *e.g.*, the push notification on iOS, Android, Windows Phone. Understanding the access patterns of apps on device, OS can add some flexibility to apps and optimize the resource usage. For example, if a user frequently resorts to a certain sleep aid app, then OS may allocate less resource to those apps that may interrupt the user's sleep.

Certain genres of smartphone apps have different characteristics, which may be taken advantage by apps designers. We observe that news and weather apps have distinctive diurnal patterns. Since the content of these apps usually are very time dependent and content fetching time is very predictable, apps designer can implement some prefetching mechanism to reduce the latency perceived by users. Similarly, the content of social networking apps can be prefetched before dinner time.

6. CONCLUDING REMARKS

In this study, we comprehensively investigated the diverse usage patterns of smartphone apps via network measurements from a national level tier-1 cellular network provider in the U.S. Our study is the first attempt in addressing the lack of how, where and when smartphone apps are used at the scale of the entire U.S.

We observed that a considerable fraction of popular apps (20%) are local because their content are expected to serve local users such as news and radio apps. This suggests that there is significant possibility for content optimization in LTE and WiFi access networks where the flexibility of placing content is high.

We also found out that there are similarities across apps in terms of geographic coverage, diurnal usage patterns, *etc.* Certain apps have a high likelihood of co-occurrence – that is, (i) when a user uses one app, he is also likely to use another one; or (ii) users use alternatives for the same type of interests, *e.g.*, multiple news apps, bank apps. These observations suggest that some apps should be treated as a "bundle" when trying to optimize for their user experience. There may be opportunities for integrating these apps together.

Diurnal patterns of smartphone apps can be remarkably different. For instance, news apps are much more frequently used in the early morning while sports apps are more frequently used in the evening. These findings suggest that content providers (*e.g.*, hosted on cloud) can leverage distinct usage patterns in classes of apps to maximize the utilization of their resources.

Many social networking and games apps are more frequently used when users are moving around. Mobility affects connectivity and performance, so bandwidth sensitive content that are mobile may need to consider techniques to compensate for bandwidth variability.

We believe that our findings on the diverse usage patterns of smartphone apps in spatial, temporal, user, device dimensions will motivate future work in the mobile community.

7. REFERENCES

[1] Apple. Apple's App Store Downloads Top 10 Billion. http://www.apple.com/pr/library/2011/01/22appstore.html.

[2] A. Balasubramanian, R. Mahajan, and A. Venkataramani. Augmenting Mobile 3G Using WiFi: Measurement, System Design, and Implementation. In *Proc. ACM MOBISYS*, 2010.

[3] X. Bao and R. Roy Choudhury. MoVi: mobile phone based video highlights via collaborative sensing. In *Proc. ACM MOBISYS*, 2010.

[4] I. Constandache, X. Bao, M. Azizyan, and R. R. Choudhury. Did you see Bob?: human localization using mobile phones. In *Proc. ACM MOBICOM*, 2010.

[5] E. Cuervo, A. Balasubramanian, D. ki Cho, A. Wolman, S. Saroiu, R. Ch, and P. Bahl. MAUI: Making smartphones last longer with code offload. In *Proc. ACM MOBISYS*, 2010.

[6] W. Enck, P. Gilbert, B.-G. Chun, L. P. Cox, J. Jung, P. McDaniel, and A. N. Sheth. TaintDroid: an information-flow tracking system for realtime privacy monitoring on smartphones. In *USENIX Symposium on Operating Systems Design and Implementation (OSDI)*, 2010.

[7] H. Falaki, D. Lymberopoulos, R. Mahajan, R. Govindan, S. Kandula, and D. Estrin. Diversity in Smartphone Usage. In *Proc. ACM MOBISYS*, 2010.

[8] H. Falaki, D. Lymberopoulos, R. Mahajan, S. Kandula, and D. Estrin. A first look at traffic on smartphones. In *Proc. ACM SIGCOMM IMC*, 2010.

[9] Federal Emergency Management Agency. Tornado Activity in the United States. http://www.fema.gov/plan/prevent/saferoom/tsfs02_torn_activity.shtm.

[10] M. Ficek, T. Pop, P. Vláčil, K. Dufková, L. Kencl, and M. Tomek. Performance study of active tracking in a cellular network using a modular signaling platform. In *Proc. ACM MOBISYS*, 2010.

[11] A. Gember, A. Anand, and A. Akella. A Comparative Study of Handheld and Non-Handheld Traffic in Campus WiFi Networks. In *Proc. International Conference on Passive and Active Network Measurement (PAM)*, 2011.

[12] Google. Eric Schmidt at Mobile World Congress 2011. http://www.youtube.com/watch?v=ClkQA2Lb_iE&feature=related.

[13] B. D. Higgins, A. Reda, T. Alperovich, J. Flinn, T. J. Giuli, B. Noble, and D. Watson. Intentional networking: opportunistic exploitation of mobile network diversity. In *Proc. ACM MOBICOM*, 2010.

[14] J. Huang, Q. Xu, B. Tiwana, Z. M. Mao, M. Zhang, and P. Bahl. Anatomizing Application Performance Differences on Smartphones. In *Proc. ACM MOBISYS*, 2010.

[15] R. Keralapura, A. Nucci, Z.-L. Zhang, and L. Gao. Profiling users in a 3g network using hourglass co-clustering. In *Proc. ACM MOBICOM*, 2010.

[16] K. A. Li, T. Y. Sohn, S. Huang, and W. G. Griswold. Peopletones: a system for the detection and notification of buddy proximity on mobile phones. In *Proc. ACM MOBISYS*, 2008.

[17] Y. Liu, A. Rahmati, Y. Huang, H. Jang, L. Zhong, Y. Zhang, and S. Zhang. xShare: supporting impromptu sharing of mobile phones. In *Proc. ACM MOBISYS*, 2009.

[18] G. Maier, F. Schneider, and A. Feldmann. A first look at mobile hand-held device traffic. In *Proc. International Conference on Passive and Active Network Measurement (PAM)*, 2010.

[19] National Hurricane Center. National Hurricane Center. http://www.nhc.noaa.gov/pdf/TAFB_Trifold.pdf.

[20] F. Qian, Z. Wang, A. Gerber, Z. M. Mao, S. Sen, and O. Spatscheck. Characterizing radio resource allocation for 3G networks. In *Proc. ACM SIGCOMM IMC*, 2010.

[21] F. Qian, Z. Wang, A. Gerber, Z. M. Mao, S. Sen, and O. Spatscheck. Profiling Resource Usage for Mobile Applications: a Cross-layer Approach. In *Proc. ACM MOBISYS*, 2010.

[22] I. Trestian, S. Ranjan, A. Kuzmanovic, and A. Nucci. Measuring serendipity: connecting people, locations and interests in a mobile 3G network. In *Proc. ACM SIGCOMM IMC*, 2009.

[23] I. Trestian, S. Ranjan, A. Kuzmanovic, and A. Nucci. Taming User-Generated Content in Mobile. Networks via Drop Zones. In *Proc. IEEE INFOCOM*, 2009.

[24] Wikipedia. High-Speed Downlink Packet Access. http://en.wikipedia.org/wiki/High-Speed_Downlink_Packet_Access.

[25] Wikipedia. High-Speed Uplink Packet Access. http://en.wikipedia.org/wiki/High-Speed_Uplink_Packet_Access.

[26] W. Woerndl, C. Schueller, and R. Wojtech. A Hybrid Recommender System for Context-aware Recommendations of Mobile Applications. In *Proc. IEEE ICDE*, 2007.

[27] Q. Xu, A. Gerber, Z. M. Mao, and J. Pang. Acculoc: Practical localization of peformance measurement in 3g networks. In *Proc. ACM MOBISYS*, 2011.

[28] Q. Xu, J. Huang, Z. Wang, F. Qian, A. Gerber, and Z. M. Mao. Cellular data network infrastructure characterization and implication on mobile content placement. In *Proc. ACM SIGMETRICS*, 2011.

[29] B. Yan and G. Chen. AppJoy: Personalized Mobile Application Discovery. In *Proc. ACM MOBISYS*, 2011.

[30] L. Zhang, B. Tiwana, Z. Qian, Z. Wang, R. P. Dick, Z. M. Mao, and L. Yang. Accurate online power estimation and automatic battery behavior based power model generation for smartphones. In *Proc. IEEE/ACM/IFIP CODES+ISSS*, 2010.

Summary Review Documentation for

"Identifying Diverse Usage Behaviors of Smartphone Apps"

Authors: Q. Xu, J. Erman, A. Gerber, Z. Mao, J. Pang, S. Venkataraman

Reviewer #1

Strengths: This is an excellent paper that I enjoyed much reading. The paper is vey well organized, reads easily and the main results are backed up by a solid methodology as well as strong intuitions and justifications. This is the first paper that I am aware of which goes one step further in understanding smartphone usage, i.e., they open up the space of the smartphone applications segment.

Weaknesses: The strength of the paper resides in the smartphone apps and how they are grouped together, but little is said on how they are identified and grouped. I would have loved to understand the details on what the authors have exactly done to appreciate the robustness and reliability of their findings.

Comments to Authors: The authors mentioned that they have used the string reported in the USER-AGENT field of the HTTP protocol to identify the specific application name. But, to the best of my knowledge, many of these applications use a default string that is indicative of the company releasing the specific application rather than the specific application in question. For example, any game released by Zynga is labeled with Zynga (at least from the packet traces I have played with in the past) and not the specific game. If a company may offer distinct apps for different categories, then the overall accuracy of the application classification and grouping will be questionable. I would strongly advice the authors to add a paragraph or even more to explain exactly how this is done as this is a vital aspect of the entire paper. Same story on how they do application grouping. Their explanation is very short and surely deserves more room in the paper. Not clear after reading it twice whether they are using the exact method proposed by Erman et all in "Network-Aware forward Caching" based on the filed CONTENT-TYPE or use a grouping like the one done in the "Profiling users in a 3g network using hourglass co-clustering" by Keralapura et all (ACM Mobicom 2010). This should be explained in more details.

Reviewer #2

Strengths: Uncovers many aspects of how people use smartphones. While none of the results are terribly surprising, these authors are the first to do this kind of analysis and the results have interesting implications of network and content provisioning.

Weaknesses: The results are mostly along expected lines. Some of the analysis methods are not rigorous enough to be conclusive (although I still think the results will hold)

Comments to Authors: Let me first comment on the lack of rigor in the analysis. I'll pick examples from Sections 4.4 and 4.5, but a similar lack of consideration for random processes is missing from other sections as well.

In Section 4.5, you should draw confidence intervals for individual hours. This is important to reliably draw the kinds of conclusions you are drawing, given that the curves are pretty jumpy and you only have 7 data points per hour. The intervals will show if the differences that you are commenting on are statistically significant.

In Section 4.4, you need to compare the results to a uniform random process to put them in perspective. Even if there was no correlation in how a user acquires applications but if instead the acquisition of each application was a uniform random process, you would see dependency ratios higher than one. How much higher depends on the subscribers of the application.

I still believe that your findings will hold, but it is a matter of using the right tools and drawing correct conclusions from them.

What is the impact of focusing analysis on only popular apps on your estimates of how many apps are local? The filter you apply is more likely to filter out local apps, because of their inherent handicap in attracting a large number of users. What if you identified top apps by traffic volume per user (not total traffic, as you appear to do in Figure 4), so local apps are not disadvantaged?

In Table 3, you mention news, weather, and entertainment as locally popular apps in the same breath. That seems like you are selling a pre-conceived notion, because the numbers show that its basically just news. The raw numbers for music are in fact higher than weather. Perhaps you are basing your claim based on comparison with the aggregate PDF for popular apps in Table 1. In that case, it would be good to directly show that comparison.

I love Figure 8!

The travel area analysis of Section 4.3.3 is highly unsatisfying in the way it is done. There is not much useful I can conclude from it, besides some apps travel.

I suggest dropping the Jaccard similarity index analysis in Section 4.4. It does not add anything that is not already covered by the succeeding dependency ratio analysis. The latter analysis is more direct. (It is closer to what I was hoping for when I originally read the Jaccard analysis, modulo the appropriate normalization comment above.)

Did you attempt to cluster users based on the applications they use or the genres of applications they use? It will be very interesting if only a few clusters (e.g., heavy news users, games and music users, etc.) exist.

In Section 4.6, were "similar" set of apps being used across the three devices?
Out of curiosity, how did you simultaneously guarantee exactly one anonymized identifier per distinct device and non-reversibility of anonymous identifiers?

Reviewer #3

Strengths: With 3G data traffic rising faster than any other network traffic and most of this being due to smart-phone apps the paper is right on target in terms of relevance. The dataset is quite impressive and the analysis sound and extensive.

Weaknesses: The paper never goes deep in any of the topics that it touches.

Comments to Authors: This paper is a nice read and I am mostly positive about it, but it stays way too high in its treatment of the problem. At no place the paper goes deep to drill on a particular topic and make a sound contribution that goes beyond interesting, but rather general observation. What I am missing here is additional work in some part of the results in order to make a concrete connection between the measurement part and the uses discussed but not demonstrated at the end of the paper. If the authors would have used the data and their analysis to improve some aspect of either the network or the devices that run smart-apps then the paper would really be stellar.

Given that the data are not made available nor there is any re-usable model derived from them for others to use, I am wondering how much these works really contribute beyond anecdotal facts that do not however connect directly with some advancement in the field.

In Section 4.1 you state that the top app generates 50% of the total traffic volume but in Fig 1a there does not seem to be any category with 50% contribution. Something is wrong there.

Section 4.4 (especially at the end where it discusses the correlations between different apps) is really hand wavy. The paper is in general full of unsubstantiated claims and theories to the point that it really hurts rigor.

Reviewer #4

Strengths: - Unprecedented scales of data in terms of spatial application usage.
- The paper is clearly written.

Weaknesses: The paper dilutes the study into a "one by one" dimension study, with very little derivation of a real consequence. All results are finally formulated in a qualitative form that is completely expected (generally immediately explained by obvious intuition on what drives traffic) and not related to some of the implications in a precise way. It makes the observations very weak.
- No effort to position this paper in the area of results known on apps usage, it's not clear what is a confirmation and what is a surprising result, even relatively.

Comments to Authors: I think the paper goes a bit far in stating that scale and diversity is the final word to judge empirical results. Comparison and insights are also a primary need. Some studies have been made of smart usage and, in addition to that, one can easily develop some intuition on how apps behave. This paper is a full confirmation of each using a massive collection of data. It chooses not to compare to any previous study, even preliminary ones that had more limitations, so it seems like a brand new start, but without a real point of incremental knowledge to grasp.

I feel it is a debate we should have in IMC to see what to do with such submission. My personal bias goes in accepting this paper for its strengthening of our understanding and also gives priority to work that would, in the short time of a conference, have a chance to bring more important research in our community.

The paper chooses to ignore topics/questions that one would expect to see addressed.

1) First of all, a comparison of the findings with previous studies of popularity of websites, wired network, etc. It is not like spatial locality and access of data from different category happen on a network.

2) Second, a comparison of the findings with the "plethora of study" mentioned in related work about apps usage. Truly these studies concluded using a much more limited set of data, still it would matter to understand what we know better from this point on.

3) Third, how are the quantitative findings present in the data set turn into operational numbers? A good example is the "locality" of 20% of the application. Unfortunately, it seems that, although the applications were carefully selected to avoid obvious degenerate cases (very unpopular applications), it is not clear how much traffic this represents (especially with massive applications like the "social utility" responsible for huge amounts of traffic).

Another example is the presence of co-occurence and temporal variation. The paper states that this property can be exploited (which is obvious). The qualitative statement that this property exists brings little and no more work to translate them in concrete savings. Note in particular that the exploitation of the temporal variation is quite obscure.

4) Statement of contributions are too vague to attract real attention ("presenting results." "present aggregate results" is all that can be found in the abstract. The introduction concludes with a "We believe our study makes an important step".)

5) The following hypothesis seems an ad-hoc simplification used to highlight the importance of the result: "We do not expect users ... as a function of their geographical location": That would be true only if looking at equivalent users. Right now, it is clear that obvious variations of demographics (rural, urban, access to city) explain a lot of spatial variation, even without any location embedded in the actual application itself.

6) Implications are narrowed and remained vague or somewhat out of the blue ("if a user resort to a certain sleep aid ...": This seems not at all a spatial property, but a quite customized option to add to a phone as an add-on to be made by the users. It is very unclear what the provider should be doing that from the network (in terms of resource location).

Reviewer #5

Strengths: The traces analyzed are unique and large in scale, very different from what's been in the literature.

Weaknesses: The analyses are fairly standard.

Comments to Authors: The paper performs extensive analysis of a very interesting dataset. The analyses include popularity of applications, spatial distributions, their joint access patterns, temporal distribution, difference across platforms. Most analysis results are as we would expect. Certainly it is useful to confirm our intuition using real data. On the other hand, it would be nice to also see some unexpected results from the analysis, e.g., are there anomalies in any of these access patterns? How often do you see deviation and what are possible reasons for them?

In Section 4.2 "Popular smartphone applications": I found the filtering analysis not compelling. Why do you filter out applications just because it does not have too many users? Will such filtering prevent deployment of new applications as they all start with a small number of users?

It is good that the paper has a section on implications. The section could be strengthened by going beyond the obvious improvement. For example, placing content closer to the users certainly makes a lot of sense. But how accurately can we predict the user access pattern to support efficient content placement? In general, if you could have some concrete numbers about the potential saving, that would be very helpful.

Response from the Authors

1. We manually checked more smartphone apps to validate the correctness of querying the marketplace API with the USER-AGENT to categorize smartphone apps.
On Table 1, we manually check top 10, 20, 50, 100, 200, and 500 apps. We are confident on the correctness of the majority of smartphone apps. Among the top 500 apps, 427 apps are considered as correct by our manual check; 14 of them are considered as misclassified into the wrong category; and 69 of are considered as "unknown" because either we are uncertain on the correctness or querying the marketplace API responds with empty.

2. We differentiated and clarified the usage of "app" and "application". "app" is used in the context of individual programs running on smartphones, such as YouTube player, Google maps; while "application" is more abstract and general, such as "push notification", "content delivery service", etc.

3. We embedded more examples in the implication section. We add more examples make our implication more concrete and more convincing. For instance, In Section 5.1, we mention "...for national apps, the distribution of geographic coverage is still very dependent on the genre (e.g., weather apps are highly used in the south-eastern U.S), even the app's name (e.g., the news app headquartered in CHICAGO), etc..."

4. We calculated the contribution of traffic volume by local apps. In our submission, we mentioned that 20% apps are local; however, we didn't mention the contribution of these local apps, i.e., whether they are significant to cellular network operators. In total, these 20% local apps contribute 2% of the total traffic volume in the smartphone apps category.

5. We agree with these comments from Reviewer #2 on taking more consideration on "random process", but we didn't go that far. The main reason is that we didn't consider the "correlation" across apps at the granularity as fine as "happen before" relationship or "causality". Given a pair of apps (A, B), we simply counted how many users used both A and B, and how many users used either A or B.

6. We addressed these minor issues:
- In Section 4.1, "the top app generates 50% of the total traffic volume" is changed to "the top app generates 50% of the total traffic volume of the smartphone apps category".
- In Section 4.1, "86% of the total network access time" is changed to "86% of the total network access time of the smartphone apps category".

YouTube Everywhere: Impact of Device and Infrastructure Synergies on User Experience

Alessandro Finamore
Politecnico di Torino
finamore@tlc.polito.it

Marco Mellia
Politecnico di Torino
mellia@tlc.polito.it

Maurizio M. Munafò
Politecnico di Torino
munafo@tlc.polito.it

Ruben Torres
Purdue University
rtorresg@purdue.edu

Sanjay G. Rao
Purdue University
sanjay@purdue.edu

ABSTRACT

In this paper we present a complete measurement study that compares YouTube traffic generated by mobile devices (smart-phones, tablets) with traffic generated by common PCs (desktops, notebooks, netbooks). We investigate the users' behavior and correlate it with the system performance. Our measurements are performed using unique data sets which are collected from vantage points in nation-wide ISPs and University campuses from two countries in Europe and the U.S.

Our results show that the user access patterns are similar across a wide range of user locations, access technologies and user devices. Users stick with default player configurations, e.g., not changing video resolution or rarely enabling full screen playback. Furthermore it is very common that users abort video playback, with 60% of videos watched for no more than 20% of their duration.

We show that the YouTube system is highly optimized for PC access and leverages aggressive buffering policies to guarantee excellent video playback. This however causes 25%-39% of data to be unnecessarily transferred, since users abort the playback very early. This waste of data transferred is even higher when mobile devices are considered. The limited storage offered by those devices makes the video download more complicated and overall less efficient, so that clients typically download more data than the actual video size. Overall, this result calls for better system optimization for both, PC and mobile accesses.

Categories and Subject Descriptors

C.2 [**Computer-Communication Networks**]: Miscellaneous; C.4 [**Performance of systems**]: Measurement techniques

General Terms

Measurement, Performance

Keywords

Internet Measurement, YouTube, Video Streaming, Mobile Performance, Quality of Experience.

1. INTRODUCTION

Created in 2005 and bought by Google in November 2006, YouTube is the most popular and bandwidth intensive service of today's Internet: it accounts for 20-35% of the Internet traffic [6, 9, 8] with 35 hours of videos uploaded every minute and more than 700 billion playbacks in 2010 [15, 16]. With such a high popularity, it presents a challenge both for the system itself and for the Internet Service Providers (ISP) that need to offer good quality of service for video streaming demands. Therefore the YouTube phenomenon attracted the interest of the research community, with several works [7, 17, 3, 4, 1, 11, 13] focusing on either video characterization, infrastructure, or user behavior.

A second recent change in the way people access the Internet is due to the exploding popularity of mobile devices. Smartphones and Internet tablets are today commonly used both at home and at public places, and the phenomenon is still growing in popularity. Recent estimates forecast that within a few years mobile devices will be the users' preferred choice for accessing the Internet [10] while according to [9, 12] multimedia content represents already a big share of the mobile traffic, with YouTube as the main contributor. Still, mobile operators are struggling with the intrinsically limited capacity of mobile access technologies.

The mix of the two phenomena has serious implications for both content providers and ISPs. Indeed, while YouTube is already commonly accessible on mobile devices from 3G/4G networks, the video encoding rate (and quality) is, by design, much more limited than the one offered to PCs. At the same time, mobile ISPs adopt tariff plans with the explicit goal to limit the amount of traffic a device can consume, a trend that is becoming popular among wired ISPs as well.

In this paper, we focus on the differences and similarities of YouTube usage when accessed from a regular "PC player" or from a "mobile player". The first category includes accesses performed from a regular web browser equipped with the Adobe Flash plugin on a standard PC, e.g., a desktop, a notebook, or a netbook. The second category includes accesses performed through the special mobile version of the YouTube portal, or through the custom application found on devices running Apple iOS, Google Android, or other smartphone operating systems. By dissecting the YouTube traffic observed in operational networks, we explore the impact of devices and corresponding infrastructure synergies on the user experience and the network. Our data sets span over three different countries, including customers in both the United States and Europe, both campus and residential networks, with very different access technologies, i.e., high speed campus LANs, WiFi hot-spots and home Access Points, ADSL and Fiber-To-The-Home links. In each vantage point, we monitored all YouTube traffic for a one-week long period of time.

Our paper exposes the fact that YouTube is highly optimized to deliver video to PC users and considerably more inefficient in serving requests from mobile devices.

To the best of our knowledge, this is the first work to present an in-depth analysis of the YouTube system accessed from mobile devices. Moreover, performing a systematic comparison respect to common PCs, and taking advantage of our unique and heterogeneous data sets, we derive a comprehensive set of results. Our key findings are:

Users access content in the same manner independently of the device used:

i) content downloaded has the same characteristics both in size and duration in all vantage points;

ii) the type of device does not modify the way people watch YouTube videos. Most of the watched videos are interrupted within the first 40 seconds, with only 10% of them lasting more than 50% of the actual video duration;

iii) people stick with default parameters, with negligible voluntary change of video resolution, and marginal fraction of views in full screen mode.

YouTube adopts different mechanisms according to the device used: the download is highly optimized for PC based players, while mobile players show consistently worse performance. This is related to the limited capabilities of the mobile devices but results show that the mechanisms used by YouTube to serve this type of devices cause i) higher access time, ii) lower download rate, iii) more bursty traffic which impair the quality achieved by mobile players.

The amount of traffic downloaded by clients but not used by the player is large:

i) due to aggressive buffering policies, 25-39% of downloaded traffic is useless when PCs are used; this fraction grows to 35-48% when mobile devices are considered;

ii) due to a possibly unoptimized implementation in the mobile players, the amount of data transferred exceeds the actual video size in 15-25% of the cases.

The last two findings are striking, and call for a possible system improvement, especially for mobile players. This is of crucial importance considering the growing popularity of mobile devices. Although our data set does not include 3G/4G mobile access clients, we believe this is even more critical for those operators for which the lack of bandwidth is and will be always a bottleneck.

The remaining of the paper is organized as follows: Sec. 2 provides a high level description of the YouTube protocols; the data sets are described in Sec. 3; details on the YouTube traffic characteristics are shown in Sec. 4; Sec. 5 and Sec. 6 detail the user behavior and performance, respectively; related work is discussed in Sec. 7, and a summary of our findings in Sec. 8.

2. YOUTUBE PRIMER

In this section we provide a high level description of the protocol used to retrieve the video content. In general, two phases can be distinguished: 1) content look-up, 2) content download and playback. The first phase is typically performed using a web browser or a custom application running on the local client and querying regular websites (e.g., youtube.com, or a website that embeds a YouTube video). The second phase starts after the user selects the video of interest. This involves resolving the video server hostname and subsequently downloading the video stream from the server. YouTube employs DNS-based mechanisms to direct clients to a server in a data center close to the user. However, in some cases, HTTP-based signaling can be exploited to further redirect the user to other video servers (e.g., in the case of server congestion, or content unavailability) [13]. In this paper, we focus our analysis on the second phase.

YouTube can be accessed from a wide range of devices, each with different capabilities and hardware constraints. Depending on the client device, two mechanisms are used to retrieve the video content:

• PC-player: the client is a regular PC running either a web browser with the Adobe Flash plugin or HTML5 compliant browser[1]. We performed experiments with several browsers and operating systems and found no difference in the traffic they exchange during the second phase. Hence, we will refer to them as PC-player without further distinction[2].

• Mobile-player: the client is a smartphone, an Internet tablet or a set-top-box which uses a custom application[3]. Also in this case we tested different combination of devices running both Apple iOS, Google Android and other operating systems. While several differences are found when considering the first phase, they all behave similarly in the second phase. Therefore, we will refer to them as Mobile-player.

Fig. 1 sketches the temporal evolution of the HTTP messages exchanged between the client and the YouTube servers. The top plot refers to the PC-player while the bottom plot refers to the Mobile-player. Clients exchange messages either with a *front-end server*, *web content servers* or *video servers*. The front-end handles the access to the YouTube portal (www.youtube.com and m.youtube.com), the web content servers provide thumbnails or other content while the video servers are in charge of the streaming. In the HTTP requests the downloaded video is identified by its *videoID* - a unique 11 characters long identifier. In the following we detail the HTTP messages that will be considered in our analysis to study the evolution of a download.

2.1 PC-player

Let us consider a client accessing the www.youtube.com web site from a regular PC using a browser as shown in Fig. 1 (top). We can split the interaction between the browser and the YouTube servers in three steps: (1) video web page retrieval, (2) video prefetch and (3) video download.

During (1), the client downloads the web page describing the video. The HTML document contains a combination of text and other "objects" (e.g., the Adobe Flash player)

[1]http://www.youtube.com/html5

[2]Notebooks and netbooks using regular browsers belong to the PC-player category.

[3]Even if set-top-boxes and TV appliances are hardly mobile, they use the same access mechanism as smartphones, so we consider them in the Mobile-player category.

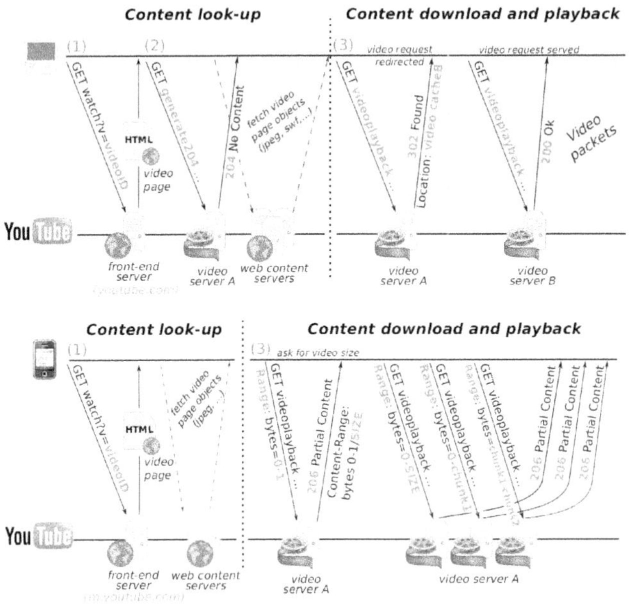

Figure 1: YouTube video download mechanisms. Example of possible evolution when accessing to *youtube.com* from a PC (top) and *m.youtube.com* from a smartphone (bottom).

that the browser needs to fetch to properly display the page. Among the different objects, a Javascript function triggers a `generate204` request sent to the video server that is supposed to serve the video. This starts the video prefetch (2), which has two main goals: first, it forces the client to perform the DNS resolution of the video server hostname. Second, it forces the client to open a TCP connection toward the video server. Both help to speed-up the video download phase. In addition, the `generate204` request has exactly the same format and options of the real video download request, so that the video server is eventually warned that a client will possibly download that video very soon. Note that the video server replies with a `'204 No Content'` response, as implied by the command name, and no video content is downloaded so far.

At this point, the browser handles the control to the Flash player which will manage the actual video download (3). The player sends a HTTP `videoplayback` request to get the video. Note that the same TCP connection previously opened during (2) can be used if HTTP persistent capability is supported between the browser and the Flash plugin. Because of server congestion or lack of content, the server can *redirect* the client to other servers [13]. In this case, the video server replies with a HTTP `'302 Found'` response which specifies the hostname of another video server to contact. The player then resolves the hostname, and sends a new `videoplayback` request. This process can repeat until a valid video server is found. The final video server of the chain replies with the usual HTTP `'200 OK'` response, which initiates the stream of video data to the client.

We highlight that the `generate204` request is a specific optimization that is found only when accessing a video through www.youtube.com. YouTube videos embedded in regular HTML pages do not exploit this, so the player have to resolve the video server hostname yet before sending the first `videoplayback` request.

2.2 Mobile-player

Mobile devices use a different protocol as shown in bottom part of Fig. 1. First, no prefetch message is sent in the content look-up phase. Second, differently from the PC-player case, the video content is downloaded in "chunks", each one requested in a separate TCP connection, using the HTTP `Range` header field to specify the requested portion of the video. The video server then replies with a `'206 Partial Content'` response.

This mechanism is possibly the result of a design choice that tries to cope with the tighter constraints in terms of storage availability for mobile devices. In fact, the mobile devices can hardly buffer the entire video so the player progressively requests portions according to the evolution of the playback.

In the following sections we will investigate the impact of the different mechanisms both on the user experience and on the system infrastructure.

3. DATA COLLECTION

In this section we first introduce the tool we use to collect the traffic, giving a high level description of the algorithms employed to classify the YouTube traffic. Then, we present the collected data sets that we used for the analysis.

3.1 Collection tool

To inspect the network traffic we relied on Tstat [5, 14], an Open Source packet sniffer with Deep Packet Inspection (DPI) capabilities, which implements both traffic classifiers and fine-grained flow-level statistics. Tstat is able to rebuild TCP flows by monitoring packets that are sent and received by clients. Leveraging on this, we improved Tstat so as to identify and we distinguish all possible HTTP messages that can be observed when a client downloads a YouTube video. In this paper, we focus only on the `videoplayback` and `generate204` requests from the client, and distinguish among all possible server replies (HTTP 200, 204, 206, 302 responses). By parsing the URL of the HTTP messages, we can identify PC-player and Mobile-player accesses[4] and extract specific video information, such as the videoID and the video format. We also extract other video related information from the video header, such as the resolution, total duration and size of the video.

In addition to the video properties, we also collect several TCP flow-level statistics, such as the total number of packets and bytes transmitted and received, the total flow duration and the average RTT[5]. Further information on Tstat capabilities as well as the source code can be obtained from [5, 14].

3.2 Data sets

We collected data sets at five vantage points spread across three countries including both Points-of-Presence (PoP) in nation-wide ISPs and University campuses. These data sets

[4]URL requests from mobile devices contain `app=youtube_gdata` or `app=youtube_mobile`. We do not make any further distinction on the type of browser or mobile device used.

[5]RTT is estimated by leveraging TCP acknowledgements [5, 14]

Name	Type	Flows	Vol.[GB]	SrcIP	Videos
US-Campus	Campus	2,172,250	10,898	20,455	446,870
EU1-Campus	Campus	173,024	714	1,203	50,205
EU1-ADSL	Home	740,330	2,615	8,154	189,788
EU1-FTTH	Home	135,907	480	1,136	33,762
EU2-ADSL	Home	830,476	3,688	5,826	205,802

Table 1: Data sets collected.

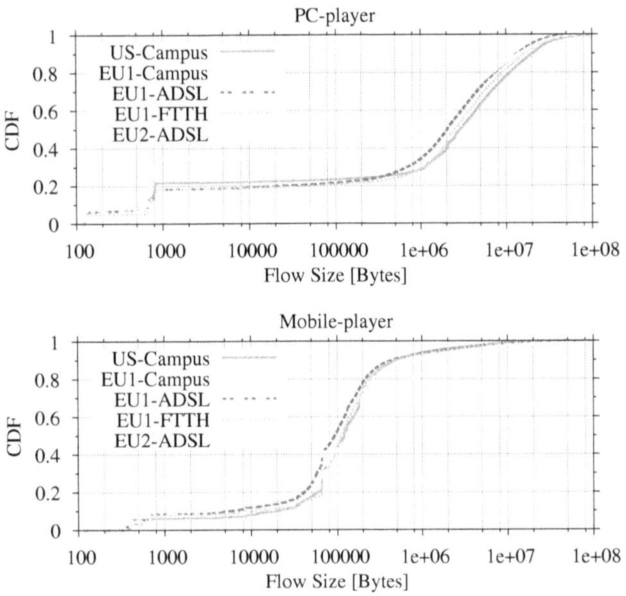

Figure 2: Distribution of the TCP flow size.

represent a unique heterogeneous mix of users and technologies. At each vantage point, we installed a *probe* consisting of a high-end PC running Tstat and monitoring all traffic generated by local clients.

This paper focuses on one-week long traces, collected simultaneously at the five locations, starting at 12:00 AM (local time) on February 25th, 2011. Table 1 summarizes the data sets reporting the name, the type of customers, the total number of YouTube video flows and the corresponding volume of bytes, the number of distinct client IP addresses and the number of videos downloaded. Overall, the data sets account for more than 16 TB of traffic, more than 900,000 videos, and more than 35,000 different client IP addresses.

The Home data sets have been collected from nation-wide ISPs of two different European countries. EU1-ADSL and EU1-FTTH correspond to two different PoPs within the same ISP aggregating users with ADSL and Fiber-To-The-Home (FTTH) access technology. The campus data sets are collected in two different University campus networks, one in the United Stated and the other in Europe. To confirm the popularity of YouTube service, we observe that in all monitored networks the volume of traffic generated by YouTube videos accounts for more than 25% of the total traffic during peak time. Finally, note that the mobile traffic collected in our data sets refers to devices accessing the Internet via WiFi access networks and not via 3G/4G ISPs.

4. FLOW AND VIDEO CHARACTERISTICS

We begin our analysis by giving an overview of the traffic generated by PC-player and Mobile-player clients. Fig. 2 reports the Cumulative Distribution Function (CDF) of TCP flow sizes, i.e., number of bytes (B) received by the client in a flow. Let us focus on the PC-player traffic (top plot). Steps in the CDF clearly show the presence of flows of typical size corresponding to specific HTTP messages: `'204 No Content'` flows are about 120 B long, `'302 Found'` flows are in the [800-1000] B range, while flows containing the `200 OK` responses are typically longer than 80 kB since they contain the actual video data. Interestingly, the initial part of the distribution is different for different probes, with EU1-Campus and EU2-ADSL suffering a higher fraction of redirections (`'302 Found'`) messages. However, the tail of the distribution looks rather similar, suggesting that the size of videos downloaded in the networks monitored is similar. We will detail this better in Sec. 5.

Looking at results for Mobile-player (bottom plot), we observe that the flow size is similar across data sets, with EU1-Campus and EU2-ADSL still exhibiting higher fraction of redirection messages. However, comparing PC-player and Mobile-player we observe interesting differences: (i) the absence of the prefetching phase causes the `'204 No Content'` responses, of size 120B, to disappear in Mobile-player; (ii) the abundant presence of the HTTP requests using the `Range` header field causes the flows carrying the video data to be one order of magnitude shorter than in PC-player. This is a direct artifact of the video chunking mechanisms and not a difference in the actual video duration and size (see Fig. 3 and Fig. 4). Interestingly, the 500B long flows are due to `'206 Partial Content'` replies to the first `videoplayback` request using the `'Range: bytes 0-1'` header which Mobile-player uses to discover the actual video size from the HTTP response field (see Sec. 2.2).

The effect of the chunking mechanism adopted by Mobile-player has clearly an impact on the number of flows generated by mobile devices to download the content. Table 2 quantifies this by reporting the fraction of flows and bytes that are due to Mobile-player for the different data sets. We can notice that, while Mobile-player traffic is a small fraction of the total volume, it accounts for a much larger fraction of flows. This might pose performance issues on flow-based devices, like NAT boxes or full-state firewalls which keep per-flow state.

Name	%Flows	%Bytes
US-Campus	32.5	3.5
EU1-Campus	15.6	2.8
EU1-ADSL	27.2	3.9
EU1-FTTH	42.2	6.6
EU2-ADSL	4.2	1.6

Table 2: Fraction of flows and bytes due to mobile terminals.

Consider now the volume of bytes. Unexpectedly, only less than 6% of YouTube traffic is due to users from mobile devices. The networks we consider offer both wired and WiFi access with large penetration of smartphones, especially in the campus networks. Therefore, one would expect that a large fraction of YouTube accesses is done from such terminals. Our measurements contrast this intuition. Moreover, some recent studies [6, 9] show that multimedia content is responsible for more than 40% of the total volume due to wireless terminals, with YouTube as the main contributor. Our results show that this traffic is little compared to the volume

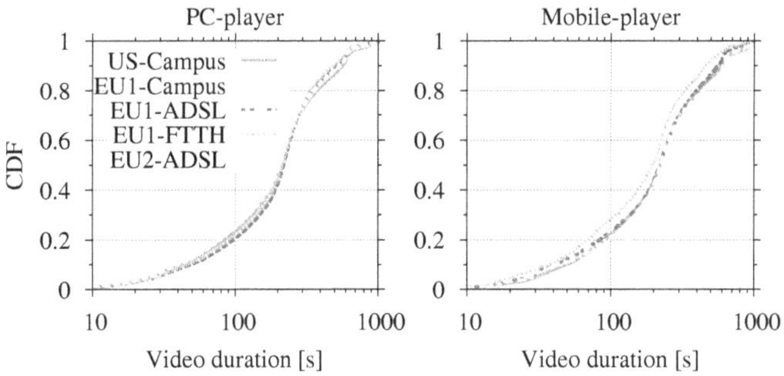

Figure 3: CDF of video duration.

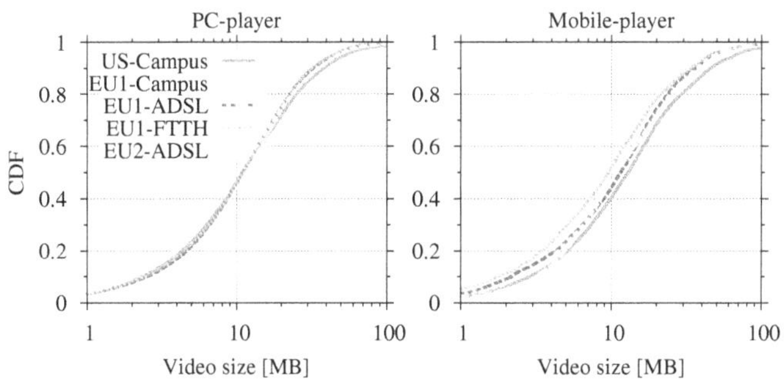

Figure 4: CDF of video size.

generated by wired networks. A possible explanation for this is the fact that wireless users in our networks still prefer to access YouTube videos from standard PC browsers, because of the better user experience compared to smartphones.

4.1 Video content duration and size

Fig. 3 reports the duration, in time, of videos for both PC-player (left) and Mobile-player (right). Note that this corresponds to the duration of the complete video and not to the portion of video watched by the user[6]. Considering the PC-player scenario, and comparing the measurements from the different data sets, we notice that there is great similarity across vantage points so that it is impossible to distinguish among them. For example, in all vantage points, 40% of the videos last less than 3 min, and less than 5% of the videos last more than 10 min.

Consider now the Mobile-player case. We observe a slightly moderate difference among the video duration accessed from different probes (notice the log-scale on the x-axis). Still, 40-50% of all videos accessed from mobile terminals are shorter than 3 minutes, and 5% of videos last more than 10 minutes. Indeed, the Mobile-player and the PC-player CDFs are very similar among them too.

This result shows that people with very different cultural bias (e.g., Europeans vs Americans, students vs residential users), using very different terminals (smartphones vs PCs) and with different Internet access bandwidth (ADSL vs FTTH vs WiFi vs Ethernet) produce and consume the same type of content: short videos which can be quickly watched from YouTube. At the aggregation level that we

[6]This information is extracted from the video metadata.

ID	Video Codec	Audio Codec	Container	Res.	Name
13	H.263	AMR	3GP	144p	others
17	MPEG-4 ASP	AAC	3GP		others
5	FLV1	MP3	FLV	240p	240p-Fl
36	H.264	AAC	3GP		others
34	H.264	AAC	FLV	360p	360p-Fl*
18	H.264	AAC	MP4		360p-Mp+
43	VP8	Vorbis	WebM		others
35	H.264	AAC	FLV	480p	480p-Fl
44	VP8	Vorbis	WebM		others
22	H.264	AAC	MP4	720p	720p-Mp
45	VP8	Vorbis	WebM		others
37	H.264	AAC	MP4	1080p	others
38	H.264	AAC	MP4	3072p	others

(*) PC-player default format , (+) Mobile-player default format

Table 3: YouTube supported video formats.

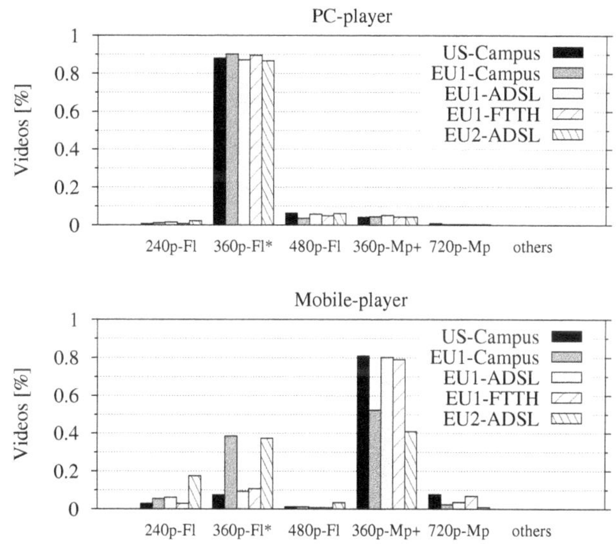

Figure 5: Fraction of videos for popular video format.

study, this reflect the distribution of video duration of the YouTube service.

Fig. 4 reports the total video size in bytes of the videos that have been seen in our data sets. We find very similar results across traces and devices. This is counterintuitive, since we would expect the distribution to be more variable, e.g., due to the availability of videos with different resolutions, and different encoding formats. In addition, intuition would suggest that the video size would be larger for PC-player than for Mobile-player, to better accommodate the limited resources of smartphones. But this is also not clear in the graph. To understand this better, in the next section we dig into the impact of video codecs and resolutions.

4.2 Video format characterization

A "video" is a complex object that multiplexes encoded video and audio streams. Encoding is done according to different algorithms, and the result is then organized into a container of different type. The combination of the encoding algorithm, video resolution, and the type of container defines the *video format*. A plethora of video formats are available, some of which are proprietary while others are standard.

YouTube supports the formats listed in Table 3. Each format is identified by a unique ID corresponding to the `itag` parameter in the video request. Each ID corresponds to a unique combination of video codec, audio codec, container and resolution. The last column shows the naming convention we used in this paper to identify each format. A marker highlights the YouTube default video format.

The variety of formats reflects the evolution of the system and technology over the last years. In the early days, only Flash Video (FLV) content was supported only at 240p resolution. In 2007 the MP4 container was introduced along with resolution 360p. This switch was driven by the introduction of new devices that did not support FLV videos (e.g., Apple iOS devices). There are also 3GP formats, which are specific for mobile devices, and the more recent WebM formats [15], which are part of the HTML5 specifications. As of today, H.264 video codec is the most widely adopted standard. Note that when the user uploads a new video, the system automatically generates the different video formats and makes them available to download.

At playback time, the user can eventually choose among multiple resolutions via the player graphical user interface. For PCs, the Adobe Flash player presents a menu button listing the available resolutions, e.g., 240p, 360p and 480p. Some Mobile-players instead present a toggle button with the choices of "high" and "low" quality, without explicit indication of the resolutions.

The supported formats do not have the same popularity. Fig. 5 reports the breakdown of video formats considering PC-player and Mobile-player data sets on top and bottom plots, respectively. There is a clear difference respect to the device used to access the video: Flash based formats are largely preferred by PC-player, while MP4 is the preferred container for Mobile-player. This is not surprising considering that Apple iOS products (e.g., iPhone, iPad, iPod touch) cannot handle FLV content. The higher fraction for Flash based formats in the Mobile-player data sets in EU1-Campus and EU2-ADSL may be related to different popularity of devices among certain users (e.g., students) to prefer smartphones running the Android operating system or Windows Mobile which support Flash content.

The default video resolution offered to PC-player is 360p, while Mobile-players tries to retrieve the best available quality according to the network/device capabilities. This causes 720p format (also known as High Definition - HD) to be more popular for Mobile-player than PC-player and this difference is the result of a system design choice.

The previous findings hold true independent from the vantage point, showing the ubiquitousness of the YouTube service. We expect this to change in 3G/4G networks, where the 3GP formats are known to be used and low resolution videos are offered by default.

4.3 Video encoding bitrate

Given a codec and a video resolution, the video quality has a strict relation with the *video encoding bitrate*. It is therefore interesting to observe what is the typical encoding bitrate of YouTube videos. Fig. 6 reports the CDF of the video encoding bitrate for the most important video formats. Each curve aggregates statistics from all videos of the data sets (each single data set presents the same distribution, being this a system choice). MP4-based formats are highlighted by line-points patterns. In general, the actual encoding bitrate is the minimum between the maximum allowed bitrate, and the bitrate that allows to achieve the desired quality. The latter depends on the video content, e.g., more static video sequences allow to reach lower encoding bitrate. This is reflected in the curves. For example, consider 240p-Fl (FLV) videos. The sharp knee around 300 kbps is the effect of the maximum bitrate limit, which is reached by 70% of videos. About 30% of videos are instead quality limited. Similarly, 360p-Mp (MP4) videos are configured to not exceed 600 kb/s, with most of the videos being quality limited. In some cases, the maximum bound of the video encoding rate can be violated as shown for example for the 10% of 240p-Fl videos. This can be due to a change in the encoding parameters that happened at some time.

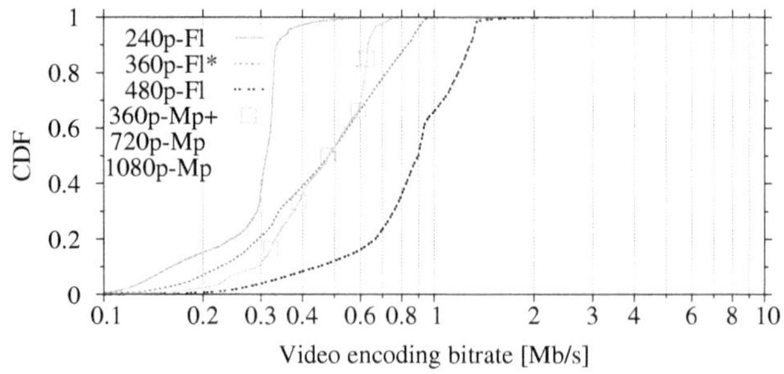

Figure 6: CDF of video encoding bitrate.

It is known that the higher is the resolution, the higher is the bitrate. For example, the 360p videos (currently the default choice) do not exceed 1 Mb/s video rate, while 480p video bitrate goes up to 1.5 Mb/s. 720p and 1080p require up to 3 Mb/s and 6 Mb/s respectively. This allows to speculate on the impact of YouTube switching to higher resolution by default. For example, defaulting to 480p would correspond to almost double the amount of traffic due to YouTube, with possibly large impact on both the YouTube CDN and on ISP networks. Going to 720p as the default choice would correspond to multiply by a factor of 4 the offered traffic. Given that YouTube already accounts for more than 20% of Internet traffic and assuming the user demand remains the same, this would correspond to a critical traffic surge that might impair the YouTube service itself.

5. USER BEHAVIOR AND IMPLICATIONS

In this section we focus our attention on the way people watch videos from the YouTube system, observing if they interact with the GUI, e.g., switching resolution or going in full screen mode, and which portion of the video people actually watches. Both have interesting implication on the workload the system has to handle and the efficiency it achieves in serving the requests. We first introduce the concept of *video session* which is required to characterize the user's behavior.

5.1 Methodology

As we have already seen in Sec. 4, video can be downloaded in multiple TCP connections, which is predominantly the case for Mobile-player. To illustrate this, Fig. 7 shows

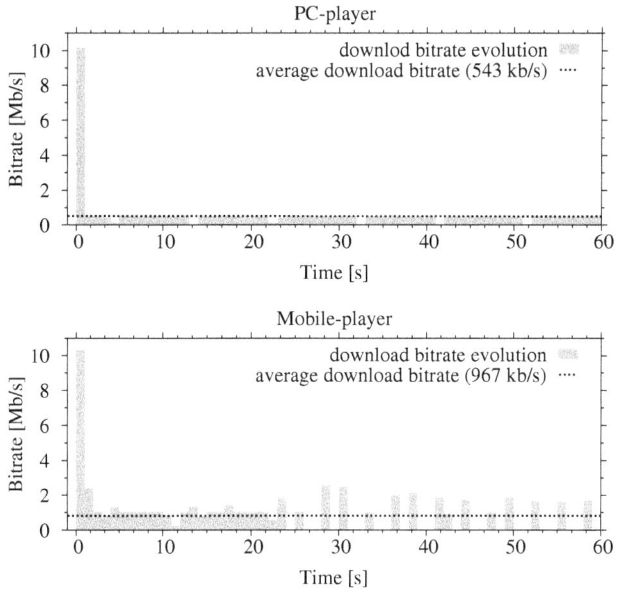

Figure 7: Evolution over time of the download bitrate for a video encoded at 540 kb/s.

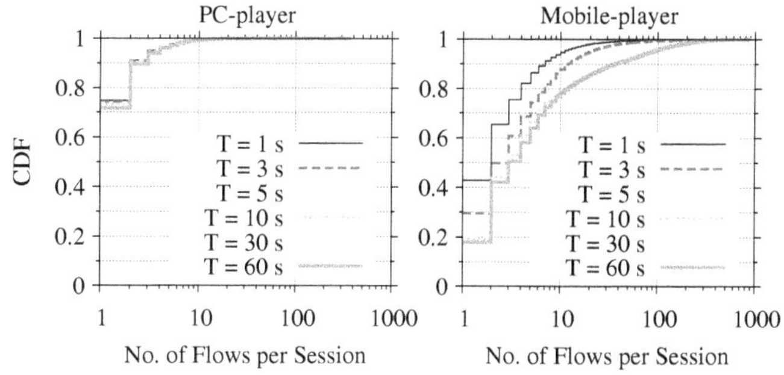

Figure 8: Sensitivity of the number of TCP connections per session for different values of T. EU1-ADSL data set.

	PC-player			Mobile-player		
Data set	0	1	>1	0	1	>1
US-Campus	95.10	4.60	0.30	99.75	0.19	0.05
EU1-Campus	96.62	3.12	0.27	99.28	0.61	0.10
EU1-ADSL	95.27	4.45	0.28	99.63	0.28	0.09
EU1-FTTH	95.73	3.99	0.28	99.39	0.42	0.19
EU2-ADSL	95.14	4.40	0.46	98.07	1.36	0.57

Table 4: Percentage of resolution switch.

the bitrate evolution obtained downloading the same video from a PC (top) and a mobile device (bottom) inside the EU1-Campus network. In both cases, the server starts sending an initial burst of data at a very fast rate to quickly fill the play-out buffer at the player. This mechanism is conventionally called "fast-start". The server then starts shaping the rate as observed in [2]. Note that this is a server-based shaping mechanism in which the client has no role (neither application layer nor TCP flow control messages are sent). For PC-player, after the initial burst, the download proceeds within the same single TCP connection, whose throughput is practically equal to the average video encoding rate (dotted line). Note that the average download rate is computed discarding the initial burst.

For Mobile-player instead, the bitrate evolution is more bursty. This is a consequence of leveraging different TCP connections to download chunks of video. Indeed, from second 23 and on, the mobile terminal aborts the ongoing TCP connection, and starts requesting chunks of video on separate TCP connections. They last about 1 second and are separated in time by about 2 seconds of silence. Since a new TCP connection is used, the server enters the "fast-start" phase, which is early interrupted when the client aborts the underlying TCP connection. We believe this mechanism is due to a client-side buffer management policy which abruptly interrupts the TCP connection when the play-out buffer is filled up. The client then re-starts the download when the buffer depletes below a certain threshold. This results in an inflation of TCP connections, and a possible inefficient download.

The early abortion of the TCP connection can be due to other causes as well. For example, a resolution change or a fast-forward in the video are handled by aborting the current download and starting a new one for both PC-player and Mobile-player. Finally, the initial control messages possibly sent on separate TCP connections are also fundamentals to capture the dynamics of the download.

To capture the variety of behaviors for downloading a video, we use the concept of "video session", i.e., a mechanism to group all connections related to the download of the same content. More specifically, a video session corresponds to the set of TCP connections that i) share the same source IP address and *videoID* and ii) are separated by a silence period shorter than T seconds. For instance, two connections c_1 and c_2 belong to the same session if the difference in time between the beginning of c_2 (time of the TCP SYN packet) and the end of c_1 (time of the last packet observed) is smaller than T.

Fig. 8 reports the number of connections per session for different values of T. The EU1-ADSL data set is considered, but other data sets show identical results. The choice of T is not critical for PC-player, while $T > 5$ s is required to properly aggregate Mobile-player connections. In the following, we set $T = 60$ s, a conservative choice to better capture users actions that could happen after the download has been completed but while the playback is still running.

Fig. 8 also shows the impact of the Mobile-player mechanisms in the number of connections per session. While for PC-player, only 2% of the sessions have more than 6 connections, for Mobile-player more than 4% of the sessions involve more than 100 connections.

5.2 Resolution switch

Given the above definition of a session, a change of video resolution is easily detected by observing requests with the same *videoID*, but different video format.

Table 4 reports the percentage of sessions involving zero, one or more than one resolution switch for both PC-player and Mobile-player. Surprisingly, results show that a resolution switch happens for less than 5% of PC-player sessions. This is an example of inertia, where users stick with the default video format. This also shows that users are possibly

Data set	Low-to-High	High-to-Low
US-Campus	95.7	4.3
EU1-Campus	86.1	13.9
EU1-ADSL	93.9	6.1
EU1-FTTH	90.5	9.5
EU2-ADSL	83.6	16.4

Table 5: Percentage of resolution switch breakdown for PC-player.

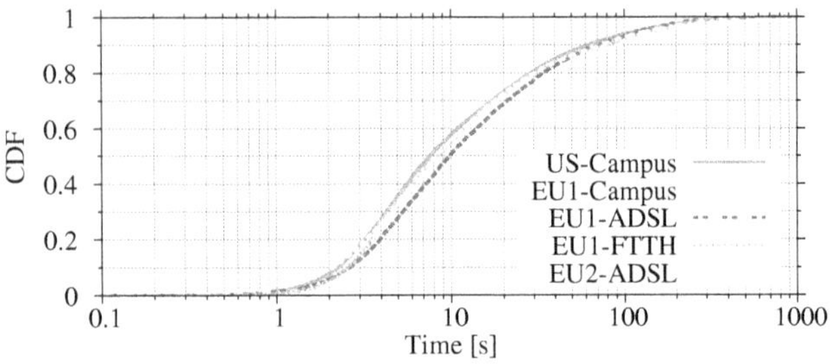

Figure 9: Time at which Low-to-High resolution switch happens.

not interested in this feature or they are unaware of it. For Mobile-player the choice of resolution is either hidden or not available, and a marginal fraction of users exploit it.

We can further classify the resolution changes in "Low-to-High" and "High-to-Low" considering the involved video resolution. Table 5 reports the breakdown. We can see that the Low-to-High resolution switch is largely predominant, with more than 80% (for all traces) being a 360p-Fl to 480p-Fl switch. Interestingly, when the full screen playback is enabled, the Flash player automatically switches from 360p-Fl to 480p-Fl (the converse is not true). Combining Tables 4 and 5, we can conjecture that full screen mode is not popular, but it is the main cause of resolution switch.

As final note, the largest majority of High-to-Low switch are 360p-Fl to 240p-Fl. This suggests that those are triggered by the user because of bad performance. EU2-ADSL and EU1-Campus show a slightly larger High-to-Low switch fraction. As we will see in the following, those are the two vantage points with slightly worse performance.

To complete the analysis, we investigate when the resolution switch is triggered. Fig. 9 shows the CDF of the time between the session start and Low-to-High resolution switch. Due to buffering at the player, this is an overestimate of the actual switch time. 50% of these events happens in the first 10 seconds, while only 10% of users trigger them after 1 minute. In terms of video size, more than 80% of the switches happens in the first 20% of the video data download while only 5% occurs in the second half of the video. The same consideration holds for High-to-Low changes. Overall we can conclude that resolution changes are usually performed at the very beginning of the playback.

We find surprising that results are practically identical in all data sets despite differences in users habits and cultures.

5.3 Fraction of watched video

We now focus our attention on the time a user spends watching a video. To measure this, we leverage the fact that the player abruptly aborts the video download if the user changes the web page on the browser (or custom player).

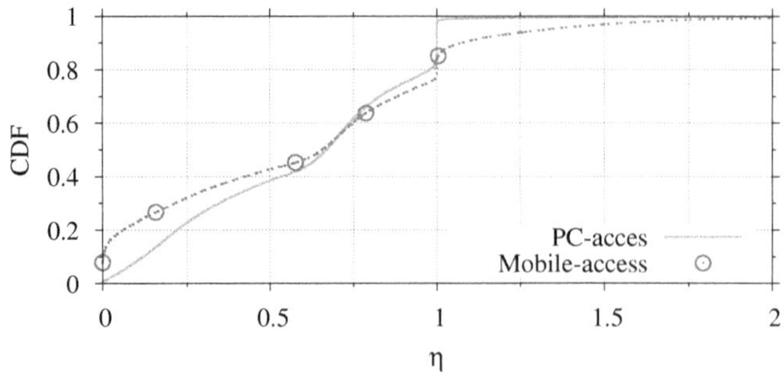

Figure 10: CDF of the fraction of downloaded video bytes. EU1-ADSL data set.

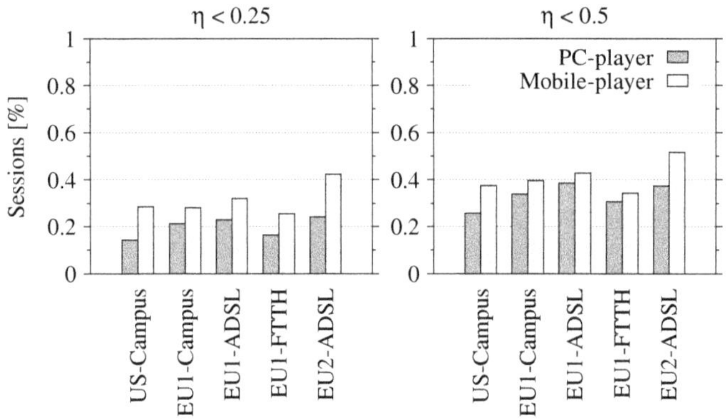

Figure 11: Fraction of video downloads having $\eta < 0.25$ and $\eta < 0.50$

Let η be the fraction of downloaded video within a session with respect to the actual video size. If $\eta < 1$, then the user did not watch the entire video[7].

Fig. 10 shows the CDF for η for EU1-ADSL data set. Two observations hold: i) about 80% of video sessions are abruptly interrupted; ii) Mobile-player results show that the player can download *more* data than the video size ($\eta > 1$). We will investigate this better next.

To better compare results, Fig. 11 details the fraction of video downloads having $\eta < 0.25$ and $\eta < 0.5$ for different data sets. Interestingly, results are similar for all vantage points, with users on Mobile-player consistently aborting earlier than users on PC-player. Fig. 12 details the absolute and relative time at which the user stops watching the video on the left and right plots, respectively. It shows that people tend to abort the playback very soon, with 60% of videos being watched for less than 20% of their duration. This can be due to a mismatch between the users' interests and the content they find on YouTube. Notice that this is also an interesting fact that could be exploited to better handle the content distribution among the CDN nodes, e.g., caching only some portion of each video. The impact of Mobile-player versus PC-player is very limited, testifying

[7]By checking the `Range` header field for requests, we filter out those sessions in which the user fast-forward the playback to a position outside the already buffered portion of the video.

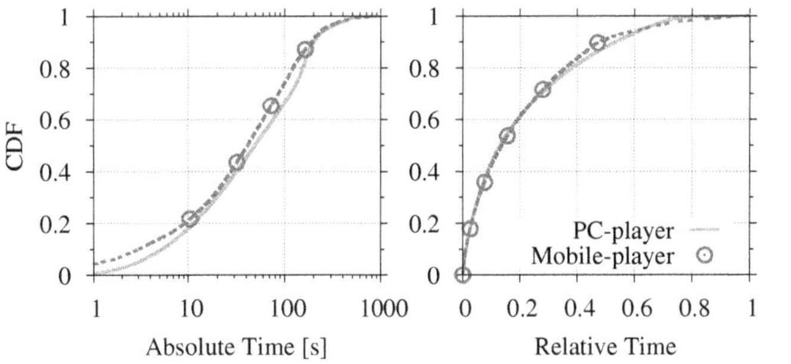

Figure 12: CDF of absolute (left) and relative (right) portions of watched videos for sessions with incomplete downloads. EU1-ADSL data set.

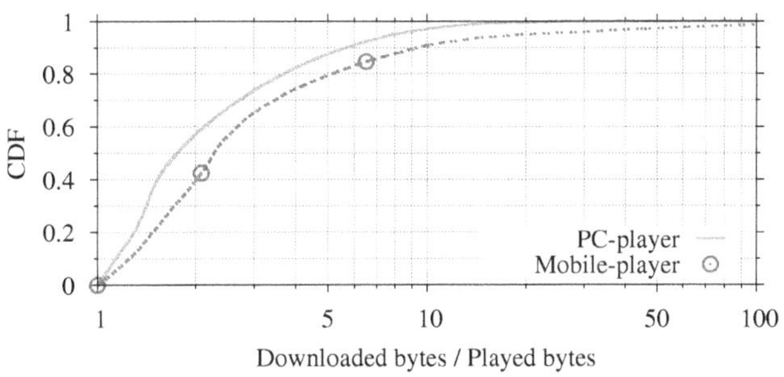

Figure 13: CDF of ratio between downloaded bytes and played bytes. EU1-ADSL data set.

that the probability of aborting the playback is not biased by the device but it is related to users' habits.

5.4 Impact of buffering policy and user early abort

Consider now all video data already buffered at the player at the time the user aborts the playback. That data has been downloaded in vain. Fig. 13 precisely quantifies this by reporting the ratio among downloaded bytes and the amount of bytes possibly consumed by the player. The latter is evaluated as $session\_duration * average\_encoding\_bitrate$, assuming that the playout started immediately after the first byte has been received, and that data is consumed at the video encoding bitrate. Since the initial buffering is neglected, our estimation can be considered as a lower bound. Notice also that we cannot evaluate the amount of wasted data for sessions which already have completed the download.

In spite of this, results are dramatic for PC-player: 40% of sessions download more than two times the amount of data that was possibly watched. This is the result of aggressive buffering policies adopted by YouTube servers (recall that server-side shaping is adopted) [2]. Even worse, the Mobile-player waste is higher, with 20% of sessions downloading more the 5 times the amount of possibly watched data.

This waste could be reduced by implementing better streaming policies, e.g., the server sends chunks of the video by explicitly request by the client. Alternatively, a more accurate prediction of the fraction of the video that a user will watch can be leveraged to avoid transferring useless data.

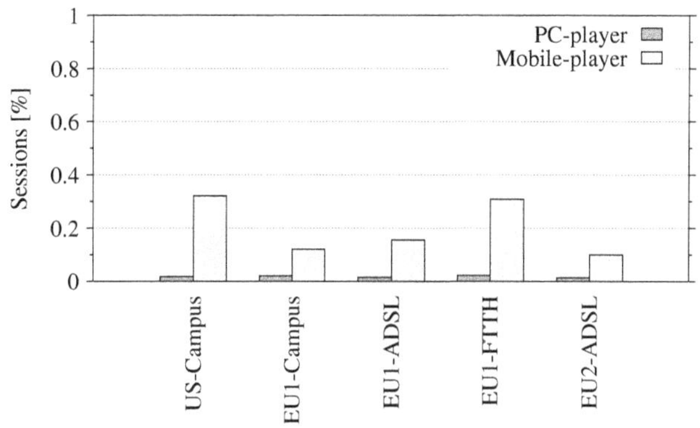

Figure 14: Fraction of sessions downloading more than the entire video.

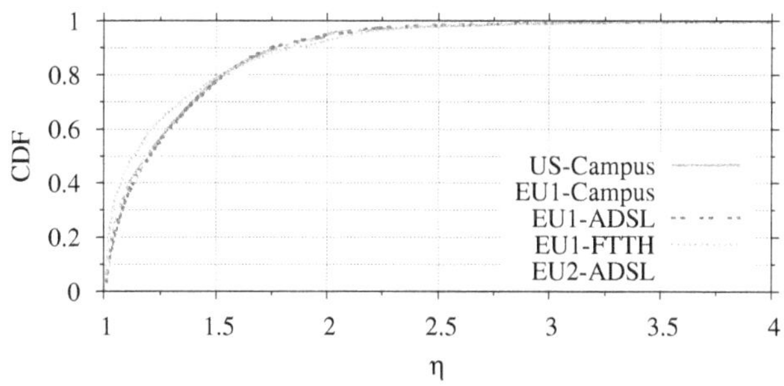

Figure 15: Ratio of downloaded data versus video size for sessions with $\eta > 1$. Mobile-player.

5.5 Sessions downloading more than the video size

Let us now focus on sessions where $\eta > 1$. Intuitively, those should be very limited, since one would expect that the player should not download more data than the total video size. Fig. 14 shows the fraction of sessions for which this happens. Only sessions with no resolution switch are considered. For PC-player, less than 2% of sessions show this phenomenon. We have found that the exceeding amount of volume is possibly related to users watching the same video multiple times causing the player to re-download the video. Overall, this effect is marginal.

For Mobile-player instead we observe that 15-30% of sessions download more than the actual video size. Performing some active experiments, we have confirmed at least two causes for this: 1) in case of backward seeks, the player has to re-download the same content because it has been already discarded from the player's local buffer. This does not happen for PC-player which caches the entire video; 2) the aggressive chunk-based download mechanism is source of inefficiency: the Mobile-player often requests chunks bigger than needed, i.e., requesting from a desired position x up to the end of the video. The server then sends data from position x at a high rate, quickly filling up the Mobile-player buffer, e.g., up to position y. Being the buffer full, the player application abruptly closes the underlying TCP connection. However TCP had already received some data at the transport-layer receiver buffer up to position $y' > y$. The data $y' - y$ is thus discarded. When the application buffer

Data set	PC-player	Mobile-player
US-Campus	39.17	47.9
EU1-Campus	36.91	38.1
EU1-ADSL	24.93	38.7
EU1-FTTH	38.43	53.5
EU2-ADSL	29.27	35.6

Table 6: Average percentage of wasted bytes considering peak hour with respect to useful data.

depletes, the player requests data from position y and not from position y'. Considering the download of $y' - y$, the aggressive server buffering policy coupled with player limited buffering capabilities is thus origin of inefficiency.

To quantify the waste of traffic due to this, Fig. 15 reports the CDF of the ratio of downloaded data versus nominal video size for sessions with $\eta > 1$. 50% of sessions download 25% more data, and 4% of the sessions downloads more than the twice of the video size.

5.6 Wasted video data

Table 6 quantifies the overall percentage of wasted bytes with respect to useful data. It includes both the effect of aggressive buffer management and of chunk based video retrieval mechanisms. Measurements refer to the peak-hour time, when YouTube traffic peaks to several hundreds of Mb/s in most vantage points. Results show that the amount of traffic downloaded by clients but not used by players is comparable with the useful data traffic. For example, for US-Campus, the wasted traffic in a single hour amounts to 28.8 GB and 1.5 GB for PC-player and Mobile-player, respectively, corresponding to more than 67 Mb/s of constant waste. This is a large amount of wasted bandwidth both from the perspective of the ISP and the YouTube CDN.

We have performed experiments on mobile devices connected to a 3G network using both iOS and Android devices. The problem shows up exactly in the same way, with clients downloading a lot more data than the video played and the video size. We did not observe differences among different devices or operating systems. This is an issue that might be particularly critical given the increasing popularity of YouTube accesses from mobile devices in 3G/4G networks.

6. STREAMING PERFORMANCE

In this section we focus on the streaming performance considering two metrics that reflect the user experience: *startup latency* and *bitrate ratio* between download rate and video encoding rate. We then pinpoint possible causes that can impair them.

6.1 Startup latency

We define the startup latency as the time elapsed between the first `videoplayback` request and the first received packet containing actual video payload. This corresponds to a lower bound of the delay experienced before the actual video playback starts since the initial buffering time at the player is ignored. The latter indeed is implementation dependent and hard to know. We prefer thus to focus on a simpler, more precise and accurate measure.

Fig. 16 reports the fraction of sessions with the startup latency higher than a certain threshold. Given that we are interested in studying the user experience, we selected

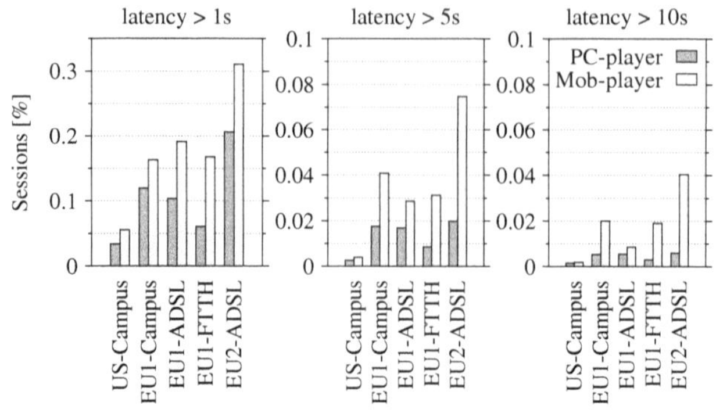

Figure 16: Fraction of sessions with high startup latency. Note the different y-axis across plots.

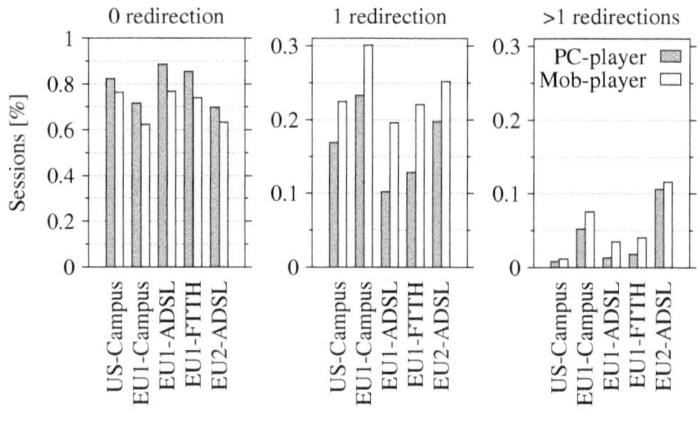

Figure 17: Fraction of sessions suffering redirections. Note the different y-axis across plots

threshold values that can be appreciated by the user, i.e., 1, 5 and 10 s. Results show that the performance is heterogeneous across the data sets, with Mobile-player suffering larger delays. For example, in the US-Campus less than 5% of sessions suffer a startup latency higher than 1 s. In the EU1-Campus instead, more than 10% of sessions start after 1 s with 2% of them suffering a startup latency higher than 5 s.

We found that the delay is due to a combination of causes. **Redirections**: Video sessions can suffer from a different number of redirections. Each redirection involves i) a DNS query to resolve the hostname of the next video server, ii) the opening of a new TCP connection, iii) a new video query. The network distance between the client and the server plays also a significant role, since YouTube CDN is likely to direct clients to video servers with the closest RTT. However, in case of redirections, the final server may not be the closest one in RTT.

Fig. 17 reports the fraction of sessions affected by redirections. More than 70% of PC-player session does not suffer from redirections in all data sets, while Mobile-player sessions are more likely to be redirected. Understanding why this is happening is difficult. A possible cause of redirection is due to cache miss. [13] already showed that a cache miss at the closest data center, may cause a redirection to a farther away data center. However, following requests for the same content are directly served by the clos-

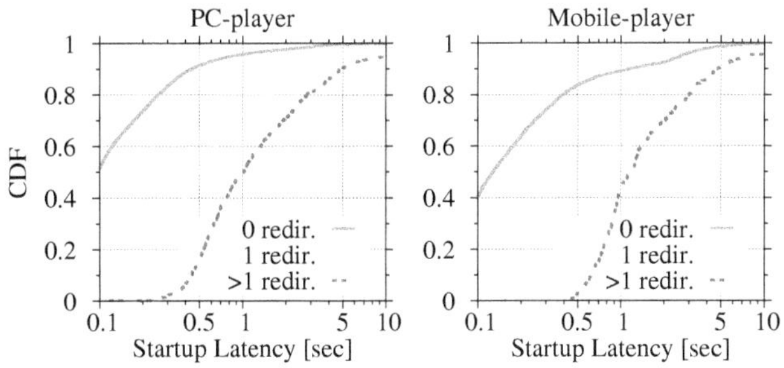

Figure 18: CDF of startup latency for different number of redirections. EU1-ADSL data set.

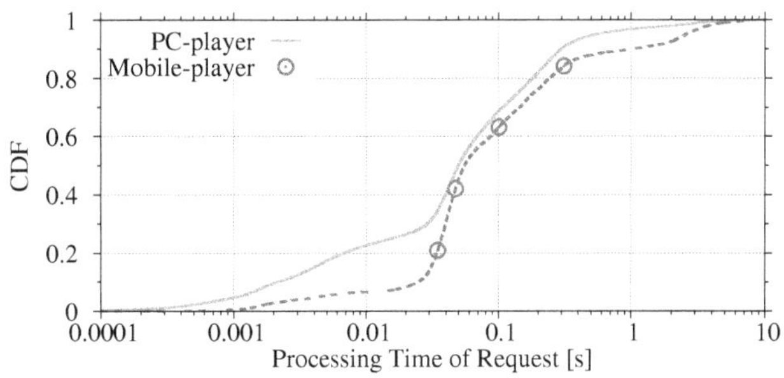

Figure 19: CDF of the video query processing time. EU1-ADSL data set.

est cache. This hints to a caching mechanism based on pull schemes. Since Mobile-player videos are less frequently requested than PC-player videos because of the different video format adopted, a cache miss is possibly more likely to happen. Thus more redirections can occur.

Fig. 18 depicts the impact of the redirections on the startup latency. We can see that the higher is the number of redirections in the video session, the higher is the startup delay. Considering PC-player (left plot), 92% of sessions that do not suffer redirections exhibit a startup latency smaller than 500 ms. When one redirection is faced, only 50% of sessions start within 500 ms. If more than 1 redirection is faced, more than 82% of sessions have a startup latency of at least 500 ms, with 10% of sessions suffering a latency higher than 5 s. Trends are similar for mobile player (right plot) where in general startup latencies are higher than in the case of PC-player.

Video request processing time: Another possible cause of large startup time can be the server processing time, i.e., time needed by the video server to process a video request. To estimate it, we compute the time between the last `videoplayback` request sent by the client and the first video packet sent by the server. To eliminate the network delay we subtract the RTT.

Fig. 19 reports the CDF of the estimated processing time for both PC-player and Mobile-player in the EU1-ADSL data set. Other data sets show similar trends. We can see that 50% of the requests are served within < 50 ms. A sharp knee around 30 ms is present and a heavy tail is found with processing time growing up to 5 s. The distribution reflects the time required by the cache to retrieve the requested content from the back-end before serving it. Very low latencies can be related to the video being already cached in the server memory; values in [30,300] ms can be related to disk access latency; finally values larger than 300 ms can be due to congestion in the back-end or to packet loss recovered by lengthy TCP timeout, or to rare content that has to be fetched from some slower storage system. The fact that Mobile-player responses require higher processing time can again be explained by the less frequent requests of Mobile-player video content. Note also that the prefetching mechanism implemented by PC-player could also speed-up the content retrieval (see Sec. 2).

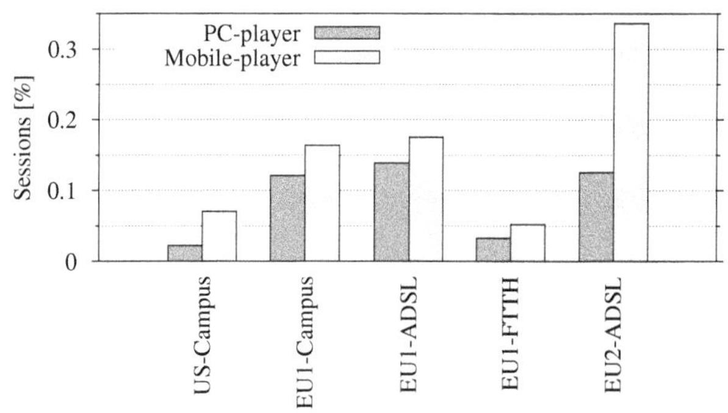

Figure 20: Fraction of sessions with bitrate ratio$<$ 1.

6.2 Bitrate ratio

The download bitrate of the video has a fundamental role in defining the quality of the video playback. In fact, if data is not received fast enough, buffer "under-run" events will be suffered, causing the video playback to pause. To measure the smoothness of the playback, we define the *bitrate ratio* as the ratio between the average session download bitrate and the video encoding bitrate. The first corresponds to the total amount of bytes downloaded aggregating flows of the same video session, divided by the time between the first and the last video packet. According to this definition, a bitrate ratio smaller than 1 is a clear sign of impaired performance.

Fig. 20 reports the fraction of sessions with a bitrate ratio lower than one. Some interesting observations hold: first, the access technology has a clear impact on the performance with the ADSL networks performing worst for more than 10% of the downloads with respect to the other networks. For instance, compare EU1-ADSL and EU1-FTTH (the latter offers 10Mb/s full duplex access capacity). Both refer to customers of the same ISP in the same city. Still, EU1-ADSL customers suffer worse performance. Unexpectedly, EU1-Campus performs also quite bad. Further investigation revealed that this is the result of a local University network policy that limits the bandwidth of subnets of some dorms. Most of the sessions having poor performance are indeed coming from those subnets. Fig. 20 shows that Mobile-player presents consistently lower performance than PC-player. This can be due to the presence of a WiFi network that is used by Mobile-player devices. The shared WiFi connection can indeed impair the download throughput. This is the case for US-Campus.

Other causes of reduced performance can be related to the YouTube infrastructure performing worst when serving Mobile-player requests. Consider EU2-ADSL, in which more

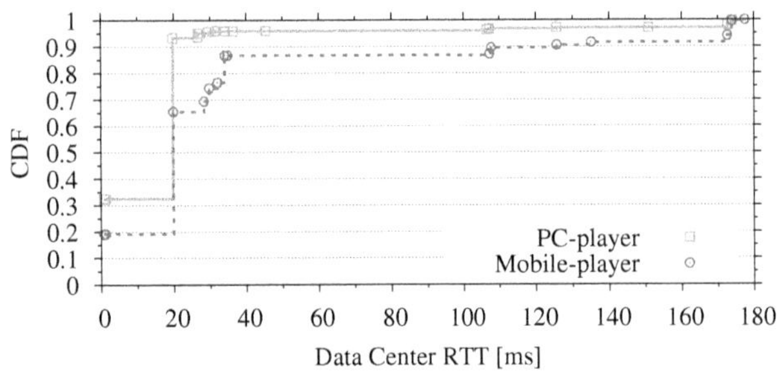

Figure 21: CDF of the fraction of bytes delivered by each data center. EU2-ADSL data set.

than 32% of Mobile-player sessions are performing poorly versus less than 13% of PC-player sessions. We pinpoint that Mobile-player impaired performance is related to the YouTube system. Consider Fig. 21. It reports the CDF of the fraction of bytes downloaded by different video servers respect to the RTT to the EU2-ADSL vantage point. Each point in the figure aggregates video servers that belong to the same CDN data center as in [13]. We found that EU2-ADSL clients can use a data center which is very close to the vantage point (RTT < 1 ms). However, it can only serve 35% of the PC-player sessions. The majority of sessions are indeed served by a second data center which is 20 ms far from the vantage point. For PC-player, these two data centers handle 96% of video requests. However, due to the lower popularity of Mobile player accessed content, 35% of Mobile-player sessions are served by other data centers, 10% of which are found outside Europe and suffer RTT > 100 ms. These sessions can be impaired by network congestion and can exhibit lower download bitrate. Finally, recall the Mobile-player chunking mechanism. The cost of opening a new TCP connection to request a new chunk becomes significant when the RTT is in the order of hundreds of ms, impairing the download bitrate too.

Overall, measurements presented in this section show that Mobile-player performance result generally less efficient than PC-player. The intrinsically smaller popularity of Mobile-player accessed videos poses additional challenges to the YouTube CDN infrastructure, which results highly optimized for PC-player as of now.

7. RELATED WORK

We consider three categories of works related to us.

YouTube Videos Characterization: These works have focused on characterizing various aspects of YouTube videos as well the usage patterns. On the one hand, [7] and [17] characterized video popularity, durations, size and playback bitrate, as well as usage pattern statistics such as day versus night accesses and volume of traffic considering a campus network. On the other hand, [3] and [4] crawled the YouTube site for an extended period of time and performed video popularity and user behavior analysis. Further, [3] compares YouTube to other video providers such as Netflix and [4] investigates social networking in YouTube videos. In contrast, our work is focused on the comparison between PC-player and Mobile-player downloads and goes deeper in the characterization of the content also taking advantage of the heterogeneous set of users and networks monitored.

YouTube Infrastructure Studies: These works characterize the YouTube video delivery infrastructure [1, 11, 13]. [11] shows that most YouTube videos are distributed from a single data center in the U.S. [1] shows that a few data centers in the U.S. were in charge of distributing the videos around the world. Finally, [13] shows that data centers spread around the world are in charge of distributing the video, and that latency between clients and servers plays a role in content server selection. In contrast, our work is focused on understanding the difference on video delivery between mobile devices and PCs. In particular, we show how mobile devices control the video download rate while in the case of PC-player, the download rate is controlled by the server [2].

User Behavior on Mobile Devices: More recently, there have been several works characterizing high level usage patterns of mobile devices [9, 6, 12]. [9] shows that the number of mobile devices doubled between 2009 and 2010 and that more than 80% of mobile devices traffic is HTTP, with multimedia traffic alone accounting for more than 30% of HTTP. [6] compares the content and flow characteristics of mobile devices and PCs traffic. Using a DPI tool, the authors are able to show that YouTube alone accounts for more than 35% of the Internet traffic. In contrast to these works, we go much deeper into the behavior and performance of users accessing YouTube from mobile devices. In addition, we highlight problems caused by the YouTube infrastructure when delivering videos to mobile devices.

8. CONCLUSIONS

Considering a large and heterogeneous data set of YouTube traces, we have presented our findings about user behavior when watching videos and how the type of user device and infrastructure influence the performance of the playback.

Interestingly, users access YouTube in a very similar manner, independent of their location, the device they use, and the access network that connects them. In addition, they typically watch only a small portion of the video, and stick to default player configurations.

While YouTube guarantees very good playback quality by means of aggressive buffering policies, we pinpointed sources of unnecessary data transfer, and the potential for future performance optimization. For example, a less aggressive buffering mechanism could be used to limit the amount of unnecessary traffic transferred to users' devices but never played back due to early abort by the users. For mobile devices, besides the adoption of the prefetching scheme that is useful to speed-up the video playback, a more precise control of the buffering is essential to avoid duplicate transmission of data. Finally, CDN caching schemes can be improved by leveraging the fact that only a fraction of videos are actually watched by users.

As future work, we aim at extending our conclusions by including traces collected from 3G/4G networks to precisely quantify the impact of YouTube traffic in such environments. Indeed, the issues we highlighted observing wireline access networks could be even more critical for 3G/4G wireless access networks, where bandwidth is precious. Similarly, an interesting direction of future research is to extend our analysis to consider other popular video streaming content distributors.

Acknowledgments

This work was funded in part by NSF Cybertrust 0715833 and by the European Union through the FIGARO project (FP7-ICT-258378). We would like to thank the ISPs and the IT Department of both campuses for their support, and also the shepherd and the anonymous reviewers for their constructive comments.

9. REFERENCES

[1] V. K. Adhikari, S. Jain, and Z.-L. Zhang. YouTube Traffic Dynamics and its Interplay with a Tier-1 ISP: an ISP Perspective. In *IMC '10: Proceedings of the 10th ACM Internet Measurement Conference*, pages 431–443, Melbourne, Australia, 2010.

[2] S. Alcock and R. Nelson. Application Flow Control in YouTube Video Streams. *SIGCOMM Computer Communication Review*, 41:24–30, April 2011.

[3] M. Cha, H. Kwak, P. Rodriguez, Y.-Y. Ahn, and S. Moon. I Tube, You Tube, Everybody Tubes: Analyzing The World's Largest User Generated Content Video System. In *IMC '07: Proceedings of the 7th ACM Internet Measurement Conference*, pages 1–14, San Diego, California, USA, 2007.

[4] X. Cheng, C. Dale, and J. Liu. Statistics and Social Network of YouTube Videos. In *IWQoS '08: 16th International Workshop on Quality of Service*, pages 229–238, Enschede, The Netherlands, 2008.

[5] A. Finamore, M. Mellia, M. Meo, M. M. Munafò, and D. Rossi. Experiences of Internet Traffic Monitoring with Tstat. *IEEE Network*, 25(3):8–14, 2011.

[6] A. Gember, A. Anand, and A. Akella. A Comparative Study of Handheld and Non-Handheld Traffic in Campus Wi-Fi Networks. In *PAM '11: Proceedings of the 12th International Conference on Passive and Active Measurement*, pages 173–183, Atlanta, Georgia, USA, 2011.

[7] P. Gill, M. Arlitt, Z. Li, and A. Mahanti. YouTube Traffic Characterization: A View From The Edge. In *IMC '07: Proceedings of the 7th ACM Internet Measurement Conference*, pages 15–28, San Diego, California, USA, 2007.

[8] C. Labovitz, S. Iekel-Johnson, D. McPherson, J. Oberheide, and F. Jahanian. Internet Inter-Domain Traffic. In *SIGCOMM '10: Proceedings of the ACM Special Interest Group on Data Communication*, pages 75–86, New Delhi, India, 2010.

[9] G. Maier, F. Schneider, and A. Feldmann. A First Look at Mobile Hand-Held Device Traffic. In *PAM '10: Proceedings of the 11th International Conference on Passive and Active Measurement*, pages 161–170, Zurich, Switzerland, 2010.

[10] The Mobile Internet Report. `http://www.morganstanley.com/institutional/techresearch/mobile_internet_report122009.html`.

[11] M. Saxena, U. Sharan, and S. Fahmy. Analyzing Video Services in Web 2.0: a Global Perspective. In *NOSSDAV '08: Proceedings of the 18th International Workshop on Network and Operating Systems Support for Digital Audio and Video*, pages 39–44, Braunschweig, Germany, 2008.

[12] M. Z. Shafiq, L. Ji, A. X. Liu, and J. Wang. Characterizing and Modeling Internet Traffic Dynamics of Cellular Devices. In *SIGMETRICS '11: Proceedings of the ACM International Conference on Measurement and Modeling of Computer Systems*, pages 305–316, San Jose, California, USA, 2011.

[13] R. Torres, A. Finamore, J. R. Kim, M. Mellia, M. M. Munafò, and S. G. Rao. Dissecting Video Server Selection Strategies in the YouTube CDN. In *ICDCS '11: Proceedings of the 31th IEEE International Conference on Distributed Computing Systems*, pages 248–257, Minneapolis, Minnesota, USA, 2011.

[14] Tstat Home Page. `http://tstat.polito.it`.

[15] YouTube Blog: Mmm mmm good - YouTube videos now served in WebM. `http://youtube-global.blogspot.com/2011/04/mmm-mmm-good-youtube-videos-now-served.html`.

[16] YouTube Press Room, `www.youtube.com/t/press_statistics`.

[17] M. Zink, K. Suh, Y. Gu, and J. Kurose. Characteristics of YouTube Network Traffic at a Campus Network - Measurements, Models, and Implications. *Computer Networks*, 53(4):501–514, 2009.

Summary Review Documentation for

"YouTube Everywhere: Impact of Device and Infrastructure Synergies on User Experience"

Authors: A. Finamore, M. Mellia, M. Munafò, R. Torres, S. G. Rao

Reviewer #1

Strengths: Well written and clear paper that answers most of the questions in each areas covered: video content characterization, user behavior and performance.
Brings attention to a critical point about current waste in bytes downloaded.

Weaknesses: Three additional points are not covered:
- Behavior on cellular networks
- Differences between devices/clients within a category (e.g. iPhone vs. Android)
- How is this different from other content providers (e.g. daily motion)?

Comments to Authors: Great paper! Not only is the paper doing a good job at characterizing YouTube traffic, I am particularly pleased to see that attention is brought to the wasted network resources caused by applications.

As mentioned in the weaknesses, your paper would be stronger, if you could get your hands on traces from a cellular network to do a more comprehensive study. A comparison with other similar content provider would be interesting, but this would be another paper.

However the point about comparison with different devices or clients within a category could be covered. You mention at the beginning are typically similar. But are there any differences? For instance, regarding the duplicate range request that leads to waste that might be due to a video buffer size. Do we see the same issue for Apple and Android smart phones? You might see differences there and it would be critical to point it out.

Figure 2, flow size: you are saying that PC vs. smartphone is not an apple to apple comparison because smart phones use range requests and the video will be split into multiple TCP flows. What about you stitch together each video and then compare the video sessions size in bytes?

Resolution switch: you mention users that are not aware of the feature. I think this is just another example of inertia, people always use the default settings (similar to the opt in / opt out results for organ donations).

Resolution switch: you claim that full screen mode is the main cause of resolution switch. You have not proved that to the reader. Is this your assumption?

Fraction of video watched: you should also highlight that once a video is fully downloaded, you assume that it is fully watched, right? Because at that point, you have no way of knowing what the user does. If that is the case, your estimates of wasted bytes are a lower bound. To be fair, you should point out that you cannot bring the number of wasted bytes down to zero because you still have to do buffer some of the data.

Video wasted data with duplicate content: FWIW I have personally noticed the same behavior on apple devices on cellular networks in the US across many providers (not just YouTube). You might want to make this clearer in Section 5.5 (test it by yourself), that this is not limited to YouTube.

Reviewer #2

Strengths: The paper does a nice study of YouTube experience on mobile and PC-based devices. The effort collects data from multiple vantage points, observes a significant number of flows, and makes some interesting observations with the data.

Weaknesses: Some of the conclusions appear more conjectures than reality and are not validated.

Comments to Authors: I thought the effort to characterize YouTube performance over different platforms is quite commendable. The authors did a very nice job of exploring different aspects of user behavior when watching these videos. Some of the observations, e.g., wasted bytes, use of default player configs, etc. are quite nice to learn about.

However, there were also a few observations that seem unclear:
- For instance, the authors point out that mobile devices use more flows than PC-based devices, and this might lead to poor performance at NATs or other stateful firewalls. Is this really true? Is the bulk on mobile device traffic video, and do such divides really get impacted?
- The authors claim that people from different locations (US and Europe) and with diverse Internet access speeds like to watch the same type of video, i.e., short videos. I wonder what is the real cause and effect. Is it not likely that most of the videos on YouTube are short videos? I would be careful about the conclusions being drawn from the data.
- The authors point out that students prefer cheaper phones, e.g., Android or Windows based. Are they really much cheaper than the iOS phones? Is this validated well?

Despite these issues, I thought the paper does make some very nice observations about video consumption on different platforms. The issue of resolution switch and the high download of bytes is interesting and I would encourage the authors to communicate this to the device vendors or operators involved. If this happens in

cellular networks, it is really an unfortunate waste of resources and should be fixed.
Overall, a nice paper and an interesting read.

Reviewer #3

Strengths: The authors analyze five very interesting and appropriate data sets. They identify interesting properties of YouTube delivery on the two studied platforms. More importantly, to me, they show that today's YouTube content delivery mechanisms are wasteful since in a large number of cases they lead to the download of more data than the video size itself. And this waste is more amplified for the mobile player.

Weaknesses: I would have loved to see similar analysis on mobile platforms - the authors only have a small experiment on this. Other than that, I think the paper makes a nice contribution.

Comments to Authors: There has been a tremendous amount of work on the characterization of the YouTube service. As such this paper falls in a rather well-published area in the measurement community. However, what this paper does, which has not been done in the past, is to study how the delivery of the YouTube service differs depending on the client platform used. And the authors clearly demonstrate that the YouTube application on mobile or set top box platforms, and the PC equivalent actually can lead to some differences in terms of performance.

The findings from the characterization study are not that impressive, I would say. Yes, the content consumed appears to be similar, with the exception of the resolution. But, interestingly to me, the authors clearly demonstrate that the performance DOES depend on the platform itself. And of course the mobile player needs to be able to deal with far more variability in the transmission medium than its PC equivalent.

Even more interestingly, it appears that the selected content delivery mechanism on mobile player can introduce significant waste, in some cases leading to the download of twice as much content as the video size itself!!!! That to me is an important aspect of YouTube that certainly deserves more attention especially when we target networks scarce in resources, like wireless networks.

The one thing I would have liked to see is a similar dataset collected on 3G/4G phones, but I think the authors have done enough. And they do have a small experiment on this aspect anyway.

Finally, I really liked the latency impact studied in the last subsection of 6.

All in all, I find that this work makes a significant contribution and I do hope that the authors find a way to reach YouTube and communicate their findings on the behavior of Mobile Player.

More detailed comments:
- Section 5.2 - the authors have not really proved that the main cause for resolution switch is full screen. At least not in the first paragraph after Figure 9. You need to study it in a little more detail before you can reach such a conclusion.
- In Section 5.6 you introduce y and y'. I would have liked to see the results on this section based on those metrics y and y' for a more precise specification of the quantity under study. For instance, is the waste of traffic in Fig 15 the sum of y'-y?

Reviewer #4

Strengths: Interesting comparison of PC vs mobile-device characteristics on Youtube across a number of dimensions. The paper also exposes how mobile devices are handled by YouTube.

Weaknesses: Unclear whether all mobile devices/applications behave the same. Some of the main observations claimed by the authors are probably misguided. The paper presentation and writing could be better.

Comments to Authors: Overall, I believe that this is an interesting paper that provides evidence on the differences of how desktop versus mobile devices are handled by YouTube, which is a significant fraction of traffic.

The paper highlights that a significant fraction of downloaded bytes may be wasted since many views are aborted before the end of the video. Further, the paper shows that mobile devices suffer higher latencies mainly due to redirection, although to me it is unclear why this is happening - the authors argue that this is due to the popularity of mobile videos but this is never truly examined in the paper and does not appear as a convincing argument.

There are a number of things that remain unclear in my opinion:

- You group all mobile devices together, but you never really examine that all mobile applications or clients do behave in a similar fashion. You claim in several places within the paper that indeed this is the case, but this is not truly verified but rather appears as author intuition.

- Why is the claim that users across institutions and devices do watch similar type of videos significant? At the aggregation level that you study the service, this simply reflects the distribution of video durations and sizes in the YouTube service. It is not a user-specific property as it is clearly shown by your results. Hence, I find Section 4 of limited interest.

There are several problems with the paper writing throughout the paper, especially grammatical and syntax mistakes.

In Section 2, you mention that you observe "no differences" regarding the second phase. Differences with respect to what?

Section 4.1: There is something wrong with the text here. Figures do not show differences but the text claims "slightly large difference", unless I missed something.

Section 4.3: I find the arguments that the network might not be able to handle better encodings a bit far-fetched. Please provide concrete evidence, or tone down the arguments.

Section 5.3: What about stop events without moving to another web page? Can you observe these?

Section 5.5: I could not really follow your discussion here towards the end of the second paragraph. It needs re-writing.

Section 5.6: Without concrete evidence on 3G performance it is hard to follow the argument that performance is the same. Since you don't have 3G data I would avoid providing vague arguments without concrete numbers on what the experiments and results were.

Section 6.1: How was the RTT measured?

Reviewer #5

Strengths: - There are a couple of interesting observations in this paper (access of YouTube is independent from the type of device and access technology, the study of flow control/adaptation mechanism of YouTube for different devices, the observation that bulk data is delivered in vain to the end-users). Despite the fact that there are a couple of anecdotal evidences it is nice to monitor how YouTube works in a systematic fashion.
- Diverse sets of devices, access technologies and locations of users and solid measurement methodology.
- A large number of downloads was considered.

Weaknesses: I like the analysis of the datasets, but there are a few aspects that have to be considered (please check my comments to the authors).

Comments to Authors: In the wireless setting, both the bandwidth and the energy are scarce resources. You may want to add a few references and comment on this in your study. Here are a few references that might be of your interest:

- "Energy consumption of mobile YouTube: quantitative measurement and analysis, in Proceedings of the Second International Conference on Next Generation Mobile Applications, Services and Technologies" NGMAST '08.
- "Cellular Data Network Infrastructure Characterization and Implication on Mobile Content Placement" Proc. SIGMETRICS 2011.

There are a couple of measurement studies that unveil how YouTube delivers bulk data to end-users; in the beginning there is a burst and then the bandwidth in throttled. For example see this paper:

- "Application Flow Control in YouTube Video Streams", ACM CCR April 2011.

You may want to comment on these results and elaborate why you observe that the amount of traffic downloaded by clients that is not used by them is significant. Is this due to the fact that the download speed is higher than the watch speed, or is it due to the fact that the mechanism cannot accurately estimate (overestimate) the minimum bandwidth that is needed so that the end-users will not complain about the quality of the video.

Did you observe special cases where the application flow mechanism of YouTube is not accurate? Does this happen for popular or unpopular content? Is this related to the proximity of the YouTube server to end-user?

You should comment on the time-of-day effect in your datasets. Do you observe that users stop the session faster during the peak hours than during non-peak hours? How does the flow control behave during the peak hours and the non-peak hours?

The related work is not very well written and should go over a few more iterations.

Response from the Authors

We would like to deeply thank the reviewers for their valuable comments. In the final version of the paper, we have integrated most of the reviewers' suggestions. In the following, we highlight the major changes.

We updated some figures adding the y-label as to better express the reported measurements. We also clarified some statements in our paper, rewrote sentences and smoothed claims by making them more conjecture-like as suggested by the second reviewer. In some cases, as for the full screen resolution switch, we provided further numbers to support our conclusions.

A common suggestion was to investigate further the impact of different mobile operating systems and to verify if the problem related to the amount of wasted data downloaded is similar considering different devices. In the original data sets, we are not able to distinguish the O.S. or the device used. This does not allow us to precisely quantify the differences. However, we performed active experiments, as reported in Sec. 5.6, with both Android and iOS devices, and concluded that they exhibit similar behavior and suffer from similar deficiencies.

All reviewers suggested improvements to the paper by including measurements collected from 3G/4G cellular networks. We agree with this requirement and we are actively pursuing the issue with mobile operators as possible partners but unfortunately we do not have such data set for now. However, in the final version of the paper we have strengthened the results by performing other active measurements using mobile phones. Findings confirm the trends already observed in the paper.

Finally, we have added a paragraph to the conclusion section, discussing some of the interesting avenues for future work. In particular, besides the analysis of 3G/4G cellular networks, we have left the assessment of the impact on our results if we consider measurements of different devices, time-of-day effects and the comparison with other streaming services as future analysis.

Broadcast Yourself: Understanding YouTube Uploaders

Yuan Ding[†], Yuan Du[†], Yingkai Hu[†], Zhengye Liu[‡], Luqin Wang[†],
Keith W. Ross[†], Anindya Ghose[⋆]

[†]Computer Science and Engineering, Polytechnic Institute of NYU
[‡]AT&T Labs, San Ramon
[⋆]Stern School of Business, New York University

{dingyuan1987, duyuanvvv, yingkaihu, zhengyeliu, lukelwang}@gmail.com
ross@poly.edu, aghose@stern.nyu.edu

ABSTRACT

YouTube uploaders are the central agents in the YouTube phenomenon. We conduct extensive measurement and analysis of YouTube uploaders. We estimate YouTube scale and examine the uploading behavior of YouTube users. We demonstrate the positive reinforcement between on-line social behavior and uploading behavior. Furthermore, we examine whether YouTube users are truly broadcasting themselves, via characterizing and classifying videos as either user generated or user copied.

Categories and Subject Descriptors

C.4 [[**Performance of Systems**]: General—*measurement techniques*; C.2.3 [**Computer-Communication Networks**]: Network Operations—*network monitoring, public networks*

General Terms

Measurement, Performance

Keywords

YouTube, system scale, social network, content classification

1. INTRODUCTION

YouTube is a major Internet phenomenon. Driving YouTube's success are its *uploaders* – the millions of users who upload content to the YouTube site. YouTube uses the slogan "Broadcast Yourself" to highlight its unique feature of allowing ordinary Internet users to freely distribute videos. By encouraging users to upload content and broadcast themselves, YouTube has transformed Internet users from video consumers to video producers.

Due to its remarkable success, there have been several recent studies about YouTube [13, 4, 6, 10, 12, 1, 2, 3, 7, 19, 17, 14, 16, 18], providing important insights into YouTube videos, viewers, social behavior, video traffic, and recommendation system. However, the YouTube uploaders – who are at the core of the YouTube phenomenon – have yet to be studied carefully. In this paper, we provide a large-scale, comprehensive measurement study of YouTube uploaders. Such a study is important, as a big-picture understanding of YouTube must take into account its uploaders. Our contributions are as follows:

- **Analysis of YouTube uploaders:** All the videos in YouTube are uploaded by users. The most fundamental question is *who are the uploaders and what are their characteristics*. To this end, we carefully design crawling, sampling and analysis methodologies. Estimating the scale of YouTube, we find that there are approximately 47.3 million uploaders, having uploaded 448 million of videos (with an aggregated length of 2,649 years), and having attracted more than 1.5 trillion of views. To our knowledge, this represents the only modern (and systematic) estimate of YouTube scale currently available. We find that the top 20% of the uploaders (in terms of number of uploaded videos) contribute 72.5% of videos, while the top 20% of most popular uploaders attract approximately 97% of views. We find that uploaders belonging to the social network are more active than those not belonging, and upload on average more than twice as many videos. We study the uploading behavior of users with different gender, age, and geographic locations.
- **UGC vs. UCC:** YouTube is designed for sharing user generated content. However, many videos in YouTube are simply copied from other places – such as from movies, TV shows, and other professional video websites – rather than being originally generated by ordinary Internet users. We classify videos as UGC and UCC and investigate the properties of UGC and UCC videos from three different groups of representative uploaders. We make the critical observation that most uploaders consistently upload either UGC or UCC videos.

2. YOUTUBE UPLOADERS

In the jargon of YouTube, each subscribed user has its own *channel*. Throughout this paper we use the term *user* and *channel* interchangeably. Each channel has a channel profile that includes the channel name and (optionally) personal information about the user, such as the user's name, gender, age, interests and homepage (outside of YouTube). A user is said to be an *uploader* if it has uploaded at least one video. Each channel also includes links to all of the user's uploaded videos, links to users favorite videos, links to the users friends, and links to its subscribers and subscriptions.

IMC'11, November 2–4, 2011, Berlin, Germany.

2.1 Methodologies and Datasets

In this paper we use the related video graph to crawl the uploaders. Specifically, for a given uploader, we first obtain the list of uploaded videos. For each of its uploaded videos, we crawl the related videos and determine all the corresponding uploaders, which we refer to as the *related uploaders*. We then repeat the process. Unlike most other social network measurement studies, where typically a small part of the social graph is crawled, and the results are highly dependent on the sampling methodologies, we attempt to crawl the entire related video graph to avoid any assumptions underlying the sampling methodologies that may not be held for the related video graph. After crawling the entire related video graph, we then randomly select a subset of uploaders and conduct deeper investigation.

Using a depth-first-search (DFS) of the related uploader graph, we crawled approximately 44.8 million unique uploader IDs over a 90-day period (from 9/22/2010 to 12/22/2010). In order to crawl such a large number IDs in a 90-day period, we did not download the channel page for each ID; instead we simply collected the ID for each uploader. In the last weeks, our crawler, based on related videos, continued to see a large number of uploaders every hour; but, the number of new IDs per hour dropped off dramatically. To verify that the 44.8 million uploader IDs nearly fully cover the YouTube uploaders, we conducted another independent crawl via the YouTube friend social network. The related video network and the social network are two separate networks. The social network is created by the YouTube users, and the related video network is created by YouTube. Using DFS of the friend social network, we crawled 100,000 YouTube social uploaders. We found that 94,737 of the social uploaders (94.7%) were found in our set of 44.8 million uploaders. Given that crawling rate dramatically dropped in the last weeks of our crawl, and that the resulting set contained 94.7% of the uploaders from an independent crawl, we believe that the crawl is representative and nearly complete over all YouTube uploaders. From the 44.8 million IDs, we randomly selected 100,000 uploaders and then fully crawled all their channel information. We call this dataset `UploadSam`.

2.2 Scale of YouTube

In this subsection, by measuring and analyzing the YouTube uploaders, we estimate the scale of YouTube, including the total number of uploaders, the total number of videos, the aggregate length of YouTube videos, the total number of views. YouTube currently does not make this information public. To our knowledge, there has not been any systematic attempt to estimate the scale of YouTube in the past several years.

First, we estimate the total number of uploaders in YouTube. Since we claim that most uploaders in YouTube have been crawled, the number of uploaders can be simply estimated as 44.8/0.947=47.3 million. We then define a *scale factor* for 473 by comparing the total number of uploaders and the number of uploaders in `UploadSam`. We now estimate the total number of videos and aggregate length in YouTube. We find that there are 947,960 videos uploaded by the uploaders in `UploadSam` and the aggregate length of these videos is 5.6 years. Using the same scaling factor of 473, we therefore estimate that, up to December 2010, the total number of videos published to be 448 million and the aggregate video length to be 2,649 years.

We can also estimate the total number of views and the total viewing time in YouTube. The total number of views of the videos in `UploadSam` is approximately 3.1 billion. Because we also know the length of individual videos and their view times for the videos in `UploadSam`, we can calculate the total viewing time on these videos, which is 20,891 years. Once again using the scale factor of 473, we can estimate the total number of views to be 1.5 trillion and total viewing time to be 9.9 million years. Table 1 summarizes the scale of YouTube.

Table 1: Estimated YouTube Scale

Number of uploaders	47.3 million
Number of videos	448 million
Aggregate video length	2,649 years
Number of views	1.5 trillion
Aggregate view time	9.9 million years

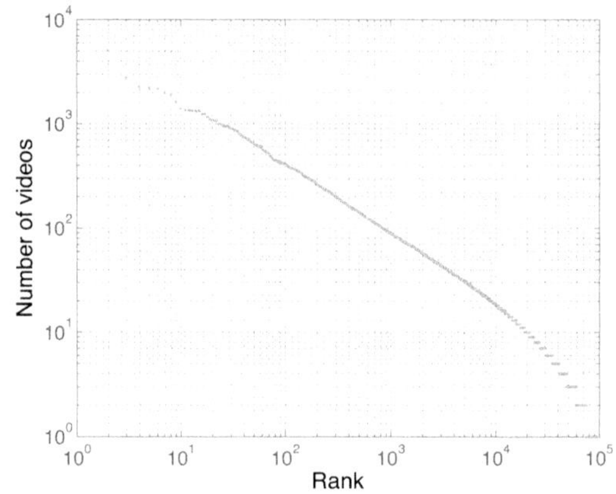

Figure 1: YouTube uploaders rank ordered by number of uploaded videos.

2.3 Uploading Behavior

Having investigated the scale of YouTube, we now investigate the behavior and characteristics of YouTube uploaders. To our knowledge, this is the first study of YouTube uploaders. We first investigate the distribution of the number of videos uploaded by the uploaders. As shown in Figure 1, the number of uploaded videos clearly follows a Zipf distribution. The maximum, mean, and median of uploaded videos are reported in Table 2. *Among these uploaders, the most active 20% of the uploaders contribute 72.5% of the videos, which largely follows the famous 80-20 rule [11].*

We further investigate the uploading pattern of YouTube uploaders. We observe that many uploaders upload very infrequently, but when they upload, they often upload several videos at the same time. An uploader who uploads multiple videos may only upload once during its life time. We investigate the "active time" of uploaders in different time scales. For example, if the time scale is one day, and if an uploader uploads at least one video, we consider this uploader active in that day, no matter how many videos it uploads. Figure 4 plots the PDF of active times of uploaders, with time scales of one day, one calendar month, and one calendar year. We eliminate the uploaders that newly joined and only consider the 83,769 uploaders that joined YouTube before 2010. We observe that 32.5%, 40.0%, and 56.1% of uploaders have been active for only one day, one month, and one year, respectively. Thus, less than half of the uploaders have been active for a period extending over one year.

We now examine whether a YouTube uploader tends to upload videos into a small number of categories. To this end, for each

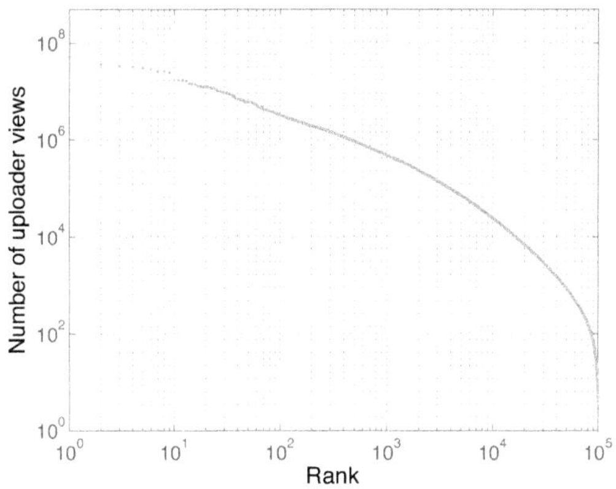

Figure 2: YouTube uploaders rank ordered by popularity.

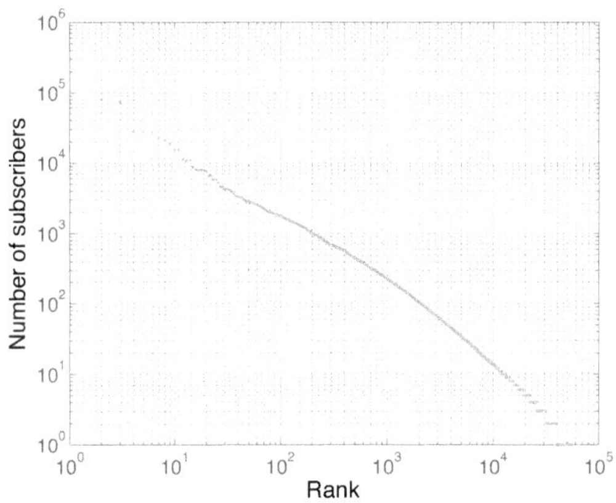

Figure 3: Distribution of number of subscribers.

uploader, we rank the categories based on the number of videos uploaded to each category, and calculate the fraction of its videos in the top category. We refer to this measure as the *top-category ratio*. If all the videos of an uploader belong to a single category, then its top-category ratio is 1. Similarly, we define the top-three-category ratio, which is the fraction of videos belonging to the top three categories of the uploader. To have a yet more comprehensive measure of upload category diversity, we introduce the category entropy for uploader i, which is expressed mathematically as:

$$e_i = \frac{-\sum_{k=1}^{K} \frac{u_{ik}}{u_i} \ln \frac{u_{ik}}{u_i}}{\ln K}, \quad (1)$$

where K is the number of categories, u_{ik} is the number of uploaded videos from user i to category k, and $u_i = \sum_{k=1}^{n} u_{ik}$ is the total number of uploaded videos of user i. If an uploader uploads all videos to a single category, then its category entropy will be 0; while if an uploader uploads uniformly to all 15 categories, then its category entropy will be 1. Note that category entropy takes into account the videos uploaded to all categories for individual uploaders, unlike the ratio of the top category (and the top three categories) which only takes into account the top categories.

Figure 5 illustrates the category uploading behavior. We consider three groups of uploaders, namely, the uploaders that upload more than one, 10, and 100 videos respectively. Figure 5 (a) shows the

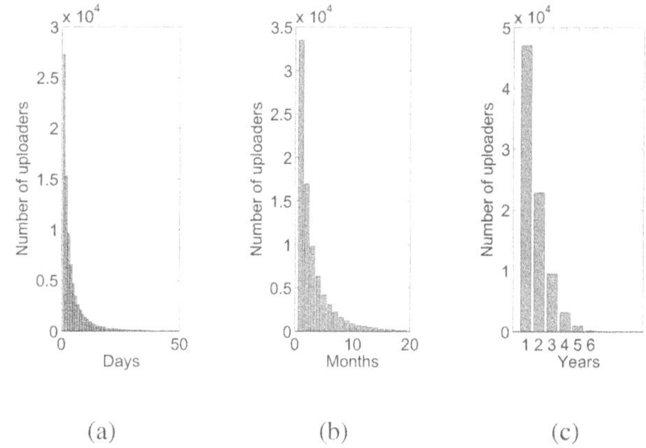

Figure 4: Distribution of active times with different time scales. (a) one day; (b) one month; (c) one year.

Table 2: Basic statistics of uploaders

	Maximum	Mean	Median
Number of videos	11,323	9.5	3
Number of views	61,130,983	31,143	847
Number of subscribers	138,583	19.6	1

CDF of the top-category ratio. Focusing on the uploaders who upload more than 100 videos, we see that about 20% of the uploaders only upload to a single category, and more than 85% of uploaders upload more than 50% of their videos to their top category. By considering the relatively large number of videos uploaded by this group of uploaders, *we see there is a strong tendency to concentrate videos in a small number of categories*. These can be further demonstrated in Figure 5 (b) and (c). As shown in Figure 5 (b), more than 70% of uploaders upload more than 80% of their videos to the top three categories. As shown in Figure 5 (c), more than 80% of uploaders have a category entropy less than 0.5. Interestingly, the category concentration trend appears to be independent of how active the uploader is. All three groups present similar behavior no matter how many videos the uploaders upload.

2.4 Uploader Views and Subscribers

In YouTube, some uploaders are more popular than others, with more users viewing their uploaded videos. YouTube incentivizes the very popular uploaders by sharing its ad revenue with them. To some extent, the number of views of an uploader influences its motivation to upload. We investigate the number of views on individual uploaders in the dataset `UploadSam`.

Figure 2 plots the uploader rank ordered by the number of uploader views in the dataset `UploadSam`. Surprisingly, *the number of views does not follow a Zipf distribution*. Our conjecture is that uploader popularity has been tuned by YouTube intentionally by YouTube's recommendation system (that is, the related videos). On one hand, there are fewer unpopular uploaders than there would be in a Zipf distribution. Specifically, more than 47% of uploaders attract more than 1,000 uploader views, implying that YouTube uploaders enjoy good visibility, even for those who upload a very small number of videos. Thus, YouTube's recommendation system (that is, related videos) seems to be somewhat biased towards less popular uploaders. On the other hand, among all uploaders, the most popular 20% of the uploaders attract 97.0% of views, which does not follow the 80-20 rule. Thus YouTube's recommendation

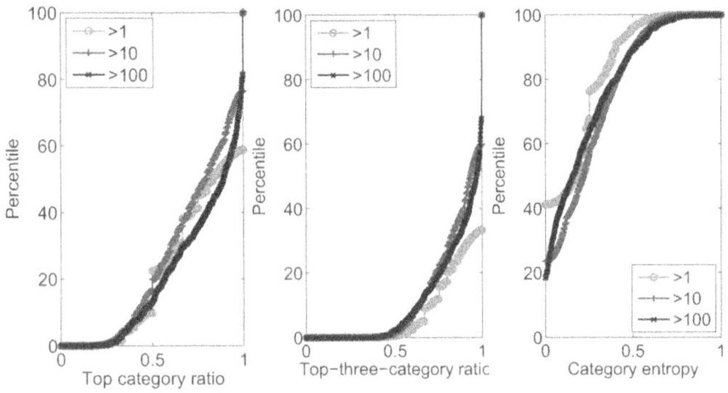

(a) (b) (c)

Figure 5: Category-concentrated uploading. (a) uploaded video ratio of the top category; (b) uploaded video ratio of the top-three categories; (c) uniformed category entropy.

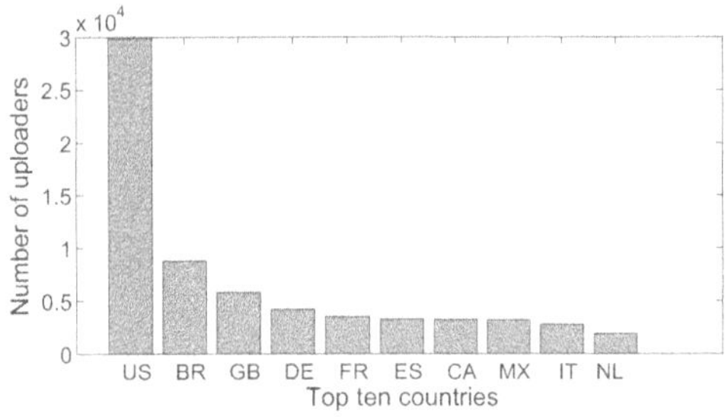

Figure 6: Distribution of geographic location .

system seems to be also biased to the very popular uploaders. The maximum, mean, and median of uploaded videos are reported in Table 2. We briefly remark that there are also many very unpopular uploaders in our random sample: 13.5% of the 100,000 uploaders have less than 100 views (aggregated across all of the uploader's videos).

Figure 3 plots the uploader rank ordered by the number of subscribers in dataset `UploadSam`. We observe that the number of subscribers follows a Zipf distribution. *Therefore, although a recommendation system may be able to shape uploader views, it is harder to change Internet users preference when it comes to subscriptions, which is a more active action than having a "quick view" upon a recommendation.* The maximum, mean, and median of number of subscribers are reported in Table 2.

2.5 Gender, Age and Location

YouTube uploaders may provide gender information in their profiles. In `UploadSam`, 97.9% of uploaders specify their gender information, 91.2% specify their ages, and 90.0% specify both. *We find that there are more than three times the number of male uploaders than female uploaders.* Consistent with the number of uploaders, male uploaders contribute more than three times the number of videos and attract more than three times the number of views than female uploaders. We also observe that the uploaders with ages from 20 to 30 are the most active uploaders, contributing approximately 40.0% of YouTube videos.

YouTube is a US-based Internet application, but it is widely used all over the world. We investigate the geographic location of the YouTube uploaders. The YouTube API provides the uploaders' country information. We carefully examine the geographic location information for the uploaders in dataset `UploadSam` and eliminate 4,137 uploaders whose location information is noisy.

Figure 6 shows the number of uploaders from the top ten countries. As expected, the US is the top country in terms of number of uploaders, accounting for 31.1% of the total YouTube uploaders. The other top nine countries account for more than 43.7%, while the remaining countries account for 25.2%. In addition to the US, YouTube is very popular in Europe and South America. However, it is less popular in Japan and Korea, which is surprising since these two countries have high Internet usage. YouTube is not accessible from Mainland China.

2.6 Social Uploaders

Some YouTube users join this social network (who we call *social users*), while others are not (who we call *non-social users*). We now study how the YouTube social network influences uploader behavior. We first ask, what fraction of the social users are uploaders, and what fraction of YouTube users on the whole are uploaders? To this end, using breath-first search, we crawl a large number of YouTube users (10,000,000) in the YouTube friend social network. We then randomly select a subset of 100,000 users (named `SocUsr`) to investigate whether these social users are uploaders. We find that 43% of the 100,000 social users in `SocUsr` have uploaded at least one video. To estimate the fraction of YouTube users on the whole who are uploaders, we assume that there are totally 135 million U.S. YouTube users. Note that this is a very conservative estimate, since it has been reported that 135 million unique U.S. viewers viewed YouTube videos in December 2009 [8]. Recall that approximately 31.1% of the uploaders are from the U.S. and that there are around 47.3 million uploaders in YouTube. By considering both social and non-social YouTube users, we estimate the fraction of YouTube users who are uploaders to be at most $\frac{47.3}{135} * 0.311 = 0.109$. In summary, whereas at most 10.9% of the YouTube users are uploaders, 43% of the social users are uploaders. *Thus, social users are much more inclined (at least four times more!) to be uploaders than the average YouTube users.*

To compare the behavior of the social uploaders and non-social uploaders, we re-visit the dataset `UploadSam` and group the uploaders into social uploaders and non-social uploaders, based on whether an uploader belongs to the social network. Figure 7 (a) plots the rank of uploaders ordered by the number of uploaded videos. Figure 7 (b) plots the rank of uploaders ordered by the number of uploader views. *These figures clearly show that social uploaders upload more videos and receive more views – on average twice as many – than their non-social counterparts.*

There are two possible reasons why social uploaders upload significantly more than non-social uploaders. On one hand, there is a feedback loop: when a social uploader publishes a new video, it will likely be viewed by many of the uploader's friends; this positive feedback incentivizes the social user to upload even more. On the other hand, users who upload a lot are more likely to join the social network, since they are already very active in YouTube. Without actually interviewing the uploaders, it is difficult to say which of these two reasons weighs more heavily in user behavior. However, it is reasonable to believe that these two reasons together explain why social uploaders are more driven to contribute.

3. USER GENERATED OR USER COPIED?

With its slogan "Broadcast Yourself", YouTube has been designed for sharing user generated content. However, a significant fraction of videos are not originally from YouTube, but are instead simply copied from other places, such as movies, TV shows, and other professional video websites. Thus, content on YouTube can

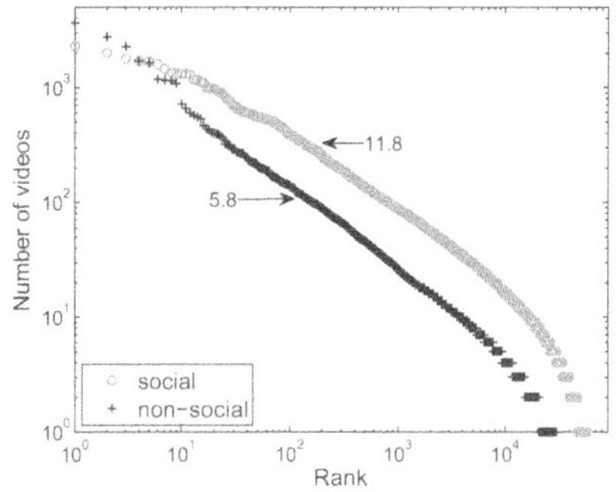

(a)

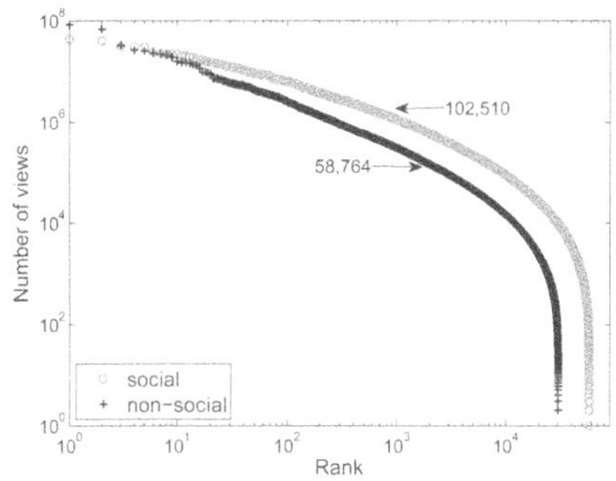

(b)

Figure 7: Social uploaders vs. non-social uploaders. (a)Number of uploaded videos; (b) number of uploader views.

be classified as User Generated Content (UGC) or User Copied Content (UCC). In this section, we seek to classify each uploader as a UGC uploader, a UCC uploader, or a combined UGC/UCC uploader. As a consequence of the classification, we will be able to estimate the importance of UCC content in YouTube.

The classification of a video as either UGC or UCC is not always black and white. We begin this analysis by defining UGC and UCC videos:

- **UCC:** A contiguous snippet of a video that was originally distributed outside of YouTube. For example, a snippet of a movie, of a TV show, or of anything originally broadcasted over TV. This also includes videos created by professional video producers, such as NBC. These professional uploaders publish these videos on their own websites, and then on YouTube to broaden their visibility.
- **UGC:** A video that is originally generated for YouTube-like video sharing websites. This not only includes videos captured with user's digital cameras and webcams, but also mashups of copied video snippets.

We now manually classify uploaders and videos as either UGC or UCC. We first create a dataset for three groups of uploaders:

- **Popular uploaders:** This group contains the 100 most popular uploaders, as explicitly presented in the YouTube website. Although it is unclear to us exactly how YouTube decides which uploaders to include in this list of 100 uploaders, in general, each of these uploaders attracts a large number of uploader views.
- **Social uploaders:** This group contains 100 randomly chosen uploaders from the YouTube social network. As shown in Section 2.6, the uploaders in the YouTube social network are in general more active than those not in the social network.
- **Random uploaders:** This group contains 100 randomly selected uploaders from `UploadSam`. This group represents the typical behavior of YouTube uploaders.

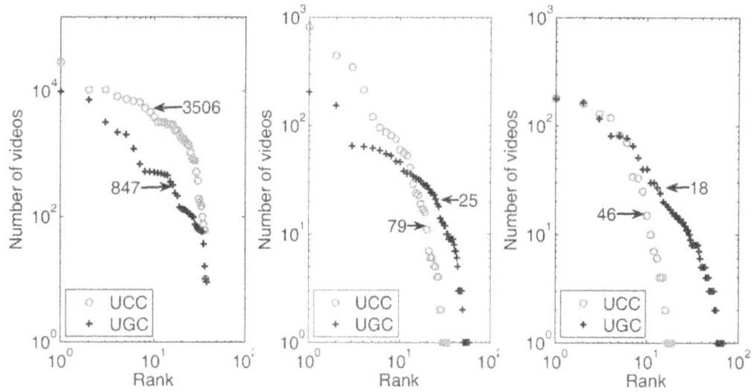

(a) (b) (c)

Figure 8: UCC uploaders vs. UGC uploaders in terms of number of uploaded videos. (a) Popular uploaders; (b) Social uploaders; (c) Random uploaders.

Table 3: Manual classification on uploaders

	UCC	UGC	non-dominate
`Popular:`	63	36	1
`Social:`	34	61	5
`Random:`	20	77	3

3.0.1 *UGC or UCC Uploader?*

We first examine whether YouTube uploaders upload mostly UGC content or mostly UCC content, but not both types of content. We say an uploader is a UCC (respectively, UGC) uploader if more than 90% of its videos are UCC (respectively, UGC).

As shown in Table 3, for each of the three groups, *more than 95% of the uploaders are either UGC uploaders or UCC uploaders.* This is a critical observation. One immediate application of this finding is, for automatically classifying videos as UGC or UCC, in addition to the features of individual videos (e.g., number of video views, video title, video category, etc.), one can indirectly classify the video by classifying its uploader. Thus, the uploader information provides useful features for automatic video classification.

Although the fraction of non-dominant uploaders is small for the three groups, the relative fractions of UCC/UGC uploaders is strikingly different among the three groups. Observe that 77% of the random uploaders are UGC uploaders. Thus most of the users in YouTube are indeed publishing user generated content. However, in the popular group, 63% of uploaders are UCC uploaders, implying that *the majority of the most popular uploaders are not uploading user generated content!* We mention that many (but not all) of the uploaders in the popular group are professional video producers, such as NBC.

3.0.2 *Number of uploaded videos*

We now investigate the detailed properties of UCC/UGC uploaders. For both UGC and UCC uploaders, and for each of the three groups, Figure 8 plots the uploader rank ordered by number of up-

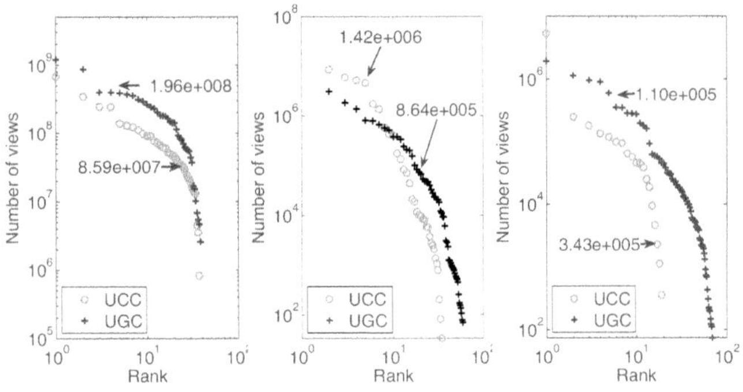

(a) (b) (c)

Figure 9: UCC uploaders vs. UGC uploaders in terms of number uploader views. (a) Popular uploaders; (b) Social uploaders; (c) Random uploaders.

loaded videos. The figure also indicates the average number of uploaded videos for each curve. We observe that, on average, *UCC uploaders upload many more videos than UGC uploaders.* This is probably because it is much easier for a UCC uploader to generate video clips from movies and TV shows than it is for a UGC uploader to generate original content. This figure clearly shows that video content influences an uploader's uploading behavior.

3.0.3 Views and subscribers

We have shown that UCC uploaders generally upload more videos than UGC uploaders. This does not necessarily mean, however, that UCC uploaders are more popular than UGC uploaders in terms of number of views. Figure 9 plots the uploader rank ordered by number of views for UCC/UGC uploaders in different groups. Similarly, we indicate the average number of views for each curve. Surprisingly, *in the popular group, the UGC uploaders on average attract more than twice as many views as the UCC uploaders, even though many of the popular UCC uploaders publish professionally generated videos and upload more videos.* This demonstrates that ordinary Internet users are capable of creating more interesting and popular channels than the professional producers! A similar observation can be made for the uploaders in the social network group and the random group: except for the top uploaders, UGC uploaders are in general more popular. However, UCC uploaders are on average more popular than the UGC uploaders in the social network group and the random group, because the very top UCC uploaders attract significantly more views than the very top UGC uploaders.

We have seen that several video features (video category and video title) and several video uploader features (number of uploaded videos, number of active times, maximum number of uploaded videos in a day, gender, and uploader dominant category) provide hints about whether a particular video is UGC or UCC. In future work, we will explore using machine learning with these features for automatic classification of videos as UGC and UCC.

4. RELATED WORK

As mentioned in the Introduction, there are several studies on measuring and analyzing YouTube. Mislove *et al.* investigated several on-line social networks, including YouTube [13]. Their study mainly focuses on the properties of social graphs, e.g., the power-law, small-world, and scale-free properties. Cha *et al.* comprehensively studied YouTube from the perspective of YouTube videos and viewers [4]. The authors studied the popularity life-cycle of videos, the statistical properties of requests and their relationship with video age, and the level of content aliasing and illegal content. From the system design perspective, they also discuss the potential of using P2P in UGC VoD systems. Similar to [4], Cheng *et al.* investigated the video properties of YouTube [6]. They found that the related video network forms a small world network. Leveraging the small world property, Cheng *et al.* optimized P2P system design to effectively distribute videos for YouTube [7]. Zhou *et al.* study the view sources of YouTube videos, and find that related video recommendation is one of the most important sources [18].

Gill *et al.* [10] investigated YouTube from the perspective of YouTube traffic. They examined YouTube usage patterns, file properties, and transfer characteristics. They also investigated the YouTube video properties, such as video popularity and referencing behaviors. Zink *et al.* also investigated YouTube from the perspective of YouTube traffic [19], with a focus on measurement methodology and modeling.

Benevenuto *et al.* investigated the user behavior in a social network created by video interactions, and characterized a social network created by the video interactions among users in YouTube [2]. They identified typical user behavior patterns and showed evidence of anti-social behavior such as self promotion and content pollution. Benevenuto *et al.* considered the problem of detecting video spammers, and applied machine learning to provide a heuristic for classifying an arbitrary video as either legitimate or spam [3]. Qiu *et al.* [15] and Cha *et al.* [5] studied the user behavior in large scale IPTV systems. Cuevas *et al.* [9] studied the user behavior of content publishers in BitTorrent.

With its slogan "Broadcast Yourself," YouTube has been designed for sharing user generated content, where uploaders play the critical role. Surprisingly, to our knowledge, none of the prior studies carefully examines YouTube uploader properties in a systematic and comprehensive way. Our study fills this gap and paints a precise picture of YouTube uploaders.

5. CONCLUSION

As Internet researchers, we are interested in the characteristics and behavior of the content creators, arguably the most important entities in the Internet phenomenon. By identifying which uploaders in the near future will likely attract many views, advertisers can make more informed decisions. Google currently makes little information publicly available about the scale of YouTube. To understand YouTube's relative importance in the Internet landscape, we need to have estimates of it scale, which are provided in this paper.

In this paper, we provide a comprehensive study on YouTube uploaders, the central agents in the YouTube phenomenon. We conduct extensive measurement and analysis and obtain an in-depth understanding of YouTube uploaders. We estimate YouTube scale and examine the uploading behavior of YouTube users. Furthermore, we examine whether YouTube users are really broadcasting themselves, via characterizing and classifying user generated videos and user copied videos. Moreover, we demonstrate the positive reinforcement between on-line social behavior and uploading behavior.

Perhaps the most surprising result in the paper is the discovery that much of the content in YouTube is not user generated. We found that 63% of the most popular uploaders are primarily uploading UCC content, and that UCC uploaders on average upload many more videos than UGC uploaders. The results and observations in Section 3 can be used as a first step towards an automatic algorithm for classifying UGC and UCC content.

6. REFERENCES

[1] BALUJA, S., SETH, R., SIVAKUMAR, D., JING, Y., YAGNIK, J., KUMAR, S., RAVICHANDRAN, D., AND ALY, M. Video suggestion and discovery for youtube: Taking random walks through the view graph. In *WWW* (2008).

[2] BENEVENUTO, F., DUARTE, F., RODRIGUES, T., ALMEIDA, V., ALMEIDA, J., AND ROSS, K. Understanding video interactions in youtube. In *ACM Multimedia* (2008).

[3] BENEVENUTO, F., RODRIGUES, T., ALMEIDA, V., ALMEIDA, J., ZHANG, C., AND ROSS, K. W. Identifying video spammers in online social networks. In *Fourth International Workshop on Adversarial Information Retrieval on the Web* (2008).

[4] CHA, M., KWAK, H., RODRIGUEZ, P., AHN, Y., AND MOON, S. I tube, you tube, everybody tubes: Analyzing the world's largest user generated content video system. In *IMC* (2007).

[5] CHA, M., RODRIGUEZ, P., CROWCROFT, J., MOON, S., AND AMATRIAIN, X. Watching television over an ip network. In *IMC* (2008).

[6] CHENG, X., DALE, C., AND LIU, J. Statistics and social networking of youtube videos. In *IEEE IWQoS* (2008).

[7] CHENG, X., AND LIU, J. Nettube: Exploring social networks for peer-to-peer short video sharing. In *INFOCOM* (2009).

[8] COMSCORE. http://comscore.com/.

[9] CUEVAS, R., M.KRYCZKA, CUEVAS, A., KAUNE, S., GUERRERO, C., AND REJAIE, R. Is content publishing in BitTorrent altruistic or profit-driven? In *ACM CoNext* (2010).

[10] GILL, P., ARLITTZ, M., LI, Z., AND MAHANTIX, A. Youtube traffic characterization: a view from the edge. In *IMC* (2007).

[11] KOCH, R. *The 80/20 Principle: The Secret to Success by Achieving More with Less*. Broadway Business, 1999.

[12] LANGE, P. G. Publicly private and privately public: Social networking on youtube. *Journal of Computer-Mediated Communication 13*, 1-2 (2007).

[13] MISLOVE, A., MARCON, M., GUMMADI, K. P., DRUSCHEL, P., AND BHATTACHARJEE, B. Measurement and analysis of online social networks. In *IMC* (2007).

[14] PAOLILLO, J. C. Structure and network in the youtube core. In *HICSS* (2008).

[15] QIU, T., GE, Z., LEE, S., WANG, J., XU, J., AND ZHAO, Q. Modeling user activities in a large IPTV system. In *IMC* (2009).

[16] SAXENA, M., SHARAN, U., AND FAHMY, S. Analyzing video services in web 2.0: A global perspective. In *NOSSDAV* (2008).

[17] SIERSDORFER, S., PEDRO, J. S., CHELARU, S., AND NEJDL, W. How useful are your comments?- analyzing and predicting youtube comments and comment ratings. In *WWW* (2009).

[18] ZHOU, R., KHEMMARAT, S., AND GAO, L. The impact of youtube recommendation system on video views. In *ACM IMC* (2010).

[19] ZINK, M., SUH, K., GU, Y., AND KUROSE, J. Characteristics of youtube network traffic at a campus network - measurements, models, and implications. *Journal of Computer-Mediated Communication 53*, 4 (2009).

Summary Review Documentation for

"Broadcast Yourself: Understanding YouTube Uploaders"

Authors: Y. Ding, Y. Du, Y. Hu, Z. Liu, L. Wang, K. Ross, A. Ghose

Reviewer #1

Strengths: Amazing result on the ability of user generated content to compete directly with professionally produced content.

Very nice results on the (estimated) size of the YouTube universe. I particularly liked the methodology for doing that (high level scalable crawl of IDs, detailed profiling of a subset, and then final extrapolation from the combination of the two).

Excellent insight on the impact of recommendation on number of views and its relatively less strong impact on number of subscribers.

The fact that uploaders tend to be highly concentrated (specializing) in very few categories is also new and gives interesting insights into the behavior of uploaders of YouTube.

Weaknesses: The paper fails to cite a highly related reference: R.Cuevas, M.Kryczka, A. Cuevas, S. Kaune, C. Guerrero and R. Rejaie, "Is Content Publishing in BitTorrent Altruistic or Profit-Driven?", Proc. ACM CoNext 2010.

Comments to Authors: Not much to add. I greatly enjoyed reading this paper. My sincere compliments to the authors.

The only glitch that I see (more of a wish probably) is that the authors do not put Youtube uploaders in context by comparing them with the uploaders of other systems eg BitTorrent or 1-click hosting sites (rapidshare). For BitTorrent there exists a recently published paper (Is Content Publishing in BitTorrent Altruistic or Profit-Driven?) and I believe that there have also been some studies of 1-click hosting.

In Section 2.1: during the last weeks of the crawler when you saw a drop on new ID's returned per hour did you also see a drop in the overall number of ID's that you saw per hour. If yes then this might mean that YouTube was rate limiting your crawler, leaving open the possibility that you have not seen all the uploaders.

Reviewer #2

Strengths: While significant studies have been done on YouTube, the paper finds a new angle.

Weaknesses: The paper focuses on the data analysis and falls short on the implication of the analysis results. Most of the findings are expected.

Comments to Authors: The paper is well written and has solid analysis of the interesting youtube data. Most of the findings are expected, such as socially active users tend to upload more, males tend to upload more than female, and significant user generated content being uploaded.

The paper studies the content based on the videos uploaded by 100 users selected in three different ways. How representative are the data given it's still very small percentage of the users? Perhaps increasing the number of users to be studied or having some sensitivity analysis by using a different number of users and see if the same conclusions hold.

It'd be great to see some more applications about the findings.

Reviewer #3

Strengths: Reasonably well executed measurement study, rather useful results, well written paper.

Weaknesses: Measurement methodology has some problems and do not seem to capture proper datasets which affects accuracy of presented results.

Comments to Authors: This paper presents a measurement study for characterizing youtube uploaders. The presented analysis is sound and the results are somewhat interesting. However, authors do not in general describe implications of their findings (with a couple of exceptions).

The main concern with this paper is the soundness of its measurement methodology that affects the accuracy of its datasets (samples) and thus the correctness of the presented results. Here are more details on this problem with the methodology:

Authors select a seed user, collect her uploaded video, crawl all the related videos and then identify their uploaders. They repeat this process by selecting a new seed user. The key question is how these seed users are selected? If these seeds are randomly selected, then the authors are likely to have a reasonably complete set of uploaders. Otherwise, the captured uploaders are likely to be a (possibly small) fraction of uploaders. Authors do not describe their strategy for seed selection and it does not seem trivial to select a random user since user IDs do not have numerical forms. It appears that authors selected known users as seed. Therefore, this approach is likely to capture only the uploaders in the largest connected component, and is going to miss uploaders in other components and singleton ones. The conducted test for completeness via comparison with DFS crawl of social network is not reliable because the seeds were selected in the same region of the graph and do not reveal other components of the graph. Youtube does not seem to have a strong social network (like facebook or other social networks). Therefore it is very likely that this approach misses a large number of uploders. This could significantly affect the presented results that are the main contributions of this paper.

It would be useful that authors provide some information about the speed of crawling and key factors that may affect this. The crawling rate seems to be around 21K users/hour, which is modest.

Using BFS approach to crawl YouTube friendship network also reveals only high degree users in SocUser dataset. It is not clear why authors use just 100K samples from SocUsers. Since there is not need for further data collection for SocUSers, it seems useful to consider all of them for related analysis.

It is odd to see that there are no uploaders with a small (<100) number of views in Fig 2, this suggests that data mostly has captured bigger (and more visible) uploaders, which relates to the problem with data collection mentioned earlier.

In section 3, clearly determining whether a video is UCC or UGC is difficult and requires a manual approach. But it is not clear that this can be done reliably even in a manual fashion, For example how do you know whether a mash-up video is created for Youtube or it already used in a tv program. Authors do not elaborate on difficulties related to classification of videos into these two classes including the reasons for their inability to classify a few videos in each dataset.

The provided reasons for various findings in the paper are mostly intuitive guesses without any evidence to back them up.

Reviewer #4

Strengths: This is a new take on a well-mined problem -- looking at uploaders instead of videos etc.

Weaknesses: I find the motivation for this work rather weak -- I dont see a good reason why understanding uploaders is interesting other than a simple curiosity-driven study (and the authors don't really point out any either). Also, many parts of the paper seem to be rehashing well known or well-expected results.

Comments to Authors: This is a reasonably nice and in-depth study of the uploader behaviors as a self-contained topic. My biggest problem with the paper as is I am not sure why we should care about this uploader behavior beyond a "curiosity" result! I would really like to see more implications or motivation for these results - how would your findings change the behavior dynamics of Youtube, viewing patterns, content caching, etc?

Section 2.1: How do you bootstrap the initial uploader list before you do the crawl?

Maybe I don't understand what is happening here, but I found the "sampling" towards the end rather puzzling. Arguably, you have down the hard work of collecting the entire graph, why do you need to down sample it; 43 million users should be pretty easy to analyze using a beefy machine? Put another way, if you were going to do this sampling anyway, why go through the trouble of collecting the full user list?

Section 2.2: For the numbers you report in Sec 2.2 - I remember seeing a bunch of nice Youtube stats at this URL earlier: http://www.youtube.com/t/fact_sheet; but Google seems to have removed this content now.

Also, given this "heavy-tail" behavior is the "linear scaling" justified?

Section 2.3: I was also mildly annoyed by your references to the 80-20 rule; that to me is just a "heuristic" observation not a golden rule for every human-driven system. So the references to "X follows this but Y does not" seem to be out of place. All of them are skewed distributions and the data shows that; whether its 80-20 or 90-20 or 70-20 to me seems somewhat secondary.

How do you identify the "Categories" - I am particularly worried that the "concentration" in category you observe is merely an artifact of incorrect categorization or Youtube tagging it automatically into some default category.

Section 2.4: I find your claim that "Youtube's related video recommendation seems to be biased toward unpopular" pretty darn speculative. I can imagine a whole slew of other causes for this; e.g., most of these uploaders are video spammers, many of the views are from click bots, Youtube also posts a bunch of recent most videos on the home page (maybe many views come from that?)

The italicized conclusion at the end of this section too seems a bit doubtful in this light.

Section 2.5: What is SamRanUpl -- a new/different dataset? Why does age/gender matter?

Section 2.6: Maybe this reflects my ignorance, but what exactly do you mean by "the social network" or "join" here? Is it someone explicitly invoking a friend relation to another user?

Also, this could just be a wording issue, but some of your conclusions at the end of Sections 2.6 and 3.0.2 seem to suggest an implicit "causal" relationship, when there could be hidden variables or the causality could in fact be reverse, e.g., social users are more inclined - it could be that "active" users tend to be social and upload more. That's the hidden causality!

Section 3: Two high-level comments about this section. First, I dont really understand how you classify UGC vs UCC; the text is vague about this. Second, I am not sure I agree with what you call UCC; NBC uploading trailers or snippets are not "copying" anything - I got the feeling you wanted to distinguish content that the user "authored" herself vs. content that the user "borrowed" from others and reposted? Your definition of copying (which is vague, btw) seems the muddle these two.

Section 4: do you apply the techniques for detecting spammers/video spam to filter your dataset. I wonder if the results will change if you do that.

Reviewer #5

Strengths: - Interesting analysis of the uploaders' profile (to the best of my knowledge, it is the one of the first studies at this level on Youtube uploaders)
- The paper reads pretty well.

Weaknesses: - The analysis is somewhat superficial, should be more careful before drawing conclusions. Assessing that the number of views/subscribers does not/does follow a Zipf distribution needs some more rigorous justification than a graphical plot.
- There may be a bias in the sampling process to construct the dataset, and the paper does not present compelling sanity checks on this point.

Comments to Authors: The paper presents an interesting set of observations, but suffers from two main problems in my view:

1. The claims about distributions are made by visual inspection of cdf plots, which is not rigorous (e.g, that Figure 2 shows that the number of views does not follow a Zipf distribution but that Figure 3 shows that the number of subscribers does follow a Zipf distribution). QQ plots, and even better, hypothesis testing, should be conducted to have a more quantitative validation. Given the emphasis given to these observations in the paper, this more rigorous validation is needed.

2. The sampling process may be biased and corrupt the analysis, for example in the way you "randomly (that is, uniformly over the set of all users?) select a subset of uploaders and conduct deeper investigation". In addition DFS adds a bias favoring high degree nodes of the graph (but which fades away if the coverage is large, see Kurant et al's paper on unbiased sampling, IEEE JSAC, 2011). The paper does not convince the reader that the proper sanity checks have been made in order to be sure that these measurement biases do not invalidate the results.

Response from the Authors

We would like to thank the reviewers for their insightful comments. We included the suggested reference but otherwise did not make any significant changes to the paper.

As Internet researchers, we are interested in the characteristics and behavior of the content creators, arguably the most important entities in the Internet phenomenon. By identifying which uploaders in the near future will likely attract many views, advertisers can make more informed decisions. As mentioned by one of the reviewers, Google currently makes little information publicly available about the scale of YouTube. To understand YouTube's relative importance in the Internet landscape, we need to have estimates of it scale, which are provided in this paper.

We are confident that we crawled the majority of the Youtube uploaders. In the last weeks, our crawler, based on related videos, continued to see a large number of uploaders every hour; but, as indicated in the paper, the number of previously un-observed uploaders dropped off dramatically in the final weeks. Most importantly, we validated our claim by examining the overlap with YouTube's social network. The related video network and the social network are two separate networks. The social network is created by the YouTube users, and the related video network is created by YouTube. We acknowledge that there may be some singleton uploaders who are not included. We also did some small studies (not reported in paper) with some low-view uploaders (the authors and their friends) and found that they were all included in our crawl. Also, 13.5% of the 100,000 uploaders have less than 100 views in our data set.

Perhaps the most surprising result in the paper is the discovery that much of the content in YouTube is not user generated. We defined UCC content in the submitted paper as: A contiguous snippet of a video that was originally distributed outside of YouTube. We believe this definition is quite clear. We manually examined all of the videos from 300 uploaders (100 from each of the three categories), a very laborious and painstaking process. Of course, we would prefer to use a larger sample size. We found that 63% of the most popular uploaders are primarily uploading UCC content, and that UCC uploaders on average upload many more videos than UGC uploaders. The results and observations in Section 3 can be used as a first step towards an automatic algorithm for classifying UGC and UCC content.

Counting YouTube Videos via Random Prefix Sampling

Jia Zhou, Yanhua Li, Vijay Kumar Adhikari, and Zhi-Li Zhang
Department of Computer Science and Engineering
University of Minnesota
Minneapolis, MN 55414, USA
{jzhou,yanhua,viadhi,zhzhang}@cs.umn.edu

ABSTRACT

Leveraging the characteristics of YouTube video *id* space and exploiting a unique property of YouTube search API, in this paper we develop a *random prefix sampling* method to estimate the *total* number of videos hosted by YouTube. Through theoretical modeling and analysis, we demonstrate that the estimator based on this method is *unbiased*, and provide bounds on its variance and confidence interval. These bounds enable us to judiciously select sample sizes to control estimation errors. We evaluate our sampling method and validate the sampling results using two distinct collections of YouTube video *id*'s (namely, treating each collection as if it were the "true" collection of YouTube videos). We then apply our sampling method to the *live* YouTube system, and estimate that there are a total of roughly 500 millions YouTube videos by May, 2011. Finally, using an *unbiased* collection of YouTube videos sampled by our method, we show that YouTube video view count statistics collected by prior methods (e.g., through crawling of related video links) are highly skewed, significantly under-estimating the number of videos with very small view counts (< 1000) ; we also shed lights on the bounds for the total storage YouTube must have and the network capacity needed to delivery YouTube videos.

Categories and Subject Descriptors

H.3.5 [**Information Storage and Retrieval**]: Online Information Services

General Terms

Measurement

Keywords

Online social networks, Sampling, YouTube

1. INTRODUCTION

As the world's largest video sharing website, YouTube hosts a large number of mostly user-generated videos that are viewed by millions of users each day. For example, based on its own counting [26], YouTube states that it serves a total of more than 2 billion views a day. According to a recent study [15], YouTube traffic contributes to a significant portion of inter-domain network traffic; some estimate [1] places it at 10% of the total Internet traffic. Estimating the total number of videos hosted by YouTube and other statistics associated with them, e.g., number of view counts per day or the number of users uploading videos, is of great interest and import from both technical and social perspectives. For instance, knowing the total number of videos and view counts per day can shed light on the total amount of storage as well as the network capacity needed to store and deliver YouTube videos.

Unfortunately, these statistics regarding YouTube videos are *not* made available publicly by YouTube. Obtaining such statistics through other means (e.g., sampling) is not an easy and straightforward task for a variety of reasons. For example, while each YouTube video is identified by a unique *11-character* identifier (thereafter referred to as YouTube video *id*) that is randomly generated, the video id space is extremely large, of the order $O(64^{11})$ (see Section 3 for details). Hence any *brute-force* survey of the entire YouTube video population will be too costly; nor will any direct application of *(uniform) random sampling* to the video id space, e.g., by querying randomly generated video id's *a la* [7, 24], be effective. Existing methods for *collecting* YouTube videos rely on crawling the YouTube website and following the "related videos" links embedded in the web pages via either breadth-first or depth-first search [4, 9, 17]. While these methods provide an effective way to collect a sample of YouTube videos (or video id's), they produce a biased sample. Estimating YouTube statistics (e.g., view counts) using such biased samples can produce very skewed results (see Section 3). More sophisticated (graph-based) sampling methods [11, 14, 16] to circumvent or correct the bias require that the underly graph be *undirected*, whereas the graph formed by YouTube related videos is *directed* (see Section 2 for further discussion on this point and other related work).

Leveraging the characteristics of YouTube video *id* space and exploiting a unique property of YouTube search API, in this paper we propose and develop a *random prefix sampling* method to estimate the *total* number of videos hosted by YouTube. YouTube provides an API to allow users to perform keyword search to find videos they are interested in. One unique property of YouTube search API that we accidentally stumble on is that when searching using a keyword string of the format "`watch?v=xy...z`" (including the quotes) where "`xy...z`" is a prefix (of length L, $1 \le L \le 11$) of a possible YouTube video id which does not contain the literal "-" in the prefix, YouTube will return a list of videos whose id's begin with this prefix followed by "-", if they exist. The search may also return some videos whose id's do not contain the prefix, but the title, description or other fields happen to contain the entire search string (including "watch?v="). When the prefix is short (e.g., 1 or

IMC'11, November 2–4, 2011, Berlin, Germany.

2), it is more likely that the returned search results may contain such "noisy" video ids; with longer prefix length, the probability that this happens becomes zero or extremely small. On the other hand, using a prefix that is too long may result in a no-hit, i.e., no video id's being returned. Hence when performing random prefix sampling, the prefix length needs to be carefully selected to balance this trade-off (see Section 4 for details).

Taking advantage of this unique property of YouTube search API that allows us to perform random prefix sampling, we develop a theoretical model to derive an *unbiased* estimator for estimating the total number of YouTube videos, and provide bounds on its variance and confidence interval. These bounds enable us to judiciously select sample sizes to control estimation errors. The model and theoretical analysis are presented in Section 5. In Section 6, we evaluate our sampling method and validate the sampling results using two distinct collections of YouTube video *id*'s (namely, treating each collection as if it were the "true" population of YouTube videos). We then apply our sampling method to the *live* YouTube system, and estimate that there are a total of roughly 500 millions YouTube videos by May, 2011. Further, using an *unbiased* collection of YouTube videos sampled by our method, in Section 3 we show that YouTube video view count statistics collected by prior methods (i.e., through crawling of related video links) are highly skewed, significantly under-estimating the number of videos with very small view counts (< 1000). Finally, we show the bounds for the total storage YouTube must have and the network capacity needed to delivery YouTube videos, which is important for us to understand the impacts of YouTube to the Internet.

2. RELATED WORK

There are a number of recent studies on estimating the size and other properties of on-line social networks. In [20], Rejaie *et al.* estimate the number of users for MySpace and Twitter, where the key technique used is based on the observation that user id's are generated sequentially in an increasing order. This method is not applicable to YouTube, as video id's are randomly generated from a large id space. The authors of [25] propose a method to estimate the number of nodes in a given connected graph, and applies to a YouTube *related video* (sub)graph obtained using a sample YouTube video dataset from [17]. This method cannot be used to estimate the *total* number of YouTube videos. Graph-based methods such as snowball sampling [23] or random walks [19, 21, 22] have been widely used for collecting a *sample* of a large online social network, and this sample is then used to estimate other properties (e.g., degree distribution) of the social networks. To ensure this sample is unbiased (with respect to statistics of interest) or to correct the bias inherent in the sample, several variations of variations of random walk sampling methods such as Metropolis-Hastings random walk [11] and reweighting random walk [16] have been proposed. These methods cannot directly be used to estimate the *total size* of the underlying network. In a more recent work [14], the authors develop a novel random-walk based method to estimate the total number of users in an online social networks. This as well as the previously cited graph-based sampling methods all assume that the underlying network is *undirected*. Unfortunately, we have tested several YouTube datasets and found that the commonly used YouTube related video network is highly *asymmetrical*: for a given video v, on average more than 50% of its related videos do not list v as their related videos. The study in [8] propose several sampling methods via a search engine API to generate a "near-uniform" sample of documents (under certain plausible assumptions about the search engine). These methods, however, do not provide an estimate of the total size of the underlying document space.

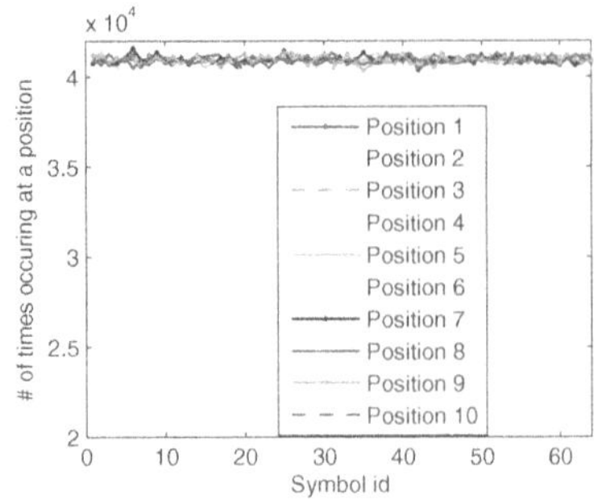

Figure 1: Frequencies at a given position of a video ID

3. YOUTUBE VIDEO ID SPACE

In this section, we present some characteristics of YouTube ids, which motivates us to propose the random prefix sampling method, that can retrieve uniform YouTube video samples.

Each YouTube id consists of 11 characters denoted by $v = [v_1, \cdots, v_{11}]$. The first 10 characters of a valid id contain any of the characters in $S = \{0-9, \_, -, A-Z, a-z\}$, i.e., $v_i \in S$ $(i = 1, \cdots, 10)$. The last (11-th) character v_{11} only comes from $T = \{0, 4, 8, A, E, I, M, Q, U, Y, c, g, k, o, s, w\}$, namely, $v_{11} \in T$[1]. The size of video id space is, therefore, $10^{64} \times 16$. We also observe that YouTube video ids are not generated in any sequence. Instead, YouTube picks an unused random id from this pool for each new video that is uploaded.

To show that YouTube video is randomly generated from the id space, we show that each valid character shows up at i-th position of an id with the same probability. We use a set of 2 million video ids collected via breadth first search using related video links. The result is shown in Fig. 1. In this figure, X-axis represents different positions of an id, and Y-axis shows the number of times a specific character shows up at that position. For any given position, we can see that all the characters are chosen with nearly equal probability. Moreover, if we fix the character(s) in one or multiple positions and count the number of appearances of characters in other positions, we can also see that all the characters are chosen with nearly equal probability for the rest positions. So the chosen of characters in different positions are also independent.

4. RANDOM PREFIX SAMPLING VIA YOUTUBE SEARCH API

In this section, we discuss how we use the YouTube API to perform a random prefix search on the YouTube video id space.

4.1 Random Prefix Search

One unique property of YouTube search API we find is that when searching using a keyword string of the format "`watch?v=xy...z`" (including the quotes) where "`xy...`" is a prefix (of length L, $1 \leq L \leq 11$) of a possible YouTube video id which does not contain the literal "-" in the prefix, YouTube will return a list of videos whose id's begin with this prefix followed by "-", if they exist. The search may also return some videos whose id's do not contain the prefix, but the title, description or other fields happen to contain the entire search string (including "watch?v="). When the prefix is short (e.g., 1 or 2), it is more likely that the returned search results may contain such "noisy" video ids; also, the short prefix may match a large number of videos and YouTube API can only return

[1]Video ids with other characters in 11th position represent copies of other videos (e.g. xG0wi1m-89p is just a copy of xG0wi1m-89o)

some of them in the result, as YouTube limits the number of returned results for any query. In contrast, if the prefix is too long (e.g., 6 or 7), no result may be returned by the search engine.

Note that YouTube search is not case sensitive, so both 'abcd' and 'AbcD' will return the same set of results. If we include a "-" in the prefix or try to search use some other format, the results returned by YouTube may contain many unrelated videos (not beginning with the prefix expected) and hard to explain. We find that querying prefixes with a prefix length of four (with all returned ids having a "-" in the fifth place) provide a big enough result set so that each prefix returns some results and small enough to never reach the result limit set by the API.

4.2 Completeness of the Returned Results

In this section, we show that our prefix based search is nearly complete. We use prefix length four for this validation. Since, by design, our queries only return videos where the fifth character is a "-", we need to show that any video id that has its first "-" in the fifth position can be found by querying YouTube API using our method and using the first 4 characters as the query string. In fact, a "-" is generally used as a separator in URLs for Google search [2] [3].

We use three real datasets to validate these results. The first one is generated using breadth first search (BFS) method based on related YouTube videos [6]. The second one provides all the videos in Entertainment category by December 21, 2006 [9]. The third one with video ids is obtained by searching different keywords and their combinations from a dictionary. In each of these cases, we see whether any video id with "-" in its fifth character observed in these dataset can be also obtained by our method. Table 1 summarizes our findings. We see that in the worst case, there are not more than 0.3% of the ids that are seen in other dataset but cannot be found using our method. More than 99.6% of the video ids with "-" in fifth position can be obtained using our method. After we carefully checked each of those missing videos, we found that those videos are missing all due to the following reasons: a) it is a very new video; b) the video is blocked due to copyright, violence, and sexual issues; c) it is already deleted or configured to be a private video by the uploader. All in all, the prefix search is indeed able to retrieve a complete video id set.

Note that, searching the same prefix in different geographical locations, in general, may return results in different order based upon local popularity. However, since we select our query string carefully to have each query match only a small set of videos, the ordering does not matter much. Moreover, we find that we see the same set of results (albeit sometimes in a different order) when we queried the YouTube API using our method from a large number of Planetlab [18] nodes.

5. RANDOM PREFIX SAMPLING: THEORETICAL ANALYSIS

An estimator is a function of a set of samples which produces an estimate of an unknown characteristic. In this section, we introduce our estimator of the total number of YouTube videos. In addition, we also analyze the variance for the proposed estimator, and develop its confidence interval. Note that the proposed methodology can also be applied to other online social systems as long as those systems satisfy: a) a new generated ID is uniformly selected from ID space; b) entries in those systems can be enumerated by ID prefix searching.

5.1 Estimator of the total number of videos

Using the unbiased random prefix sampling method, now we propose an estimator $\hat{N}$ for the total number of YouTube videos.

Table 1: Prefix search via YouTube API can return a complete set of YouTube videos.

.	Size	$N1$	$N2$	$N3$
Dataset #1 [6]	932763	13864	41	0.30%
Dataset #2 [9]	1687506	24576	66	0.27%
Dataset #3	6692429	99887	122	0.12%
$N1$	Number of IDs with "-" at the 5-th position			
$N2$	Number of IDs with "-" at the 5-th position, but are not in search result			
$N3$	Percentage of IDs with "-" at the 5-th position, but are not in search result			

The observations presented in previous section indicate that 1) the entire YouTube id space can be represented as $\mathcal{S} = S^{10} \times T$, where $S = \{0\text{–}9, \_, -, A\text{–}Z, a\text{–}z\}$ and $T = \{0, 4, 8, A, E, I, M, Q, U, Y, c, g, k, o, s, w\}$; 2) when a YouTube video is uploaded, the probability that a randomly generated id matches a given L-length prefix is a constant, $1 \leq L \leq 11$. Let p_L denote this probability and we have

$$p_L = \begin{cases} \frac{1}{|S|^L} & \text{if } L = 1, \cdots, 10 \\ \frac{1}{|S|^{10}|T|} & \text{if } L = 11 \end{cases} \tag{1}$$

(2)

To estimate N, we randomly generate m prefixes with length L, $1 \leq L \leq 11$, and query them using YouTube API. Each query returns a sample value X_i^L, $1 \leq i \leq m$, representing the total number of YouTube videos with that particular prefix. Then, the total number of YouTube videos can be estimated using these m samples, as stated in Theorem 1.

THEOREM 1 (Estimator of the Total Number of Videos). *Given m samples X_i^L, $(1 \leq i \leq m)$ by querying randomly generated prefixes of the same length $1 \leq L \leq 11$, we have the* unbiased *estimator*

$$\hat{N} = \frac{\bar{X}^L}{p_L} = \frac{1}{mp_L}\sum_{i=1}^{m} X_i^L. \tag{3}$$

for the total number of YouTube videos, where p_L is defined as above.

PROOF. We consider the process of how all N YouTube video ids are generated.

Based on our observations discussed in previous section, each YouTube video is generated uniformly and independently from the id space $\mathcal{S}$. Given a prefix of length L, let I_k^L $(1 \leq k \leq N)$ be an indicator variable for the k-th YouTube video id, where $I_k^L = 1$ if the k-th ID belongs to that prefix, and $I_k^L = 0$ otherwise. Clearly, $I_k^L(k = 1, \cdots, N)$ are all independent and they all follow the same Bernoulli distribution with successful probability as p_L. Then, the random variable

$$X^L = \sum_{k=1}^{N} I_k^L \tag{4}$$

captures the number of videos with a prefix of length L, and satisfies binomial distribution $Binomial(N, p_L)$ (since it is a sum of N random variables with the same Bernoulli distribution).

The random variable X^L can be sampled by querying randomly generated prefixes with length $1 \leq L \leq 11$. Each outcome from a query is the total number of videos with a particular prefix of length L. If we take m $(1 \leq m \ll 1/p_L)$ queries, we have m samples as

$$X_i^L \sim Binomial(N, p_L), \qquad i = 1, \cdots, m. \tag{5}$$

Then each of them has expectation value $E[X_i^L] = Np_L$.

Define the variable $\bar{X}^L = \frac{1}{m}\sum_{i=1}^{m} X_i^L$, which indicates the sample mean. The expectation of $\bar{X}^L$ satisfies

$$E[\bar{X}^L] = E[\frac{1}{m}\sum_{i=1}^{m} X_i^L] = \frac{1}{m}\sum_{i=1}^{m} E[X_i^L] = Np_L$$

Hence the estimator $\hat{N}$ can be derived as follows

$$\hat{N} = \frac{\bar{X}^L}{p_L} = \frac{1}{mp_L}\sum_{i=1}^{m} X_i^L. \quad (6)$$

Then from eq. (6), the expectation of $\hat{N}$ satisfies

$$E[\hat{N}] = E[\frac{\overline{X^L}}{p_L}] = N, \quad (7)$$

which proves that $\hat{N}$ defined in eq. (3) is unbiased. □

5.2 Variance Analysis and Confidence Interval

In this part, we provide some analytical results for our estimator, i.e., its variance and the confidence interval. According to eq. (3), the variance of $\hat{N}$ is

$$\begin{aligned} Var[\hat{N}] &= Var[\frac{\overline{X^L}}{p_L}] = \frac{1}{p_L^2 m^2} Nmp_L(1 - mp_L) \\ &= N(\frac{1}{mp_L} - 1), \end{aligned} \quad (8)$$

which indicates that two key factors, i.e., the prefix length L and the number of samples m determine the variance (or the accuracy) of the estimator $\hat{N}$. When m increases, the variance decreases linearly, and when L increases, the variance increases exponentially. In the next subsection, we will discuss how to choose the parameters m and L to minimize the variance.

Now we switch to find the confidence interval for our estimator, where the following Theorem 2 states the result.

THEOREM 2 (Confidence Interval of the Estimator $\hat{N}$). *Given any $0 < \epsilon \ll 1$ and $0 < \alpha \leq 1$, the confidence interval for our estimator $\hat{N}$ as below*

$$Pr[N(1 - \epsilon) \leq \hat{N} \leq N(1 + \epsilon)] = 1 - \alpha,$$

can be guaranteed when

$$m \geq \frac{z_{\alpha/2}^2}{p_L(\epsilon^2 N + z_{\alpha/2}^2)},$$

where $z_{\alpha/2}$ is the $100(1 - z_{\alpha/2})$-th percentile of the standard normal distribution $\mathcal{N}(0, 1)$.

PROOF. Since each random variable X_i^L follows the same binomial distribution, their sum $\sum_{i=1}^{m} X_i^L$ also follows a binomial distribution $Binomial(N, mp_L)$. When both Nmp_L and $N(1 - mp_L)$ are larger than 10, $\sum_{i=1}^{m} X_i^L$ can be well approximated by a normal distribution [13]. Then, we have the random variable

$$Y_m^L = \frac{\frac{1}{m}\sum_{i=1}^{m} X_i^L - Np_L}{\sqrt{\frac{Np_L}{m}(1 - mp_L)}} \quad (9)$$

approximate to the standard normal distribution $\mathcal{N}(0, 1)$. Then for a given confidence level $1 - \alpha$, $0 < \alpha < 1$, we have

$$Pr(-z_{\alpha/2} \leq Y_m^L \leq z_{\alpha/2}) = 1 - \alpha, \quad (10)$$

where $z_{\alpha/2}$ is the $100(1 - z_{\alpha/2})$-th percentile of the standard normal distribution. Then, from eq. (9) and eq. (10), we have

$$N(1 - \epsilon) \leq \hat{N} \leq N(1 + \epsilon) \quad (11)$$

$$\epsilon = \frac{z_{\alpha/2}}{p_L}\sqrt{\frac{p_L(1 - mp_L)}{mN}} \quad (12)$$

where from eq. (12), we know that eq. (11) holds true when the sample size m satisfies

$$m \geq \frac{z_{\alpha/2}^2}{p_L(\epsilon^2 N + z_{\alpha/2}^2)}.$$

□

5.3 How to Choose the Prefix Length L and Sample Size m

Now we are in a position to show how to choose m and L in practice. We use the relative root mean square error (RRMSE) as a metric to quantify the accuracy of the estimation, which is defined as below

$$RRMSE(\hat{N}) = \sqrt{E[(\frac{\hat{N} - N}{N})^2]}. \quad (13)$$

Table 2: Minimal number of samples for different RRMSE and L. Each entry represents corresponding minimum m value for a particular tuple (RRMSE, L)

RRMSE \ L	1	2	3	4	5	6	7
0.05	1	1	1	7	430	27488	1759218
0.10	1	1	1	2	108	6872	439805
0.15	1	1	1	1	48	3055	195469
0.20	1	1	1	1	27	1718	109952

In Table 2, we can see that as L increases, RRMSE increases exponentially. Hence, we will choose L as small as possible to minimize the variance. However, in practice, a prefix of length $L < 5$ contains usually more than one hundred results, and YouTube API can only return at most 30 ids for each prefix query. On the other hand, based on our experimental results, a prefix with length $L = 5$ always contains less than 10 valid ids. Therefore, a prefix length of 5 is a good choice in practice. With this prefix length, from Table 2 we can see that to achieve an RRMSE of 0.05, 0.10, 0.15 and 0.20, we need to have at least $m = 430, 108, 48, 27$ samples, respectively.

6. EXPERIMENTAL RESULTS

In this section, we examine how correctly and efficiently our method works with actual data. Since we do not know the actual video counts for YouTube, we use a "synthetic data" approach. We take a subset of YouTube video ids as "ground truth" and try to see how correctly our method can estimate it. In particular, we study the error rates, and confidence intervals as they change when we change the sample size etc. To justify that the estimated results are unbiased and accurate, we perform cross validations in "synthetic dataset" and in real YouTube. We next apply our method to estimate the total number of actual YouTube videos. Finally, we also present results that show how we can construct a more realistic picture of the view-count distribution of YouTube videos using our unbiased samples.

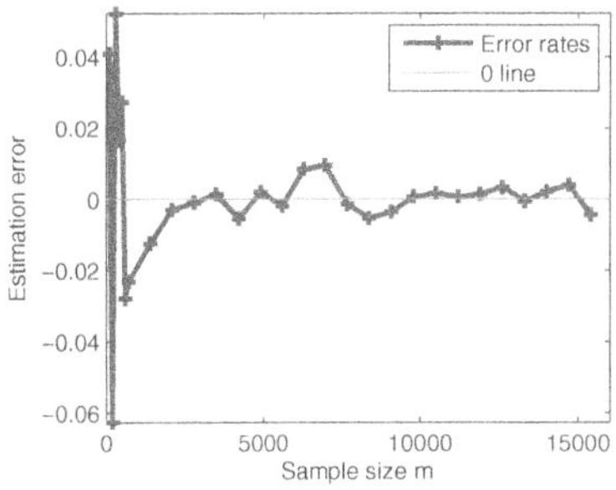

Figure 2: Error rate over Ground Truth, when $L = 3$

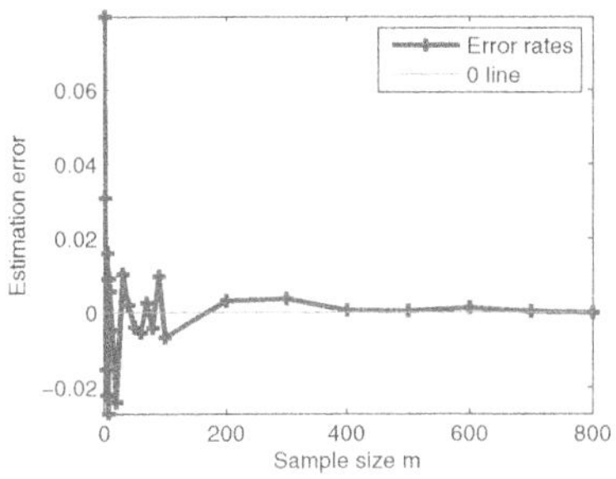

Figure 3: Error rate over Ground Truth, when $L = 4$

6.1 Validating the Theory

We first evaluate our sampling method and validate the theoretical results using two distinct collection of YouTube video id's (Datasets I and II in Table 1), treating each collection as if it were the "true" collection of YouTube videos. Using Dataset II and with $L = 3$ and $L = 4$ respectively, Fig. 2 and Fig. 3 show the estimation errors as a function of the sample size m. We see that in both cases, the estimation error converges quickly to 0, when the sampling size m increases. Further, for smaller prefix length, e.g., $L = 3$, more samples are needed to reach the same level of error rate as that of $L = 4$. These results confirm our theoretical analysis. Fix the prefix length as $L = 3$, Fig. 4 shows the estimation accuracy as a function of the sample size with different confidence interval levels, $\alpha = 5\%, 25\%, 75\%, 95\%$. We see that as we increases the sample size, the confidence interval narrows as expected.

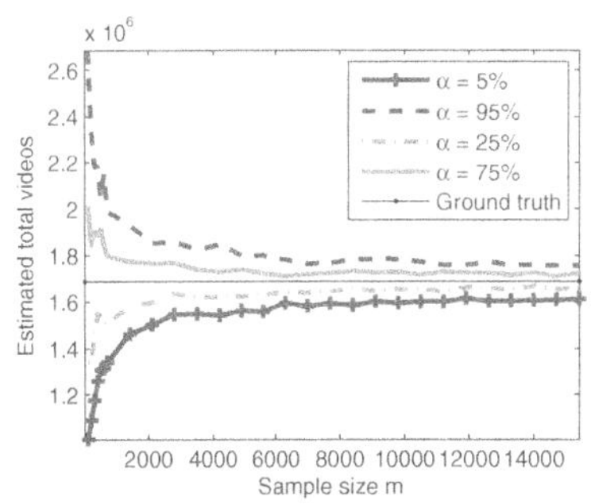

Figure 4: Confidence interval

6.2 Estimating the Total Number of YouTube Videos

We now apply our method to the *live* YouTube website and estimate the total number of YouTube videos. We set $L = 5$ and randomly generate prefixes of length 5 to perform random prefix sampling using the YouTube search API. In Fig. 5, for each $x = 0, 1, \ldots$, we plot the number of (randomly generated) prefixes (the y-axis) that the YouTube search yields exactly x video id's matching the prefix – this plot provides an approximation to the distribution of X^L. Clearly, the curve is bell-shaped, resembling a Gaussian distribution, as predicted by our theoretical model: for large N, the binomial distribution of X^L (see eq.(5) can be approximated by a Gaussian distribution with the same mean and variance.

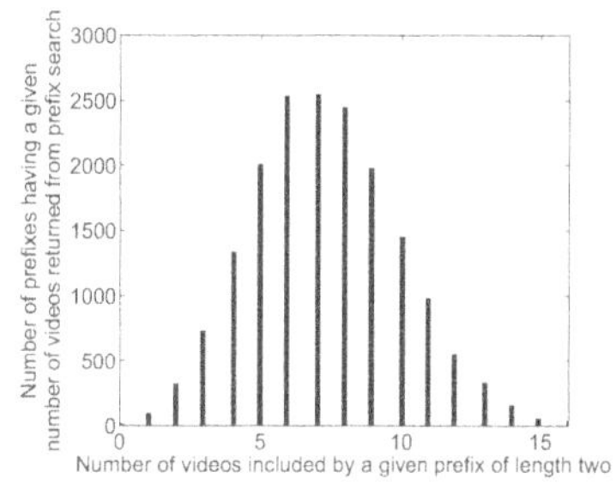

Figure 5: The distribution of the prefixes of length $L = 5$, over number of returned videos

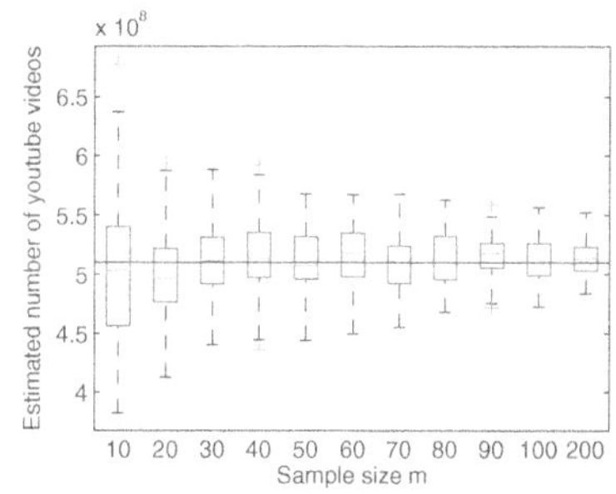

Figure 6: Estimated number of YouTube videos by 05/12/2011

For a fixed sample size m, we can estimate the total number of YouTube videos using the estimator in eq.(7), and bound the variance of the estimation using eq.(8). Fig. 6 plots the estimation results as we vary the sampling size m. We see that as the sampling size m increases, the estimated total number of YouTube videos converges to 5.02×10^8 (502 millions).

Since we do not know the *ground truth* about the total number of YouTube videos, we perform the following simple cross-validation using the sample YouTube video datasets listed in Table 1. We take $N = 5.02 \times 10^8$ as if it were the ground truth, and for a fixed L, generate the *theoretical* distribution of X^L using eq.(5). We then use the sample YouTube datasets to generate the *empirical* distribution of X^L. For $L = 2$, Fig. 7 compares the theoretical and empirical distributions of X^L using Dataset I. The two distributions match surprisingly well, indicating that our estimated total number of YouTube videos is likely within the ballpark of the real ground truth.

6.3 Impact on View Counts

Our random prefix sampling method not only enables us to estimate the total number of YouTube videos; it also produces an *unbiased* sample of YouTube videos. To illustrate the importance of such an *unbiased* sample in estimating other important YouTube video statistics, we take the total *view count* distribution as an example. Fig. 8 plots the total view count distributions obtained from

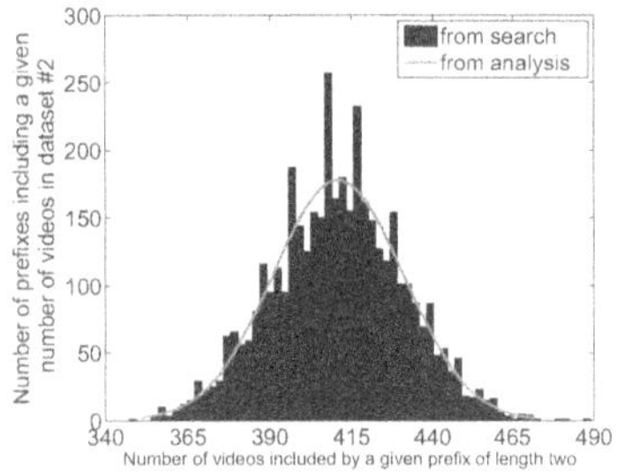

Figure 7: The distribution of the prefixes of length $L = 2$, over number of returned videos

Datasets I and II (two "biased" collections via crawling related videos via breadth-first search) as well as the sample video collection using our random prefix search. In this figure, the x-axis represents the percentage of the videos and the y-axis represents the total view counts. It is clear that the two biased datasets overestimate the total view counts of YouTube videos. For example, our dataset indicates that only 14% of videos have a total view count of more than 1000 (the straight line), whereas 89% and 52% percentage of videos in Datasets I and II have at least 1000 view counts. So Datasets I and II significantly underestimate the number of videos with extremely small total view counts (< 1000). As a result, Datasets I and II significantly inflate the average view counts: the average view count from Dataset I, Dataset II and our dataset are 32046, 9928, and 3898 respectively.

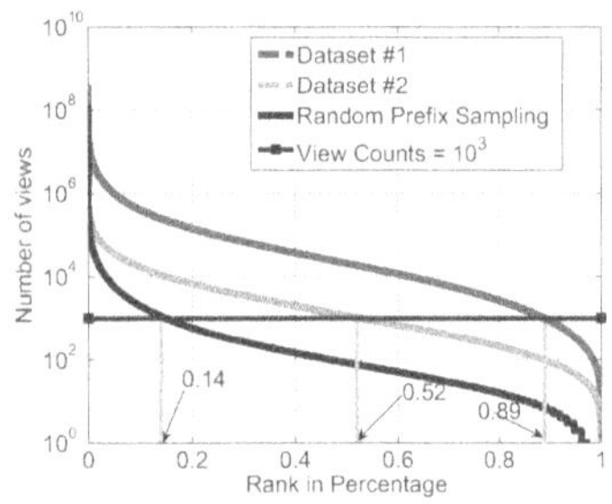

Figure 8: Views counts by different data sets

7. ESTIMATING THE TOTAL STORAGE AND NETWORK CAPACITY REQUIREMENTS OF YOUTUBE

In this section, using an *unbiased* collection of YouTube videos sampled by our method, we provide an estimation of the minimal total amount of storage needed to store YouTube and the total network capacity needed per day to delivery YouTube videos.

To begin with, we first calculate the average file size of YouTube videos. To do this, we analyze the length fields of HTTP responses for the corresponding sampled videos. The average size we obtained is 9.87MB, which is similar to that in [12]. Multiplying this average size with the total number of YouTube videos by May 2011 , we obtain an estimate of the minimal total storage needed to store all YouTube videos by then, which is around 5 Petabytes (PBs) $\approx$ 10MB $\times 0.5 \times 10^9$. Note that for each video, YouTube in general stores multiple (at least 4 [5]) copies and several different formats [10]. So the actual storage capacity needed is likely far bigger; perhaps multiplying a factor of 10 would give us a closer estimate to the real order of magnitude.

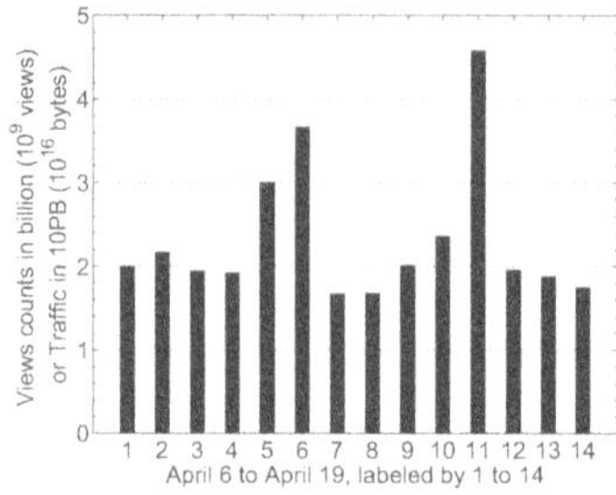

Figure 9: Views counts by different data sets

Further, using an unbiased sample of YouTube videos and examining their view counts over time, we calculate an estimation of the total YouTube video counts per day, and by multiplying it by the average video file size (10 MBs), we obtain an estimated amount of total network capacity needed to carry YouTube videos over the Internet each day. For a two-week period from April 5th to April 18th, the results are shown in Fig.9. From Fig.9, we see that the total view counts range from around 1.7 billion/day to 4.6 billion/day, and the resulting traffic (network capacity) ranges from 17 PBs/day to 46 PBs/day. Note that users may not download and watch the entire video during each viewing and YouTube has different video formats (e.g., formats used by mobile players on smart phones); on the other hand, there are also "wasted" network capacity in YouTube delivery [10]. The above simple "rule-of-thumb" estimation does not capture these effects. Nonetheless, we believe that our results provide a "ballpark estimate" of the actual amount of total YouTube traffic per day.

8. CONCLUSION

In this paper, we introduce a random prefix sampling method via YouTube API, that can uniformly collect YouTube ids, which enables us to design an unbiased estimator of the total number of YouTube videos, as well as in depth analysis on its variance and confidence interval in terms of the sample size and prefix length. Extensive experimental results demonstrate that our sampling and estimation methods provide unbiased estimation of total number of YouTube videos, and total view counts, which discloses a high inherent bias in the results obtained by existing biased sampling methods. We also shed lights on the bounds for the total storage YouTube must have and the network capacity needed to delivery YouTube videos. The proposed random prefix sampling provides a way to unbiasedly study characteristics of YouTube Videos.

As part of our future work, we are interested in using this method to further study how the statistics, such as the total number of YouTube videos, view counts evolve over time, which would give us a dynamic view of traffic by YouTube.

9. ACKNOWLEDGMENTS

We would like to thank the anonymous reviewers and our shepherd, Ratul Mahajan, for their helpful feedbacks on this paper.

We gratefully acknowledge the support of our sponsors. The work is supported in part by the NSF grants CNS-0905037, CNS-1017092 and CNS-1017647.

10. REFERENCES

[1] Ellacoya data shows web traffic overtakes peer-to-peers as largest percentage of bandwidth on the network. http://www.ellacoya.com/news/pdf/2007/NXTcommEllacoyaMediaAlert.pdf.

[2] Google test : hyphen and underscore. http://www.prweaver.com/blog/2004/08/26/2-hyphen-and-underscore/.

[3] Word separators used by google. http://www.internetofficer.com/seo/google-word-separator/.

[4] V. K. Adhikari, S. Jain, Y. Chen, and Z.-L. Zhang. Reverse Engineering the YouTube Video Delivery Cloud. In *HotMD'11*.

[5] V. K. Adhikari, S. Jain, Y. Chen, and Z.-L. Zhang. Vivisecting youtube: An active measurement study. Technical report. http://www.cs.umn.edu/research/technical_reports.php?page=report&report_id=11-012.

[6] V. K. Adhikari, S. Jain, and Z.-L. Zhang. Youtube traffic dynamics and its interplay with a tier-1 isp: an isp perspective. In *Proceedings of the 10th annual conference on Internet measurement*, IMC '10, pages 431–443, New York, NY, USA, 2010. ACM.

[7] Y. Ahn, S. Han, H. Kwak, S. Moon, and H. Jeong. Analysis of topological characteristics of huge online social networking services. In *Proceedings of the 16th International Conference on World Wide Web*, Alberta, Canada, 2007.

[8] Z. Bar-yossef and M. Gurevich. Random sampling from a search engine's index. In *WWW '06: World Wide Web Conference*, pages 367–376.

[9] M. Cha, H. Kwak, P. Rodriguez, Y.-Y. Ahn, and S. Moon. I tube, you tube, everybody tubes: analyzing the world's largest user generated content video system. In *Proceedings of the 7th ACM SIGCOMM conference on Internet measurement*, IMC '07, pages 1–14, New York, NY, USA, 2007. ACM.

[10] A. Finamore, M. Mellia, M. Munafo, R. Torres, and S. R. Rao. YouTube Everywhere: Impact of Device and Infrastructure Synergies on User Experience. In *IMC '11*.

[11] W. R. Gilks, S. Richardson, and D. J. Spiegelhalter. Markov chain monte carlo in practice. In *Operations Research*, 1996.

[12] P. Gill, M. Arlitt, Z. Li, and A. Mahanti. Youtube traffic characterization: a view from the edge. In *Proceedings of the 7th ACM SIGCOMM conference on Internet measurement*, IMC '07, pages 15–28, New York, NY, USA, 2007. ACM.

[13] I. Hacking. *An Introduction to Probability and Inductive Logic*. Cambridge University Press, 2001.

[14] L. Katzir, E. Liberty, and O. Somekh. Estimating sizes of social networks via biased sampling. In *Proceedings of the 20th international conference on World wide web*, WWW '11, pages 597–606, New York, NY, USA, 2011. ACM.

[15] C. Labovitz et al. Internet inter-domain traffic. In *SIGCOMM'10*.

[16] L. Lovász. Random walks on graphs: A survey. *Combinatorics Paul Erdos is Eighty*, 2(1):1–46, 1993.

[17] A. Mislove, M. Marcon, K. P. Gummadi, P. Druschel, and B. Bhattacharjee. Measurement and analysis of online social networks. In *Proceedings of the 7th ACM SIGCOMM conference on Internet measurement*, IMC '07, pages 29–42, New York, NY, USA, 2007. ACM.

[18] PlanetLab. An open platform for developing, deploying, and accessing planetary-scale services. http://www.planet-lab.org.

[19] A. Rasti, M. Torkjazi, R. Rejaie, N. Duffield, W. Willinger, and D. Stutzbach. Respondent-driven sampling for characterizing unstructured overlays. In *Proceedings of IEEE INFOCOM 2009 Mini-Conference*, April 2009.

[20] R. Rejaie, M. Torkjazi, M. Valafar, and W. Willinger. Sizing up online social networks. *Network, IEEE*, 24(5):32 –37, 2010.

[21] B. Ribeiro and D. Towsley. Estimating and sampling graphs with multidimensional random walks. In *Proceedings of the 10th annual conference on Internet measurement*, IMC '10, pages 390–403, New York, NY, USA, 2010. ACM.

[22] D. Stutzbach, R. Rejaie, N. Duffield, S. Sen, and W. Willinger. On unbiased sampling for unstructured peer-to-peer networks. In *Proceedings of the 6th ACM SIGCOMM conference on Internet measurement*, IMC '06, pages 27–40, New York, NY, USA, 2006. ACM.

[23] S. Wasserman and K. Faust. *Social Network Analysis. Methods and Applications*. 1994.

[24] C. Wilson, B. Boe, A. Sala, K. Puttaswamy, and B. Y. Zhao. User interactions in social networks and their implications. In *EuroSys*, pages 205–218, 2009.

[25] S. Ye and F. Wu. Estimating the size of online social networks. In *Social Computing (SocialCom), 2010 IEEE Second International Conference on*, pages 169 –176, 2010.

[26] YouTube. YouTube statistics. www.youtube.com/t/press_statistics.

Summary Review Documentation for

"Counting YouTube Videos via Random Prefix Sampling"

Authors: J. Zhou, Y. Li, V. Adhikari, Z. Zhang

Reviewer #1

Strengths: Nice paper that exploits some interesting practical observations. Well written with very careful and thorough analysis.

Weaknesses: Estimating total number of videos in Youtube appears to be a relatively narrow problem. The approach itself is quite simple and did not particularly strike me as a fundamentally.

Comments to Authors: I like this paper's methodology, careful experimentation and attention to detail. I was however underwhelmed by the goal of just counting YouTube Videos. To me, that was too narrow a goal.

I guess things like view count distributions are interesting to estimate, but that has so little real estate devoted in this paper. I wish I had seen a bit more treatment of such more detailed analysis where the power of the proposed scheme may be a bit more relevant and important.

The authors argue vehemently in the intro that existing approaches offer skewed and biased results. I am not sure I saw in the paper what the total video count results are using those method compared to the proposed method.

I could not completely follow the view count distribution results. The authors mention they use Datasets I and II obtained by BFS crawling of YouTube as the total collection. Then they compare Random Prefix Sampling with other biased methods that again use BFS. So, this is BFS over BFS crawled data, which makes it a bit hard to digest what the implications are.

Why not plot the actual distribution in Figure 8 instead of showing one point alone ?

Reviewer #2

Strengths: A nice, short paper that provides both a way to randomly sample youtube videos and shows the bias in current datasets.

Weaknesses: The results may be short-lived. Perhaps youtube will change their id assignment mechanism tomorrow.

Inufficient evidence that the id assignment mechanism has been reverse engineered correctly.

Comments to Authors: Your entire paper hinges on you having correctly reverse-engineered the video id assignment mechanism. Yet, it wasn't clear to me that the evidence you present of its correctness in the paper is sufficient. Your evidence is essentially the experiment behind Figure 1, which shows that each symbol is equally likely to occur at each position.

Aren't there other id assignment mechanisms that lead to the same distribution (e.g., some multi-letter codes)? It appears that you need a more detailed experiment that shows that each position is filled independently.

Why do you think '-' is treated as a special character in the search? Is that an attempt to accommodate for accidental hyphenation (e.g., by email readers) or something else is going on?

Reviewer #3

Strengths: A piece of work with a clear purpose and a significant technical contribution that provides new insight into YT.

Weaknesses: The work and proposed methodology is YT-specific and unlikely to apply to other online social media systems. There is also little room for follow-up work.

Comments to Authors: This is a nice short paper. while it is exclusively focused on YT, the work does provide new insight into YT as a system and how it is being used.

While theorems 1 and 2 are rather standard, it's nice to see a careful treatment of the proposed estimator before it is applied in practice.

Some discussion about YT-like systems where the proposed methodology may also applicable (what key ingredients are required?) would be helpful.

Reviewer #4

Strengths: The analysis for any sampling bias is the paper's main strength.

Weaknesses: There is little point to the analysis for sampling bias; it is not clear why one should expect there to be significant bias, it is not clear how (much more difficult) measurements of social network size via crawling are precedent for this relatively straightforward count of objects in a uniform ID space.

Comments to Authors: The main problem in this paper is lack of motivation. Why does it matter how many videos are in youtube? Why is your technique interesting for networking researchers in general? Now that I know there are 500 million youtube videos, what am I going to do with that number? Your introduction states (without support) "estimating the total number of videos hosted by youtube and other statistics associated with them ... is of great interest and import from both technical and social perspectives". I don't see it. Sure, you can guess about how much total storage youtube must have, but not really understand the network capacity needed, since the number of videos is not representative of the popularity of videos. And what's the "import" from a social perspective?

At a lower level, again the problem is motivation; assuming I care about how many youtube videos exist, why do I need all the analysis of how a hashed ID space uniformly distributes objects so that counting the number of objects in a portion of the uniform space estimates the occupancy of the whole? Why not do something more interesting? Why not answer the questions posed in the introduction of how much total storage youtube must have or how much network capacity is needed? It would seem to be simple arithmetic when youtube is happy to provide view counts and file sizes.

Thus, the beginning of section 2 (the topic sentence of the only paragraph in the section) seems unnecessary. I can understand what challenges may befall a project that wishes to estimate the size of a graph based on the properties of a random walk. I cannot understand what those challenges have to do with estimating the size of a bag based on the properties of regions of ID space.

The work appears very well done, which leads to my relatively high rating of the paper. Yet, this exhaustive analysis of a relatively simple trick (that is likely to be disabled if youtube wants to keep the total number of videos a secret) seems more appropriate for a journal than for IMC.

Reviewer #5

Strengths: An unexpected application of prefix sampling.

Weaknesses: The problem domain is narrow and it is not clear how important to count YouTube videos. I'd like to see more interesting applications besides this one.

Comments to Authors: The paper shows an unexpected application of random sampling technique to count YouTube videos. However, the problem domain is too narrow and not well motivated. Some of the proposed techniques are tailored this context that YouTube happened to return its videos that begin with a given prefixes. Such interfaces are bound to change, and the exact ID assignment are also subject to change, which renders the approach no longer work.

I'd like to see other applications of your approach beyond this problem or give me some interesting analyses that you can perform with the knowledge of video counts.

Response from the Authors

We are grateful to the anonymous reviewers and our shepherd, Ratul Mahajan, for their helpful feedback on this paper. We have carefully revised our paper with respect to these comments and we think that as a result, the quality of the paper has been considerably improved. We highlight the major changes as follows.

1. One common concern among reviewers is that it is a relatively narrow goal if this paper only considers estimating the total number of YouTube videos. One of the major goals of this paper is to understand how much storage and network capacity YouTube needs to store and deliver its videos. Therefore, as a response to this concern, we add section 7 discussing the total storage and the network capacity needed to delivery YouTube videos. Specifically, after an estimation of average file size and the total number of YouTube videos, we compute a lower bound for the storage YouTube must have. Additionally, after a sampling and estimating of view counts per day, we compute the total traffic generated by YouTube video delivery. This new section sheds lights on the direct impacts of YouTube to the Internet traffic, demonstrating an important application of counting YouTube videos.
2. Another common concern is that a change of YouTube will render the methodology no longer work. We admit that the proposed method needs certain interfaces to work. However, the insights gained by our method, such as uncovering the possible biases introduced by previous BFS sampling and the impacts of YouTube videos to the Internet traffic, is still important.
3. A third concern is that the proposed methodology may not work for other online social systems. We add a discussion pointing out that the proposed methodology can also be applied to other online social systems as long as those systems satisfy: a) a new generated id is uniformly select from id space; b) entries in those systems can be enumerated by id prefix searching.
4. Finally, for other specific technical concerns, we point out each id position is filled independently. We validate this by fixing the symbol(s) in one or multiple positions and counting the number of appearances of symbols in other positions. For the symbol "-", we provide references showing that it is generally used as a separator in URLs for Google search and we also carefully validate the YouTube case using Datasets I, II and III in Section 4.

On Word-of-Mouth Based Discovery of the Web

Tiago Rodrigues
Universidade Federal de Minas Gerais, UFMG
Belo Horizonte, Brazil
tiagorm@dcc.ufmg.br

Fabrício Benevenuto
Universidade Federal de Ouro Preto, UFOP
Ouro Preto, Brazil
fabricio@iceb.ufop.br

Meeyoung Cha
Graduate School of Culture Technology, KAIST
Daejeon, Korea
meeyoungcha@kaist.edu

Krishna P. Gummadi
Max Planck Institute for Software Systems, MPI-SWS
Saarbrucken, Germany
gummadi@mpi-sws.org

Virgílio Almeida
Universidade Federal de Minas Gerais, UFMG
Belo Horizonte, Brazil
virgilio@dcc.ufmg.br

ABSTRACT

Traditionally, users have discovered information on the Web by browsing or searching. Recently, *word-of-mouth* has emerged as a popular way of discovering the Web, particularly on social networking sites like Facebook and Twitter. On these sites, users discover Web content by following URLs posted by their friends. Such word-of-mouth based content discovery has become a major driver of traffic to many Web sites today. To better understand this popular phenomenon, in this paper we present a detailed analysis of word-of-mouth exchange of URLs among Twitter users. Among our key findings, we show that Twitter yields propagation trees that are wider than they are deep. Our analysis on the geo-location of users indicates that users who are geographically close together are more likely to share the same URL.

Categories and Subject Descriptors

J.4. [**Computer Applications**]: Social and behavioral sciences Miscellaneous; H.3.5 [**Online Information Services**]: Web-based services

General Terms

Human Factors, Measurement

Keywords

Word-of-mouth, information diffusion, social networks, web content discovery

IMC'11, November 2–4, 2011, Berlin, Germany.

1. INTRODUCTION

Recently online social networking sites like Facebook and Twitter have emerged as a popular way of discovering information on the World Wide Web. In contrast to traditional methods of content discovery such as browsing or searching, content sharing in social networking sites occurs through *word-of-mouth*, where content spreads via conversations between users. For instance, users share links to content on the web with personal recommendations like "This is a must-see video."

While such word-of-mouth based content discovery existed long before in the form of emails and web forums, online social networks (OSNs) have made this phenomenon extremely popular and globally reaching. In fact, today social networking sites are known to be a major driver of traffic to many web sites [40]. For certain web sites, Facebook and Twitter drive, respectively, 44% and 29% of the traffic [35]. These OSNs are sharing tens of millions of web links every day, [41] and we expect that the amount of information exchanged by word-of-mouth in OSNs will grow over time.

In this paper, we present a detailed analysis of the word-of-mouth based content discovery on the web, by analyzing the web links (URLs) shared on a popular social platform, Twitter. We used the Twitter data in [14], which comprises 54 million user profiles, 1.9 billion follow links, and all 1.7 billion tweets posted by Twitter users between March 2006 and September 2009. Twitter is an ideal medium to study word-of-mouth based discovery of web content for several reasons. First, the core functionality provided by Twitter, *tweeting*, is centered around the idea of spreading information by word-of-mouth. Second, Twitter provides additional mechanisms like *retweet* (act of forwarding other people's tweet), which enable users to propagate information across multiple hops in the network through word-of-mouth. Third, thanks to URL shortening services, sharing URLs has become a common practice in Twitter. In fact, nearly a quarter of all tweets in our data contained URLs, and a total of 208 million URLs were shared during the three year period.

In order to study how the 54 million users in Twitter collaboratively discovered and spread web links, we built an information propagation tree for every URL that was shared during a random week in 2009. We considered both explicit (e.g., retweets) and implicit information flows (e.g., when a user shares a URL that has already been posted by one of the contacts she follows, without citing the original tweet). By accounting for implicit information flows, our methodology produces much denser trees than previous work that considers only explicit links [27,44]—the number of edges in a tree has increased by a factor of 23.9.

Based on the propagation trees of URLs, we try to answer several key questions that are fundamental to understanding word-of-mouth based web discovery. The questions we ask include: Can word-of-mouth reach a wide audience? What kinds of content are popular in social media as opposed to the web in general? Does word-of-mouth give all content, including those published by unpopular domains, a chance to spread? What are the typical structures of word-of-mouth propagation trees? We discuss the implications of our findings for the design of word-of-mouth based marketing strategies and the role of social media.

The key findings of our work can be summarized as follows:

1. Word-of-mouth can be used to spread a single URL to a large portion of the user population, in some cases even to an audience of several million users.

2. Popular URLs spread through multiple disjoint propagation trees, with each of the propagation trees involving a large number of nodes.

3. Domains whose URLs or content is spread widely by word-of-mouth tend to be different from the domains that are popular on the general Web, where content is found primarily through browsing or searching. Our analysis shows that word-of-mouth gives all content—including those published on relatively unpopular domains—a chance to be propagated to a large audience.

4. Word-of-mouth in Twitter yields propagation trees that are wider than they are deep. Our finding is in sharp contrast to the narrow and deep trees found in Internet chain letters.

5. Our analysis of the geo-location of users reveals a significant correlation between propagation and physical proximity. Moreover, content tends to spread for short distances only on the first hops away from the content creator.

The rest of the paper is organized as follows. Section 2 describes the data and our methodology for constructing information propagation trees. In Section 3 we examine what kinds of content is popular in word-of-mouth discovery of the Web. In Section 4 we characterize several aspects of word-of-mouth propagation. Section 5 presents an study of the geo-location of users and how far word-of-mouth content travels around the globe. We discuss implications of findings in Section 6 and present related work in Section 7. Finally, we conclude in Section 8.

2. METHODOLOGY

Twitter is a prime example of an OSN where users discover Web content through word-of-mouth. In this paper, we used the Twitter dataset gathered in [14] and study the properties of word-of-mouth based Web discovery.

2.1 The Twitter Dataset

Data collection utilized the official Application Programming Interface (API) of Twitter and took over a month using 58 servers in Germany [14]. We had these servers whitelisted by Twitter so that they can send API requests rapidly. The data comprises the following three types of information: profiles of 54,981,152 users, 1,963,263,821 directed follower links among these users, and all 1,755,925,520 public tweets that were ever posted by the collected users. The oldest tweet in our dataset is from March 2006, when the Twitter service was publicly launched. The dataset does not include any tweet information about a user who had set his account private (8% of all users). Our dataset is near-complete because user IDs were sequentially queried from all possible ranges (0–80 million) at the time of data collection in September 2009. Therefore, it provides a unique opportunity to examine the largest word-of-mouth based URL propagation event in Twitter.

A Twitter user might follow another user to receive his tweets, forming a social network of interest. The node in-degree and out-degree distributions measured on this network are heavy-tailed, and the network topology is similar to those of other OSNs like Facebook. They can be fit well with a Power-Law distribution with exponents 2.19 for in-degree and 2.57 for out-degree (R^2=0.05–0.09%). While a very small fraction of users have an extremely large number of neighbors, the majority of users have only a few neighbors; 99% of users have no more than 20 in- or out-degree neighbors. The most popular users include public figures like Barack Obama, celebrities like Oprah Winfrey, as well as media sources like BBC. A social link in Twitter is directional. Unlike other OSNs, the Twitter network exhibits extremely low reciprocity; only 23% of all links are bidirectional, which means that high in-degree nodes are not necessarily high out-degree nodes.

2.2 URLs in tweets

We treat a URL as a clean piece of information that spreads in Twitter. The number of tweets containing URLs has increased rapidly over the years, as shown in Figure 1. Since 2009, on average 22.5% of tweets contain URLs, and as of September of 2009 more than 30% of tweets contain URLs. This is equivalent to sharing 1.3 million distinct URLs per day in 2009. The URL usage is even higher in retweeets: 47%. Interestingly, the number of retweets grew abruptly after July of 2008. This is because retweeting became a convention between users around this time [13].

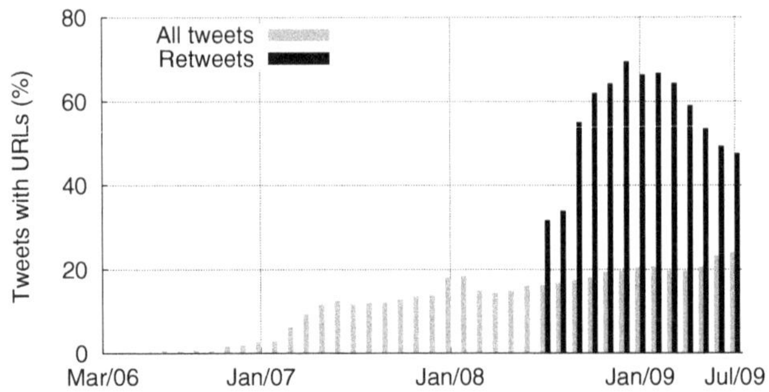

Figure 1: Usage of URLs on tweets over time

	Period	Distinct URLs	Tweets	Retweets	Users
Dataset 1	Jan 1, 2009 – Jan 7, 2009	1,239,445	6,028,030	295,665	995,311
Dataset 2	Apr 1, 2009 – Apr 7,2009	4,628,095	17,381,969	1,178,244	2,040,932

Table 1: Statistics of the two Twitter datasets analyzed

In analyzing the web links within tweets we found that the majority of the URLs (nearly 75%) were from URL shortening services (e.g., *bit.ly*), which substantially shorten the length of any web link. Hence we had to take into account several possible confounding factors such as when multiple short URLs refer to the same long URL or when the short URLs are recycled after not being used for some time (e.g., when there is no human visitor for 120 days, some URL shortening services allow a short URL to point to a new content). Therefore, we picked a large pool of URLs over several short time periods (so that these URLs refer to identical content), then resolved all the short URLs to the long URLs for data analysis in this paper.

Table 1 displays the summary of datasets we analyzed. Each week period contains several million distinct URLs. Because the samples are from a one week period, certain URLs were already in the process of word-of-mouth propagation. Hence, we scanned the entire tweet dataset to find all tweets that contain the URLs in Table 1 and additionally considered them in our analysis. We made sure that none of the added URLs were recycled. Due to space constraints, in the rest of the paper, we present results only for Dataset2 in Table 1. All the conclusions hold for Dataset1 as well.

2.3 Modeling information cascades

Below, we describe the model of URL propagation.

2.3.1 Hierarchical tree model

We build information propagation paths based on Krackhardt's hierarchical tree model [25]. A hierarchical tree is a directed graph where all nodes are connected and all but one node, namely the *root*, have in-degree of one. This means that all nodes in the graph (except for the root) have a single parent. Hence, an edge from node A to node B is added to the tree only when B is not already a part of the tree. An edge from node A to node B means that a piece of information was passed from A to B. While each hierarchical tree has a single root, there may be multiple users who independently share the same URL. In this case, the propagation pattern of a single URL will contain *multiple* trees and form a *forest*.

While we assume there is only a single parent for any intermediate nodes, in real life there may be more than one source who passed the same piece of information to a given user. In order to resolve the tie, we resort to the pattern seen in explicit links in our data. We found that, when users have multiple sources, more than 80% of them cite their last source. We attribute this pattern to the timeline interface of Twitter, which work as a stream, showing the last 200 tweets to the user, chronologically ordered. Hence, we assumed that each user received a URL from the most recent source. Our model is different from that proposed by Sun *et al.* [38], where they considered all friends who joined the same group on Facebook within the last 24 hours as valid sources.

Following the definitions proposed in [42], we call the users in the root of a hierarchical tree **initiators**. These users are the ones who independently shared URLs. We call all other nodes who participated in URL propagation **spreaders**. Initiators and spreaders make up the hierarchical tree. We call users who simply received a URL but did not forward it to others **receivers**. Later when we refer to the hierarchical tree structure, we do not include these users. For convenience, we collectively call all three types of users who potentially read the URL as its **audience**. Figure 2 depicts this relationship.

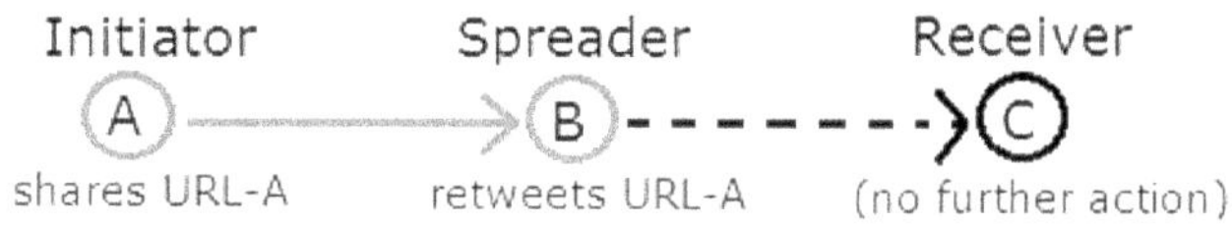

Figure 2: Terminology

2.3.2 Explicit vs implicit links

There are two major ways to reconstruct information propagation paths. One approach is to rely solely on the retweet convention. A retweet typically contains the original tweet content by someone else along with a "RT @username" or "via @username" text that cites the person who posted the tweet. Citation sometimes extends to the intermediary persons who also retweeted the same message. Identifying information propagation based on explicitly retweeted links has been a popular approach in previous work [27, 44]. Another approach, which we take in this paper, is to consider implicit links as well. As opposed to the former approach, implicit URL propagation occurs when a user, without necessarily citing the information source, shares a URL that has already been shared by one of his followees. In other words, an implicit URL propagation occurs when a user A publishes a URL after receiving it from a user B, but user A does not explicitly cite user B.

Since retweeting was not a built-in mechanism in Twitter in 2009 but was a convention that people started adopting over time, some Twitter users did not use the retweeting convention and even when they did, there were many forms of citation (e.g., via, retweeting, RT). Thus, ignoring these implicit links resulted in a sparsely connected graph as shown in Figure 3, which is based on a real example from our tweet data. In fact, we found that considering implicit links (as opposed to using only explicit retweet links) increases the number of edges in the information propagation paths by a factor of 23.9.

In order to verify the impact of using implicit links, we did some experiments varying the way in which the implicit link is chosen. Some examples include getting a random source (when the user received the URL from multiple sources) and considering an implicit link as valid only if it occurs within a specific time interval as valid (for example, if the retweet occurs within 24 hours of the tweet). In all the experiments we found similar results as the ones presented in this paper. As more than 80% of the users usually retweet (explicity link) their most recent source, we decided to consider the most recent source in implicit links. Furthermore, as some retweets happen after a long time interval (for example, more than a month after the original tweet), we did not use any time interval limit.

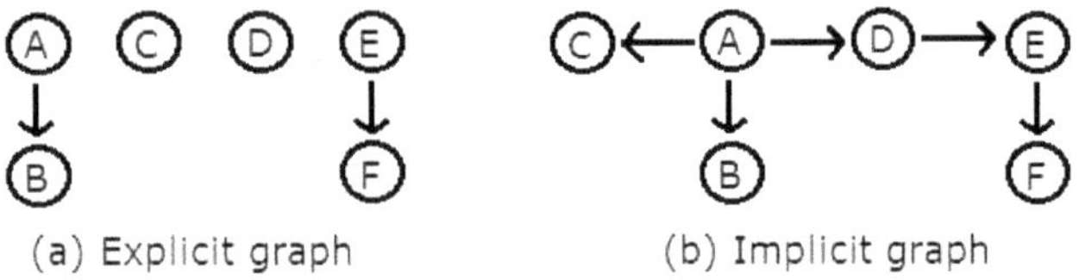

Figure 3: Explicit vs implicit graphs

3. WHAT CONTENT IS POPULAR

In this section, we examine which URL shortening services are widely used in Twitter, which web domains these short URLs point to, and what kinds of content is popular in word-of-mouth discovery of the Web.

3.1 URL shortening services

URL shortening services make it easy for Internet users to share web addresses by providing a short equivalent [9]. For example, a web link `http://topics.nytimes.com/top/news/business/companies/twitter/` can be shortened to `http://nyti.ms/1VKbrC` by a commercial service Bit.ly [2], which will redirect any request access to the original NYTimes website. URL shortening services allow otherwise long web addresses to be referred to in various OSNs like Twitter that often impose character limit in tweets and comments. There are hundreds of commercial URL shortening services. Hence, the same web address can have several short alternatives in services like tinyURL [6] and Ow.ly [4].

In order to identify whether a given web address is a short or long URL, we took a heuristic approach. We wrote a Python script to resolve a URL in a tweet by sending a web access request to that URL and comparing the domain of the original URL with that of the resolved URL. If the two domain names were different, we considered the URL in the tweet to be a short URL, otherwise, we considered it a long URL.

A total of 30 URL shortening services were in use from 2006 to summer 2009 in Twitter. Table 2 displays the top 10 services and their share of tweets. Usage of the top two services tinyurl.com and bit.ly make up more than 90% of the total usage. Between January to April of 2009, we find that bit.ly doubled its presence. The 3rd ranked service is.gd also continued to gain presence in Twitter.

3.2 Popularly linked web domains

We next checked whether URLs popularly shared on Twitter come from major web domains in the Internet (such as nytimes.com or google.com). Our motivation is to verify a widely held belief that word-of-mouth can help popularize niche or esoteric information from domains that are not otherwise very popular. We used the translated long URLs for this analysis and the rest of the paper, and grouped the URLs based on their domain names.

Rank	Web Domain	Dataset2	Dataset1
1	tinyurl.com	4,398,940 (68.2%)	1,883,032 (81.4%)
2	bit.ly	1,530,613 (23.7%)	262,171 (11.3%)
3	is.gd	493,124 (7.6%)	142,497 (6.2%)
4	snipurl.com	27,146 (0.4%)	24,606 (1.1%)
5	hugeurl.com	1,578 (0.0%)	841 (0.0%)
6	url.ca	1,116 (0.0%)	451 (0.0%)
7	xrl.in	361 (0.0%)	250 (0.0%)
8	u.nu	282 (0.0%)	139 (0.0%)
9	simurl.com	216 (0.0%)	6 (0.0%)
10	doiop.com	101 (0.0%)	90 (0.0%)

Table 2: Top 10 URL shortening services in 2009

In total, there were 4,638,095 long URLs that came from 429,551 distinct web domains. The top 20% of the web domains accounted for 95% of these URLs. We ranked the domains based on the number of distinct URLs that belong to the domain as well as the total size of the audience reached by URLs belonging to the domain. Experiments using both ranking methods had similar results. We compared the list of top domains in the resulting rankings with the list of top ranked domains in the general Web published by Alexa [1]. Table 3 displays the top-5 domains based on the number of URLs, their description, the fraction of all URLs that belong to the domain, and their rank from Alexa.com.

Rank	Top list	Description	URLs	Alexa rank
1	twitpic.com	photo sharing	8.5%	103
2	blip.fm	music sharing	3.0%	6,736
3	youtube.com	video sharing	2.1%	3
4	plurk.com	social journal	2.1%	1,146
5	tumblr.com	blog	1.4%	100

Table 3: Top-5 domains in Twitter (April, 2009)

The most popular domain, twitpic.com, accounted for 8.5% of all URLs in the tweet data. The coverage of the other top domains quickly drops with decreasing rank. The Alexa ranking shows that the top-5 domains are quite different from the top list in the Web. Only youtube.com is within the top 10 sites from alexa.com. The top-5 list in Alexa includes major portals and search engines (Google) and portals (Yahoo, Live). We also found that Twitter users often share user-generated content, as seen in the table. Twitter users share photos (twitpic.com), videos (youtube.com), blog articles (techcrunch.com), as well as participate and promote social events (abolishslavery.com and earthday.net).

Figure 4 shows the fraction of top-K domains that also appear in the top-K domain list from Alexa.com for various values of K. The bar plot also shows a comparison to the top URLs identified by the size of the audience reached within Twitter (including initiators, spreaders, and receivers. The overlap is minimal; fewer than 30% of the top-K domains in Twitter overlap with that of the general Web, for all ranges of K=100,$\cdots$,1000. This finding suggests that as word-of-mouth becomes a dominant source of discovering information, a different set of domains might become popular in the Web in the near future.

A recent work characterizing the usage of short URLs on Twitter also presented an analysis comparing the popularity of domains on Twitter and on the general Web [9]. Although the authors of that work considered only the domains pointed by short URLs, which differs from our analysis, they also found that the most popular domains shared on Twitter differs significantly from the general Web case.

Rank	URL domain	Audience	Description
1	wefollow.com	28M	Social application that suggests list of users to follow
2	facebook.com	14M	Social network (warning page)
3	abolishslavery.org	4.5M	Social organization dedicated to combating human traffic (initial page)
4	twitpic.com	4.5M	Photo sharing (photo published by famous actor Ashton Kutcher)
5	youtube.com	4.5M	Video sharing (popular comedy video with title "David After Dentist")
6	tweetvalue.com	4.3M	Application that measures the value of a Twitter account (initial page)
7	techcrunch.com	3.6M	Blog (article with rumors about Google in talks to buy Twitter)
8	earthday.net	3.3M	Social organization dedicated to the Earth's natural environment (initial page)
9	twibes.com	3M	Application to find people with similar interests on Twitter (initial page)
10	latenightwithjimmyfallon.com	2.4M	TV Show from NBC (initial page)

Table 4: Top 10 URLs domains in terms of the audience size reached by the most popular URL

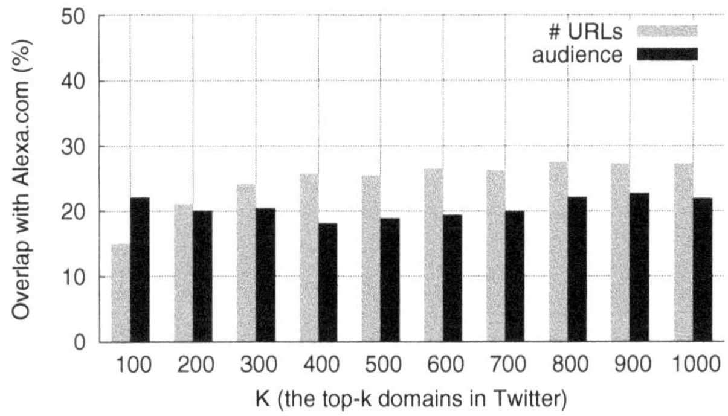

Figure 4: Popular domains in Twitter and Alexa rank

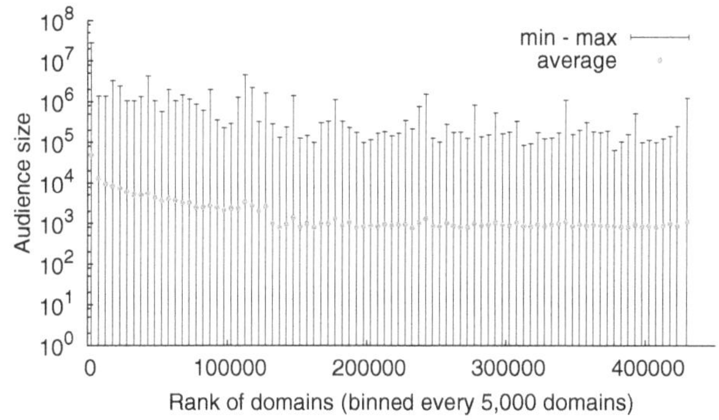

Figure 5: Audience size across the domain ranks

3.3 Popular individual URLs

Next we focus on popularity of individual URLs within domains. Of particular interest to us is the hypothesis that word-of-mouth gives all URLs and content a chance to become popular, independent of popularity of the domain it comes from. The hypothesis is rooted in the observation that anyone could identify an interesting URL and start a viral propagation of the URL, independent of the reputation or popularity of the domain where it is published.

To verify this hypothesis, we computed the size of the audience reached by individual URLs within each domain. Figure 5 plots the minimum, the average, and the maximum size of the audience for individual URLs within each domain. Given the large number of domains (over 400,000 of them) we ranked the domains based on number of URLs, grouped them into bins of 5,000 consecutively ranked domains and plotted one data point for each bin. It is striking to observe that URLs from some unpopular domains beyond the rank of 300,000 reached an audience that is comparable to the size of the audience reached by URLs from the most popular domains. On average, URLs in the top 5,000 domains reached 49,053 users, while URLs from the bottom 5,000 domains reached 1,107 users. Although URLs from top domains reached a 44 times larger audience than those from bottom domains, there do exist individual URLs from bottom domains that reach as large as audience as the most popular URL from the top domains.

Thus, word-of-mouth does offer a chance for all content to become popular, independent of the domain it is published in. Previous work on book and DVD recommendations [29] showed that viral marketing is effective for niche products compared to mass marketing. Our analysis suggests a similar trend.

3.4 Content types

With millions of URLs published per day on Twitter, several different types of contents are shared. A natural question that arises from this observation is whether the type of content affects the word-of-mouth propagation dynamics.

In order to identify the content type, we first select several interest categories based on Open Directory Project (DMOZ), which is a human-edited directory of the Web [3]. DMOZ's content classification relies on the fact that a domain name has a hierarchical structure. So, a domain name of a web address could potentially be used to identify the specific content category, given the list of predefined classifications for many web domains as in the DMOZ service. For example, nytimes.com is classified in the news category; last.fm is classified as the music category.

Among various categories DMOZ supports, we picked 5 categories of interest: photo sharing, videos, music, news, and applications, and downloaded the list of web domains in each of these categories. In total, the DMOZ listing contained 343 domains across all five categories. For the application category, we used the list of applications that are widely used within Twitter, such as tweetdeck.com and wefollow.com.[1]

Table 5 displays the share of each topical category in Dataset2. Matching the domains of the URLs in Dataset2 with the domains listed in these five categories in DMOZ, we were able to successfully categorize 17.6% of websites, although a much larger fraction of users (43.7%) were cov-

[1] http://www.dmoz.org/Computers/Internet/On_the_Web/Online_Communities/Social_Networking/Twitter/

ered. The most popular category is photo sharing, which has 458,662 URLs, posted by 271,138 users on 735,137 tweets. The average audience reached by each photo's URL is 436 users. The second most popular category is music, followed by videos, news and applications.

While photo sharing seems a dominant activity in Twitter as opposed to news or application sharing, the set of most popular individual URLs are from a diverse set of topical categories as shown in Table 4. The most popular URL was the social application, wefollow.com, which reached an audience of 28 million (i.e., nearly half of the entire Twitter network).

Although our analysis the different content types shared on Twitter is an interesting aspect of our study, we note that our methodology has some limitations. First, we were able to categorize only 17.6% of the URLs, which might not be representative. Second, DMOZ is often criticized for its lacks of representativeness and transparency [7], but it is not easy to categorize content to begin with, and we manually checked the list of web domains in each category we used from DMOZ. Moreover, our main interest in the URL categorization is at understanding the similarities and differences between the propagation of different content types on Twitter. We are not trying to say that Twitter users share more photos than videos or news, for example.

4. THE SHAPE OF WORD-OF-MOUTH

This section presents an analysis of the size and shape of word-of-mouth based URL propagation patterns in Twitter.

4.1 How large is the largest word-of-mouth?

We examine the skew in popularity across different URLs. Figure 6(a) shows the size distribution of spreaders and audience for URL propagations in Twitter. An average URL was spread by three users and gained an audience of 843 users through word-of-mouth. In contrast, the most popular URL engaged 426,820 spreaders and reached an audience of 28 million users, which is more than half of the entire Twitter network. The power of word-of-mouth extends beyond the few most popular URLs. Each of the 100 most popular URLs reached an audience of more than 1 million users and 15% of the URLs reached an audience of over 1000 users.

The difference between the number of spreaders and the size of the audience is nearly two orders of magnitude, for popular URLs as well as niche URLs that have only a few spreaders. This demonstrates the potential of word-of-mouth in reaching a large audience. As opposed to a typical web page that is viewed by individual visitors, content shared in word-of-mouth fashion is *collaboratively* shared by other visitors who liked it and can reach a much larger audience.

Both of the distributions for spreaders and audience exhibit power-law behavior (a straight line waist in a log-log plot). The best fit power-law exponents of these distributions $y = cx^{-\alpha}$ were $\alpha = 1.71$ for spreaders, and $\alpha = 1.98$ for audience, indicating that the skew in popularity among the most popular and the least popular URL became slightly more severe due to audience.

4.2 The role of initiators

We classified users into three types based on their position within a cascade: initiators, spreaders, and receivers (Figure 2). Initiators are at the root of each cascade tree and share URLs to others independently in Twitter. In this subsection, we investigate the role of initiators in particular and ask the following questions: To what extent can initiators alone reach a large audience (without the help of spreaders)? How many initiators share the same URL? Is having multiple initiators essential for yielding a large cascade?

In Twitter, nearly 90% of all URLs are introduced only by initiators without involving any spreaders. URLs that were propagated further by spreaders went multiple hops in the Twitter social graph and gained a 3.5 times larger audience than those spread by initiators. This implies that while initiators' role is dominant and that most URLs propagate only 1-hop in the network, multi-hop propagation by spreaders can extend the readership of URLs by a significant amount.

Next we investigated the relationship between the num-

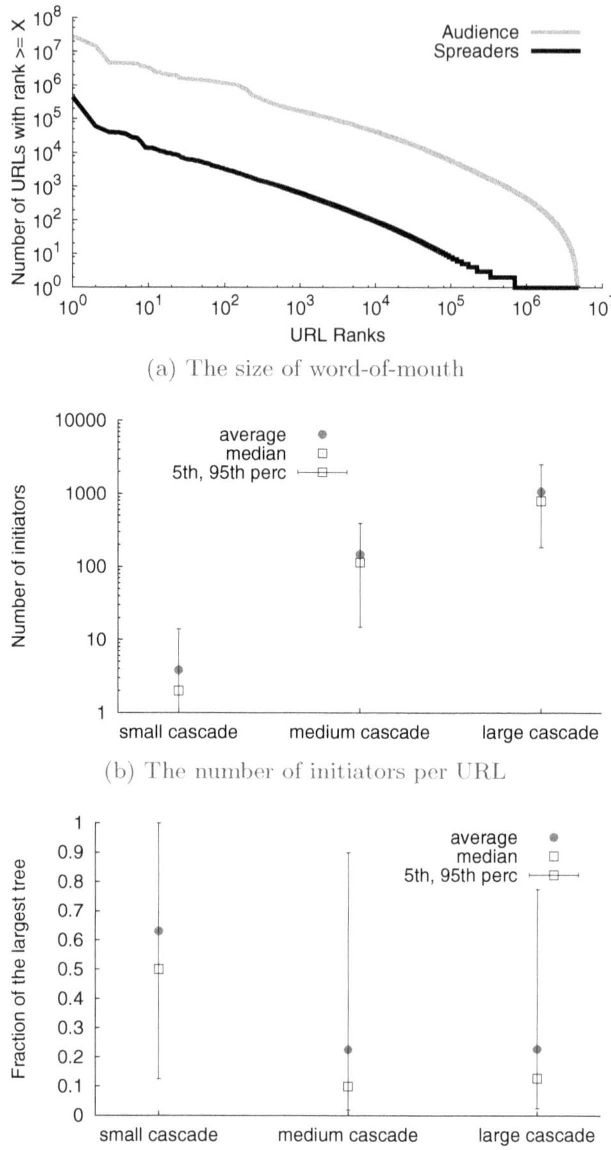

(a) The size of word-of-mouth

(b) The number of initiators per URL

(c) Roles of initiators by the largest subtree

Figure 6: Characteristic shape of word-of-mouth information propagation in Twitter

Category	URLs	Users	Tweets	Audience
Photos	458,662 (9.7%)	271,138 (13.3%)	735,137 (4.0%)	436
Music	181,676 (3.8%)	46,483 (2.3%)	338,654 (1.8%)	316
Videos	123,412 (2.6%)	261,081 (12.8%)	509,975 (2.8%)	877
News	58,467 (1.2%)	113,667 (5.6%)	305,911 (1.7%)	2,492
Applications	15,223 (0.3%)	198,499 (9.7%)	370,047 (2.0%)	3,285

Table 5: Summary information of categories of URLs

ber of initiators and cascade size. In order to focus on URLs with multiple initiators, we focus on URLs with at least two participants (i.e., initiators or spreaders). We group URL cascades into three types: small (1,10), medium [100,1000), and large [1000,∞). Figure 6(b) shows the number of initiators per URL for the three types of cascades. The plot shows the 5th percentile, median, average, and 95th percentile values. The number of initiators are orders of magnitude larger over the cascade size. The median number of initiators is 2, 114, and 792 for small, medium, and large cascades, respectively. Furthermore, a very few URLs (0.2%) had more than 100 initiators who independently shared the same URL. While certain large cascades only involved a single initiator, the plot indicates that the number of initiators does affect the size of the cascade for most URLs—larger cascades likely involve more users who independently share the URL.

While there seems to be a relationship between the number of initiators and cascade size in general, it is not clear whether all of the initiators contributed equally in obtaining audience, or whether a few major initiators played a significant role. Figure 6(c) investigates the fraction of the largest subtree for each URL over cascade size. The plot shows much variability, shown by the wider range of the 5th and 95th percentiles. Nonetheless, the median and the average data points shows a clear trend.

For small cascades, the fraction of total audience reached in the largest subtree (i.e., by a single major initiator) is nearly 50%. For larger cascades, however, the fraction of the largest subtree is marginal (10-20%). This implies that a single initiator's role is likely limited in these cases and that popular content usually propagates through several different propagation trees. In fact, we observed a strong positive correlation between the number of initiators and the total size of the audience (Pearson's correlation ρ=0.7171).

On Digg, a social news aggregator that allows users to submit links to and vote on news stories, a story of general interest usually spreads from many independent seed sites, while a story that is interesting to a narrow community usually spreads within that community only [28]. This observation might also be true in the case of URLs propagated in Twitter, but we leave the investigation for future works.

4.3 The shape of word-of-mouth

Having investigated the size of URL cascades, we next examine the overall shape of URL propagations. We define the following terminology. We refer to the maximum hop count from root to any of the leaf nodes as the *height* of the tree. We define the *width* of the tree as the maximum number of nodes that are located at any given height level. For instance, a two-node cascade graph has height of 2. The cascade graph in Figure 3(b) has a width of 3 and a height of 4 (i.e., the longest path being A-D-E-F). Because a single URL propagation may have multiple tree structures, we consider only the largest propagation tree for each URL and examine its width and height.

Figure 7(a) shows the distributions of height and width for all URLs. Nearly 0.1% of the trees had width larger than 20, while only 0.005% of the URLs had height larger than 20. This suggests that cascade trees in Twitter are wider than they are deep. In fact, the maximum observed width of any propagation tree was 38,418, while the maximum observed height was 147—a difference of two orders of magnitude.

Figure 7(b) shows the relationship between the width and height level, as the 10th, 50th (median), and 90th percentile width over every height level. We grouped trees based on their size (according to the number of spreaders). Small trees with fewer than 100 spreaders tend to have a very narrow shape of width 1 or 2 throughout the height level. Larger trees with more than 100 spreaders were widest at low heights and the width decreased slowly towards the leaf nodes. Interestingly, the median width remained near 10 even at heights above 80. A visualization revealed that these large trees occasionally included bursts at all height levels, i.e., the branch out factor is suddenly large at particular spreaders. We found not one but multiple such bursts for every popular URL.

Finally, Figure 7(c) shows the size of a typical cascade for the five different types of URLs: photos, music, videos, news and applications. We find several interesting differences across content types. Videos propagations likely involve a larger cascade tree; more than 30% of videos URLs involved at least two participating users who shared the URL. News and applications propagation also involved multiple users (28% and 23%, respectively), while photos and music were mostly shared by a single initiator (90% and 97%, respectively). These observation indicates that the type of content affects the potential of the eventual cascade size. The probability of involving 10 or more users in spreading is around 10% for news, applications and videos, while it is only 1% for photos and music.

4.4 Comparison of cascade shapes

A large difference between the height and width in Figure 7(a) indicates that cascade trees are likely shallow and wide. This word-of-mouth propagation pattern is in stark contrast to other patterns of cascade.

Recent work [31] demonstrated that massively circulated Internet chain letters proceed in a narrow but deep tree-like pattern, continuing for several hundred propagation hops. The Internet chain letter on the circulation of a petition on the US-Iraq war reached 18,119 users with a median height of 288 and the maximum width of 82. Table 6 shows a comparison between the height and width of Internet chain letters and the Twitter propagation graph. We estimated the size of smaller Internet chain letters following the model

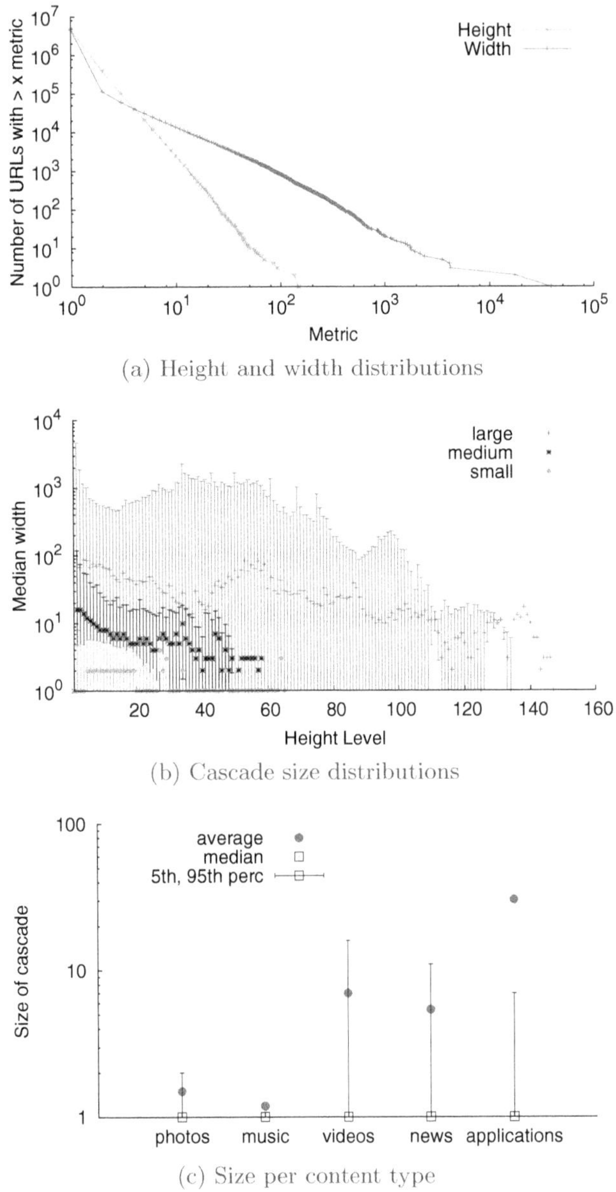

(a) Height and width distributions

(b) Cascade size distributions

(c) Size per content type

Figure 7: Height and width of the largest cascade subtree

described in [5, 31]. In the table, we grouped Twitter propagation graphs of similar sizes (900-1100 nodes and 100-300 nodes) and showed the average height and width of those trees.

Twitter cascades are much wider than they are deep, unlike those of the Internet chain letters. We believe the broadcast design of Twitter directly influence such difference. As an example, consider that 5 friends (namely, A, B, C, D and E) want to exchange messages. On e-mail systems, the sender of each message needs to choose all receivers for that message. In our example, user A might send an e-mail to B and C, who decides to forward it to D and E. In this case, the tree is of height 3 and width 2. What happens on Twitter is exactly the opposite: the receivers choose all senders from whom they want to receive messages automatically. The senders just need to send the messages and a huge audience is reached quickly. In our simple example, if B, C, D and E follow user A, if A send a tweet all of them will receive it at once. In this case the tree is of height 2 and width 4. Another possible explanation for wider cascades on Twitter is the size of the messages. As Twitter allows only 140 characters, users can quickly read and forward a message. If people receive a long email, it is possible that a lot of recipients will not read and, consequently, not forward it. We leave in-depth investigation of the reasons for when wide cascades occur in Twitter as future work.

Data Source	Nodes	Height	Width
PNAS [31]	18,119	288 (med)	82
Twitter	26,227	23 (max)	17,255
PNAS (estimated)	980	16 (med)	4
Twitter (900-1,100)	980±0.02	20±0.25	398±0.27
PNAS (estimated)	162	3 (med)	1
Twitter (100-300)	162±0.02	10±0.03	86±0.03

Table 6: Shape comparison between Internet Chain letter and the Twitter propagation graph

5. CONTENT DISTRIBUTION

So far we investigated several key characteristics of word-of-mouth based URL propagation in Twitter. The observed propagation patterns have direct implications on systems, especially on content distribution and caching strategies. In this section, we revisit some of these observations and use geo-location information of users to examine how far word-of-mouth content travels around the globe.

For this, we need to know the location of users who post and receive tweets. The location information written in user profiles of Twitter is in free text form and often contains invalid location like "Mars" making it difficult to automate the process. We filtered out invalid locations and inferred plausible locations of users by using the Google Geocoding API [21], which converts addresses or city names written in free text form into geographic coordinates of latitude and longitude. In total, we identified the location of 1,096,804 users. In the remainder of this section, we only consider the network and the URL propagation patterns among these one million users.

5.1 Content producers and consumers

We first investigate physical proximity between content producers and consumers in Twitter. Here, a content producer represents a user who posts a URL independently of others (i.e., root nodes in any cascade tree) and a content consumer represents all other nodes in a cascade tree. Figure 8 shows the distribution of physical distance between any two users in the word-of-mouth URL propagation. Physical distance is computed based on the latitude and longitude information of two users. The distance is in units of 10km, representing a local community. The graph shows the probability distribution function for each distance d, which is the physical distance among all user pairs (u, v), where either (1) user u explicitly retweeted the URL that another user v shared or (2) user u follows another user v and shared the same URL after v posted it on Twitter. If either of these two conditions holds, we say that there is a *propagation* link from user u to user v.

For comparison purposes, Figure 8 also shows the distance distribution for two users who have a (unidirectional) follow link between them. We call this a *friendship* link. The friendship links represent the full potential of content distribution through word-of-mouth (i.e., when every follower actively reads or consumes the URL she receives from others).

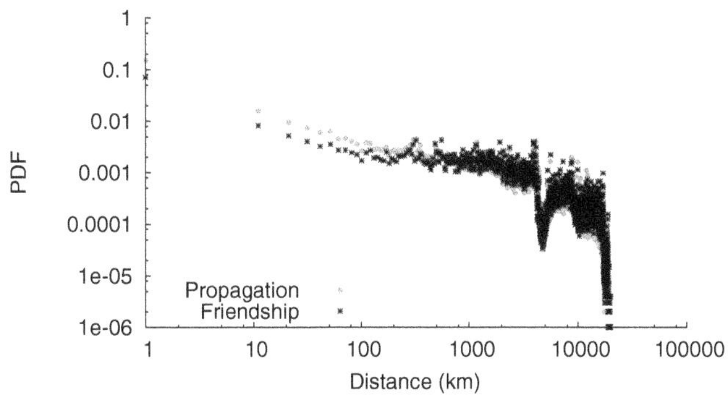

Figure 8: Physical distance of Twitter friendship links and URL propagation links

We observe a significant correlation between the content propagation probability and physical proximity of users. That is, users within a short geographical distance (e.g., 10 km) have a higher probability of posting the same URL than those users who are physically located farther apart. The current OSN infrastructures could exploit this physical proximity between content producers and consumers. Moreover, a significant correlation between the friendship and physical proximity is also observed. This is expected as users tend to interact more with other users who are physically nearby. Liben-Nowell *et al.* [32] previously found a strong correlation between friendship and geographic location among LiveJournal users.

Interestingly, the correlation between the content propagation probability and physical proximity of users is slightly higher than that observed for having a friendship link. This might be explained by the fact that Twitter users follow not only their friends, but also media companies and celebrities, as well as distant users that post content that is valuable to them. However, when it comes to retweeting other users' messages, Twitter users chose tweets posted by those geographically nearby.

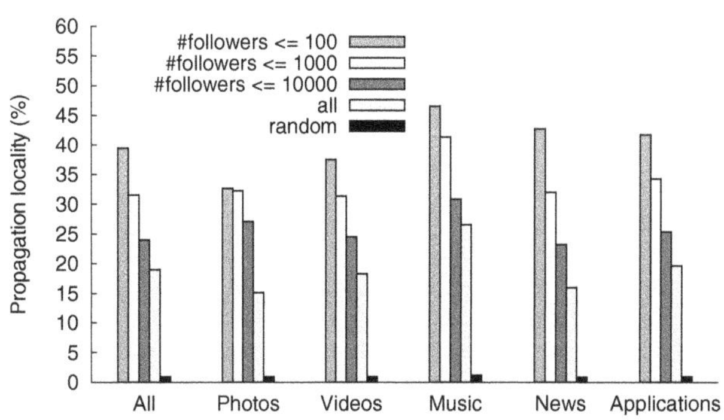

Figure 9: Distribution locality across content types

We tested if the level of locality changes according to the popularity of content producers and different content types. The first set of bars in Figure 9 shows the probability that content producers and consumers are located within a distance of 50km, which roughly represents a large metropolitan area. In order to separate out the impact of producer popularity, we grouped content producers into three groups based on their in-degree. Also, in order to see the representativeness of the results, we randomized the location between all users in our dataset by shuffling the location tags of users and computed the distance between them (shown as 'random' in the figure).

First, we focus on the impact of content producer's popularity on distribution locality and examine the first set of bars labeled 'All' content type in the x-axis. Overall, about 24% of the users who propagated content are physically close to very popular content producers who had more than 1000 followers, 32% are close to content producers with between 100 and 1000 followers, and 39% are close to content producers with less than 100 followers. This result indicates that producers with a small number of followers tend to incur content propagations to geographically nearby locations. On the other hand, content producers with a large number of followers tend to be celebrities or well-known people and incur content propagations across wider areas.

Next, we focus on the impact of content types on distribution locality. Figure 9 also shows the result for different types of content (photos, videos, music, news and applications). Interestingly, the locality for photos is the lowest, while the locality for music is the highest. News and applications had much stronger local appeal than photos and videos. Overall, a non-negligible fraction (15-25%) of content propagated locally. We do not know the reasons for why certain content type has more local appeal than the others. We leave investigating these reasons as exciting future work.

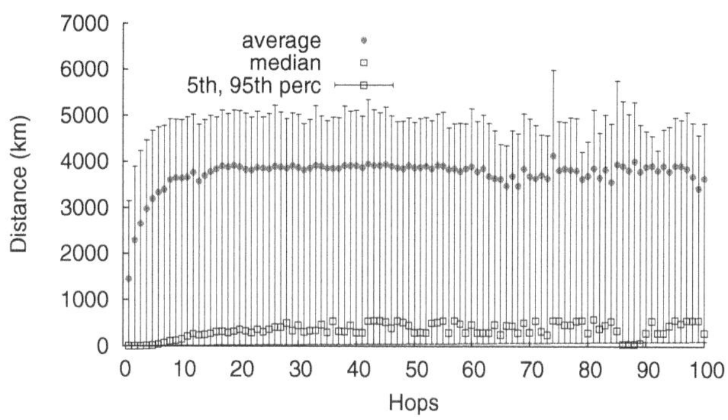

Figure 10: Distance between initiators and spreaders

Motivated by the overall high content locality at 1-hop users, we look at the distance a URL travels as it is further propagated by users within 2- and 3-hops away from the content creator. Figure 10 shows the geographical distance related to the content creator (initiator) as a function of the height level of spreaders on the hierarchical trees. Clearly, content tends to spread short distances on the first hops. As soon as friends-of-friends join the cascade and shares the same URL, it reaches users located in different regions and, consequently, reach distant locations.

The observations that social content produced by users

Rank	Country	Users	Tweets	Rank	U.S. State	Users	Tweets
1	United States	613,458 (55.9%)	6,319,585 (34.1%)	1	California	86,532 (19.7%)	910,379 (21.1%)
2	United Kingdom	86,613 (7.9%)	856,318 (4.6%)	2	Texas	36,509 (8.3%)	358,013 (8.3%)
3	Canada	54,021 (4.9%)	525,869 (2.8%)	3	Florida	24,389 (5.5%)	238,558 (5.5%)
4	Brazil	51,047 (4.7%)	395,433 (2.1%)	4	New York	21,191 (4.8%)	194,971 (4.5%)
5	Australia	31,963 (2.9%)	276,762 (1.5%)	5	Illinois	18,070 (4.1%)	167,597 (3.9%)
6	Germany	27,069 (2.5%)	283,733 (1.5%)	6	Washington	17,352 (3.9%)	165,495 (3.8%)
7	Iran	15,827 (1.4%)	149,887 (0.8%)	7	Georgia	16,842 (3.8%)	144,895 (3.4%)
8	Netherlands	15,812 (1.4%)	208,046 (1.1%)	8	Massachusetts	16,817 (3.8%)	159,464 (3.7%)
9	Japan	14,087 (1.3%)	222,825 (1.2%)	9	Pennsylvania	16,027 (3.6%)	142,265 (3.3%)
10	India	12,750 (1.2%)	140,124 (0.8%)	10	Ohio	13,064 (3.0%)	126,457 (2.9%)

Table 7: Summary information of geographical location of users

with a small number of followers is usually consumed by users that are located within a small physical distance of the content creator could be exploited for caching design and content delivery networks (CDNs).

5.2 Expected traffic pattern

Finally, we study the potential traffic pattern of content that is produced and consumed by users in the Twitter dataset. In Dataset2, 56% of the users are from the United States. In order to conduct a more detailed analysis of the traffic pattern, we inferred a finer grained geo-location information of these U.S. users. We used publicly available data from the U.S. National Atlas and the U.S. Geological Survey to map the inferred latitudes and longitudes into their respective county and state within the United States. In total, we were able to obtained county-level information for 440,036 users.

Table 7 displays the distribution of users and their tweets for the 10 most populated countries and the 10 most populated states in the U.S. based on our Twitter data. Users from United States are well distributed among the states, as the most popular, California, contain no more than 19.7% of all U.S. users.

We then estimated the volume of traffic generated from the U.S. through Twitter by focusing on the subset of URLs linking to photos and videos. In particular, we focused on two most popular services: twitpic.com and youtube.com. For all URLs linking to these services in Dataset2, we collected information about the exact size of each twitpic.com photo and the duration of each youtube.com video. We could not get the exact size of the videos through the YouTube API, hence we estimated the size of each video based on the play length and the video encoding rate of each video. Table 8 shows the statistics for the 10 states that generated the highest traffic volume. The traffic volume was calculated by multiplying the size of each photo or video with the number of tweets from users of each state who posted the URL of the content.

Although the traffic pattern shown in Table 8 is based on our estimation, we conjecture that the real traffic distribution would look similar because we conservatively chose active content consumers who actually looked at the content and decided to share it further. We observe similar distributions of traffic pattern for both photos and videos. The most popular state, California, is responsible for 24.2% and 23.9% of the traffic of photos and videos, respectively. While this number is slightly higher than the user population (19.7%), we find that content producers are located widely across different states. In fact, 9 out of the 10 most populated states appear in Table 8.

Considering that content in Twitter is typically produced by geographically-diverse users but consumed locally, one could allow users to upload content to a local server in the corresponding geographical area, like a server located in a city center, instead of a national server like in the current distribution architecture. Such a content distribution mechanism could significantly reduce the amount of wide-area bandwidth needed to upload the same URL to a centralized, remote server. Additionally, the trend towards local consumption and the fact that users are uniformly distributed across different locations indicates that placing a server in every region can reduce the amount of cross-region traffic.

5.3 Summary

Information dissemination among individuals located within a short physical proximity has been used to explain a number of phenomena in society, such as the proliferation of specific industries in a certain region [36] and individuals employment status [39]. Here, we were particularly interested in understanding how far and over what distance social content is generated and consumed. Given that OSNs use the infrastructure originally designed for web workloads to deliver social content, understanding geographical aspects of word-of-mouth propagation patterns can unveil potential opportunities for improving the current designing of OSN content delivery [34].

6. DISCUSSION

In this paper, we made several key observations. For two of these observations we would like to provide additional explanations. First, we showed that word-of-mouth could reach a large audience. Second we noted that the shape of the word-of-mouth propagation tree is more wide than deep.

- **The power of word-of-mouth**

In Section 3, we showed that URLs could reach a wide audience of several tens of million users through word-of-mouth. Most word-of-mouth events, however, involved a single user who shared URLs and reached only a small audience. This finding conforms to the observation by Watts [43] that global cascades are rare, but by definition are extremely large when they do occur.

In studies of information propagation, a great amount of attention has been devoted to the cascade size distribution and the underlying mechanism that shapes it. Unfortunately, due to a lack of empirical data detailing such cascade size distributions, synthetic distributions have been used to describe the phenomenon [43]. Largely, power-law and bimodal distributions imply the trend of large events occurring infrequently, although these distributions are quite different

Photos				Videos			
Rank	U.S. State	Traffic (GB)	Tweets	Rank	U.S. State	Traffic (hours)	Tweets
1	California	2,411 (24.2%)	32,395 (24.6%)	1	California	854 (23.9%)	11,813 (24.1%)
2	Texas	985 (9.9%)	13,481 (10.2%)	2	Texas	345 (9.6%)	4,549 (9.3%)
3	Florida	688 (6.9%)	8,951 (6.8%)	3	Florida	209 (5.8%)	2,755 (5.6%)
4	Washington	517 (5.2%)	6,190 (4.7%)	4	Illinois	178 (5.0%)	2,425 (4.9%)
5	Georgia	452 (4.5%)	5,473 (4.2%)	5	Washington	155 (4.3%)	2,093 (4.3%)
6	Illinois	411 (4.1%)	5,571 (4.2%)	6	Massachusetts	152 (4.3%)	2,223 (4.5%)
7	Pennsylvania	392 (3.9%)	5,340 (4.1%)	7	Pennsylvania	148 (4.1%)	1,978 (4.0%)
8	Ohio	338 (3.4%)	4,362 (3.3%)	8	Georgia	140 (3.9%)	2,023 (4.1%)
9	Massachusetts	282 (2.8%)	3,800 (2.9%)	9	Ohio	115 (3.2%)	1,631 (3.3%)
10	Arizona	275 (2.8%)	3,588 (2.7%)	10	Oregon	97 (2.7%)	1,316 (2.7%)

Table 8: Total volume of traffic potentially initiated by Twitter on each state (United States), for Twitpic photos and YouTube videos

and represent different underlying mechanisms. In this respect, the Twitter data provides a first opportunity to study size distributions.

The size distribution of word-of-mouth was best fit with the power-law distribution $y = cx^{-\alpha}$. In contrast to the exponents α of 2.19–2.56 seen in the in-degree and out-degree distributions of the topology, the exponents 1.71–2.23 observed in cascade sizes are smaller. This difference may be due to the collaborative act of sharing in Twitter. If each user were to share a URL without the help of any other user, then the size distribution for such a cascade should be the same as the in-degree distribution. However, when users collaboratively spread the same URL, the gap between the most popular user and the least popular user (based on in-degree of a user) becomes less important to the success of cascades, hence yielding a smaller exponent.

• The shape of propagation trees in Twitter

In Section 4, we analyzed the shape of propagation trees and found that word-of-mouth in Twitter yields trees that are much wider than they are deep. Our finding is in sharp contrast to the narrow and deep trees exhibited by Internet chain letters, as found by Liben-Nowell and Kleinberg [31]. Internet chain letters showed a narrow tree shape (width=82) that went several hundred levels deep (height=288) for a large cascade that involved 18,119 spreaders.

A possible explanation for this discrepancy might be the difference in the way the two systems work. Twitter does not allow its users to restrict the recipients of tweets; tweets are broadcast to all a user's followers. On the other hand, emails can be forwarded to a selective set of users, restricting the propagation to only a fraction of the friends, which creates narrower and deeper cascades.

Related to the temporal dynamics of word-of-mouth, we observed that certain URLs spread for several months (or even several years) in Twitter. This finding could indicate that social media like Twitter and Flickr encourage the interaction of Internet users with media content by forming communities of interest in the World Wide Web. The social media act as channels for distributing content, where users can generate content themselves, discuss it, and rediscover old content. Compared to Flickr or blogs, Twitter showed a much shorter time span for content propagation. The mean time for information to cross each social link was much shorter: 53% of the retweets occurred within a day.

This observation on the long delay is unexpected from the topological structure of the network. Most social networks exhibit the "small-world" property [33], where the average path length between people is so small that every pair of users can be connected in a few hops even when the size of the network reaches planetary-scale. Hence, in theory, this structural property allows new information to spread quickly and widely in the network. The question of which underlying mechanisms lead to such a long delay remains to be answered. We expect to gain insight about such mechanisms from the studies on the bursty dynamics of human behavior [11] and the limited attention span of users [17].

7. RELATED WORK

Throughout the paper, we have discussed the references that closely relate to our work. As our work covers a broad spectrum of topics from information flow models to viral marketing, in this section, we briefly summarize the related work on these topics.

A rich set of theoretical work explains the interplay between the social network structure and information flow. Granovetter [22] proposed a linear threshold model, where someone will adopt an innovation only if a large enough proportion of his neighbors have previously adopted the same innovation. Dodds and Watts [16] studied this model in the field of disease spreading in an epidemiological setting. Watts [43] proposed a mathematical model of global cascades based on sparse Erdős-Rényi random networks and found that global-scale cascade could occur even with few early adopters. Watts examined the conditions for when such cascade happens under homogenous thresholds of user susceptibility. Karsai *et al.* [26] followed the time evolution of information propagation in small-word networks and showed that the slowing down of spreading is found to be caused mainly by weight-topology correlations and the bursty activity patterns of individuals. Steeg *et al.* [37] analyzed information cascades on Digg and concluded that the highly clustered structure of the Digg network limits the final size of cascades observed, as most people who are aware of a story have been exposed to it via multiple friends.

With the advent of OSN data, a number of researchers have presented data-driven analysis and measured patterns of information spreading across social network links. Gruhl *et al.* [24] studied the diffusion of information in the blogosphere based on the use of keywords in blog posts. They presented a pattern of information propagation within blogs using the theory of infectious diseases to model the flow.

Adar and Adamic [8] further extended the idea of applying epidemiological models to describe the information flow and relied on the explicit use of URL links between blogs to track the flow of information. Bakshy *et al.* [10] studied content propagation in the context of the social network existent in Second Life, a multi-player virtual game. By examining cascade trees they find that the social network plays a significant role in the adoption of content.

More recently, Leskovec *et al.* [30] developed a framework for tracking short, distinctive phrases that travel relatively intact through online media. They observed a typical lag of around 2.5 hours between the peak of attention to a phrase in the news media compared to blogs. Similarly, Sun *et al.* [38] also found long chains by studying cascades on Facebook pages, but also showed that these diffusion chains on Facebook are typically started by a substantial number of users. In contrast to these works, our study unveils different aspects of word-of-mouth information, such as not only of the shape of cascades, but also the impact of publishers and subscribers of content. Gomez-Rodriguez *et al.* [20] investigated the problem of tracing paths of diffusion and influence and proposed an algorithm to decide a near-optimal set of directed edges that will maximize influence propagation. Ghosh and Lerman [19] compared a number of influence metrics over Digg.com data and suggested that a centrality-based measure is the best predictor of influence. Scellato *et al.* [34] studied how geographic information extracted from social cascades can be exploited to improve caching of multimedia files in a Content Delivery Network. Their evaluation showed that cache hits can be improved with respect to cache policies without geographic and social information. Wang *et al.* [42] found that social and organizational context significantly impacts to whom and how fast people forward information.

Finally, several recent papers focus on characteristics of the Twitter topology, user influence, and spam. Kwak *et al.* [27] studied the Twitter topology, finding a non-power-law follower distribution, a short effective diameter, and low reciprocity. They also studied approaches for ranking influential users based on the Twitter social network structure. Cha *et al.* [14] showed that highly influential users are not necessarily the most followed users, meaning that aspects of the Twitter topology are not sufficient to capture a user's influence. Galuba *et al.* [18] propose a propagation model that predicts which users are likely to mention which URLs in Twitter. Recent efforts identified different forms of spam [12,23] and phishing [15] disseminated on Twitter and obfuscated by URL shortening services.

Compared to this body of work, our interest is in investigating the fundamental properties of word-of-mouth-based Web discovery by focusing on URL propagation in OSNs.

8. CONCLUSION

We have presented a first-of-a-kind analysis of word-of-mouth Web discovery using large data gathered from Twitter. Acquisition of such a rich dataset enabled us to reconstruct the cascade processes of various Web URLs and study the role that world-of-mouth based propagation played in making those web links popular within Twitter. Our analysis highlights several important aspects of word-of-mouth based URL discovery, including its impact on URL popularity, dependence on users with a large number of followers, and effect on the diversity of information discovered by users.

There are various directions in which our work can evolve. First, we would like to leverage our findings to improve ranking of actual search engines for real-time content based on the spread patterns of word-of-mouth propagation of URLs. Second, we would like to be able to determine the topological structure of initiators that will speed up the propagation of content in a social network. Such tools would have an important impact in the commercial world, such as advertising and political campaigns, as well as for Web users in general.

9. ACKNOWLEDGEMENTS

Tiago Rodrigues acknowledges the MPI-SWS people for all their support during his summer internship, when this work was done. Meeyoung Cha was supported by Basic Science Research Program through the National Research Foundation of Korea (NRF) funded by the Ministry of Education, Science and Technology (Grant no. 2011-0012988). We also would like to thank our shepherd Vyas Sekar and our anonymous reviewers.

10. REFERENCES

[1] Alexa. *http://www.alexa.com.*

[2] Bit.ly. *http://www.bit.ly.*

[3] Open directory project. *http://www.dmoz.org.*

[4] Ow.ly. *http://www.ow.ly.*

[5] Rule of three (mathematics) - wikipedia. *http://en.wikipedia.org/wiki/Rule_of_three_(mathematics).*

[6] tinyurl. *http://www.tinyurl.com.*

[7] Why the open directory (dmoz) is not so open? *http://www.dmozsucks.org/why-the-open-directory-is-not-so-open.php.*

[8] E. Adar and L. A. Adamic. Tracking Information Epidemics in Blogspace. In *ACM Int'l Conference on Web Intelligence*, 2005.

[9] D. Antoniades, I. Polakis, G. Kontaxis, E. Athanasopoulos, S. Ionnadis, E. P. Markatos, and T. Karagiannis. we.b: The web of short URLs. In *Int'l World Wide Web Conference (WWW)*, 2011.

[10] E. Bakshy, B. Karrer, and L. A. Adamic. Social Influence and the Diffusion of User-Created Content. In *ACM Conference on Electronic Commerce (EC)*, 2009.

[11] A.-L. Bárabási. The Origin of Bursts and Heavy Tails in Humans Dynamics. *Nature*, 435:207, 2005.

[12] F. Benevenuto, G. Magno, T. Rodrigues, and V. Almeida. Detecting spammers on twitter. In *Annual Collaboration, Electronic messaging, Anti-Abuse and Spam Conference (CEAS)*, 2010.

[13] D. Boyd, S. Golder, and G. Lotan. Tweet, Tweet, Retweet: Conversational Aspects of Retweeting on Twitter. In *Annual Hawaii International Conference on System Sciences (HICSS)*, 2010.

[14] M. Cha, H. Haddadi, F. Benevenuto, and K. Gummadi. Measuring User Influence in Twitter: The Million Follower Fallacy. In *Int'l AAAI Conference on Weblogs and Social Media (ICWSM).*

[15] S. Chhabra, A. Aggarwal, F. Benevenuto, and P. Kumaraguru. Phi.sh/$ocial: The phishing landscape through short urls. In *Annual Collaboration, Electronic messaging, Anti-Abuse and Spam Conference (CEAS)*, 2011.

[16] P. Dodds and D. Watts. A Generalized Model of Social and Biological Contagion. *Journal of Theoretical Biology*, 2005.

[17] R. I. M. Dunbar. Coevolution of Neocortical Size, Group Size and Language in Humans. *Behavioral and Brain Sciences*, 16(4):681?35, 1993.

[18] W. Galuba, K. Aberer, D. Chakraborty, Z. Despotovic, and W. Kellerer. Outtweeting the twitterers - predicting information cascades in microblogs. In *USENIX Conference on Online Social Networks (WOSN)*, 2010.

[19] R. Ghosh and K. Lerman. Predicting Influential Users in Online Social Networks. In *AAAI Int'l Conference on Weblogs and Social Media (ICWSM)*, 2010.

[20] M. Gomez-Rodriguez, J. Leskovec, and A. Krause. Inferring Networks of Diffusion and Influence. In *ACM SIGKDD Conference on Knowledge Discovery and Data Mining (KDD)*, 2010.

[21] Google Geocoding API. `http://code.google.com/intl/en/apis/maps/documentation/geocoding/`.

[22] M. Granovetter. Threshold Models of Collective Behavior. *American Journal of Sociology*, 83(6):1420–1443, 1978.

[23] C. Grier, K. Thomas, V. Paxson, and M. Zhang. @spam: The underground on 140 characters or less. In *ACM conference on Computer and communications security (CCS)*, 2010.

[24] D. Gruhl, R. Guha, D. Liben-Nowell, and A. Tomkins. Information Diffusion Through Blogspace. In *Int'l World Wide Web Conference (WWW)*, 2004.

[25] R. Hanneman and M. Riddle. *Introduction to Social Network Methods*. Digital form at http://faculty.ucr.edu/~hanneman/, 2005.

[26] M. Karsai, M. Kivelä, R. K. Pan, K. Kaski, J. Kertész, A.-L. Barabási, and J. Saramäki. Small but slow world: How network topology and burstiness slow down spreading. *Phys. Rev. E*, 83(2):025102, Feb 2011.

[27] H. Kwak, C. Lee, H. Park, and S. Moon. What is Twitter, a Social Network or a News Media? In *Int'l World Wide Web Conference (WWW)*, 2010.

[28] K. Lerman and A. Galstyan. Analysis of social voting patterns on digg. In *ACM SIGCOMM Workshop on Social Networks (WOSN)*, 2008.

[29] J. Leskovec, L. A. Adamic, and B. A. Huberman. The Dynamics of Viral Marketing. *ACM Trans. on the Web (TWEB)*, 2007.

[30] J. Leskovec, L. Backstrom, and J. Kleinberg. Meme-Tracking and the Dynamics of the News Cycle. In *ACM SIGKDD Conference on Knowledge Discovery and Data Mining (KDD)*, 2009.

[31] D. Liben-Nowell and J. Kleinberg. Tracing Information Flow on a Global Scale using Internet Chain-Letter Data. *Proc. Natl. Acad. Sci. USA*, 2008.

[32] D. Liben-Nowell, J. Novak, R. Kumar, and P. R. A. Tomkins. Geographic Routing in Social Networks. *Proc. of the Nat. Academy of Sciences (PNAS)*, 102:11623–1162, 2005.

[33] S. Milgram. The Small World Problem. *Psychology Today*, 1(3), 1967.

[34] S. Scellato, C. Mascolo, M. Musolesi, and J. Crowcroft. Track Globally, Deliver Locally: Improving Content Delivery Networks by Tracking Geographic Social Cascades . In *Int'l World Wide Web Conference (WWW)*, 2011.

[35] E. Schonfeld, Facebook Drives 44 Percent of Social Sharing On The Web, *TechCrunch*, 2010. *http://techcrunch.com/2010/02/16/facebook-44-percent-social-sharing/*.

[36] O. Sorenson. Social networks and industrial geography. *Journal of Evolutionary Economics*, 13(5):513–527, 2003.

[37] G. V. Steeg, R. Ghosh, and K. Lerman. What Stops Social Epidemics? In *AAAI Int'l Conference on Weblogs and Social Media (ICWSM)*, 2011.

[38] E. Sun, I. Rosenn, C. Marlow, and T. Lento. Gesundheit! Modeling Contagion Through Facebook News Feed. In *AAAI Int'l Conference on Weblogs and Social Media (ICWSM)*, 2009.

[39] G. Topa. Social interactions, local spillovers and unemployment. *Review of Economic Studies*, 68(2):261–95, 2001.

[40] A. Campbell. Social Activity Becomes Significant Source of Website Traffic, *Small Business Trends*, 2009. *http://smallbiztrends.com/2009/03/social-activity-significant-source-website-traffic.html*.

[41] L. Rao, Twitter Seeing 90 Million Tweets Per Day, 25 Percent Contain Links, *TechCrunch*, 2010. *http://techcrunch.com/2010/09/14/twitter-seeing-90-million-tweets-per-day/*.

[42] D. Wang, Z. Wen, H. Tong, C.-Y. Lin, C. Song, and A.-L. Barabasi. Information Spreading in Context. In *Int'l World Wide Web Conference (WWW)*, 2012.

[43] D. J. Watts. A Simple Model of Global Cascades on Random Networks. *Proc. of the Nat. Academy of Sciences (PNAS)*, 2002.

[44] Z. Yang, J. Guo, K. Cai, J. Tang, J. Li, L. Zhang, and Z. S. Understanding Retweeting Behaviors in Social Networks. In *ACM Conference on Information and Knowledge Management (CIKM)*, 2010.

Summary Review Documentation for

"On Word-of-Mouth Based Discovery of the Web"

Authors: T. Rodrigues, F. Benevenuto, M. Cha, K. Gummadi, V. Almeida

Reviewer #1

Strengths: Timely, interesting problem. Great dataset. Well organized. Interesting insights.

Weaknesses: I was less convinced about the tie-in to networking/systems. Also, its hard to judge the novelty given that most of the work in this area happens outside core IMC/networking venues.

Comments to Authors: This paper was a lively interesting read, with well motivated questions. I do not see any major problems, but have some minor comments/issues:

1. My understanding was that the Twitter API only allows a "random" sample approximately 5% of the tweets. Is your data sampled in any way; if yes how does that bias the findings? Or did you obtain a more exclusive access; if so please clarify.

2. The fact that implicit links uncover 24X more links raises a few red flags; can you provide some more analysis/insights into why this is the case or at least validate this better?

3. "58 whitelisted servers" – I do not follow what you mean here; maybe this is related to (1)

4. The exponents for indegree/outdegree seem to be very similar; this is surprising since all anecdotal evidence suggests that the twitter graph is highly asymmetric (maybe there is no discrepancy here because the power law exponent does not tell anything structurally, but I was intrigued).

5. Early on in the paper, you refer to "trees", when in fact the propagation structure is a forest; maybe you want to be more careful.

6. Again, I found that 80% of people retweet the most recent post weird; is this an effect of specific user interface effects or human behavior in "batching" access to reading tweets?

7. Maybe this is obvious (e.g., look at timestamps?), but it would help to spend a small section describing your heuristic for identifying "implicit" links. Also, I assume that the 80% is for explicit retweets -- does that extrapolation also apply to the implicit links also?

8. I do not understand why you specifically look at the largest tree in Sec. 4.3; why not look at all propagation trees instead of just the largest component in the forest?

9. I had a tough time understanding the discussion in the first 2 paragraphs on page 11. At one point you say most retweets occur on day 1, but then the next paragraph talks about long delay. What timescales are you talking about here?

Reviewer #2

Strengths: Interesting observations are presented and the paper is well written. The difference in the popular domains on Twitter and on the web is presented. The result verifies that Twitter create chances for niche URLs to become popular. The results on content locality of the spreads are new.

Weaknesses: Some of issues have been studied in the paper of WSDM2011 by Bakshy et al., e.g., type of URL vs. cascade size, content category vs. cascade size, height of the cascades.

Comments to Authors: There are overlaps between this paper and the WSDM paper mentioned above. This paper also includes new results, which are interesting considering the location aspects. It is interesting to see that the audience size of less popular domains can be comparable to those of the popular ones, which suggests that niche URLs can be popular on Twitter.

The claim that as twitter becomes popular source of information, niche website can be popular. However, it is not clear that despite the popularity of twitter, web search might still be important and dominate source of web content discovery.

Some more comments:

- Regarding Section 5.2 the expected traffic pattern, why videos traffic are considered in hours and not the exact size of the videos? Also, the suggestion about the local server for content distribution may need further investigation as Twitter is not the only source of traffic for websites.

- Section 6 (1), the third paragraph discussing the relationship between the in-degree distribution and cascade size distribution is hard to follow. What does "collaborative act of sharing" mean? How does it relate to the two distributions?

- Section 6.1, in the last paragraph discussing the redundant information, the authors say that for URLs with > 100 spreaders, at least one users receive the URL multiple time. This does not seem significant in comparison with the case when the URLs with fewer spreaders. Is there stronger support?

Reviewer #3

Strengths: Information propagation has become an important area in OSNs and hence the paper is interesting in that respect. The authors argue that Twitter propagation trees may be different than what previous work has shown for more traditional media such as email. The paper is well written.

Weaknesses: The paper appears more as a preliminary study of URL forwarding without going deep into the topic. No justifiable explanations or models are explored for the particular observations (i.e., width of propagation trees), while the data is there. Some parts of the paper are known observations from previous work.

Comments to Authors: This is a well-written, easy to follow paper on an interesting topic - content propagation in Twitter. The main point of reference is forwarding of URLs which indeed is a major component in Twitter.

The paper does present a couple of novel observations, with the most interesting of those being the fact that twitter propagation trees are more wide than deep. Similarly, the analysis on content distribution based on location is interesting - although projecting this to traffic patterns does not appear as convincing. In my view, from the 5 key findings listed in the introduction, the 4th and 5th are the most interesting (and novel) ones.

However, it is disappointing that the paper only remains superficially at these observations without delving deeper regarding the factors that lead to these observations. For example, the authors should have examined what contributes most to this effect (i.e., large width), and for which types of users - instead only conjectures are made referring to the follower-mechanism of twitter as the main cause.

Besides this, I have a couple of other reservations with the paper:

First, the authors concentrate a lot on the differences observed in the height and width of the propagation trees, when compared to the chain-letter work by Nowell and Kleinberg [30] (key finding number 4 in the introduction). While indeed the differences appear true, the methodologies generating the corresponding propagation trees in each case are different. It is thus unclear how much this comparison makes sense. The authors assume that each node's parent is the last node sending the content, while in [30] a spanning tree algorithm is run. Does this result to any differences in the shape of the trees? Could the authors use the same tree generation algorithm as in [30] and then compare the observations?

Second, the authors present a number of observations that have been presented in previous work, without however the authors sufficiently comparing or referring to it. Two examples here include: 1) The fact that distinct initiators result in large cascades (section 4.1) has been observed before in Digg (WOSN 2008, Lerman et al. - not cited in the paper). 2) URL propagation in twitter was also studied in the context of short URLs in [9] with newer datasets. [9] observes exactly the third key finding of the authors mentioned in the introduction. In fact, the analysis in most of Section 3 is the same as in [9] (without this being mentioned), but the findings are quite different in some cases (e.g., percentage of bit.ly URLs) which might reflect the change between 2009 (traces used in the paper) and 2010 (data in [9]). It would be interesting to cross-reference the results of the two papers, which is avoided in the paper. Yet, the fact remains that these are not as novel observations as the ones regarding the propagation trees.

Other comments:

The discussion section is quite lengthy and it is unclear that it offers much information for the rest of the paper.

Section 2.1: It would be nice to provide definitions for the in-degree and out-degree.
Section 2.2: What do you mean by URL recycling, and where is the "120 days of inactivity" coming from? Reference?

Section 3.4: Is the 17% sample enough for this categorization? DMOZ is often criticized for its representativeness.

Section 4.1: It would be nice to provide also the p-value for the correlations.

Section 4.3: It would be interesting to see the results with other definitions of width besides the maximum.

Section 4.4: The example in the last paragraph is not convincing to me, since if the email is forwarded to all A-E, the resulting tree the same as in twitter. People do have e-mail lists where they forward fun and other stuff (e.g., images, Youtube links etc), where the resulting propagation trees might be similar to what you observe for Twitter. This goes back to the main comment on the paper - the origins of the width are not sufficiently examined.

Section 5.2: How do you know that users indeed looked at the content and not blindly re-tweeted?

Reviewer #4

Strengths: - Large data set that is studied from many angles.
- Study of impact of geolocation on propagation.

Weaknesses: - No study of the propagation time.
- Data set is almost 2 years old.

Comments to Authors: This is a clear paper that is nice to read. I think you did a good job at looking at the data set from different angles to characterize word of mouth; the main dimension that is absent is a study of the propagation time of these words of mouth. But the results are really incremental.

It is expected that when you have a broadcast mechanism available like Twitter, you will create a tree that is wider than if you forward a chain letter and have to choose who you want to forward the email to.

What would make the paper more exciting is to compare, if possible, the word of mouths of different OSNs: e.g. Twitter vs. Facebook.

I like your comparison of popular content with Alexa and your study of word of mouth for different content type.

How would Figure 5 look like if the ranking of domains would also be based on the overall audience instead of the number of links. I am not sure that I am convinced that it makes sense to have a ranking based on the number of URLs. You should first study the correlation between overall audience and number of links.

"Considering that content in Twitter is typically produced by geographically-diverse users but consumed locally, one could allow users to upload content to a local server in the corresponding geographical area, like a city. Such a mechanism could significantly reduce the amount of wide-area bandwidth needed compared to an upload to a centralized, remote server. Additionally, the trend towards local consumption and the fact that users are uniformly distributed across different locations indicates that placing a server in every region can reduce the amount of cross-region traffic." - You are simply saying that CDNs would make the distribution more efficient which is not really surprising, and companies like YouTube/Google are already doing that.

Reviewer #5

Strengths: The topic is interesting, as it works toward to goal of understanding what makes content propagate quickly/widely in a social network. The paper confirms some widely held beliefs, and is well written and well executed.

Weaknesses: I quite dislike two aspects of this paper. First, it is too long. I would have much preferred the findings in a crisp 7-pager than the given 14 pages. Second, the paper is typical for IMC in that a lot of the findings are not surprising at all yet the authors tend to make it sound like they are.

Comments to Authors: "Can word of mouth reach a wide audience?" Obviously. It is called viral marketing. I find it similarly obvious that widely spread URLs can originate on unpopular websites - it matters who spreads the content and how, not where it comes from. That too is central to viral marketing. It is scientifically completely valid to confirm the intuition, but there is no reason to sound surprised (e.g. "it is striking", "interestingly") when you do.

The analysis of Table 4 is brief. You say it covers a diverse set of topics. I would argue that it reflects rather clearly that you're looking at Twitter, given that around half of the top 10 are clearly related to it. What is #2, the Facebook warning page? (Change the caption to "Top 10 URL domains [...]".)

In subfigure 6a, how can the rank of a URL be 1/10, i.e., less than 1? How many initiators did the most popular URL from that plot have?

How often is the initiator the contributor of the widest point in a cascade? I.e., does Lady Gaga find new stuff, or merely retweet?

The comparison to chain letters feels tedious. Email and Twitter are substantially different communication media; it is completely clear that chain letters are more narrow yet deeper. As you are saying, Twitter is inherently broadcast, but chain letters typically explicitly ask for forwards to a given (small!) number of people.

I wanted the paper to end on page 9 -- everything except for the related work section after it feels like it is inflating the paper to full length. I really do not see how Sec 6.1 is part of "Discussion". I think a terrific way to make this a better full paper would have been to integrate the analysis of the social structure of the graph into the URL propagation patterns. That would shed some light into *why* content propagates, not merely what content, and how.

Response from the Authors

We thank all the reviewers for their great suggestions. We tried to incorporate these suggestions in the camera ready version whenever possible. In particular, we fixed small mistakes and clarified description of the analyses throughout the paper. We cited the related works suggested, comparing with our analysis whenever possible (e.g., in sections 3.2 and 4.2). We also reduced the discussion section as one of the reviewers suggested. We believe these changes increased the quality of our paper.

In some parts of the suggestions the reviewers did not agree among themselves, in which case we decided not to apply any change. For example, reviewer #3 suggested that we extend the analysis on the comparison of cascade shapes with that of the Internet chain-letters, while reviewers #4 and #5 commented that the differences are obvious and expected.

We also left some of the suggestions (e.g., providing new models of cascades, adding new deeper analysis on cascade shapes) as future work, as they are interesting but there was not time to make these changes. We plan to address these suggestions when we extend our work for a journal submission.

In conclusion, we appreciate all the important suggestions the reviewers provided in helping us prepare a high quality ACM IMC paper.

GQ: Practical Containment for Measuring Modern Malware Systems

Christian Kreibich
ICSI & UC Berkeley
christian@icir.org

Nicholas Weaver
ICSI & UC Berkeley
nweaver@icsi.berkeley.edu

Chris Kanich
UC San Diego
ckanich@cs.ucsd.edu

Weidong Cui
Microsoft Research
wdcui@microsoft.com

Vern Paxson
ICSI & UC Berkeley
vern@cs.berkeley.edu

Abstract

Measurement and analysis of modern malware systems such as botnets relies crucially on *execution* of specimens in a setting that enables them to communicate with other systems across the Internet. Ethical, legal, and technical constraints however demand *containment* of resulting network activity in order to prevent the malware from harming others while still ensuring that it exhibits its inherent behavior. Current best practices in this space are sorely lacking: measurement researchers often treat containment superficially, sometimes ignoring it altogether. In this paper we present GQ, a malware execution "farm" that uses explicit containment primitives to enable analysts to develop containment policies naturally, iteratively, and safely. We discuss GQ's architecture and implementation, our methodology for developing containment policies, and our experiences gathered from six years of development and operation of the system.

Categories and Subject Descriptors

C.2 [**Computer-Communication Networks**]: NETWORK ARCHITECTURE AND DESIGN

General Terms

Design, Measurement, Reliability, Security

Keywords

Malware containment, malware execution, honeyfarm, botnets, command-and-control

1. INTRODUCTION

Some of the most challenging Internet measurement studies today concern analyzing malicious distributed systems such as botnets. Such measurement often relies crucially on *execution*: "letting loose" malware samples in an execution environment to study their behavior, sometimes only for seconds at a time (e.g., to understand the bootstrapping behavior of a binary, perhaps in tandem with static analysis), but potentially also for weeks on end (e.g., to conduct long-term botnet measurement via "infiltration" [13]).

This need to execute malware samples in a laboratory setting exposes a dilemma. On the one hand, unconstrained execution of the malware under study will likely enable it to operate fully as intended, including embarking on a large array of possible malicious activities, such as pumping out spam, contributing to denial-of-service floods, conducting click fraud, or obscuring other attacks by proxying malicious traffic. On the other hand, if executed in full isolation, the malware will almost surely fail to operate as intended, since it cannot contact external servers via its command-and-control (C&C) channel in order to obtain input data or execution instructions.

Thus, industrial-strength malware measurement requires *containment*: execution environments that on the one hand allow malware to engage with the external world to the degree required to *manifest* their core behavior, but doing so in a highly controlled fashion to *prevent* the malware from inflicting harm on others. Despite the critical importance of proper containment, measurement researchers often treat the matter superficially, sometimes ignoring it altogether. We perceive the root cause for this shortcoming as arising largely from a lack of technical tools to realize sufficiently rich containment, along with a perception of containment as a chore rather than an opportunity. To improve the state of affairs, we present *GQ*, a malware execution "farm" we have developed and operated regularly for six years. GQ's design explicitly focuses on enabling the development of precise-yet-flexible containment policies for a wide range of malware. Drawing upon GQ's development and operation over this period, we make three contributions:

First, we develop an architecture for malware measurement and analysis that provides a natural way to configure and enforce containment policies by means of *containment servers*. These scalable decision points remain logically and physically separate from the system's gateway, and establish first-order primitives for effecting containment on a per-flow granularity. We began our work on GQ during the peak of the "worm era" [9], and initially focused on capturing self-propagating network worms. Accordingly, we highlight both the system's original architectural features that have "stood the test of time," as well as the shortcomings the emerged as our usage of GQ began to shift towards broader forms of malware.

Second, we describe a methodical—albeit largely manual—approach to the development of containment policies to ensure prevention of harm to others. Our goal here is to draw attention to the issue, highlight potential avenues for future research, and point out

IMC'11, November 2–4, 2011, Berlin, Germany.

that far from being a chore, containment development can actively *support* the process of studying malware behavior.

Third, we present insights from our extensive operational experience [4, 9, 13, 18, 19, 25, 21, 3] in developing containment policies that serve to illustrate the effectiveness, importance, and utility of a methodical approach to containment.

We begin by reviewing the approaches to containment framed in previous work (§ 2), which provides further context for our discussion of the issue of containment (§ 3). We then present GQ's design goals (§ 4), architecture (§ 5), and implementation (§ 6), illustrating both initial as well as eventual features as a consequence of our continued desire to separate policy from mechanism and increase general applicability of the system. Finally, we report on our operational experiences over GQ's lifetime (§ 7), and offer concluding thoughts, including discussion of containment's general feasibility (§ 8).

2. RELATED WORK

A large body of prior work focuses on malware execution for the purpose of understanding the modi operandi of binary specimens. Historically, "honeyfarms" were the first platforms supporting large-scale malware execution. These systems focused in particular on *worm* execution, with the "honey" facet of the name referring to a honeypot-style external appearance of presenting a set of infectible systems in order to trap specimens of global worm outbreaks early in the worm's propagation. The predecessor [9] of today's GQ platform represents a typical example of this line of work. In contrast to our current platform, its containment policies were fully hardwired and specific to the goal of capturing worms. Vrable et al. designed the Potemkin honeyfarm [29] as a (highly) purpose-specific prototype of a worm honeyfarm that explored the scalability constraints present when simulating hundreds of victim machines on a single physical machine. Their work also framed the core issue of containment, but leveraged a major simplification that worms can potentially provide, namely that one can observe worm propagation even when employing a very conservative containment policy of redirecting outbound connections to additional analysis machines in the honeyfarm. Jian and Xu's Collapsar [11], a virtualization-based honeyfarm, targeted the transparent integration of honeypots into a distributed set of production networks. The authors focused on the functional aspects of the system, and while Collapsar's design supports the notion of assurance modules to implement containment policies, in practice these simply relied on throttling and use of "Inline Snort" to block known attacks.

With the waning of the "worm era," researchers shifted focus from worm-like characteristics to understanding malware activity more broadly. Bayer et al. recognized the significance of the containment problem in a paper introducing the Anubis platform [2], which has served as the basis for numerous follow-up studies: "*Of course, running malware directly on the analyst's computer, which is probably connected to the Internet, could be disastrous as the malicious code could easily escape and infect other machines.*" The remainder of the paper, however, focuses on technical aspects of monitoring the specimen's interaction with the OS; they do not address the safety aspect further.

The CWSandbox environment shares the dynamic analysis goals of Anubis, using virtualization or potentially "raw iron" (non-virtualized) execution instead of full-system emulation [31]. The authors state that CWSandbox's reports include "*the network connections it opened and the information it sent*", and simply acknowledge that "*using the CWSandbox might cause some harm to other machines connected to the network.*"

The Norman SandBox [23] similarly relies on malware execution in an instrumented environment to understand behavior. As a proprietary system, we cannot readily infer its containment model, but according to its description it emulates the "*network and even the Internet.*"

Chen et al. [7] presented a "universe" management abstraction for honeyfarms based on Potemkin, allowing multiple infections to spread independently in a farm. Their universes represent sets of causally related honeypots created due to mutual communication. GQ provides such functionality in a more general fashion via its support for independently operating subfarms. In contrast to Potemkin's universes, GQ's subfarms do not imply that malware instances executing within the same subfarm necessarily can communicate.

More recently, John et al. presented Botlab [12], an analysis platform for studying spamming botnets. Botlab shares commonalities with GQ, including long-term execution of bot binaries, in their case particularly for the purpose of collecting spam campaign intelligence. They also recognize the importance of executing malware safely. In contrast to GQ, the authors designed Botlab specifically to study email spam, for which they employed a static containment policy: "*[T]raffic destined to privileged ports, or ports associated with known vulnerabilities, is automatically dropped, and limits are enforced on connections rates, data transmission, and the total window of time in which we allow a binary to execute.*" In addition, the authors ultimately concluded that containment poses an intractable problem, and ceased pursuing their study: "*Moreover, even transmitting a "benign" C&C message could cause other, non-Botlab bot nodes to transmit harmful traffic. Given these concerns, we have disabled the crawling and network fingerprinting aspects of Botlab, and therefore are no longer analyzing or incorporating new binaries.*"

Researchers have also explored malware execution in the presence of complete containment (no external connectivity). These efforts rely on mechanisms that aim to mimic the fidelity of communication between bots and external machines. The SLINGbot system emulates bot behavior rather than allowing the traffic of live malware on the commodity Internet [10]; clearly, such an approach can impose significant limits on the obtainable depth of analysis. The DETER testbed [22] relies upon experimenters and testbed operators to come to a consensus on the specific containment policy for a given experiment. Barford and Blodgett's Botnet Mesocosms run real bot binaries, but emulate the C&C infrastructure in order to evaluate bot behavior without Internet connectivity [1]. Most recently, Clavet et al. described their in-the-lab botnet experimentation testbed with a similar containment policy to Botnet Mesocosms, but with the capability of running thousands of bot binaries at one time [5]. While all of these systems guarantee that malicious traffic does not interact with the commodity Internet, they required substantial effort for enabling a useful level of operational fidelity and, in the process, necessarily sacrifice the fidelity that precisely controlled containment can offer.

3. ADDRESSING THE PROBLEM OF CONTAINMENT

The frequently light treatment of the central problem of executing malware *safely* is to some extent understandable. Established tool-chains for developing containment do not exist, so the resulting containment mechanisms are ad-hoc or suboptimal, leaking undesirable activity or preventing desired activity. This deficiency renders containment implementation and verification a difficult, time-consuming problem—one that frequently gets in the way of conducting the intended experiment. GQ aims to fill this gap by making containment policy development a natural component of the malware analysis process: per-flow containment decisions form central, explicit notions reflected in much of the system's architecture.

Development of precise containment requires a balance of *(i) allowing* the outside interactions necessary to provide the required realism, *(ii) containing* any malicious activity, all while *(iii)* convincingly *pretending* to the sample under study that it enjoys unhampered interaction with external systems. Lacking rigor in this process raises ethical issues, since knowingly permitting such activity can cost third parties significant resources in terms of cleaning up infections, filtering spam, fending off attacks, or even financial loss. It also may expose the analyst to potential legal consequences, or at the very least to abuse complaints. Finally, technical considerations matter as well: prolonged uncontained malicious activity can lead to blacklisting of the analysis machines by the existing malware-fighting infrastructure. Such countermeasures can prevent the analyst from acquiring unbiased measurements, as these responses can lead to filtering of key activity elsewhere in the network, or because the malware itself changes its behavior once it detects suspiciously diminishing connectivity. We might consider full containment as a viable option for experiments such as "dry-runs" of botnet takedowns [5], but we find that frequently the dynamically changing nature of real-world interactions and the actual content of delivered instructions holds central interest for analysis.

Thus, we argue for the importance of avoiding the perception of containment as a resource-draining chore. Indeed, we find that developing containment from a default-deny stance, iteratively permitting understood activity, in fact provides an excellent way to understand the behavioral envelope of a sample under study.

GQ currently does not by itself help to automate the development of containment policies. However, it provides the basis for a methodical approach to containment policy development. When deploying new malware samples, we employ the following strategy. Beginning from a complete default-deny of interaction with the outside world, we execute the specimen in a subfarm providing a "sink server" that accepts arbitrary traffic without meaningfully responding to it, and to which the containment server reflects all outbound traffic. We thus understand the extent to which the specimen comes alive, and can inspect the nature of the attempted communication and in the best case infer the precise intent, or at least distinguish C&C traffic from malicious activity. We can then whitelist traffic believed-safe for outside interaction, in the most narrow fashion possible. For example, we might only allow HTTP GET requests, seemingly for C&C instructions, that have a similar URL path structure. Generally opening up HTTP would be overzealous, as malware might use HTTP both for C&C as well as a burst of SQL injection attacks. We then iterate the process over repeated executions of the specimen until we arrive at a containment policy that allows just the C&C lifeline onto the Internet, while containing malicious activity inside GQ.

Finally, we emphasize that we do not mean for GQ to replace the use of static or dynamic malware analysis tools. Rather, we argue that researchers should deploy cutting-edge malware analysis tools *inside* a system such as GQ, to provide a mature containment environment in which they can employ sophisticated malware instrumentation safely and robustly.

4. INITIAL & EVENTUAL DESIGN GOALS

As we mentioned above, our initial design for GQ targeted a worm-oriented honeyfarm architecture. Over the past years, we focused on evolving the system into a generic *malware farm*—a platform suitable for hosting all manner of malware-driven research safely, routinely, and at scale. In the following we outline our original design goals as well as those we came to formulate at later stages of building the system.

Versatility. In contrast to previous work, GQ must serve as a platform for a broad range of malware experimentation, with no built-in assumptions about inmates belonging to certain classes of malware, or acting exclusively as servers (realizing traditional honeyfarms) or clients (realizing honeycrawlers [30]). Our initial focus on worms imposed design constraints that became impractical once we wanted to experiment with non-self-propagating malware. Similarly, focus on a particular class of botnets (say those using IRC as C&C, or domain generation algorithms for locating C&C servers via DNS), restricts versatility.

Separation of policy and mechanism. This goal closely relates to the former, but we needed to invest considerable thought in order to achieve it in an effective fashion. In our original honeyfarm architecture we tightly interwove mechanism (a highly customized packet forwarder) and policy (worm containment) in forwarding code that we could adapt only with difficulty and by imposing system downtime. At the time, the need for greater containment flexibility when running arbitrary kinds of malware had not yet become clear to us. GQ must clearly separate a comparatively stable containment *enforcement mechanism* from an adaptable containment *policy definition*.

Verifiable containment. GQ must provide complete control over all inbound and outbound communication. This remains as true now as it was at the outset of GQ's development. Depending on a flow's source, destination, and content the system must allow dropping, reflecting, redirecting, rewriting, and throttling the flow flexibly according to current execution context. Moreover, ideally mechanisms would exist to *verify* that developed policies operate as intended; we have not implemented such, a deficiency of our current system.

Multiple execution platforms. Malware frequently checks the nature of its execution platform in order to determine whether it likely finds itself running in an analysis environment or as a successful infection in the wild. For example, malware often considers evidence of virtualization a tell-tale sign for operation in a malware analysis environment [8] and ceases normal operation. Independently of potential virtualization, malware also might only execute correctly on certain operating system types, versions, or patch levels, so we need to ensure support for a diverse range of such configurations. For these configurations, GQ must support virtualized, emulated, and raw iron execution as desired, on a per-inmate granularity, in a fashion transparent to the containment process.

Multiple experiments. While extending GQ we increasingly encountered the need for running multiple malware-driven setups at the same time. The original *single-experiment* design made it difficult to accommodate this. For GQ, we aim to provide a platform for independently operating experiments involving different sets of machines, containment policies, and operational importance. For example, we have found it exceedingly useful to run both "deployment" and "development" setups for studying spambots; one for continuously harvesting spam from specimens for which we have developed mature containment policies, the other one for developing such policies on freshly obtained samples.

Infection strategy & threat model. We need to consider the way in which machines on our inmate network become infected, as well as the behavioral envelope once a machine has become infected. Regarding the former, if an experiment so desires, GQ fully supports the traditional honeyfarm model in which external traffic

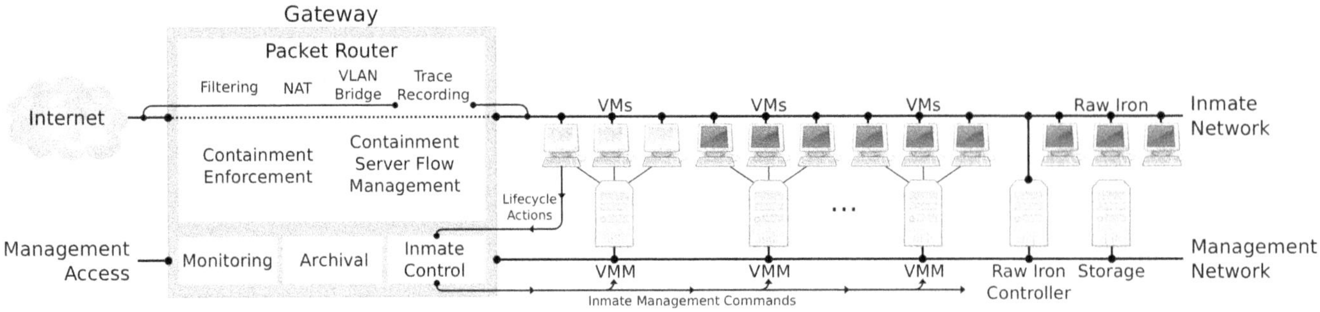

Figure 1: GQ's overall architecture.

directly infects honeypot machines. Today, we find *intentional infection* with malware samples collected from external sources more relevant and useful. We describe our mechanism for facilitating such infections in § 6.6. Regarding post-infection behavior, we adopt the position of other systems executing malware in virtualized environments and assume that the program cannot break out of the virtual environment. The malware may corrupt user and kernel space on the infected host arbitrarily and conduct arbitrary network I/O.

5. GQ'S ARCHITECTURE

5.1 Overall layout

We show GQ's architecture in Figure 1. A central *gateway* sits between the outside network and the internal machinery, separating it into an *inmate network* on which we host infected machines—*inmates*—and a *management network* that we use to access virtual machine monitors (VMMs) and other farm control infrastructure.

Within the gateway, custom packet forwarding logic enables and controls the flow of traffic between the farm and the outside network, as well as among machines within the farm. This takes several forms. First, a custom learning VLAN bridge selectively enables crosstalk among machines on the inmate network as required, subject to the containment policy in effect. Its ability to learn about the hosts present reduces the configuration overhead required to bootstrap the inmate network. Second, we devote the majority of the forwarding logic for redirecting outgoing and incoming flows to a *containment server*, which serves two purposes. First, it decides what containment policies to enforce on a given flow, and second, for some containment decisions it also proceeds to enforce the containment. (We describe this further in § 5.4.) Finally, a *safety filter* ensures that the rate of connections across destinations and to a given destination never exceeds configurable thresholds.

5.2 Inmate hosting & isolation

We employ three different inmate-hosting technologies: full-system virtualization (using VMware ESX servers), unvirtualized "raw iron" execution (more on this in § 6.4), and QEMU for customized emulation [4]. The hosting technology we employ for a given inmate remains transparent to the gateway.

GQ enforces inmate isolation at the link layer: each inmate sends and receives traffic on a unique VLAN ID. VLAN IDs thus serve as handy identifiers for individual inmates. Physical and, where feasible, virtual switches (for simplicity not shown in Figure 1) behind the gateway enforce the per-inmate VLAN assignment, which our inmate creation/deletion procedure automatically picks and releases from the available VLAN ID pool.

The gateway's packet forwarding logic enables connectivity to the outside Internet when permissible, while selectively enabling inmate crosstalk as required.

5.3 Network layout

We use network address translation for all inmates. The packet forwarder dynamically assigns internal addresses from RFC 1918 space, triggered by the inmates' boot-time chatter. It maps source addresses in inside→outside flows to configurable global address space, and depending on configuration either drops outside→inside flows (emulating typical home-user setups) or forwards them on, rewriting destination addresses to the corresponding internal ones (thus providing Internet-reachable servers). This provides one level of indirection and allows us to keep the inmate configuration both simple and dynamic at inmate boot time. To facilitate this, the inmate network provides a small number of *infrastructure services* for the inmates, including DHCP and recursive DNS resolvers. The gateway places these services into a restricted broadcast domain, comprising all machines the inmates can reach by default. In addition, infrastructure services include experiment-specific requirements such as SMTP sinks, though these do not belong to the broadcast domain.

5.4 Containment servers

GQ's design hinges crucially on the notion of an explicit *containment server* that determines each flow's containment policy. Having such a separate component represents a major improvement over existing systems. Our original design included no equivalent; instead, the packet router in the gateway alone implemented the containment policy. The current design results from our desire to reduce the gateway's forwarding logic to an infrequently changing *mechanism* to the greatest extent possible, while keeping containment *policies* configurable and adaptable. This contrasts starkly with our initial design, which intermixed a fixed nine-step containment policy with the mechanisms for enforcing that policy, all inside the gateway.

The containment server is both a machine—typically a VM, for convenience—and a standard application server running on the machine. Conceptually, the combination of the gateway's packet router and the containment server realizes a transparent application-layer proxy for all traffic entering and leaving the inmate network. The gateway's packet router informs the containment server of all new flows to or from inmates, enabling it to issue *containment verdicts* on the flows.[1] Our implementation (§ 6.2) ensures that race conditions cannot occur. The router subsequently enforces these verdicts, which enable both *endpoint control* and *content control*.

[1] Note that this approach parallels the architecture of OpenFlow [20] devices to some extent. However, our implementation predates OpenFlow's wide availability.

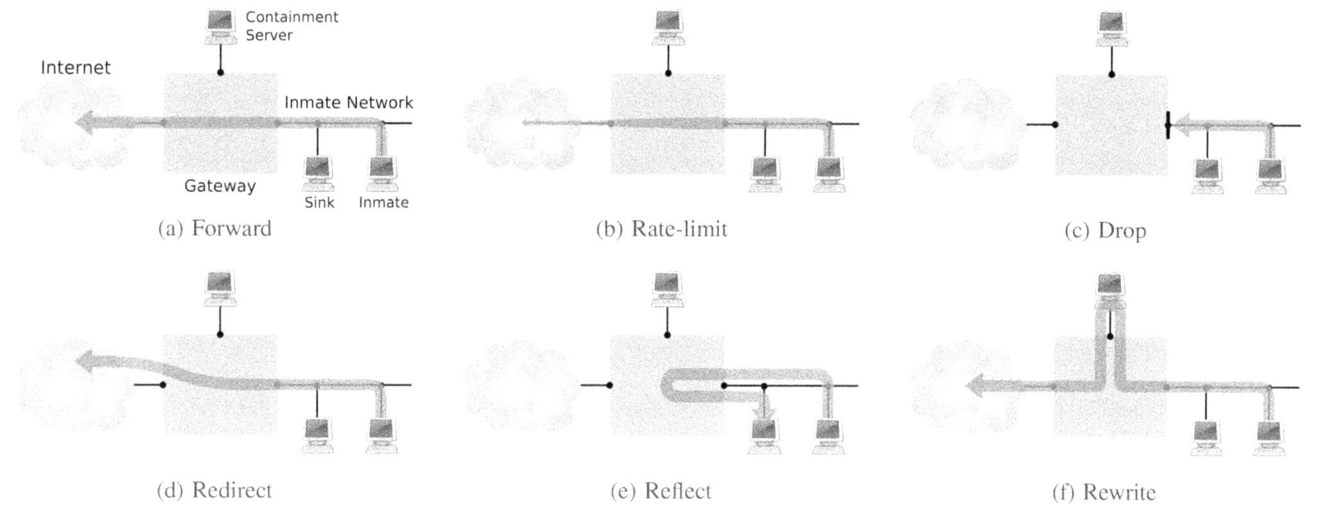

(a) Forward (b) Rate-limit (c) Drop (d) Redirect (e) Reflect (f) Rewrite

Figure 2: GQ's flow manipulation modes, illustrated on flows initiated by an inmate.

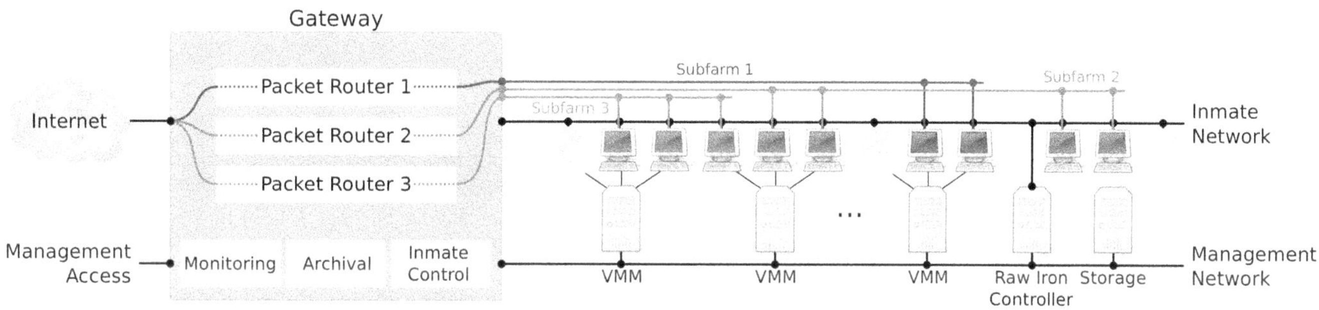

Figure 3: A possible subfarm scenario in GQ: three independent routers handle disjunct sets of VLAN IDs, thus enabling parallel experiments. For sake of clarity, we do not show per-subfarm infrastructure services individually.

Endpoint control happens at the beginning of a flow's lifespan and allows us to (*i*) forward flows unchanged, (*ii*) drop them entirely, (*iii*) reflect them to a sink server or alternative custom proxy, (*iv*) redirect them to a different target, or (*v*) rate-limit them. Once the gateway has established connectivity between the intended endpoints, it alone enforces endpoint control, conserving resources on the containment server. Content control, on the other hand, remains feasible throughout a flow's lifespan, and works by fully proxying the flow content through the containment server. We can thus (*i*) rewrite a flow, (*ii*) terminate it when it would normally still continue, or (*iii*) prolong it by injecting additional content into a flow that would otherwise already terminate. Note that the connection's destination need not necessarily exist: the containment server can simply *impersonate* one by creating response traffic as needed. Endpoint and content control need not mutually exclude each other; for example, it can make sense to redirect a flow to a different destination while also rewriting some of its contents. Figure 2 illustrates the flow manipulation modes. Note how the containment server remains passive during containment enforcement except in case of content rewriting (Figure 2(f)).

Besides flow-related containment management, the containment server also controls the inmates' *life-cycle*. As the containment server witnesses all network-level activity of an inmate, it can react to the presence—and absence—of such *network events* using activity *triggers*. These triggers can terminate the inmate, reboot it, or revert it to a clean state for subsequent reinfection. For example, a typical life-cycle policy for a spambot might automatically restart the bot once it has ceased spamming activity for more than an hour. Another common policy is to terminate an inmate that has begun sending a particular recipient more than a certain number of connection requests per minute.

5.5 Inmate control

To facilitate inmate life-cycle control, we require a component in the system that can create inmates, expire them, or adjust their life-cycle state by starting, stopping, or reverting them to a clean snapshot. In GQ's architecture, the containment servers issue life-cycle actions to an *inmate controller* located centrally on the gateway. [2] Since we keep containment servers logically and physically separate from the gateway, we require a mechanism allowing them to communicate with the inmate controller. We do so by maintaining an additional network interface only on "maintaining ... only on" reads peculiarly –VP the containment servers that allows them to interact directly (out-of-band of the inmate-related network activity), with the gateway via the management network. This controller understands the inmate hosting infrastructure and abstracts physical details of the inmates, such as their hosting server and whether they run virtualized or on raw iron. The controller requires only the

[2] Conceptually, we could place the controller on a separate server. For practical reasons, including immediate access to all VMMs and the Raw Iron Controller (see 6.4), we decided to keep it on the gateway.

inmate's VLAN ID in order to identify the target of a life-cycle action. The thin arrowed line in Figure 1 illustrates the trigger–action flow from the containment server to the hosting infrastructure.

The combination of central gateway and inmate network parallelizes naturally: instead of a global packet forwarding logic handling the entire range of VLAN IDs on the inmate network, multiple instances of the packet router process traffic on disjoint sets of VLAN IDs. This creates independent, self-contained, non-interfering habitats for different experiments. We call these habitats *subfarms*. Subfarms generally have their own containment server (thereby distributing load and allowing other subfarms to continue operating while we tune a given subfarm's configuration) and infrastructure services, but can vary widely in experiment-specific additional services. Shared network resources, as mentioned by Chen et al. [7], are possible, but we have not found them necessary in practice—the very reason for creating independent subfarms is typically the need to configure systems differently or record separate data sets. Figure 3 illustrates subfarms.

5.6 Monitoring and packet trace archival

We use a two-pronged packet trace recording strategy. First, the gateway's packet routers record each subfarm's activity from the inmate network's perspective, i.e., with unroutable addresses for the inmates. Using these local addresses has the benefit of providing some degree of immediate anonymity in the packet traces, simplifying data sharing without the risk of accidentally leaking our global address ranges. Second, system-wide trace recording happens at the upstream interface to the outside network, thus capturing all activity globally and as seen outside of GQ.

6. IMPLEMENTATION

6.1 Packet routing

We implement the subfarm's packet routers on the gateway using the Click modular router [16]. We separate each subfarm's Click configuration into a module containing invariant, reusable forwarding elements shared across all subfarms (400 lines), and a small (40 lines) configuration module that specifies each subfarm's unique aspects, including the external IP address ranges, set of VLAN ID ranges from the inmate network, and logfile naming. The custom Click elements for the VLAN bridge, NAT, containment server flow handling, and trace recording comprise around 5,000 lines of C++.

6.2 Containment server

We wrote the containment server in Python, using a pre-forked, multi-threaded service model. The server logic comprises roughly 2,200 lines, with 600 lines for the event-trigger logic. The containment policies, including content rewriters, add up to 1,000 lines.

Shimming protocol. To couple the gateway's packet router to the containment server, we need a way to map/unmap arbitrary flows to/from the single address and port of the containment server. We achieve this mapping using a *shimming protocol* conceptually similar to SOCKS [15]: upon redirection to the containment server, the gateway injects into the flow a *containment request* shim message with meta-information. Figure 4 summarizes the message structure.

The containment server expects this meta-information and uses it to assign a containment policy to the flow. The containment server similarly conveys the containment verdict back to gateway using a *containment response* shim, which the packet router strips from the flow before relaying subsequent content back to the endpoint. For TCP, the shim is sent as a separate TCP packet injected into

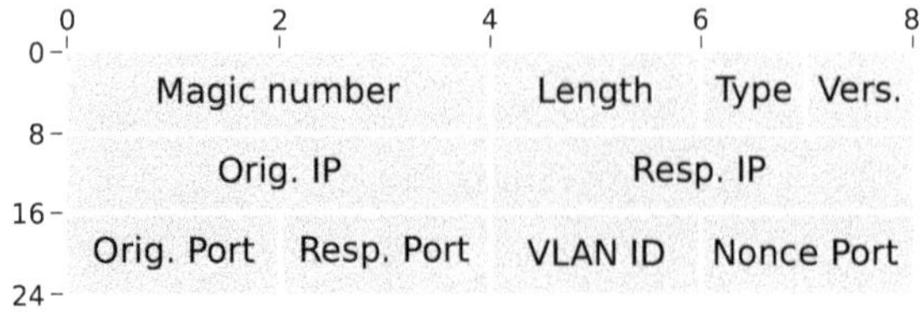

(a) Request Shim

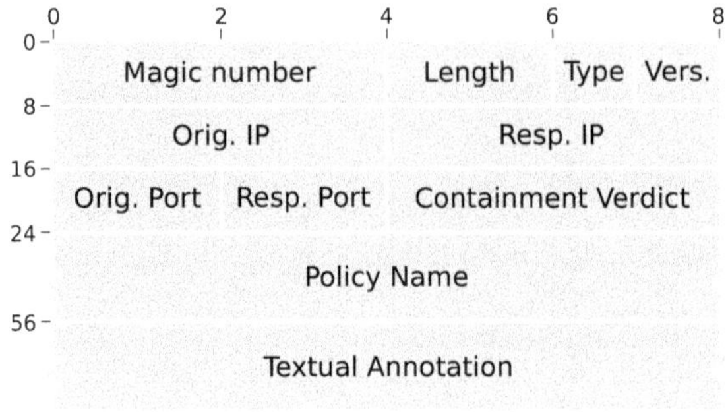

(b) Response Shim

Figure 4: The shim protocol message structure.

the sequence space, so adding and removing shim packets requires bumping and unbumping of sequence and acknowledgement numbers; for UDP it requires padding the datagrams with the respective shims.[3] The request shim occupies 24 bytes and begins with a preamble of 8 bytes containing a magic number (4 bytes), the message length (2 bytes), a message type indicator (1 byte), and a shim protocol version number (1 byte), followed by the original flow's endpoint four-tuple ($2 \cdot 4$ bytes plus $2 \cdot 2$ bytes), the VLAN ID of the sending/receiving inmate (2 bytes) and a nonce port (2 bytes) on which the gateway will expect a possible subsequent outbound connection from the containment server, in case the latter needs to rewrite the flow continuously. The response shim can vary in length and requires at least 56 bytes, consisting of a similar preamble (8 bytes), the resulting endpoint four-tuple (12 bytes), the containment verdict (`FORWARD`, `LIMIT`, `DROP`, `REDIRECT`, `REFLECT`, or `REWRITE` as per Figure 2, possibly in combination when feasible) expressed as a numeric opcode (4 bytes), a name tag for the resulting containment policy (32 bytes), and an optional annotation string to clarify the context in which the containment server decided the containment verdict.

We show an example of this containment procedure in Figure 5. An inmate initiates the TCP handshake for an upcoming HTTP request (❶), which the gateway redirects to the containment server's fixed address and port, synthesizing a full TCP handshake. Upon completion, the gateway injects into the TCP stream the containment request shim (❷). The containment server in turn sends a containment response shim (❸) including the containment verdict for the flow, in this case a `REWRITE`. To serve as a transparent proxy rewriting the flow content, it also establishes a second TCP connection to the target via the gateway and the nonce port received as part of the containment request shim. The gateway forwards this TCP `SYN` to the target and relays the handshake between target and inmate (❹). The inmate completes its connection establishment and sends the HTTP request, which the gateway relays on to the containment server as part of the same connection that it used to exchange containment information, bumping the sequence num-

[3]For large UDP datagrams, this can require fragmentation.

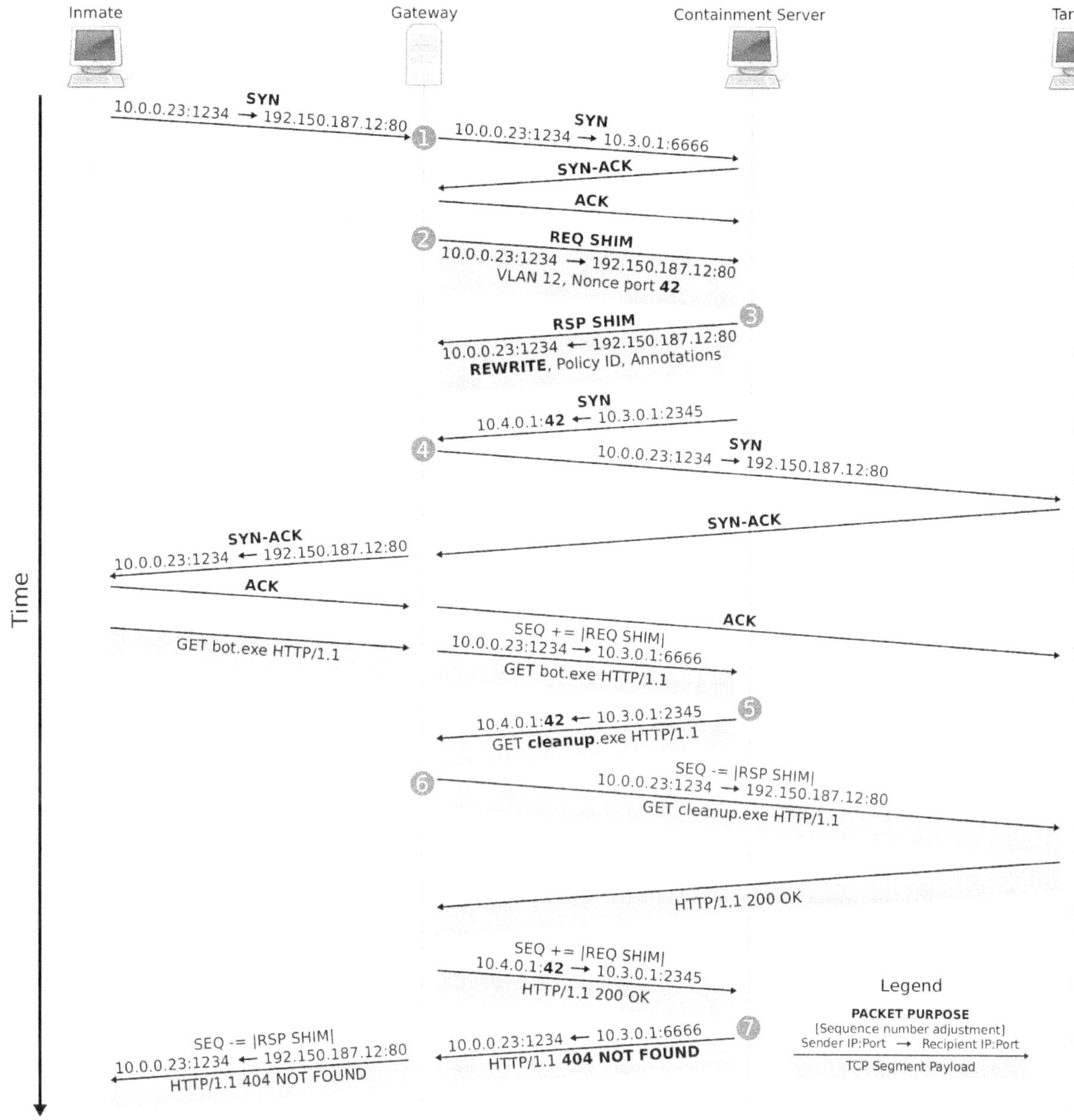

Figure 5: TCP packet flow through gateway and containment server in a `REWRITE` containment. See § 5.4 for details.

ber accordingly (❺). The containment server rewrites the request as needed (here changing the requested resource to another one) and forwards it on to the target, via the gateway (❻). The target's response travels in the opposite direction and arrives at the containment server, which again rewrites it (here to create the illusion of a non-existing resource) and relays it back to the inmate (❼). (For brevity, we do not show the subsequent connection tear-downs in the figure.)

Policy structure. We codify containment policies in Python classes, which the containment server instantiates by keying on VLAN ID ranges and applies on a per-flow basis. We base endpoint control upon the flow's four-tuple, and content control depends on the actual data sent in a given flow. Object-oriented implementation reuse and specialization lends itself well to the establishment of a hierarchy of containment policies. From a base class implementing a default-deny policy we derive classes for each endpoint control verdict, and from these specialize further, for example to a base class for spambots that reflects all outbound SMTP traffic. The containment server simply takes the name of the class implementing the applicable containment policy into the response shim (recall Figure 4(b)) in order to convey it to the gateway.

Configuration. The codified containment policies are customizable through a configuration file. This file serves four purposes. It specifies: (*i*) the initial assignment of a policy to a given inmate's traffic, (*ii*) the individual or set of malware binaries with which we would like to infect a given inmate over the course of its life-cycles,[4] (*iii*) activity triggers (e.g., revert and reinfect the inmate once the containment server has observed no outbound activity for

[4]As indicated earlier, we typically specify precisely which sample to infect an inmate with. However, GQ equally supports traditional

```
[VLAN 16-17]
Decider = Rustock
Infection = rustock.100921.*.exe

[VLAN 18-19]
Decider = Grum
Infection = grum.100818.*.exe

[VLAN 16-19]
Trigger = *:25/tcp / 30min < 1 -> revert

[Autoinfect]
Address = 10.9.8.7
Port = 6543

[BannerSmtpSink]
Address = 10.3.1.4
Port = 2526
```

Figure 6: Example of a containment server configuration file: GQ will infect the inmates on VLAN IDs 16 and 17 iteratively with binaries from the `rustock.100921.*.exe` batch, using the "Rustock" containment policy. It will apply similar policies to inmates with VLAN IDs 18 and 19, for Grum. On all four VLAN IDs a lifecycle trigger reverts inmates to a clean state whenever the number of flows to TCP port 25 in 30 minutes hits zero. The last two sections specify the location in the subfarm of an auto-infection server and of an SMTP sink, respectively.

30 minutes) and (*iv*) IP addresses and port numbers of infrastructure services in a subfarm (e.g., where to find a particular SMTP sink or HTTP proxy). Figure 6 shows a sample configuration snippet.

6.3 Inmate controller & sinks

We structure the inmate controller as a simple message receiver that interprets the life-cycle control instructions coming in from the containment servers. We use a simple text-based message format to convey the instructions. At startup, the controller scans the VMMs deployed on the management network to assemble an inventory of inmates and their VLAN IDs. We implement the controller in 470 lines of Python. The support scripts for managing inmate VMs and raw iron machines abstract concrete virtualization platforms (such as VMware's ESX control scripts), in 2,000 lines of script code. We likewise implement GQ's sink servers in Python. Our simplest *catch-all* server accepts arbitrary input and requires a mere 100 lines of code, while our most complex sink constitutes a fidelity-adjustable SMTP server that can grab greeting banners from the actual target and randomly drop a configurable fraction of connections. It needs 800 lines, using the same pre-forked multithreaded back-end as the containment server.

6.4 Raw iron management

Researchers have long known of the use of VM-detecting anti-forensics capabilities in malware toolkits [8]. Using a variety of techniques, the malware attempts to identify virtualized execution, which it perceives as a tell-tale sign of attempted forensic analysis. Rather than attempt to develop specific countermeasures (such as renaming interfaces or hiding other VM artifacts), GQ bypasses this problem by providing a group of identically configured small form-factor x86 systems running on a network-controlled power sequencer to enable remote, OS-independent reboots. Like our virtualized inmates, each raw iron system uses its own exclusive VLAN. From the gateway's viewpoint, the only difference in the inmate hosting platform is the presence of an additional DHCP service and a separate reimaging process, executed by a dedicated Raw Iron Controller.

The raw iron systems' boot configuration alternates between booting over the network (leading to a subsequent OS image transfer and installation) and booting from local disk when network booting fails (leading to normal inmate execution). The Raw Iron Controller has a network interface on a VLAN trunk which includes all raw iron VLAN IDs. The controller runs a separate Click configuration which creates a virtual network interface that multiplexes and demultiplexes traffic across the VLAN trunk, enabling unmodified Linux servers, including DHCP, TFTP, and NFS, to access the raw iron VLANs transparently.

To reimage a system, we configure the controller's DHCP server to send PXE boot information in reply to DHCP requests from the inmate. The power sequencer then reboots the inmate and the subsequent network boot installs a small Linux boot image (we use Trinity Rescue Kit [14]). This image, once booted, downloads a compressed Windows image and writes it to disk using NTFS-aware imaging tools. Next, the controller disables network-booting in the DHCP server and again power-cycles the raw iron inmate. The subsequent reboot yields a local booting of the locally installed OS image. This process takes around 6 minutes per reimaging cycle, which we find sufficiently fast for hosting bots or other malcode. An alternate version restores the image from a hidden second Linux partition on the system's main disk. This version is slightly slower (around 10 minutes) but supports efficient reimaging of all raw-iron systems simultaneously. We use a similar mechanism to capture disk images from a suitably configured OS image.

6.5 Reporting

We implemented the reporting component using Bro [24]. We developed an analyzer for the shimming protocol to keep track of all containment activity on the inmate network, and track specific additional classes of traffic as needed (for example, we leverage Bro's SMTP analyzer to track attempted and succeeding message delivery for our spambots). Bro's log-rotation functionality then initiates activity reports on an hourly and daily basis. The reports break down activity by subfarm, inmate, and containment decision, allowing us to verify that the gateway enforces these decisions as expected (for example, an unusual number of `FORWARD` verdicts might indicate a bug in the policy, and absence of any C&C `REWRITE`s would indicate lack of botnet activity). We also pull in external information to help us verify containment (for example, we check all global IP addresses currently used by inmates against relevant IP blacklists). Figure 7 shows part of a report. The reporting setup extracts all of the per-inmate textual information from network activity.

6.6 Auto-infection & batch processing

Automating the infection (and re-infection, after a revert to clean state) of inmates is a key ingredient for saving us time operating GQ. We have implemented an auto-infection routine as follows. We configured auto-infection inmate master images to run a custom infection script at first boot (subsequent reboots should not trigger reinfection, as some malware intentionally triggers reboots itself). This script then contacts an HTTP server at a preconfigured address and port, requests the malware sample, and executes it, thus completing the infection. Note that we can realize the HTTP server as a `REWRITE` containment, simplifying the implementation substan-

honeypot constellations in which dynamic circumstances (such as a web drive-by) determine the nature of the infection.

```
Inmate Activity
===============

Active subfarms: Botfarm, Clickbots

Subfarm 'Botfarm' [Containment server VLAN 11]
--------------------------------------------------------

  Grum [xxx.yyy.0.170/10.3.9.241, VLAN 18]
  ------------------------------------------------------
  FORWARD
  - C&C port                 target        port   #flows
           50.8.207.91.SteepHost.Net      http      682

  REFLECT
  - full SMTP containment    target        port   #flows
                             *.*.*.*       smtp   144997

  REWRITE
  - autoinfection 6f007d640b3d5786a84dedf026c1507c
                             target        port   #flows
                             10.9.8.7      6543        6

  SMTP sessions                                    93340
  SMTP DATA transfers                              93112


  Rustock [xxx.yyy.0.164/10.3.9.247, VLAN 7]
  ------------------------------------------------------
  FORWARD
  - C&C port                 target        port   #flows
                             *.*.*.*       https     287

  REFLECT
  - simple SMTP containment  target        port   #flows
                             *.*.*.*       smtp   280620

  REWRITE
  - C&C filtering            target        port   #flows
                             *.*.*.*       http      788

  - autoinfection 0740eb0e408ea0b6cfa95981273f89bb
                             target        port   #flows
                             10.9.8.7      6543       21

  SMTP sessions                                   182653
  SMTP DATA transfers                             284765
```

Figure 7: Section of actual report generated by the monitoring setup, for the "Botfarm" subfarm, for inmates contained using the "Grum" and "Rustock" policies, respectively. The `REWRITE`s show that the containment server employs auto-infection (§ 6.6), along with the MD5 hashes of the actual executables. The number of SMTP flows `REFLECT`ed differs from the total number of SMTP sessions because we configured the SMTP sink to drop connections probabilistically. (Global inmate IP addresses anonymized.)

tially: the containment server observes the attempted HTTP connection anyway, and can thus proceed to impersonate the simple HTTP server needed to serve the infection. We implement this as a separate containment class that serves as a base class for all policies that operate using auto-infection. Again, VLAN IDs drive the selection of a malware sample, as the configuration in Figure 6 illustrates. Processing batches of malware samples follows as a simple generalization: instead of serving the same sample repeatedly, we maintain the batch as a list of files and serve them sequentially.

6.7 External network address space

In practice we operate GQ using a set of five /24 networks. We use one network only to make externally available our experiments' control infrastructure (at least each subfarm's containment servers, potentially also sink servers and other machinery), leaving four networks for our inmate population. The size of these allocations forms an upper bound on the number of inmates we can accommodate at any given time, but so far has proved sufficient: we experience no blacklisting of our inmates' global IP addresses, and thus no need to move inmates around in our address range to preserve their functionality. This general absence (with rare exceptions, which we cover in the next section) of blacklisting speaks for the quality of our containment policies.

7. OPERATIONAL EXPERIENCES

We now report on experiences gained over the course of our work on GQ. In particular, we focus on practical lessons learned while developing containment policies, and on insights on the general scalability of the system.

7.1 Containment-derived insights

While containment policy development can easily feel like a chore, we have found that developing tight containment often forms a key step for understanding the behavior of a sample under study. Examples of such insights learned during containment development include:

Absence of activity. During our operation of GQ as a worm-capturing honeyfarm at the beginning of 2006, we captured 66 distinct worms belonging to 14 different malware families (according to classification by Symantec's anti-virus products at the time). Table 1 summarizes the captures. Note the high variation in incubation times: nine infection classes required more than *three minutes* on average for a propagation. This illustrates the importance of long-duration execution to observe the desired behavior, even in infections that supposedly act quickly.

Unexpected visitors. During our infiltration of the Storm botnet in 2008 [13, 18, 19] we developed sufficiently complete understanding of this particular malware family that a containment policy seemed to follow naturally. For the C&C-relaying proxy bots in the middle of the Storm hierarchy, we preserved outside reachability of the bots (the requirement for their becoming relay agents as opposed to spam-sourcing drones) and redirected all outgoing activity other than the HTTP-borne C&C protocol to our standard sink server. In June, however, we noticed apparent FTP connection attempts arriving at our sink server. Closer investigation revealed the attempted use of our Storm bots for iframe injection. An upstream botmaster attempted to use the bots' ability to receive and process SOCKS [15] message headers to initiate FTP connections to specific hosts, authenticate and log in with known credentials, download a specific HTML file and re-upload it with a malicious iframe tag inserted. At the time, articles on Storm frequently stated that its proxy bots did not themselves engage in malicious activity, and a correspondingly loose containment policy would have allowed these attacks to proceed unhindered.

Mysterious blacklisting. While deploying spambots of the Waledac family [27] in June 2009, we noticed to our surprise that the Composite Blocking List (CBL) [6] listed our inmates—a strong indication of a possible containment failure. However, the only outside interaction we had permitted was a single test SMTP message, sent to a GMail server, because redirection to our default SMTP sink caused the bots to cease further activity due to the lack of their receiving the Google SMTP banner in response to their attempts. Subsequent independent testing revealed that the bots themselves used a recognizable HELO greeting string (`wergvan`), that Google detected its presence, and that they informed blacklist providers of the IP addresses of SMTP speakers employing the

Executable	Worm name	# Events/ # Conns	Incubation period (s)
a####.exe	W32.Zotob.E	4 / 3	29.0
a####.exe	W32.Zotob.H	9 / 3	25.2
a####.exe	—	1 / 3	**223.2**
cpufanctrl.exe	Backdoor.Sdbot	1 / 4	111.2
chkdisk32.exe	—	1 / 4	134.7
dllhost.exe	W32.Welchia.Worm	297 / 4 or 6	24.5
enbiei.exe	W32.Blaster.F.Worm	1 / 3	28.9
msblast.exe	W32.Balster.Worm	1 / 3	43.8
lsd	W32.Poxdar	11 / 8	32.4
NeroFil.EXE	W32.Spybot.Worm	1 / 5	**237.5**
sysmsn.exe	W32.Spybot.Worm	3 / 3	79.6
MsUpdaters.exe	W32.Spybot.Worm	1 / 5	57.0
RealPlayer.exe	W32.Spybot.Worm	2 / 5	95.4
WinTemp.exe	W32.Spybot.Worm	1 / 5	178.4
wins.exe	W32.Spybot.Worm	1 / 5	118.2
msnet.exe	W32.Spybot.Worm	1 / 7	**189.4**
msgupdates.exe	W32.Spybot.Worm	2 / 5	125.3
ntsf.exe	—	1 / 5	**459.4**
scardsvr32.exe	W32.Femot.Worm	4 / 3	46.2
scardsvr32.exe	W32.Femot.Worm	1 / 3	66.5
scardsvr32.exe	W32.Femot.Worm	55 / 3	96.6
scardsvr32.exe	W32.Femot.Worm	2 / 3	179.6
scardsvr32.exe	W32.Femot.Worm	1 / 5	49.3
scardsvr32.exe	W32.Femot.Worm	4 / 3	41.4
scardsvr32.exe	W32.Femot.Worm	1 / 3	41.1
scardsvr32.exe	W32.Valla.2048	1 / 5	32.2
scardsvr32.exe	—	1 / 7	54.8
scardsvr32.exe	W32.Pinfi	1 / 3	**180.8**
x.exe	W32.Korgo.Q	17 / 2	6.6
x.exe	W32.Korgo.T	7 / 2	9.5
x.exe	W32.Korgo.V	102 / 2	6.0
x.exe	W32.Korgo.W	31 / 2	5.9
x.exe	W32.Korgo.Z	20 / 2	6.6
x.exe	W32.Korgo.S	169 / 2	6.6
x.exe	W32.Korgo.S	15 / 2	8.6
x.exe	W32.Korgo.V	2 / 2	24.4
x.exe	W32.Licum	2 / 2	7.9
x.exe	W32.Korgo.S	3 / 2	10.4
x.exe	W32.Pinfi	1 / 2	**329.7**
x.exe	W32.Korgo.V	6 / 2	11.3
x.exe	W32.Pinfi	5 / 2	20.1
x.exe	W32.Pinfi	5 / 2	24.9
x.exe	W32.Pinfi	2 / 2	27.5
x.exe	W32.Korgo.V	1 / 2	27.5
x.exe	W32.Pinfi	1 / 2	63.1
x.exe	W32.Korgo.W	1 / 2	76.1
x.exe	W32.Korgo.S	1 / 2	18.0
x.exe	W32.Pinfi	1 / 2	58.2
x.exe	W32.Korgo.S	1 / 2	**210.9**
xxxx...x	Backdoor.Berbew.N	844 / 2	9.4
xxxx...x	W32.Info.A	34 / 2	7.2
xxxx...x	Trojan.Dropper	685 / 3	10.0
xxxx...x	W32.Pinfi	1 / 3	32.5
xxxx...x	W32.Pinfi	3 / 2	34.2
n/a	W32.Korgo.C	3 / 2	4.8
n/a	W32.Korgo.L	1 / 2	7.0
n/a	W32.Korgo.G	8 / 2	4.1
n/a	W32.Korgo.N	2 / 2	5.3
n/a	W32.Korgo.G	3 / 2	5.4
n/a	W32.Korgo.E	1 / 2	5.6
n/a	W32.Korgo.gen	1 / 2	5.0
n/a	W32.Korgo.I	15 / 2	4.3
n/a	W32.Korgo.I	1 / 2	5.4
multiple	W32.Muma.A	2 / 7	**186.7**
multiple	W32.Muma.B	2 / 7	**208.9**
multiple	BAT.Boohoo.Worm	1 / 72	**384.9**

Table 1: Self-propagating worms caught by GQ in early 2006. Events correspond to total infections during the course of the experiment with the same executable. Next come the numbers of connections needed per infection to complete the propagation, and incubation times (the delay from initial infection in our farm to subsequent infection of the next inmate). We show delays of over 3 minutes in bold.

string. This caused us to stop the policy of allowing even seemingly innocuous non-spam test SMTP exchanges.

Satisfying fidelity. It soon turned out that Waledac was not the only spambot family whose members paid close attention to the greeting banners returned by the SMTP servers. As a consequence, we upgraded our SMTP sink to support *banner grabbing* for select connections: SMTP requests to a hitherto unseen host now caused the sink to actually connect out to the target SMTP server and obtain the greeting message, relaying it back to the spambot. The more closely malware tracks whether the responding entity behaves as expected, the more likely we are to get drawn into an arms race of emulating and testing fidelity.

Protocol violations. On several occasions during our ongoing extraction of spam from spambots [18], our spam harvest accounting looked healthy at the connection level (since many connections ensued), but, upon closer inspection, meager at the content level (since for some bot families no actual message body transmission occurred). Closer investigation revealed that our SMTP sink protocol engine followed the SMTP specification [26] too closely, preventing the protocol state machine from ever reaching the DATA stage. The protocol discrepancies included such seemingly mundane details as repeated HELO/EHLO greetings or the format of email addresses in MAIL FROM and RCPT TO stanzas (with or without colons, with or without angle brackets).

Exploratory containment. Containment policy development need not always try to facilitate continuous malware operation. To better understand a sample, we frequently find it equally important to create specific environmental conditions under which the sample will exhibit new behavior. In preparing for our infiltration of Storm, we tried to understand the meaning of the error codes returned in Storm's delivery reports [18] using a dual approach of live experimentation, in which we exposed the samples to specific error conditions during SMTP transactions, and binary analysis. Interestingly, neither approach could individually explain all behavior, but by iterating alternation of the two—live experimentation confirming conjectures developed during binary analysis, and vice versa—we eventually identified the error codes' meanings. We used this approach again during our infiltration of the MegaD botnet [4]. Here, live experimentation allowed us to confirm the correct functionality of the extracted C&C protocol engine. During a recent investigation of clickbots [21] we used the approach to understand the precise HTTP context of some of the bots' C&C requests.

Unclear phylogenies. When we take specimens supposedly belonging to malware family X and subject them to a corresponding containment policy, we implicitly assume that this family membership is in fact correct and that other samples belonging to family X will exhibit behavioral similarity. We find this assumption increasingly violated in practice. We have repeatedly observed third parties labeling samples inconsistently, including cases of split personalities in malware: in February 2010 we encountered a specimen that at times showed MegaD's C&C behavior, and at other times behaved like a member of the Grum family. While tight containment ensures that our operation causes no harm when containment policy and observed behavior mismatch, it casts doubt on the appealing idea of developing a library of containment policies from which we can easily pick the appropriate one. A batch-processing setup that enables some extent of automated family classification is thus an important tool to have. To this end, we reflect all outgoing network activity to our catch-all sink and apply network-level fingerprinting on the samples' initial activity trace. We have successfully used this approach to classify approximately 10,000 unique malware samples that we harvested from pay-per-install distribution servers [3].

7.2 System scalability

Traditional honeyfarms such as Potemkin [29] place a strong emphasis on scalability of the inmate population: these systems quickly "flash-clone" new inmates to provide additional infectees as needed. For the worm model this made sense—it requires infectee chains to reliably identify infections, and the assumption that any incoming flow may constitute a potential worm infection implies the need to set aside resources potentially for each sender of traffic received in the honeyfarm's IP address range. Today's requirements for malware execution have shifted. Self-propagating malware infections are not extinct, but play less of a role in today's landscape, and typically use entirely different vectors (such as the user's activity on specific websites, as in the case of Koobface [28]). Correspondingly, careful filtering and resource management related to unsolicited, inbound traffic has become less pressing, particularly when considering the typical scenario of home-user machines deployed behind network address translators. We find it more important to achieve scalability in terms of providing independent experiments at varying stages of "production-readiness" (including development of the farm architecture itself) with moderate requirements of inmate population size, and convenient mechanisms for intentional, controlled infection of the inmate population. GQ's architecture reflects these considerations.

The architecture we outlined in § 5 constrains scalability as follows. First, VLAN IDs are a limited resource. The IEEE 802.1Q standard limits the VLAN ID to twelve bits, allowing up to 4,096 inmates. However, physical switches frequently support less. Naturally, we can avoid this limitation by moving to multiple inmate networks and prepending a gateway-internal network identifier to VLAN IDs for purposes of identifying inmates. Second, with a large number of inmates in a single subfarm, a single containment server becomes a bottleneck, as it has to interpose on all flows in the subfarm. We can address this situation in a straightforward manner by moving to a cluster of containment servers, managed by the subfarm's packet router. We would simply need to extend the router's flow state table entries to include an identifier of the containment server responsible for the flow. Several containment server selection policies come to mind, such as random selection under the constraint that the same containment server always handles the same inmate. Third, similarly to the containment server, the central gateway itself becomes a bottleneck as the number of inmates and subfarms grows. To date, we have not found this problematic: the same 3Ghz quad-core Xeon machine with 5GB of memory that we deployed six years ago still serves us well today, running 5-6 subfarms in parallel with populations ranging from a handful to a dozen of inmates. Fourth, our globally routable IP address space is of limited size, creating an incentive to avoid blacklisting and leaking of our actively used addresses to reduce the rate at which we "burn through" this address space. Currently we find our address allocations sufficient. Should this change, we may opt to use GRE tunnels in order to connect additional routable address space available in other networks (provided by colleagues or interested third parties) to the system.

8. CONCLUSION

The GQ malware farm introduces containment as a first-order component in support of malware analysis. In building and operating GQ for six years, we have come to treat containment itself as a tool that can improve our understanding of monitored malware. While modern malware increasingly resists longitudinal analysis in completely contained environments, GQ not only allows but encourages flexible and precise containment policies while maintaining acceptable safety. With ongoing development, we anticipate it continuing to provide core functionality for monitoring malware and botnet operation well into the future.

We fully acknowledge the manual and—depending on the specimen at hand—time-consuming nature of this process. But, crucially, GQ makes this process both explicit and feasible. While recent work on automated C&C protocol extraction from binaries [4, 17] could aid in understanding the significance of individual flows, these automated approaches currently cannot provide the understanding that human-driven analysis of an inmate's traffic produces. The language in which we express containment policies in the containment server forms another area of future work. The primary reason for our current use of Python is experience and convenience, but the general-purpose nature of the language complicates the creation of a tool-chain for processing policies. For example, a traffic generation tool that can automatically produce test cases for a given concrete containment policy would strengthen confidence in the policy's correctness significantly. A more domain-specific, abstract language (like in Bro [24]) could simplify this.

It behooves us to contemplate the consequences of a containment arms race, in which malware authors explicitly try to defeat our approach to containment. It is easy to see—as mentioned by John et al. [12]—that botmasters can construct circumstances in which malware will cease to function as desired, despite our best efforts. For example, spam campaigners could scatter control groups of email addresses among the spam target lists and require successful delivery of messages to these addresses to keep a bot spamming. However, we remain optimistic about the feasibility of providing safe containment for new malware types. First, in practice the majority of specimens we encounter still possesses readily distinguishable C&C protocols. Second, we note the conceptual difference between achieving the desired goal of executing malware (say, longitudinal harvesting of spam messages) and tight containment preventing harm to others. While the former may fail, in our experience we can guarantee the latter, given tight containment. We thus believe that we can operate malware safely to the point of attack and control traffic becoming so blended that we can no longer meaningfully distinguish them.

Acknowledgements

This work has spanned many years, and would not have been possible without the support of many parties. We wish to thank the U.S. Department of Energy's ESnet, Hewlett/Packard, Microsoft, and VMware for their generous in-kind donations used to construct and operate GQ. We particularly wish to thank Randy Bush, Eli Dart, Chris Grier, Craig Leres, Stefan Savage, Helen Wang, and our colleagues at the Lawrence Berkeley National Laboratory and the University of California, San Diego, for assistance and feedback during GQ's five years of operation. This work was supported in part by National Science Foundation grants NSF-0433702, CNS-0831535, and CNS-0905631, and by the Office of Naval Research MURI grant N000140911081. Any opinions, findings, and conclusions or recommendations expressed in this material are those of the authors and do not necessarily reflect the views of the funders.

9. REFERENCES

[1] P. Barford and M. Blodgett. Toward botnet mesocosms. In *Proceedings of the First Workshop on Hot Topics in Understanding Botnets*, Berkeley, CA, USA, 2007. USENIX Association.

[2] U. Bayer, C. Kruegel, and E. Kirda. TTAnalyze: A tool for analyzing malware. In *15th Annual Conference of the*

European Institute for Computer Antivirus Research (EICAR), 2006.

[3] J. Caballero, C. Grier, C. Kreibich, and V. Paxson. Measuring Pay-per-Install: The Commoditization of Malware Distribution. In *Proceedings of the 20th USENIX Security Symposium*, San Francisco, CA, USA, August 2011.

[4] J. Caballero, P. Poosankam, C. Kreibich, and D. Song. Dispatcher: Enabling active botnet infiltration using automatic protocol reverse-engineering. In *Proceedings of the 16th ACM CCS*, pages 621–634, Chicago, IL, USA, November 2009.

[5] J. Calvet, C. R. Davis, J. M. Fernandez, J.-Y. Marion, P.-L. St-Onge, W. Guizani, P.-M. Bureau, and A. Somayaji. The case for in-the-lab botnet experimentation: creating and taking down a 3000-node botnet. In *Proceedings of the 26th ACSAC Conference*, pages 141–150, New York, NY, USA, 2010. ACM.

[6] CBL. Composite Blocking List. `http://cbl.abuseat.org`, 2003.

[7] J. Chen, J. McCullough, and A. C. Snoeren. Universal Honeyfarm Containment. Technical Report CS2007-0902, UCSD, September 2007.

[8] X. Chen, J. Andersen, Z. Mao, M. Bailey, and J. Nazario. Towards an understanding of anti-virtualization and anti-debugging behavior in modern malware. In *Proceedings of the 38th Conference on Dependable Systems and Networks (DSN)*, pages 177–186. IEEE, 2008.

[9] W. Cui, V. Paxson, and N. Weaver. GQ: Realizing a System to Catch Worms in a Quarter Million Places. Technical Report TR-06-004, International Computer Science Institute, September 2006.

[10] A. W. Jackson, D. Lapsley, C. Jones, M. Zatko, C. Golubitsky, and W. T. Strayer. SLINGbot: A System for Live Investigation of Next Generation Botnets. In *Proceedings of the 2009 Cybersecurity Applications & Technology Conference for Homeland Security*, pages 313–318, Washington, DC, USA, 2009. IEEE Computer Society.

[11] X. Jiang and D. Xu. Collapsar: A VM-based architecture for network attack detention center. In *Proceedings of the 13th USENIX Security Symposium*, page 2. USENIX Association, 2004.

[12] J. John, A. Moshchuk, S. Gribble, and A. Krishnamurthy. Studying spamming botnets using Botlab. In *Proceedings of the 6th USENIX Symposium on Networked Systems Design and Implementation*, pages 291–306. USENIX Association, 2009.

[13] C. Kanich, C. Kreibich, K. Levchenko, B. Enright, G. M. Voelker, V. Paxson, and S. Savage. Spamalytics: An empirical analysis of spam marketing conversion. In *Proceedings of the 15th ACM Conference on Computer and Communications Security*, pages 3–14, Alexandria, Virginia, USA, October 2008.

[14] T. Kerremans and B. Verstricht. Trinity Rescue Kit. `http://trinityhome.org`.

[15] D. Koblas. SOCKS. In *Proceedings of the 3rd USENIX Security Symposium*. USENIX Association, September 1992.

[16] E. Kohler, R. Morris, B. Chen, J. Jannotti, and M. Kaashoek. The Click modular router. *ACM Transactions on Computer Systems (TOCS)*, 18(3):263–297, 2000.

[17] C. Kolbitsch, T. Holz, C. Kruegel, and E. Kirda. Inspector Gadget: Automated extraction of proprietary gadgets from malware binaries. In *2010 IEEE Symposium on Security and Privacy*, pages 29–44. IEEE, 2010.

[18] C. Kreibich, C. Kanich, K. Levchenko, B. Enright, G. M. Voelker, V. Paxson, and S. Savage. On the Spam Campaign Trail. In *Proceedings of the First USENIX Workshop on Large-scale Exploits and Emergent Threats (LEET)*, San Francisco, USA, April 2008.

[19] C. Kreibich, C. Kanich, K. Levchenko, B. Enright, G. M. Voelker, V. Paxson, and S. Savage. Spamcraft: An inside look at spam campaign orchestration. In *Proceedings of the Second USENIX Workshop on Large-scale Exploits and Emergent Threats (LEET)*, Boston, USA, April 2009.

[20] N. McKeown, T. Anderson, H. Balakrishnan, G. Parulkar, L. Peterson, J. Rexford, S. Shenker, and J. Turner. OpenFlow: Enabling Innovation In Campus Networks. *ACM SIGCOMM Computer Communication Review*, 38(2):69–74, 2008.

[21] B. Miller, P. Pearce, C. Grier, C. Kreibich, and V. Paxson. What's Clicking What? Techniques and Inovations of Today's Clickbots. In *Conference on Detection of Intrusions and Malware & Vulnerability Assessment (DIMVA)*. Springer, July 2011.

[22] J. Mirkovic, T. V. Benzel, T. Faber, R. Braden, J. T. Wroclawski, and S. Schwab. The DETER project: Advancing the science of cyber security experimentation and test. In *IEEE Intl. Conference on Technologies for Homeland Security (HST)*, page 7, November 2010.

[23] Norman ASA. Norman SandBox. `http://www.norman.com/security_center/security_tools/`.

[24] V. Paxson. Bro: A System for Detecting Network Intruders in Real-Time. *Proceedings of the 7th USENIX Security Symposium*, pages 31–51, 1998.

[25] A. Pitsillidis, K. Levchenko, C. Kreibich, C. Kanich, G. Voelker, V. Paxson, N. Weaver, and S. Savage. Botnet Judo: Fighting Spam with Itself . In *Proceedings of the 17th Annual Network and Distributed System Security Symposium (NDSS)*, San Diego, CA, USA, March 2010.

[26] J. Postel. Simple Mail Transfer Protocol. RFC 821, August 1982.

[27] G. Tenebro. W32.Waledac Threat Analysis. `http://www.symantec.com/content/en/us/enterprise/media/security_response/whitepapers/W32_Waledac.pdf`, 2009.

[28] N. Villeneuve. Koobface: Inside a Crimeware Network. `http://www.infowar-monitor.net/reports/iwm-koobface.pdf`, November 2010.

[29] M. Vrable, J. Ma, J. Chen, D. Moore, E. Vandekieft, A. Snoeren, G. Voelker, and S. Savage. Scalability, fidelity, and containment in the potemkin virtual honeyfarm. *ACM SIGOPS Operating Systems Review*, 39(5):148–162, 2005.

[30] Y. Wang, D. Beck, X. Jiang, and R. Roussev. Automated Web Patrol with Strider Honeymonkeys: Finding Web Sites that Exploit Browser Vulnerabilities. In *Proceedings of the 13th Annual Network and Distributed System Security Symposium (NDSS)*, San Diego, CA, USA, March 2006.

[31] C. Willems, T. Holz, and F. Freiling. Toward automated dynamic malware analysis using CWSandbox. *IEEE Security & Privacy*, pages 32–39, 2007.

Summary Review Documentation for

"GQ: Practical Containment for Measuring Modern Malware Systems"

Authors: C. Kreibich, N. Weaver, C. Kanich, W. Cui, V. Paxson

Reviewer #1

Strengths: GQ is very useful for studying malware. The authors discuss some experiences from operating the farm for six years, which could be interesting for future farm developers.

Weaknesses: The work does not provide new insights into the design of containment policies. The main take-away message is that policies should be implemented manually from a deny-all starting point, which does not add something new. The paper focuses heavily on GQ implementation and configuration low-level details. It was not clear what research challenges this work addresses.

Comments to Authors: At some points I felt the paper reads a bit like a software configuration/implementation guide. The authors should try to make it more interesting to read, perhaps, by explaining better the challenges they address and their design options/choices.

Previous work [Botlab] found the problem of containment intractable because allowing even a benign msg could cause third-party bots to transmit harmful traffic. I wonder what is the opinion of the authors, is the problem really intractable? I do not see how GQ solves this problem.

The authors mention "GQ [...] making containment policy development a natural component of the malware analysis process". It would be nice if it was a bit more clear what "natural component" means.

In Section 4, I didn't understand what the paper means with "separation of policy with mechanism". Is the point that the two entities should be physically separated to avoid resource contention?

In the conclusion the authors talk about "flexible and precise" containment policies, but there is almost nothing in the paper about containment policies.

Reviewer #2

Strengths: The design is excellent and demonstrates the authors' familiarity with practical, real-world malware analysis. The platform seems versatile enough to study most kinds of existing malware at the level of detail that is required while maintaining fine control over the damage that the malware can inflict upon the world at large.

Weaknesses: The need for rigor in designing a containment platform is somewhat lessened by the fact that malware analysis is still going to be a very manual process. Moreover, the evolution of their platform is an indicator that the authors are stuck in an arms race; the publication of this work could make the work itself obsolete.

Comments to Authors: The GQ platform is quite impressive and I have no complaints about the technical contributions of the paper. The weaknesses I mentioned above are a) acknowledged by the authors, and b) fundamental to the problem space.

The title and the text are a bit mismatched. The title involves "practical", yet "practical" does not appear in the paper. What makes GQ "practical"? Conversely, the text asserts a "principled approach" to containment policies, yet then fails to describe any actual "principles". Perhaps there is a methodology... Or perhaps the principles are described and the reader is supposed to figure out that this constitutes a "principled approach". However, it seems an unnecessary oversell of an engineering feat, as well as an implied knock against prior work that seems no less principled, and I am disappointed by it. Eventually, in the conclusion, the authors admit "[GQ] provides the basis for a principled approach to containment policy development" -- which appears to be a step back from the principled approach promised in the introduction.

As someone relatively unfamiliar with malware research, I wonder just what having GQ will provide malware researchers, given that each piece of malware still requires so much manual analysis. Is it helpful for avoiding causing external damage? The section "Mysterious blacklisting" suggests that mistakes can still be made and that human error is still a substantial hurdle. There's no clear metric for measuring how much easier it is to safely analyze malware with GQ than without, and the results are all anecdotal.

The paper could be a bit more readable. Section 6 (6.2 in particular) was perhaps too detailed to be interesting, unlike the rest of the paper. Section 8 was particularly important; it answered a lot of questions that I had lingering in my head since the introduction, so I feel like it should really be moved closer to the introduction if possible. The last sentence in section 8 is accurate, insightful, and deeply troubling.

Reviewer #3

Strengths: The paper presents a real system that does something useful and challenging. The design is nice.

Weaknesses: However, it does not introduce any new ideas, or bring any new understanding to how malware works. Also, I think that it promises more than it delivers (but this is a matter of presentation).

Comments to Authors: There is no denying that the presented system is useful. Also, assigning the implementation of the containment policies to separate containment servers sounds like a great design choice that would make it significantly easier to experiment with new policies.

But, despite appreciating all the hard and useful work done by the authors, it is not clear how this paper advances the state of the art. As far as I can tell, the design does not include any novel technique. The resulting system still requires manual trial and error to determine what containment policy to use for each flow. The results that the authors obtained using this system have been published in separate reports.

A complaint regarding presentation: Imo, the paper overclaims. In particular, the title talks about *practical* containment; I don't think that manual trial and error qualifies as practical. The introduction talks about "principled containment", which made me expect a set of principles that would guide researchers in choosing containment policies; the only principle advocated in the paper is to separate containment policy from enforcement.

A couple of minor questions: In Section 5.5, why is the inmate controller located centrally on the gateway? Couldn't it be implemented on a separate server? In the same section, it says that subfarms have their own containment servers, "thereby providing subfarm-specific containment policies." I found this statement confusing. It implies that you would need separate servers to implement separate policies, which is not the case, right?

Reviewer #4

Strengths: Great topic, important for the community. Major questions are covered: architecture, implementation, lessons learned / creation of policies.

Weaknesses: Not enough information shared on past containment policies. Didn't explain how this is different from your past publications (e.g. reference 9). Didn't cover performance implications.

Comments to Authors: Nice paper! Containment is indeed seen as a chore and it is great to bring attention to this issue. I'm not sure if I'm convinced that it will no longer be a chore with your system, but at least containment will be easier to do and be implemented in a well thought manner.

Did you think about whether it would make sense to release the tool (e.g. gateway + containment server) to the community?

The only disappointment is that I was hoping to see more info about the past containment policies that you have used. It's great though to see your last section on recommendations about the creation of containment policies.

While this paper contains new material, you are still expected in your reference section to explain how your work is not only different from the work of other people, but also how this is different from your 2006 paper (reference 9).

In terms of readability, I had some difficulties at the beginning to separate the role of the containment server from the role of the gateway and understand how they communicate. You cover this later in the paper, but you should already mention earlier in the paper, that you will cover how they communicate.

Could you also explain what is the impact of your system on the performance of the communications? e.g. how much delay is added?

Reviewer #5

Strengths: The paper presents a long running deployment experiment of a malware measurement and containment system. The system has been operational for the last 5 years, and there are many useful insights presented in the work.

Weaknesses: The evaluation and anecdotal part of the system was a little light --- for a 5 year study, I would have expected the measurement part to be particularly central to the paper. Instead the authors present such operational experience in about 3 pages in this 14 page paper.

Comments to Authors: I thought the problem domain and the proposed solution was quite an important one. Clearly the approach proposed in this paper is a useful one and continues to have significant impact in the world of network security. There were some interesting nuggets presented in the paper, e.g., their system got blacklisted in June 2009, which they subsequently fixed.

Since I do not have strong expertise in this area, I am unable to judge the relative novelty of the contributions. However, given this is a measurement paper, I was surprised at the lightness of the measurement results presented. There were a few interesting nuggets mentioned, but the paper seems much more about a potential system design and less about the measurement study itself.

Response from the Authors

Multiple reviewers suggested that the research question we address is unclear, and that technically the paper provides little new. We offer in response that we view the main contribution to be that GQ makes containment *development* (as opposed to relying on preconceived, fixed filtering policies) a first-grade component of the malware experimentation process.

To address Reviewer #1's concerns, we have expanded our commentary on the theoretical intractability of the containment problem, which we originally only mentioned in passing at the end of the paper. We have also clarified what we mean by policy development becoming a "natural component".

We acknowledge Reviewer #2's criticism that even given GQ, the containment development process remains largely manual. As stated in the paper, we do not think this is necessarily a bad thing. In many situations one needs to understand what the monitored malware is doing. We think the task of iteratively developing a suitable containment policy is in fact a natural way for gaining this understanding, at least until binary analysis tools that strive to extract the semantics of malware executables become significantly more powerful. We have strengthened this argument in the paper. We regret that this reviewer (and also, in part, Reviewer #3) perceived that we overstated the degree to which GQ makes developing containment policies principled and practical. Our main perspective is that it does so in relative terms compared with existing work/approaches; we recognize that there is a good ways to go in absolute terms.

Regarding Reviewer #4's question as to whether we would consider releasing gateway and containment server code to the community, we indeed considered this. However, in our experience malware execution platforms differ substantially, and it would likely be hard to make our code work in a variety of environments. In addition, we lack the support to commit to the maintenance necessary for such a public release to be effective.

We have improved our treatment of related work, as requested by Reviewer #4, and clarified the distinction of gateway and containment server.

Regarding Reviewer #5's comments, we would like to say that we felt the way in which the current GQ architecture *enables* policy development is more important than reporting in detail on past containment policies, which by the very nature of malware turn out to be quite individual and generally ephemeral.

Finally, we have improved wording throughout the paper, hopefully addressing various reviewer requests for clarification.

Measurement and Evaluation of a Real World Deployment of a Challenge-Response Spam Filter

Jelena Isacenkova, Davide Balzarotti

Eurecom, Sophia Antipolis, France

{isachenk,balzarotti}@eurecom.fr

ABSTRACT

Despite the number of existing solutions, spam still accounts for a large percentage of the email traffic on the Internet. Both the effectiveness and the impact of many common anti-spam techniques have already been largely studied and evaluated against multiple datasets. However, some of the less known solutions still lack a proper experimental validation. For example, Challenge-Response (CR) systems have been largely discussed, and often criticized, because they shift the effort to protect the user's mailbox from the recipient to the sender of the messages. In addition, these systems are believed to produce a lot of backscattered emails that further deteriorate the global Internet situation.

In this paper we present the first comprehensive measurement study of a real anti-spam system based on a challenge-response technique. In our work we analyze a large amount of data, collected for a period of six months from over forty companies protected by a commercial challenge-response product. We designed our experiments from three different point of views: the end user, the system administrator, and the entire Internet community. Our results cover many different aspects such as the amount of challenges sent, the delay on the message delivery, and the likelihood of getting the challenge server blacklisted.

Our aim is neither to attack nor to defend CR-based solutions. Instead, we hope that our findings will shed some light on some of the myths about these kind of systems, and will help both users and companies to take an informed decision on the topic.

Categories and Subject Descriptors

C.4 [**Performance of Systems**]: Measurement techniques, Performance attributes

General Terms

Experimentation, Measurement

Keywords

Spam, whitelist, challenge-response, blacklisting

1. INTRODUCTION

Despite the considerable effort and the large amount of proposed solutions to detect and filter unsolicited emails, according to the MessageLabs Intelligence Annual Security Report [35] published by Symantec, in 2010 spam still accounted for 89.1% of the emails on the Internet. Even worse, according to the same Symantec's report, in 2010 the spam volume increased by 1.4% compared with the previous year.

Traditional anti-spam solutions are based on two common techniques: filtering emails based on their content, or filtering them based on their senders. The first category includes content-based text classification techniques [15, 19, 32, 33] that aim at finding (often using supervised learning) the tokens commonly associated to spam messages. The second category includes instead detection methods based on some properties of the sender [24, 30, 31], of his reputation [11, 36], or of the domain from which the email is delivered [18, 22, 36].

Even though these two categories cover most of the widely adopted techniques, a number of other solutions have also been proposed to fight spam. One notable example is represented by Challenge-Response (CR) filters [21, 29], a solution based on the observation that the large majority of good emails are delivered from senders that are already known to, and trusted by, the recipient. The name of the approach comes from the fact that, whenever the sender of an email is unknown (i.e., not yet in the user's personal whitelist), the system temporarily quarantines the email and automatically sends back a message to the sender, asking him to solve a simple *challenge* to verify his legitimacy. This technique somehow changes the traditional approach of treating incoming emails, shifting the delivery responsibility from the recipient to the sender of the message.

Since their first introduction, CR-based techniques have been considered an extremely controversial solution [13, 2]. On the one hand, they seem to be able to completely block any unsolicited email, but, on the other hand, they also have a number of side-effects that can seriously hamper their adoption on a large scale.

In particular, it is possible to group the main criticisms against CR systems around three main points. First, the *social* and *usability* issues that, on one side, are related to the efforts required from the user to maintain a proper whitelist, and, on the other, to the annoyance for the sender that has to invest time to solve a challenge in order to have his message delivered. Previous studies, in particular Erickson et al. [21], have already studied the usability of CR systems in controlled experiments. Their study concludes that such systems are very effective when accompanied with already existing anti-spoofing techniques. The authors also measure that CR solutions outperform traditional systems like SpamAssassin, generating on average 1% of false positives with zero false negatives.

The second point against CR systems concerns the fact that they can introduce a (possibly conspicuous) delay in the emails delivery due to the quarantine period applied to previously unknown senders. Finally, the last (and one of the main) critique against CR systems is due to the challenge emails sent in response to spam messages. Since unsolicited emails often contain spoofed sender addresses, the challenges are often delivered to non-existing recipients or to innocent users. These misdirected messages (often referred as "backscattered" spam) pollute the Internet with unnecessary traffic and damage other users that may receive challenges for emails they never sent. From this point of view, CR antispam filters seem to literally bounce the spam back towards other innocent users. However, supporters of the CR approach often rebut by saying that well-designed systems only send back a challenge to a few percents of the spam messages they receive. Therefore, considering the fact that real forged addresses are not too common, normal users are very unlikely to often receive misdirected challenges. Unfortunately, since both sides lack real data to support their own hypothesis, it is hard for users and companies to tell which is the truth and take a conscious decision.

To the best of our knowledge, this paper presents the first study on both the effectiveness and the impact of a real-world deployment of a challenge-based antispam solution. In our work we measure and analyze a large amount of data collected for a period of six months from 47 companies protected by a commercial CR-based antispam product.

In particular, we conduct our measurements to analyze the behavior of CR systems from three different perspectives:

1. From the *end user* point of view, to measure how this technique affects the delivery of both spam and normal messages to the end user's mailbox;

2. From the *server's administrator* point of view, focusing on some of the problems of maintaining a CR installation in a real company;

3. From the *Internet* point of view, to measure the amount and the impact of backscattered messages and misdirected challenges.

It is important to stress the fact that the purpose of this study is neither to attack nor to defend CR-based solutions. Instead, our goal is to provide real-world figures and statistics that can help both users and companies to take an informed decision based on our study. Our results can also help to shed some light on some of the myths related to CR antispam techniques.

The rest of the paper is organized as follows. In Section 2 we introduce our data collection methodology and the dataset we used in our measurements. Section 3 presents a study of the amount of challenges sent by a CR system. Section 4 describes the effectiveness of CR systems in distinguishing spam from legitimate messages. Section 5 introduces some of the problems related to maintaining this type of antispam filter. Then, we summarize our findings in Section 6, present a survey of related work in Section 7, and finally conclude the paper in Section 8.

2. DATA COLLECTION

In this section, we describe the dataset we used in our experiments and we provide a short overview of our data collection methodology.

System Overview

Our study has been carried out within a company providing an anti-spam solution based on a challenge-response technique. Figure 1 presents the overall system architecture and a "weighted" lifecycle of the incoming emails. The *CR filter* consists of two main components: a message dispatcher and a set of additional spam filters.

The dispatcher receives the incoming messages from the company's Incoming Mail Transfer Agent (MTA-IN) server. Some of the email servers were configured to work as *open relays*, serving emails also for a *restricted* number of domains that are different from the ones in which the systems are installed. This configuration allows the server to accept messages not targeting to, or originating from, known users in the system.

The MTA-IN server first checks if the email address is well formed (according to RFC822 [17]) and then if it is able to resolve the incoming email domain. In addition, if the server is not configured as an open relay, it also verifies that the recipient exists in the system.

Our study shows that this first layer of simple checks is responsible to drop more than 75% of the incoming messages (see Figure 2), while open-relay systems pass most of the messages to the next layer. These results are perfectly in line with similar values reported by the other analysis of spam delivery rate [34, 26]. The reasons behind the dropped messages are summarized in the following table:

Dropped Percentage	Reason
0.06%	Malformed email
4.19%	Unable to resolve the domain
2.27%	No relay
0.03%	Sender rejected
62.36%	Unknown Recipient

The second check point for the incoming emails is at the internal email dispatcher. This component is the core of the CR infrastructure and it is the one responsible for deciding to which category the email belongs to: white, black or gray.

The white and black spools are controlled by the user's *whitelist* and *blacklist*. Emails in the black category are dropped immediately, while emails from senders in the whitelist are delivered to the user's INBOX. Emails matching none of the previous lists fall in the gray category. These messages are then filtered with additional antispam techniques (e.g., virus scan, reverse DNS and IP blacklisting). If an email passes the filters, then dispatcher sends a challenge-response message to the original sender containing a request to solve a CAPTCHA. Otherwise, the email is considered spam and it is dropped.

Figure 1 also reports the average number of messages for each spool, assuming that 1,000 emails are received by the MTA-IN. The figures are computed by aggregating the data of all the monitored servers not configured as open relay.

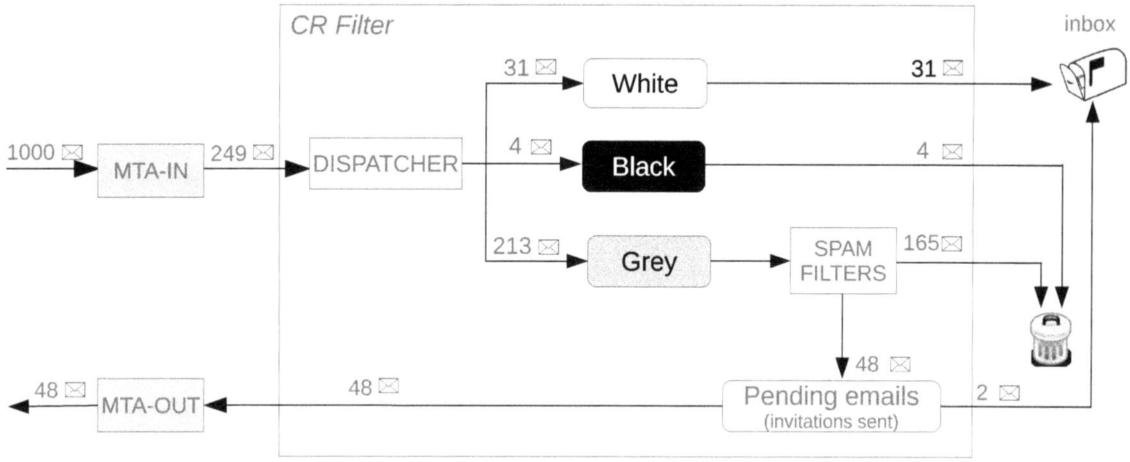

Figure 1: Lifecycle and distribution of incoming emails

Figure 3 shows that the other spam filters included in the CR engine drop on average 54% of the gray emails. Challenge messages are instead generated for 28% of emails. In the open relay cases, the engine filters have a lower performance rate, and the number of challenges sent increases by an extra 9%. This shows that, in an open relay configuration, the CR system receives more junk messages and it is more likely to reply with a challenge to illegitimate emails.

Whitelisting process

The process of email whitelisting involves both parties: the sender and the recipient. There exist several alternative ways for the email address to get added to a user's whitelist. In particular, the system we tested in our experiments supported the following mechanisms:

- The sender solves a challenge sent by the CR system as a response to one of his messages;
- The user authorizes the sender from the daily message digest;
- The address is manually added to the whitelist by the user;
- The user previously sent an email to that address.

In the general scenario, suppose that Alice sends an email to Bob, a user protected by a challenge-response system. If this is the first communication between Alice and Bob, the system temporarily stores the email in a "gray" spool and sends back a message to Alice. The message includes a link to a webpage that contains a CAPTCHA (the challenge) that Alice has to solve to get her email delivered and her address added to Bob's whitelist. After this simple authentication step, Alice's address is considered trustworthy, and the CR system will not interfere in any future communication between the two users, promptly delivering to Bob any further message coming from Alice.

If Alice does not solve the challenge, the email stays in the gray spool for a period of 30 days, after which it is dropped by the system. Bob also receives a daily digest that summarizes the quarantined messages, so that he can manually authorize them or delete them from the list.

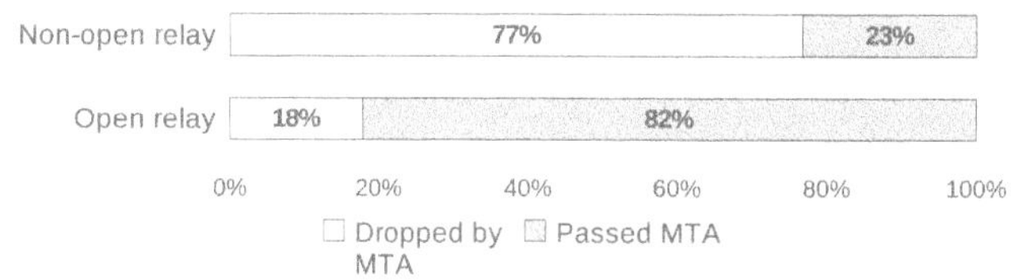

Figure 2: MTA-IN email treatment

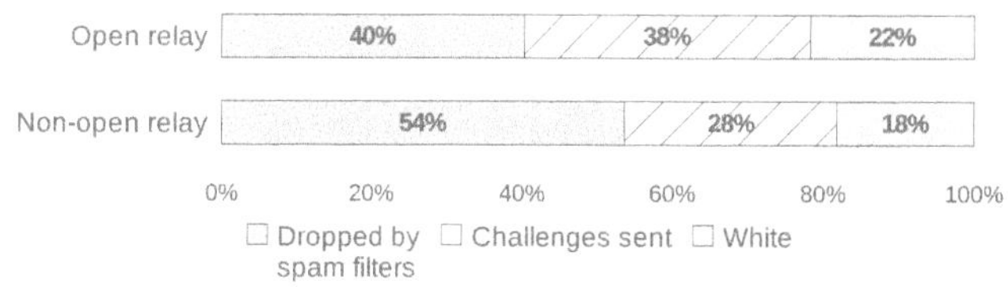

Figure 3: Message category at the internal email processing engine

General Statistics

In our experiment we collected statistical data about a commercial system deployed in 47 companies of different sizes. The monitoring period lasted for 6 months, between July and December 2010. For some of the servers we had access to the data for the entire time frame, while for other companies our collection was limited to a shorter period of time (with a minimum of 2 months).

In total we collected statics for 90 millions of incoming emails. All the results were sanitized to protect both the end users and the companies privacy. In particular, we never got access to the message bodies and we stored only aggregated figures obtained from the automated analysis of the email headers.

The data collection was performed on a daily basis by analyzing the logs of the MTAs and of the challenge-response engines. In addition, information about the solved CAPTCHAs was collected by analyzing the access logs of the web-server serving the challenges. The extracted information was stored

General Statistics

Number of Companies	47	Challenge Sent	4,299,610
Open Relays	13	Emails Whitelisted from digest	55,850
Users protected by CR	19,426	Solved CAPTCHAs	150,809
Total incoming emails	90,368,573	Messages Dropped because of:	
Messages in the Gray spool	11,590,532	reverse DNS filter	3,526,506
Messages in the Black spool	349,697	RBL filter	4,973,755
Messages in the White Spool	2,737,978	Antivirus filter	267,630
Total Messages Dropped at MTA	75,690,366	Total Messages Dropped by filters	7,290,922

Daily Statistics

Emails (per day)	797,679	Challenges sent (per day)	53,764
Messages in the White spool (per day)	31,920	Total number of days	5,249

Table 1: Statistics of the collected data

in a Postgres database and later analyzed and correlated by a number of Python scripts.

Table 1 shows some general statistics about the dataset we collected. Each company's server was configured to protect certain users with the challenge-response system, while protecting other accounts by traditional anti-spam techniques. In this paper we limit our analysis to the 19,426 users protected by the CR solution (this number includes normal users as well as administrative accounts and other rarely used email addresses). The table also shows the total number of the messages that we analyzed, the breakdown in the different spools (white, black, and gray), and some statistics about the effectiveness of the other spam filters included in the system (discussed in more details in Section 5).

Finally, since the number of days in which we were able to collect data varies between companies (for a total of 5,249 analyzed days), the table also report some *daily* statistics.

3. PART I: THE INTERNET POINT OF VIEW

In this section we focus on the consequences of adopting CR spam filters from a global point of view. In particular, we present an evaluation of the amount of challenge emails sent out by a challenge-response system during normal operation.

These *backscattered messages* are often criticized for two main reasons: the fact that misdirected challenges can be delivered to innocent users, and the fact that a large amount of useless messages are poured into the Internet, thus increasing the global traffic and overloading third parties email servers.

In the rest of the section we provide real-world measurements to estimate the impact of these two phenomena.

3.1 Email Backscattering

From an external point of view, a challenge response system can be approximated by a black box that receives emails from the Internet and separates them in three categories: some (the *white* set) are delivered to the users Inbox, while others (the *black* set) are immediately flagged as spam and discarded. The remaining messages (the *gray* set) are the ones for which the system is unable to take a decision. Therefore, for each email in this set, the system sends back to the sender another email containing a challenge to be solved. In this simplified model, a challenge-response system can be seen as a software that receives a certain amount of emails, and "reflects" a fraction of them back to the senders. This fraction, that we call *Reflection Ratio* $\mathcal{R}$, is an important parameter of a CR system.

By using the numbers in Figure 1, it is easy to compute the average reflection ratio: $\mathcal{R} = 48/249 = 19.3\%$ for the emails reaching the CR filter (or, $\mathcal{R} = 48/1000 = 4.8\%$ if we consider all the emails reaching companies' MTA-INs).

Understanding the Reflection Ratio

Is 19.3% a good value for $\mathcal{R}$? If not, what would be a reasonable value?

Unfortunately, it is very hard to answer these questions since it is not clear how to estimate which is an acceptable range for the reflection ratio.

To explain why, let us consider two extreme cases. In the first case, the CR system does not contain any other spam detector or blacklist mechanism. Therefore, the amount of challenges it sends is roughly the same as the amount of spam it receives, currently estimated between 80 and 90% [35] of the total email traffic. Values of $\mathcal{R}$ close to this range are obviously unacceptable, since, from a global point of view, the system would just act as a spam multiplier.

In the second scenario, the CR system has been carefully configured and it has been associated with another perfect spam detector. In this case, the system never replies to spam and only sends back challenges to legitimate messages whose senders are not already in the recipients whitelist. In this case (represented by very low values of $\mathcal{R}$) the system does not generate any backscattered emails. Therefore, it may seem to be the final goal to reach in a perfect CR system.

Unfortunately, a very low value of $\mathcal{R}$ also corresponds to a completely useless system. In fact, if the internal spam filter can already distinguish good messages from spam, there is no need to add a challenge response system on top of it. In other words, in order to be useful a CR system has to be able to "substantially" reduce the amount of spam received by the users. However, this can only happen if the system sends back an equivalent "substantial" number of backscattered messages.

To conclude, the reflection ratio is a good indicator of the amount of challenges generated by a CR system. At the same time, it is important to be extremely careful to use this value alone to draw conclusions about the quality of such systems.

3.2 Misdirected Challenges

So far, we focused on the amount of challenges generated by a CR system. However, this value only measures the *amount* and not the real *impact* of the generated emails. In fact, not all the challenges are the same. Some of them reach the real senders and, despite being a little nuisance, could be tolerated as an acceptable price to pay for fight-

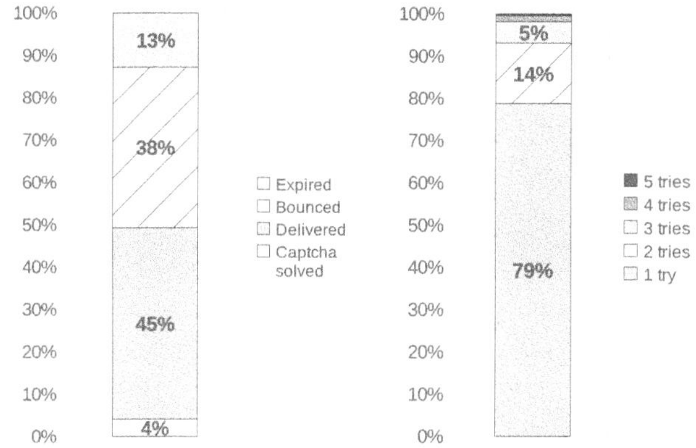

(a) Challenge delivery status distribution (b) Tries required to solve CAPTCHA

Figure 4: Challenge statistics

ing spam. We refer to them as *legitimate challenges*. A second class of them is directed to non-existing addresses, and, thus, constitutes garbage traffic on the network. Finally, some misdirected challenges are delivered to existing spoofed email addresses, therefore reaching other innocent users. This category is much more harmful, and it is often referred to as *backscatter spam* (note that not all the backscattered *messages* are spam).

In order to distinguish the three categories of challenges, we analyzed the status of the challenge delivery in the servers' logs. In the systems under analysis, we found that only 49% of the challenges were successfully delivered to the destination servers. The remaining 51% were either bounced, or expired after many unsuccessful attempts (see Figure 4(a)). In the bounced set, a small portion has been stopped because the server that sent the challenges has been temporarily blacklisted (the problem will be discussed in more details in Section 5), while the large majority (71.7%) has been bounced due to the fact that the recipient address did not exist. This value provide a reasonable estimation of the amount of challenges that belong to the second category.

Another piece of the puzzle can be found by measuring the number of challenges that were actually solved. Previous work [21], conducted in a controlled environment, estimated that about 50% of the challenges were never solved. Unfortunately, our study shows a completely different picture. According to the web servers' logs of the companies we analyzed, on average 94% of the CAPTCHA URLs included in the delivered challenges were never even opened. The remaining were either solved (4%) or were visited by the user but not solved (0.25%). Figure 4(b) also shows the average number of attempts required to solve the CAPTCHAs. The fact that we never observed more than five attempts support the fact that probably there are still no real cases of attack against CR systems based on trying to automatically solve the challenges.

So far, we estimated the legitimate challenges to be at least 4% and the ones sent to non-existing recipients to be around 36.6% (71.7% of the 51% of undelivered messages). The third category, i.e., the backscattered spam, can instead be approximated with the number of challenges correctly delivered but never solved, i.e. somewhere between 0 and 45 %.

By combining the percentage of backscattered spam with the reflection ratio we presented before, we obtain the *Backscattered Ratio* β, i.e., the ratio of incoming emails for which the CR system sends back a misdirected challenge to the wrong user. In our experiments, we obtain, in the worst case, $\beta = 8.7\%$ (at the CR filter) or 2.1% (at the MTA-IN).

However useful, these figures must be considered only approximate upper bounds. For example, it is possible that challenge messages get dropped by some spam filter after being successfully delivered, or that real users ignore or intentionally decide to not solve a particular challenge. Finally, there are automatically generated emails (notifications from websites, mailing lists, receipts of purchase, ...) to take into account. When a user expects to receive such messages, he should either use an email address not protected by the CR system (functionality provided by the commercial product we have evaluated), or manually add the address to the whitelist.

Unfortunately, this is not always the case. In fact, we measured that around 2% of the message addresses in the gray spool have been whitelisted manually by the users from the daily digest. In other words, the challenge was not delivered or it was not solved, but the user recognized that the message was not spam and he manually added the sender to his whitelist to allow future communications.

3.3 Traffic Pollution

The reflection ratio only measures the number of messages, without taking into account their size. Therefore, it is not a very accurate indicator to estimate the amount of traffic generated by a challenge response system. For that purpose, we need to extend the previous definition by introducing the *ReflecteD Traffic ratio* $\mathcal{R}_T$, that represents the ratio between the amount of traffic received by the system and the amount of email traffic generated for the challenges.

To measure this new value, we deployed to all the servers a new sensor that extracts from the email headers the total size of the incoming messages and the total size of the outgoing challenges. Over a month period, the average ratio we measured at the CR filter was $\mathcal{R}_T = 2.5\%$. Unfortunately, we could not get a similar measure at the entrance of the MTA-IN servers. However, since the number of messages at MTA-IN is in average four times bigger than at the CR filter (see Figure 1), we can estimate that a large scale deployment of challenge-response spam filters would increase the email traffic on the Internet of around 0.62%.

3.4 Data Variability

In previous sections we reported aggregated figures for a number of different factors that can be used to estimate the "external" impact of a CR system.

In order to preserve the companies' privacy, each value was obtained by combining together the data collected from all the monitored installations. However, it is interesting to investigate what the variance of those values is, and if the size of the company affects in some way the presented indicators. For instance, it could be the case that CR filters work better for small companies, but fail to scale well to larger installations.

Figure 5 shows a scatter plot of five variables: the number of protected accounts (`users`), the amount of emails re-

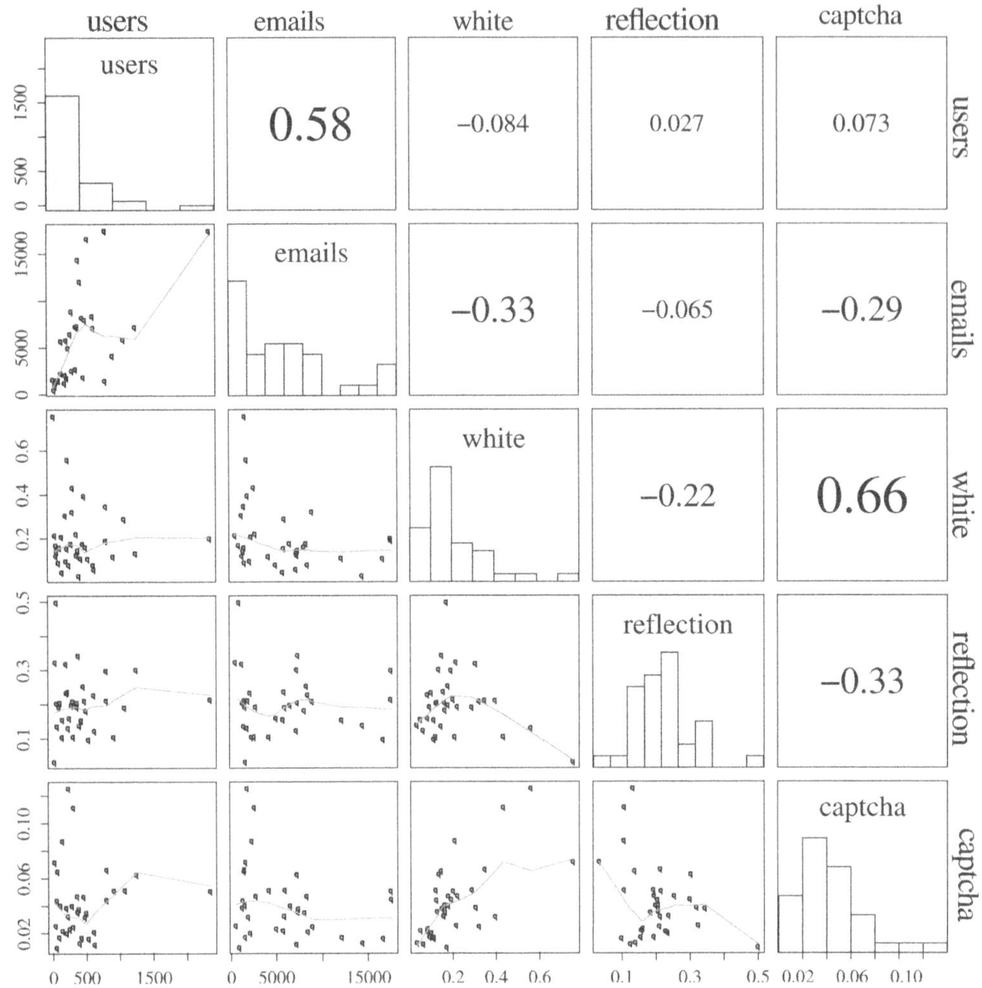

Figure 5: Histograms and correlations between different dimensions. Graphs on the diagonal represent the data histogram. Below the diagonal are the plots of the correlation between every pair of variables, summarized by the correlation values reported above the diagonals.

ceived daily (`emails`), the percentage of emails delivered in the white spool (`white`), the reflection ratio at the CR filter (`reflection`), and the percentage of challenges solved (`captcha`).

This graph represents a very efficient way to convey a large amount of information about the five variables. On the diagonal, it shows the histograms of the values of each variable. For example, the first element on the diagonal shows that most of the companies have less than 500 users, with few exceptions that have more than 2,000 users. Some values have a very high variability, such as the percentage of white emails that varies from less than 10% to over 70%. However, the two main coefficients we have measured in this Section, i.e. the reflection ratio and the percentage of solved challenges, seem to stay constant between different installations. The percentage of solved challenges only varies between 2% and 12%, and the reflection ratio stays in the range of 10% to 25%.

In Figure 5, the plots below the diagonals show the correlation between every pair of variables, while the upper part of the graph reports the corresponding correlation values (the font size allows to immediately focus on the higher values). Notably, the percentage of challenges sent by a CR system (`reflection`) is not correlated to the size of the companies (`users`) or to the amount of emails received. Not surprisingly, a small inverse correlation exists instead with the percentage of white emails. In other words, servers that receive a large amount of white emails (and therefore a lower amount of spam), tend to send less challenges and vice versa.

The rate of solved challenges (`captcha`) shows more correlations with other values, and in particular it is also strongly correlated with the white percentage. However, as the histogram shows, the variability of the `captcha` variable is so small that it can be considered almost a constant between the different installations.

4. PART II: THE USER POINT OF VIEW

Despite the backscattering phenomenon described in the previous section, CR systems are often considered one of the most effective ways to protect users from spam. In theory, if the challenge-response system is properly configured, these systems should be able to achieve a 100% detection rate, thus blocking all unsolicited emails. However, previ-

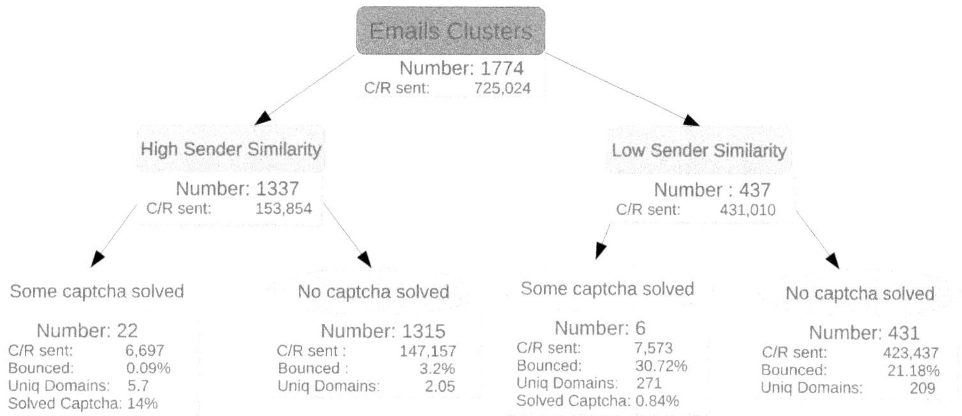

Figure 6: Spam clustering statistics

ous studies [21] that confirmed this value were conducted on prototype systems evaluated in a controlled environment.

In this section we measure if this is actually the case in a real-world installation, and we evaluate the real impact for the end users protected by a CR system. In particular, we measure the delay introduced in the legitimate emails delivery, and the amount of spam that is able to reach the final users despite the CR filter. In addition, we also measure the change rate of the users' whitelists, one of the foundations of this kind of antispam solution.

4.1 Spam Protection

The main purpose of a CR system is to block all automatically generated emails coming from addresses previously unknown to the recipient. The first obvious consequence of this approach is that CR solutions are ineffective by design against targeted attacks, i.e., attacks in which the attacker manually composes a malicious message to target a particular individual. In fact, if the attacker receives back the challenge message, he can easily solve it and have his message delivered to the recipient. However, a recent Symantec report [35] estimated that only one out of 5,000 spam messages contains a targeted attack. In addition, all the existing anti-spam mechanisms can be easily evaded by targeted attacks, and, therefore, we can consider this threat beyond reach of all existing anti-spam solutions.

Unfortunately, targeted attacks are not the only ones that can pass through a CR filter. By studying a dataset of bounced challenges, we noticed that a large number of messages had the same subject and the same size. Per se, this is not surprising. However, a closer look revealed that while most of the messages were bounced or dropped by the filter, in some cases one of those emails was successfully delivered to the final user's mailbox.

To better investigate the reason behind this sporadic phenomenon, we decided to analyze the behavior, in terms of challenges and delivered messages, of a number of large spam campaigns.

For our experiment we applied standard clustering algorithms to the subject of the messages in the gray spool (i.e., the ones for which the system generated a challenge message). In particular, we put in the same cluster the messages with the same subject, limiting the analysis to the ones at least 10 words long. Finally, we discarded the clusters containing less than 50 emails. These very conservative thresholds were adopted to greatly reduce the risk of misclassification. In reality, the large majority of emails (including spam) have much shorter subjects, or they have enough variability to elude our simple comparison algorithm. However, our target was not to be able to cluster and identify all the incoming emails or all the spam campaigns, but just to identify a number of them with a low percentage of false positives.

The results obtained over a three month monitoring period are summarized in Figure 6. Our system identified 1,775 clusters, containing between 50 and 3696 messages each. In the next step, we divided the clusters in two categories, based on the sender email similarity. In the first group we put all the clusters where emails are sent by a very limited number of senders, or in which the sender addresses are very similar to each other (for example, `dept-x.p@scn-1.com`, `dept-x.q@scn-1.com`, and `dept-x.p@scn-2.com`). These clusters are likely associated to newsletters or marketing campaigns. The second group contains instead the clusters with a very low sender similarity, i.e., the ones in which most of the emails originate from different domains and different senders' addresses. This behavior is very common in spam campaigns sent by malware infected machines.

Figure 6 shows that only 28 out of 1774 clusters contain at least one solved challenge. Moreover, these few clusters have very different characteristics, depending on whether they belong to the first or the second category. The ones with high sender similarity have a higher rate of solved challenges (some clusters as high as 97%) and almost no bounced emails. The clusters with low sender similarity have instead on average 31% of emails bounced because of non-existing recipient, and only one or two captchas solved each.

This second category is particularly interesting for our study. Each cluster in this group contains hundreds of emails, coming from many different domains, and often from non-existing sender addresses. However, out of these messages, sometimes one of the challenges was solved and, therefore, the email got whitelisted and delivered to the recipient's mailbox. These spam messages that are able to pass through the CR defense are likely a side effect of backscattered challenges that are sometimes erroneously delivered to innocent users. As a result, it is possible that one of these users solves a challenge for a mail he never sent. This phenomenon is,

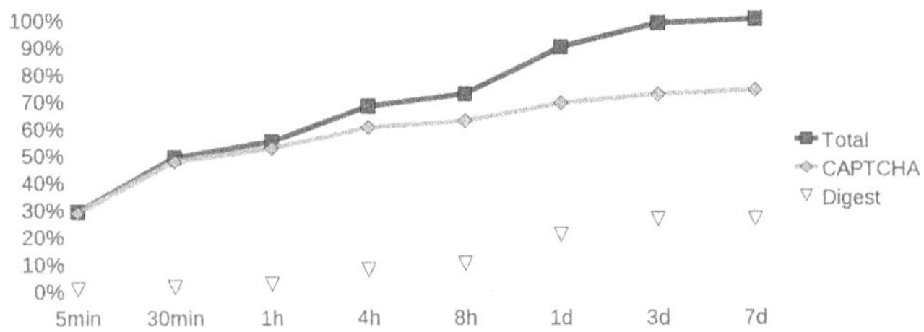

Figure 7: Cumulative effect of Captcha and Digest whitelisting

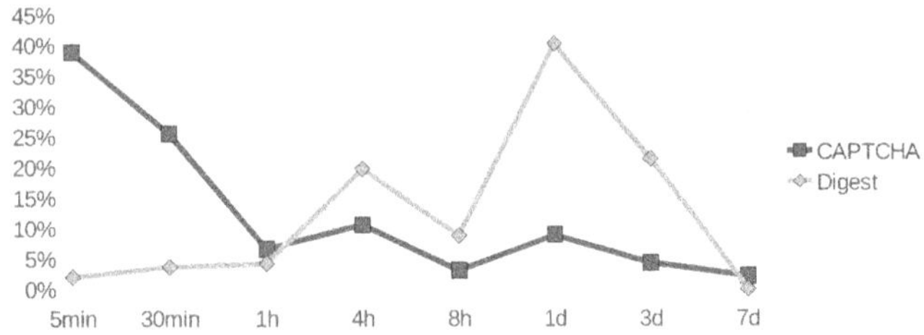

Figure 8: Time distribution of whitelisted messages

however, extremely rare. According to our measurements, we estimate that this kind of spurious spam delivery occurs ~1 every 10,000 challenges sent. According to Table 1, this rate translates to an average of five spam delivery a day, over the 47 companies in our dataset. Excluding these isolated cases, CR systems are actually able to block all incoming spam messages.

4.2 Impact on Messages Delivery

Another consequence of blocking automatically generated emails is the fact that also normal emails can get blocked and remain in the user's graylist waiting for the corresponding challenges to be solved. This can happen for two reasons: because the sender still has to solve the challenge, or because the email is sent by an automatic system and the challenge is, therefore, dropped or never delivered. In both cases, the user fails to receive a (maybe important) email.

Figure 7 shows the CDF of the messages that were moved from the graylist to the whitelist in the monitored servers. The two curves report the percentage of messages that were whitelisted because the sender solved the challenge, and the ones that were whitelisted manually by the user from the daily digest. According to the graph, 30% of the messages are delayed less than 5 minutes, and half of them are delivered in less than 30 minutes. However, if the challenge was not solved after 4 hours, then it is likely that it will not be solved at all (Figure 8). In those cases, the user has to manually select the messages from the digest, with a delivery delay that is on average between 4 hours and 3 days.

Combining the values from these figures with the number of white and whitelisted emails (31 and 2 respectively) in Figure 1, we can conclude that:

- 31/33 = 94% of the emails in the user's INBOX are sent from addresses already in the whitelist, and, therefore, are delivered instantly.
- Out of the remaining 6% (2/33) of the messages that are quarantined in the gray spool, half of them are delivered in less than 30 minutes because the sender solved the challenge.
- Only 0.6% (10% of the 6%) of the messages were delivered with more than one day of delay.

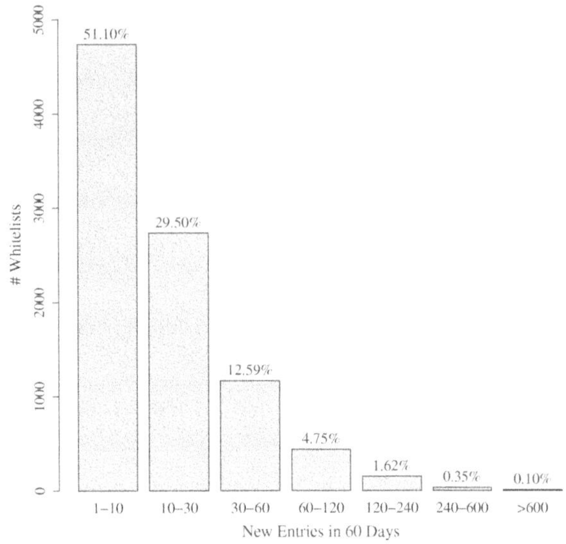

Figure 9: Distribution of the number of changes in users' whitelist

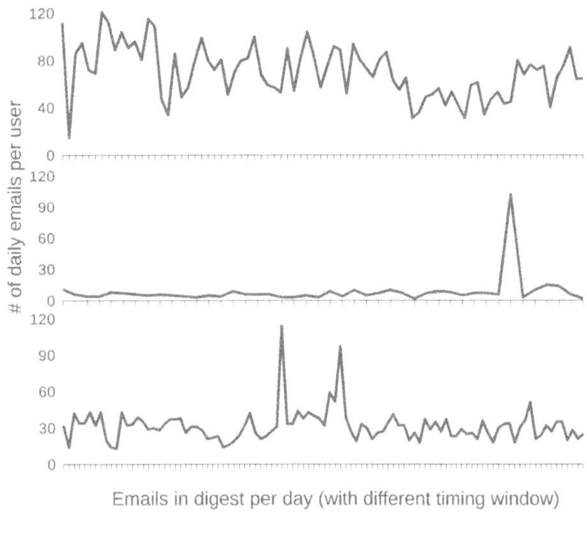

Figure 10: Daily pending email distribution of 3 different users

4.3 Whitelists' Change Rate

We conclude this section on the user point of view with an analysis of the rate at which the users' whitelists change over time. For this experiment we monitored the number of changes in the users' whitelists for a period of two months. Email addresses can be added to a whitelist in four different ways, two manual and two automated. A user can manually import a new entry or he can whitelist a certain address from the digest. Automatically, new entries are included when the user sends a mail to those addresses or when the senders solve the challenges generated by the CR system.

During the monitored period, 9267 whitelists were modified at least once. Out of them, only 6.8% had at least 1 new entry per day (on average), and the percentage drops even further when we look at higher changing rates (2.1% of the whitelists had at least 2 new entries per day, and 0.2% at least 5). Figure 9 presents a more detailed histogram of the frequency of changes. The graph shows how the large majority of the whitelists are, in fact, constantly in a steady state.

Finally, we monitored the amount of new messages present in the daily digest. This value varies greatly between users and also between different days. Figure 10 shows examples extracted from three different users. Some of them have constantly a large number of messages in the gray spool, while others have normally very small daily digests with anomalous peaks in conjunction to particular user behavior or unusually large amount of spam messages.

Again, a large size of the digest is at the same time a good and a bad factor for a CR system. In fact, a high number of messages means that the system is blocking a substantial amount of spam that would have been otherwise delivered to the user (remember that these are messages that successfully pass through the antivirus, reverse DNS, and the SpamHouse blacklist). On the other side, a large digest is also a negative factor as it increases the amount of work for the user that has to manually verify its content to double-check that he did not miss any important message. Finally, this also demonstrates that the degree to which CR system works depends a lot on the interplay of users' involvement. Some recipients may diligently weed out their digest, while others may let it grow hoping for the senders to respond to the challenges.

5. PART III: THE ADMINISTRATOR POINT OF VIEW

In this section we analyze some of the issues related to maintaining challenge-response systems from the system administrator point of view. In particular, we focus on the effort required to maintain the challenge-response infrastructure, and on the additional antispam techniques that can be integrated in the system to reduce the backscattering effect.

5.1 Server Blacklisting

As we already described in Section 4, when a CR system sends a challenge in response to a message with a spoofed sender's address, the challenge is delivered to a recipient that may not exist. As a result, these challenge-response messages can hit a spam trap [31], i.e., a set of email addresses that are maintained and distributed with the sole purpose to lure spam.

The emails collected by those traps are often adopted by popular services (e.g., SpamHaus [11], SORBS [7], SpamCop [10]) to update their blacklists. Hence, the IP used to send the challenges can itself get blacklisted as a result of the backscattered spam it sends. In order to reduce the impact of being blacklisted, one third of the systems we tested in our experiments were configured to rely on two MTA-OUT servers (with different IP addresses): one to send the challenges and another to send the outgoing user emails.

Our initial hypothesis was that the probability that a

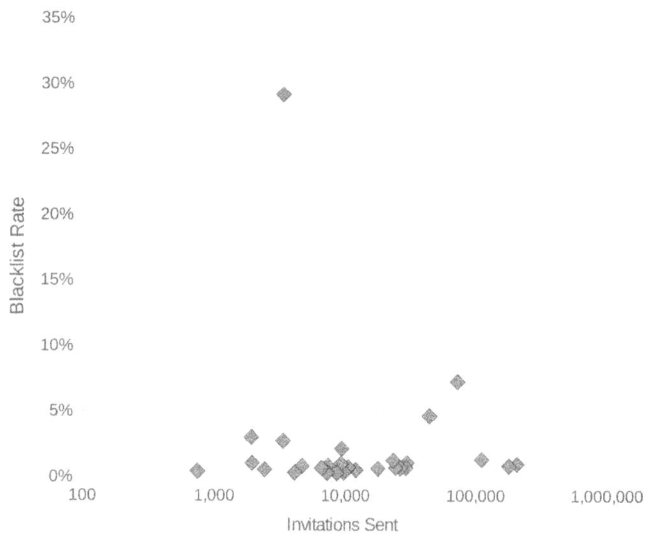

Figure 11: Server blacklisting rate

server has to get blacklisted should have been somehow proportional to the size of the email server, represented either by the number of users, or by the number of the received emails. In other words, we expected that systems sending more challenges were blacklisted more often, thus making CR solutions more difficult to maintain for large companies.

Surprisingly, our experiments proved us wrong. Using the data we collected we were able to estimate the rate at which various challenge server IPs get blacklisted. In particular, we followed two parallel approaches. In the first, we analyzed one month of data for 32 companies, measuring the ratio between the number of challenges sent and the number of blacklist-related error messages received from the challenge-response recipients. The result, summarized on a logarithmic scale in Figure 11, shows that while most of the servers had no problem at all with blacklisting, some of them were often blacklisted, even for a few days in a row. However, there seems to be no relationship between the server blacklisting ratio and the number of challenges it sends.

The main problem with this approach is that the error messages received when delivering the challenges were not always very accurate, providing results that may not be completely reliable. Therefore, we decided to complement our analysis with a second technique, based on an automated script that periodically checked for the IP addresses of the CR servers in a number of services that provide an IP blacklist for spam filtering. In particular, our tool queried the blacklists provided by Barracuda [1], SpamCop [10], SpamHause [11], Cannibal [9], Orbit [4], SORBS [7], CBL [3], and Surriel [5]. The queries were performed every 4 hours for a period of 132 days (between September 2010 and January 2011).

The results of this second analysis confirm our previous finding. In more than four months, 75% of the servers never appeared in any blacklists. Few servers were blacklisted for less than one day, while the remaining four servers experienced some serious problems, appearing in at least one of the blacklists for many consecutive days (17, 33, 113, and 129 respectively). Again, between the top 3 server (according to the traffic and the number of challenges sent) none appeared

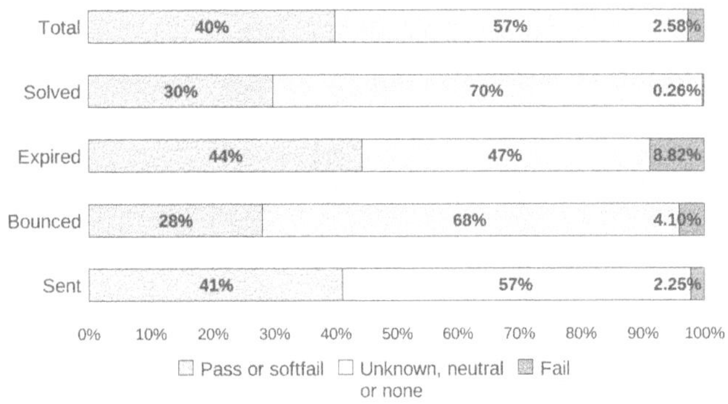

Figure 12: SPF validation test

in any of the blacklists during our experiment. Thus, proving again that there is no direct link between the number of times a server gets blacklisted and the server size.

5.2 Combining CR Systems with Other Spam Filters

Our final evaluation focuses on the combination of CR systems with other antispam solutions. As we already mentioned in Section 2, the product we analyzed in our experiments includes three other spam filters in order to reduce the number of useless challenges sent in response to spam messages. It employs a traditional antivirus to scan the emails, an IP blacklist provided by SpamHause [11] to filter out known spammers, and a reverse DNS lookup to exclude suspicious origins.

According to Table 1 and Figure 1, the combination of these filters was responsible for dropping 77.5% of the messages in the gray spool. One may argue if this is good enough, or if a much better result could be obtained by introducing other antispam techniques. This is a difficult question to answer, since the main drawback of adding new filters is that they also introduce false positives, to avoid which CR systems were introduced in the first place.

However, we decided to experiment with one additional spam filter based on the verification of the Sender Policy Frawework [36] (SPF). SPF was introduced to detect source address spoofing, that is one of the main problems of CR systems. Since SPF checks were not included in the product we evaluated in this paper, we decided to evaluate the potential impact of this filter by using an offline tool to automatically test all the emails in the gray spool. Figure 12 shows the results of our experiment, grouped by different message categories. For instance, by dropping the emails for which the SPF test fails, it would be possible to reduce by almost 9% the challenges that cannot be delivered (`expired`), and 4.10% of the bounced ones. The overall result shows that SPF can further reduce the number of "bad" challenges by 2.5%, at the cost of loosing 0.25% of the challenges that are actually solved by the sender.

6. DISCUSSION

Even though the aim of this work is neither to attack nor to defend challenge-response systems, it may be natural to ask what conclusions about this class of antispam solutions could be drawn from our measurements.

In the rest of this section we summarize the main findings we presented in the previous three sections.

Whitelist Assumptions

All approaches based on white-lists share two main assumptions: first, that the large majority of the "good" emails come from senders already in the recipient's whitelist, and, second, that these lists eventually reach a steady state where changes do not occur very often.

Both claims are supported by our experiments. In fact, over 43 companies, only $2/33 = 6.1\%$ of the incoming emails delivered to the users' INBOX require a challenge-response phase (see Figure 4) and 2% require the user to manually pick the message from the digest.

The stability of the whitelists was already evaluated by Erickson et al. [21], showing that the major burden on the user is concentrated in the first three weeks, after which the number of changes drops on average to one per day. Our experiments show that, in a real deployment, there are on average 0.3 new entry per user per day (excluding new users). Only 6.8% of the users had at least one daily change in their whitelists.

Delivery Delay

Another common critique of CR systems is due to the fact that the challenge-response step introduces a delay in the incoming email delivery. This is obviously an unavoidable side-effect, but our measurements show that it also has a limited impact. In fact, according to our study, it concerns only 4.3% of incoming emails and in half of the cases the delay is below 30 minutes. Even though the remaining 2.15% may still be an unacceptable inconvenient for certain users, we believe that for most of the users it would be a reasonable price to pay to protect against spam.

Challenge Traffic

Most of the criticisms against CR systems, and most of the hassles for the system administrators, come from the challenges that are sent to the wrong recipients. If they correspond to existing email accounts, the misdirected challenges become a spam for other users. On the other hand, if the addresses do not exist, the challange may hit a spamtrap. And on top of that, they constitute useless traffic over the Internet.

Our study shows that, on average, a CR system sends back one challenge for every 21 emails it receives (see Section 3), accounting for a traffic increase of less than 1%. These figures depend on the amount of spam received by the server, and seems to be more or less constant between small and large servers.

Unfortunately, the large part of the challenges sent are indeed useless (only about 5% of them are solved). But, as we already explained in the paper, these challenges are "required" to justify the system. In other words, without useless challenges, it would be the CR system to be useless. Therefore, this can be considered an intrinsic and unavoidable limitation of systems based on a challenge-response approach.

Our findings confirm that the backscattered phenomenon is the main problem of solutions based on challenge-response technique. Each installation must be carefully configured in order to minimize the impact of misdirected challenges on other real users. The administrator also has to decide which other additional antispam techniques should be combined with the CR filter to maximize the benefits and, at the same time, to reduce the side effects and the risk of having the servers' IP blacklisted. However, the backscattered phenomenon is intrinsic in the behavior of a CR system and cannot be completely eliminated. From a company, the single most negative argument against the adoption of CR system is the fact that the challenge server can occasionally get blacklisted. Even worse, an attacker could intentionally forge malicious messages with the goal of forcing the server to send back the challenge to spam trap addresses, thus increasing the likelihood of getting the server IP added to one or more blacklist.

Other Limitations

This paper does not cover all aspects related to the adoption of a challenge-response system. We focused on performing a set of measurements based on real installations that were not under our direct control. Therefore, we intentionally excluded from our studies any evaluation of potential attacks against CR systems (like trying to spoof the sender address using a likely-whitelisted address).

In addition, in order to protect the users and the companies' privacy, we limited our study to the statistical information that can be automatically extracted from the headers of the messages. This ruled out other potentially interesting experiments that would have required access to the email bodies.

7. RELATED WORK

Most of the spam blocking techniques proposed by previous research fall into two categories: content-based and sender-based filtering. Content-based spam filtering techniques rely on signatures and classification algorithms applied to the emails content [32, 14, 19, 15, 33]. Although content-based filters were initially very effective and provided an acceptable defense against spam [27], with the evolution of the spam sophistication they became less effective over time.

Sender-based spam filtering techniques aim instead at blocking spams by analyzing information about the sender. To date, a wide range of sender-based filtering solutions has been proposed, including sender authentication (e.g., SPF [36], DMIK [18], and Occam [22]), sender IP reputation [11], network-level feature categorization, sender whitelisting, and detecting anomalies on the sender's behavior.

Sender authentication techniques authenticate the sender either by verifying it's domain [36, 18] or by providing a protocol to authenticate the server at each message delivery [22]. These kind of solutions are quite effective to prevent email spoofing, a phenomenon that is very common among spammers.

Approaches based on IP reputation [11, 25] rely on whitelists or/and blacklists of IP addresses that are known either to send spam or to be a trusted source. Therefore, these approaches are effective against static spammers and open-relay servers used for spam distribution. On the other hand, they are not able to provide the same degree of protection against spam sent through botnets, since botnets can change the sender's IP address by using a large number of different infected machines to deliver the messages.

Behavior-based solutions, like the ones proposed by Pathak et al. [30] or Ramachandran et al. [31], and network-level detection techniques, like the one proposed by Hao et al. [24], tend to react faster to spam campaigns and have a lower number of false-positive. However, these kind of solutions block only part of illegitimate emails, and, therefore, they have to be used in combination with other filters.

Beside the more common techniques presented so far, a number of other solutions have been proposed to protect users against spam. For example, fine-grained approaches have been proposed based on personal white and blacklists. The assumption behind such techniques is that users communicate mainly with a list of contacts that does not change much over time [16, 20, 21].

In this case, the main problem is to provide an automated way to populate and maintain the users whitelist. Garris et. al. [23] proposed a solution to this problem based on the idea of sharing the whitelist content with the user's friends on social networks. Their cryptographic solution addresses also the sender spoofing problem, and the protection of the privacy of the users during the friend list sharing process. The main limitation of their system is the fact that it requires a large-scale adoption by many social networking users.

One of the most wide-spread approaches for building and maintaining a list of trusted senders is based on the adoption of a challenge-response technique [28, 29, 8, 12, 6], already largely described in the rest of the paper.

Although challenge-response schemes are extremely successful in blocking spam, they also have a number of limitations that makes them disadvantageous over other solutions [21]. Additionally, CR solutions received a great amount of critiques from the anti-spam community [13, 2], often because of the amount of challenge emails they generate.

To the best of our knowledge, the only empirical study that analyzes challenge-response based whitelisting systems is presented by Erickson et.al. [21]. The authors focus on the deployment and the usability of such systems. The results of their evaluation support the usability of CR systems, but also show their limitations in coping with automatically generated legitimate emails, such as newsletters and notifications. On the other hand, the authors concluded that challenge-response systems are very successful to prevent spam and have lower false positives and false negatives rates compared to traditional content filtering techniques like SpamAssassin.

Our work aims instead to present a comprehensive study of a real-world whitelisting challenge-response antispam system, evaluating it's effectiveness and it's impact on the end-users, Internet, and server administration.

8. CONCLUSIONS

In this paper we present the first measurement study of the behavior of a real world deployment of a challenge-response antispam system. The experiments lasted for a period of six months, covering 47 different companies protected by a commercial CR solution.

In particular, we measure the amount of challenges generated by these systems and their impact in terms of traffic pollution and possible backscattered messages delivered to innocent users. We then measure the amount of emails that are delayed due to the quarantine phase, and the amount of spam that is able to pass through the filter and reach the users mailboxes. Finally, we focus on a problem that is less known, i.e., the fact that the invitations sent by these systems can accidentally hit a spamtrap and cause the email server to be blacklisted.

Our findings can be used to evaluate both the effectiveness and the impact of adopting this class of techniques. We hope that the figures provided in this paper may help to settle the long debate between advocates and opponents of CR systems.

9. REFERENCES

[1] Barracuda. `http://www.barracudacentral.org/`.

[2] Challenge-Response Anti-Spam Systems Considered Harmful. `http://linuxmafia.com/faq/Mail/challenge-response.htm`.

[3] Composite Blocking List. `http://cbl.abuseat.org/`.

[4] ORBITrbl. `http://www.orbitrbl.com/`.

[5] Passive Spam Block List. `http://psbl.surriel.com/`.

[6] Sendio. `http://www.sendio.com/`.

[7] Spam and Open-Relay Blocking System. `http://www.sorbs.net/`.

[8] Spam Arrest. `http://www.spamarrest.com/`.

[9] Spam Cannibal. `http://www.spamcannibal.org/`.

[10] SpamCop. `http://www.spamcop.net/`.

[11] The spamhaus project. `http://www.spamhaus.org/`.

[12] Total Block. `http://www.totalblock.net/`.

[13] Why are auto responders bad? `http://spamcop.net/fom-serve/cache/329.html`.

[14] I. Androutsopoulos, J. Koutsias, K. Chandrinos, G. Paliouras, and C. Spyropoulos. An evaluation of naive bayesian anti-spam filtering. 2000.

[15] A. Bergholz, J. Chang, G. Paaß, F. Reichartz, and S. Strobel. Improved phishing detection using model-based features. In *Proc. of the Conference on Email and Anti-Spam (CEAS)*, 2008.

[16] D. Bernstein. Internet mail 2000 (IM2000).

[17] D. Crocker. RFC822: Standard for ARPA Internet Text Messages. *Retrieved April*, 7:2008, 1982.

[18] M. Delany. Domain-Based Email Authentication Using Public Keys Advertised. In *the DNS (DomainKeys)", RFC 4870*, 2007.

[19] H. Drucker, D. Wu, and V. Vapnik. Support vector machines for spam categorization. *IEEE Transactions on Neural Networks*, 10(5):1048–1054, 1999.

[20] Z. Duan, Y. Dong, and K. Gopalan. Diffmail: A Differentiated Message Delivery Architecture to Control Spam. Technical report, 2004.

[21] D. Erickson, M. Casado, and N. McKeown. The Effectiveness of Whitelisting: a User-Study. In *Proc. of Conference on Email and Anti-Spam*, 2008.

[22] C. Fleizach, G. Voelker, and S. Savage. Slicing spam with occamâĂŹs razor. *CEASâĂŹ07*, 2007.

[23] S. Garriss, M. Kaminsky, M. Freedman, B. Karp, D. Mazieres, and H. Re. Reliable email. In *Proc. of NSDI*, 2006.

[24] S. Hao, N. Syed, N. Feamster, A. Gray, and S. Krasser. Detecting spammers with SNARE: Spatio-temporal network-level automatic reputation engine. In *Proc. of the 18th conference on USENIX security symposium*, pages 101–118. USENIX Association, 2009.

[25] J. Jung and E. Sit. An empirical study of spam traffic and the use of DNS black lists. In *Proc. of the 4th ACM SIGCOMM Conference on Internet measurement*, pages 370–375. ACM, 2004.

[26] C. Kanich, C. Kreibich, K. Levchenko, B. Enright, G. Voelker, V. Paxson, and S. Savage. Spamalytics: An empirical analysis of spam marketing conversion. In *Proceedings of the 15th ACM conference on Computer and communications security*, pages 3–14. ACM, 2008.

[27] D. Lowd and C. Meek. Good word attacks on statistical spam filters. In *Proc. of the second conference on email and anti-spam (CEAS)*, pages 125–132, 2005.

[28] R. Mastaler. Tagged message delivery agent. `http://www.tmda.net/`.

[29] M. Paganini. ASK: active spam killer. In *Proc. 2003 Usenix Annual Technical Conference*, 2003.

[30] A. Pathak, Y. Hu, and Z. Mao. Peeking into spammer behavior from a unique vantage point. In *Proc. of the 1st Usenix Workshop on Large-Scale Exploits and Emergent Threats*, pages 1–9. USENIX Association, 2008.

[31] A. Ramachandran, N. Feamster, and S. Vempala. Filtering spam with behavioral blacklisting. In *Proc. of the 14th ACM conference on computer and communications security*, pages 342–351. ACM, 2007.

[32] M. Sahami, S. Dumais, D. Heckerman, and E. Horvitz. A Bayesian approach to filtering junk e-mail. In *Learning for Text Categorization: Papers from the 1998 workshop*, volume 62, 1998.

[33] G. Sakkis, I. Androutsopoulos, G. Paliouras, V. Karkaletsis, C. Spyropoulos, and P. Stamatopoulos. A memory-based approach to anti-spam filtering for mailing lists. *Information Retrieval*, 6(1):49–73, 2003.

[34] B. Stone-Gross, T. Holz, G. Stringhini, and G. Vigna. The underground economy of spam: A botmasterˇ2019s perspective of coordinating large-scale spam campaigns. In *USENIX Workshop on Large-Scale Exploits and Emergent Threats (LEET)*, 2011.

[35] Symantec's MessageLabs Intelligence. Messagelabs intelligence annual security report, 2010.

[36] M. Wong and W. Schlitt. Sender policy framework (SPF) for authorizing use of domains in e-mail, version 1. Technical report, RFC 4408, April, 2006.

Summary Review Documentation for

"Measurement and Evaluation of a Real World Deployment of a Challenge-Response Spam Filter"

Authors: J. Isacenkova, D. Balzarotti

Reviewer #1

Strengths: Real world data of a deployed system; spam is still a hot topic.

Weaknesses: In an effort to be objective, the authors (willfully?) avoid some fairly obvious conclusions about challenge-response systems. Intuitively, the throughput numbers per company and per day seem low, so I wonder about the generality of the study.

Comments to Authors: High-level: interesting paper that goes in-depth to a less often studies spam fighting technique. Despite the author's claims, I believe that this data actually speaks quite negatively about CR-style systems, and as a result, will be of interest to the community looking to provide numbers to what it (likely) already intuitively believes.

Specifically, in S5.1, I agree with your conclusion that there is not a good correlation of challenges sent to number of servers blacklisted, but I feel like this is missing the point. Any system that could result in your outgoing mail server being black listed seems inherently like a bad idea. You say that 75% of servers never appeared in a blacklist, but that means that 25% did get blacklisted at some point! This typically requires some amount of proactive work on the part of the admin to unblacklist the mail server, or worse, debug why the outgoing mail is getting filtered by the destination. It is nice to quantify what that probability is, but my guess is that these blacklisting rates will be enough to scare off most administrators. Further, the reality is that someone could maliciously trick a CR system into getting black listed with 100% certainty, which is even worse.

My belief is the back-scatter *rate* is a little bit of a red herring. Emails are ultimately very small volume in terms of bits on the wire relative to other Internet services. What's more of interest is the number of messages that actually annoy non-CR participating senders. Have you considered doing a user-survey to try to estimate this?

Judging from back-of-the-envelope numbers from talking to local campus mail admins, 90M mails in 6 months for 20K people seems on the low end (~25 emails per person day, including spam, so at 90% spam, ~3 non-spam messages/person/day?). How does your study compare in terms of scale (emails per person per unit time) of non-CR previous work?

The data in figure 9 would have been nice to see also as a time series to understand how bursty white list changes are.

Reviewer #2

Strengths: Real world data; detailed analysis of a less understood spam fighting

Weaknesses: Strong conclusions from insufficient.

Comments to Authors: I was most concerned about the server blacklisting, 25% seems high. Isn't that the most negative argument against CR systems? 25% of mail servers means a lot of email delays,and lots of offline work to get them off the blacklist.

Even if there is a large amount of backscatter challenges being sent to innocent users, is it really such a big deal from a network traffic point of view? I would be more worried about other costs to the innocent users, rather than unwanted traffic volumes.

Reviewer #3

Strengths: The results presented in the paper help to illustrate the impacts of using Challenge-Response system with real-world data. It provides useful information for making decision on adopting the system.

Weaknesses: While analyzing real-world data, authors shy away from drawing any conclusion and stop at providing numbers. Some of analysis is incomplete and lacks depth. See below for detail.

Comments to Authors: Overall, this paper is written well. It is interesting to see the results presented from the viewpoints of a user, a system administrator, and the Internet.

In section 3.1, on understanding backscattered ratio, clearly it depends on the effectiveness of spam filter. It is not clear the result of 19.3% backscattered ratio reflects the spam filter or the effectiveness of the CR system. On the other hand, CR system and spam filter collectively fight spams. High backscattered ratio will bother many "innocent senders". The tradeoff between accuracy of spam filter and backscatter spam will be interesting.

As part the message or conclusion of the measurement result, I find that only 4% of challenges to be legitimate bothersome (section 3.2). Furthermore, 45% of challenges seem to belong to the case that the challenges are sent to "innocent senders". This effectively introduces spams to the system. Furthermore, how would spam filter treat these newly introduced spams. Could it be that the spam filter has already filtered those challenge questions?

Figure 5 is a bit confusing to read. The plots below diagonals should be explained further.

Reviewer #4

Strengths: The main strength of this paper is that it is the first study of real world deployment of challenge response spam filters. The evaluation covers a lot of data accumulated from different sources (47 companies of different sizes).

Weaknesses: The main weakness of the paper is that it presents the results while reserving judgment on the results. The paper would have been stronger if the authors explained how some results were good or bad when using CR systems. Also, in addition to evaluation of an existing CR system, the authors should have presented how certain design choices affect the results, and how CR systems could be improved.

Comments to Authors: This paper is a good first step in understanding the impact of CR systems in real world. The paper can be made stronger by providing guidance/insights regarding choices to make in design/deployment that will alleviate the problems of CR systems.

Reviewer #5

Strengths: Cool dataset, and analysis that provides some helpful numbers where people have often speculated. The paper looks at most aspects that came to mind while I read the paper.

Weaknesses: The studied systems are a niche solution and unlikely ever to make a real difference (which, to their credit, the authors acknowledge right from the start). The paper's execution is pretty rough at times and the presentation confusing.

Comments to Authors: In Section 2, it would help if you could describe your datasets earlier. I found it confusing to read about results of open/non-open relays before you describe the actual dataset. Similarly, it'd be nice to see the CR's architecture before presenting any results.

What size are the companies that have deployed the system? In which country/countries are they located?

90 million messages isn't exactly "almost 100 million", as you're stating in the "General Statistics" subsection. In Table 1, percentages would help; same for Figure 3.

In 3.1, separate notation for the two notions of R (accepted deliveries vs attempted deliveries) would help.

You need to define clearly what you mean by backscattered emails. In Section 3, you first describe them as "challenge emails sent out by a challenge-response system". Later it becomes clear that you mean only *misdirected* challenge messages. Then you conflate reflection ratio and backscatter ratio (which you mention in 3.1 but don't define until 3.2), etc. I found this quite frustrating.
I'm not sure whether looking at Figure 5 I should be in awe or send the information visualization police and have you all arrested on the spot. For sure, it's far too complicated and busy, because I keep needing to go back and forth between text and plot to understand what it shows. For example, I remained confused about how negative numbers could possibly represent a ratio until you explain that the numbers in fact are correlations. All I learn about the sizes of the companies in your dataset is that most (I can't tell the percentage, given the useless y-axis label) have less than 500 employees -- that's really rather coarse information. The alternating axis label locations are the icing on the cake. You have room in the paper, why not break the chart apart into individual, semantically coherent ones?

The description of Figure 7 in 4.2 doesn't match what Figure 7 shows in any straightforward way. I don't see how your observations regarding Figures 7 and 8 affect the numbers you report in the three bullet points ending Section 4.2.

I like 4.3. It reflects that the degree to which CR works depends a lot on the interplay of users' involvement, on *both* sides. Some recipients may diligently weed out their digest, while others may let it grow and hope for the senders to solve the problem by solving the CAPTCHAs. The flip-side applies to the senders -- why would they solve the CAPTCHA right away when there's a chance that the recipient is diligent and will see it in the digest anyway?

In Section 5 you start speaking about invitations. Are you referring to challenge messages?

The writing needs a lot of work. Fix: "the same Symantec's report" -- do you mean "the same year's Symantec report"? "1% of false positive", "possible conspicuous", "users that may [...] receives", "we collected statics", "let's", "challenge messages were never open", "between every pairs", "one of the most effective way", "withelists", "messages where bounced". Broken reference (or cut'n'paste bug?) in 4.2. :("SpamHause", "do not exists", "a challenge-response systems").

Response from the Authors

First of all, we want to thank all the reviewers for their insightful comments on our work. According to most of them, the main weakness of the paper was the lack of conclusions based on the performed experiments. Even though our main goal was to present and discuss the data, and not to draw personal conclusions, we decided to address the reviewers' comments by adding some overall conclusions to the discussion section.

Another point raised by two reviewers was that Figure 5 was hard to understand. We took this comment into account by better presenting those results and by adding a detailed description of each part of the figure.

We also found extremely useful all the suggestions about the ways in which we could improve the paper presentation and the description of the data. In particular, according to the authors comments, we completely reorganized section 2, corrected the confusing definitions of the backscattering and reflection ratios, and clarified the results on the impact on emails delivery (Section 4.2). Furthermore, we stressed some of the points (e.g., the fact that misdirected challenges could be filtered out by spam filters) and we added more precise comments on possible inaccuracy of some of the presented figures.

The first reviewer mentioned the fact that 90M emails for 20K accounts seems on the very low end. This misunderstanding is probably due to the fact that the 20K accounts also include a large number of internal mailboxes used for administrative purposes, accounts of previous employees, and mailboxes that were inactive during the period of our experiments. Additionally, as we already mentioned in the paper, not all of the servers were monitored for 6 months (the period during which we had access to the data varied between 2 and 6 months). And lastly, some of the accounts received hundreds of emails per day, while others only few per week, thus accounting for the low average mentioned by the reviewer.

Finally, we could not address few comments (e.g., about the size and physical location of the companies) in order to preserve the privacy of the data providers. In some cases we were not able to evaluate some of the reviewers proposals (e.g., by trying different spam filters) that, even though extremely interesting, would have required us to change the production servers.

The SSL Landscape – A Thorough Analysis of the X.509 PKI Using Active and Passive Measurements

Ralph Holz, Lothar Braun, Nils Kammenhuber, Georg Carle
Technische Universität München
Faculty of Informatics
Chair for Network Architectures and Services
{holz,braun,kammenhuber,carle}@net.in.tum.de

ABSTRACT

The SSL and TLS infrastructure used in important protocols like HTTPs and IMAPs is built on an X.509 public key infrastructure (PKI). X.509 certificates are thus used to authenticate services like online banking, shopping, e-mail, etc. However, it always has been felt that the certification processes of this PKI may not be conducted with enough rigor, resulting in a deployment where many certificates do not meet the requirements of a secure PKI.

This paper presents a comprehensive analysis of X.509 certificates in the wild. To shed more light on the state of the deployed and actually used X.509 PKI, we obtained and evaluated data from many different sources. We conducted HTTPs scans of a large number of popular HTTPs servers over a 1.5-year time span, including scans from nine locations distributed over the globe. To compare certification properties of highly ranked hosts with the global picture, we included a third-party scan of the entire IPv4 space in our analyses. Furthermore, we monitored live SSL/TLS traffic on a 10 Gbps uplink of a large research network. This allows us to compare the properties of the deployed PKI with the part of the PKI that is being actively accessed by users.

Our analyses reveal that the quality of certification lacks in stringency, due to a number of reasons among which invalid certification chains and certificate subjects give the most cause for concern. Similar concerns can be raised for other properties of certification chains and also for many self-signed certificates used in the deployed X.509 PKI. Our findings confirm what has long been believed – namely that the X.509 PKI that we use so often in our everyday's lives is in a sorry state.

Categories and Subject Descriptors

C.2.2 [**Computer-Communication Networks**]: Network Protocols—*SSL, TLS, X.509*; C.2.3 [**Computer-Communication Networks**]: Network Operations—*SSL, TLS, X.509*; E.3 [**Data Encryption**]: Public key cryptosystems, Standards, SSL, TLS, X.509; H.4.3 [**Information Systems Applications**]: Communications Applications—*Electronic mail, Information browsers, SSL, TLS*

General Terms

Security, Measurement, Human Factors

Keywords

SSL, TLS, HTTPS, X.509, Certificates, Public Key Infrastructure

1. INTRODUCTION

Security, privacy and data integrity are important properties of today's Internet applications and protocols. As the Internet is being used for many commercial activities, such as shopping, online banking, or electronic trading, the value of data has increased. Networking protocols and applications are therefore increasingly expected to protect critical data by providing encryption, data integrity, and, most importantly, entity authentication. As these security goals are difficult to attain, application developers and protocol designers often rely on well-established security layers below their own protocols. The SSL and TLS protocol suites are used by many applications and protocols to provide a certain level of security, as they build on well-understood and thoroughly-analyzed cryptographic algorithms. Authentication is done using a public key infrastructure (PKI) built with the X.509 standard.

Cryptographic algorithms can be mathematically analyzed with respect to the security they offer, and implementations of these algorithms can be checked for correctness. Hence, it is possible to estimate the level of security they provide with a fair amount of confidence. In contrast, X.509 infrastructures depend not only on cryptography, but also on various organizations and entities that are required to conduct their work in conformance with abstract process descriptions. Certification Authorities (CAs), for example, certify the identities and public keys of other entities in an X.509 certificate. CAs need to conduct an identity check at a certain level of thoroughness before issuing a certificate. However, these CA-internal work processes are difficult to assess from the outside, and thus users need to place their trust into the correct working of a CA. As many of these processes involve human work, factors such as negligence or malice can introduce problems – yet entity authentication relies completely on the correct execution of identification processes. Web clients are a good example for this: browser vendors decide which CAs are included in their so-called Root Stores, i.e., their lists of trusted CAs. This reveals a classic dilemma: although this method removes control from end-users, it is difficult to imagine a better method, as it would likely be too much to ask of users themselves to assess the trustworthiness of CAs. However, the number of trusted CAs has grown very large (more than 150 in the case of Mozilla Firefox). This raises the question: can we assess the quality of the PKI that has thus been established? Although we cannot verify the implementation of work processes within a CA from outside, we can observe and analyze the results of these processes: the deployed X.509 public key infrastructure.

This paper conducts a thorough analysis of the currently deployed and practically used X.509 infrastructure for TLS/SSL and examines its security-related properties. To obtain an overall picture of the deployed PKI, we collected X.509 certificates over a time-span of more than 1.5 years, and from several measurement points. Furthermore, we used passive traffic measurements on a 10Gbps link to obtain a picture of which parts of the PKI are actually used. We observed about 250 million TLS/SSL sessions over a four-week time span and extracted certificates from these sessions. We then evaluated the security-relevant properties of all acquired certificates. Last, but not least, we included data from previous third-party work into our analysis to be able to extend our view and compare our work with previous evaluations.

Contributions. Using these data sets, we evaluated the state of the currently deployed infrastructure and estimated its quality as encountered by users. We can show how often popular hosts offer TLS/SSL and what the negotiated ciphers and key lengths are. Most importantly, we present a number of results that show the certification infrastructure to be broken at several points: certification chains are often invalid, host names in subjects are frequently incorrect, and many certificates are re-used on too many hosts. This leads to a very low number of certificates that are accepted by e.g., a Web browser: only one out of five certificates can be counted as absolutely valid. Even then, some of these certificates exhibit weaknesses like weak signature algorithms. We also show which errors in certification chains are most common, how long these chains are, and the surprisingly small number of distinct chains that are actually used. Furthermore, we assess the properties of public keys and signature algorithms. We also include an analysis of occurrences of cryptographically weak keys. Thanks to the long-time observations and the geographic distribution, we are able to capture and describe the rather slow development of the X.509 PKI.

Organization. The remainder of this paper is organized as follows: Section 2 introduces X.509 and the structure of the PKI that is built upon the standard. We highlight relevant security parameters and properties, possible flaws in the processes that are responsible for setting these parameters, and the security implications of such errors. Section 3 presents related work that previously analyzed the X.509 infrastructure, and discusses how our work differs and extends these previous evaluations. Our data sets, their properties and the active and passive measurement methodology that we used to obtain the data are presented in Section 4. Section 5 presents the actual analysis of security-related PKI properties based on these data sets. Our paper concludes with a discussion in Section 6.

2. X.509 PUBLIC KEY INFRASTRUCTURE

This section introduces the public key infrastructure that is used by SSL and TLS. We describe those parts of X.509 that are relevant for this paper.

X.509 is an ITU-T standard for a public key infrastructure (PKI) and has been adopted by the Internet Engineering Task Force (IETF) as the PKI for several IETF protocols [1]. Thus, X.509 certificates are an integral part of the SSL and TLS protocol suites [2]: most often, they are used for server authentication in TLS/SSL, where the server presents its certificates to the client. Certificates are thus important for various protocols such as HTTPs, IMAPs, SMTPs and POP3s.

X.509 defines a somewhat complex certification infrastructure. Certification Authorities (CAs) are issuers of certificates, which are essentially a cryptographic binding of identity and public key. The binding is achieved with a digital signature. The identity is stored

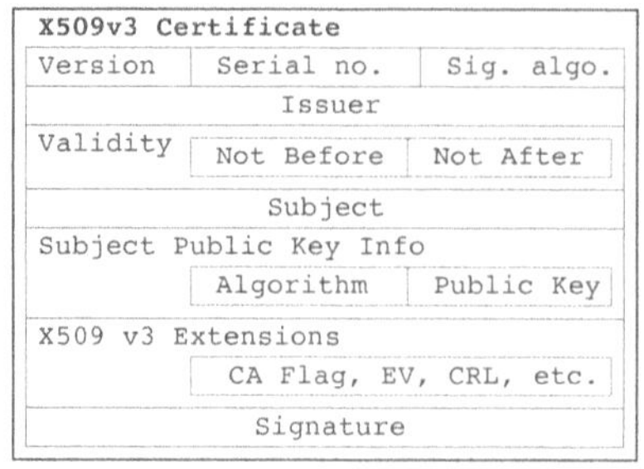

Figure 1: Schematic view of an X.509v3 certificate.

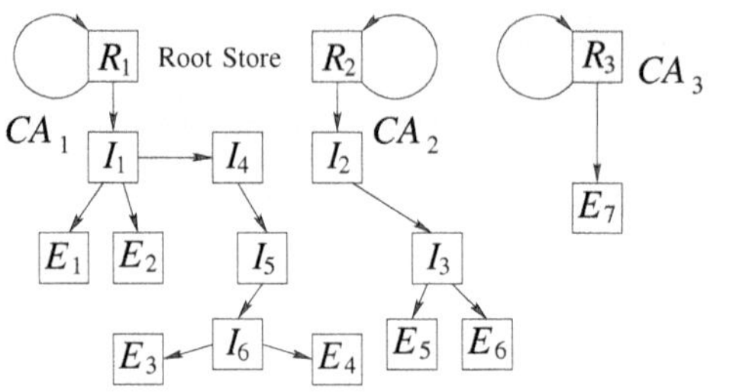

Figure 2: X.509 certificate chain examples.

in the so-called *subject* field of the certificate (Fig. 1). Every CA must ensure it only issues a certificate to the correct entity that is identified in the subject. This is most commonly a DNS host name.

As certificates contain information about communication peers, they are commonly exchanged at the beginning of a session setup. A communication peer must analyze its peer's certificate in order to determine whether it considers it to be the desired communication partner. To this end, it checks whether the certificate was issued and signed by a CA that it has trust in. Then, it checks if the information in the certificate identifies the other peer as the intended communication partner. In the example of the WWW, a browser needs to check if the domain in the certificate really is the domain it intends to connect to. Apart from identity and public key information, a certificate contains further important data, e.g., a validity period.

The X.509 PKI can be viewed as a tree or, since many CAs exist, a forest. Figure 2 displays a toy example for such a forest. CAs reside at the top and issue certificates. For this purpose, they issue certificates to themselves (*self-signed certificates*), so-called *Root Certificates* (R_x). These are then used for signing, i.e., issuing certificates. Instead of issuing certificates directly to end-entities (E_x), it is allowable – and in practice often done – that CAs issue intermediate certificates (I_x) that are then used for further signing processes. There are several reasons for this. First, it allows CAs to delegate the identification process to other authorities. This is especially useful for globally operating CAs as it spreads the workload to local registrars, who are supposedly also more competent at local identification procedures. However, intermediate certificates do not necessarily identify other authorities. They can also be used for security reasons: they allow a CA to sign an intermediate certificate with their Root Certificate. The intermediate certificate can then be used in the CA's online issuing business and can be replaced or revoked at any time, whereas the Root Certificate (R_1, R_2) is kept safe off-line. An intermediate certificate may be used to sign further intermediate certificates. The result is a so-called *trust chain* or *certification chain*, which may (in theory) be arbitrarily long.

The number of intermediate authorities and certificates thus increases the number of points for attack. It also removes some con-

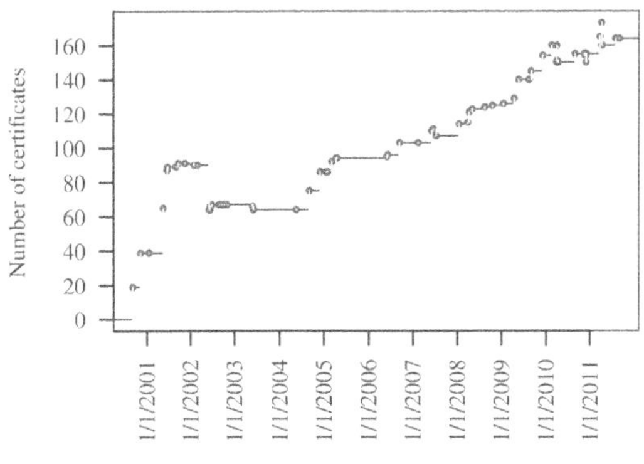

Figure 3: Growth of the NSS/Mozilla Root Store.

trol from the client – it is debatable if users would trust all intermediate authorities even if they knew about them. To understand the extent of the problem, it is important to realize that *any* CA can issue a certificate for *any* domain name.

For certificate checking to work, Root Certificates have to be known to the verifying party. This is solved in Web browsers by shipping a so-called *Root Store*, which contains the Root Certificates of selected CAs. In our example, R_1 and R_2 are in the Root Store while R_3 is not; hence the browser would reject E_7 as untrusted and display a warning message. An interesting case is *cross-signing*, where a CA also has a certificate (I_4) that has been actually signed by a Root Certificate of another CA. This is useful if the other CA is contained in a Root Store in which the cross-signed CA is not contained. However, Root Stores have a very undesired effect. If a CA or any of the subordinate intermediates it cooperates with becomes compromised, the attacker can issue certificates for *any* domain. It has been documented that this has happened several times [3, 4] in 2011: an attacker (purportedly the same) hacked several CAs such that he was able to issue certificates for several high-value domains to himself. In the first case [3], the number of issued certificates was low, and browser vendors responded by blacklisting the forged certificates. In the latter case [4], the number of forged certificates exceeded 500, and there were claims that the certificates had been used on a state level in a Man-in-the-middle attack. This led to the removal of the affected Root CA from the Root Store, an unprecedented step in the history of the X.509 PKI for the WWW.

CAs are included in the Root Store by vendor-specific processes. In the case of Mozilla, this is an open forum; but this is not the case for large companies like Microsoft or Apple. It should be noted that the number of Root CAs in browsers has been growing for a long time. We verified this for Mozilla Firefox, whose Root Store comes with the NSS crypto library that it uses. Figure 3 shows the development of the NSS Root Store since the year 2000. Starting out with about only a handful of certificates, the number has greatly increased over the years. Until December 2010, the number has grown to 160, the latest Root Store we used for this paper.

In order to be valid, a certificate must fulfill several properties, which we will present in detail later. These properties have different security implications for the overall security of the TLS/SSL connections. Also, it should be noted that users are today very used to browser warnings when certificates or trust chains are found to be broken. Studies like [5] showed that, for various reasons, the typical reaction is to ignore warnings and continue with the connection. All in all it is quite correct to conclude that the X.509 PKI is a very fragile construction. In fact, criticism has been voiced by prominent researchers [6, 7].

3. RELATED WORK

We are aware of two previous contributions on certificate analysis for TLS/SSL. Both were given as talks at hacking symposia, but have not been published as articles. Between April and July 2010, members of the Electronic Frontier Foundation (EFF) and iSEC Partners conducted a scan of the entire IPv4 space on port 443 and downloaded the X.509 certificates. Initial results were presented at [8] and [9]. A second scan was conducted in August 2010. The authors focused on determining the certification structure, i.e., number and role of CAs, and several noteworthy certificate properties like "weird" subjects (e.g., `localhost`) or issuers.

Ristic conducted a similar scan like EFF in July 2010 and presented some results in talks at BlackHat 2010 [10] and again (now including the EFF data) at InfoSec 2011 [11]. The initial scan was conducted on 119 million domain names, and additionally on the hosts on the Alexa Top 1 Million list [12]. He arrived at about 870,000 servers to assess, although the exact methodology cannot be derived from [10, 11]. However, the information about certificates and ciphers collected is the same as in our scans, and together with the EFF data set, our data sets provide a more complete coverage.

Lee et al. also conducted a scan of TLS/SSL servers [13]. In contrast to our work, they did not investigate certificates but focused on properties of TLS/SSL connections (i.e., ciphers, MACs, etc.) and the cryptographic mechanisms supported by servers. The number of investigated servers was much lower (20,000).

Yilek et al. investigated the consequences of the Debian OpenSSL bug of 2008 [14]. A bug in the OpenSSL implementation had caused very weak randomness in key generation, and it was possible to pre-compute the affected public/private key combinations. The authors traced the effect of the error over a time of about 200 days and scanned about 50,000 hosts.

The problem with scans is generally that hosts are included that are not intended to be accessed with TLS/SSL and thus provide invalid (and often default) certificates. The percentages given in [8, 9, 10, 11] thus need to be treated with caution. Our actively obtained data sets concentrate on high-ranked domains from the Alexa Top 1 Million list, and observe these domains over a long time period. Note that high-ranked domains can be assumed to be more aimed at use with TLS/SSL. This should at least be true for the top 1,000 or top 10,000. Our monitoring does not suffer significantly from this problem. Thanks to it, we are not only able to estimate the deployment of the TLS/SSL infrastructure, but to analyze which parts of the PKI are actively used and therefore seen by users. Furthermore, our view on the TLS/SSL deployment is not a single snapshot at an arbitrary time, but includes changes that operators have conducted in 1.5 years. Moreover, by analyzing TLS/SSL data that has been obtained from all over the world, we can even estimate how users see the TLS/SSL-secured infrastructure in other parts of the world. Finally, we include the EFF data from the mentioned related work into our own evaluation, and are therefore able to enhance previous results by applying our own evaluation algorithms, providing more comparability between our work and theirs.

4. DATA SETS

This section presents the various data sets that we obtained for our analyses. Section 4.1 presents our approach and the tools we used to perform our active TLS/SSL scans. Our setup and tool chain for our passive measurement of TLS/SSL traffic is explained in Section 4.2. All data sets that we use in our analyses, including the data sets from related work, are described in Section 4.3. Table 1 gives an overview of all data sets for this work. The data sets

Short Name	*Location*	*Time (run)*	*Type*	*Certificates (distinct)*
Tue-Nov2009	Tübingen, DE	November 2009	Active scan	833,661 (206,588)
Tue-Dec2009	Tübingen, DE	December 2009	Active scan	819,488 (205,700)
Tue-Jan2010	Tübingen, DE	January 2010	Active scan	816,517 (204,216)
Tue-Apr2010	Tübingen, DE	April 2010	Active scan	816,605 (208,490)
TUM-Sep2010	Munich, DE	September 2010	Active scan	829,232 (210,697)
TUM-Nov2010	Munich, DE	November 2010	Active scan	827,366 (212,569)
TUM-Apr2011	Munich, DE	April 2011	Active scan	829,707 (213,795)
TUM-Apr2011-SNI	Munich, DE	April 2011	Active scan with SNI	826,098 (212,229)
Shanghai	Shanghai, CN	April 2011	Active scan	798,976 (211,135)
Bejing	Beijing, CN	April 2011	Active scan	797,046 (211,007)
Melbourne	Melbourne, AU	April 2011	Active scan	833,571 (212,680)
İzmir	İzmir, TR	April 2011	Active scan	825,555 (211,617)
São Paulo	São Paulo, BR	April 2011	Active scan	833,246 (212,698)
Moscow	Moscow, RU	April 2011	Active scan	830,765 (213,079)
Santa Barbara	Santa Barbara, USA	April 2011	Active scan	834,173 (212,749)
Boston	Boston, USA	April 2011	Active scan	834,054 (212,805)
MON1	Munich, DE	September 2010	Passive monitoring	183,208 (163,072), Grid: 47% (51.94%)
MON2	Munich, DE	April 2011	Passive monitoring	989,040 (102,329), Grid: 5.72% (24.40%)
EFF	EFF servers	March–June 2010	Active IPv4 scan	11,349,678 (5,529,056)

Table 1: Data sets used in this work.

that we acquired by active scans ourselves will be released to the scientific community at [15].

4.1 Active Scans

As a base for our scans, we used the Alexa Top 1 Million Hosts list [12] that was current at the time of the respective scan. This list contains the most popular hosts of the WWW as determined by the ranking algorithm of Alexa Internet, Inc. These are thus sites that many users are likely to visit. Although its level of accuracy is disputed [16], it nevertheless is appropriate for our need to identify popular hosts. Since the list's format is somewhat inconsistent, we emulated browser behavior by expanding each entry to two host names: one with `www` prefix and one without.

Every scan was preceded by `nmap` scans on TCP port 443 to filter out hosts where this port was closed. The actual certificate scans thus started two weeks after obtaining the Alexa list. Our SSL scanning tool itself uses OpenSSL. It takes a list of host names as input and attempts to conduct a full TLS/SSL handshake on port 443 with each of them. Where successful, the full certificate chain as sent by the server is stored, along with further data, such as TLS/SSL connection properties.

4.2 Passive Monitoring

We monitored all TLS/SSL traffic entering and leaving the *Munich Scientific Research Network* (MWN) in Munich, Germany. The network interconnects three major universities as well as affiliated research institutions in the greater Munich area and provides Internet access to their users via a 10 Gbit/s link to the German research network DFN. It serves about 120,000 users with approximately 80,000 devices. During busy hours, the average link load amounts to approximately 2 Gbit/s inbound and 1 Gbit/s outbound traffic (as of April 2011). We obtained passive monitoring data in two runs. One problem we had to cope with was the high link speed. We improved our monitoring software setup between the first and second run, whereas the hardware (a four-core Intel Core i7 with hyper-threading using an Intel 10 GE network interface with 82598EB chipset) remained the same.

In order to deal with the huge amount of traffic, both runs used a sampling algorithm that samples the first n bytes of each bi-flow [17]. This is sufficient, as the handshake messages including the X.509 certificates are exchanged at the beginning of a TLS/SSL session setup.

For our first monitoring run, we used a process similar to the one used by the *Time Machine* [18]: we captured the beginning of every observed bi-flow and dumped all sampled packets to disk, starting a new file as soon as a dump file reached 10 GB. Whenever a dump file was finished, the TLS/SSL connections were extracted offline. Due to disk I/O and disk space limitations, we were only able to sample the first 15 kB of each bi-flow.

The second monitoring run in April 2011 was conducted using online TLS/SSL analysis. We used an optimized capturing setup, including our improvement presented in [19], based on TNAPI [20] to build a multi-core aware online analysis system. We now were able to run six instances of our monitoring application in parallel. Each instance employed a sampling process that sampled the first n kB of each bi-flow. Using this parallelization technique, we were able to analyze for each bi-flow up to 400 kB of traffic data while suffering less than 0.003% overall packet loss.

As the TLS/SSL processing tool, we used the intrusion detection and protocol parsing system Bro [21] in both monitoring runs. Using Bro's dynamic protocol detection feature [22], we were able to identify TLS/SSL in a port-independent way. We used Bro-1.5 with some applied patches to the Bro code, which fix some issues and allow us to extract and store complete certificate chains from the monitored connections.

4.3 Data Properties

Table 1 summarizes the locations, dates and number of certificates in the different sets. Table 2 provides additional details for the monitoring runs. Our data sets can be grouped into four classes.

First, we conducted scans from hosts that were located in Germany at the University of Tübingen and at TU München. These scans were carried out between November 2009 and April 2011, thus spanning a time interval of about 1.5 years. In April 2011, we performed an extra scan with SNI enabled. SNI is a TLS extension to address virtual HTTP hosts. With SNI, the host name is passed in the TLS handshake so the server can select an appropriate certificate to deliver (note that the TLS/SSL handshake takes place *before* the client sends the HTTP header).

The second group of data sets was obtained in April 2011. We employed PlanetLab [23] nodes from different countries, in order to obtain a geographically distributed picture of the TLS/SSL deployment. We wanted to determine whether location-dependent factors like content distribution networks (CDNs), which use DNS to route clients to different computing centers depending on the geographic location of the client, would also result in different certificates. This can yield information on the state and practice of certificate deployment in CDNs. Furthermore, we had the hope that, as a side effect, we might be able to determine whether certain locations actively interfere with TLS/SSL traffic by swapping end-host certificates during connection establishment (Man-in-the-middle).

The third group of data sets was obtained by passively monitoring live TLS/SSL traffic. The important distinction between certificates obtained from passive monitoring and those obtained by scans is that these certificates reflect that part of the PKI infrastructure that is not only deployed but also actually used due to user access to sites. We extracted all observed certificates in TLS/SSL traffic over each two-week period. In September 2010, we were able to observe in total more than 108 million TLS/SSL associations, resulting in over 180,000 certificates, of which about 160,000 were distinct. Our second run observed, during a similar time span of two weeks, more than 140 million TLS/SSL connections, which were responsible for about 990,000 certificates, of which about 100,000 were distinct.

As the MWN is a research network that hosts several high-performance computing clusters, we observed much Grid-related traffic secured by TLS/SSL. Although most TLS/SSL connections are due to HTTPs, IMAPs and POPs (see Table 2 for details), we encountered a rather large number of Grid certificates, as Grid certificates were often replaced (their median validity period was just 11 hours). As Grid-related certificates are not comparable to those used on the WWW, we filtered them out in our analysis of certificate properties. We explain this in Section 4.4.

Finally, we included a data set from related work into our analysis. This data set was obtained using a different scanning strategy. The EFF data set is based on scanning the entire assigned IPv4 address space, which took a few months. This results in a higher number of observed certificates, but does not provide a mapping onto DNS names. Hence, the data set cannot be verified in terms of a matching subject for a host name, since information about which domain was supposed to be served with a given certificate is not contained. In contrast, our own data sets provide this information.

4.4 Data Pre-Processing

The International Grid Trust Federation [24] operates an X.509 PKI that is separate from the one for HTTPs and other TLS/SSL-related protocols. Their Root Certificates are not included in the Firefox Root Store, but are distributed in Grid setups.

Our setup stored certificates without a reference to the (potentially many) TLS/SSL connections during which it was observed. Although we cannot filter out Grid traffic in our analysis of TLS/SSL connections to hosts (Section 5.1), we were still able to identify some properties of Grid traffic by correlating the encountered IP addresses with those of known scientific centers.

For our analysis of certificate properties (Section 5.2), however, it is possible to identify Grid-related certificates and filter them out. Our filter mechanism is rather coarse: we simply check whether or not a certificate contains the word 'Grid' in the issuer field. We acknowledge this is imperfect, but it is much less expensive to conduct than verifying if a certificate chains up to one of the Grid Root CAs. We tested our certificate filter by checking the certification chains in the sub-data set of Grid certificates. Indeed, 99.95% of them could not be found to chain to a CA in the Firefox Root Store, and not one of them had a valid certification chain (as is to be expected due to the use of a different PKI setup). At the same time, the values for validity of certification chains of non-Grid certificates was in the same range as with our active scans.

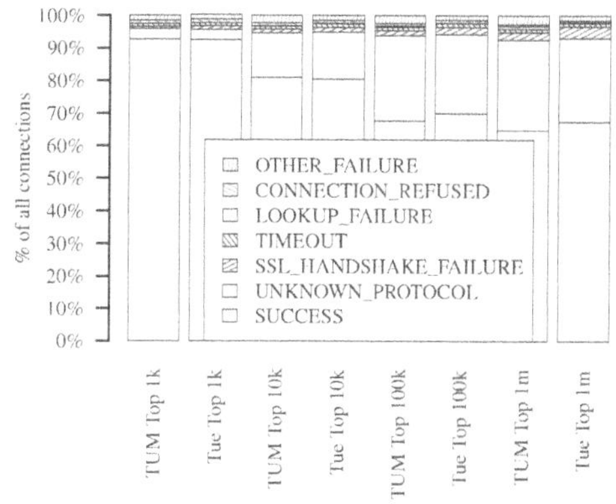

Figure 4: TLS/SSL connection errors for Tue-Nov2009 and TUM-Apr2011 scans, in relation to Alexa rank.

We thus conclude that our filter has removed most of the Grid certificates and the remaining bias is tolerable.

5. RESULTS OF OUR INVESTIGATIONS

We now describe results from our analyses, going item-wise through each question that we address. For each item, we explain its relevance for the security of the TLS/SSL infrastructure.

An important distinction that we sometimes make is whether we analyzed certificates of the full set or just the *distinct* certificates in the data set. The difference is that the former refers to the deployment as we have seen it and includes duplicate certificates, i.e., certificates that are used on more than one host. The latter is a pure view at certificates as they have been issued.

5.1 Host Analyses

Before investigating actual certificates, we first present some properties of the TLS/SSL hosts that we either contacted through active scanning, or whose connections we monitored passively.

Host Replies with TLS/SSL. A very central question is how many hosts actually support TLS/SSL and allow TLS/SSL connections on ports that are assigned to these protocols. To determine how many hosts offer TLS/SSL on the HTTPs port, we evaluated replies to our OpenSSL scanner described in Section 4.1. Figure 4 shows results for the scans in November 2009 and April 2011. It gives an overview on all queried hosts, the top 1,000, the top 10,000, and the top 100,000. As can be seen, the numbers do not change significantly over time, neither for the overall picture nor for the top 1,000. Two thirds of all queried hosts offer TLS/SSL on port 443, and more than 90% of the top 1,000 do so, too.

The number of cases where an unknown protocol was used on the HTTPs port is surprising, however. We therefore re-scanned all hosts that had previously shown this result and analyzed samples of the re-scan traffic manually. In all samples, the servers in question offered plain HTTP on the TLS/SSL port. As can be seen, this unconventional configuration is less popular with highly ranked servers.

Handshake failures during TLS/SSL setup can also result in failure of the association setup. However, the overall number of handshake failures and the number of other (i.e., not grouped otherwise) failures is rather low.

All in all, only about 800,000 hosts from the expanded Alexa list allowed successful TLS/SSL handshakes on the HTTPs port. Since a number of important sites (Google, Facebook, Twitter, ...)

Property	MON1	MON2
Connection attempts	108,890,868	140,615,428
TLS/SSL server IPs	196,813	351,562
TLS/SSL client IPs	950,142	1,397,930
Different server ports	28,662	30,866
Server ports ≤ 1,024	91.26%	95.43%
HTTPs (port 443)	84.92%	89.80%
IMAPs and POPs (ports 993 and 995)	6.17%	5.50%

Table 2: TLS/SSL connections in recorded traces.

have switched to offer TLS/SSL by default, we find it surprising that there does not seem to be a marked change in the overall deployment in the past 1.5 years either.

Our passive monitoring data shows quite a large number of TLS/SSL-enabled servers. This is related to Grid traffic, which we did not filter out for this analysis. The numbers changed markedly between the monitoring intervals in September 2010 and April 2011, although both runs were conducted over a period of two weeks and both time intervals were during university semester breaks. We found differences in the number of observed TLS/SSL connections, and in the number of clients and servers that were involved in this communication. These differences are summarized in Table 2. The number of connections between the first and second monitoring runs increased from 108 million to 140 million connections. Both the number of TLS/SSL servers and the number of the observed TLS/SSL clients have increased. The increase in observed TLS/SSL servers is also the main factor responsible for the increase in the observed certificate numbers in Table 1. The vast majority of observed TLS/SSL traffic used well-known ports ($< 1,024$), especially HTTPs, IMAPs and POPs. We can show that the remaining traffic was Grid-related on several occasions as the involved IP addresses are assigned to scientific computing centers.

Negotiated Ciphers and Key Lengths. The strength of the cryptographic algorithms and the length of the involved symmetric keys determine the cryptographic protection of the TLS/SSL connection. From our monitoring data, we obtained statistics on the ciphers and key lengths used to encrypt TLS/SSL connections. Data from active scans was not involved: it has only limited validity here, as the negotiated ciphers highly depend on what a client supports; hence, all results from active scans would be biased.

Figure 5 presents the most frequently negotiated ciphers, key lengths and digests encountered in the monitoring runs. Generally, strong ciphers (AES, Camellia, RC4) were selected with appropriate key lengths, sometimes offering a very good safety margin (256 bit). 3DES is still used, but not in the majority of cases. The use of MD5 for Message Authentication Codes, although not problematic at this time, is not encouraged [2]. However, it is still extensively used: the most popular cipher/digest combination (`RSA_WITH_RC4_128_MD5`) in September 2010 employed MD5 hashes for digest calculation. Fortunately, we can see that the popularity of this combination is decreasing: while it is still the most popular combination in April 2011, we can see an increasing share of SHA-based digest algorithms.

When comparing our results to those from 2007 in [13], we find that while the two most popular algorithms remain AES and RC4, their order has shifted. In 2007, AES-256, RC4-128 and 3DES were the default algorithms chosen by servers, in that order. In our data, we find the order is RC4-128, AES-128 and AES-256. It is difficult to give a compelling reason here. It could be that more clients support TLS/SSL now and their cipher support is different; but it could also be that more servers support TLS/SSL now and

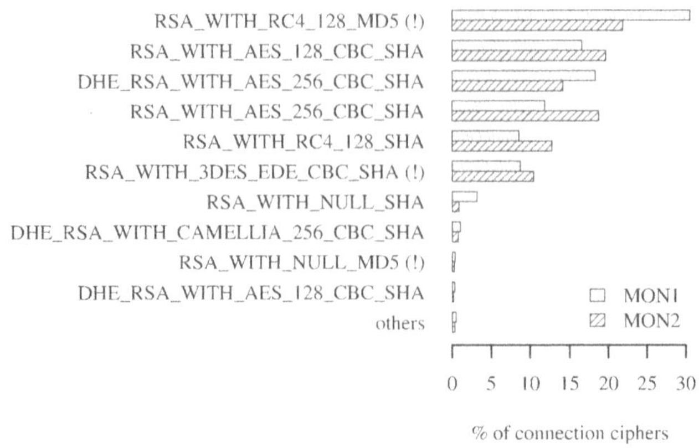

Figure 5: Top 10 chosen ciphers in passive monitoring data.

their default choice is the very fast RC4 at lower key length. If so, this is a debatable choice: although RC4 is secure, great care must be taken to avoid certain attack vectors [25].

Furthermore, we can see that some of the connections, albeit a minority, chose no encryption for their user traffic during the handshake. Such `NULL` ciphers were observed for 3.5% of all connections in MON1, and in about 1% of all connections in MON2. Again, we can show that the corresponding IP addresses are assigned to computing centers, and the connections are likely Grid traffic. Our hypothesis is that TLS/SSL is only used for authentication purposes, whereas encryption is omitted due to performance reasons.

5.2 Certificate Properties

We investigated several security properties of the X.509 PKI that are related to properties of certificates and certification chains. In this analysis, we filtered out Grid-related certificates in the data we had obtained from passive monitoring.

Certificate Occurrences. Ideally, every host should have its own certificate to allow TLS/SSL connections. Since the SNI extension does not enjoy real deployment, however, it is quite common that a certificate is issued for several domain names. This is not the only reason: it may be less costly to buy a certificate from a CA that includes several host names than to buy certificates for each host name. It may also be less time-consuming for the operator. However, as the private key for every certificate must also be stored with the public key, this can potentially increase the attack surface if a certificate is used on more than one physical machine.

We thus checked how often the same certificate is reused on several hosts. Figure 6 shows the complementary cumulative distribution function (CCDF) of how often the same certificate was returned for multiple different host names during the active scan of September 2010, in the middle of our observation period. We can see that the same certificate can be used by a large number of hosts (10,000 or more), although the probability for this is significantly less than 1:10,000. However, the probability that a certificate is reused rises quickly for a smaller number of reuses. It is not uncommon (about 1% of the cases) that 10 hosts share the same certificate.

We thus investigated which hosts are particularly prone to reuse a certificate. Hosts are identified by the domain names in the certificate's subject field. Figure 7 shows these for the certificates that we found most often. Most of these are identifiable as Web hosters – but only the certificates for `*.wordpress.com` were actually valid

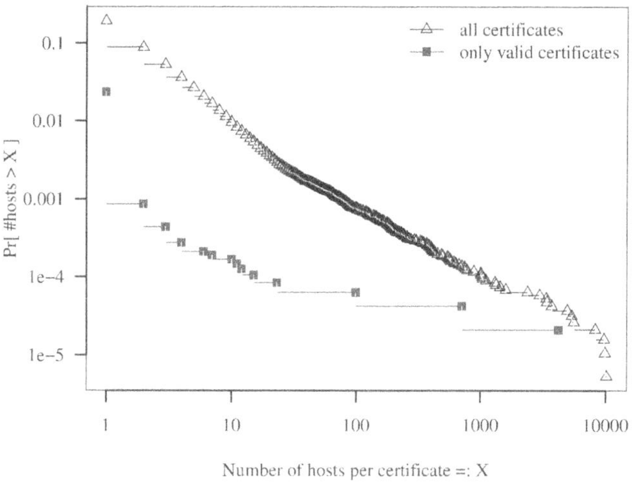

Figure 6: Certificate occurrences: CCDF for number of hosts per distinct certificate.

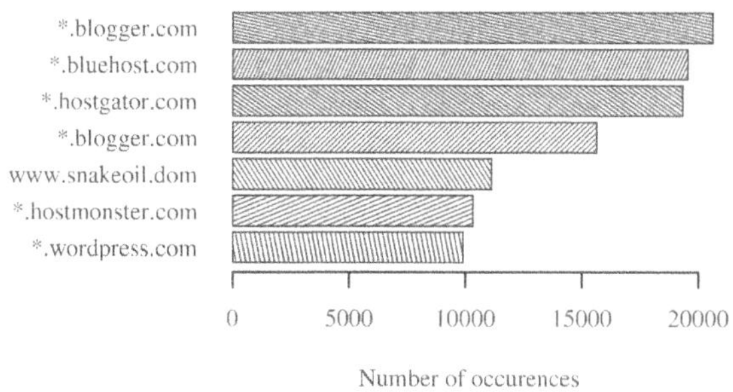

Figure 7: Domain names appearing in subjects of certificates most frequently used on many hosts.

(correct chain, correct host name). This is a rather poor finding, considering how popular some of these hosters are.

`www.snakeoil.dom` is a standard certificate for the Apache Web server, possibly appearing here because of Apache servers that run a default configuration (but probably are not intended to be accessed via HTTPs). We continued to investigate host names for those certificates that occurred at least a 1,000 times, and found that these seemed to be primarily Web hosting companies. We explore the issues of domain names in the subject fields and correctness of certificates in the sections below.

Validity of Certification Chains. There are several factors that determine whether a browser should accept a certificate as correct or not. The first one is whether the certification chain presented by a server is correct, i.e., the chain is complete and leads to a Root Certificate in the browser's Root Store, no certificate in the chain has expired and all signatures in the chain verify, etc.

There are a number of causes for a broken chain. We thus investigated the correctness of chains with respect to the Firefox Root Store from the official developer repositories at the time of the scan or monitoring run. Note that a missing Root Certificate only means that the certificate is not valid in a default Firefox, but the Root Store of a client can be reconfigured to contain the required Root Certificate. Moreover, some CAs have not yet been included in Root Stores, although a number of people consider them trustworthy. A prominent example is CACert.org, a community-driven non-profit CA.

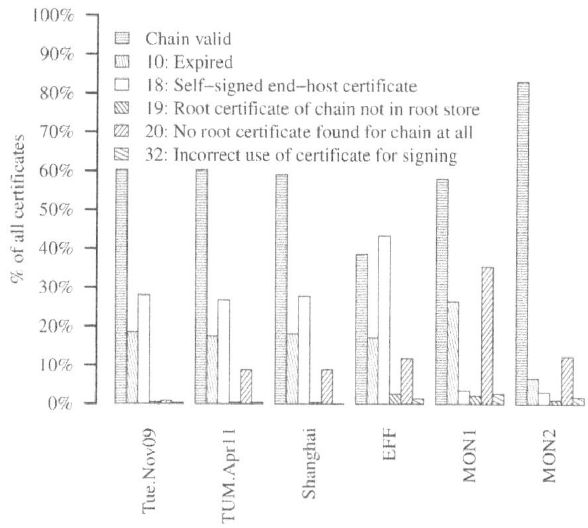

Figure 8: Error codes in chain verification for various data sets. Multiple errors can cause the sums to add up to more than 100%.

We used OpenSSL's `verify` command to check certification chains. Our check verified the full certification chain. This step does not check whether the subject in the certificate has a certain value (e.g., the correct host name) – this has to be checked separately. We examined which errors occurred how often in the validation of a certification chain (N.B.: a single chain can report multiple errors). Figure 8 presents our results for a selection of our data sets. The error codes are derived from OpenSSL error codes. In each case, a browser would display a warning to the user (usually with the option to override the alert). Depending on the vendor, additional user clicks are necessary to determine the exact cause. Error code 10 indicates the end-host certificate was expired at the time we obtained it. For the monitoring runs, we allowed a grace period here until the end of the run, as we had not logged timestamps due to disk space limitations. Expired certificates can be considered in two ways: either as completely untrustworthy, or just as less trustworthy than certificates within their validity period. The latter would account for human error, i.e., failure to obtain a new certificate. Error code 18 identifies an end-host certificate as self-signed. This means no certification chain at all is given, a user has to trust the presented certificate and can only determine its validity out-of-band (e.g., by manually checking hash values) [1]. Error codes 19–21 indicate a broken certification chain. Error code 19 means a correct full chain was received, but the Root Certificate is not in the Root Store and thus untrusted. This error can occur, for example, if a Web site chooses to use a Root Certificate that has not been included in a major browser. As explained, certain organizations (like some universities) sometimes use Root CAs of their own and expect their users to manually add these Root Certificates to their browsers. If this is not done securely out-of-band, its value is very debatable – we have anecdotal experience of university Web sites asking their users to 'ignore the following security warning', which would then lead them to the 'secured' page. Error code 20 is similar: there was a certificate in the sent chain for which no issuing certificate can be found, neither in the sent chain nor in the Root Store. Error code 21 means that only one certificate was sent

[1]Certificate pinning has been suggested as useful here. The idea is to imitate the trust model of SSH where a host key is viewed as correct on first encounter and its key remembered by the client for verification upon revisit.

(i.e., no chain) and there is no Root Certificate in the Root Store that would match the issuer of the end-host certificate. Error code 32 is interesting: it means that one or more certificates in the chain are marked as not to be used for issuing other certificates.

Some certificates found in all scans were found to have broken or nonsensical validity periods. Since there are less than 10 occurrences in any scan, we did not investigate them further. We also found cases where signatures are wrong and cannot be verified. Ratios were between 0.01% and 0.1%.

Figure 8 reveals that trust chains were valid in about 60% of cases when considering the active scans and over all certificates. Expired certificates (about 18%) and self-signed certificates (about 25%) are by far the most frequent errors found. The number of valid certificates does not change significantly when considering distinct certificates only. This means that issuing *and* deployment of certificates with valid trust chains are in line, which is a positive finding. Between November 2009 and April 2011, however, these numbers also remained constant. The same can be said for expired certificates: their number also remained around 18%. Note that the entries on the Alexa list had greatly differed by then; more than 550,000 hosts in April 2011 had not been on our expanded list in November 2009. We can thus say that even while the popularity of Web sites may change (and new sites likely enter the stage), the picture of this PKI with respect to valid certificates remains the same. This is a rather poor finding, as no improvement seems to occur.

Error code 20 increased in frequency: the number rose to around 8% in April 2011. We do not know a reason. Error codes 19 and 32 occurred very rarely. For our scans from Germany, we can thus conclude expired certificates and self-signed certificates are the major cause for chain verification failures. We compared our findings to the vantage points in Santa Barbara and Shanghai (Fig. 8; only Shanghai data shown) and found the perspective from these vantage points is almost the same.

Figure 8 also shows the findings for MON1 and MON2. Here, the situation is somewhat different. Although the number of valid chains was similar in MON1 (57.94%), it was much higher in MON2 (83.07%). We can also see that the number of errors due to expired certificates or with Error 20 has decreased. This does not mirror the findings from our scans. We did not find an immediate explanation for this phenomenon and will monitor it further.

We consequently also compared our results with the full data set of the EFF, which represents the global view for the IPv4 space. We found differences. First of all, the ratio of self-signed certificates is much higher in the EFF data set. This is not surprising, given that certification costs effort and often money – operators on not so high-ranking sites may opt for self-issued certificates, or just use the default certificates of common Web servers like Apache.

On the whole, however, the fact that about 40% of certificates in the top 1 million sites show broken chains is discouraging, even when considering that self-signed certificates are so common.

Correct Host Name in Certificate. The second major factor to determine whether a certificate should be accepted is the correct identification of the certified entity. The application itself needs to check if the subject of the certificate matches the entity it has contacted. The common practice on the WWW (but also for IMAPs and POPs) is that the client verifies that the subject certified in the certificate matches the DNS name of the server. In X.509 terminology and syntax, the subject field must be a *Distinguished Name* (DN). A *Common Name* (CN) is part of the DN. Very commonly, a DNS name is stored in the CN. Instead of writing the DNS name into the subject field, an alternative is to put it in the certificate's *Subject Alternative Name* (SAN) field. This can actually be viewed as desirable, as this is the intended purpose for this field [1]. It is, however, the less common practice. We checked if the CN attribute in the certificate subject matched the server's host name. Then, we checked if the SAN matched. We call certificates with correct chains where CN or SAN match 'absolutely valid'. Where the CN or SAN fields were wild-carded, we interpreted them according to RFC 2818 [26], i.e., `*.domain.com` matches `a.domain.com` but not `a.b.domain.com`. One exception was to count a single `*` as not matching, in accordance with Firefox's behavior. Note that we can conduct this investigation only for data sets from our scans, as neither data from monitoring nor the EFF data contain an indication of the requested host name.

In TUM-Apr2011, we found that the CNs in only 119,648 of the 829,707 certificates matched the host name. When we allowed Subject Alternative Names, too, this number rose to 174,620. However, when we restrict our search to certificates that also had correct chains, the numbers are 101,238 (correct host name in CN) and 149,900 (correct host name in CN or in SAN). This corresponds to just 18.07% of all certificates. We checked whether the picture changed for the data set of April 2011 where we had SNI enabled. This was not the case. The number of certificates with both valid chains and correct host names remained at 149,451 (18.09%). We deduce from this that client-side lack of SNI support is not the problem. We also determined the numbers for Tue-Nov2009, Tue-Apr2010 and TUM-Sep2010: they are 14.88%, 15.88% and 16.88%, respectively. This indicates a weak but positive trend.

Our findings mean that only up to 18% of certificates can be counted as absolutely valid according to the rules implemented in popular browsers – in a scan of the top 1 million Web sites. More than 80% of the issued certificates lead to a browser warning – we are not surprised that so many people are used to security warnings. These are major shortcomings that need to be addressed. However, we also have to add a word of caution here: while a poor finding, it is likely that many of these hosts are actually not intended to be accessed via HTTPs and thus neglect this critical configuration. Normal users may therefore never encounter the misconfigured site, even in the case of very popular sites. Still, omitting support for TLS/SSL does not increase security, either.

Unusual Host Names in the Common Name. We encountered a few unusual host names. In 60,201 cases (TUM-Apr2011-SNI, i.e., SNI enabled), we found the string 'plesk' as a CN. Our hypothesis was that this is a standard certificate used by the Parallels/Plesk virtualization and Web hosting environment. We tested this by rescanning the hosts, hashing the HTTP reply (HTML) and creating a histogram of this that counted how often which answer occurred. Just 8 kinds of answers were responsible alone for 15,000 variants of a Plesk Panel site, stating "site/domain/host not configured" or the like. As there are standard passwords for the Plesk Panel sites readily available via simple Google search, we find it problematic that such entry points cannot be authenticated in so many cases. A further favorite of ours are certificates issued for `localhost`, which we found 38,784 times. Fortunately, neither certificates with 'plesk' nor `localhost` were ever found to have valid chains.

However, by far the most answers occurred on relatively few hosts (2–10). We sampled some of these and found that HTTP redirections to normal HTTP sites were common after the TLS/SSL session establishment.

Host Names in Self-Signed Certificates. Server operators may opt to issue a certificate to themselves and act as their own CA.

EV Status	*Tue-Nov2009*	*TUM-Sep2010*	*TUM-Apr2011*	*Shanghai*	*Santa Barbara*	*Moscow*	*İzmir*
Yes	1.40%	2.10%	2.50%	2.56%	2.49%	2.51%	2.50%
No	98.60%	97.90%	97.50%	97.44%	97.51%	97.49%	97.50%

Table 3: Deployment of EV certificates over time and from Germany; and the same for April 2011 from Shanghai, Santa Barbara, Moscow and İzmir.

Hence, no external, responsible Certification Authority exists. This saves the costs for certification, but requires users to accept the self-signed certificate and trust it. The value of self-signed certificates is debatable: some view them as useful in a Trust-On-First-Use security model, as successfully used in the popular SSH protocol; others view them as contrary to the goals of X.509. Our own view is that self-signed certificates can be useful for personally operated servers, or where it is safe to assume that a Man-in-the-middle attack in the first connection attempt is unlikely. In the data set with enabled SNI (TUM-Apr2011-SNI) we checked if the self-signed certificates have a subject that matches the host name. The result is sobering: 97.78% of CNs do not match. Subject Alternatives Names matched in 0.5% of cases, but were rarely used (1.65% of certificates). Interestingly, the top 3 account for more than 50% of the different CNs. 'plesk' occurred in 27.30% of certificates, `localhost` or `localhost.localdomain` in 25.39%. The remaining CNs in the top 10 were usually in the range of 0.5–3%. The bulk of CNs is made up of entries that do not occur more than 1–4 times. Our conclusion is that self-signed certificates are not maintained with respect to host name. This does not make them useless in the above mentioned security model, but it certainly makes them puzzling when encountered by the average user.

Extended Validation (EV). Technically, a user should not only verify that the domain in the CN or SAN matches, but that other information in the certificate correctly identifies the entity on an organizational level, e.g., that it is really the bank he intended to connect to – and not a similar-looking phishing domain. This is the purpose of so-called Extended Validation certificates, which have been introduced several years ago. EV certificates are meant to be issued under the relatively extensive regulations described by the CA/Browser-Forum [27]. An *object identifier* in the certificate identifies it as EV. A browser is meant to signal EV status to the user (e.g., via a green highlight in the address bar).

We analyzed how often EV certificates are used; Table 3 shows the results. One can see that there is a light trend towards more EV certificates. We inspected the top 10,000 hosts in TUM-Apr2011 more closely and found that the ratio of EV certificates was 8.93%. For the top 1,000 hosts it was 8.11%, and for the top 100, 8.33%. Surprisingly, for the top 50 it was 5.17%. We found two explanations for this. First, Google sites dominate the top 50 (almost half of all hosts), and Google does not use EV. Second, a number of well-known Web sites (e.g., Amazon and eBay) use different hosts to let users log in. These are not in the top 50, but use EV.

Our conclusion here is that EV certificates are not very widespread, even though they can be very useful for sensitive domains (one may count Google's services among those, but also any bank). Since they are commonly more expensive than standard certificates, which are just issued against a domain name, this is somewhat to be expected. Even then, this is a sad finding.

Length of Certification Chain. As explained in Section 2, probabilities for negligence and errors can be assumed to increase with a high number of intermediate certificates if these are not subject to the same control as within the Root CA, e.g., if they are used by Intermediate CAs outside the direct control of the Root CA. Furthermore, servers sometimes sent more certificates than needed to build a valid chain. This can potentially reduce performance.

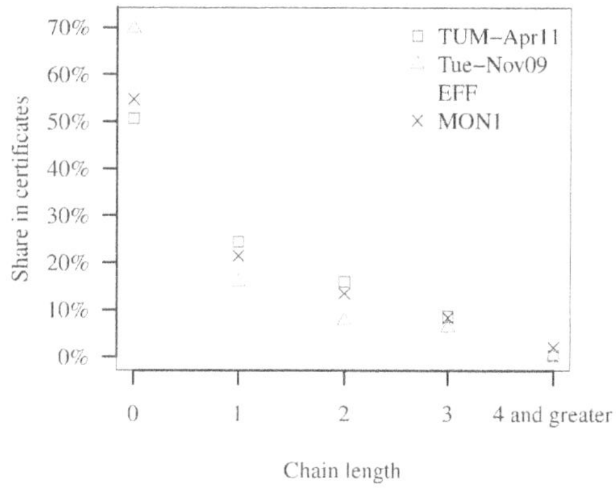

Figure 9: Chain characteristics for two scans, one monitoring run, and the EFF data. If no intermediate certificates are sent, the chain length is 0.

We thus computed the length of certification chains by only counting those certificates in the chain that were neither the end-host certificate, nor Root Certificates, nor self-signed intermediate certificates[2]. The latter cannot possibly contribute to an otherwise *valid* certification chain.

Figure 9 shows the result for two scans and one monitoring run from Germany, and a comparison with the EFF data set. We see that the vast majority of certificates is verified through a chain of length ≤ 3. For the EFF data, which was obtained in the first half of 2010, this cutoff is even at a length of ≤ 2. At the other end, more than half of the certificates have a chain length of 0. An explanation for this can be the relatively large fraction of self-signed certificates. When comparing Tue-Nov2009 to TUM-Apr2011, we see that the share of chains of length 0 has greatly decreased while the share of chains with length ≥ 1 has significantly increased by about 20%. The graph, as well as the increased average chain length (0.52 for Tue-Nov2009 vs. 0.67 for TUM-Apr2011) point to a weak tendency in the past 1.5 years to employ more intermediate certificates, not less. Overall, however, certification chains have remained remarkably short. Considering the trade-off of too many intermediate certificates vs. the benefits of using them, this seems more a positive development than a negative one.

The maximum length of chains found in scans is 16-17; in the EFF data, it is 18; whereas in the monitoring data, it is only 11 and 12, respectively. The scans thus have detected hosts with very unusual chain lengths (outliers), whereas most certificate chains are actually relatively short. In summary, we note that the chain length distributions of the four data sets do not exhibit very large differences.

Concerning how often unneeded self-signed certificates were included in the server's response, we only found 1,727 occurrences

[2] The minimum chain length was naturally 0, as some end-host certificates are self-signed or do not require intermediate certificates.

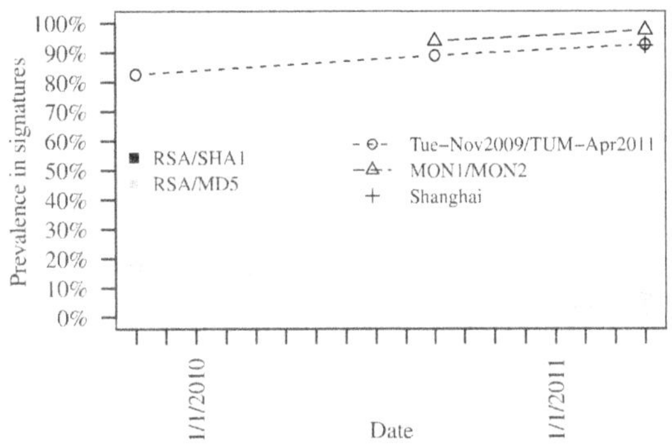

Figure 10: Popular signature algorithms in certificates.

in Tue-Nov2009 and 2,057 in TUM-Apr2011 where this was the case. As this is an unexpectedly low number, we also checked the EFF data set. Here, we find 63,290 occurrences in 4,375,901 valid chains. Our conclusion is that unneeded self-signed intermediate certificates in chains are rare. This is a good finding for performance.

Signature Algorithms. Cryptographic hash algorithms have come under increasing pressure in the past years, especially MD5 [28]. Even the stronger SHA1 algorithm is scheduled for phase-out [29]. When researchers announced in 2008 they could build a rogue CA using MD5 collisions [30], a move away from MD5 was expected to begin.

We thus extracted the signature algorithms in certificates. Figure 10 shows the results for TUM-Apr2011 and Tue-Nov2009, MON1 and MON2 (for all certificates and distinct ones), and Shanghai. We have omitted the rare cases (less than 20 occurrences altogether) where we found the algorithms GOST, MD2 and SHA-512 (a variant of SHA). The algorithms SHA256 and SHA1 with DSA were also only rarely found, in 0.1% of cases or less.

In our active scans, 17.3% of certificates were signed with a combination of MD5 and RSA in 2009. In 2011, this has decreased by 10% and SHA1 has risen by about the same percentage. The view from the monitoring data was slightly different. Most importantly, MD5 usage numbers were lower, both for all certificates and only for distinct ones. Between September 2010 and April 2011, the number had even fallen further.

Our conclusion here is that while MD5 is still sometimes used, it is indeed being phased out and does not play an import role in this PKI any longer.

Public Key Properties. It is quite evident that the ciphers used in certificates should be strong, and keys should be of a suitable length to achieve the desired security. Otherwise the certificate might be crackable by an attacker: RSA with 768 bit was factored in 2009 [31]. With the security margin of RSA-1024 shrinking, a move towards longer ciphers was recommended [32]. Furthermore, there should be no duplicate keys between different certificates, at least if the key owners are not the same.

We thus investigated the public keys in certificates. Concerning the ciphers, the result is very indicative. In the active scans Tue-Nov2009 and TUM-Apr2011, which span 1.5 years, the percentage of RSA keys on all queried hosts was always around 99.98%. DSA keys made up the rest. Counting only distinct certificates, the percentages remained the same. The values for the monitoring runs are practically identical. In these two scans, we also found a movement towards longer RSA key lengths: the percentage of

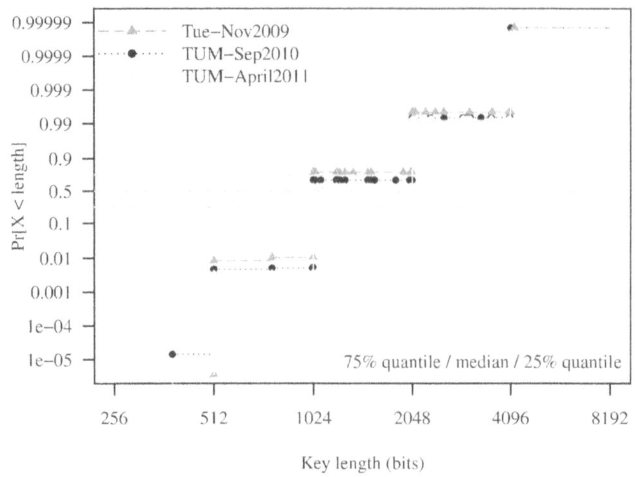

Figure 11: Cumulative distribution of RSA key lengths. (Note the unusual atanh scaling (double-ended pseudo-log) of the y axis.)

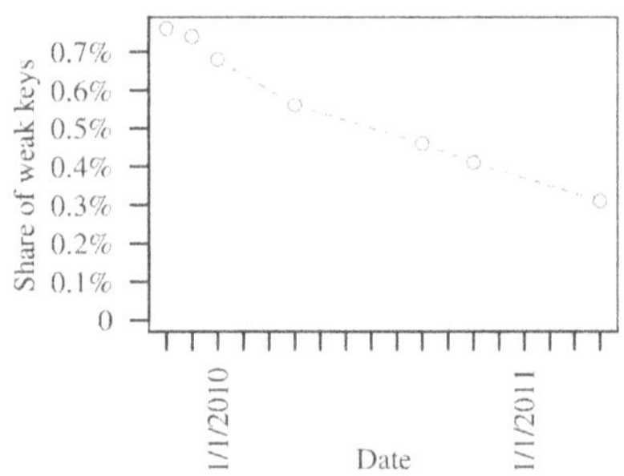

Figure 12: Debian weak keys over the course of 1.5 years in the scans of the Alexa top 1 million.

keys with more than 1,024 bit increased by more than 20% while the percentage of 1,024 bit keys fell by about the same. The general trend towards longer key lengths can be seen in Fig. 11: the newer the data set, the further the CDF graph is shifted along the x axis. This shows that the share of longer key lengths has increased while shorter key lengths have become less popular, with the notable exception of 384 bit keys that were found in the crawls from 2010 and 2011, but not in the 2009 data (left-hand side). The small triangles/circles/lozenges along the curves indicate the jumps of the CDF curves; hence they reveal furthermore that there is a significant number of various non-canonical key lengths, i.e., key lengths that are neither a power of 2 (e.g., 2,048) nor the sum of two powers of 2 (e.g., 768). However, their share is extremely small, as the CDF lines do not exhibit any significant changes at these locations.

An exponent and modulus make up the public key together; and there is only one private key for every public key. Concerning RSA exponents, the most frequent RSA exponent we found in Tue-Nov2009 was 65,537, which accounts for 99.13% of all exponents used. The next one was 17, which accounts for 0.77% of exponents.

There are two caveats to watch out for in public/private keys. The first refers to the Debian OpenSSL bug, which we have described in Section 3. We determined the number of certificates with weak keys of this kind by comparing with the official blacklists that come with every Debian-based Linux distribution. Figure 12 shows the results for our scans of the last 1.5 years. We can see that the number of affected certificates is clearly diminishing, and our numbers fit well with where the investigation in [14] left off. Furthermore,

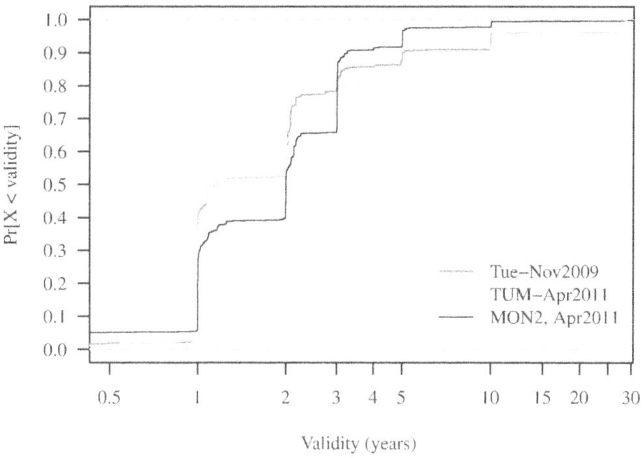

Figure 13: Comparison of certificate validity periods.

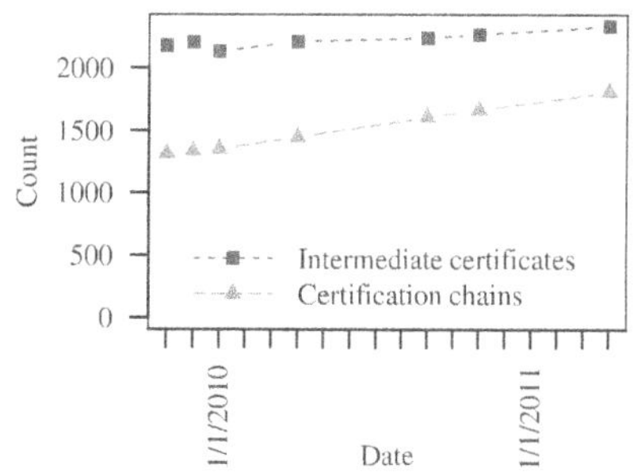

Figure 14: Temporal development of the number of distinct intermediate certificates (squares) and the number of distinct certification chains (triangles) across the scanning data sets.

the percentage of affected certificates was four times less in our monitoring data (about 0.1%) – this is a very good finding, as it shows that the servers that most users deal with are generally unlikely to be affected. However, we also found that a number of weak yet absolutely valid certificates (correctly issued by CAs, correct host names etc.) is still in use, but the number is very small: such certificates were found on about 20 hosts in the last scan.

The second caveat is that no combination of exponent and modulus should occur twice in different certificates. However, in TUM-Apr2011 we found 1,504 distinct certificates that shared the public/private key pair of another, different certificate. In Tue-Nov2009, we found 1,544 such certificates. The OpenSSL bug could be a cause for this, but we found that only 40 (Tue-Nov2009) and 10 (TUM-Apr2011) of the certificates fell into this category. We found one possible explanation when we looked up the DNS nameservers of the hosts in question. In about 70% of cases, these pointed to nameservers belonging to the same second-level domain. In about 28% of cases, these domains were `prostores.com` and `dnsmadeeasy.com`. We can only offer a hypothesis here, namely that some Web space providers issue a kind of default certificate and reuse the public/private keys. We do not know a reason for this practice, but it does not seem commendable: it means some private key owners are theoretically able to read encrypted traffic of others. They can even use a scanner to find out which domain to target.

Our conclusion here is that shorter key lengths are still encountered too often, but the trend is very positive. RSA keys should not be issued anymore at less than 2,048 bit. The Debian OpenSSL vulnerability has become rare in certificates. The cases of duplicate keys are curious, but not very frequent.

Validity Period. Certificates contain information for how long they are valid. This validity period is also a security factor. If a certificate is issued for a very long period, advances in cryptography (especially hash functions) can make it a target for attack.

When we analyzed the validity period for the certificates we encountered in our scans, we found that the majority of the certificates is issued with a life span of 12–15 months, i.e., one year plus a variable grace period. Other popular lifespans are two years, three years, five years, and ten years. This can be seen from the cumulative distribution function of the certificate life spans depicted in Fig. 13. Comparing Tue-Nov2009 to TUM-Apr2011, we can see that the share of certificates with an expiry time of more than 2 years has increased, in particular the share of certificates lasting 10 years. The curve for MON2 reveals that that the life spans typically encountered by users is either one, two, or three years, plus some grace period. In particular, certificates with life spans of more than five years seem to be used only rarely. What the figure does not show are the extremal values for the certificate life span: we encountered life spans on a range from two hours up to an optimistic 8,000 years. On the whole, however, the validity periods of certificates do not seem to be a major cause for concern.

Intermediate Certificates and Certification Chains. As explained in Section 2, many CAs do not issue certificates directly from their Root Certificates, but from an intermediate certificate (or a series thereof) that is signed by their Root Certificate. While beneficial for security, it also means that if too many intermediate certificates are used in a chain, the undesired result can be that the attack surface increases, as there are more keys that can be attacked. This is particularly true if intermediate certificates are accessible by regional resellers of CAs. We thus investigated the number of distinct intermediate certificates and the distinct certification chains that are built with them.

Figure 14 shows the development of the intermediate certificates. For the active scans from Germany, we see about 2,300, with a trend to increase. Compared to the size of the Root Store in Firefox, this means that, on average, every CA would use more than 10 intermediate certificates. However, we already know that the average chain lengths are much smaller, so this points to a very skewed distribution. The number of distinct intermediate certificates in the EFF data set is even higher, almost grotesque: 124,387. The ratio of certificates/intermediate certificates for the top 1 million hosts is about 335 (TUM-Apr2011); in contrast, it is about 91 for the whole IPv4 space. This means that the top 1 million hosts use less intermediate certificates than hosts in the whole IPv4 space do.

To analyze chains, we computed a unique ID for every distinct certification chain we found. For this, we discounted any self-signed intermediate certificate in a chain as a potential Root CA. The remaining intermediate certificates were sorted, concatenated and hashed. Recall that the number of intermediate certificates is very small compared to the number of end-host certificates. Correspondingly, we found only a small number of certification chains. This means that the X.509 certification 'tree' (end-hosts are leaves) shrinks rapidly from a wide base to very few paths leading to the Root CAs. In the EFF data set, we find an unexpected number of different chains: 17,418, which is much higher than the number in our scans. The number of distinct intermediate certificates in the active scans was always close in magnitude to the number of distinct certification chains (Fig. 14), whereas for the EFF data, the

Scan	*Suspicious certificates*	*Differences to TUM-Apr2011*
Santa Barbara	1,628	5,477
São Paulo	1,643	6,851
Melbourne	1,824	7,087
İzmir	2,069	7,083
Boston	2,405	5,867
TUM-Apr2011	3,245	—
Shanghai	10,194	9,670
Bejing	10,305	9,901
Moscow	10,986	11,800

Table 4: Occurrences of suspicious certificates per location, and number of certificates different to those seen from TUM.

number of different chains is smaller by a factor of 10. This indicates that the convergence to very few certification paths is much more expressed for the global IPv4 space than for the popular Alexa hosts. In other words, there is more relative variance in Root CAs in the top 1 million than in the whole IPv4 space.

Overall, our finding here is that too many intermediate certificates are encountered (leading to an unnecessary attack surface), even though it seems they are usually not needed for the (shorter) certification chains. In the top 1 million hosts, the situation is better than in the IPv4 space as a whole.

Different Certificates between Locations. We investigated how many downloaded certificates were different between locations. Our motivation was two-fold. A Web site operator may offer duplicated or different content depending on geographic region; Content Distribution Networks (CDNs) are a large-scale example of this. In this case, it is possible that certificates are bought from different CAs. It is also possible that an operator has switched CAs but not propagated the move to all sites yet.

Another possible reason can be of a malicious nature: a router can intercept traffic and swap certificates transparently on the fly. Through this Man-in-the-middle attack, the attacker knows the private key of the swapped certificate and is thus able to read the encrypted traffic. We labeled hosts as 'suspicious' when their certificate was identical from most locations and only differed at 1–3 locations. Table 4 shows the results from each vantage point.

Although the suspicious cases seem to occur particularly often with respect to hosts scanning from China and Russia, this might as well be the result of localized CDN traffic. We thus examined differences between Shanghai and TUM-Apr2011. The number of different certificates between these two locations was 9,670, which is about 1% of all certificates in TUM-Apr2011. Only 213 of the corresponding sites were in the top 10,000; the highest rank was 116. We can surmise that if operators of high-ranking sites use CDNs for their hosting in these regions, then they correctly deploy the same certificates. From manual sampling, we could not find a Man-in-the-middle interception from our vantage points.

We checked how many of the certificates from Shanghai were actually valid (correct chain, CN etc.). This yielded just 521 cases – and only in 59 cases, the certificate was absolutely valid in TUM-Apr2011 but not in Shanghai. We checked the corresponding domains manually; not one of them could be identified as highly sensitive (e.g., politically relevant, popular Web mailers, anonymization services). About a quarter of certificates were self-signed but different in Shanghai and TUM-Apr2011. The reason for this is unknown to us, but we do not think it is related to an attack.

While we are reluctant to offer compelling conclusions here, we do wish to state the following. First, there are not many differences between locations. High-ranked domains using CDNs seem to properly distribute their certificates. Maybe this is the most interesting finding, given the overall administrative laxness that is revealed by the many badly maintained certificates. Second, the number of different certificates was significantly higher from the vantage points in China and Russia. However, we found no indication of an attack. Rather, the findings seem to point at administrative difficulties. Third, we emphasize that we did not manually investigate all domains – we will thus publish the data sets where certificates were different so others can investigate them, too.

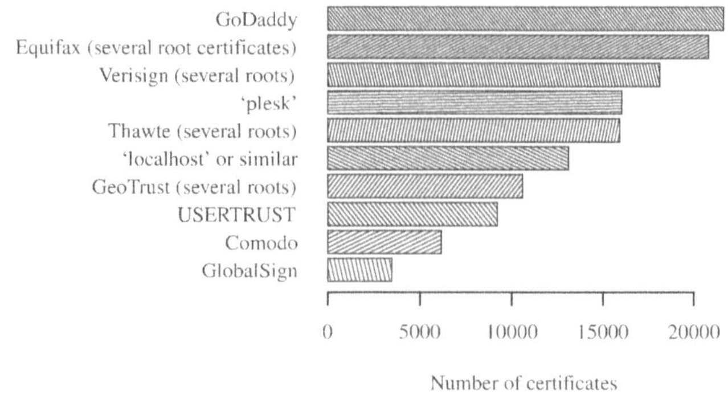

Figure 15: Top ten of issuers in TUM-Apr2011.

Certificate Issuers. We were interested to see which issuers occur most commonly, since the corresponding CAs are attack targets of higher value, due to the higher value of the customer database. We therefore determined the most common issuers for certificates in the data set TUM-Apr2011 (distinct certificates). There were 30,487 issuers in total.

Then, we concentrated on issuers that were found in at least 2,000 certificates. In total, these issuers accounted for 135,011 certificates – this is more than half of all distinct certificates. Figure 15 presents the top ten. Note, however, that there are close to 200 Root Certificates in the Firefox Root Store, and several CAs have actually more than one Root Certificate in there. Where possible, we thus identified issuers as companies with subsidiaries not grouped together. Obviously, two entries are not companies: as was explained before, 'plesk' as the issuer is an indication of virtualization, and `localhost` or similar entries were always issuers in self-signed certificates.

Further Parameters. We inspected the serial numbers in valid certificates and looked for duplicates by the same issuing CA. We did not find any in the last three scans, TUM-Apr2011, TUM-Nov2010 and TUM-Sep2010. This is a good finding, as a certificate's serial number is intended to be a unique identifier (in fact, blacklisting of certificates in so-called revocation lists is done via the serial numbers).

We also investigated a certificate property that is not security-relevant, but interesting nonetheless: X.509 Version 1 is outdated, and there is no reason to use it anymore. The current version is X.509 Version 3. We investigated data sets Tue-Nov2009 and TUM-Apr2011 in this regard. In November 2009, 86.01% of certificates were Version 3, 13.99% were Version 1. In April 2011, 85.72% were Version 3 and 14.27% Version 1.

Although our first guess was that this is an artifact of measurement, we found that 33,000 certificates with Version 1 had not been seen in any previous scan. None of them had valid certification chains, however, and 31,000 of them were self-signed. Of the others, the biggest issuer was a Russia-based company. We investi-

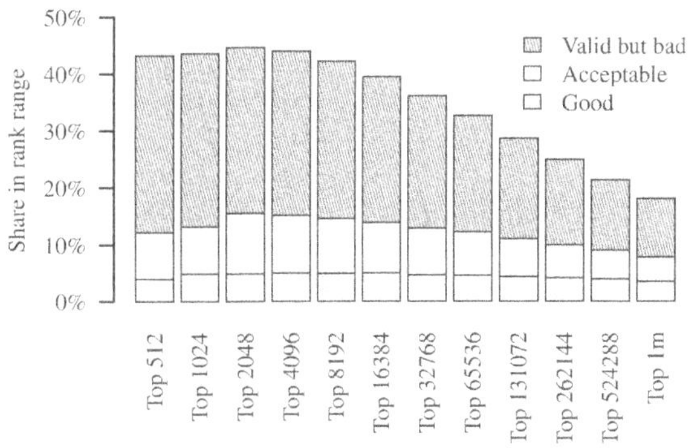

Figure 16: Certificate quality in relation to Alexa rank.

gated all issuers that had issued more than 2 certificates and found that all of them seemed to employ a PKI of their own, but without Root Certificates in Firefox. The reasons for this use of Version 1 are unknown to us, but plausible causes are software default settings or an arbitrary choice to use the simpler format of Version 1.

Certificate Quality: A Summarizing View.

We conclude our analysis with a summarizing view of certificate quality. Figure 16 reveals that the share of valid certificates (=total height of the bars) is negatively correlated with the Alexa rank. This does not come as a surprise, since operators of high-profile sites with a higher Alexa rank can be expected to invest more resources into a working HTTPs infrastructure. What is surprising, however, is that even in the top 512 or 1,024 – i.e., truly high-ranking sites – only just above 40% of certificates are absolutely valid. The figure also shows a classification of the certificates in three categories, which we have termed 'good', 'acceptable' and 'valid but bad'. *Good* certificates have correct chains, correct host names, a chain length of 2 at most, do not use MD5 as a signature algorithm, use non-weak keys that are either DSA keys or RSA keys of more than 1024 bit, and have a validity of at most 13 months (a year plus a grace period). For *acceptable* keys, we require the same but allow a chain length of 3 and validity is allowed to be up to 25 months. *Valid but bad* keys represent the remainder of keys (with correct chains and host names, but that otherwise fail our criteria). Interestingly, although high-profile sites are more likely to deliver valid certificates, the share of bad certificates among their valid certificates is much higher (about two thirds) when compared to that of all sites (about half). The conclusion we have to draw here is that even among the absolutely valid certificates the number of certificates with strong properties is disappointingly low.

6. DISCUSSION AND CONCLUSION

By combining and evaluating several actively and passively obtained data sets, which were in part also obtained over 1.5 years, we were able to derive a very comprehensive picture of the X.509 infrastructure as used with TLS/SSL. Our analysis supports with hard facts what has long been believed: that the X.509 certification infrastructure is, in great part, in a sorry state.

The most sobering result is probably the percentage of certificates that a client using the Mozilla Root Store would accept without a warning: just 18%. This can be traced to both incorrect certification chains (40% of all certificates exhibit this problem), but even more so to incorrect or missing host names in the subject or subject alternative name. With self-signed certificates, where conscientious operators would have an incentive to use the correct host name, the situation was much worse. The only positive point is that the percentages of absolutely valid certificates have increased since 2009, but then again only very slightly. Recall that these numbers refer to the top 1 million hosts – the percentage of certificates where the chains are correct is lower for the full IPv4 space than for the top sites, as we found by examining the EFF data set.

Moreover, many certification chains showed more than one error. Expired certificates were common, and so were certificates for which no Root Certificate could be found. A further problematic finding is that all our data sets reveal a high number of certificates that are shared between a large number of hosts. This is even the case for high-profile Web hosters – and often, the host names do not match the certificates there, either. Although offered by several CAs, Extended Validation certificates do no seem to be in wide use.

This truly seems a sorry state, and it does not come as a surprise that users just click away warnings, thus adding to the general insecurity of the WWW. As few CAs are responsible for more than half of the distinct certificates, one should think the situation should be better or at least easier to clean up.

There are some more positive tendencies that should be mentioned, however. Our evaluation shows that the more popular a given site is, the more likely it supports TLS/SSL at all, and the more likely it shows an absolutely valid certificate. On the whole, key lengths seem not to constitute a major problem. The same is true for signature algorithms. Keys with short bit lengths are becoming fewer, and the weak MD5 algorithm is clearly being phased out, too. Over the past 1.5 years, we also found an increase in the use of intermediate certificates while chain lengths remained remarkably short. This is a good development, as end-host certificates should not be issued by a Root Certificate that is used in online operations. However, use of intermediate certificates can be overdone and sometimes is. The latter will add to the already complex certification infrastructure that we have encountered, with a high number of distinct certification chains.

Concerning our passive monitoring, the data we obtained allowed us to evaluate negotiated properties of TLS/SSL associations, which cannot be obtained by active scans. We were able to determine the negotiated ciphers and digest mechanisms. Our observations lead us to conclude that most connections use secure ciphers with acceptable key lengths, and that key lengths are even increasing over time, with a good security margin. This is in line with the corresponding trends in certificate keys. However, MD5 is still commonly used to compute Message Authentication Codes (MACs). This is not really dramatic at the moment – even now, collision attacks take at least some seconds, and preimage attacks much longer. An attacker's time window is likely too short for a useful on-the-fly attack at this time (note that TLS/SSL uses a replay protection for the payload, too). However, we cannot see a compelling reason to continue using MD5 for MACs (except possibly for some very old legacy clients). We feel it should be discouraged and phased out.

With the above mentioned problems in certificates, however, we have to conclude that the positive movements do not address the most pressing problem, which is the certification structure itself. Unfortunately, the general state seems to persist as made evident by the fact that several critical factors like validity of certification chains, correct host names in certificates, or plainly the number of hosts that offer TLS/SSL do not seem to change. As this work has focused on the top 1 million hosts (scans) and the PKI as accessed by users (monitoring), this seems to indicate a pressing need.

7. ACKNOWLEDGEMENTS

We thank Nathan Evans and the Leibniz-Rechenzentrum (LRZ) in Munich for assisting us with obtaining the data. We especially thank Helmut Reiser of LRZ for his valuable feedback. This work has been partially funded by the European Union within the EU FP7 project ResumeNet (FP7-224619).

8. REFERENCES

[1] D. Cooper, S. Santesson, S. Farrell, S. Boeyen, R. Housley, and W. Polk, "Internet X.509 public key infrastructure certificate and certificate revocation list (CRL) profile," RFC 5280 (Proposed Standard), May 2008.

[2] T. Dierks and E. Rescorla, "The transport layer security (TLS) protocol version 1.2," RFC 5246 (Proposed Standard), Aug. 2008, updated by RFCs 5746, 5878, 6176.

[3] J. Appelbaum, "Detecting certificate authority compromises and Web browser collusion," Blog entry: https://blog.torproject.org/blog/detecting-certificate-authority-compromises-and-web-browser-collusion, 2011, [online; last retrieved in May 2011].

[4] Mozilla Security Blog, "DigiNotar removal follow up," https://blog.mozilla.com/security/2011/09/02/diginotar-removal-follow-up/ [online; last retrieved in September 2011], 2011.

[5] C. Herley, "So long, and no thanks for the externalities: the rational rejection of security advice by users," in *Proc. 2009 Workshop on New Security Paradigms*. New York, NY, USA: ACM, 2009.

[6] C. Ellison and B. Schneier, "Ten risks of PKI: What you're not being told about public key infrastructure," *Computer Security Journal*, vol. 16, no. 1, 2000.

[7] P. Gutmann, "PKI: It's not dead, just resting," *IEEE Computer*, vol. 35, no. 8, August 2002.

[8] P. Eckersley and J. Burns, "An observatory for the SSLiverse," Talk at Defcon 18., July 2010, [last retrieved in May 2011]. [Online]. Available: https://www.eff.org/files/DefconSSLiverse.pdf

[9] P. Eckersley and J. Burns, "Is the SSLiverse a safe place?" Talk at 27C3. Slides from https://www.eff.org/files/ccc2010.pdf [online; last retrieved in May 2011], 2010.

[10] I. Ristic, "Internet SSL Survey 2010," Talk at BlackHat 2010. Slides from https://media.blackhat.com/bh-us-10/presentations/Ristic/BlackHat-USA-2010-Ristic-Qualys-SSL-Survey-HTTP-Rating-Guide-slides.pdf, 2010, [online; last retrieved in May 2011].

[11] I. Ristic, "State of SSL," Talk at InfoSec World 2011. Slides from http://blog.ivanristic.com/Qualys_SSL_Labs-State_of_SSL_InfoSec_World_April_2011.pdf, 2011, [online; last retrieved in May 2011].

[12] Alexa Internet Inc., "Top 1,000,000 sites (updated daily)," http://s3.amazonaws.com/alexa-static/top-1m.csv.zip, 2009–2011, [online; last retrieved in May 2011].

[13] H. K. Lee, T. Malkin, and E. Nahum, "Cryptographic strength of SSL/TLS servers: Current and recent practices," in *Proc. 7th ACM SIGCOMM Conference on Internet Measurement (IMC)*, San Diego, CA, USA, October 2007.

[14] S. Yilek, E. Rescorla, H. Shacham, B. Enright, and S. Savage, "When private keys are public – results from the 2008 Debian OpenSSL vulnerability," in *Proc. 9th ACM SIGCOMM Conference on Internet Measurement (IMC)*, Chicago, Illinois, USA, Nov. 2009.

[15] Data sets of active scans, http://pki.net.in.tum.de, 2011.

[16] A. Croll and S. Power, *Complete Web Monitoring*. O'Reilly Media, 2009.

[17] L. Braun, G. Münz, and G. Carle, "Packet sampling for worm and botnet detection in TCP connections," in *Proc. IEEE/IFIP Network Operations and Management Symposium (NOMS)*, Apr. 2010.

[18] S. Kornexl, V. Paxson, H. Dreger, A. Feldmann, and R. Sommer, "Building a time machine for efficient recording and retrieval of high-volume network traffic," in *Proc. 5th ACM SIGCOMM Conference on Internet Measurement (IMC)*, Berkeley, CA, USA, Oct. 2005.

[19] L. Braun, A. Didebulidze, N. Kammenhuber, and G. Carle, "Comparing and improving current packet capturing solutions based on commodity hardware," in *Proc. 10th ACM SIGCOMM Conference on Internet Measurement (IMC)*, Nov 2010.

[20] F. Fusco and L. Deri, "High speed network traffic analysis with commodity multi-core systems," in *Proc. 10th ACM SIGCOMM Conference on Internet Measurement (IMC)*, Nov 2010.

[21] V. Paxson, "Bro: a system for detecting network intruders in real-time," *Computer networks*, vol. 31, no. 23-24, 1999.

[22] H. Dreger, A. Feldmann, M. Mai, V. Paxson, and R. Sommer, "Dynamic Application-Layer Protocol Analysis for Network Intrusion Detection," in *Proc. USENIX Security Symposium*, Apr. 2006.

[23] Planet Lab, "Planet Lab Web site," https://www.planet-lab.org [online; last retrieved in May 2011].

[24] The International Grid Trust Federation, "IGTF Web site," http://www.igtf.net/ [online; last retrieved in May 2011].

[25] A. Klein, "Attacks on the RC4 stream cipher," *Designs, Codes and Cryptography*, vol. 48, 2008.

[26] E. Rescorla, "HTTP over TLS," RFC 2818 (Informational), 2000.

[27] CA/Browser Forum, "EV SSL certificate guidelines version 1.3," http://www.cabforum.org/Guidelines_v1_3.pdf, 2010, [online; last retrieved in May 2011].

[28] M. Stevens, A. Lenstra, and B. de Weger, "Chosen-prefix collisions for MD5 and colliding X.509 certificates for different identities," in *Advances in Cryptology – EUROCRYPT 2007*, ser. LNCS. Springer Berlin / Heidelberg, 2007, vol. 4515.

[29] NIST, "Approved Algorithms," http://csrc.nist.gov/groups/ST/toolkit/secure_hashing.html, 2006, [online; last retrieved in May 2011].

[30] A. Sotirov, M. Stevens, J. Appelbaum, A. Lenstra, D. Molnar, D. A. Osvik, and B. de Weger, "MD5 considered harmful today," http://dl.packetstormsecurity.net/papers/attack/md5-considered-harmful.pdf, 2008, [online; last retrieved in May 2011].

[31] T. Kleinjung, K. Aoki, J. Franke, A. Lenstra, E. Thomé, J. Bos, P. Gaudry, A. Kruppa, P. Montgomery, D. Osvik, H. te Riele, A. Timofeev, and P. Zimmermann, "Factorization of a 768-bit RSA modulus," in *Advances in Cryptology – CRYPTO 2010*, ser. Lecture Notes in Computer Science. Springer Berlin / Heidelberg, 2010, vol. 6223.

[32] NIST, "Special publications (800 Series)," http://csrc.nist.gov/publications/PubsSPs.html, 2011, [online; last retrieved in May 2011].

Summary Review Documentation for

"The SSL Landscape – A Thorough Analysis of the X.509 PKI Using Active and Passive Measurements"

Authors: R. Holz, L. Braun, N. Kammenhuber, G. Carle

Reviewer #1

Strengths: The paper examines some extensive data sets. It compares and contrasts the information gleaned via active and passive measurements. The paper is (generally speaking) presented in a manner that makes the work appealing to a broad audience. The paper is on an important topic, and the results may help improve the security of the Internet.

Weaknesses: In places, the presentation needs improvement (i.e., some sections seem like they were written hastily). The paper needs to more clearly distinguish between Internet and Grid certificates.

Comments to Authors: Abstract: The location of the clients used in the active measurements did not.seem to have much effect on the results (nor would I have expected any), so I would not highlight that in the abstract, I would only mention it briefly in the methodology section. The abstract should summarize the key results, not make vague statements about being able to "perform additional analyses" (this is one example where the text seems to have been hastily written).

Introduction: Negligence is not the only possible reason for problems; malice, blackmail, etc. are some of the others. The fact that "several measurement points" were used is stated/implied multiple times, but since it really did not have an effect on the results, I would de-emphasize this. Immediately prior to describing the "remainder of the paper", summarize the key findings of your study.

Section 2: Provide a diagram of a certificate (i.e., that shows the common information fields contained in a certificate). I would include a "conceptual" diagram of PKI; figure 1 is a bit detailed to start off with. Unless you can cite a credible source regarding the source of the CA attack, delete the statement "supposedly from Iran" (it is not relevant to the issue any way); also, please clarify that the attacker gained the signing authority of the CA. Rather than just providing the number of root CAs in the root store for August 2009 to December 2010, it would be interesting to look at much older versions of Netscape/Mozilla, and plot the growth.

Section 3: One paper to add is H. Lee, T. Malkin and E. Nahum, "Cryptographic strength of SSL/TLS servers: current and recent practices", IMC 2007. (if not in this section, than in Section 5.2). Clarify that Ristic gave a talk at InfoSec 2011, rather than had a paper there

Section 4: Where will the data be released? Clarify which nmap scan was done, and why that type of scan(s) was chosen. Please clarify why a new scanning tool was developed; Lee et al. developed one that likely would have provided all of the required features (perhaps it is not publicly available), and workload generation tools like httperf also have the ability to do what is described in this section. Please clarify how much encrypted "Internet" was on non-standard ports (rather than encrypted "Grid" traffic); was it really worth trying to analyze all ports? Have the Bro patches been shared with Bro developers? Again, multiple client sites are mentioned; but it doesn't seem like this mattered, so why keep mentioning it?

Section 5: Create a separate subsection for the discussion of filtering Grid-related certificates (e.g., "5.1 Data Pre-processing"). Although the few few paragraphs discuss filtering the Grid-related certificates, there is still discussion later in the paper about Grid traffic; this is confusing to the reader; please either completely filter it from the data set, or skip the discussion of filtering, and then do a more exhaustive job of describing the results for "Internet" certificates versus "Grid" certificates.

Reviewer #2

Strengths: The Web PKI is a critical component of the Internet, timely given the uptick in HTTPS, and as far as I am aware there is no comprehensive empirical characterization of it that matches this paper. If true that is reason enough to accept it. The results themselves are perhaps not very surprising in retrospect (lots of certificates are expired or have other problems!) but there are some gems (like 1000 different certificates that have duplicate private keys!) and it is valuable to see how much minor dysfunction is below the surface.

Weaknesses: Well, it's a bit of a dry characterization that is not surprising for the most part. However, it is still valuable unless it has been reported previously.

Comments to Authors: Thanks for an interesting read - I've always wondered about certificates.

Please include your key results / contributions in the abstract and introduction. What are they? For instance, near the end of the paper it says "the more popular a site, the more likely it supports SSL, and the fewer the problems". I did not get this from the results I read, perhaps because there are so many small results that it's hard to keep the overall thrust together.

I was confused about self-certs. You describe these as for a host, but I believe it is common enough for an organization like a university to self-cert themselves as a root. Is this true, and can you separate this from other "missing root" errors? Basically, it is likely not an error for the users.

Can you tell us for each error what is common browser behavior? This would help to put the errors in perspective; I wasn't sure if they would all result in a user alert, or not.

The error that surprised me most was that mismatches between CN and domain are very common. Surely this is a significant security problem? Please say more about what it means in practice.

Can you sketch a little more of the TLS mechanics wrt certificates? You imply that a server sends the certificate chain on SSL connect. I thought it was a multi-step process.

Reviewer #3

Strengths: It's good to have quantitative numbers on what everyone already suspects: that the x509 system is badly deployed and vulnerable.

Weaknesses: There are no surprises or take-away points from this paper that are not already published.

Comments to Authors: The main benefit of this paper in my mind is to more completely quantify what people already know and have previously studied [4,7,9]. That said, it's not clear to me that a more in-depth study of something that's known to be broken will be of interest to the IMC audience.

The text in S4.1 makes it sound like you scanned 1M _clients_ on port 443; you really scanned 1M popularly advertized web servers, right? The "acceptable use" clause in the CFP would make the former a Bad Thing, so you may want to consider making this more clear.

For this paper to be accepted, I would really like to see a more concrete example of the impact on users: are the sites with broken certificates still being visited (and thus people are just ignoring the "security") or are these just accidental clicking or probes. One thing that was not clear was the frequency distribution of certs: how common are the most common certs and what does that tail look like? Are there any very common certs that are broken and people keep using them?

I don't understand why multiple geographic locations at the same time is a benefit for your active probing or why different locations have different results: where there really connectivity problems or where you exploiting CDN phenomena? Fig 6 seems to show that the results were mostly comparable, no?

Figures 5 (a), 5(b) and 6 should probably be collapsed down to a single "stacked" bar graph for ease of comparison and space savings.

I thought that the explanation of the x509 protocol in in S2 was something that most people knew and could probably have been removed.

In general, I think a lot could have been done to shorten descriptions in the paper and make better use of space: maybe this points to this data being presented in a short paper format?

Reviewer #4

Strengths: The authors processed very large sets of collected data, a impressive amount of work. The results present an overall picture of the x509 certificate deployment, with various pieces of interesting results.

Weaknesses: The goal of the paper seems a bit unclear to me. After reading the paper one ends with lots data but a vague picture of the current stage of affairs. The paper started by claiming that "it always has been felt that the certification processes of this (x509) PKI may lack in stringency, resulting in a deployment where many certificates do not meet the requirements of a secure PKI.", but did not offer a concrete conclusion at the end with regard to that statement, i.e. does/not the deployment lack stringency? If so, what may be the causes of the problems? What need to change?

Comments to Authors: In this paper the authors processed impressive amount of collected data, and collected a variety of interesting stats regarding the deployment of x509 certificates (e.g. fig-3, the decreasing use of MD5; fig-4, more than 100K hosts sharing one single certificate?! Fig-5 & fig-6, percentages of different errors--but some inconsistency between the figures and text, see below).

High level comment: the overall results seem just like a collection, a bit lacking of stringency and focus.

The paper stated that "we evaluated our datasets with respect to the properties of certificates and certification chains, also correlating this with specific host properties (e. g. popularity)" Maybe the paper could be made stronger by first nailing down exactly what kinds of "properties" of the certificates that the paper would want to *focus* on, and for what purpose (e.g. is the goal to examine the effectiveness of the certificates in protecting the data).

Without a clearly defined focus, the results look rather diverse.

Reviewer #5

Strengths: The first study of X.509 Certificates in the wild for the purpose of determining the strength of PKI certification that focus on highly ranked domains and performed live monitoring of SSL/TLS to focus on used certificates, aiming at filtering out invalid certificates. The study reveals several pressing problems of the PKI infrastructure.
Extensive implementation and setup to capture SSL flows at a high speed and to comprehensively study deployed X.509 certificates. The authors successfully combined multiple tools (TNAPI, Bro, SNI, PlanetLab etc), which requires a substantial amount of effort.
Well written paper. Clearly explains the motivation of their study and their methodology.
Interesting statistics on the types of ciphers and their frequency used in SSL/TLS. Interesting statistics on how many times the same certificate occurs on multiple hosts.
Interesting statistics on the validity of the certificate chains. Some unexpected errors were found. 60% of trust chains were valid. It's good to have quantitative numbers on what everyone already suspects: that the x509 system is badly deployed and vulnerable.

Weaknesses: The methodology is quite straight forward and used a technique introduced in [13,14,15,16]. No innovative techniques were introduced.

It would be great if the authors were able to motivate all the statistics presented in the paper. For example, knowing the frequency with which ciphers appear in SSL would help us do ...

Related work: Mishari Al Mishari, Emiliano De Cristofaro, Karim El Defrawy and Gene Tsudik, "Harvesting SSL Certificate Data to Mitigate Web-Fraud", another large scale study of certificates.

Comments to Authors: Overall, I enjoyed reading the paper, I learned aspects of the real PKI deployment and obtained several statistics regarding the PKI. The authors could do a better job motivating the use of their statistics. It is a good paper. Its main weakness is that it is not introducing any non-obvious measurement techniques. But it is asking good questions and the answers the authors obtain are satisfactory.

Response from the Authors

In the following, we describe the major changes we have made to our original submission, as requested by the reviewers. The focus of the paper was improved by stating our goals and contributions in the introduction, as well as listing properties that we concentrate on. We restructured the paper to improve the storyline: basically, we mimic the steps that a client executes while validating a certificate (errors in certificate chains, host names etc.). This is followed by an investigation of certificate properties that impact the security of a SSL/TLS association (e.g., hash algorithms and public keys). Finally, we turn to deployment issues and discuss the security relevance of our findings. For every certificate property that we discuss, we added an introductory explanation that describes the importance of the property in question, and how a correct certificate should look like in this respect. At several points, we highlight typical client behavior when encountering a faulty certificate, in particular bad certification chains and self-signed certificates. As requested by the reviewers, we clarified the distinction between Grid and non-Grid certificates. Grid certificates are now only discussed when presenting the properties of SSL/TLS traffic, whereas they are filtered out from the discussion of certificate properties. As was proposed, we extended the discussion of data in some sections and reduced it in others. For example, we shortened the discussion of certificates from different locations where the results are not surprising. However, we disagree with the reviewers in the point that globally distributed scans should not be expected to show differences in the result; therefore, we added a section that outlines interesting differences encountered between our scanning locations. Further discussions of issuers of the most frequent certificates or keys affected by the Debian OpenSSL vulnerability have been added. The validity of certificates and host names contained therein is presented in greater detail, with reference to the effects in clients. We highlight that only about 18% of all certificates are actually counted as valid in a client. To make the paper more accessible, we furthermore updated the background section and added more information about X.509. In light of recent attacks on CAs (StartCom, DigiNotar), we moreover included descriptions of these attacks. Last but not least, we would like to thank our anonymous reviewers for their valuable feedback, and wish to particularly highlight the work of reviewer A.

On the Prevalence and Characteristics of MPLS Deployments in the Open Internet

Joel Sommers
Colgate University
jsommers@colgate.edu

Brian Eriksson
Boston University
eriksson@cs.bu.edu

Paul Barford
University of Wisconsin-Madison and Qualys, Inc.
pb@cs.wisc.edu

ABSTRACT

Multi-Protocol Label Switching (MPLS) is a mechanism that enables service providers to specify virtual paths through IP networks. The use of MPLS in the open Internet (*i.e.*, public end-to-end paths) has important implications for users and network neutrality since MPLS is frequently used in traffic engineering applications today. In this paper we present a longitudinal study of the prevalence and characteristics of MPLS deployments in the open Internet. We use path measurement data collected over the past 3.5 years by the CAIDA Archipelago project (Ark), which consist of over 10 billion individual traceroutes between hosts throughout the Internet. We use two different techniques for identifying MPLS paths in Ark data: direct observation via ICMP extensions that include MPLS label information, and inference using a Bayesian data fusion methodology. Our direct observation method can only identify uniform-mode tunnels, which very likely underestimates MPLS deployments. Nonetheless, our results show that the total number of tunnels observed in a given measurement period has varied widely over time with the largest deployments in tier-1 providers. About 7% of all autonomous systems deploy MPLS and this level of deployment has been consistent over the past three years. The average length of an MPLS tunnel has decreased from 4 hops in 2008 to 3 hops in 2011, and the path length distribution is heavily skewed. About 25% of all paths in 2011 cross at least one MPLS tunnel, while 4% cross more than one. Finally, data observed in MPLS headers suggest that many ASes employ some types of traffic classification and engineering in their tunnels.

Categories and Subject Descriptors

C.2.3 [**Network Operations**]: Network management, Network monitoring; C.2.5 [**Local and Wide-Area Networks**]: Internet (*e.g.*, TCP/IP; C.4 [**Performance of Systems**]: Measurement Techniques

General Terms

Algorithms, Design, Experimentation, Measurement, Performance

IMC'11, November 2–4, 2011, Berlin, Germany.

Keywords

MPLS, `traceroute`, traffic engineering, tunnels

1. INTRODUCTION

In the late 1990's, the limitations and inflexibility in IP routing and forwarding coupled with the on-going quest to improve switching performance led to the development of Multiprotocol Label Switching (MPLS). Label switching[1] was envisioned and designed as a simple mechanism that would operate between layers 2 and 3 in the standard Internet protocol stack, and enable efficient lookups at each hop on a designated path. Standardization efforts in the IETF began in 1997 [14] and have resulted in an assortment of drafts and RFCs that define and specify the protocol. Today, MPLS is a standard feature in routers and is available on a wide variety of platforms from many different vendors.

Along with improved switching speeds, MPLS was quickly recognized as a highly useful protocol for traffic engineering [10]. MPLS affords the ability to configure multi-hop tunnels that supersede shortest path routes for definable traffic aggregates. It enables service providers to operate their infrastructures in a fashion that more directly addresses their business and operational requirements. Anecdotal reports suggest that MPLS is currently used by service providers in a variety of ways including facilitating traffic engineering, implementation of multi-service networks (including virtual private networks), and improving robustness [34]. Despite its appeal and implications of its broad use, to the best of our knowledge there are no studies to date that provide a systematic empirical assessment of MPLS deployments in the Internet.

In this paper, we present a longitudinal analysis of MPLS deployments in the open Internet (*i.e.*, paths that are not part of virtual private networks). The goal of our work is to establish a broad empirical baseline for MPLS since tunnels have a direct impact on traffic behavior and measurement, and have significant implications for network neutrality, which is an increasingly active topic of conversation. We seek to answer questions such as: How many networks use MPLS? Has the use of MPLS grown over time? What are the characteristics of individual MPLS tunnels? How likely is it that my traffic will encounter an MPLS tunnel? To address these questions, we require measurements of a large set of Internet paths conducted over a period of years.

Studies of Internet-wide phenomena related to end-to-end, router-level path properties typically rely on active probe-based measurement tools such as `traceroute` for gathering data. At first glance, MPLS appears to present an insurmountable challenge to standard TTL-limited active probing methods that rely on layer 3 messaging

[1] Originally it was called "tag switching" [30] and had roots in Ipsilon's flow management protocol [29].

since MPLS is not a layer 3 protocol. However, relatively recent extensions to the ICMP protocol [12] that enable it to include the entire MPLS label stack overcome this challenge (as long as the measurement tool and target routers implement the extensions and the router is not configured to hide the tunnel). Traceroute-style path measurements that include MPLS label stacks are the starting point for our work.

We use data collected by the Ark project [22], which, since 2008 includes MPLS label stacks wherever they are in use and visible on an end-to-end path. Network operators can configure MPLS tunnels in such a way as to hide them from `traceroute`. Thus, our work relies on tunnels that are configured in uniform (visible) mode, which we describe below. The Ark infrastructure and methodologies have been designed to efficiently measure all routable /24's in the Internet. Since its inception, Ark has conducted over 10B individual `traceroute` measurements, and as such offers are a compelling source of data for our longitudinal study.

Our analysis of MPLS labels in Ark path measurement data reveals a broad set of characteristics about the deployment and use of the protocol. In particular, we find that the total number of tunnels observed in any measurement period has varied widely over time from a low of about 200K in '09 to a recent high of around 350K. Curiously, we find that the variability of tunnel deployments correlates closely with key economic indicators. Roughly 7% of all autonomous systems use MPLS on some subset of their paths with the largest deployments in tier-1 providers. This level of deployment has been relatively stable over the past three years. We also find that the average length of an MPLS tunnel has decreased from 4 hops in 2008 to 3 hops in 2011. The tunnel length distribution is heavily skewed with over 90% of tunnels at 7 hops or less, however some tunnels extend beyond 15 hops. Approximately 25% of all paths in 2011 cross at least one MPLS tunnel, while 4% cross more than one, and data observed in MPLS headers suggest that many ASes employ some kinds of traffic classification and engineering in their tunnels.

While label-based analysis enables a compelling characterization of MPLS path properties, it precludes analysis of other path measurement data archives (*e.g.*, Skitter [13]) that do not include labels. Analysis of data sets that lack the ICMP extension information could expand our perspective and enable a more comprehensive longitudinal analysis. To address this problem we develop an MPLS tunnel identification method that is based on analysis of round trip time measurements instead of labels. The observation is that with some MPLS configurations, when a packet's TTL expires, the ICMP time exceeded message will be encapsulated in an MPLS header and forwarded *to the end of the tunnel* prior to being sent back to the source host. This observation is the basis for a Bayesian inference method that we show to be effective for identifying MPLS tunnels. Applying this method to additional data sets to gain a broader view of MPLS deployments over time is a goal for future work.

A summary of the key findings our work are as follows. First, the increasing trend in deployments over the past three years and the wide use by tier-1 providers means that it is increasingly likely that packets will encounter an MPLS tunnel. Second, tunnels are likely to span the entire edge-to-edge distance of a transit provider, with typical transit times on the order of 10s of milliseconds. Third, our examination of the use of traffic classifiers indicates that while multiple classes are not uncommon, the diversity of classes has not changed over the past three years.

The remainder of this paper is organized as follows. In Section 2, we provide an overview of MPLS, how MPLS interacts with `traceroute`, and our label-based method for identifying MPLS hops on an end-to-end path. In Section 3, we provide details on the Ark data set and report the details of our label-based MPLS deployment study. In Section 4, we describe our inference-based method for identifying MPLS paths and report our findings on applying this method to the Ark data. We summarize our work and describe next steps in our study in Section 6.

2. MPLS AND TRACEROUTE

MPLS is typically thought of as a protocol that exists between layers 2 and 3 of the Internet protocol stack. Fundamentally, it is path-based encapsulation and forwarding protocol that adds a 32-bit header to packets as they enter an MPLS tunnel, or label-switched path (LSP). We use the terms tunnel and LSP interchangeably in this paper. The MPLS header consists of a 20-bit label, 8-bit time-to-live (TTL) field, 3-bit traffic class field, and a 1-bit end of label stack field.

Specific labels are applied to packets based on forwarding equivalence class (FEC), which is a generalization of longest-prefix match. As packets traverse an MPLS tunnel, forwarding decisions are made based on *exact* matching of the MPLS label. Labels are only locally significant between a pair of routers, so as packets traverse a tunnel, labels are swapped (overwritten) prior to forwarding. Hierarchies of tunnels can also be created (*i.e.*, an already-tunneled packet can enter a new tunnel); stacks of MPLS headers can be used for this purpose.

MPLS tunnels must be configured (and labels distributed) on each label switch router (LSR) along a designated path (series of LSRs), and supersede layer 3 routes. The flexibility to define paths through a network not simply based on shortest paths makes MPLS highly attractive for traffic engineering tasks. Details on MPLS can be found in [31], and several other IETF RFCs.

Our work relies on recent modifications to routers and `traceroute` programs that implement extensions to ICMP specified in RFC 4950. These extensions permit the inclusion of the entire MPLS label stack (*i.e.*, *all* MPLS header information) in the ICMP message that is returned to a source host [12]. Thus, it is this information included in ICMP time exceeded messages that are generated as part of the `traceroute` process that allows us to positively identify a router as participating in an MPLS tunnel.

There are two basic ways in which the IP time-to-live (TTL) field is processed in the presence of an MPLS tunnel. These are referred to as *uniform mode* and *pipe mode* [9], and they determine whether an MPLS tunnel is visible to a public user of `traceroute` or not[2]. Figure 1 illustrates these two modes of operation.

In pipe mode, the MPLS tunnel is not exposed to a `traceroute` user. At LSR B in Figure 1, the IP TTL is decremented by one and inspected upon router ingress. After that, the packet is encapsulated in an MPLS header and forwarded to the next LSR along the path. The MPLS header that is constructed at the first LSR is initialized with a prespecified TTL value, typically 255. Upon egress from a pipe mode tunnel, the MPLS header is removed and the TTL value in the IP header is unchanged. Thus, the MPLS TTL field has no relationship to the IP TTL in a pipe-mode tunnel, and the IP TTL is only decremented by one regardless of the number of LSRs that switch the packet through the tunnel.

Note that with the pipe model, the first router of an MPLS tunnel is visible, but the ICMP time exceeded response generated from the

[2]Note that the uniform and pipe modes more commonly refer to tunneling models to support differentiated services in MPLS networks [19]. We use these terms similar to the way in which they are used to describe TTL processing in MPLS networks in RFC 3443 [9].

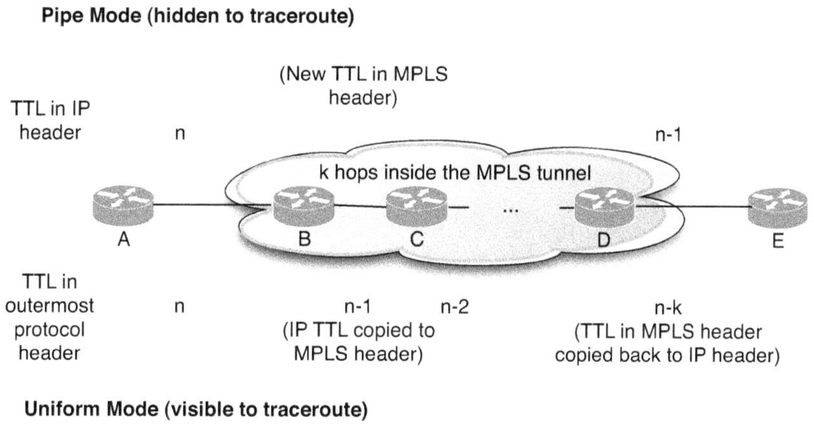

Figure 1: Two modes of IP header TTL processing in the presence of an MPLS tunnel: pipe and uniform.

router (if the IP TTL is decremented to zero) does not indicate that the packet expired at the edge of a tunnel, since it has not actually entered one yet. Thus, there is no indication to a `traceroute` user that an MPLS tunnel is traversed, and only the ingress router is visible at all. (Note that penultimate hop-popping (PHP) does not affect this picture from the standpoint of `traceroute` [9]. We discuss PHP further in § 3.3.) The upshot is that identifying pipe mode tunnels with end-to-end measurements remains a significant measurement challenge and one that we do not address in this paper.

In uniform mode, the LSRs along an MPLS tunnel are visible to a `traceroute` user. At the first LSR (B in the figure), the IP TTL is decremented by one and inspected upon router ingress, just as in the pipe model. Upon encapsulation in an MPLS header, however, the IP TTL is copied into the MPLS header. At each LSR along the tunnel, the TTL in the MPLS header is decremented by one. Upon egress from a uniform mode tunnel, the MPLS TTL field is copied back to the IP header. If the TTL falls to zero at any router along the tunnel, an ICMP time exceeded message will be generated and sent back to the source of the original packet. Thus, *all* routers in the tunnel are visible to a user of `traceroute`. Importantly, only if the router implements MPLS extensions for ICMP [12] will a `traceroute` user be able to clearly identify the fact that the packet's TTL expired while inside an MPLS tunnel.

Interestingly, uniform mode is the default mode of operation for Cisco and Juniper routers (among others) [4, 5]. This behavior is likely due to language in the MPLS architectural RFC (3031) that specifies that the total number of hops through a tunnel `SHOULD` be reflected in the IP TTL when the packet emerges from the tunnel. Also, it is important to note that pipe and uniform mode TTL processing can be configured on a per-LSP basis. Even nested tunnels can have different visibility characteristics (*i.e.*, while the innermost tunnel may be visible via `traceroute`, a nested tunnel may not be). From a practical perspective, this means that network operators must explicitly configure routers *not* to propagate the IP TTL to the MPLS header, thus hiding tunnels from the public's eye.

Another important impact that MPLS tunnels can have is on delay measurements of individual `traceroute` packets. When the TTL of a packet is decremented to zero inside an MPLS tunnel (in uniform mode, since that is the only way that an outsider can observe an MPLS tunnel), the ICMP time exceeded message may need to be re-encapsulated in an MPLS header and forwarded to the end of the tunnel [8]. If the LSR at which the ICMP packet is generated does not have sufficient information (*e.g.*, routes imported via BGP), the packet will be re-encapsulated and traverse the entire length of the tunnel. At the end of the tunnel, the ICMP message can be routed back to the source host. The result is that the `traceroute` output will show roughly equivalent delay for the series of hops along the MPLS tunnel. In that case, we would measure the latency across the tunnel to be approximately zero. This observation is the starting point for our tunnel inference method described in Section 4.

While we focus on measurement of MPLS tunnels from outside a service provider's network, internal network operators can use other mechanisms for measuring and troubleshooting MPLS LSPs. For example RFC 4379 describes MPLS-based versions of ping and traceroute for this purpose [24].

3. ARK DATA ANALYSIS

In this section we present our analysis of MPLS tunnels and their characteristics as observed in the CAIDA IPv4 Routed /24 AS Links Dataset [22]. Our focus in this section is on characteristics of MPLS tunnels that can be directly observed through ICMP extension information.

3.1 Data and Limitations

Since we do not have insight into the ways in which labels have been assigned, or generally how MPLS has been configured in a given provider network, we use a pragmatic definition of *tunnel* in our data analysis. Our goal in the present work is not to try to identify *how* different MPLS tunnels have been configured, but rather to report and analyze their observed characteristics. Our working definition of *tunnel* is any consecutive series of label-switched routers within the same autonomous system[3]. As described in Section 2, we can identify LSRs by the presence of MPLS extension information in an ICMP time exceeded message from a router. Note that with this definition, the length of a tunnel refers only to the innermost label switched path (*i.e.*, the length of the tunnel identified by the sequence of labels at the bottom of the label stack) and does not consider nested LSPs. (We comment on nested tunnels and nested tunnel lengths below.) Note also that within an AS, we may see some number of layer 3 (IP) hops before entering a tunnel. We

[3]In our analysis, we detected no instances of a tunnel that spanned multiple ASes.

may also see some number of layer 3 hops *after* exiting a tunnel, as we discuss below.

The data that we use are collected as part of the Archipelago (Ark) project, and include `traceroute` measurements to all routed /24 prefixes in the IPv4 Internet, initiated from a set of widely distributed probing hosts. The probing tool used in Ark is Scamper [26], and the specific `traceroute` method used is ICMP Paris [28]. The Ark project was initiated in 2007, and data are available starting from September of that year. However, the version of Scamper used at that time did not support the ICMP extensions for MPLS. Support for those extensions was introduced into Scamper in early 2008, and a version of Scamper with support for ICMP extensions for MPLS was rolled out to Ark in mid-May of 2008[4] [21, 27]. For that reason, we restrict our analysis in this section to the Ark data from June 2008 to August 2011. Lastly, rather than analyzing *all* the available Ark data from June 2008 onward, we selected the first full set of data available for each month resulting a corpus of over 250M individual `traceroute` measurements. Investigating MPLS deployment dynamics at finer levels of granularity is a topic for future study. In our analysis below, the scope of our characterizations is bounded by the Ark measurement data, and placement of probing nodes. However, the Ark project has gone to great lengths to be comprehensive and we believe it provide an important and representative view of Internet structure.

Along with the Ark data, we used the CAIDA IPv4 prefix to autonomous system (AS) mapping data, which is based on analysis of Routeviews data [1]. We also use UCLA Cyclops data to classify a given AS as a tier 1, large ISP, small ISP, or stub network [2]. We use these data to perform AS-specific analyses, and to identify the number and characteristics of ASes that appear to be employing MPLS for traffic management. Since the prefix-to-AS mapping data are based on a measured perspective of Internet routing activity, there are imperfections and complications. In our analyses, we omit any `traceroute` paths that have IP addresses for which we do not know the AS number, and any IP addresses that have multiple ASes identified in the prefix-to-AS mapping. We do this to simplify our analyses of specific ASes. We note that the overall amount of data discarded is small (under 1%), thus we do not believe this materially affects our overall results.

For many analyses in this section, we wanted to identify the set of *unique* tunnels within an AS. We found that either using the sequence of IP addresses of the LSRs, or using the sequence of MPLS labels at the bottom of the label stack gave virtually equivalent results (differences were under 0.01% of the total number of observed tunnels).

Finally, as we discuss above, our analysis relies on the presence of ICMP extension information to positively identify MPLS LSRs. Thus, our analysis is limited to MPLS tunnels that have been configured in uniform mode. While we are certain that there are tunnels configured in pipe mode that evade our analysis, we have no way to presently quantify or characterize these tunnels. Indeed, there are ISP-published maps of MPLS networks for which we do not see any (or exceedingly few) LSRs in our data (*e.g.*, see Sprint's [6] network map and other maps available at the Internet Topology Zoo project [7]). Moreover, we have no visibility into any MPLS virtual private networks since our measurements are taken from hosts attached to the public Internet.

[4]The roll-out of a new version of Scamper corresponded to the passing of the Internet Measurement Conference paper deadline that year.

3.2 MPLS Prevalence

We begin by examining the prevalence of MPLS tunnels, and how many ASes appear to use MPLS. We turn first to the total number of ASes that we observe to use MPLS. In the top plot of Figure 2, we see this number has remained fairly steady over the past 3 years, at around 7%.

The bottom plot of Figure 2 shows the fraction of ASes, classified by AS type, that are empirically observed to employ MPLS. We use the UCLA Cyclops data to perform the AS classification [2]. (Note that these classification data are only available starting in October 2008.) We observe that nearly all tier 1 providers use MPLS (in October 2008 there were 8 tier 1 providers, and in August 2011 there were 11). We observe a lesser percentage of large ISPs (50–55%), an even smaller percentage of small ISPs (25–30%), and few stub networks (around 5%) to use MPLS. Because there are so many stub networks (13817 in August 2011), the overall percentage of ASes using MPLS is rather low (again, around 7%).

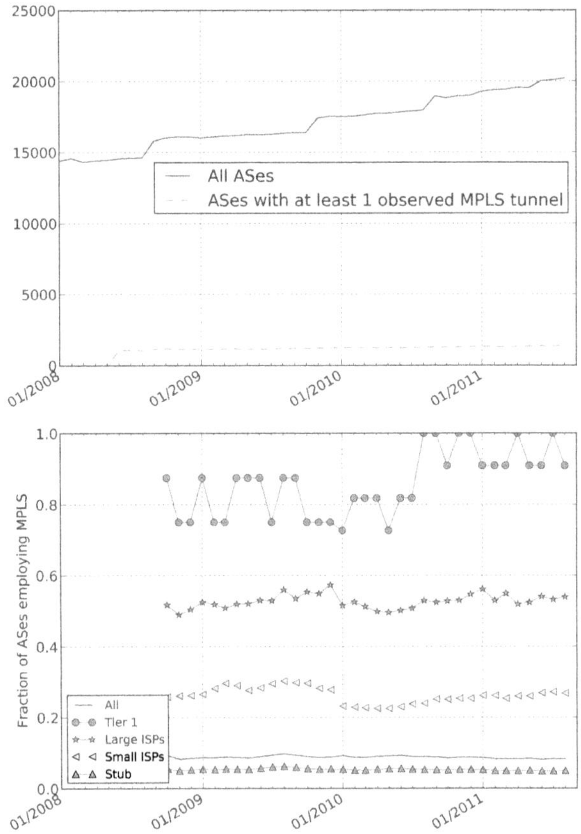

Figure 2: Comparison of the total number of ASes seen in our Ark dataset versus the number of ASes for which at least 1 MPLS tunnel is observed (top), and the fraction of ASes by AS type that employ MPLS (bottom).

Figure 3 plots the total number of unique tunnels observed in a given measurement period over the past three years. The figure shows a significant dip in the total number of tunnels beginning in '08, a rebound in mid '09 and a steady increase to the current peak of nearly 350K tunnels. For comparison, we also plot the Dow Jones Industrial Average in the figure[5]. Interestingly, the total number of MPLS tunnels over time appears to indirectly track this eco-

[5]Data obtained from `http://finance.yahoo.com/`.

nomic indicator (and other, similar indicators such as the S&P 500, not shown). So, while it is apparent from Figure 2 that the sheer number of ASes using MPLS is independent of economic activity, the deployment of tunnels *within* these ASes roughly correlates with economic conditions. Our conjecture is that this phenomenon reflects merger and acquisition activity within the telecom industry. We have engaged ISPs to better understand the underlying reasons behind our observations, and we hope to report on our findings in the future.

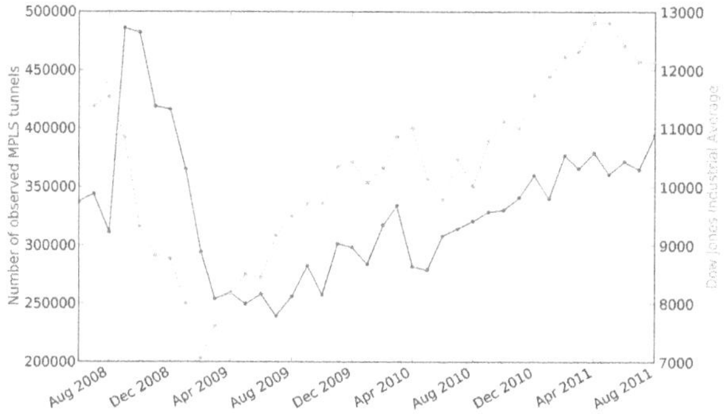

Figure 3: The total number of visible MPLS tunnels over time (solid line). The Dow Jones Industrial Average is plotted (dotted line) for reference over the same time period.

Figure 4 shows the number of unique tunnels deployed by a small set of ASes over the past three years. First, we see a sharp drop in the number of tunnels deployed by AS7018. This drop mirrors the drop in the total number of tunnels seen in Figure 3. We see from the figure that other ASes show some variability over time in the number of deployed tunnels. For example, AS1273 emerges in early 2010 from very few (nearly zero) observed tunnels. On the other hand, the number of tunnels observed from AS3320 drops to zero in mid-2010. We conjecture that in addition to economic factors, there are likely AS policy decisions (*e.g.*, to change tunnels to "invisible" pipe mode, or to reveal previously hidden tunnels) that play a role in the observed variability.

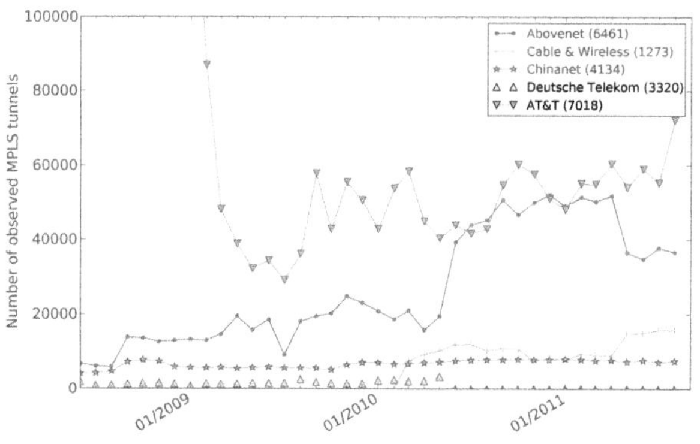

Figure 4: Number of observed MPLS tunnels over time across selected ASes.

Figure 5 provides another perspective on the number of deployed tunnels per AS. The figure shows empirical cumulative distribution functions of the number of observed tunnels per AS for six-month time intervals over the measurement period. We see that 20% of all ASes have fewer than 10 tunnels. We also see that 80% of ASes are observed to have under 200 tunnels, and that about 10% of ASes have at least 1000 tunnels.

Table 1 identifies the numbers and names of the top 10 ASes in terms of the number of observed MPLS tunnels. The table shows the top 10 ASes for six month periods starting from mid-2008. These results support the intuition and evidence in the bottom plot of Figure 2 that larger and more complex infrastructures are more likely to use MPLS tunnels.

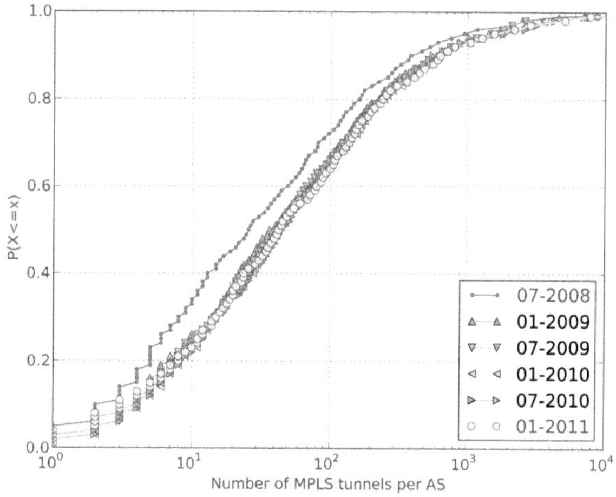

Figure 5: Empirical cumulative distribution functions of the number of visible MPLS tunnels per AS. CDFs are plotted for six month periods starting 6/2008. (Note that the x-axis is on log scale.)

Lastly, we examine the fraction of paths probed by Ark that include one or more MPLS tunnels. Figure 6 shows the fraction of probing paths that cross *at least* 1 MPLS tunnel, and the fraction of paths that cross exactly 1, 2, or 3 tunnels. Interestingly, although only about 7% of all ASes are observed to use MPLS, about 25% of all probing paths crossed at least 1 tunnel in the most recent measurement data. Approximately 4% of all paths cross more than one MPLS tunnel; this observation holds across the three years. We can see that the increase in likelihood of crossing at least 1 MPLS tunnel from about 20% in June 2008 to about 25% in August 2011 is primarily due to higher occurrences of encountering a single tunnel on a path. This result is consistent with the fact that larger networks are more likely to appear on end-to-end paths and are more likely to deploy MPLS.

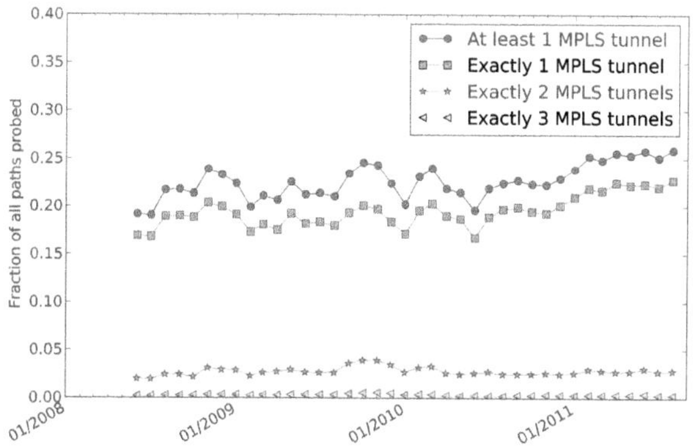

Figure 6: Fraction of paths with some MPLS.

Table 1: MPLS heavyweights: the top 10 ASes in terms of number of observed MPLS tunnels.

Rank	7–12/2008	1–6/2009	7–12/2009	1–6/2010	7–12/2010	1–6/2011
1	7018 AT&T	7018 AT&T	7018 AT&T	7018 AT&T	7018 AT&T	7018 AT&T
2	6389 Bellsouth	6389 Bellsouth	6461 Abovenet	6461 Abovenet	6461 Abovenet	6461 Abovenet
3	6461 Abovenet	6461 Abovenet	6389 Bellsouth	19262 Verizon	4837 China-169	6830 UPC
4	6453 Tata	3269 Telecom Italia	3269 Telecom Italia	6389 Bellsouth	6453 Tata	6453 Tata
5	3292 TDC	6453 Tata	19262 Verizon	6453 Tata	1273 CW	174 Cogent
6	4134 Chinanet	19262 Verizon	6453 Tata	4837 China-169	6830 UPC	1273 CW
7	4230 Embratel	4230 Embratel	4230 Embratel	4230 Embratel	4134 Chinanet	4837 China-169
8	19262 Verizon	4134 Chinanet	4837 China-169	4134 Chinanet	19262 Verizon	4134 Chinanet
9	5462 Virgin	4837 China-169	4134 Chinanet	6774 Belgacom	6774 Belgacom	4230 Embratel
10	4837 China-169	2914 NTT	2914 NTT	1273 CW	4230 Embratel	10318 Cablevision SA

Surprisingly, there were some probing paths that crossed 7 MPLS tunnels, which was the maximum we observed. Also surprisingly, within a single AS we observed multiple, separate tunnels in a single probing path. That is, from the `traceroute` output, we observed a series of MPLS LSR hops within an AS, followed by one or more "normal" IP hops, followed by another series of MPLS LSR hops. The frequency of occurrence of either many tunnels (> 4) on a single path, or multiple tunnels within a single AS was quite rare (about 0.3% of all paths in May 2011).

3.3 MPLS Tunnel Characteristics

We now examine characteristics of observed MPLS tunnels, both globally and within different ASes.

We first examine first-order path length statistics in ASes. We consider three segments of a path through an AS: IP hops *before* a tunnel is entered, hops *within* a tunnel, and IP hops *after* a tunnel, prior to exiting the AS. For this analysis, we omitted any paths through an AS that contained multiple separate tunnels. Figure 7 shows the average number of pre-tunnel, post-tunnel, and in-tunnel hops over the past three years. We see that the average length of an MPLS tunnel has decreased over the measurement period from just over 4 hops, to around 3 hops. This change likely is due to changes in operational policy or underlying infrastructure. We also see that the average number of pre- and post-tunnel hops has remained roughly constant over the past three years, at around 1 hop and 1.8 hops, respectively.

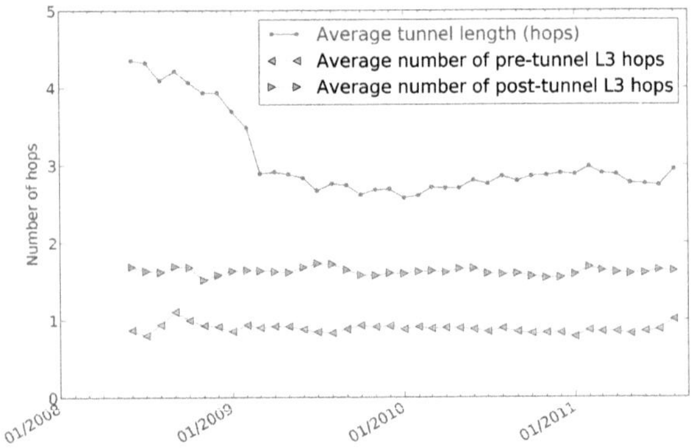

Figure 7: Average number of hops before, inside, and after MPLS tunnels for all ASes.

Figure 8 plots average tunnel lengths over time for 4 different ASes. We observe a variety of behaviors. While the average length of a tunnel in AS7018 has decreased by around 1 hop over the past three years, the average length of a tunnel in AS6461 has increased by around 2 hops. The average length of a tunnel in AS4230 has increased, but is quite short, and the plot for AS3320 shows that tunnels in that AS are currently an average of about 1 hop long.

An interesting phenomenon suggested by Figure 8 is that of very short 1-hop MPLS tunnels. In Figure 9, we show the fraction of tunnels over time that consist of one hop, for a set of ASes and globally across all tunnels. We again see a variety of behaviors. While most ASes have very few tunnels of just 1 hop, the majority of tunnels in AS4134 consist of only one hop, and tunnel lengths in AS3320 have decreased to close to a single hop.

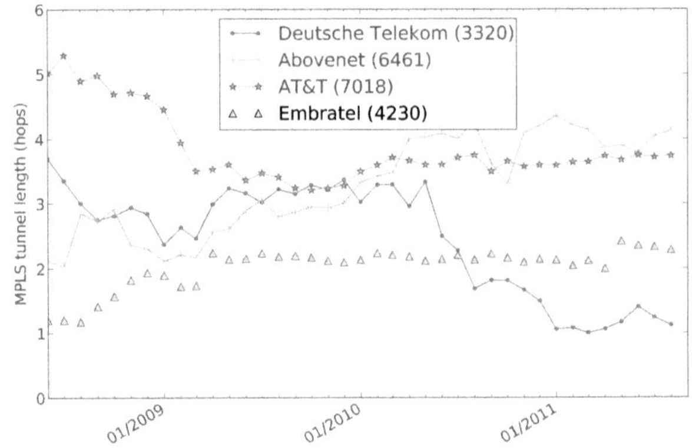

Figure 8: Average MPLS tunnel lengths for selected ASes over time.

While there are certainly operational policy decisions and other configuration factors which may lead to the observation of 1-hop tunnels (*e.g.*, there may be nested tunnels that are configured in pipe mode, making some segment of the tunnel invisible to `traceroute`), one simple reason we might see such short tunnels is the following. Consider the network in Figure 1, and assume that there are only three LSRs in the tunnel (B, C, and D). When a packet enters the tunnel at LSR B, it will be encapsulated in an MPLS header and forwarded to C. C might then do a label switch and forward it to D. At that point, the label is popped and the IP packet emerges from the MPLS tunnel.

In `traceroute` output, router B would appear to be a "normal" layer 3 hop since the packet has not yet been encapsulated, and routers C and D would appear to be MPLS routers. Thus, we would observe a tunnel of length 2.

Consider, however, if the ISP has configured routers to do penultimate hop-popping (PHP), which is basically an optimization to avoid encapsulating a packet that has only one more hop in a tunnel [31], and to reduce label stack popping load on a tunnel egress router. In this case, we would only observe router C to employ MPLS; D would appear as a "normal" layer 3 hop. Given our definition of MPLS tunnel, we consider this to be a one-hop tunnel,

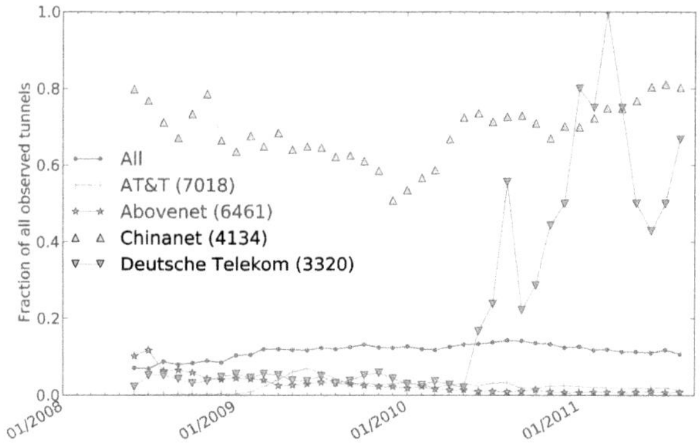

Figure 9: Fraction of tunnels that consist of one hop, over time.

though it is arguable whether this is, in fact, a two-hop tunnel. Given the measurements at hand, we cannot say for certain that an ISP is doing PHP, so the best we can say is that the tunnel is of length 1, and there was one more IP hop in the AS prior to egress.

Next, we examine the distribution of tunnel lengths, both in terms of number of hops, and in latency (milliseconds). Figure 10 shows complementary CDFs for all tunnels, and for three ASes. Note that the y-axis is log scale. Lines in each plot correspond to six month periods, starting in January 2009. We choose this form of plot to emphasize the tail of the distribution. We see that the distribution is skewed: for all tunnels, 90% are 7 hops or fewer, but there are instances of long tunnels, even beyond 15 hops. Plots for individual ASes are somewhat similar to the plot for all ASes. Interestingly, we observe some inflation in path lengths over time for AS6461.

Figure 11 shows similar complementary cumulative distribution function plots of tunnel lengths for all tunnels and the same three ASes, but now considering length in terms of milliseconds. Again, note that the y-axis is log scale. Lines in each plot correspond to six month periods, starting in January 2009. We observe that half of all tunnel lengths are approximately *zero* milliseconds in length, 90% are 150 milliseconds or less. (Refer to Section 2 for an explanation of why we may see close to zero latency across a tunnel.) We also see that some tunnels exceed 300 milliseconds in length. Tunnel latency distributions for the three ASes differ more obviously than the tunnel hop-length distributions. While the majority of tunnels in ASes 7018 and 6461 are relatively short, 10% of the tunnels in the most recent six months for AS6453 exceeded 340 milliseconds.

The above analysis considers only the length of inner-most tunnels, *i.e.*, not nested tunnels. In Figure 12 we plot the distribution of lengths of nested tunnels for all ASes for six time periods (*cf.* the upper left plot in Figure 10). Interestingly, while there is no clear distributional trend in the similar plot in Figure 10, it appears from Figure 12 that nested tunnels appear to be growing longer.

Lastly, we examine the use of multiple depths of label stacks, and the use of different traffic class identifiers. The main uses of label stacking are for supporting VPN services, for more sophisticated traffic engineering, and for LSP protection ("fast reroute") in the event of link or router failure [34]. Since it is highly unlikely that the label stacks we observe are due to VPN services since the Ark nodes are connected to the public Internet, we hypothesize that observed uses of label stacking are due to traffic and network resilience engineering. Figure 13 shows the fraction of tunnels using up to three MPLS labels. Six separate months are shown for all tunnels and for three selected ASes. We see that typically just over 80% of all tunnels have used a stack of only one label, and virtually no ASes use stacks of three labels. (We observed only a single instance of a label stack of four labels, which was AS3549 in April 2011.) The three ASes shown exhibit much different behavior. While AS7018 used only single-level labels in the earliest measurement period, the majority of its tunnels now employ stacks of two labels. AS2119 was one of the few ASes we observed to employ label stacks of depth 3 (we never observed more than 10 ASes to use 3-deep stacks). We also see that it has very few tunnels that have just a single label on the stack. Lastly, we see that AS19262 has made roughly equal use of label stacks with 1 or 2 labels. In future work we hope to gain insight into the operational practices that lead to these observed behaviors.

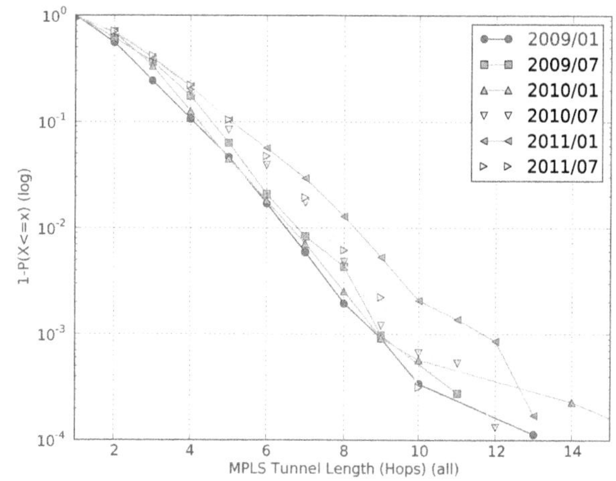

Figure 12: Complementary CDF of the length of all *nested* tunnels (measured in hops). Note that the y-axis is log scale.

The MPLS header contains a 3-bit traffic class field, which can be used by ISPs for implementing different quality of service policies and for prioritizing LSPs. Table 2 shows the fraction of ASes employing different unique traffic class identifiers, over the first month of the past three years. We see that in January 2009, 68% of all ASes used a single traffic class, 22% used two classes, and about 10% used more than two classes. We also see that traffic class identifier usage was roughly the same in January 2010 and 2011.

Table 2: Fraction of ASes employing a given number of traffic class identifiers.

Traffic class labels in use	01/2009	01/2010	01/2011
1	0.682	0.649	0.651
2	0.223	0.224	0.283
3	0.063	0.091	0.033
4	0.010	0.010	0.007
5	0.006	0.006	0.004
6	0.004	0.003	0.003
7	0.005	0.007	0.003
8	0.006	0.006	0.010

Figure 14 shows cumulative probabilities of using one of the 8 traffic class identifiers across all ASes (left) and in selected ASes (right). We see, similar to Table 2, that the majority of ASes used a single identifier of 0. However, a number of ASes used a variety of traffic class identifiers. Indeed, we see that AS6799 and AS6834 used the traffic class identifiers with what appears to be almost equal probability. This is surprising, given the fact that the

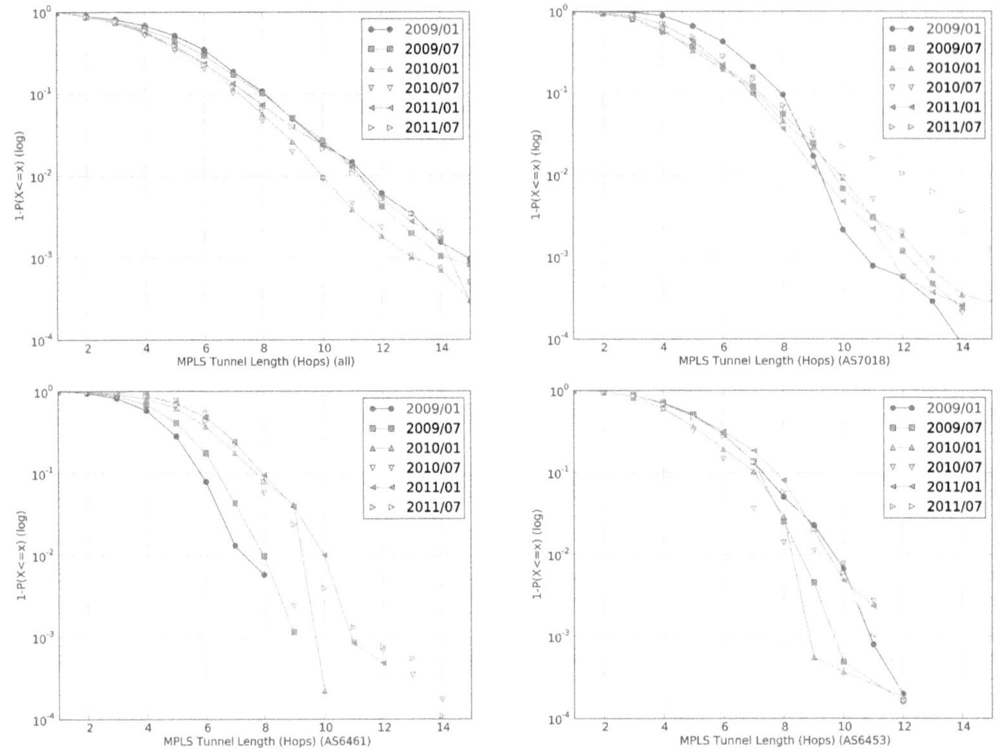

Figure 10: Complementary CDF of length of MPLS tunnels in terms of hops. Note that the y-axis is log scale. Plots shown for all tunnels (upper left) and three selected ASes (7018, 6461, and 6453).

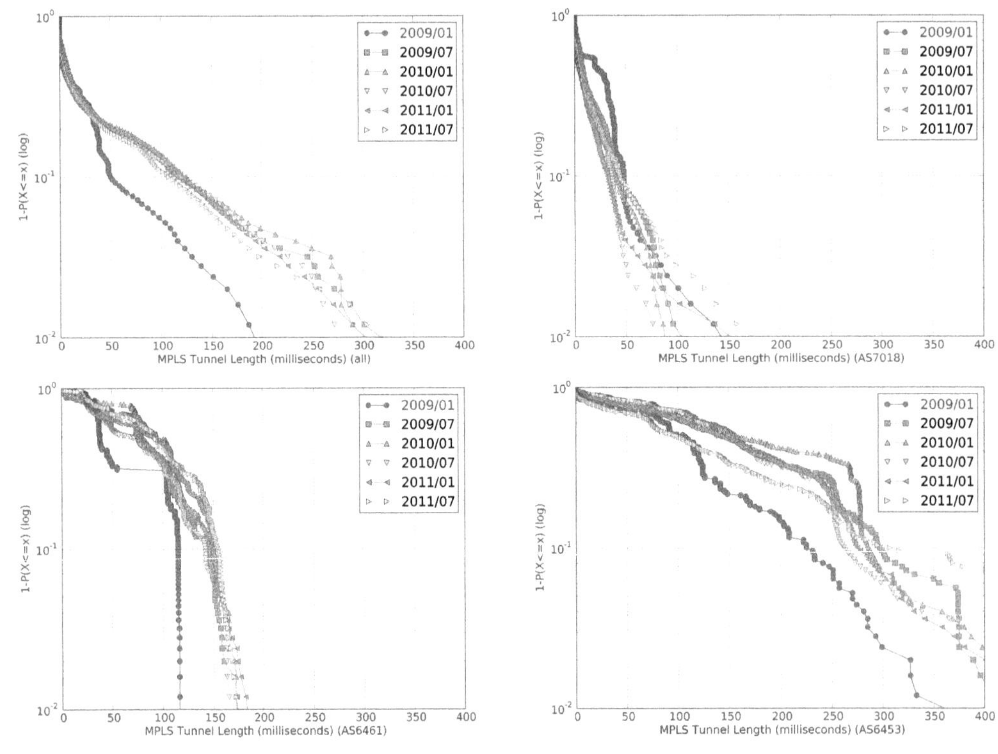

Figure 11: Complementary CDF of length of MPLS tunnels in terms of latency (milliseconds). Note that the y-axis is log scale. Plots shown for all tunnels (upper left) and three selected ASes (7018, 6461, and 6453).

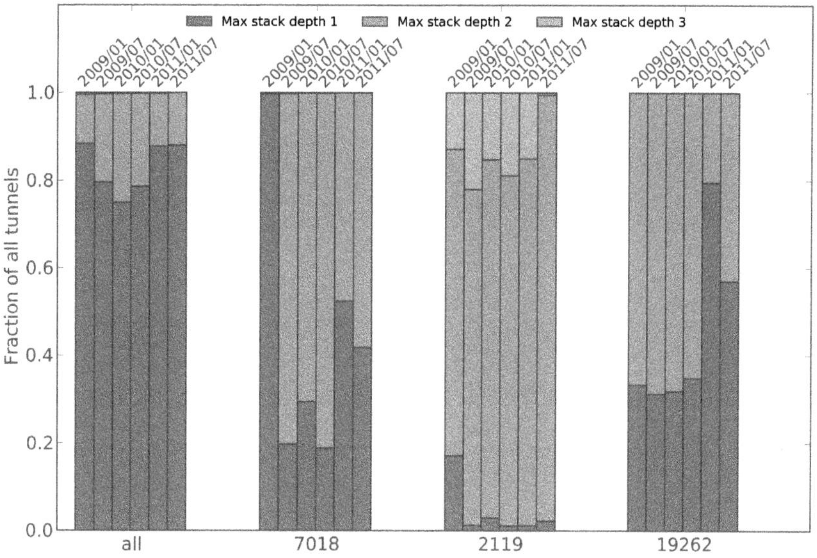

Figure 13: Fraction of tunnels employing different label stack depths, for all tunnels and three selected ASes. Bars for each group are produced from data from one month, as labeled in the plot.

`traceroute` measurements we analyze are produced using the ICMP-paris method over the entire data collection period, *i.e.*, a single type of source traffic provokes different traffic classifications within the same AS. Taken together, the use of label stacks greater than 1 label and more than 1 traffic class identifier by many ASes suggests that they employ some types of traffic classification and traffic engineering methods. While the details of these methods are not clear, in the future we hope to examine these issues more closely by emitting hop-limited packets using different transport protocols and application payloads along paths that contain MPLS tunnels.

4. TUNNEL INFERENCE

Although ICMP extensions enable direct identification of MPLS tunnels in a network, sole reliance on these labels limits the scope of our study. In order to examine the prevalence of MPLS in a wide range of network topologies lacking these MPLS annotations (*e.g.*, the Skitter [13] dataset), this requires the construction of an MPLS inference methodology. We demonstrate how to exploit observable characteristics of MPLS tunnels across various measurement features in order to accurately estimate which paths in a network go through an MPLS tunnel. Note that in this analysis we can only hope to identify tunnels that have been configured in uniform mode, but for which we do not have ICMP extension information to clearly identify the router as being part of an MPLS tunnel.

4.1 MPLS Tunnel Features

Consider observable characteristics of a network path which may indicate a particular router interface is in an MPLS tunnel. Assuming `traceroute`-like probes, we focus on three path properties: latency, hop count, and the IP subnet.

First, consider observations of round-trip time along a `traceroute` path. As previously described, uniform mode MPLS deployments are configured such that the expiration of a packet within a tunnel causes the packet to be forwarded to the end of the tunnel prior to being routed back to the source host. Intuitively, this results in latency observations for interfaces in the same tunnel that are all roughly equal. From mining the Ark dataset, we observe the difference in latency between the interfaces under consideration and the next consecutive interfaces in an observed path. Using kernel density estimators [20], we approximate the probability of observed latency given an interface in an MPLS tunnel (*i.e.*, $\widehat{P}_{lat}^{(k)}(\ell \mid \text{MPLS})$, where ℓ is the observed latency between the interface under consideration and the k-hops away interface in the observed path) and the probability of observed latency given that an interface is *not* in an MPLS tunnel (*i.e.*, $\widehat{P}_{lat}^{(k)}(\ell \mid \text{MPLS}^C)$). In Figure 15, we clearly demonstrate for the April 2011 MPLS-labeled Ark data that MPLS annotated interfaces have different latency characteristics than non-MPLS interfaces. Specifically, for all three figures we find that MPLS interfaces have pairwise latency closer to zero compared with non-MPLS interfaces, which matches our intuition.

We further assume that interfaces in the same MPLS tunnel will be allocated with similar IP addresses, since all the tunnels we observed reside in the same AS. Therefore, two interfaces consecutively found in a path are more likely to be in an MPLS tunnel if they are closer in IP space (*e.g.*, two interfaces in the same /24 are more likely to be in an MPLS than two interfaces in the same /4). In Figure 16, we plot the MPLS-labeled April 2011 Ark mined kernel density estimates with respect to the observed IP subnet with the k-th consecutive interface in observed paths (*i.e.*, $\widehat{P}_{IP}^{(k)}(s \mid \text{MPLS})$, where s is the observed IP subnet between the interface under consideration and the k-hops away interface in the observed path) and the probability the interface is *not* in an MPLS tunnel (*i.e.*, $\widehat{P}_{IP}^{(k)}(s \mid \text{MPLS}^C)$) Again, we find a difference in characteristics between MPLS interfaces and non-MPLS interfaces in this Ark dataset, with MPLS interface having higher IP address subnet compared with non-MPLS interfaces.

Notice that while both of these features show different characteristics for MPLS and non-MPLS interfaces, neither are powerful enough to accurately classify using a single component of information alone. This motivates fusing multiple observed characteristics from the observed path measurement. Specifically, we exploit

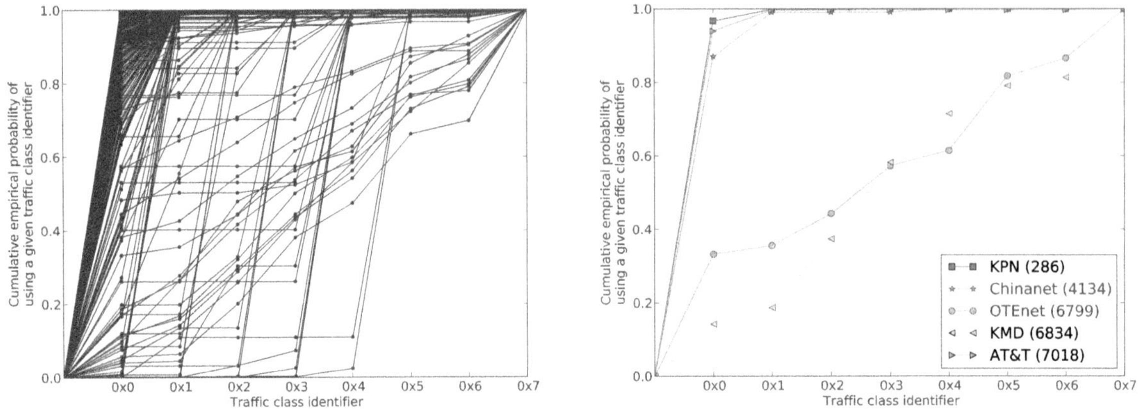

Figure 14: Cumulative empirical probabilities of using different traffic class identifiers for all ASes (left) (each curve corresponds to one AS) and for tunnels in selected ASes (right).

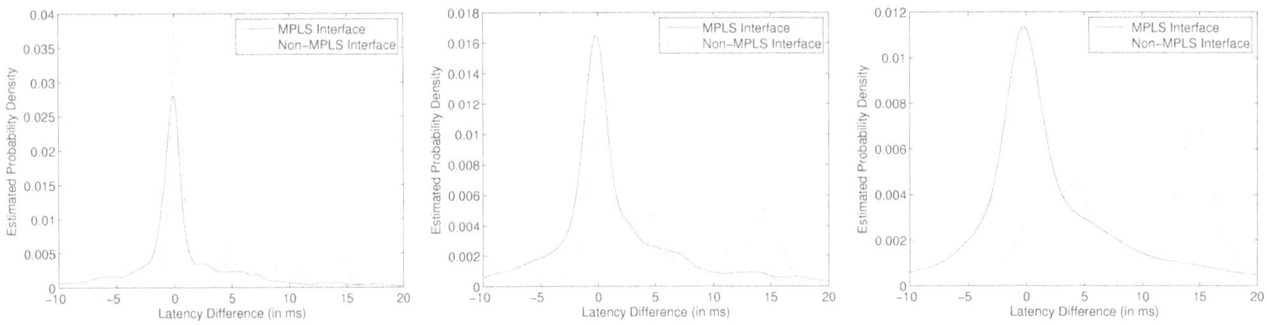

Figure 15: Estimated latency-based distributions between non-MPLS and MPLS interfaces, $\widehat{P}_{lat}^{(k)}(\ell \mid \textbf{MPLS})$ and $\widehat{P}_{lat}^{(k)}(\ell \mid \textbf{MPLS}^C)$, respectively. Where ℓ is the latency between interfaces separated by k hops in observed `traceroute` paths. (Left) interfaces separated by one hop, $k = 1$, (Center) interfaces separated by two hops, $k = 2$, and (Right) interfaces separated by three hops, $k = 3$.

the continuous property of MPLS tunnels in terms of observed hop count. For example, for a path with three interfaces in the same MPLS tunnel, all three of these interfaces must be observed consecutively. This property both reinforces our classification and helps us distinguish between MPLS tunnels and simply an observation of co-located routers in the same PoP along a `traceroute` path.

4.1.1 *Bayesian Data Fusion Methodology*

We state the probability of an interface i being in an MPLS tunnel given our observed measurements ($\mathcal{M}_i$, the collection of latencies and IP subnets) for this interface, $P(\text{MPLS} \mid \mathcal{M}_i)$, as

$$\begin{aligned} P(\text{MPLS}_i) &= P(\text{MPLS} \mid \mathcal{M}_i) \\ P(\text{MPLS}_i) &\propto P(\mathcal{M}_i \mid \text{MPLS})\, P(\text{MPLS}) \end{aligned}$$

Using Bayes Rule (*i.e.*, $P(A|B) = \frac{P(B|A)P(A)}{P(B)}$) and where $\mathcal{M}_i$ is the set of observed features from the K interfaces found before and after the interface i in the observed path.

We do not argue that these are the only features that can distinguish MPLS paths; there may indeed be others. This issue is a topic for future investigation.

Unfortunately, as more information is brought to bear on this problem (*i.e.*, the set of features, $\mathcal{M}_i$, grows), the higher the dimension of the probability distribution $P(\mathcal{M}_i \mid \text{MPLS})$ becomes, which results in a computationally intractable problem [20]. In addition, to exploit multiple characteristics from interfaces along the path, it is necessary to fuse together disparate data types (*i.e.*, latency, IP subnet, etc.), for which many off-the-shelf density estimation procedures were not designed. To avoid these limitations, we look to a *Naive Bayesian* data fusion approach. The Naive Bayesian approach converts the problem from estimating one M-dimensional density (which may be computationally intractable) to estimating M one-dimensional densities, such as those estimated in Figure 15 and Figure 16.

Using Naive Bayes, the resulting log-likelihood estimated probability for an interface i being in an MPLS tunnel is formulated as:

$$\log \widehat{P}(\text{MPLS}_i) = \sum_{k=-K}^{K} \log \widehat{P}_{lat}^{(k)}\left(\ell_{i,i+k} \mid \text{MPLS}\right) + \sum_{k=-K}^{K} \log \widehat{P}_{IP}^{(k)}\left(s_{i,i+k} \mid \text{MPLS}\right) \quad (1)$$

While the log-likelihood estimated probability for an interface *i not being* in an MPLS tunnel is formulated as :

$$\log \widehat{P}(\text{MPLS}_i) = \sum_{k=-K}^{K} \log \widehat{P}_{lat}^{(k)}\left(\ell_{i,i+k} \mid \text{MPLS}^C\right) + \sum_{k=-K}^{K} \log \widehat{P}_{IP}^{(k)}\left(s_{i,i+k} \mid \text{MPLS}^C\right) \quad (2)$$

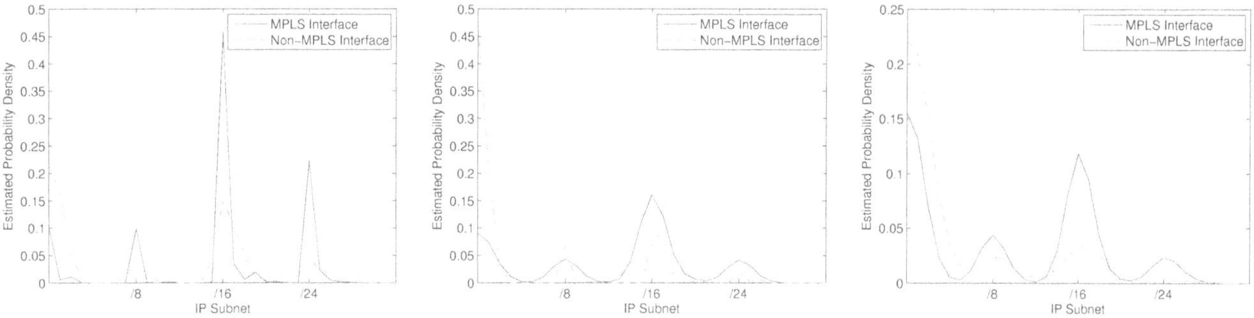

Figure 16: Estimated IP subnet-based distributions between non-MPLS and MPLS interfaces, $\widehat{P}_{IP}^{(k)}(s \mid \text{MPLS})$ and $\widehat{P}_{IP}^{(k)}(s \mid \text{MPLS}^C)$, respectively. Where s is the IP subnet between interfaces separated by k hops in observed `traceroute` paths. (Left) interfaces separated by one hop, $k = 1$, (Center) interfaces separated by two hops, $k = 2$, and (Right) interfaces separated by three hops, $k = 3$.

Where K is the number of hops in the observed `traceroute` path that we examine with respect to the interface i.

From this formulation, we see that the computational complexity of this methodology for each interface is only $O(M)$, where M is the number of path features under consideration. On a reasonably equipped host, we find that to resolve the estimated MPLS probability for every interface along a path takes on average 6 milliseconds.

Prior work on using Naive Bayes methodologies on Internet measurements have been explored in the context of IP geolocation in [18]. Our approach differs here through the use of path-based measurements (as opposed to only end-to-end measurements in the prior work) and application (MPLS identification vs. geolocation). We direct the readers to this prior work for a detailed introduction to the Naive Bayes approach.

4.2 Inference Experimental Results

We now consider the ability to estimate MPLS tunnels on an Ark dataset from April 2011 containing over 9 million `traceroute` paths. Due to the use of our learning-based Naive Bayesian inference approach, hold out cross validation [36] is performed to avoid potential bias in our results. This is performed by holding out 5% of the observed paths (randomly selected) as training data, learning the MPLS characteristics using kernel density estimators, then testing our Bayesian inference method on the remaining 95% of the observed paths. The detection accuracy results presented are with respect to this held-out test set.

4.2.1 MPLS Interface Detection

First, we consider the performance of our methodology with respect to detecting if an interface is in an MPLS tunnel given an observed path containing that interface. Using our Naive Bayesian approach, we fuse together latency, hop count, and IP subnet information to estimate the log-likelihood probability an interface is in an MPLS tunnel. In order to classify our test set of interfaces, we consider a simple thresholding approach between the estimated probability the interface is in an MPLS, against the estimated probability it is not in an MPLS tunnel. The intuition is that the more likely an interface is to be in an MPLS tunnel, the larger this margin will be. Given a set threshold λ, an interface i is assigned,

$$i \in \begin{cases} \text{MPLS} & : \log \widehat{P}(\text{MPLS}_i) - \log \widehat{P}(\text{MPLS}_i^C) \geq \lambda \\ \text{MPLS}^C & : \log \widehat{P}(\text{MPLS}_i) - \log \widehat{P}(\text{MPLS}_i^C) < \lambda \end{cases}$$

Using hold-out cross validation on our set of over 9 million paths, the false alarm/detection characteristics for detecting if interfaces in our test set are in MPLS tunnels can be seen in Figure 17. The figure shows the region operating characteristics (ROC) curve of our classifiers across all feasible values of the threshold λ (where each point in the figure represents a different value of λ and the associated false alarm and detection rate). These results include our full Naive Bayes data fusion technique (using both latency and IP subnet information), Naive Bayes using only IP subnet information, and Naive Bayes using only latency information. We find that our full technique can detect over 55% of the MPLS interfaces with only declaring 10% of the non-MPLS interfaces incorrectly, a significant improvement over using a single characteristic.

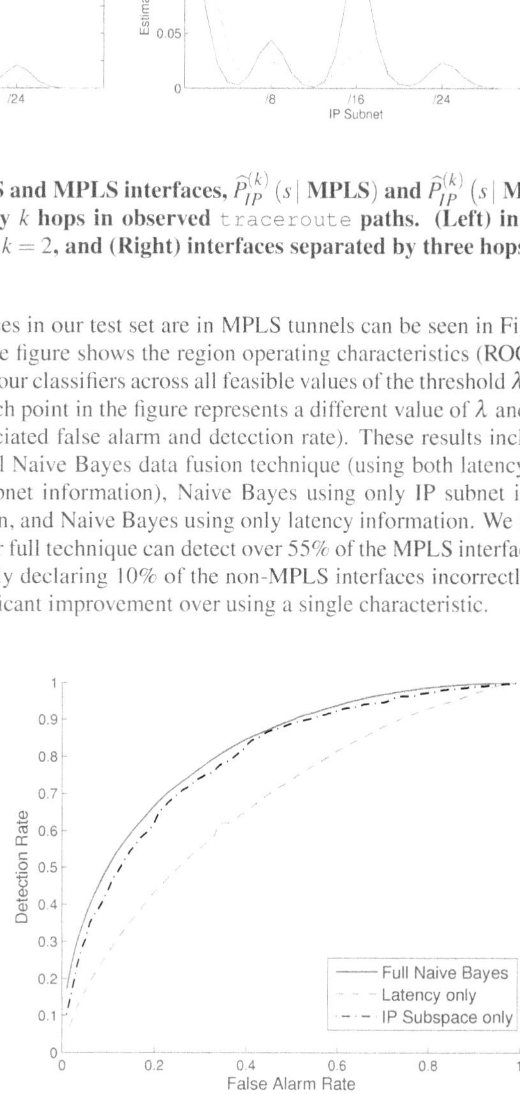

Figure 17: Comparison of the full Naive Bayesian methodology with using only latency or IP subnet to detect MPLS interfaces using `traceroute` paths from the April 2011 Ark Dataset.

4.2.2 MPLS Path Detection

More valuable to a network operator may be knowledge of whether or not a given `traceroute` path has traversed an MPLS tunnel. In order to classify each observed path as an *MPLS path* (*i.e.*, a path that crossed an MPLS tunnel) or a *non-MPLS path*, we consider using the characteristics inferred on each of the interfaces along the observed path. Specifically, we consider aggregating the interface information in the form of the maximum interface log-likelihood probability. Such that, for an observed path

$\mathbf{p}_j = \{p_1, p_2, ..., p_M\}$ we find,

$$\log \widehat{P}\left(\text{MPLS}_{\mathbf{p}_j}\right) = \max_{i=\{1,2,...,M\}} \left(\log \widehat{P}\left(\text{MPLS}_{p_i}\right) - \log \widehat{P}\left(\text{MPLS}^C_{p_i}\right)\right)$$

Again we threshold these margin values against a parameter λ to classify each path as MPLS or non-MPLS. As expected, the length of the MPLS tunnel is directly related with the ability to detect if the path does or does not go through an MPLS tunnel. Separating out with respect to MPLS tunnel length, we find the detection characteristics in Figure 18 across the specified April 2011 Ark dataset and all feasible values of λ.

For MPLS tunnels of length greater than or equal to 4, we can detect roughly 80% of the MPLS paths with only a 10% false alarm rate. This is in contrast to considering all MPLS tunnels, where we only detect 35% of the tunnels for the same false alarm rate.

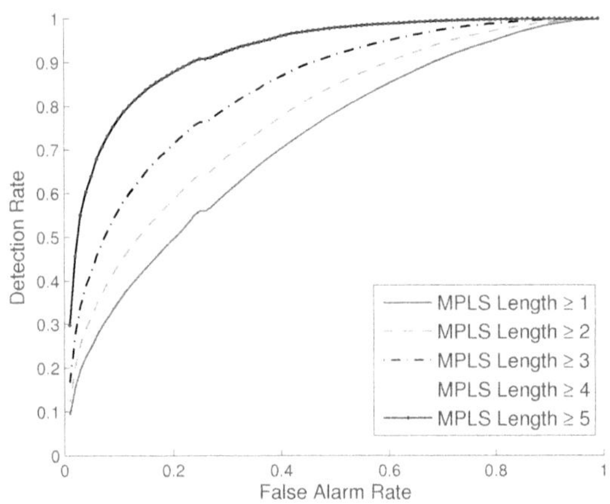

Figure 18: Comparison of the MPLS path detection methodology with respect to the length of the MPLS tunnel using the April 2011 Ark Dataset.

4.3 Unlabeled MPLS Path Estimation

Finally, we examine the performance on prior Ark data that does not have MPLS labels. We train our classifier using a subset of labeled June 2008 Ark data, and then test on the prior months (March, April, and May 2008) for which we have no ground truth. We present our results with respect to the four most frequently encountered ASes in our training set. In Table 3, we find the results of our MPLS path detection in terms of the percentage of observed paths for a given autonomous system that we estimate to include an MPLS tunnel. The table shows the percentage of inferred MPLS tunnels as gross characteristics consistent with the labeled June 2008 data. The level of variability in our inference is consistent with the variability that we see in the labeled MPLS data.

While our pre-June 2008 data does not contain uniform-mode MPLS labels, we do have the ability to examine paths that are found in *both* unlabeled pre-June 2008 data and labeled June 2008 data. Using the June 2008 MPLS labels as ground truth, we can examine performance of our inference methodology on an intersection of these two sets. Figure 19 shows the performance of our inference technique on unlabeled Ark data from March, April, and May 2008. As expected, the classifier performance is more accurate for time frames closer to the labeled set (*i.e.,* May dataset), when compared with the more temporally distant unlabeled set (*i.e.,* March dataset).

Table 3: Comparison of estimated percent of MPLS paths for unlabeled Ark data.

	Estimated Paths with Tunnels				Obs. Data
AS	03/08	04/08	05/08	06/08	06/08
7018	60.7%	59.2%	76.7%	62.5%	69.2%
6389	54.2%	67.5%	66.4%	69.5%	71.0%
4134	7.1%	8.1%	8.5%	3.1%	0.4%
4230	35.5%	27.0%	29.8%	29.4%	25.8%

5. RELATED WORK

The literature on MPLS largely falls into three categories. The first are studies that describe methods for expanding and enhancing MPLS beyond the original RFCs describing the protocol. Examples include methods for improving reliability and fault tolerance (*e.g.,* [15, 25]) and extension for a wide range of label switched paths including photonic networks (*i.e.,* GMPLS [11]) and wireless networks (*e.g.,* [23]). The second category are studies that describe methods for employing MPLS to meet various operational objectives within a given network infrastructure. The most prominent among these are studies that describe a wide variety of traffic engineering methods based on MPLS (*e.g.,* [17, 37]). In the third category are studies describing new routing algorithms that can be used in conjunction with MPLS to establish paths with target characteristics (*e.g.,* [35]).

Details of the MPLS protocol are described in various RFCs which are all linked from the IETF's MPLS working group homepage [3]. The main MPLS architectural reference is RFC 3031 [31], and the most relevant standards document to our study is RFC 4950, which defines the ICMP extensions that enable label stacks to be returned to clients [12]. Beyond RFC documents, Davie and Rekhter wrote a comprehensive textbook reference on MPLS that broadly treats the protocol [16]. There are also numerous online references and notes on practical aspects of MPLS configuration and management (*e.g.,* [34])

We are aware of no prior studies on Internet-wide MPLS deployment characteristics. Perhaps the most relevant empirical studies were by Sherwood *et al.* in [32, 33]. The former study describes a method for measuring router-level topologies that includes the capability to discover MPLS nodes using ICMP extensions. That study provides a small set of measurements on routers that respond with MPLS labels. The latter study also discusses certain aspects of MPLS, again in the context of router-level topology discovery. Our study differs from theirs in its specific focus on MPLS and the longitudinal characterization of its deployment.

6. SUMMARY AND CONCLUSIONS

MPLS offers compelling capabilities for traffic engineering, multi-services networks and improved network robustness. In this paper, we describe a longitudinal study of the prevalence and characteristics of MPLS deployments in the open Internet. The goal of our work is to establish a comprehensive baseline for the evolution and current status of MPLS deployments since they have important implications for issues such as quality of service and network neutrality. We use the large `traceroute` archive from the Ark project as the basis for our work. Over the past 3 years, this data set has included MPLS label stacks, which enable direct evaluation of MPLS tunnels configured in uniform mode. We note again that our direct observations likely underestimate MPLS deployments due to the inability to empirically identify pipe-mode tunnels.

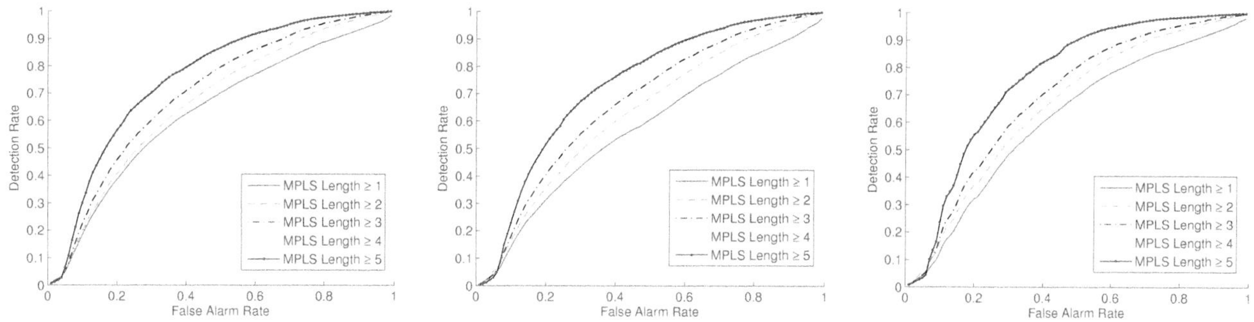

Figure 19: Comparison of the MPLS path detection of unlabeled data using June 2008 labels. (Left) - March 2008 Ark Dataset, (Center) - April 2008 Ark Dataset, (Right) - May 2008 Ark Dataset

The summary findings of our analysis show an increasing trend in MPLS deployments over the past three years and the wide use by tier-1 providers, implying that it is increasingly likely that packets will encounter an MPLS tunnel on end-to-end paths. We also find that tunnels are likely to span the entire edge-to-edge distance of a transit provider, with typical transit times on the order of tens of milliseconds. Lastly, our examination of the use of traffic classifiers indicates that while multiple classes are not uncommon, the diversity of classes has not changed over the past three years.

We develop an MPLS tunnel inference method that is based on the observation that for certain configurations, RTTs for internal hops will all be similar. Our inference method uses Bayesian data fusion to efficiently identify MPLS paths based on RTTs. Using the labeled data, we demonstrate that this method can indeed identify MPLS paths with high accuracy.

In future work, we plan to investigate MPLS deployments in additional `traceroute` data archives using our Bayesian inference method. A short term target is the Skitter data set, which would give us the opportunity to investigate MPLS deployments over a longer time period. We also plan to expand our survey by conducting more targeted investigations using distributed infrastructures such as Planetlab.

7. ACKNOWLEDGMENTS

This work was supported in part by NSF grants CNS-0716460, CNS-0831427 and CNS-0905186, and NSF CAREER award NSF-1054985. Any opinions, findings, conclusions or other recommendations expressed in this material are those of the authors and do not necessarily reflect the view of the NSF.

Support for the IPv4 Routed /24 AS Links Dataset is provided by the NSF, the US Department of Homeland Security, the WIDE Project, Cisco Systems, and CAIDA Members. We sincerely thank CAIDA for making these high quality data available to the community.

8. REFERENCES

[1] Routeviews Prefix to AS mappings Dataset (pfx2as). http://www.caida.org/data/routing/routeviews-prefix2as.xml.

[2] Cyclops. http://irl.cs.ucla.edu/topology/data/, Accessed August 2011.

[3] IETF Multiprotocol Label Switching (mpls) Working Group. http://datatracker.ietf.org/wg/mpls/charter/, Accessed August 2011.

[4] Junos OS MPLS Applications Configuration Guide. http://www.juniper.net/techpubs/en_US/junos11.1/information-products/topic-collections/config-guide-mpls-applications/config-guide-mpls-applications.pdf, Accessed August 2011.

[5] Multiprotocol Label Switching on Cisco Routers. http://www.cisco.com/en/US/docs/ios/12_1t/12_1t3/feature/guide/rtr_13t.pdf, Accessed August 2011.

[6] Sprint IP/MPLS Network Maps. https://www.sprint.net/network_maps.php, Accessed August 2011.

[7] The Internet Topology Zoo. http://www.topology-zoo.org/, Accessed August 2011.

[8] The Traceroute Command in MPLS. http://www.cisco.com/en/US/tech/tk436/tk428/technologies_tech_note09186a008020a42a.shtml, Accessed August 2011.

[9] P. Agarwal and B. Akyol. RFC 3443: Time to Live (TTL) Processing in Multi-Protocol Label Switching (MPLS) Networks. http://www.ietf.org/rfc/rfc3443.txt, January 2003.

[10] D. Awduche, J. Malcolm, J. Agogbua, M. O'Dell, and J. McManus. RFC 2702: Requirements for Traffic Engineering Over MPLS. http://www.ietf.org/rfc/rfc2702.txt, September 1999.

[11] L. Berger. RFC 3473: Generalized Multi-Protocol Label Switching (GMPLS) Signaling Resource ReserVation Protocol-Traffiic Engineering (RSVP-TE) Extensions. http://www.ietf.org/rfc/rfc3473.txt, January 2003.

[12] R. Bonica, D. Gan, D. Tappan, and C. Pignataro. RFC 4950: ICMP Extensions for Multiprotocol Label Switching. http://www.ietf.org/rfc/rfc4950.txt, August 2007.

[13] CAIDA. The Skitter Project. http://www.caida.org/tools/measurement/skitter/, Accessed August 2011.

[14] R. Callon, P. Doolan, N. Feldman, A. Fredette, and G. Swallow. Draft: A Framework for Multiprotocol Label Switching. `http://tools.ietf.org/html/draft-ietf-mpls-framework-00`, May 1997.

[15] H. Chengcheng, V. Sharma, and K. Owens. Building Reliable MPLS Networks Using a Path Protection Mechanism. *IEEE Communications Magazine*, 40(3), March 2002.

[16] B. Davie and Y. Rekhter. *MPLS: Technology and Applications*. Morgan Kaufmann, 2000.

[17] A. Elwalid, C. Jin, S. Low, and I. Widjaja. MATE: MPLS Adaptive Traffic Engineering. In *Proceedings of IEEE INFOCOM '01*, April 2001.

[18] B. Eriksson, P. Barford, J. Sommers, and R. Nowak. A Learning-based Approach for IP Geolocation. In *Proceedings of Passive and Active Measurements Conference*, April 2010.

[19] F. Le Faucheur *et al.* RFC 3270: Multi-Protocol Label Switching (MPLS) Support of Differentiated Services. `http://www.ietf.org/rfc/rfc3270.txt`, May 2002.

[20] T. Hastie, R. Tibshirani, and J. Friedman. *The Elements of Statistical Learning*. Springer, 2001.

[21] Y. Hyun. Personal communication, May 2011.

[22] Y. Hyun, B. Huffaker, D. Andersen, E. Aben, M. Luckie, kc claffy, and C. Shannon. The IPv4 Routed /24 AS Links Dataset: January 2008–August 2011. `http://www.caida.org/data/active/ipv4_routed_topology_aslinks_dataset.xml`.

[23] H. Kim, K. Wong, W. Chen, and C. Lau. Mobility-aware MPLS in IP-based Wireless Access Networks. In *Proceedings of IEEE Globecom '01*, November 2001.

[24] K. Kompella and G. Swallow. RFC 4379: Detecting Multi-Protocol Label Switched (MPLS) Data Plane Failures. `http://www.ietf.org/rfc/rfc4379.txt`, February 2006.

[25] S. Lee and M. Gerla. Fault Tolerance and Load Balancing in QoS Provisioning with Multiple MPLS Paths. In *Proceedings of the 9th International Workshop on Quality of Service*, June 2001.

[26] M. Luckie. Scamper: a Scalable and Extensible Packet Prober for Active Measurement of the Internet. In *Proceedings of ACM SIGCOMM Internet Measurement Conference*, November 2010.

[27] M. Luckie. Personal communication, May 2011.

[28] M. Luckie, Y. Hyun, and B. Huffaker. Traceroute probe method and forward IP path inference. In *Proceedings of ACM SIGCOMM Internet Measurement Conference*, pages 311–324, October 2008.

[29] P. Newman, W. Edwards, R. Hinden, E. Hoffman, C. Liaw, T. Lyon, and G. Minshall. RFC 1953: Ipsilon Flow Management Protocol Specification for IP. `http://www.ietf.org/rfc/rfc1953.txt`, May 1996.

[30] Y. Rekhter, B. Davie, D. Katz, E. Rosen, and G. Swallow. RFC 2105: Cisco's Tag Switching Architecture Overview. `http://www.ietf.org/rfc/rfc2105.txt`, February 1997.

[31] E. Rosen, A. Viswanathan, and R. Callon. RFC 3031: Multiprotocol Label Switching Architecture. `http://www.ietf.org/rfc/rfc3031.txt`, January 2001.

[32] R. Sherwood, A. Bender, and N. Spring. Discarte: a disjunctive internet cartographer. In *Proceedings of ACM SIGCOMM '08*, pages 303–314, August 2008.

[33] R. Sherwood and N. Spring. Touring the Internet in a TCP Sidecar. In *Proceedings of ACM SIGCOMM Internet Measurement Conference*, pages 339–344, October 2006.

[34] R. Steenbergen. Nanog Tutorial: MPLS for Dummies. `http://www.nanog.org/meetings/nanog49/presentations/Sunday/mpls-nanog49.pdf`, June 2010.

[35] B. Wang, S. Xu, and C. Chen. A New Bandwidth Guaranteed Routing Algorithm for MPLS Traffic Engineering. In *Proceedings of ICC '02*, April 2002.

[36] L. Wasserman. All of nonparametric statistics (springer texts in statistics). Springer, May 2007.

[37] X. Xipeng, A. Hannan, B. Bailey, and L. Ni. Traffic Engineering with MPLS in the Internet. *IEEE Network*, 14(2), March/April 2000.

Summary Review Documentation for

"On the Prevalence and Characteristics of MPLS Deployments in the Open Internet"

Authors: J. Sommers, B. Eriksson, P. Barford

Reviewer #1

Strengths: First large scale Internet wide study of the deployment of MPLS.
Proposal of a reasonable approach to detect some of the hidden tunnels.

Weaknesses: Some of the MPLS deployments can be completely transparent to traceroutes even with the proposed methodology to detect some cases of hidden deployments. Comparison of routing data with stock market data...

Comments to Authors: I am glad to see that finally someone spends time on this topic; it is an important topic that has been neglected for a long time.

Figure 2 and general comments about the deployment of MPLS: you should really break down the statistics by AS type. For instance, you could use the "Cyclops" classification and provide stats for Tier 1 ISPs, Large ISPs or stub ASs. I think this would provide a better view about the extent of the deployment of MPLS. My guess is that your 7% would significantly increase if you were to look at Tier 1 ISP or large ISPs. You might want to summarize it as at least 7% of all ASs and X% of large ISP or Tier 1 ISPs.

While you do a good job in the paper of explaining the caveats (there are cases where you can simply not detect MPLS), I think you need to highlight this also better in the abstract, intro and conclusion. This is all the more important as you propose a heuristic to detect MPLS deployments, so some readers might think that your heuristic covers all the cases and your 7% is a good approximation.

In the intro, you should also mention that multi service networks go beyond MPLS VPNs, MPLS also enables IPv6 and VPLS.

PLEASE remove Fig 3. Don't compare routing data to the stock market (or the weather!). Trying to correlate the two doesn't make any sense to me. Furthermore, Fig 4 already shows that AT&T experiences a significant drop in early 2009 (how significant?). How would Fig 3 look like without AT&T? It seems that you simply detected a major architecture change within AT&T around that period.
Did you contact Deutsche Telekom to explain what you are observing on Fig 4?

You mention the issue of PHP and how it impacts the length of the tunnel. That's a great observation. But it seems to me that you could go further and try to detect the use of PHP by looking at traces within an ISP in 2 opposite directions (the path will be asymmetrical so it will complicate things but I'm sure you can work something out).

On traffic classes: you should highlight again that this is for public Internet traffic. It is possible that ISPs use one class for their Internet traffic but use another 3 other classes for otehr services like MPLS VPN that you cannot detect.

Regarding AS6799 and AS6834: you should check if the traffic class for these ISPs depend on the the previous AS hop: maybe the traffic class is X if the traffic enters from AS Y and traffic class Z if the traffic enters from AS A because one is a peer and one is a customer. Just an idea.

You claim that you can detect 80% of the MPLS paths that are longer than 4. Is Fig 4 not showing that most of the MPLS paths are shorter than 4 hops? Could you quantify it here?

Reviewer #2

Strengths: Internet topology studies have ignored MPLS until now. Only anecdotal evidence about MPLS deployment was discussed in the community. This study is among the first that try to measure how many ASes use MPLS and also how it is used. The paper give a detailed introduction into the methodology and the measurement pitfalls.

This paper is critical to every researcher working on any traceroute-based topology measurements.

Weaknesses: The study is a bit premature. While it nicely discusses methodology and in how many ASes MPLS has been detected. it relies on CAIDA's ARK data, which collects traceroutes from a set of specific locations. This results in measurements, which are heavily biased towards those observation points. The authors do not provide any insights into how suitable this dataset is for studying MPLS deployment and what the limitations are. The paper does not make any effort into addressing this issue at all (e.g., not even as an explanatory warning to the reader). Many observations in this paper are described in relation to "number of observed MPLS tunnels". This, of course heavily relies on the used data and is of little insight to the reader in what it really means.

Comments to Authors: This is a very well written paper, and relevant for everyone who is trying to understand the Internet topology. While the paper could do a better job in explaining what the authors know about the limitations and the measurement bias, this is overall a well done study. It includes an excellent introduction into what is relevant to know for a measurement researcher if he/she wants to include MPLS measurements into their work.

As mentioned above, it is difficult to get a good feeling for the data. Talking about 350K MPLS tunnels or hearing that 20% of all ASes have fewer than 10 tunnels, is relatively meaningless overall. For a different set of observation points those numbers could look different. The reader lacks a bit perspective of how relevant or irrelevant this is. The paper provides little topological information, and it remains unclear what the quality or suitability of using CAIDA's probing is for the purpose of this study.
Admitted, the authors are not able to do things differently, as this would easily lead into areas of pure speculations and could introduce a strong bias in the data. However, the authors could have added a section that gives a bit more intuition about the CAIDA ARK data. For example, AT&T relies heavily on MPLS (as the paper shows), but could there be a region in Asia which uses as much MPLS at AT&T, but due to the lack of measurement points this might not be detectable?

It remained a mystery to me why the authors develop the MPLS detection method in "regular" traces, validate it, and then study 3 additional month in 2008. This data does not add any new insights! What would have been nice is a long-term analysis of, for example skitter data; and trying to detect properties of the early adaptors.

Reviewer #3

Strengths: Longitudinal, high-quality data of something the IMC community should know more about, but does not. The high deployment rate of MPLS underscores the importance of this type of work.

Weaknesses: None? The text failed to properly emphasize that all data here is inherently a lower bound on MPLS deployments due to the measurement technique.

Comments to Authors: Great paper - MPLS is a big blind spot for the academic community and this paper does a lot to try to address it. First and foremost, this paper quantifies how prevalent MPLS deployments are. I would have loved to have seen the deployment numbers broken down by tier-1 (perhaps defined by http://en.wikipedia.org/wiki/Tier_1_network#List_of_tier_1_networks, for a common definition), tier-2, etc.

I suspect that the numbers presented here (i.e, 25% of all hops go through an MPLS tunnel) is in fact a significant underestimate due to pipe-mode tunnels, so I suggest the authors next try to work on this for their future work. As a basis, one could consider extending the Bayesian classifier to look at more characteristics of MPLS vs. non-MPLS links, as suggested in the text. Also, note that L1 often imposes physical limitations on real link lengths that would appear violated by an MPLS-tunnel, so that might be another direction to look.

Regarding MPLS-usage tracking the DOW, my guess is that if you were to do the homework, you would find that your data better correlated with ISP mergers or out-right bankruptcies, which transitively tracks the DOW, rather than some more direct interaction. You should be able to correlate this in your data by looking at unique ASes in the same period. Interesting in any case.

The break down of tunnels by class is a very interesting addition, and should be listed as a first class contribution. The authors might consider correlating it with existing traffic studies or talking to the operators directly to discover what the traffic classes are used for, e.g., VoIP, IPTV, best-effort, etc. I suspect that if you do so, you might be able to dig more information from the data, e.g., quantify the extent of IP-TV deployments or some such.

From the text, it was not clear if the techniques in S4 were being applied to both pipe-mode and uniform-mode tunnels. If both, then can you quantify the fraction of pipe vs. uniform tunnels? That is, the fraction of paths that according to the classifier appear to be going through an MPLS tunnel, but don't have the ICMP MPLS information? This might help shed some light on the pipe vs. uniform deployments.

Reviewer #4

Strengths: Despite its importance as one of the most important new lower level technologies of the evolved Internet, I am not aware of another large scale measurement study of MPLS on the open Internet.
Clear quantifications: 7% ASes employing MPLS, average length of tunnels 3-4 hops, 25% of paths crossing at least one tunnel, ~30% of tunnels employing more than 1 traffic class.
The tunnel inference method based on roundtrip times and TTLs is smart but it is not clear how many tunnels fall in this category (uniform mode but without MPLS extensions enabled.)

Weaknesses: Although the reports are clear and the inference technique interesting the paper is rather flat in terms of conclusions. The connection to net neutrality is rather superficial and overall the authors fails to connect the reported numbers with any bigger questions about the state of the current Internet and the dilemmas regarding its evolution.

Comments to Authors: Good solid paper with interesting numbers and a bit of methodological contribution on inference based on deep understanding of the workings of the protocol. Two issues mainly for me: I wish the paper connected better its findings with some more general questions about the Internet (e.g., to what extent MPLS, covers design goals claimed as motivation for clean slate re designs). Also, I find the paper a bit sparse in terms of results. Maybe it would have been more interesting as a short paper. Also I would like to have seen some more discussion regarding the limitations of the measurement (e.g., an estimation of the MPLS tunnels in pipe mode that go unnoticed).

Reviewer #5

Strengths: - Well written and first of the kind study of MPLS.
- The authors observe interesting technical challenges in detecting these MPLS tunnels and propose new solutions to overcome such problems.

Weaknesses: - Some of the problems involving visibility are fundamental and the heuristics proposed work only for a limited set of scenarios.
- Due to lack of ground truth, some of the reasons mentioned are largely speculative and there is no way to verify.

Comments to Authors: There are a lot of reasons to accept this paper. (1) The paper focuses measurement-based characterization of MPLS prevalence, which has not received too much attention in the past. (2) The paper does a good job exposing and outlining what information can be observed about MPLS tunnels using traceroute data already collected by the Ark project. (3) Some of the findings of this study are interesting, although the paper does not confidently specify the reasons, but that's okay.

One constructive criticism: This study would tremendously benefit from engaging some large ISP into the mix. The authors have lot of contacts from their prior research with research labs that may provide this necessary angle. For example, the authors look at the MPLS tunnels in the AT&T network; it might be interesting to get some operational insight into what the operational reasons for the increase/decrease/variation of the number of tunnels and other characteristics.

I like Section 2 that provides a good overview of the MPLS state-of-the-art and stuff. The section however focused on measurement techniques from outside the AS. I believe there are more direct tools at the MPLS layer for measurement within the AS (for example, for ISPs to troubleshoot) such as the MPLS trace route. It would be good to mention some of those as well in this section, although I understand we, as researchers, cannot obtain that data unless we collaborate with the ISP.

There was some mention of the ISP MPLS maps, but comparisons are largely missing. It would be helpful to see if the findings in this paper are consistent with those MPLS maps.

In Sec. 3.2, the statement "While the rate of increase in ASes that use MPLS is greater than the rate of increase of all ASes, the fraction of ASes employing MPLS has remained roughly constant at 7%" is absurd. If the numerator changes at a faster rate than the denominator, how can the ratio remain fixed? The correlation with Dow Jones is quite interesting! The statement "So, while it is apparent from Figure 2... roughly correlate with economic conditions" is quite confusing and appears quite absurd. Please elaborate on this.

Figure 8: It would be nice if you discussed with one of the ISPs to see what the operational reasons might be.

I found the description of the nested tunnels devoid of any intuition. It would be good to give some reasons or intuition why somebody would opt for nested tunnels of depth 2-3 (or even 4). Also, are the outer labels reused across two LSPs?

Response from the Authors

We thank the reviewers for their comments and suggestions.

In response to the reviews, we have (1) emphasized in additional places in the paper that our results are limited to uniform-mode tunnels and that it is almost certain (though impossible to quantify) that we underestimate MPLS deployments, (2) added analysis of MPLS deployments by AS type (i.e., tier 1, large ISP, small ISP, and stub networks), (3) expanded our inference analysis to include more unlabeled Ark data and (4) fixed a number of minor textual issues raised. Moreover, we have extended the time period over which we analyzed Ark data to August 2011 in order to provide the most up-to-date view of MPLS activity possible within the time constraints.

We stand by our conjecture that the number of MPLS tunnels deployed over time is related to merger and acquisition activity, and indirectly tracks economic indicators. We believe that Figure 3 makes a compelling case and that this observation could lead to further work on relationships between economics and network configurations. We are in discussions with ISPs to better understand and validate our observations. We emphasize that we merely hypothesize a relationship between MPLS deployments and economic conditions; it is not our intent (as is implied by the word conjecture!) to make a solid claim at this time. Indeed, there may be several reasons behind the observed number of MPLS tunnels over time and it is our hope to better understand these reasons in future work.

Latency Inflation with MPLS-based Traffic Engineering

Abhinav Pathak
Purdue University
pathaka@purdue.edu

Ming Zhang
Microsoft Research
mzh@microsoft.com

Y. Charlie Hu
Purdue University
ychu@purdue.edu

Ratul Mahajan
Microsoft Research
ratul@microsoft.com

Dave Maltz
Microsoft Research
dmaltz@microsoft.com

ABSTRACT

While MPLS has been extensively deployed in recent years, little is known about its behavior in practice. We examine the performance of MPLS in Microsoft's online service network (MSN), a well-provisioned multi-continent production network connecting tens of data centers. Using detailed traces collected over a 2-month period, we find that many paths experience significantly inflated latencies. We correlate occurrences of latency inflation with routers, links, and DC-pairs. This analysis sheds light on the causes of latency inflation and suggests several avenues for alleviating the problem.

Categories and Subject Descriptors

C.4 [**Performance of Systems**]: Performance Attributes

General Terms

Measurement, Performance

Keywords

MPLS, LSP, Autobandwidth, Latency

1. INTRODUCTION

Traffic engineering (TE) is the process of deciding how traffic is routed through the service provider network. Its goal is to accommodate the given traffic matrix (from ingress to egress routers) while optimizing for performance objectives of low latency and loss rate. Effective TE mechanisms are key to efficiently using network resources and maintaining good performance for traffic.

The importance of TE has motivated the development of many schemes (*e.g.*, [5, 7]), but little is known today about the effectiveness or behavior of schemes that have been deployed in practice. Much of the prior work is based on various forms of simulations and emulations rather than based on real measurements taken from an operational network.

In this paper, we present a case study of the behavior of TE as deployed in a large network. This network (MSN) is the one that connects Microsoft's data centers to each other and to peering ISPs.

IMC'11, November 2–4, 2011, Berlin, Germany.

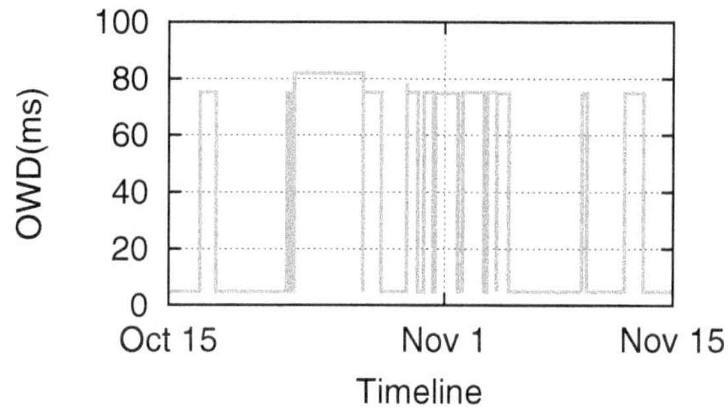

Figure 1: Tunnel latency during one month period

MSN uses MPLS-based TE, which is perhaps the most widely used TE mechanism and is supported by major router vendors such as Cisco and Juniper. Although we use MSN as a case study, we believe that our findings are general because the behaviors we uncover are tied to the MPLS-TE algorithms themselves rather than to MSN. The contribution of our work lies in uncovering and quantifying problems with MPLS-TE in a production network, as a first step towards improving the TE algorithms.

Our interest in studying the behavior of MPLS-TE was not purely academic but was motivated by anomalous behavior observed by the operators of Bing Search which uses the MSN network. During the period of our study, Bing Search experienced incidents of unexpectedly high latencies between two of its DCs from time to time. Because these two DCs are in the same city, Bing's operations expected the latency between them to be negligible. In fact, this assumption is also made by Bing's planning team when they chose to distribute Bing's backend services across the two DCs.

Figure 1 plots the latency of a tunnel (also known as LSP for label switched path) between the two DCs during a month period. We describe how MPLS-TE works in more detail later; but briefly, it works at the granularity of tunnels between ingress and egress routers. There can be multiple tunnels between a pair of routers. MPLS-TE uses a greedy algorithm that periodically finds the shortest path that can accommodate the tunnel's estimated traffic demand. The figure shows that the tunnel latency switched frequently between 5 and 75 ms. It stayed at 75 ms for almost half of the time, which adversely impacted Bing's backend services.

Our systematic evaluation using data from a 2-month period in 2010 reveals that it is not these two DCs that are impacted. 22% of the DC pairs experience significant latency spikes. 20% of the tunnels exhibit more than 20 ms of latency spikes. Over 5% of the tunnels experience high latency inflation for a cumulative duration of over 10 days in the 2 months.

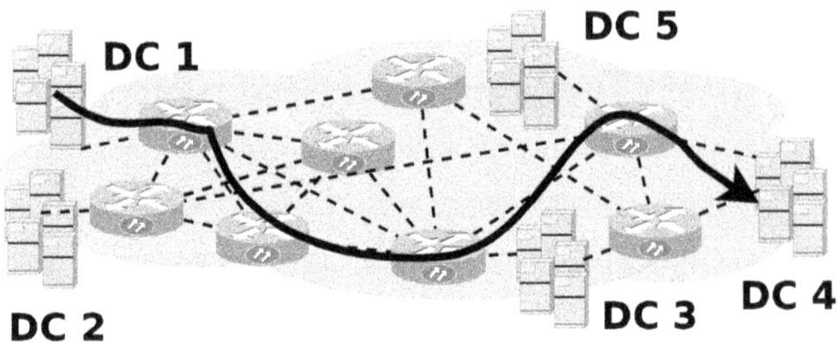

Figure 2: OSP network topology

To gain insight into the causes for latency inflation, we correlate such occurrences with specific links, routers, and DC pairs. Our analysis shows that 80% of latency inflation occur due to changes in tunnel paths concentrated on 9% of the links, 30% of the routers, and 3% of the active DC-pairs. This confirms traffic load changes exceeding the capacity of a small set of links along the shortest paths of tunnels as the primary culprit. MSN operators have since added capacity along these paths to alleviate the problem.

But to understand the effectiveness of MPLS at using available resources, we compare the latency with MPLS-TE to that with an optimal strategy based on linear programming. We find that the weighted and the 99th percentile byte latency under MPLS-TE are 10%-22% and 35%-40% higher than that under optimal routing strategy, respectively, suggesting there exists room for improvement under MPLS-TE.

We identify several problems caused by sub-optimal setting of MPLS parameters but leave as future work automatic parameter setting and *on-the-fly* LSP split as two methods to fix the latency inflation problem.

2. BACKGROUND

A service provider network is composed of multiple points-of-presence (PoPs). Our work is in the context of an online service provider (OSP), where these PoPs serve as data centers (DCs) for hosting services as well as peering with neighboring transit ISPs (Internet service provider). The distinction between an OSP and ISP is not important for our work, though we note that the nature of traffic may be different in these two kinds of networks and there is a higher premium placed on latency reduction in OSP networks.

Figure 2 illustrates the topology of a large OSP network. It comprises multiple DCs at different geographical locations to serve users around the world. To save inter-DC bandwidth cost, these DCs are often interconnected with dedicated or leased links, forming a mesh-like topology.

2.1 MPLS-TE Basics

A growing number of OSPs and ISPs have adopted MPLS networks which offer more TE [2] flexibility than the traditional IGPs such as OSPF and IS-IS. The former allows traffic to be arbitrarily distributed and routed between a source and a destination while the latter only allows traffic to be evenly distributed and routed on the shortest paths. Such restriction may cause IGP TE to be far from optimal under certain circumstances.

LSP: Label Switched Path. An LSP is an one-way tunnel in MPLS network over which data packets are routed. Packets are forwarded using MPLS labels instead of IP addresses inside LSP tunnels. The labels are inserted into packets according to local policy at ingress routers, which are later stripped by egress routers. Unlike in IGP routing, an LSP tunnel does not have to follow the shortest path from an ingress to egress. In an OSP network, each DC pair is provided with multiple LSPs in either direction to leverage path diversity in the underlying physical network. Traffic between the same DC pair can be split among different LSPs either equally or unequally.

An LSP has several attributes such as the current path, allocated bandwidth, priority, *etc.*. There are two types of LSP: static and dynamic. The former is allocated a static bandwidth and path at setup stage which remains the same thereafter. The latter continually monitors the traffic rate flowing through the tunnel and adapts its allocated bandwidth accordingly. It may also switch path when there are changes in its own allocated bandwidth or the available bandwidth in the network.

2.2 MPLS-TE algorithms

An LSP path is either configured manually or computed using Constrained Shortest Path First Algorithm (CSPF). After a path is selected, the LSP reserves the required bandwidth at the outgoing interface of each router along the path. Each router outgoing interface maintains a counter for its current reservable bandwidth. The reservable bandwidth information along with network topology (also called Traffic Engineering Database (TED)) is periodically flooded throughout the network.

Priority and preemption. Each LSP is configured with two priority values: *setup priority* and *hold priority*. Setup priority determines whether a new LSP can be established by preempting an existing LSP. Hold priority determines to what extent an existing LSP can keep its reservation. A new LSP with high setup priority can preempt an existing LSP with low hold priority if: (a) there is insufficient reservable bandwidth in the network; and (b) the new LSP cannot be setup unless the existing LSP is torn down.

CSPF. CSPF sorts LSPs based on their priority and uses a greedy algorithm to select the shortest path for each LSP. Starting with the highest priority LSP, it prunes the TED to remove links that do not have sufficient reservable bandwidth or do not satisfy a preconfigured access control policy. It then assigns the shortest path in the pruned TED (using tie-breaking if multiple) to the LSP and updates the reservable bandwidth on the relevant links. This process continues until no LSP is left.

Re-optimization. CSPF is run periodically based on a configurable timer to reassign each LSP a better path if possible.

Autobandwidth. MPLS does not have a bandwidth policing mechanism — an LSP may carry any traffic demand irrespective of its reserved bandwidth. Instead, router vendors (Cisco, Juniper) supporting MPLS, provides *autobandwidth* which permits an LSP to adjust its reserved bandwidth according to current traffic demand. To use autobandwidth, an LSP needs several additional parameters (Table 1), including minimum/maximum bandwidth, adjustment threshold, adjustment interval and sampling interval. Once every sampling interval (*e.g.*, 5 minutes), an LSP measures the average traffic demand flowing through it. Once every adjustment interval (*e.g.*, 15 minutes), it computes the maximum of the average traffic demand measured in each sampling interval. If the maximum traffic demand differs from the current reserved bandwidth by more than the adjust threshold and is within the minimum and maximum bandwidth, the LSP will invoke CSPF with the maximum traffic demand as the new reserved bandwidth.

3. EXPERIMENTAL METHODOLOGY

To study how MPLS-TE algorithms affect inter-DC traffic, we collected various types of data from October 15 to December 5 2010 from a portion of Microsoft's intercontinental production network (MSN), one of the largest OSP networks today. This portion of MSN comprises of several tens of DCs interconnected with

Table 1: Autobandwidth parameters

Parameter	Description
Subscription factor	% of interface bandwidth that can be reserved
Adjust interval	Time interval to trigger autobandwidth
Adjust threshold	% of change in reserved bandwidth to trigger autobandwidth
Min/max bw	Bandwidth limits of an LSP
Setup/hold priority	Priorities for determining LSP preemption

high-speed dedicated links with the core of network in US. All the inter-DC traffic is carried over 5K LSPs, each using autobandwidth, with 1-32 LSPs between each pair of DC. The data contains network topology and router and LSP configurations. For each LSP, it also contains each path change event and traffic volume in each 5-minute sampling interval.

Measuring LSP latency is a challenging task for two reasons (a) LSPs are unidirectional; as a result a simple ping would return One-Way Delay (OWD) latencies of two LSPs (the forward LSP and the reverse direction LSP). Separating out the two latencies would require strict time synchronization between the probers across DCs (b) Traffic between a DC pair is load balanced using hashing algorithms on all the LSPs (between 1 to 30) between the DCs. Hash functions are based on IP/TCP or even application level headers. As a result, to probe all the LSPs between a DC pair using simple ping, we must have one prober covering all the possible IP ranges allocated as well as a applications running in DCs.

Another way to measure LSP latency is to use LSP ping [6, 9]. However, because LSP ping is disabled in MSN , we choose to estimate LSP latency based on the geographical locations of the routers along an LSP path. Given an LSP, we calculate the great-circle distance between each pair of intermediate routers and sum it up to obtain the total geographical distance of the LSP. We then dividing the total distance by the speed of light in fiber to obtain the LSP latency. We verified for a few LSPs that the conversion indeed estimates correct delay with minimal error. Note that LSP is unidirectional, as a result, the latency measured in this mechanism is One-Way-Delay (OWD) estimation.

4. LSP LATENCY INFLATION

In this section we first describe the severity of the latency problem in an MPLS based network and then correlate latency inducing LSP path changes with dc pairs, routers and links in the network.

4.1 How badly is latency inflated?

Prevalence of latency inflation To quantify how widespread latency inflation is, we compute the difference between the minimum and maximum latency for each LSP during the 50-day period. Figure 3 plots the CDF of latency difference of all LSPs. We observe that a substantial number of LSPs encounter severe latency inflation. 20% (over 1K) of the LSPs experience latency inflation of over 20 ms. Moreover, the latency of 10% (over 500) of the LSPs is inflated by more than 40 ms! Because a single user request may trigger many round trips of inter-DC communication, such latency inflation could noticeably impair user-perceived performance.

To systematically measure the frequency and duration of latency inflation, we define a *latency spike* as the contiguous period of time during which the latency of an LSP is at least x ms *and* y% more than the minimum latency observed for the LSP. These two conditions capture the significance of latency inflation in both absolute and relative terms. As shown in Figure 4, a spike starts when both conditions are met and ends when either condition becomes false.

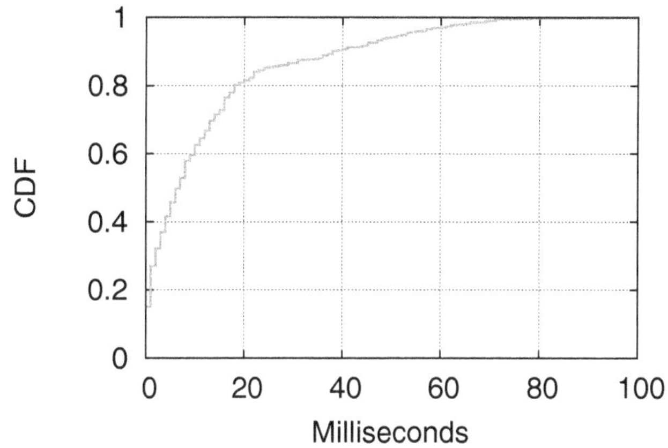

Figure 3: LSP latency difference (max-min) CDF

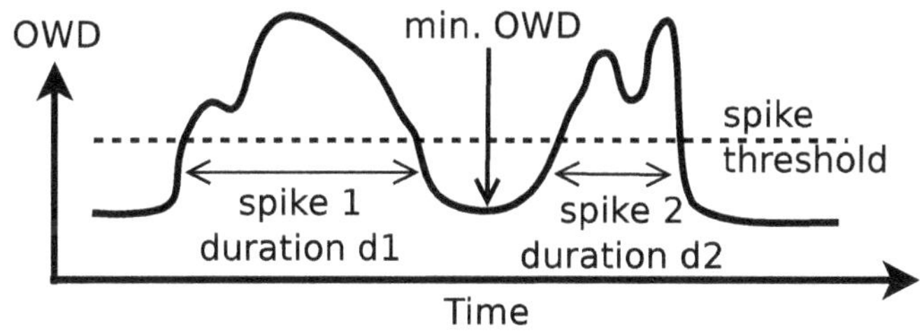

Figure 4: Definition of $spike(x, y)$

Figure 5 and 6 plot the CDF of total number and cumulative duration of latency spikes for each LSP. We observe that latency inflation is quite common. Under the (20ms, 20%) spike threshold, roughly 18% (over 900) of the LSPs experience at least one latency spike during the 50-day period. For 10% (over 500) of the LSPs, the cumulative duration of latency spikes is over 1 day. This problem becomes even more severe for the top 5% (250) of the LSPs whose cumulative spike duration is more than 10 days! This indicates persistent latency problem for the inter-DC traffic carried by those LSPs. Figure 5 and 6 also show similar curves under a more aggressive spike threshold of (30ms, 30%), where the total number and duration of latency spikes are only slightly smaller. This suggests the latency inflation experienced by many of the LSPs is indeed quite significant.

The traffic in the core of MSN network consists of only the traffic generated by inter-DC communications. All the 5K LSPs in the network use autobandwidth algorithms to manage paths and reserve bandwidth. Inter-DC links in the core of network exhibit over 99.9% of availability [4]. However, most LSPs exhibits long cumulative durations in spikes in order of days(figure 6). This suggests that severe LSPs spikes are caused by autobandwidth instead of failures.

Comparison with optimal TE strategy Although we have shown many LSPs encounter latency spikes frequently, so far it is unclear if those spikes are caused by insufficient network capacity or by inefficiency of MPLS-TE algorithms. To answer this question, we compute the *optimal* TE strategy that minimizes the weighted byte latency($\sum_{\forall LSP} lat. * bw$ / $\sum_{\forall LSP} bw$) for all inter-DC traffic. Given the network topology and traffic matrix, this can be formulated as a multi-commodity flow problem and solved using linear programming (LP) [8, 3, 1]. Note that although it is relatively easy to find the optimal TE strategy offline, the problem is much harder

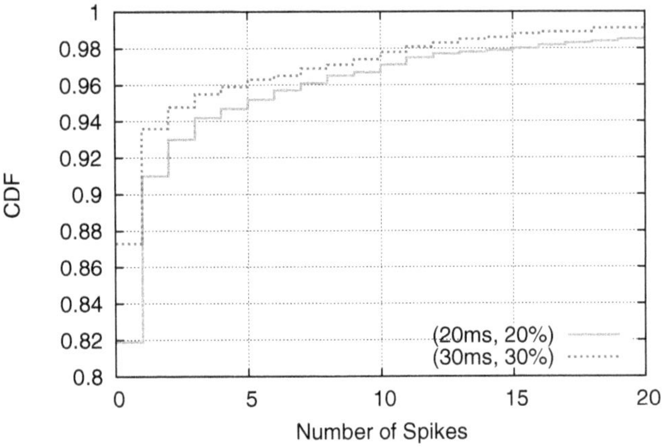

Figure 5: CDF of number of spikes observed by LSPs for different values of spikes

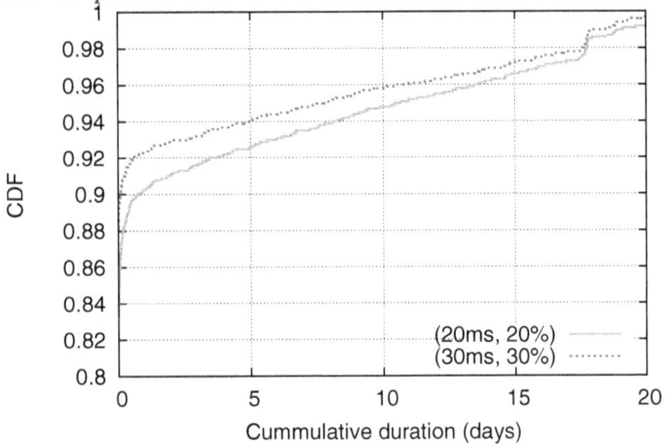

Figure 6: CDF of cumulative duration of spikes observed by LSPs for different values of spikes

to tackle online due to the of size of the topology (resulting in million variable LP) and volatility traffic demand.

We divide the time into 5-minute intervals and compute the optimal TE strategy for each interval using the method stated above. Compared to optimal routing, we found that MPLS based routing incurs an overall 10% to 22% increase in weighted byte latency over different snapshots spanning over a one day period. Figure 7 compares the latency at different traffic volume percentile under the optimal and MPLS-TE in a typical interval. There is substantial latency gap between the two TE strategies — the relative latency difference stays above 30% (y2 axis) at 50th, 90th, 95th, and 99th-percentile of traffic volume. Figure 8 plots the latency at the 99th-percentile of traffic volume under both TE strategies during an entire day. Except between midnight and early morning hour, the latency under MPLS-TE is consistently 20 ms (35%-40%) larger than that under the optimal TE, leaving enough space for improvement.

4.2 Is there a pattern in latency inflation?

LSP latency inflation is triggered by an LSP switching from a short to a long path. We now study the patterns of LSP path changes to see if they cluster at certain links, routers, DC pairs or time periods. Although there are many LSP path changes, we consider only those that cause a latency spike (*e.g.,*, latency jumps by more than 20 ms and 20%) and call them LLPC's (large latency path changes). We ignore the remaining path changes since they either have little

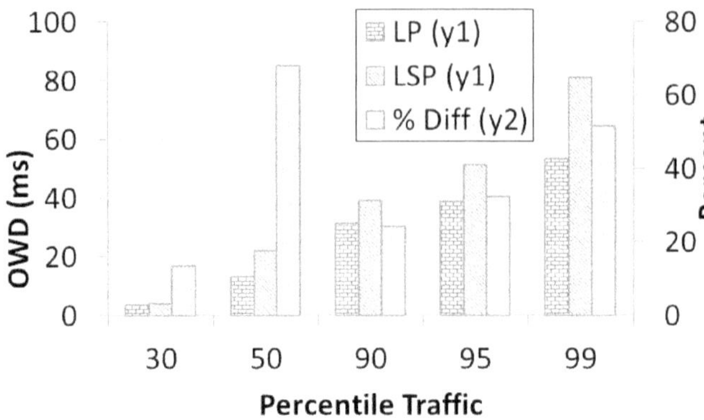

Figure 7: Byte latency bar chart for LSP and LP

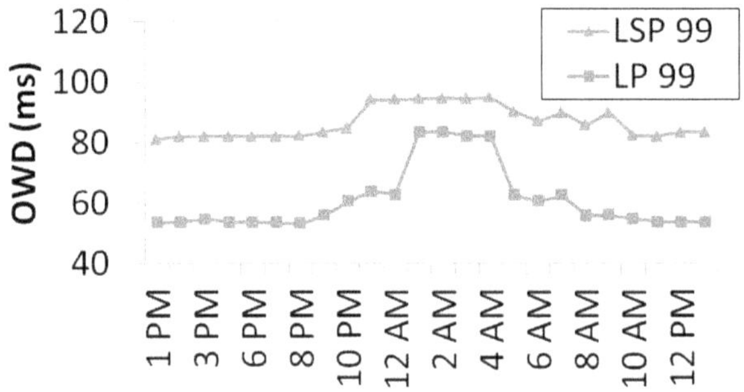

Figure 8: 99th percentile byte latency under MPLS (LSP) and Optimal Routing (LP)

impact on latency or reduce latency. For an LLPC, we attribute it to the old path rather than the new one because it is triggered by insufficient bandwidth on the former.

Correlation with links, routers and DC pairs. We first correlate each LLPC with the links, routers, and DC pair the corresponding LSP traverses. In Figure 9(a), the y-axis on the left shows the number of LLPC's per link sorted in an increasing order and the y-axis on the right shows the cumulative fraction of LLPC's observed by the links. The x-axis is normalized to anonymize the total number of links in MSN . Figure 9(b) and 9(c) plots similar curves for routers and DC pairs respectively. From these figures, we find that the LLPC's occur mostly at a small fraction of links and DC pairs — the top 10% of links and DC pairs account for 80% and 95% of the LLPC's respectively. This pattern is true for routers as well, although less pronounced. Our analysis suggests that the latency inflation problem could be significantly alleviated by adding capacity to a small subset of links.

Correlation with time. Next we correlate LLPC's with time. We divide the time into 1-hour bins and compute the number of LLPC's observed per (link, time-bin) pair. Figure 10(a) plots the number of LLPC's of each (link, time-bin) pair in an increasing order and the cumulative fraction of LLPC's of all the pairs. It shows the LLPC's are highly concentrated both at certain links and in certain time. 1% of the (link, time-bin) pairs witness 80% of the LLPC's. This distribution is even more skewed than that in Figure 9(a). Since bandwidth change is the primary cause of LSP path changes (§2.2), this is likely due to dramatic traffic surge in those (link, time-bin) pairs. We observe similar patterns for (router, time-bin) and (DC-pair, time-bin) pairs which are illustrated in Figure 10(b,c) respectively.

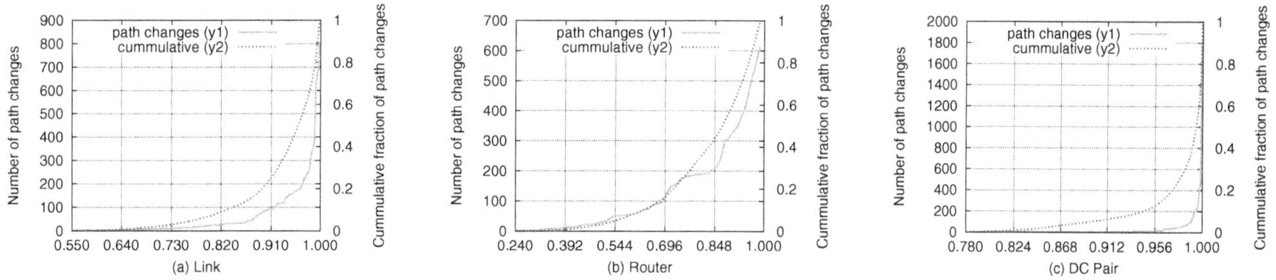

Figure 9: Histogram and cumulative path change per link, router and dcpair

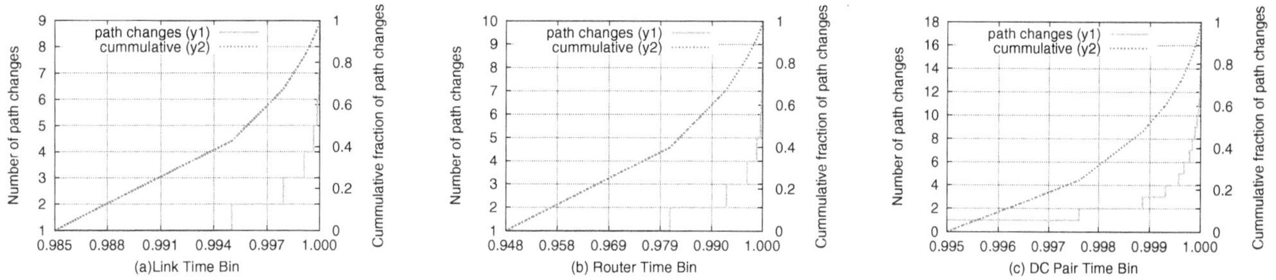

Figure 10: Histogram and cumulative path change per time bin per link, router and dcpair

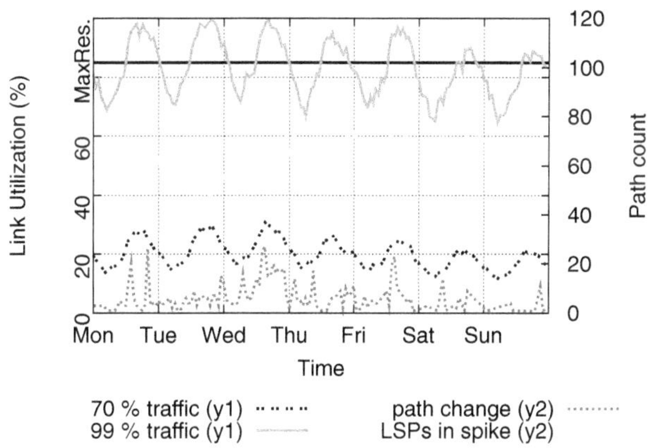

Figure 11: Link utilization and path change count as a function of time of day for one week period

Correlation with link utilization. Finally we study the impact of link utilization on LLPC's and latency inflation. Again we divide the time into 1-hour bins. In Figure 11, the left y-axis shows the 70th and 99th-percentile link utilization in each time bin during one week (the MaxRes line shows the maximum allowed reservation in links: configured at 85%). The right y-axis shows the number of LLPC's and the number of LSPs in latency spike in each time bin during the same period. We observe that although MSN is generally over-provisioned (70th-percentile link utilization is only around 20%), there are always certain links which are fully saturated (99th-percentile link utilization is around 100%). This is somewhat surprising because we would expect the traffic load is more evenly distributed during off-peak hours when there is abundant spare capacity. However, remember that in autobandwidth each LSP greedily looks for the shortest path, therefore it is possible that many LSPs are competing for just a few "critical" links even though other links are left idling.

Figure 11 also illustrates the number of LLPC's and number of LSPs in latency spike are strongly correlated with link utilization while all of them exhibit a clear time-of-day pattern. This conforms to our expectation since more LSPs will be forced to switch to longer path when the overall network utilization becomes higher.

Table 2: Impact of MPLS autobandwidth parameters

Parameter	Low	High
min bw	Large # of path changes	reserved bw wastage
max bw	No guarantee of traffic delivery if high requirement	harder to find new path (same as static LSP)
setup priority	Harder to find better path	Easy to find better path
hold priority	Easily give up current path	Stick to current path
adjust thres.	High # of path changes	LSP growth is harder
subscription	Less headroom for LSPs	Resource wastage
# of LSPs	High traffic per LSP	High LSP overhead

5. EFFECT OF AUTOBW PARAMETERS

LSP path changes and corresponding latency spikes are the direct consequences of both the autobandwidth algorithm and individual LSP's configuration parameters. Given the large number of LSPs in an OSP network, it is a common practice for operators to manually configure the LSP parameters with some static values which rarely change thereafter. In many cases, operators simply use the default values set by router vendors, *e.g.,* Cisco and Juniper. We study the impact of different LSP parameters on LSP latency spikes and summarize our findings in Table 2.

LSP priority We studied a few large latency spikes in LSPs traversing nearby DCs (as in figure 1). In this set of latency spikes, the LSPs, instead of traversing the direct shortest path between the DCs, traverse a considerably longer path (across the US). This was because the reserved bandwidth of the direct shortest path between the DCs was exhausted by another sets of LSPs with (mostly) equal or higher priority. Some of these LSPs traversed long distance and had several different path options available. Their decision to choose the particular link resulted in saturation of its reserved bandwidth. Later due to a bandwidth increase of a nearby DC LSP, autobandwidth moved the LSP to a much longer path. The situation gets complicated when several such improper path selections form a chain of dependencies.

The spike in cases like these could have been mitigated by increasing the priority of the LSP between the nearby DCs. But setting priority across thousands of LSPs to globally minimize latency in the network is a hard problem. Further, it is also unclear whether a static set of priorities would be sufficient to reduce the problem. As a future work, we plan to investigate how to automatically adjust priorities for the LSPs in latency spike in an online manner, to force them to switch to a shorter path, while ensuring minimal impact on other LSPs.

"All or nothing" autobandwidth policy The second cause for latency spikes in LSPs stems from the 'all-or-nothing' policy of autobandwidth algorithm. This severely impacts high-volume LSPs. A bandwidth increase of an LSP, running on a short path, where at least one of the links is close to its reservation limit, forces the entire LSP to another, long latency path. This results in the entire LSP traffic to traverse the long path even though the short path is capable of carrying most of the traffic.

As a part of future work, we plan to devise algorithms to split LSPs in such cases (currently done manually in some networks [10]). When an entire LSP will be forced to switch to a long path due to its traffic demand increase, we could subdivide the LSP (*on-the-fly* LSP split up) into two smaller ones so that only the increased traffic traverses longer path.

Minimum/maximum bandwidth Minimum and maximum bandwidth specify the bounds of the LSP bandwidth. A low minimum bandwidth value, renders an LSP fickle, triggering large number of path changes (minimal latency difference) since a small increase in bandwidth (a few 100KBs is sufficient) is now sufficient to trigger the bandwidth threshold. LSPs in this case change their path even though current path has sufficient available bandwidth because the autobandwidth tie-breaking algorithms (random, least filled, most filled) forces them to migrate to another equal cost path. A high value of minimum bandwidth wastes reservable bandwidth in the network.

A lower maximum bandwidth bounds the LSP bandwidth reservation forcing the fate of additional traffic on LSP to be uncertain and requires larger number of LSPs to be setup between the DC pair to accommodate the entire traffic. Each LSP incurs additional overhead in terms of computation and storage on ingress router and on the network. A large value for maximum bandwidth parameter makes LSP immobile, since during load, it gets harder for LSP to find path with free large reservable bandwidth. The 'all-or-nothing' policy causes further complications

Bandwidth threshold and subscription factor Bandwidth threshold dictates when should the autobandwidth algorithm be triggered. A small value renders and LSP to be fickle while a large value makes the LSP less responsive and requires larger headroom on link to absorb additional bandwidth. Similarly subscription factor which determines what fraction of link capacity must be reserved, play an important role. A small value wastes network capacity, while a large value diminishes the headroom for LSPs to grow so that autobandwidth gets triggered.

As a part of future work we will study how to adjust the autobandwidth parameters automatically. Also, so far, we have assumed all the LSPs and traffic are equally important. However, in an OSP network, different application traffic usually have distinct latency requirement. For instance, the traffic of most web applications is latency-sensitive, but the traffic of backup and replicate applications is not. A "smart" TE strategy would optimize latency only for the former while provisioning sufficient bandwidth for the latter. Such strategy could be implemented by classifying application traffic into delay-sensitive and delay-tolerant LSPs and assigning higher priority to the former type of LSPs. We will study effectiveness of such classification as our future work.

6. CONCLUSION

In this paper, we presented the first study of the effectiveness of MPLS-TE in a multi-continent production network connecting tens of data centers. Using detailed LSP traces collected over a 2-month period, we showed that a substantial number of LSPs encounter severe latency inflation. We further showed that 80% of latency inflation occur due to LSP path changes concentrated on 9% of the links, 30% of the routers, and 3% of the active DC-pairs. Our analysis confirms traffic load changes exceeding the capacity of a subset of links along the shortest paths of LSPs as the primary root cause of latency inflation but also uncovers poor configuration of MPLS-TE's autobandwidth algorithms in the studied network as a source of inefficacy. As future work, we are developing guidelines and automatic schemes to adjust autobandwidth configurations to changing traffic loads.

Acknowledgments

We thank the program committee and reviewers for their helpful comments, and especially our shepherd, K. Papagiannaki, whose detailed feedback significantly improved the paper and its presentation

7. REFERENCES

[1] D. Applegate and E. Cohen. Making intra-domain routing robust to changing and uncertain traffic demands: Understanding fundamental tradeoffs. In *Proc. of SIGCOMM*. ACM, 2003.

[2] D. Awduche, L. Berger, D. Gan, T. Li, V. Srinivasan, and G. Swallow. RFC 3209: RSVPâĂŤTE: exâĂŤtensions to RSVP for LSP tunnels. 2001.

[3] D. Bertsekas and R. Gallager. *Data networks*. Prentice-hall New York, 1992.

[4] P. Gill, N. Jain, and N. Nagappan. Understanding network failures in data centers: measurement, analysis, and implications. In *Proc. of SIGCOMM*. ACM, 2011.

[5] S. Kandula, D. Katabi, B. Davie, and A. Charny. Walking the tightrope: Responsive yet stable traffic engineering. In *Proc. of SIGCOMM*. ACM, 2005.

[6] K. Kompella and G. Swallow. RFC 4379: Detecting multi-protocol label switched (MPLS) data plane failures. 2006.

[7] H. Wang, H. Xie, L. Qiu, Y. Yang, Y. Zhang, and A. Greenberg. COPE: traffic engineering in dynamic networks. In *Proc. of SIGCOMM*. ACM, 2006.

[8] Y. Wang, H. Wang, A. Mahimkar, R. Alimi, Y. Zhang, L. Qiu, and Y. Yang. R3: Resilient routing reconfiguration. In *Proc. of SIGCOMM*. ACM, 2010.

[9] LSP Ping: MPLS LSP ping/traceroute for LDP/TE, and LSP ping for VCCV. `http://www.cisco.com/en/US/docs/ios/12_4t/12_4t11/ht_lspng.html`.

[10] MPLS for dummies, 2010. `http://www.nanog.org/meetings/nanog49/presentations/Sunday/mpls-nanog49.pdf`.

Summary Review Documentation for

"Latency Inflation with MPLS-based Traffic Engineering"

Authors: A. Pathak, M. Zhang, Y. Hu, R. Mahajan, D. Maltz

Reviewer #1

Strengths: MPLS traffic engineering mechanisms are likely in wide use. Understanding how some of these mechanisms work in practice, and some of their pitfalls is likely to be of interest and value to the measurement community. Measurements are from a well-known online service provider (MSN).

Weaknesses: A key implication of the work is that MPLS TE deployments that use autobandwidth also experience the kinds of problems identified in the paper, though it is not clear that that is the case.

Comments to Authors: MPLS is used widely in the Internet these days, and it's nice to see a empirical study of the effectiveness (problems!) of some of traffic engineering mechanisms. Since many ISPs don't reveal much of anything about their MPLS networks, this study is likely to be useful and to spur additional work in this area. I appreciate the fact that MSN was willing to air a bit of dirty laundry, because some of the inter-DC latency numbers are pretty ugly (i.e., Fig 1).

There's an apparent mismatch in the caption of Figure 3 and the text describing it. In the caption, it refers to spike magnitudes (and spikes haven't yet been defined). In the text, it refers to the CDF of the latency difference for all LSPs. Which is it? It seemed to me that the description of latency spikes might be best described first, before any of the results in that section.

In the all-or-nothing discussion in \S 5, you might mention that some ISPs are already doing some manual splitting of LSPs. See, e.g.,http://www.nanog.org/meetings/nanog49/presentations/Sunday/mpls-nanog49.pdf

There are a number writing and presentation issues that should be addressed. The writing and presentation were, for me, the very weakest aspects of the paper. While these are all basically "minor" issues, addressing them would help greatly in making the paper more readable and useful. There are precious few references to related work. In particular, there are *zero* citations of any IETF RFCs that specify the behavior of MPLS, RSVP-TE, or any of the other protocols or mechanisms that you describe. RFC 3209 should at least be cited, and it should be mentioned that the autobandwidth algorithms are (as far as I understand) vendor-specific (i.e., not standardized), though Cisco and Juniper implement them similarly. Also, ref [6] should really be a reference to RFC 4379 rather than a ref to a proprietary Cisco document: MPLS Ping is a standard mechanism. It might also be helpful to have references to both Cisco and Juniper (perhaps others) documents that specify how to configure autobandwidth parameters.

There are a number of instances of the phrase "LSP Path", which is of course redundant. There are a number of cases in which it is stated that "the LSP reserves the required bandwidth" (\S 2.2), or an "[LSP] continually monitors the traffic rate" (\S 2.1), or some other, similar statement that assigns action to the LSP. An LSP is simply the label switched path. It isn't a router or any other "active" agent. In a number of places, you could simply say that the label edge router, or LSR, or simply router, performs a specific action. In Section 5, LSPs are referred to as "fickle" (twice), which also is a bit of anthropomorphising.

Section 5 is really a general discussion section rather than specifically a discussion on autobandwidth parameters (that is, you discuss issues beyond those parameters). Might it be better to simply name this section "Discussion"?

Reviewer #2

Strengths: Latency between data centers is a critically important topic as is MPLS TE. The results are not surprising but are critically important for operators.

Weaknesses: The experimental methodology uses geographic information to approximate latency instead of active probing to infer the real latency.

Comments to Authors: Good short paper. This paper confirms what many including myself have expected that MPLS-TE is not optimal, quantifies the added delay, and attributes the root cause of delay to the hard-coded MPLS autobandwidth parameters. I believe this is an important result (read: we now have data that there really is a problem and it's degree) and I encourage the authors to follow through on their future plans to come up with a good solution.

My one big quibble with the paper was the experimental methodology. If I understand S3 correctly (it was a bit terse for a measurement paper), you did not do any active probing but rather summed the geographic distances between points in the MPLS tunnel -- is that correct? This methodology fails to account for delay inherent to store and forward devices or to the fact that fibers layouts have addition constraints (mountains, roads, private property, etc.) and are not always able to take the shortest path between two points. None of this contradicts your results, but in your followup work, I would recommend that you present some active probing data to better validate your claim that this is a reasonable approximation of latency (I found the one sentence disclaimer "We verified with a few LSPs that..." a bit of a red flag). Ok, so Microsoft doesn't use LP ping... just use standard ping from inside the data centers - it shouldn't be too hard to setup a vantage point in each data center.

Fig 9c: it seems like a very small number of DC-pairs are causing a lot of the flapping -- did you talk to the operators about this? If yes, what was the response? Is this simply that these nodes are more heavily loaded, under-provisioned, or because they are sub-optimally configured? Adding feedback from the operators could improve this paper.

Another point to look (likely in follow up work) at is the 5 minute timer that autobandwidth uses to recalculate routes: if that were decreased and the algorithms made more responsive, is there any additional benefit?

Reviewer #3

Strengths: The first look into MPLS-TE in practice. Nice dataset. Paper shows some problems with current TE implementations that should lead to further research.

Weaknesses: The measurements of latency are not direct and some of the analysis could be a little deeper.

Comments to Authors: This paper presents an interesting study of MPLS-TE. To the best of my knowledge this is the first study of a large-scale production network running MPLS-TE. I feel that I've learned more about MPLS-TE and the issues that can arise in practice. I just have a few comments.

From your introduction, it is clear that OSP operations have strict requirements for latency between data centers, could you give some numbers of the ranges of acceptable latencies? It would help people who want to find solutions to the problems you are pointing out.

When you present the network in Sec. 3, it would be nice to give an idea of the geographical spread. You only say that it is intercontinental in the conclusion.

At the last paragraph of Sec. 3, it would be nice to add a small explanation of how you verify that your latency estimation actually matches latency. It is a little disappointing that you can't get direct measurements of latency (why not just do pings from the data centers?), at least elaborating on the validation would help.

Why do label Figures 4, 7, and 8 with OWD, if earlier you've defined latency and that is what you use in the text?

People usually use the term stretch to refer to latency inflation.

Sec. 4.2 talks about correlation, but it uses no metric of statistical correlation. One can kind of see the correlation in the example week in Fig. 11, but the numbers would be more general.

Reviewer #4

Strengths: This is the first paper I know that demonstrates the impact of MPLS TE on latency across a network. The authors show a good understanding of how MPLS TE works and discuss possible reasons behind such a phenomenon.

Weaknesses: Unfortunately, the paper does not really prove that the reason behind the latency increase is the way autobandwidth works. The correlation with utilization is weak at best and there is no significant analysis performed to convince that this is the case - for that reason my assessment would be between a 2 and a 3 with a technical correctness at similar levels.

Comments to Authors: I find that this paper makes an attempt to look into a very interesting problem - that of the performance of traffic engineering mechanisms like MPLS TE. Providers have deployed such a solution in the hope that they will be able to better handle performance in their network, but as the authors mention very little is known as to how successful the employed mechanisms actually are. Moreover, as the authors demonstrate these mechanisms are typically accompanied by a number of thresholds that network operators rarely change - and reasonably so, since nobody could really estimate the impact of those changes.

Interestingly, this paper shows that employing MPLS-TE can lead to significant increases in latency as compared to shortest paths. A large number of paths inside Microsoft's Online Service Network are showing spikes in latency, thus affecting the performance of the provided services.

The authors have studied the magnitude of latency increases, the number of data centers that they affect, as well as routers. They have further attempted to correlate it with link utilization with the goal to demonstrate that such latency increases may be due to the reaction of autobandwidth mechanism in high load conditions. Unfortunately, that point is never really proven. I would really have liked to see the authors formulating a hypothesis and testing it according to their data. Showing the result on Figure 11 is by no means a proof of that point. For each time bin they have identified the 70% and 99% percentile load across the network and then counted the number of path changes. They claim that the correlation is high but the presented figure is far from conclusive. I would like to have seen something more precise, where the authors track utilization across the network, the LSP messages that will be triggered for sure if autobandwidth kicks in, and then the precise correlation of that LSP change with the utilization increase in one of the links of the LSP. Otherwise, you have not really shown what you claim.

For that reason, i would say that this paper should only be accepted conditionally and published only if the authors manage to properly demonstrate such a correlation of remove that claim from the paper. You need to define the several causes that could lead to a path change (such as failure, etc) and then clearly test the hypothesis of link utilization being the culprit. Given the novelty of the data set and the rest of the analysis I would not say that this paper is a straight reject.

Finally, the authors compare MPLS TE latency with that obtained through an optimization problem that is never precisely defined. I think it is worth spending some space trying to make the paper self-consistent. What is byte weighted latency.

Reviewer #5

Strengths: This is the very first paper that I have read on the measured performance of MPLS networks. These results would be interesting to network operators.

Weaknesses: The paper simply reported the results in a straightforward way. Rather than just scratching the surface of the problem (hey look the paths are not optimal), I wish the paper had gone deeper to analyze the causes of why these sub-optimal paths.

Comments to Authors: This is an interesting paper, perhaps the first one, to report MPLS path quality in a real, large operational network. The specific measurement results would be interesting to people in operations and perhaps also in research (to understand why sub-optimal paths occurring from time to time).

However as someone who knows a bit about MPLS, the paper did not seem that exciting. I think a main reason is perhaps the result is a bit shallow. MPLS is simply a means to balance traffic flows across network, this measurement study shows that the decision process (on the path selection and dynamic adjustment of MPLS circuits) does not pick the best decision all the time -- this is expected (I actually thought the performance was not bad:). To me the more interesting bit is not how bad the delay can be inflated, but to explain why MPLS picked sub-optimal paths from time to time.

Response from the Authors

We mention the two important points raised by the reviewers and how we addressed them in our paper.

1. The paper does not prove directly that autobandwidth is the root cause of latency spikes

MSN comprises tens of DCs interconnected with a dedicated network. All the traffic in MSN is carried over LSPs which are managed by autobandwidth algorithm.

- Most inter-dc links have three 9's availability (figure 9(c) in sigcomm'11 paper (Understanding Network Failures in Data Centers: Measurement, Analysis, and Implications)).

- Three 9's for 50 days is 1.2 hours. However, about 82.8% of LSPs which show severe spikes have cumulative spike durations more than 1.2 hrs. Also, about 98.9% of global cumulative LSP spike duration (sum of all severe LSP spikes across all LSPs) is originated from LSP spikes where individual spikes are more than 1.2 hrs.

This suggests that LSPs spikes which are severe are caused by autobw instead of failures. We confirmed similar LSP spikes in MPLS simulations.

2. Use of geographical distances to estimate latency instead of directly measuring it.

We currently cannot obtain the data for direct LSP latency measurement. The MSN operators do not provide LSP ping. It is also difficult to associate end-to-end ping data with an individual LSP due to load-balancing across multiple LSPs between the same DC pair. The latency estimate based on great-circle distance and speed-of-light is the best approximate we can get.

We have included the above details in the paper.

ShaperProbe: End-to-end Detection of ISP Traffic Shaping using Active Methods*

Partha Kanuparthy, Constantine Dovrolis
School of Computer Science, Georgia Institute of Technology
partha@cc.gatech.edu, constantine@gatech.edu

ABSTRACT

We present an end-to-end measurement method for the detection of traffic shaping. Traffic shaping is typically implemented using token buckets, allowing a maximum burst of traffic to be serviced at the peak capacity of the link, while any remaining traffic is serviced at a lower shaping rate. The contribution of this paper is twofold. First, we develop an active end-to-end detection mechanism, referred to as ShaperProbe, that can infer whether a particular path is subject to traffic shaping, and in that case, estimate the shaper characteristics. Second, we analyze results from a large-scale deployment of ShaperProbe on M-Lab over the last 24 months, detecting traffic shaping in several major ISPs. Our deployment has received more than one million runs so far from 5,700 ISPs.

Categories and Subject Descriptors

C.2.3 [**Computer-Communication Networks**]: Network Operations—*Network monitoring*

General Terms

Measurement, Performance

Keywords

Active probing, traffic shaping, inference

1. INTRODUCTION

The increasing penetration of broadband access technologies, such as DSL, DOCSIS and WiMAX, provides users with a wide range of upstream and downstream service rates. Broadband users need to know whether they actually get the service rates they pay for. On the other hand, ISPs now have an extensive toolbox of traffic management mechanisms they can apply to their customers' traffic: application classifiers, schedulers, active queue managers etc. In this paper we focus on a class of such mechanisms referred to as *traffic shapers* or *traffic policers*.[1]

A traffic shaper is a single-input single-output packet forwarding module that behaves as follows: Consider a link of capacity C bps, associated with a "token bucket" of size σ tokens. Whenever the bucket is not full, tokens are generated at a rate ρ tokens per second, with $\rho < C$. The link can transmit an arriving packet of size L bits only if the token bucket has at least L tokens - upon the transmission of the packet, the shaper consumes L tokens from the bucket. So, if we start with a full token bucket of size σ tokens, and with a large burst of packets of size L bits each (suppose that σ is an integer multiple of L for simplicity), the link will be able to transmit k of those packets at the rate of the capacity C, with $k = \frac{\sigma/L}{1-\rho/C}$. After those k packets, the link will start transmitting packets at the token generation rate ρ. Usually ρ is referred to as the "shaping rate", the capacity C is also referred to as the "peak rate", while σ is referred to as the "maximum burst size". Another way to describe a traffic shaper is by specifying that the *maximum number of bits* that can be transmitted in any interval of duration τ, starting with a full token bucket, is:

$$\hat{A}(\tau) = \min\{L + C\tau, \sigma + \rho\tau\}$$

The difference between a traffic shaper and a traffic policer is that the former has a buffer to hold packets that arrive when the token bucket is empty [6, 23]. A policer simply drops such "non-conforming" packets. In other words, a shaper delays packets that exceed the traffic shaping profile (σ, ρ), while a policer drops them.[2] Policers can cause excessive packet losses and so shapers are more common in practice - we focus on the latter in the rest of the paper.

Why would a residential ISP deploy traffic shaping? First, to allow a user to exceed the service rate that he/she has paid for, for a limited burst size. In that case the user pays for ρ bps, with the additional service capacity $C - \rho$ marketed as a free service enhancement. This is, for instance, how Comcast advertises their PowerBoost traffic shaping mechanism [5]. Second, an ISP may want to limit the service rate provided to the aggregate traffic produced or consumed by a customer, or to limit the service rate consumed by a certain application (e.g. BitTorrent). This form of shaping is relevant to the *network neutrality* debate. Third, certain ISPs prefer to describe their service rates as upper bounds

*This work was supported by a research gift from Google Inc.

IMC'11, November 2–4, 2011, Berlin, Germany.

[1] When it is not important to distinguish between shaping and policing, we will simply refer to such mechanisms as "traffic shapers" or just "shapers".

[2] A shaper also drops packets once its droptail buffer is full.

for what the user will actually get, e.g., a downstream rate of *at most* 6Mbps. In that case, a shaper can be used to enforce the upper bound of the service rate.

The contribution of this paper is twofold. First, we develop an *active end-to-end detection mechanism*, referred to as *ShaperProbe*, that can infer whether a particular path is subject to traffic shaping, and in that case, estimate the shaper characteristics C, ρ and σ. Second, we analyze results from a large-scale deployment of ShaperProbe on M-Lab [11] since May 2009, detecting traffic shaping in several major ISPs. Our deployment received about one million runs over the last two years from more than 5,700 ISPs; we currently see 2,000-3,000 runs per day (see Figure 1). All data collected through ShaperProbe runs is publicly available through M-Lab [8].[3]

Traffic shaping detection and estimation methods can be used in different ways: *as a library (API)*; and as a *service* that enables users/administrators to detect or verify their SLAs/shaping configurations. In this paper, we focus on the latter. The ShaperProbe client is a download-and-click userspace binary (no superuser privileges or installation needed) for 32/64-bit Windows, Linux, and OS X; a plugin is also available for the *Vuze* BitTorrent client. The non-UI logic is about 6000 lines of open source native code.

There are several challenges that one needs to tackle when designing an active measurement service that can scale to thousands of users per day, including *accuracy*, *usability* and *non-intrusiveness*. Even though these challenges are often viewed as not significant, at least from the research perspective, they have greatly influenced several design choices and parameter values in ShaperProbe.

Related work. Lakshminarayanan *et al.* recorded initial observations of traffic shaping in residential ISPs in 2003 [18]. Dischinger *et al.* found downstream traffic shaping in a 2007 study [13] using a 10s flow at 10Mbps; they did not find evidence of upstream traffic shaping. More recently, two studies [12, 21] focused on the effects of PowerBoost in cable ISPs. Recent research efforts on detecting traffic discrimination in ISPs [14, 16, 19, 20, 22, 24, 25] compliment our work, since we consider the problem of detecting traffic shaping independent of differentiation. In particular, Glasnost [14] uses aggregate throughput of an emulated application and compares it with a baseline to *detect* throughput differences. Weinsberg *et al.* infer queue weights of a discriminatory scheduler [24].

In the rest of the paper, we describe the active detection method (§2), implementation and deployment of ShaperProbe (§3), and look at ShaperProbe data using case studies of four ISPs (§4).

2. ACTIVE PROBING METHOD

The active probing method is an end-to-end process in which one end-host $\mathcal{SND}$ sends packets on the network path to the receiver $\mathcal{RCV}$. We detect the presence of traffic shaping in the path $\mathcal{SND} \rightarrow \mathcal{RCV}$ at $\mathcal{RCV}$.

Suppose that the narrow link's capacity on the path is C, and that the sender probes at a *constant bit rate* $R_s = C$. The ShaperProbe capacity estimation process is described in

[3]We log per-packet send and receive timestamps and sequence numbers for all probing phases, and client IP address and server timestamp (UTC) for each run.

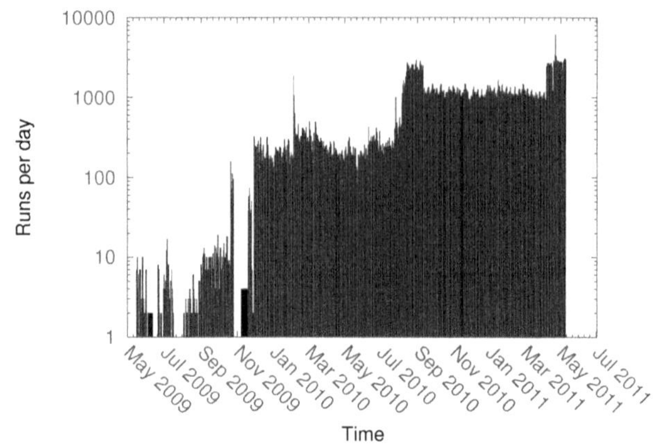

Figure 1: ShaperProbe: volume of runs. The gaps in time show downtime due to tool enhancements.

the Tech Report [17]. The receiver $\mathcal{RCV}$ records the received rate timeseries $R_r(t)$. We compute $R_r(t)$ by discretizing time into fixed size non-overlapping intervals of size Δ. For simplicity, assume that the probing starts at $t = 0$, and that intervals are numbered as integers $i \geq 1$. The i'th interval includes all packets received in the interval $[(i-1)\,\Delta, i\Delta)$, where packet timestamps are taken at $\mathcal{RCV}$ upon receipt of each packet. The discretized received rate timeseries $R_r(i)$ is estimated as the total bytes received in interval i divided by Δ. Note that this estimator of $R_r(t)$ can result in an error of up to $\epsilon = \pm S/\Delta$ where S is the MTU packet size. By choosing a reasonably large Δ, we can reduce the magnitude of ϵ relative to the true received rate.

In the presence of a token bucket traffic shaper (or policer) on $\mathcal{SND} \rightarrow \mathcal{RCV}$, there exists a value of $i > 1$ at which the received rate timeseries $R_r(i)$ undergoes a *level shift to a lower value*. Our goal is to detect the presence of a level shift, and estimate the token bucket parameters using $R_r(i)$.

2.1 Detection

We want to detect a level shift in R_r in *real-time*, i.e., as we compute the received rate for each new interval. Note that the receiver $\mathcal{RCV}$ is also receiving new packets during the level-shift detection process, and so our method should be fast and computationally light-weight to avoid the introduction of timestamping jitter. The detection method is rather simple and relies on nonparametric rank statistics of R_r so that it is robust to outliers [15].

We compute ranks online. Suppose that we have estimated n values of R_r so far. At the start of the new interval $n+1$ (i.e., after the receipt of the first packet in that interval), we compute $R_r(n)$ and update the ranks $r(i)$ of $R_r(i)$ for $i = 1 \ldots n$. We identify τ as the *start of level shift* if it is the first interval index that satisfies the following three conditions.

First, all ranks at the left of τ are *equal to or higher* than all ranks at the right of τ:

$$\min_{i=1\ldots\tau-1} r(i) \geq \max_{j=\tau+1\ldots n} r(j) \quad (1)$$

Second, we have observed a minimum time duration before and after the current rate measurement:

$$n_L < \tau < n - n_R \quad (2)$$

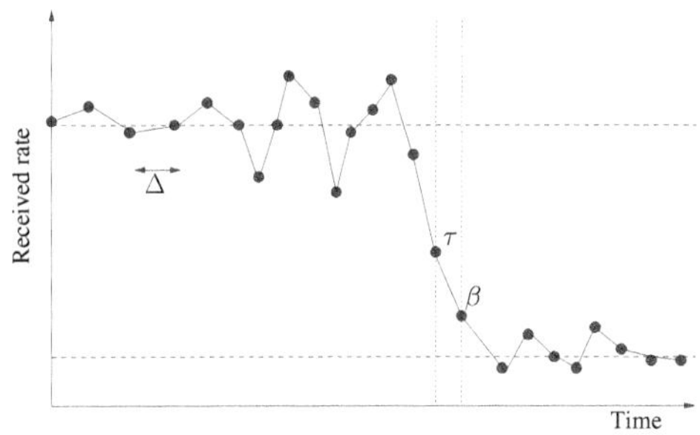

Figure 2: Active probing: Level shift detection.

The value of n_L is chosen based on empirical observations of typical burst durations in ISP deployments, and n_R is a sanity check to ensure that the drop in rate is not just a temporary variation (e.g., due to cross traffic).

Third, we require that there is a *significant drop* in the median rate at point τ:

$$\underset{i=1\ldots\tau}{\tilde{R}_r(i)} > \gamma \underset{j=\tau\ldots n}{\tilde{R}_r(j)} \tag{3}$$

where $\tilde{R}_r$ denotes the median, and γ is a suitable threshold. We select γ based on empirical observations of ISP capacities and shaping rates in practice (see Section 2.3).

Similarly, we detect the *end of a level shift* index β such that $\beta \geq \tau$ and β is the *last* point which satisfies the rate condition in Equation 1. Figure 2 illustrates the two level shift indices.

2.2 Estimation

After the detection of a level shift, we estimate the token bucket parameters from the rate timeseries R_r as follows. The token generation rate (shaping rate) ρ is estimated as the *median* (to be robust to outliers) of the received rate measurements *after* β:

$$\hat{\rho} = \underset{i=\beta+1\ldots n}{\tilde{R}_r(i)} \tag{4}$$

We estimate the token bucket depth (burst size) σ based on the number of bytes sent till the τ'th time interval. We estimate a range for σ, since we discretize time in to intervals of size Δ, based on the estimate $\hat{\rho}$ of ρ and the received rates:

$$\hat{\sigma} = \sum_{i=1}^{\tau} [R(i) - \hat{\rho}]\Delta \pm \frac{[R(i) - \hat{\rho}]\,\Delta}{2} \tag{5}$$

2.3 Parameter Selection

As in any other measurement tool that is used in practice, there are some parameters that need to be tuned empirically. In ShaperProbe, the key parameters are the factor γ, the probing duration Λ, and the interval duration Δ. We have selected the values of these parameters based on the detection of actual shaper deployments in broadband ISPs for which we knew the "ground truth".

Figure 3 shows the ratio of the capacity over the shaping rate C/ρ and the maximum burst duration (in seconds) for 36 advertised traffic shaper deployments at Comcast and Cox in metro Atlanta in October 2010. Note that all tiers have a capacity-to-shaping rate ratio of 1.1 or higher; in the current implementation of ShaperProbe we use $\gamma = 1.1$.

The probing duration Λ should be sufficiently long so that it can detect as many ISP shaping configurations as possible,

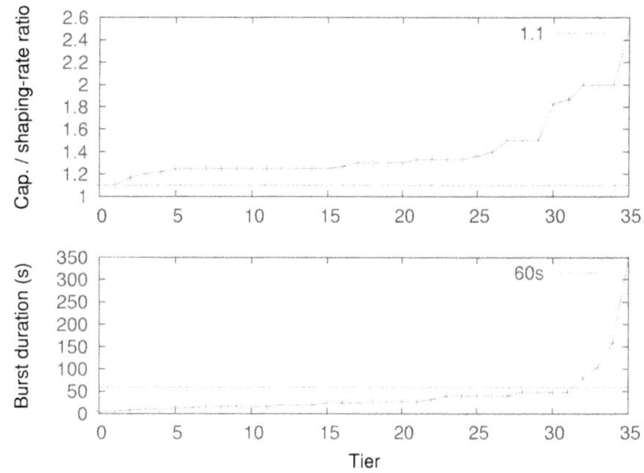

Figure 3: Advertised Comcast, Cox tiers: required γ and Λ.

while at the same time keeping the total probing duration reasonably short when there is no shaping. Figure 3 shows that the burst duration is at most 48s, except for 4 out of 36 configurations. Λ is set to 60s in the current implementation. A typical ShaperProbe residential run lasts for 2-3 minutes.

The averaging window size Δ should be sufficiently large to keep the estimation noise in R_r low, and sufficiently short so that Λ includes several rate samples. We have performed 100 trials in the upstream direction of a Comcast residential connection, whose SLA we know (4.5Mbps shaped to 2Mbps). We found that for $\Delta \geq 50$ms, the shaping detection rate is 100%; as Δ approaches the inter-packet gap, the detection rate drops significantly. We set Δ to 300ms so that we can detect shaping even in low capacity links.

3. SHAPERPROBE IMPLEMENTATION

The design of a tool that works well on a wide variety of network conditions, OS platforms and broadband link technologies is challenging. A first challenge is that ShaperProbe requires a fast and accurate estimate of the narrow-link capacity between the sender and receiver; this estimate is the ShaperProbe probing rate. ShaperProbe uses packet train dispersion for estimating capacity; it additionally probes using a longer train to be robust to wireless link effects. Second, the probing method should be able to generate traffic at a *constant rate*, even with a coarse-grained userspace OS timer granularity. At the same time, the transmission of packets should not impose heavy load on the CPU resources at the sender. ShaperProbe sends small periodic packet trains, and times the inter-train gaps such that busy-wait loops are minimized. Third, the ShaperProbe client should be non-intrusive. The client and server abort the probing process if they observe losses on the path. Finally, cross traffic on the path may lead to temporary drops in the received rate R_r; we need to incorporate a filtering mechanism that can remove *outliers* from R_r. ShaperProbe filters outliers using recorded observations from the local neighborhood of the R_r timeseries. The Tech Report [17] describes how ShaperProbe addresses the previous challenges and implementation details.

We currently run load-balanced ShaperProbe server replicas on 48 M-Lab hosts connected directly to tier-1 ASes. For measurement accuracy, we allow only one client at each server replica at any time.

ISP	Upstream (%)	Dwnstrm. (%)
Comcast	**71.5** (34874)	**73.5** (28272)
Road Runner	6.5 (7923)	**63.9** (5870)
AT&T	10.1 (8808)	10.9 (7748)
Cox	**63** (5797)	**47.4** (4357)
MCI-Verizon	5.6 (8753)	8.4 (7733)

Table 1: Shaping detections: top-5 ISPs in terms of ShaperProbe runs. For each ISP we show percentage of runs with detected shaping and number of total runs.

C (Mbps)	ρ (Mbps)	σ (MB)	Burst duration (s)
3.5	1	5	16.7
4.8	2	5, 10	15.2, 30.5
8.8	5.5	10	25.8
14.5	10	10	18.8

(a) Upstream.

C (Mbps)	ρ (Mbps)	σ (MB)	Burst duration (s)
19.4	6.4	10	6.4
21.1	12.8	10	10.1
28.2	17	20	14.9
34.4	23.4	20	15.3

(b) Downstream.

Table 2: Comcast: detected shaping properties.

4. RESULTS

In this section, we take a first look at results from the ShaperProbe deployment at M-Lab. We first examine accuracy using two ISPs for which we know the shaping ground truth and from emulation experiments.

Accuracy. We test the latest version of ShaperProbe on two residential ISPs, AT&T and Comcast, at two homes in metro Atlanta. We use the High-Speed Internet service of Comcast, and the DSL service of AT&T. At the time of these experiments, the Comcast configuration was: {10Mbps up, 22Mbps down} shaped to {2Mbps up, 12Mbps down} [5], while the AT&T configuration did not use shaping ({512Kbps up, 6Mbps down}) [2]. Out of 60 runs, we did not observe any shaping detection errors in either direction at the AT&T connection, while we observed two upstream false negatives at the Comcast connection due to capacity underestimation.

We also emulated token bucket shaping on a wide-area path between a residential Comcast connection and a server deployed at the Georgia Tech campus. We use the LARTC `tc` tool on Linux with a 2.6.22 kernel on a dual-NIC 1GHz Celeron router with 256MB RAM. Over 20 experiments for each token bucket configuration and 10 configurations, we found that ShaperProbe detects the traffic shaper in all (200) experiments; it also accurately estimates the shaping rate and bucket depth for all configurations.

Data preprocessing. In the following, we analyze data collected from the ShaperProbe M-Lab service. First, we consider runs from the latest ShaperProbe release, collected between 20th October 2009 and 9th May 2011 (total of 845,223 runs). Each run's trace contains per-packet timestamps and sequence numbers for the upstream and downstream probing "half runs". Second, we say that a half run is "unfinished" if no shaping was detected and the run lasted for less than 50s - we discard such runs. All completed half runs which are not diagnosed as shaping are considered *no-shaping* cases. Recall that ShaperProbe probes each direction for 60s, and terminates a half run if it either detected shaping or if it observed packet losses during probing. A half run can also be unfinished if the user aborted the client before it could run to completion. After preprocessing, we have a total of 281,394 upstream and 236,423 downstream finished half runs.

Next, we cluster AS numbers into ISPs using their `whois` AS names. The AS information was obtained from Cymru's whois database in May 2011. Runs which passed the preprocessing checks come from 5,167 distinct ISPs. The top five ISPs in terms of the number of runs as well as the fraction of shaping detections are shown in Table 1.

It should be noted that there are several factors that influence the fraction of shaping detections in an ISP. First, ISPs provide multiple tiers of service; some tiers may not use shaping, while service tiers change frequently. Second, an ISP may not deploy shaping in all geographic markets. Third, the access link type can be a factor: a DSL provider can dynamically change the link capacity instead of doing shaping, while a cable provider is more likely to use shaping since DOCSIS provides fixed access capacities. Fourth, for a given connection, the shaping parameters can be dynamically adjusted based on time or load conditions in the ISP. Fifth, an ISP A can originate the BGP prefixes of a smaller ISP B that deploys shaping (while A does not) - we cannot distinguish A from B based on BGP prefix-to-ASN mapping. We study some of these factors in ISP case studies next. Some ISPs disclose their traffic shaping configurations; in such cases, we can validate our observations.

4.1 Case Study: Comcast

Comcast offers Internet connectivity to homes [5] and enterprises [3], and uses two types of access technologies: cable (DOCSIS 3.0) and Ethernet. In each access category, it offers multiple tiers of service. Comcast shapes traffic using the PowerBoost technology [4].

Shaping profiles. We observed many shaping configurations at Comcast between October 2009 and May 2011. Figure 4 shows the shaping configuration of each run (ordered by capacity). For each run, designated by an "ID", we plot two points in the top panel for the capacity and the shaping rate; and a point in the bottom panel for the burst size. The capacities form an *envelope* of the shaping rate points. We see that there are strong *modes* in the data; Table 2 is a summary of these modes. For higher capacities, we see a larger number of modes in the shaping rate. However, at the tail of the capacity distribution there is only one shaping rate that corresponds to the highest service tier provided by Comcast. We verified our observations with the Comcast website listings [3, 5]. Note that we may not observe all service tiers in that web page, depending on the number of ShaperProbe users at each service tier. We also observe two or three burst sizes that are used across all tiers; the PowerBoost FAQ mentions 10MB and 5MB burst sizes [4].

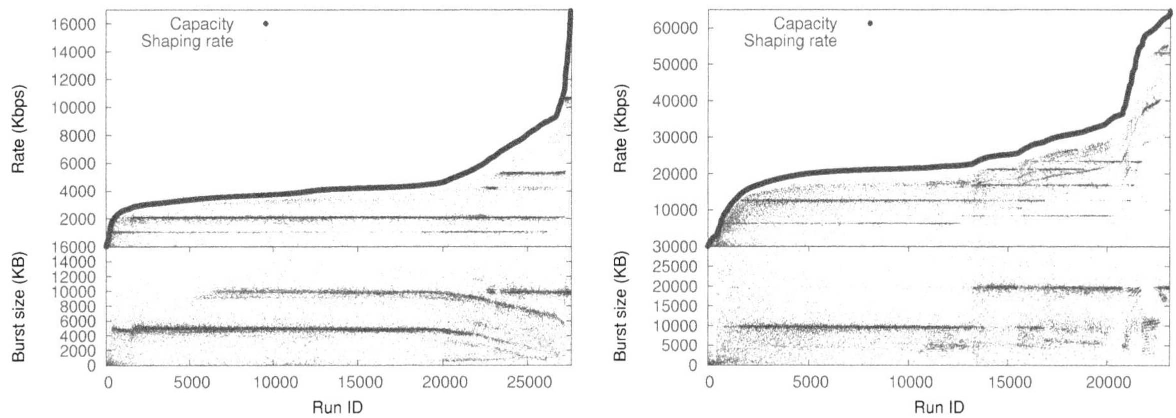

(a) Upstream. (b) Downstream.

Figure 4: Comcast: Shaping characteristics.

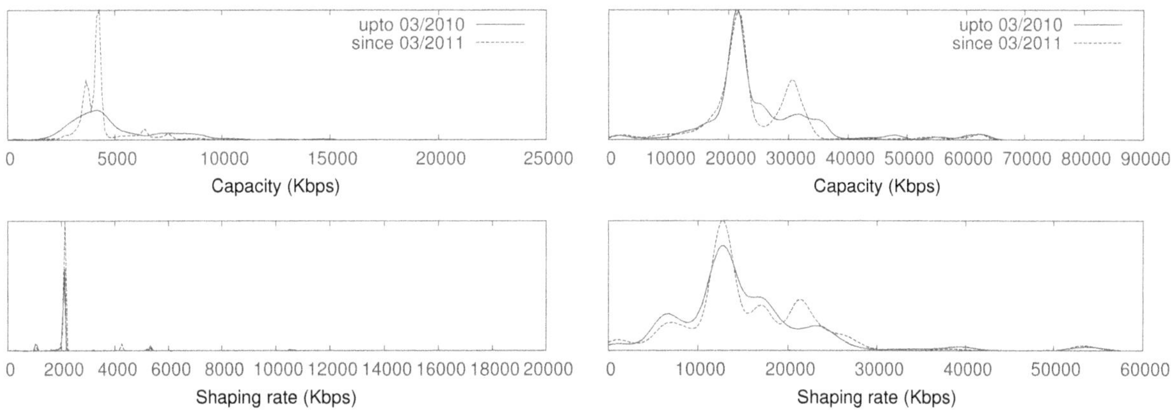

(a) Upstream. (b) Downstream.

Figure 5: Comcast: histogram of bandwidth with time.

Note that the capacity curves do not show strong modes, unlike the shaping rates. This is due to the underlying DOCSIS access technology. The cable modem uplink is a non-FIFO scheduler; depending on the activity of other nodes at the CMTS, the capacity can vary due to customer scheduling and DOCSIS concatenation. A DOCSIS downlink can also influence the dispersion-based capacity estimates under heavy traffic load conditions because it is a broadcast link.

Did shaping configurations change during the last two years?. We compare data from Comcast collected in October 2009-March 2010 and in March-May 2011. Figure 5 shows estimates of the capacity and shaping rate distributions using a Gaussian kernel density estimator. In the upstream direction, the capacity and shaping rates (the modes of the corresponding distributions) have not changed significantly. The downstream links show a new capacity mode of 30Mbps and a shaping rate mode of 22Mbps in 2011. We did not find significant changes in the burst size during the last two years.

Non-shaped runs. We examine runs in which ShaperProbe did not detect shaping. Figure 6 compares the capacity distribution in such runs with the shaping rate distribution in shaping runs. The non-shaped capacity distributions are *similar* to the shaping rate distributions. Non-shaping runs occur due to the following two reasons. First, Comcast provides service tiers that do not include PowerBoost, but have capacities similar to PowerBoost service tiers (e.g., the Ethernet 1Mbps and 10Mbps business service). Second, it is possible that cross traffic resulted in an empty token bucket at the start of the measurement, and so the capacity that ShaperProbe estimated was equal to the shaping rate; we would not detect shaping in that case.

4.2 Case Studies: Road Runner and Cox

Road Runner (RR) is a cable ISP. A unique aspect of RR is that we have found evidence of downstream shaping, but *no evidence* of upsteam shaping in any service tier on their web pages. The ShaperProbe measurements for RR support this observation - 94% of the upstream runs *did not* detect shaping, while 64% of the downstream runs did. Another interesting aspect of RR is that shaping depends on

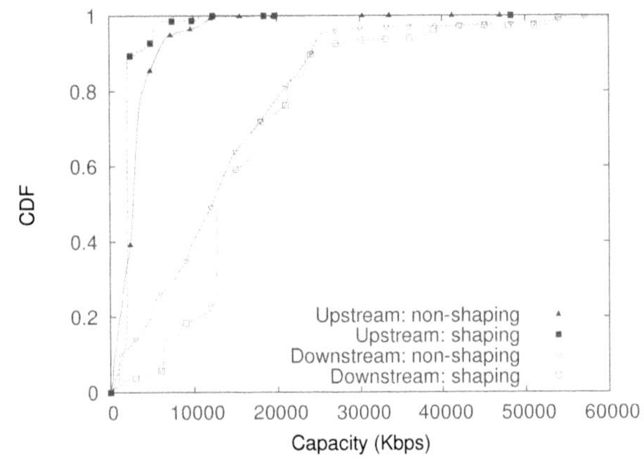

Figure 6: Comcast: distribution of capacities in non-shaping and shaping rate in shaping runs.

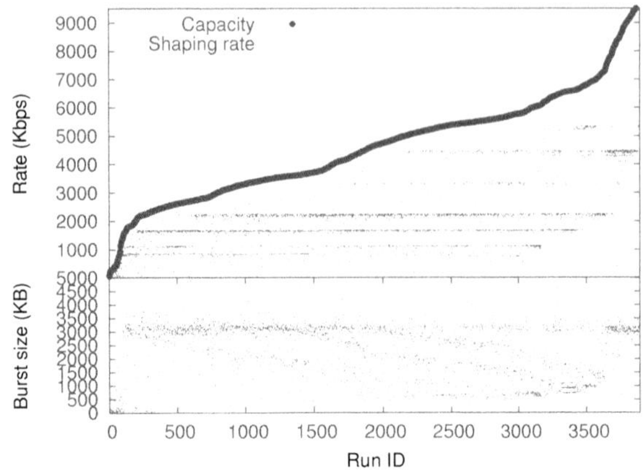

Figure 7: Cox: Upstream shaping.

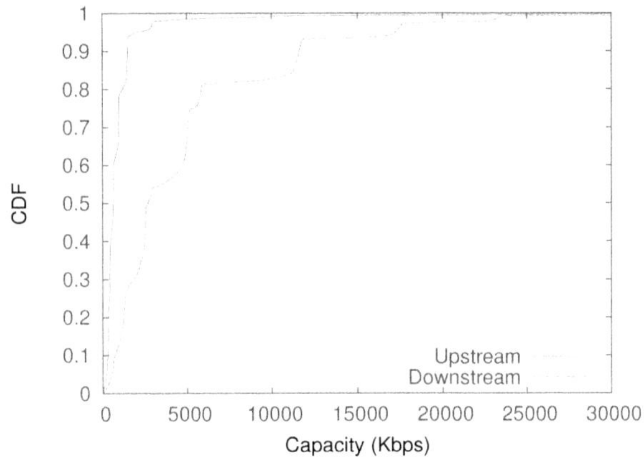

Figure 8: AT&T: Capacity of non-shaping runs.

the geographic region of the customer; for example, in Texas, RR provides four service tiers: the lower two are not shaped while the upper two are shaped [10]. Under the hypothesis that RR does not shape upstream traffic, we can say that our false positive detection rate for their upstream links is about 6.4%. The capacity distribution of non-shaped RR runs shows that, unlike Comcast, the downstream capacity mode of 750Kbps is not equal to any of their shaping modes (figure omited due to space constraints; see [17]).

Cox provides residential and business Internet access using cable and Ethernet access. The website [7] mentions that the residential shaping rates and capacities depend on the location of the customer. We gathered residential shaping configurations from the residential pages [7]. The upstream shaping properties of Cox runs in Figure 7 agree with some of the ground truth information we found: (C, ρ)Mbps: (1, 0.77), (1.3, 1), (2, 1.5), (2.5, 1), (2.5, 2), (3, 2), (3.5, 3), (5, 4) and (5.5, 5). Note that the previous ground truth was collected in October 2010, while the ShaperProbe data covers two years. We also found a single burst size mode.

4.3 Case Study: AT&T

Our final case study is that of an ISP for which we do not see frequent shaping detections (10% or less). AT&T provides Internet access to a wide range of customers, from homes and small businesses to enterprises (including other ISPs). Their residential service includes four DSL service tiers [1, 2]. We did not find any mention of traffic shaping in the AT&T service descriptions [1, 2].

Capacity. We first look at the 90% of the runs that did not see shaping. The capacity distribution of non-shaped runs is shown in Figure 8. Given the point-to-point nature of DSL links, ShaperProbe estimates the narrow link capacity more accurately than in cable links. The capacity distributions show several modes: {330Kbps, 650Kbps, 1Mbps, 1.5Mbps} upstream, and {1Mbps, 2.5Mbps, 5Mbps, 6Mbps, 11Mbps, 18Mbps} downstream. We did not observe significant changes in the capacity modes between 2009-2011.

Shaping runs. We look at the 10% of AT&T runs that were *probably mis-diagnosed* as shaping. We found that about a third of these runs exhibit strong shaping rate modes and an associated burst size mode (for figure, see [17]). About 80% of 333 runs that have the shaping rate modes come from hostnames that resolve to the domain `mchsi.com`, owned by the cable ISP Mediacom [9]. So, it is possible (though we can not be certain) that these shaping detections were *not* errors afterall.

5. CONCLUSION

In this work, we presented an end-to-end active probing, detection, and estimation method of traffic shaping in ISPs. Our evaluation using controlled experiments and in two known ISP deployments shows that ShaperProbe has false positive and false negative detection rates of less than 5%. We presented a first large-scale study of shaping at four large ISPs, and validated some of our observations using ISP advertised tier data. A strong modality of shaping rates and burst sizes suggests that ISPs typically deploy a small set of shaping configurations. We found some shaping detections for which the ISPs do not mention shaping in their service descriptions[4]. Lack of publicly-available information, however, does not necessary imply that these are false detections. We are currently working on passive shaping detection methods (for preliminary results, see [17]).

[4]ISPs, however, typically mention in their SLAs that "listed capacities may vary".

6. REFERENCES

[1] *AT&T FastAccess Business DSL Plans (May 12, 2010).* http://smallbusiness.bellsouth.com/internet_dsl_services.html.

[2] *AT&T FastAccess DSL Plans (May 12, 2010).* http://www.bellsouth.com/consumer/inetsrvcs/inetsrvcs_compare.html?src=lftnav.

[3] *Comcast Business Class Internet (May 12, 2010).* http://business.comcast.com/internet/details.aspx.

[4] *Comcast High Speed Internet FAQ: PowerBoost.* http://customer.comcast.com/Pages/FAQListViewer.aspx?topic=Internet&folder=8b2fc392-4cde-4750-ba34-051cd5feacf0.

[5] *Comcast High-Speed Internet (residential; May 12 2010).* http://www.comcast.com/Corporate/Learn/HighSpeedInternet/speedcomparison.html.

[6] Comparing Traffic Policing and Traffic Shaping for Bandwidth Limiting. *Cisco Systems: Document ID: 19645.*

[7] *Cox: Residential Internet (May 12, 2010).* http://intercept.cox.com/dispatch/3416707741429259002/intercept.cox?lob=residential&s=pf.

[8] *Data from M-Lab Tools (May 2011).* http://www.measurementlab.net/data.

[9] *Mediacom: Hish-speed Internet (May 12, 2010).* http://www.mediacomcable.com/internet_online.html.

[10] *Road Runner cable: central Texas (May 12, 2010).* http://www.timewarnercable.com/centraltx/learn/hso/roadrunner/speedpricing.html.

[11] *ShaperProbe (M-Lab).* http://www.measurementlab.net/measurement-lab-tools#tool5.

[12] S. Bauer, D. Clark, and W. Lehr. PowerBoost. In *ACM SIGCOMM HoneNets workshop*, 2011.

[13] M. Dischinger, A. Haeberlen, K. Gummadi, and S. Saroiu. Characterizing residential broadband networks. In *ACM IMC*, 2007.

[14] M. Dischinger, M. Marcon, S. Guha, K. Gummadi, R. Mahajan, and S. Saroiu. Glasnost: Enabling End Users to Detect Traffic Differentiation. In *USENIX NSDI*, 2010.

[15] M. Hollander and D. Wolfe. Nonparametric statistical methods. 1973.

[16] P. Kanuparthy and C. Dovrolis. DiffProbe: Detecting ISP Service Discrimination. In *IEEE INFOCOM*, 2010.

[17] P. Kanuparthy and C. Dovrolis. End-to-end Detection of ISP Traffic Shaping using Active and Passive Methods. *Technical Report, Georgia Tech*, 2011. http://www.cc.gatech.edu/~partha/shaperprobe-TR.pdf.

[18] K. Lakshminarayanan and V. Padmanabhan. Some findings on the network performance of broadband hosts. In *ACM SIGCOMM IMC*, 2003.

[19] G. Lu, Y. Chen, S. Birrer, F. Bustamante, C. Cheung, and X. Li. End-to-end inference of router packet forwarding priority. In *IEEE INFOCOM*, 2007.

[20] R. Mahajan, M. Zhang, L. Poole, and V. Pai. Uncovering performance differences among backbone ISPs with Netdiff. In *USENIX NSDI 2008*.

[21] S. Sundaresan, W. de Donato, N. Feamster, R. Teixeira, S. Crawford, and A. Pescapè. Broadband Internet performance: a view from the gateway. In *ACM SIGCOMM*, 2011.

[22] M. Tariq, M. Motiwala, and N. Feamster. NANO: Network Access Neutrality Observatory. In *ACM Hotnets Workshop 2008*.

[23] G. Varghese. *Network Algorithmics: an interdisciplinary approach to designing fast networked devices.* Morgan Kaufmann, 2005.

[24] U. Weinsberg, A. Soule, and L. Massoulie. Inferring traffic shaping and policy parameters using end host measurements. In *IEEE INFOCOM Mini-conference*, 2011.

[25] Y. Zhang, Z. Mao, and M. Zhang. Detecting traffic differentiation in backbone ISPs with NetPolice. In *ACM IMC*, 2009.

Summary Review Documentation for

"ShaperProbe: End-to-End Detection of ISP Traffic Shaping Using Active Methods"

Authors: P. Kanuparthy, C. Dovrolis

Reviewer #1

Strengths: Traffic shaping is a timely problem; residential networking is interesting in general. The paper is relatively well-written. Collecting a taxonomy of service tiers is significant.

Weaknesses: Very mature work; references to a tech report that would seem to have the interesting components of the tool's design; unsurprising conclusions and no clear statement about traffic shaping as good or evil. No experimentation into per-application (or port) shaping.

Comments to Authors: This work is complete enough to get press coverage, therefore it is complete enough to have a full paper worth of submission and not be presented as an abstract of a longer tech report. It does not fit the description "Short papers (up to 7 two-column pages) can convey work that is less mature but shows promise, articulating a high-level vision, describing challenging future directions, critiquing current measurement wisdom or offering results that do not merit a full submission."

http://arstechnica.com/tech-policy/news/2011/05/new-shaperprobe-tool-detects-isp-traffic-shaping.ars

The one paragraph "ShaperProbe Implementation" section was most disappointing. To understand the quality of your tool, I don't need an equation for the median (2.2); I do need a sense for the tradeoffs in parameters: what if I believe that the buckets are just too small for you to detect? How do you generate traffic at a truly constant rate? How do you filter? Submit the 12-14 pager; it might be more interesting. Conversely, perhaps your passive shaping detection method (conclusion section) would be a good topic for a 6 page submission.

Reviewer #2

Strengths: Interesting and timely topic; publicly release tool; real-world data; interesting findings.

Weaknesses: Some graphs are a bit hard to read.

Comments to Authors: This is great work with almost everything one could ask for.

I really appreciate you making the tool available to the Internet at large and collecting data from real users for your analysis.

The presentation is also very well done; I only have some minor issues with some of the graphs in page 5 and 6. Fig. 4 and 7 are hard to parse; it would help if you could "read" one of them when you introduce them in page 4. You jump too quickly to the tables that summarize the data but the figures, if explained, offer an interesting perspective.

How common would you expect cross traffic to result on an empty token bucket and make it impossible for ShaperProbe to detect shaping?

Reviewer #3

Strengths: The paper presents a clear method to detect traffic shaping. A large data set is available to the authors. There is a comparison with ground truths.

Weaknesses: This should have been a long paper: not enough details about the methodology (e.g. detection of C, the capacity) and not enough results shared (e.g. you got results about 5700 ISPs and you only discuss 4 ISPs. In how many ISPs did you detect traffic shaping?). The false positive rate claimed in the conclusion is not backed up by content in the paper. Where does the number come from?

Comments to Authors: I tried your tool. I liked it; it was simple and clear to use.

You mentioned that the data collected is publicly available. Where is it? I couldn't find the data. Maybe I missed something, you should make it more clear where it is located.

You have a 14 page version on your homepage, you should have submitted it. This is mature work, and there are enough questions to answer and enough data for a full evaluation to fill up 14 pages. The 6 page paper skips a lot of them.

What happens if the bucket size is really small? Wouldn't you simply not detect traffic shaping with your methodology?

In the intro, you mention "services up to 6 Mbps". This is typically for DSL services and has nothing to do with traffic shaping. I wouldn't make that third point.

You may want to better articulate the differences with Glasnot in the related work section

In the active probing method, you mention that Rs=C without explaining how you measure C and more importantly whether your method of measuring C could be influenced by traffic shaping in place or not. If some settings of traffic shaping could influence your detection of C, then you could have a lot of false negatives.

You don't discuss enough the robustness of your tool to the impact of cross traffic.

I am really pleased to see a parameter selection section! I like it.

How can some burst last 5mn in traffic shaping environments on figure 3? Is that really traffic shaping?

Your results section doesn't discuss your millions of results from 5700 ISPs. You go through 4 ISPS as case studies. Case studies are great after you present your overall results which are missing. For instance, were all your cases of traffic shaping for cable providers (good point about DSL vs. cable)?

"non shaped runs": while you say the distributions are similar. It is interesting to note that you see a step function for the capacity of the shaped traffic.

The AT&T case study seems to be an issue where you include traffic from multiple ISPs (Mediacom). If that's the case, why don't you just present the results per ASN? This should solve the issue. AT&T would probably not use the same ASN for its own subscribers and for the subscribers of companies, such as Mediacom, buying transit from its tier 1 network.

The false positive and false negative rates are important when presenting these kinds of results. You claim specific rates in the conclusion (less than 5%), yet you didn't explain how you came up with these numbers.

Reviewer #4

Strengths: Reasonable tool and design. Lots of great data from the wild to work with. Confirmation of at least some of the results, which suggests that the tool is fairly accurate.

Weaknesses: A more serious and extensive evaluation of the tool in a controlled setting would improve confidence in it, and help to better understand its weaknesses.

Comments to Authors: Fun paper. I've used the tool a couple different times in the past (it wasn't able to detect known shaping in my campus network, fwiw). I like the presentation of results in the form of case studies.

In most cases it appears that shaperprobe detects the right thing, but there are clearly some fraction of runs in which the tool is wrong. It would have been nice to have some experiments in a controlled setting using "real" routers and other devices, along with some cross traffic, to get a better sense of the tool's limitations. The minimal Linux experiments are nice, but aren't terribly enlightening since they're run in a setting in which you don't have control to create conditions that could be problematic for the tool, e.g., congestion somewhere on the path that might cause a level shift-like event.

Reviewer #5

Strengths: A method to detect and infer the parameters of "token bucket" mechanism employed in most of today shapers. Analysis of a large scale measurement of the tool that provides interesting information about today's networks.

Weaknesses: The method is susceptible to cross traffic. More extensive evaluation of the tool under different cross-traffic settings is needed.

Comments to Authors: I like the idea of detecting and inferring parameters of the packet shapers. Your effort in implementing and performing large scale validation of your tools is commendable. Below are detailed comments.

Section 2, by having large Δ you will need long measurement time. How does the measurement time affect the accuracy of your estimations?

Section 2.1, The receiving rate highly depends on cross-traffic, not just the shapers. How does cross traffic affect the received rate, hence your estimations? I would like to see more evaluation of the method with regards to the cross traffic.

Section 2.3, You mention in Section 2.1 that N_L and n_R will be selected from the ISP data, but you do not actually explain how do you set these parameters in your measurements. Furthermore, you set the other parameters, e.g. γ, using data from some specific ISPs. You then use these parameter values for measurements on other networks. As networks are different, you should really change these parameters for different networks too.

Section 4.1, you mention that you verify your results with Comcast listings. Where are the results of the verification? In general, it is very hard to verify the results in Section 4 as ground-truth data is not available. You should consider cross validation. Using a subset of measurements for inference and another subset to validate the inference results.

Section 5, where does the accuracy result come from?

Response from the Authors

Regarding the ``long versus short paper'' issue: there is indeed a longer version of this work that includes, first, more detail about the implementation of the tool, and second, a method to detect traffic shaping passively given packet-level traces. The passive estimation algorithm is significantly different than ShaperProbe, and its evaluation also follows a different approach. So, we decided to split the work in two papers: this IMC short paper and a second paper (passive detection) that will be published later. This short IMC paper cannot describe all the implementation details of ShaperProbe -- if we would include those details in a long paper, we suspect that most readers would find them uninteresting. Additionally, we note that it is not true that IMC short papers are not ``less mature'' than long papers. IMC has published many short but mature research papers in the last few years, which is great. Not every significant research contribution requires 12 pages.

We have revised the paper to address the presentation problems that the reviewers identified. Additionally, we have added a bit more information in Section 3 about how the tool works.

There are also some comments that we could not address (e.g., additional validation results or a more thorough study of the robustness with respect to cross traffic). Due to space constraints, we focus here on two comments that appear in several reviews:
(1) It is true that if the token bucket is too small we may not be able to detect it. However, such a traffic shaper would not make much performance difference at the first place. In practice, we see that Cable-access ISPs typically use a bucket size of at least 5-10MB, and ShaperProbe can detect that.
(2) If the path has significant cross traffic, ShaperProbe will abort the measurements (because it will detect packet losses). So, even though it is true that cross traffic can cause the token bucket to be non-full, ShaperProbe will avoid producing erroneous results in that case.

Sketching the Delay: Tracking Temporally Uncorrelated Flow-Level Latencies

Josep Sanjuàs-Cuxart
UPC BarcelonaTech
Jordi Girona 1-3
Barcelona 08034, Spain
jsanjuas@ac.upc.edu

Pere Barlet-Ros
UPC BarcelonaTech
Jordi Girona 1-3
Barcelona 08034, Spain
pbarlet@ac.upc.edu

Nick Duffield
AT&T Labs–Research
180 Park Avenue
Florham Park, NJ 07932
duffield@research.att.com

Ramana Rao Kompella
Dept. of Computer Science
Purdue University
West Lafayette, IN 47907
kompella@cs.purdue.edu

ABSTRACT

Packet delay is a crucial performance metric for real-time, network-based applications. Obtaining per-flow delay measurements is particularly important to network operators, but is computationally challenging in high-speed links. Recently, passive delay measurement techniques have been proposed that outperform traditional active probing in terms of accuracy and network overhead. However, such techniques rely on the empirical observation that packet delays across different flows are temporally correlated, an assumption that is not met in presence of traffic prioritization, load balancing policies, or due to intricacies of the switch fabric.

We present a novel data structure called Lossy Difference Sketch (LDS) that provides per-flow delay measurements without relying on any specific delay model. LDS obtains a notable accuracy improvement compared to the state of the art with a small memory footprint and network overhead. The data structure can be sized according to target accuracy requirements or to fit a low memory budget.

We deploy an actual implementation of LDS in an operational research and education network and show that it obtains higher accuracy than temporal correlation-based techniques without exploiting any knowledge about the underlying delay model.

Categories and Subject Descriptors

C.2.3 [**Computer-Communication Networks**]: Network Operations—*network monitoring*; C.4 [**Performance of Systems**]: General—*measurement techniques*; G.3 [**Probability and Statistics**]: General—*Probabilistic algorithms*

General Terms

Algorithms, Measurement

Keywords

One-way packet delay, network latency, network measurement, delay sketch

1. INTRODUCTION

Packet delay has become a key network performance metric, together with other metrics such as throughput and packet loss. This growth in importance of packet delay is mainly due to the emergence of a new class of network-based applications that demand extremely low end-to-end latency. For instance, algorithmic trading applications require end-to-end latencies to not exceed few microseconds, otherwise they may lose significant amount of revenue in the form of lost arbitrage opportunities [21]. High-performance computing applications form another class of such applications with message latencies directly impacting the amount of time it takes for the job (e.g., weather simulation) to be finished. Finally, modern data center applications have soft real-time deadlines [3] that typically are in the order of milliseconds, but once backend computation requirements are factored in, very little time is left for network delays.

Now, consider a network operator that is running and managing a network environment that supports low-latency applications, such as a data center network. Typically, many data centers host several thousands of machines connected via a network fabric that is often constructed out of commodity networking equipment (e.g., switches and routers). Depending on the requirements (e.g., full bi-section bandwidth), the network is often connected in a multi-rooted tree topology (e.g., a fat-tree) with several thousand switches providing multiple paths between servers for load-balancing purposes. Further, the cluster itself may be shared across several tens to hundreds of customers running tens to hundreds of different applications with potentially very different network usage patterns. Given the complexity stemming from the sheer number of network elements as well as the variety of networking-based applications, it becomes extremely difficult to debug and troubleshoot latency anomalies (such as delay spikes) throughout the network *without* proper latency measurement tools at various points in the network.

Traditionally, such measurements have been obtained using active probing in wide-area ISP networks [5, 24, 6, 28]. However, end-to-end network delays are an order of magnitude smaller in data center networks—order of *microseconds* compared to milliseconds. To capture delay dynamics at such microsecond granularity, high probing frequency (e.g., 10,000Hz [17]) is required, which makes this approach prohibitively expensive in practical scenarios. Further, diagnosing end-to-end delay anomalies requires measurements at various vantage points in the network—ideally, at each pair of interfaces within each switch in the network, so that the root cause can be localized down to a router or a switch. The network operator could then conduct a more extensive analysis, such as study the set of customers or applications that may be routed through that switch to carefully investigate the root cause of the problem.

Unfortunately, native switch/router support for packet delay measurements is sorely lacking. Today, NetFlow and SNMP form the two main measurement solutions that a router supports. Neither, however, focuses on delay measurements. In some environments such as the London Stock Exchange, operators resort to specialized measurement boxes (e.g., Corvil [1]) that can detect these delays at high fidelity. However, because of the high costs and the hassles of administering a new box in the network, such an approach does not scale well. The complexity of packet latency measurements comes fundamentally from the fact that we cannot easily just store a packet timestamp at two monitoring points, without incurring high storage and communication complexity, since the complexity is linear in the number of packets. It is therefore important to overcome the linear relationship between number of collected timestamps and network overhead for any solution to be scalable.

Recent work [17] proposed the lossy difference aggregator (LDA) to overcome the linear relationship between sample size and network overhead by intelligently aggregating timestamps between the two measurements points. LDA, however, provides only aggregate latency estimates *across* all packets, which may be inadequate for diagnosing customer-specific or application-specific latency issues [18]. As pointed out by prior work [18], flows may exhibit significant diversity in their latency characteristics at a given router, and hence, per-flow measurements are important for network operators. Unfortunately, the problem of measuring per-flow delay is harder in the environments we consider, since the number of flows can be quite large; collecting and exchanging per-flow state becomes prohibitively expensive.

The problem of measuring per-flow delay has been very recently explored in [18, 19]. Both papers exploit the *key observation* that packets exhibit significant temporal delay correlation in specific settings, i.e., packets that are transmitted close in time experience similar delays, even if they do not belong to the same flow. RLI [18], the most recent of the two, exploits this observation to inject simple active probes periodically and uses linear interpolation to estimate per-packet delay. At the downstream monitoring point, these estimated per-packet delays can be aggregated into per-flow latencies using only three counters per-flow.

While the assumption that packets exhibit temporal correlation is valid in a restricted subset of systems, this assumption *does not* hold true in more general scenarios where there is prioritization across packets with two or more parallel queues. For example, many modern routers support different queuing for prioritizing real-time traffic (e.g., VoIP, video) over regular data transmissions (e.g., Web). Thus, in these cases, there exists very little correlation between the delays of packets that end up traversing two different queues. Similarly, in many modern data center networks, packets are routinely load balanced across multiple paths using ECMP—temporal delay correlation may potentially exist across any given path but *certainly not* across paths. Finally, modern switch fabrics (e.g., Clos-network-based switch fabrics used in Juniper's T-Series routers [2]) are often composed of intermediate stages of switching with each packet being sent to a random intermediate location; the latency of a packet through the router may be different depending on the path within the router. (In such switches, packets are re-sequenced back because TCP does not interact well with reordering, but such reordering needs to be only on a per-flow basis.)

Thus, the assumption of temporal delay correlation is not universally applicable; unfortunately, schemes such as RLI will produce grossly inaccurate latency estimates if the assumption does not hold, posing a major hurdle for deploying RLI on a global basis. Switch vendors do not wish to be bothered about the specifics of the deployment scenario, and instead would like to have one scheme that is universally applicable across *all* possible scenarios. Our objective in this paper is to accomplish this task. Specifically, we focus on devising a scalable *delay-model-agnostic mechanism* to obtain per-flow latency measurements at microsecond granularity across two measurement points in the network.

In this paper, we propose a technique called lossy delay sketching (LDS) that essentially combines the model independence nature of LDA with sketching techniques that do not rely on per-flow state to obtain model-free and scalable per-flow delay estimation. LDS essentially maintains a series of hash buckets, with each bucket consisting of a timestamp sum and the number of packets that hash to the bucket (similar to an LDA bucket). In accordance with the spirit of sketching, LDS maps each flow to a random *subset* of buckets, that are potentially shared (partially or fully) by other flows. To minimize the effect of interference, we randomize the fate-sharing by maintaining different banks of buckets, similar to a sketch, with a different hash function.

While the basic idea of blending LDA with sketches makes intuitive sense, several problems must be overcome to design such a data structure. For instance, flows may differ in their delay properties as well as their sizes significantly. It is important to ensure the interference due to collisions does not impact the accuracy of the flow's latency estimates. We present theoretical analysis on determining the size of LDS in order to reduce this interference.

Thus, the main contributions of this paper are as follows.

- We propose a new data structure called LDS that *obtains per-flow delay estimates* and that does not rely on delay models (Section 2). It blends LDAs that are model independent with sketching techniques that provide per-flow measurements without per-flow state.

- We present a comprehensive theoretical analysis of the data structure and show how to size it to achieve the desired accuracy (Section 3).

- We introduce a series of practical enhancements to LDS that allow network operators to fine-tune the data structure for the specifics of an actual deployment scenario (Section 4).

- We evaluate LDS with real traffic collected at a large academic network (Section 5). Our results indicate that sketching is superior to existing techniques when temporal correlation is not present. Sketching is particularly accurate for large flows, even in the presence of loss. Additionally, the accuracy of a selected subset of flows can be easily incremented.

Finally, Section 6 covers the related work in the literature, while Section 7 concludes the paper.

2. DELAY SKETCHING

Our main goal is to measure the one-way delay introduced by a network between two measurement points on a per-flow basis. While we can typically support any definition of flow, usually, this will consist of the 5-tuple formed by source and destination IP addresses, originating and destination ports, and protocol. We mainly focus on obtaining per-flow average latency, but we also outline in Sec. 4 how we can obtain second moments as well.

Our architecture is oblivious to what locations exactly constitute the measurement points. Thus, we can imagine obtaining per-flow measurements within a switch or a router across an ingress and egress interface. Alternately, we can obtain measurements across two different routers. Note that both measurement locations are merely viewpoints along the path that packets follow, and do not need to be (although they could be) the emitter or final destination of the traffic. We call the first measurement point *sender*, and the second, *receiver*. We consider the reverse path measurements separately with the *receiver* becoming the *sender* and vice versa.

2.1 Assumptions

Single stream. We assume that the sender and receiver observe the same stream of packets. In general, this is highly dependent on the particular scenario. For instance, suppose we consider an ingress (egress) switch interface as the sender (receiver). The receiver (sender) may obtain (transmit) packets from (to) many different ingress interfaces. Thus, we assume there is a simple way to filter out the packets that travel from the sender to the receiver. Note that we do not assume packets flow through a single queue, or even in a FIFO order—just that we have a way to separate out packets that appear at both the sender and the receiver. Within switches, there are often internal headers that contain the port at which they originated and the port to which they are headed to, that we can use for this purpose. Across routers, we can leverage prefix-based filtering to identify the set of packets that travel through one given path (forwarding is prefix-based). Such routers do not need to be co-located or close in terms of network hops.

Packet loss. We assume packets can be lost between the sender and receiver. Depending on the scenario, the packet loss rates may differ significantly. For example, in a financial trading network, we may imagine the network to suffer from minimal packet loss. However, in a real backbone network, packet loss may be slightly more common. Typically, while some amount of loss resilience is required in our data structures, we assume the loss rates are still quite low (say $<1\%$) as TCP may not work well under higher loss rates.

Time synchronization. We also assume the clocks of the sender and receiver are synchronized. This is a common requirement of one-way packet delay measurement techniques [17, 19, 18]. Although techniques have been proposed that do not require clock synchronization (e.g., [25, 22, 29]), removing this assumption was out of the scope of this paper. To achieve fine grained precision, packet timestamping clocks can be synchronized to the GPS signal (i.e., using Endace DAG cards), or using the IEEE 1588 protocol [16]. Both these methods are capable of sub-microsecond precision and thus suitable for our needs [10]. (In our evaluation, we obtained traces from a production network that already uses IEEE 1588 protocol to synchronize measurements.)

Embedding timestamps in packets. Similar to prior work [17, 18], we assume that it is *not* possible to embed timestamps within IP packets because existing IP headers do not have a placeholder for timestamps, and it would require significant changes to router forwarding paths and other third-party components making it difficult. We note however that our solutions are important even in the context where router vendors can put a timestamp in a packet, as the number of flows may be still large.

In fact, for ease of exposition, we present a simple data structure called SDS using the *timestamp assumption*, i.e., assuming packets can be embedded with timestamps. We will, however, get rid of this assumption in Sec. 2.3 when we describe our main data structure LDS.

2.2 Simple Delay Sketch (SDS)

As mentioned before, we initially assume the sender can embed a timestamp into the packets to be measured for easy exposition of the delay sketching idea. (We will relax this in the next section.) Thus, the receiver can obtain delays for each packet, but still need a scalable mechanism to store per-flow latencies, which is obtained by the data structure we describe in this section. The main idea of our technique is to explore sketching techniques that have been studied before in the literature to obtain measurements without maintaining per-flow state, and requiring very few memory accesses per packet. Such techniques will allow us to compute a comparatively smaller compressed summary of the traffic that allows recovering approximate measurements. We assume measurements are performed in fixed time intervals, which we refer to as *measurement intervals*.

A canonical sketch data structure that we can exploit in our setting is the multi-stage filter [13]. In this data structure, each stage has C associated counters, which are initialized to zero. Then, for each incoming packet, a hash of its flow identifier is used to determine which counter will be updated in the 1st stage. If, for example, one wishes to measure flow sizes, then the packet size is added to that counter. Since every flow always hashes to a particular position, its associated counter can be queried to obtain an upper bound on its size (only an upper bound, since other flows can hash to the same position, i.e., can collide). Additional stages can then be added that are independent replicas of this scheme, thus randomizing collisions. Then, the estimated size of a given flow is the minimum of all of its associated counters in each stage. The Count-Min Sketch [9] is also based on a similar approach.

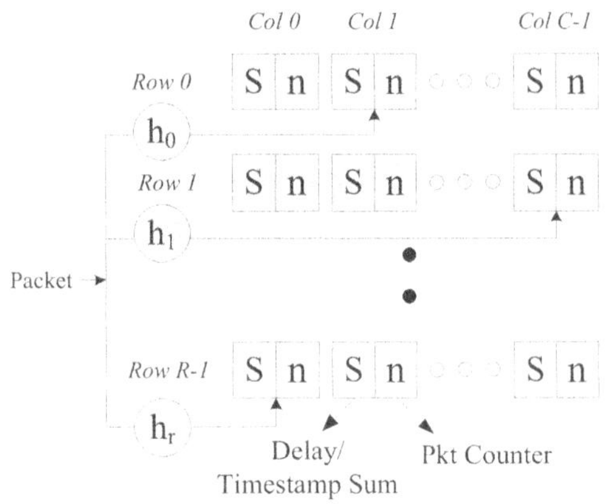

Figure 1: Basic data structure. In each cell, s stores the sum and n the number of packets that hash to that cell.

```
procedure UPDATE STATE(flow, τ)
    for i=1, R do
        j ← (hash(i, flow)%C)          ▷ Compute ith hash
        SDS[i][j].S ← SDS[i][j].S + τ
        SDS[i][j].N ← SDS[i][j].N + 1
    end for
end procedure
```

Figure 2: SDS – Per-packet operations

Our initial idea is to use this sketching technique for per-flow delay measurement. The data structure we propose called Simple Delay Sketch (SDS) contains a series of cells organized in a matrix of R rows and C columns. Each row r has an associated pseudo-random hash function h_r that returns a value in the range $[0, C-1]$. Each cell of the matrix contains a tuple of values $<s,n>$, with s storing the sum and n the number of packets that hash to that cell. The data structure is graphically depicted in Figure 1.

Update. When a packet that belongs to a flow with identifier f arrives, for each row r, a position in the matrix is determined using its hash function h_r, which yields position $(r, h_r(f))$. Then, the cells in these positions are updated as follows. The s values of each cell are increased by the delay of the packet (i.e., the current time at *receiver* minus the timestamp embedded in the packet at *sender*), while n values are increased by one (i.e., maintains a count of the packets that hashed to that cell). In other words, s values contain the sum of all packet delays that hit that cell, while n values represent packet counts. Note also that the per-packet cost of this measurement scheme is, for each row, a hashing operation and two counter updates. The full algorithm is described in Figure 2.

Delay Estimation. If the data structure were single-row and infinitely large, and the hash functions were perfectly random, each non-empty cell would measure the average delay of the packets of a particular flow. That is, the data structure would be collision-free, since two flows would not hash to the same position. Therefore, to obtain the (exact) average delay of flow with identifier f, one would simply divide the s and n values of cell $(0, h_0(f))$.

```
procedure ESTIMATE DELAY(flow, SDS)
    N_min = ∞
    for i=1, R do
        j ← hash(i, flow)               ▷ Compute ith hash
        if SDS[i][j].N < N_min then
            N_min = SDS[i][j].N
            S_min = SDS[i][j].S
        end if
    end for
    return S_min/N_min
end procedure
```

Figure 3: SDS – Delay estimation algorithm

However, in practice, rows cannot be large enough, and there is a non-zero probability of several flows colliding (i.e., hashing to the same cell in one or more rows). When several flows collide, the value obtained by dividing the s and n values is a weighted average of the delays experienced by said flows, where weights correspond to the number of packets of each flow. Therefore, in practice, flow delays can not be exactly obtained, but only estimated from the data structure. To minimize the impact of collisions over measurement accuracy, it is desirable to have a large number of rows. For a given flow, we can obtain one estimate of its average delay for each of the rows, to then choose the one that is least contaminated by other flows.

Several strategies can be devised to obtain the estimates. For example, one could produce a final estimate by combining several cells, such as taking the mean or the median of the available estimates, like other sketching techniques do (e.g., see [9]). In our case, using the average would be problematic for flows that collided with larger ones in *any* of the cells, because the weight they would carry in their estimates would be small. This would invalidate the advantages of provisioning multiple rows to randomize collisions. Likewise, using the median would tend to drag each estimate towards the median delay of all flows.

We find it best to choose the cell that has the lowest n value to produce an estimate. This has two interesting properties. First, if one of the cells is collision free, the algorithm will choose it and, thus, produce an error-free result. Otherwise, it will pick the cell where the fewest amount of packets have collided, i.e., the one where the measured flow carries the highest possible weight. The full algorithm is described in Figure 3.

Of course, the cell with the smallest n will not necessarily produce the best estimate among all cells. For example, it may have collided, in one cell, with a large flow that has an extremely similar average delay. However, this strategy always chooses, among all the cells, the one where the measured flow carries the highest possible weight. In Sec. 3, we analyze the accuracy that this data structure offers, and provide guidelines to dimension and parametrize it.

The SDS data structure we presented in this section is a first-cut approach to blending the ideas of LDA with sketching techniques. However, SDS is only applicable if we assume embedding timestamps within packets—an assumption which is hard to achieve in practice, at least in the short term if not in the longer term. We now study a new data structure LDS that relaxes this assumption.

2.3 Lossy Difference Sketch (LDS)

In this section, we discuss our main data structure called lossy difference sketch (LDS) to obtain per-flow latency measurements *without* requiring the timestamp assumption. The LDS data structure starts with the basic SDS data structure, and uses the following ideas to make it practical:

1. To get rid of the timestamp assumption, the sender and receiver maintain separate copies of the data structure (described in the previous section), and the sender periodically transmits its copy to the receiver. The receiver then post-processes both sketches to obtain the delays of all packets that hash to each cell (Sec. 2.3.1). We need the sender and receiver to use consistent hashing (same hash function) to ensure packets hash to the same cell in both cases.

2. Since packet losses and reordering can occur between the sender and receiver, this may make the cells inconsistent across the sender and receiver. We detect losses easily since the number of packets does not match across the sender and receiver cells. We detect reordering using a separate field in each cell that stores a stream digest for each cell, similar to prior work [27, 20] (Sec. 2.3.2).

3. To handle packet losses, we map packets that belong to the given flow across several contiguous cells in essence forming a virtual LDA for each flow. We also use a stage of sampling to reduce the probability of a packet loss completely corrupting all cells for a given flow. We randomize the set of flows that collide in each row so as to randomize the fate-sharing. This randomization allows us to minimize the interference of other colliding flows on the estimates for any particular flow (Sec. 2.3.3).

The following subsections will discuss these ideas in detail.

2.3.1 Removing the Timestamp Assumption

The main problem when measurement points cannot embed a timestamp in the packets is that we cannot compute the packet delay at *receiver*. Thus, neither can we directly aggregate delays in the data structure as described in Sec. 2.2. However, we can achieve the same effect by using a simple, yet extremely powerful technique introduced in [17]. Ref. [17] states that to measure average delay of a set of packets, one does not need to embed a timestamp in the packet or transmit individual timestamps between *sender* and *receiver*. Instead, we can proceed as follows. In both measurement points, compute the sum of all packet timestamps, and maintain a packet count. Then, to compute average delay, compare the aggregate timestamps and divide over the total number of packets.

We leverage this idea in designing LDS as follows: In both measurement nodes, we maintain a sketch as the one described in Sec. 2.2, where each position aggregates the packet timestamps observed at each point, instead of packet delays. Both measurement nodes use the same hashing functions in order to map flows to the same counter positions. Then, at the end of the measurement interval, one of the resulting sketches is sent to the other measurement point. The aggregate timestamps at *sender* are subtracted from those at *receiver*. The result is exactly equivalent to a sketch that aggregates packet delays.

After this step, the average delay of the packets that hit a cell can be simply obtained by dividing its s and n, where s is now the sum of timestamps kept in each cell, instead of the aggregate packet delays. Assume a series of packets $p_1, p_2 \dots p_k$, with timestamps $t_1, t_2, \dots t_k$ at *sender* and $t'_1, t'_2 \dots t'_k$ at *receiver*. The delay of the ith packet is then $t'_i - t_i$. Our data structure calculates $\frac{s}{n} = \frac{\sum_{i=0}^{k} t'_i - \sum_{i=0}^{k} t_i}{k} = \frac{\sum_{i=0}^{k} t'_i - t_i}{k}$, i.e., the average packet delay.

Note that, while we focus on average delay estimation, other useful estimates, including per-flow delay standard deviation, can also be mined from the data structure as described later in Sec. 4.

2.3.2 Detecting Losses and Reordering

When packets are lost some of the n fields in *receiver* would be smaller than those obtained by *sender*. This is an important problem, because our data structure relies on the difference of s values at *sender* and *receiver* to calculate average packet delays, as explained in Sec. 2.2; using cells where the set of packet delays aggregated in each measurement point differs introduces severe error [17]. In general, when packet counts n do not match, the set of timestamps aggregated in the corresponding s fields will not be consistent. Thus, in LDS, we do not use such cells for delay measurement.

Packet reordering poses an additional challenge: n fields can match, while the set of aggregated packet timestamps might differ. This is a problem that is analyzed in more detail in [20]; in summary, at the boundaries of measurement intervals, packets might jump to the next (or previous) interval. This, coupled with loss, can easily cause matching packet counts, and mismatching sets of packet timestamps. As introduced in [27, 20], this problem can be solved by attaching, to each sketch position, a small digest d of the packets that hit such cell, which can be achieved simply with an extra hashing operation as follows.[1]

In LDS, thus, each cell will consist of the additional d field along with s and n for each cell. This value contains a digest of all packets that hashed to a cell. We require digests to be computationally lightweight, and to provide a means to detect loss and packet reorders with high probability. As discussed in [27, 20], an easy way to achieve this is to cumulatively XOR the hashes of the packet contents. This scheme guarantees that, using b bit hashes, mismatches will be detected with probability $1 - 2^{-b}$.

It is easy to see that, with this basic data structure, no accurate delay estimates can be produced for (i) those flows that experience even a single loss or reordering, and (ii) for those that collide with flows that have experienced such conditions. For such flows, packet digests (and often, n values) in *sender* will not match those at *receiver*, and thus will always be invalidated. We next discuss the mechanism used in LDS to make the flow estimates more robust to packet losses or reordering.

2.3.3 Robustness against Loss and Reordering

To make LDS more robust to losses and reordering, we leverage the basic idea used in LDA, which consists of partitioning each flow's packets into k sub-streams, and mapping

[1]In the final data structure described in Sec. 2.3.4, the hash value provided by h' is used, thus saving this extra hashing operation.

each packet to one of k different cells *in every row*. To coordinate both measurement nodes, the cell that a given packet will hit is also determined by a hash function, although this time of the full packet instead of only headers, so that successive packets of the same flow are scattered across the k cells.

This way, if one cell is hit by lost or reordered packets, only a subset of packets that belong to the flow are thrown away. The remaining cells to which the flows' packets are mapped will possibly remain intact, thus providing with reasonable estimates for the flow. To reduce the chances of losing cells to losses and reordering, we additionally place a packet sampling stage that will reduce the absolute number of packet losses, but also reduce the number of good estimates (similar to LDA). As analyzed in detail in [14], the LDA operates optimally when the sampling rate p is set to L/k, where L corresponds to the absolute number of losses in the packet stream. In Sec. 4.2 explores how to configure sampling rates in real deployments.

Now, we have two choices for the k cells. First, we can essentially replace each counter in the SDS data structure with k different cells. Second, we can allocate k (contiguous or random) cells in the counter matrix independently to each flow. If the k cells are contiguous, we can think of them as overlapping virtual LDAs (vLDA) per-flow, but they are not dedicated per-flow. In LDS we use this second approach, since it has the advantage of allowing a larger k without reducing the number of cells, thus increasing the robustness against loss at the cost of introducing extra collisions in the data structure.

2.3.4 Final Data Structure

The final data structure LDS is formally described as follows. LDS contains a matrix of R rows and C columns. Each cell of the matrix contains a tuple of values $<s,n,d>$, which keep aggregate timestamps, packet counts, and packet digests respectively. Both the sender and receiver maintain separate LDS copies, that is transmitted by the sender at the end of the measurement interval. Each row r has now *two* associated pseudo-random hash functions h_r and h'_r. While h_r returns a value in the range $[0, C-1]$, h'_r returns a value in the range $[0, k-1]$, where k is a configuration parameter of our algorithm that, as we shall see, represents the length of the virtual LDAs in our data structure. Once a packet that arrives at time t hits a cell, its s is increased by t, n is incremented by 1, and d is XORed with the digest of the new packet.

Update. When a packet with payload x and flow identifier f arrives at time t, for each row r, a position in the matrix given by $(r, (h_r(f)+h'_r(x)) \, mod \, C)$ is determined. That is, the flow hash is used to obtain a base position in each row, while the packet payload's hash determines an offset to that position in the range $[0, k-1]$. Thus, the packets of a given flow are randomly distributed among the neighboring cells. To coordinate this randomization between sender and receiver, they both use, again, the same pre-arranged (consistent) hash functions. Figure 4 presents a diagram of this scheme, while Fig. 5 formally describes this algorithm.

This scheme has the advantage of, while not introducing the full overhead of embedding a LDA in each cell, still obtains its advantages, by spreading the packets of each flow across several cells thus gaining protection against loss or reordering. If a flow experiences losses, they will invalidate

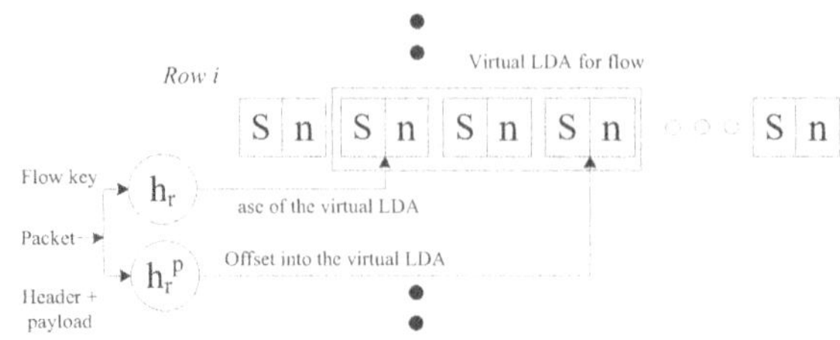

Figure 4: Virtual LDA extension to the data structure (d fields are not depicted).

```
procedure UPDATE STATE(pkt, f, τ)
    ph ← hash_packet(pkt)%k                ▷ k is vLDA size
    for i=1, R do
        fh ← (hash(i, f))
        j ← ((fh + ph)%C)
        LDS[i][j].S ← LDS[i][j].S + τ
        LDS[i][j].N ← LDS[i][j].N + 1
        LDS[i][j].D ← LDS[i][j].D ⊕ pkthash
    end for
end procedure
```

Figure 5: LDS – Per-packet operations

some, but not necessarily all of the counters, which gives the algorithm a chance to recover its delay. As will be discussed in Sec. 3, this feature increases the amount of collisions. Therefore, to support the same number of flows, it still has to be larger than the basic data structure presented in Sec. 2.

Delay Estimation. When producing an estimate of a given flow, all associated usable vLDA cells are initially selected. After this step, the question of how to estimate flow delays arises. The algorithm now has to choose among the usable cells to produce an estimate. In the event that, for a flow, none of its cells are invalidated, it has Rk cells that can produce delay estimates (for each row, all cells of the flow's vLDA).

Again, several strategies could be used to select which cells are going to be used for estimation. For example, one could aggregate all usable cells of each row into a single one, thus obtaining one candidate delay estimation per row and, like in the previous data structure, choose the one with the least amount of packets.

Such a strategy is impractical, because it unnecessarily gives up the advantages of having the packets spread across several positions in the data structure. Instead, it is beneficial to selectively discard specific positions with high measurement interference.

We thus adopt the following strategy. First, among all cells, we choose the one with the smallest number of packets. Assuming that each vLDA cell contains $1/k$th of the packets of the measured flow, this is the cell that has experienced least colliding packets. Let the number of packets aggregated in this cell be n. Then, from the rest of the cells, we select those that contain, at most, $n(1+\alpha)$ packets, where α is a configuration parameter that reflects a maximum percentage of tolerable interference. Too large an α leads to the inclusion of interfering packets, while setting it too small discards valid samples. We empirically found

```
procedure DELAY ESTIMATION(f, L1, L2)
    N_min = ∞
    for i=1, R do
        fh ← hash(i, f)
        for j = fh, (fh + k)%C do          ▷ k is vLDA size
            if L1[i][j].N == L2[i][j].N &&
                    L1[i][j].D == L2[i][j].D then
                cell = {L2[i][j].S − L1[i][j].S, L1[i][j].N}
                S = S ⋃ cell               ▷ Stores all valid cells
                N_min = min{N_min, cell.N}
            end if
        end for
    end for
    for cell ∈ S do
        if cell.N < (1 + α)N_min then
            S_sum+ = cell.S
            N_sum+ = cell.N
        end if
    end for
    return S_sum/N_sum
end procedure
```

Figure 6: LDS – Delay estimation algorithm

$\alpha = 0.1$ to represent a good trade-off between these two factors in our setting.

Then, the resulting set of cells are aggregated to produce a final estimate. Since, within each vLDA, packets are randomly distributed across cells, the possibility of double counting packets exists. Note that this is not problematic for the measurement of average delay.

The pseudocode in Fig. 6 captures our delay estimation mechanism more formally. Here $L1$ and $L2$ are the sender- and receiver-side LDSes. Note that k refers to the configured vLDA size for each flow. Also, we assume both $L1$ and $L2$ have already been updated with the same hash functions $hash(i)$, $i = 1 \ldots R$.

3. ANALYSIS

In this section, we analyze our data structure and provide guidelines on how to dimension it in order to obtain the desired level of accuracy. We start with the analysis of SDS and then extend it to the more general case of LDS.

3.1 Simple Delay Sketch

One could hope to dimension the data structure so that measurements are error-free with high probability, i.e., flows are highly likely to be free from collision in, at least, one of the cells. Unfortunately, this would require a great deal of memory since, for example, when using a single row with as many counters as flows, the probability that a given flow is collision free is only e^{-1} (as in a standard Bloom filter with a single hash function). In order for this probability to grow beyond 95%, we require a number of counters that is well above of the number of flows we want to measure.

As explained, in our data structure, colliding flows cause interfering measurements, and estimates produced by each row are an average delay weighted by the number of packets of the colliding flows. In other words, in practice, larger flows tend to have less error, since they will most often collide with small flows, rather than larger ones.

In order for a flow to be accurately measured, the total number of packet in flows that collide with it must be sufficiently small so as not to significantly impact its delay estimate. Specifically, we say that a flow suffers *only small collisions* if the number of colliding packets is no more than some threshold x. To compute the probability Q of small collisions we consider first the number of flows colliding with a given flow, and then the number of packets that they bring. Letting K_i denote the probability of i colliding flows, and S_i the probability that these i flows bring no more that x packets in total, then $Q = \sum_{i=0}^{n} K_i S_i$, assuming n background flows. By definition, $S_0 = 1$, since a flow is always correctly measured when it is free from collision.

We aim to dimension the data structure in a way that the probability Q of only small collisions stays high. Assuming a uniform distribution of hash values, K_i is probability of obtaining i items under the Binomial distribution $B(n, 1/C)$, yielding a mean number n/C of colliding flows. To compute S_i we need to assume some distribution of flow sizes. We will assume Pareto distributed flow sizes. This distribution is often used to model flow sizes (e.g., [15, 23]) and can be fitted to the characteristics of the network data we use in the evaluation in Sec. 5. The sub-exponential property of the Pareto distribution implies that, if T_k is the sum of the sizes of k flows, then $\Pr[T_k > x] \approx k \Pr[T_1 > x]$ for large x at fixed k. In other words, when T_k is very large, this tends to be because one entry in the sum is very large, not because several are moderately large. Using this property, we obtain $Q \approx \sum_{i=0}^{n} K_i(1 - iP) = 1 - \frac{n}{C} * P$, where $P = \Pr[T_1 > x]$ under the (fitted) Pareto distribution. The accuracy of approximation increases for small n/C and large x.

Using this analysis, we can adapt the size of our data structure to obtain the desired probabilistic accuracy bound. For example, using Pareto parameters that match our traffic (see Sec. 5), we obtain a probability $Q \approx 91\%$ of small collisions comprising at most 50 packets, with half as many counters as flows ($n/C = 2$), structured in 1 row. This means that, for example, flows with 1000 or more packets have a 91% probability of small collisions comprising no more than 5% of their packets. Incidentally, a numerical computation of Q without the subexponential approximation differed by a few tenths of absolute percent in this example.

The formulation of this example illustrates a key requirement to measure a flow accurately: not only must it suffer only small collisions but the flow itself must be large. (How large depends on the delay distribution.) To simplify the analysis, we stipulate a large flow to be one with at least x packets, where x is the threshold total packets for small collisions. With this formulation, we call a flow *survivable* in storage if it is both large, and suffers only small collisions. What then, is the maximal storage capacity of survivable flows? Suppose n flows are stored. The average number of large flows is nP and so the average number of survivable flows is $nPQ = nP(1 - nP/C)$. This expression is maximized at $n = C/(2P)$, yielding $C/4$. This is reminiscent of the collision free capacity C/e of the standard Bloom filter. The difference is that the proposed structure can store up to $C/4$ *survivable* flows out of a potentially far larger $C/(4P)$ that are presented for storage.

In fact we do not expect the operating regime to accommodate the maximal number of flow because the probability of *large* (i.e., not small) collisions is $1 - Q = nP/C = 1/2$. We now investigate operating regimes with rare large collisions in the generality of multiple $R \geq 1$ rows. We assume the primary design aim is to limit the probability of large collisions, with a secondary aim of maximizing the number of survivable flows under that constraint. In the case of multiple rows, a large flow is survivable if it has small collisions in at least one row. With R rows, the total resources C are divided up evenly between rows, and so substituting C/R for C in Q, the relevant survival probability is $Q(R) = 1-(1-Q)^R = 1-(nP/CR)^R$. For a cleaner analysis it is convenient to change variables from n to $z = nP/C$, which can be thought of as the offered load of large flows per unit storage. Then $Q(R) = q(z, R) := 1 - (zR)^R$.

As a function of R for fixed z, $q(z, R)$ is maximized at $R = 1/(ez)$. But only $R \geq 1$ are physical. (In this analysis we omit consideration of integrality; in practice we round to an integer at the end). Thus $\max_{R\geq 1} q(z, R) = q(z) := q(z, \max\{1, 1/(ez)\})$. $q(z)$ is a decreasing function of z which takes the value $1 - z$ for $z > 1/e$ (corresponding to $R = 1$) and $1 - e^{-1/(ez)}$ for $z \leq 1/e$ (corresponding to the case $R > 1$). Assuming we wish a small probability $\varepsilon < 1/e \approx 0.63$ of large collisions, then we should be in the small $z < 1/e$ regime, so we would want to chose z such that $\varepsilon > e^{-1/(ez)}$, which corresponds to the choice $R = -\log(\varepsilon)$, modulo discretization, then making sure the offered load z is less than $z_{max} = -1/(e \log(\varepsilon))$. The relative gain of allowing multiple rows can be seen as follows: under the constraint $R = 1$, achieving the same bound on the probability of large collisions would require $z = 1 - q(z, 1) \leq \varepsilon$. Hence allowing $R > 1$ allows us to increase the offered load by a ratio $-1/(e\varepsilon \log(\varepsilon)) > 1$ for target $\varepsilon < 1/e$. Conversely, maintaining the same load achieves a dramatic reduction in the frequency of large collisions. In the previous example $z = nP/C = 0.0875$, so we are in the regime $z \leq 1/e$, leading to optimal $R = 4.20$. Rounding to the nearest integer $R = 4$, we obtain $q(4, z) = 0.9850$, as compared with the previous $q(1, z) = 0.91$.

3.2 Lossy Difference Sketch

The introduction of the Virtual LDAs in the LDS has several side effects. The principal consequence of further spreading flow packets across the data structure is that fewer positions remain unused and, more importantly, more collisions occur. However, this is to some extent compensated by the fact that every flow is spread across k positions, and, thus, collision randomization is higher. In this section, we will investigate how these factors change the previous analysis.

The Virtual LDA divides up the packets of a flow amongst k locations in each of R rows. Accurate estimation of a given flow depends on having only small collisions in at least one of these locations. Thus we adapt our notion of survivability as follows for general k: A given flow is *survivable* if it is large (the number of packets exceeds some value x) while at the same time suffers only small collisions (of size no more than x/k) at at least one of the Rk locations it occupies in the Virtual LDA.

In this section we examine a simplified model of the Virtual LDA that admits an extension to the analysis of Section 3.1 to approximate the probability of survivability. This shows that, from the collision survivability point of view, the Virtual LDA is no worse than the multirow data structure described in Section 3.1, and is actually expected to be better. This property, coupled with the superior loss resilience of the Virtual LDA, recommends it as the better choice.

Our model and analysis are as follows. For a specific flow, let U_ℓ be the number of its packets hashed to a location ℓ, and V_ℓ the number of packets from all other flows that are mapped to that location. The estimation algorithm first determines the location ℓ of minimal $U_\ell + V_\ell$. Since we are concerned principally with the case that the specific flow has some large number u of packets, our first simplification is to ignore the sampling variability amongst the U_ℓ and approximate the U_ℓ as taking the same value (i.e., the average u/k). Thus the problem of minimizing $U_\ell + V_\ell$ is thus reduced to that of minimizing the V_ℓ.

Because the locations allocated to a given flow in a row are contiguous, the V_ℓ are in general dependent, because if packets from a background flow hash to location ℓ, the other packets from the same flow are more likely to collide at a neighboring location ℓ'. This dependence leads to positive correlations amongst the V_ℓ, meaning that the joint probability of collisions occurring at all locations of a flow is greater than the product of the marginal probability of collisions occurring at each site. Conversely, the corresponding survival probability is bounded below by that of a model where collisions are independent: it is conservative to use this as our second simplification. Thus we model the distribution K_i of the number of colliding flows as a Bernoulli $B(nk, R/C)$ random variables.

For our final simplification, we note that under our Pareto model, the probability that the number $T(k)$ of packets sampled from a background flow to each of the k locations in a row exceeds a level x obeys $\Pr[T(k) \geq x] \approx \Pr[T_1 \geq kx]$ for large x, where T_1 the length of the background flow; see [26]. Coupled with the subexponential approximation for sums of flow lengths, we approximate the probability of a small number of packets (at most x/k) due to i colliding flows at some site ℓ as $S_i = \Pr[V_\ell < x/k | \text{i colliding flows}] \approx 1 - iP$ where $P = \Pr[T_1 > x]$ under the (fitted) Pareto distribution.

Thus, under our simplifications, the probability of small collisions is $Q(Rk) = 1 - (nkRP/C)^{Rk}$. The optimization and dimensioning strategy is then immediate by comparison with Section 3.1: (i) choose a value k based on targets for loss resilience; (ii) for a given small target survivability rate $1 - \varepsilon$, calculate the number of rows by rounding $\max\{1, -\log(\varepsilon)/k\}$ to the nearest integer.

4. PRACTICAL ENHANCEMENTS

In this section, we introduce a series of enhancements to the LDS data structure that make it more practical for real deployment. We start by defining a mechanism to boost the accuracy for a selected subset of flows of particular interest to network operators. We then investigate how to parametrize the sampling rates to support a wide range of loss ratios. Finally, we note that the data structure contains additional information that can be used to mine other interesting metrics, including per-flow packet loss and heavy hitter detection.

4.1 Weighting of Flows

As formally analyzed in Sec. 3, the LDS intrinsically produces better estimates for large flows. This is due to the fact that, when flows collide, estimates are average delays of said flows, weighted by the amount of packets.

However, often times, small flows are of interest (a notable example are DNS flows, which usually consist of only one packet per direction). On the other hand, operators might be particularly interested in measuring a particular set of flows with higher accuracy. For example, one could increase the accuracy for certain subnetworks where critical services are hosted, or where troubleshooting activities call for precise examination of network delays (a practical use case for flow weighting is presented in Sec. 5).

We provide a mechanism to raise the accuracy of flows at will. This can be very simply accomplished by weighting flows according to some pre-defined policies driven by the operator's desires. Such policies can define a flow's weight according to any information present on packet headers. The default weight for non-policed flows is defined as 1 for simplicity.

These weights are taken into consideration straightforwardly by slightly modifying the update procedure. When a packet of a flow f arrives, its headers are examined and a weight w is determined according the existing weighting policies. Then, a cell of each row is selected as explained in Sec. 2.3.4. For each of the cells, their s value is increased by w times the packet timestamp, while n values are increased by w (recall that, previously, s values were increased by the timestamp and n values by 1).

No modification is required to the estimation procedure. When all flow weights are equal, the estimates are identical to those of Sec. 2.3.4. Otherwise, flows are weighted by their number of packets times their weight. It shall be noted, however, that this extra accuracy will always come at expense of the accuracy of the estimates for flows with lesser weight. Thus, it is not advisable to heavily increase the weight of a large percentage of flows, as it will dramatically reduce the accuracy for all the others. We will analyze the effect of weighting from a practical standpoint in Sec. 5.

4.2 Multi-Bank LDS

As explained in Sec. 2.3.3, to maximize the collection of delay samples in front of packet loss, each vLDA should sample the incoming packet stream at rate L/k, where L corresponds to its associated number of losses and k to its length. However, in a real scenario, the absolute number of losses that each flow will experience is unpredictable, which raises the question of how to set the sampling rate. On the one hand, a reasonable amount of loss has to be supported, which calls for low sampling rates. On the other, aggressive sampling will miss small flows and fail to collect enough packets for those that do not experience loss.

Inspired by [17], we propose dividing the counters of the LDS in several banks, and have each bank sample the incoming packets at a different rate. This way, at least one of the banks will suit the actual loss rate of each flow.

A natural way to divide counters in banks is to set a different sampling rate on a per-row basis. In the evaluation provided in Sec. 5, we show that configuring one row for worst-case loss scenarios, and maintaining increasingly higher sampling rates in the other rows, does not sacrifice accuracy in normal scenarios with low loss, while still providing protection against high loss. When a flow surpasses the target worst-case threshold, the LDS will be unable to provide delay estimates for that flow. In such a case, however, the data structure can provide an estimate for its number of lost packets, as will be explained in Sec. 4.3.

This variant of the LDS requires very few changes to the algorithms detailed in Sec. 2.3. Now each row has an associated sampling stage, which is also implemented using pseudo-random hashing to coordinate measurement nodes, while the estimation procedure only needs to be modified to be aware of the sampling rate that each cell has applied. In particular, packet counts need to be inverted before deciding which LDS cell will be selected to produce a final estimate. After the cell selection procedure, delay estimates are produced normally.

4.3 Mining Other Estimates

The LDS data structure can be mined to extract additional information of practical interest to network operators. Firstly, the data structure can provide per-flow delay variance estimates by examining the differences across the delays recorded in buckets dedicated to a given flow. The procedure to obtain this estimate was originally proposed and is thoroughly described in [17]. Our data structure has a comparatively smaller number of buckets per flow, but the same method could be applied to obtain rough delay variance estimates. This additional estimate can be extremely useful in practice to detect unexpected delay variations, such as jitter or delay peaks.

If we ignore the s fields and focus only on the n fields of each cell, the data structure behaves similarly to a Count-Min Sketch [9]. Consequently, an estimate of the length of a given flow can be obtained as follows. For each row, aggregate all vLDA cells to obtain a packet count. Then, take the minimum of such values. This is the final estimate. It can be easily shown that this estimate is, at best, error free, and, in the presence of collisions, it can only be greater than the actual value. This is an interesting property for certain problems and, especially, for heavy hitter detection. The accuracy of this technique is analyzed in greater detail in [9].

Simply by attaching another counter to each cell, where packet sizes are aggregated, we can also estimate flow sizes in bytes. Both these new counters and the existing could be used for heavy hitter detection in terms of bytes or packets respectively. Additionally, one could obtain crude estimates for the average packet sizes. In this paper we divide the aggregate delay over the number of packets to estimate average flow delays. Likewise, total flow sizes could be used to obtain a per-flow average packet size. Finally, we note that per-flow packet loss can be obtained by comparing the n fields of our data structure as collected in *sender* and *receiver*.

5. EVALUATION

With the objective of evaluating the LDS data structure in a realistic scenario, we deployed two network monitors in an operational network. For the sake of reproducibility, we collected a packet delay trace, rather than directly processing live traffic. We then ran a series of experiments using LDS and two state of the art techniques that will be described in Sec. 5.1. We note, however, that all the traffic measurement procedures, including LDS and both reference techniques, were fast enough to run on-line and, therefore, the results we present are completely equivalent to live traffic analysis.

The first monitor was deployed in a 10 Gb/s link that connects a large research and educational networking consortium to the rest of the Internet. The second was located in the 1 Gb/s access link of one University part of this consortium. We obtained a copy of the traffic that traversed both links in both directions and used Endace DAG

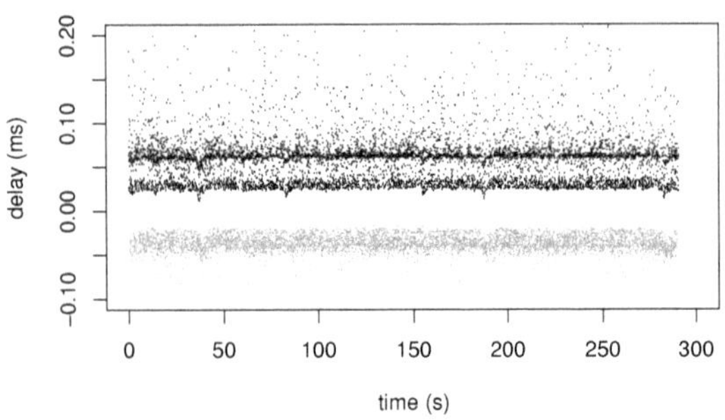

Figure 7: Timeseries of a sample of the packet delays, with outbound delays portrayed as negative values.

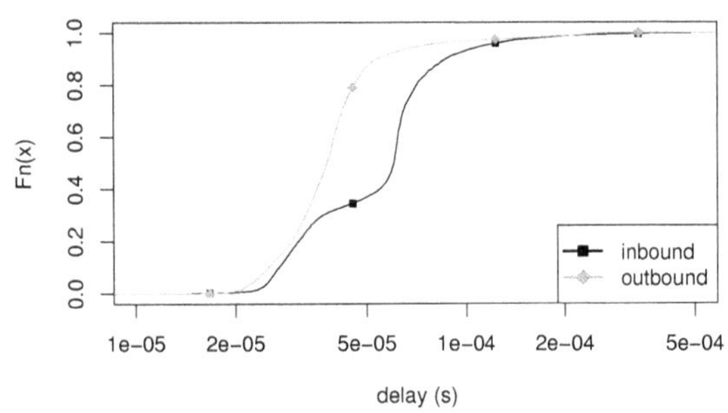

Figure 8: CDF of the delays for inbound and outbound packets.

cards [12] to simultaneously capture packets in both measurement points. We synchronized DAG clocks using the PTP protocol, which reportedly provides sub-microsecond accuracies [10] and thus is accurate enough for fine grained delay measurement.

We then wrote a CoMo module [4] to analyze the trace and extract, for each packet, its flow identifier, packet identifier, and exact one-way delay. The trace averages 27Kpkts/s and contains around 7.76 million packets that belong to approximately 146000 flows.

Figure 7 shows a time series of a sample of the packet delays for each traffic direction. Two features are apparent from this figure that make inbound traffic (i.e., destined towards the University network) more interesting. First, inbound packet delays present higher variability. Second, two delay modes are clearly appreciable in the inbound traffic, as can be also confirmed in the CDF of the packet delays presented in Figure 8. Therefore, unless otherwise noted, the experiments presented next in the evaluation are performed on the inbound traffic.

5.1 Comparison with Existing Methods

The objective of this section is to compare the accuracy of LDS with the state-of-the-art on per-flow delay measurement. We choose the NetFlow Multi-Point Estimator (MPE) [19] and the Reference Latency Interpolation (RLI) [18] as representatives of a recently introduced class of techniques that exploit temporal delay correlation to refine measurements from a few samples.

The Multi-Point Estimator is conceived as an extension to NetFlow, and requires routers to use coordinated sampling. Under this assumption, for each sampled flow, there exist two delay samples from which to estimate the flow delay (NetFlow records include a timestamp of the first and last packet). Additionally, based on the empirical observation that packets that travel close in time experience similar delays, the method can interpolate the delay between these two samples using the NetFlow records of other flows that start or end within the duration of the measured flow. The main difference between MPE and RLI is that, while MPE relies on a modified version of NetFlow, RLI injects active probes to obtain the necessary delay samples and assumes that packets between two probes experience the same delay.

We evaluate LDS with three different configurations: one that provisions half as many counters as flows ($n/C \approx 2$) (to obtain a configuration that, as will be discussed, is comparable with MPE), while the other two are 10 times larger and smaller than this reference LDS. Consistently with the example in Sec. 3, we structure the sketch in 4 rows, which yields a sketch of 17500×4 counters for the first configuration. Given that loss is negligible in our scenario, we set the vLDA length $k = 1$, and the sampling rate $p = 1$. We analyze the impact of loss in detail in Sec. 5.2.

Figure 9 plots the CDF of the relative error obtained by each flow in the traffic, for different flow sizes. The figure includes the accuracy of MPE with a sampling rate of 1% and 10%,[2] RLI with 1KHz probing, and a simple method that estimates the delay of each flow to be the average delay of all packets. The figure shows that LDS greatly outperforms both MPE and RLI. The increase in accuracy compared to MPE can be explained by two primary causes. First, MPE completely misses a large number of small flows (e.g., more than 50% with 10% sampling). For these flows, we estimate their delay as the average delay of all packets, instead of simply assigning an error of 1. In contrast, LDS can always obtain an estimate for all flows. Second, for the flows it does collect, it interpolates the delays using other flows, but in our case these are not necessarily correlated, as can be observed in Figure 8. While RLI outperforms MPE, its accuracy is also far from LDS, especially for large flows, and requires significantly more memory and state maintenance.

Figure 9 (left) shows that, as predicted by the analysis, large flows are very accurately measured. A still notable accuracy for flows of 100 or more packets is also observed in the middle plot. Figure 9 (right) shows the per-flow accuracy for all flows, including also those with less than 100 packets. According to the analysis in Sec. 3, these flows are not considered to be survivable, since they tend to experience large collisions. These flows however only account for 20% of the packets in our trace. Even in this case, the accuracy of LDS is consistently above the state of the art. This result shows that the estimate of LDS for unsurvivable flows is in practice more accurate than just using the average delay of all packets.

LDS also features better memory usage. For example, with 10% sampling, MPE captures around 70000 flows, so (generously disregarding the fact that NetFlow stores flow keys) it consumes roughly as much memory as the 17500×4 LDS. Thus, with the same memory budget, LDS clearly outperforms MPE in terms of measurement accuracy. Note also that, even when LDS uses 10 times less memory than MPE ($C = 1750 \times 4$), it obtains significantly higher accuracy, especially for medium sized to large flows. LDS also outperforms

[2] Note that MPE uses sampling to control the memory usage, while for LDS sampling is only a measure against packet loss.

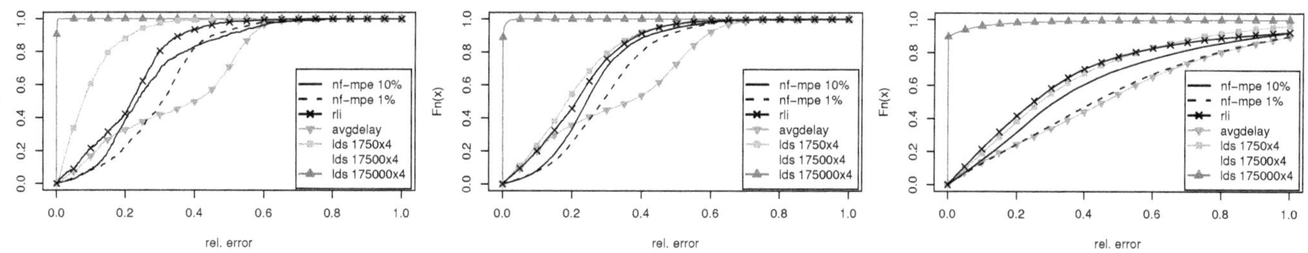

Figure 9: CDF of the relative error of various measurement methods for flows with > 1000 pkts. (left), with > 100 pkts (center) and all flows (right).

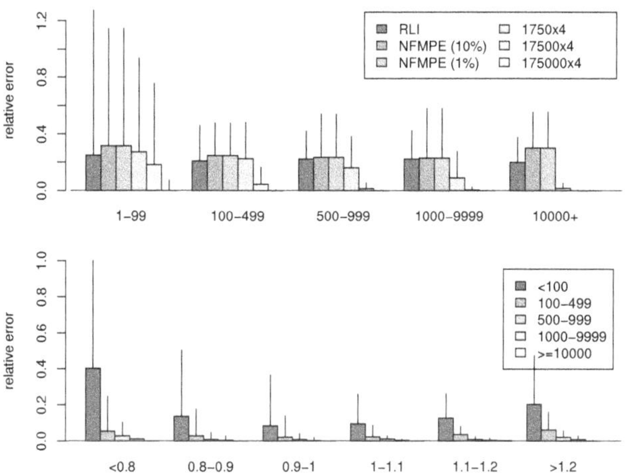

Figure 10: Median and 95-pct of relative error, binning flows by number of packets (top) and number of packets and average delay (relative to avg. flow delay; bottom).

RLI, which requires even more memory than MPE, since it maintains per-flow state.

Figure 10 (top) plots the median and 95-percentile of the relative error of flows binned by size. Consistently with the analysis of Sec. 3, the figure shows that larger flows are more accurately measured. Our method compares extremely favorably to both MPE and RLI. Only with 7,000 counters we obtain significant improvements for flows larger than 1,000 packets. When using 70,000 counters, which take about 1MB, flows with 500 to 999 packets obtain 1.2% median relative error, which falls to 0.4% and 0.06% for the larger size bins.

Figure 10 (bottom) bins flows both by size and average delay with a fixed sketch size of 70,000 counters. The figure shows how the errors are slightly larger as delay deviates in extreme values for the mean. This happens because smaller flows show more extreme values, but interferences tend to drag measurements toward the mean.

5.2 Measurement under Packet Loss

We now analyze the effect of packet loss to our data structure. Under small loss rates, it is desirable to keep the vLDA length parameter k small, since increasing it increments the number of collisions in the sketch. However, increasing k provides higher protection against loss. Additionally, sampling helps contain loss, since a large number of losses in a single flow can potentially invalidate the k counters.

We wish to dimension our data structure to support a given maximum number of losses per flow. The main intuition behind this approach is that, when flows experience a large amount of losses, performance degradation is more a consequence of loss than delay; thus, delay measurements cease to be meaningful (note that LDS can be mined to estimate per-flow loss, as explained in Sec. 4.3).

In this experiment, we arbitrarily set a target number of losses of 500 packets per flow. However, we also wish the LDS to be able to capture a large sample size if losses are much lower. Thus, we use a multi-bank configuration of LDS, as described in Sec. 4.2. We provide 4 rows with $k = 5$ vLDA buckets, like in the previous scenario, increase the size of each row of the sketch by a factor of k, and set $\alpha = 0.1$. We then pick suitable packet sampling rates for each row. With $k = 5$, each vLDA cell needs to support 100 losses, according to our target number of losses. This means that the sampling rate should be set to 0.01 to support this worst-case loss. Then, we wish the rest of the banks to tolerate lower loss in order not to sacrifice the accuracy of LDS in the normal case. We set the rest of the banks with increasing sampling rates of 0.1, 0.5 and 1 to tolerate up to 50, 10 and 5 losses respectively. For comparative purposes, we also set two LDS with a fixed sampling rate in all rows of 0.05 and 1.

Since, in our scenario, losses are negligible, we introduce random, uniform loss to test such configurations. Consistently with the assumptions made in Sec. 2.1, we perform 3 series of experiments with loss rates 0.1%, 0.5% and 1%. It should be noted that uniform loss is one of the most harmful loss models to LDS, for three main causes. First, losses are spread among a large number of flows, instead of being contained within a few. Second, the absolute number of losses that hit each bucket heavily varies according to the lengths of the involved flows. Recall from Sec. 2.3 that the optimal sampling rate for each bucket depends on its absolute number of losses. Third, this loss model penalizes large flows, which are precisely those that our method can measure most accurately.

Figure 11 shows the results we obtained. We start by noting that neither 5% nor 100% sampling single-bank LDSs perform satisfactorily. The former maintains its accuracy under higher loss, but is too conservative and underperforms on low loss. Conversely, 100% sampling is too optimistic and does not offer protection against loss. Thus, its cells become

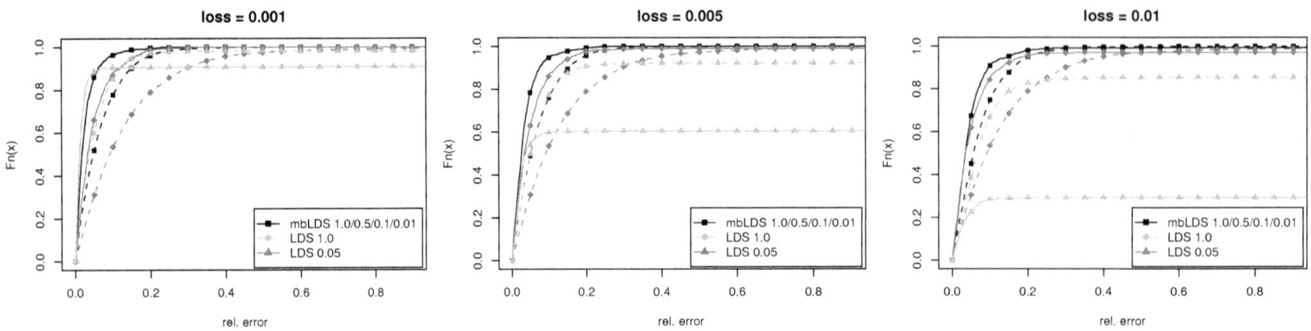

Figure 11: CDF of the relative of several LDS parametrizations under varying uniform loss rates. Solid lines represent flows with at least 10^3 packets, while dashed lines, flows with more than 100 packets.

too quickly invalidated under increasing loss, causing measurements to be lost.

In contrast, the multi-bank LDS performs consistently well under all loss rates. This desirable behavior is a consequence that, in all three scenarios, most flows experience losses that are well tolerated by at least one of the banks. Therefore, very seldom a flow invalidates all of its buckets, and accurate measurements are always produced.

The accuracy of LDS in Fig. 11 is still above that of RLI and MPE without loss (as presented in Sec. 5.1). However, MPE and RLI are more robust to loss. Hence, in scenarios with high loss and temporal correlation, we expect MPE and RLI to be a better choice.

5.3 Flow Weighting

We now test a more realistic use case of our technique. We envision a data center that hosts network services for a series of customers. Not all customers, though, are equally sensitive to network delay. We group the hosted services in three classes. First, bronze customers are not overly concerned about packet delays in the data center. For example, those could include bulk data transfer applications, such as backup, static web content serving, e-mail relaying, or computing intensive tasks.

Second, silver customers are somewhat dependent on network delay, but they do not require strict compliance of low-delay QoS requirements. A class that would fit these well are interactive services, such as remote shells, highly interactive web applications (e.g., Google is known to seek low delay to enhance the user's browsing experiences of AJAX-powered web applications), or web services for third party applications.

Finally, gold customers host applications that are extremely sensitive to delay, and wish to closely track the QoS of the services they are offering. Perfect examples for this class of applications involve multi-media streaming, audio/video conferencing, or remote gaming. Financial services such as automated trading could also fit this category, although, given that, in their case, low-delay data transmission is critical, they are unlikely to be hosted in shared infrastructure.

Since we do not have access to network traffic from a data center that hosts such applications, we adapt our scenario as follows. We randomly assign each flow to one of the categories. Bronze customers take 90% of the flows; silver customers, 9%, and gold customers, 1%. This approach ensures that the results are not an artifact of flow sizes, since large flows tend to be more accurately measured. In a real setting, these weights can be adjusted to the specific characteristics of the traffic under measurement.

We experiment with different sizings of the data structure, and various weights for each of the customer classes. Figure 12 shows the result of a series of experiments. We have tested two reference configurations. One that uses 40,000 counters (first row), an another that uses 100,000 counters and provides greater accuracy (second row). The first configuration fits in 625KB, and the second, in around 1.5MB. As for flow weights, we have tested three different configurations, which can be observed in each column: assigning weights of 1, 25 and 100 (first); 1, 10 and 100 (second), and, 1, 50 and 2500 (third).

The figure shows the relative error for the full set of flows (solid lines) and only for flows with more than 100 packets (dashed lines). Besides the error of each customer class, the figure also shows, as a reference, the result of applying no weighting. An important observation to be made is that flows from classes that have higher weights obtain significantly greater accuracy. The accuracy boost greatly depends on the actual weights; for example, when gold customers carry weight 2500, they obtain extreme accuracy. However, this penalizes the accuracy of bronze customers. In this case, we have ensured that the accuracy of bronze customers is not highly penalized, because few flows belong to higher priority classes. If, otherwise, the number of flows in each class was more balanced, the only option to increase accuracy for the flows of a given class without significantly diminishing that of a lower priority class would be to increase the sketch size. In other words, this method is only applicable to increase the accuracy of a small subset of flows.

6. RELATED WORK

One-way packet delay has been measured both using passive and active schemes. Active monitoring methods (e.g., [5, 24, 6, 28]) are based on injecting probe traffic in the network under study, and inferring one-way delay from the delays incurred by such probes. In contrast, passively monitoring network delays has been traditionally accomplished by recording packet timestamps in two measurement points, and exchanging such timestamps for comparison. Because these techniques generate huge data volumes, they require aggressive sampling to reduce the overhead. Further, packet sampling has to be coordinated across nodes, since the timestamps recorded at both measurement points must corre-

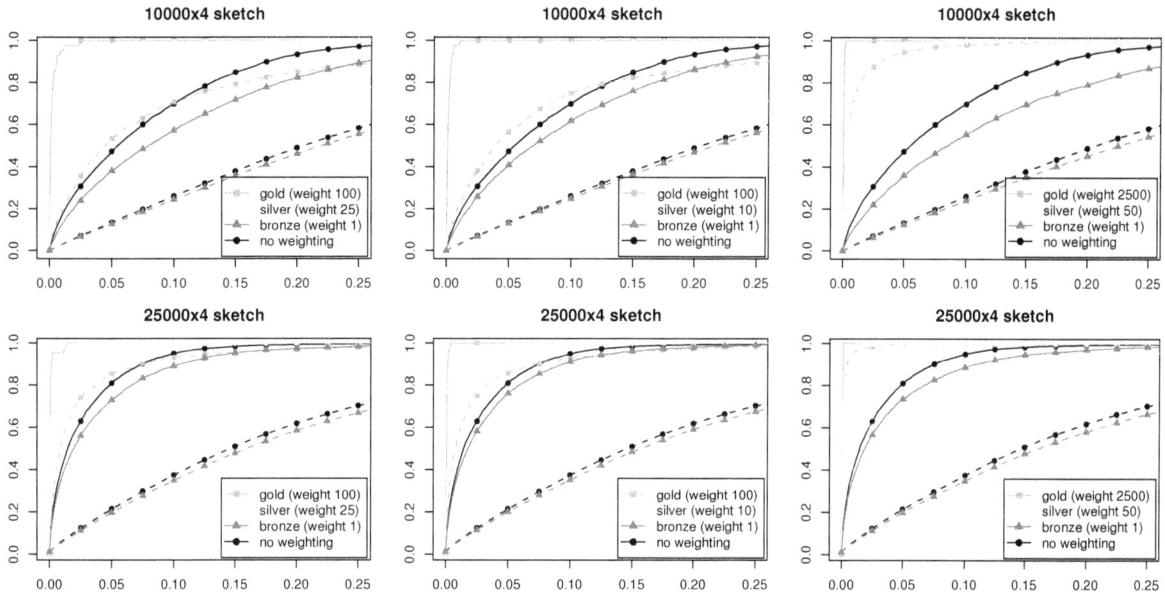

Figure 12: CDFs of the relative error with various flow weights and sketch sizes. Solid lines correspond to flows with more than 100 packets, while dashed lines include the full set of flows.

spond to an equal subset of all packets. This effect can be achieved using consistent hashing, i.e., using same prearranged hash function—an idea used before in trajectory sampling [11]).

More recently, LDA [17] has been proposed as a mechanism to overcome the linear relationship between sample size and overhead. LDA has been further analyzed in [27, 14] as well. Since our paper borrows some of the ideas of LDA, we have discussed this idea in great length. The problem of obtaining per-flow latency estimates in a scalable fashion, which is exactly the problem we attempted to solve in this paper, has received recent attention [18, 19]. [19] proposes modifying NetFlow [7] to allow measurement of one-way delay. If NetFlow samples packets using consistent hashing, the first and last timestamp fields of NetFlow records can be used to obtain two delay samples of a given flow that can be refined from using samples from other flows in between these two timestamps. The core idea of temporal delay correlation forms the basis for Reference Latency Interpolation [18], that we also discussed in detail in the paper. The biggest difference between RLI and our work is that we do not assume temporal correlation of packet delays. Removing the dependence on this assumption is beneficial in many ways, as explained in Sec. 1.

Besides packet delay measurement techniques, sketching is also very relevant to this work. Most relevant to us are two similar data structures: Multi-Stage Filters [13], which are designed for elephant flow detection, and the Count-Min Sketch [9], which can provide per-flow estimates with probabilistic accuracy guarantees. Other sketching techniques are reviewed and compared in [8].

7. CONCLUSIONS

We have presented a sketch-based data structure capable of producing per-flow one-way delay estimates. Although sketching naturally produces the best estimates for larger flows, this data structure can enhance the accuracy of arbitrary flows. For measurement in networks with packet loss, we have combined our sketching technique with a recently appeared data structure called Lossy Difference Aggregator.

State-of-art techniques rely on temporal correlation of delays to produce their estimates. However, in practice, routers can use various queueing policies for different kind of traffic, which greatly reduces the effective of said techniques. In our evaluation, we show how our technique achieves higher accuracy than such techniques when using a similar amount of memory, even in the presence of packet loss.

We have also presented a practical deployment scenario where our technique and its ability to improve measurement for arbitrary flows could be very useful. In particular, our technique could very well cater a data center with shared resources, where various applications present diverse degrees of dependency on network delay. In such a scenario, our technique can be used to obtain extremely precise measurements for the most critical applications, while still providing an acceptable degree of accuracy for other applications.

8. ACKNOWLEDGMENTS

This research was funded by the Spanish Ministry of Science and Innovation under contract TEC2011-27474 (NOMADS project), and by the *Comissionat per a Universitats i Recerca del DIUE de la Generalitat de Catalunya* (ref. 2009SGR-1140).

9. REFERENCES

[1] Corvil. `http://www.corvil.com/`.

[2] Juniper Networks T series Core Routers Architecture Overview. `www.juniper.net/us/en/local/pdf/whitepapers/2000302-en.pdf`.

[3] M. Alizadeh, A. Greenberg, D. A. Maltz, J. Padhye, P. Patel, B. Prabhakar, S. Sengupta, and

M. Sridharan. Data center TCP (DCTCP). In *Proc. of ACM SIGCOMM*, 2010.

[4] P. Barlet-Ros, G. Iannaccone, J. Sanjuàs-Cuxart, D. Amores-López, and J. Solé-Pareta. Load shedding in network monitoring applications. In *Proc. of USENIX Annual Technical Conf.*, 2007.

[5] J. Bolot. Characterizing end-to-end packet delay and loss in the internet. *Journal of High Speed Networks*, 2(3):289–298, 1993.

[6] B. Choi, S. Moon, R. Cruz, Z. Zhang, and C. Diot. Practical delay monitoring for ISPs. In *Proc. of ACM CoNEXT*, 2005.

[7] Cisco. NetFlow. http://www.cisco.com/web/go/netflow.

[8] G. Cormode and M. Hadjieleftheriou. Methods for finding frequent items in data streams. *The VLDB Journal*, 19(1):3–20, 2010.

[9] G. Cormode and S. Muthukrishnan. An improved data stream summary: the count-min sketch and its applications. *Journal of Algorithms*, 55(1):58 – 75, 2005.

[10] L. De Vito, S. Rapuano, and L. Tomaciello. One-way delay measurement: State of the art. *IEEE Transactions on Instrumentation and Measurement*, 57(12):2742–2750, 2008.

[11] N. Duffield and M. Grossglauser. Trajectory sampling for direct traffic observation. *IEEE/ACM Transactions on Networking*, 9(3):280–292, 2001.

[12] Endace. DAG network monitoring cards. http://www.endace.com.

[13] C. Estan and G. Varghese. New Directions in Traffic Measurement and Accounting: Focusing on the Elephants , Ignoring the Mice. *ACM Transactions on Computer Systems*, 21(3):270–313, 2003.

[14] H. Finucane and M. Mitzenmacher. An improved analysis of the lossy difference aggregator. *ACM SIGCOMM Computer Communication Review*, 40(2):4–11, 2010.

[15] S. Fred, T. Bonald, A. Proutiere, G. Regnie, and J. Roberts. Statistical bandwidth sharing: a study of congestion at flow level. In *Proc. of ACM SIGCOMM*, 2001.

[16] IEEE. IEEE/ANSI 1588 standard for a precision clock synchronization protocol for networked measurement and control systems, 2002.

[17] R. Kompella, K. Levchenko, A. Snoeren, and G. Varghese. Every microsecond counts: tracking fine-grain latencies with a lossy difference aggregator. In *Proc. of ACM SIGCOMM*, 2009.

[18] M. Lee, N. Duffield, and R. Kompella. Not all microseconds are equal: fine-grained per-flow measurements with reference latency interpolation. In *Proc. of ACM SIGCOMM*, 2010.

[19] M. Lee, N. Duffield, and R. Kompella. Two samples are enough: opportunistic flow-level latency estimation using netflow. In *Proc. of IEEE INFOCOM*, 2010.

[20] M. Lee, S. Goldberg, R. Kompella, and G. Varghese. Fine-grained latency and loss measurements in the presence of reordering. In *Proc. of ACM SIGMETRICS*, 2011.

[21] R. Martin. Wall street's quest to process data at the speed of light. `www.informationweek.com/news/infrastructure/showArticle.jhtml?articleID=199200297`.

[22] S. Moon, P. Skelly, and D. Towsley. Estimation and removal of clock skew from network delay measurements. In *Proc. of IEEE INFOCOM*, 1999.

[23] K. Park, G. Kim, and M. Crovella. On the relationship between file sizes, transport protocols, and self-similar network traffic. In *Proc. of International Conference on Network Protocols*, 2002.

[24] V. Paxson. Measurements and analysis of end-to-end Internet dynamics. Technical Report CSD-97-945, University of California at Berkeley, 1998.

[25] V. Paxson. On calibrating measurements of packet transit times. In *ACM SIGMETRICS Performance Evaluation Review*, volume 26, pages 11–21. ACM, 1998.

[26] C. Y. Robert and J. Segers. Tails of random sums of a heavy-tailed number of light-tailed terms. *Insurance: Mathematics and Economics*, 43(1):85 – 92, 2008.

[27] J. Sanjuas-Cuxart, P. Barlet-Ros, and J. Solé-Pareta. Validation and Improvement of the Lossy Difference Aggregator to Measure Packet Delays. *Traffic Monitoring and Analysis Workshop*, 2010.

[28] J. Sommers, P. Barford, N. Duffield, and A. Ron. Accurate and efficient SLA compliance monitoring. In *Proc. of ACM SIGCOMM*, 2007.

[29] L. Zhang, Z. Liu, and C. Honghui Xia. Clock synchronization algorithms for network measurements. In *Proc. of IEEE INFOCOM*, 2002.

Summary Review Documentation for

"Sketching the Delay: Tracking Temporally Uncorrelated Flow-Level Latencies"

Authors: J. Sanjuas-Cuxart, P. Barlet-Ros, N. Duffield, R. Kompella

Reviewer #1

Strengths: Entire scheme has been implemented and tested on real traces.
Reasonable analysis of data structure space requirements and accuracy.

Weaknesses: Relatively incremental approach. Scheme requires O(#flows) state; perhaps this is unavoidable. Some claims (accuracy/state requirement) in paper are inflated. The paper does not describe how to set many different parameters.

Comments to Authors: The assumption of synchronized clocks is big, but is not paid due attention. The accuracy of the algorithm depends entirely on the synchronization of the sender and receiver clocks: how expensive are the DAG cards used to timestamp packets? How does this cost compare to the high frequency active probes mentioned in the Introduction?

The LDS algorithm is a relatively simple merge of existing techniques. Handling lost/reordered packets is the most difficult problem, and that is dealt with, rather inelegantly, by smearing the measurements over multiple buckets and hoping that some measurements survive.

The virtual LDS scheme is not likely to be effective if some flows incur heavy losses, as might be the case with best effort flows. The evaluations only assume <1% loss, which is overly conservative.

How is the \alpha parameter set? Does choosing a small \alpha lead to high variance in results?

The x parameter (threshold of collision by number of packets) ignores per-flow variability. If a low latency flow gets mapped to flows with less than x packets but each with much higher latency, then the low latency flow's estimates will be affected disproportionately. It is not clear why the number of interfering packets is chosen as the measure of interference.

Evaluation:

The base parameters use half as many counters as flows. Is the total memory used not sufficient to maintain per flow statistics? Some of the experiments use 10 times more counters than flows - might as well keep per-flow state?

In general, the parameters in the experiments are chosen given the trace statistics, which says nothing about how one would set the parameters on a live network.

The experiments were performed, post-hoc, on a trace. Is it possible to perform experiments, live, on a high speed link? The other methods, NetFlow MPE for instance, are operating on a live link, and a offline comparison does not seem fair. Especially when the comparison requires O(#flow) state to provide a per-flow measure of latency.

Nits:

Section 2.3.3: How are individual packets mapped to one of k cells?

Figure 7: how many cells were used in the experiments?

The paper is unnecessarily long: A lot of the simple ideas presented in pseudocode can be removed.

Reviewer #2

Strengths: The authors provide nice and intuitive algorithmic optimizations to advance the state of the art in delay estimation at the flow level.

Weaknesses: The work appears too incremental to a large body of prior work by some of the authors.

Comments to Authors: The paper does a nice job of building up a nice algorithmic solution to the problem proposed. The results indicate the performance advantages of the proposed scheme and its accuracy.

However, my understanding of the paper is that it is very incremental to prior work. The LDS scheme as described, appears to be the LDA scheme enhanced with some sketch based data structures to track flows better. Seems like a very simple optimization beyond prior work.

Unfortunately, I am unable to judge how this paper is a significant enhancement over prior art.

Reviewer #3

Strengths: -cute idea
- relevant problem
- extensive evaluation with real traces
- well written.

Weaknesses: - fairly incremental to the authors' own prior work
- not sure how feasible the synchronization assumption is

Comments to Authors: How feasible is microsecond level synchronization? The paper depends quite heavily on it. I imagine that it should be fine, given that such synchronization is regularly achieved in some systems (e.g. cellular wireless networks). But what is the cost?

Some of the parameters in the experiments are unclear. For example, how is the \alpha parameter set?

What happens if packets are lost? Does it not distort the measurements?

Reviewer #4

Strengths: - Novel approach for estimating delays in the network, even when there is no assumption on the temporal dependencies of the flows.
- Experimental evidence shows the improvement over state of the art approaches in realistic scenarios.

Weaknesses: There are not enough theoretical guarantees on error that validate the goodness of the LDS approach.

Comments to Authors: 1. This paper removes the assumption of temporal correlation but the flows are not necessarily "uncorrelated".

2. In Section 3.2, it is not clear why the minimization problem (U_l + V_l) is reduced to minimization problem of V_l. Is it practical to make the assumption?

3. Under packet loss scenario, the result shows the MB-LDS performs better than LDS. But it does not have any comparison with other state of the art approaches.

4. How MB-LDS performs under higher packet loss scenario?

5. In Figure 8, the bronze customers' accuracy does not look affected with the higher weights in gold and silver. The proportion of flows is the reason. It will be interesting to first see how the proportion are affecting the bronze customers when they are not that asymmetric.

Reviewer #5

Strengths: A more practical and effective technique for per-flow delay measurement; solid presentation; good evaluation.

Weaknesses: Evaluation focuses on average delay.

Comments to Authors: The paper present LDS, a new sketching-based technique and associated data structure to obtain per-flow latency measurements. LDS does not rely on model assumptions about the relation between delays across flows, has lower memory requirement and network overhead than existing techniques and a data structure that can resized based on necessary accuracy.

I expected to see but did not find references to papers that evaluate the impact of prioritization, load balancing, etc on the effectiveness of other techniques.

The presentation of LDS is well done, with a step-by-step introduction of the ideas starting with SDS and relaxing assumptions to introduce LDS, flow weighting and multibank-LDS.

The presentation includes results from an evaluation of LDS using data collected from links connecting a research and a university networks to (rest of) the Internet. The evaluation section does a pretty good job at presenting the advantages and potential issues with the technique.

I did not see an analysis of the effectiveness of the technique in capturing other estimates than average. Sec. 4.3 briefly discusses how other information could be mined but there is no follow-up in the evaluation on the effectiveness of the approach to capture, for instance, delay variations.

It would be good to drop an example of number of flows that makes collecting and exchanging per-flow state prohibitively expensive

Response from the Authors

The first and third reviewers raise concerns over the assumption of clock synchronization. This assumption is common to many one-way delay measurement methods, including active techniques based on probing. The authors agree that it is an assumption that raises difficulties, even if they can be solved with the methods presented in the paper. Removing this assumption was out of the scope of this paper. We have provided references to papers that specifically deal with the clock synchronization issue.

The paper introduces a "half as many counters as flows" configuration since it has the advantage that results make for a fair comparison with other methods that require similar memory usage (e.g., MPE). The evaluation also tests a configuration with fewer counters satisfactorily (fig. 5). We further stress that LDS still outperforms the competition using 10% of this amount of memory.

The reviewers raise the question of whether LDS works under higher loss. Low loss is an assumption of our paper (Sec. 2.1). We argue that delay measurements might not be particularly interesting when loss is very high, since TCP does not work under high loss. We now point that under such conditions, other loss-tolerant methods might be a better option than LDS, since k should be larger and would require more memory.

The number of packets in each bucket provides an assessment of the amount of interfering packets (x) although the reviewers raise the valid point that the measurements can be damaged if delays differ largely in magnitude. While other alternatives exist (e.g., combining multiple cells), we defend our choice in Sec. 2.2. Also, we have extended the discussion on how to map packets to each virtual LDA cell (Sec. 2.3.3)

In the evaluation, we have included our choice of the α parameter. We also explain that the results of the experiments are equivalent to an on-line setting, that LDS can actually run on-line, and discuss the accuracy of reference methods under loss. The evaluation also acknowledges that weighting is only useful to increase the accuracy for a small set of flows.

We ensured that other less critical concerns raised by the reviewers were discussed in the paper to our best ability.

The Evolution of Network Configuration: A Tale of Two Campuses

Hyojoon Kim
Georgia Tech
Atlanta, GA, USA
joonk@gatech.edu

Theophilus Benson
University of Wisconsin
Madison, WI, USA
tbenson@cs.wisc.edu

Aditya Akella
University of Wisconsin
Madison, WI, USA
akella@cs.wisc.edu

Nick Feamster
Georgia Tech
Atlanta, GA, USA
feamster@cc.gatech.edu

ABSTRACT

Studying network configuration evolution can improve our understanding of the evolving complexity of networks and can be helpful in making network configuration less error-prone. Unfortunately, the nature of changes that operators make to network configuration is poorly understood. Towards improving our understanding, we examine and analyze *five years* of router, switch, and firewall configurations from two large campus networks using the logs from version control systems used to store the configurations. We study how network configuration is distributed across different network operations tasks and how the configuration for each task evolves over time, for different types of devices and for different locations in the network. To understand the trends of how configuration evolves over time, we study the extent to which configuration for various tasks are added, modified, or deleted. We also study whether certain devices experience configuration changes more frequently than others, as well as whether configuration changes tend to focus on specific portions of the configuration (or on specific tasks). We also investigate when network operators make configuration changes of various types. Our results concerning configuration changes can help the designers of configuration languages understand which aspects of configuration might be more automated or tested more rigorously and may ultimately help improve configuration languages.

Categories and Subject Descriptors

C.2.3 [**Computer-Communication Networks**]: Network Operations—*Network management*

General Terms

Management, Measurement

Keywords

Network configuration, Network evolution, Longitudinal analysis

1. INTRODUCTION

The behavior of a communications network depends in part on the configuration of thousands of constituent network devices, each of which is configured independently. In this sense, network configuration is a large, distributed program. Despite its importance in dictating the overall behavior of the network, we understand very little about the nature of configuration. Today, network operators implement high-level network tasks with low-level configuration commands; operators frequently make mistakes when making changes to network configuration [6, 14]. Although some studies have examined properties of configuration "snapshots" (*e.g.*, [15]), we have little understanding of how network configuration *evolves* over time.

Studying the evolution of network configuration over time can offer unique insights that cannot be learned from a single static snapshot. First, such a study can shed light on how network functions evolve over time: for example, we can learn more about how network configuration evolves, and which network tasks contribute to the growth in complexity. Second, because configuration changes are the cause of many errors, understanding the nature of how configuration changes over time—and what tasks configuration changes are associated with—can better inform configuration testing by helping create targeted test cases. Third, knowledge about configuration changes also offers valuable information about the parts of network configuration where operators spend time, which may help designers of configuration languages and configuration management systems design a better environment to make these tasks easier.

Towards these goals, this paper presents the first long-term longitudinal study of the evolution of network configuration, for two large campus networks: Georgia Tech and the University of Wisconsin. Comparing the evolution of network configuration across two different large campuses allows us to identify trends that are common across campuses, as well as practices that are specific to a particular network. We study the changes that operators make to the configurations of all routers, switches, and firewalls in these networks over a five-year period. We study the following questions:

- How does network configuration size evolve over time? How many of the changes are additions, modifications, or deletions? Do changes tend to occur at a specific time of day or day of the week?
- Which network-wide factors contribute most to configuration evolution?

- What parts of the configuration change most frequently, and why?
- Are there dependencies and correlations in changes to network configuration, and why?

We perform our analysis on two campus networks. Although the results may not generalize beyond these two campuses, they represent a case study and a first attempt to perform extensive longitudinal analysis on campus networks. Our study also complements previous studies, which have focused on enterprise and backbone networks [7, 18].

We find that configurations continue to grow over time, and a variety of factors—infrequent ones, such as, infrastructure expansion and policy changes, and more frequent ones, such as customer addition/modification—contribute in interesting ways to configuration evolution. We find that routers experience configuration changes more frequently, and that changes to routers involve a broader range of network configuration tasks than the changes that operators make to switch and firewall configurations. Given that there are far fewer routers than firewalls or switches in both networks, the relative frequency of configuration changes to routers highlights that many crucial day-to-day network operations tasks center around router configurations. Third, although there are many similarities in the configurations between the two campuses—both in the amount of configuration devoted to each configuration task and to the nature of the configuration changes—the network operators for each campus do have distinct practices (*e.g.*, the use of static ARP entries) that tend to appear on more general purpose devices, such as core routers. In contrast, devices that are more special-purpose such as firewalls tend to exhibit more common configuration change patterns. Finally, we note that configuration changes to switches and routers are sometimes correlated, suggesting the possibility for better configuration tools that can assist operators by automatically recognizing these dependencies.

Our findings suggest possible areas for improvement in configuration management and testing. For example, our findings concerning correlated changes across configurations can suggest improvements to the configuration process: a configuration management system could observe correlations in configuration changes and suggest changes that operators might make to low-level configuration constructs based on observations of past correlated changes for different high-level tasks. The management system can similarly help with debugging erroneous changes to configuration. Our observations regarding the high frequency of router configuration updates—which are often manual and hence error-prone—suggest the need for automated network-wide configuration management systems targeted specifically toward routers.

The rest of the paper is organized as follows. Section 2 presents background on network configuration, and on the configuration management systems used to make changes to network configuration. Section 3 describes the datasets that we use for this study and our approach. Section 4 describes our results for routers, switches, and firewalls. In each case, we observe characteristics for a snapshot of the network configuration; we also perform a longitudinal analysis of configuration changes over the five years of our study. Section 5 discusses possible future research directions for our results, including suggestions for how they might be used to improve configuration management and testing. Section 6 concludes.

2. BACKGROUND AND RELATED WORK

We use an archived history of network configuration files to analyze the nature and causes of configuration changes to switches, routers, and firewalls in the Georgia Tech and University of Wisconsin campus networks. In this section, we describe the common configuration management systems used by the networks studied.

```
1   ...
2   1.51
3   log
4   @Fri Feb  5 15:04:28 EST 2010
5   @
6   text
7   @a141 1
8    port-object range bootps bootpc
9   a160 4
10  object-group service 12-123-12-13-any-udp udp
11   port-object range bootps bootpc
12  object-group service 12-123-12-14-any-udp udp
13   port-object range bootps bootpc
14  d173 16
15  a188 9
16  object-group service 13-14-15-16-any-udp udp
17   port-object range bootps bootpc
18  object-group service 14-15-16-17-any-udp udp
19  ...
20  @
```

Figure 1: RCS file showing changes to network configuration.

2.1 Configuration Management

Both campus networks use a configuration management tool called RANCID [17] for tracking and monitoring network device configurations. RANCID's main function is to construct a catalog of devices, pull the current configurations, and store them in a version control system, which can allow network operators to track changes in the configurations to network devices. In addition to device configurations, RANCID also pulls hardware information (*e.g.*, cards, serial numbers). RANCID operates with devices from many vendors, including Cisco, Juniper, Foundry, and HP. More details can be found on the RANCID Web site [17].

In addition to accepting input from RANCID, the version control system also allows network operators to manually checkpoint and commit changes to the repository. Just as programmers use revision control to track changes to source code, network operators have adopted revision control to manage network devices by tracking changes to device configuration files. The CVS repository tracks changes by giving each revision of the configuration file a unique revision number and by storing metadata along with this revision, such as the time of change, comment, author of the change, and the sets of lines changed.

CVS stores all the metadata along with revisions for each configuration file in a single Revision Control System (RCS) file. Figure 1 shows an excerpt from an RCS file. The current revision number is on the top (line 2), followed by *log* (lines 3–5), which contain comments provided by the operator or RANCID explaining the nature and cause of the change (the revision date in this case). The *text* (lines 6–20) lines document the location, number and nature of the change; these lines allow us to track additions and deletions to the network configuration. We interpret an addition immediately followed by a deletion as a modification if the sum of the line number and the number of line changes of deletion is equal to the line number of addition added by one. For example, in Figure 1, lines 14–15 shows a modification (173+16 = 188+1).

2.2 Related Work

We provide a brief overview of related work. We first discuss various prior work on static analysis of network configuration to better understand network properties and to characterize or diagnose network configurations. Although the networking community has seen only limited work on analyzing configuration *changes*, the software engineering community has performed extensive studies of changes to source code that relate to our study.

Static analysis. Previous work has performed static analysis of network configurations to study network properties and to help network operators diagnose misconfigurations in their networks. Caldwell *et al.* propose a system to automatically discover configuration templates and rules [2]. Maltz *et al.* performed a study of many enterprise network configurations to gain insights about the design and use of network configuration in enterprise networks [15]. The *rcc* tool performs network-wide static analysis of router configurations to detect configuration errors in BGP [6]. There is much other previous work on identifying and detecting misconfiguration [10, 14], but these tools focus on static analysis. Other work has used static analysis of router configuration to understand how operators configure specific functions (*e.g.*, route redistribution [12] and access control [19]), as well as to identify sources of configuration complexity [1]. The NetDB system pulled router configurations from the AT&T backbone network into a database for analysis of configuration snapshots [7]. Gottlieb *et al.* used NetDB to perform static analysis of network configuration to discover and construct configuration templates to help network operators automatically configure new sessions for ISP customers [8]; a follow-up system, Presto, constructs network configurations based on configuration templates [5]. These systems rely on operators to manually specify network configuration templates; ultimately, the type of analysis we perform in this study might help automatically identify common tasks and configuration idioms that could be automated.

Dynamic analysis. Other projects have explored the changes in configuration over time, albeit for smaller sets of network configuration, or over shorter periods of time. Sung *et al.* examined changes in stanzas over time for five enterprises VPN customers. They study which sets of stanzas change most often [18]. Chen *et al.* also examine the dependencies between configuration stanzas by analyzing changes [3]. Le *et al.* [11] aim to automatically generate rules to determine commands that a given stanza should contain. This approach requires pre-processing and domain knowledge to determine how to represent the commands as attributes of stanza; it also does not explore configuration changes over time.

Mining software repositories. The field of software repository mining, a sub-area of software engineering, mines version control systems to discover artifacts that are produced and archived during the evolution of a software program. Several studies have explored the longitudinal evolution of software. Lehman *et al.* studied the evolution of source code in several IBM products between 1969 and 2001 [13]. Eick *et al.* studied the phenomenon of code decay, whereby changes to a software system become increasingly difficult over its lifetime [4]. Those studying changes to software repositories focus on both changes to high-level *properties*, such as software complexity or maintainability; and on changes to *artifacts*, which is typically done by analyzing differences between versions in the version control system itself. A specific approach to mining software repositories called *source code differencing*, pioneered by Raghavan *et al.*, examines difference data in software repositories to look for additions, deletions, and modifications to source code over time [16]. This approach is similar to that which we take in this paper, where we explore additions, deletions, and modifications to network configuration files to understand changes to software artifacts. Kagdi *et al.* provide an excellent survey and taxonomy of the large body of work in mining software repositories [9].

	Routers	*Firewalls*	*Switches*	*Total*
Georgia Tech	16	365	716	1097
Wisconsin	53	325	1246	1624

Table 1: Number of devices for each device type.

3. DATA AND ANALYSIS

We describe the configuration data that we use in our study and our approach for postprocessing and analyzing the data.

3.1 Data

Both Georgia Tech (*GT*) and University of Wisconsin (*UW*) manage their network configurations with RANCID and CVS, the tools described in the previous section. We have collected five years of archived configuration files from all network devices (*i.e.*, routers, firewalls, and switches) in the two networks. Table 1 shows the number of network devices currently deployed in both networks for each device type. We note that both networks comprise mostly Cisco devices; configurations are stored in the RCS format. Our analysis tools thus focus on parsing Cisco's configuration language and the RCS format. The border routers in both networks are Juniper routers. Because the configuration language syntax differs significantly from Cisco's configuration language, we omit the border routers from our analysis for both networks. We now describe the design of each network and how they use RANCID and CVS in more detail.

Georgia Tech. Figure 2a shows the topology of the Georgia Tech network. The Internet connection originates from two multi-homed border routers; two physical firewalls are deployed close to the border. Departments, research groups, and residence halls are divided into separate subnets and assigned unique virtual LANs (VLANs). Each subnet has different access control policies, enforced with a separate virtual firewall. The network has hundreds of virtual firewall instances that are not shown in the figure. Hosts are connected to the network via switches at the edge. RANCID pulls the latest configuration files every three hours and saves the snapshot of the files. A CVS "commit" only occurs when the system detects a change in the latest configuration. In this network, the operators rarely make manual backups of the configurations; as such, most revisions in the repository are created by RANCID.

University of Wisconsin. The *UW* network, shown in Figure 2b, is similar to *GT* in many aspects; like the *GT* network, the *UW* network topology is hierarchical, with Internet traffic entering through two border routers and redirected through two major border firewalls for access control. Border routers are distinct from core routers, and they reside one level higher than the core routers. Figure 2b does not show the border routers. The *UW* network contains four tiers: the core and node layers, which primarily comprises routers; and the radial and access layers, primarily comprising switches. The access switches connect computers in the different departments to the network. Unlike *GT*, the RANCID setup at *UW* pulls snapshots for only firewall configurations. Similarly, commits to firewall configuration files only happen when the system detects a change to the latest configuration. Operational policies and tools at *UW* force operators to manually snapshot and commit all other configuration changes before they can be pushed to the devices. As such, most revisions are created by operators. This different approach does not affect our results, as it simply reflects a difference in the mechanism on who pulls snapshots, detects changes and commits to the repository.

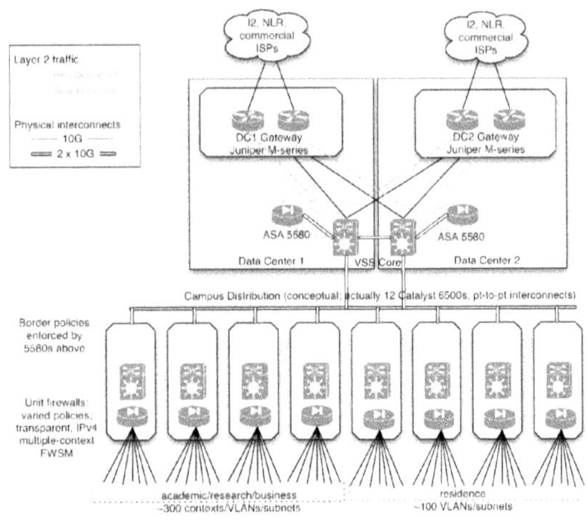

(a) Georgia Tech

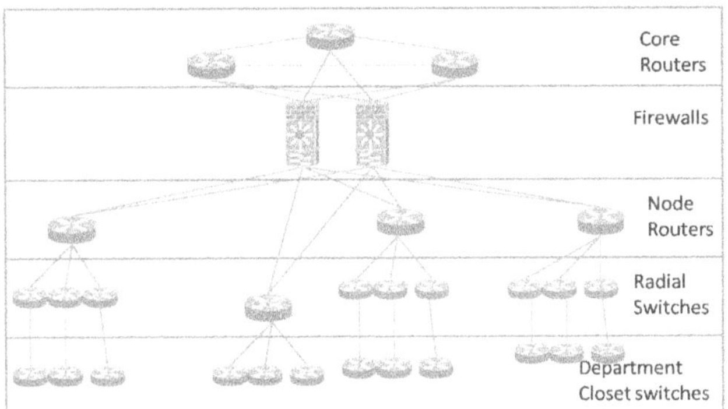

(b) University of Wisconsin

Figure 2: GT and UW campus networks.

3.2 Analysis

We analyze the evolution of network configuration changes by analyzing the RCS files for changes and extracting information about how each configuration file changes over time. This section describes our analysis, which has two major parts: (1) abstracting higher-level operator tasks from low-level configuration changes; (2) performing change analysis on the RCS files.

3.2.1 Developing abstractions for functionality

The first task in analyzing the network configuration is to derive abstractions of high-level functions and tasks from low-level configuration commands. This helps us more readily identify the types of tasks that network operators most commonly perform when making changes to the network configuration and the amount of configuration devoted to each task. We do so by manually associating each command in the configuration language with a unique function. Table 2 shows the list of the functions we use in our analysis, with several example commands for each of the categories. Given this categorization, we construct a database that maps configuration commands to one of these functions. Due to the abstraction we apply to the configurations, we do lose fine-grain information that can be valuable to our study, but the goal of this work is to offer a high-level analysis of network configuration and its evolution.

Although our categorization is extensive, the mapping does not cover all configuration commands: some commands are difficult to classify or do not map to any particular function (*e.g.*, commit checksum values, comments, banners, start/end markers, and version info). Although not complete, we believe our functionality map is extensive enough to cover 93% of all configuration commands and 91% of all configuration changes in University of Wisconsin, and 98% of all commands and changes in Georgia Tech, thus complete enough to shed light on how operators devote time to various high-level tasks.

	Meaning	Examples
mgt	device management settings	username, password, telnet, ssh, logging, aaa, clock, console, radius-server
l1	interface/port settings	interface definition, bandwidth, switchport, description, duplex
l2	layer 2 settings	arp x.x.x.x, mac-address, ip proxy-arp, arp timeout, spanning-tree
vlan	VLAN settings	vlan definition, switchport mode trunk, switchport mode access vlan, set vtp, set vmps
l3	layer 3 related	ip address x.x.x.x , ip gateway x.x.x.x, ip route x.x.x.x, nat, router bgp/ospf/rip, router-id, neighbor
acl	access control	object define, access-list, permit, deny
sec	security related	vpn, ipsec, crypto, webvpn, anyconnect, ssl, tunnel-group, flood-guard
cflt	control filtering	prefix-list
qos	QoS	policy-map, class-map, service-policy, port-channel load-balance, set qos

Table 2: Functionality map. We map each command to a specific functionality to effectively analyze configuration files.

To abstract configuration changes that involve multiple lines of configuration, we group configuration into *stanzas*, each of which is the largest contiguous block of commands that encapsulate a piece of the network functionality. Cisco's configuration language provides special symbols ("!") for separating stanzas. We analyze configuration changes according to how stanzas change in total.

3.2.2 Change analysis

After developing abstractions for the configuration tasks and grouping configuration commands by stanza, we perform three types of analysis on the configuration changes to better understand how configuration evolves over time:

- *Snapshot and change analysis.* As a baseline for understanding the composition of network configuration in the two networks, we analyze a snapshot of the network configuration for each network and examine the number of lines of configuration devoted to each function. To understand where operators devote their efforts when modifying network configuration, we then study the extent to which network configuration changes are associated with different functions that the configuration performs. We also explore how many of the changes corresponded to additions, deletions, and modifications. We use a Python library called *difflib* to infer what constitutes an addition, deletion, or modification, by comparing two consecutive revisions and producing a "diff" in a context format. We evaluate the size of the diff in terms of number of lines. We assume the library is able to correctly identify additions, deletions, and modifications. We also correlate the line number difference from the first version to the

Georgia Tech	*add*	*del*	*mod*	Total
Routers (16)	31,178	27,064	262,216	326,458
Firewalls (365)	249,595	118,571	171,005	539,171
Switches (716)	216,958	20,185	116,277	353,420
Rtr avg. per device	2,324	1,692	16,389	20,404
FW avg. per device	684	325	469	1,477
Swt avg. per device	303	28	162	494

Table 3: Number of add/del/mod for all devices and average per device for each device type in *GT*.

UW-Madison	*add*	*del*	*mod*	Total
Routers (53)	79,202	38,288	154,407	271,897
Firewalls (325)	193,499	73,827	161,863	429,189
Switches (1246)	1608,512	213,910	1,768,384	3,590,806
Rtr avg. per device	1,494	722	2,913	5,130
FW avg. per device	595	227	498	1,321
Swt avg. per device	1,291	172	1,419	2,882

Table 4: Number of add/del/mod for all devices and average per device for each device type in *UW*.

last revision to verify that the numbers of line additions, deletions, and modifications derived are consistent.

- *Longitudinal analysis.* To understand how the network configuration has evolved over time, and the primary factors underlying different evolution patterns, we perform a longitudinal analysis of configuration changes, using five years of RCS files from each network.
- *Correlation analysis.* To understand whether certain aspects of the network configuration frequently change together, we perform a correlation analysis to determine network configuration tasks that operators commonly perform together.

Our toolkit parses each RCS file and aggregates information for the snapshot and basic change analysis, such as how many lines of configuration are devoted to each function, how many changes occur and what types of changes (*i.e.*, addition, deletion, modification) occur, when and where these changes happen. It also parses the data and author information from the RCS files determine the frequency of changes made on certain days, times, and by certain authors. The toolkit then inserts this information into a database that performs the longitudinal and stanza analysis. Correlation analysis requires additional software functionality, beyond gathering first-order statistics. To perform this analysis, the toolkit parses the RCS files and extracts every version of the configuration file. The configuration files are parsed, and stanzas from each configuration file are stored in a database, using which we can study correlated changes.

4. THE EVOLUTION OF CONFIGURATION

We now present results on network configuration evolution in the two campus networks. In the process, we identify change characteristics that the campuses share in common and those where they differ. We augment our analysis with operator discussions to shed light on the impact of operational practices on configuration evolution in the respective campuses.

4.1 Overview

What types of changes occur? We begin by measuring the number of configuration commands changed for each device type and normalize the results by the number of devices, as shown in Tables 3 and 4.

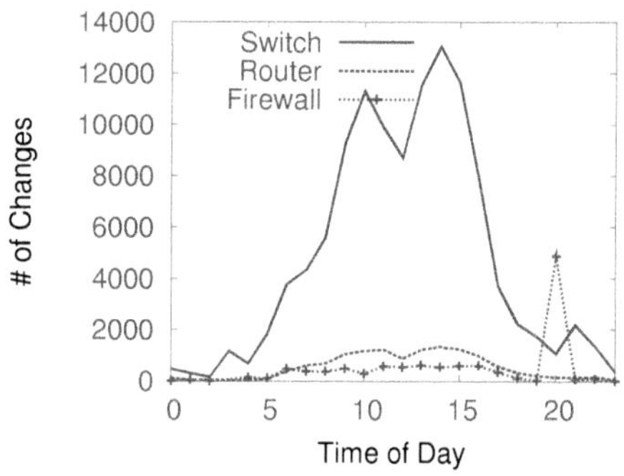

Figure 3: Changes to the *UW* network configuration over a day.

We make the following high-level observations. First, the networks have a similar number of firewalls, but *UW* has nearly four times as many routers and almost twice as many switches. Second, although most changes happen in firewalls and switches (with changes on switches dominating), routers, which are far fewer in number, tend to have many more configuration changes per device (on average) in both the *GT* and *UW* networks. We delve into router configuration changes in Section 4.2. Third, we find interesting differences between the two networks: in *UW*, switches clearly undergo a large number of modifications relative both to other devices in the same network, and to switches in the *GT* network. *GT* has relatively more changes to its firewall devices than *UW*. We delve into firewall and switch configuration evolutions across the two campuses in Sections 4.3 and 4.4, respectively.

When do changes occur? Figure 3 shows how configuration changes are distributed across hours of the day for *UW*. The pattern shows that most changes to switches and routers are made during the work hours. However, many of the configuration changes to firewalls happen later, as shown by a large increase in commits around 8 p.m. In contrast to routers and switches, the firewall configurations are often managed by a department-specific system administrator and then transferred to a member of the campus IT staff, who checks them for consistency and eventually uploads the files to the firewalls and commits them toward, or after the end of, working hours. Figures 4a and 4b show how changes to network configuration are distributed across the months of the year in the two networks. We observe that the number of configuration changes peaks during August. Our conversations with operators revealed that, in both networks, large network-wide changes are put off until the summer when many of the users are away and disruptions might have the least detrimental effect on users of the network.

Table 5 summarizes the main findings from our analysis of these two campus networks. We note several interesting characteristics that may ultimately help understand network configuration and its evolution better, and ultimately devise better methods or tools for device configuration and management. The rest of this section discusses these findings and others in more detail.

4.2 Routers

We first focus our analysis on routers. The main function of routers in the network is to support layer-3 routing, but, interestingly, many of the configuration changes on routers are associated with tasks other than layer 3 routing.

4.2.1 *Snapshot and change analysis*

Commands other than those involving routing change frequently over time. Figures 5a and 5b present the results from

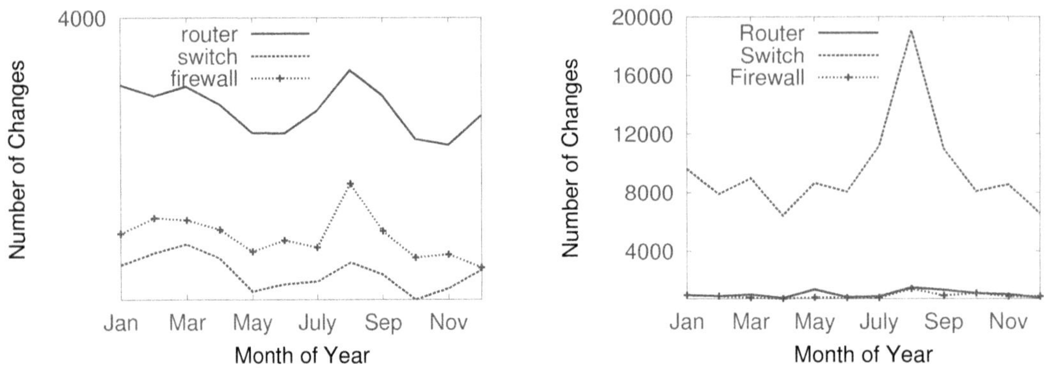

(a) GT (b) UW

Figure 4: Changes to the *GT* and *UW* configurations over one year. Changes to the configuration increase dramatically before the start of the academic year.

Many changes in routers are security-related. Bulk changes in routers come from security-related tasks, and different campuses use different mechanisms, thus showing dissimilar patterns of changes.	§4.2.1, §4.2.2, Figure 5, Figure 6
Deployment location matters. Where the device is placed within the network , *e.g.*, border vs edge, have significant influence on the size of change and what changes. Intuitively, devices at the border undergo a lot more changes than edge devices. In addition, the changes are more restrictive at borders and are more closely monitored.	§4.2.1: Figure 6, §4.3.1: Figure 9
Variety of network-wide tasks contribute to changes in devices. This includes network expansion, change of policy, addition of new features or modification of existing, and provisioning new customers or deleting subnetworks.	§4.2, §4.3, §4.4
Specialized devices are similar across different networks. Highly specialized network appliances, like firewalls, tend to have very similar traits when it comes to configuration and its evolution.	§4.3.1, §4.3.2
Correlated changes in firewall devices occur within the *acl* command. In firewalls, commands are highly concentrated on *acl* stanzas. However, we found highly correlated behavior within the *acl* stanza, namely object definition and actual access lists.	§4.3.3
Switch configuration is highly port-centered. Switches are configured port-by-port, and batch changes on interfaces is frequent. *l1* has a variety of subcommands, hence large correlation occur among commands in switches, although they differ by network and tasks assigned.	§4.4, §4.4.3

Table 5: Main results, and where they are described.

analyzing a snapshot of recent configuration files from all routers from each campus. Figures 5c and 5d present the changes occurring in both networks over five years for the routers in each campus. In both campuses, the *l1* and *l3* commands are added, deleted, or modified most frequently. In the *GT* network, *l2* changes are extremely frequent, due to changes to static ARP entries, which we will explain in more detail later. There are many more modifications to the *UW* network in general, many of which result from modifications to the existing *l1*– *l3* and *vlan* commands. Further investigation shows that VLAN interface definitions in *UW* router configurations are constantly changing due to addition, update and removal of "customers" of the *UW* network (departments or groups of users with specific needs, each group with its own VLAN). This explains the large amount of the *l1*, *l2* and *vlan* configuration changes. As we show later, the changes in *l3* are due to security related changes to a particular router.

Distinct security-related practices are found. Notably, many configuration changes to routers involve security-related tasks, although the mechanisms that each network uses differ. Each campus has security practices that use specific router configuration commands. The significant amount of the *l2* command changes in Figure 5c shows one example. Further inspection reveals that this is due to *static ARP* entries in routers deployed in residence halls in the *GT* network. The *GT* network maps each end host machine's MAC address to a static IP address in residence halls. The main goal is to provide better security and more fine-grained monitoring. This part of the configuration constantly undergoes changes as residents come and go. We examine changes to the stanzas in the routers for the different networks in Figures 6a and 6b. Our analysis shows that, on average, most routers in the *UW* network have configuration changes that reflect a consistent breakdown across functions, regardless of the router. The exception to this pattern is device 6, which has significantly more layer-3 changes than other devices. Upon further examination, we discovered that router is a *blackhole* device. Blackhole filtering, or null routing, provides a firewalling service with minimal impact on performance, by routing certain traffic to nowhere, and not providing any information regarding what happened to the traffic sources (no "no route to destination" reported back; hence the term blackhole). This practice uses "static routes" to manipulate the blackhole behavior; thus, we see constant changes to *l3* stanzas in this router device. This is another example of using specific router configuration commands to achieve certain security goals. The *GT* network also has routers with changes that are distinct from one another. Devices 5, 6, 7, and 8 are "resnet" routers in the campus dormitories with static ARPs.

Number of changes in core routers are noticeably larger than non-core routers. In Figure 6a, devices 1, 2, and 3 in the *GT* network have many *l1* and *vlan* changes, which are distinct from other routers. These three routers are core routers through which many VLANs are trunked. Core routers are responsible for routing traffic between the upper border gateway and subnets at the edge. Many VLANs for edge subnets are aggregated (or trunked) at these routers, so changes in each subnet can result in substantial changes

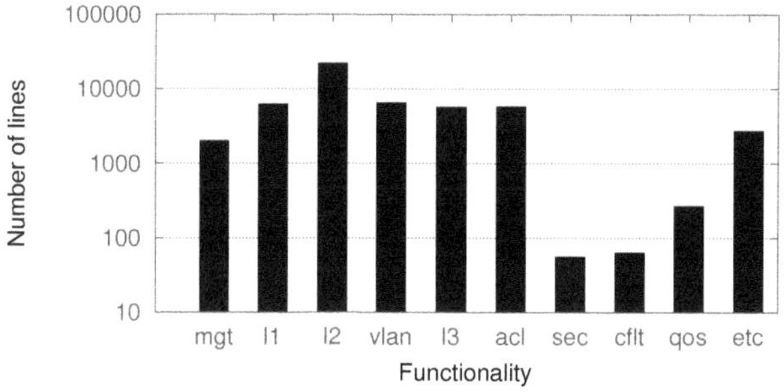

(a) Static analysis of latest snapshot (logscale) - *GT*

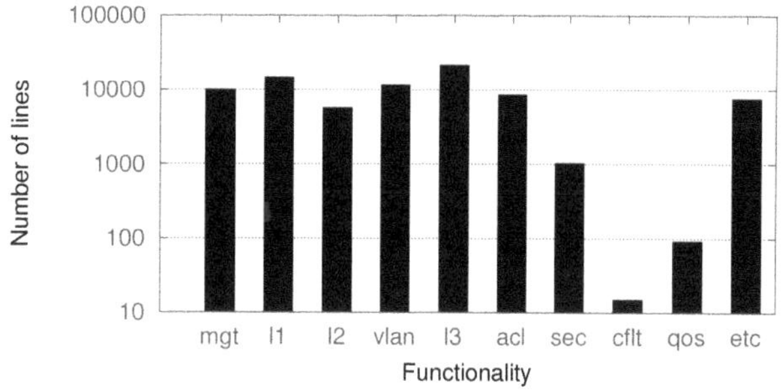

(b) Static analysis of latest snapshot (logscale) - *UW*

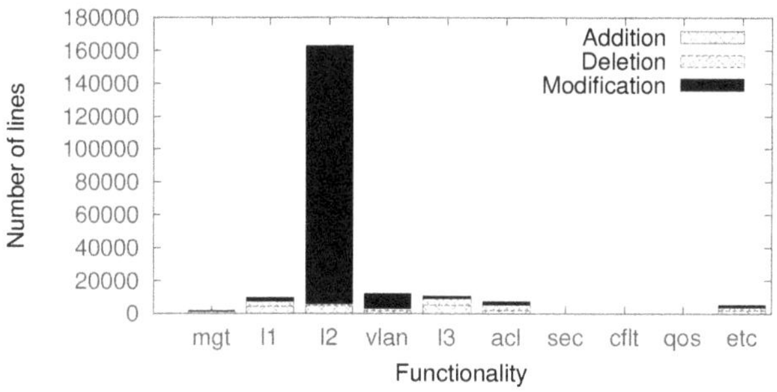

(c) Change characteristic over five years - *GT*

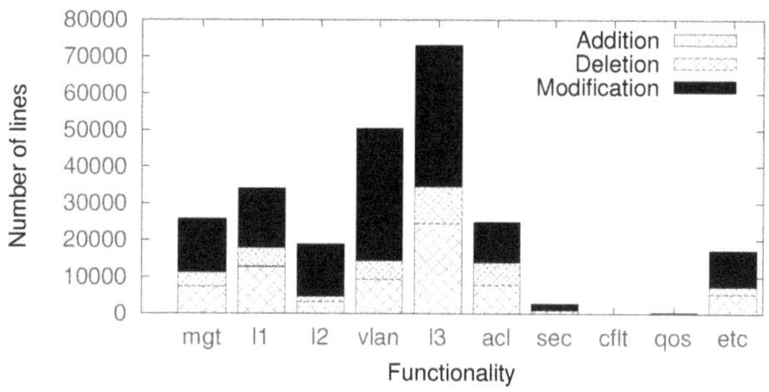

(d) Change characteristic over five years - *UW*

Figure 5: Static analysis and change analysis for routers. (a) and (b) shows a static analysis of the latest router configurations all combined for each campus. (c) and (d) shows the number of additions, deletions and modifications of each command in a row-stacked fashion, all devices combined over 5 years.

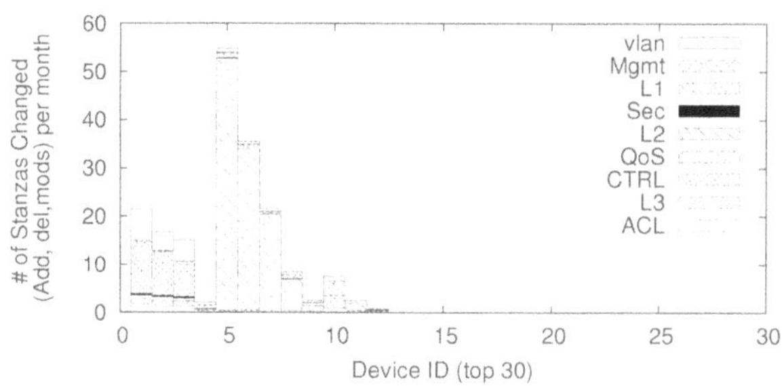

(a) *GT*

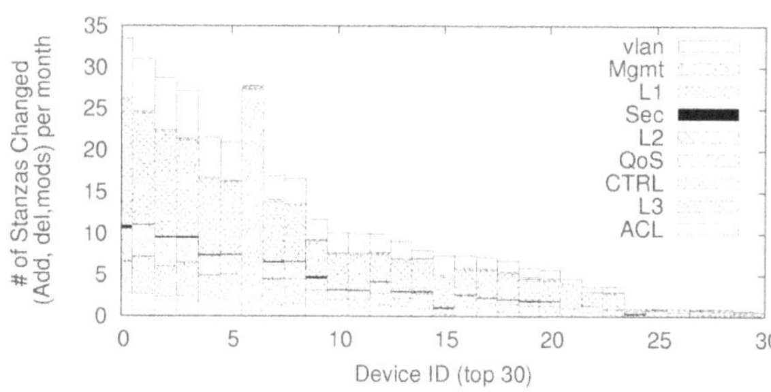

(b) *UW*

Figure 6: Number of changes to each router per month for the *GT* and *UW* networks.

at the core router. This characteristic is apparent in the *UW* network as well, as shown in Figure 6b. Devices aligned on the left of the figure (device 0-5) are the core routers, which are identified by their device names. The number of changes per month for these routers are significantly larger than other non-core routers. The changes are concentrated on *l1* and *vlan* stanzas.

This analysis shows that, depending on the function of the router and its placement in the network, the changes to its configuration may differ significantly. Different design and operational practices in two networks result in distinct change patterns in routers.

4.2.2 *Longitudinal analysis*

Network expansion causes steady increase in configuration size. Figures 7a and 7d show how the number of lines changes, for each router function. The figures account for all routers that were deployed in the network at a single time epoch. There is a gradual increase in overall number of lines in *UW* routers while it is quite steady for the *GT* routers. This growth appears to be caused by devices being added to the network, as shown in Figures 7c and 7f. The number of *GT* routers has grown relatively slowly over the past five years, while the *UW* network has added many routers over the time period. In 2007, there are 7 cores, 10 nodes, and 6 devices playing miscellaneous roles. By 2010, however, there are 9 cores, 12 nodes, 4 radial and hot spares, 1 VPN router, and several access routers. There is one considerable period of growth in routers in the *GT* campus network around July 2008 (Figure 7c), which caused a significant increase in *l2*, as shown in Figure 7a. This growth in routers corresponded to the expansion of the "resnet" network in *GT*.

Adding features, modifying existing commands and provisioning new customers using VLANs cause a lot of changes. We now examine the evolution of a typical router configuration. We calculate the median number of lines of each function among all

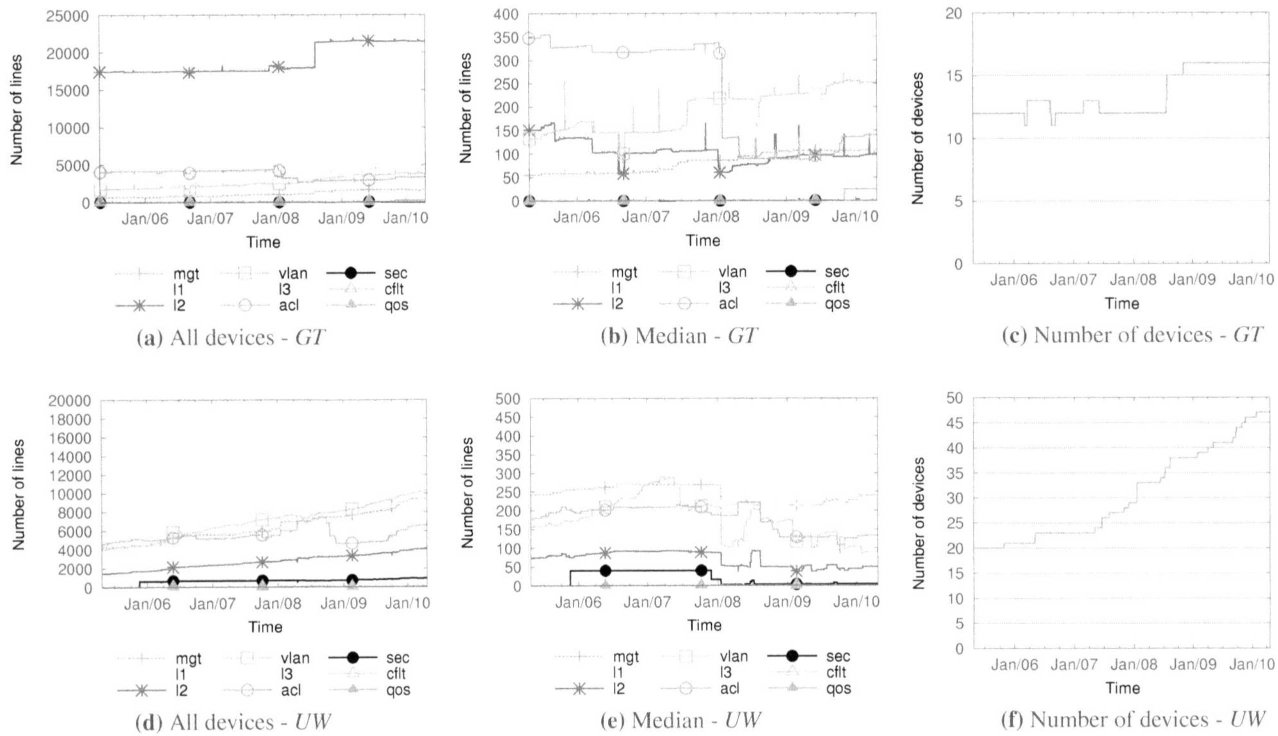

Figure 7: Longitudinal analysis of routers over five years. The graphs show the total number of lines of configuration for all devices, the median number of lines of configuration per device, and the total number of devices over time.

routers at every time epoch. Results are shown in Figure 7b and 7e. For the *GT* network, *l1* is increasing over time, while *l3* stays relatively steady. The sudden increase of *l1* seems to be caused by new routers added to the network, again around July 2008. This is understandable, as new router devices would have a bulk of ports defined and opened when first deployed. A sudden drop in *acl* around January 2008 was caused by a major configuration clean-up: several core routers purged hundreds lines of access control lists, and disabled *AppleTalk* routing and related instances. Several subnets were removed from the network at this point, causing hundreds of *acl* to be obsolete. For the *UW* network, the number of *vlan* and *l3* lines for the median device generally decreases over time as new devices are added, mainly because the newly added devices have far fewer lines with these functionalities. The exception to this is the period from from Jan 2008 to Jun 2008, where there is growth in the configuration constructs for these two functions. There are two reasons for this: first, the median device remains the same over this period; as more VLANs are added, there is a steady growth in *vlan* statements; and second, the introduction of multicast related configuration and new filters *acl* result in a sharp jump in *l3* and *acl* configuration lines.

On the whole, we find that a variety of network-wide factors contribute to configuration changes: network expansion, addition of new features or modification of existing ones, and provisioning of new customers. No one factor appears to be the dominant reason for configuration changes, although the impact of the first two factors, and the configuration changes that result from them, appear less often.

UW		GT	
Correlated Stanzas	%	Correlated stanzas	%
l1, vlan	35%	l1, vlan	26%
l1, l2, l3	13%	l1, l2	18%
l1, l3	14%	acl, l1	10%
acl, l1, l2, l3	7%	l1, l3	9 %
acl, l1	5%	l1, l3, acl	5%

Table 6: Correlated stanza changes for routers.

4.2.3 Correlation analysis

We first examine the extent to which changes to certain configuration constructs are correlated with others. To perform a certain high-level operational task, an operator has to change (add, delete, or modify) many different stanzas simultaneously. Indeed, we found that a fraction of changes—13% and 10% of all change events in *UW* and *GT*, respectively—are indeed performed in a correlated fashion, involving two or more stanza types. Such correlation has implications for the design of configuration management and debugging tools, as we discuss in Section 5.

Table 6 enumerates the five most common types of correlated stanza changes. The two campuses agree in three of the five: (1) *l1* and *vlan*: Although routers provide routing capabilities, they also have to control reachability (i.e., offer basic connectivity between, as well as ensure separation of, multiple subnets), which is often achieved through the use of VLANs. Thus, a considerable amount of change to *l1* and *vlan* occurs; (2) *l1* and *acl*: These change together because adding, deleting, or modifying networks (an *l1* change) often causes access control lists corresponding to the networks to be added, deleted, or modified to ensure consistency; and

(3) *l1* and *l3*: These correlated changes occur because modifying interfaces and subnets in the routing stanzas permits redistribution of reachability information.

Correlated *l1* and *l2* changes (the second most common in the *GT* network) occur when defining interfaces and setting a spanning-tree protocol for that interface for which each port has a variety of options. Similarly, correlated *l1*, *l2* and *l3* changes in *UW* occur when interfaces are added, the spanning tree is modified for the interfaces, and the routing protocol is changed to include the subnet or to setup routing protocol/peering adjacency over the interface.

4.3 Firewalls

A firewall's main function is to perform access control. As expected, we find that configuration changes are concentrated on *acl* statements (Figures 8c and 8d). Therefore, we focus most of our analysis instead on how firewalls are used in the respective campuses and the similarities and differences in how they are used. We find that, despite the highly specialized nature of firewalls, their usage across the two campuses is similar (see Figures 8 and10).

4.3.1 Snapshot and change analysis

The change characteristics are similar between two campuses. Figures 8a and 8b show the static analysis of the latest firewall configuration snapshot. As expected, most of the configuration is dedicated to access control (note that graphs are in log scale). This characteristic holds for changes as well, as shown in Figure 8c and 8d. Most changes are dedicated to access control while other types are mostly insignificant. High similarity in snapshot and change analysis between two different campus networks is intriguing. These similarities also appear in the longitudinal analysis shown in Figure 10. This similarity seems to result from the fact that devices like firewalls are designed to provide specific functionality to the network. Most changes involve *acl* for both campus networks. The actual content of commands will still differs, since network policies from two distinct networks are far from similar.

Deployment location matters. Figure 9 shows the top 30 firewall devices sorted in terms of number of stanza changes per month. Again, the graph shows that changes are heavily concentrated on *acl* stanzas. The number of changes per firewall is skewed, with a few firewalls experiencing many more changes and a large set of remaining firewalls experiencing minimal changes per month. Upon closer examination, we find that the top firewalls in the *GT* network (Figure 9a) are close to the border, and are physical devices where multiple virtual firewall instances actually spawn from. All changes to the virtual firewalls are reflected on these border firewalls, hence showing a lot of changes compared to others. This is true for the *UW* network as well. We also found a practice in the *GT* network that close-to-border firewalls are periodically backed up and commit to the CVS every six hours, while unit firewalls which are deployed closer to the edge are not managed that intensively. We assume this is due to the higher reliability requirement for the border firewalls compared to the unit firewalls; failure or misconfiguration on border firewalls can bring destructive consequences to the whole network.

Distinct practice using *sec* stanzas is captured. There are some noticeable *sec* stanzas on the *UW* network in Figure 9b. Inspection of the actual commands changed show that operators are turning off failover for the interfaces (internal and external). This prevents the virtual firewalls from failing over when the interfaces or connected devices are taken down. The anomalies occur in the firewalls used primarily by the campus IT department.

In summary, the two campus networks show very similar configuration change and usage patterns when it comes to firewalls. The majority of the changes occur at the border firewalls, where the changes on virtual firewalls are aggregated to. Border firewalls are also managed more intensively compared to simple unit firewalls at the edge.

4.3.2 Longitudinal analysis

Figure 10 shows the longitudinal view of firewall configuration evolution over a span of five years. The number of lines for *acl* commands increases sharply over five years. For the *GT* network, there was a factor of six increase. In the case of the *UW* network, firewalls were deployed starting in January 2006, and around 260 firewalls were added through April 2010.

Figures 10b and 10e show how the configuration of a typical firewall evolves over time. The small spike in the *GT* network around July 2007 is caused by adding new firewall machines and moving a substantial amount of access control lists to those firewalls. ACL configurations in previous firewalls are removed several days after the migration occurs. A slight increase of *qos* commands occurs around July 2008. Further inspection in the configuration shows a global policy map, which includes default inspection ports and Session Initiation Protocol (SIP) ports, is defined and inserted into around 40 firewalls. This policy map enforces further inspection on the specified services. In the *UW* network (Figure 10e), we observe a similar increase in *qos* commands around January 2008. These define two class maps: one for SIP ports as with the *GT* network, and one for a specific list of management services, ranging from DNS and rsh to SunRPC.

The decrease of *mgt* commands around January 2008 is due to the removal of the "pdm" (PIX Device Manager) commands from all firewalls. This command allows the device to determine who will have access to the management GUI for the firewalls. The removal of these commands prevents access to the GUI and forces the departments to submit all changes to the campus IT team, reflecting a new campus-wide security policy instituted in *UW* in 2008.

As with routers, we observe that a variety of network-wide factors, ranging from infrastructure expansion, to policy changes, and addition/modification of features, contribute to firewall configuration evolution.

4.3.3 Correlation analysis

Correlation analysis on firewall devices has not shown any specific correlated change behavior on stanzas, as most changes are solely made to *acl* stanzas. Clearly, the functionality abstraction we employ in this paper is too high-level for correlation analysis on firewalls. We do witness many correlated changes within the *acl* commands. Specifically, if there is a change in the network object group definition (where operators can combine multiple IP addresses, ports, subnets to separate groups), there are also changes in the actual access control lists which reference that particular network object. More fine-grained classification of commands within the *acl* stanza may show interesting correlated change behavior. For example, there might be correlated changes within the access control lists; such an exploration would make a good direction for future work.

4.4 Switches

In this section, we study changes in switch configurations. We find: (i) interface definition and related subcommands dominate the changes in switches (Figures 11c and 11d); and (ii) extensive correlated changes (Table 7).

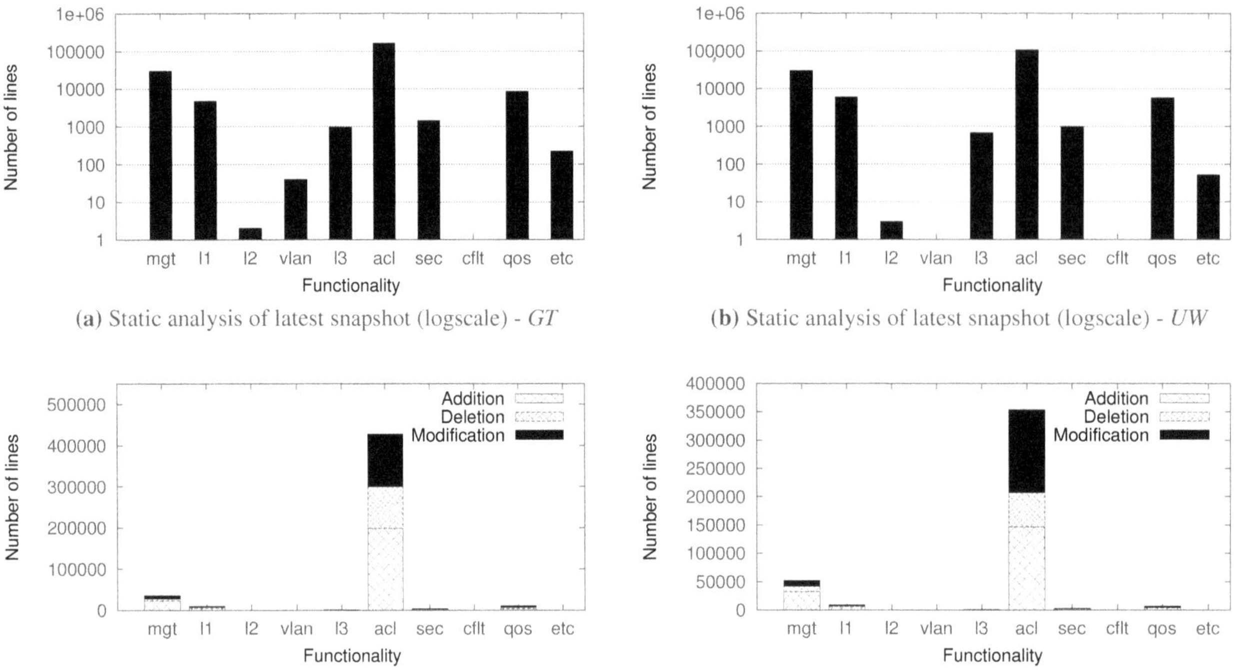

(a) Static analysis of latest snapshot (logscale) - *GT*

(b) Static analysis of latest snapshot (logscale) - *UW*

(c) Change characteristic over five years- *GT*

(d) Change characteristic over five years- *UW*

Figure 8: Static analysis and change analysis for firewalls. (a) and (b) shows a static analysis of the latest firewall configurations all combined for each campus. (c) and (d) shows the number of additions, deletions and modifications of each functionalities in a row-stacked fashion, all devices combined over 5 years.

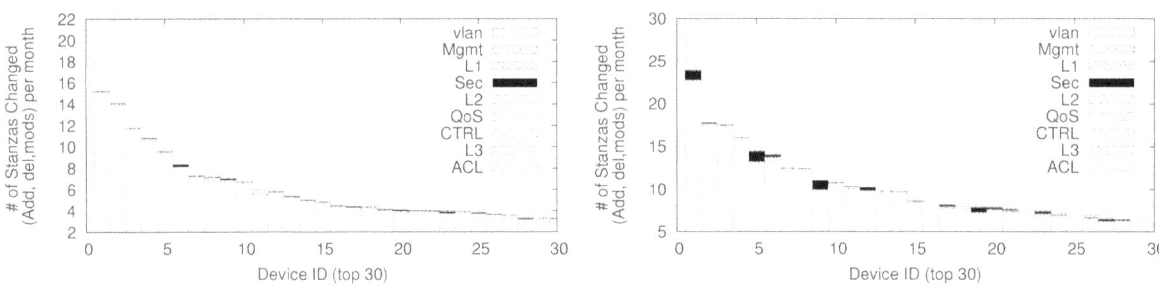

(a) *GT*

(b) *UW*

Figure 9: Number of changes to each firewall device per month for the *GT* and *UW* networks.

4.4.1 Snapshot and change analysis

Many changes involve *management, layer 1, layer 2* and *VLAN* commands. Figure 11 shows the static snapshot and change analysis of switches from both campuses. If we focus on changes of the configuration, Figures 11c and 11d show that there are many *mgt*, *l1*, *l2* and *vlan* command changes. Note from Figures 11a and 11b that these lines also constitute a majority of any given switch configuration snapshot. As seen previously, *l1* and *vlan* changes occur together naturally. *l2* changes are understandable as switches can offer layer 2 connectivity. The abnormality seems to be the significant number of changes in *mgt* commands. A majority of *mgt* changes in switch devices are in fact *snmp trap* and *logging* commands; *snmp trap* is for sending events to the SNMP server when particular conditions are met, and *logging* configures the logging behavior for the interface. The default is to define SNMP trap and logging commands along with the port configuration in the *UW* network. This induces the bulk of the *mgt* and *l1* changes to the network.

Certain practices shape how switch configuration evolves. The *GT* network has many additions, while the *UW* network experiences many modifications. Most of the changes in the *GT* network are actually due to additions in *l1* and *vlan*, followed by *mgt* and *l2* commands. However, the *UW* network looks different; there are a lot of modifications in general, with changes in *mgt* and *l1* followed by *vlan* appearing to dominate the changes. We found that this resulted from a large number of modifications that operators made to a majority of switches in the *UW* network, including interface and their subcommands, *snmp trap* and *logging*. From this behavior, it appears as though operators of the *UW* network have decided to uniformly enable or disable some functions on ports across most of its switches.

Specialized switch devices can be identified by their distinct

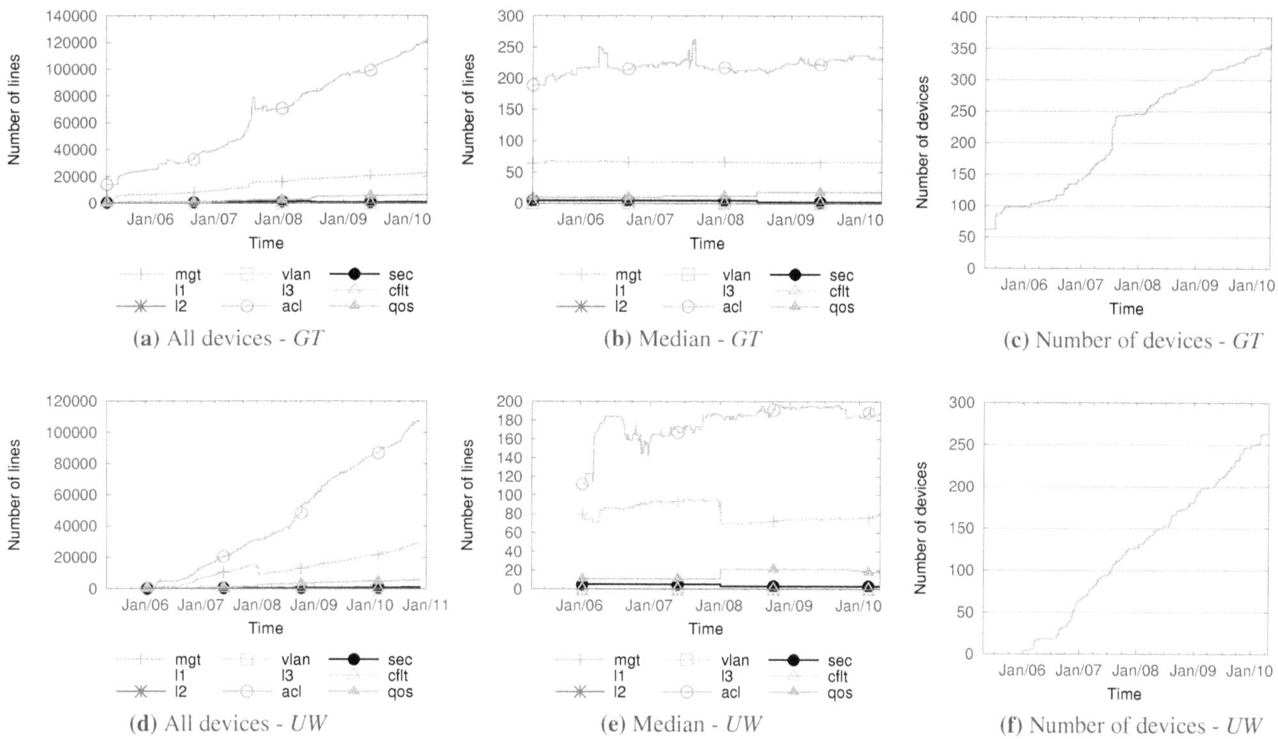

Figure 10: Longitudinal analysis of firewalls over five years.

patterns. Figure 12 presents the number of changes per stanza type, for each of the top 30 switches in both networks. The switches in *UW* are similar, in that most of the changes are in the interface commands, with a few devices having a significant amount of VLAN additions. Unlike *UW*, *GT* switches have several different patterns. *mgt* accounts for a significant amount for Device 1. This device is a switch for the SoX (Southern Crossroads) deployed within the Georgia Tech campus, and the changes to *mgt* are due to changes to the device authentication configuration, namely aaa, radius-server, and file stanzas. This can be caused by the fact that multiple users manage this device. There is also a group of devices (devices 25–29) that have a lot of *sec* stanzas. Further inspection shows these devices are *VPN* boxes with many *ipsec* changes. These devices can be classified as specialized switches that provide unique functions of secure connection establishment between the internal and external network.

4.4.2 *Longitudinal analysis*

Evolution trend is heavily influenced by how switches are added, removed or swapped, as well as their initial configuration. Figures 13a and 13d show a gradual increase in the total number of configuration lines, for both networks. The increasing trend is mainly due to the increase in number of switch devices, as shown in Figures 13c and 13f. An abnormal spike appears around September 2010 in Figure 13a, when 150 new switches were added to the *GT* network. In Figure 13b, the *l2* command experiences several decreases and increases. Inspection of the switch configurations reveals that around February 2006, a set of new switches with 24 ports was added to the network; older switches had more ports and hence had more verbose configuration. The other increases and decreases are of the same nature: the trend depends on what type of switches are added to the network with specific initial configurations. This phenomenon is similar to the decreasing number of *vlan* commands in Figure 13b; switches with small *vlan* instances are being added to the network continuously.

Distinct practices and decisions in *UW*. Turning to *UW*, in Figures 13d and 13e, we see that in January 2008, the number of lines for *sec* doubles and *mgt* decreases. Additions to *sec* commands occurred due to changes to all interfaces on all switches to make the network more resilient to bursty traffic, by installing a limiting mechanism. The *mgt* drop in Jan, 2008 is due to operators removing the SNMP feature from all interfaces. In both cases, the large changes reflect updates to all switches in the network.

We find that operational and network expansion practices of individual networks play an important role in shaping how the switch configuration evolves; understanding this evolution can facilitate the design of better network management tools.

4.4.3 *Correlation analysis*

In Table 7, we examine the set of correlated stanzas for the switches across the two campuses. Most changes in *UW* include either *l1* or *mgt* whereas most changes in *GT* include either *vlan* or *l1*. However, both networks agree on a set of correlated changes: (1) *vlan* and *l1*, (2) *acl* and *l1*, and (3) *mgt* and *l1*. As with other devices, interface definition and VLAN configuration commands have high correlation, as do ACLs that reference certain interfaces. *l1* and *mgt* correlates well in switches, because many default interface configuration in switches have *snmp trap* and *logging*. The *UW* network has an additional *l2* correlation with *l1* and *mgt*. This is due to heavily using spanning-tree related subcommands on interfaces. Although not shown, *UW* does in fact contain *mgt* and *vlan* correlations; *UW* contains half as many correlated occurrences of *mgt* and *vlan*. In addition to those, *GT* includes a unique combi-

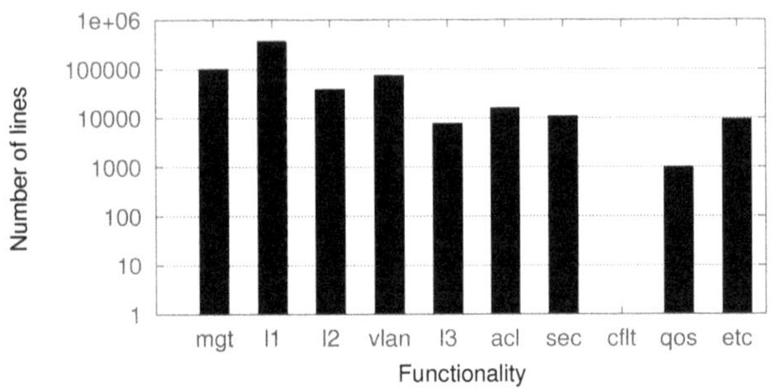

(a) Static analysis of latest snapshot (logscale) - *GT*

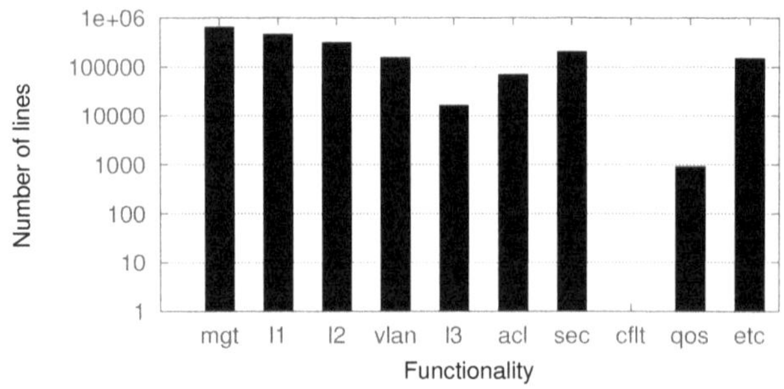

(b) Static analysis of latest snapshot (logscale) - *UW*

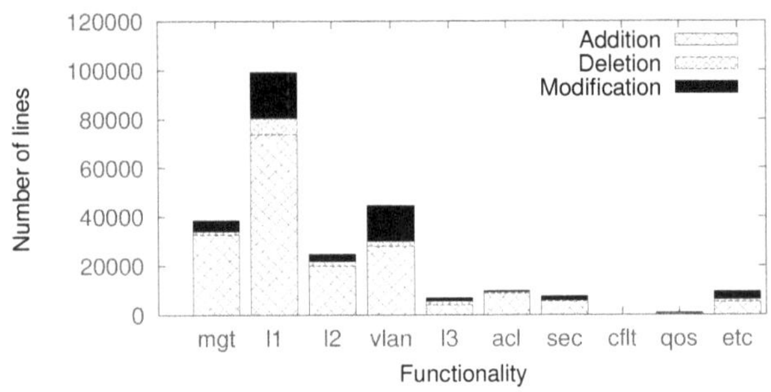

(c) Change characteristic over five years - *GT*

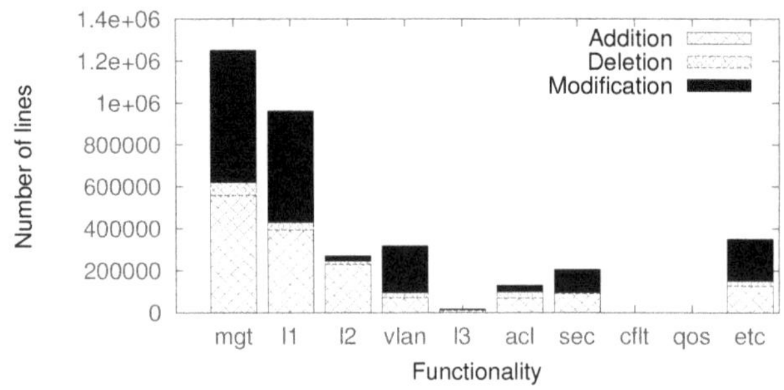

(d) Change characteristic over five years- *UW*

Figure 11: Static analysis and change analysis for switches. (a) and (b) shows a static analysis of the latest configurations all combined for each campus. (c) and (d) shows the number of additions, deletions and modifications of each functionalities in a row-stacked fashion, all devices combined over 5 years.

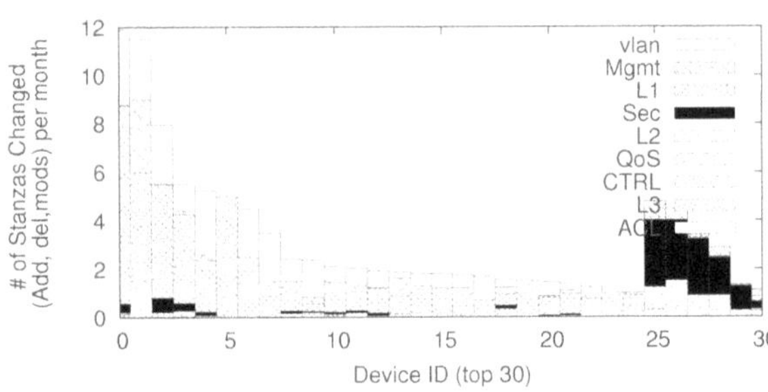

(a) *GT*

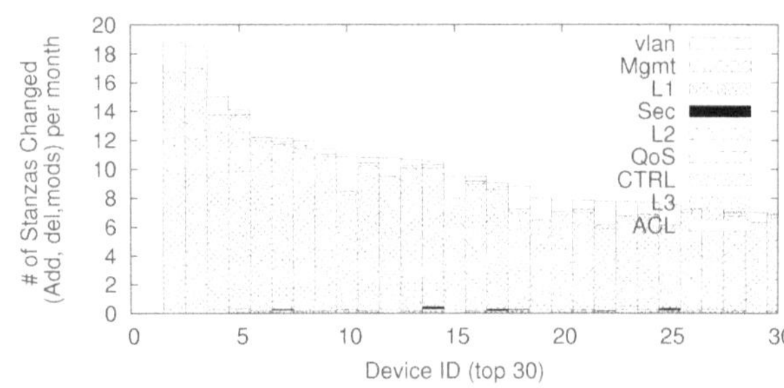

(b) *UW*

Figure 12: Number of changes to each switch per month for the *GT* and *UW* networks.

nation *sec* and *qos*, this combination can be attributed to the usage of VPN devices, which are unique to *GT*. The *l1*,*l2*, and *mgt* combinations are unique to the *UW* campus; similar commands change as with the *l1* and *mgt* combination.

On the whole, we find significant evidence of correlated changes to stanzas, although the specific sets of stanzas that change depend on the network in question. As such, when using correlations to drive configuration management (*e.g.*, in providing guidance on configuration changes to install, as discussed in Section 5), we must first design techniques that learn the correlations prevalent in a given network.

UW		GT	
Correlated Stanzas	%	Correlated Stanzas	%
acl, l1	24%	*mgt, l1*	15%
l1, vlan	11%	*l1, vlan*	13%
l1, l2, mgt	11%	*acl, l1*	11%
mgt, l1	10%	*mgt, vlan*	6%
vlan, mgt	9%	*sec, qos*	6%

Table 7: Correlated stanza changes for switches.

5. DISCUSSION

We now discuss how our observations can help augment existing and proposed configuration tools and mechanisms.

First, it may be possible to provide recommendations or suggestions to the operator concerning changes, based on the previous historical change logs. For example, we have found that *l1* and *l3* stanzas change the most in routers, while *l1* and *vlan* stanzas changes together frequently in switches. Based on the what the operator is changing, a system could provide feedback or possible changes associated with currently updated stanzas. For example, in firewalls, if there is a change in network object group defini-

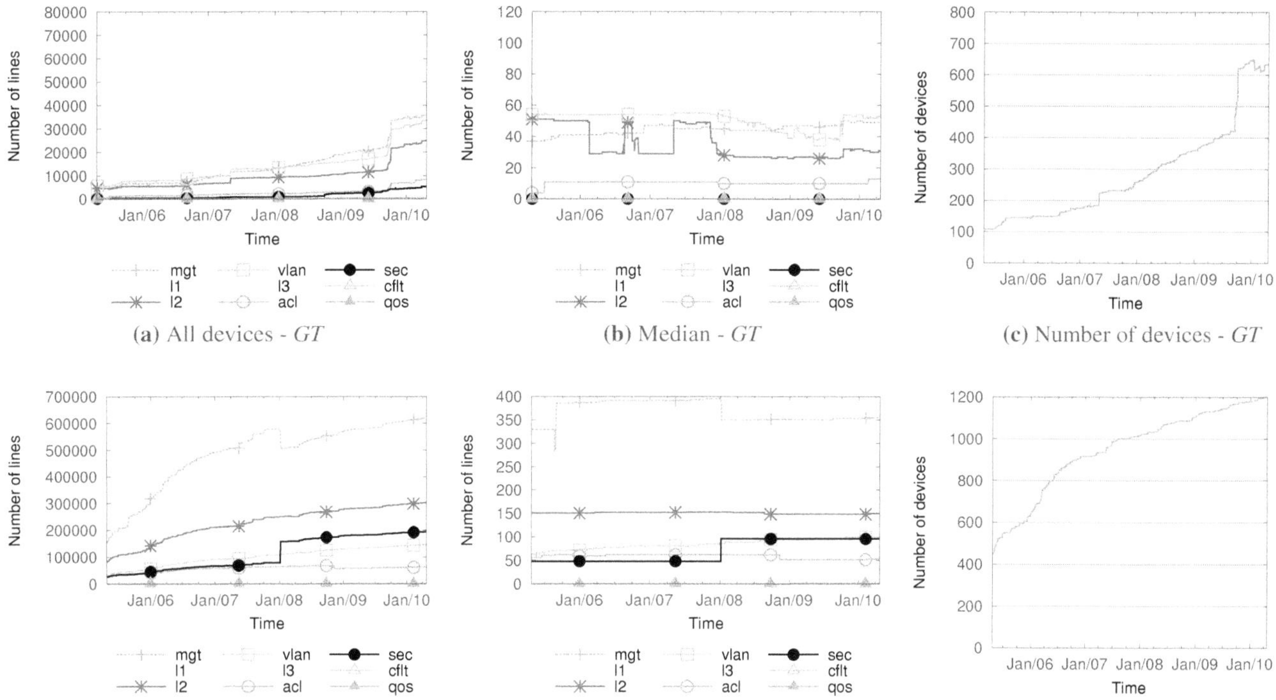

(a) All devices - *GT* (b) Median - *GT* (c) Number of devices - *GT*

(d) All devices - *UW* (e) Median -*UW* (f) Number of devices - *UW*

Figure 13: Longitudinal analysis of switches over five years.

tions, the system can recommend the operator to also consider the ACLs where that group is used. A tool could also proactively offer *negative* recommendations. If the operator attempts to change a line or stanza of the network configuration that is not frequently changed, the configuration system could discourage the modification by raising an alert, forcing the operator to go through multiple confirmation steps, or blocking a low-rank operator from making changes.

Knowledge of network configuration changes also helps point designers of configuration automation tools to parts of the configuration that could be automatically generated, for various types of devices. Our results reveal that network operators make different types of configuration changes, depending on the network device type and, hence, point to possibilities for customizing these configuration change templates based on the type of device. Highly specialized devices like firewalls are distinct, where most configuration is dedicated to access control, and the changes mostly happen on that specific area as well. For switches, a template that enables batch-modification on ports and VLAN configurations would be helpful.

Our work also opens many possible avenues for studying configuration changes in more detail. One possibility would be to look for changes to network configuration that were later reverted or changed again. Such changes might point to cases where operators made errors when configuring the network; knowledge about where in the configuration these errors occur could improve configuration testing methods. Another possibility would be to analyze the configuration for "copy-paste" behavior, as is done in software engineering studies of "code clones". Identifying parts of configuration that are commonly copied might also inspire design templates for configuration update.

6. CONCLUSION

We presented a longitudinal analysis of network configuration and its evolution over five years for two large campus networks. We focused on capturing configuration characteristics and common practices by examining change patterns from CVS commit log data, in contrast to earlier studies, which have mostly examined a single configuration snapshot. In contrast to earlier studies, which have focused mostly on router configuration, we also study configuration changes for firewalls and switches, which comprise a significant portion of the networks. Our study unearths a variety of important aspects regarding configuration evolution: we study the frequency and extent of configuration updates, showing the similarities and differences across networks; identify the prevalence of correlated changes; and shed light on how various network-wide factors affect evolution.

Our work is a first step toward understanding configuration evolution in more depth. Just as mining software repositories has emerged into a mature field in software engineering for assisting programmers understand software engineering better, we believe that mining network repositories for configuration changes can help deepen our understanding of configuration and design practices. A better understanding of this process is imperative, as it is a cornerstone for improving current methods of configuring and managing network devices, easing the pain of network operators by providing recommendations, offering better templates, reducing misconfiguration and, ultimately, enabling automation.

Acknowledgements

We thank the campus network operators who provided us with network configuration data. We especially thank Dan Forsyth and Dale Carder for answering many questions about network management and configuration practices. We should also like to thank Lixia Zhang (our shepherd) and the anonymous reviewers for their insightful feedback. This work is supported in part by NSF grants CNS-0643974, CNS-0746531, CNS-1017545, CNS-1018021, and CNS-1050170.

REFERENCES

[1] T. Benson, A. Akella, and D. Maltz. Unraveling Complexity in Network Management. In *Proc. 6th USENIX NSDI*, Boston, MA, Apr. 2009.

[2] D. Caldwell, A. Gilbert, J. Gottlieb, A. Greenberg, G. Hjalmtysson, and J. Rexford. The cutting edge of IP router configuration. In *Hotnets-II*, Cambridge, MA, Nov. 2003.

[3] X. Chen, Z. Mao, and J. Van der Merwe. Towards automated network management: network operations using dynamic views. In *INM 07*.

[4] S. Eick, T. Graves, A. Karr, J. Marron, and A. Mockus. Does code decay? assessing the evidence from change management data. *IEEE Transactions on Software Engineering*, 27(1):1–12, 2001.

[5] W. Enck, T. Moyer, P. McDaniel, S. Sen, P. Sebos, S. Spoerel, A. Greenberg, Y. Sung, S. Rao, and W. Aiello. Configuration management at massive scale: system design and experience. *IEEE Journal on Selected Areas in Communications*, 27(3):323–335, 2009.

[6] N. Feamster and H. Balakrishnan. Detecting BGP Configuration Faults with Static Analysis. In *Proc. 2nd USENIX NSDI*, Boston, MA, May 2005.

[7] A. Feldmann and J. Rexford. IP network configuration for intradomain traffic engineering. *IEEE Network*, Sept. 2001.

[8] J. Gottlieb, A. Greenberg, J. Rexford, and J. Wang. Automated Provisioning of BGP Customers. *IEEE Network*, 2003.

[9] H. Kagdi, M. Collard, and J. Maletic. A survey and taxonomy of approaches for mining software repositories in the context of software evolution. *Journal of Software Maintenance and Evolution: Research and Practice*, 19(2):77–131, 2007.

[10] S. D. Krothapalli, X. Sun, Y.-W. E. Sung, S. A. Yeo, and S. G. Rao. A toolkit for automating and visualizing vlan configuration. SafeConfig '09, pages 63–70, New York, NY, USA, 2009. ACM.

[11] F. Le, S. Lee, T. Wong, H. Kim, and D. Newcomb. Minerals: using data mining to detect router misconfigurations. In *Proc. MineNets '06*, pages 293–298, Pisa, Italy, Sept. 2006.

[12] F. Le, G. Xie, D. Pei, J. Wang, and H. Zhang. Shedding Light on the Glue Logic of the Internet Routing Architecture. Aug. 2008.

[13] M. Lehman. Programs, life cycles, and laws of software evolution. *Proceedings of the IEEE*, 68(9):1060–1076, 1980.

[14] R. Mahajan, D. Wetherall, and T. Anderson. Understanding BGP misconfiguration. In *Proc. ACM SIGCOMM*, pages 3–17, Pittsburgh, PA, Aug. 2002.

[15] D. Maltz, G. Xie, J. Zhan, H. Zhang, G. Hjálmtýsson, and A. Greenberg. Routing Design in Operational Networks: A Look from the Inside. In *Proc. ACM SIGCOMM*, Portland, OR, Aug. 2004.

[16] S. Raghavan, R. Rohana, D. Leon, A. Podgurski, and V. Augustine. Dex: A semantic-graph differencing tool for studying changes in large code bases. 2004.

[17] Really Awesome New Cisco Conflg Differ (RANCID). `http://www.shrubbery.net/rancid/`, 2004.

[18] Y. Sung, S. Rao, S. Sen, and S. Leggett. Extracting Network-Wide Correlated Changes from Longitudinal Configuration Data. In *Proc. PAM*, Seoul, South Korea, Apr. 2009.

[19] G. Xie, J. Zhan, D. Maltz, H. Zhang, A. Greenberg, G. Hjalmtysson, and J. Rexford. On static reachability analysis of IP networks. In *IEEE INFOCOM*, volume 3, pages 2170–2183, 2005.

Summary Review Documentation for

"Understanding the Evolution of Network Configuration: A Tale of Two Campuses"

Authors: H. Kim, T. Benson, A. Akella, N. Feamster

Reviewer #1

Strengths: The paper claims this to be the first, detailed longitudinal study of network configuration, and it provides a good deal of empirical data on how network element configurations change at the macro level (at least for these kind of networks). It is also well written and on the whole well executed.

Weaknesses: I'm not sure that I could tell you what the key takeaways from the study if you cornered me. There are lots of facts and characterizations of changes, but it is not clear whether this data is useful for anything in particular. That said, I come down in favor of this work as a step ahead (and see comments below).

Comments to Authors: The best way to improve your paper would be to sharpen the problem that you are investigating. Right now the paper reads like an open-ended exploration of network configuration. The abstract, in particular, is vague and has no results, and the introduction is quite general in places. On the plus side it delivers on exactly what the title says by describing what happened to the configurations over time :)

If you could identify some key questions or hypotheses to investigate (what did you expect, going in?) this might give more of a point to the paper. It would also help us to understand whether the data you are presenting is useful. For example, I suspect that it will be necessary to look more deeply than the change in the number of configuration lines per element for different functions to uncover much of value, and that the overall statistics are not very helpful. But I also acknowledge that I don't yet have a good sense of what to look for more deeply, and I hope this would be part of the conversation should your paper be accepted. I see your paper as an advance in moving this conversation ahead rather than a conclusive study.

Consider an operator survey in addition to your config file analysis. This might help you work out where to focus.

Another main point: you describe a method for parsing log files to infer additions / deletions / changes. How well does that method work? Errors in the inference will affect your results. So I would have liked you to specify the inference process more carefully and evaluate how well it worked and the likely impact of inference errors. If the process is always correct by definition then say that (but I don't see how this can be the case if addition / deletion / change is defined from the point of view of the operator).

What is the size in lines of the additions / deletions / modifications? I don't have a sense and was surprised that this didn't come out.

End of 3.1: how does the lack of RANCID for GT routers/switches impact the results? 4.1: seems like you should say explicitly that GT has many router mods. Many of your graphs are unreadable in black and white and/or too small. See Fig 4 as an example.

Reviewer #2

Strengths: This paper represents a thorough study of configuration changes over a long period of time. The analysis is rigorous and the results are intuitive.

Weaknesses: The research focuses only on two university networks, which have many specific properties that cannot be generalised to other more interesting networks such as ISPs, enterprises

Comments to Authors: I like the thoroughness of your analyses and the conclusions drawn from these. However, I find that the data is a bit limited with only two university networks and it will be hard to generalise these findings. More datasets would solve this problem. Of course, I understand the difficulty in obtaining good datasets. Towards that end, you should consider making the data public.

By grouping commands into functions, you lose the fine-grain information from the configuration files. For the high-level analyses you provide in this paper that is good enough. But I would like to see more low level analyses for example, root-cause analysis of some l3 configuration changes. You actually observed this loss of information in Section 4.3 for Firewalls, in particular ACL stanzas.

Section 4.2, regarding configuration changes in routers, you seem to observe more correlations than [18]. It would be good if you can compare your results against those in [18]. The difference could be that you analyse changes at higher-level than those in [18].

While I like your thorough analyses of the data, most of your analyses are elementary. It would provide a lot more insight into the configuration management problems if more advanced statistical techniques are used in addition to those already used in this paper.

Reviewer #3

Strengths: To this reader's limited knowledge, this paper seems the first of its kind, i.e. using longitude data to gain a deeper understanding of exactly what is going on with network configurations, as first step towards improving it.

Weaknesses: Although the paper suggested a few ways that can benefit from this study, I still wish the authors could have gone a little deeper in interpreting the results.

One example: I was intrigued by the observation that "devices that are more special-purpose such as firewalls tend to exhibit more common configuration change patterns", while more general purpose boxes like core routers would have distinct practices. This seems a bit counter-intuitive to me. But the paper merely just mentioned it.

Comments to Authors: None.

Reviewer #4

Strengths: Well-written with a detailed account of network evolution in GT and UW campuses.

Weaknesses: Not generalizable - Not sure what to make out of the comparisons between UW and GT campuses.

Comments to Authors: I think the paper does a good job writing and articulating what happened to the UW and GT campus network configurations over the past 5 years. I think the authors seem to have spent some time investigating various causes for kinks in the network evolution, which is definitely good. Unfortunately, however, I found this paper quite boring to read, to be completely honest. There are a lot of graphs that convey nothing too insightful, and the paper contains many conclusions either not generalizable or left me wondering `so what' most of the time.

To be clear, I understand the challenges in obtaining such configuration data and I do appreciate and commend the effort of the authors in obtaining such data. However, I think the study was a bit too focused on statistics reporting and did not have a clear goal of what it was trying to find. Most of the time, the paper talks about things like, "there were changes because new routers were added into the network", or "a security policy decision was made to remove certain protocols", or "changes at layer X and Y correlated for some reason 20% of the time".

I did not know what to make out of these results, since there is always something going on in an enterprise network with new policies, updates and so on. The statistics reported and the graphs in this paper unfortunately are not generalizable outside of the two networks. If we take two random networks, and do such a study, they may agree on a few things and may disagree on a few others. Unfortunately, there is nothing much I learned from that that I can take away and apply it elsewhere.

There is one paragraph in the discussion which tried to argue where the results are useful. I found those to be quite far-fetched. Recommending the network operators that X and Y are correlated some Z% of the time is not sufficient to keep popping to the network operator that if he changes X, he ought to be considering changing Y. Others were equally far-fetched unfortunately.

Reviewer #5

Strengths: Longitudinal studies of this type seem really valuable. This is done in detail and with some care.

Weaknesses: These are just case studies, and they are limited to two Universities. There is a question about how representative they are. However, this is the sort of case study that can only really be done on a case by case basis.

Comments to Authors: There are a couple of issues with the paper.

At times it seems like something of a data dump. I guess its nice to display the same information for each view, but it gets a bit tedious by the end.

Paragraph 2 uses the word complexity a large number of times without defining it. It would be nice to have a meaningful metric of complexity here, instead of an entirely heuristic one.

Response from the Authors

Despite widespread agreement that simplifying network management tasks is critically important, there has been relatively little work towards improving this state of affairs. An important first step towards simplifying network configuration management is systematically analyzing how network operators configure networks. Studying the changes to network configuration is the most direct way to study these phenomena. Along these lines, this paper opens new directions in the field of ``network configuration mining" - the process of analyzing network configuration (and, additionally, *changes* to network configuration) to better understand the tasks that network operators perform. As with any first paper in an area, some of the findings may seem somewhat first-order. In the future, more fine-grained analysis will certainly reveal more interesting traits and lessons about network configuration.

For this paper, our goal is to obtain a high-level view of network configuration and its evolution over time. Therefore, a certain level of abstraction is necessary. We do have interesting discoveries, and we have highlighted those points more explicitly in the final version. We expect that this paper will spawn interesting follow-up papers with deeper analysis. We performed the analysis described in the paper on both the Georgia Tech and Wisconsin campus networks, which are two large campus networks, and we noted the differences in configuration changes across these two networks and explained why discrepancies in the types of changes might arise. Because of our efforts to explain these discrepancies, network operators who read this paper should easily be able to determine the aspects of the paper that apply to their network. We do not claim that this study generalizes either how a typical network's configuration looks like or how it evolves. This research is a case study, and a first attempt to perform extensive longitudinal analysis on campus networks. We should also note that a detailed, accurate log of changes to network configuration across a long time is difficult to obtain, but we are happy to help other network operators or researchers repeat this analysis on other datasets that they might have access to that record configuration changes. Our analysis tools can be applied to any network configuration changes that are represented as Revision Control System (RCS) logs.

To address reviewer concerns, we have also added more details concerning how we derive certain results, and how errors or omissions in data affect the final outcome. We have also added more discussion of previous work.

Understanding and Characterizing PlanetLab Resource Usage for Federated Network Testbeds

Wonho Kim
Department of Computer Science
Princeton University
wonhokim@cs.princeton.edu

Ajay Roopakalu
Department of Computer Science
Princeton University
aroopaka@cs.princeton.edu

Katherine Y. Li
Department of Computer Science
Princeton University
klfive@cs.princeton.edu

Vivek S. Pai
Department of Computer Science
Princeton University
vivek@cs.princeton.edu

ABSTRACT

Global network testbeds are crucial for innovative network research. Built on the success of PlanetLab, the next generation of federated testbeds are under active development, but very little is known about resource usage in the shared infrastructures. In this paper, we conduct an extensive study of the usage profiles in PlanetLab that we collected for six years by running CoMon, a PlanetLab monitoring service. We examine various aspects of node-level behavior as well as experiment-centric behavior, and describe their implications for resource management in the federated testbeds. Our main contributions are threefold: (1) Contrary to common belief, our measurements show there is no tragedy of the commons in PlanetLab, since most PlanetLab experiments exploit the system's network reach more than just its hardware resources; (2) We examine resource allocation systems proposed for the federated testbeds, such as bartering and central banking schemes, and show that they would handle only a small percentage of the total usage in PlanetLab; and (3) Lastly, we identify factors that account for high resource contention or poor utilization in PlanetLab nodes. We analyze workload imbalance and problematic slices in PlanetLab, and describe the implications of our measurements for improving overall utility of the testbed.

Categories and Subject Descriptors

C.4 [**Performance of Systems**]: Design studies, Performance attributes

General Terms

Measurement, Design, Performance

IMC'11, November 2–4, 2011, Berlin, Germany.

Keywords

PlanetLab, Network Testbeds, Characterization

1. INTRODUCTION

Building on the unprecedented success of PlanetLab [23], the next generation of testbeds have been under active development recently. In its design phase, the GENI [14] project aims to federate multiple testbeds that are owned and operated by autonomous organizations. It plans to cover diverse networks including PlanetLab-like wide-area testbeds, fiber optics, and even sensor grids. To coordinate resource management across the organizational boundaries, the federated infrastructure suite needs an extensive policy framework and incentive system. However, very little is known about resource usage in the federated frameworks, which is required for designing future policy engines.

In this paper, we analyze resource usage in PlanetLab and discuss its design implications for the emerging federated testbeds. We note that PlanetLab itself is a federated platform. The nodes in PlanetLab are managed by a trusted intermediary named PlanetLab Central (PLC), but each site retains ultimate control over its own nodes. Since it was launched in 2002, PlanetLab has tried to balance fairness and the utility of the system without imposing strict resource controls [6, 22]. Thus, we believe that understanding resource usage in PlanetLab can help shape the policy decisions of future testbeds that have similar design requirements. Since planned testbeds such as GENI have architectures similar to PlanetLab, the lessons we have learned from our analysis can be generalized beyond PlanetLab to many federated systems that need to control shared resources donated by autonomous organizations.

Characterizing PlanetLab's resource usage is challenging because it is highly dynamic and evolves with changes in the underlying platform. For example, some experiments are active year-round and consume an almost constant amount of resources while many other experiments show heavy and bursty demand over short time periods. As a result, large-scale, long-term analysis is necessary to capture usage patterns and their evolution.

To address this challenge, we have collected detailed statistics on every online PlanetLab node and the active experiments running on the node since August 2004 through the PlanetLab monitoring system CoMon [20]. The collected datasets have detailed information about both node-centric and experiment-centric data at five minutes granularity. In addition to passively recording OS-provided metrics, CoMon also actively gathers information about each node's status by periodically running a set of test programs. In this paper, we analyze six years of PlanetLab usage, from 2005 to 2010. Our three main observations follow:

No tragedy of the commons Conventional wisdom suggests that network testbeds should suffer from a tragedy of the commons, and this belief has led to much development on PlanetLab, including two deployed resource reservation schemes [16, 27], two deployed resource discovery systems [1, 2], and papers investigating resource allocation and migration [12, 19]. This belief has even shaped the requirements of testbeds like GENI, which are devoting much attention and software development cost to resource reservation systems [13].

However, we observe no indication of the tragedy of the commons on PlanetLab, and we find several measurements indicating that these kinds of network testbeds are unlikely to suffer such effects. Unlike compute clusters where users try to utilize every available resource, most PlanetLab users are not aggressive in using resources in the testbed. While PlanetLab hosts some long running services, most PlanetLab experiments have bursty resource consumption, and this resource consumption is tied to network activity. As a result, the resource consumption shows bimodal distributions along many axes. The primary reason for the non-aggressive behavior of PlanetLab users is that the main utility of PlanetLab comes from its wide network vantage points, not the aggregate amount of resources.

Limitations of market-based resource allocation Using data-driven analysis, we explore the effectiveness of two representative resource allocation schemes proposed for PlanetLab-like federated systems: pair-wise bartering and market-based banking. We find that the bartering and banking systems can account only for 3% and 14% of the total resource usage respectively, because most resource usage is from sites that do not donate the same amount of resources. Since the remaining 83% of the resources need to be allocated, market-based allocation approaches are not sufficient for network testbeds, and some mechanism must be employed to ensure that the bulk of the testbed's resources are used appropriately.

Improving utility of PlanetLab We examine factors that degrade the overall utility of PlanetLab, and discuss how to mitigate their impact. We find that workload is persistently unbalanced among PlanetLab nodes, resulting in high system lags in overloaded nodes as well as inefficient resource usage. Several factors are responsible for this imbalance, ranging from users staying with known-good nodes to node utility being degraded due to DNS failures, node unreliability, bandwidth limitations, and other reasons. We also find unstable experiments consume a disproportionately high share of the resource, typically dwarfing stable long-running services. We simulate pruning the problematic experiments to measure their impact on other well-behaved experiments in PlanetLab.

The rest of this paper is structured as follows. In Section 2, we describe some background on PlanetLab and CoMon datasets. We analyze per-slice characteristics in Section 3, and examine several resource allocation systems in Section 4. We examine the workload imbalance problem in Section 5, and discuss policing of slices in Section 6. We compare our observations with related work in Section 7. Section 8 concludes the paper.

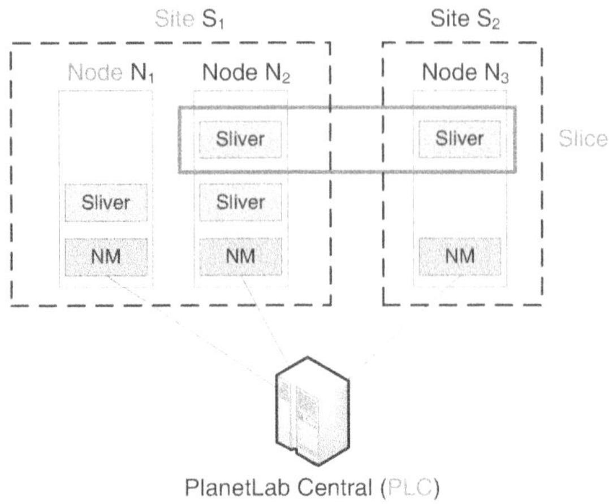

Figure 1: Overview of PlanetLab Architecture.

Year	Nodes	Slices	LiveSlices	Size
2005	354 (62)	215 (14)	106 (8)	164.8 GB
2006	433 (33)	278 (38)	136 (18)	232.9 GB
2007	438 (77)	371 (54)	133 (21)	260.7 GB
2008	474 (85)	254 (66)	139 (25)	291.2 GB
2009	613 (55)	349 (103)	145 (19)	430.1 GB
2010	683 (67)	421 (62)	158 (15)	503.9 GB
Total				1883.6 GB

Table 1: Summary statistics for CoMon datasets. Each row contains means and standard deviations of online nodes, in-memory slices, and live slices per day in each year.

2. BACKGROUND AND DATASETS

To better understand the analysis in this paper, some background on PlanetLab and its terminology is provided here. Figure 1 illustrates the architecture of PlanetLab and its components. When organizations join PlanetLab, they host physical servers at one or more locations. Each location is called a *site*, and the servers are called *nodes*. All account creation and node management is handled by a centralized database, called PlanetLab Central (PLC). Users create accounts on one or more PlanetLab nodes to perform their experiments. The nodes host one virtual machine per account, and users can run any number of processes within their own slivers. The virtual machines are called *slivers*, and the set of virtual machines assigned to one account is called a *slice*. PlanetLab is a shared testbed, so multiple slivers are running on the same node at any given time.

We classify a sliver as an *in-memory* sliver if it contains at least one instantiated process, regardless of whether the process is running or blocked. An in-memory sliver is called a *live* sliver if it uses more than 0.1% of the CPU per day[1]. A slice that has at least one live sliver is called a live slice. We say that a slice *uses* a node if the slice has in-memory slivers in the node. A node is considered to be live if it responds to CoMon requests.

[1]0.1% is the minimum CPU time that CoMon measures for a sliver's CPU usage at any given time.

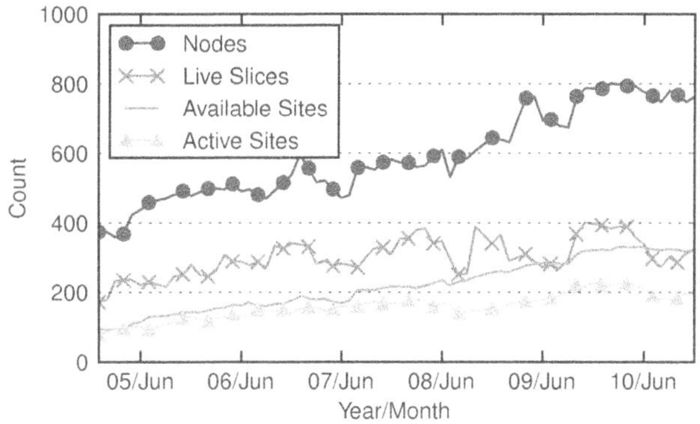

Figure 2: The scale of PlanetLab over time. PlanetLab node and live slice counts have increased as more researchers have joined the testbed in general.

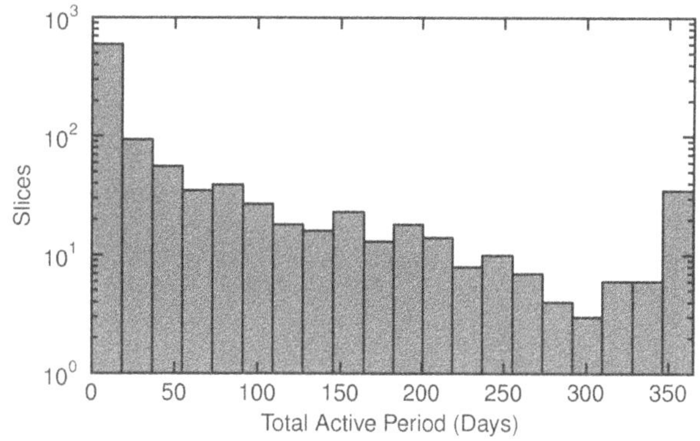

Figure 3: The distribution of slice total active period. While most slices are short-lived, a number of slices were active for an entire year.

In this paper, we analyze six years (2005 to 2010) of data from CoMon, a scalable monitoring system for PlanetLab. Since August 2004, CoMon has collected and reported statistics on PlanetLab nodes to help PlanetLab users monitor their services and spot problems. CoMon runs daemons in every PlanetLab node to gather values that are provided by operating systems, and values that are actively measured by means of test programs running on the nodes. A central CoMon server collects data from all PlanetLab nodes every 5 minutes.

CoMon monitors and collects *node-centric* and *slice-centric* data. The node-centric datasets consist of 51 fields that represent node health and aggregate resource consumption, including CPU utilization, memory usage, timing behavior, DNS resolver behavior, bandwidth consumption, etc. The slice-centric data contains information about each sliver's resource usage on its node, which is an aggregate resource used by all processes within the sliver in the node. The measured metrics include CPU usage, memory consumption, and transmit/receive bandwidths.

Table 1 shows the basic statistics about our datasets. The sizes of the datasets have increased over time because PlanetLab's node count has increased and more metrics have been added to CoMon over time. The slice-centric datasets contain resource usage of each sliver, and can be aggregated into slices as needed. Since CoMon fetches data from all PlanetLab nodes in parallel, the aggregated values estimate the total amount of resources that a slice uses across multiple nodes at a given time. We associate the two kinds of datasets to study the effect of an experiment's behavior on a node's status, and vice versa.

CoMon's task has grown over time as the testbed itself has expanded, since CoMon tries to monitor information about every sliver in the system. Figure 2 presents the numbers of online nodes, live slices, sites running online nodes (labeled as "Available Sites"), and sites having live slivers in other remote nodes ("Active Sites") per month. We find that the scale of the testbed has persistently increased over the time period (2005 to 2010) that we examine. The number of available sites and their nodes has increased by 179% and 82%. The active site count has increased at a slower rate (95%) because most PlanetLab users intermittently run their experiments in the testbed, and their usage of the testbed is spread over time. Similarly, the number of live slices has increased by 48%. In particular, it is notable that live slice count has been fluctuating over time, which implies that resource demands on PlanetLab are synchronized to some degree with external events such as conference submission deadlines. Sliver count has increased at a faster rate (123%) than slices because slivers counts grow as a result of slice growth and node growth. Most slices only create slivers on a fraction of the nodes, but some slices, particularly those related to infrastructure, are typically created on every node in the system.

3. SLICE RESOURCE USAGE

Examining the slice resource usage in PlanetLab allows us to determine how experiments are using the system, and the patterns of resource consumption on the testbed. We find that PlanetLab experiments are typically bursty along several dimensions, and that most use relatively few resources at any given time. This likely stems from the network-centric experiments on PlanetLab – their resource consumption is tied to their network activity, rather than the total resource pool on PlanetLab.

3.1 Active Periods

Since PlanetLab slices share nodes, we begin our per-slice analysis by examining how long slices tend to run and actively use resources. We define a sliver's *active period* to be the number of hours during which the sliver is continuously live on its node. Experimenters typically leave slivers instantiated on nodes for long periods of time, and only use the slivers when actively performing experiments, resulting in multiple active periods separated by idle periods in CoMon datasets. We consider a slice active if any of its slivers are active, even if sliver count changes over time.

We find that slice activity is largely bimodal, with a great many short-lived slices and a number of very long-lived slices, as shown in Figure 3. The number of short-lived slices is not surprising, since many classes use PlanetLab for hands-on measurement projects and short assignments. It is also notable that there are 26 slices that were live longer than 360 days in 2010. These slices include 6 management slices (e.g., root and SliceStat [28]), and 20 long-running services that run on PlanetLab [7, 8, 11, 15, 21].

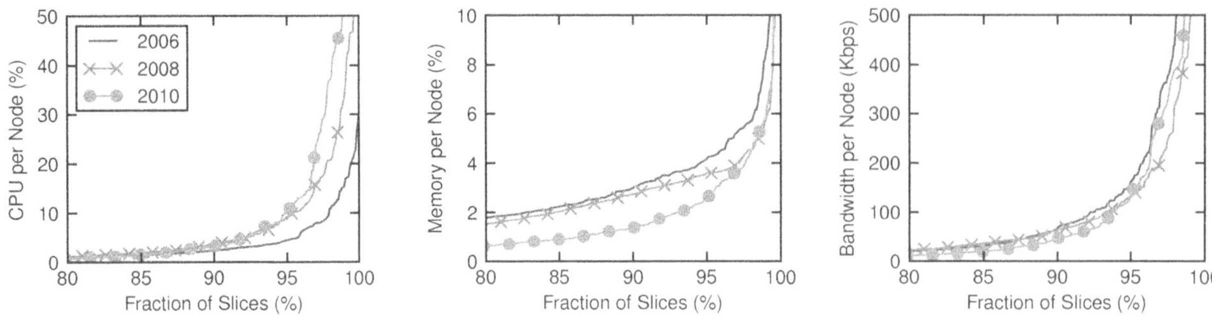

(a) CPU (b) Memory (c) Bandwidth

Figure 4: Per-sliver usage of CPU, memory, and bandwidth for slices in 2006, 2008, and 2010. Most slices have low resource consumption except for the heaviest 5% of slices. The CPU usage shows the heaviest slices gaining a larger share over time, while memory usage shows flatter curves. The heaviest bandwidth consumers typically provide services to large external user populations.

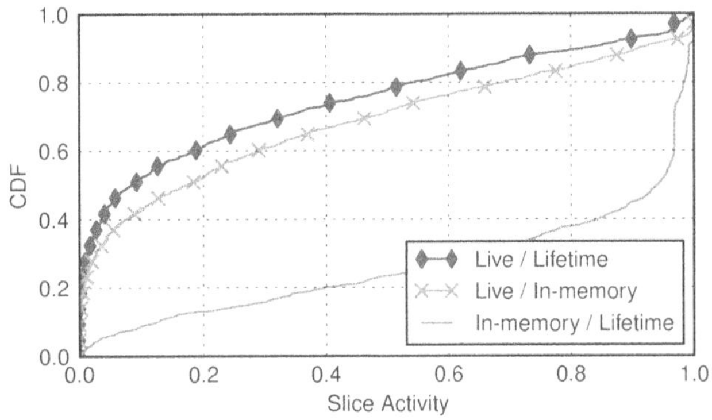

Figure 5: CDFs of the relative activity of slices over their lifetimes. Versus their lifetimes, most slices have relatively small periods of activity (Live/Lifetime). The ratio of activity is even low when compared to the time a slice is instantiated (Live/In-memory).

One possible observation from this data is that short-lived slices are an important aspect of PlanetLab usage, and that it may serve as a training facility for future developers. As such, all of the setup overhead on PlanetLab may be an issue for this class of user, who has to perform these tasks and then amortizes that effort over a relatively short usage. Testbed designers may be well advised to focus on simplicity as a way of gaining usage.

The other implication of this result is that most slices do not use a significant amount of resources, even when they are active. Shown in Figure 5 is that the total active periods of the slices is often spread over a much longer slice lifetime (Live/Lifetime), so many of those slices are idle for most of their lifetimes. The ratio of activity is even low when compared to the time a slice is instantiated (Live/In-memory). Slices often tend to also disappear and re-appear over time, with large gaps in time when they are not present at all on the testbed. Any attempt at introducing heavyweight resource allocation mechanisms would therefore have two side effects – it would burden the users of most slices, and it would often require resource overcommitment anyway in order to ensure that the resources are being used.

3.2 Local Resource Consumption

Understanding the distribution of slice resource usage and its change over time provides insight into the workload profiles of PlanetLab experiments. We focus on three resources – CPU, memory, and network bandwidth, and examine them on a per-sliver basis when the sliver is active. We do not include disk usage in our analysis because PlanetLab disk space is partitioned into per-sliver quotas (5 GB), and not shared by multiple users in a node.

Since most slivers have fairly low resource consumption, we focus only on the heaviest quintile of resource consumers, shown in Figure 4. The three graphs have similar characteristics, in that the aggregate resource consumption is a few percent at most, and increases sharply as we approach the heaviest 5% of slices. However, important differences are apparent when examined in closer detail. The CPU usage, for example, shows the heaviest slices gaining a larger share over time, while memory usage shows the exact opposite.

We believe these differences are a result of PlanetLab policy and the changes in hardware over time. PlanetLab uses a modified CPU scheduler [22], which allocates CPU evenly across slices (not threads/processes), and then allocates any unused CPU on demand. Over time, as more machines enter the PlanetLab testbed, and more powerful machines enter the system, the aggregate CPU in the system increases. As a result, more slices can have their CPU demands met, and the remaining CPU is used by the heaviest consumers. However, these heavy CPU consumers are not heavyweight long-running services, but instead are classified as spin-loop slivers that consume many CPUs but do not generate any network traffic, which we cover in more detail in Section 6. This result suggests that CPU contention in PlanetLab has been decreasing over time.

The CDF of memory consumption differs in that the curves are much flatter, and that the opposite effect occurs over time, with the heaviest consumers using less of the testbed. One reason that partly explains both features is that PlanetLab's policy for memory allocation is that when a node runs out of swap space, the heaviest consumer of physical memory is killed on that node. As a result, slices have a tendency to police their own memory usage to avoid being the heaviest consumer, leading to a flatter memory consumption profile among slices. Over time, as the memory capacities of the

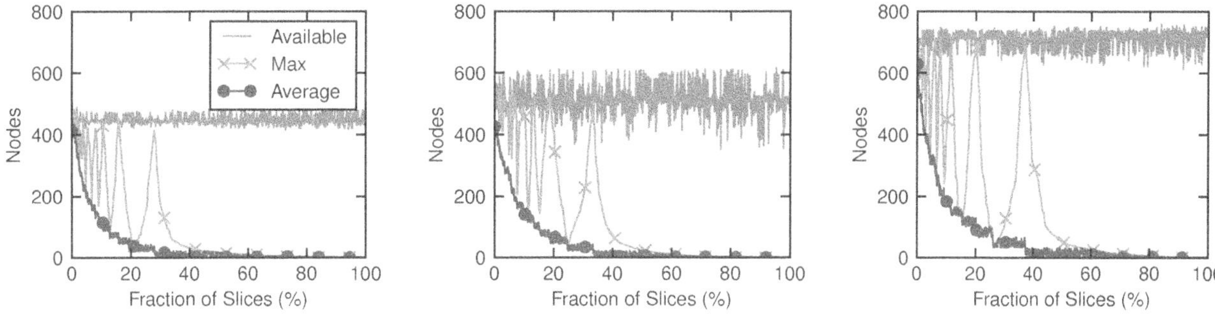

(a) 2006 (b) 2008 (c) 2010

Figure 6: The average and maximum daily sliver counts for slices in 2006, 2008, and 2010. Most slices have a low average number of slivers, but a large number of them have relatively high maximum sliver counts in their lifetimes.

nodes have increased, the self-policing behavior introduced by the memory-killing policy results in slices consuming a smaller fraction of memory over time.

Bandwidth consumption is related to the testbed itself – for those experiments without a large user population, bandwidth consumption is driven by the experiment itself and whatever bandwidth caps the nodes have been assigned. The heaviest bandwidth consumers typically involve large external (non-PlanetLab) user populations, such as content distribution networks or peer-to-peer systems, and the consumption of these systems is not captured on this graph.

3.3 Slice Sizes and Dynamics

As we have seen that PlanetLab's resource distribution and slice distribution has many bimodal properties, it is worth investigating whether PlanetLab is monopolized by only a handful of researchers, or whether it has a broader utility to the community. As we believe that PlanetLab's main differentiator versus other testbeds is its network reach, one measure of this utility would be to see how different slices use PlanetLab's scale.

To visualize the range of sliver usage within slices, we want to view the average and maximum daily sliver counts for the slices. However, viewing this data sorted by only one of these values results in garbled images since the average and maximum values are not necessarily correlated. To address this problem, we divide slices into 20 groups by their daily average sliver counts. We then sort slices within each group by their maximum sliver counts. The sort order alternates between ascending and descending for the different groups for aesthetic appeal. The results for 2006, 2008, and 2010 are shown in Figure 6.

These graphs show a number of interesting features – the first is that most slices have a relatively low average number of slivers, with 75% of the slices using less than 7% of the available nodes on average, and only 4% use more than half the available nodes on average. However, we also see that the maximum number of nodes used approaches the total size of PlanetLab for virtually every range of average node counts. This result suggests that while much of the development of experiments may happen at low sliver counts, many researchers are in fact expanding their experiment to a large fraction of the available nodes at some point in the slice's lifetime.

This usage pattern becomes more apparent when we aggregate the slices into the sites that created them, and then examine network reach, as shown in Figure 7. For each site, we combine the locations of all slivers created by researchers from that site, and examine the locations of those slivers, by site and continent. We find that 105 sites were purely donating resources in 2010, and did not run any slices of their own on the rest of the network. At the same time, 132 sites (35%) used more than 200 remote sites (53%). Taking the inactive sites into account, this result implies that 50% of all active sites used more than half of all available sites for their experiments, which would be impossible without PlanetLab-like global testbeds. Similarly, 73% of all active sites used nodes in every accessible continent (North America, South America, Europe, and Asia) in PlanetLab.

Combined, these two results demonstrate the main utility of PlanetLab – it allows researchers much larger network reach than they would have from just their own sites. Snapshots over small time periods are likely to understate this usage, since most experiments run on a small number of nodes for most of their lifetimes, but a large number of them expand to over half the testbed at some point in their lifetimes. This kind of utilization of the network is not likely to be captured by examining CPU or memory resources, as would be appropriate for computer clusters.

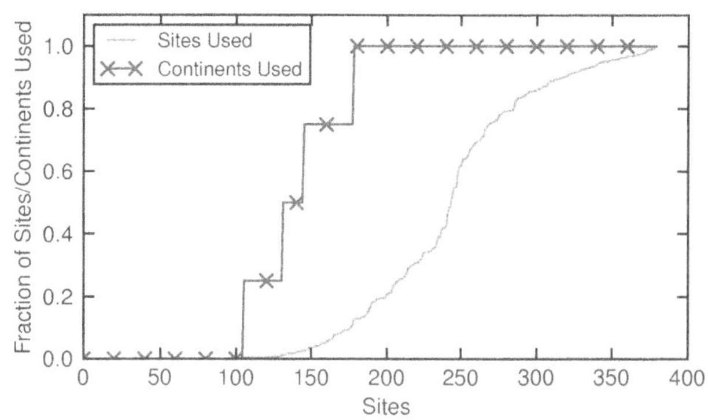

Figure 7: The distribution of network reach that PlanetLab sites used in 2010. More than 50% of all active sites used remote nodes in half of all available sites and every accessible continent in PlanetLab.

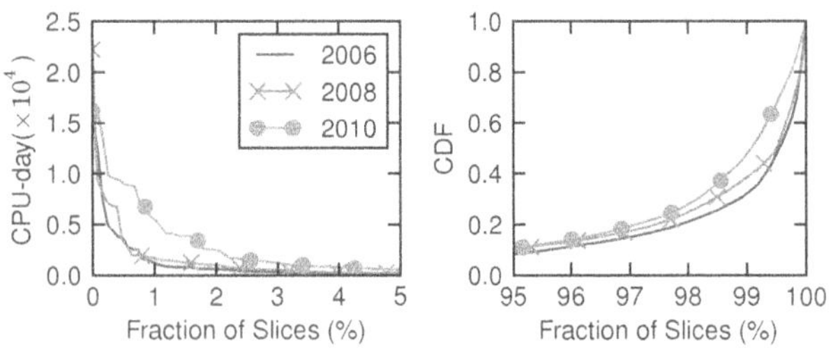

(a) Per-slice CPU usage (b) CDF of total CPU usage

Figure 8: Total CPU consumptions by slices in 2006, 2008, and 2010. Only 3% of all slices can account for 80% of all CPU usage in PlanetLab.

3.4 No Tragedy of the Commons

From the details presented earlier in this section, we find no measurement-based support for the idea that there is a tragedy of the commons on PlanetLab. Most experiments are relatively small most of their lifetimes, and use a large fraction of the testbed in a bursty manner. Likewise, resource consumption is relatively low for most slices, and the fact that the largest CPU consumers are runaway processes suggests that many more slices could get more CPU if needed.

The related question is that if PlanetLab appears to have excess capacity, why is that capacity not being (even surreptitiously) tapped by non-networking researchers? We believe that several PlanetLab policies make it unappealing for compute-intensive researchers. The first is that PlanetLab is organized with a small number of nodes (typically 2) per site, and a large number of sites. This model is different from compute grids, which have a large number of nodes per site connected with high-bandwidth local-area networks. In comparison, the external bandwidth capacity at many PlanetLab sites is in the range of 1-10 Mbps, so the ratio of CPU to bandwidth is much different than compute grids. Not only does PlanetLab have a worse bisection bandwidth than LANs, but the latency between nodes is much higher due to the physical distance. The other issue is the available memory – a large memory footprint increases the chances of a sliver being killed, so memory-intensive compute applications are not well-matched to PlanetLab. This combination of high CPU and low bandwidth is typical of certain bag-of-tasks parallel applications, such as SETI@home [26], but volunteers can provide far more CPUs than are available on PlanetLab.

4. RESOURCE ALLOCATION

Since the usage behavior of PlanetLab experiments is very different from compute-intensive testbeds, decisions on resource allocation policy are likely to also be impacted. In this section, we use the historical usage data to examine the resource allocation systems that have been proposed for federated network testbeds.

4.1 Total Resource Consumption

To understand the impact of resource allocation proposals, we must first understand resource consumption, which has many dimensions, such as node count, length of running time, resource consumption per node, etc. To capture the different usage patterns and to reduce the dimensions of the problem, we focus on the contended resources, CPU and memory, and aggregate per-slice usage across time and across the entire testbed.

We represent a slice's total resource usage in units of *CPU-day* and *MEM-day*. A CPU-day means the total CPU time that a single CPU core provides per day. Likewise, we define a MEM-day as the total memory space that a node provides per day. If a sliver uses 20% of CPU time and 10% of memory space in 10 nodes for 2 days, its total resource usage is 4 CPU-days and 2 MEM-days.

Figure 8a presents the distributions of per-slice total CPU usage in decreasing order. The top 1% of slices use more than 10^3 CPU-days while the medians are below 0.1 CPU-days in the years that we examined. PlanetLab slices consumed in total 0.9×10^5, 1.2×10^5, 2.2×10^5 CPU-days in 2006, 2008, and 2010 respectively. Figure 8b presents a detail from the CDFs of the total CPU usage. We find that only 3% of all slices can account for more than 80% of all CPU usage in PlanetLab. Memory usage has a similar pattern, with 4% of all slices account for more than 80% of all memory usage.

4.2 Resource Usage by Experiment Type

To understand what kinds of slices are creating resource demands and the extent of their demands, we categorize slices into several groups and compare their aggregate resource usages.

We first divide slices along two axes, the variability in the number of slivers and the lifetime of the slice. Using these groupings, we would expect an infrastructure service to have a long live and a stable sliver count, while a bursty experiment would have a short life and a variable sliver count. Figure 9 plots each slice's total active period and variability

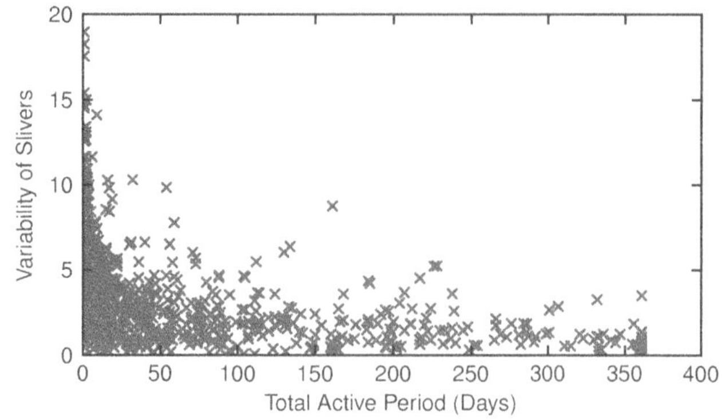

Figure 9: The distribution of each slice's total active period and coefficient of variation in its sliver count over time. Long-running slices show relatively lower variability than short-lived slices.

Slice group name	Slice count	Percentage
Short	718	56
Medium	370	29
Long-intermittent	171	13
Long-continuous	16	2
Total	1275	100

Table 2: The distribution of slice groups. The majority of slices are in the short or medium slice groups.

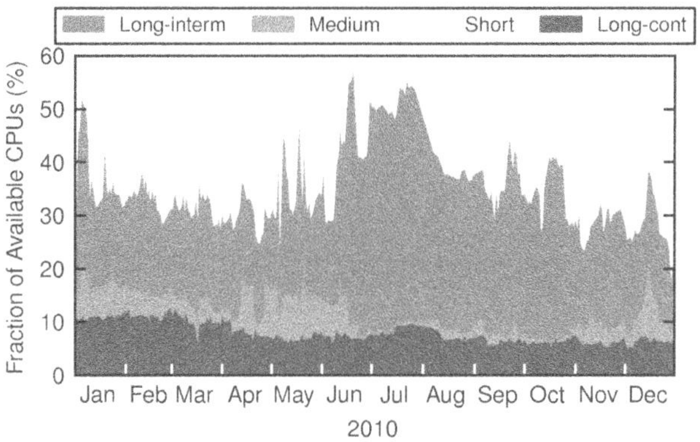

Figure 10: Time series of the distributions of CPU usage by each slice type in 2010. The y-axis represents the fraction of available CPUs consumed by slices per day. The Long-intermittent slices consume the largest amount of the resources with high variation.

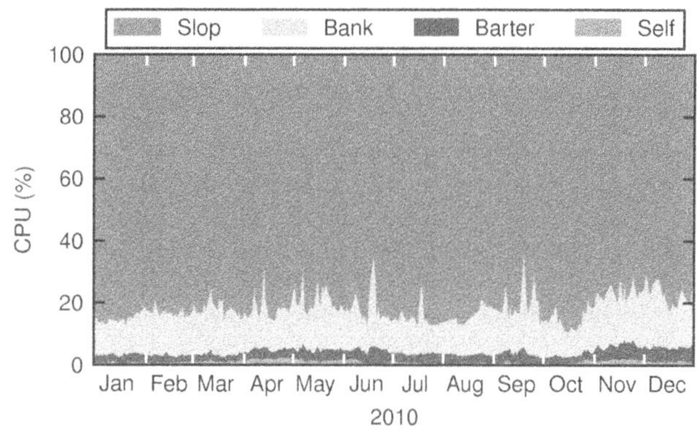

Figure 11: Time series of the distributions of CPU usage that could be addressed by several resource peering schemes. Barter and Bank can account for only 17% of the total CPU usage on PlanetLab because most CPU usage is from Slop.

of its slivers. The variability of slivers is measured as the coefficient of variation in a slice's sliver count over time. We find that long-running services show relatively lower variability than short-lived slices in general. For simplicity, we pick some break points, with Short slices have less than a week of total activity per year, Medium slices having between one week and 100 days of activity, and Long slices as have more than 100 days. We further divide the long slices into continuous or intermittent based on the normalized deviation of sliver count, with continuous slices having a deviation of less than 0.25. The number of slices in each of these groups is shown in Table 2.

Daily aggregate CPU usage across the testbed, divided by the slice types, is shown in Figure 10. We first calculate the total CPU usages by all slices per day. The Short slices, despite being over half of all slices, show virtually no CPU usage, while the Long-continuous slices, at 2% of all slices, consume roughly 5-12% of all available CPUs over time. The Medium and Long-intermittent slices are much more bursty in their CPU usage, with the Medium slices showing the least activity during the summer months and the start of the academic year. This behavior would correlate with PlanetLab being used for coursework and projects during the academic year.

Upon closer inspection of the slice groups, we find that the slices in the Long-continuous group run infrastructure services. The slices provide package management [7], monitoring [17, 20, 28], or scalable file distribution services [11, 21, 30]. These slices, while often heavy bandwidth consumers, are surprisingly not a huge impact on PlanetLab CPU, presumably because a production-quality service that has external users must take some care to run stably. On the other hand, the Long-intermittent slices are the primary source of the fluctuation in the workloads of the testbeds. For example, we find that many spin-loop slices, described in Section 6, belong to this group.

4.3 Resource Allocation Systems

We extend our analysis to explore the effectiveness of alternative resource allocation schemes in PlanetLab. Among the various resource allocation systems proposed for federated platforms, we focus on two representative approaches in this section: *pair-wise bartering* and *centralized banking*. Other schemes, such as chaining resources among a subset of the nodes [12], would fall between these two extremes. We examine how well the PlanetLab workload could be addressed by the alternative resource allocation systems if they were widely deployed in PlanetLab.

The two schemes we have selected represent the envelope of resource allocation schemes, since pair-wise barter is the most restrictive and banking is the most permissive. The two schemes assume that users trade their resources with each other, or bid their resources to reserve remote resources in other sites. In bartering, a site A grants a certain units of A's resources to site B in exchange for access to the same units of B's resources. This peering enables the sites to trade their resources without central agreement. In the central banking system, a site earns virtual currency budgets based on the amount of its donated resources, and obtains remote resources by spending its balance.

To calculate the amount of the PlanetLab workload that could be addressed by the resource peering schemes, we break each site's total resource usage into four categories: Self, Barter, Bank, and Slop. If a slice from site A runs on nodes owned by the same site A, we classify the slice's resource usage as *Self*. In bartering, each site keeps separate balances for the other sites. Site A's balance for site B, bal_{AB} increases when B uses resources at A's nodes, and decreases when A consumes B's nodes over time. If A uses r_{AB} resources at B, we classify $min(r_{AB}, bal_{AB})$ as *Barter* at a given date. In banking, each site has a balance across the testbed. A's balance, bal_A increases when other sites use resources at A's nodes. If A consumes r_A resources in total at other sites, then we classify $min(r_A, bal_A)$ as *Bank* at the given date. Lastly, the remaining resource usage is called *Slop*, which is the amount of resources that sites used beyond what they contributed.

For simplicity and generality, we make a number of assumptions about the resource allocation schemes, but these do not lead to a loss of generality in the results. For bartering schemes, we assume a uniform exchange rate, rather than a dynamic exchange rate proposed by some systems [4, 9, 16], since the dynamic rate would only restrict some of the exchanges we observe. Similarly, in central banking, we do not impose any upper limit on resource balances, which allows us to capture all exchanges that could be performed in a central banking model. We consider the effect of resource limits later in this section.

Figure 11 presents the amount of testbed-wide CPU usage addressed by each category. As expected, the percentage of Self usage is low, since sites would have little reason to join PlanetLab and use solely their own machines. The Barter approach handles on average less than 3% of the CPU usage on PlanetLab, and the Bank approach handles an additional 14% beyond Barter. The vast majority of the CPU usage, however, cannot be handled by any of these approaches, and is allocated from Slop. This implies that, no matter the underlying exchange rate mechanism, there is not much demand for resource that the resource peering schemes are able to handle. It also means that there has to be a policy to handle allocation when bartering or banking fails since most resources will be allocated via Slop. For memory usage, the Bank and Barter schemes show slightly higher percentages (19% total) than for CPUs, but the results are consistent with CPU usage in that most memory usage also comes from Slop. The underlying cause of these results is that CPU demand is unbalanced, with most sites using a large network reach but relatively little CPU. Schemes that attempt to allocate resources must contend with the fact that, for the vast majority of users, CPU is in relatively low demand.

We extend our simulation of the pair-wise bartering scheme to examine the effectiveness of resource routing in PlanetLab, which enables sites to access resources in more remote sites through some transitive ticket redemption paths. If site A has a ticket to claim on B's resources and B has a ticket to claim on C's resources, A could request C's resources using the chained redemption of its ticket to B ($A \rightarrow B \rightarrow C$). For conservative evaluation, we assume that every site has the global knowledge of the distribution of tickets at a given time, and we set no limit on the length of the path that can be used to claim resources.

We find that such resource routing enables PlanetLab sites to find 3.2 times more CPUs than with the pair-wise bartering scheme, but that the total usage addressable by chained approaches is still less than 7% of total CPU usage. Even with unlimited chain lengths, the chained bartering schemes have a result that is much closer to pair-wise bartering than to central banking, which suggests that the chains are likely to be fairly short. Indeed, we find that the maximum length of the used path was 18 hops, but most of the CPU addressed (85% of the 7%) in bartering was found in sites within 4 hops.

Despite the Bank approach addressing only 14% beyond Barter, any feasible implementation would achieve even less since some limit has to be placed on the balances each site can accumulate. Using the data for January 2010, we examine the bank balance growth in Figure 12, and show the effect of various limits. With no limit on balances, the total bank balances grow quickly and exceed the daily capacity of PlanetLab ("Available CPUs") within three days. Beyond this limit, the virtual currency becomes inflated, as more currency is accumulated than can ever be spent. With balance limits enforced, the total balance converges at certain points. We find that five CPU-days limit (or lower) can prevent the total balances from growing beyond what PlanetLab can serve. Since most nodes in PlanetLab are dual-core or quad-core machines (82%), the five CPU-days correspond to two physical machines, which is what each site typically provides.

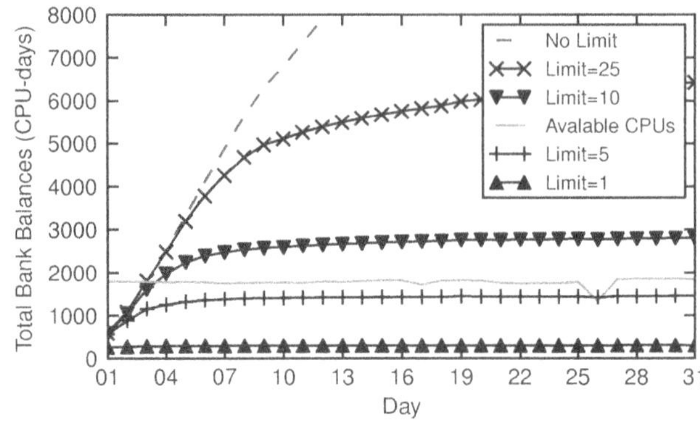

Figure 12: The total balances amassed at all sites. Without balance limits, the total balances will exceed the daily capacity of PlanetLab within 3 days, leading to inflation of virtual currency.

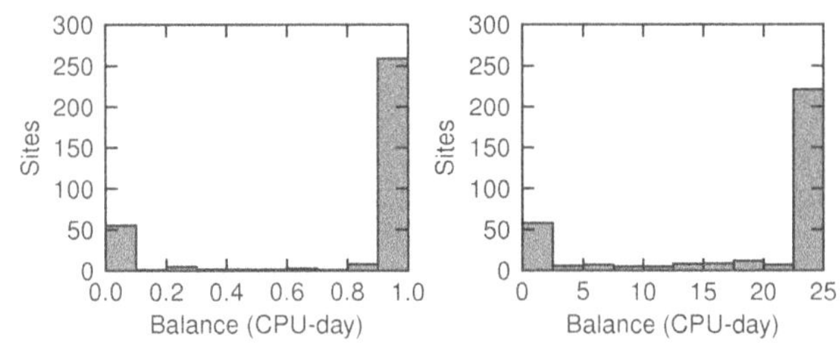

(a) 1 CPU-day Limit (b) 25 CPU-day Limit

Figure 13: The distribution of bank balances among sites. There are bimodal distributions with most sites being near the limits.

Even if the total balance is bounded, the utility of banking and resource auctions depends on users willing to outbid each other in order to get access to resources. However, we find that bank balances tend toward bimodal distributions, as shown in Figure 13. The majority of sites hit the balance limit, and a fraction of sites are constantly at a zero balance, with similar patterns at balance limits of 1 CPU-day and 25 CPU-days.

If banking is intended to solve the problem of demand before external events, such as conference submission deadlines, this bimodal wealth distribution suggests that auctions will fail, since all sites have the same amount of currency to bid on the same resource, and the utility of the resource presumably drops to zero after the paper submission deadline.

Conversely, when no external deadline exists, the bank balances provide little benefit, since PlanetLab already has most of its resources being allocated via Slop. So, a banking scheme would allow all of the current demand to be satisfied, without providing any additional benefit beyond what is currently present.

If banking were employed to reduce the resources being allocated via Slop, then a policy decision has to be made regarding the testbed. From our earlier examination of consumption, the Long-continuous slices were responsible for far less CPU consumption than the Long-intermittent slices.

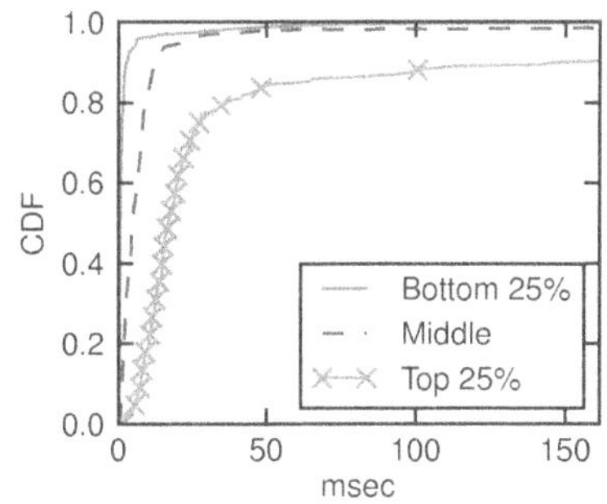

(a) ServTest-max

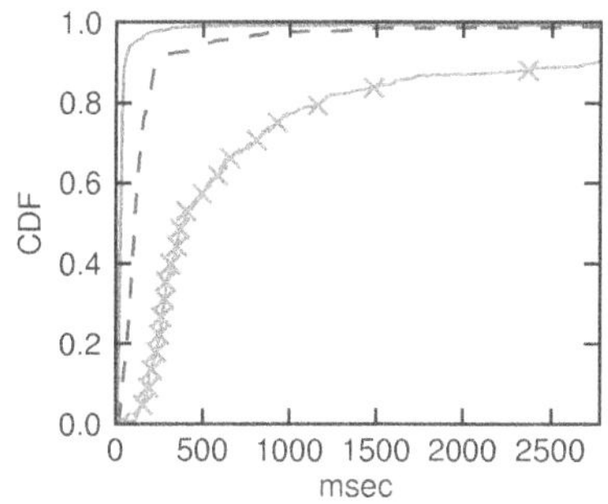

(b) Timer-max

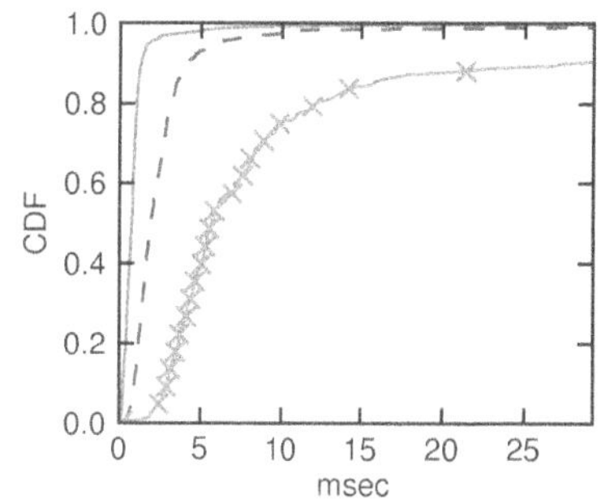

(c) SleepLoop

Figure 14: CDFs of system lags in nodes grouped by their average CPU load.

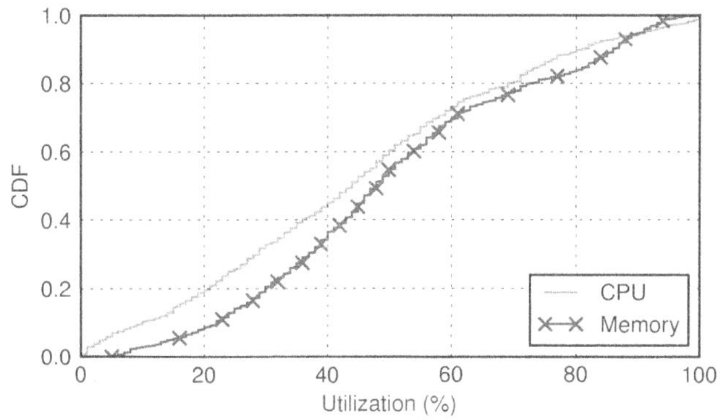

Figure 15: CDFs of average CPU/Memory utilization of all PlanetLab nodes in 2010.

One may decide that Slop should be allocated preferentially to continuously-running services in order to increase the visibility (internally and externally) of PlanetLab. In any case, the decision becomes how to allocate the Slop, not how to use banking, suggesting that banking by itself provides little utility.

5. WORKLOAD IMBALANCE

Despite the availability of resources on PlanetLab, some level of contention does occur from the testbed being shared, leading to workload imbalance. In this section, we examine the workload distribution in 2010, and analyze the degree of imbalance in PlanetLab and its effects on the system. We analyze some reasons for the distribution, and explore solutions based on these observations.

By measuring average CPU and memory utilization by node, we can see a persistent difference during the year, as shown in Figure 15. The effects of this imbalance are also quantifiable, using CoMon's metrics regarding system lag and timing. These metrics are related to the responsiveness of networked systems, so load-induced timing problems would degrade PlanetLab's overall utility. The metrics used are

- **ServTest** – Measure latency to make a loopback connection and receive a byte from it. Calculate maximum and average values over previous 60 runs. Used to measure connectivity responsiveness.

Field	CPU-Low	Med	High
ServTest-max	2.71	12.95	150.57
ServTest-avg	0.29	0.62	3.66
Timer-max	38.02	282.75	3247.94
Timer-avg	10.35	10.62	15.01
SleepLoop	1.28	4.15	27.72
SpinLoop	0.49	0.98	7.48

Table 3: The 90th percentile values (in milliseconds) of the system lag metrics in nodes with low, medium, and high CPU load.

- **Timer** – Measure latency in wake-ups from 10 msec sleeps. Calculate maximum and average values over last 60 runs. Used to measure load on the scheduler.

- **SleepLoop** – Run 11 spin-loops with 10 msec sleeps in-between. Measure gaps between the loops and calculate (max - min) of the gaps. Used to simulate the behavior of low-rate measurement activity.

- **SpinLoop** – Run 11 spin-loops without sleeps. Calculate a diff value like SleepLoop. Used to simulate the behavior of high-rate measurement activity.

We divide PlanetLab nodes into three groups based on their CPU load shown in Figure 15: top 25%, bottom 25%, and the remaining 50% of all nodes. Then we compare the values of the lag-related metrics between the groups (Figure 14). It is noticeable that the nodes with high CPU load show two orders of magnitude of increase in the metrics compared to other lightly loaded nodes. This latency may degrade responsiveness of network services or add measurement noise to running experiments. Table 3 summarizes the 90th percentile values of all the metrics in each group. We observe similar results in the nodes grouped by their memory load. Such timing increases complicate experiment design and add noise to measurements. On the positive side, long-running services will have to develop mechanisms to deal with these issues, which are also likely to occur in the real world, thereby making their services more robust outside of testbed environments.

5.1 Origins of Imbalance

While one may expect that a certain amount of workload imbalance is naturally to be expected in a large testbed, we believe that the imbalance on PlanetLab has other more

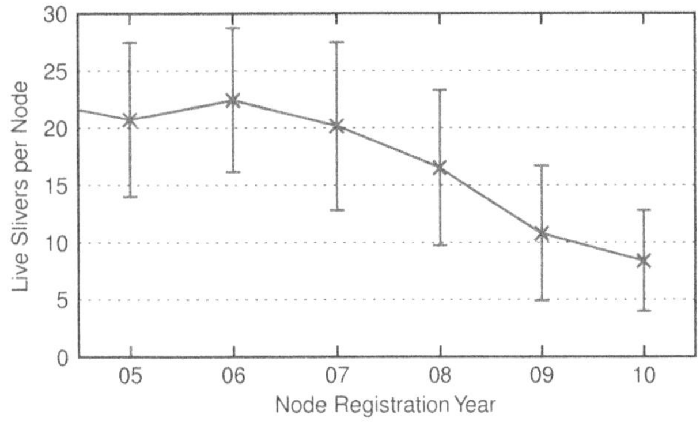

Figure 16: The number of live slivers per node in 2010. The recently registered nodes serve lower number of live slivers than older nodes. The error bars represent standard deviations.

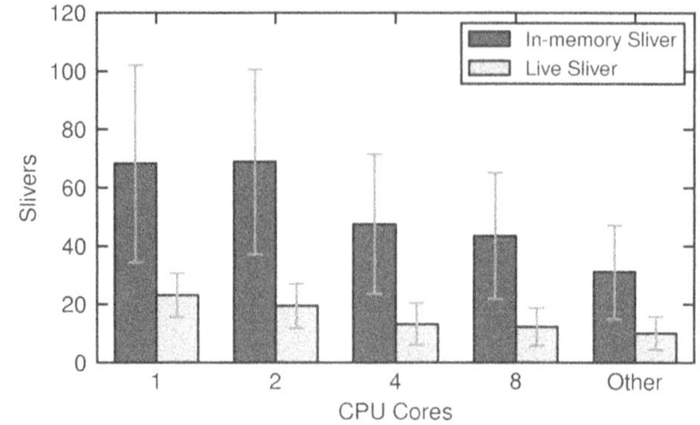

Figure 17: The distribution of slivers in nodes based on the number of CPU cores per node. The number of in-memory and live slivers shows a generally decreasing trend as the number of cores increases, which is responsible for some of the measured workload imbalance. The error bars represent standard deviations.

identifiable causes. Identifying these causes can help researchers in improving the resources their experiments use, and it can help future testbed operators determine policies that would help alleviate imbalance.

One of our observations regarding PlanetLab nodes is that newer, more powerful nodes are often very lightly used, and that older, less capable nodes are in heavy demand, which is the opposite behavior of what one would expect from researchers seeking out the most available CPU resources. We can quantify this behavior by examining the sliver counts on different nodes. Figure 16 shows the number of live slivers per node, broken down by the year the node entered PlanetLab. We see that the older nodes have more than twice as many slivers as the newer nodes, and this metric understates the difference, since these sliver counts include many of the long-running services.

The same behavior is evident if we examine the type of machine involved, since older nodes would tend to have fewer CPU cores, and newer machines would have more cores. Figure 17 plots the numbers of slivers in nodes, based on the number of CPU cores per node. The trend is clear – not only do fewer slices run on the more powerful machines, but even if we look at just the instantiated slices (the in-memory slivers), fewer of those exist on the more powerful machines. Even the most powerful nodes (labeled as "Other") are the least popular among the nodes. This breakdown is even more apparent when calculated the slivers per core, with the 8-core nodes serving only 1.53 slivers per core at a given time while single-core machines were busy with running 23.16 slivers.

We observe similar patterns in memory usage when compared to node memory size. Figure 18 shows the average memory usage of nodes, grouped by the memory size of the node. We see that nodes with more memory see relatively little extra usage of that memory. We believe that the reason that more memory is not used is because experiments that are deployed across multiple nodes have to plan for the lowest common denominator, and therefore restrict their memory usage to avoid being killed. At the same time, the reason we see any growth in memory usage on larger nodes is likely due to more memory-intensive experiments avoiding the smaller nodes, perhaps as a result of having found their

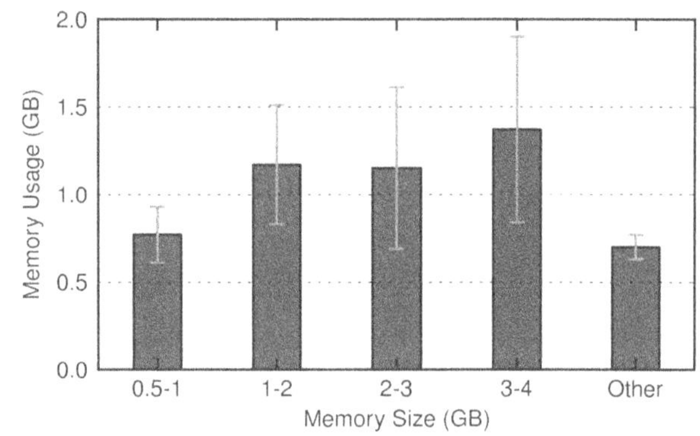

Figure 18: The memory usage by node memory size. The nodes with more memory see relatively little extra usage of that memory. The error bars represent standard deviations.

slivers killed on those nodes. Regarding live sliver counts, we see some of the same trends observed for the node's CPU cores. The nodes with the largest memory space ("Other") host only 6.64 live slivers on average while the most memory-constrained nodes ("0.5 - 1GB") are busy with running 20.14 live slivers.

Several possible explanations can explain this behavior, ranging from the history of PlanetLab to human nature. One may expect that users obtain a list of working nodes, and do not regularly update their lists, leading to a bias against newly-introduced nodes. Older nodes may also reflect more established hosting sites that joined PlanetLab earlier since they had more active network research groups. These sites may have a larger user population keeping their nodes well-maintained, and may be connected to the Internet using better-quality links. Users may also flock to more busy nodes precisely because other users have found them desirable – knowing nothing else about two nodes, the one with more active users may actually be the better node to use, because other users have already found the node to be more useful for their experiments.

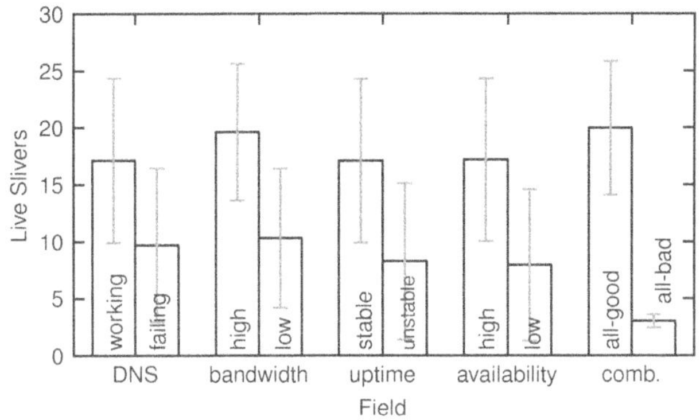

Figure 19: Popularity of nodes based on failure modes. PlanetLab users avoid nodes with high DNS failures, low bandwidth, and unstable operation. The error bars represent standard deviations.

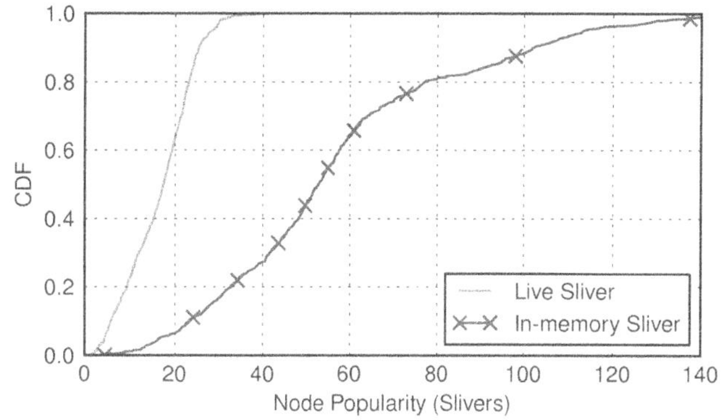

Figure 20: CDFs of node popularity. Each node's popularity is measured as its sliver count.

5.2 Nodes with Failures

While it may be argued that there is little harm letting users flock to known-good nodes, it can also be useful to explore why users avoid other nodes. From a policy perspective, the testbed itself has reasons to encourage a flatter load balance, because it can increase the capacity of the testbed, reduce experimental variance, and alleviate congestion. The testbed operators may also want to ensure that the participating sites are really contributing resources of value, instead of pro-forma resources that are useless to the rest of the testbed.

Since resource pressure on a node is not a main concern for users, we focus on the types of failures that could significantly limit network experiments on the node. CoMon records a set of metrics about node health. Among them, we selected four fields that we believe users are likely to correlate with the stability and the quality of network connections that a node provides. They are DNS failure rates, provisioned bandwidth, system uptime, and availability of each PlanetLab node.

We define several failure modes for nodes. A node is considered to have a non-working DNS system if its DNS failure rate is over 90% on average in the node. A node has low bandwidth if its 90th percentile of the achieved bandwidth in the node is less than 1 Mbps. For stability, we define a node to be unstable if its average system uptime is less than a week. Lastly, a node's availability is classified as low if the node was online for less than a month in total during 2010. These choices are meant to be conservative, in that users may still prefer higher quality values than our thresholds.

We classify PlanetLab nodes based on each failure mode that we define, and compare their popularity using sliver counts as a proxy. Figure 19 presents the average number of live slivers in both failed nodes and healthy nodes. In contrast to resource availability, we find that PlanetLab users do react to the failures in the nodes. We find that healthy nodes have twice as many live slivers compared to failing nodes, and since many of these slivers are due to infrastructure services, the difference in experimental slivers is likely to be even higher. The "all-bad" nodes in the combination failures (labeled as "comb.") represent nodes that exhibit all the four failures. Those nodes had only 3 live slivers while other healthy nodes hosted 18.5 live slivers on average. Figure 20 plots the distribution of node popularity measured as live slivers per node and in-memory slivers per node. We find that the all-bad nodes are in the bottom 3% of the unpopular nodes. Roughly 65% of nodes were "all-good" nodes that do not have any failures. Those nodes serve 20 live slivers on average, which is in the 64th percentile in node popularity.

5.3 Alternative Experiment Placement

In the previous sections, we showed that PlanetLab users seem to stay with the nodes they have been known to work well over time while avoiding non-working nodes for their experiments. However, this conservative placement strategy can collectively lead to inefficient resource allocation and undesirable system lags in the popular nodes. Also, the manual deployment prevents a new participant's nodes from being adopted by existing users, which can hamper the growth of the testbed in the long term.

We examine how the workload would change if researchers were to deploy their systems in a different manner. In PlanetLab, heavily loaded nodes are easily avoidable because there are available services to help users identify such nodes. CoMon provides a set of interfaces to allow users to pick lightly loaded nodes based on web-based queries. Similarly, CoMon provides interfaces to filter out failing nodes in using various metrics. Some available execution management systems [1, 2] locate resources based on high-level queries in XML given by users.

We consider a "what if" scenario that all PlanetLab users query a CoMon-like monitoring systems to find the set of lightly loaded *all-good* nodes when they deploy their experiments. We simulate the scenario using the CoMon data of 2010. We assume that a sliver is placed on the node selected by a monitoring service only when it is started, and that continuously live slivers do not migrate between nodes in our simulation.

Figure 21 plots the distribution of slivers with several alternative service-placement policies. *Original* plots the number of live slivers per core that we observed in the datasets. *BestFit* represents a policy that places a new sliver in the least loaded all-good node regardless of its location. However, it is not always desirable to deploy services in this way, because users may want to deploy their experiments at a certain range of network vantage points. *Continent* and

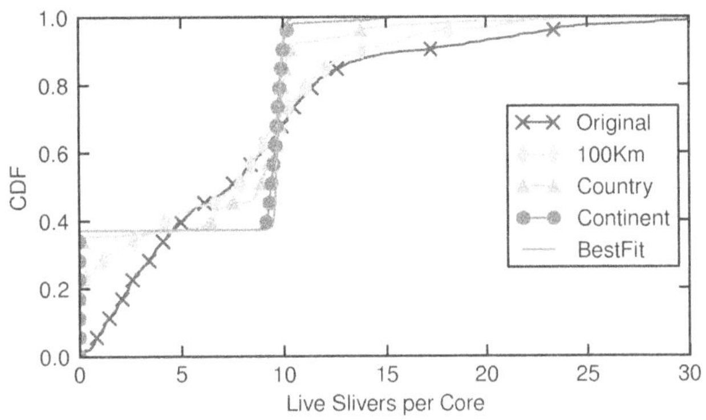

Figure 21: CDFs of live slivers per core in simulations of alternative node placement policies. Since lightly loaded and all-good nodes are selected, the workload is well balanced among nodes while any undesirable failures are avoided.

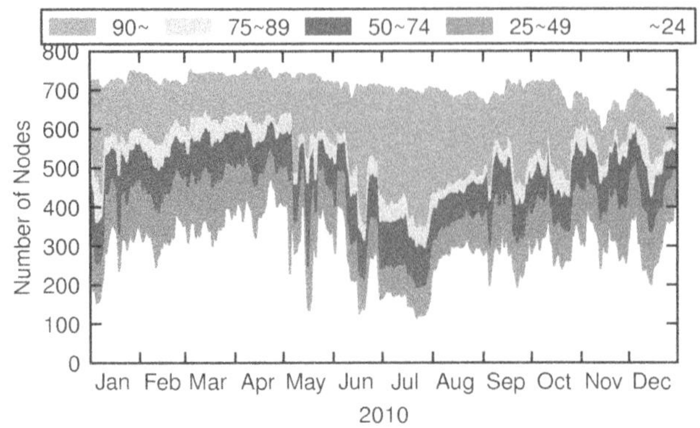

Figure 22: The distribution of per-day CPU loads on PlanetLab nodes in 2010. Each day, nodes are divided into five categories according to their per-day CPU usage. The nodes with more than 90% CPU usage account for up to 49% of all PlanetLab nodes (July 22).

Country represent policies that find nodes from the same continent or the same country as its original node in the dataset, respectively. Lastly, since some countries have a large number of nodes, we simulate a policy to find a node for a sliver within a configurable distance, 100 Kilometers, from its initial node. We compare against an ideal policy, BestFit, in which all good nodes host an equal number of slivers, and any nodes that exhibit failures (201 in total) are avoided entirely.

Our simulation result shows that the dynamic experiment placement could greatly improve the load balancing in PlanetLab while still largely avoiding problematic nodes. The 90th percentile of per-node live slivers decreases from 16.1 to 13.7 (in 100 km) and 10.3 (in Country). As the placement restrictions are loosened, not only does it become possible to more evenly distribute load, but it also becomes more likely that the bad nodes are avoided entirely. The 100-km policy still allocates a substantial fraction of nodes from the bad set, whereas continent-level placement avoids them almost entirely. If a user wants to use a set of specific nodes, she should be able to deploy her service on the nodes, but many other users could benefit from the intelligent service placement. The primary reason for the improved load-balancing is that most experiments are short-lived (Section 3), so the dynamic experiment placement can help spread well the load over available nodes.

6. POLICING OF SLICES IN PLANETLAB

In this section, we show that PlanetLab's resources are affected by a few problematic slices. We examine the impact of those slices on PlanetLab and consider the implications for policing of resource usage in the testbed. We also explore how PlanetLab's workloads would change if stricter form of policing is introduced in PlanetLab.

6.1 Spin-loop Slices in PlanetLab

PlanetLab is a shared infrastructure, and while it provides some mechanisms to prevent experiments from interfering with each other, it also relies on the cooperation of researchers. For example, local tests and incremental rollouts are recommended before a new service is fully deployed in PlanetLab [29]. We observed that most slices follow this

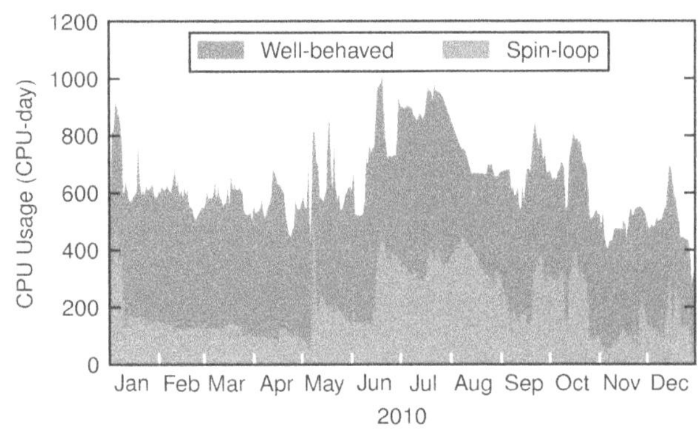

Figure 23: The CPU consumption of spin-loop slices in 2010. Although there are only a few spin-loop slices (4.8 slices among 152.7 live slices per day), the average CPU consumption of the spin-loop slices accounts for 31% of the total CPU usage of all slices.

practice well in Figure 6. To minimize centralized control, PlanetLab typically does not police resource usage of a slice unless there are significant risks of system crashes or security concerns that need to be addressed immediately.

However, some experiments may behave poorly because of design or implementation flaws, and negatively affect many other well-behaved experiments. We analyze the problem using CoMon data collected in 2010. We divide nodes into several categories according to their per-day CPU usage, and observe the distribution of the nodes over time. Figure 22 presents the distribution of per-day CPU loads on PlanetLab nodes in 2010. In this analysis, we define a node to be *overloaded* on a given date if its per-day CPU usage is over 90%, and up to 49% of all live PlanetLab nodes are overloaded. The number of overloaded nodes varies over time, but we did not find any noticeable correlation between the numbers of overloaded nodes and live slices a day (the graph is omitted for brevity). This implies that the overloaded nodes are not caused by the increase of active users.

The largest testbed-wide CPU consumers are often a few slices that use many aggregate CPU cycles without gen-

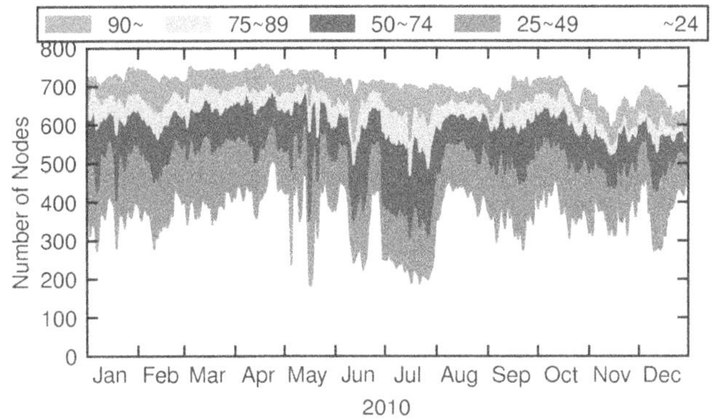

Figure 24: Time series of the updated distributions of per-day CPU loads after pruning spin-loop slices. The number of overloaded nodes is reduced by 71% (150 to 43) on average.

erating network traffic. We define a *spin-loop sliver* as a sliver that consumes more than 20% of a CPU and has an average bandwidth consumption (Tx + Rx) below a minimum value, 1 Kbps a day. We classify a slice as a *spin-loop slice* if the majority of its slivers are spin-loop slivers. Figure 23 presents the CPU consumption of the spin-loop slices in 2010. We find that the problematic slices accounted for on average 31% of the total CPU across all of PlanetLab. Since spin-loop slices average 4.8 per day among the 152.7 live slices per day, the 31% resource consumption is significantly large.

6.2 Pruning Spin-loop Slices

We simulate pruning the spin-loop slices to measure their impact on other slices. For a spin-loop slice, we subtract its sliver's CPU consumption from the node's CPU usage. If a spin-loop sliver had been pruned by PlanetLab, more CPUs might have been available to non-spinloop slivers in the node. Therefore, for each non-spinloop sliver, we select the larger of its CPU usage in a day or the median of its CPU usage throughout the year, to recompute the node's CPU usage after pruning.

Figure 24 plots the updated distribution of CPU load after spin-loop slices are pruned by PlanetLab. We find that the number of overloaded nodes is reduced from 150 to 43 nodes by policing only 4.8 spin-loop slices a day on average. It is notable that there are still some overloaded nodes even after pruning all identified spin-loop slices on PlanetLab nodes. We examine the nodes in order to understand what other factors made them remain overloaded. We find that 56% of the overloaded nodes are single core machines, which represent only 13% of all PlanetLab nodes.

7. RELATED WORK

Several resource management frameworks have been proposed for PlanetLab-like federated distributed computing infrastructures. In Sharp [12], multiple autonomous parties can exchange their resources using tickets. A ticket represents the holder's claim over a certain amount of resources in other peers, which can be issued, delegated, and redeemed in a cryptographically secure manner. Millennium [10], Mirage [9], Tycoon [16], and Bellagio [4] propose market-based mechanisms for trading resources in an economically efficient way. The systems focus on maximizing the values delivered to users by providing a means to express their valuation of resources. In Bellagio, participating users receive virtual currency budgets based on their resources that they contributed, and submit their preferences in the form of auction bids. The market-based systems are not widely deployed in PlanetLab because user valuation of resources is useful in the systems where resource demand exceeds resource supply (e.g., sensor network testbed). We expect that our analysis results will provide insights into user behavior in the federated infrastructures, which is required for designing similar economic resource allocation models.

Previous studies in traditional cluster resource management largely focused on resource utilization for compute-intensive applications in time-sharing or batch-queue systems. The job scheduling and resource allocation in the systems are designed to improve performance metrics such as throughput and mean response time. Distributed batch queue systems (Condor [18], Matchmaking [25]) provide resource sharing across loosely coupled pools of distributively owned machines. Load balancing systems (MOSIX [5], LSF [24]) balance CPU load across nodes in cluster by actively migrating processes across cluster machines. However, these cluster resource management systems do not address non-aggressive user behavior in wide-area network testbeds that are much different from compute clusters.

Our work relates to research projects that help PlanetLab users monitor and locate resources in the testbed. SWORD [2] is a resource discovery service deployed in PlanetLab. In SWORD, users describe desired resources such as per-node characteristics in XML and submit the queries, and then the service locates an appropriate set of resources for the user based on the given specification. CoMon [20] provides a comprehensive view of statistics about every node and slice in PlanetLab. It also provides a mechanism to select nodes based on queries provided by users. Also, several execution management systems [1, 3, 7] are available to provide GUI interfaces to help users deploy and monitor their systems across multiple remote nodes.

8. SUMMARY

In this work, we conduct an extensive and in-depth analysis of six years of PlanetLab measurements to understand and characterize PlanetLab's resource usage. Based on our analysis, we discuss the implications for designing resource management policies in new federated network testbeds. We find that the usage is much different from shared compute clusters, that conventional wisdom does not hold for PlanetLab, and that several properties of PlanetLab as a network testbed are largely responsible for this difference. We find that experiments typically utilize PlanetLab to expand their network reach, and that this metric of utility is a far better indicator of PlanetLab's effectiveness than compute-oriented metrics like CPU utilization.

We also find that approaches focusing on compute-oriented metrics are likely to be inapplicable to PlanetLab-like workloads. In particular, we find that resource usage is very bursty, and that the vast majority of experiments consume very little resources over much of their lifetimes. Based on the measurement of total resource usage, we explore the effectiveness of several resource allocation systems, and find that both pair-wise bartering and centralized banking systems can address only a small percentage of total resource usage. This result implies that resource management systems in federated network testbeds still need policies to fairly allocate available resources for the vast majority of the workload. We examine some policies for better resource discovery and, node management, and pruning of runaway experiments.

9. ACKNOWLEDGMENTS

We would like to thank our shepherd, Olaf Maennel, as well as the anonymous IMC reviewers. We also thank KyoungSoo Park, Michael Golightly, and Sunghwan Ihm for several beneficial discussions and comments on earlier drafts of this paper. This research was partially supported by the NSF Awards CNS-0615237 and CNS-0916204.

10. REFERENCES

[1] J. R. Albrecht, R. Braud, D. Dao, N. Topilski, C. Tuttle, A. C. Snoeren, and A. Vahdat. Remote control: Distributed application configuration, management, and visualization with Plush. In *Proceedings of USENIX Large Installation System Administration Conference (LISA)*, 2007.

[2] J. R. Albrecht, D. L. Oppenheimer, A. Vahdat, and D. A. Patterson. Design and implementation trade-offs for wide-area resource discovery. *ACM Transactions on Internet Technology (TOIT)*, 8(4), Sept. 2008.

[3] AppManager. `http://appmanager.berkeley.intel-research.net/`.

[4] A. AuYoung, B. N. Chun, A. C. Snoeren, and A. Vahdat. Resource allocation in federated distributed computing infrastructures. In *Workshop on Operating System and Architectural Support for the Ondemand IT Infrastructure (OASIS)*, 2004.

[5] A. Barak and O. Laadan. The MOSIX multicomputer operating system for high performance cluster computing. *Future Generation Computer Systems*, 13(4-5), Mar. 1998.

[6] A. Bavier, M. Bowman, B. Chun, D. Culler, S. Karlin, S. Muir, L. Peterson, T. Roscoe, T. Spalink, and M. Wawrzoniak. Operating system support for planetary-scale network services. In *Proceedings of USENIX NSDI*, 2004.

[7] J. Cappos, S. Baker, J. Plichta, D. Nyugen, J. Hardies, M. Borgard, J. Johnston, and J. H. Hartman. Stork: Package management for distributed VM environments. In *Proceedings of USENIX Large Installation System Administration Conference (LISA)*, 2007.

[8] J. Cappos, I. Beschastnikh, A. Krishnamurthy, and T. Anderson. Seattle: A platform for educational cloud computing. In *Proceedings of ACM Technical Symposium on Computer Science Education*, 2009.

[9] B. N. Chun, P. Buonadonna, A. AuYoung, C. Ng, D. C. Parkes, J. Shneidman, A. C. Snoeren, and A. Vahdat. Mirage: A microeconomic resource allocation system for sensornet testbeds. In *Proceedings of IEEE Workshop on Embedded Networked Sensors*, 2005.

[10] B. N. Chun and D. E. Culler. User-centric performance analysis of market-based cluster batch schedulers. In *Proceedings of IEEE International Symposium on Cluster Computing and the Grid*, 2002.

[11] M. J. Freedman, E. Freudenthal, and D. Mazières. Democratizing content publication with Coral. In *Proceedings of USENIX NSDI*, 2004.

[12] Y. Fu, J. S. Chase, B. N. Chun, S. Schwab, and A. Vahdat. SHARP: an architecture for secure resource peering. In *Proceedings of ACM SOSP*, 2003.

[13] GENI Aggregate Manager API. `http://groups.geni.net/geni/wiki/GeniApi/`.

[14] GENI: Global Environment for Network Innovations. `http://www.geni.net/`.

[15] T. Isdal, M. Piatek, A. Krishnamurthy, and T. Anderson. Privacy-preserving P2P data sharing with OneSwarm. In *Proceedings of ACM SIGCOMM*, 2010.

[16] K. Lai, L. Rasmusson, E. Adar, L. Zhang, and B. A. Huberman. Tycoon: An implementation of a distributed, market-based resource allocation system. *Multiagent and Grid Systems*, 1(3), Aug. 2005.

[17] S.-J. Lee, P. Sharma, S. Banerjee, S. Basu, and R. Fonseca. Measuring bandwidth between PlanetLab nodes. In *Proceedings of Passive and Active Measurement Conference (PAM)*, 2005.

[18] M. J. Litzkow, M. Livny, and M. W. Mutka. Condor - a hunter of idle workstations. In *Proceedings of IEEE International Conference on Distributed Computing Systems (ICDCS)*, 1988.

[19] D. Oppenheimer, B. Chun, D. Patterson, A. C. Snoeren, and A. Vahdat. Service placement in a shared wide-area platform. In *Proceedings of USENIX Annual Technical Conference*, 2006.

[20] K. Park and V. S. Pai. CoMon: A mostly-scalable monitoring system for PlanetLab. *ACM SIGOPS Operating Systems Review*, 40(1), Jan. 2006.

[21] K. Park and V. S. Pai. Scale and performance in the CoBlitz large-file distribution service. In *Proceedings of USENIX NSDI*, 2006.

[22] L. Peterson, A. Bavier, M. E. Fiuczynski, and S. Muir. Experiences building PlanetLab. In *Proceedings of USENIX OSDI*, 2006.

[23] PlanetLab. `http://www.planet-lab.org/`.

[24] Platform Computing Load Sharing Facility (LSF). `http://www.platform.com/`.

[25] R. Raman, M. Livny, and M. H. Solomon. Matchmaking: Distributed resource management for high throughput computing. In *Proceedings of IEEE International Symposium on High Performance Distributed Computing (HPDC)*, 1998.

[26] SETI@home. `http://setiathome.berkeley.edu/`.

[27] Sirius: A Calendar Service for PlanetLab. `https://snowball.cs.uga.edu/~dkl/pslogin.php/`.

[28] SliceStat: Slice monitoring sensor on PlanetLab. `http://codeen.cs.princeton.edu/slicestat/`.

[29] N. Spring, L. Peterson, A. Bavier, and V. Pai. Using PlanetLab for network research: Myths, realities, and best practices. *ACM SIGOPS Operating Systems Review*, 40(1), Jan. 2006.

[30] L. Wang, K. Park, R. Pang, V. S. Pai, and L. Peterson. Reliability and security in the CoDeeN content distribution network. In *Proceedings of USENIX Annual Technical Conference*, 2004.

Summary Review Documentation for

"Understanding and Characterizing PlanetLab Resource Usage for Federated Network Testbeds"

Authors: W. Kim, A. Roopakalu, K. Li, V. Pai

Reviewer #1

Strengths: This is a very unique, extensive, and interesting dataset. PlanetLab as a platform has been a tremendous boost to networking/measurement research and a retrospective measurement study of usage there is very relevant. The problem of how a federated test bed will be used is important and timely given the interest in deploying more of these.

Weaknesses: I do not see any strong weaknesses in terms of techniques/results, other than the description of some of the results can be improved and I would like to see some more in-depth analysis of a few more interesting aspects of the problem instead of too many figures making the same, somewhat obvious observations.

Comments to Authors: In the introduction, I would tone down some of the claims about "conventional wisdom"/"tragedy of commons" etc, because it seems fairly obvious that the workloads for PlanetLab are very different from traditional compute clusters!

I found Section 3.2 very confusing. Maybe this is a terminology/writing problem – you have "slice" but really you are doing a "sliver"/node level analysis here. The writing goes back and forth and its confusing me a bit. Also, what is the "average" being computed over - across time for each sliver or across nodes?
Would it also be useful to just look at average over "active periods" instead of the overall average?

In Section 3.2, how you generate this visualization is very confusing.

I agree with the observation made in Section 3.4, but I feel that you are overselling the analysis by saying that this flies in the face of conventional wisdom etc.

When you calculate the timeseries of bank/barter/slop etc. – are these based on "instantaneous" measurements or over a sliding window or cumulative over history?

Fig 14 seems to suggest that most sites are incredibly altruistic – i.e. that they have a huge balance that they have not claimed. I wonder if you can correlate this with papers/projects that the sites have generated that use PlanetLab to verify.

In Section 5.2, I found your choice "memory" imbalance very puzzling. I imagine that most PlanetLab workloads are not really memory bound, so it's not terribly surprising that there is a memory imbalance. I would much rather see the corresponding result for network resources or CPU.

I agree with the overall notion of dynamic experiment placement; an obvious concern is w.r.t repeatability/correctness when you end up choosing different nodes over different runs of the same experiment/measurement. E.g., you could see network latency/congestion effects from different nodes being different. In fact, I am guessing this could be one motivation for manually choosing nodes. Could you comment on this, or try a dynamic-but-stable strategy, where the system also tries to find sites that overlap with the prior choice?

Also, I have heard and seen anecdotal evidence that people manually choose nodes because many nodes are inherently "unreliable". Can you comment on this?

You have an amazing dataset! I really hope that this dataset will be made public. I would try to cut some of the figures that are making more obvious points to try and fit in other aspect. Here are some potential directions to increase the depth of analysis that I could think of:

1. I wonder if you could characterize the slices into common buckets of "operating models". The goal is that if we have a few standard "configuration modes" and an interface for choosing these, then researchers could choose from these typical use cases for an easy to use dynamic resource allocation strategy.

2. There are two dimensions to your analysis space: Space (nodes) and Time. Would it help to try different ways of combining these — you have chosen specific points to e.g., average over time or max over time of sum over nodes etc. For example, it could be useful to look max over time max over nodes? I.e., when a slice is active does it hog a particular node?

3. Are there "runaway" experiments or slices that people have forgotten to turn off long after a deadline?

Reviewer #2

Strengths: PlanetLab is widely used. For every researcher working on PlanetLab there is a need to know what bias the system introduces. The paper looks at CPU and memory workloads.

Weaknesses: The study is more a sophisticated sysadmin report for the PlanetLab central administration, than a measurement paper for the research community.

Comments to Authors: In the current form the paper is written more from a system administration perspective and not for a user point of view. The authors study mainly CPU-days and Memory-days of users using the system. The authors warn several times of measurement errors that could be created by an overloaded system. For example, on page 10, the authors say: "This latency may degrade responsiveness of network services or add measurement noise to running experiments".
Admittedly, it is a very difficult task to estimate any boundaries on network performance errors that might be created due to an overloaded system, but it would have been nice to see some form of quantification.

It is certainly up to the experimenter to critically review the measurement results and understand the bias introduced by the system, but for a research paper it would have been nice to give at least an anecdotal flavor for what the upper bounds might be.

Reviewer #3

Strengths: Very cool data set, and an interesting topic. Clearly future testbeds can benefit from improved understanding of how PlanetLab has been put to use and working out over the past years.

Weaknesses: I find the authors discuss basic findings in too much depth, from too many angles, for too long, with too many plots, while I have a hard time following some of the more interesting analyses because of their resulting terseness.

Comments to Authors: My main problem with this paper is that I find some elementary findings eating too much space at the cost of interesting things that ended up overly terse. For example, one can sum up virtually all of Section 3 by the 80/20 rule - a small number of heavy users, along all dimensions, while everything else is intermittent. Do you really need 4 pages for that? Most of the paper is similarly one-dimensional.

When it matters, I found things brief and superficial. Your analysis of barter and banking systems for resource management, while interesting, feels quite simplistic. I feel that instead of adding a plot for virtually every paragraph of text, the paper would be a more productive experience for the reader if you had left out a good handful of plots and instead integrated analyses that go a bit beyond your dataset.

I disagree with your suggested expectation of a Tragedy of the Commons in PlanetLab. That model simply does not apply. General lack of resource-hogging is very much what I expected to see, simply from PlanetLab's intended purpose.

It would really help if instead of the overlong Sections 3 and 4 you put in a little more background on PlanetLab. If it is clear from the outset that experimenters pick nodes manually, you are eliminating a lot of the guesswork.

I find Figures 11 and 12 unsurprising. It seems unreasonable to expect a single site to contribute equal amounts of resources as it consumes in the entire remaining network, so clearly the slop fraction is highest. Surely you could come up with better banking schemes that factor this imbalance into the budget earning/spending calculation?

I do not understand your definition of bank. A provides resources in its nodes, and consumes resources elsewhere. Why is "bank" the minimum of the two, and not the difference? Any normal balance can be positive or negative. Did you just pick really unfortunate terminology?

I don't understand Figure 13. So PlanetLab's available CPU capacity was around 1,800 CPU-days per day, throughout. You also have the CPU consumptions accumulating at each node over the course of a month. I see no explanation on how the limits you mention would result in the curves you show. Is this simulation, as you are mentioning it in the next paragraph? I find the rest of that section too compressed to follow.

In Section 6.2 you refer back to Section 3, stating that you discussed how experiments follow the guideline of testing in-the-small and expanding gradually for d-day. You do not actually show that; you say it is true for one slice doing IPOP experiments (in Sec. 3.3).

Figure 23 is not surprising. If a program spins instead of blocking on I/O or otherwise behaving "nicely", then obviously its CPU contribution skyrockets.

It would have been nice to see some orthogonal analyses. For example, do people signing up actually run experiments? How often do they succeed in deploying something long-running? How often was that actually the goal? PlanetLab requires experimental descriptions for the studies it hosts. Does this fit with high CPU consumption at all? I.e., do they suggest obvious bugs, or are they openly declared CPU crunching?

Reviewer #4

Strengths: Fantastic dataset; thorough analysis of resource usage and slice classes; resource management in federated distributed testbeds is an important and persistent problem.

Weaknesses: Nothing obvious.

Comments to Authors: This is a great piece with many interesting findings on the use of PlanetLab and the effectiveness of policies and potential algorithms. There are a few issues with the presentation here and there, but all of them could be addressed in a camera-ready version.

It is surprising not to see references to all the work done in cluster-based and grid systems in you related work section (and only one in your overall reference list); particularly given your comments about how this is different from what you see in PlanetLab. A quick web search points to Hart's paper on measuring TeraGrid, which would seem appropriate even if to say how they were different. What is the length of the measurement period (less than 5', I know, but what). Is 0.1% CPU utilization a magic number? Seems alright to me but I tend to dislike these sort of constants.

There seem to be a neat shift in CPU usage over the three years and I wonder if there is a learning process there.

Fig 5 took me a while partially due to the short and unclear discussion and the heavy reliance on color. The reading of slices with more than 200 nodes helps a bit but it may be better to pick another point as well, perhaps the 200 slices that use over 200 nodes 50% of the time (or something like that).

"fly in the face of the common expectations" seems to be a bit too strong; if you are going to make this claim I think you should have references to work arguing this. It is either that or you soften your lines. And you probably want to speak 'of common expectations' and not 'of the common expectations'.

I agree with the reading in p. 8-9 about the effectiveness of different resource management systems. It is surprising and a bit disappointing, however, that a service aimed to the whole research community seems to be driven by a small set of synchronized deadlines.

I really like the analysis of Sec. 5.2, particularly the simulation-based study of alternative placement policies.

The paper seems to need a summary of findings as a way of closing a long list of interesting findings. For instance, I would like to see there a discussion of how your observations can be generalize to other federated systems and what would be the potential issues with those generalizations.

Reviewer #5

Strengths: Extensive characterization of resource usage based on long term and detailed measurement.

Weaknesses: Implications of some of the findings are not clear.

Comments to Authors: The paper examines a wide range of characteristics of resource usage. Overall, this paper is well organized and well written. The main issue for this reviewer is the limited discussion on the implications of some of the findings.

Response from the Authors

Most of the comments that we received from the reviewers were questions about our measurement results presented in the paper. We revised our descriptions of the results to answer those questions and make them clearer. To address the comment "...anecdotal evidence that people manually choose nodes because many nodes are inherently unreliable.", we added a new result in Section 5 to show that PlanetLab users seemingly avoid nodes in exhibiting various failure modes. At the same time, we also demonstrated other biases that may not be entirely appropriate. For a deeper analysis of bartering/banking systems, we extended the analysis by adding resource routing to bartering system. We discussed the effectiveness of the resource routing in PlanetLab by comparing the enhanced bartering with simple pair-wise resource exchange in Section 4. Besides resource consumption, we analyzed each site's usage of network reach in terms of remote sites and continents. The added result helps better explain the usage patterns seen and the reason why a tragedy of commons is not visible in PlanetLab.

vPF_RING: Towards Wire-Speed Network Monitoring Using Virtual Machines

Alfredo Cardigliano[1]
Luca Deri[1,2]
ntop[1], IIT-CNR[2]
Pisa, Italy
{cardigliano, deri}@ntop.org

Joseph Gasparakis
Intel Corporation
Hillsboro, USA
joseph.gasparakis@intel.com

Francesco Fusco
IBM Research
Rüschlikon, Switzerland
ffu@zurich.ibm.com

ABSTRACT

The demand of highly flexible and easy to deploy network monitoring systems has pushed companies toward software based network monitoring probes implemented with commodity hardware rather than with expensive and highly specialized network devices. Deploying software probes under virtual machines executed on the same physical box is attractive for reducing deployment costs and for simplifying the management of advanced network monitoring architectures built on top of heterogeneous monitoring tools (i.e. Intrusion Detection Systems and Performance Monitoring Systems). Unfortunately, software probes are usually not able to meet the performance requirements when deployed in virtualized environments as virtualization introduces severe performance bottlenecks when performing packet capture, which is the core activity of passive network monitoring systems.

This paper covers the design and implementation of vPF_RING, a novel framework for efficiently capturing packets on virtual machines running on commodity hardware. This solution allows network administrators to exploit the benefits of virtualization such as reduced costs and centralized administration, while preserving the ability to capture packets at wire speed even when deploying applications in virtual machines. The validation process has demonstrated that this solution can be profitably used for multi-gigabit network monitoring, paving the way to low-cost virtualized monitoring systems.

Categories and Subject Descriptors

C.2.2 [**Computer-Communication Networks**]: Network Protocols—Measurement; C.2.3 [**Network Operations**]: Network monitoring—Performance.

General Terms

Measurement, Performance.

Keywords

Virtualization, Packet Capture, Passive Traffic Monitoring.

1. INTRODUCTION AND MOTIVATION

In the past years, one of the industry trends is to optimize rack space and power consumption while simplifying administration by migrating physical servers onto Virtual Machines (VMs).

In the context of network monitoring, the idea of running multiple monitoring systems on independent VMs deployed on the same physical box is definitely appealing. By running software probes in virtualized environment network administrator can delegate certain tasks (i.e. performance management) to third persons, each having full access and control over specific virtual machines. VMs are often used for implementing monitoring on demand: namely activate monitoring facilities on specific network locations whenever certain network conditions happen (e.g. security alert). In addition, virtualization provides substantial deployment benefits in all the cases where multiple monitoring applications require access to the entire (or a subset of) the network traffic for performing different analysis tasks. By running heterogeneous monitoring software on the same box the complexity of deploying systems responsible to simultaneously dispatch the traffic towards multiple network analysis boxes can be completely avoided.

Since traffic splitting or dispatching is usually implemented by deploying advanced hardware based multi-port network taps and management networks, virtualization in the context of network monitoring allows to substantially reduce the deployment costs of advanced multi-probe monitoring architectures.

Unfortunately, running multiple monitoring systems in virtualized environments is desirable but not yet a common practice mostly due to the severe performance bottlenecks that virtualization introduces in application performing network monitoring. The most critical performance bottleneck introduced by virtualization when used for network monitoring is caused by the inefficient implementation of packet capture, which is the most important building block for most network monitoring applications. In fact, passive network monitoring systems strongly depends on packet capture, which is the process of accessing the stream of packets flowing on a network link. The packet stream is captured for performing several tasks, including network troubleshooting, traffic accounting, security breaches detection, and performance monitoring. Depending on the number of monitoring systems and on their nature, the same packet have to be captured several times. For instance an intrusion detection system (IDS) and a traffic accounting application might need the same packets for accomplishing their respective monitoring tasks. Depending on the criteria these systems use for classifying traffic [1], they might be interested in capturing all packets independently from their nature and content, or only a subset of packets that match specific filtering rules (e.g. all UDP packets sent by server 192.168.1.1) usually specified using BPF filters [2] or hardware-assisted filtering rules supported by modern network adapters [21].

The following figure shows the packet capture performance (packets are just captured and not processed) of a single VM running on a Kernel-based Virtual Machine (KVM) [3] while capturing packets using VirtIO-Net [4] on a quad-core Xeon system.

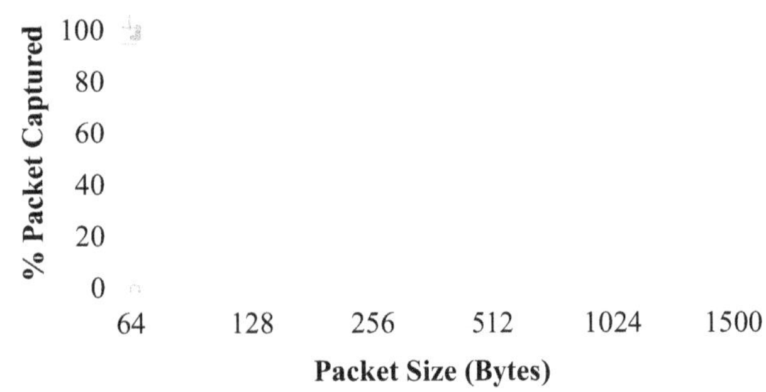

Figure 1. Packet Capture Rate at 1Gbit using KVM

Since packet capture performance under a KVM virtualized host is poor for small packets and acceptable only for medium/large packets, KVM virtual machines are not suitable for running network monitoring applications.

In the past years, the authors have developed PF_RING [5] [45], a Linux kernel module implementing a framework that can be profitably used for simplifying the development of efficient monitoring applications requiring high speed packet capture. PF_RING substantially accelerates packet capture under the Linux operating system and for this reason is widely used on specific field such as for accelerating IDS/IPS and for passively monitoring network traffic using flow-based tools. Unfortunately, the framework does not provide packet capture acceleration under virtualized environments. In this work, we introduce virtual PF_RING (vPF_RING), an high performance packet capture solution optimized for virtualized environments that solves the performance bottlenecks present in KVM when used for deploying multiple monitoring applications on the same physical box. To improve the packet capture performance the authors capitalize on vNPlug, a novel framework that provides hypervisor bypass.

The rest of the paper is structured as follows. In section 2, we discuss how networking has changed with the advent of virtual machines. In section 3, we cover the design of vNPlug a framework that implements support for hypervisor-bypass. In section 4, we describe how vNPlug has been successfully used to create vPF_RING, an extension of PF_RING for virtualized environments. Finally in section 5, vPF_RING performance is evaluated.

2. RELATED WORK

2.1 Networking in Virtual Machines

Virtualization is appealing for the industry as it simplifies administrative tasks, while reducing costs and increasing scalability [29] [40]. In the past few years there have been many efforts to improve network performance on VMs [33] [34], both with hardware [37] and software solutions [36]. However, with the only exception of Endace, which offers the virtual DAG capture device (vDAG [18]), there are no other companies addressing the problem of using VMs for high-performance network monitoring but just for general network operations. A popular solution for bypassing the hypervisor during network operations is to map the network adapters directly inside the VM such as VMware VMDirectPath [31] [43]. We believe that this solution is sub-optimal for traffic monitoring because:

- Each VM would need a physical network port, thus increasing:
- Each VM would need a physical network port, thus increasing:
    - The operational costs due to the need of private per-VM ports.
    - The number of monitoring ports.
    - The complexity required during live VM migration and reconfiguration, being each VM bound to a specific network port on which traffic to be analyzed is received.
- If multiple VMs running on the same host need to analyze the same traffic with different goals (e.g. run a VM with an IDS and another VM with a NetFlow probe), it is necessary to use specialized hardware for duplicating the packets to be dispatched to each adapter.
- As packet capture is a costly activity in terms of CPU cycles required, capturing the same packet multiple times on various VMs running on the same hosts is more expensive than capturing the packet once and dispatching it to multiple VMs especially when having high throughputs and small packets.
- As hardware adapters are accessed directly by VMs, it is necessary to install native drivers into the guests, adding an extra constrain to live migration with respect to virtualized adapters.
- Physical and virtual IRQ sharing, and device assignment dependencies [43] can jeopardize the performance of the system and make this solution effective only on specialized servers.

Paravirtualization [19] has been the first attempt to reduce the overhead of emulating real network devices. By implementing paravirtualization, the guest operating system is aware of being virtualized, and cooperates with the hypervisor to virtualize the underlying hardware. In other words, the guest uses custom drivers that use a direct path for communicating with the hypervisor. Taking the example of VirtIO-Net [4], the paravirtualized network device in KVM, the burden on the hypervisor is reduced, and some optimizations, such as the VHost-Net support, attempt to reduce the number of system calls thus improving latency. Unfortunately the packet journey is not reduced as packets flow through virtual bridges and virtual TAP devices, and twice through the operating system.

Recently, network equipments manufactures have introduced technologies for enhancing networking on virtualized environments. For example, some Intel server class network interface cards (NICs) implement the Intel VMDq (Virtual Machine Device Queues) technology [8]. To abstract the network device and share it across multiple VMs, the hypervisor has to implement a software network switch, which usually introduce severe performance penalties. As shown in Figure 2, VMDq-aware NICs implement all this in hardware thus preventing the in-software switching overhead. By combining this technology with optimized paravirtualization techniques, it is possible to achieve high networking performance in VMs [9] [10]. Unfortunately packet capture cannot benefit from it, as VMDq basically partitions the NIC into several virtual NICs but it does not feature mechanisms for:

- Accelerating packet capture.
- Capturing packets from all virtual queues, rather than from just the one assigned to the VM.

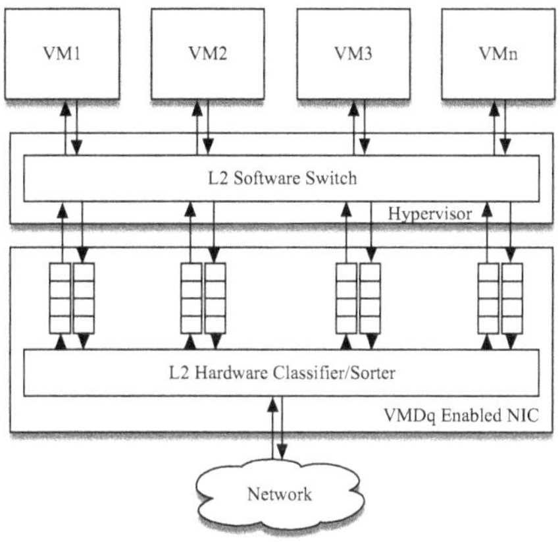

Figure 2. Intel VMDq Technology

Along the path of VMDq, the Single Root I/O Virtualization technology [11] is a way of sharing a device in a virtualized environment, bypassing the hypervisor involvement in data movement. As depicted in Figure 3, with this technology a single Ethernet port can be configured by the hypervisor to appear as multiple independent devices, each one with its own configuration space. The hypervisor assigns each Virtual Function (VF, lightweight PCIe functions) to a VM, providing independent memory space and DMA streams. PCIe PF (Physical Functions) is the physical device seen by the hypervisor on the host. Memory address translation technologies based on IOMMUs [12] [13], such as Intel VT-d [14] and AMD IOMMU, provide hardware assisted techniques to allow direct DMA transfers bypassing the hypervisor, while keeping isolation between host and VMs [30].

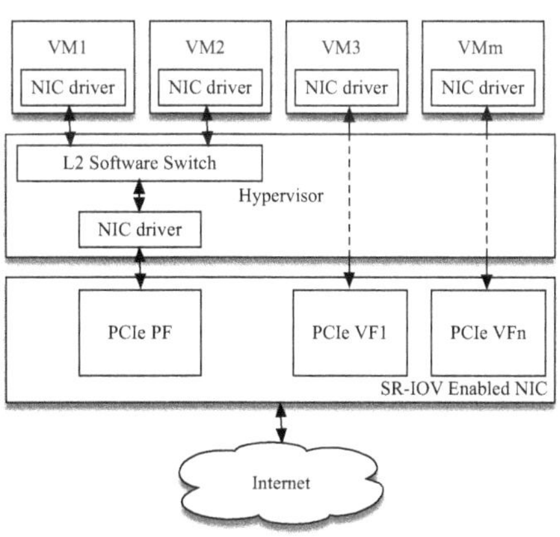

Figure 3. SR-IOV Technology

There are several projects following the same approach of the SR-IOV, with different designs of self-virtualized devices for direct I/O [15] [16] [17]. All these techniques represent good solutions for common connectivity but, besides efficiency, they do not provide assistance in accelerating packet capture.

2.2 Packet Filtering

The previous section has shown various alternatives to implement efficient networking inside VMs. With paravirtualization, packets pass through virtual bridges and virtual TAP devices if hardware support such as VMDq is not present. Using VMDq-aware network devices or self-virtualized devices [11] [15] [16] [17], packet filtering still happens in software as hardware filtering used by VMDq usually provides only MAC-address filtering and thus in-NIC bridging that is disabled when the NIC is set in promiscuous mode. The result is that both with/without VMDq, packet filtering has to happen in software as modern NICs do not provide assistance for filtering packets when used in virtualized environments.

Early packet filtering is necessary to prevent packets from being discarded late in their journey to the VM, after that they have passed through several components. This is because filtering on guest OS means that the packet has already reached the VM and thus that in case of packet not satisfying any filter it would result in wasted CPU cycles.

Another side effect of in-VM filtering, is that all received packets need to be copied to each VM, whereas in case of early filtering, just the packets matching the filters will be forwarded to VMs.

For specific application domains such as lawful interception, filtering at the VM level represents a major performance issue. This is because network operators usually provide a shadow copy of all packets flowing through a link where several hundred users are connected, but only a small portion of them belong to users that need to be intercepted; the result is that most packets will be discarded except those belonging to the targets (i.e. those users that are being intercepted). This problem is even more visible if the same input traffic needs to be passed to various VMs, each performing a different type of analysis. For this reason early packet discard on the physical machine is very important as it avoid VMs to be over flood with packets that will be discarded later on. Lawful interception is a good example where the physical host receives all packets, and it both filters and dispatches to the VMs only those packets matching the individual filters set by each VM.

A possible solution to the problem is to replace virtual bridges with virtual switches such as Open vSwitch [26] [27]. Open vSwitch implements standard Ethernet switching, while providing high flexibility with full control on the forwarding table by implementing a superset of the OpenFlow protocol [28]. However, as mentioned in [26], the problem is that these switches cause high CPU utilization when switching packets, so latency and overhead of the paravirtualization solutions increases. On the contrary, hardware based OpenFlow switches [42], can potentially offload the VMs from packet filtering. This approach allows the load on VMs introduced by packet filtering to be reduced [29] [41], but limits the flexibility offered by virtualized environments (e.g. the migration of VM across physical machines is compromised) and limits filtering to what is offered by the switches.

In order to implement efficient VM filtering, it is necessary to discard packets in the physical machine as close as possible to the physical NIC. This way, only packets matching the filtering rules will continue their journey to the VMs, whereas others will be dropped immediately as depicted in Figure 4. In a nutshell, early packet filtering in the context of network monitoring is a key requirement for achieving a high performance.

Discarding packets on the physical machine leveraging on the PF_RING filtering support would be very useful in security when IDS (Intrusion Detection Systems) are used. We have developed a PF_RING module, part of the PF_RING code distribution, for the popular snort IDS named PF_RING DAQ (Data AcQuisition library) [46]. This module is responsible for receiving packets from PF_RING and dispatching them to snort. For each packet, snort emits a verdict that can be drop/pass and also white/black-list. In the latter case, it would be very desirable to have a snort instance running on a VM able to set filtering rules inside the PF_RING kernel module running on the physical host by means of this DAQ module. The advantage is that unwanted packets/flows are discarded by PF_RING and never hit the VM. This would be a great advantage of early packet discarding that we want to offer inside the vPF_RING framework.

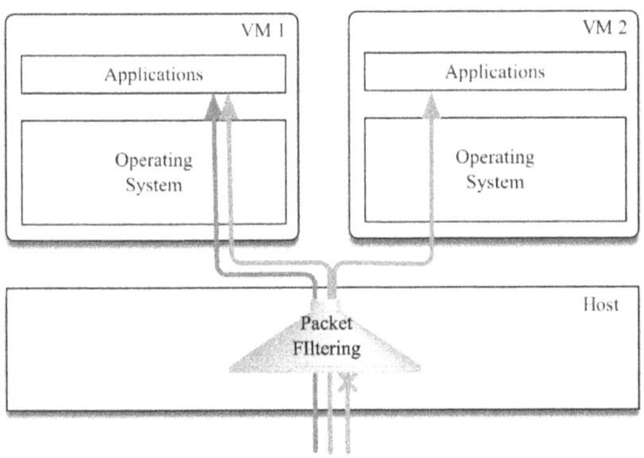

Figure 4. Early Packet Filtering

2.3 PF_RING and Operating System Bypass

PF_RING is a kernel-based extensible traffic analysis framework, that significantly improves the performance of packet capture. It reduces the journey of captured packets from wire to user-space, and features a flexible packet filtering system and an extensible plugin-based architecture for adding new functionality at runtime.

PF_RING can use both vanilla Linux drivers and PF_RING-aware drivers. The main difference is that the latter can push captured packets directly to the PF_RING kernel module thus reducing the packet journey with respect to Linux native packet capture. PF_RING supports a rich set of packet filtering mechanisms that allow users to specify actions (e.g. dump a packet to disk), whenever incoming packets match the filtering rules. It also supports hardware filtering and packet steering capabilities when packet capture happens on modern network adapters, such as the Intel 82599 [21] and the Silicom PE210G2RS [22]. With those adapters packets are filtered inside the NIC without any assistance from the main CPU as it happen with software packet filtering. Hardware and software packet filtering, allow efficient applications processing packets directly inside the kernel to be easily implemented. Kernel based packet processing is more efficient than user-space packet processing as packets do not have to be copied from kernel to user-space in case they don't match any configured filter.

The PF_RING framework provides a user-space library that exposes an easy-to-use API for implementing monitoring applications. As depicted in Figure 5, through this library, ring buffers on which PF_RING is based, are directly mapped from kernel-space into user-space by using *mmap()*, reducing overheads and the number of data copies.

When an application wants to read a new packet, the library checks the ring:

- If there are new packets available, they get processed immediately.
- When no packets are found, a *poll()* is called in order to wait for new packets. When the *poll()* returns, the library checks again the ring for new packets.

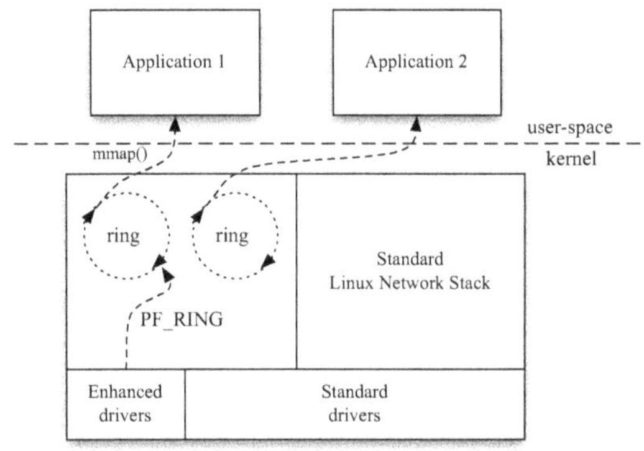

Figure 5. PF_RING Architecture

In order to reduce the number of *poll()* calls and thus a continuous *poll()*-wake up-*poll()* transition, the PF_RING kernel module implements a dynamic polling mechanism that can be configured by packet capture applications. The *poll()* system call returns when at least X packets are available, where X can range from one to several thousand, or when the call times out, usually this is set to 10 msec. This mechanism allows CPU cycles to be preserved for those applications that do not need to process packet immediately, but it also enables low-latency applications to be implemented setting X to one.

As described above, the approach followed by PF_RING is to create a straight path for packets bypassing the operating system standard mechanisms by means of a memory-map from kernel-space to the address space of the monitoring application. With this solution, system calls other than the *poll()* are completely avoided. The operating system bypass approach is adopted in many research projects [23] [24] as well as commercial products such as those manufactured by companies such as Endace and Napatech, most of all in areas requiring intense I/O activity, and where low latency and high bandwidth are vital.

2.4 Hypervisor Bypass

The hypervisor involvement in all the VM I/O accesses ensures isolation and system integrity, 4uti t also leads to longer latency and higher overhead compared to native I/O accesses in non-virtualized environments, thus becoming a bottleneck for I/O intensive workloads.

In this paper, we propose a model that extends the PF_RING's operating system bypass approach to the context of virtual environments, thus creating a direct mapping between the host kernel-space and the guest user-space. This approach aims to perform operations that require intensive workloads such as packet capture using a direct VM-to-physical host path, without the involvement of the hypervisor except during the setup phase. It is worth to note that as in native PF_RING, this does not mean that the hypervisor is completely bypassed in all operations, but just for those that are computationally expensive such as packet capture while it is still used for implementing packet polling. In this view, hypervisor overhead does not affect packet capture performance because this component is fully bypassed when packets are read from the PF_RING ring sitting on the host.

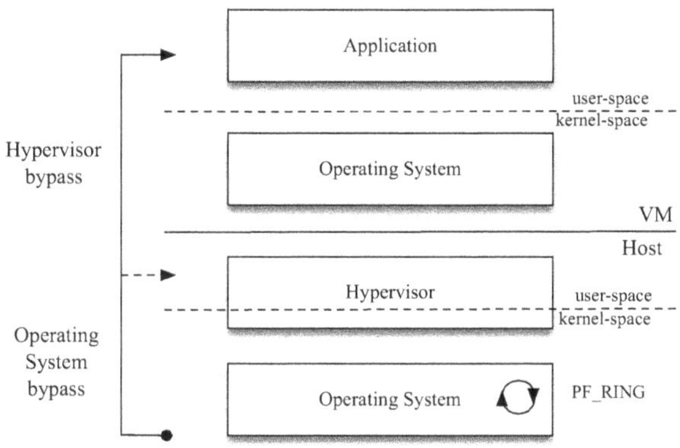

Figure 6. Hypervisor Bypass

The hypervisor-bypass approach is not a novel idea: self-virtualized devices for direct I/O, such as SR-IOV [35] capable ones, are an example. There are also some studies in the context of High Performance Computing (HPC) [6] [7] that have demonstrated that the hypervisor-bypass method can represent a very good solution in order to remove bottlenecks in systems with high I/O demands, especially those equipped with modern low latency and high bandwidth network interconnects.

3. vPF_RING DESIGN PRINCIPLES

In this section, we present the design and implementation of Virtual PF_RING (vPF_RING), that is based on vNPlug, a framework implementing the hypervisor-bypass, also developed by the authors. Although the work presented on this paper addresses general issues that are not dependent on a specific virtualization framework, the authors focus only on KVM as it leverages Linux kernel capabilities, such as scheduling and memory management. KVM is a small and relatively simple software, present out-of-the-box on the majority of Linux distributions, contrary to other similar solutions such as Xen that is not integrated into the mainstream kernel. Proprietary solutions such as VMware [38], which is widely accepted in the industry, have not been taken into account due to their license restrictions and because of the source code not being open and available [20].

KVM implements a kernel-based virtual machine on top of the Linux kernel, and exploits a modified version of QEMU [25] for emulating I/O devices. Implemented as kernel module, KVM supports native code execution by exploiting hardware virtualization extensions such as Intel VT and AMD Secure Virtual Machine. Common tasks, such as scheduling and memory management, are delegated to the Linux kernel. VMs run as conventional user-space processes making Linux unaware of dealing with a virtual system.

vPF_RING, described later in section 3.2, does not strictly depend on KVM but it mostly relies on PF_RING APIs. Instead, as described in the next section, the vNPlug framework has been designed on top of KVM for implementing the hypervisor-bypass approach (mapping memory, exchanging control messages, notifying events). Porting vNPlug to another hypervisor such as Xen, requires a complete code rewrite, contrary to the vPF_RING code that should not be modified.

3.1 vNPlug Framework

The vNPlug framework exploits the hypervisor-bypass approach for achieving high packet capture performance in virtualized environments. It has been designed to be general enough for being used by every monitoring application and not just vPF_RING. For instance, the Linux native socket type PF_PACKET is quite similar to PF_RING as both use memory mapped buffers to exchange packets between kernel and user-space. Porting PF_PACKET on top of vPF_RING-vNPlug is thus just a matter of time as it does not seem to have any technical challenge being the two socket types pretty similar.

The framework follows a paravirtualization-like design, guests are aware of being virtualized and consequently the architecture is logically split in a guest and an host side block.
The framework is logically divided into two main components. The first component, *vNPlug-Dev*, is responsible for:

- Mapping memory between the host kernel-space and the guest user-space.
- Implementing an efficient event notification that is necessary for VM/Host communications.

The second component, *vNPlug-CTRL*, is responsible for coordinating the host and guest side of applications by means of a control communication channel. The channel is required, for example, when an application needs to instrument its host-side back-end for filtering specific packets.

As can be seen, applications built on top of the framework can access physical host resources that are usually not available in virtualized environments. In case of vPF_RING, applications executed under VMs can capture packets not only from VM's network interfaces, but also from physical host interfaces. This feature can be offered by building vPF_RING on top of the vNPlug framework.

vNPlug is implemented as a QEMU patch on the host side, and a Linux kernel module (vnplug.ko), based on both vNPlug-Dev and vNPlug-CTRL components, on the guest OS.

3.1.1 vNPlug-Dev

The original PF_RING maps kernel ring buffers to user-space via memory-map. vNPlug-Dev allows to further memory-map these virtual memory areas to virtual machines. The initial memory-mapping happens through the hypervisor, whereas all packets are exchanged directly between the VM and the PF_RING sitting on the host without any hypervisor support. This mapping is performed dynamically attaching additional blocks of memory via virtual PCI devices whenever a vPF_RING is created. Inside the VM, these memory regions can be accessed by *ioremap()*, and mapped in virtual memory areas via the vnplug.ko kernel module that creates character devices that can be memory-mapped. Figure 7 depicts the vNPlug-Dev architecture.

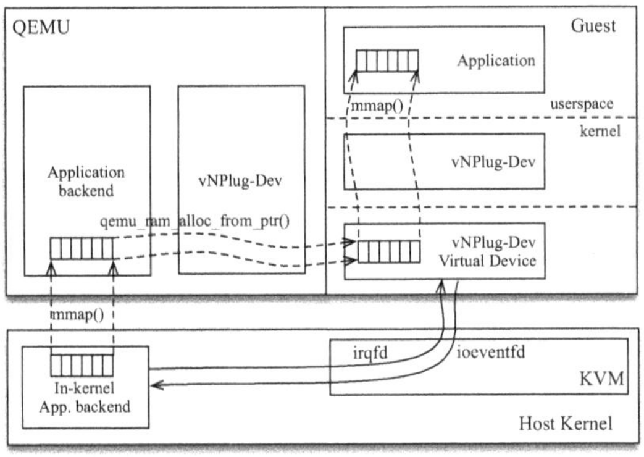

Figure 7. vNPlug-Dev Architecture

vNPlug-Dev is dynamic by design as it allows dynamic memory-mapping to take place by means of virtual PCI devices. Therefore, the number of rings is not limited as it happens, for instance, in BSD systems where packets are captured from a limited number of statically allocated capture devices (/dev/bpfX).

The PCI hotplug support allows devices to be dynamically attached and removed from a running system. Even if hotplug is rarely used in practice, basic hotplug support is provided by the majority of modern operating systems, making hot-plugged devices immediately usable with limited effort. By exploiting the hotplug, it is possible to dynamically attach memory mappings to guests whenever necessary, making vPF_RING a very flexible system that does not have any limitation in terms of functionality and flexibility with respect to native PF_RING.

The event signaling functionality of the framework takes advantage of the *irqfd* and *ioeventfd* supports of KVM in order to provide a two-way notification mechanism, from host-to-guest and from guest-to-host. Both of them are based on the *eventfd* file descriptor for event notification, that is quite powerful yet flexible as it can be used from both user-space and kernel-space in order to signal/wait events.

Using the *irqfd* support it is possible to send interrupts to the VM without passing through the QEMU process, which is responsible to emulate the device on which interrupts are dispatched. In fact, since virtual interrupts are injected to the guest via KVM, the *irqfd* support allows the latter to directly translate a signal on an *eventfd* into an interrupt, thus ensuring efficiency. At the same time, the MSI (Message Signaled Interrupt) support ensures flexibility, by using multiple vectors that simplifies the notification mechanism when several events are required. On the guest side, the framework has been inspired by the *eventfd* approach that uses a blocking *read()* on a character device for notifying user-space applications that an interrupt has been received.

ioeventfd is used to register arbitrary addresses of a MMIO (Memory-Mapped I/O) region belonging to a virtual device, along with a unique value and an *eventfd*. On the guest side, these MMIO regions are mapped in user-space. Whenever the guest OS writes a value to such MMIO region, if the written value matches the registered value, then an event is triggered on the corresponding *eventfd*. This mechanism is quite efficient as it allows a lightweight exit (long enough to signal an *eventfd* in kernel-space by means of a KVM service routine), while a normal I/O operation on an emulated virtual device requires a costly VM exit.

3.1.2 vNPlug-CTRL

The component implements a message based communication channel that allows control messages to be exchanged between the guest side of the monitoring application and its back-end. For instance it can be used by an application to request the back-end to setup a new memory-mapping, or to filter packets.

The vNPlug-CTRL component has been introduced for having a control channel totally independent from network communications, and, as such, not susceptible to unintentional network configuration changes.

As depicted in Figure 8, the vNPlug-CTRL component implementation is based on the VirtIO interface for paravirtualization that is efficient and ensures low response times, but required a little more effort at development time compared to a network communication implementation. The two-way communication channel over VirtIO uses two *virtqueue's*, one for host-to-guest messages and one for the opposite direction. In order to send and receive messages from the guest user-space, the framework exposes common file operations (*read* and *write*) on a character device.

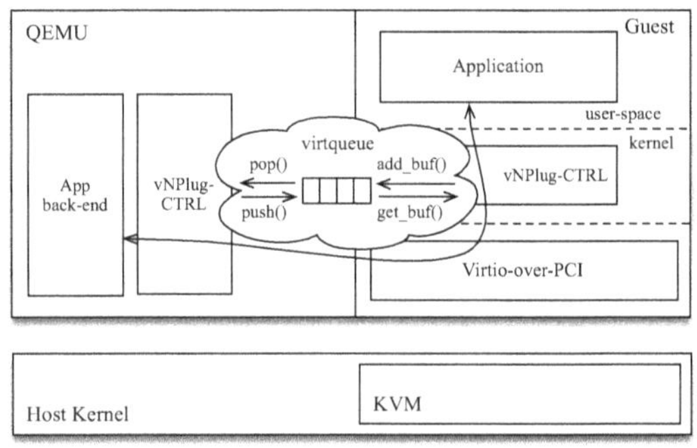

Figure 8. vNPlug-CTRL Component

Through this communication channel, the framework routes messages between the host-side and guest-side of applications. As multiple applications are supported, each with multiple virtual devices, the framework uses a minimal and yet efficient protocol stack, depicted in Figure 9. At the bottom of the stack, the VirtIO transport mechanism takes place, providing a two-way point-to-point communication channel between the two sides of the framework: guest and host side. At the second layer, a framework-level header allows the framework to distinguish between messages addressed to itself and those addressed to an application. At the third layer, an application-level header allows the framework to identify the application to which such message has to be delivered. From the fourth layer on, all is managed by the application, in order to identify internal operations and address virtual devices.

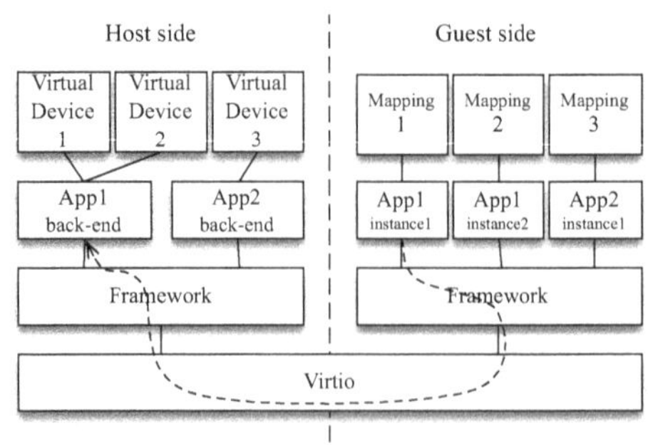

Figure 9. vNPlug-CTRL Message Routing

3.1.3 vNPlug API

In order to simplify the development of monitoring applications, the framework provides a simple API, that implements an abstraction layer on top of the implemented functions. Framework's components get abstracted through two subsets of the interface: the host side API and the guest side API.

The main features the interface provides:

- Host Side
  - Registration and unregistration of the application back-end.
  - Control messages reception and transmission.
  - Virtual devices, for memory-mapping, creation and tear-down.
- Guest Side
  - Control messages transmission and reception.
  - Shared memory-mapping and unmapping in the virtual address space of the application.
  - Event signaling/waiting functionalities.

3.2 vPF_RING

vPF_RING is an extension of PF_RING for virtualized environments built on top of vNPlug. The design of original PF_RING lent itself particularly well to be adapted to the vNPlug framework. In fact, on the host side, it only needed a few enhancements, keeping both the kernel module and the user-space library fully backward-compatible with the original version. As the PF_RING library uses memory-mapping for exporting the packet capture ring from kernel-space into user-space, the virtual memory address returned by *mmap()* can be used by the framework to map it into the guest. In a nutshell, PF_RING is responsible for making this memory area available to the guest user-space.

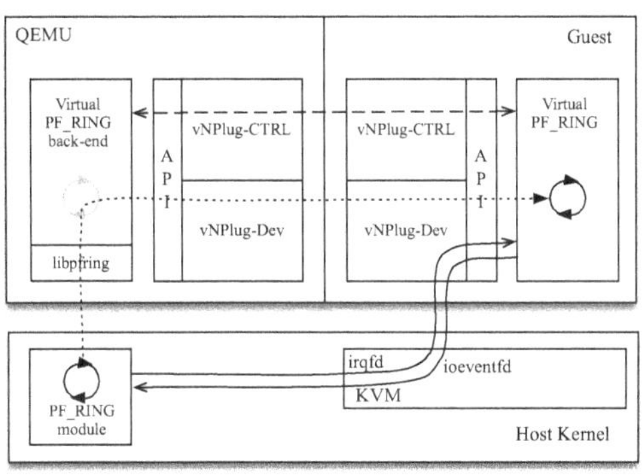

Figure 10. vPF_RING Design

The two-way event signaling support of the framework has been used for replacing the *poll()* calls used by PF_RING applications for being waken-up when new incoming packets are available. When an application on the guest-side has to read a new packet, but no packets are ready to be read, the library on the guest-side informs the host side. This way, the host-side knows that if there are unread packets, or when a new one arrives, it has to send an interrupt to the guest-side that is waiting for packets. Furthermore an algorithm similar to the adaptive sleep of the PF_RING native library is used, in order to avoid many *poll*-equivalent calls.

A new and thin library has been created on the guest-side for:

- Translating each call to the PF_RING library into control messages over the communication channel provided by the framework.
- Memory-mapping and event signaling/waiting mechanisms just described.

The vPF_RING back-end on the host-side, is also responsible of translating guest-to-host control messages into calls to the PF_RING library. It allows monitoring applications running on guests to:

- Read packets from kernel via memory-map and not through read() system calls as it happens with VirtIO.
- Access host network interfaces in addition to guest network interfaces.
- Setup packet capture filters directory on the host PF_RING, thus implementing early packet filtering.
- Seamlessly develop applications, that can run unchanged both on physical or virtualized environments, easing the move towards a virtualized monitoring environment.

In a nutshell vPF_RING has been designed to be transparent to application developers, both in terms of features and packet capture speed. The only visible difference is the device name from which packets are captured. With native PF_RING it is possible to capture packets just from physical interfaces. Using vPF_RING, it is possible to capture packets from both the VM's virtual Ethernet device, and the physical host interface. In the former case, vPF_RING operates as PF_RING when capturing packets from a host adapter (in this case from the VM virtual adapter). In the latter case, vPF_RING is not capturing from the VM's interface but from the host's physical interface. As vPF_RING's API is unchanged with respect to PF_RING, a special device naming convention has been used in order to instruct the framework to capture packets from the host interface. This is because host interfaces are not visible to the VM via standard Linux commands such as ifconfig, and also because interface name present on both the VM and host might be the same (e.g. eth0). For this reason in vPF_RING the following naming convention has been used: interface names with a "host:" prefix indicate host interface. For instance when a VM opens "eth0" it means that it wants to open the virtual VM eth0 interface; instead "host:eth0" means the eth0 physical host interface.

vPF_RING honors all PF_RING capture extensions. For instance applications can capture traffic from a specific RX queue of a multi-queue adapter when using PF_RING-aware driver [32], and specify filtering and packet steering rules in hardware on adapters such as Intel 82599 [21]. On one hand, these are interesting features to have as for instance a VM having to analyze HTTP traffic, can capture traffic on RX queue X on which it has configured a hardware filter that sends to such queue only HTTP packets. On the other hand, like most kernel bypass technologies (e.g. the same PF_RING), must be used properly as they circumvent some protection mechanisms, such as the insulation of the VM from host environment.

4. vPF_RING VALIDATION

vPF_RING validation and performance evaluation tests have been performed on a simple test bed, where an IXIA 400 traffic generator has been used for sending packets to a server powered by an Intel Xeon X3440, running Linux kernel 2.6.36 and equipped with a dual Intel 82576 Gigabit Ethernet controller. The IXIA 400 traffic generator is connected to the server via the two gigabit ports, and can generate network traffic at configurable rates, including the wire-rate, on both port regardless of the packet size. For 10 Gigabit tests we have used a home-grown tool named *pfsend* with PF_RING DNA (Direct NIC Access) [47] for reproducing traffic at wire speed previously captured on a network backbone. This has allowed us to test vPF_RING under various conditions and with both synthetic and real network traffic. For the tests described later on this section, have been used forged packets in order to evaluate this work with different packet rates and sizes.

The performance of vPF_RING has been compared with the performance of native PF_RING 4.6.x running on a physical (non virtualized) host and PF_RING running on a virtual KVM environment (using the VirtIO-Net support with the VHost-Net optimization). vPF_RING performance has also been positionedagainst VMware ESXi (using VMXNET 3, the latest version available of the VMware paravirtualized network device). All the VMs used during the evaluation have a single-core virtual CPU and also run Linux kernel version 2.6.36.

The device driver used on the server on the host-side is the *igb*, developed by Intel, which is included in the Linux kernel. It is worth to remark that, although PF_RING supports PF_RING-aware optimized drivers to bypass the standard operating system's mechanisms, we decided not to use them in order to evaluate our work on the worst case (i.e. without any packet capture acceleration exploiting specific network cards features). This is because we want to compare native VirtIO-Net agains vPF_RING, without accounting any vPF_RING performance benefit due to these optimized drivers.

Before describing the evaluating results, it is important to understand how the packet size affects the benchmarks. This parameter is relevant because the maximum packet rate that can be injected on a link depends on the packet size. As shown in Table 1, at wire-rate, small packet sizes corresponds tohigher packet rates. The packet capture performance is affected by the packet rate, which can be as high as 1.4 Million of packets per seconds (Mpps) when the packet size is 64 bytes (minimum packet size) on Gigabit links, 14.880 Mpps on 10 Gigabit.

Table 1. Maximum Packet Rates

Line Speed	Rates Per Frame Size (Kpps)				
	64 Byte	128 Byte	256 Byte	512 Byte	1024 Byte
1 Gigabit	1488	844	452	234	119
10 Gigabit	14880	8445	4528	2349	1197

Another aspect worth to mention, is that with vPF_RING it is possible to use efficient packet filtering techniques within the host (in kernel-space or even in hardware), to further increase the performance. In fact, through the efficient communication channel provided by the vNPlug-CTRL component, vPF_RING is capable to instrument the PF_RING module for setting a variety of efficient filters. However, as we are interested in evaluating our work in the worst case scenario, packet filtering has not been used.

Benchmarks have been done using *pfcount*, a simple packet capture application implemented on top of the PF_RING API. The application captures packets, updates some statistics, and then discards packets without doing any further processing.

In the first test we evaluate the packet capture performance when a single instance of pfcount processes the traffic injected at wire rate with different packet sizes on a single Gigabit link.

In Figure 11 we show that vPF_RING, similar to PF_RING on a native environment, is able to process packets at wire-rate (without packet loss), for every packet size, up to the maximum rate (1.488 Mpps per port). From the same figure we can observe that by using PF_RING in a virtual environment with the VirtIO-Net support (i.e. without the assistance of our framework), it is possible to efficiently capture without packet loss only medium/large packets, when packet rates are not more than a few hundred Kpps. In fact, with small packets severe packet drops can be observed. Results are slightly better when using PF_RING on a VMware ESXi virtual environment, but we can still notice severe packet drops for high rates.

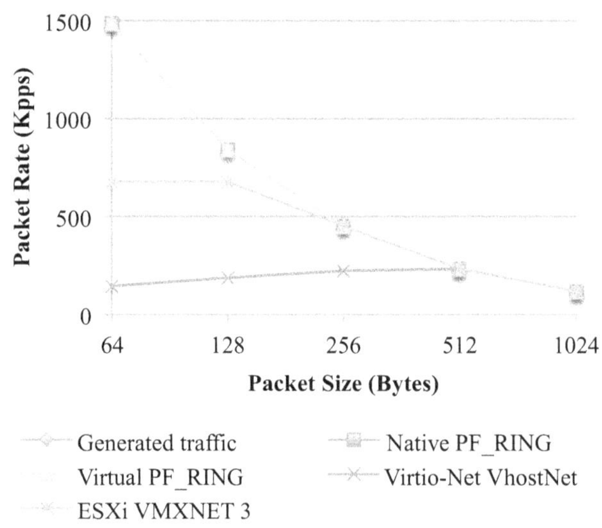

Figure 11. Packet Capture Rate (1 Gbit)

In addition to packet capture, we evaluate the percentage of CPU idle time as reported by the *top* command utility. In this way, we can have an indication of the free CPU cycles available for packet processing.

Figure 12 shows that vPF_RING can cope with high packet rates while keeping the CPU relatively idle, almost the same percentage as the native solution. Instead, with the VirtIO-Net support, there is an higher overhead even if fewer packets per second are processed.

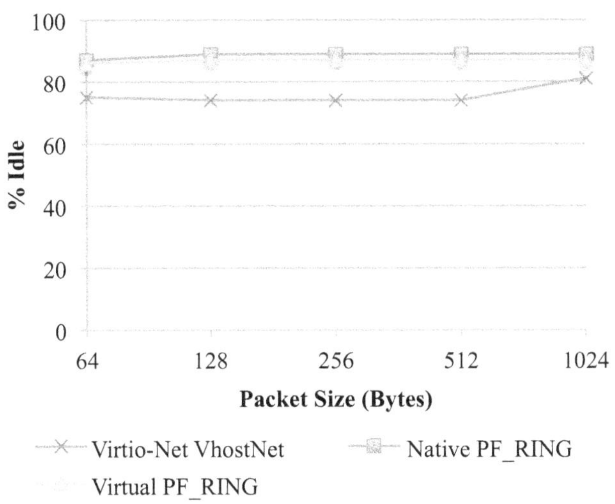

Figure 12. Idle CPU % During Capture On Host As Reported By top (1 Gbit)

Figure 13 depicts the packet loss percentage that pfcount reports when using different capture mechanisms. The result highlights that both vPF_RING and PF_RING allows packets to be captured without observing any packet loss for all packet sizes, including the minimum packet size corresponding to the highest packet rate (1.4 Mpps for 64 byte packets). On the contrary, when using VirtIO-Net, the packet loss percentage is significant (as high as 90% in the case of 64 bytes packets), making it unsuitable for applications where 100% packet capture is required. A lower packet loss percentage can be observed when VMware ESXi is used; however also this solution cannot guarantee no packet loss.

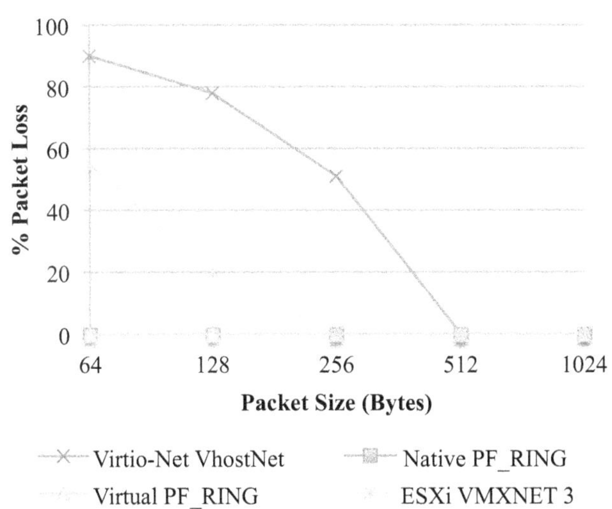

Figure 13. Packet Loss Percentage (1 Gbit)

A second test has been performed to evaluate the performance when two instances of the *pfcount* application, running on the same VM, process the traffic injected on two different Gbit interfaces.

Figure 14 shows the aggregated packet capture rate that is achieved by running the two *pfcount* instances. Both vPF_RING and PF_RING are able to process up to nearly two million packets per second without packet loss (with an average of one million per instance). When the packet rate on the wire increases further (with 64-byte packets at wire-speed) both capture mechanisms lose packets. However native PF_RING processes about half a million more than vPF_RING.

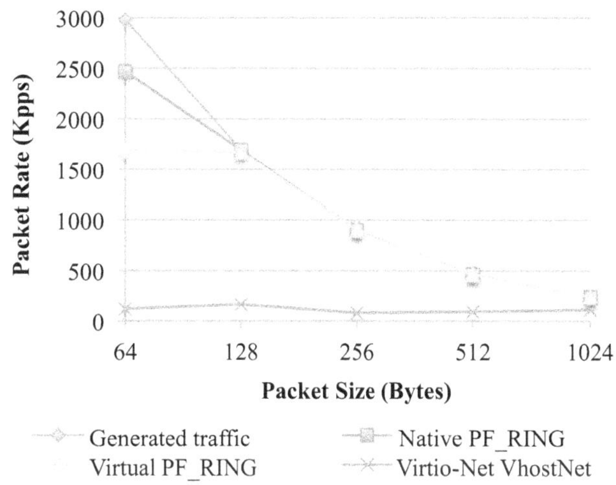

Figure 14. Total Captured Packets By Two pfcount Instances Running On The Same VM

As the virtual machine where the two instances of pfcount have limited CPU resources, this result does not necessarily mean that vPF_RING offers a worse scalability than the native PF_RING. In fact, while the two instances of *pfcount* of the native solution can run concurrently on different cores of the same processor, we know that a virtual CPU, where the two application instances of the virtual solution are scheduled on, is itself scheduled as a normal thread by the host operating system.

Regarding the virtual solution without the framework, using the VirtIO-Net support, performance are similar or even worse to the previous, with up to one hundred thousand packets per second processed by each application instance. The conclusion is that even with large packets, packet loss is pretty severe.

Figure 15 depicts the percentage of CPU idle time, and it confirms that vPF_RING keeps the CPU relatively idle, even more that native PF_RING. This is because the native PF_RING is more efficient than the virtual version, thus it consumes packets more quickly hence calls *poll()* much more often that contributes to reduce the idle time. Instead the solution based on VirtIO-Net requires more CPU time even with a very low percentage of captured packets.

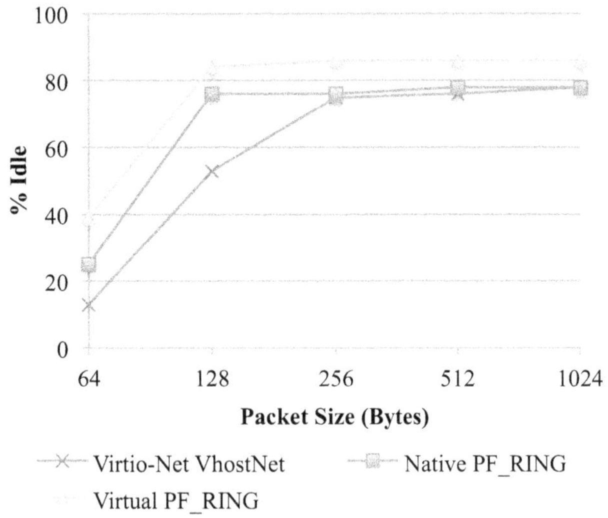

Figure 15. Idle CPU % When Two pfcount Instances Are Running On The Same VM

Another test has been conducted for evaluating the performance of two instances of the application, each one processing one Gigabit of traffic on a different interface, but this time each running on a different VM.

As shown in Figure 16, the total number of captured packets by both application instances has that same trend as in the previous test. The only difference is that in this case for 64-byte packets the capture rate of vPF_RING is basically the same of the native PF_RING. This, once again, confirms our hypothesis about scalability. In fact, in this case we have two virtual CPUs scheduled on the host, one for each VM, and on each virtual CPU an application instance is scheduled.

The solution based on VirtIO-Net, this time, seems to scale for large packets but, at high rates, performance is similar to the one observed in the previous tests.

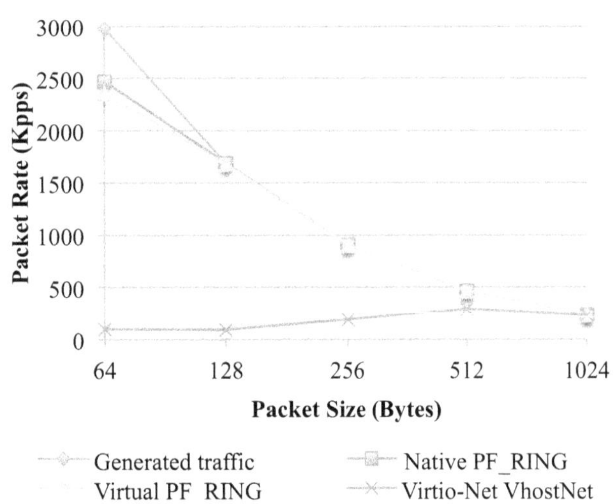

Figure 16. Total Captured Packets By Two pfcount Instances Running On Different VMs

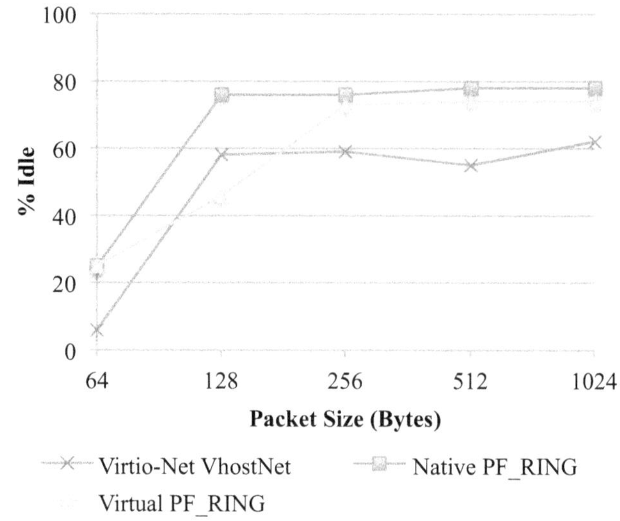

Figure 17. Idle CPU % When Two pfcount Instances Are Running On Different VMs

Figure 17 shows the percentage of CPU idle time. As one would guess, vPF_RING overhead is higher than the native PF_RING. The solution based on VirtIO-Net still requires many more CPU cycles, even if its packet capture performance is lower.

Another series of tests has been performed in order to compare the packet capture performance offered by vPF_RING when capturing from a 10 Gigabit link, to the performance provided by the native PF_RING. *pfsend* on top of PF_RING DNA has been used to generate traffic at wire speed. An Intel 82599 based Gigabit Ethernet interface has been used as a capture device. The server used is still an Intel Xeon X3440 running Linux kernel 2.6.36. The device driver used for these tests, on the host-side, is a PF_RING-aware version of the *ixgbe*, which is able to copy packets directly to PF_RING my means of Linux NAPI packet polling.

In the first of these tests, we evaluated the performance with a single application instance. Figure 18 shows that vPF_RING is able to match the packet capture performance offered by the native PF_RING.

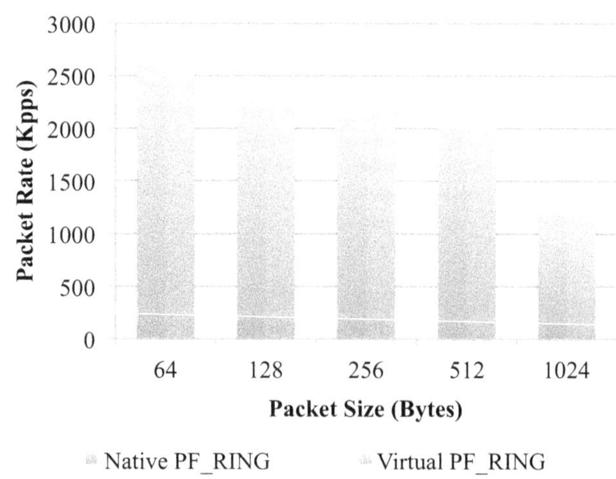

Figure 18. Packet Capture Rate (10 Gigabit)

A second test has been performed to evaluate the scalability, with two instances of *pfcount* capturing packets from the same interface, balancing the traffic across applications by means of RSS (Receive-Side Scaling) queues. In the virtual case, each *pfcount* instance is running on a different VM. As shown in Figure 19, also in this case, packet capture performance offered by vPF_RING is close to the one offered by the native PF_RING.

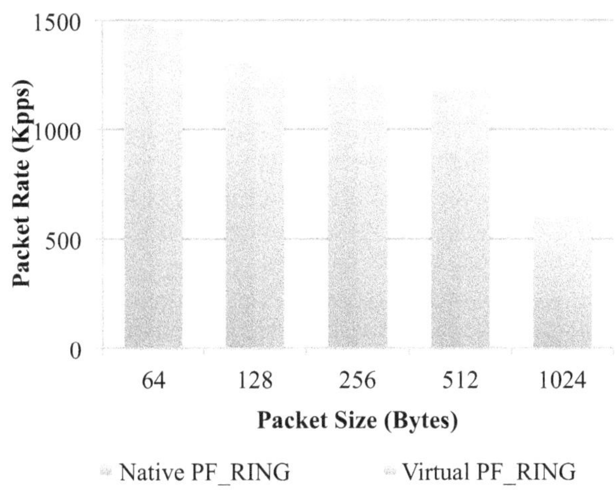

Figure 19. Captured Packets By Each Of the Two pfcount Instances Running On Different VMs (10 Gigabit)

In order to further evaluate the scalability, another test has been conducted with four instances of *pfcount*. As in the previous test, the *pfcount* instances capture packets from the same interface.

As depicted in Figure 20, vPF_RING offers packet capture performance comparable to the one provided by the native PF_RING.

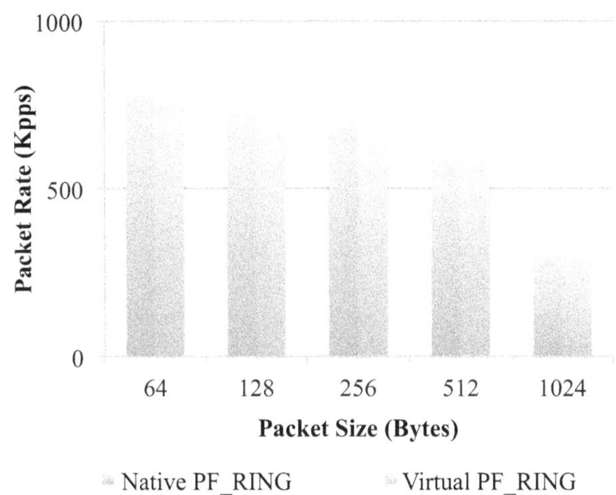

Figure 20. Captured Packets By Each Of The Four pfcount Instances Running On Different VMs (10 Gigabit)

In summary using vPF_RING has no performance penalty relative to native PF_RING (Figures 11,12). Relative to PF_RING in a VM:

- vPF_RING is more than an order of magnitude faster with respect to the performance achieved by vanilla KVM. This means that thanks to vPF_RING it is finally possible to effectively perform traffic monitoring inside KVM-based VMs.
- For all packet sizs, vPF_RING and PF_RING have comparable performance (Fig 14, 18).

5. OPEN ISSUES AND FUTURE WORK

The work described on this paper is an efficient and flexible solution to effective packet capture on VMs. Nevertheless there are a few areas where extra work is needed.

The main issue is live VM migration, as the hypervisor does not have knowledge of the resources allocated by the applications. This is in contrast to traditional device virtualization approaches, where the hypervisor is involved and it can suspend all the operations when live migration starts. While developing the framework we mostly focused on achieving high packet capture performance and we did not consider additional virtualization features, such as live migration. In the future we plan to address the issue for further increasing the flexibility offered by our solution.

Furthermore, it would be interesting to perform more detailed tests, look for further performance improvements, and evaluate the framework on VMs with multiple virtual CPUs investigating on scheduling and resource management.

6. FINAL REMARKS

In the past few years there have been many efforts to improve network performance on VMs, both with hardware and software solutions. However, none of the available solution addresses the problem of using VMs for high-performance network monitoring.

This paper used a well-known approach named hypervisor-bypass, which allows packets to follow a straight path from kernel to VMs, thus avoiding per-packet overhead due to the hypervisor and system calls. This mechanism has been successfully applied for implementing vPF_RING, a kernel-based extensible traffic analysis framework developed by the authors. The validation phase has confirmed that it can drastically improve packet capture performance, often achieving packet capture rates and CPU usage close to those that can be obtained on bare hardware. This reducing the dropped packet rate up to 90% on Gigabit links with respect to preexisting open source software solutions, 55% with respect to commercial solutions such as VMware (or even more on faster links).

The outcome is that it is now possible to efficiently run multiple VMs on commodity hardware, each monitoring the same traffic for different purposes, without packet loss and with plenty of CPU cycles available for processing the captured traffic.

7. CODE AVAILABILITY

This work is distributed under the GNU GPL license and is available at the ntop home page http://www.ntop.org/products/pf_ring/vpf_ring/.

8. ACKNOWLEDGEMENTS

Our thanks to Silicom Ltd. that has greatly supported this research work and provided network equipment used during tests.

9. REFERENCES

[1] F. Baboescu and G. Varghese, Scalable packet classification, Proc. of ACM Sigcomm, 2001.

[2] S. McCanne and V. Jacobson, The BSD Packet Filter: A New Architecture for User-level Packet Capture, Proc. of USENIX Conference, 1993.

[3] A. Kivity, Y. Kamay, D. Laor, U. Lublin, and A. Liguori, kvm: the Linux virtual machine monitor, Proc. of 2007 Ottawa Linux Symposium, July 2007.

[4] R. Russell, VirtIO: Towards a De-Facto Standard for Virtual I/O Devices, SIGOPS Operating Systems Review, Vol. 42, Issue 5, July 2008.

[5] L. Deri, Improving Passive Packet Capture: Beyond Device Polling, Proc. of SANE 2004, 2004.

[6] W. Huang et al., A case for high performance computing with virtual machines, Proc. of the 20th annual international conference on Supercomputing, 2006.

[7] J. Liu et al., High performance VMM-bypass I/O in virtual machines, Proc. of USENIX annual conference, 2006.

[8] R. Hiremane and S. Chinni, Virtual Machine Device Queues: An Integral Part of Intel Virtualization Technology for Connectivity that Delivers Enhanced Network Performance, Intel Corporation, White Paper, 2007.

[9] K.K. Ram et al., Achieving 10 Gb/s using safe and transparent network interface virtualization, Proc. of the 2009 ACM SIGPLAN/SIGOPS international conference on Virtual execution environments, 2009.

[10] J.R. Santos et al., Bridging the gap between software and hardware techniques for i/o virtualization, Proc. of USENIX 2008 Annual Technical Conference on Annual Technical Conference, 2008.

[11] PCI-SIG, Single Root I/O Virtualization and Sharing Specification, Revision 1.0, 2007.

[12] M. Ben-Yehuda et al., Utilizing IOMMUs for virtualization in Linux and Xen, Proc. of the 2006 Ottawa Linux Symposium, 2006.

[13] M.D. Hummel et al., Address translation for input/output (I/O) devices and interrupt remapping for I/O devices in an I/O memory management unit (IOMMU), US Patent 7'653'803, 2010.

[14] S. Muthrasanallur et al., Intel Virtualization Technology for Directed I/O, Intel Corporation, 2006.

[15] J. LeVasseur et al.,Standardized but flexible I/O for self-virtualizing devices, Proc. of the First conference on I/O virtualization, USENIX Association, 2008.

[16] H. Raj and K. Schwan, High performance and scalable I/O virtualization via self-virtualized devices, Proc. of the 16th international symposium on High performance distributed computing, ACM, 2007.

[17] J. Shafer et al., Concurrent direct network access for virtual machine monitors, Proc. of IEEE 13th International Symposium on High Performance Computer Architecture, 2007.

[18] Endace, OSm 4.2 vDAG (Virtualized DAG), http://www.endace.com/endace-operating-system-for-network-monitoring-osm.html, June 2011.

[19] L. Youseff at al., Paravirtualization for HPC Systems, Proc. of Workshop on Xen in High-Performance Cluster and Grid Computing, 2006.

[20] K. Adams and O. Agesen, A Comparison of Software and Hardware Techniques for x86 Virtualization, International Conference on Architectural Support for Programming Languages and Operating Systems (ASPLOS), 2006.

[21] L. Deri et al., Wire-Speed Hardware-Assisted Traffic Filtering with Mainstream Network Adapters, Proc. of NEMA 2010 Workshop, October 2010.

[22] Silicom Ltd., PCIe Packet Processor Server Adapter PE210G2RS, http://www.silicom-usa.com/default.asp?contentID=2144, 2010.

[23] A. Biswas, A High Performance Real-time Packet Capturing Architecture for Network Management Systems, Masters Thesis, Concordia University, 2005.

[24] L. Degioanni and G. Varenni, Introducing Scalability in Network Measurement: Toward 10 Gbps with Commodity Hardware, Proc. of IMC '04, 2004.

[25] F. Bellard, QEMU, a Fast and Portable Dynamic Translator, Proc. of the USENIX Annual Technical Conference, FREENIX Track, 2005.

[26] J. Pettit et al., Virtual Switching in an Era of Advanced Edges, 2nd Workshop on Data Center – Converged and Virtual Ethernet Switching (DC-CAVES), Sept. 2010.

[27] B. Pfaff et al., Extending networking into the virtualization layer, Proc. of HotNets, October 2009.

[28] N. McKeown et al., OpenFlow: enabling innovation in campus networks, ACM SIGCOMM Computer Communication Review 38.2 (2008).

[29] A. Greenhalgh et al., Flowstream Architectures, Proc. of WowKiVS 2009 Conference, 2009.

[30] Intel Corporation, 82599 10GbE Controller Datasheet, Revision 2.3, April 2010.

[31] Intel Corporation and VMware Inc., Enabling I/O-Intensive Applications for Server Virtualization, White Paper, 2009.

[32] Luca Deri et al., High Speed Network Traffic Analysis with Commodity Multi-core Systems, Proc. of IMC 2010, November 2010.

[33] B. Plaff et al., Extending Networking into the Virtualization Layer, Proc. of 8th HotNets Workshop, October 2009.

[34] N. Chowdhury and R. Boutaba, Network virtualization: state of the art and research challenges, IEEE Communications Magazine, July 2009.

[35] Y. Dong at al., SR-IOV networking in Xen: architecture, design and implementation, Proc. of WIOV'08, 2008.

[36] S. Rixner, Network Virtualization: Breaking the Performance Barrier, ACM Queue Magazine, Vol. 6 Issue 1, Jan./Feb 2008.

[37] D. Unnikrishnan et al., Scalable network virtualization using FPGAs, Proc. of ACM FPGA '10, 2010.

[38] E. L. Haletky, VMware ESX Server in the Enterprise: Planning and Securing Virtualization Servers, ISBN 0132302071, 2008.

[39] J. Wiegert et al., Challenges for Scalable Networking in a Virtualized Server, Proc. of 16th ICCCN Conference, 2007.

[40] N. Niebert et al., Network Virtualization: A Viable Path Towards the Future Internet, Strategic Workshop, 2007.

[41] R. Sherwood et al. FlowVisor: A Network Virtualization Layer. Technical Report Openflow-tr-2009-1, Stanford University, 2009.

[42] R. Sherwood et al., Carving research slices out of your production networks with OpenFlow. ACM SIGCOMM Computer Communication Review, 2010.

[43] VMware Inc.,Configuration Examples and Troubleshooting for VMDirectPath, Technical Note, 2010.

[44] L. Deri, nCap: Wire-speed Packet Capture and Transmission, Proc. of E2EMON Workshop, 2005.

[45] L. Braun et al., Comparing and Improving Current Packet Capturing Solutions Based On Commodity Hardware, Proc. of. IMC '10, November 2010.

[46] Russ Combs, Snort 2.9 Essentials: The DAQ, http://vrt-blog.snort.org/2010/08/snort-29-essentials-daq.html, August 2010.

[47] ntop, PF_RING DNA, http://www.ntop.org/products/pf_ring/dna/, September 2011.

Summary Review Documentation for

"vPF_RING: Towards Wire-Speed Network Monitoring Using Virtual Machines"

Authors: A. Cardigliano, L. Deri, J. Gasparakis, F. Fusco

Reviewer #1

Strengths: A software framework for hypervisor bypass to improve passive packet capture performance in virtualized environments.

Weaknesses: Limited novelty of the system (hypervisor bypass has been proposed and implemented in other intensive I/O settings)

Comments to Authors: The vPF_RING framework proposed and evaluated by the authors is a nice, albeit unsurprising, adaptation of hypervisor bypass to improve passive network measurement performance. The work is valuable and likely to see wide use and adaptation in other hypervisors, e.g., VMWare, Hyper-V, and Xen. The specific technical contributions and evaluation, however, are somewhat limited and the paper would have perhaps been better formulated as a short submission. The writing (especially related work) is quite verbose and could have been substantially tightened. Indeed, I believe the paper would have been a stronger submission had it been a short paper.

In Figure 17, there's no explanation for the poor relative performance of vPF_RING for packet size of 128 B.

Reviewer #2

Strengths: The work is technically sound and well presented.

Weaknesses: Given that the solution builds on the author's previously existing tool to accomplish performance sensitive I/O tasks in virtualized environments, it's not clear how to value the marginal contribution of this work. It seems like the most performance benefit relative to native PF_RING is only realized when the average packet size is < 128 bytes - is this true? Also, there are missing points that could have improved the evaluation.

Comments to Authors: There was not a clear "X% better" statement in the paper. Digging a bit, I think I have come up with the following candidates: if you agree, you should repeat them many times in the paper, likely both in the introduction and the conclusion:
- relative to PF_RING, in a VM, vPF_RING reduces the dropped packet rate from x% to y% for packet rates above z PPS (1 Gbps/128 byte packets?). For packet rates below z, vPF_RING and PF_RING have comparable performance (Fig 14)
- using vPF_RING in native (non-VM) mode has no performance penalty relative to PF_RING (figs 11,12)

As it stands, particularly from graph 14, it looks like there is no benefit to using vPF_RING if your average packet size is above 128 bytes: is that really true? If so, that definitely limits the utility of this work.

I would have really liked to see a *quantatitive* comparison of your work against the more naive solutions in either VMWare or Xen. Particularly with closed source applications, quite often high-level algorithmic arguments about why solution X is better than Y (as you claim in the related work section) are not correct simply because the algorithms are trade secrets and not published.

It's a shame that you didn't also compare against PF_RING optimized drivers. It's good to understand both the common and the worst case. Given that PF_RING seems to preform comparable to vPF_RING for medium sized packets, it makes me wonder what the utility would be with an optimized driver.

The focus on PF_RING as a base software-capture tool is a bit dated. Please see the following paper (and its references) for more cutting edge software-capture technologies: Lothar Braun, Alexander Didebulidze, Nils Kammenhuber, Georg Carle, "Comparing and Improving Current Packet Capturing Solutions based on Commodity Hardware", Proc. IMC 2010.

How much work would it take to extend your work from PF_RING to PF_PACKET? Would vPF_RING need to be rewritten completely for each new capture architecture?

Reviewer #3

Strengths: Systems that use virtual machines are more common every day and we currently have no efficient way to do packet captures in these systems. The libraries designed in this paper should be useful in practice.

Weaknesses: The writing mixes implementation details with design principles making it hard to understand the key ideas. The paper also lacks a clear motivation and set of use cases for this type of measurement.

Comments to Authors: This paper presents the thorough design and evaluation of a framework to capture packets at high speeds on virtual machines. Given the prevalence of systems using virtualization, the concepts to make packet capture work on VMs introduced here are an important contribution to the community. In my view, the paper has two main contributions: (i) the design principles and (ii) the tool itself, which serves as a proof-of-concept and works only for KVM. It is not clear from the paper whether the tool will be available to the community, but I assume it is. The first contribution is not easy to get from the current version of the paper because of the presentation.

There are two main changes that can help improve the presentation:

1. The paper never clearly articulates the scenarios in which one would need to monitor packets in virtualized environments. Often when applications are running in different VMs it is because they need isolation, so the idea that one VM can tap another VM's traffic is not conventional. It would be helpful to have examples of systems that need this kind of capability. Having clear use cases from the start can also help motivate and kind the evaluation. The evaluation section could be much more interesting if you had some case studies motivated by the use cases from your introduction.

2. The discussion in Sec. 3 presents details first and the overall idea after. The functionality discussion that is currently in Sec. 3.2 helps set the stage for why you need the APIs and functions described in Sec. 3.1. In general, this section goes into a lot of detail, but it doesn't clearly separate the design principles. It would be helpful to have some conceptual discussion of the hooks you need in the kernel, the kinds of interrupts, memory-mapping, then you can discuss more specific implementation (anything that is specific to KVM and your implementation). In fact, it is OK to only implement the framework for one virtualization technique, but it is important to discuss which parts of the framework are specific for KVM and what is general.

The paper would benefit from a careful proof reading.

In Sec. 4, it is not clear where the traces are coming from. The first paragraph of Sec. 4 says that you capture traces with the Endace card on a network backbone (if this is the case, can you give some details on the traces? Dates of collection, length of the trace, the type of network it was collected, how many bytes in the trace). However, the results in this section seem to indicate that traces were generated synthetically with different packet sizes at fixed bandwidth.

Reviewer #4

Strengths: Timely, relevant work, impressive performance numbers. Very nicely written to put the work in context of other related work.

Weaknesses: My major concern was whether PF_RING itself was widely adopted or used, and what the value of porting it to virtualized environments is.

The evaluation was a bit too repetitive - I would have liked to see more results on (a) the effects of running multiple monitoring applications on different VMs and (b) the benefits of early packet capture.

Comments to Authors: I really liked this paper - it addresses a timely problem with a well-engineered system implementation that has very good performance.

I don't really know how widely used PF_RING is, and what the merits of this exercise are in terms of practical deployments etc. Some numbers/statistics on how PF_RING is deployed would add to your motivation a lot.

I liked Section 2 - the authors have done a nice job of putting their work in perspective of the various proposed optimizations in the literature (e.g., hypervisor bypass, dedicated NICs per VM etc).

The figures were very helpful, but they dont seem to be referred to or explained in the text and I found them to be lacking in context at times; e.g., in Figure 3 what's the difference between the PCIePF and PCI-e VFI?

Sec 2.2 - the comment about lawful interception -- I dont understand this paragraph.

Are you worried about accidental privacy leakage?

Sec 2.3 - is the main difference between a modified hardware and a vanilla hardware the ability to offload filtering to the NIC?

Figure 5 - can standard drivers not write to the PF_RING data structure, the text seems to suggest otherwise, but the figure is confusing me?

Section 3 - some examples of how different applications could "subscribe" to different subsets of traffic filters would be very helpful here. An end-to-end example of how a monitoring application can use vPFRing would be very useful here.

Section 4 - the results are impressive, but I would have liked to see a bit more "breadth" in the experiments. Right now, you go deep into a single VM performance in the worst case, but what about running multiple applications, what's the impact on say an application like Snort, how can packet filtering at early stage help etc?

Section 5 - I don't think I followed the concerns about live migration here. Is this specific to vPF-Ring or any approach that does bypass or paravirtualization?

Section 6 - "introduced a mechanism named hypervisor bypass" - didn't you tell me that this was well known.

Reviewer #5

Strengths: The development of a highly accurate packet capture for virtual machines is important for using them in network measurements. This paper presents an important step toward reducing cost and improving coverage of traffic monitoring systems.

Weaknesses: This new method builds on an existing PR_RING framework and provides little innovation for a full paper. The evaluations are limited to only one architecture and do not consider multiple virtual CPUs.

Comments to Authors: I find your work extremely interesting as it allows for using virtual machines to measure networks. This solution will then enable us to reduce deployment and management cost of a shared measurement platforms. However, the innovation in by-passing hypervisor was already considered in previous work, including [5]. The evaluation is also limited.

Some detailed comments on the paper:

The related work section (Section 2) is a bit too long and you have not used all the available space for the paper. There are spaces to present more validations to fully understand the limitations of the proposed solution.

Section 4, the comparisons between vPF_RING and PF_RING show that vPF_RING performs almost as good as PF_RING, which is expected. However, comparisons with other packet capture techniques both on virtual machine and on real hardware are needed to understand the potentials and limitations of the techniques used in both vPF_RING and PF_RING.

Response from the Authors

- We have analyzed all reviewer's comments and taken them into account. We have not found a single comment that was out of scope, thus all of them have been addressed in the new paper version. The main changes include:
- Positioned out work against other VMs (Xen) as well commercial VMs (VMware). We have also extended the figures so that we have depicted also the performance of VMware with respect to our work.
- Clarify some statements that were not fully correct, or not easy to understand
- Added some sentences about how difficult would be to port out work to other hypervisors.
- Added a few examples where our work could be used, including (as requested) security and snort, a popular IDS/IPS.
- Better described our statement about the use of VMs in lawful interception.
- Explained some technical terms we used in the text but that are not very common.
- Moved/rewritten some sentences to simplify the text.

Going Viral: Flash Crowds in an Open CDN

Patrick Wendell*
U.C. Berkeley
Berkeley, CA, USA
pwendell@eecs.berkeley.edu

Michael J. Freedman
Princeton University
Princeton, NJ, USA
mfreed@cs.princeton.edu

Abstract

Handling flash crowds poses a difficult task for web services. Content distribution networks (CDNs), hierarchical web caches, and peer-to-peer networks have all been proposed as mechanisms for mitigating the effects of these sudden spikes in traffic to under-provisioned origin sites. Other than a few anecdotal examples of isolated events to a single server, however, no large-scale analysis of flash-crowd behavior has been published to date.

In this paper, we characterize and quantify the behavior of thousands of flash crowds on CoralCDN, an open content distribution network running at several hundred POPs. Our analysis considers over four years of CDN traffic, comprising more than 33 billion HTTP requests. We draw conclusions in several areas, including (i) the potential benefits of cooperative vs. independent caching by CDN nodes, (ii) the efficacy of elastic redirection and resource provisioning, and (iii) the ecosystem of portals, aggregators, and social networks that drive traffic to third-party websites.

Categories and Subject Descriptors: C.4 [**Performance of Systems**]: Measurement Techniques

General Terms: Measurement, Performance

Keywords: content distribution networks, flash crowds

1. INTRODUCTION

Volatile request rates complicate the delivery of Internet services. Most websites experience significant diurnal fluctuations in request volume. Over shorter time scales, traffic may fluctuate due to the changing popularity of content or localized events. The most severe (and least predictable) type of volatility are *flash crowds*, which occur when services see sudden, large, and often unforeseen increases in request rates. Flash crowds are infamous for overwhelming even well-provisioned services, causing HTTP clients to timeout when trying to access starved server resources.

*Work performed while author was studying at Princeton University.

IMC '11, November 2–4, 2011, Berlin, Germany.

To insure themselves against the risk of a flash crowd, sites can outsource static content distribution to CDNs such as Akamai, which distribute traffic surges over a global network of content caches. This strategy, however, does not generally address dynamically generated content, where CPU cycles are required to construct user-customized pages. To fill this gap, services are increasingly using cloud infrastructure (such as Amazon EC2) to scale dynamic content creation in a similar fashion. Provisioning new resources in the cloud, while not instantaneous, can be done orders-of-magnitude more quickly than purchasing and installing new hardware.

While flash crowds have long been used as anecdotal motivation for elastic-computing platforms, little research exists characterizing such events in an operational CDN. To address this limitation, this paper analyzes flash crowds based on four years of data from CoralCDN [4, 5], an open CDN comprised of globally cooperating proxies. Using data from thousands of flash crowds detected amongst hundreds of thousands of domains, it answers several questions about the nature of flash crowds, both from the perspective of an online service and from that of a large content distributer.

This paper uses flash-crowd data to shed light on three broad aspects of online service delivery.

Cooperative Caching. In the best case, websites use a global network of caches to prevent origin overload during flash crowds. Whether distributed caches benefit from cooperation, as opposed to each cache fetching content individually from the origin, depends on the rate of requests and their distribution over caches. Section 3 evaluates the benefits of cooperative caching for real crowds.

Request Redirection and Elastic Provisioning. When unprecedented surges of traffic hit a service, it is often necessary to provision new resources or re-allocate existing ones to handle the requests. Services that operate on cloud infrastructure, for instance, might want to spin up additional virtualized instances to further spread load. Large content distributors with a fixed infrastructure may wish to allocate a greater portion or number of their caches to a particular customer [6]. Peer-to-peer systems may wish to build distribution trees to replicate content quickly [5, 10, 13]. In Section 4, we analyze how much time these parties might have to adapt their computing footprint in the face of flash crowds.

Source Attribution. Third-party portals such as Slashdot are often thought to be the primary drivers of flash crowds. These sites operate as centralized "bulletin boards," sharing a small set of links amongst large numbers of simultaneous viewers. In Section 5, we briefly consider how often these portals play a role in flash crowds and assess whether decentralized, peer-to-peer link sharing (such as Facebook or Twitter updates) creates equivalent request surges.

Before performing such analysis, we first describe our CoralCDN data set and provide the working definition of a flash crowd that we use throughout our analysis.

1.1 4 Years of Data from CoralCDN

CoralCDN is a open, cooperative content distribution network, designed to proxy content requests for heavily loaded services. It operates on a set of globally distributed machines that act as caching proxies. Users fall broadly into three categorical use cases. First, HTTP clients can explicitly access a piece of content through CoralCDN by "Coralizing" an existing URL (appending `nyud.net` to any URL's domain). This is a popular practice for links posted on major portals, as the Coralized link helps prevent the origin server from becoming overwhelmed by referred traffic. Second, some sites persistently use these URLs for their embedded content, so that static files are transparently requested via CoralCDN. Third, some sites use HTTP redirects to offload traffic to CoralCDN during periods of heavy load. When possible, we distinguish between these scenarios.

CoralCDN proxies persistently log data for each HTTP request they service. The logs include the URL being accessed, any HTTP referrers, the client IP address, and several other request attributes. The results in this paper are drawn from four years of aggregated CoralCDN logs, from 2007 to early 2011. These logs cover 33,354,760,349 individual HTTP requests and represent a complete (not sampled) trace of all CoralCDN traffic during this period. That said, a small number of logs are missing due to periodic failures of CoralCDN proxies and its logging subsystem [4].

CoralCDN sees a biased cut of HTTP traffic, and in some cases, this limits our exploration of the data. Since websites might use CoralCDN intermittently, for instance, we cannot readily perform longitudinal analysis across individual domains, *e.g.*, to characterize the frequency and scale of flash crowds that an average domain would experience over the course of a year. We leave such analysis to future work and carefully limit the scope of our inference.

2. DEFINING FLASH CROWDS

While the term "flash crowd" is in widespread use, prior work has generally not defined what constitutes such a crowd (systems proposals can be qualitative, and previous measurement studies [8] only had traces of one or two such crowds). To detect crowds in such a large dataset, we were pressed to craft a working mathematical definition of "flash crowd." We present this definition both to describe our own methodology and to standardize future research efforts.

2.1 Defining Flash Crowds

We define a *flash crowd* as a period over which request rates for a particular *fully-qualified domain name* are increasing exponentially. Call r_{t_i} the average per-minute request rate over a particular time period t_i. We say a domain is experiencing a flash crowd if

$$r_{t_i} > 2^i \cdot r_{t_0}, \quad \forall i \in [0, k]$$

and

$$\max_i r_{t_i} > m \quad \wedge \quad \max_i r_{t_i} > n \cdot r_{avg}$$

where constant m is a minimum per-minute request rate, and the constant n specifies how much more the maximum sustained rate must be than the service's average rate. Effectively, this requires that the crowd has occurred over a modest number of periods (at least k) and resulted in a larger terminal rate (m) that is many times the mean (n). Choices of k, m, and n are subjective, although in this study, we use $k = 3$, $m = 500$ reqs/min, and $n = 15$. The use of such constants may seem ad-hoc, but they are necessary in any derivative-based definition in order to filter out small fluctuations. We continue to add subsequent periods until we have seen τ periods ($\tau = 3$) for which

$$r_{t_j} \cdot 2^{-1} < r_{t_{j+1}} < r_{t_j} \cdot 2$$

Many unique URLs may belong to the same crowd, *e.g.*, they represent embedded content in a web page. However, because they may be served by different origin servers or CDNs, we conservatively consider requests to different fully-qualified domains (*e.g.*, a.example.com and b.example.com) as belonging to distinct crowds.

2.2 Request Rate Epochs and Crowd Speed

Thus far, we have not specified the granularity at which we measure request rates. Adjusting the epoch period for request rate calculations affects the type of crowd we detect. At shorter epochs, such as 60 seconds, we detect crowds that increase very rapidly but have a limited duration. For instance, if r_{t_0} were to be just 1 req/min, a crowd lasting 30 minutes must have a terminal request rate $r_{t_{30}}$ of more than one billion requests per minute to satisfy this definition. On the other hand, crowd detection with longer epochs will present a less extreme growth rate.

In this study, we consider crowds using six different epoch periods: 1, 2, 5, 10, 30, and 60 minutes. (Crowds detected using shorter epochs provide less time for a service to react to its increased demand, a problem explored in Section 4.) Using these definitions, we identify 3,553 crowds in the CoralCDN trace. Of these, 1,052 crowds originate from fewer than 10 client IP addresses each; manual inspection of some of these traces uncovered various undesired uses, such as attempted password cracking. Crowds of this nature likely would not occur in a closed, commercial CDN, given their increased security protections. Consequently, with the exception of Figure 3, our subsequent analysis filters out these crowds and only considers the remaining 2,501.

3. FLASH CROWD CACHEABILITY

3.1 Caching Challenges

During flash crowds, a CDN often acts as an intermediary between a large distributed base of clients and a small number of origin servers; ensuring efficient communication with both of these parties poses distinct challenges. On the demand side, CDNs need to proportionately distribute thousands of simultaneous requests across a network of caches. Simultaneously, a CDN must judiciously fetch content from the origin server(s), being careful to avoid simply relaying the brunt of the load to the origin.

How large are the flash crowds that CoralCDN observes and how amenable are they to caching? At the minimum, each unique URL must be fetched at least once from the origin. Crowds with many unique URLs—for example, due to different URLs representing distinct dynamic content—can incur greater origin load. Figure 1 plots the flash crowds analyzed in this study, comparing the number of unique URLs per crowd (given on the x-axis) with their peak request rate to CoralCDN (given on the y-axis). If a crowd is identified under more than one epoch size (per Section 2.2), we record it multiple times in this analysis. The upper right quadrant of the figure represents crowds that are both massive in scale and distributed over large numbers of URLs.

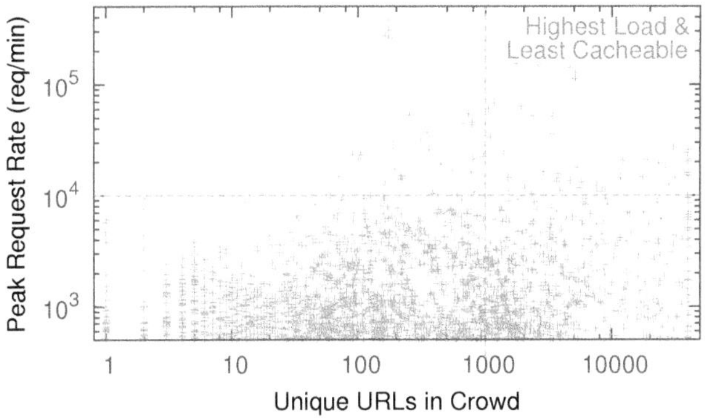

Figure 1: Size and cacheability of 2,501 flash crowds.

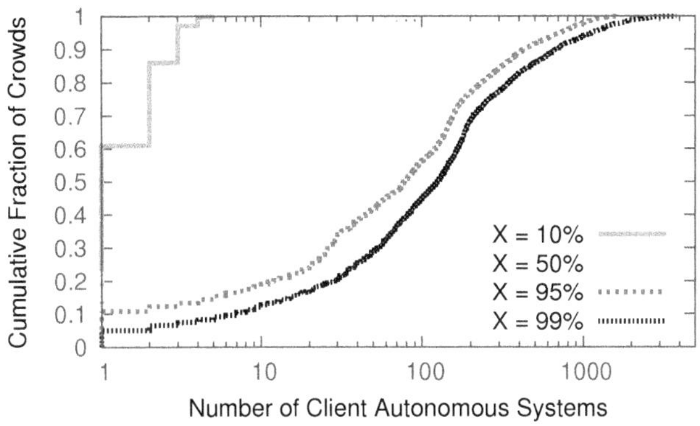

Figure 2: AS-level clustering of client requests. Each line plots a CDF of the number of ASes with clients that generate *X*% of crowds' requests.

3.2 Comparison of Caching Strategies

To minimize origin load and decrease client perceived latency, CDNs cache content widely across their networks. While they may employ a variety of caching strategies, one fundamental choice is the degree to which caches coordinate in fetching origin content. CoralCDN uses *cooperative caching*, where proxies discover and fetch content from other caching proxies, before requesting content from the origin. CoralCDN uses a distributed hash table for global content discovery, while earlier cooperative approaches were based on more static cache hierarchies [2]. In contrast, many commercial CDNs, including Akamai [9, 14], primarily use *non-cooperative caching*, where each remote proxy (or proxy cluster) independently fetches content from the origin site. A continuum of caching strategy exists with varying degrees of cache coordination. For clarity of comparison, however, we restrict our analysis to these two extremes.

Cooperative caching yields strictly fewer requests to the origin server than non-cooperative approaches, since all but the first request for each URL are served from cache. At the same time, cooperation increases system complexity and adds coordination overhead. In this section, we evaluate the performance benefit of cooperative caching in observed crowds. We also identify factors which influence how much benefit cooperative caching will provide to a particular crowd.

First, the client distribution over proxies plays an important role. When clients are concentrated at a small number of proxies (perhaps due to their locality), relatively few distinct caches fetch content from the origin, diminishing the benefits of cooperation. On the other hand, crowds distributed over large numbers of caches pose a higher risk of overloading the origin if caches do not cooperate.

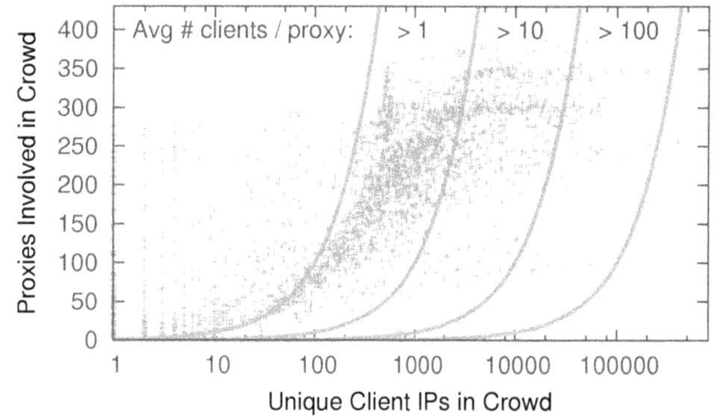

Figure 3: Number of proxies and clients involved in each flash crowd. Guide lines plot the curves for 1, 10, 100, and 1000 clients per proxy.

Our crowd traces support the latter scenario—clients are distributed across many network locations—suggesting that cooperation could be helpful. To illustrate, Figure 2 shows the clustering of clients based on network topology. While 20% of crowds have half of their requests originate from clients within a single Autonomous System (AS), crowds commonly involve hundreds of ASes. Similarly, many CoralCDN proxies are involved in serving a crowd, as shown in Figure 3, and requests are well distributed over them. This unfiltered figure shows all 3,553 crowds, including those with only a few clients, likely malicious, accessing large numbers of proxies.

The concentration of a crowd's URLs can also affect its cooperative cacheability. To characterize this less intuitive factor, we calculate the number of requests seen by each crowd's origin under both non-cooperative and ideal cooperative caching (under the latter, the origin sees a single hit per URL). In this analysis, we make the simplifying assumption that caches do not evict a crowds' content during its lifetime. CoralCDN typically operates at around 300 servers world-wide (spread over around 150 POPs), and the arrival of clients to each server was drawn directly from actual crowd traces. Since the distribution of requests amongst caches determines cache locality, using real request traces is necessary for correct evaluation.

Figure 4 demonstrates that content dynamism (the number of unique URLs) has a significant impact on the relative benefits of cache cooperation. The top graph plots the fraction of cache hits under cooperative and non-cooperative strategies, as a function of URL distribution. The lower graph plots the difference in these numbers, highlighting the normalized reduction in origin load under cooperation. Its shape reveals an interesting pattern: In crowds with a small number of unique URL's, cooperative caching provides relatively little incremental benefit, since each cache retrieves the critical set of URLs from the origin in a small number of hits. On the other extreme, crowds with mostly unique URLs—typically dynamic content differentiated for each client—receive no additional benefit from cooperative caching. Such crowds are fundamentally uncacheable, since no URL is ever repeated.

The lower graph in Figure 4 reveals a "sweet spot" for cooperative caching. In this region, cooperation has the potential to decrease origin load substantially, often by more than half the size of the crowd itself. These results suggest that the decision to introduce cooperation in CDNs should depend on the types of crowds that a CDN expects to handle. If it is somehow known *a priori* that crowds will be concentrated over just a small number of unique objects, then cooperation is likely unnecessary. Figure 5 illustrates these results in CDF form: about 30% of crowds see less than a 10% reduction

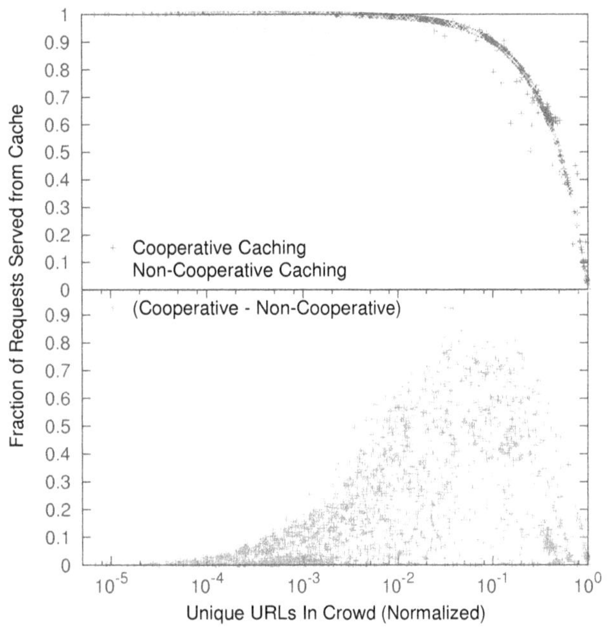

Figure 4: *Top:* Percentage of request served from cache using cooperative (dark blue) and non-cooperative (light green) caching strategies. *Bottom:* Fractional increase in cache hits from cache cooperation.

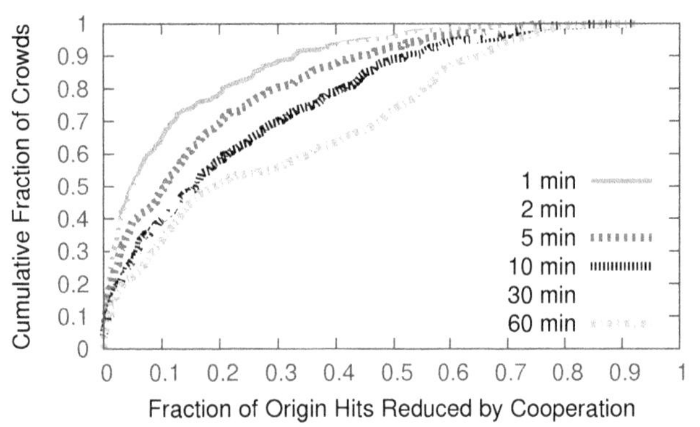

Figure 5: Origin load reduction from cooperation, as a fraction of total requests, for crowds defined by different epoch lengths.

in origin load, while 20% see between a 20% and 55% reduction in origin load. Further, slower-building flash crowds saw greater benefits from cooperative caching.

4. ELASTIC RESOURCE ALLOCATION

During flash crowds, services need to allocate additional resources to meet surging HTTP traffic. The nature of such allocation depends on whether the crowd is composed of static or dynamic content.

Crowds for a small number of unique URLs are easily served from cache. As a result, the primary resource allocation challenge falls to the CDN, which must direct clients to its wide-area proxies handling the requested domain (typically during DNS resolution). CDNs may also (re)allocate additional cache resources to particular crowds or popular content; to do so, they must observe that existing proxies are getting overloaded [6].

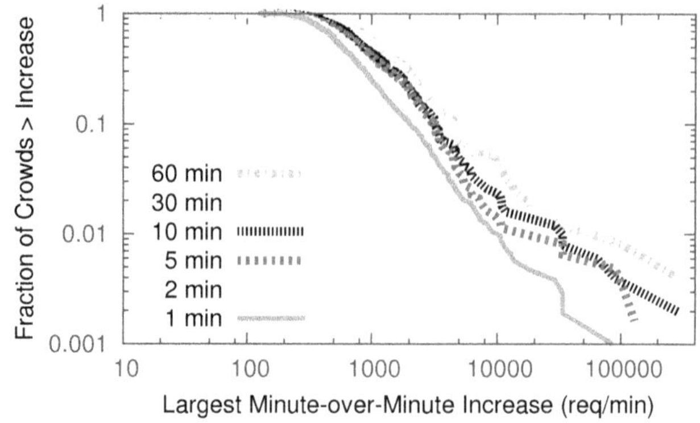

Figure 6: Complementary CDF of the largest request rate increase between successive minutes, for sets of crowds defined by different epoch lengths.

The situation is more complex when crowds are for dynamic or otherwise uncacheable content. In the face of flash crowds, poorly provisioned services can use fall-back mechanisms to reduce server functionality (for instance, disabling php execution on a web server). This approach reduces the computational load per request, but at the cost of losing personalization, analytics, or other beneficial services. It also fails to guarantee availability, since servers may be overwhelmed even under reduced functionality.

A second option is to push the problem of scaling computation (rather than the normal communication) to the CDN. This approach is supported by a set of "edge computing" APIs, which allow partial distribution of application logic to remote cache sites [3]. Unfortunately, not only does such a solution constrain application developers to a particular set of (non-standardized) service APIs, but it also fails to address the common situation where application logic requires back-end communication with a coordinating, more centralized database (which also must scale rapidly during crowds).

Only recently has a general-purpose solution arisen to the problem of scaling a dynamic application. The introduction of elastic computing platforms, such as Amazon's EC2, enables web services to spin-up new resources on demand in multiple global datacenters. Simultaneously, a litany of scalable back-end datastores—such as MongoDB, Cassandra, and HBase—scale quickly with the addition of new hardware resources (which also can be allocated in a virtualized environment).

Whether the resource allocation is delegated to a CDN or performed in-house using elastic-computing resources, the responsible service must have adequate time to react: Can such resource allocation be performed fast enough in the face of flash crowds? This section analyzes the rate of flash crowds and evaluates the efficacy of dynamic resource allocation.

4.1 Measuring Rate Increases

Figure 6 presents the complementary CDF of the maximal minute-over-minute increase in request rate observed during each crowd. A separate CCDF is plotted for each epoch time.

We observe that a handful of crowds experience extremely large surges in request rates, increasing by tens of thousand of requests in successive minutes. Further investigation determined that such volatility is caused by a particular usage scenario: such sites use HTTP 302 redirects to relay traffic to CoralCDN only during extremely loaded periods. Such elastic load shedding presents an

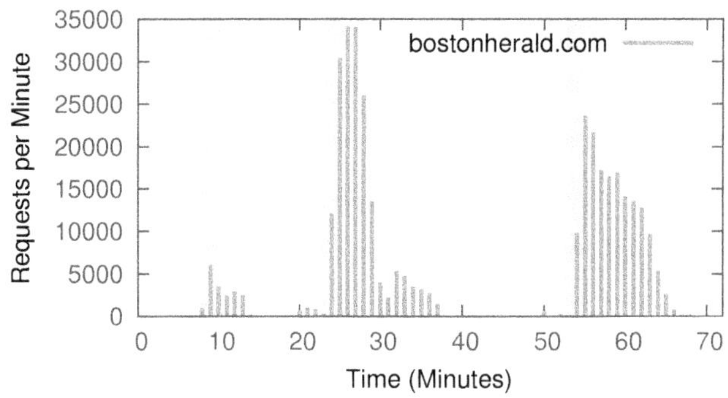

Figure 7: Surging request rates caused by intermittent 302 redirection from *The Boston Herald*.

attractive proposition for resource-constrained websites: the ability to use third-party content distribution only when local resources are oversubscribed. However, it also eliminates the traditional request build-up that can serve as an "early warning sign" for CDNs.

As an example of such rapid increases, Figure 7 plots the number of requests per minute to CoralCDN during a flash crowd experienced by *The Boston Herald* over roughly one hour. The three distinct traffic surges (grey background regions) occur just after the website switches on redirection, likely in response to a local load-shedding policy. As a result, CoralCDN sees thrashing and unpredictable request rates.

While instantaneous flash crowds to CoralCDN are still a small fraction of its total use, they still point to the important concept of resource elasticity. Under such scenarios, it can be difficult for CDNs and origins to respond quickly to dramatic load increases.

4.2 Effectiveness of Elastic Scaling

Crowds for static or dynamic content require distinct resource allocation mechanisms. Using cloud-computing platforms such as Amazon EC2, origin sites can "spin up" new virtual nodes to handle increased demand for dynamic or uncacheable content. Alternatively, CDNs can satisfy request spikes for static content by adapting the set of proxies handling a particular domain, possibly within seconds. In either case, the service must measure resource utilization and determine when to allocate new resources to address flash crowds.

To examine whether either environment can adapt rapidly enough, we simulated dynamic resource allocation strategies against the crowd traces. In our experiments, we assume that each proxy or compute node can handle a fixed request rate. We further consider a desired utilization ratio across all nodes. Production services often target an average utilization ratio that is well below 100% to ensure that spare capacity exists during unpredicted fluctuations in demand. Lower utilization provides a better hedge against rate increases, at the price of higher operational cost.

In our simulation, a service begins with a sufficient number of nodes to handle 5% of the crowd's peak load at the desired utilization. After each 10-second interval, during which time the request rate can increase, the service initializes zero or more new nodes to bring its utilization below the desired target. There is a delay of d seconds before a new node can service requests (d = 10, 60, 600). In this experiment, a service never decreases its number of active nodes.

Our main considerations are how often this simple strategy leaves the service oversubscribed (that is, more than 100% utilized) and how sensitive any oversubscription is to the speed of resource allocation.

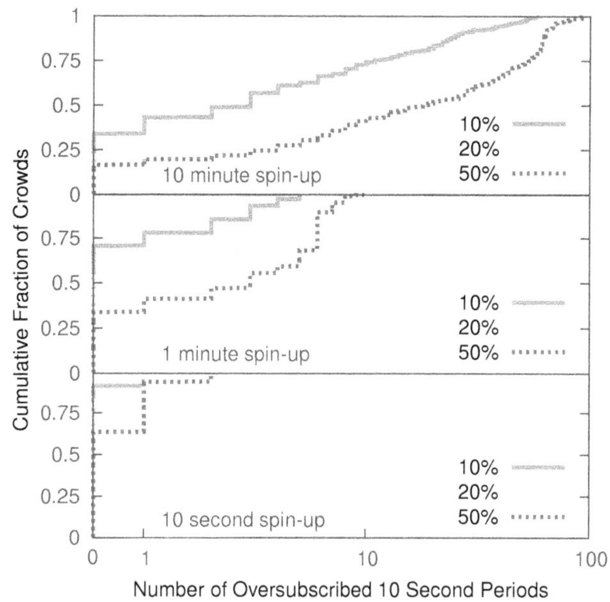

Figure 8: CDFs of the number of oversubscribed (>100% utilization) periods when resources are dynamically scaled during flash crowds. Plots differ by the spin-up delay *d* needed to bring resources online, each evaluating several target utilizations.

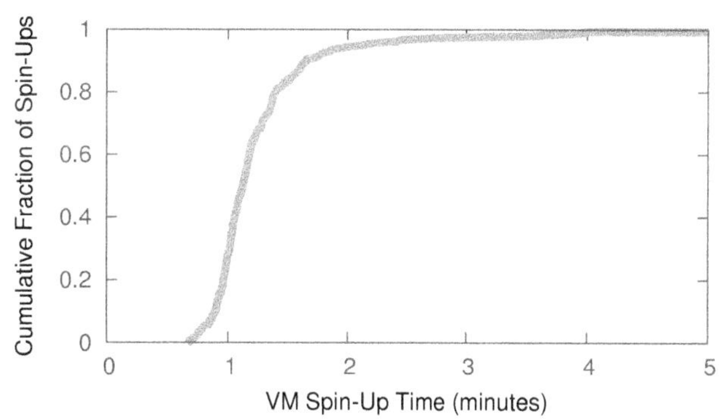

Figure 9: CDF of spin-up times for EC2 virtual instances.

Figure 8 plots a CDF of the number of oversubscribed 10-second intervals during each experiment (for each of the 2,501 crowds) for various target utilizations (10%, 20%, and 50%). We find that sub-minute resource allocation is required to prevent oversubscription in most flash crowds. For instance, if allocating new VMs requires ten minutes, 66% of all crowds experience at least one period of oversubscription, even under the most conservative target of 10% utilization. While this experiment is highly simplified, it motivates the need for further study on the effectiveness of resource allocation policies in the face of load volatility.

To characterize the delay for allocating new resources in the cloud, we profiled Amazon EC2. Our experiment measured the time required to spin-up a new VM, repeating the process in three different datacenter locations each hour over the course of one day (August 31, 2011). Figure 9 plots the CDF of spin-up times observed on EC2: The majority of instances became available within 1-2 minutes. Given these delays, avoiding dropped requests for the majority of observed crowds requires the most aggressive provisioning strategy.

Referer	# Crowds	Referer	# Crowds
digg.com	123	facebook.com	10
reddit.com	20	duggmirror.com	8
stumbleupon.com	15	duggback.com	5
google.com	11	twitter.com	4

Figure 10: Domains that are common referrers for crowds.

5. SOURCE ATTRIBUTION

While flash crowds may seem unpredictable and random to service providers, they are often explained by human factors. The "Slashdot Effect," for instance, refers to the spike in popularity witnessed by sites linked to by the Slashdot website. Increasingly, social networks are facilitating the *viral* sharing of links between acquaintances, which can lead to explosive growth in content popularity. This section qualifies the role of third-party portals in creating flash crowds.

5.1 Causal Inference for Source Attribution

We determine the cause of flash crowds through HTTP Referer headers. The Referer header, when present, indicates that a user has arrived at a particular URL by means of a link from another URL, or that the URL represents content embedded in a parent webpage. In many cases, a complex web of referrers arises when a user accesses a web page, fetches embedded content, and then further browses the trending website. We use the set of pair-wise referral links to reverse-engineer a user's HTTP session (with referral links that form a directed acyclic graph). This allows us to attribute their subsequent traffic to as small a set of originating referrers as possible.

5.2 Effects of Portals, Networks, and Tweets

Figure 10 lists referring domains that contributed heavily and frequently to flash crowds. We consider a domain as a heavy referrer if it originates more than a third of a crowd's requests. Well-known Internet portals, (in)famous for causing flash crowds, top this list. These findings confirm the perception that online portals are a common source for flash crowds. The term "Slashdot Effect" may be a slight misnomer, however: While Coralized URLs were posted on the Slashdot homepage several times during the trace, very few generated sufficient traffic to meet our crowd threshold. Still, these findings are predisposed by user behavior: CoralCDN appears to be more commonly used by digg readers than those of Slashdot.

Perhaps more surprising is the presence of crowds referred from Facebook and other social networking sites. Unlike centralized content portals, these sites disseminate links through social connections, spreading virally via pairwise, decentralized exchange. A link posted on Twitter is shared with direct followers, then re-tweeted and propagated through the social graph, for instance. Recent work [11] has considered the role of user location in predictively caching content for such crowds. We confirm that project's hypothesis that social-network activity can generate meaningful flash crowds.

A handful of crowds arose with even less explicit coordination: those whose primary referrer was search traffic from sites such as Google, Yahoo!, and Bing. These crowds relied on no central portal or coordinating website, instead growing through some type of out-of-band communication, *e.g.*, e-mail, word of mouth, etc. Still, through the "zeitgeist," search engines generated exponential traffic increases to particular websites, and ultimately to CoralCDN.

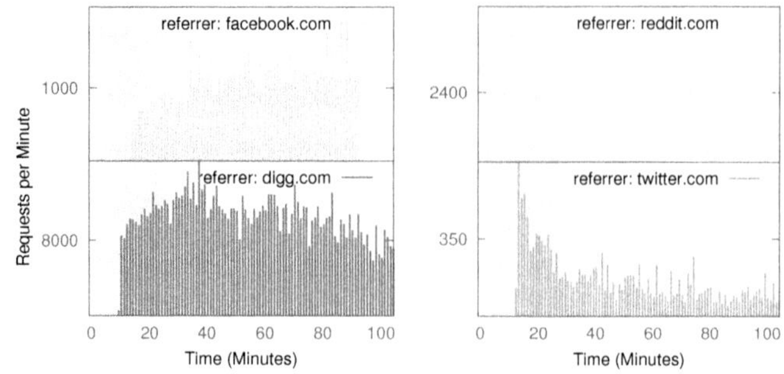

Figure 11: Referral traces from third parties. Each plots a distinct crowd, but timing of each surge (grey regions) are aligned.

To illustrate the traffic patterns from a few example crowds, Figure 11 plots the requests rates from a variety of referring websites, including social media sites and content portals.

6. RELATED WORK

Several research projects have focused on mitigating the effects of flash crowds. A number of papers explore the use of peer-to-peer protocols to cooperatively address traffic surges [5, 10, 12, 13]. Work on request redirection in traditional CDNs has also considered flash crowds, reallocating demand among back-end proxies during periods of high load [6]. Still other work has focused on detecting and pruning flash crowds within local networks, before traffic ever reaches a bombarded service [1, 7]. None of these studies consider traces or offer analysis of real flash crowds observed across the wide area. A notable exception is Jung *et al.* [8], which draws conclusions from a small number of flash crowds against a single web server. That study focuses on distinguishing flash crowd traffic from denial-of-service attacks, a topic we only briefly address in this paper. Very recent work has considered using social network information, such as user location, to determine cache policy during flash crowds [11]. That work restricts its analysis to user-level observations of twitter crowds, however, and it lacks information about the true network location of users and caches. Our analysis is complementary, profiling the actual distribution of users amongst caches in an operational CDN and characterizing cache locality during real crowds.

7. CONCLUSIONS

This paper finds that flash crowds, even when conservatively defined, are quite commonplace in a popular, open CDN. We initiate the study of flash-crowd dynamics using logs of several thousand such crowds. Our measurements show that crowds vary in their amenability to effective caching, and that cooperation between caching proxies minimizes origin load for some crowds, but not all. Further, we find that some crowds can grow too quickly for dynamic resource allocation to keep up with demand; cloud-based approaches of spinning up new VM instances can sometimes fare poorly in preventing oversubscription. Finally, we confirm anecdotal evidence that third-party portals contribute to substantial numbers of crowds, and document that the sharing of links through social media and the uncoordinated use of search engines lead to flash crowd formation as well.

Acknowledgments. We thank Stefan Saroiu and Kay Ousterhout for their helpful comments about this work. This work was supported by the National Science Foundation under Award CNS-0904860.

REFERENCES

[1] P. Barford and D. Plonka. Characteristics of network traffic flow anomalies. In *Proc. Internet Measurement Workshop (IMW)*, Nov. 2001.

[2] A. Chankhunthod, P. Danzig, C. Neerdaels, M. Schwartz, and K. Worrell. A hierarchical Internet object cache. In *Proc. USENIX Annual Technical Conference*, Jan. 1996.

[3] A. Davis, J. Parikh, and W. E. Weihl. EdgeComputing: Extending enterprise applications to the edge of the Internet. In *Proc. World Wide Web Conference (WWW)*, May 2004.

[4] M. J. Freedman. Experiences with CoralCDN: A five-year operational view. In *Proc. Networked Systems Design and Implementation (NSDI)*, Apr. 2010.

[5] M. J. Freedman, E. Freudenthal, and D. Mazières. Democratizing content publication with Coral. In *Proc. Networked Systems Design and Implementation (NSDI)*, Mar. 2004.

[6] L. Wang, V. Pai, and L. Peterson. The effectiveness of request redirection on CDN robustness. *SIGOPS Operating Systems Review*, 36, Dec. 2002.

[7] R. Mahajan, S. M. Bellovin, S. Floyd, J. Ioannidis, V. Paxson, and S. Shenker. Controlling high bandwidth aggregates in the network. *Computer Communications Review*, 32(3), July 2002.

[8] J. Jung, B. Krishnamurthy, and M. Rabinovich. Flash crowds and Denial of Service attacks: Characterization and implications for CDNs and web sites. In *Proc. World Wide Web Conference (WWW)*, May 2002.

[9] E. Nygren, R. K. Sitaraman, and J. Sun. The Akamai network: A platform for high-performance Internet applications. *SIGOPS Operating Systems Review*, 44, Aug. 2010.

[10] V. N. Padmanabhan and K. Sripanidkulchai. The case for cooperative networking. In *Proc. Intl. Workshop on Peer-to-Peer Systems (IPTPS)*, Mar. 2002.

[11] S. Scellato, C. Mascolo, M. Musolesi, and J. Crowcroft. Track globally, deliver locally: Improving content delivery networks by tracking geographic social cascades. In *Proc. World Wide Web Conference (WWW)*, Mar. 2011.

[12] S. Shakkottai and R. Johari. Demand-aware content distribution on the Internet. *IEEE/ACM Trans. Networking*, 18(2), Apr. 2010.

[13] T. Stading, P. Maniatis, and M. Baker. Peer-to-peer caching schemes to address flash crowds. In *Proc. Intl. Workshop on Peer-to-Peer Systems (IPTPS)*, Mar. 2002.

[14] B. Maggs. Personal communication, 2009.

Summary Review Documentation for

"Going Viral: Flash Crowds in an Open CDN"

Authors: P. Wendell, M. Freedman

Reviewer #1

Strengths: Very interesting topic. Talk of flash crowds can be found all over the area of content distribution but surprisingly it is almost always anecdotal whereas there is very little systematic work on characterizing them.
The connection to elastic (cloud based) scaling is very relevant and interesting.
The fact that flash crowds can also arise in an epidemic, OSN-based, manner is also very interesting and rather unexpected.

Weaknesses: The comparison between cooperative and non-cooperative caching is rather dull and misleading.
Fails to cite and compare against related work on early detection of social cascades, e.g. Salvatore Scellato, Cecilia Mascolo, Mirco Musolesi, Jon Crowcroft "Track Globally, Deliver Locally: Improving Content Delivery Networks by Tracking Geographic Social Cascades", Proc. of 20th International World Wide Web Conference (WWW 2011), Hyderabad, India. March 2011. You also need to explain the novelty with respect to [3].

Comments to Authors: Very interesting and timely work.

Main concern: You NEED to comment and put your work in context with respect to the papers mentioned above. Your work is not the only measurement work in the area.

Some additional suggestions:

Sec. 3.2 "Comparison of Caching Strategies" is rather boring compared with the rest of the paper. I would say that the matter is also a bit exaggerated since the difference between cooperative and non-cooperative caching is rather trivial in terms of the load reaching the origin server. The maximum difference in number of requests hitting the origin server cannot exceed the size of the caching group. Since the number of hits of a flash crowd is in the order of thousands per minute whereas for most CDNs the number of servers/PoPs is in the order of hundreds, it does not really matter if you get |size of caching group| fewer requests at the origin server. The comparison makes sense for long tail content where individual items see a few requests but is totally secondary for flush crowds. The "flash crowds" that see some difference are indeed the smallest ones. The paper totally bloats its importance in my opinion.

I wish you could nail down a little bit more the elastic scaling section. For instance, run an example in EC2 and automate the purchase process. Report the metrics under real VM purchasing delays.

Reviewer #2

Strengths: - The problem of identifying and mitigating flash crowds in CDNs is timely.
- To the best of my knowledge this is the first paper that formally defines flash crowds.
- The authors use large scale measurements of an operational CDN to identify and characterize flash crowds. This can be a good reference paper.
- The conclusions of this paper are very important for the design and dimensioning of CDNs.
- The paper is well written and easy to follow.

Weaknesses: None.

Comments to Authors: In Section 3.2, you may want to refer to the following paper: S. Triukose, Z. Al-Qudah, and M. Rabinovich, "Content Delivery Networks: Protection or Threat?", in ESORICS, 2009. In this paper the authors show that it is easy to take advantage of the hierarchical cache structure in order to attack the original server by utilizing CDN nodes. Thus, a collaborative scheme is not only robust to flash crowds, but to DDoS as well.

Can you correlate the time zone of the AS and the time-of-day that flash crowd is observed? Can you verify that the majority of flash crowds take place on the peak time of the time zone of ASes with the highest population of users? Do you see that users that belong to ASes in different time zones are participating in a follow-up flash crowd?

It would be nice if you comment on the delay penalty that end users pay due to flash crowd. Is it the case that users from US are re-directed to Europe or Asia during flash crowds using your collaborating caching scheme?

As a second reference for the Akamai architecture, you may want to this the following reference: "The Akamai Network: A Platform for High-Performance Internet Applications" ACM SIGOPS Operating Systems Review, Vol. 44, No.3, July 2010.

A minor comment when working with CoralCDN: It seems that applications that depend on location information may have problems. For example when you are browsing http://www.google.com.nyud.net/ in France you may be redirected to the front page of Czech Google. It seems that collaborative caching may mitigate flash crowds but can also be unfriendly to location-based services.

Reviewer #3

Strengths: This is a solid measurement paper with interesting results.

Weaknesses: I wish the paper would have gone down one step deeper, for example use some specific examples to more vividly describe the creation and impact of flash crowds. The current paper only has rather aggregated curves.

Comments to Authors: One problem I had with reading this paper is that I"m not familiar with CoralCDN, to know exactly how it works or who are its user communities.

I also have a slightly different opinion regarding the role of cooperative vs. independent caching by CDN nodes. The paper argued that CDN nodes collaboration would be needed to help reduce origin server workload. However deployed CDN systems can use URL hashing to assure that the requests for the same data go to the same nodes, achieve the goal without the overhead of collaboration.

Reviewer #4

Strengths: Nice paper, which presents a formal definition of flash crowds and examines their effect on caching and a case-study showing whether cloud services can help. Interesting to see that social network activity leads to significant flash crowds.

Weaknesses: Only minor problems with the paper.

Comments to Authors: I enjoyed reading the paper, and I would actually like to see more from the analysis, especially regarding the sources of flash crowds.

The paper is also well written.

You introduce a number of hard constants in your model, which seem to come out of nowhere. It would be nice to present some intuition first on why these are the right numbers (e.g., number of reqs/min as a lower threshold).

I really have no context on what type of users CoralCDN serves. Some description here would help.

Regarding the analysis of the sources, it would be interesting to see the relative intensity across different types of flash crowds and their characteristics. For example, I would like to see similar figures to 1-3, but conditioning on the source of the flash crowd.

Reviewer #5

Strengths: - The CoralCDN dataset collected over a 4 years time-period.

- Interesting observations on the effect of flash crowds for designing and operating CDNs.

Weaknesses: - The definition of flash crowd is meant to be formal, but looks very ad hoc.

- The work is quite preliminary, but this is OK for a short paper.

Comments to Authors: It is nice to have a formal definition of flash crowds, but this definition looks quite ad hoc to me. First, why are k = 3 (minutes, I guess) enough, the exponential rate of increase during these 3 minutes at least 2 (and nothing else), on which duration is the max taken when comparing it m = 500 and 15*average_rate?

I do not understand how you obtain the 3 curves superimposed on the cloud of points in Figure 3. An explanation would help.

Response from the Authors

We thank the reviewers for their careful consideration. We identify three primary topics expressed in these reviews: (i) commentary on the caching observations in the paper, (ii) issues with the definition of "flash crowd" used to detect crowds, and (iii) confusion about CoralCDN's design and user population.

Reviewers #1 and #3 offered distinct criticisms of the caching section. In the first case, the reviewer asserted that the number of origin requests was limited to the size of caching group, which is small enough to be inconsequential even in the worst case. In fact, those requests are bounded by (the size of caching group * number of unique URLs), hence the important of content dynamism discussed in section 3. In the second case, the reviewer suggested that simply designating a small number of caches responsible for a particular crowd could prevent origin overload. This is not always a desired solution: some of today's CDNs run on tens of thousands of servers located in thousands of networks, specifically so that content is cached near to geographically disparate clients.

Reviewers #4 and #5 took issue with the paper's formal definition of a flash crowd. These reviewers pointed to the use of some constant terms as somewhat ad-hoc. Our intent in defining a "flash crowd" was to provide a reasonable working definition for our analysis and future projects. We couldn't find any quantitative definition of flash crowds in prior work (likely because they considered a single or small number of events), and we needed some way to classify crowds from amongst the 4 years of traces we analyzed. That said, we altered the text to better frame this definition and explained its constants in some more detail.

Several reviewers requested more information about the details of particular crowds and about CoralCDN. Our intention in writing this paper was to describe aggregate data on crowds, rather than in-depth analysis of any particular crowd (readily available in prior work). Thus, given space constraints, we have not elected to include detailed or anecdotal discussions of particular crowds. We have also added a little more information about CoralCDN in the text, although readers wanting more information about CoralCDN can consult its two referenced papers, which describe its design and operation in depth.

Finally, a few reviewers referred us to recent related work; we added references to these publications where appropriate

Characterizing Roles of Front-end Servers in End-to-End Performance of Dynamic Content Distribution

Yingying Chen, Sourabh Jain, Vijay Kumar Adhikari, Zhi-Li Zhang
Department of Computer Science & Engineering
University of Minnesota - Twin Cities
Minneapolis, MN 55414, USA
{yingying,sourj,viadhi,zhzhang}@cs.umn.edu

ABSTRACT

This paper investigates the roles of front-end (proxy) servers in improving user-perceived performance of *dynamic* content distribution. Using Bing and Google search services as two case studies, we perform extensive network measurement and analysis to understand several key factors that affect the overall user-perceived performance. In particular, we develop a simple model-based inference framework to indirectly measure and quantify the (directly unobservable) "frontend-to-backend fetching time" comprised of the query processing time at back-end data centers and the delivery time between the back-end data centers and front-end servers. We show that this fetching time plays a critical role in the end-to-end performance of dynamic content delivery.

Categories and Subject Descriptors

C.4 [**Performance of Systems**]: Performance attributes

General Terms

Measurement, Performance

Keywords

Dynamic content distribution, Search service, TCP-splitting

1. INTRODUCTION

More and more content on the Internet is now stored at powerful, large-scale data centers in the cloud. A significant portion of this content is *dynamic* in that in response to a user's request for content, the content returned to her is generated dynamically and sometimes personalized. Web search is one common example of such dynamic content generation. With the emergence of cloud computing and cloud-based services, we expect that more data will be stored in the cloud, and more dynamic content will be generated on the fly in response to user requests. Because of the sheer scale and cost of building and operating large-scale powerful data centers, their number is few and far between. Hence they are generally far away from a large majority of users.

One way to mitigate this effect and improve the user-perceived performance (e.g., the overall response time) is to deploy "proxy" servers – hereafter we refer to them as *front-end* (FE) servers – closer to users. The usefulness of such an approach for *static* content distribution (e.g., video) is obvious because of *content caching*. FE servers can also be exploited to improve the *user-perceived* performance of *dynamic* content distribution due to the following two key aspects [9,11]: i) a portion of the (dynamic) content may be static; thus can be cached and delivered immediately from the FE servers; and more importantly, ii) via *split* TCP connections, a FE server can establish a *persistent* TCP connection with the data center which not only eliminates the effect of TCP slow-start congestion window ramp-up on the throughput of the TCP connection between the FE server and the back-end (BE) data center, but also mitigates such effect on the throughput of the TCP connection between the user and the FE server (due to the reduced RTT). Nonetheless, the *overall* user-perceived *end-to-end* performance likely depends on a confluence of various factors such as RTT, loss rate and throughput of the connections between users and FE servers and between FE servers and BE data centers, the load on FE servers, the processing time at BE data centers to generate user-requested dynamic content, and so forth.

To investigate the roles of FE servers in improving user-perceived end-to-end performance of *dynamic* content distribution, we conduct an active measurement-based *comparative* study of Google and Microsoft Bing web search services. Both services utilize a number of FE servers that are placed closer to users to assist *dynamic* content (i.e., search results) distribution: Google deploys a set of its own FE servers, whereas Bing relies on Akamai's content distribution network (CDN). Using the PlanetLab nodes, we perform extensive measurements of Google and Bing search services by emulating and generating a variety of keyword search queries of varying popularity, granularity and complexity, and collect a large amount of dynamically generated content and application-layer measurement data. Through *content analysis* and *temporal clustering* of packet-level events, we confirm that both Bing and Google search results contain a *static* portion, such as the HTTP header, HTML header, etc., which is cached and delivered immediately by the FE servers upon receiving a user request. As the effect of the aforementioned second key aspect cannot be *directly* measured, we develop a novel *model-based* inference framework: we classify and separate the content (i.e., search results) into

IMC'11, November 2–4, 2011, Berlin, Germany.

two parts – the *static* portion that is cached and directly delivered by FE servers, and the *dynamic* portion that is generated by the BE data centers and then passed onto the FE servers for delivery. We define several *directly measurable* parameters to characterize and *predict* the delivery performances of static and dynamic portions. These predictions are indeed borne out by our measurement data, and thus enable us to deduce that despite that one utilizes a third-party CDN (as FE servers) and the other does not, both Bing and Google employ FE servers in a similar fashion.

Furthermore, our inference framework allows us to *bound* the *FE-BE fetch time* (T_{fetch}) of dynamic content – namely, the overall time it takes for a FE server to forward user query to a BE data center, for the data center to dynamically generate the user-requested content and deliver it to the FE server – we note that *this time cannot be directly observed and measured at the end systems.* Comparing Bing and Google search services, we find that the fetch time between Google FE servers and BE data centers tends to be smaller and more stable for Google; in contrast, the fetch time between the Akamai FE servers and Bing data centers tends to be larger and shows higher variability. Hence, despite Akamai FE servers are generally placed closer to users (and their number is larger than that of Google FE servers), user-perceived performance of the Bing search service tends to vary significantly from queries to queries. While it is known that placing FE servers closer to users can generally improve the user-perceived performance (e.g. [9]), our study demonstrates a critical trade-off between placement of FE servers and the FE-BE fetch time which limits this improvement: there is a *distance threshold* within which placing FE servers further closer to users is no longer helpful; instead, the end-to-end performance is now determined solely by the FE-BE fetch time. Thus, to improve the end-to-end performance, it is also crucial to optimize the FE-BE fetch time. Lastly, we develop heuristics to factor the FE-BE fetch time so as to estimate the back-end processing time (T_{proc}) and the BE-FE round-trip delivery time (RTT_{be}) separately.

Related Work. Most prior works in this area focus on understanding the distribution of static content. For instance, in [5], authors study the assignment of clients to the CDN edge servers, in order to maximize the performance for each user. Similarly, several other studies such as [4,6,7] develop techniques to use a peer-to-peer based model to distribute the content, which is assumed to be static. In [10] authors study the various caching mechanisms used by CDN networks. Besides, a recent OSN study [12] show that placing more proxy servers can enhance the content distribution for Facebook users sharing similar interests. However, the focus of the study was to exploit the redundancy in the data accessed by users in a given geography, and reduced the user-perceived delay by caching the content at nearby proxy servers. A study [9] that is more closely related to our work compares the performance of cloud service with and without tcp-splitting, and therefore dealt with only the indispensability of TCP-splitting. On the other hand, in this paper, by reverse engineering the strategies used by Google and Bing to distribute the dynamic content, we shed light on the trade-offs among different underlying factors in designing TCP-splitting for dynamic content distribution.

2. PROBLEM SETTING & A SIMPLE MODEL

In this section, we describe the basic infrastructure with FE servers for dynamic content distribution, and present a simple abstract model to capture the interactions between users and FE servers and between FE servers and BE data centers. This model will guide us in the measurement and analysis of dynamically generated search results from Bing and Google.

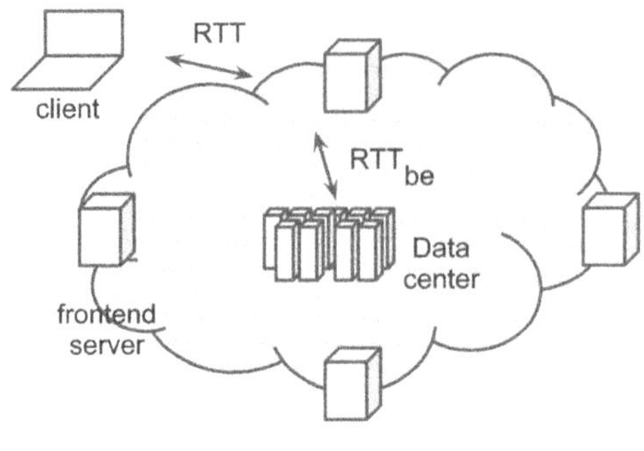

Figure 1: Content distribution infrastructure.

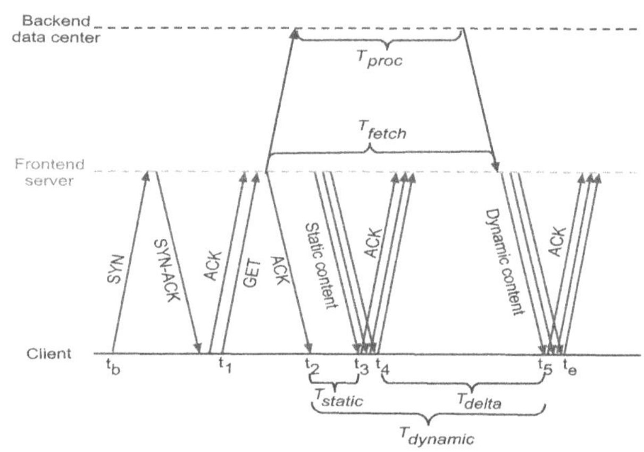

Figure 2: Modeling search query timeline.

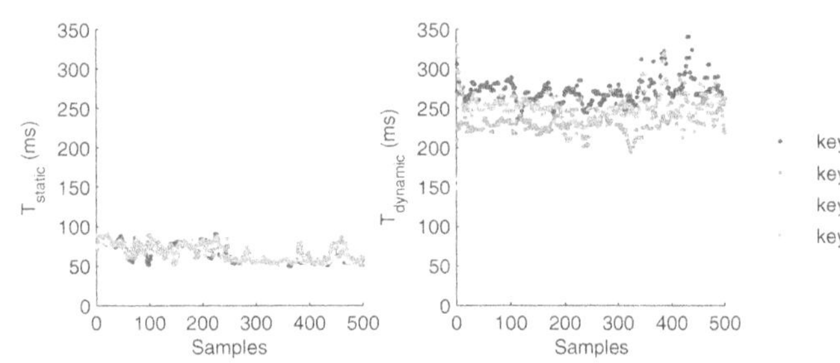

Figure 3: T_{static} and $T_{dynamic}$ for different keywords.

Figure 1 depicts a typical infrastructure set-up for dynamic content delivery consisting of FE servers that are deployed at the "edge of the cloud" (thus relatively closer to users) and BE data centers "deep in the cloud". When serving static content, FE servers often function as caches. When serving dynamic content, FE servers can play two key roles: i) they can cache certain portion of static content that is common to all dynamically generated content, and deliver it immediately upon receiving a user's request; ii) by splitting the end-to-end TCP connection, FE servers can establish persistent TCP connections with BE data center to speed up the delivery of the dynamically generated content between them.

Unlike the static content distribution, there are several key factors affecting the user-perceived performance of dynamic content distribution: the latency or round-trip time (RTT), available bandwidth and loss rate between a user and a FE server, the load on a FE server, the latency or round-trip time, available bandwidth and loss rate between a FE server and the BE data center, the processing time at the data center to generate dynamic content in response to a user's request, the load on servers at the data centers, and so forth. Unfortunately most of these latter factors cannot be *directly observed and measured at the end hosts*. To address this, we develop a novel inference framework which allows us to indirectly measure and quantify the overall (search query) processing and delivery time between the data center and a FE server.

As shown in Figure 2, we model the packet-level generation and reception process and define several (*measurable*) parameters to capture the events of the *static* and *dynamic* portions of the content distribution. The process starts at t_b with a TCP three-way handshake[1]. At time t_1, a user (client) sends an HTTP GET request, and receives the ACK packet from the FE server after one RTT at t_2. At t_3 the client receives the first packet containing the *static* portion of the content, and at t_4 receives the last packet containing the static content. At time t_5, the first packet containing dynamic content is received, and at time t_e, the final packet of the entire content is received. The correctness of the model is validated in later sections, and is also quite consistent with the descriptions given in [8, 9, 11].

In our model, the time when the first and last packets of the *static* content portion are received should, *by definition*, hinge on the factors involving only the FE server and client, namely, they are independent of the BE data center. We define $T_{static} := t_4 - t_2 (= t_4 - t_1 - RTT)$ which bounds the processing and delivery of the static content portion *at the FE server side* (assuming a constant RTT). We define $T_{dynamic} := t_5 - t_2$ and $T_{delta} := t_4 - t_2$. Then $T_{dynamic}$ upper-bounds the overall fetch time T_{fetch}, while $T_{delta} := t_5 - t_4$ serves as a (potentially loose) lower-bound on this overall time. Meanwhile, T_{fetch} is mainly consisted of the time it takes for the FE server to send the user request to a BE data center, for the data center to process and dynamically generate a response (the *dynamic content* portion) to the user request, and deliver it to the FE server. Namely,

$$T_{delta} \leq T_{fetch} \leq T_{dynamic} \qquad (1)$$

$$T_{fetch} = T_{proc} + C * RTT_{be} \qquad (2)$$

where C is constant, which depends on the TCP window size on the BE data center. Moreover, fixing a FE server, T_{fetch} should be a constant, assuming the variability introduced by FE server and data center loads, the available bandwidth between them, etc., is small and negligible relative to the RTT between the FE server and a client. In other words, the time it takes for the FE server to receive the delivery of the *dynamically generated* portion of the content from the BE server is (roughly) a constant. On the other hand, the delivery time ($t_4 - t_3$) for the static content is a function of RTT. Hence our model predicts that as RTT increases, T_{delta} decreases. With sufficiently large RTT, $T_{delta} = 0$; thus the last packet of the static content portion and the first packet of the dynamic content portion will be delivered back-to-back or even coalesce as a single packet.

[1]DNS resolution time is not included, as it is negligible as compared to the overall user-perceived response time.

3. ACTIVE MEASUREMENT & CONTENT ANALYSIS

For our study, we develop an in-house user search query emulator, which performs exactly the same functionality as the web-based search box. We deploy the emulator on globally distributed[2] PlanetLab nodes as well as on our lab and home machines. The number of Planetlab nodes participating in each of our experiments ranges from 200 to 250, depending on their reachability at the time being. We conduct extensive measurements by submitting the same search queries to both Bing and Google search engines, and collect detailed TCPdump with full application-layer payloads. We perform two sets of experiments: 1) In the first set, search queries are launched from all measurement nodes to their *default*[3] FE servers every 10 seconds. 2) In the second set, we fix one FE server (of Bing or Google respectively) at a time, and launch queries from all measurement nodes to this server. We repeat these two sets of experiments using different sets of keywords and over different times. We refer to the data collected in the first set/type of experiments as *Datasets A*, and the second as *Datasets B*. Due to space limitation, we omit the details of the active measurement platform and experiment design and execution.

Parsing Application-Layer Packet Traces and Identifying the Static Content Part. Using the packet traces collected via TCPdump, we perform detailed application layer content analysis as well as transport layer temporal classification of packet generation and reception events. We find that in the search results returned by both Bing and Google, there is a portion of the content that is *static*, namely, independent of the search keywords submitted. This *static* content portion includes the HTTP header, HTML header, CSS style files, and the static menu bar, e.g. "Videos," "News," "Shopping," etc. that are placed on top of each search result page. The remaining *dynamic* portion includes the *keyword-dependent* dynamic menu bar, search results and ads. The temporal analysis of the packet-level events confirms that this static content portion is most likely cached at FE servers and delivered immediately, as its delivery time is largely a function of RTT, and does not vary significantly with, say, the types and complexity of search queries as does the dynamic content portion (see below and Section 4).

Choice and Effect of Search Queries. Since the dynamically generated content portion is search query dependent, we use different sets of search keywords with varying *popularity, granularity, and complexity*. For instance, the Bing main page provides a list of most popular keywords at the current time. In terms of granularity, we generate search queries with concatenated keywords which gives us increasingly refined search results (e.g., "Computer Science Department" and "Computer Science Department at University of Minnesota"). In terms of complexity, we use long and com-

[2]Although users are distributed globally, the size of the returned search results are quite similar.

[3]The default server is whatever server IP address the DNS resolution returns to the client.

plex search queries and mixtures of keywords that are not highly correlated (e.g., "computer *and* potato").

As an example, Fig. 3 illustrates the effect of 4 search keywords of different types on the Bing search performance: the left and right panels plot T_{static} and $T_{dynamic}$, respectively, for the 500 sample queries made in chronological order. As the performance is susceptible to short-term fluctuations, we plot the moving median with the sample window size being 10. (The results using Google have similar distributions.) We observe that $T_{dynamic}$ varies significantly with the types of search keywords used, whereas T_{static} is mostly insensitive to the search keywords used.

Do FE Servers Cache Search Results? To answer this question and mitigate the effect of this type of caching on our measurement analysis, we conduct a series of experiments. First, we collect a list of commonly searched keywords (e.g., "mobile cloud computing") as listed in the drop-down "search suggestion box" used by both Bing and Google. We also generate a list of search words not listed by the suggestion bar. A total of 40,000 keywords are used in the experiments. We perform two sets of experiments. In the first set, all measurement nodes submit the same search query sequentially to a fixed FE server. In the second set, each node submits a different search query to a fixed FE server. We repeat the experiments with different search queries and vary the FE server used. Analysis and comparison of the measurement results (in particular, the characteristics and distributions of $T_{dynamic}$) suggest that FE servers do *not* appear to cache any (dynamically generated) search result. This may not be too surprising, as most search engines attempt to *personalize* search results for individual users.

4. DISSECTING END-USER PERFORMANCE

In this section, we present the analysis of search query traces collected by us using Bing and Google. In particular, we use the model described in Sec. 2 to extract the T_{static} and $T_{dynamic}$ from the traces. We present our methodology to understand how the round trip delay between user and FE web servers affects the distribution of T_{static} and $T_{dynamic}$.

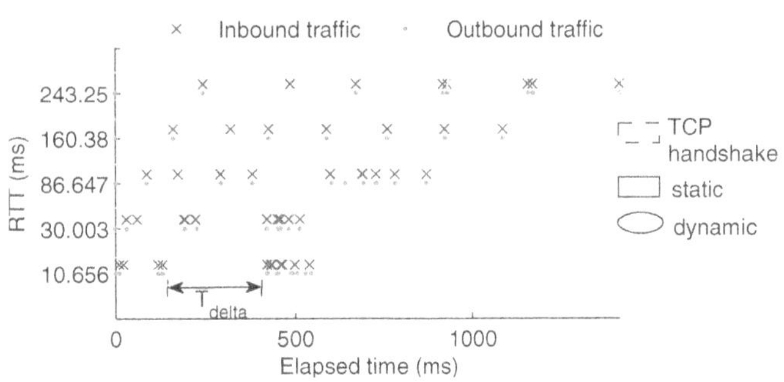

Figure 4: Inbound and outbound traffic events triggered by a single search query.

4.1 Extracting & Analyzing T_{static} and $T_{dynamic}$

Guided by the basic abstract model in Sec. 2, we perform temporal analysis of the packet-level events at the user (client) side using the collected packet traces. Figure 4 plots five sample timelines of packet generation and reception events at the client side, where five PlanetLab nodes are used as clients, each submitting the same search query to the Bing FE server. The x-axis represents the elapsed time since the start of the session, when the first TCP SYN packet is sent to the FE web server. The y-axis represents the round trip time (RTT) between the client and the FE server. Each horizontal array of dots/markers represents the timeline of packet-level events, where each blue cross/red dot marker indicates the sending/receiving time of a TCP packet. When RTT values are small, the temporal clusters of packet events are clearly visible: correlating with the application-layer packet payloads, we find that the first cluster represents the three-way TCP handshake between the client and the FE server; the second and third cluster represent the delivery of static and dynamic contents, respectively, from the server to the client. As the RTT increases, the gap between the end of the second and the beginning of the third clusters decreases, and eventually the two are lumped together, as predicted exactly by our model.

Using the *datasets B* collected via the second type of experiments (see Sec. 3) conducted for both Bing and Google, we extract and analyze the parameters T_{static}, $T_{dynamic}$ and T_{delta}. Figure 5 shows the distribution of these parameters using a sample of measurement data for one Bing FE server (IP address 198.189.255.208) and one Google FE server (IP address 74.125.224.18), where 720 repeated experiments using the same search query are performed over time at each PlanetLab node. In these plots, x-axis represents the RTT between a PlanetLab node and the FE server, while y-axis represents the *median* value of T_{static}, $T_{dynamic}$ and T_{delta} observed at each of the PlanetLab nodes. With a few outliers, the leftmost plot shows that for both Bing and Google, T_{static} is relatively stable and is largely independent of the PlanetLab node that had sent the query. Similarly, $T_{dynamic}$ is roughly a constant when RTT is small. However, when RTT is large, $T_{dynamic}$ increases linearly with RTT. In the case of T_{delta}, when RTT is small, it decreases linearly with RTT; and it becomes zero when RTT is beyond a certain threshold (for Google, this threshold is around 50ms to 100ms, for Bing, around 100ms to 200ms).

All these observations can be explained using our simple abstract model. First note that in the definition of T_{static}, we have subtracted the (initial) effect of RTT. Hence T_{static} depends mostly on the time to generate and deliver the (same) static content portion at the FE server (assuming the available bandwidth and the server load seen by all the PlanetLab node is roughly the same). When RTT is small, the delivery of the static content portion will be finished before the FE receives the dynamically generated search result from the BE data center (the time at which this is received at the FE server is independent of where the client is). Hence when RTT is small, $T_{dynamic}$ is roughly a constant while T_{delta} decreases as a function of RTT. When RTT increases beyond a certain threshold, the dynamic content portion will be received by the FE server before the static content portion is entirely delivered to the client. Hence $T_{dynamic}$ increases as a function of RTT (due to the TCP window mechanism), while T_{delta} becomes zero. The observations therefore match the prediction by our simple abstract model. Our analysis also suggests that below a certain threshold, reducing the RTT further will not drastically improve the overall user perceived performance.

4.2 Comparing Bing & Google Performances

We now compare the performances of Bing and Google by

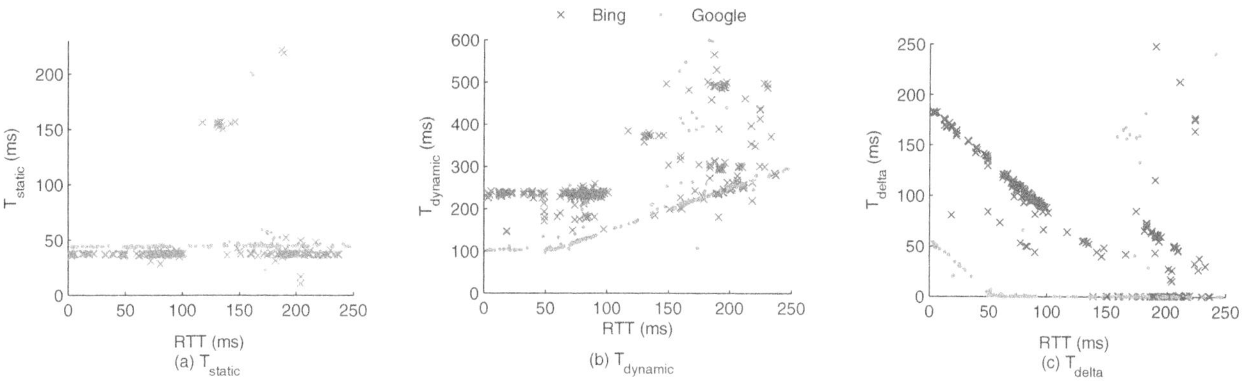

Figure 5: Distribution of T_{static}, $T_{dynamic}$, and T_{delta}.

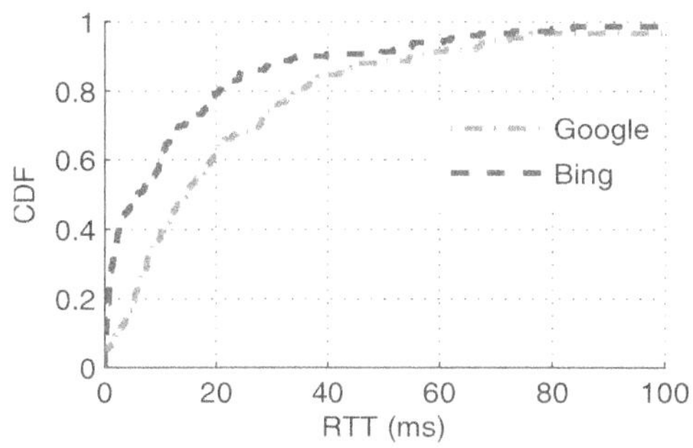

Figure 6: RTT distribution.

examining various factors and time components in affecting the overall user-perceived response times using the *datasets A* collected via the first type of experiments (see Sec. 3).

Comparing RTT Distributions. In Figure 6, we compare the RTTs between the PlanetLab nodes and their *default* FE servers (as determined by the DNS resolution). As seen in this plot, in general, Bing has FE servers (Akamai CDN servers) which are closer to PlanetLab nodes than for Google. In particular, more than 80% of PlanetLab nodes observe an RTT of less than 20ms for reaching the Bing FE servers. On the other hand, only 60% of PlanetLab nodes observe this latency for Google.

Comparing T_{static} and $T_{dynamic}$ Distributions.

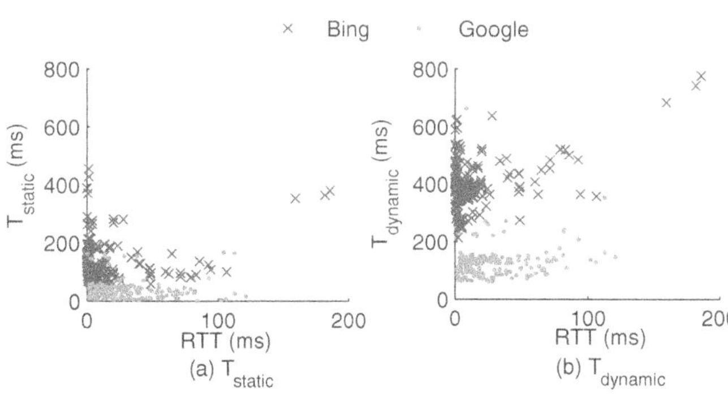

Figure 7: T_{static} and $T_{dynamic}$ for Planetlab nodes using default frontend servers.

Next, we extract and analyze T_{static} and $T_{dynamic}$ seen by each client when the default FE server is used for search queries. Figure 7 shows the distribution of T_{static} and $T_{dynamic}$ for both Google and Bing. As seen in this figure, although the Bing FE servers are generally closer to the clients (PlanetLab nodes), it has significantly higher value of T_{static} and $T_{dynamic}$ than Google. In contrast, Google has slightly farther FE servers from the clients, but has significantly lower T_{static} and $T_{dynamic}$. In addition, Bing exhibits more *variable* performance (i.e., higher variances) in the measured values of T_{static} and $T_{dynamic}$ than Google. These results illustrate that placing FE servers closer to clients does not necessarily reduce T_{static} and $T_{dynamic}$. We speculate that a plausible reason that Bing has higher and more variable T_{static} values may be due to the higher and more variable loads at the Akamai FE servers, as they are shared with a number of other services; while that Google FE servers have smaller and more stable T_{static} values may be attributed to the fact that these servers are likely dedicated to distribution of search results. Similarly, the $T_{dynamic}$ values for Bing FE servers are larger, and have more variability. The contributing factors may involve the processing capability and load fluctuations on the BE data centers, the search algorithm being used, the quality of the connection between FE and BE servers, e.g. loss rate, jitter, throughput, etc. A dedicated connection between FE and BE servers via "internal" network usually provides better connection than that built on the general Internet connections.

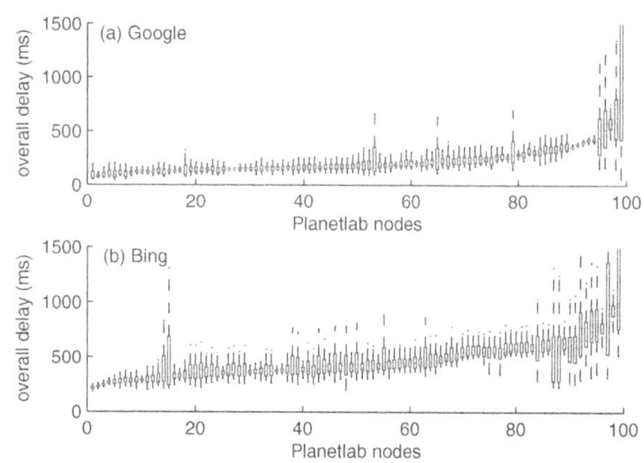

Figure 8: Overall delay performances.

Comparing Overall User Search Experiences. Finally, we compare the overall responsive time for individual search queries performed on both Bing and Google, as shown in Figure 8. The x-axis represents the PlanetLab nodes, and the y-axis represents the box-plot for the distribution for different samples. The results show that comparing Google, users using the Bing search service tend to experience slightly longer and more variable overall response times. In conclusion, our study shows that simply placing FE servers closer to users may not be entirely effective in improving the overall user-perceived performance in dynamic content distribution. Other key factors such as the processing time, server loads at both FE servers and BE data centers as well as the (physical and TCP) connections between them also play a critical role. Improving and optimizing these factors are therefore important in improving the overall user-perceived performance in dynamic content distribution such as dynamic generation of search results in response to user queries.

5. FACTORING FE-BE FETCH TIME

As discussed in Sec. 2, T_{fetch} consists of two key components, namely, T_{proc} and RTT_{be}. They represent the search query processing time at the BE data center and the delivery time of search results from the BE server to the FE server respectively. As part of our ongoing work, we are exploring various mechanisms to separate these two components.

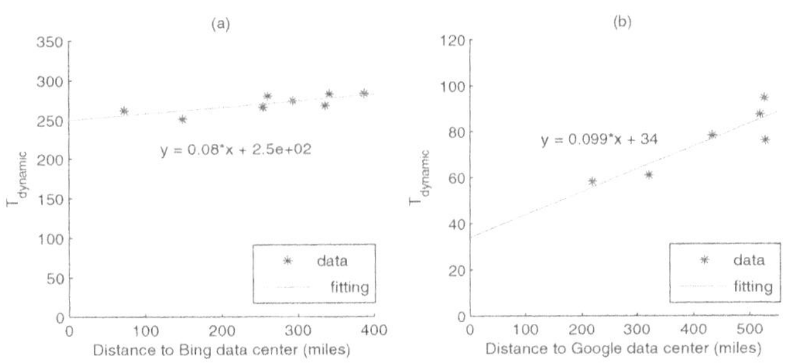

Figure 9: Correlating $T_{dynamic}$ and the distance to BE data center.

To get a better understanding of these components we conducted the following analysis. We first get a list of possible locations for Bing and Google data centers from [1, 2]. Next for each of these data centers we consider the geographically closest FE servers, and plot the distribution of $T_{dynamic}$ with respect to geographical distane between FE and BE. As explained in Sec 4 for smaller values of RTT, $T_{dynamic}$ can be considered as an approximation for the T_{fetch}. Figure 9 shows the distribution of T_{fetch} time for Bing and Google with respect to the geographical distance between the FE and BE locations. For this plot, we consider the Bing data center located in Virginia (US), while we pick the Lenoir, North Carolina data center for Google. As seen in these figures, the T_{fetch} time increases linearly as the distance between BE and FE increases. We perform a linear regression to fit a straight line for these data points, which is shown using the red continuous lines in the figure. As seen in this figure the Y-intercept for the regression is 260ms for Bing, while it is only 34ms for Google data center. This intercept actually represents the computation time for a given search query for Bing and Google data centers. Similarly, the slope of the line represents the contribution of network delay in T_{fetch}, which are similar for both Bing and Google. For the different keywords used in our search queries, we get very similar slope, but pretty ydifferent intercept values. Though our initial results show interesting characteristics of factors affecting the FE-BE fetch time, we are currently conducting extensive experiments and analysis to gain a better understanding behind the factors affecting the FE-BE fetch time, and thus will potentially guide us in designing better content placement and delivery strategies for dynamic content distribution.

6. DISCUSSIONS

In this paper we have focused on the roles of frontend servers on the end-to-end performance of search queries using the standard search fucntions of search engines. More recently, some search engines such as Google has introduced more advanced search features such as the *interactive* "search as you type" feature. Our preliminary investigation of this new feature shows that our basic model and key observations still hold. We find that using the interactive search feature, after each letter a user has typed, a separate query (using a *new* TCP connection) is sent to the FE server. The delivery of each query hence still fits our basic model; although we believe it is likely that the search query processing times at the BE data centers are generally reduced because the subsequent queries are highly correlated with previous queries. We are in the process of conducting more thorough measurements and analysis on this and other search features.

As most Planetlab nodes are located within or close to the University campus networks (and it is known that some Akamai frontend servers are placed closer to University campus networks), we realize that using the PlanetLab as the testbed may introduce some biases. For instance, the RTT between PlanetLab and Akamai FE servers may not be of all users. In addition, in our measurements we do not see any significant packet losses. In an environment where the loss rates are high (e.g., in a wireless network), placing FEs closer to users in fact may significantly improve the user-perceived end-to-end performance by reducing the total time needed to deliver the query result (that has been delivered to the FE server from a BE data center) to a user. As part of ongoing work, in addition to the PlanetLab, we are utilizing other testbeds (e.g., Seattle testbed [3]). We are also investigating the trade-offs between RTTs and loss rates (e.g., in a WiFi environment) in the placement of FE servers.

7. CONCLUSIONS

In this paper we investigated the roles of FE servers in improving the user-perceived performance of dynamic content distribution. Using Bing and Google search services as case studies, we conducted extensive application-layer active measurement and data analysis. Our results demonstrate that there is a critical trade-off between the placement of FE servers and the FE-BE fetch time. While placing FE servers closer to users can help reduce latency, other key factors such as processing times and loads at both FE servers and BE data centers as well as the quality of (physical and TCP) connections between them also play a critical role in determining the overall user-perceived performance.

Acknowledgments

This work is supported in part by the NSF grants CNS-0905037, CNS-1017092 and CNS-1017647.

8. REFERENCES

[1] Google data centers. `http://www.google.com/corporate/datacenter/locations.html`.

[2] Microsoft online services data center locations. `http://www.championcloudservices.com/data-center-locations/`.

[3] Seattle. `https://seattle.cs.washington.edu/html/`.

[4] S. Androutsellis-Theotokis and D. Spinellis. A survey of peer-to-peer content distribution technologies. *ACM Computing Surveys (CSUR)*, 36(4):335–371, 2004.

[5] M. Bateni and M. Hajiaghayi. Assignment problem in content distribution networks: unsplittable hard-capacitated facility location. In *Proceedings of the twentieth Annual ACM-SIAM Symposium on Discrete Algorithms*, pages 805–814. Society for Industrial and Applied Mathematics, 2009.

[6] M. El Dick, E. Pacitti, R. Akbarinia, and B. Kemme. Building a peer-to-peer content distribution network with high performance, scalability and robustness. *Information Systems*, 2010.

[7] H. Jiang, Z. Wang, A. Wong, J. Li, and Z. Li. A replica placement algorithm for hybrid CDN-P2P architecture. In *2009 15th International Conference on Parallel and Distributed Systems*, pages 758–763. IEEE, 2009.

[8] D. Lewin, A. Davis, S. Gendler, M. Kagan, J. Parikh, and W. Weihl. Dynamic content assembly on edge-of-network servers in a content delivery network, July 6 2010. US Patent 7,752,258.

[9] A. Pathak, Y. Wang, C. Huang, A. Greenberg, Y. Hu, R. Kern, J. Li, and K. Ross. Measuring and evaluating TCP splitting for cloud services. In *Passive and Active Measurement*, pages 41–50. Springer, 2010.

[10] J. Ravi, Z. Yu, and W. Shi. A survey on dynamic Web content generation and delivery techniques. *Journal of Network and Computer Applications*, 32(5):943–960, 2009.

[11] M. Tariq, A. Zeitoun, V. Valancius, N. Feamster, and M. Ammar. Answering what-if deployment and configuration questions with wise. In *Proceedings of the ACM SIGCOMM 2008 conference on Data communication*, SIGCOMM '08, pages 99–110, New York, NY, USA, 2008. ACM.

[12] M. Wittie, V. Pejovic, L. Deek, K. Almeroth, and B. Zhao. Exploiting locality of interest in online social networks. In *CoNEXT*, page 25. ACM, 2010.

Summary Review Documentation for

"Characterizing Roles of Front-end Servers in End-to-End Performance of Dynamic Content Distribution"

Authors: Y. Chen, S. Jain, V. Adhikari, Z. Zhang

Reviewer #1

Strengths: Simple and clear model that is then confirmed by measurements. Comparison of 2 different search engines, instead of just applying the model to one.

Weaknesses: It is surprising to see such differences in the slope of the lines in figure 8, you would expect them to be roughly the same. Model doesn't take into account new search engine webpages where dynamic content is continuously updated as people type and try different searches.

Comments to Authors: Short and clear paper.

1. Introduction: you should mention that the load on the client side might also impact the overall performance
2. As mentioned in your weaknesses, your model assumes a single search when search engines have now dynamic webpages where the static content is initially downloaded and the dynamic content is continuously updated as the user type and try different searches.
3. Do you have any references about the front end architecture for Bing and Google?
4. In section 2, I assume that you define Tdelta as t5-t4 and not t4-t2
5. Did you also observe protocol manipulations when you compared the 2 search engines? Did you see for instance differences in initial congestion windows?
6. I like your section 5 but I'm puzzled by it and by figure 8. I was expecting indeed a different Y-intercept for both search engines. However I don't understand how we can observe a difference of a factor of 3 between the slopes of the lines in the 2 figures. You would expect these numbers to be pretty similar.

Reviewer #2

Strengths: The problem of inference the frontend-to-backend delay is an important one. The paper can be a good reference. Solid measurement methodology and analysis of measurements. Large scale experiments. I like the trade-off between placing caches very close to the user vs. put caches close enough to the datacenters to reduce fetching time. The paper is well-written.

Weaknesses: In section 3 it is not clear how you generate the queries. Queries and answers may very per region, this issue was not enough discussed in the paper. The authors used only PlanetLab nodes; there are other available testbeds that were not utilized.

Comments to Authors: (1) In section 3 you have to elaborate more on how you generate the queries. I guess that the fetching time depends on the complexity of the query. You should expect low fetching time for very popular queries and a higher fetching time for complex queries. It would be nice to present results on this. You may want to evaluate if there is a correlation between the fetching time and the number of words used in the query.

(2) You have to provide evidence that your queries are quite representative for users located in different regions. It is known that queries and answers in both Google and Bing highly depend on the user region, you have to address this issue.

(3) It is also known that both Google and Bing also optimize based on user profile. In your study this can not be simulated. Do you think that this may increase the fetching time you observe?

(4) It is not clear what is the popularity of your queries. Do you expect that the answers are pre-cached or you always receive a fresh answer for dynamic content?

(5) Despite the fact that this is a short paper, you have to provide information for the active measurement platform.

(6) Did you observe any fetching activity if the autocompletion feature is activated?

(7) You may also want to compare the fetching time with the DNS resolution time.

(8) You may want to repeat your experiments using the Seattle testbed (https://seattle.cs.washington.edu/html). The bandwidth limitations should not be a problem for your measurements.

Reviewer #3

Strengths: Very timely and relevant problem. Nice methodology in terms of measurement, model building and validation. Useful reported results. Very good presentation.

Weaknesses: Some missing related work.

Comments to Authors: I really enjoyed reading this paper, my compliments to the authors.

1. Please take a look at: Exploiting Locality of Interest in Online Social Networks, Mike P. Wittie et al., ACM CoNEXT'10. From the title it does not seem that relevant but it is about OSNs FE used to split the TCP connection to the OSN BE and as well cache static parts ... Please discuss how your work compares to this paper.
2. A suggestion: Why don't you use a virtual coordinates system to estimate the RTT between FE and BE servers and then take

this and Tstatic+RTT out from Tdynamic in order to say something about Tproc at the datacenter?

3. Additionally, I think that you can improve (or maybe report if you have already done) the study around the effect of particular queries to the observed results. For example you should explain more clearly at least the two extremes, simple queries for which the answer will come very quick (might be cached at the BE) and more complicated ones.
4. Another thing, in your model I cannot see how the the interactive "search as you type" offered by google the last 1-2 years would fit.
5. Also I think you need to improve the positioning of your work and contributions. Cite more papers on tiered internet services, optimization of intra datacenter communications between FE and BE, etc. There is work here that you don't mention.

Reviewer #4

Strengths: This is a very timely topic as dynamic service delivery is emerging as the next big business for CDNs, after video delivery. the paper's model and evaluation concurre and validate each other. the results on the differences from Bing using Akamai and Google using their own CDN are interesting too.

Weaknesses: The model does a good job at capturing delays between edge and back servers, processing times, and delivery times. however, it lacks a more fundamental study of the impact that losses can have in TCP splicing and thus the position of the servers. you assume that FE server position is only worth it to have enough pipelining such as to ensure that no idle time exists, and in the case of high processing time, placing servers closer to the user may not have any effect. this is true, as long as there are no losses since splitting TCP connections under losses can have a secondary effect, i.e. that of increasing the throughput of the connection. for instance look at this paper: "TPOT: Translucent Proxying of TCP". P. Rodriguez, S.Sibal, O.Spatscheck, WCW'00, International Caching Workshop.

Comments to Authors: None.

Reviewer #5

Strengths: Nice observations about content delivery performance.

Weaknesses: Study from planetlab only, so RTT is probably not representative but the message should still be valid when measured from other end-hosts.

Comments to Authors: A latency of 20ms even to Akamai is really low. DSL end-hosts would have higher latency, even to Akamai. Maier et al. Characteristics of residential traffic. IMC 2009, showed that often 30 ms is added just by the DSL interleaving, so the latencies you found are certainly not realistic, not even mentioning mobile devices. Your observations are due to Akamai having caches in academic networks and large ISPs. This is not always the case and greatly varies across networks, both academic and commercial. Despite the methodological limitations, this paper is of great interest to Akamai, send it to them.

Response from the Authors

We thank the anonymous reviewers for providing valuable comments and feedback on our paper. We have addressed a majority of them in this final version of the paper, and few others are listed as future work. Rest of the comments contain interesting suggestions, but unfortunately are out of the scope of this paper.

We add one separate discussion section to discuss the major concerns raised by the reviewers. One such concern is that we only dealt with the traditional search engine, in which advanced features such as the interactive search, autocomplete function are not considered. To address this problem, we elaborate on how these features work, and how they still fit our basic model.

Some reviewers suggest that the use of Planetlab may not be representative of the typical RTT between the users and the FE servers. Also, the loss rate might be another factor that should be taken into consideration in placing the FE servers. In particular, with the increasing popularity of wireless users, the loss rate at the last hop can be a major issue. We discuss these issues in the discussion section, and also list them as our ongoing work.

Some reviewers asked for clarification about the results presented in the last section, i.e. factoring FE-BE fetch time. The slope values shown in the last figure was quite different. To validate the correctness of our results, we repeat the same measurements described in that section for different keywords, and only consider front-end servers close enough to the BE servers, and new results are reported in the final version of the paper.

To address concerns that the impact of the DNS resolution time, and the personalization of the search results generated for users in different regions were not explicitly mentioned, we put several footnotes in the final version of the paper to better clarify them. We also added some of the citations suggested by the reviewers, and fixed several typos.

Overclocking the Yahoo! CDN for Faster Web Page Loads

Mohammad Al-Fares[1,2], Khaled Elmeleegy[2], Benjamin Reed[2], and Igor Gashinsky[3]

[1]Computer Science and Engineering, UC San Diego [2]Yahoo! Research [3]Yahoo! Inc.

malfares@cs.ucsd.edu {khaled, breed, igor}@yahoo-inc.com

Abstract

Fast-loading web pages are key for a positive user experience. Unfortunately, a large number of users suffer from page load times of many seconds, especially for pages with many embedded objects. Most of this time is spent fetching the page and its objects over the Internet.

This paper investigates the impact of optimizations that improve the delivery of content from edge servers at the Yahoo! Content Delivery Network (CDN) to the end users. To this end, we analyze packet traces of 12.3M TCP connections originating from users across the world and terminating at the Yahoo! CDN. Using these traces, we characterize key user-connection metrics at the network, transport, and the application layers. We observe high Round Trip Times (RTTs) and inflated number of round trips per page download (RTT multipliers). Due to inefficiencies in TCP's slow start and the HTTP protocol, we found several opportunities to reduce the RTT multiplier, e.g. increasing TCP's Initial Congestion Window (ICW), using TCP Appropriate Byte Counting (ABC), and using HTTP pipelining.

Using live workloads, we experimentally study the micro effects of these optimizations on network connectivity, e.g. packet loss rate. To evaluate the macro effects of these optimizations on the overall page load time, we use realistic synthetic workloads in a closed laboratory environment. We find that compounding HTTP pipelining with increasing the ICW size can lead to reduction in page load times by up to 80%. We also find that no one configuration fits all users, e.g. increasing the TCP ICW to a certain size may help some users while hurting others.

Categories and Subject Descriptors

C.4 [**Performance of Systems**]: measurement techniques, performance attributes; C.2.3 [**Computer-Communication Networks**]: Network Operations—*network monitoring, public networks*

General Terms

Measurement, Experimentation, Performance

Keywords

Content Delivery Networks, Traffic Analysis, Web Page Load Time, TCP tuning

1. INTRODUCTION

For web sites to maintain high user satisfaction, their web pages need to load quickly. However, web pages are becoming more content rich over the past few years. They include many embedded images, scripts, and style sheets. Consequently, page load times are getting higher. As we will see in Section 4.1.2, many users can experience tens of seconds of load time for popular web pages like Yahoo!'s front page.

Our measurements and previous research show that virtually all of this time is spent in the network stack downloading the web page and its embedded objects [14,20,25]. Two main factors contribute to the long download time. The first is the network RTT from the user to the web server. Second, a page download typically takes tens of round trips to download the web page data and all its embedded objects. The number of round trips involved is called RTT multiplier.

Long network RTTs can be due to a combination of long Internet routes, route misconfigurations, and long queuing delays at routers along the packets' path. To alleviate this problem, CDNs are deployed across the globe by companies like Akamai, Facebook, Microsoft, Google, and Yahoo! These CDNs bring content closer to users across the world, hence reducing their network RTTs. However, this study and previous work by Krishnan *et al.* [16] have shown that even with globally deployed CDNs, many users experience hundreds of milliseconds RTTs. To alleviate this high RTT problem, Krishnan *et al.* proposed a tool, *WhyHigh*, that attempts to identify routing misconfigurations leading to inflated network RTTs. This helps fix these misconfigurations and reduce round trip times.

Inflated RTT multipliers are mainly due to inefficiencies during TCP slow start and in the HTTP protocol. TCP slow start probes the available link capacity by exponentially growing the transfer rate per RTT until a packet is lost (or the slow-start threshold is reached). This probing is fairly conservative, as it starts from a modest ICW, with a default value of three in most networks. Hence, it wastes many network round trips before the full available network bandwidth is utilized. Similarly, HTTP is used inefficiently in practice as it requests a single object at a time wasting a network round trip per object. For a page with tens of small embedded objects, this is very wasteful.

Two key optimizations were proposed by the IETF and industry [7,11]: First, TCP should start probing from a larger ICW size.

Dukkipati *et al.* [11] argue for using an ICW of 10 segments. Using traffic measurements from Google's users, they argue that this would reduce object load time with virtually no downside. Second, TCP should open up the congestion window size at a higher rate per round trip. TCP slow start increases the congestion window by one for every acknowledgment received. However, delayed acknowledgments, which are pervasively deployed in the Internet, make the receiver send an acknowledgment for every other packet received. This causes TCP congestion window to increase by a factor of 1.5 instead of 2 per network round trip during slow-start. To remedy this problem, ABC [3, 5], was introduced to increase the window based on the number of bytes acknowledged instead of the number of acknowledgments received.

HTTP pipelining [12] was introduced to optimize HTTP downloads reducing the number of round trips. It allows for sending HTTP requests for new objects, while responses from earlier requests have not yet been recieved. As seen in Figure 1, HTTP pipelining saves RTTs reducing overall web page load time. Unfortunately, HTTP pipelining is not available by default in major web browsers. For example, Internet Explorer, the dominant web browser, does not support it. [1] And while Firefox supports it, it is disabled by default.

This paper is concerned with the delivery of content from edge servers from the Yahoo! CDN to the users. To this end, we collect packet traces of 12.3 million TCP connections from users of Yahoo! across the world. Using these traces, we present an in-depth cross-layer study of different factors affecting web page load times. Then, we study different cross-layer optimizations and their interplay aimed at reducing the RTT multiplier. Specifically, we study varying the ICW size, TCP ABC, and HTTP pipelining using live and realistically-inspired synthetic workloads.

The contributions of this paper are three fold:

1. Characterize the connections from users' to the Yahoo! CDN web servers at the IP, TCP, and HTTP layers.

2. Study TCP optimizations to reduce web page load times – most notably changing the ICW. We find that many users benefit significantly (up to 38%) from increasing the ICW size. However, in contrast to previous work, we show that no one size for the ICW fits all the users as increasing the ICW for some users can increase packet loss hurting the overall page load time. Moreover, we show that, in some cases, increasing the ICW size can be unfair to other flows in the network. We believe that currently this result is especially important given the efforts at IETF to increase TCP's ICW size to the fixed size of 10 [10].

3. Study and quantify the performance gains from HTTP pipelining using realistic workloads. In addition, quantify the gains when HTTP pipelining is used in conjunction with optimum ICW size. These gains can reach 80% reduction in the page load time.

The rest of this paper is organized as follows. Section 2 presents the background and previous related work. Section 3 characterizes the traffic observed at the Yahoo! CDN. Section 4 presents our study of different optimizations to reduce the RTT multiplier to reduce the web page load time. Section 5 discusses our findings. Section 6 concludes the paper.

[1] The main reason Microsoft gives is that pipelining is not universally implemented, e.g. head-of-line blocking with buggy proxy servers.

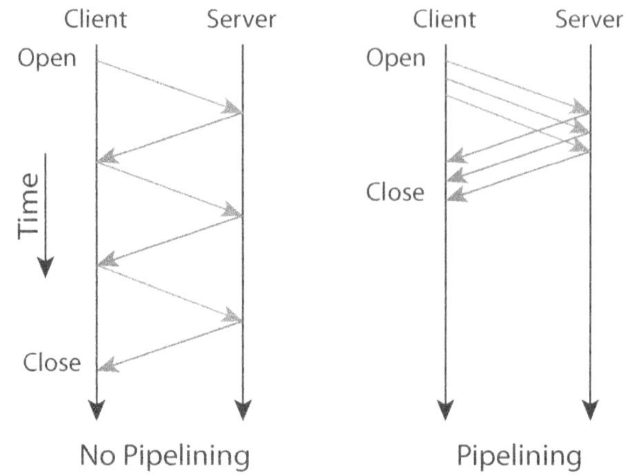

Figure 1: Non pipelined vs. pipelined HTTP connection. The client arrows indicate GET requests.

2. BACKGROUND AND RELATED WORK

In this section, we explain how content delivery networks work. We also present some of the related work aimed at optimizing content delivery at CDNs, more specifically optimizations to the network stack.

2.1 Content Delivery Networks

CDNs are usually built as a network of geographically diverse sites. Each site hosts a cluster of servers caching content and delivering it to users. The geographical diversity serves two purposes. First, it brings content closer to the users reducing network latency. Second, it provides redundancy to tolerate failures of individual sites.

In a nutshell, a CDN typically works as shown in Figure 2. When the user tries to fetch an object from a particular URL, it first performs a DNS lookup. The DNS server returns the IP address of a server near the user. The user then contacts the server to fetch the object. If the server has the object locally, it serves it to the user from its cache. Otherwise, the server contacts a back-end server, usually over a fast private network, to fetch the object into its cache and then serve it to the user.

There are multiple CDNs deployed worldwide. Some companies run and use their own private CDNs like Google, Facebook, and Yahoo!. Others use third party CDNs like Akamai [19] and CoralCDN [13].

In this paper, we study the delivery aspect of the Yahoo! CDN. At a high level, the Yahoo! CDN operates as described above.

2.2 Round Trip Times

Krishnan *et al.* [16] studied the network round trip latencies in the Google CDN. They reported that latencies are generally high and that 40% have round trip times higher than 400ms. They argued that adding more CDN sites is not always the best solution as this high latency is sometimes due to queuing delays and routing misconfigurations. They then introduced a new tool, *WhyHigh*, that tries to identify prefixes suffering from inflated latencies. Finally, this tool attempts to diagnose the causes for this inflated latency by using multiple active measurements, using different tools like *ping* and *traceroute*, and correlating inflated subnet latencies to common AS paths for example.

In this paper, we also studied round trip latencies, and also found latencies to be high (on the order of a few hundred milliseconds in the developing world). However, the latency distributions we observed were significantly lower than those reported in [16].

2.3 Optimizing the Network Stack

Previous work have argued for increasing TCP's initial window size [7, 10, 11]. Dukkipati *et al.* [11] recently argued for increasing the window size to 10 segments in order to decrease page load time. They argued that this reduces page load time with virtually no downside. In contrast, although we find that many users benefit from larger initial window size in this study, we also observe a subset of users who suffer due to increased packet loss.

Qian*et al.* [23], have studied the Internet backbone traffic and shown that up to 15% of large-flows already violate the ICW limit set by the spec ($min(4 * MSS, max(2 * MSS, 4380)$, which equals 3 for a Maximum Segment Size (MSS) of 1460) [7]), and values up to 9KB have been observed in the wild.

Allman [4] studied traffic to and from a single web server. He characterized different settings of the protocols used (TCP and HTTP) by this traffic. For example, he studied the deployment of TCP features like selective acknowledgments. Like other studies, Allman too reported long RTTs for studied connections. This study is over 10 years old though and only studied 751K connections at a single web server at a single geographic location. Moreover, unlike this paper, Allman only relied on passive measurements and did not try to measure different performance metrics in response to changing different protocol settings.

To allow for increasing the ICW while not hurting users with poor connectivity, Chu [10] *et al.* argued that users with poor connectivity can can advertise a smaller receive window sizes. In theory this can fix the problem. However, in practice, modifying the network stacks of existing users with poor connectivity to dynamically detect their network conditions and consequently adjusting their corresponding receive window sizes is challenging.

A different line of research proposed multiplexing several small streams on top of TCP to reduce web page load time, e.g. SPDY [2] and Stream Control Transmission Protocol [24]. However, both protocols are still experimental and not used at a large scale in the web. In contrast, we aim to optimize existing protocols to achieve best possible performance without breaking backward compatibility.

On the HTTP and application layer front, Leighton [17] advocates several optimizations such as pre-fetching embedded content, pre-caching popular objects at the edge, and using compression and delta-encoding of popular web pages. The argument being that, in contrast to a decade ago when the last-mile connection to the user was likely the bottleneck, the *middle-mile*'s capacity growth has not kept pace and become the new bottleneck, and that these techniques would all contribute to alleviating web traffic on the backbone and faster page loads.

3. STUDYING YAHOO! CDN TRAFFIC

In this section, we present our study of the traffic characteristics at the Yahoo! CDN edge servers. Specifically, we wanted to analyze and dissect network connections on multiple levels to answer questions as follows:

- Routing Layer (IP): What is the distribution of RTTs? Are some ISPs suffering from exceptionally high RTT to the nearest CDN node?

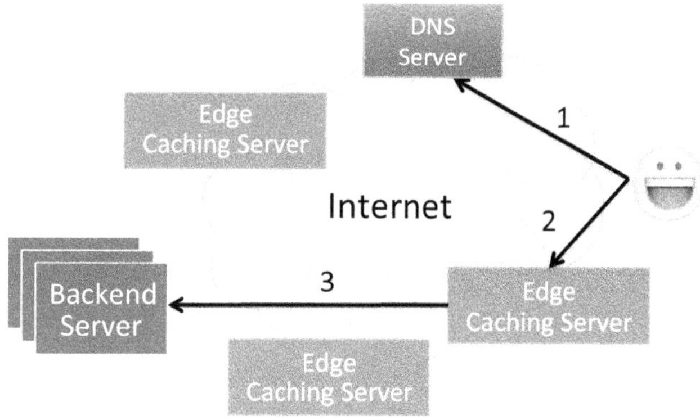

Figure 2: An HTTP request to a CDN. First, the DNS resolves the server's name to a nearby edge server. Then, the client sends the request to the nearby caching edge server. On a cache miss, the edge server contacts the back end servers to fetch the missing content and then deliver it to the user.

- Transport Layer (TCP): What level of packet retransmission rates do different users experience? What is the distribution of bytes transfered per connection? What is the distribution of the connection lifetime?
- Application Layer (HTTP): How many web objects are fetched per TCP connection? What is the distribution of the sizes of objects fetched?

3.1 Methodology

For this study, we used 1-hour long *tcpdump* traces collected from edge servers in the Yahoo! CDN across the world. We selected an edge server at each of the following sites: Chicago, Germany, Singapore, and India. These sites were chosen to span different important regions of the world with diverse connection characteristics. We have verified that the traffic characteristics at one server are representative of its corresponding site. We did this by collecting traces from different servers at the same site and comparing their characteristics and verifying they are virtually the same. Consequently, we only report results from one server per site. These servers run Linux with 2.6 kernels. Moreover, these servers were configured with default kernel settings for the TCP stack. The packet traces were collected at 1 p.m. local time, which previous studies at Yahoo! have shown to be traditionally the peak load time on these servers. We have also verified that traffic at other times of the day has qualitatively similar characteristics.

We used a combination of of *tcpsplit* [6] and *tcptrace* [21] to analyze every TCP connection we captured (12.3M connections). This provided a detailed report on a multitude of key connection characteristics; connection duration, number of bytes transferred, average roundtrip time estimates, retransmitted packets, etc. In addition, we used the HTTP module in *tcptrace* to parse HTTP layer information such as request arrival, response initiation, and completion timestamps, objects requests and their sizes, etc. Finally, we used Yahoo!'s proprietary internal data sets for geo-locations, connection speeds, and subnet prefixes in conjunction with information extracted from the traces to complete this study.

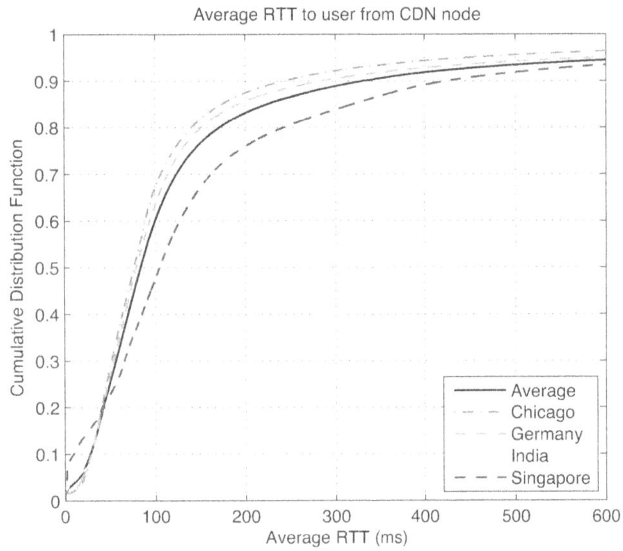

Figure 3: Average RTT distribution across the four Yahoo! CDN nodes.

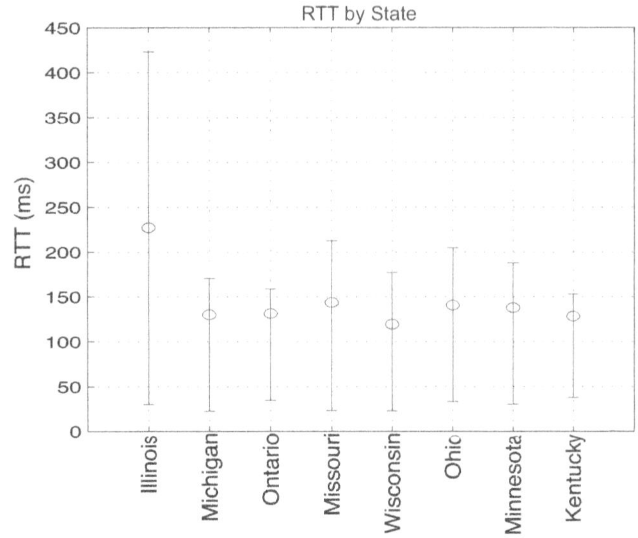

Figure 6: RTTs of top 8 most-frequent user origin states. Showing the median, 10th and 90th percentiles.

3.2 Results

3.2.1 RTT Characterization

In this section, we study the RTTs experienced by different users at the four sites.

Figure 3 shows the RTT distributions for the 4 sites. We note that the distributions for the Chicago and the Germany sites are considerably better than the Singapore and the India sites. As reported by previous work [16], we note that RTTs are generally high even though CDN nodes are geographically distributed to be close to the users. However, in contrast to [16], which showed that 40% of the user connections had greater than 400ms RTT, in our workload, only 10% of the user connections experience 400ms or more RTT.

Figures 4 and 5 breakdown the data by the users' source network (this applied clustering is similar to studies such as [15], which grouped web-clients based on source network, among other factors). They show the median, 10th, and 90th percentiles of RTT and packet retransmission rates of users' connections per source subnet for their corresponding sites. They also show the connection counts per subnet. Both figures only show the top-100 subnets with respect to the number of connections arriving from each subnet. Since both the Germany and the Chicago sites had similar connectivity characteristics, we chose to show one example of them only – Chicago. Similarly, we chose the Singapore site as an example of the other two sites. In both figures, we note that there is a wide range of RTTs with some subnets having connections experiencing multi-second RTT. Also, we notice a wide range of packet retransmission rates with some subnets having connections experiencing over 50% packet retransmission rate.

Figure 6 shows the RTT distribution of the 8-most frequent states connecting to the Chicago node. We note that even though these states are very close geographically to Chicago, big fraction of their connections experience hundreds of milliseconds RTT (This could be due to many reasons including long queueing delays). Hence, one can conclude that adding more CDN sites with geographical proximity to the users does not guarantee to significantly reduce their RTTs. This is consistent with observations and conclusions made by previous work [16].

Figure 7 shows the RTT distribution by connection type. Note that *Broadband* represents connections having high speed, yet their connection type is unknown. Also, note that mobile connections have significantly high RTT. Given the growth of mobile networks, improving the RTT multiplier for these connections becomes more pressing so that mobile users can have acceptable web page load times.

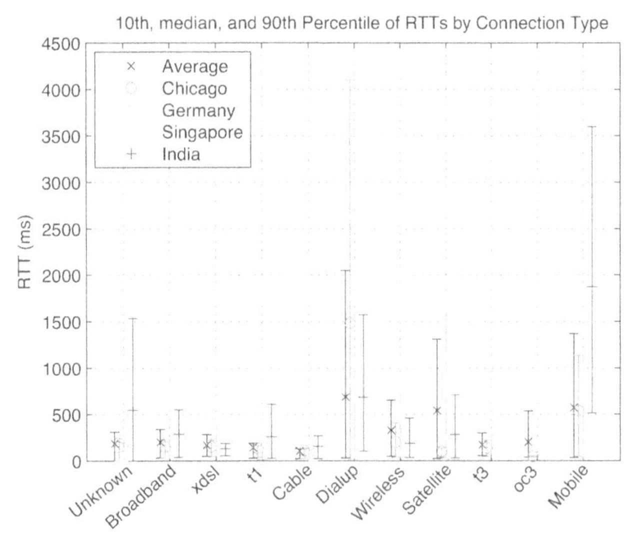

Figure 7: Median, 10th and 90th percentiles of RTTs, by connection speed.

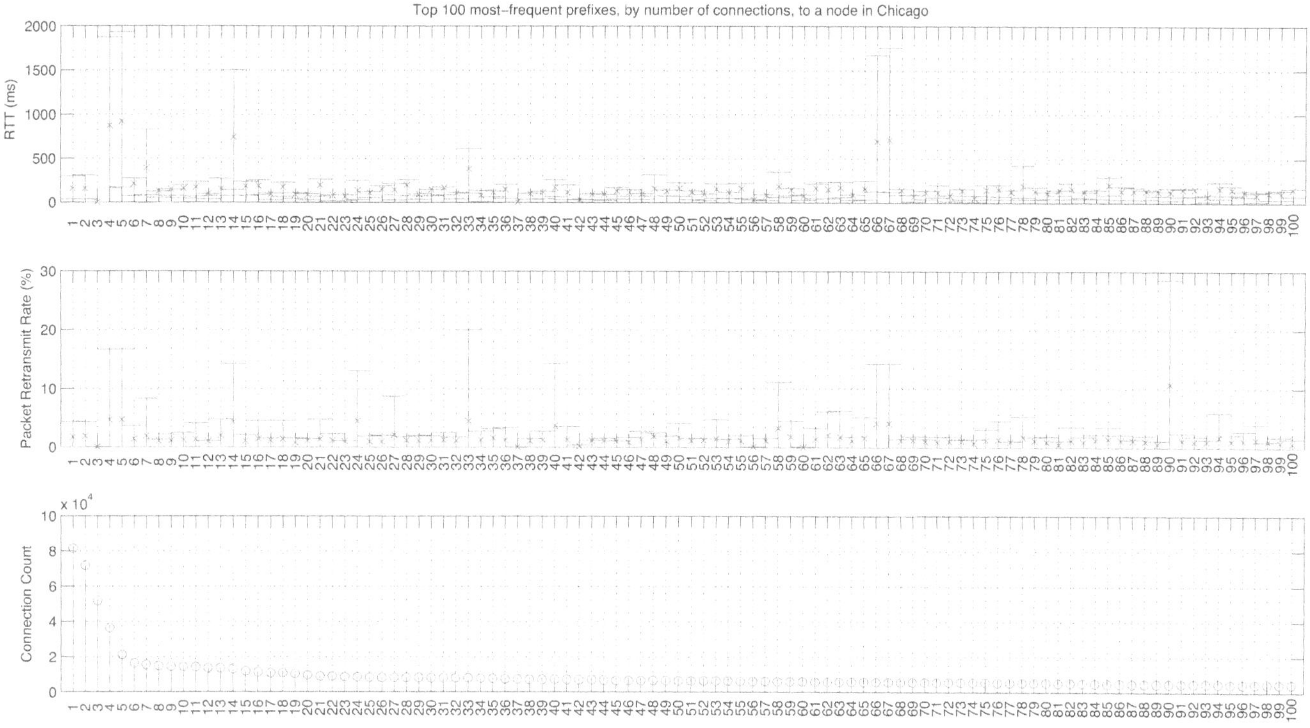

Figure 4: Median, 10th and 90th percentile RTTs, by user prefix, retransmission rate, and connection count to Yahoo! CDN node in Chicago.

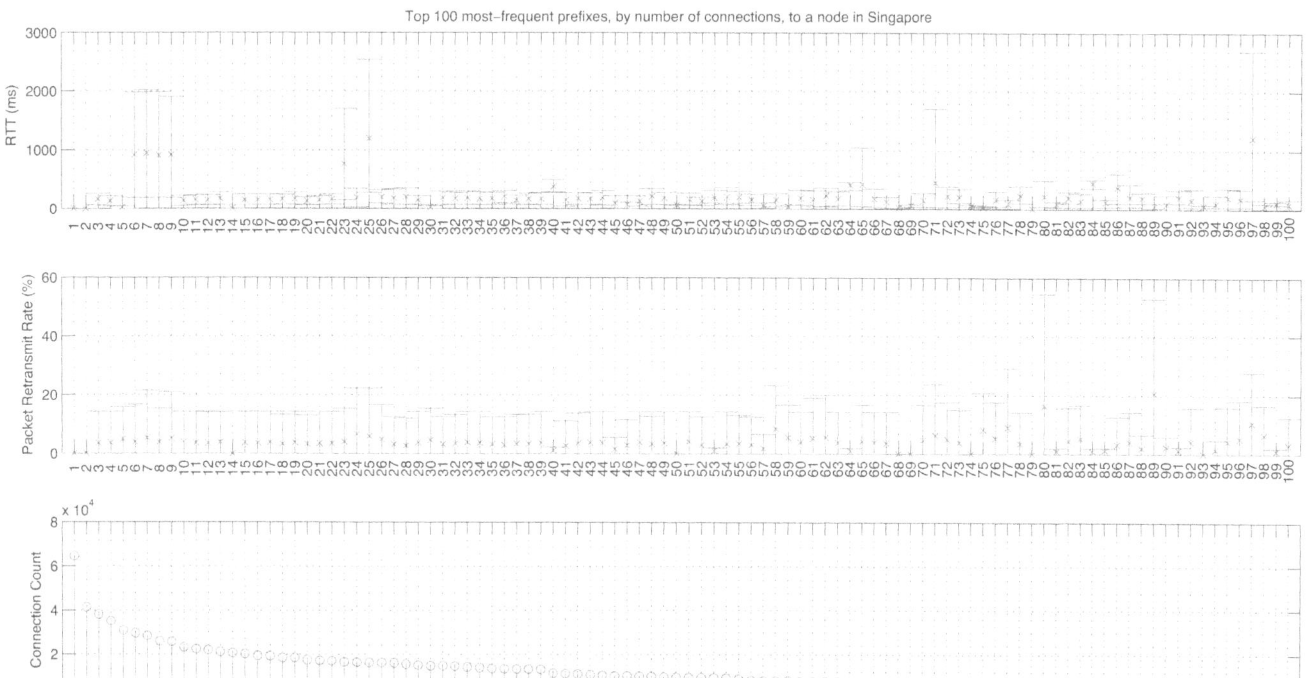

Figure 5: Median, 10th and 90th percentile RTTs, by user prefix, retransmission rate, and connection count to Yahoo! CDN node in Singapore.

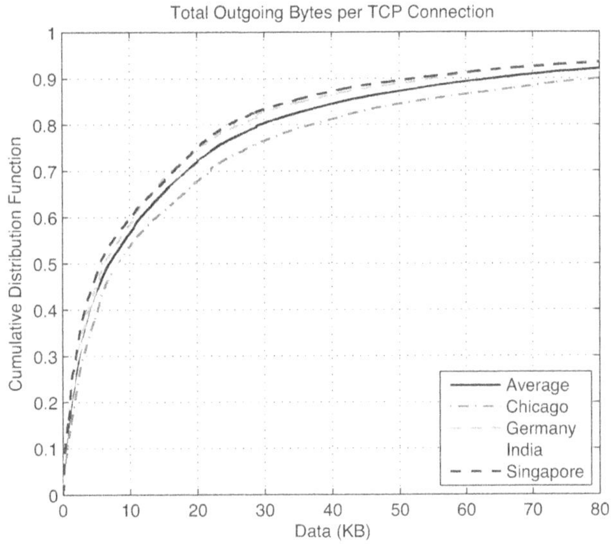

Figure 8: Bytes transferred per TCP connection.

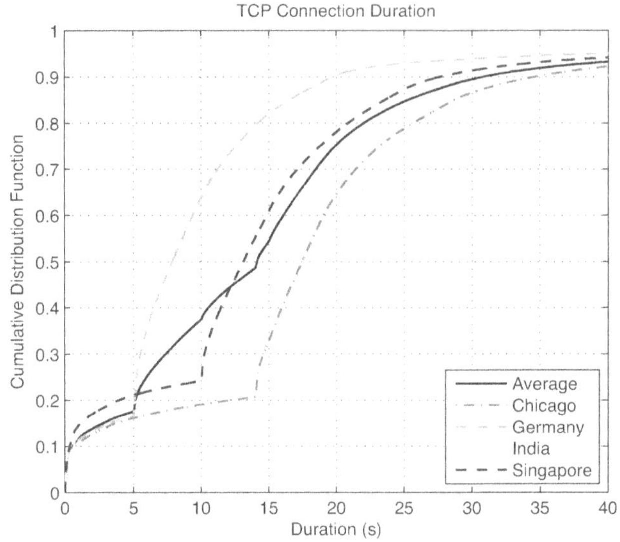

Figure 9: TCP connection duration.

3.2.2 TCP Connection Characterization

In this section we study different characteristics of users' TCP connections to the Yahoo! CDN.

Figure 8 shows the distribution of the total number of bytes transferred to the user per connection. We see that about 90% of connections download less than 64KB of data. Note that TCP Reno, the default TCP flavor at many operating systems including Linux, has 64KB as the default value for TCP's initial *ssthresh* (Slow Start Threshold). One important consequence of this is that 90% of the connections, barring loss, would never enter TCP's congestion avoidance phase and the transfer is done entirely in the slow-start phase.

Figure 9 shows the distribution of connection duration at the four servers. The different knees in the graphs correspond to the server's connection timeout setting, which reflects differences in the local server configurations. Note that this does not correspond to active transfer times; due to the typical size of objects requested, and the small number of objects in a persistent connection, as we will see in Section 3.2.3, a typical connection is idle most of the time.

To study packet loss for these connections, we use a metric that is measurable from the packet traces we collected, i.e. retransmission rate. This retransmission rate is an upper bound on the packet loss rate. Since most users use selective acknowledgments, retransmissions establish a tight upper bound. Figure 10 shows the distribution of packet retransmission rates per connection. Note that, in India for example, over 70% of the connections see no retransmissions; however, over 17% of connections have retransmit rates above 10%. Similarly, in Figures 4 and 5, we see that some subnets experience very little retransmissions, while others experience substantial retransmission rates that sometimes reach 50%. As we see in Section 4.1.2, overall page load time is extremely sensitive to the packet-loss rate, especially during connection setup, where a SYN timeout is on the order of seconds. This is compounded for networks where RTTs are significantly higher, and it is not uncommon to see total page load time in the range of 10-120 seconds for the Yahoo! frontpage.

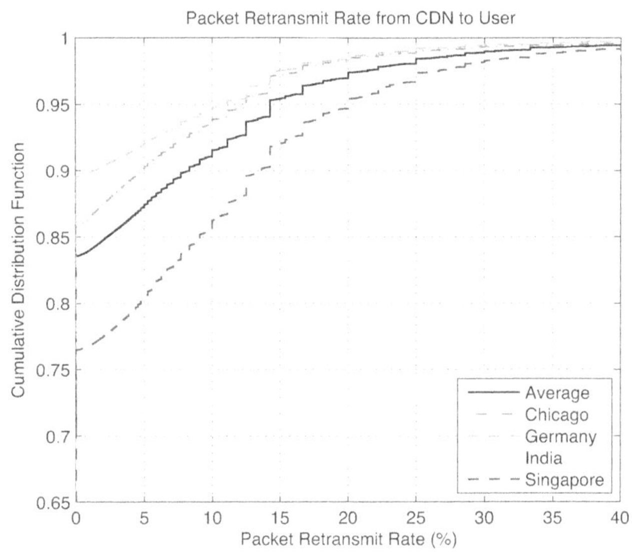

Figure 10: Packet retransmission rate.

3.2.3 HTTP Workload Characterization

In this section we study different properties of the downloaded web objects at the Yahoo! CDN. We can see the distribution of requested object sizes in Figure 11, which shows around 90% of objects are smaller than 25KB (17 segments). Figure 12 shows the distribution of the number of HTTP requests per connection to see the effect of persistent connections. The mean is only about 2.4 requests per connection, with the majority of connections requesting only one object. The reason for having a small number of requests per connection in spite of typical web pages having tens of objects is because web browsers typically use multiple concurrent TCP connections per domain per web page. Putting together Figures 11 and 12 tells us that even when requesting multiple objects back-to-back, objects are so small and so few that a typical connection does not have enough time to take advantage of opening up the congestion window. Hence, most of the time is spent ramping up in slow-start.

In Figure 13, we show the distribution of the time between HTTP requests within the same connection (so-called "think-time"). We observed that the overall majority, about 80% of back-to-back requests, occur in under one second, and therefore unlikely to be the result of user-clicks, but rather the browser fetching objects.

Linux 2.6 kernels also provide a setting called *tcp_slow_start_-after_idle*, which resets the congestion window to the ICW and moves TCP back to the slow-start phase if there is no data to send after a given idle period, defined as one retransmission timeout (RTO). This is *on* by default. In Figure 13, we also plot the distribution of the difference between the inter-request time and our estimate of of the RTO, calculated using the standard Jacobson estimator: $RTO = RTT_{average} + 4 * RTT_{variance}$. We find that approximately 10% of back-to-back object requests are seperated by more than one RTO. All these users have to go through slow start again when downloading the following object spending expensive network round trips to probe the network for bandwidth again.

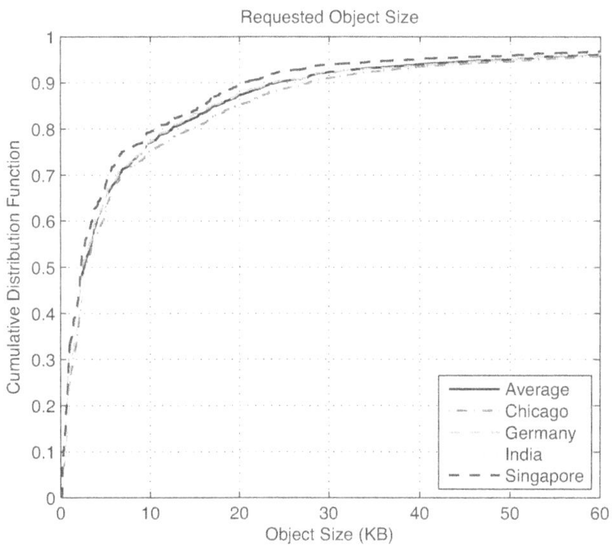

Figure 11: HTTP object size distribution.

Figure 14 shows the distribution of the fraction of the total number of bytes downloaded via objects with certain sizes. For example, we note that 50% of the total bytes downloaded come from objects with sizes of 60KB or greater. Looking at Figure 11, we note that less than 5% of the web objects downloaded have sizes of 60 KB or more. Hence, one can conclude that less than 5% of the web objects downloaded account for 50% of the bytes downloaded.

4. IMPACT OF DIFFERENT OPTIMIZATIONS ON WEB PAGE LOAD TIME

In Section 3, we saw that RTTs are generally high. They are even higher for the up-and-coming segment of users – mobile users. For CDN operators, little can be done about this to significantly change the picture. This means that the bigger opportunity to reduce the web page load time lies in reducing the RTT multiplier. In this section, we study different optimizations to reduce this multiplier.

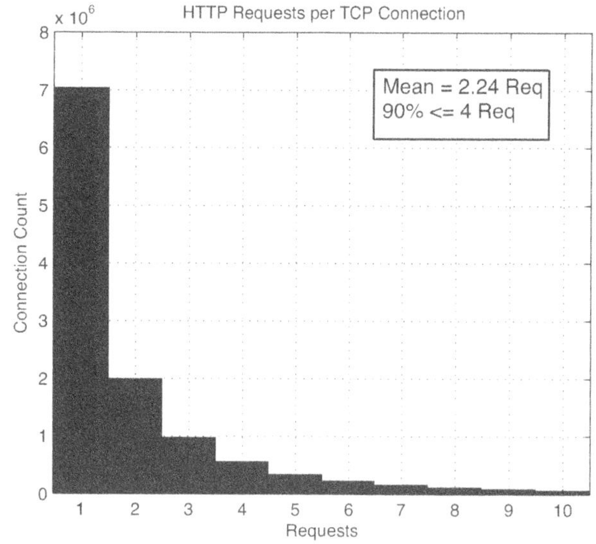

Figure 12: HTTP requests per connection.

Two of these optimizations attempt to reduce the number of round trips during TCP slow start.

The first optimization is increasing TCP ICW size, which attempts to make TCP slow start begin transmitting data at a rate closer to the maximum available bandwidth. Hence, it can use fewer round trips to reach optimal window size that achieves the maximum transmission rate. Section 4.1 studies the effects of using larger ICW sizes.

The second optimization is opening up the congestion window at a higher rate during slow start. TCP slow start increases the congestion window by one for every acknowledgment received. However, delayed acknowledgments, which is pervasively deployed in the Internet, makes the receiver send an acknowledgment for every other packet received. This causes TCP congestion window to increase by a factor of 1.5 instead of 2 (as originally intended) per round trip. To remedy this problem, Appropriate Bytes Counting (ABC) was introduced. ABC increases the window based on the number of bytes acknowledged instead of just counting the number of acknowledgments received. In Section 4.2, we study the effectiveness of ABC in reducing page load time.

Finally, in Section 4.3 we study the effectiveness of HTTP pipelining in reducing the RTT multiplier. Moreover, we study its interplay with increasing the ICW size.

For these different optimizations, we experimentally evaluated their effectiveness using live traffic from real users. Moreover, we used macro benchmarks to evaluate their overall effects on web page load times in a closed laboratory environment. In these macro benchmarks, we constructed our synthetic workloads based on measurements from the live traces.

4.1 Initial Congestion Window (ICW)

We have seen that the vast majority of Yahoo! CDN connections transfer very few, and very small objects, which means that TCP spends most of its time in the slow-start phase. For this reason, improving the efficiency of this phase is crucial. When a new TCP connection starts probing for available bandwidth, the Linux TCP implementation follows RFC 3390 [7], which specifies an ICW of 3 segments for networks having a MSS of 1460 bytes, which is the

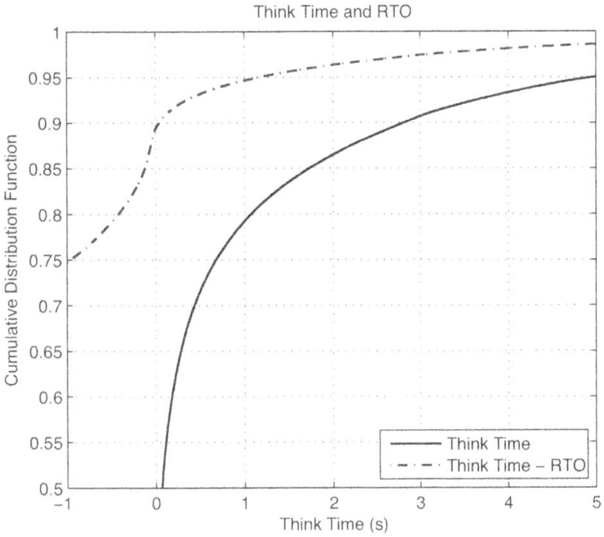

Figure 13: Inter-request time and retransmission timeout (RTO).

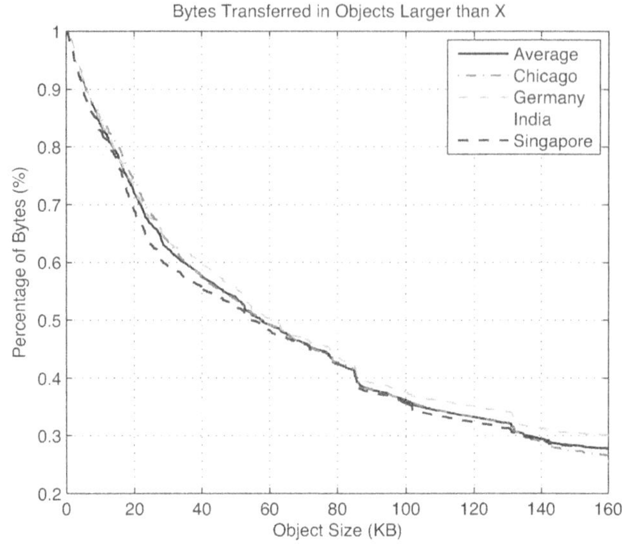

Figure 14: Percentage of overall bytes transferred across all objects vs. object size.

most common MSS. By increasing this ICW, small objects stand to be transferred in fewer RTTs, which when compounded across all objects on a page can cut down the total page load time significantly.

Obviously, TCP at the server end would not send more unacknowledged data than is allowed by the client's advertised receive window so as not to overflow the client's receive buffer (The receive window is dynamically allocated on most operating systems and advertised throughout the connection). Luckily, on popular operating systems (except Linux which has a much smaller receive window), the initial receive window is quite large (64KB-256KB), which would allow for utilizing a larger ICW. According to [11], more than 90% of user connections have receive windows large enough to utilize an ICW of 10. Hence, increasing TCP's ICW can be beneficial.

4.1.1 Evaluation Using Live Traffic

To test the effects of increasing the ICW size, we chose one of our CDN sites – Singapore. We chose it due to the diversity of its connections qualities as seen in Figure 5. There, we varied this setting and captured traces for each ICW size.

We show in Figure 15 the distribution of object transfer time normalized by the connection's average RTT. This normalization allows us to compare transfer times of objects over connections having different RTTs. We observe a reduction of 32% in object transfer time overall at the 80th percentile when going from an ICW of 3 to 16. However, increasing the ICW sees diminishing returns beyond that point. Because the effects of increasing the ICW would be more evident during the beginning of a TCP connection, we show in Figure 16 the same metric for the *first* HTTP request only, where the improvement is a 38% reduction in transfer time. Subsequent HTTP requests benefit less as the TCP window is usually opened up at the first request. Note that in both Figures 15 and 16 there is a fraction of the objects that are downloaded in under one average RTT. The reason for this is that the average RTT is measured across all round trips measured in the lifetime of a connection. By examining the traces, we observed that sometimes round trip times vary significantly within a single connection. Hence, within a single connection an RTT can be less than the connection's average RTT.

A potential side effect of increasing the ICW is an increase in retransmission rates, which we did observe as shown in Figure 17. Note that while over 70% of connections see no retransmissions, increasing the ICW from 3 to 16 increases the retransmit rate from 17% to 25% for about 10% of connections. As we will see later in this section, this will have a significant impact on the overall page load time as it is highly sensitive to packet-loss.

To study the effects of increasing the ICW size on the tail of the distribution of object transfer times on a per-subnet basis, we show in Figure 18 the 80th percentile of the average object transfer times per network prefix. In this figure, for each subnet, 7 data points, corresponding to 7 different ICW sizes, are presented. Each point represents the average object transfer time normalized by the average RTT. In the figure, we can observe that most subnets benefit from increasing the ICW and see dramatically lower object transfer times. We also note that for these 20% of the objects, maximum benefit is achieved at an ICW of 16. After that, for ICW of 32, object transfer time goes higher. In contrast, other objects are not hurt by larger ICW sizes as seen in Figure 15. Note that we chose the *80th* percentile to show that a significant portion of the connections in the tail of the distribution can suffer from using larger ICW size.

4.1.2 Studying Page Load time

While the previous section studied traces of individual HTTP requests in the wild, we also wanted to capture the effects of tuning the TCP ICW size on the overall page load time. Since a full web page encompasses many objects, any straggling object download will delay the overall web page download time, especially if this straggling download is for the HTML file. Studying whole page load times in the wild is very difficult though. This is because when using packet traces, there is no notion of a full page download as the objects in a page likely span multiple connections that are difficult to tie together in a postmortem analysis. Moreover, these objects are often at different servers. Hence, no one server

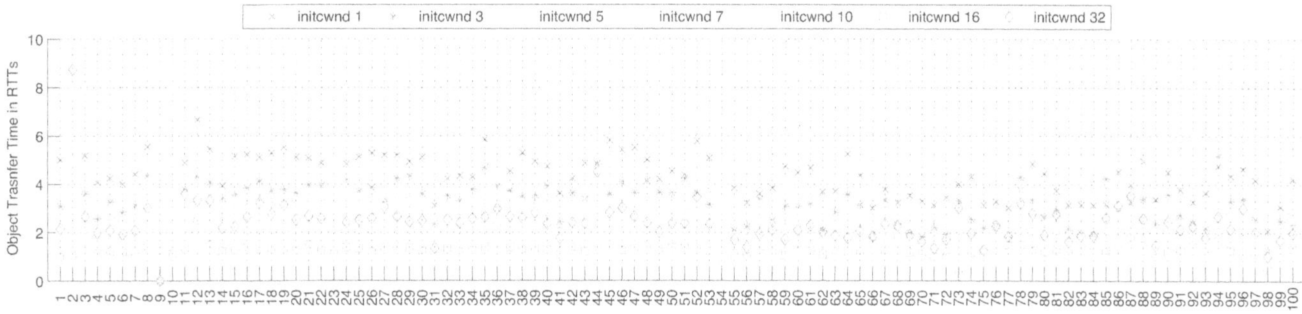

Figure 18: The 80th percentile of object transfer times in RTTs per network prefix for the top 100 prefixes, for different ICW sizes.

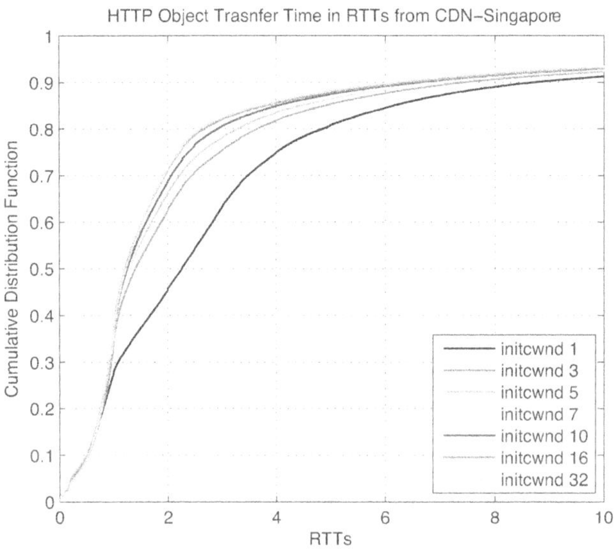

Figure 15: Overall object transfer time in RTTs.

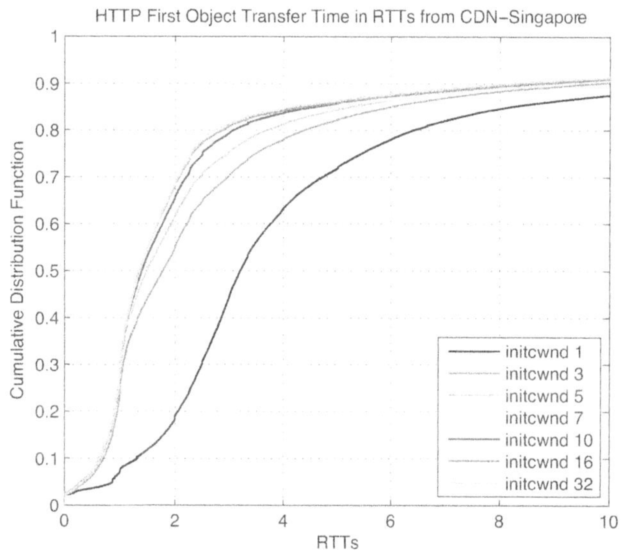

Figure 16: First-object transfer time in RTTs.

trace can contain full page downloads. For this reason, this section studies the overall page load time in a controlled environment in the lab using real workloads and realistic network conditions. These simulated network conditions (latency and packet loss rates) are based on connections' profiles from previous sections. These network conditions represent links' latecy and congestion due to cross traffic in the internet.

Experimental Setup

We captured a snapshot of the Yahoo! front page, by far the most popular Yahoo! web page, and fairly representative of the measured traffic workload. We hosted this page and its resources locally such that all object requests are directed to a local server.

In this setup, the client browser is 3.6.9 Firefox running on Mac OS X 10.5.8. Apart from disabling caching, all other browser and TCP settings are set to their default. Most notably, delayed ACKs are enabled, and for Firefox, six maximum simultaneous connections per domain were used.

The server is a guest VM on the same machine, running CentOS 4.8 release with an updated 2.6.29.5 linux kernel and the apache 2.0.52 web server. We used the *ipfw* command to setup dummynet pipes in order to control the perceived RTT and packet-loss rates from and to the server. During the experiments, no hardware resource was saturated, which guaranteed that request latencies were only due induced RTTs and packet loss. The web page had 30 objects distributed across two domains. Thus, we created two IP aliases at the server representing the two domains.

We had the client repeatedly request the front page. The embedded links , which represented the static content on the page, namely images, Javascript, and stylesheets, were replaced to point to IP aliases on the local server. Firefox fetched 30 objects distributed across two domains via six concurrent connections per domain resulted in an average of 2.5 objects per connection, very close to the average number of objects per connection measured in live traces shown in Figure 12.

We wanted to measure the total page load time, which we define as the time difference between the first packet of the first HTTP request and the final ACK of the last object fetched (Page rendering time is negligible compared to the download time). We captured the tcpdump trace of the request at the client, and reported the page load time between the first outgoing request and the last object ACK. For every parameter combination we reported, we gave the geometric mean of five requests for the Yahoo! front page.

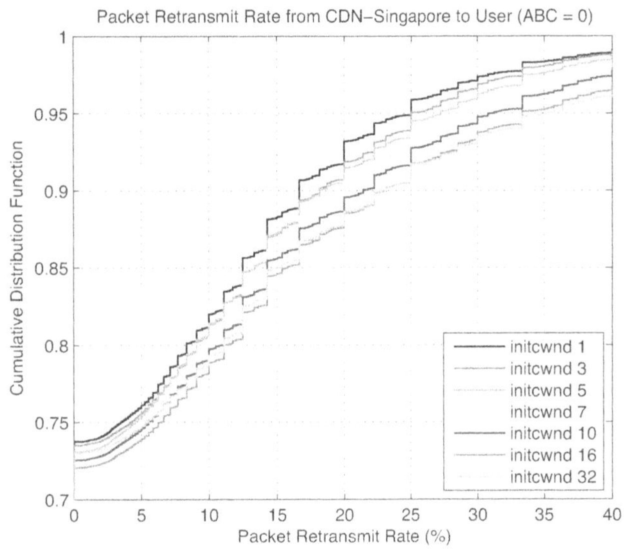

Figure 17: Packet retransmit rate.

Results

Figure 19 shows the total page load time for different values of RTT and different values of ICW sizes. We find that the relative reductions in page load times were relatively consistent; ranging from 27%-38% when going from an ICW of 3 to 16.

When taking packet loss into account, we show in Figure 20 the different page load times for different loss rates and different ICW sizes and an RTT of 100ms (the median for Singapore). We find that page load times and their variance appear to be superlinear and very sensitive to packet loss; increasing the loss rate from 5% to 10% *increases* page load time by 63% for an ICW of 3.

However, as seen in Figure 17, increasing the ICW can increase packet loss, especially for users with congested links. This raises important questions. First, can increasing the ICW hurt the overall page load time for some connections? Second, if the answer to the previous question is *yes*, is there a single optimum value for ICW with respect to page load time that fits all connections?

To study whether there are cases where increasing the ICW size can hurt the overall web page load time, we need to consider users that would suffer from increased packet loss due to increasing the ICW. For such users, we need to estimate the increase in packet loss due to the increase in ICW. Then, based on the estimated packet loss and the corresponding ICW, we should measure the corresponding page load time. To this end, we use a user connection in the 90% percentile of retransmission rate in Figure 17 as an example. We assume that the measured retransmission rate is equal to packet loss rate. Moreover, we assume that increasing the ICW size for this connection will follow the same increases in retransmission rates observed for the 90th percentile connection in Figure 17. The pairs of the ICW sizes and the corresponding packet loss rates are listed in the first two columns of Table 1. Finally, we assumed that this connection has the median RTT for the Singapore site – 100ms. We measured the page load times using the experiment described above for every ICW size and its corresponding packet loss rate listed at Table 1 and recorded it in the table at the third column. We note that for the 90th percentile connections (with respect to packet retransmission rates), increasing the ICW can lead to significant increase of page load time. The same would apply to other connections with higher percentile retransmission rates. We see that for the connection in the 90th percentile, it first benefits from increasing the ICW size up to seven, then by increasing the ICW size more, the page load time starts increasing until it reaches 70% more than the minimum load time achieved at an ICW size of 7.

Conversely, looking at the right side of Table 1 (columns 4 and 5) with zero packet loss rate (representing the 70th percentile retransmission rate of all connections) we see the benefits from increasing the ICW size all the way to 32.

Consequently, one can conclude that no one ICW choice would benefit all users.

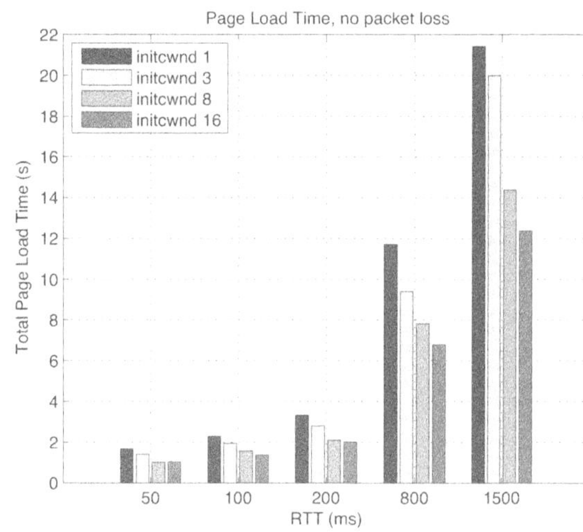

Figure 19: Page load time for different ICWs with no loss.

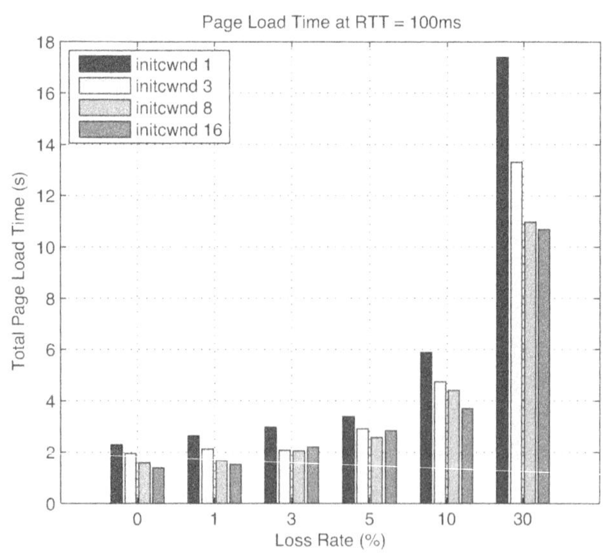

Figure 20: Page load time for different ICWs, packet loss rates, and an RTT of 100ms (median for Singapore).

	loss (%)	Time (s)	loss (%)	Time (s)
initcwnd 1	17	8.56	0.00	2.36
3	18	8.06	0.00	1.87
5	18	7.29	0.00	1.72
7	20	6.32	0.00	1.56
10	22	6.92	0.00	1.50
16	25	10.22	0.00	1.32
32	25	10.87	0.00	0.96

Table 1: Yahoo! front page load times for an RTT of 100ms (median for Singapore) with increasing ICWs and their corresponding loss rates from Figure 17. Right columns show times with no loss for comparison.

4.1.3 *Impact on TCP Fairness*

When making changes to TCP, we need to make sure that it remains fair to other TCP flows in the network. In this section, we study the impact of increasing the ICW on TCP fairness.

Increasing TCP ICW size can be unfair to longer flows, sharing the same bottleneck with short flows. If the network is congested and experiencing significant packet loss, increasing the ICW will increase packet loss. This loss may cause the congestion window to shrink by half each round trip until it may eventually reach one. Moreover, the sender could even experience timeouts. Hence, for a long lived flow, the sender can end up sending at a rate lower than one packet per round trip. Conversely, for a short flow, e.g. a web object download, packet loss will only extend the transmission by a few round trips and the window size may not drop to one by then. Hence, the *average* window size for the whole transfer can be significantly higher than that for a large transfer.

To demonstrate this point, we conducted the following experiment using the setup described at Section 4.1.2. We configured the connection between the host machine and the virtual machine to have the profile of connections in the 95th percentile from Figure 10, i.e. 100ms of RTT and 25% packet loss rate. Also, we configured the ICW to be 32.

First, we ran *iperf* for 5 minutes between the two machines representing a long flow. This transfer achieved a bandwidth of 12.6KB/s – less than 1 segment per RTT (14.3KB/s). For the second experiment, we downloaded a 48KB (32 segments) file off the web server. The measured bandwidth for this second transfer was 59.1KB/s. Note that as discussed in Section 3.2.3, although 48KB is the 95th percentile of downloaded web object sizes, it is the 50th percentile with respect to objects contributing to overall bytes downloaded from the Yahoo! CDN web servers.

Moreover, given that a recent study has shown that 52% of the internet traffic is web traffic [8] and given that increasing the ICW can increase packet loss and congestion for users with poor connections as shown in Fig. 17, we conclude that increasing the ICW can be more unfair for longer flows for users having poor connectivity.

Furthermore, one can conclude that increasing the ICW will be unfair to other short flows that remain using small ICW – e.g. the current default value of 3.

We conclude that if the TCP standard is changed advocating larger ICW sizes, this will be unfair to some flows, e.g. long flows having high packet loss.

4.1.4 *Discussion*

In this section, we have seen that varying ICW size can have a significant impact on web page load times. While a big fraction of users benefit from larger ICW sizes, others may suffer. Moreover, the level of benefit or suffering can vary across users according to their connection quality. Consequently, to achieve best performance, different users should have different values of ICW depending on their connection quality. Hence, we argue that a dynamic mechanism for configuring the ICW per connection is needed.

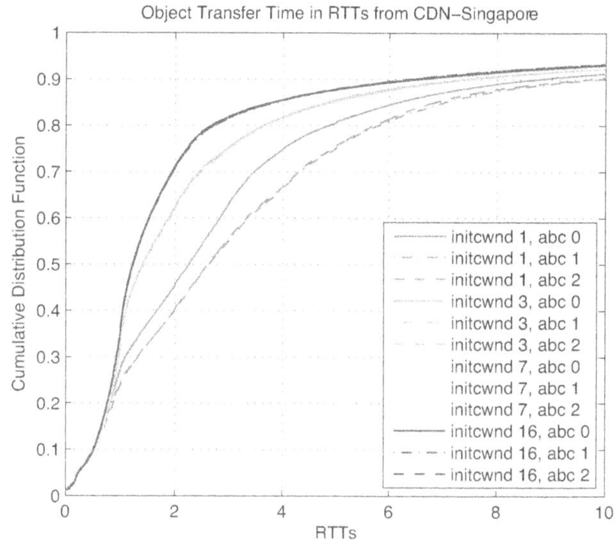

Figure 21: First object transfer time in RTTs, for different ICW and ABC settings.

4.2 Appropriate Byte Counting (ABC)

As explained above, the deployment of *delayed acknowledgments* is pervasive. This leads to the congestion window growing only by a factor of 1.5 per round trip. ABC mitigates this effect by relying not on ACK arrival but on the number of bytes acknowledged instead to increase the window size. This results in the congestion window doubling during slow-start every round trip as it was intended in the original TCP design. Linux allows 3 ABC settings: 0 turns off ABC; 1 increments the window by one for each acknowledged full segment; 2 increments the window by two for each acknowledgement received.

4.2.1 *Evaluation Using Live Traffic*

We varied the ABC settings at the server and show their effect in Figure 21. From these results we find that turning this feature on has a positive, but limited, effect on object transfer times.

4.2.2 *Studying Page Load time*

To study the effects of TCP ABC on overall web page load time, we used the same setup used in 4.1.2, except we used an RTT of 100ms and packet loss of zero and measured the page load time with the ABC optimization turned on and off. As shown in Figure 22, turning on the ABC optimization has marginal effects on the overall web page load time. The reason for this is that the effects of ABC will only be noticeable after many round trips. However, each TCP connection downloads very small number of little objects, and thus it requires only few packets and few round trips. Hence, there is not much difference in transmission time.

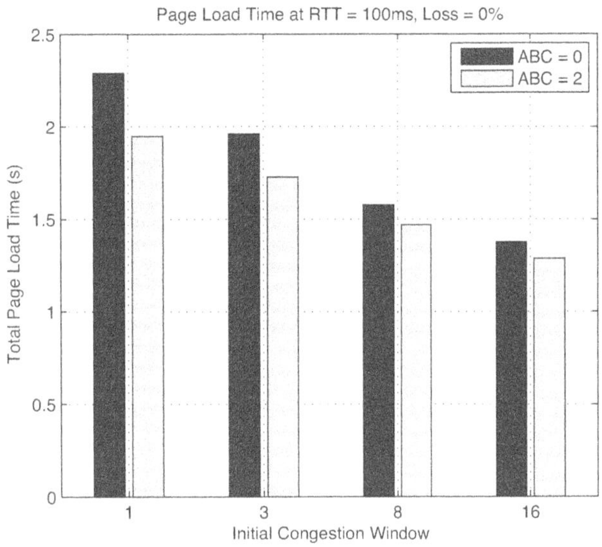

Figure 22: Page load time, for different ICW and ABC settings.

4.3 HTTP Pipelining

HTTP pipelining is known to deliver better performance. In this section, we quantify the performance gains from using HTTP pipelining using realistic workloads. We also study the interplay of HTTP pipelining with lower layers optimizations like increasing the ICW size.

HTTP 1.0 only supported downloading a single object per connection. This was inefficient especially for high delay networks as at least two network round trips are spent per object download – one for TCP connection establishment and another for downloading the object. Moreover, web pages are typically composed of multiple small objects, making HTTP 1.0 even less efficient for latency purposes. Later, HTTP 1.1 supported persistent connections spanning multiple object downloads. Furthermore, it allowed for pipelined HTTP requests over the same TCP connection as shown in Figure 1.

HTTP pipelining can eliminate multiple expensive network round trips from a web page download. This is because the client can request multiple objects without waiting for the corresponding responses to arrive from the server as seen in Figure 1.

Furthermore, pipelining allows web downloads to utilize much larger TCP ICW sizes leading to faster downloads. As seen in Section 4.1, currently the vast majority of web downloads cannot utilize TCP ICW larger than 16, even if the web user has more network bandwidth available. This is because web browsers download one object at a time. As seen in Figure 11, 90% of objects downloaded from the Yahoo! CDN are less than 24KB, i.e. they can fit in a TCP window of 16. In contrast, with pipelining, multiple objects with much larger aggregate sizes are downloaded concurrently. Hence, much larger windows can be utilized to reduce the number of network round trips per download.

Unfortunately, most web browsers do not support HTTP pipelining. For example Internet Explorer, the most popular browser [1], does not support it. Firefox, the second most popular browser, claims to support pipelining but has it switched off by default. As of today, these two browsers control more than 74% of the web browser market [1]. We tried to verify the level of pipelining supported by Firefox. We turned pipelining on, configured Firefox to use a single connection to download objects from each domain, and then downloaded Yahoo!'s front page. By looking at packet traces of the download, we realized that only a few object downloads were pipelined – at most two at time. This is in spite the fact that the web page had many objects per domain – up to 15 objects.

A main reason for not supporting pipelining by web browsers is that some web proxies in the Internet do not support it. However, this problem can be overcome if web browsers are modified to probe a well known web server, at start time, to check if it is connected to the server via a faulty proxy or not [18]. If no faulty proxy is found, pipelining is used, otherwise, it is not.

To study the effectiveness of HTTP pipelining and its interplay with TCP ICW size, we evaluated it experimentally. We built a simple web client that implements HTTP pipelining. It first downloads the HTML files. Then, it connects to the domains hosting the different web page objects. All objects per domain are downloaded in a pipelined fashion over a single persistent TCP connection. We used the setup in Section 4.1.2 having Yahoo!'s front page as our workload. The page objects span multiple domains. The domain with the maximum aggregate objects' size had 14 objects with total aggregate size of 445KB. To allow for a single network round trip download, we set the TCP ICW size at the server to 300 ($\sim$450KB). We also set the web client's receive buffer to 450KB. Under these settings, the web page download took 4 round trip times. The first two round trips were to connect to the server then download the HTML file. Once the HTML file is downloaded, its embedded objects and their locations are identified. The client then starts parallel connections to all the domains involved, one connection per domain. For each domain, HTTP pipelining is used to fetch all the objects in question at this domain. Hence, The two last round trips are for connecting to the domain, then fetching all the objects. This is well below the minimum number of round trips obtained in Section 4.1 – 8 round trips.

It is worth mentioning that this minimal number of network round trips can be also achieved by downloading all the web page objects concurrently each via a separate TCP connection. Current web browsers are moving in this direction by having multiple TCP connections per domain. This is why we see in Figure 12 that the average number of object downloads per TCP connection is 2.4. However, this approach has many shortcomings. First, it limits TCP's ability to control congestion as TCP controls congestion within single connection. So, if many connections start transmitting packets concurrently congestion collapse can happen, especially if the connections have high ICW. In this case a separate congestion manager [9] may be needed to control congestion across all the connections, which increases the system's complexity. Second, having multiple concurrent connections consumes more resources, e.g. the per connection TCP state and the CPU cycles to maintain this state. That is why most web browsers cap the number of concurrent connections used for objects download. For example, by default, Firefox caps the number of persistent connections per domain to 6 and caps the total number of connections to 30. Web browsers for mobile phones use less concurrent connections, e.g. Safari for the iPhone uses 4 connections. While the load from 6 connections per domain may be not that significant for most clients, it is certainly significant on web servers. It effectively means that they have to handle 6 times more connections and their corresponding overhead. Finally, using multiple TCP connections per application can be unfair to other applications and users that use a single connection per application.

5. DISCUSSION AND FUTURE WORK

As we have seen in the previous sections tuning the initial congestion window size can have a great impact on web page load time, especially if used in conjunction with HTTP pipelining. In Section 4.3, we have seen that web page load time can benefit from huge ICW sizes measured in hundreds of packets. Whereas, we see in Figures 18 and 17 that some users suffer from having much smaller ICW sizes.

This wide range of optimal initial TCP window sizes calls for a dynamic scheme for setting this size per connection as there is no one size that fits all. The right size depends on the connection characteristics, e.g. available bandwidth. This information can be learned from history of connections coming from the same location. TCP Fast Start [22] was proposed to allow a new connection to a host to reuse the state of older connections to the same host. It also included a mechanism to modify intermediate routers to identify packets from hosts using Fast Start and give these packets lower priority in the event of congestion. This is to account for the fact that Fast Start may be using stale cached information. It is questionable though how effective this reuse will be. A typical host does not reconnect to the same other host very frequently. Hence, *per-host* cached information is likely to be stale. Moreover, maintaining persistent state per client may be very expensive for a server serving millions of clients. Finally, the requirement for modifying intermediate routers is a significant hurdle to adoption.

We believe that the right approach to setting the initial TCP congestion should rely on previous history as well. However, a more effective approach tailored for web servers is needed. We leave this as future work.

Finally, because of its effectiveness, we advocate supporting pipelining in web browsers and implementing techniques, like [18], to overcome faulty proxies. Moreover, it will allow for taking full advantage of larger ICW sizes.

6. CONCLUSION

In this paper, we first characterized the traffic workload observed at the edges of Yahoo!'s content distribution network. We noticed that many connections have high RTTs. Some had significant retransmission rates. Based on this, we suggested and evaluated, both in the wild and in the lab, the effects of several optimizations at the TCP and HTTP layers with the goal of reducing overall page-load time. These included a combination of TCP Appropriate Byte Counting, increasing the slow-start ICW, and HTTP pipelining.

Overall, we find that, based on our traffic studies, a majority of users would see significant benefit from increasing the ICW – up to 38% reduction in page load time. However, for clients in poorly connected networks with high packet loss-rates, performance is likely to suffer when using high ICW sizes. For this reason, we conclude that no "optimal" setting exists that satisfies all users. We also found that HTTP pipelining is very effective, especially if used in conjunction with large ICW sizes. This combination can reduce page load time by up to 80%.

7. REFERENCES

[1] Global web stats. `http://www.w3counter.com/globalstats.php`, 2010.

[2] SPDY: An Experimental Protocol for a Faster Web. `http://dev.chromium.org/spdy/spdy-whitepaper`, 2010.

[3] ALLMAN, M. Tcp byte counting refinements. *SIGCOMM Comput. Commun. Rev. 29* (July 1999), 14–22.

[4] ALLMAN, M. A web server's view of the transport layer. *SIGCOMM Comput. Commun. Rev. 30* (October 2000).

[5] ALLMAN, M. TCP Congestion Control with Appropriate Byte Counting (ABC). RFC 3465, IETF, 2003.

[6] ALLMAN, M. tcpsplit. `http://www.icir.org/mallman/software/tcpsplit/`, 2010.

[7] ALLMAN, M., FLOYD, S., AND PARTRIDGE, C. Increasing TCP's Initial Window. RFC 3390, IETF, 2002.

[8] ARBOR NETWORKS. 2009 Internet Observatory Report. `http://www.nanog.org/meetings/nanog47/presentations/Monday/Labovitz_ObserveReport_N47_Mon.pdf`, 2010.

[9] BALAKRISHNAN, H., RAHUL, H. S., AND SESHAN, S. An integrated congestion management architecture for internet hosts. In *Proceedings of SIGCOMM '99* (New York, NY, USA, 1999), ACM.

[10] CHU, J., DUKKIPATI, N., CHENG, Y., AND MATHIS, M. Increasing TCP's Initial Window. `http://tools.ietf.org/html/draft-ietf-tcpm-initcwnd-01`, 2011.

[11] DUKKIPATI, N., REFICE, T., CHENG, Y., CHU, J., HERBERT, T., AGARWAL, A., JAIN, A., AND SUTIN, N. An argument for increasing tcp's initial congestion window. *SIGCOMM Comput. Commun. Rev. 40* (June 2010).

[12] FIELDING, R., GETTYS, J., MOGUL, J., FRYSTYK, H., MASINTER, L., LEACH, P., AND BERNERS-LEE, T. Hypertext Transfer Protocol – HTTP/1.1, 1999.

[13] FREEDMAN, M. J., FREUDENTHAL, E., AND MAZIÈRES, D. Democratizing content publication with coral. In *Proceedings of NSDI '04* (Berkeley, CA, USA, 2004), USENIX Association.

[14] HOPKINS, A. Optimizing Page Load Time. `http://www.die.net/musings/page_load_time/`, 2010.

[15] KRISHNAMURTHY, B., AND WANG, J. On network-aware clustering of web clients. In *Proceedings of SIGCOMM '00* (New York, NY, USA, 2000), ACM.

[16] KRISHNAN, R., MADHYASTHA, H. V., SRINIVASAN, S., JAIN, S., KRISHNAMURTHY, A., ANDERSON, T., AND GAO, J. Moving beyond end-to-end path information to optimize cdn performance. In *Proceedings of IMC '09* (New York, NY, USA, 2009), ACM.

[17] LEIGHTON, T. Improving Performance on the Internet. *Commun. ACM 52* (February 2009).

[18] NOTTINGHAM, M. Making HTTP Pipelining Usable on the Open Web. `http://tools.ietf.org/html/draft-nottingham-http-pipeline-00`, 2010.

[19] NYGREN, E., SITARAMAN, R. K., AND SUN, J. The akamai network: a platform for high-performance internet applications. *SIGOPS Oper. Syst. Rev. 44* (August 2010).

[20] OLSHEFSKI, D., AND NIEH, J. Understanding the management of client perceived response time. In *Proceedings of SIGMETRICS '06/Performance '06* (New York, NY, USA, 2006), ACM.

[21] OSTERMANN, S. tcptrace. `http://www.tcptrace.org/`, 2010.

[22] PADMANABHAN, V. N., AND KATZ, R. H. TCP Fast Start: A Technique For Speeding Up Web Transfers. In *IEEE Globecom* (1998).

[23] QIAN, F., GERBER, A., MAO, Z. M., SEN, S., SPATSCHECK, O., AND WILLINGER, W. Tcp revisited: a fresh look at tcp in the wild. In *Proceedings of IMC '09* (New York, NY, USA, 2009), ACM.

[24] R. STEWART, E. Stream Control Transmission Protocol. RFC 4960, IETF, 2007.

[25] SOUDERS, S. High-performance web sites. *Commun. ACM 51* (December 2008).

Summary Review Documentation for

"Overclocking the Yahoo! CDN for Faster Web Page Loads"

Authors: M. Al-Fares, K. Elmeleegy, B. Reed, I. Gashinsky

Reviewer #1

Strengths: The results of the paper show Web performance as perceived by real clients and shed light on TCP dynamics and the likely impact of various well-known refinements. For example, the paper uses its data to show that uniformly increasing the initial congestion window to 10 segments helps most connections but at the cost of longer downloads (due to increased loss) for a fraction of the connections.

Weaknesses: The data in the paper is great, but it is mostly straightforward reporting of performance for a few different options, and so perhaps the paper is not a large contribution compared to other work. It just depends on the submission pool.

Comments to Authors: Thanks for an inside look at Web performance an enjoyable read! I really had very few comments while reading, as you paper was very explanatory and well supported.

The main way I thought you could improve your paper was to look more deeply into what happens when the page load latency is larger than expected (higher RTT multiplier). You do have a latency distribution, but I think this combines many effects even though it is RTT-normalized, like objects of different sizes. How and why does latency vary for a fixed RTT and object size? If you could answer this, it might suggest the most important refinements.

Fig 15, etc.: how can the transfer time be smaller than one RTT something like 30% of the time?

Reviewer #2

Strengths: The data set used to evaluate ICW, ABC and HTTP pipelining is new and is collected from an operational CDN. The performance evaluation of ICW, ABC and HTTP in this data set is detailed.

Weaknesses: Techniques such increase of TCP congestion window, ABC and HTTP pipelining are not new, and have been already used in major CDNs. There is no in-depth analysis of the assignment of end-users to nodes. High RTT might be an artifact of the mis-location of users. The data set used collected in only four nodes of the Yahoo CDN and for only 1-hour operation. The argument that the peak activity of all nodes is on 1 pm local time is weak. Some of the results are not well explained and raise questions on the validity of the results.

Comments to Authors: Many CDNs are already using increased TPC congestion window ABC and HTTP pipelining, see e.g., "Improving Performance on the Internet" Communications of ACM 2009, "The Akamai Network: A Platform for High-performance Internet Applications". SIGOPS Oper. Syst. Rev." 2010. You may want to include these references in your paper.

Yahoo CDN has more than four nodes. You have to argue why you selected just four of them. It is because you have access to only four of them? If you perform the same study in the other nodes do you conclude to the same results?

You have to provide enough evidence why 1 pm local time is the peak time in all nodes.

You have to evaluate to which degree the high RTT as well as the different values of RTTs in a session are due to the fact that users are assigned to nodes based on the LDNS location and not the end-user. There are many references in the literature that show the mis-match between end-user and CDN nodes, e.g.,"A Precise and Efficient Evaluation of the Proximity Between Web Clients and Their Local DNS Servers" USENIX ATC 2002, "Comparing DNS Resolvers in the Wild" IMC 2010.

It is somehow suspicious that users in Illinois (a state that hosts one of the CDN nodes -- in Chicago) has the highest median RTT as shown in Figure 6.

You also have to explain how you infer the access technology used by different users (x-axis in Figure 7).

The structure of the paper and the presentation of the figures have to be improved (eg. Figure 4 and 5 are difficult to follow).

A better way to characterize the perceived performance to users is to use cluster them based on their network locations and characteristics as proposed in: "On Network-Aware Clustering of Web Clients", SIGCOMM 2000.

In Figures 18 and 19, you show indeed that there is no single optimal value of congestion window. Can you correlate your results with the size of requested object and the location of the end-user in order to give some hints on how the size of the congestion window can be tuned?

Reviewer #3

Strengths: The most interesting part of this paper is the traces from a live CDN provider with a lot of traffic and popular web properties. The rest of the analysis both in terms of transport level optimizations as well as application level optimizations is of lesser value.

Weaknesses: This is a very well researched and studied area and it is hard for a paper of this type to bring new or unexpected results. Both academia as well as industry have provided solutions and measured the performance results obtained by such optimizations. In fact, moderm CDNs provide separate solutions to accelerate Dynamic Web sites, which include TCP optimizations including TCP splicing and protocol parameter's tuning, application level optimizations such as compression and content transformation, and http level improvements including proxy2proxy pipelining and reduction of RTTs. Companies such as Netli, later bought by Akamai, have been doing this for over a decade.

The value of the paper resides more on the evalution of a few of those techniques. However, the ones picked are the ones better researched, e.g. congestion control window, and http pipelining. Other than saying that a single ICW does not work well across all clients, the paper does not bring much more interesting info.

In terms of methodology or new measurement techniques the paper is also very thin.

Comments to Authors: See above.

Reviewer #4

Strengths: Nice data: packet traces from for Yahoo! CDN in four different countries. Interesting results on some of the aspects that impact web page load times and discussions on how proposed optimizations should work given the Yahoo! workload.

Weaknesses: The paper lacks more analysis and discussions of the biases of the results.The evaluation of the optimizations is not thorough.

Comments to Authors: The paper lacks a discussion on the biases and limitations of the results. Yahoo! is a large web provider, so it does carry different content types. The paper should analyze the content that is being measured. Is this only Yahoo!'s main site? After a discussion of the content types studied, then it should be possible to put these results into perspective. How does this workload compare with other large web providers' workload? Is there anything that is particular to Yahoo!? Similarly, does the locality of the CDN nodes or the upstream connectivity bias the results in any way?

In Sec. 3.2.1, why are RTTs for Yahoo! smaller than those observed for the Google CDN? Is it that the Yahoo! nodes are better connected or that the RTTs improved in general since their study? It would be nice to have a bit more explanation of these differences.

The discussion of Fig. 6 focuses a lot on geography. Clearly, geographical proximity should reduce the RTTs, but the geographical proximity of the two end-hosts doesn't imply that the network path stays within a limited area. It also depends on the network-level connectivity. You could run traceroutes from the server to the IPs to verify whether you can explain some of the differences because of the network level path.

In Fig. 7, how do you determine the connectivity type?

The results in Fig. 8 should vary depending on the type of web content. It would be nice to have a small characterization of the content types you study.

How do results in Fig 9 correlate to Fig 8?

What is presented in Fig. 14? Is this a CCDF? Not sure this figure and discussion is really needed for the story in this paper.

First paragraph of Sec. 4 says that we can't do much to improve RTTs. Is this true? If you are Yahoo! it is easier to work on TCP or HTTP, but it is possible to improve RTT at the access.

The results in Sec. 4.1.2 are a bit of speculation. It would have been better to test this in some live connections for some hosts you control.

The discussion in Sec. 4.1.3 makes sense, but the experiments are not conclusive. It is just one example. The argument at the of this section is a little hard to follow. The conclusion is expected. It is unclear, the analysis is really necessary.

Sec. 4.3, paragraphs 2 and 3 are repeated from Sec. 1 and 2.

Reviewer #5

Strengths: The paper reports measurement results collected from yahoo's global CDN network. It reports various interesting stats that other researchers may find useful to know (for example fig-10 on retransmissions, even for India clients 70% of connections see no retransmissions! Fig-11, HTTP object size distribution).

Weaknesses: Despite its value the paper does not really report something that seems exciting. It is not the problem of writing but the topic itself -- how TCP settings affect download delay.

Comments to Authors: A small nit on the writing: I like papers that tell the reader the goal of the paper upfront. But for this paper the first page is all about general description of well known issues and ongoing work about TCP in IETF. Not until the second page, the paper stated "This paper is concerned with the delivery of content from edge servers from the Yahoo! CDN to the users." (the wording is still a bit too narrowly scoped, e.g. how would this work be interesting to community as a whole to be worth publishing at IMC?)

It seems that the findings of this paper would be highly interesting to the operational community (e.g. fig-6 results seem highly relevant to yahoo operations, why the RTT so high), and to IETF (e.g. ICW value impact, as IETF is mid of discussing recommended new settings).

The ICM value selection change reflects changes in the underlying network infrastructure capacity and traffic load patterns, and hence engineering tuning of operational parameters; I am not sure that represent some highly interesting issues to the research community.

The finding that no one size for the ICW fits all the users is also not surprising, given data is collected from a global network, it is only expected that in some places the network resources are still not up to the newly tuned value for other places.

Response from the Authors

First off, we would like to thank the reviewers for their feedback.

One of the common high-level comments was about the novelty of the techniques used to reduce the web page load times. We do not claim novelty inventing or using any of these techniques. The contribution of this paper is studying the impact of these techniques in the wild using real workloads and evaluating the interplay of these techniques. We will try to make this clearer in the camera-ready version.

Another high-level comment was about only using four CDN nodes and one hour of traffic. We would like to point out that each of these four nodes belongs to a different site in a different region of the world. We believe that traffic at these regions is representative of Yahoo! traffic from across the world. We have verified that traffic at nodes in the same site have similar characteristics; hence we only report traffic from a single node per site. Also, we have verified that traffic during other times of the day qualitatively has the same characteristics as that in the afternoon. Moreover, we would like to point out that the traffic we analyzed contains over 12 million connections spanning hundreds of gigabytes of traces, which we believe to be a reasonable sample to give a general idea about Yahoo!'s CDN traffic characteristics.

About the comment that the high RTTs measured could be due to misrouting users to wrong CDN nodes because of a mismatch between end users and their DNS resolvers as shown in previous work, we do not believe that this is the case. We use a different proprietary technique to route users that we believe to be accurate. Moreover, our results are qualitatively in line with results reported by another study (Krishnan et. al. 2009) over another CDN.

We addressed most of the other lower level comments in the camera-ready version. The things we could not address properly are requests for comparisons with other CDNs. We do not have access to the CDNs of other companies, so we cannot speculate.

Web Content Cartography

Bernhard Ager
T-Labs/TU Berlin
bernhard@net.t-labs.tu-berlin.de

Wolfgang Mühlbauer
ETH Zurich
muehlbauer@tik.ee.ethz.ch

Georgios Smaragdakis
T-Labs/TU Berlin
georgios@net.t-labs.tu-berlin.de

Steve Uhlig
T-Labs/TU Berlin
steve@net.t-labs.tu-berlin.de

ABSTRACT

Recent studies show that a significant part of Internet traffic is delivered through Web-based applications. To cope with the increasing demand for Web content, large scale content hosting and delivery infrastructures, such as data-centers and content distribution networks, are continuously being deployed. Being able to identify and classify such hosting infrastructures is helpful not only to content producers, content providers, and ISPs, but also to the research community at large. For example, to quantify the degree of hosting infrastructure deployment in the Internet or the replication of Web content.

In this paper, we introduce *Web Content Cartography*, i. e., the identification and classification of content hosting and delivery infrastructures. We propose a lightweight and fully automated approach to discover hosting infrastructures based only on DNS measurements and BGP routing table snapshots. Our experimental results show that our approach is feasible even with a limited number of well-distributed vantage points. We find that some popular content is served exclusively from specific regions and ASes. Furthermore, our classification enables us to derive content-centric AS rankings that complement existing AS rankings and shed light on recent observations about shifts in inter-domain traffic and the AS topology.

Categories and Subject Descriptors

C.2.5 [**Computer-Communication Networks**]: Local and Wide-Area Networks—*Internet*

General Terms

Measurement

Keywords

Content delivery, hosting infrastructures, measurement, DNS

The measurement traces are available from
`http://www.inet.tu-berlin.de/?id=cartography`

1. INTRODUCTION

Today's demand for Web content in the Internet is enormous, reflecting the value Internet users give to content [18]. Recent traffic studies [15, 12, 22, 27] show that Web-based applications are again very popular. To cope with this demand, Web-based applications and Web content producers use scalable and cost-effective hosting and content delivery infrastructures. These infrastructures, which we refer to as *hosting infrastructures* throughout this paper, have multiple choices on how and where to place their servers.

Leighton differentiates between three options for Web content delivery [24]: *(i)* centralized hosting, *(ii)* data-center-based content distribution network (CDN), *(iii)* cache-based CDNs. Approaches *(ii)* and *(iii)* allow to scale content delivery by distributing the content onto a dedicated hosting infrastructure. This hosting infrastructure can be composed of a few large data-centers, a large number of caches, or any combination. In many cases, DNS is used by the hosting infrastructure to select the server from which a user will obtain content [20, 37, 7, 30].

The deployment of hosting infrastructures is dynamic and flexible in multiple ways, e.g.: increasing the size of the existing hosting infrastructure, changing peerings with ISPs, placing parts of the infrastructure inside ISP networks. Therefore, being able to identify and classify hosting infrastructures in an automated manner is a step towards understanding this complex ecosystem, and an enabler for many applications. Content producers can benefit from understanding the footprint of hosting infrastructures to place content close to their customer base. For CDNs, a map of hosting infrastructures can assist them in improving their competitiveness in the content delivery market. For ISPs, it is important to know which hosting infrastructures deliver a specific content and at which locations to make relevant peering decisions. The research community needs a better understanding of the evolving ecosystem of hosting infrastructures, given its importance as a driver in the evolution of the Internet.

As demand drives hosting infrastructures to make a given content available at multiple locations, identifying a particular hosting infrastructure requires sampling its location diversity. Previous work has attempted to discover specific hosting infrastructures in an extensive manner, e. g., Akamai [36, 35, 17]. Such studies rely on the knowledge of a signature that identifies the target infrastructure, e. g., CNAMEs in DNS replies or AS numbers. Labovitz et at. [22] inferred that a small number of hosting infrastructures are responsible for a significant fraction of inter-domain traffic. Unfortunately, this study observes only the traffic crossing AS boundaries, not traffic delivered directly from inside the monitored ISPs. As a consequence, important CDNs such as Akamai as well as data-centers deployed inside ISP networks are under-represented.

In this paper, we introduce *Web Content Cartography*, i. e., the identification and classification of hosting infrastructures. We propose a lightweight and fully automated approach to discover hosting infrastructures based on DNS measurements and BGP routing table snapshots. Compared to previous work, our method is able to identify and classify new as well as existing hosting infrastructures without the need of a priori knowledge of their operation or deployment. To achieve such a degree of generality, we rely on the information that hosting infrastructures expose to end-users when requesting hostnames through DNS. We construct mappings between requested hostnames and IP addresses returned, and cluster the hostnames into hosting infrastructures with the help of network information such as IP addresses, prefixes and AS numbers.

Our contributions can be summarized as follows:

- *Identification of hosting infrastructures:* We propose a lightweight and fully automated approach to discover hosting infrastructures, based on DNS measurements and BGP routing table snapshots.
- *Classification of hosting infrastructures:* We classify individual hosting infrastructures and their different deployment strategies based on their network and location footprint.
- *Content replication:* We quantify the degree of content replication in the Internet and its impact on local content availability in different regions of the world. We introduce the *content monopoly index* that reflects the content an organization hosts, either replicated or exclusively hosted.
- *Revisiting AS rankings:* We derive content-centric AS rankings that complement existing AS rankings and shed light on recent observations about shifts in inter-domain traffic and the AS topology.

The remainder of this paper is structured as follows. We present our methodology in Section 2 and discuss our measurements in Section 3. In Section 4, we provide our results, and discuss the implications of our work in Section 5. We present related work in Section 6 and summarize the paper in Section 7.

2. METHODOLOGY

In this section we describe our approach to identify and classify hosting infrastructures in the Internet. The key idea is to collect the IP addresses that DNS returns for various popular and unpopular hostnames from geographically diverse vantage points. We use this information for several purposes: *(i)* to find the geographic location where popular content is available from, *(ii)* to find the network locations, e. g., prefixes and ASes, where content is available, and *(iii)* to find out by which hosting infrastructure a hostname is served.

2.1 Design Goals

To achieve our goals of mapping content and identifying hosting infrastructures, we design measurements tailored to our specific needs: *(i)* we target the hosting infrastructures that host content and *(ii)* we sample the network footprint of each of these hosting infrastructures in order to be able to classify them and study aspects such as content replication. We now elaborate on our choices and explain why they ensure that our measurements allows us to achieve the above goals.

Hosting Infrastructure Coverage.

To satisfy the first requirement, i. e., obtaining a wide coverage of popular hosting infrastructures in terms of traffic volume, one approach is to sample all possible hostnames. However, due to the sheer size of the Web – an estimated 92 million active domains only for the .COM top-level domain [6] – querying all host names in the Internet would be way too cumbersome from a measurement perspective. Fortunately, there is high variation in the popularity of Web content. Given that Internet traffic at various levels of aggregation is consistent with Zipf's law [13, 40, 38, 10], the hosting infrastructures that serve popular hostnames are likely to be responsible for a major part of today's Internet traffic. Despite a lack of definitive figures about how many hosting infrastructures are responsible for most of the Web traffic, we believe that it is reasonable to assume that a limited number of highly popular Web sites is sufficient to cover the hosting infrastructures responsible for the majority of the HTTP traffic in the Internet. For example, Akamai claims to deliver about 20 % of the total Web traffic in the Internet [30]. Labovitz et al. [22] attribute up to 10 % of all Internet traffic to Google, more than 15 % to the top 10 hosting infrastructures and more than 40 % to the top 100.

Network Footprint.

The second goal—sampling the network footprint of hosting infrastructures—asks for measurements from multiple vantage points. By running measurements from vantage points that reside in different networks and countries, we benefit from the way hosting infrastructures use DNS to select the server from which a user obtains the requested content [20, 35, 36, 7]. CDNs rely on the network location of the recursive DNS resolver to determine the IP address returned by DNS [30, 28, 37]. In many cases, the hosting infrastructure assumes that the DNS resolver is close to the client and optimizes based on this assumption. Therefore, to sample the locations from which a given hosting infrastructure serves content, our approach relies on volunteers to sample from different networks, ASes, and countries around the world.

2.2 Network Features

The way hosting infrastructures are deployed in the Internet is not homogeneous. In Section 2.3 we leverage the "network footprint" of hosting infrastructures to map them. Now, we discuss features that can be used to distinguish between different deployment strategies of hosting infrastructures.

To this end, we extract the IP addresses obtained within the DNS replies, from geographically dispersed vantage points. The set of IP addresses returned for a particular hostname reveals the degree to which the corresponding hosting infrastructure is network-wise and geographically distributed. Hence, the natural choice for our features are *prefix*, *AS* and *location* of an IP address. For example, small data-centers will be located within a single AS in a single geographic location, having a limited number of /24 subnetworks, and a large number of IP addresses. A massively distributed CDN will rely on multiple ASes. Evidently, these features are correlated, and potentially differ in their power to discriminate between different types of hosting infrastructures. We leave this for further investigation, and prefer to rely on all features for now.

Throughout the paper, we rely on both the granularity of BGP prefixes as well as /24 subnetworks. /24 subnetworks have the advantage of better representing the actual usage of the address space by highly distributed hosting infrastructures such as Akamai. BGP prefixes on the other hand indicate at which granularity routing is performed and more closely match the address space usage of centralized hosting infrastructures such as data-centers.

To determine the AS for a given IP address, we use BGP routing information from RIPE RIS [4] and RouteViews [33], and assume that the last AS hop in an AS path reflects the origin AS of the prefix.

To infer the geographical location of an IP address, we rely on

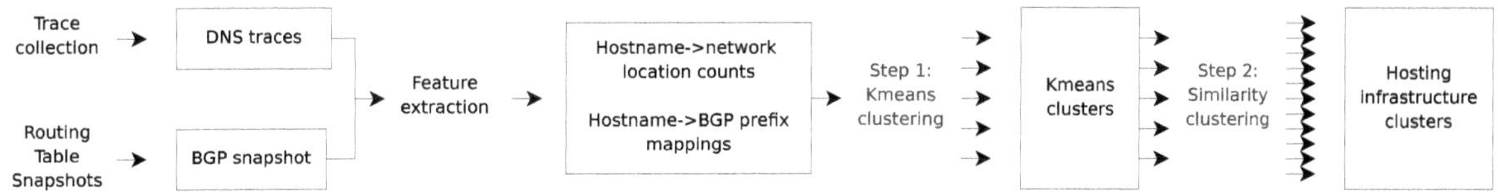

Figure 1: High level view of our approach.

the Maxmind geolocation database [29]. We are aware that geolocation databases suffer from limited accuracy. However, they have been shown to be reliable at the country-level [32].

2.3 Clustering Algorithm

Our goal is to detect where hosting infrastructures are located by AS and country, and classify them according to their network footprint. The key idea is to cluster all hostnames that are served by the same hosting infrastructure. To this end, we rely on the assumption that each hostname is served by a single hosting infrastructure.

We are aware that counter-examples exist: Meebo, an instant messenger aggregator, which is running its own meta-CDN, distributes the content demand across different CDNs by using a DNS server under their control. Another case is Netflix, which offers video-on-demand streams and relies on both Level 3 and Limelight. Our approach accommodates such counter-examples by putting the respective hostnames into separate clusters.

By examining the resolved CNAME records for various hostnames, it is sometimes already possible to identify the CDN that delivers the respective content. For example, a CNAME to `akamai.net` clearly points to the Akamai CDN. Yet, finding content providers would require an extensive a-priori database. In addition, some CDNs do not use CNAMEs, and CNAMEs are also used in different contexts than CDNs. In contrast, our clustering approach achieves the important goal of identifying hosting infrastructures in the wild, and could be used to help build such a database. Moreover, our agnostic approach is able to separate hosting infrastructures if they are actually maintained by the same administrative entity (e.g., the Akamai CDN), but treat various hostnames differently in terms of replication.

In the rest of the section we present our algorithm that identifies hosting infrastructures based on our data. We choose a two-step algorithm as depicted in Figure 1. During the first step, we ensure that the prominent hosting infrastructures are identified. It also gives an upper bound on the size of the clusters. In the second step, the algorithm merges clusters that share network features. The first step prevents the second one from clustering small hosting infrastructures with large ones. This may happen for example when infrastructures share address space with others.

Step 1: Separating Large Hosting Infrastructures.

The goal here is to separate large hosting infrastructures from the rest. We rely on three network-based features: *(i)* the number of IP addresses, *(ii)* the number of /24 networks and *(iii)* the number of ASes a hostname is resolved to. We use the k-means algorithm [26] to partition the hostnames in up to k clusters in the feature space. The choice of the value of k is discussed at the end of this subsection. Clusters whose features have high values relate to widely-deployed infrastructures. On the other hand, smaller infrastructures that use very few /24 subnetworks and IP addresses are not sufficiently different, and therefore, can be found in the same cluster. Increasing the value of k in the clustering algorithm does not lead to improvements, as the feature space simply does not allow to differentiate them.

Step 2: Distinguishing Small Hosting Infrastructures.

The pre-clustering of hostnames in Step 1 does not take into account the actual network locations from where content is served, but only features that reflect the *size* of the hosting infrastructures. The goal of the second step is to build sub-clusters within each k-means cluster by identifying the hostnames that are hosted on similar network locations in terms of IP address space. To this end, we take into account the set of BGP prefixes the hostname maps to. Based on the similarity between the sets of prefixes of two similarity-clusters, we decide if they belong to the same hosting infrastructure, and if so we merge these clusters. For this, we define the similarity between two sets s_1 and s_2 as follows:

$$similarity(s_1, s_2) = 2 \cdot \frac{|s_1 \cap s_2|}{|s_1| + |s_2|} \quad (1)$$

where $|.|$ denotes the size of the set. The purpose of the factor 2 is to stretch the image of the similarity function to the interval $[0, 1]$.

The second step of the algorithm is performed for each k-means cluster separately. Initially, we put each hostname contained in the current k-means cluster into its own sub-cluster, called a similarity-cluster. Then, we perform a pairwise comparison of all similarity-clusters of the current k-means cluster and merge them according to their similarity. We iterate the process until convergence to a fixed point. At this stage, each similarity-cluster identifies all hostnames used by a single content delivery infrastructure.

Tuning.

Generally, choosing k too high will lead to split large hosting infrastructures into smaller clusters, while choosing it too low may result in significant overlap between hosting infrastructures. As part of our case study in Section 4 we examine how sensitive the outcome of our clustering is to the choice of k. We find that the whole interval $20 \leq k \leq 40$ provides reasonable and similar results according to our verification, and therefore we decide to choose $k = 30$. Extensive tests reveal that merging thresholds of 0.7 on the similarity between two similarity-clusters work well for the second phase of the algorithm. We leave it for future work to advance our clustering techniques and to optimize the choice of parameters, and rather focus on the methodology for analyzing hosting infrastructures in the following.

2.4 Metrics: Content Potential and Monopoly

Now, we propose metrics and rankings that allow us to compare the obtained hosting infrastructures. We will use these metrics and corresponding rankings later (Section 4) to get insight about the geographic properties of content replication as well as the role of different organizations in the hosting of Web content, e. g., which organizations exclusively host content.

Content Delivery Potential.

Our goal is to provide intuition on the amount of content that is available for download in a geographic region (e. g., country, continent) or an AS. To this end, we define the *content delivery potential* as the fraction of hostnames that can be served from either a geographic region or an AS. Values close to 1 suggest that a major part of popular content is available locally. The disadvantage of the content delivery potential is that replicated content is counted as many times as there are different locations where it is hosted, introducing a bias in favor of replicated content.

Normalized Content Delivery Potential.

Therefore, we introduce the *normalized content delivery potential*, which takes into account the total number of locations from where content is available. Intuitively, a location does not exclusively deliver content, if the content has been replicated to a large number of locations. To take this into account, we calculate the normalized content delivery potential of a hostname as follows. First, we determine the weight of a hostname, which is 1 divided by the number of all hostnames. Second, we check how many different ASes, subnetworks, or regions serve this count, henceforth referred to as *replication-count*. To assess the contribution of a particular hostname to the normalized content delivery potential of an AS, subnetwork, or region, we take the weight from the first step and divide it by replication-count. The benefit of the normalized content delivery potential is a more balanced ranking in terms of hosted content, as it spreads the weight of distributed content infrastructure across all ASes, regions, or subnetworks that serve their hosted content.

Content Monopoly Index.

To distinguish between locations (ASes, geographic regions) that have exclusive content and those that host replicated content, we introduce the *Content Monopoly Index* (CMI). We define it as the ratio between the normalized content potential and the non-normalized content potential. An AS with a large CMI hosts a large number of hostnames that are not available in another AS.

3. MEASUREMENTS

In this section we present our approach to collect traces, i. e., active DNS measurements, in order to evaluate our methodology. To achieve our goal of identifying hosting infrastructures we compile a list of diverse hostnames and analyze DNS traces when resolving these hostnames as collected by end-users in commercial ISPs. Our experimental results advocate that our methodology is able to identify a significant fraction of hosting infrastructures network footprints, even with a small number of well-distributed vantage points.

3.1 Hostname Selection

To obtain a good coverage of the largest hosting infrastructures, we decide to include in our hostname list the top ranked ones according to Alexa [1]. Alexa relies on statistical sampling and determines its ranking by counting how many pages were visited by Internet users who have downloaded their toolbar. Note, Alexa itself is already accounting for various sampling biases of its user list[1]. In order to check for potential differences and to scrutinize replication of content also for less popular hosts, we further add hosts that are at the bottom of Alexa's ranking.

Moreover, many web-pages contain embedded content, e. g., images, videos, and advertisements that the browser of the user has to download from different servers. In our study, such embedded content has to be taken into account, as it might be served from servers other than those serving the front page of a popular hostname. To give an example, the front page of `facebook.com` is served from Facebook datacenters, but the logo and other embedded objects such as the profile photo is served from the Akamai content distribution network. In addition, to increase the chance of detecting the relevant infrastructures, we extracted hosts that are likely to be hosted on hosting infrastructures from the ranks 2001 to 5000 of the Alexa list. We identify such hosts by checking if they have CNAME records in their DNS answers.

Overall, we keep the 2,000 most popular and 2,000 from the least popular hostnames according to the Alexa ranking. Moreover, we include more than 3,400 embedded hostnames and 840 hostnames because of CNAMEs. This list leads to four subsets which we will refer to as TOP2000, TAIL2000, EMBEDDED, and CNAMES, respectively, for the remainder of the paper. Note, that several hostnames are used to deliver both embedded objects as well as popular websites. This leads to an overlap of 823 hostnames between TOP2000 and EMBEDDED.

3.2 Measurement Approach

Our measurement approach relies on volunteers to run a program that is publicly available for download on our project web-page along with instructions on how to perform the experiment. We initially announced the project during the IMC 2010 conference. In addition, we made a public call in several DNS-related mailing lists and invited friends to participate. This resulted in a total of 484 traces. Participants in our study run the program locally on their end-hosts. The program queries the locally configured DNS resolver, a Google Public DNS resolver and an OpenDNS resolver for the list of over 7400 hostnames, and stores the full DNS replies in a *trace* file. The traces collected with our program do not interact with any of the browsing or download history and activity of the user.

In addition to the DNS data, we collect meta-information that helps in sanitizing the measurement and in debugging. We report the Internet-visible IP address of the client every 100 DNS queries by asking a web-server running a custom script, and store information such as the operating system and the timezone, as well as the IP addresses of the DNS resolvers in use.

To sanitize the measurements, we check that the locally configured resolver is not a 3rd-party resolver such as Google Public DNS or OpenDNS. This information cannot always be derived from the resolver IP address, as the recursive resolver may hide behind a DNS forwarding resolver. Therefore, we perform queries for 16 additional names to domains under our administrative control. Their authoritative name servers are configured to reply to queries with the IP address of the querying resolver. This gives us the IP addresses of the resolvers directly, without having to further correlate logs from our authoritative name servers with the traces. To avoid receiving cached copies of the entries, we construct the names on-the-fly with the help of microsecond resolution timestamps and the Internet-visible IP address of the client.

The program is designed to collect all of the above data once every 24 hours, and write it to a trace file, until stopped by the user. This implies that there may be multiple traces per *vantage point*. We identify vantage points through the information contained in the trace files as well as meta information provided by the end-user running the program when uploading the trace files.

3.3 Data Cleanup

We perform a thorough cleanup process on the raw traces. We check for the following measurement artifacts.

We do not consider traces if the vantage point roams across ASes during the experiment, as we cannot determine the exact impact of the change. If the DNS resolver of the host returns an excessive number of DNS errors, or is unreachable, we do not consider the trace. If the DNS resolver of the host is a well-known third-party

[1]`http://alexa.com/help/traffic_learn_more`

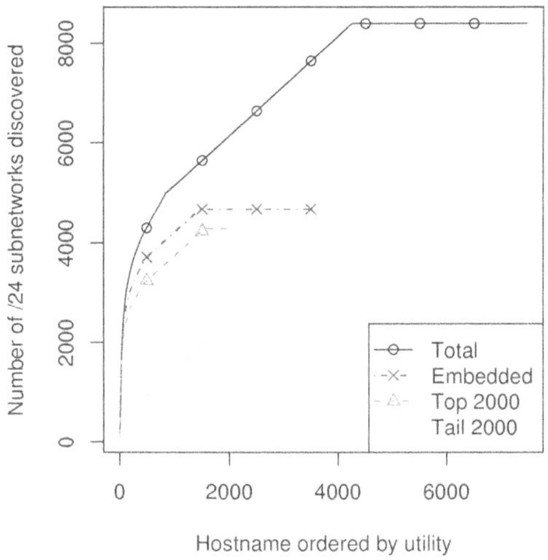

Figure 2: /24 subnetwork coverage by the hostname list.

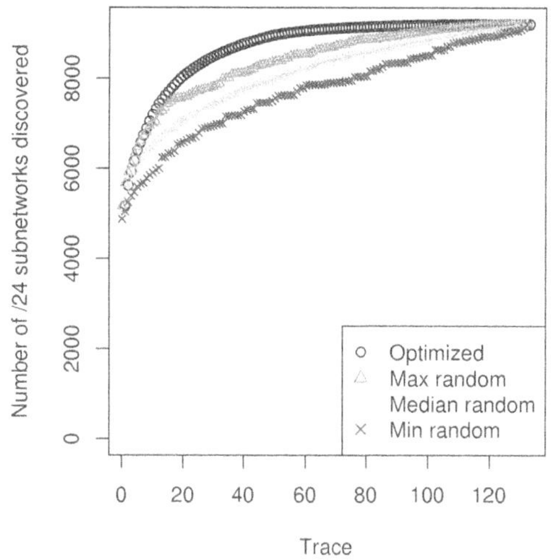

Figure 3: /24 subnetwork coverage by traces.

resolver, e. g., OpenDNS, Google Public DNS, we do not consider the trace. We showed in previous work that using third-party resolvers introduces bias by not representing the location of the end-user [7].

When a vantage point provides us with repeated measurements over time, we only use the first trace that does not suffer from any other artifact to avoid over-representing a single vantage point. This is important to avoid bias when quantifying the content potential (cf. Section 2.4).

After removing all traces with the above artefacts, we have 133 clean traces that form the basis of this study Note, the cleanup process has limited impact on our hosting infrastructure coverage and sampling of the network footprint.

3.4 Data coverage

We next investigate the coverage that our hostnames and vantage points provide.

3.4.1 Network and Geographic Footprint of Vantage Points

We map the IP addresses of vantage points of the 133 clean traces to ASes and countries using the mapping methodology described in Section 2.2. This leads to a coverage of 78 ASes and 27 countries that span six continents. Our experiments include traces from major residential ISPs, e. g., AT&T Internet Services, Comcast, Verizon, Road Runner, Telefonica, Deutsche Telekom, British Telecom as well as smaller residential ISPs and some university and research networks.

3.4.2 Network Coverage by Hostname

Previous studies [17, 35, 36] were able to achieve an exhaustive coverage for a limited number of well known hosting infrastructures. In our study, we strive to achieve a wide coverage of the prevalent hosting infrastructures without targeting a-priori known hosting infrastructures. Thus, we investigate the scope of the network coverage of our study. For this, we analyze to which degree replies for different parts of our hostname list result in different network coverage. To identify the IP ranges utilized by hosting infrastructures we aggregate the returned IP addresses over /24 subnetworks. We argue that this is the right granularity as hosting infrastructures tend to deploy server clusters for resilience and load balancing. Aggregation on the prefix of the returned IP addresses may lead to overestimation of the coverage, yet another indication why aggregation on /24 subnetworks is justified.

Figure 2 shows the total number of discovered /24 subnetworks when we stepwise add hostnames from our list (see Section 3.1) according to their utility. By utility we mean the number of new /24 subnetworks that are discovered by a hostname. The y-axis shows the total number of discovered /24 subnetworks as a function of the number of traces considered on the x-axis. In addition to the full list, we differentiate between three types of hostnames introduced in Section 3.1: TOP2000, TAIL2000, and EMBEDDED.

The curves in Figure 2 can be separated into three regions: a steep slope on the left, followed by a region with a slope of 1, and a flat region at the end. The steep slope region identifies hostnames with a high utility. These hostnames should be included to discover a significant fraction of the content infrastructure with limited probing effort. The region having a slope of 1 results from hostnames that positively contribute to the coverage but the utility is much lower than hostnames on the left. The third and flat region corresponds to hostnames that return redundant information about the hosting infrastructure, compared to the first two regions.

Let us now turn to the pairwise comparison of the three types of hostnames. While the hostname lists of TOP2000 and TAIL2000 are of equal size, the /24 subnetworks observed by TOP2000 and TAIL2000 exhibit a difference by a factor of more than two in the number of subnetworks they uncover. This unveils that popular content is served from more widely distributed hosting infrastructures than this of less popular content. Most of the difference in the cumulative utility between TOP2000 and TAIL2000 stems from a small number of popular hostnames. Furthermore, we observe that the hosting infrastructures that serve hostnames in EMBEDDED are well distributed.

To estimate the utility of additional hostnames we calculate the median utility of 100 random hostname permutations. We find that when adding the last 200 hostnames, the average utility is 0.65 /24 subnets per hostname, and 0.61 /24 subnets when adding the last 50 hostnames.

3.4.3 Network Coverage by Trace

Hosting infrastructures rely on geographic hints to serve content from servers close to the end user [24, 30]. We expect that traces in diverse regions of the world sample different parts of the host-

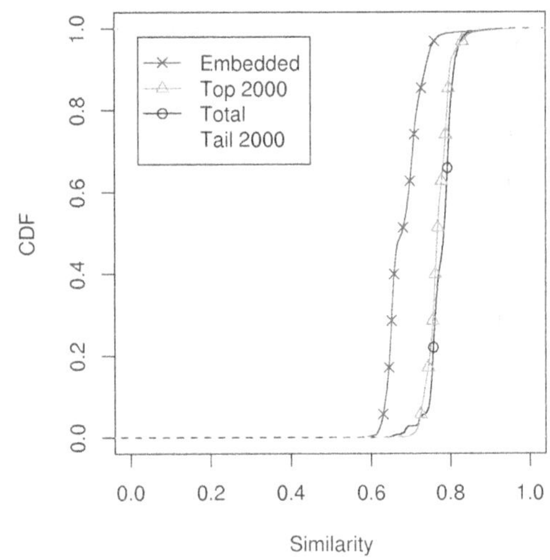

Figure 4: CDF of similarities for answers across different traces, for different sets of hostnames.

ing infrastructures. Therefore, we address now the utility of traces obtained from different vantage points.

Figure 3 displays the number of discovered /24 subnetworks of hosting infrastructures when we stepwise add traces from our dataset, see Section 3.2. The x-axis indicates the number of used traces while the y-axis shows the cumulative number of /24 subnetworks that can be identified based on these traces. The four curves of Figure 3 provide the results for different sequences in which we stepwise add traces: to obtain the curve with the black circles, we add in each step the trace that adds most additional /24 subnetworks to the set of already identified subnetworks ("Optimized"). In addition to the optimized cumulative utility (black circles) Figure 3 shows the maximum, median, and minimum cumulative utilities for 100 random permutations of the 133 traces.

In total, we find more than 8000 /24 subnetworks that are utilized by hosting infrastructures. We observe that every trace samples about half of these subnetworks (4800). About 2800 of these subnetworks are found in all traces. This relatively high fraction of common subnetworks among traces is the consequence of our choice of hostnames. It is not biased towards any given hosting infrastructure.

To estimate the potential benefits by including additional vantage points, we study the slope of the median curve (green crosses). Extrapolating the utility of the last 20 traces yields approximately ten /24 subnetworks per additional trace.

Furthermore, we notice that the traces that provide the highest utility (traces corresponding to the leftmost side in Figure 3), are actually located in different ASes and countries. For example, the first 30 traces belong to 30 different ASes in 24 different countries. The first 80 traces belong to 67 different ASes and 26 countries. This highlights the importance of utilizing vantage points that are geographically diverse and are hosted in different ASes.

To better understand both the need for diversity in vantage points as well as the underlying reasons behind the limited additional network coverage of hosting infrastructures by each trace, we perform a direct comparison of the traces. For this we re-use the similarity concept defined by Equation 1. For the same hostname, we define the /24 subnetwork similarity between two DNS replies as the similarity between their respective sets of /24 subnetworks. For two traces, we define their similarity as the average of /24 subnetworks similarities across all hostnames.

In Figure 4 we show the cumulative distribution of the similarity across all pairs of traces (TOTAL). We also show the similarity across traces when considering only one of the three subsets of the hostname list (EMBEDDED, TOP2000, TAIL2000). The high baseline value of similarity (always above 0.6) highlights the need for diversity to sample hosting infrastructures. It also confirms the slow increase in the utility of the traces shown in Figure 3.

As expected, the similarity for TAIL2000 is very high, indicating the limited location diversity for the corresponding hosting infrastructure. This is contrasted with the similarity for EMBEDDED, that is the lowest among the four curves. A low similarity for EMBEDDED is the consequence of the nature of the corresponding objects: typically they have a long lifetime and often are large. This makes them prime candidates for being hosted on distributed infrastructures, e. g., CDNs. TOP2000 lies in-between TAIL2000 and EMBEDDED. This indicates that the corresponding hostnames are hosted on a mix of centralized and distributed hosting infrastructures.

3.4.4 *Summary*

Our choice of a mix of different hostnames enables us to estimate the effect of our hostname list on sampling hosting infrastructures. Popular hostnames and embedded objects contribute most to discovering networks used by hosting infrastructures. Overall, studying data coverage we find that our set of popular and embedded hostnames is unlikely to miss large hosting infrastructures. The diversity of vantage points in terms of geographic and network location, however, is crucial to obtain good coverage.

4. RESULTS

In this section we examine our data set. First, based on the IP addresses we investigate where content can be obtained from. Next, we apply our clustering algorithm to characterize the resulting hosting infrastructure clusters. We gain insight on the deployment and hosting strategies of different infrastructures. We utilize our insight to derive content-centric AS-rankings and compare them with existing ones.

4.1 A Continent-level View of Web Content

Before delving into characteristics of hosting infrastructures, we want to understand which parts of the world serve Web content. In this section we choose the granularity of a continent, for two reasons: *(i)* the results directly reflect the round trip time penalty of exchanging content between continents, and *(ii)* our sampling is not dense enough to support country-level statistics. We quantify to which degree a user can find content in her own continent. This provides a view on the relative importance of different continents for Web content delivery as well the degree of replication of content.

4.1.1 *Geographic Replication of Content*

We first examine the relationship between the locations of content requester and content location as identified by DNS answers. We focus on TOP2000 in this section, and compare with other content types in the following section. Each line of Table 1 summarizes requests that originate from a given continent. Columns of Table 1 break down the requests among the continents from which the requested hostname is served. Each line adds up to 100 %, while columns do not as they reflect the global importance of a continent. The shade of each entry of Table 1 is a visual aid, directly indicating its value (the darker the higher is the value).

At least 46 % of the popular hostnames can be served from North America, 20 % from Europe and 18 % from Asia. The other three

Requested from	Served from					
	Africa	Asia	Europe	N. America	Oceania	S. America
Africa	0.3	18.6	32.0	46.7	0.3	0.8
Asia	0.3	26.0	20.7	49.8	0.3	0.8
Europe	0.3	18.6	32.2	46.6	0.2	0.8
N. America	0.3	18.6	20.7	58.2	0.2	0.8
Oceania	0.3	20.8	20.5	49.2	5.9	0.8
S. America	0.2	18.7	20.6	49.3	0.2	10.1

Table 1: Content matrix for TOP2000. Each line provides the percentage of all requests that originate from a given content. Columns indicate the continent from where content is served.

Requested from	Served from					
	Africa	Asia	Europe	N. America	Oceania	S. America
Africa	0.3	26.9	35.5	35.8	0.3	0.6
Asia	0.3	37.9	18.3	40.1	1.1	0.6
Europe	0.3	26.8	35.6	35.6	0.4	0.6
N. America	0.3	26.5	18.4	52.9	0.3	0.6
Oceania	0.3	29.2	18.5	38.7	11.3	0.6
S. America	0.3	26.4	18.2	39.3	0.3	14.2

Table 2: Content matrix for EMBEDDED. Each line provides the percentage of all requests that originate from a given continent. Columns indicate the continent from where content is served. The diagonal is more pronounced than for TOP2000 (Table 1).

continents, namely Africa, Oceania, and South America, do not appear to serve a lot of popular hostnames.

Another observation from Table 1 is a strong diagonal in the matrix, indicating that at least part of the hostnames are fetched from the same continent. Subtracting the minimum of a column from the corresponding element in the diagonal reveals that up to 11.6 % of the hostname requests are served from their own continent. This locality of hostnames availability provides evidence that a considerable fraction of content is replicated in different regions of the world. Note, by choosing the granularity of countries, the existing diversity within continents is hidden. In addition, we observe an almost identical behavior for hostnames requested from Africa and Europe. Two factors are likely to cause this behavior: *(i)* a limited number of traces from Africa and *(ii)* the fact that Internet connectivity in Africa is mostly provided via Europe coupled to the lack of local content replication infrastructure. Oceania and Asia localize to a lesser degree than either Europe or North America.

4.1.2 Content-dependent Replication

Content varies in both popularity and type. This is the reason why we distinguish not only popular and less popular hostnames, but also different types of embedded objects (see Section 2). In this section, we refine the previous analysis of the relationships between the locations of content requester and content origin by comparing with the other two subsets of hostnames: TAIL2000 and EMBEDDED.

Surprisingly, the content delivery matrix for TAIL2000 (not shown) is almost identical to the one for TOP2000 (Table 1). The largest difference is a stronger concentration towards North America, with up to 1.4 % points higher entries for TAIL2000. This indicates that the degree to which replicated hosting infrastructures are used in TOP2000 and TAIL2000 is very similar. How does that relate to the fact that top content has a far better utility in sampling large amounts of the address space than TAIL2000, cf. Section 3.4.2? The hosting infrastructures of highly popular content

Rank	#hostnames	#ASes	#prefixes	owner	content mix
1	476	79	294	Akamai	
2	161	70	216	Akamai	
3	108	1	45	Google	
4	70	35	137	Akamai	
5	70	1	45	Google	
6	57	6	15	Limelight	
7	57	1	1	ThePlanet	
8	53	1	1	ThePlanet	
9	49	34	123	Akamai	
10	34	1	2	Skyrock OSN	
11	29	6	17	Cotendo	
12	28	4	5	Wordpress	
13	27	6	21	Footprint	
14	26	1	1	Ravand	
15	23	1	1	Xanga	
16	22	1	4	Edgecast	
17	22	1	1	ThePlanet	
18	21	1	1	ivwbox.de	
19	21	1	5	AOL	
20	20	1	1	Leaseweb	

Table 3: Top 20 hosting infrastructure clusters by hostname count. The order of bars in the *content mix* column is: only on TOP2000, both on TOP2000 and EMBEDDED, only on EMBEDDED, and TAIL2000.

are distributed to a larger degree within each continent, when compared to hosting infrastructures predominantly used for less popular content.

When comparing the matrix of EMBEDDED (Table 2) with the others (TAIL2000 not shown, TOP2000 in Table 1), we observe that the diagonal is more pronounced for EMBEDDED. This indicates that embedded objects are, on a continent-level, more locally available than content from the other sets. We notice that Asia appears stronger for EMBEDDED compared to TOP2000 and TAIL2000, while North America appears weaker.

4.1.3 Summary

In this section, we analyzed the relative weights of Web content in different continents. We showed the prevalence of North America, Europe, and Asia in Web content presence, and how each region relies on each other. We observed a considerable local availability of content in most continents, implying that a considerable fraction of content is replicated across multiple continents.

4.2 A Portrait of Hosting Infrastructures

We turn our attention to the independent hosting infrastructures that are serving the hostnames from our list. In this section we identify the prominent hosting infrastructures, detect where they are actually located by AS and country, and classify them according to their network location footprint. Moreover, we study the geographic properties of hosting infrastructures and provide a ranking of countries according to their capability of serving popular Web content.

4.2.1 Clustering Validation

As first step, we validate the output of our algorithm of Section Section 2.3. Table 3 presents the top 20 clusters by hostname count. We find out by manually cross-checking that, indeed, all top 20 clusters correspond to networks that host large amounts of content.

Moreover, we leverage additional information about the Akamai and Limelight hosting infrastructures. In the case of Akamai we know the names present in the A records at the end of the CNAME chain inside DNS replies, which follow typical patterns. In the

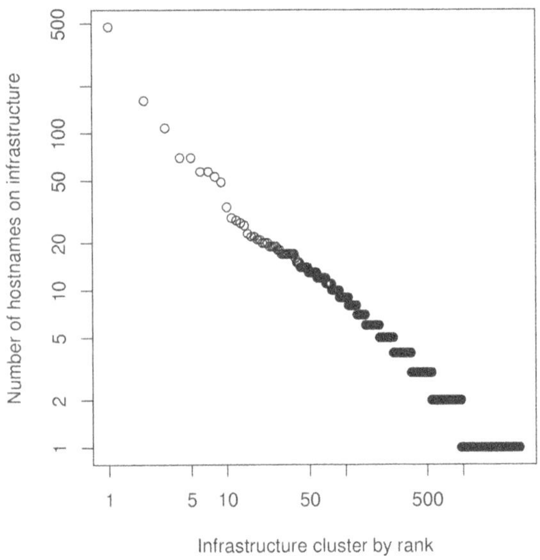

Figure 5: Number of hostnames served by different hosting infrastructure clusters.

case of Limelight, we can use the same approach, and also verify that IP addresses belong to the AS number of Limelight. Scrutinizing this additional source of information, we find a few hostnames that are not included in the top clusters of Table 3. Typically, such hostnames are only available at a very small subset of the whole infrastructure, and are therefore separated in the first step of the clustering algorithm (Section 2.3) due to their unusual features. We conjecture these hostnames are intentionally treated differently by the hosting infrastructures.

4.2.2 *Clustering Results*

Overall, the output of our algorithm leads to the identification of more than 3000 potentially distinct hosting infrastructures. Figure 5 shows, for each hosting infrastructure cluster, the number of hostnames from our list that are served by the hosting infrastructure of that cluster, on a log-log scale. Hosting infrastructure clusters are ranked in decreasing order of hostname count. We observe that a few hosting infrastructure clusters are serving a large number of hostnames. Most of the hosting infrastructure clusters serve a single hostname. Hosting infrastructure clusters that serve a single hostname have their own BGP prefix. We infer that these are likely to be located in a single facility and in most of the cases serve non-replicated content. The top 10 largest hosting infrastructures clusters are serving more than 15 % of the hostnames from our list. The top 20, still less than 1 % of all clusters, are serving about 20 % of the hostnames.

The resulting clustering allows us to make qualitative observations, namely that well-known hosting infrastructures are represented. Table 3 lists the top 20 clusters in terms of the number of hostnames from our list. Among them, we find well distributed CDNs such as Akamai, "hyper-giants" such as Google, and data-centers, such as ThePlanet. Note the different deployment strategies as coined by Leighton [24].

As can be seen in Table 3, we find multiple hosting infrastructure clusters run by the same infrastructure authority. Possible explanations include the observation that different types of services are hosted by hosting infrastructures, the geographic disparity of the infrastructure deployment, and acquisition or mergers. For Akamai and Google, the network footprints of their clusters are different enough to be separated by the k-means step (first step) of the clustering algorithm (Section 2.3), while the ThePlanet clusters are only separated by the similarity step (second step).

For Akamai, the top two clusters have about twice as many locations as the other two clusters. Further investigation reveals that the first two Akamai clusters correspond to servers in the `akamai.net` second level domain (SLD), and the latter two are hosted on servers in the `akamaiedge.net` SLD.

Similar observations are made for the two Google clusters. The cluster with rank 3 is used for the standard Google services including Web search and the YouTube front page. The hostnames in this cluster are served from more than 200 IP addresses. The cluster with rank 5 hosts `doubleclick.net`, `googleapis.com`, `blogspot.com`, and several other Google related SLDs, which are served by 40 to 130 IP addresses each.

For ThePlanet, hostnames rarely map to more than one IP address. The clusters only emerge in step 2 of the clustering algorithm (Section 2.3), because the content is hosted on different BGP prefixes.

In addition, Table 3 shows the content-mix that is hosted on different hosting infrastructure clusters as bar-plot. We add CNAMES (which come out of the Alexa Top 5000) to TOP2000 and report it as top content. In addition, we separate hostnames which are on both TOP2000 and EMBEDDED into a category of its on, top and embedded, to facilitate the interpretation of the content mix bar-plot. The order of the categories in the bar-plot (cf. caption of Table 3) is crafted to allow visually adding content of the top and embedded category to either the TOP2000 or the EMBEDDED category.

As expected, embedded content is prevalent on the top hosting infrastructures. Several hosting infrastructure clusters even almost exclusively serve embedded content, e. g., Limelight, Skyrock, Xanga, Edgecast, and the ad-service ivwbox.de. On others, e. g., the Akamai clusters, the first Google cluster, and AOL, top content accounts for a large fraction of the served hostnames. Some hosting infrastructure clusters serve mainly tail content, e. g., Wordpress, ThePlanet, and the second Google cluster. This may appear surprising at first, but it is a result of content consolidation. For example, blogs hosted by Google and Wordpress can be found amongst this content. This highlights how helpful less popular content can be in identifying and classifying the hosting infrastructures. The above mentioned results show that separating the hosting infrastructure of certain organizations into multiple clusters is both justified and necessary, because the infrastructures are not used homogeneously [30].

4.2.3 *Geographic Deployment of Hosting Infrastructures*

The clustering of the hosting infrastructures presented in the previous section is agnostic with respect to geographic locations. To provide insight about the geographic deployment of the different clusters as well as to better understand the degree of co-location in the content infrastructure, we map the clusters to the geographic locations of their prefixes.

Distinguishing between content infrastructures that rely on a few ASes or prefixes is tricky, especially because we do not have a priori knowledge about their signature in terms of ASes and prefixes. Indeed, some of these clusters might very well be present in a single location but for administrative reasons split their infrastructure into multiple ASes or use multiple prefixes due to multi-homing. One known example is Rapidshare [8], that relies on multiple ASes and prefixes yet whose facility is a single data-center.

Therefore, we estimate the number of countries in which a host-

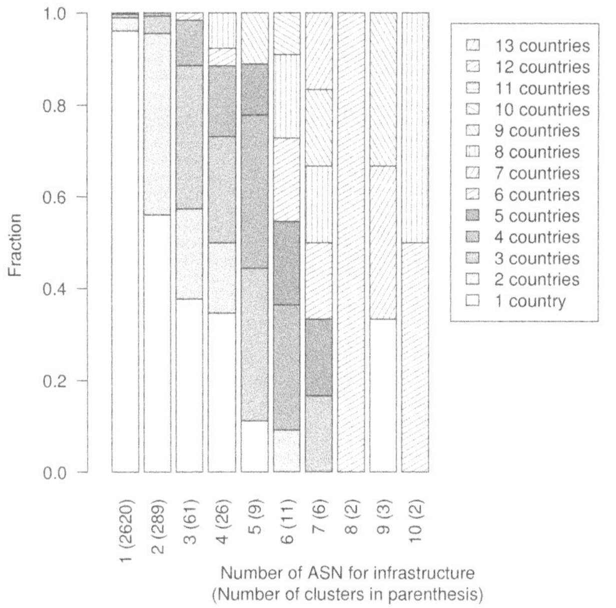

Figure 6: Country-level diversity of content infrastructure clusters.

Rank	Country	Potential	Normalized potential
1	USA (CA)	0.254	0.108
2	China	0.128	0.107
3	USA (TX)	0.190	0.061
4	Germany	0.183	0.058
5	Japan	0.163	0.051
6	France	0.146	0.034
7	Great Britain	0.157	0.030
8	Netherlands	0.144	0.029
9	USA (WA)	0.135	0.027
10	USA (unknown)	0.164	0.027
11	Russia	0.038	0.027
12	USA (NY)	0.130	0.026
13	Italy	0.122	0.018
14	USA (NJ)	0.125	0.016
15	Canada	0.028	0.015
16	USA (IL)	0.116	0.014
17	Australia	0.118	0.013
18	Spain	0.116	0.013
19	USA (UT)	0.111	0.012
20	USA (CO)	0.113	0.012

Table 4: Geographic distribution of content infrastructure, ranked by the normalized potential.

ing infrastructure cluster is present based on geolocation information. For each cluster we check onto how many countries it is deployed. Figure 6 shows the resulting relationship in the form of a stacked bar-plot. On the x-axis, we show the number of ASes in which clusters are discovered. We annotate the number of different clusters found for a given number of ASes in parenthesis. On the y-axis, we show the fraction of clusters whose prefixes are located in a given number of countries (see legend).

As shown in Figure 6, most of the hosting infrastructure clusters that use a single AS are present in a single country. As a cluster's footprint is on more ASes, the likelihood that it is present in multiple countries increases. At the same time, a significant fraction of hosting infrastructure clusters using multiple ASes are located in a single country. Because of the limited number of content infrastructure clusters located in 5 or more ASes (33 clusters), the fraction for these clusters in Figure 6 simply reflects a few instances of particular hosting infrastructures. Most of these clusters are present in several countries, thus, are probably CDNs.

4.2.4 Summary

In this section, we used our clustering algorithm to identify hosting infrastructures based on network features. We validate our classification based on additional information for two large CDNs. We present evidence of how Akamai and Google slice up their hosting infrastructures for different hosting purposes, and show which content is hosted on which hosting infrastructures. We distinguish between smaller hosting infrastructures based on both their features and their geographic deployment. We find a relationship between the number of ASes on which a hosting infrastructure is present and the multiplicity of its locations, giving a hint about their deployment strategy.

4.3 Mapping Hosting Infrastructures

To find out the geographic location of the hot-spots that serve most hostnames from our list, we compute both content potentials on a per country basis. Table 4 shows the results for both potentials. Note, for the USA only, we provide the state level. The lines of Table 4 are ranked by decreasing normalized content delivery potential and show the top 20 hosting infrastructures.

Despite the division into states, the USA leads the ranking with its hosting infrastructure in California. Indeed, in total 9 US states are among the top 20. On the second place we find China. Directly comparing California with China reveals that China's delivery potential is a lot lower than California's, yet the values of their normalized potential are quite close. Comparing China's potential with its normalized potential indicates that a large fraction of the content served from China is only available in China. In total, China and California together count for over 23 % of hostnames of our list in the normalized potential. Besides USA and China, 7 European countries are among the top 20, as well as Japan, Australia and Canada. In total we see content being delivered from 122 countries/US states, or 77 countries. The top 20 countries/US states presented here are responsible for 70 % of all hostnames in our study.

4.4 Revisiting AS Rankings

Geographic hot-spots are insightful in that they reflect where large chunks of the hosting infrastructures are. However, they provide little insight to understand how content is delivered to Internet users. Therefore, we investigate where content resides at the AS-level.

To map hosting infrastructure clusters to ASes, we rely on the same approach as in Section 4.2.3. For each cluster, we take the prefixes from which it serves content, and map each prefix to an AS number using BGP data. This gives us a set of AS numbers for each cluster. Recall that a hosting infrastructure cluster is defined by a set of hostnames it serves. We reuse the notion of content delivery potential, as introduced in Section 2.4, but where "locations" are now ASes. The content delivery potential of an AS is the fraction of hostnames it can potentially serve from all the clusters that are hosted on this AS.

Figure 7 provides the top 20 ASes in terms of their content delivery potential. Unexpectedly, we find mostly ISPs in this top 20. Note that the CMI (cf. Section 2.4) is very low for all the top ranked ASes. The two genuine content hosters in the list are Akamai and Bandcon. There are two main factors explaining the unexpected top

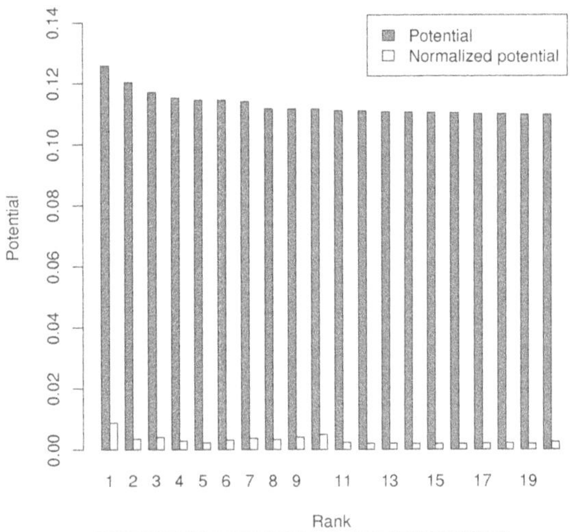

Rank	AS name	CMI
1	NTT America	0.070
2	Tinet	0.029
3	Global Crossing	0.034
4	KDDI	0.025
5	Akamai Europe	0.019
6	TeliaNet Global	0.027
7	Deutsche Telekom	0.033
8	Korea Telecom	0.030
9	Qwest	0.036
10	Bandcon	0.045
11	Cable and Wireless	0.021
12	SingTel Optus	0.019
13	Akamai	0.018
14	France Telecom - Orange	0.017
15	Internode	0.017
16	Comcast	0.017
17	StarHub	0.018
18	nLayer	0.020
19	Beyond The Network	0.018
20	TATA	0.023

Figure 7: Top 20 ASes in content delivery potential.

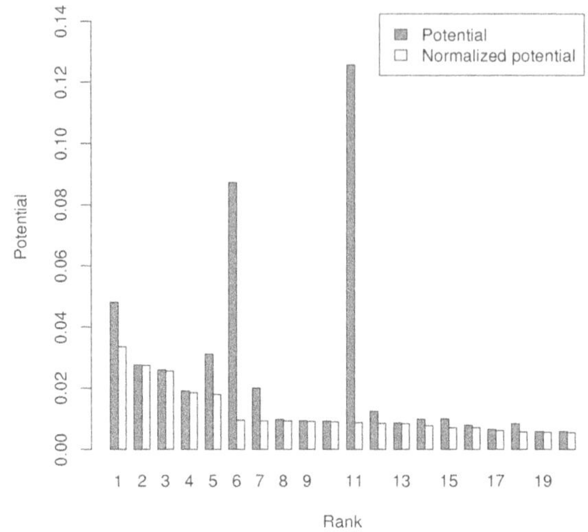

Rank	AS name	CMI
1	Chinanet	0.699
2	Google	0.996
3	ThePlanet.com	0.985
4	SoftLayer	0.967
5	China169 Backbone	0.576
6	Level 3	0.109
7	China Telecom	0.470
8	Rackspace	0.954
9	1&1 Internet	0.969
10	OVH	0.969
11	NTT America	0.070
12	EdgeCast	0.688
13	GoDaddy.com	0.969
14	Savvis	0.785
15	China169 Beijing	0.706
16	Amazon.com	0.895
17	LEASEWEB	0.942
18	Cogent	0.687
19	Hetzner Online	0.962
20	AOL	0.932

Figure 8: Top 20 ASes in normalized content delivery potential.

20: *(i)* all these ASes host Akamai caches that boost their content delivery potential and *(ii)* all these ASes host some content that no other AS can provide. Given the widespread deployment of Akamai caches in carriers, the second factor is actually more important and explains why some ASes appear among the top and why others do not. A content-centric AS-ranking should be able to cope with the bias introduced by the deployment of highly distributed hosting infrastructures within ASes.

An AS-ranking based on the normalized content delivery potential does exactly this. It spreads the weight of distributed content infrastructure across all ASes that serve their hosted content. Figure 8 provides the top 20 ASes in terms of normalized content delivery potential. Our first observation is that the only overlap with the non-normalized ranking is NTT. The ASes that appear on the top of the normalized ranking do so because of the exclusiveness of the content they host as reflected by their CMI values. As expected, Google is among the top ranked ASes due to its importance in popular content. We also see data-center content infrastructures: ThePlanet, SoftLayer, Rackspace, 1&1 Internet, OVH, Amazon, Leaseweb, and Hetzner Online. A limited number of ISPs in China seem to have a monopoly on a considerable fraction of popular content.

When comparing the normalized potential for all hostnames with TOP2000 and EMBEDDED, two more ASes enter the picture, Abitcool China and China Networks Inter-Exchange. In addition, slight re-rankings can be observed.

4.4.1 *Content vs. Traditional AS Rankings*

Many topology-driven rankings have been proposed [5, 22, 3, 2]. In this section we compare content-based rankings, described in the previous section, with topology-driven ones. Among the most well-known AS rankings are two from CAIDA [5]: one based on AS-degree and another on the size of the customer cone of an AS. Fixed Orbit [2] calculate an the Knodes Index, a centrality based metric. Labovitz et al. [22] provide an AS ranking based on the amount of traffic by monitoring inter-domain traffic from 110 ASes.

Table 5 compares seven different AS rankings: the CAIDA AS-degree (CAIDA-degree) and customer cone (CAIDA-cone) rankings [5], a ranking similar to CAIDA's by Renesys (Renesys) [3], the Knodes Index (Knodes) as reported by Fixed Orbit [2], the traf-

Rank	CAIDA-degree	CAIDA-cone	Renesys	Knodes	Arbor	Potential	Normalized potential
1	Level 3	Level 3	Level 3	Level 3	Level 3	NTT	Chinanet
2	Cogent/PSI	AT&T	Global Crossing	Cogent	Global Crossing	Tinet	Google
3	AT&T	MCI	Sprint	Global Crossing	Google	Global Crossing	ThePlanet
4	MCI	Cogent/PSI	NTT	Sprint	*	Deutsche Telekom	SoftLayer
5	Hurricane	Global Crossing	Savvis	Tinet	*	KDDI	China169 backbone
6	Qwest	Sprint	TeliaSonera	NTT	Comcast	Telia	Level 3
7	Sprint	Qwest	Tinet	AT&T	*	Akamai	Rackspace
8	Global Crossing	Hurricane Electric	Verizon	Swisscom	*	Bandcon	China Telecom
9	tw telecom	tw telecom	AT&T	Hurricane	*	Cable and Wireless	1&1 Internet
10	INIT7	TeliaNet	China Telecom	Telia	*	Qwest	OVH

Table 5: Topology-driven AS rankings against traffic-driven and content-based AS rankings.

fic exchanges-based ranking by Labovitz et al. [23][2] (Arbor), and finally our content-based rankings (potential and normalized potential). The purely topological rankings like the ones from CAIDA and Renesys tend to rank large transit carriers high. Besides the case of Google and Comcast, the top of Arbor's ranking leads to similar results to topological rankings. Our content infrastructure-driven rankings on the other hand give more weight to those ASes that deliver a large amount of content. We notice that our normalized potential leads to similar top ranked ASes as topological and traffic-based rankings, while of course favoring ASes that host content.

We argue that no AS ranking captures all relevant aspects of the importance of an AS. All aspects of the Internet are important, i. e., topology, traffic, and content, and need to be taken into consideration to understand the Internet ecosystem.

4.4.2 Summary

We proposed two different ways to rank ASes based on their content potential. We showed that these rankings reveal different aspects of content hosted by ASes: replicated content and content exclusively hosted by a given AS. We proposed an index, called the content monopoly index, which measures the degree to which an AS hosts content not available elsewhere, compared to content that is replicated in other ASes. Finally, we related our content-centric rankings to those presented in the literature.

5. DISCUSSION

The deployment of hosting infrastructures is dynamic in multiple ways, e. g., by growing their existing infrastructure, by changing their peerings with ISPs, or by placing part of the infrastructure inside ISP networks. Our methodology is an automated tool that makes it possible to monitor the state of hosting infrastructures deployment in the Internet at a given point in time. Given the changing nature of the hosting infrastructures ecosystem, as observed by Labovitz et al. [22], it is important to have tools that allow the different stakeholders in the Internet to better understand the space in which they evolve.

With the commoditization of the content delivery and hosting landscape, content producers have more and more choice as to where they can place their content, for example to better target their user base. With the rise of user-generated content, e. g., through Facebook, Twitter, and YouTube, content producers also need to deliver a mix of different media for which multiple suitable content delivery platforms might be available. Meta-CDNs such as Meebo, an instant messenger aggregator, or Conviva[3], a video delivery platform, distribute the content demand across different CDNs. To understand the trade-offs involved in their business decisions, content producers need to be able to measure the actual server diversity visible to different users from different places in the world, as well as the performance delivered by different CDNs. Our work is a step in this direction.

Given the already wide deployment of hosting infrastructures around the world, existing and new CDNs need to understand the marginal utility of deploying more infrastructure. Indeed, competition among CDNs is intense, and exacerbated by the fact that ISPs have already deployed and are deploying more hosting infrastructures inside their network. The recently created Content Delivery Networks Interconnect (CDNi) [25] working group at the IETF, aimed at standardizing interconnection between CDNs, is a proof of the maturity of the CDN market that now considers collaboration.

Some ISPs nowadays deploy their own CDN, data-centers, caches, or even CDN boxes such as those from Akamai. The increased availability of content caching and hosting with ISP networks further complexifies the current and future hosting infrastructures landscape. With the significant server diversity from which a given content can be obtained [31], both outside and inside their network, the traffic engineering task of ISPs is becoming even more challenging. Separating intradomain traffic engineering from peering engineering is indeed becoming less and less relevant. ISPs need to think globally about the network and understand what content can be obtained from where before making traffic engineering and peering decisions. Web content cartography, combined with a better understanding of content delivery performance, can help ISPs to an adequate strategy to deliver content to their customers.

It is worth mentioning the critical role of virtualization for hosting infrastructures. Virtualization is one of the highly disruptive enablers that we believe will change the hosting infrastructures landscape in the near-future. Indeed, virtualization technology offers flexibility that can be exploited by content producers and providers, as well as ISPs, to dynamically move content. By exploiting virtualization, we expect to see a hosting infrastructures market that is richer, that better utilizes the available resources, and better serves end-users. Virtualization has both a positive and a negative impact on Web content cartography. On the negative side, the use of virtualization, together with collaboration between CDNs and meta-CDNs, will pose challenges to Web content cartography. On the positive side, it will make it more necessary to keep track of the dynamic mapping of content onto hosting infrastructures.

The research community also needs an understanding of the evolving ecosystem of hosting infrastructures, given its importance as a driver in the evolution of the Internet. In light of the recent observations by Labovitz et al. [22] that showed significant changes in the whole Internet ecosystem, it is important for the research community to be able to foresee the impact of hosting infrastructures to work on the most relevant technical challenges that the future Inter-

[2]Some of the entries of the Arbor ranking were intentionally omitted by [22].

[3]`http://www.conviva.com/`

net may face. Our work is a first step in the direction of creating a comprehensive map of the whole Internet ecosystem that includes hosting infrastructures. A map of hosting infrastructures combined with a corresponding view of the paths (and their performance) to the end-users, would constitute a significant step forward in our understanding of Internet content delivery.

6. RELATED WORK

Our work on Web content cartography is motivated by recent studies that provide evidence in support of the significant rise of Web content traffic [15, 12, 22, 27]. Two major reasons are the growth of video traffic and the increasing penetration of broadband access. To cope with these changes, large-scale content distribution networks are being deployed [24, 30]. In addition, applications, such as file sharing, that used to rely on peer-to-peer delivery are nowadays increasingly served from data-centers [21], or One-click Hosters [8].

Labovitz et al. [22] observed consolidation of Web content traffic as well as a significant shift in peerings to better facilitate connectivity to content providers. They analyzed inter-domain traffic over a two year period, relying on data from 110 commercial ISPs and content providers. They detect global shifts in inter-domain traffic and the AS ecosystem. Our approach is complementary and focuses on hosting infrastructures, not inter-domain traffic. The advantage of our approach is our extensive coverage of popular hosting infrastructure, whose importance may be underestimated when analyzing only inter-domain traffic. For example, a significant fraction of the traffic delivered by a highly distributed infrastructure such as Akamai as well as data-centers located within ISPs, does not cross AS boundaries.

Shue et al. [34] observed, by looking at the `.com` and `.net` domains, that a vast majority of Web servers are co-located. Our results, on a more diverse set of domains, confirm that there is co-location of servers as well as hosting infrastructures.

Huang et al. [17], Su et al. [35], and Triukose et al. [36] leverage DNS requests to understand the distribution of Web content. However, their work is restricted to the study of specific CDNs, and does not try to detect different types of hosting infrastructures. Utilizing DNS replies of popular content in order to identify the location of hosting infrastructures shares similarities with work by Ager et al [7], by Krishnamurthy et al [20], by Feldmann et al. [14], and by Chang et al. [9]. Yet, their focus was on studying the performance of DNS resolvers [7, 20] or on deriving empirical models of inter-domain traffic matrices [14, 9], rather than leveraging DNS for Web content cartography.

Other approaches have been proposed to identify hosting infrastructures. Gill et al. [16] performed traceroutes towards large hosting infrastructures from distributed vantage points. They relied on DNS resolution from a single vantage point inside a university, providing a limited view of the network footprint of hosting infrastructures. Recently, Wang et al. [39] proposed a measurement methodology to estimate the distance between end-users towards two large CDNs. They rely on embedded measurement scripts within multiple websites and collect the measurements performed by the end-users. Our approach differs in that we do not require the targeted hosting infrastructure to be known a priori.

Clustering has been used in the past in different contexts, e. g., to group end-users from the perspective of routing [19] or DNS resolution [11]. Our approach does not focus on clustering of end-users, but rather on the identification and clustering of hosting infrastructures in the Internet.

7. CONCLUSION

In this paper, we introduce Web content cartography. We propose a lightweight and fully automated approach to discover Web content hosting and delivery infrastructures based only on DNS measurements and BGP routing table snapshots. To the best of our knowledge this is the first attempt to identify hosting infrastructures based on DNS replies and routing information, rather than relying on pre-identified signatures such as CNAMES. The advantage of this method is that is general enough to identify new hosting infrastructures as well as cluster them based on their operation as revealed by DNS.

Our results show that by utilizing traces from a small number of well distributed vantage points it is possible to make qualitative observations for the deployment of hosting infrastructures and content replication. A key insight of our study is that a significant fraction of the content is exclusively delivered by hosting infrastructures such as Google or geographical regions, e. g., China. Furthermore, by deriving content-centric AS rankings that complement existing AS rankings we shed light on recent observations about shifts on the AS topology.

Our work is an important step towards answering crucial questions for content producers, content providers, ISPs, and the research community. For ISPs, knowing the locations from which popular content can be obtained is a key factor in peering decisions and network dimensioning. For content producers, geographic and network footprint of a CDN is an important factor in choosing how to deliver content best to their customer base. For content providers, Web content cartography can help them improve their competitiveness in the content delivery market. Moreover, the research community needs to understand and track the evolving ecosystem of hosting infrastructures, given their importance as a driver in the evolution of the Internet. Web content cartography is complementary to other maps of the Internet, e. g., router-level and AS-level maps, and enables further investigation of the shaping forces of the Internet. In particular it will allow researchers to investigate the interplay of content infrastructures with the Internet topology.

Acknowledgments

We want to thank the numerous submitters of DNS trace files.

8. REFERENCES

[1] Alexa top sites. `http://www.alexa.com/topsites`.
[2] Fixed Orbit Knodes Index. `http://www.fixedorbit.com/metrics.htm/`.
[3] Renesys Market Intelligence. `http://www.renesys.com/products_services/market_intel/`.
[4] RIPE Routing Information Service. `http://www.ripe.net/ris/`.
[5] The CAIDA AS Ranking. `http://as-rank.caida.org/`.
[6] Whois Source – Domain Counts & Internet Statistics. `http://www.whois.sc/internet-statistics/`.
[7] B. Ager, W. Mühlbauer, G. Smaragdakis, and S. Uhlig. Comparing DNS Resolvers in the Wild. In *Proc. ACM IMC*, 2010.
[8] D. Antoniades, E. Markatos, and C. Dovrolis. One-click Hosting Services: A File-Sharing Hideout. In *Proc. ACM IMC*, 2009.
[9] H. Chang, S. Jamin, M. Mao, and W. Willinger. An Empirical Approach to Modeling Inter-AS Traffic Matrices. In *Proc. ACM IMC*, 2005.

[10] K. C. Claffy and N. Brownlee. Understanding Internet Traffic Streams: Dragonflies and Tortoises. *IEEE Commun. Mag.*, 2002.

[11] C .D. Cranor, E. Gansner, B. Krishnamurthy, and O. Spatscheck. Characterizing Large DNS Traces Using Graphs. In *Proc. ACM IMW*, 2001.

[12] J. Erman, A. Gerber, M. Hajiaghayi, D. Pei, and O. Spatscheck. Network-aware Forward Caching. In *Proc. WWW*, 2009.

[13] W. Fang and L. Peterson. Inter-AS Traffic Patterns and their Implications. In *Proc. IEEE Global Internet*, 1999.

[14] A. Feldmann, N. Kammenhuber, O. Maennel, B. Maggs, R. De Prisco, and R. Sundaram. A Methodology for Estimating Interdomain Web Traffic Demand. In *Proc. ACM IMC*, 2004.

[15] A. Gerber and R. Doverspike. Traffic Types and Growth in Backbone Networks. In *Proc. of OFC/NFOEC*, 2011.

[16] P. Gill, M. Arlitt, Z. Li, and A. Mahanti. The Flattening Internet Topology: Natural Evolution, Unsightly Barnacles or Contrived Collapse? In *Proc. of PAM*, 2008.

[17] C. Huang, A. Wang, J. Li, and K. Ross. Measuring and Evaluating Large-scale CDNs. In *Proc. ACM IMC*, 2008.

[18] V. Jacobson, D. Smetters, J. Thornton, M. Plass, N. Briggs, and R. Braynard. Networking Named Content. In *Proc. CoNEXT*, 2009.

[19] B. Krishnamurthy and J. Wang. On Network-aware Clustering of Web Clients. In *Proc. ACM SIGCOMM*, 2001.

[20] B. Krishnamurthy, C. Wills, and Y. Zhang. On the Use and Performance of Content Distribution Networks. In *Proc. ACM IMW*, 2001.

[21] R. Krishnan, H. Madhyastha, S. Srinivasan, S. Jain, A. Krishnamurthy, T. Anderson, and J. Gao. Moving Beyond End-to-end Path Information to Optimize CDN Performance. In *Proc. ACM IMC*, 2009.

[22] C. Labovitz, S. Lekel-Johnson, D. McPherson, J. Oberheide, and F. Jahanian. Internet Inter-Domain Traffic. In *Proc. ACM SIGCOMM*, 2010.

[23] C. Labovitz, D. McPherson, and S. Iekel-Johnson. Internet observatory report, 2009. http://www.nanog.org/meetings/nanog47.

[24] T. Leighton. Improving Performance on the Internet. *Commun. ACM*, 52(2):44–51, 2009.

[25] Kent Leung and Yiu Lee. Content Distribution Network Interconnection (CDNi) Requirements. IETF draft, work in progress, draft-ietf-cdni-requirements-00, Sep 2011.

[26] S. Lloyd. Least Squares Quantization in PCM. *IEEE Trans. Information Theory*, 1982.

[27] G. Maier, A. Feldmann, V. Paxson, and M. Allman. On Dominant Characteristics of Residential Broadband Internet Traffic. In *Proc. ACM IMC*, 2009.

[28] Z. M. Mao, C. Cranor, F. Douglis, M. Rabinovich, O. Spatscheck, and J. Wang. A Precise and Efficient Evaluation of the Proximity Between Web Clients and Their Local DNS Servers. In *Proc. Usenix ATC*, 2002.

[29] MaxMind. http://www.maxmind.com/app/ip-location/.

[30] E. Nygren, R. K. Sitaraman, and J. Sun. The akamai network: a platform for high-performance internet applications. *SIGOPS Oper. Syst. Rev.*, 44:2–19, August 2010.

[31] I. Poese, B. Frank, B. Ager, G. Smaragdakis, and A. Feldmann. Improving Content Delivery using Provider-aided Distance Information. In *Proc. ACM IMC*, 2010.

[32] I. Poese, S. Uhlig, M. A. Kaafar, B. Donnet, and B. Gueye. IP geolocation databases: unreliable? *ACM CCR*, 41:53–56, 2011.

[33] University of Oregon Route Views Project. http://www.routeviews.org/.

[34] C. .A. Shue, A. J. Kalafut, and M. Gupta. The Web is Smaller than it Seems. In *Proc. of IMC*, 2007.

[35] A. Su, D. Choffnes, A. Kuzmanovic, and F. Bustamante. Drafting Behind Akamai: Inferring Network Conditions Based on CDN Redirections. *IEEE/ACM Trans. Netw.*, 17(6):1752–1765, 2009.

[36] S. Triukose, Z. Wen, and M. Rabinovich. Measuring a Commercial Content Delivery Network. In *Proc. WWW*, 2011.

[37] P. Vixie. What DNS is Not. *Commun. ACM*, 52(12):43–47, 2009.

[38] J. Wallerich, H. Dreger, A. Feldmann, B. Krishnamurthy, and W. Willinger. A Methodology for Studying Persistency Aspects of Internet Flows. *ACM CCR*, 2005.

[39] Y. A. Wang, C. Huang, J. Li, and K. W. Ross. Estimating the Performance of Hypothetical Cloud Service Deployments: A Measurement-based Approach. In *Proc. IEEE INFOCOM*, 2011.

[40] Y. Zhang, L. Breslau, V. Paxson, and S. Shenker. On the Characteristics and Origins of Internet Flow Rates. In *Proc. ACM SIGCOMM*, 2002.

Summary Review Documentation for

"Web Content Cartography"

Authors: B. Ager, W. Mühlbauer, G. Smaragdakis, S. Uhlig

Reviewer #1

Strengths: - Novel approach that covers a neglected aspect of the Internet topology.
- Well thought through metrics such as content monopoly index and normalized potential.

Weaknesses: - The same weight is given to each hostname.
- Small data set, only 100 clean traces.
- Lack of ground truth.
- Rely on Alexa ranking to identify hostnames.

Comments to Authors: Your approach makes sense but it has some serious flaws:
- The same weight is given to each hostname: if your ASN ranking gives the same weight to google.com, yahoo.com, netflix.com and random websites. Will your AS ranking or the size of each continent mean anything? As you write, the internet traffic is following a Zipf's law.
- You are not using any ground truths (yes you validated Akamai). Is there a way to collect Netflow data in one or two ISPs and use it to do some validation?

Sec. 2.2: you mention that a data center based CDN may rely on multiple ASes and a massively distributed CDN may rely on a large number of ASes. I would leave out the last part of the sentence. The distinction does not really make sense and very large CDNs like Limelight don't use a large number of ASNs.

Sec. 2.3: your assumption that a hostname is served by a single hosting infrastructure has a lot of exceptions. I know companies that for instance use both Akamai and Limelight. For instance, in the US, NEtflix, the largest source of traffic is using multiple CDNs (Akamai, Limelight and Level 3).

Sec. 4.1.1 is surprising. I was expecting more content to be served locally (e.g. only 5.9% for Oceania!). You should highlight that North America still seems to dominate.

Table 3 shows the top 20 hosting infrastructures. Did you investigate the tail further to see if it makes sense? Did you try to run reverse lookups inside BGP prefixes to see if there are any interesting patterns that might confirm or reject your classification?
What is Skyrock doing as number 10? Isn't that Internet Radio? That does not seem to make sense. Is it a bias introduced by the fact that you are counting hostnames and maybe Internet radios have many different hostnames registered? You actually write that there is no false positive. This looks like a false positive to me.

In your summary, you claim that your approach is "accurate". I would not make this claim and present this as a novel methodology with some flaws for a challenging problem.

Reviewer #2

Strengths: - Simple methodology to identify hosting infrastructures.
- The analysis on content delivery potential per country and AS is interesting.

Weaknesses: - It is unclear how accurate the methodology presented is as the validation is quite limited and manual.
- While the authors claim that cartography can be used by ISPs and content providers to profile infrastructures, it is unclear how this can be achieved.

Comments to Authors: This is an interesting paper that attempts to characterize hosting and content delivery infrastructures. The proposed methodology is simple but novel and appears to work to some extent at least.

I liked the metrics of content delivery potential that provide some basic characterization on where content is generated and delivered.

There are three main points of criticism for the paper in my view:

First, the authors claim that ISPs and content providers can benefit from this characterization of hostnames and infrastructures. This is only vaguely discussed and it is quite unclear to me how this high-level profiling can assist providers or ISPs in their decisions.

Second, how much can one learn by just examining the hostname? Some hostnames are pretty straightforward to map to infrastructures. You methodology most probably provides a better grouping, but you could at least examine how much one can do by just looking at the hostnames.

Third and most important, I really have no intuition of what type of clusters your methodology provides, to what extent the grouping of various hostnames together is valid or not (or just a side-effect of your similarity metrics), and whether it makes sense. I am not sure how you can answer these questions, but your validation process is quite manual and the analysis does not really help clarifying these points. This also holds for the various thresholds and parameters used during the clustering.

Some parts of your paper are quite vague. For example, the summary in Sec. 3.4.4 notes that "more hostnames might reveal other infrastructures", or other similar arguments. It would be better to try and quantity the claims here.

How many clusters are created at each step of your algorithm? What is the relative importance and sensitivity of the two steps?

In Tables 1 and 2, it would be nice to quote the number of samples per continent so that we get a feeling of their relative importance.

Summary 4.2.4 is really over-stretching the discussion during the section. The classification method is hardly validated, and some hints are only presented for the hosting infrastructures.

There are some problems with the writing throughout the paper.

Reviewer #3

Strengths: The paper is mostly well written and thorough. I like the separation of embedded content (assuming I am understanding it right), as it seems a good discriminator in the nature of the CDN-hosted content.

Weaknesses: In general, I find "web content cartography" overstates what the paper achieves - but it is a cute term.

The dataset is weak -- 132 resulting sessions aren't all that great, and the argument that more sessions would not improve things substantially seems not quite true. 4.1, in particular, should really be at the country level, as I find the continent granularity quite un-insightful.

A breakdown of which kinds of content (in terms of news, entertainment, blogs, search, etc) are most distributed would be insightful. Perhaps it's hard to find differences, but I saw no mentioning of this aspect.

I suppose the big CDNs host too many of the names in the looked-up list, but it would still help to get a sense of "what's hosted where", which I found somehow lacking.

Comments to Authors: I mostly like this paper and spent quite a bit of time on it. My biggest complaint is the size of your dataset. 484 traces are not particularly diverse to begin with, and the fact that you only provide continent-level granularity in 4.1 is a pity. Did you not talk with people who have distributed infrastructures out there? Ono, Netalyzr, PlanetLab?

I also wonder about parts of your clustering approach. It is certainly interesting, but another approach comes to mind, namely looking at the resulting CNAMEs, authorities, and reverse lookups and identifying the CDNs from that directly. How different would those results be? Could you use it to cross-check your classifier?

Thanks for the summary subsections at the end of each section, they helped a lot.

Detailed comments:

- Why the factor of two in your similarity metric (Sec 2.3), and why did you not just use Jaccard?

- In the Normalized Content Delivery Potential section (Sec 2.4) you speak of the weight of a hostname, which you have not defined yet. In general, it would help a lot to provide examples here or clarify further, because Sec 4.3 becomes hard to follow with the relatively abstract notion of normalized Content Delivery Potential.

- In Sec. 3.1, be clearer what you mean by "embedded hostname"
- I suppose third-party sites referenced in a page's HTML source?

- What about intra-AS hosting differences? Is it a given that customers of very large ISPs see the same hosting infrastructures throughout? That seems doubtful.

- I'm not a fan of the writing in Sec 3.4.2, which I found particularly hard to follow. I read this paragraph a bunch of times and was still not sure what you're talking about: "To quantify the value of a hostname in relation to a set of hostnames we define its hostname utility as the number of /24 subnetworks it adds to the set of /24 subnetworks discovered by the set of hostnames." Too many hostnames in there! Figure 2 speaks of utility, which you do not define. The section mentions coverage, which you also do not define.

- The finding in Sec. 3.4.3 that geographic diversity is required in order to find lots of network prefixes that names resolve to is obvious, though good to see confirmed.

- In Sec. 4.2.1, say "misclassification" instead of "false positive", as you classification is not Boolean.

- Why don't you list (normalized) content delivery potentials in them in Tables 7 and 8 (which should replace Figures 7 and 8)?

Reviewer #4

Strengths: Timely problem, reasonably sound measurements.

Weaknesses: The clustering technique in Section 2 is a bit hard to understand and validate. Also, the paper oversells the lightweight/dynamic aspect of the measurement/methodology.

Comments to Authors: I do not have any serious criticism of this work, except that the clustering algorithm seems to be poorly explained and validated. I do have a bunch of questions/suggestions for the authors:

1. Section 2 seems a bit out of place and hard to understand. I was constantly wondering what the hostnames were, what exactly is being clustered, what the clustering is trying to do, and so on. Maybe moving 3.1/3.2 earlier so that the reader has context for what is happening would be useful.

2. Why do you need user volunteers -- why not use Planetlab? Also, given that you discarded most users/measurements, it raises the question of why you imposed this unnecessary load on the users when you intended only to take 1 measurement snapshot per user? Also, I found the "discarding" a bit ill motivated -- all you want is "diversity", why not treat different roaming locations of the same user as different geographically isolated points?

3. Sec 2.2 -- "small data centers ... and a large number of IP addresses" – This seems like an incorrect generalization -- Many webservers sit behind a single IP address but use load balancers/anycast within the data center.

4. It would really help to have more concrete examples in Sec 2.3 -- the writing is verbose and unclear at the same time.

5. Sec 3 -- what do you mean by bottom of Alexa -- bottom 2000 in the top-million? Also, it seems that the hostnames in the top-2000/tail-2000 are served by "origin" servers (e.g., cnn.com) that are not typically served by hosting infrastructures or cdns etc, so I found this choice of hostnames puzzling - the only thing that really makes sense here are the embedded content. Is your goal is to study how these origin servers are being hosted as well?

6. How exactly do I read the breakdown in Table 3?

7. Sec 4.4 was the part of the paper I found most interesting (the rest of the results were largely expected). Maybe it would be useful to speculate or try out some "unified" ranking across the different kinds of ranks (e.g., simple avg rank) to see what the top ASes would be?

8. Related work --One missing but closely related reference: The Web is smaller than it seems – conferences.sigcomm.org/imc/2007/papers/imc124.pdf

Reviewer #5

Strengths: A first broad, systematic attempt to uncover the hosting infrastructure in the Internet.

Weaknesses: While there is a lot of analysis in this paper, in the end, I cannot really tell what I learnt from this paper (which I did not know before- e.g., North America hosts a lot of content, etc.). Part of the problem is that the paper focuses too much on numbers and rankings, and less on drawing interesting conclusions from their data.

Comments to Authors: I am little puzzled by your methodology. If I understand things correctly, to identify embedded hostnames you fetched the content of Top 5K and Tail 2K Alexa sites once and from one location. But what if the embedded hostnames different for different locations and/or change with time? Some content providers dynamically decide when to offload content serving to third parties and use them only during peak usage hours.

I cannot tell what sort of bias may be introduced using your method of getting the embedded hostnames only once. I suppose the reason you do not ask your vantage points to fetch content and instead have them only do lookups is to keep the vantage point load low and the probing quick. But perhaps you want to validate if this optimization leads to different results than the full measurements.

Somewhat related to the above, I am also puzzled by the metrics you introduce in Section 2.1 and then use to understand the importance of countries and ASes. The metrics are based on fraction of hostnames that can be served from a given entity. But a user is not interested in hostnames, but the content behind the hostname, which may be served by multiple entities. You seem to be equating hostname and content.

The other thing that is missing from your metrics is a sense of what content is popular where. As you measure things, North America seems very important from the perspective of Africa (say), but if most Africans are only visiting African/European sites, then that reliance on North America is a lot weaker. Do you stats on what sites are popular where, to enable you to modulate your metrics?

Questions about methodology and metrics aside, the most disappointing part of the paper for me was the analysis. It rattles off a bunch of statistics that look at data from various perspectives, but does not go deep enough to provide any new insights. When I was done with reading the paper, nothing stuck in terms of your results. The sense I got was, yeah, there are a lot of good numbers here and I will look at the paper if I ever needed those numbers.

You claim in a couple of places that your methodology is fully automated. But recruiting volunteers doesn't seem automatic.

I think a study like yours is really valuable if it can provide a longitudinal perspective on how the hosting infrastructure is evolving. So, I would encourage you to fully automate your methods and periodically repeat your measurements and analysis.

Section 5 is not a discussion. It is repeating the motivation of your work, and the arguments are identical to the intro. I expected higher-level reflection on your findings and experience here..

Response from the Authors

- Methodology: Our methodology provides an automated way to identify hosting infrastructures in the wild. To the best of our knowledge this is the first attempt to identify hosting infrastructures based only on the DNS replies and routing information, rather than relying on pre-identified signatures, such as CNAMES. The advantage of this method is that it general enough to identify new hosting infrastructures as well cluster hosting infrastructures based on their operation, as long as they rely on DNS.

It is important to understand that our study is a qualitative, and not quantitative, study of the geographic and AS-level footprint of content infrastructures. The focus of this paper is to identify the existence and deployment of content infrastructures, not to quantify their relative utilization, e.g., the amount of traffic each infrastructure carries.

- Traces: It is true that the geographic coverage of our traces can be improved. However, we show that by utilizing traces from a small number of well-distributed vantage points, it is possible to make qualitatively correct conclusions. The expected implication of adding more traces is to highlight even more the difference between our content-related metrics. Furthermore, adding more traces will ease the classification task of the clustering. We disagree that using PlanetLab is the right way to improve the diversity of the vantage points, because our diversity aims at sampling the commercial Internet.

- Benefits for ISPs and CPs: For ISPs, knowing the locations from which popular content can be obtained is a key factor in peering decisions. For content producers, the locations of candidate CDNs tell them how best to deliver their content to their customer base. For CDNs, content cartography can help them improve their competitiveness in the content delivery market.

- Take-home message: A key inside of our study is that a significant fraction of the content is exclusively delivered by hosting infrastructures (e.g. Google) or geographical regions (e.g. China). By deriving content-centric AS rankings, that complement existing AS ranking, we shed light on recent observations about shifts on the AS topology.

- Future work: Our work is the initial step towards understanding the always changing deployment of content infrastructures. As such, it enables further investigation and can be refined to answer specific questions. In particular, it will allow us to investigate the interplay of content infrastructures with the Internet topology.

Author Index

www.ingramcontent.com/pod-product-compliance
Ingram Content Group UK Ltd.
Pitfield, Milton Keynes, MK11 3LW, UK
UKHW051241300926
15471UKWH00015B/1650

9 781450 313988